PEARSON

mymarketinglab™

mymarketinglab helps you clearly identify what you know, and learn the topics you don't know using:

- **Personalized study plans**

- **Self assessments**

- **Videos**

- **eBook**

- **Flashcards**

- **Downloads for your ipod**

www.mypearsonmarketinglab.com

Marketers are key to any successful company —creative, innovative people who make tough decisions about the best way to develop a new product, or about how to make a product so irresistible it flies off store shelves.

Will you become one of these people?

Maybe you already are—after all, you **market yourself** every day:

to your **family**, your **friends**, and your **teachers**.

What's important to know about this textbook is that it's the only one to present marketing from the perspective of the **people** who do marketing. In the pages ahead, you will meet real **marketers**— the people who make marketing decisions at leading companies every day.

This book is for students who want to be marketers as well as those who don't. If you fall into the first category, we'll teach you the basics so you can understand how marketers contribute to the creation of **value** . If you fall into the second category, maybe at the end of the term you'll change your mind and move into the first! Even if you don't, we're going to show you how the principles of marketing **apply** to many other fields—everything from the arts to accounting. However you choose to use this course, we've worked hard to make the material come alive with our focus on decision making.

Your won't just **read**  about it—**you'll do it**.

marketing 6E

real
people
choices

marketing 6E

real people choices

Michael R. Solomon
SAINT JOSEPH'S UNIVERSITY

Greg W. Marshall
ROLLINS COLLEGE

Elnora W. Stuart
THE UNIVERSITY OF SOUTH CAROLINA UPSTATE

PRENTICE HALL

UPPER SADDLE RIVER, NJ 07458

Library of Congress Cataloging-in-Publication Data
Solomon, Michael R.
  Marketing : real people real choices / Michael R. Solomon, Greg W. Marshall, Elnora W. Stuart.
— 6th ed.
    p. cm.
  ISBN 978-0-13-605421-4 (pbk.)
  1. Marketing—Vocational guidance. I. Marshall, Greg W. II. Stuart, Elnora W. III. Title.
  HF5415.35.S65 2009
  658.8—dc22

                         2008038437

AVP/Executive Editor: Melissa Sabella
VP/Editorial Director: Sally Yagan
Product Development Manager: Ashley Santora
Editorial Project Manager: Melissa Pellerano
Editorial Assistant: Karin Williams
Media Project Manager: Denise Vaughn
Marketing Manager: Anne Fahlgren
Marketing Assistant: Susan Osterlitz
Senior Managing Editor: Judy Leale
Production Project Manager: Ana Jankowski
Permissions Coordinator: Charles Morris
Senior Operations Specialist: Arnold Vila
Creative Director: John Christiana
Interior and Cover Design: Blair Brown
Senior Art Director: Blair Brown

Director, Image Resource Center: Melinda Patelli
Manager, Rights and Permissions: Zina Arabia
Manager, Visual Research: Beth Brenzel
Manager, Cover Visual Research & Permissions: Karen Sanatar
Image Permission Coordinator: Annette Linder
Photo Researcher: Rachel Lucas
Composition: GEX Publishing Services
Full-Service Project Management: GEX Publishing Services
Printer/Binder: Courier/Kendallville
Typeface: 9/13 Palatino

Credits and acknowledgments borrowed from other sources and reproduced, with permission, in this textbook appear on appropriate page within text.

Pearson Education Ltd., London
Pearson Education Singapore, Pte. Ltd
Pearson Education Canada, Inc.
Pearson Education–Japan
Pearson Education Upper Saddle River, New Jersey

Pearson Education Australia PTY, Limited
Pearson Education North Asia Ltd., Hong Kong
Pearson Educación de Mexico, S.A. de C.V.
Pearson Education Malaysia, Pte. Ltd.

Prentice Hall
is an imprint of

10 9 8 7 6 5 4 3 2
ISBN-13: 978-0-13-605421-4
ISBN-10: 0-13-605421-8

www.pearsonhighered.com

To Gail, Amanda, Zachary, Alexandra, Orly, Squishy,
and Kelbie Rae— my favorite market segment

—M.S.

To Patti and Justin

—G.M.

To Sonny, Patrick, Gabriela, and Marge

—E.S.

▶Brief Contents

▶Contents

PART 3 Create the Value Proposition 230

PART 4 Communicate the Value Proposition   366

CHAPTER 12: Catch the Buzz: Promotional Strategy and Integrated Marketing Communication....................366

CHAPTER 13: Advertising, Sales Promotion, and Public Relations..............398

▶ **Preface**

WHAT'S **NEW** IN THE 6TH EDITION?

To keep you on top of the world of marketing, we've **updated** and **expanded** our coverage of countless marketing topics. Here's just a sample of what's new (new concepts are in **bold**):

CHAPTER 1:
The triple bottom line
The accelerating importance of social networks in marketing
Open source business models
Microcelebrity
Instapreneurs
The power of crowds
A new section to address some common criticisms of marketing

CHAPTER 2:
Integration of the crucial issue of sustainability into our overall discussion of the marketing planning process

CHAPTER 3:
We've refocused the entire chapter around global issues. As many of our adopters requested, we've significantly beefed up our coverage of ethical issues in every chapter rather than focusing on these concerns in a stand-alone section.

CHAPTER 4:
We've linked the emerging practice of behavioral targeting to database marketing.
We've added more examples specific to on-line research and connections to on-line communities to gather consumer intelligence.
Prediction markets

CHAPTER 5:
Tribal marketing
Shopmobbing
Metrosexuals
Greenwashing

CHAPTER 6:
Additional clarity on differences in B2B versus B2C and why the differences matter
An enhanced treatment of stages in the organizational buyer decision-making process
Customer reference programs

CHAPTER 7:
More focus on Gen Y than before, and on teens and children
Additional attention to psychographic and behavioral segmentation
Overall enhancement of CRM section
Customer experience management (CEM)

CHAPTER 8:
More focus on gaming, technology, and telecom products

CHAPTER 9:
New discussion of the "dark side" of having too many brands in a family

CHAPTER 10:
More focus on technology-related services
More coverage of gaps in service quality

CHAPTER 11:
Hybrid EDLP
Freenomics
Network externalities
Prestige pricing and the price-placebo effect

CHAPTER 12:
Expanded coverage of consumer-generated media
Experiential marketing
Share of customer

CHAPTER 13:
We've revised our section on media to include material on indirect forms of advertising such as product placement and advergaming.

CHAPTER 14:
Enhanced attention to technology issues in personal selling
Opt-in services for mail catalogs

CHAPTER 15:
We've added new material on electronic distribution issues.
On-line distribution piracy
We've added more emphasis on new technologies related to the supply chain.

CHAPTER 16:
RFID in-store information
Video enabled expert advice through in-store kiosks
Updated e-commerce data
Merging on-line and in-store sales
Downloading movies
What's new in vending machines
Pop-up motels
High fashion e-commerce
Blue-light specials on-line
E-menus
Activity stores
Extended coverage of ethical issues in retailing: shrinkage due to shoplifting, employee theft, retail borrowing, and ethical treatment of customers

Features of the 6th Edition of Real People, Real Choices

Meet Real Marketers

Many of the "Real People, Real Choices" vignettes are new to this edition, featuring a variety of decision makers, from CEOs to brand managers. Here is just a sample who we feature:

- Julie Cordua, (RED)
- Thomas Connerty, NutriSystem
- Thomas J. Petters, Petters Group Worldwide/Polaroid
- Lara L. Price, The Philadelphia 76ers
- Walter (Walt) F. Judas, Tourism Vancouver
- Joe Chernov, BzzAgent

NEW! Ethics in Marketing

Because the role of ethics in business and in marketing is so important, we focus on ethics not just in a single chapter but in EVERY CHAPTER of the book, providing coverage in two distinct ways:

- Topical coverage of ethical issues integrated with relevant content within every chapter.
- In every chapter, you have an opportunity to make a decision based on an ethical dilemma that we have "pulled from the headlines." Each "Ethical Decisions in the Real World" feature is based on a recent news story about an ethical or unethical decision.

Here's a sample of our chapter by chapter coverage of ethics:

- In Chapter 1, we begin with a discussion of the Relationship Era of marketing, the social marketing concept and sustainability.
- In Chapter 2, we discuss business ethics in general and how firms develop codes of ethics.
- Chapter 3 covers differences in both the perception and practice of ethical business behavior in different parts of the world and discusses how bribery and extortion are special problems in global marketing.
- We discuss consumerism, the Consumer Bill of Rights, and environmental stewardship in Chapter 5.
- Chapter 9 includes coverage of legal and ethical issues in packaging and labeling, gray goods, product knockoffs, and intellectual property rights.
- We discuss ethical issues in pricing in Chapter 11 including bait-and-switch tactics, price-fixing, price discrimination, and predatory pricing.
- Chapter 12 discusses ethical issues in buzz marketing.
- In Chapter 13 we consider some of the criticisms of advertising (that advertising is manipulative, is deceptive, creates stereotypes, and causes people to buy things they don't need). We also discuss corrective advertising and puffery.
- In Chapter 16, we talk about shrinkage due to shoplifting, employee theft, and retail borrowing, and about the ethical treatment of customers.

An Easy-to-Follow Marketing Plan Template

Chapter 2 includes a pullout template of a marketing plan you can use as you make your way through the book. The template provides a framework that will enable you to organize marketing concepts by chapter and create a solid marketing plan of your own. On the back of the template is a world map. We encourage you to keep this pullout as a handy reference after the class.

NEW! Consumer-Generated Value: By the People, for the People

One of the most significant (and still evolving) marketing stories today is the avalanche of consumer-generated marketing activity. Largely because of advances in technology, everyday people are involving themselves with companies as they seek to become part of a dialogue with marketers rather than just passive recipients of information. Consumers are voting on new product designs, submitting their own amateur commercials, and writing reviews of products and services on thousands of Web sites, blogs, and social networking applications like Facebook. So that students understand all the ways that marketing activities are changing and will continue to change as this trend continues, we've introduced a new chapter feature we call "By the People, for the People." Each box highlights a current example relevant of a marketing activity that originates with material that customers, rather than company employees, generate.

Measuring the Value of Marketing through Marketing Metrics

Just how do marketers add value to a company and can that value be quantified? More and more, businesses demand accountability and marketers respond as they develop a variety of "scorecards" that show how specific marketing activities directly affect their company's ROI—return on investment. And on the job, the decisions that marketers make increasingly come from data and calculations and less from instinct. Throughout the book you'll find numerous *Metrics Moment* boxes that provide real-world examples of the measures marketers use to help them make good decisions.

Learning How to Market Yourself: Brand You

You are a product. That may sound weird, but we often talk about ourselves and others in marketing terms. It is common for us to speak of "positioning" ourselves for job interviews, or to tell our friends not to "sell themselves short." You'll learn more about the most effective way to market yourself by following the advice provided in a dynamic and helpful *Brand You* handbook. You'll find concrete advice you can use today that will help you to thrive in a competitive marketplace tomorrow.

All New and Updated End-of-Chapter Cases in this Edition

Each chapter concludes with an exciting "Marketing in Action" mini-case about a real firm facing real marketing challenges. Questions at the end let you make the call to get the company on the right track.

Student Resources
PEARSON mymarketinglab™

mymarketinglab gives you the opportunity to test themselves on key concepts and skills, track your own progress through the course and use the personalized study plan activities—all to help you achieve success in the classroom.

Features Include:

- Personalized study plans—Pre and Post Tests with remediation activities directed to help you understand and apply the concepts where you need the most help.

- Self-assessments—Prebuilt self-assessments allow you to test yourself.

- Interactive Elements—A wealth of hands-on activities and exercises let you experience and learn firsthand. Whether it is with the on-line ebook where you can search for specific keywords or page numbers, highlight specific sections, enter notes right on the ebook page, and print reading assignments with notes for later review or with other materials including Real People Real Choices Video Cases, online End of Chapter activities, Active Flashcards and much more.

- iQuizzes—Study anytime, anywhere iQuizzes work on any color-screen iPod and are comprised of a sequence of quiz questions, specifically created for the iPod screen

www.mypearsonmarketinglab.com

Study Guide

The study guide is a one-of-a-kind companion for students. It includes detailed chapter outlines and student exercises, as well as solutions. This guide serves as a great review tool in preparing for exams.

VangoNotes

Study on-the-go with VangoNotes. Just download chapter reviews from your text and listen to them on any MP3 player. Now wherever you are—whatever you're doing—you can study by listening to the following for each chapter of your textbook:

- Big Ideas: Your "need to know" for each chapter

- Practice Test: A gut check for the Big Ideas—tells you if you need to keep studying

- Key Terms: Audio "flashcards" to help you review key concepts and terms

- Rapid Review: A quick drill session—use it right before your test

VangoNotes are flexible; download all the material directly to your player, or only the chapters you need. And they're efficient. Use them in your car, at the gym, walking to class, wherever. So get yours today and get studying. **www.VangoNotes.com**.

Brand You Handbook

Products aren't alone in benefiting from branding—people can benefit, too. Branding strategies help professionals get noticed and position them for exciting new career opportunities. Prepared by Kim Richmond of Saint Joseph's University, the *Brand You* handbook gives you concrete advice on how to thrive in a competitive marketplace and provides a hands-on approach to achieving career success. *Brand You* boxes appear throughout this textbook to help you plot your own branding strategies. This separate *Brand You* supplement can be purchased at **www.mypearsonstore.com**.

▶About the Authors

Michael R. Solomon, Elnora W. Stuart, Greg W. Marshall

MICHAEL R. SOLOMON

MICHAEL R. SOLOMON, PhD, joined the Haub School of Business at Saint Joseph's University in Philadelphia as Professor of Marketing in 2006, where he also serves as Director of the Center for Consumer Research. From 1995 to 2006, he was the Human Sciences Professor of Consumer Behavior at Auburn University. Prior to joining Auburn in 1995, he was Chairman of the Department of Marketing in the School of Business at Rutgers University, New Brunswick, New Jersey. Professor Solomon's primary research interests include consumer behavior and lifestyle issues; branding strategy; the symbolic aspects of products; the psychology of fashion, decoration, and image; services marketing; and the development of visually oriented on-line research methodologies. He currently sits on the editorial boards of the *Journal of Consumer Behaviour, the European Business Review*, and the *Journal of Retailing*, and he recently completed a six-year term on the Board of Governors of the Academy of Marketing Science. In addition to other books, he is also the author of Prentice Hall's text *Consumer Behavior: Buying, Having, and Being*, which is widely used in universities throughout the world. Professor Solomon frequently appears on television and radio shows such as *The Today Show, Good Morning America*, Channel One, the *Wall Street Journal* Radio Network, and National Public Radio to comment on consumer behavior and marketing issues.

GREG W. MARSHALL

GREG W. MARSHALL, PhD, is the Charles Harwood Professor of Marketing and Strategy in the Crummer Graduate School of Business at Rollins College, Winter Park, Florida. Prior to joining Rollins, he served on the faculties of Oklahoma State University, the University of South Florida, and Texas Christian University. He earned a BSBA in Marketing and an MBA from the University of Tulsa, and a PhD in Marketing from Oklahoma State University. Professor Marshall's research interests center on issues surrounding sales force and sales manager performance, decision making by marketing managers, and intraorganizational relationships. He currently serves on the editorial boards of the *Journal of the Academy of Marketing Science, Journal of Business Research*, and *Industrial Marketing Management*, and he is editor of the *Journal of Marketing Theory and Practice* and former editor of the *Journal of Personal Selling & Sales Management*. Professor Marshall is President-Elect of the Academy of Marketing Science, Past-President of the American Marketing Association Academic Division, and a Fellow and Past-President of the Society for Marketing Advances. His industry experience prior to entering the academe includes product management, field sales management, and retail management positions with firms such as Warner-Lambert, the Mennen Company, and Target Corporation.

ELNORA W. STUART

ELNORA W. STUART, PhD, is Professor of Marketing at the University of South Carolina Upstate. Prior to joining USC Upstate in 2008, she was Professor of Marketing and the BP Egypt Oil Professor of Management Studies at the American University in Cairo, Professor of Marketing at Winthrop University in Rock Hill, South Carolina, and on the faculty of the University of South Carolina. She is also a regular visiting professor at Instituto de Empresa in Madrid, Spain. She earned a BA in Theatre/Speech from the University of North Carolina at Greensboro and both a Master of Arts in Journalism and Mass Communication, and a PhD in Marketing from the University of South Carolina. Professor Stuart's research has been published in major academic journals including the *Journal of Consumer Research, Journal of Advertising, Journal of Business Research*, and *Journal of Public Policy and Marketing*. For over 25 years she has served as a consultant for numerous businesses and not-for-profit organizations in the United States and in Egypt.

▶ Acknowledgments

We feature many talented marketers and successful companies in this book. In developing it, we also were fortunate to work with a team of exceptionally talented and creative people at Prentice Hall. Melissa Sabella, Executive Editor, was instrumental in helping us solidify the vision for the 6th edition, and her assistance with decisions about content, organization, features, and supplements was invaluable. Anne Fahlgren also contributed great ideas from a marketing perspective. Melissa Pellerano spearheaded the revision and deserves kudos for keeping us honest and on time while still managing to be nice about it, and Karin Williams's upbeat attitude and efficiency helped as well. Ana Jankowski did yeoman work to smoothly integrate all the pieces of this project into one book. Kelly Morrison of GEX worked with us patiently to produce the final product.

A special note of appreciation goes to Paul Borges of the Crummer Graduate School of Business at Rollins College for all his great work in helping assemble chapter materials to ensure this edition is as fresh and timely as possible.

No book is complete without a solid supplements package. We extend our thanks to our dedicated supplement authors who devoted their time and shared their teaching ideas.

Finally, our utmost thanks and appreciation go to our families for their continued support and encouragement. Without them this project would not be possible.

Many people worked to make this 6th edition a reality. The guidance and recommendations of the following professors and focus group participants helped us update and improve the chapters and the supplements:

REVIEWERS

Robert Cosenza, University of Mississippi
Brent Cunningham, Jacksonville State University
Kimberly D. Grantham, University of Georgia
Janice M. Karlen, LaGuardia Community College
Sandra J. Lakin, Hesser College
Timothy R Mittan, Southeast Community College
Jakki Mohr, University of Montana
Michael Munro, Florida International University
Jeff B. Murray, University of Arkansas
Mohammed Rawwas, University of Northern Iowa
Steven A. Taylor, Illinois State University
Sue Umashankar, University of Arizona
Mark Young, Winona State University

FOCUS GROUP PARTICIPANTS

Roy Adler, Pepperdine University
Gerald Athaide, Loyola College
Carole S. Arnone, Frostburg State University
Christopher Anicich, California State University- Fullerton
Nathan Austin, Morgan State University
Xenia Balabkins, Middlesex County College
Fred Beasley, Northern Kentucky University
Jas Bhangal, Chabot College
Silvia Borges, Miami Dade CC - Wolfson Campus
Tom Boyd, California State University- Fullerton
Henry C. Boyd III, University of Maryland-College Park
Val Calvert, San Antonio College
Richard Celsi, California State University-Long Beach
Swee-Lim Chia, LaSalle University
Paul Cohen, Florida Atlantic University
Brian Connett, California State University-Northridge
Patricia Doney, Florida Atlantic University
Rita Dynan, LaSalle University
Jill S. Dybus, Oakton Community College
Joyce Fairchild, Northern Virginia Community College
Joanne Frazier, Montgomery College

David Hansen, Texas Southern University
Manoj Hastak, American University
Dorothy Hetmer-Hinds, Trinity Valley Community College
Gary Hunter, Florida International University
Annette Jajko, Triton College
Gail Kirby, Santa Clara University
David Knuff, Oregon State University - Cascades
Kathleen Krentler, San Diego State University
Linda N. LaMarca, Tarleton State University
Freddy Lee, California State University-Sacramento
Ron Lennon, Barry University
Marilyn Liebrenz-Himes, George Washington University
Cesar Maloles, California State University-East Bay
Norton Marks, California State University-San Bernardino
Kelly Duggan Martin, Washington State University
Carolyn Massiah, University of Central Florida
Linda Morable, Richland College
Linda Newell, Saddleback College
Eric Newman, California State University-San Bernardino
David Oliver, Edison College
Beng Ong, California State University- Fresno
North Harris Montgomery Community College District–Cy-Fair College
Lucille Pointer, University of Houston- Downtown
Bruce Robertson, San Francisco State University
Leroy Robinson, University of Houston-Clear Lake
Barbara Rosenthal, Miami Dade Community College-Kendall Campus
Behrooz Saghafi, Chicago State University
Ritesh Saini, George Mason University
Marcianne Schusler, Prairie State College
Susan Silverstone, National University
Melissa St. James, California State University-Dominguez Hills
Frank Svestka, Loyola University of Chicago
James Swartz, California State Polytechnic University-Pomona
Kim Taylor, Florida International University-Park Campus
Steven Taylor, Illinois State University

Sal Veas, Santa Monica College
D. Roger Waller, San Joaquin Delta College
Kathleen Williamson, University of Houston-Clear Lake
Mary Wolfinbarger, California State University-Long Beach
Leatha Ware, Waubonsee Community College
Kim Wong, Albuquerque TVI Community College
Steve Wong, Rock Valley College
Richard Wozniak, Northern Illinois University
Mark Young, Winona State University
Marybeth Zipperer, Montgomery College

EXECUTIVES, PROFESSORS, AND STUDENTS

In addition to our reviewers and focus group participants, we want to extend our gratitude to the busy executives, professors, and students who gave generously of their time for the "Real People, Real Choices" features:

Executives Featured in "Real People, Real Choices" vignettes:

Chapter 1: Bill Bieberbach, Ron Jon Surf Shop Inc.
Chapter 2: Richard Pickering, SwapaCD.com
Chapter 3: Robert Chatwani, eBay
Chapter 4: Cindy Tungate, Plan-it Marketing
Chapter 5: Julie Cordua, (RED)
Chapter 6: Brad Tracy, NCR Corporation
Chapter 7: Tom Connerty, NutriSystems
Chapter 8: Palo Hawken, Bossa Nova Beverages
Chapter 9: Tom Petters, The Petters Group/Polaroid
Chapter 10: Lara Price, Philadelphia 76ers
Chapter 11: Danielle Blugrind, Taco Bell
Chapter 12: Walt Judas, Tourism Vancouver
Chapter 13: Joe Chernov, BzzAgent
Chapter 14: Jeffery Brechman, Woodtronics
Chapter 15: Jim Lawrence, Darden Restaurants
Chapter 16: Stan Clark, Eskimo Joe's

Faculty Featured in "Real People, Other Voices" boxes:

Robert A. Bergman, Lewis University
Koren Borges, University of North Florida
Deborah Boyce, State University of New York Institute of Technology
Gloria Cockerell, Collin County Community College
Emily Crawford, Savannah State University
Peter J. Gordon, Southeast Missouri State University
Janice M. Karlen, City University of New York, LaGuardia Community College
Debra A. Laverie, Texas Tech University
Freddy Su Jin Lee, California State University at Los Angeles
Vaidotas Lukošius, Tennessee State University
Lisa E. McCormick, Community College of Allegheny County
Mohan K. Menon, University of South Alabama
Linda K. Meyers, Baker College of Muskegon
Michael S. Munro, Florida International University
Eric Newman, California State University – San Bernardino
A.J. Otjen, Montana State University–Billings
Jeffery A. Periatt, Auburn University Montgomery
Rosemary Ramsey, Wright State University

Joseph F. Rocereto, Monmouth University
Henry H. Rodkin, DePaul University
Samuel A. Spralls III, Central Michigan University
Keith Starcher, Indiana Wesleyan University
David J. Urban, Virginia Commonwealth University
Ann Marie Vega, University of New Hampshire
Ted Wallin, Syracuse University
Wendy Wysocki, Monroe County Community College
Donna N. Yancey, University of North Alabama
Merv Yeagle, University of Maryland at College Park
Martha Zenns, Jamestown Community College

Students Featured in "Real People, Other Voices" boxes:

Brooke D. Bayer, Missouri State University
Devin Dadigan, Syracuse University
Kathleen Finlayson, San Diego State University
Peter Hodgson, Arizona State University
Dawn Hulsey, West Texas A&M University
Jordan Buck, Jamestown Community College
Michael Lee, Washington State University
Hollyanne Pronko, Saint Joseph's University
Laura Sutton, Berry College

REVIEWERS OF PREVIOUS EDITIONS

The following individuals were of immense help in reviewing all or part of previous editions of this book and the supplement package:

Ruth Clottey, Barry University
Robert M. Cosenza, Christian Brothers University
Elizabeth Ferrell, Southwestern Oklahoma State University
Jon Freiden, Florida State University
John Heinemann, Keller Graduate School of Management
Mark B. Houston, University of Missouri-Columbia
Jack E. Kant, San Juan College
Laura M. Milner, University of Alaska
John E. Robbins, Winthrop University
Kimberly A. Taylor, Florida International University
Susan L. Taylor, Belmont University
John Thanopoulos, University of Piraeus, Greece
Jane Boyd Thomas, Winthrop University
Judee A. Timm, Monterey Peninsula College
Steve Wedwick, Heartland Community College
Brent M. Wren, University of Alabama
Janice M. Karlen, LaGuardia Community College/City University of New York
Deborah Boyce, State University of New York Institute of Technology, Utica New York;
Merv Yeagle, University of Maryland at College Park
Freddy Su Jin Lee, California State University at Los Angeles;
Gloria Cockerell, Collin County Community College
Mike Gates, South Hills School of Business and Technology
A.J. Otjen, Montana State University-Billings;
Debra A. Laverie, Texas Tech University
Eric Newman, California State University-San Bernardino;
Robert A. Bergman, Lewis University
Samuel A. Spralls III, Central Michigan University

marketing 6E

real

people
choices

Chapter 1

Part 1 Make Marketing Value Decisions (Chapters 1, 2, 3)
Part 2 Understand Consumers' Value Needs (Chapters 4, 5, 6, 7)
Part 3 Create the Value Proposition (Chapters 8, 9, 10, 11)
Part 4 Communicate the Value Proposition (Chapters 12, 13, 14)
Part 5 Deliver the Value Proposition (Chapters 15, 16)

Welcome to the World of Marketing:

Create and Deliver Value

Bill
Bieberbach
Profile ▼

A **Decision Maker** at Ron Jon Surf Shop Inc.

Do you travel to Florida for spring break or like to visit a local beach during warm, sunny days? Then you probably bring along a chair, sunglasses, blanket—and, maybe a surfboard. There's a person behind the scenes who creates and markets these and other products that you buy. Let's meet one of these people.

Bill Bieberbach is Vice President of Corporate Development for Ron Jon, which operates stores in Florida, New Jersey, and California. The stores are familiar to many aspiring "beach bums" who flock to sunny vacation destinations. Bill's job includes looking at corporate expansion opportunities and strategic marketing, including market research and market analysis for all existing stores. After getting an MBA from Rollins College in Orlando, Bill started his career at Walt Disney World. Disney wanted an analyst who had a science background and business training to help ensure the massive theme park's financial and marketing success. In 1976, he went to Taft Broadcasting's amusement division as the Marketing and Planning Director. In this role, he learned a great deal about the amusement park industry and served as its spokesman for 18 months. In the early 1980s, Bill began consulting in the leisure-time industry and traveled the world working on a variety of projects from World's Fairs to the Olympics to events at Madison Square Garden. He came to Ron Jon in 1991 as a consultant on a one-year assignment, and he has been there ever since.

real people, **Real Choices**

Decision Time at Ron Jon Surf Shop

On average, more than 12,000 people visit a Ron Jon store every day, and more than 300,000 foreign tourists visit the company's Cocoa Beach and Orlando stores annually. The Ron Jon flagship store in Cocoa Beach, Florida, also known as The World's Most Famous Surf Shop, has been a tourist destination in the central Florida area for more than 40 years.

Still, Ron Jon's management began to detect a problem: The visitor market in central Florida is dominated by the large theme parks and by *Fortune* 500 companies. Disney, Universal, and Sea World are the three key Orlando visitor destinations. In 2005 more than 45 million people visited the central Florida market, making it the largest visitor market in the world. While these attractions have been a huge boon to the area, there is a downside: Over the past 20 years retailers outside the core Orlando destinations have seen declining attendance. Some of these secondary attractions have closed and/or dramatically reduced their operations. Because Cocoa Beach is 45 miles from Orlando, the store there has been affected by this overall trend. Although gross sales continued to show a modest increase, by 1998 the number of people coming to the flagship store was dropping. Bill knew that at some point the declining visitor counts would cause sales to decline. Ron Jon traditionally spends about 10 percent of its sales revenue on marketing, so a reduction in sales would, in turn, force the stores to trim their advertising and marketing expenses. These reductions might create a vicious cycle, as decreased advertising would depress sales even more.

Bill knew he had to get a better handle on the market and devise a way to boost attendance at the store. He decided to think more about how to get the Ron Jon message out to tourists when they first arrived in central Florida, so they would be more likely to include a stop in Cocoa Beach to visit the legendary store on their vacation itineraries. Of the 45 million tourists who descend on central Florida each year, 31 million come by car. Ron Jon already advertised extensively on highway billboards, using nearly 70 billboard locations in Florida and generating over 500 million advertising impressions per year because the boards are seen by 500 million people—though this number includes people who may see the boards more than once. Bill felt confident that Ron Jon was reaching motorists effectively. However, he realized that there are very few opportunities for the 13 million people arriving by air to see any Ron Jon advertising. He was particularly interested in reaching the most profitable segment that earlier research had identified as tourist families of four arriving from midwestern and northeastern states. Now, Bill had to figure out just how to advertise at airports to maximize Ron Jon's impact on these arriving passengers.

Things to remember:

The successful attractions in the Orlando area tend to draw visitors away from other locations such as Cocoa Beach where one of Ron Jon's big stores is located.

Companies need to think carefully about their customers before they make strategic decisions. It helps to conduct research with consumers whenever possible, as Ron Jon did when it tested the dioramas it placed in the Orlando Airport.

Bill considered his Options 1·2·3

Option 1
Focus advertising on rental cars by placing ads for Ron Jon on maps and mirror hangers. Of course, not all tourists arriving by air used rental cars, and renters would not be immersed with multiple impressions, which are preferable for maximum advertising impact.

Option 2
Advertise on dioramas. The Orlando airport offers advertisers a series of backlit photographs (called *dioramas*) that are wall-mounted at eye level for maximum impact. On the one hand, if Ron Jon purchased this advertising it would offer the promotional exposure Bill was seeking. On the other hand, arriving tourists may already have made their sightseeing plans, and Bill might be wasting a lot of money reaching people who already have their minds made up about whether they plan to visit the store while in Florida.

Option 3
Advertise on escalators. The Orlando airport has an arrival sequence that requires 85 to 90 percent of all visitors to descend a series of four escalator "gateways." If Ron Jon placed a series of posters/banners in these gateways, almost all air arrivals would be sure to see them. But escalators don't offer "long reads" for advertising messages, so the ads would have to make a really strong impact—and quickly—as tourists rode down toward the baggage claim. Also, the Airport Authority was not fully committed to this advertising and Ron Jon management thought it might not be available on a long-term basis. Now, put yourself in Bill Bieberbach's shoes: Which option would you choose, and why?

You Choose

Which **Option** would you choose, and **why**?
1. ☐YES ☐NO   **2.** ☐YES ☐NO   **3.** ☐YES ☐NO

See what **option** Bill chose and its success on **page 31** ⇒

3

1

OBJECTIVE

Understand who marketers are, where they work, and marketing's role in a firm.

(pp. 4–8)

Welcome to Brand You

I have a TV screen of some 32 inches
TV dinner and an easy chair
From where I view a disaster
And switch the channel fast
And thank my lucky star I wasn't there
The world's in a hurry but I don't have to worry
There's a movie on with a happy end
I've seen it before but I can see it some more
So I don't have to go out and pretend

Alex wakes up with a groan as the Heliacopters blare out a song from the next bedroom. Why does her roommate have to download these loud ringtones onto her cell phone and then leave it on so early in the morning? She throws back the Ralph Lauren sheets and rolls off of her new Sleep Number mattress. As Alex stumbles across the room in her VS Signature pajamas from Victoria's Secret, her senses are further assaulted as she catches wafts of Amanda's trademark Magic by Celine perfume. She pours herself a steaming cup of Starbucks Verona Blend coffee from the Capresso CoffeeTeam Luxe coffeemaker and stirs in a heaping mound of Splenda. As she starts to grab a Yoplait from the SubZero, she checks her BlackBerry and suddenly remembers: Big job interview with NCR Corporation today! Yeah for Monster.com! Good thing she IM'd her friends last night to get advice about what to wear so she won't have to think about it this morning. Alex does a quick scan of the *New York Times Online*, checks the forecast on weather.com, and for one last time Googles the executive who will be interviewing her. Hopefully he won't remember to check out her page on MySpace; those photos she posted from her trip to Sandals don't exactly communicate a professional image! Well, he'll be more impressed by the volunteer work she's doing with Sweatshopwatch.org to build a buzz about horrific labor conditions in developing countries. Just in case, she glances down at her wrist to be sure she's wearing her turquoise advocacy bracelet (which new cause was that for, anyway?).

Alex slips into her sleek new Ann Taylor suit, slides on her Prada shoes, grabs her Coach briefcase that was a graduation present from her parents, and climbs into her Scion. As she listens to the Coke ad blaring over the loudspeakers while she gasses up at the Exxon station, Alex finds herself looking forward to tomorrow. The pressure will be off, and she can put on the new casual outfit she picked up at Ron Jon (Pacific Legend Lani dress, Reef sandals, and Roxy Jagger shades). Then, it'll be out to that hot new bar to look for Mr. Right—or maybe a few Mr. Wrongs. Oh yes, and perhaps a quick check on Craigslist for a new roommate.

Marketing is all around us. Indeed, some might say we live in a branded world. Like Alex, you have encounters with many marketers even before you leave for the day: ads, products, TV, the Web, charitable causes, podcasts.

What's more, like Alex, *you* are a product. That may sound weird, but companies like Monster couldn't exist if you were not a product with

Check out chapter 1 **Study Map** on page 31

value. We're going to use that word a LOT in this book, so let's define it now: **Value** refers to the benefits a customer receives from buying a good or service.

You have "market value" as a person—you have qualities that set you apart from others and abilities other people want and need. After you finish this course, you'll have even more value because you'll know about the field of marketing and how this field relates to you both as a future businessperson *and* as a consumer. In addition to learning about how marketing influences each of us, you'll have a better understanding of what it means to be "Brand You"—and hopefully some ideas about what you can do to increase your value to employers and maybe even to society.

Although it may seem strange to think about the marketing of people, in reality we often talk about ourselves and others in marketing terms. It is common for us to speak of "positioning" ourselves for job interviews or to tell our friends not to "sell themselves short." Some people who are cruising for potential mates even refer to themselves as "being on the market." In addition, many consumers hire personal image consultants to devise a "marketing strategy" for them, while others undergo plastic surgery or makeovers to improve their "product images." The desire to package and promote ourselves is the reason for personal goods and services markets ranging from cosmetics and exercise equipment to resumé specialists and dating agencies.[1]

So, the principles of marketing apply to people, just as they apply to coffee, convertibles, and computer processors. Sure, there are differences in how we go about marketing each of these, but the general idea remains the same: Marketing is a fundamental part of our lives both as consumers and as players in the business world. We'll tell you why throughout this book. But first, we need to answer the basic questions of marketing: Who? Where? What? When? and Why? Let's start with Who and Where.

value
The benefits a customer receives from buying a good or service.

The *Who* and *Where* of Marketing

Marketers come from many different backgrounds. Although many have earned marketing degrees, others have backgrounds in areas such as engineering or agriculture. Retailers and fashion marketers may have training in merchandising or design. Advertising copywriters often have degrees in English. E-marketers who do business over the Internet may have studied computer science.

Marketers work in a variety of locations. They work in consumer goods companies such as Taco Bell or at service companies like Tourism Vancouver. You'll see them in retail organizations like Eskimo Joe's and at companies that manufacture products for other companies to use, like NCR Corporation. You'll see them at philanthropic companies like (RED) and at "buzz-building" public relations agencies like BzzAgent. We'll get to know these and other companies better as we make our way through this book.

And, although you may assume that the typical marketing job is in a large, consumer-oriented company like NutriSystem, marketers work in other types of organizations too. There are many exciting marketing careers in companies that sell to other businesses. In small organizations, one person (perhaps the owner) may handle all the marketing responsibilities. In large organizations, marketers work on different aspects of the marketing strategy.

No matter where they work, all marketers are real people who make choices that affect themselves, their companies, and very often thousands or even millions of consumers. At the beginning of each chapter, we'll introduce you to marketing professionals like Bill Bieberbach in a feature we call "Real People, Real Choices." We'll tell you about a decision the marketer had to make and give you the possible options he considered. Think about these options as you read through the chapter so you can build an argument for selecting an option. We'll share some other people's opinions about the featured marketer's decision in a feature we call "Real People, Other Voices"—you'll see these views pop up throughout the chapter. At the end of each chapter, we'll tell you what option the marketer chose and why in a feature called "Real People, Real Choices: How It Worked Out."

Marketing's Role in the Firm: Working Cross-Functionally

What role do marketers play in a firm? The importance organizations assign to marketing activities varies a lot. Top management in some firms is very marketing-oriented (especially when the chief executive officer comes from the marketing ranks), whereas in other companies marketing is an afterthought. However, analysts estimate that at least one-third of CEOs come from a marketing background—so stick with us!

Sometimes a company uses the term *marketing* when what it really means is sales or advertising. In some organizations, particularly small, not-for-profit ones, there may be no one in the company specifically designated as "the marketing person." In contrast, some firms realize that marketing applies to all aspects of the firm's activities. As a result, there has been a trend toward integrating marketing with other business functions (such as management and accounting) instead of making it a separate function.

No matter what size the firm, a marketer's decisions affect—and are affected by—the firm's other operations. Marketing managers must work with financial and accounting officers to figure out whether products are profitable, to set marketing budgets, and to determine prices. They must work with people in manufacturing to be sure that products are produced on time and in the right quantities. Marketers also must work with research-and-development specialists to create products that meet consumers' needs.

Where Do *You* Fit In? Careers in Marketing

Marketing is an incredibly exciting, diverse discipline brimming with opportunities. There are many paths to a marketing career; we've tried to summarize the most typical ones here. Check out Table 1.1 to start thinking about which path might be best for you.

Okay, now that you've gotten a glimpse of who marketers are and where they work, it's time to dig into what marketing really is.

Emily
Crawford

a professor at Savannah State University

My Advice for Ron Jon Surf Shop would be to choose

Option

real people, **Other Voices**

Option 1 is the best choice. Consumers who rent cars are both business-to-business and travel-oriented. These consumers are

not only looking for their destinations but interesting places to visit. This advertising strategy will bring awareness of an attraction that a car renter may not have noticed in the past. The placement of the ad on maps and mirror hangers could act as a reinforcement of billboard ads that they may see as they drive through the city. I feel that the rental car consumer is a captive audience for this type of advertising strategy. ➤

Table 1.1 | Careers in Marketing

Marketing Field	Where Can I Work?	What Entry-Level Position Can I Get?	What Course Work Do I Need?
Advertising	**Advertising agency:** Media, research, and creative departments; account work **Large corporation:** Advertising department: brand/product management **Media:** Magazine, newspaper, radio, and television selling; management consulting; marketing research	Account coordinator (traffic department); assistant account executive; assistant media buyer; research assistant; assistant brand manager	Undergraduate business degree
Brand Management	**Any size corporation:** Coordinate the activities of specialists in production, sales, advertising, promotion, R&D, marketing research, purchasing, distribution, package development, and finance	Associate brand manager	MBA preferred, but a few companies recruit undergraduates; expect a sales training program in the field from one to four months and in-house classes and seminars
Business-to-Business Marketing	**Any size corporation:** Only a few companies recruit on campus, so be prepared to search out job opportunities on your own, as well as interview on campus.	Sales representative; market research administrator; product manager; pricing administrator; product administrator; assistant marketing manager; sales administrator; assistant sales manager; sales service administrator	Undergraduate business degree. A broad background of subjects is generally better than concentrating on just one area. A technical degree may be important or even required in high-technology areas. Courses in industrial marketing and marketing strategy are very helpful.
Direct–Response Marketing	**Any size corporation:** Marketing-oriented firms, including those offering consumer goods, industrial products, financial institutions, and other types of service establishments; entrepreneurs seeking to enter business for themselves	Direct-response marketing is expanding rapidly and includes direct mail; print and broadcast media, telephone marketing, catalogues, in-home presentations, and door-to-door marketing. Seek counsel from officers and directors of the Direct Marketing Association and the Direct Selling Association	Undergraduate business degree. Supplemental work in communications, psychology, and/or computer systems is recommended.
Supply-Channel Management	**Any size corporation, including transportation corporations:** The analysis, planning, and control of activities concerned with the procurement and distribution of goods; the activities include transportation, warehousing, forecasting, order processing, inventory control, production planning, site selection, and customer service	Physical distribution manager; supply chain manager; inventory-control manager; traffic manager; distribution-center manager; distribution-planning analyst; customer service manager; transportation marketing and operations manager	Undergraduate business degree and MBA; broad background in the core functional areas of business, with particular emphasis in distribution related topics such as logistics, transportation, purchasing, and negotiation
International Marketing	**Large corporations:** Marketing Department at corporate headquarters	Domestic sales position with an international firm may be the best first step toward international opportunities.	MBA; A broad background in marketing is recommended, with some emphasis on sales management and market research.

(continues on the next page)

Marketing Field	Where Can I Work?	What Entry-Level Position Can I Get?	What Course Work Do I Need?
Marketing Models and Systems Analysis	**Large corporations:** Consult with managers who are having difficulty with marketing problems	Undergraduate: Few positions available unless you have prior work experience; graduate: market analyst, market research specialist, and management scientist	MBA; Preparation in statistics, mathematics, and the behavioral sciences
Marketing Research	**Any size corporation:** Provide management with information about consumers, the marketing environment, and the competition	Assistant market analyst or assistant product analyst level	MBA or an MS in Marketing Research although prior experience and training may improve an undergraduate's chances
New Product Planning	**Any size corporation:** Marketing of consumer products, consumer industries, advertising agencies, consulting firms, public agencies, medical agencies, retailing management	Assistant manager or director of product planning or new product development	MBA
Retail Management	**Retail corporations**	Assistant buyer positions; department manager positions	Undergraduate business degree
Sales and Sales Management	**Profit and nonprofit organizations:** Financial, insurance, consulting, and government	Trade sales representative who sells to a wholesaler or retailer; missionary sales representative in manufacturing who sells to retailers or decision makers (e.g., pharmaceutical representative); technical sales representative who sells to specified accounts within a designated geographic area	Undergraduate business degree; MBA; *Helpful courses:* consumer behavior, psychology, sociology, economics, anthropology, cost accounting, computer science, statistical analysis, communications, drama, creative writing; language courses, if you're interested in international marketing; engineering or physical science courses if you're interested in technical selling
Services Marketing	**Any size corporation:** Banking and financial service institutions, health care organizations, leisure-oriented businesses, and in various other service settings	Assistant brand manager; assistant sales manager	Undergraduate business degree; MBA; Additional course work in management policy, research, advertising and promotion, quantitative analysis, consumer behavior, and the behavioral sciences should prove useful

Source: This information was adapted from an excellent compilation prepared by the Marketing faculty of the Marshall School of Business, University of Southern California at **www.marshall.use.edu/web/marketing.cfm?doc_id=2890** (accessed May 8, 2006). For recent salary figures broken down by job type and region, visit the Aquent/AMA Compensation Survey of Marketing Professionals 2006 at **www.marketingsalaries.com/aquent/Home.form**.

2

OBJECTIVE

Explain what marketing is and how it provides value to everyone involved in the marketing process.

(pp. 8–11)

The Value of Marketing

marketing
The activity, set of institutions, and processes for creating, communicating, delivering and exchanging offerings that have value for customers, clients, partners, and society at large.

Marketing. Lots of people talk about it, but what is it? When you ask people to define **marketing**, you get many answers. Some people say, "That's what happens when a pushy salesman tries to sell me something I don't want." Other people say, "Oh, that's simple—TV commercials." Students might answer, "That's a course I have to take before I can get my business degree." Each of these responses has a grain of truth in it, but the official definition of marketing the American Marketing Association adopted in late 2007 is as follows:

"Marketing is the activity, set of institutions, and processes for creating, communicating, delivering and exchanging offerings that have value for customers, clients, partners, and society at large."[2]

The basic idea of this somewhat complicated definition is that marketing is all about delivering value to everyone who is affected by a transaction. Let's take a closer look at some of the different ideas related to this definition.

Marketing Is about Meeting Needs

One important part of our definition of marketing is that it is about meeting the needs of diverse stakeholders. The term **stakeholders** here refers to buyers, sellers, or investors in a company, community residents, and even citizens of the nations where goods and services are made or sold—in other words, any person or organization that has a "stake" in the outcome. Thus, marketing is about satisfying everyone involved in the marketing process.

One important stakeholder is you. A **consumer** is the ultimate user of a good or service. Consumers can be individuals or organizations, whether a company, government, sorority, or charity. We like to say that the consumer is king (or queen), but it's important not to lose sight of the fact that the seller also has needs—to make a profit, to remain in business, and even to take pride in selling the highest-quality products possible. Products are sold to satisfy both consumers' and marketers' needs—it's a two-way street. When you strip away the big words, try this as a bumper sticker: *Marketers do it to satisfy needs*.

Most successful firms today practice the **marketing concept**—that is, marketers first identify consumer needs and then provide products that satisfy those needs, ensuring the firm's long-term profitability. A **need** is the difference between a consumer's actual state and some ideal or desired state. When the difference is big enough, the consumer is motivated to take action to satisfy the need. When you're hungry, you buy a snack. If you're not happy with your hair, you get a new hairstyle. When you need a job (or perhaps just get mad at your boss), you check out linkedin.com.

Needs relate to physical functions (such as eating) or to psychological ones (such as wanting to look good). Levi Strauss & Company is one company that tries to meet the psychological needs of consumers to look good (as well as their basic need to be clothed). The company's research indicates that people wear Levi's jeans to say important things about themselves and their desired image. From time to time, the company even receives a beat-up, handed-down pair in the mail, with a letter from the owner requesting that the jeans be given a proper burial—that's a pretty "deep-seated" attachment to a pair of pants![3] The specific way a person satisfies a need depends on his unique history, learning experiences, and cultural environment.

A **want** is a desire for a particular product we use to satisfy a need in specific ways that are culturally and socially influenced. For example, two classmates' stomachs rumble during a lunchtime lecture, and both need food. However, how each person satisfies this need might be quite different. The first student may be a health nut who fantasizes about gulping down a big handful of trail mix, while the second person may be enticed by a greasy cheeseburger and fries. The first student's want is trail mix, whereas the second student's want is fast food (and some antacid for dessert).

A product delivers a **benefit** when it satisfies a need or want. For marketers to be successful, they must develop products that provide one or more benefits that are important to consumers. The challenge is to identify what benefits people look for and then develop a product that delivers those benefits while also convincing consumers that their product is better than a competitor's product—making the choice of which product to buy obvious. As the late management guru Peter Drucker observed, "The aim of marketing is to make selling superfluous."[4]

Everyone can want your product, but that doesn't ensure sales unless consumers have the means to obtain it. When you couple desire with the buying power or resources to satisfy a want, the result is **demand**. So, the potential customers looking for a snappy, red

---

stakeholders
Buyers, sellers, or investors in a company, community residents, and even citizens of the nations where goods and services are made or sold—in other words, any person or organization that has a "stake" in the outcome.

consumer
The ultimate user of a good or service.

marketing concept
A management orientation that focuses on identifying and satisfying consumer needs to ensure the organization's long-term profitability.

need
The recognition of any difference between a consumer's actual state and some ideal or desired state.

Bill
Bieberbach
APPLYING Needs

Bill knows that Ron Jon's success depends on its ability to meet consumers' intangible needs for status and being "cool" in addition to their tangible needs for sun block and durable swimwear.

want
The desire to satisfy needs in specific ways that are culturally and socially influenced.

benefit
The outcome sought by a customer that motivates buying behavior—that satisfies a need or want.

demand
Customers' desires for products coupled with the resources needed to obtain them.

Marketers create value for society when they help to promote worthy causes.

market
All the customers and potential customers who share a common need that can be satisfied by a specific product, who have the resources to exchange for it, who are willing to make the exchange, and who have the authority to make the exchange.

marketplace
Any location or medium used to conduct an exchange.

utility
The usefulness or benefit consumers receive from a product.

BMW convertible are the people who want the car minus those who can't afford to buy or lease one (no, stealing the car doesn't count). A **market** consists of all the consumers who share a common need that can be satisfied by a specific product and who have the resources, willingness, and authority to make the purchase.

A *marketplace* used to be a location where buying and selling occurs face to face. In today's "wired" world, however, buyers and sellers might not even see each other. The modern **marketplace** may take the form of a glitzy shopping mall, a mail-order catalog, a television shopping network, an eBay auction, or an e-commerce Web site. In developing countries, the marketplace may be a street corner or an open-air market where people sell fruits and vegetables much as they did thousands of years ago. Indeed, a marketplace may not even exist in the physical world—as players of on-line games will tell you. Residents of cyberworlds like *The Sims*, *Second Life*, and *Project Entropia* buy and sell virtual real estate—with real money. One Project Entropia player recently paid $100,000 (that's in real dollars) for a space resort he calls Club Neverdie. He plans to develop the station's facilities and sell condos for game dollars, which the project's developer converts into U.S. dollars at a 10:1 exchange rate.[5]

Marketing Is about Creating Utility

Marketing activities play a major role in creating **utility**, which refers to the sum of the benefits we receive when we use a good or service. By working to ensure that people have the type of product they want, where and when they want it, the marketing system makes our lives easier. Utility is what creates value. Marketing processes create several different kinds of utility to provide value to consumers:

- *Form utility* is the benefit marketing provides by transforming raw materials into finished products, as when a dress manufacturer combines silk, thread, and zippers to create a bridesmaid's gown.

- *Place utility* is the benefit marketing provides by making products available where customers want them. The most sophisticated evening gown sewn in New York's garment district is of little use to a bridesmaid in Kansas City if it isn't shipped to her in time.

- *Time utility* is the benefit marketing provides by storing products until they are needed. Some women rent their wedding gowns instead of buying them and wearing them only once (they hope!).

A marketplace can take many forms, such as a traditional bazaar or an upscale mall.

- *Possession utility* is the benefit marketing provides by allowing the consumer to own, use, and enjoy the product. The bridal store provides access to a range of styles and colors that would not be available to a woman outfitting a bridal party on her own.

As we've seen, marketers provide utility in many ways. Now, let's see how customers "take delivery" of this added value.

Marketing Is about Exchange Relationships

At the heart of every marketing act—big or small—is something we refer to as an "exchange relationship." An **exchange** occurs when a person gives something and gets something else in return. The buyer receives an object, service, or idea that satisfies a need and the seller receives something he feels is of equivalent value.

For an exchange to occur, at least two people or organizations must be willing to make a trade, and each must have something the other wants. Both parties must agree on the value of the exchange and how it will be carried out. Each party also must be free to accept or reject the other's terms for the exchange. Under these conditions, a gun-wielding robber's offer to "exchange" your money for your life does not constitute a valid exchange. In contrast, although someone may complain that a store's prices are "highway robbery," an exchange occurs if he still forks over the money to buy something there—even if he still grumbles about it weeks later.

To complicate things a bit more, everyone does not always agree on the terms of the exchange. Think, for example, about *music piracy*, which is a huge headache for music labels. On the one hand, they claim that they lose billions of dollars a year when consumers download songs without paying for them. On the other hand, a lot of people who engage in this practice don't feel that they are participating in an unfair exchange that deprives manufacturers of the value of their products. They argue that music piracy is the fault of record companies that charge way too much for new songs. What do you think?

The debate over music downloading reminds us that an agreed upon transfer of value must occur for an exchange to take place. A politician can agree to work toward certain goals in exchange for your vote, or a minister can offer you salvation in return for your faith. Today, most exchanges occur as a monetary transaction in which currency (in the form of cash, check, or credit card) is surrendered in return for a good or a service. Some transactions today even take the form of *virtual* exchanges—as when players of on-line games like *Second Life* "buy" property using currency the game maker issues!

Some transactions today, like those on the on-line game *Second Life*, are virtual exchanges.

exchange
The process by which some transfer of value occurs between a buyer and a seller.

When Did Marketing Begin?
The Evolution of a Concept

OBJECTIVE
Explain the evolution of the marketing concept.
(pp. 11–16)

Now that we have an idea of how the marketing process works, let's take a step back and see how this process worked (or didn't work) in "the old days." Although it sounds like good old common sense to us, believe it or not the notion that businesses and other organizations succeed when they satisfy customers' needs actually is a pretty recent idea. Before the 1950s, marketing was basically a means of making production more efficient. Let's take a quick look at how the marketing discipline has developed. Table 1.2 tells us about some of the more recent events in this marketing history.

Table 1.2 | Marketing History

Year	Marketing Event
1955	Ray Kroc opens his first McDonald's.
1956	Lever Brothers launches Wisk, America's first liquid laundry detergent.
1957	Ford rolls out Edsel, loses more than $250 million in two years.
1959	Mattel introduces Barbie.
1960	The FDA approves Searle's Enovid as the first oral contraceptive.
1961	Procter & Gamble launches Pampers.
1962	Wal-Mart, Kmart, Target, and Woolco open their doors.
1963	The Pepsi Generation kicks off the cola wars.
1964	Blue Ribbon Sports (now known as Nike) ships its first shoes.
1965	Donald Fisher opens The Gap, a jeans-only store in San Francisco.
1971	Cigarette advertising is banned on radio and television.
1973	Federal Express begins overnight delivery services.
1976	Sol Price opens the first warehouse club store in San Diego.
1980	Ted Turner creates CNN.
1981	MTV begins.
1982	Gannett launches *USA Today*.
1983	Chrysler introduces minivans.
1984	Apple Computer introduces the Macintosh.
1985	New Coke is launched; Old Coke is brought back 79 days later.
1990	Saturn, GM's first new car division since 1919, rolls out its first car.
1993	Phillip Morris reduces price of Marlboros by 40 cents a pack and loses $13.4 billion in stock market value in one day.
1994	In the largest switch in ad history, IBM yanks its business from scores of agencies worldwide and hands its entire account to Ogilvy & Mather.
1995	eBay goes on-line as an experimental auction service.
1997	McDonald's gives away Teenie Beanie Babies with Happy Meals. Consumer response is so overwhelming that McDonald's is forced to take out ads apologizing for its inability to meet demand. Nearly 100 million Happy Meals are sold during the promotion.[a]
1998	Germany's Daimler-Benz acquires America's Chrysler Corporation for more than $38 billion in stock to create a new global automaking giant called Daimler-Chrysler.[b]
2003	Amazon debuts its "Search Inside the Book" feature that allows you to search the full text of more than 33 million pages from over 120,000 printed books.
2004	On-line sales in the United States top $100 billion.[c]
2007	About 30 open source companies were purchased for more than $1 billion.[d]
2008	MySpace boasts over 225 million members worldwide. [d]

Sources: Patricia Sellers, "To Avoid Trampling, Get Ahead of the Mass," 1994, except as noted.[a] Tod Taylor, "The Beanie Factor," *Brandweek*, June 16, 1997, 22–27.[b] Jennifer Laabs, "Daimler-Benz and Chrysler: A Merger of Global HR Proportions," *Workforce*, July 1998, 13.[c] Keith Regan, "Report: Online Sales Top $100 Billion," *E-Commerce Times*, June 1, 2004, **www.ecommercetimes.com/story/34148.html**.[d] Frank Rose, "Wired Business Trends 2008," *Wired* **http://www.wired.com/techbiz/it/magazine/16-04/bz_opensource**, December 2007.

The Production Era

Many people say that Henry Ford's Model T changed America forever. Even from the start in 1908, when the "Tin Lizzie," or "flivver" as the T was known, sold for $825, Henry Ford continued to make improvements in production. By 1912, Ford got so efficient that the car sold for $575, a price even the Ford employees who made the car could afford.[6] As the price continued to drop, Ford sold even more flivvers. By 1921, the Model T Ford had 60 percent of the new-car market. In 1924, the ten-millionth Model T rolled off the assembly line. The Model T story is perhaps the most well-known and most successful example of an organization that focuses on the most efficient production and distribution of products.

Ford's focus illustrates a **production orientation**, which works best in a seller's market when demand is greater than supply because it focuses on the most efficient ways to produce and distribute products. Essentially, consumers have to take whatever is available—there weren't a whole lot of other Tin Lizzies competing for drivers in the 1920s. Under these conditions, marketing plays a relatively insignificant role—the goods literally sell themselves because people have no other choices. In the former Soviet Union, the centralized government set production quotas, and weary shoppers lined up (often for hours) to purchase whatever happened to be on a store's shelves at the time.

Firms that focus on a production orientation tend to view the market as a homogeneous group that will be satisfied with the basic function of a product. Sometimes this view is too narrow. For example, Procter & Gamble's Ivory soap has been in decline for some time because the company viewed the brand as plain old soap, not as a cleansing product that could provide other benefits as well. Ivory soap lost business to newer deodorant and "beauty" soaps containing cold cream that "cleaned up" in this market.[7]

The Sales Era

When product availability exceeds demand in a buyer's market, businesses may engage in the "hard sell" in which salespeople aggressively push their wares. During the Great Depression in the 1930s, when money was scarce for most people, firms shifted their focus from a product orientation to moving their goods in any way they could.

This **selling orientation** means that management views marketing as a sales function, or a way to move products out of warehouses so that inventories don't pile up. The selling orientation gained in popularity after World War II. During the war, the United States dramatically increased its industrial capacity to manufacture tanks, combat boots, parachutes, and countless other wartime goods. After the war, this industrial capacity was converted to producing consumer goods.

Consumers eagerly bought all the things they couldn't get during the war years, but once they satisfied these initial needs and wants they got more selective. The race for consumers' hearts and pocketbooks was on. The selling orientation prevailed well into the 1950s. But consumers as a rule don't like to be pushed, and the hard sell gave marketing a bad image.

Companies that still follow a selling orientation tend to be more successful at making one-time sales rather than at building repeat business. We are most likely to find this focus among companies that sell *unsought goods*—products that people don't tend to buy without some prodding. For example, most of us aren't exactly "dying" to shop for cemetery plots, so some encouragement may be necessary to splurge on a final resting place.

The Relationship Era

At Direct Tire Sales in Watertown, Massachusetts, customers discover an unusual sight: The customer lounge is clean, there is free coffee with fresh cream and croissants, employees wear ties, and the company will even pay your cab fare home if your car isn't ready on time. People don't mind paying 10 to 15 percent more for these extra services.[8] Direct Tire Sales has found that it pays to have a **consumer orientation** that satisfies customers' needs and wants.

As the world's most successful firms began to adopt a consumer orientation, marketers had a way to outdo the competition—and marketing's importance was also elevated in the firm. Marketers did research to understand the needs of different consumers, assisted in tailoring products to the needs of these various groups, and did an even better job of designing marketing messages than in the days of the selling orientation.

The marketing world was humming along nicely, but then inflation in the 1970s and recession in the 1980s took their toll on company profits. The marketing concept needed a boost. Firms had to do more than meet consumers' needs—they had to do this better than the competition and do it repeatedly. They increasingly concentrated on improving the quality of their products. By the early 1990s, many in the marketing community followed an approach termed **Total Quality Management (TQM)**. The TQM perspective

production orientation
A management philosophy that emphasizes the most efficient ways to produce and distribute products.

selling orientation
A managerial view of marketing as a sales function, or a way to move products out of warehouses to reduce inventory.

consumer orientation
A management philosophy that focuses on ways to satisfy customers' needs and wants.

Total Quality Management (TQM)
A management philosophy that involves all employees from the assembly line onward in continuous product quality improvement.

Girls who enter the Stardoll virtual world create fashion designs and see what they look like on their favorite celebrities.

instapreneur
A business person who only produces a product when it is ordered.

triple bottom line orientation
A business orientation that looks at financial profits, the community in which the organization operates, and creating sustainable business practices.

takes many forms, but essentially it's a management philosophy that involves all employees from the assembly line onward in continuous product quality improvement.

Indeed, rapid improvements in manufacturing processes give forward-thinking firms—even small ones—a huge edge in the marketplace because they are more nimble and thus able to create products consumers want when they want them and at the price they want. One way they do is to manufacture *on demand*—this means that they don't actually produce a product until a customer orders it. The Japanese pioneered this idea with their *just-in-time model* that we'll learn more about in Chapter 15. Today, however, even small mom and pop companies can compete in this space. Technology is creating a new class of business person that we call an **instapreneur**. All you need is a design; even amateurs can produce jewelry, T-shirts, furniture, and indeed almost anything we can imagine. They don't have to pay to store their inventory in huge warehouses and they don't need any money down. For example, the German firm Spreadshirt hosts 500,000 individual T-shirt shops. You see a design you like, place an order and bam—it gets produced and sent to your door.[9] Spreadshirt even partnered in 2008 with Stardoll, a Swedish virtual world that lets girls create fashion designs and see what they look like on virtual celebrities. Now, they can actually transfer their own designs to the real world.

The Triple Bottom Line: Make Money <u>and</u> a Contribution

Over time, many forward-thinking organizations began to see their commitment to quality even more intensely than "just" satisfying consumers' needs during a single transaction. A few realized that making monetary profit is important—but there's more to think about than just the financial bottom line. Instead, they began to focus on **a triple bottom line orientation** that meant building long-term bonds with customers rather than merely selling them stuff today.[10] This new way of looking at business emphasizes the need to maximize three components:

1. *The financial bottom line*: Financial profits to stakeholders

2. *The social bottom line*: Contributing to the communities in which the company operates

3. *The environmental bottom line*: Creating sustainable business practices that minimize damage to the environment or that even improve it

Is it possible to contribute in a positive way to society and the earth and still contribute to your paycheck? Take a look at the German conglomerate Siemens to see how. The industrial giant has seen its share price triple in the past five years, partly due to strong sales of energy-saving LED lights and wind turbines.[11] There's gold in green products.

One outgrowth of this new way of thinking was the concept of **customer relationship management (CRM)**, which involves systematically tracking consumers' preferences and behaviors over time in order to tailor

RUBBISH CAN BE RECYCLED. NATURE CANNOT.

Marketing messages like this Romanian one for the World Wildlife Fund focus on the environmental bottom line.

the value proposition as closely as possible to each individual's unique wants and needs. With the advent of the Internet, a CRM approach got a lot easier to implement as more and more firms started to rely heavily on the Web to connect with consumers. The Internet provides the ultimate opportunity for implementation of the marketing concept because it allows a firm to personalize its messages and products to better meet the needs of each individual consumer. More on this in Chapter 12.

Although dot-com companies took a beating in the marketplace, many analysts believe that this is just a preliminary shakeout—the heyday of the Internet is yet to come. More recent success stories like Google, MySpace, and **Flickr** seem to be proving analysts right. Indeed, some marketing analysts suggest that the Internet has created a *paradigm shift* for business, meaning that companies must adhere to a new model or pattern of how to profit in a wired world. They argue that we are moving toward an *attention economy*, one in which a company's success will be measured by its share of mind rather than share of market.

This means that companies must find new and innovative ways to stand out from the crowd and become an integral part of consumers' lives rather than just being a dry company that makes and sells products. For example, major consumer packaged foods companies are drawing many more customers to their Web sites than in the past. More important, the sites are "sticky," meaning that they tend to keep visitors long enough to make a lasting impression on them and motivate people to keep coming back for more.

How are they doing this? Instead of following their old strategy of simply offering product information and recipes on-line, they now offer games, contests, and other promotions that transform their Web sites into less of a grocery store and more of a carnival. For example, about a third of the people who visit Kraft's Candystand.com site, which promotes products like Lifesavers and Planters nuts, return to it again. They come back to play games like Nut Vendor, where the player assumes the role of a ballpark peanut hawker. Candystand, like other sites, gathers customers' e-mail addresses as they register for sweepstakes, and then lures them back with offers of new recipes, games, and products.[12]

Another result of this new way of long-term thinking is the **social marketing concept**, which maintains that marketers must satisfy customers' needs in ways that also benefit society while still delivering a profit to the firm. This perspective is even more important since the terrorist attacks of 2001, which led many people and firms to reexamine their values and redouble their commitments to community and country.

Many big and small firms alike practice this philosophy. Their efforts include satisfying society's environmental and social needs for a cleaner, safer environment by developing recyclable packaging, adding extra safety features such as car air bags, voluntarily modifying a manufacturing process to reduce pollution, and sponsoring campaigns to address social problems.

An important trend now is for companies to think of ways to design and manufacture products with a focus on **sustainability**, which we define as "meeting present needs without compromising the ability of future generations to meet their needs."[13] For example, the Sheraton Rittenhouse Square Hotel in Philadelphia incorporates "sustainable design" on a grand scale within an opulent setting. The hotel uses materials and finishes, such as a cut glass front desk that is 100 percent recycled and organic cotton bedding, to combine comfort with environmental responsibility. Avon Products is another firm that believes social marketing is good for its customers and good for the company. For over 10 years, Avon has supported one and only one cause: breast cancer. Since the inception of the program in 1993, Avon has raised over $400 million for breast cancer programs through a variety of fund-raising

Concerns about the environment are a driving force behind many current marketing efforts.

customer relationship management (CRM)
A strategy that involves systematically tracking consumers' preferences and behaviors over time in order to tailor the value proposition as closely as possible to each individual's unique wants and needs.

social marketing concept
A management philosophy that marketers must satisfy customers' needs in ways that also benefit society and also deliver profit to the firm.

sustainability
A product design focus that seeks to create products that meet present consumer needs without compromising the ability of future generations to meet their needs.

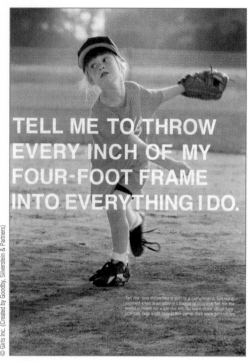

Organizations like Girls Inc. practice social marketing to promote worthwhile causes.

return on investment (ROI)
The direct financial impact of a firm's expenditure of a resource such as time or money.

popular culture
The music, movies, sports, books, celebrities, and other forms of entertainment consumed by the mass market.

4

OBJECTIVE

Understand the range of services and goods that organizations market.

(pp. 16–19)

channels. These efforts include Avon's "3-Day" event, a long-distance walking event in San Francisco, Boston, Atlanta, Chicago, Los Angeles, and New York.[14]

In addition to building long-term relationships and focusing on social responsibility, triple bottom line firms place a much greater focus on *accountability*—measuring just how much value marketing activities create. This means that marketers at these organizations ask hard questions about the true value of their efforts and their impact on the bottom line. These questions all boil down to the simple acronym of **ROI (return on investment)**. Marketers now realize that if they want to assess just how much value they are creating for the firm, they need to know exactly what they are spending and what the concrete results of their actions are.

However, it's not always so easy to assess the value of marketing activities. Many times managers state their marketing objectives using vague phrases like "increase awareness of our product" or "encourage people to eat healthier snacks." These goals are important, but their lack of specificity makes it pretty much impossible for senior management to determine marketing's true impact. Because management may view these efforts as costs rather than investments, marketing activities often are among the first to be cut out of a firm's budget. To win continued support for what they do (and sometimes to keep their jobs), marketers in triple bottom line firms do their best to prove to management that they are generating measurable value by aligning marketing activities with the firm's overall business objectives.[15]

What Can Be Marketed?

Marketers' creations surround us. It seems that everywhere we turn we get bombarded by advertisements, stores, and products that compete fiercely and loudly for our attention and our dollars. Marketers filter much of what we learn about the world, such as when we see images of rich or beautiful people on television commercials or magazines. Ads show us how we should act and what we should own. Marketing's influence extends from "serious" goods and services such as health care to "fun" things such as extreme skateboarding equipment and hip-hop music (though many people take these products as seriously as their health).

From Peas to P. Diddy

Popular culture consists of the music, movies, sports, books, celebrities, and other forms of entertainment that the mass market consumes. The relationship between marketing and popular culture is a two-way street. The goods and services that are popular at any point in time often mirror changes in the larger society. Consider, for example, some U.S. products that reflected underlying cultural changes at the time they were introduced:

- The TV dinner signaled changes in family structure, such as a movement away from the traditional family dinner hour filled with conversation about the day's events.

- Cosmetics made of natural materials and not tested on animals reflected social concerns about pollution and animal rights.

- Condoms marketed in pastel carrying cases intended for female buyers signaled changing attitudes toward sexual responsibility.

As this ad from Thailand demonstrates, virtually anything from dog food to adopting a dog can be marketed.

Marketing messages often communicate **myths**, stories containing symbolic elements that express the shared emotions and ideals of a culture. Consider, for example, how McDonald's takes on mythical qualities. To some, the golden arches are virtually synonymous with American culture.[16] These familiar structures offer sanctuary to Americans in foreign lands who are grateful to know exactly what to expect once they enter. Basic struggles of good versus evil play out in the fantasy world of McDonald's advertising, as when Ronald McDonald confounds the Hamburglar. McDonald's even runs Hamburger University, where fast-food majors learn how to make the perfect burger.

Is there any limit to what marketers can market? Marketing applies to more than just canned peas or cola drinks. Some of the best marketers come from the ranks of services companies such as American Express or not-for-profit organizations such as Greenpeace. Politicians, athletes, and performers use marketing to their advantage (just think about that $30 T-shirt you may have bought at a baseball game or rock concert). Ideas such as political systems (democracy, totalitarianism), religion (Christianity, Islam), and art (realism, abstract) also compete for acceptance in a "marketplace." In this book, we'll refer to any good, service, or idea that can be marketed as a **product**, even though what you're buying may not take a physical form.

The people we see on mass media influence our expectations about reality.

Consumer Goods and Services

Consumer goods are the tangible products that individual consumers purchase for personal or family use. **Services** are intangible products that we pay for and use but never own. Service transactions contribute on average more than 60 percent to the gross national product of all industrialized nations. Marketers need to understand the special challenges that arise when marketing an intangible service rather than a tangible good.[17]

In both cases, though, keep in mind that the consumer looks to obtain some underlying value, such as convenience, security, or status, from a marketing exchange. That value can come from a variety of competing goods and services, even those that don't resemble one another on the surface. For example, a new CD and a ticket to a local concert may cost about the same, and each may provide the benefit of musical enjoyment, so consumers often have to choose among competing alternatives if they can't afford (or don't want) to buy them all.

Business-to-Business Goods and Services

Business-to-business marketing is the marketing of goods and services from one organization to another. Although we usually relate marketing to the thousands of consumer goods begging for our dollars every day, the reality is that businesses and other organizations buy a lot more goods than consumers do. They purchase these **industrial goods** for further processing or to use in their own business operations. For example, automakers buy tons of steel to use in the manufacturing process, and they buy computer systems to track manufacturing costs and other information essential to operations.

Similarly, there is a lot of buzz about **e-commerce** and the buying and selling of products—books, CDs, cars, and so forth—on the Internet. However, just like in the off-line world, much of the real on-line action is in the area of business-to-business marketing.

Not-for-Profit Marketing

As we noted earlier, you don't have to be a businessperson to use marketing principles. Many **not-for-profit organizations**, including museums, zoos, and even churches, practice the marketing concept. Local governments are adopting marketing techniques to create more effective

myths
Stories containing symbolic elements that express the shared emotions and ideals of a culture.

product
A tangible good, service, idea, or some combination of these that satisfies consumer or business customer needs through the exchange process; a bundle of attributes including features, functions, benefits, and uses.

consumer goods
The goods individual consumers purchase for personal or family use.

services
Intangible products that are exchanged directly between the producer and the customer.

business-to-business marketing
The marketing of those goods and services that business and organizational customers need to produce other goods and services, for resale or to support their operations.

industrial goods
Goods individuals or organizations buy for further processing or for their own use when they do business.

e-commerce
The buying or selling of goods and services electronically, usually over the Internet.

Everyone's going low carb lately. We've been there since day one.

A friendly reminder from America's Peanut Farmers ™

One serving of dry roasted peanuts (30 grams) contains 12 grams of unsaturated fat and 2 grams of saturated fat, and 0 cholesterol.

Visit www.nationalpeanutboard.org for delicious recipes.

Successful marketers try to connect their products with trends in popular culture. The Peanut Board links its products to the low-carb craze.

not-for-profit organizations
Organizations with charitable, educational, community, and other public service goals that buy goods and services to support their functions and to attract and serve their members.

target market
The market segments on which an organization focuses its marketing plan and toward which it directs its marketing efforts.

taxpayer services and to attract new businesses and industries to their counties and cities. Even states are getting into the act: We've known for a long time that I ♥ NY, but recently Kentucky and Oregon hired advertising agencies to develop statewide branding campaigns (the official state motto of Oregon is now "Oregon. We love dreamers.").[18] The intense competition for support of civic and charitable activities means that only the not-for-profits that meet the needs of their constituents and donors will survive.

Idea, Place, and People Marketing

Marketing principles also get people to endorse ideas or to change their behaviors in positive ways. Many organizations work hard to convince consumers to use seat belts, not to litter our highways, to engage in safe sex, or to believe that one political system is preferable to another. In addition to ideas, places and people also are marketable. We are all familiar with tourism marketing that promotes exotic resorts like Club Med ("the antidote for civilization"). For many developing countries like Thailand, tourism may be the best opportunity available for economic growth.

You may have heard the expression, "Stars are made, not born." There's a lot of truth to that. Beyoncé Knowles may have a killer voice and Ryan Howard may have a red-hot baseball bat, but talent alone doesn't make thousands or even millions of people buy CDs or stadium seats. Entertainment events do not just happen. People plan them. Whether a concert or a baseball game, the application of sound marketing principles helps ensure that patrons will continue to support the activity and buy tickets. Today, sports and the arts are hotbeds of marketing activity. Many of the famous people you pay to see became famous with the help of shrewd marketing: They and their managers developed a "product" that they hoped would appeal to some segment of the population.

Some of the same principles that go into "creating" a celebrity apply to you. An entertainer—whether 50 Cent or Tony Bennett—must "package" his talents, identify a **target market** that is likely to be interested, and work hard to gain exposure to these potential customers by appearing in the right musical venues.

In the same way, everyday people like Alex "package" themselves by summing up their accomplishments on a resumé and distributing it at venues like Monster.com to attract potential "buyers." And this person marketing perspective is more valid than ever—now that almost everyone can find his "15 minutes of fame" on a Web site, a blog, or a YouTube video. We even have a new word—*microcelebrity*—to describe someone who's famous not necessarily to millions of people but certainly to hundreds or even thousands who follow their comings and goings on Facebook, Flickr, or Twitter. Some of these stories reveal heartbreak and despair—including the chronicle of a woman named Jennifer who described her husband's betrayal in intimate detail to the 55,000 readers of her blog, NakedJen.com. Others focus on more crucial issues like how to handle a bad hair day—Blogger.com lists over 4,000 postings that ask readers: "Should I cut my hair?" In a way, when you post some text about how you spent your day on your blog or Facebook wall, you're basically sending out a press release about yourself (we'll find out more about those in Chapter 13). So, be careful what you broadcast—you might make the news sooner than you think![19]

Not-for-profit organizations like zoos need to market themselves too.

5 The Value of Marketing and the Marketing of Value

OBJECTIVE

Understand value from the perspectives of customers, producers, and society.

(pp. 19–28)

So far, we've talked a lot about marketing delivering value to customers. As we noted at the beginning of this chapter, **value** refers to the benefits a customer receives from buying a good or service. Marketing then communicates these benefits to the customer in the form of a **value proposition**, a marketplace offering that fairly and accurately sums up the value that the customer will realize if he purchases the product. The challenge to the marketer is to create an attractive value proposition. A big part of this challenge is convincing customers that this value proposition is superior to others they might choose from competitors.

How do customers (such as your potential employers) decide how much value they will get from a purchase? One way to look at value is to think of it simply as a ratio of benefits to costs—that is, customers "invest" their precious time and money to do business with a firm, and they expect a certain bundle of benefits in return.

But here's the tricky part: Value is in the eye of the beholder, meaning that something (or someone) may be worth a lot to one person but not to another. Your mother may believe that you are the greatest person on the planet, but a prospective employer may form a different opinion. A big part of marketing is ensuring that the thing being exchanged is appreciated for the value it holds. Let's look at value from the different perspectives of the parties that are involved in an exchange: the customers, the sellers, and society.

value proposition
A marketplace offering that fairly and accurately sums up the value that will be realized if the good or service is purchased.

Value from the Customer's Perspective

Think about something you would like to buy, say a new pair of shoes. You have narrowed the choice down to several options. Your purchase decision no doubt will be affected by the ratio of costs versus benefits for each type of shoe—that is, in buying a pair of shoes, you consider the price (and other costs) along with all the other benefits (utilities) that each competing pair of shoes provides you.

As we noted previously, the value proposition includes the whole bundle of benefits the firm promises to deliver, not just the benefits of the product itself. For example, although most people probably couldn't run faster or jump higher if they were wearing Nikes versus Reeboks, many die-hard loyalists swear by their favorite brand. These archrivals are largely marketed in terms of their images—meanings their respective advertising agencies have carefully crafted with the help of legions of athletes, slickly-produced

Aquafina hopes to build demand for water as an alternative to other stylish beverage options.

commercials, and millions of dollars. When you buy a Nike "swoosh," you're doing more than choosing shoes to wear to the mall—you may also be making a statement about the type of person you are or wish you were. In addition to providing comfort or letting you run faster, that statement also is part of the value the product delivers to you.

You can probably think of possessions you own with which you've "bonded" in some way—that is, their value to you goes beyond their function. Marketers who understand this know that in the long run, their value proposition will be successful if they manage to build a relationship between their product and the people who buy it.

Value from the Seller's Perspective

We've seen that marketing transactions produce value for buyers, but how do sellers experience value, and how do they decide whether a transaction is valuable? One answer is obvious: They determine whether the exchange is profitable to them. Has it made money for the company's management, its workers, and its shareholders?

That's a very important factor, but not the only one. Just as we can't measure value from the consumer's perspective only in functional terms, value from the seller's perspective can take many forms. For example, in addition to making a buck or two, many firms measure value along other dimensions, such as prestige among rivals or pride in doing what they do well. Some firms by definition don't even care about making money, or they may not even be allowed to make money; nonprofits like Greenpeace, the Smithsonian Institution, or National Public Radio regard value in terms of their ability to motivate, educate, or delight the public.

Because value is such a complicated but important concept, now more than ever marketers search for new and better ways to accurately measure just what kind of value they deliver. They also try to learn how this stacks up to the competition, and—as we'll see next—in some cases even whether the relationship they have with a customer possesses enough value for them to continue it.

Building Value Through Customers

Smart companies today understand that making money from a single transaction doesn't provide the kind of value they desire. Instead, their goal is to satisfy the customer over and over again so that they can build a long-term relationship rather than just having a "one-night stand."

In recent years many firms have transformed the way they do business. They now regard consumers as *partners* in the transaction rather than as passive "victims." That explains why it's becoming more common for companies to host events (sometimes called *brandfests*) to thank customers for their loyalty. For example, the Ford Motor Company sponsored "The Great American Pony Drive II" in honor of devotees of its legendary Mustang. This party included a performance of the song "Mustang Sally" by Sir Mack Rice (who recorded the original version) as well as a preview of the next-generation Mustang.[20]

Ford's decision to reward Mustang owners with a party means the car company has learned an important secret: *It is more expensive to attract new customers than it is to retain current ones.* Although this notion has transformed the way many companies do business, it doesn't always hold true. In recent years, companies have been working harder to calculate the true value of their relationships with customers by asking, "How much is this customer <u>really</u> worth to us?" Firms recognize that it can be very costly in terms of both money and human effort to do whatever it takes to keep some customers loyal to the company. Very often these actions pay off, but there are cases in which keeping a customer is a losing proposition.

Nonprofit organizations such as the National Sports Center for the Disabled measure value in terms of their ability to motivate, educate, or delight the public.

This way of thinking is similar to how we may decide which friends are "worth keeping." You may do a lot of favors for two friends, only to discover that when you need something, one of them is always there for you, while the other is nowhere to be found. Over time, you may decide that maintaining a friendship with that second person just doesn't make sense. Similarly, a company may use a lot of resources to appeal to two customers and find that one returns the favor by buying a lot of its products, while the other buys hardly anything. In the long run, the firm may decide to "fire" that second customer. Perhaps you once ordered something in a catalog, and you get that catalog in your mailbox every month. If you don't order anything for a certain period of time, the company will stop sending you the catalog. In the words of Donald Trump, "You're fired!"

Companies that calculate the **lifetime value of a customer** look at how much profit they expect to make from a particular customer, including each and every purchase he will make from them now and in the future. To calculate lifetime value, companies estimate the amount the person will spend and then subtract what it will cost to maintain this relationship.

Providing Value through Competitive Advantage

How does a firm go about creating a competitive advantage? The first step is to identify what it does really well. A **distinctive competency** is a firm's capability that is superior to that of its competition. For example, Coca-Cola's success in global markets—Coke commands 50 percent of the world's soft-drink business—is related to its distinctive competencies in distribution and marketing communications. Coke's distribution system got a jump on the competition during World War II. To enable U.S. soldiers fighting overseas to enjoy a five-cent Coke, the U.S. government assisted Coca-Cola in building 64 overseas bottling plants. Coke's skillful marketing communications program, a second distinctive competency, has contributed to its global success. In addition to its television commercials, Coke blankets less-developed countries such as Tanzania with signs posted on roads and on storefronts so that even people without televisions will think of Coke when they get thirsty.

The second step in developing a competitive advantage is to turn a distinctive competency into a **differential benefit**—one that is important to customers. Differential benefits set products apart from competitors' products by providing something unique that customers want. Differential benefits provide reasons for customers to pay a premium for a firm's products and exhibit a strong brand preference. For many years, loyal Apple computer users benefited from superior graphics capability compared to their PC-using counterparts. Later, when PC manufacturers caught up with this competitive advantage, Apple relied on its inventive product designers to create another differential benefit—futuristic-looking computers in a multitude of colors. This competitive advantage even tempted many loyal PC users to take a bite of the Apple.

Note that a differential benefit does not necessarily mean simply offering something different. For example, Mennen marketed a deodorant with a distinctive feature: It contained vitamin D. Unfortunately, consumers did not see any reason to pay for the privilege of spraying a vitamin under their arms. Despite advertising claims, consumers saw

lifetime value of a customer
How much profit companies expect to make from a particular customer, including each and every purchase he will make from them now and in the future. To calculate lifetime value, companies estimate the amount the person will spend and then subtract what it will cost the company to maintain this relationship.

distinctive competency
A superior capability of a firm in comparison to its direct competitors.

differential benefit
Properties of products that set them apart from competitors' products by providing unique customer benefits.

Brooke D.
Bayer
a student at Missouri State University
My Advice for Ron Jon Surf Shop would be to choose

1
Option

real people, **Other Voices**

I would choose Option 1. People who rent cars for the most part have flexibility to go and visit where they choose once reaching their

destination. Those not renting cars most likely have pre-set travel packages and planned activities that cannot easily be changed. Thus, those who rent cars are more likely to visit the Ron Jon shop in Cocoa Beach. By placing ads and offering discounts on needed beach attire and accessories, more tourists will be drawn to the store. Also, by placing ads in maps, even those not renting a car may pick up a map in order to become more familiar with the area. These maps can be sold or given to rental car agencies, in addition to gift shops in the airports and hotels in the area. ➤

no benefit, and the product failed. The moral: *Effective product benefits must be both different from the competition and things customers want*. A firm that delivers these desired benefits provides value to its customers and other stakeholders.

Adding Value through the Value Chain

Many different players—both within and outside a firm—need to work together to create and deliver value to customers. The **value chain** is a useful way to appreciate all the players that work together to create value. This term refers to a series of activities involved in designing, producing, marketing, delivering, and supporting any product. In addition to marketing activities, the value chain includes business functions such as human resource management and technology development.[21]

The value chain concept reminds us that every product starts with raw materials that are of relatively limited value to the end customer. Each link in the chain has the potential to either add or remove value from the product the customer eventually buys. The successful firm is the one that can perform one or more of these activities better than other firms—this is its competitive advantage. The main activities of value-chain members include the following:

- *Inbound logistics*: Bringing in materials to make the product

- *Operations*: Converting the materials into the final product

- *Outbound logistics*: Shipping out the final product

- *Marketing*: Promoting and selling the final product

- *Service*: Meeting the customer's needs by providing any additional support required

For example, when you buy a new Apple iPod at your local Circuit City store, do you think about all the people and steps involved in designing, manufacturing, and delivering that product to the store? Not to mention other people who create brand advertising, conduct consumer research to figure out what people like or dislike about their mobile music players, or even make the box it comes in or those little plastic peanuts that keep the unit from being damaged in shipment?

As Figure 1.1 shows, all these companies (and more) belong to Apple's value chain. This means that Apple must make a lot of decisions. What electronic components will go into its music players? What accessories will it include in the package? What trucking companies, wholesalers, and retailers will deliver the iPods to stores? What service will it provide to customers after the sale? And what marketing strategies will it use? In some cases, members of a value chain will work together to coordinate their activities to be more efficient and thus create a competitive advantage.

We've organized this book around the sequence of steps necessary to ensure that the appropriate value exchange occurs and that both parties to the transaction are satisfied—making it more likely they'll continue to do business in the future. Figure 1.2 shows these steps. Basically, we're going to learn about what marketers do as a product makes its way through the value chain from manufacturers into your hands. We'll start with a focus on how companies decide what to make, how and where to sell it, and to whom to sell it. Then, we'll take a look at how they decide to "position" the product in the marketplace, including choices about what it should look like, how its value should be communicated to customers, and how much to charge for it. As we reach the end of our marketing journey, we'll talk about how the product actually gets delivered to consumers.

How Do We Know What's Valuable?

How do marketers measure value? Increasingly, they develop *scorecards* that report (often in quantified terms) how the company or brand is actually doing in achieving various goals. We can think of a scorecard as a marketing department's report card. Scorecards tend to be short

value chain
A series of activities involved in designing, producing, marketing, delivering, and supporting any product. Each link in the chain has the potential to either add or remove value from the product the customer eventually buys.

Figure 1.1 | A Value Chain for the Apple iPod

Inbound Logistics	Operations	Outbound Logistics	Marketing and Sales	Service
• Planar lithium battery (Sony) • Hard drive (Toshiba) • MP3 decoder and controller chip (PortalPlayer) • Flash memory chip (Sharp Electronics Corp.) • Stereo digital-to-analog converter (Wolfson Microelectronics Ltd.) • Firewire interface controller (Texas Instruments)	• Consumer research • New-product-development team • Engineering and production	• Trucking companies • Wholesalers • Retailers	• Advertising • Sales force	• Computer technicians

Source: Based on information from Erik Sherman, "Inside the Apple iPod Design Triumph," *Electronics Design Chain* (May 27, 2006), accessed at **http://www.designchain.com/coverstory.asp?issue=summer02**.

and to the point, and they often use charts and graphs to summarize information in an easy-to-read format. They might report "grades" on factors such as actual cost per sale, a comparison of Web hits (the number of people who visit an e-commerce site) versus Web transactions (the number who actually buy something at the site), a measure of customers' satisfaction with a company's repair facilities, or perhaps even a percentage of consumers who respond to a mail piece that asks them to make a donation to a charity that the firm sponsors. Throughout this book, we'll show you examples of how marketers calculate ROI based on their actions in boxes we call "Measuring Value."

Consumer-Generated Value: From Audience to Community

One of the most exciting new developments in the marketing world is the evolution of how consumers interact with marketers. In particular, we're seeing everyday people actually *generating* value instead of just buying it—consumers are turning into advertising directors, retailers, and new-product-development consultants. They create their own ads (some flattering, some not) for products and posting them on sites like YouTube. They buy and sell merchandise ranging from Beatles memorabilia to washing machines (to body parts, but that's another story) on eBay. They share ideas for new styles with fashion designers, and customize their own unique versions of products on Web sites. These changes mean that marketers need to adjust their thinking about customers: They need to stop thinking of buyers as a passive audience and start thinking of them as a community that is motivated to participate in both the production and the consumption of what companies sell. We'll talk more about this phenomenon later, but for now think about these recent examples of **consumer-generated value**:

- Kao Corp., which makes Ban deodorant, invited teenage girls to make an ad that would encourage other girls their age to buy the product. The company got almost 4,000 submissions from girls who were asked to submit an image and fill in the blank in the company's "Ban It" slogan. One entry shows four girls in similar jeans and tank tops, with their backs to the camera with the headline: "Ban Uniformity."[22]

- Rite-Solutions, a software company that builds advanced command-and-control systems for the Navy, set up an internal "prediction market," in which any employee can propose that the company acquire a new technology, enter a new

consumer-generated value
Everyday people functioning in marketing roles, such as participating in creating advertisements, providing input to new product development, or serving as wholesalers or retailers.

Figure 1.2 | Make and Deliver Value

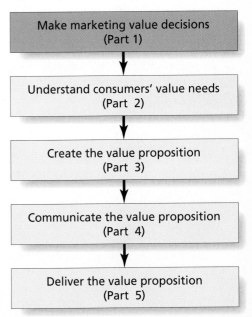

Make marketing value decisions (Part 1)

↓

Understand consumers' value needs (Part 2)

↓

Create the value proposition (Part 3)

↓

Communicate the value proposition (Part 4)

↓

Deliver the value proposition (Part 5)

Metrics Moment

An Example of a Customer Service Scorecard

Item Text	Quarterly Scores		
	1st Qtr.	2nd Qtr.	3rd Qtr.
Satisfaction with			
C1 Employee responsiveness	60%	65%	68%
C2 Product selection	60%	62%	63%
C3 Service quality	60%	62%	55%
C4 Cleanliness of facility	75%	80%	85%
C5 Knowledge of employees	62%	62%	58%
C6 Appearance of employees	60%	62%	63%
C7 Convenience of location	60%	65%	68%

Source: From C. F. Lunbdy and C. Rasinowich, "The Missing Link," *Marketing Research*, Winter 2003, p. 18. Copyright © 2003 American Marketing Association.

business, or make an efficiency improvement. These proposals become stocks, complete with ticker symbols, discussion lists, and e-mail alerts. Employees buy or sell the stocks, and prices change to reflect the sentiments of the company's engineers, computer scientists, and project managers—as well as its marketers, accountants, and even the receptionist. One "stock" resulted in the development of a new product that now accounts for 30 percent of the company's sales.[23]

- The action movie *Snakes on a Plane* starring Samuel L. Jackson (an assassin who releases hundreds of venomous snakes in the hope of killing a witness) generated a huge amount of pre-release buzz—not to mention consumer-generated Web sites, blogs, and even merchandise. The commotion started when a screenwriter (who had been invited to work on the script) blogged about the movie. The title inspired other bloggers to create songs, apparel, poster art, pages of fan fiction, parody films, and mock movie trailers. Now, posters on Internet forums use the phrase "Snakes on a Plane" to indicate that a topic doesn't make sense—sometimes the slang form SoaP substitutes for the old phrase "sh** happens."[24]

Social Networking

The tremendous acceleration of social networking is fueling this fire. The odds are you and most of your classmates checked your Facebook or MySpace page before (or during?) class today. Specialized sites like LinkedIn that reach a more targeted group already are recording strong profits as advertisers figure out that these sites are a great way to reach an audience that tunes in regularly and enthusiastically to catch up with friends, or sometimes to check out photos of what they did at that outrageous party Saturday night, proclaim opinions about political or social issues, or share discoveries of new musical artists. As consumers continue to tweak advertising and broadcast their own personal testimonials—or rants—about brands, sites like Social Vibe and Ad Roll allow users to choose brands to endorse on their pages or provide easy ways to share favorite ads with other members.[25]

Social networking is an integral part of what many call **Web 2.0**, which is like the Internet on steroids. The key difference between Web 1.0 and the new version is the interactivity we see among producers and users, but these are some other characteristics of a Web 2.0 site:[26]

Web 2.0
The new generation of the World Wide Web that incorporates social networking and user interactivity.

- It improves as the number of users increases. For example, Amazon's ability to recommend books to you based on what other people with similar interests have bought gets better as it tracks more and more people who are entering search queries.

- Its currency is eyeballs. Google makes its money by charging advertisers according to the number of people who see their ads after typing in a search term.

- It's version-free and in perpetual beta. Wikipedia, the on-line encyclopedia, gets updated constantly by users who "correct" others' errors.

- It categorizes entries according to "folksonomy" rather than "taxonomy." In other words, sites rely on users rather than pre-established systems to sort contents. Listeners at Pandora.com create their own "radio stations" that play songs by artists they choose as well as other similar artists.[27]

This last point highlights a key change in the way some new media companies approach their businesses: Think of it as marketing strategy by committee. The **wisdom of crowds** perspective (from a book by that name) argues that under the right circumstances, groups are smarter than the smartest people in them. If this is true, it implies that large numbers of (nonexpert) consumers can predict successful products.[28] For example, at Threadless.com, customers rank T-shirt designs ahead of time and the company prints the winning ideas. Every week, contestants upload T-shirts designs to the site where about 700 compete to be among the six that it will print during that time. Threadless visitors score designs on a scale of 0 to 5, and the staff selects winners from the most popular entrants. The six lucky artists each get $2,000 in cash and merchandise. Threadless sells out of every shirt it offers. This business model has made a small fortune for a few designers "the crowd" particularly likes. One pair of Chicago-based artists sold $16 million worth of T-shirts. To keep the judges and buyers coming back, the owners offer rewards—upload a photo of yourself wearing a Threadless T-shirt and you get a store credit of $1.50. Refer a friend who buys a T-shirt and you get $3. The site sells more than 1,500 T-shirts in a typical day.[29]

wisdom of crowds
Under the right circumstances, groups are smarter than the smartest people in them meaning that large numbers of consumers can predict successful products.

Open Source Business Models

Yet another related change is the rise of the **open source model** that turns some of our conventional assumptions about the value of products and services on its head. This model started in the software industry where the Linux system grows by leaps and bounds—even IBM uses it now. Unlike the closely-guarded code that companies like Microsoft use, open source developers post their programs on a public site and a community of volunteers is free to tinker with it, develop other applications using the code, then give their changes away for free. For example, the company that gives out (for free) the Mozilla internet browser that competes with Microsoft has a market value of between $1.5–$4 billion.[30] We'll talk more about this—and answer the question of how in the world you can make money from something when you give it away—in Chapter 11.

open source model
A practice used in the software industry in which companies share their software codes with anyone to assist in the development of a better product.

Value from Society's Perspective

Every company's activities influence the world around it, in ways both good and bad. Therefore, we must also consider how marketing transactions add or subtract value from society. In many ways, we are at the mercy of marketers because we trust them to sell us products that are safe and perform as promised. We also trust them to price and distribute these products fairly. Conflicts often arise in business when the pressure to succeed in the marketplace provokes dishonest business practices—the collapse of energy giant Enron and the trial of its (late) former Chief Executive Officer Ken Lay are a case in point.

By the **People**, For the **People**

The popularity of homemade videos on video-sharing sites like YouTube and Yahoo Video is soaring. The vision of a new player, Current TV, is to create a consumer-brewed TV channel and enhance grass-root communications in a public arena.

Co-founded by former U.S. Vice-President and Nobel Laureate Al Gore and lawyer Joel Hyatt in 2005, Current TV hopes to develop a platform for young adults to express their voices and ideas to the public. Since so many young adults today are avidly creating and editing their home videos and hanging out on social networking Web sites like MySpace and Facebook, they provide abundant resources to meet Current TV's programming needs. Indeed, viewers create around one-third of the programs the company broadcasts. This home-grown content not

only reduces production costs; it increases the diversity of the programming and reflects what its consumer base wants to see.

Current TV has over 50 program categories (or "POD" topics) that include action and adventure, environment, human interest, opinion and commentary, and technology. More than 50 million homes in the United States and the United Kingdom spend an average of 7.5 hours per week watching the network. Most of the viewers are affluent, college-educated young adults who tend to be influencers in their social group, so they are a very desirable audience for advertisers. So, if you don't like the programs you see on "the boob tube," make your own!

Sources: Anne Becker, "Power to the Viewer," *Broadcasting and Cable* (November 27, 2006); pp. 18; Peter Burrows, "The Wiki Cable Channel," *BusinessWeek*, Issue 4059 (November 19, 2007), pp. 64.

Did you hear the one about the fat guy suing the restaurants?

It's no joke.
He claims the food was too cheap so he ate too much!

Learn more about the erosion of personal responsibility and common sense. Go to:

ConsumerFreedom.com

Some people feel that marketers manipulate consumers, while others argue that people should be held responsible for their own choices. This ad is critical of the current trend of lawsuits brought against fast-food companies by people who blame their health problems on the fast-food industry. What do you think?

Companies usually find that stressing ethics and social responsibility also is good business, at least in the long run. Some find out the hard way. For example, the Chrysler Corporation was accused of resetting the odometers of new cars that managers had actually driven prior to sale. The company admitted the practice only after some managers tried to get out of paying speeding tickets by claiming that their speedometers—and odometers—didn't work because the cables were disconnected.[31] These actions caused the company great embarrassment, and it took years of hard work to restore the public's trust.

In contrast, Procter & Gamble voluntarily withdrew its Rely tampons from the market following reports of women who had suffered toxic shock syndrome (TSS). Although scientists did not claim a causal link between Rely and TSS, the company agreed with the Food and Drug Administration to undertake extensive advertising notifying women of the symptoms of TSS and asking them to return their boxes of Rely for a refund. The company took a $75 million loss and sacrificed an unusually successful new product that had already captured about one-quarter of the billion-dollar sanitary product market.[32]

Is Marketing Evil?

For some—hopefully not many and hopefully not <u>you</u> after you read this book—marketing is a four-letter word. The field sometimes gets attacked for a number of reasons.[33] Here are some primary ones:

Criticism: Marketing corrupts society. The marketing system comes under fire from both ends of the political spectrum. On the one hand, some members of the Religious Right believe that marketers contribute to the moral breakdown of society because they present images of hedonistic pleasure and encourage the pursuit of secular humanism at the expense of spirituality and the environment. On the other hand, some leftists argue that the same deceitful promises of material pleasure function to buy off people who would otherwise be revolutionaries working to change the system.[34]

*A Response: A **need** is a basic biological motive; a **want** represents one way that society has taught us to satisfy the need.* For example, thirst is biologically based; we are taught to want Coca-Cola to satisfy that thirst rather than, say, goat's milk. Thus, the need is already there; marketers simply recommend ways to satisfy it. A basic objective of marketing is to create awareness that needs exist, not to create needs.

Criticism: Advertising and marketing are unnecessary. Marketers arbitrarily link products to desirable social attributes, fostering a materialistic society in which people measure us by what we own.

A Response: Products are designed to meet existing needs, and advertising only helps to communicate their availability.[35] Advertising is a service for which consumers are willing to pay, because the information it provides reduces search time.

Criticism: Marketers promise miracles and manipulate consumers. Through advertising, consumers are led to believe that products have magical properties; products will do special and mysterious things for consumers in a way that will transform their lives. Consumers will be beautiful, have power over others' feelings, be successful, and be relieved of all ills.

A Response: Advertisers simply do not know enough about people to manipulate them. Consider that the failure rate for new products ranges from 40 to 80 percent. Although people think that advertisers have an endless source of magical tricks and scientific techniques to manipulate them, in reality the industry is successful when it tries to sell good products and unsuccessful when selling poor ones.[36]

The Dark Side of Marketing

Whether intentionally or not, some marketers <u>do</u> violate their bond of trust with consumers, and unfortunately the "dark side" of marketing often is the subject of harsh criticism.[37] In some cases, these violations are illegal, such as when a retailer adopts a "bait-and-switch" selling strategy, luring consumers into the store with promises of inexpensive products with the sole intent of getting them to switch to higher-priced goods.

In other cases, marketing practices have detrimental effects on society even though they are not actually illegal. Some alcohol and tobacco companies advertise in low-income neighborhoods where abuse of these products is a big problem. Others sponsor commercials depicting groups of people in an unfavorable light or sell products that encourage antisocial behavior. An on-line game based on the Columbine High School massacre drew criticism from some who say it trivializes the actions of the two teen killers.

Despite the best efforts of researchers, government regulators, and concerned industry people, sometimes consumers' worst enemies are themselves. We tend to think of ourselves as rational decision makers, calmly doing our best to obtain products and services that will maximize our health and well-being and that of our families and society. In reality, however, our desires, choices, and actions often result in negative consequences to ourselves and the society in which we live. Some of these actions are relatively harmless, but others have more onerous consequences. Some harmful consumer behaviors such as excessive drinking or cigarette smoking stem from social pressures, and the cultural value people place on money encourages activities such as shoplifting or insurance fraud. Exposure to unattainable ideals of beauty and success can create dissatisfaction with the self. Let's briefly review some dimensions of "the dark side" of consumer behavior:

Terrorism: The terrorist attacks of 2001 revealed the vulnerability of nonmilitary targets and reminded us that disruptions of our financial, electronic, and supply networks can potentially be more damaging to our way of life than the fallout from a conventional battlefield. The hours many of us spend waiting to pass through security lines in airports is but one consequence of these attacks.

Addictive consumption: **Consumer addiction** is a physiological or psychological dependency on goods or services. These problems of course include alcoholism, drug addiction, and cigarettes—and many companies profit from addictive products or by selling solutions. Although most people equate addiction with drugs, consumers can use virtually anything to relieve (at least temporarily) some problem or satisfy some need to the point that reliance on it becomes extreme. "Shopaholics" turn to shopping much the way addicted people turn to drugs or alcohol.[38] There is even a Chap Stick Addicts support group with approximately 250 active members![39]

Exploited people: Sometimes people are used or exploited, willingly or not, for commercial gain in the marketplace; these situations range from traveling road shows that feature dwarfs and midgets to the selling of body parts and babies on eBay. *Consumed consumers* are people who themselves become commodities.

Illegal activities: The cost of crimes consumers commit against businesses has been estimated at more than $40 billion per year. A survey the McCann-Erickson advertising agency conducted revealed the following tidbits:[40]

- Ninety-one percent of people say they lie regularly. One in three fibs about their weight, one in four about their income, and 21 percent lie about their age. Nine percent even lie about their natural hair color.

- Four out of ten Americans have tried to pad an insurance bill to cover the deductible.

- Nineteen percent say they've snuck into a theater to avoid paying admission.

- More than three out of five people say they've taken credit for making something from scratch when they have done no such thing. According to Pillsbury's CEO, this "behavior is so prevalent that we've named a category after it—speed scratch."

consumer addiction
A physiological or psychological dependency on goods or services.

Ethical Decisions in the Real World

For many young people, drugs are "cool"—at least partly because adults discourage their use. The media doesn't help when it glamorizes drinking, pot smoking, and other illegal drug use by featuring celebrities who use these products. Then, there's candy cigarettes, "alco-pop" drinks that look like soft drinks but pack a punch, and energy drinks that boast of the "buzz" they'll give you. For some companies that want to encourage kids to use their legal products, it's tempting to link them to illegal ones with a "nod and a wink." So, why not go a step farther and name your product in a way that directly associates it with an illegal drug—say Pot Brownie flavor ice cream, Ecstasy perfume, or even Cocaine energy drink? Your customers will probably get the "joke" but jump on the chance to sport a legal brand with a racy name. If you're a marketer looking to get the attention of young consumers in a competitive market, does this idea make sense? Would you try this—why or why not?

Ripped from the Headlines! See what happened in the Real World at **www.mypearsonmarketinglab.com**

ETHICS CHECK: ◀

Find out what other students taking this course **would do** and **why** on **www. mypearsonmarketinglab. com**

Would you give a legal product the name of an illegal drug to increase sales?

☐YES ☐NO

Shrinkage: A retail theft is committed every five seconds. *Shrinkage* is the industry term for inventory and cash losses from shoplifting and employee theft. As we'll see in Chapter 16 this is a massive problem for businesses that is passed on to consumers in the form of higher prices. Analysts attribute about 40 percent of the losses to employees rather than shoppers.

Anticonsumption: Some types of destructive consumer behavior are *anticonsumption*—events in which people deliberately deface products. This practice ranges from relatively mild acts like spray-painting graffiti on buildings and subways, to serious incidences of product tampering or even the release of computer viruses that can bring large corporations to their knees.

6 Marketing as a Process

OBJECTIVE

Explain the basics of marketing planning and the marketing mix tools we use in the marketing process.

(pp. 28–31)

Our definition of marketing also refers to *processes*. This means that marketing is not a one-shot operation. When it's done right, marketing is a decision process in which marketing managers determine the strategies that will help the firm meet its long-term objectives and then execute those strategies using the tools they have at their disposal. In this section, we'll look at how marketers make business decisions and plan actions and the tools they use to execute their plans. We'll build on this brief overview in the next chapter, where we'll also provide you with a "road map" in the form of a pullout planning template you can use to understand the planning process as you work your way through the book.

Marketing Planning

A big part of the marketing process is to engage in *marketing planning* where we think carefully and strategically about the "big picture" and where our firm and its products fit within it. The first phase of marketing planning is to analyze the marketing environment. This means understanding the firm's current strengths and weaknesses by assessing factors that might help or hinder the development and marketing of products. The analysis must also take into account the opportunities and threats the firm will encounter in the marketplace, such as the actions of competitors, cultural and technological changes, and the economy.

Firms (or individuals) that engage in marketing planning ask questions like these:

- What product benefits will our customers look for in three to five years?

- What capabilities does our firm have that set it apart from the competition?

- What additional customer groups might provide important market segments for us in the future?

- How will changes in technology affect our production process, our communication strategy, and our distribution strategy?

- What changes in social and cultural values are occurring now that will impact our market in the next few years?

- How will customers' awareness of environmental issues affect their attitudes toward our manufacturing facilities?

- What legal and regulatory issues may affect our business in both domestic and global markets?

Answers to these and other questions provide the foundation for developing an organization's **marketing plan**. This is a document that describes the marketing environment, outlines the marketing objectives and strategy, and identifies who will be responsible for carrying out each part of the marketing strategy. As we noted earlier, in Chapter 2 we'll give you a template you can use to construct your own marketing plan that will help bring this important process to life. If you want, you can even use it to develop a plan to market "Brand You!"

A major marketing decision for most organizations is which products to market to which consumers without simultaneously turning off other consumers. Some firms choose to reach as many customers as possible so they offer their goods or services to a **mass market** that consists of all possible customers in a market regardless of the differences in their specific needs and wants. Marketing planning then becomes a matter of developing a basic product and a single strategy to reach everyone.

Although this approach can be cost-effective, the firm risks losing potential customers to competitors whose marketing plans instead try to meet the needs of specific groups within the market. A **market segment** is a distinct group of customers within a larger market who are similar to one another in some way and whose needs differ from other customers in the larger market. For example, automakers such as Ford, General Motors, and BMW offer different automobiles for different market segments. Depending on its goals and resources, a firm may choose to focus on one segment. A product's **market position** is how the target market perceives the product in comparison to competitors' brands. We'll learn more about these ideas in Chapter 7.

Marketing's Tools: The Marketing Mix

When they decide upon the best way to present a good or service for consumers' consideration, marketers have to make many decisions so they need many tools. The marketer's strategic toolbox is the **marketing mix**, which consists of the tools the organization uses to create a desired response among a set of predefined consumers. These tools include the product itself, the price of the product, the promotional activities that introduce it to consumers, and the places where it is available. We commonly refer to the elements of the marketing mix as the **Four Ps**: *product, price, promotion,* and *place.* As Figure 1.3 shows, each P is a piece of the puzzle that the marketer must combine with other pieces. Just as a radio DJ puts together a collection of separate songs (a musical mix) to create a certain mood, the idea of a mix in this context reminds us that no single marketing activity is sufficient to accomplish the organization's objectives.

Although we talk about the Four Ps as separate parts of a firm's marketing strategy, in reality, product, price, promotion, and place decisions are totally interdependent. Decisions about any single one of the four are affected by and affect every other marketing-mix decision. For example, assume that a firm is introducing a superior quality product, one that is more expensive to produce than its existing line of products. The price the firm charges for this new product must cover these higher costs, but in addition the firm must create advertising and other promotional strategies to convey a top-quality image. At the same time, the price of the product must cover not only the costs of production but also the cost of advertising. Furthermore, the firm must include high-end retailers in its distribution strategy. The elements of the marketing mix therefore work hand-in-hand.

marketing plan
A document that describes the marketing environment, outlines the marketing objectives and strategy, and identifies who will be responsible for carrying out each part of the marketing strategy.

mass market
All possible customers in a market, regardless of the differences in their specific needs and wants.

market segment
A distinct group of customers within a larger market who are similar to one another in some way and whose needs differ from other customers in the larger market.

market position
The way in which the target market perceives the product in comparison to competitors' brands.

marketing mix
A combination of the product itself, the price of the product, the place where it is made available, and the activities that introduce it to consumers that creates a desired response among a set of predefined consumers.

Four Ps
Product, price, promotion, and place.

Figure 1.3 | The Marketing Mix

What marketing is all about! The marketing mix is a combination of the Four Ps—product, price, place, and promotion—that an organization uses together to satisfy customer needs.

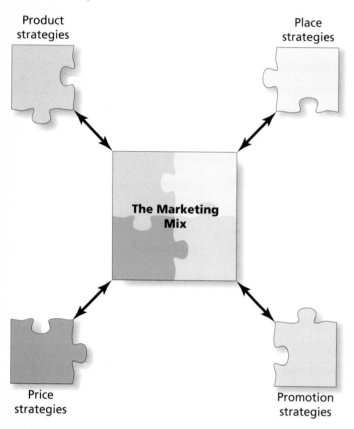

Product strategies

Place strategies

The Marketing Mix

Price strategies

Promotion strategies

price

The assignment of value, or the amount the consumer must exchange to receive the offering.

Bill
Bieberbach
APPLYING Promotion

Bill knows that 13 million visitors arrive by air to Florida each year. He needs a promotion strategy that will communicate with these passengers. ➡

promotion

The coordination of a marketer's marketing communications efforts to influence attitudes or behavior; the coordination of efforts by a marketer to inform or persuade consumers or organizations about goods, services, or ideas.

place

The availability of the product to the customer at the desired time and location.

We'll examine these components of the marketing mix in detail later in this book. For now, let's briefly look at each P to gain some insight into its meaning and role in the marketing mix.

Product

We've already seen that the product is a good, a service, an idea, a place, a person—whatever is offered for sale in the exchange. This aspect of the marketing mix includes the design and packaging of a good, as well as its physical features and any associated services, such as free delivery. So we can see that the product is a combination of many different elements, all of which are important to the product's success. For example, when the British firm Virgin introduced Virgin Cola in the United States, the company attempted to make the product stand out from the competition through its distinctive packaging. Advertising that introduced the brand told customers about the curved squeezable bottles: "If all you got is Va Va, You got to get some Voom; It's in the curvy bottle, Yeah, Virgin Drinks got Voom.... Virgin puts the Voom in your Va Va."[41] We're not quite sure what that means, but it does get your attention. Whether the focus is on the bottle or some other element, the product is an important part of the marketing mix.

Price

Price is the assignment of value, or the amount the consumer must exchange to receive the offering. Marketers often turn to price to increase consumers' interest in a product. This happens when they put an item on sale, but in other cases marketers actually try to sell a product with a <u>higher</u> price than people are used to if they want to communicate that it's high quality or cutting edge. For example, the Adidas 1 computerized running shoe got a lot of attention in the media. Some of the fuss was that the shoe was billed as the first "smart shoe" because it contains a computer chip that adapts its cushioning level to a runner's size and stride. But a lot of the press coverage also revolved around the hefty price tag of $250 per pair, which makes buying the shoe a status statement for the hard-core runner.[42]

Promotion

Promotion includes all the activities marketers undertake to inform consumers about their products and to encourage potential customers to buy these products. Promotions can take many forms, including personal selling, television advertising, store coupons, billboards, magazine ads, and publicity releases.

Place

Place refers to the availability of the product to the customer at the desired time and location. This *P* relates to a *supply chain*—the set of firms that work together to get a product from a producer to a consumer. For clothing or electronics, this channel includes local retailers as well as other outlets, such as retail sites on the Web that strive to offer the right quantity of products in the right styles at the right time.

To achieve a competitive advantage over rivals in the minds of consumers, the marketer carefully blends the four Ps of the marketing mix—that is, the organization develops product, price, place, and promotion strategies to meet the needs of its target market. These strategies may vary from one country to another, and marketers may inject them with fresh ideas over time to maintain or change the product's position.

Now that you've learned the basics of marketing, read "Real People, Real Choices: How It Worked Out" to see which strategy Bill selected to maximize the exposure of Ron Jon Surf Shop Inc. to tourists who arrive at Florida airports.

Real People, **Real Choices**

Bill
Bieberbach
Bill chose:

Option

How it Worked Out at Ron Jon Surf Shops

Bill chose Option 2. Ron Jon began with a test of dioramas it placed at a number of locations in the Orlando Airport. The company concentrated its test ads at gate arrival and baggage claims areas through which passengers flying on air carriers that served midwestern and northeastern cities would be likely to walk. Ron Jon's managers administered surveys to shoppers at its Cocoa Beach store and learned that customers did in fact seem to be noticing the ads.

In addition, Ron Jon opened a store in the Orlando market in the hope of capturing more of the market and becoming less reliant on the day travelers to Cocoa Beach. And Ron Jon even opened a small store in the Orlando Airport adjacent to the very busy food court area to capture more arrivals traffic. Surf and sales are up at Ron Jon!

How Ron Jon Measures Success

The Cocoa Beach and Orlando stores distribute surveys to 7,500 shoppers each year. The stores collect information about respondents' backgrounds, including age and gender, and place of residence. They also ask non-Florida residents how they traveled to the state (by air, auto, or bus) and which primary highway they used to get to the store. Bill and his colleagues use these results to be sure they continue to put advertising messages in places where they will make the biggest impression on tourists.

Refer back to **page 2** for Bills story ➡

Brand **YOU**!

Do you want to be a standout among all the new grads seeking their first job out of college? Learn how in the *Brand You* supplement. Discover how to realize professional success, whether it's landing a great job, getting paid what you're worth, or launching your own startup. Get started creating your own personal brand by taking a look at Chapter 1 in the *Brand You* supplement.

Objective Summary ➡ **Key Terms** ➡ **Apply**

CHAPTER 1
Study Map

1. Objective Summary (pp. 4–8)

Understand who marketers are, where they work, and marketing's role in a firm.

Marketers come from many different backgrounds and work in a variety of locations, from consumer goods companies to non-profit organizations to financial institutions to advertising and public relations agencies. Marketing's role in a firm depends on the organization. Some firms are very marketing-oriented, whereas others do not focus on marketing. However, marketing is increasingly being integrated with other business functions. Therefore, no matter what firm marketers work in, their decisions affect and are affected by the firm's other operations. Marketers must work together with other executives.

Key Terms

value, p. 5 (Metrics Moment, p. 24)

2. Objective Summary (pp. 8–11)

Explain what marketing is and how it provides value to everyone involved in the marketing process.

Marketing is the activity, set of institutions, and processes for creating, communicating, delivering and exchanging offerings that have value for customers, clients, partners, and society at large. Therefore, marketing is all about delivering value to stakeholders, that is, to everyone who is affected by a transaction. Organizations that seek to ensure their long-term profitability by identifying and satisfying customers' needs and wants have adopted the marketing concept. Marketing is also about exchanges or the transfer of value between a buyer and a seller.

Key Terms

marketing, p. 8 (Figure 1.2, p. 23)

stakeholders, p. 9

consumer, p. 9

marketing concept, p. 9

need, p. 9 (Figure 1.3, p. 30)

want, p. 9

benefit, p. 9 (Figure 1.1, p. 23)

demand, p. 9

market, p. 10

marketplace, p. 10

utility, p. 10

exchange, p. 11 (Figure 1.2, p. 23)

3. Objective Summary (pp. 11–16)

Explain the evolution of the marketing concept.

Early in the twentieth century, firms followed a production orientation in which they focused on the most efficient ways to produce and distribute products. Beginning in the 1930s, some firms adopted a selling orientation that encouraged salespeople to aggressively sell products to customers. In the 1950s, organizations adopted a consumer orientation that focused on customer satisfaction. This led to the development of the marketing concept. Today, many firms are moving toward a triple bottom line orientation that includes not only a commitment to quality and value, but also a concern for both economic and social profit.

Key Terms

production orientation, p. 13

selling orientation, p. 13 (Table 1.2, p. 12)

consumer orientation, p. 13 (Table 1.2, p. 12)

Total Quality Management (TQM), p. 13

instapreneur, p. 14

triple bottom line orientation, p. 14

customer relationship management (CRM), p. 15

social marketing concept, p. 15

sustainability, p. 15

ROI (return on investment), p. 16 (A Metrics Moment box, p. 24)

4. Objective Summary (pp. 16–19)

Understand the range of services and goods that organizations market.

Any good, service, or idea that can be marketed is a product, even though what is being sold may not take a physical form. Consumer goods are the tangible products that consumers purchase for personal or family use. Services are intangible products that we pay for and use but never own. Business-to-business goods and services are sold to businesses and other organizations for further processing or for use in their business operations. Not-for-profit organizations, ideas, places, and people can also be marketed.

Key Terms

popular culture, p. 16

myths, p. 17

product, p. 17 (Figure 1.3, p. 30)

consumer goods, p. 17

services, p. 17

business-to-business marketing, p. 17 (Table 1.1, pp. 7–8)

industrial goods, p. 17

e-commerce, p. 17

not-for-profit organizations, p. 18

target market, p. 18

5. Objective Summary (pp. 19–28)

Understand value from the perspectives of customers, producers, and society.

Value is the benefits a customer receives from buying a good or service. Marketing communicates these benefits as the value proposition to the customer. For customers, the value proposition includes the whole bundle of benefits the product promises to deliver, not just the benefits of the product itself. Sellers determine value by assessing whether its transactions are profitable, whether it is providing value to stakeholders by creating a competitive advantage, and whether it is providing value through its value chain. Customers generate value when they turn into advertising directors, retailers, and new product development consultants, often through social networking. Society receives value from marketing activities when producers and consumers engage in ethical, profitable, and environmentally friendly exchange relationships.

Key Terms

value proposition, p. 19 (Figure 1.2, p. 23)

lifetime value of a customer, p. 21

distinctive competency, p. 21 (Figure 1.2, p. 23)

differential benefit, p. 21 (Figure 1.2, p. 23)

value chain, p. 22 (Figure 1.1, p. 23)

consumer-generated value, p. 23 (By the People box, p. 25)

Web 2.0, p. 24

wisdom of crowds, p. 25

open source model, p. 25

consumer addiction, p. 27

6. Objective Summary (pp. 28–30)

Explain the basics of marketing planning and the marketing mix tools managers use in the marketing process.

The strategic process of marketing planning begins with an assessment of factors within the organization and in the external environment that could help or hinder the development and marketing of products. On the basis of this analysis, marketers set objectives and develop strategies. Many firms use a target marketing strategy in which they divide the overall market into segments and then target the most attractive one. Then they design the marketing mix to gain a competitive position in the target market. The marketing mix includes product, price, place, and promotion. The product is what satisfies customer needs. The price is the assigned value or amount to be exchanged for the product. The place or channel of distribution gets the product to the customer. Promotion is the organization's efforts to persuade customers to buy the product.

Key Terms

marketing plan, p. 29 (Figure 1.2, p. 23)

mass market, p. 29

market segment, p. 29

market position, p. 29

marketing mix, p. 29 (Figure 1.2, p. 23 & 1.3, p. 30)

Four Ps, p. 29

price, p. 30 (Figure 1.3,p. 30)

promotion, p. 30 (Figure 1.3, p. 30)

place, p. 30 (Figure 1.3, p. 30)

Chapter Questions and Activities

Concepts: Test Your Knowledge

1. Where do marketers work, and what role does marketing play in the firm?
2. Briefly explain what marketing is.
3. Explain needs, wants, and demands. What is the role of marketing in each of these?
4. What is utility? How does marketing create different forms of utility?
5. Trace the evolution of the marketing concept.
6. Define the terms *consumer goods*, *services*, and *industrial goods*.
7. To what does the *lifetime value of the customer* refer, and how is it calculated?
8. What does it mean for a firm to have a competitive advantage? What gives a firm a competitive advantage?
9. What is involved in marketing planning?
10. List and describe the elements of the marketing mix.

Choices and Ethical Issues: You Decide

1. Have you ever pirated software? How about music? Is it ethical to give or receive software instead of paying for it? Does the answer depend on the person's motivation and/or if he could otherwise afford to buy the product?
2. The marketing concept focuses on the ability of marketing to satisfy customer needs. As a typical college student, how does marketing satisfy your needs? What areas of your life are affected by marketing? What areas of your life (if any) are not affected by marketing?
3. In both developed and developing countries, not all firms have implemented programs that follow the marketing concept. Can you think of firms that still operate with a production orientation? A selling orientation? What changes would you recommend for these firms?
4. Successful firms have a competitive advantage because they are able to identify distinctive competencies and use these to create differential benefits for their customers. Consider your business school or your university. What distinctive competencies does it have? What differential benefits does it provide for students? What is its competitive advantage? What are your ideas as to how your university could improve its competitive position? Write an outline of your ideas.
5. Ideally, each member of a value chain adds value to a product before someone buys it. Thinking about a music CD you might buy in a store, what kind of value does the music retailer add? How about the label that signs the artist? The public relations firm that arranges a tour by the artist to promote the new CD? The production company that shoots a music video to go along with the cut?
6. User-generated commercials seem to be part of a broader trend toward user-generated content of all sorts. Examples include MySpace, Flickr (where users post photos and comment on others' pictures), blogging, and video-sharing sites like YouTube. Do you think this is a passing fad or an important trend? How (if at all) should marketers be dealing with these activities?
7. Some marketing or consumption activities involve the (literal) consumption of people—voluntarily or not. In one recent controversial incident, a man in Germany advertised on the Internet to find someone who wanted to be killed and eaten (we are not making this up). He actually found a willing volunteer and did just what he promised—he's now on trial for murder. If a person consents to be "consumed" in some way, is this still an ethical problem?

Practice: Apply What You've Learned

1. An old friend of yours has been making and selling vitamin-fortified smoothies to acquaintances and friends of friends for some time. He is now thinking about opening a shop in a small college town, but he is worried about whether he'll have enough customers who want these smoothies to keep a business going. Knowing that

you are a marketing student, he's asked you for some advice. What can you tell him about product, price, promotion, and place (distribution) strategies that will help him get his business off the ground?

2. Assume that you are employed by your city's chamber of commerce. One major focus of the chamber is to get industries to move to your city. As a former marketing student, you know that there are issues involving product, price, promotion, and place (distribution) that can attract business. Next week you have an opportunity to speak to the members of the chamber, and your topic will be "Marketing a City." Develop an outline for that presentation.

3. As a marketing professional, you have been asked to write a short piece for a local business newsletter about the state of marketing today. You think the best way to address this topic is to review how the marketing concept has evolved and to discuss the triple bottom line orientation. Write the short article you will submit to the editor of the newsletter.

4. As college students, you and your friends sometimes discuss the various courses you are taking. One of your friends says to you, "Marketing's not important. It's just dumb advertising." Another friend says, "Marketing doesn't really affect people's lives in any way." As a role-playing exercise, present your arguments against these statements to your class.

Miniproject: Learn by Doing

The purpose of this miniproject is to develop an understanding of the importance of marketing to different organizations.

1. Working as a team with two or three other students select an organization in your community that practices marketing. It may be a manufacturer, a service provider, a retailer, a not-for-profit organization—almost any organization will do. Then schedule a visit with someone within the organization who is involved in the marketing activities. Arrange for a short visit during which the person can give your group a tour of the facilities and explain the organization's marketing activities.

2. Divide the following list of topics among your team and ask each person to be responsible for developing a set of questions to ask during the interview to learn about the company's program:
   - What customer segments the company targets
   - How it determines needs and wants
   - What products it offers, including features, benefits, and goals for customer satisfaction
   - What its pricing strategies are, including any discounting policies it has
   - What promotional strategies it uses and what these emphasize to position the product(s)
   - How it distributes products and whether it has encountered any problems
   - How marketing planning is done and who does it
   - Whether social responsibility is part of the marketing program and, if so, in what ways

3. Develop a team report of your findings. In each section of the report, share what you learned that is new or surprising to you compared to what you expected.

4. Develop a team presentation for your class that summarizes your findings. Conclude your presentation with comments on what your team believes the company was doing that was particularly good and what was not quite so good.

Real people, **real surfers**: explore the web

Ron Jon sells clothing and other merchandise both in its stores and on its Web site (**www.ronjons.com**). Visit the Web site, and also identify the Web site of a competitor. *Hint:* You can do this by Googling the term "surfwear." Follow the links to find out as much as you can about the companies. Then on the basis of your experience, answer the following questions:

1. Which firm has the better Web site? What makes it better?

2. Do you think the firms are targeting specific market segments? If so, what market segments? What features of the Web site give you that idea?

3. What are your major criticisms of each of the Web sites? What would you do to improve each site?

Marketing Plan Exercise

A key to long-term business success lies in a firm's ability to offer value to customers through its product offerings. The task of communicating that value proposition rests largely with the company's marketers. A marketing plan not only must clarify the sources of value but also must specify how the value message gets out.

Pick a good or service you like—one that you believe has a strong value proposition. Identify the specific source(s) of value—that is, what leads you to conclude the product offers value?

1. How is that value communicated?

2. What other sources of value might be developed for the product you identified?

3. How might these new value-adding properties be communicated to customers?

Marketing in Action Case:

Real **Choices** at **Virgin** Galactic

Would you like to travel to outer space? Unless you are an astronaut or scientist conducting experiments in the weightlessness of space, is there any reason for you to undertake the risk of space travel? Sir Richard Branson, one of Britain's best-known entrepreneurs, thinks there are a lot of consumers who see outer space as the ultimate adventure holiday. In fact, up to 40 percent of people in one survey said they would like to travel to space. Branson thinks this kind of enthusiasm could lead to thousands of passengers per year hoping to go boldly where few have gone before.

Branson is so convinced of the success of Virgin Galactic that he has already ordered six spaceships, plans an initial investment of $250 million, and says he expects to turn a profit within five years of the launch in 2010. Original plans are for one flight a week but eventually up to 14 flights a week are planned.

Richard Branson is not new to creating successful businesses. He has started a number of companies under the "Virgin" brand name, including Virgin Atlantic airlines, Virgin Records, Virgin Megastores, and the Virgin Mobile phone service. To capitalize on the growing interest in space tourism that one day may be a multibillion-dollar industry, Branson created Virgin Galactic after watching *Spaceship One*, the first spacecraft designed and built by a private citizen, reach space in 2004.

The product that Virgin Galactic hopes to offer to satisfy the demand for space tourism is a ride on *Spaceship Two*, a successor space vehicle to the original *Spaceship One*. The new space vehicle will have seating for eight people and will be launched from an airplane at an altitude of 55,000 feet. Once released from the airplane, *Spaceship Two* will fire rocket engines and the aircraft will climb, almost vertically, to the edge of space, or roughly 70 miles above Earth. At this altitude, passengers will be able to leave their seats and experience a view spanning 800 miles in any direction to include the curvature of the earth and the darkness of space. After spending five minutes at this altitude, the spaceship will descend and land like a regular airplane. Before the flight, three-day preparation for the two-hour flight will include a simulation of zero-gravity environment to show travelers what it means to accelerate and decelerate quickly.

Being a space tourist will not be cheap. However, despite a fare of $200,000 per flight Virgin Galactic already has deposits of $20,000 from 38,000 people in 126 different countries. In addition, a core group of 100 tourists has paid the full $200,000 up front. Prospective passengers have to go though a long application process that includes a series of interviews with the company. Those numbers result in total revenue for the company of $780 million, a sizable amount for a start-up company to take in. And passengers won't begin flying until late 2009 or early 2010.

Obviously, space travel is not available from any existing airport. While original flights will be from Mojave, California, the company struck a deal with the State of New Mexico.

Officials from the state agreed to build a $225 million spaceport from which Virgin Galactic can launch its space tourist flights. Virgin Galactic chose New Mexico as the site because of its steady climate, high altitude, free airspace, and overall low population density. The spaceport will be built just 25 miles south of the town Truth or Consequences, which likely will see a rise in tourism spending once the space flights begin.

A final element of the marketing mix Virgin Galactic addresses is its promotion. Aside from having a well-developed Web site (**virgingalactic.com**) the company has not had to engage in much promotion yet. Because the entire space tourism industry is so new, almost any development receives extensive (and free) coverage from major news outlets such as broadcast and cable TV news, newspapers, and magazines. Promotion is one element of the marketing mix that may require greater development as the space tourism business matures.

Certainly it seems that space tourism has a promising, even if somewhat uncertain, future. Still, there is no guarantee that Virgin Galactic will be a success. While there appears to be a large untapped market for space tourism that could easily change. For instance, what might happen to the industry if an accident occurs and perhaps an entire spaceship, with its passengers and crew, is lost? Such an incident could easily lead to a drop in consumer demand and increased government regulation. And, despite the somewhat limited number of people who are willing to be a space tourist and who actually can afford the price, there's growing competition. Competitors include European firm Astrium, Blue Origin (started by Amazon.com founder Jeff Bezos), Space Exploration Technologies Corp. (created by PayPal founder Elon Musk), and Bigelow Aerospace, a venture aimed at creating space hotels by hotelier Robert Bigelow.

While most of Branson's Virgin businesses have been successful, there have been failures. Virgin Cola was a flop in the U.S. market. Virgin Galactic's management has made initial decisions about the four Ps—product, price, place, and promotion. But are these basic marketing decisions enough? What else is needed to ensure a smooth takeoff for Virgin Galactic?

You Make the Call

1. What is the decision facing Virgin Galactic?
2. What factors are important in understanding this decision situation?
3. What are the alternatives?
4. What decision(s) do you recommend?
5. What are some ways to implement your recommendations?

Based on: "Space Tourism Lures a Rising Number of US Entrepreneurs," *Agence France Presse*, March 22, 2006; Jeff Holtz, "2-Hour Flight: $200,000. The View: Priceless," *New York Times*, July 10, 2007; Melanie Lee, "Virgin Galactic Plans More Spaceships," *Reuters*, February 21, 2008, **http://uk.reuters.com/article/businessNews/idUKSP12834820080221**; Jane Wardell, "Virgin Spaceport to be Built in N.M." *Associated Press*, December 13, 2005; Ben Webster, "Space Tourists Prepare for Lift-Off 2008," *The Times* (London), March 30, 2006.

Chapter 2

Part 1 Make Marketing Value Decisions (Chapters 1, 2, 3)
Part 2 Understand Consumers' Value Needs (Chapters 4, 5, 6, 7)
Part 3 Create the Value Proposition (Chapters 8, 9, 10, 11)
Part 4 Communicate the Value Proposition (Chapters 12, 13, 14)
Part 5 Deliver the Value Proposition (Chapters 15, 16)

Strategic Market Planning: Take the Big Picture

Richard Pickering Profile ▼

A **Decision Maker** at National Book Swap

Richard received a degree in decision science (business, computer science, and math) from Berry College in Rome, Georgia, in 1984 and an MBA from Harvard University in 1989. After successfully launching and selling two other entrepreneurial businesses in electronic banking and payment, Richard was looking for a new idea and determined that a great opportunity was available through the exchange of various media in the mass market.

National Book Swap, the parent company of the first swap site PaperBackSwap.com was launched with the goal of allowing members to swap gently used paperbacks via the U.S. mail. The basic premise is simple—list the romance novels, biographies, or other books that you are willing to swap on the site's virtual library. When another member selects your book, you mail it to them and receive a book credit. Then you can use that credit to request a book from any other member in the system for free. Yes, you pay the postage, but then another member returns the favor and mails you one for free.

The company has been very successful with over 35,000 books currently being traded in an average week, and it boasts over two million books to select from in the virtual library. Expanding upon the same idea, two other companies were launched in related markets—SwapaCD.com and SwapaDVD.com. Collectively all three companies have been featured in over 200 newspaper, magazine, TV, and radio publications to date.

▼ **Q** & **A** with Richard Pickering

Q) What I do when I'm not working?
A) Ride my Harley Davidson motorcycle or '71 Ford Mustang convertible, volunteer in the community, and work with the Sheriff's Youth Homes for neglected children.

Q) First job out of school?
A) Sr. Director of Finance at a large national real estate conglomerate.

Q) Business book I'm reading now?
A) *Happier* by Tal Ben-Shahar. While not strictly a business book, the focus is on being happier in your life which encompasses your business and the people you surround yourself with every day.

Q) My motto to live by?
A) *Carpe diem*—Seize the day. We only have so long to make a difference while on this earth, so you better make the most of it!

Q) What drives me?
A) Business is like a chess game. You always set out to win and do the best you can in every decision. Plan ahead and learn from your earlier mistakes. Your game gets better every time you play.

Q) My management style?
A) Take extra care to find very talented individuals and allow them to do what they love and remember that we are all part of the same team. I want them to view me as just another team member. In other words, casual and laid back—but get the job done and do it right the first time!

Q) Don't do this when interviewing with me?
A) Interrupt by attempting to figure out what I am going to say next so that you can show me how smart you are in a given situation.

Q) My pet peeve?
A) Anyone who claims to "always be right" and does not listen to ideas or suggestions from other team members.

To read Richard Pickering's full interview, please visit **www.mypearsonmarketinglab.com**.

real people, **Real Choices**

Decision Time at PaperBackSwap

PaperBackSwap (**http://www.paperbackswap.com**) was founded with a very simple goal in mind: To become the biggest and best book club in America. The young company's business model is often referred to as *freemium*. This means that the core functionality is offered free of charge but any user can "upgrade" her experience with premium features that range anywhere from $0.27 per use to $8.00 per year. An example of a *freemium* a large company uses is Google's Gmail. By default Google gives you 2 GB of free e-mail storage space. If you need additional space it will sell it to you at a yearly rate that depends upon the block size you purchase.

PaperBackSwap is based upon the very simple premise of swapping what you no longer want for things you do want. When another member requests a book from you, you mail it to them and in turn receive a "credit" once they receive the book. A credit is good for any other book available in the club library. When you request a book to be mailed to you, you give the system a credit. The book is free and yours to keep for as long as you would like.

The typical user that PaperBackSwap initially attracted is a female, age 40 and over, who is frugal, and not very tech-savvy (in fact, 90 percent of users are women). Many of the members were young mothers and they often met with a circle of friends on a regular basis. While the club has a tremendous selection of books to choose from, the typical users read either romance or nonfiction. These users found the site primarily through either word-of-mouth or media mentions. The company's partners knew this because they asked members some questions about themselves when they first registered at the site.

Richard believed that PaperBackSwap would provide great value to its users, but getting the word out and getting people to believe that the swap service is for real and not a scam turned out to be harder than he originally thought. Once the management team began to understand who its core market was going to be, they knew that a traditional on-line model wouldn't work. If the business was going to grow, they had to come up with alternative methods to attract users and to promote the site. The management team members realized that they would have to build in a viral component, meaning that the best way to attract new users was to get current users to tell their friends about it rather than relying on traditional advertising methods that probably wouldn't reach the women they sought. One way they encouraged this word-of-mouth activity was to build in easy options for members to print off signs, flyers, and bookmarks while on the site. For example, some members post the flyers in their break room at work to let others know about the site. Members also can print their own PaperBackSwap business cards that they can hand out to others.

But this grassroots effort alone wasn't enough to build the site. After all, the book swapping network's value to users relies upon an ever-expanding group of participants; this ensures that each user has a greater selection of books they can trade with other members. Besides initially developing the site and its core functionality, promoting it was the partners' biggest problem. They didn't have a large marketing budget and, they made their money by the penny rather than by the dollar, so a major effort like TV advertising wasn't even something they could consider. Richard knew that in order to succeed he would have to carefully consider the current marketing environment and identify just which trend he might latch onto in order to propel the new service into the limelight.

Things to remember:

Core functionality is offered **free of charge**. The most popular feature upgrade is called Box-O-Books, which costs a member **$8 per year**.

90% of **users are female**, age 40 and over.

One of the biggest challenges was getting the word out and people to believe that the swap service is for real and **not a scam**.

To grow the business, they encouraged **word-of-mouth activities**. For example, some members post flyers from the site in their break room at work to let others know about the site.

To succeed they need to carefully consider the **current marketing environment** and identify which **trend** might propel the new service into the limelight.

Richard considered his **Options** 1·2·3

1 **Option**
Market the site as a way to help the environment. Find ways to take advantage of the recycling aspect of the site. With emphasis being put on recycling or cutting back in so many areas of our lives, saving a book from being thrown away seems like a logical fit. By swapping the books with each other, members get to enjoy reading a new book, but they also know that they saved that paperback from being sent to a landfill. Richard figured that with all the media buzz about the environment, this approach would appeal to a lot of people. On the other hand, maybe being seen as a green business wouldn't get the business noticed. After all, many organizations and companies are touting their green attributes (true or not), so PaperBackSwap might get lost in the shuffle.

2 **Option**
Use PaperBackSwap as a vehicle to promote literacy. Book readership among the general public is declining steadily, especially in lower income areas where access to books may be limited. Taking this angle would provide the company with a "feel-good story" that would probably be picked up by a lot of media outlets. But lower income consumers may not have reliable access to the Internet, and, in addition, they may not be willing to spend the money to mail their books to other members.

3 **Option**
Position the site as a cheap source of entertainment. People are always trying to find ways to save money yet still enjoy their favorite things. Users could "have their cake and eat it too" by reading books they like at a lower cost. On the other hand, tastes change, and if your site is viewed as an entertainment destination it may lose popularity over time as consumers move on to the next big thing.

Now, put yourself in Richard's shoes: Which option would you choose, and why?

You Choose

Which **Option** would you choose, and **why**?
1. ☐YES ☐NO   2. ☐YES ☐NO   3. ☐YES ☐NO

See what **option** Richard chose and its success on **page 61** ➡

1
OBJECTIVE

Explain the strategic planning process. (pp. 38–41)

Business Planning:
Compose the Big Picture

Richard Pickering at National Book Swap LLC, parent company of PaperBackSwap.com, understands that planning is everything—well, almost. Part of Richard's role as a planner is to define his offering's distinctive identity and purpose. Careful planning enables a firm to speak in a clear voice in the marketplace so that customers understand what the firm is and what it has to offer that competitors don't—especially as it decides how to create value for customers, clients, partners, and society-at-large.

We think this process is so important that we're launching into our exploration of marketing by starting with a discussion about what planners do and the questions they (both PaperBackSwap.com and marketers in general) need to ask to be sure they keep their companies and products on course. To make things even clearer, we're giving you a "road map" to follow later in this chapter—a pull-out marketing plan template you can use as you make your way through the book helping you to keep the big picture in mind no matter which chapter you're reading.

Whether a firm is a well-established company like NCR or Darden Restaurants (which we'll feature in later chapters) or an upstart like PaperBackSwap, planning for the future is a key to prosperity. Sure, it's true that a firm can succeed even if it makes some mistakes in planning, and there are times when even the best planning cannot anticipate the future accurately. It's also true that some seat-of-the-pants businesses are successful. But without good planning for the future, firms will be less successful than they could be. In the worst-case scenario, a lack of planning can be fatal for both large and small businesses. So, like a Boy Scout, it's always better to be prepared.

Business planning is an ongoing process of decision making that guides the firm both in the short term and the long term. Planning identifies and builds on a firm's strengths, and it helps managers at all levels make informed decisions in a changing business environment. *Planning* means that an organization develops objectives before it takes action. In large firms like Microsoft and Toyota, which operate in many markets, planning is a complex process involving many people from different areas of the company's operations. At a very small business like Mac's Diner in your home town, however, planning is quite different. Mac himself is chief cook, occasional dishwasher, and the sole company planner. With entrepreneurial firms like PaperBackSwap, the planning process falls somewhere in between, depending on the size of the firm and the complexity of its operations.

In many ways, developing great business planning is like taking a great digital photo. The metaphor works because success in photography is built around capturing the right information in the lens of your camera, positioning the image correctly, and snapping the picture you'll need to set things in motion. A business plan is a lot like that.

In this chapter, we'll look at the different steps in an organization's planning. First, we'll see how managers develop a **business plan** that includes the decisions that guide the entire organization or its business units. Then we'll examine the entire marketing planning process and the stages in that process that lead to the development and implementation of a **marketing plan**—a document that describes the marketing environment, outlines the marketing objectives and strategies, and identifies how the company will implement and control the strategies imbedded in the plan. But first, let's consider one of the most important overarching issues in planning—ethics.

Ethics and Marketing Planning

It's hard to overemphasize the importance of making ethical marketing decisions. Businesses touch many stakeholders and they need to do what's best for all of them where possible. On a more selfish level, unethical decisions usually come back to bite you later. The consequences of low ethical standards become very visible when you consider a slew of highly publicized corporate scandals that have made news headlines since the turn of the century:

- In the fall of 2001, Houston-based Enron—at that time one of the world's great energy firms—revealed a massive accounting fraud. The company had hidden hundreds of millions of dollars of debt through unethical and illegal accounting practices with the assistance of the nationally renowned accounting firm Arthur Andersen. Former Enron chairman Ken Lay was found guilty of conspiracy in 2006, but passed away before he was to go to jail. CEO Jeff Skilling was also convicted in 2006 of multiple federal felony charges relating to Enron's financial collapse, and is currently serving a 24-year and 4-month prison sentence.[1]

- In 2002, when the giant telecommunications firm WorldCom collapsed into bankruptcy after revealing it had falsified its financial statements by roughly $11 billion, the U.S. General Services Administration banned government contracts with the company, stating that WorldCom "lacked internal controls and business ethics."[2] In July 2005, CEO Bernard Ebbers was sentenced to 25 years in prison.

- Designer diva Martha Stewart went to jail in March 2005 for lying to federal investigators about receiving insider information prior to selling off ImClone stock.[3]

- The U.S. mortgage banking industry melted down in 2007 when it became apparent that lack of regulation and poor self-policing of the industry had resulted from easy access over the prior five years to "sub-prime" mortgages—loans that tantalize buyers with very low interest rates for a year or two then balloon to unaffordable payments.[4]

The fallout from these and other cases raises the issue of how damaging unethical practices can be to society at large. The business press is filled with articles about accountability, corporate accounting practices, and government regulation as the public and corporate worlds rethink what we define as ethical behavior. When major companies defraud the public, everyone suffers. Thousands of people lose their jobs, and in many cases the pensions they counted on to support them in retirement vanish overnight.

Other stakeholders are punished as well, including stockholders who lose their investments, and consumers who end up paying for worthless merchandise or services. Even confidence in our political system suffers, as was the case with allegations that the Bush administration gave favorable treatment to Halliburton when awarding contracts for the wars in Iraq and Afghanistan (former Vice President Dick Cheney was CEO of Halliburton prior to taking office). All taxpayers may wind up paying a penalty as well if the government decides to

business planning
An ongoing process of making decisions that guides the firm both in the short term and for the long term.

business plan
A plan that includes the decisions that guide the entire organization.

marketing plan
A document that describes the marketing environment, outlines the marketing objectives and strategy, and identifies who will be responsible for carrying out each part of the marketing strategy.

Major problems in the mortgage industry beginning in 2007 created economic nightmares for many consumers.

Ripped from the **Headlines**

Ethical Decisions in the Real World

For over fourteen years the U.S. Food and Drug Administration (FDA) has had a moratorium on the sale of silicone implants for breast augmentation. The moratorium occurred in response to claims in the early 1990s that the popular product caused a wide range of diseases and other negative physical reactions in users—claims that industry-leading players such as Dow Corning, 3M, Bristol-Myers Squibb, Baxter International, Allergan, Inc., and Mentor Corporation always disputed. Nonetheless, thousands of product-liability lawsuits forced Dow Corning into bankruptcy and all the rest, except Allergan and Mentor, eventually exited the business.

ETHICS CHECK: ↖

Find out what other students taking this course **would do** and **why** on **www.mypearsonmarketinglab.com**

But more recently, newer studies have quieted many critics, and in November 2007 the FDA actually lifted the ban on silicone implant sales—with a requirement that sellers provide formal written warnings of potential product risks. The combination of the product's checkered history, the fact that many women who had the implants from the 1980s–1990s era still firmly believe their health was compromised, and the potential for huge sales and profits on market re-entry make for a very difficult decision as to whether a firm should reactivate an aggressive marketing planning process for reintroducing silicone breast implants to the U.S. market. What would you do?

Ripped from the Headlines! See what happened in the Real World at **www.mypearsonmarketinglab.com**

Would you market silicone implants? Why?

☐YES ☐NO

business ethics

Rules of conduct for an organization.

code of ethics

Written standards of behavior to which everyone in the organization must subscribe.

"bail out" an industry or company (as it has done with the savings-and-loan industry, with Chrysler, and with the national passenger rail system, now known as Amtrak).

Codes of Business Ethics

Ethics are rules of conduct—how most people in a culture judge what is right and what is wrong. **Business ethics** are basic values that guide a firm's behavior. These values govern all sorts of marketing planning decisions that managers make including what goes into their products, where they source raw materials, how they advertise, and what type of pricing they establish. Developing sound business ethics is a major step toward creating a strong relationship with customers and others in the marketplace.

With many rules about doing business—written and unwritten—floating around, how do marketers know what upper management, investors, and customers expect of them? In order to answer this question definitively, many firms develop their own **code of ethics**—written standards of behavior to which everyone in the organization must subscribe—as part of the planning process. These documents eliminate confusion about what the firm considers to be ethically acceptable behavior by its people, and also set standards for how the organization interacts with its stakeholders. For example, the Dow Chemical Company's Code of Business Conduct, available in 20 different languages through its Web site at **www.dow.com**, is based on Dow's stated corporate values of integrity and respect for people. The code deals with the following issues: diversity; the environment; financial integrity; accurate company records; conflicts of interest; obligations to customers, competitors, and regulators; computer systems and telecommunications security; safeguarding important information; interactions with the public; and corporate social responsibility.[5]

To help marketers adhere to ethical behavior in their endeavors, the American Marketing Association (AMA) developed the code of ethics that we reproduce in Table 2.1. Note that this code spells out norms and expectations relating to all aspects of the marketing process, from pricing to marketing research.

Table 2.1 | AMA Code of Ethics

Ethical Norms and Values for Marketers

Preamble

The American Marketing Association commits itself to promoting the highest standard of professional ethical norms and values for its members. Norms are established standards of conduct that are expected and maintained by society and/or professional organizations. Values represent the collective conception of what people find desirable, important and morally proper. Values serve as the criteria for evaluating the actions of others. Marketing practitioners must recognize that they not only serve their enterprises but also act as stewards of society in creating, facilitating and executing the efficient and effective transactions that are part of the greater economy. In this role, marketers should embrace the highest ethical norms of practicing professionals and the ethical values implied by their responsibility toward stakeholders (e.g., customers, employees, investors, channel members, regulators and the host community).

General Norms

1. Marketers must do no harm. This means doing work for which they are appropriately trained or experienced so that they can actively add value to their organizations and customers. It also means adhering to all applicable laws and regulations and embodying high ethical standards in the choices they make.

2. Marketers must foster trust in the marketing system. This means that products are appropriate for their intended and promoted uses. It requires that marketing communications about goods and services are not intentionally deceptive or misleading. It suggests building relationships that provide for the equitable adjustment and/or redress of customer grievances. It implies striving for good faith and fair dealing so as to contribute toward the efficacy of the exchange process.

3. Marketers must embrace, communicate and practice the fundamental ethical values that will improve consumer confidence in the integrity of the marketing exchange system. These basic values are intentionally aspirational and include honesty, responsibility, fairness, respect, openness and citizenship.

Ethical Values

Honesty—to be truthful and forthright in our dealings with customers and stakeholders.

- We will tell the truth in all situations and at all times.
- We will offer products of value that do what we claim in our communications.
- We will stand behind our products if they fail to deliver their claimed benefits.
- We will honor our explicit and implicit commitments and promises.

Responsibility—to accept the consequences of our marketing decisions and strategies.

- We will make strenuous efforts to serve the needs of our customers.
- We will avoid using coercion with all stakeholders.
- We will acknowledge the social obligations to stakeholders that come with increased marketing and economic power.
- We will recognize our special commitments to economically vulnerable segments of the market such as children, the elderly and others who may be substantially disadvantaged.

Fairness—to try to balance justly the needs of the buyer with the interests of the seller.

- We will represent our products in a clear way in selling, advertising and other forms of communication; this includes the avoidance of false, misleading and deceptive promotion.
- We will reject manipulations and sales tactics that harm customer trust.
- We will not engage in price fixing, predatory pricing, price gouging or "bait-and-switch" tactics.
- We will not knowingly participate in material conflicts of interest.

Respect—to acknowledge the basic human dignity of all stakeholders.

- We will value individual differences even as we avoid stereotyping customers or depicting demographic groups (e.g., gender, race, sexual orientation) in a negative or dehumanizing way in our promotions.
- We will listen to the needs of our customers and make all reasonable efforts to monitor and improve their satisfaction on an ongoing basis.
- We will make a special effort to understand suppliers, intermediaries and distributors from other cultures.
- We will appropriately acknowledge the contributions of others, such as consultants, employees and coworkers, to our marketing endeavors.

Openness—to create transparency in our marketing operations.

- We will strive to communicate clearly with all our constituencies.
- We will accept constructive criticism from our customers and other stakeholders.
- We will explain significant product or service risks, component substitutions or other foreseeable eventualities that could affect customers or their perception of the purchase decision.
- We will fully disclose list prices and terms of financing as well as available price deals and adjustments.

Citizenship—to fulfill the economic, legal, philanthropic and societal responsibilities that serve stakeholders in a strategic manner.

- We will strive to protect the natural environment in the execution of marketing campaigns.
- We will give back to the community through volunteerism and charitable donations.
- We will work to contribute to the overall betterment of marketing and its reputation.
- We will encourage supply chain members to ensure that trade is fair for all participants, including producers in developing countries.

Implementation

Finally, we recognize that every industry sector and marketing subdiscipline (e.g., marketing research, e-commerce, direct selling, direct marketing, advertising) has its own specific ethical issues that require policies and commentary. An array of such codes can be accessed through links on the AMA Web site. We encourage all such groups to develop and/or refine their industry and discipline-specific codes of ethics to supplement these general norms and values.

The American Marketing Association helps its members adhere to ethical standards of business through its Code of Ethics.

2 The Three Levels of Business Planning

OBJECTIVE

Understand the three levels of business planning: strategic, functional, and operational.

(pp. 42–43)

We all know what planning is—we plan a vacation or a great Saturday night party. Some of us even plan how we're going to study and get our assignments completed without stressing out at the last minute. When businesses plan, the process is more complex. As Figure 2.1 shows, planning occurs at three levels: strategic, functional, and operational. The top level is "big picture" stuff, while the bottom level specifies the "nuts-and-bolts" actions the firm will need to take to achieve these lofty goals.

strategic planning

A managerial decision process that matches an organization's resources and capabilities to its market opportunities for long-term growth and survival.

- **Strategic planning** is the managerial decision process that matches the firm's resources (such as its financial assets and workforce) and capabilities (the things it is able to do well because of its expertise and experience) to its market opportunities for long-term growth. In a strategic plan, top management—usually the chief executive officer (CEO), president, and other top executives—define the firm's purpose and specify what the firm hopes to achieve over the next five years or so. For example, a firm's strategic plan may set an objective to increase total revenues by 20 percent in the next five years.

strategic business units (SBUs)

Individual units within the firm that operate like separate businesses, with each having its own mission, business objectives, resources, managers, and competitors.

Large firms, such as the Walt Disney Company, have a number of self-contained divisions called **strategic business units (SBUs)**—individual units representing different areas of business within a firm that are different enough to each have their own mission, business objectives, resources, managers, and competitors. Disney's SBUs include its theme park, movie, television network, and cruise line divisions, and strategic planning occurs both at the overall corporate level (Disney headquarters planning for the whole corporation) and at the individual business unit level (at the theme park, movie studios, television networks, and cruise line level). We'll discuss these two levels later in the chapter.

functional planning

A decision process that concentrates on developing detailed plans for strategies and tactics for the short term, supporting an organization's long-term strategic plan.

- The next level of planning is **functional planning** (sometimes called "tactical planning"). This level gets its name because the various functional areas of the firm, such as marketing, finance, and human resources get involved. Vice presidents or functional directors usually do this. We refer to what the functional planning marketers do as *marketing planning*. The person in charge of such planning may have the title of Director of Marketing, Vice President of Marketing, or Chief Marketing Officer. Marketers like

Figure 2.1 | Levels of Planning

During planning, an organization determines its objectives and then develops courses of action to accomplish them. In larger firms, planning takes place at the strategic, functional, and operational levels.

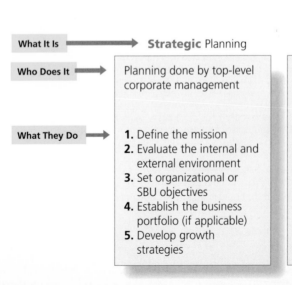

	Strategic Planning	**Functional** Planning (In Marketing Department, called Marketing Planning)	**Operational** Planning
What It Is			
Who Does It	Planning done by top-level corporate management	Planning done by top functional-level management such as the firms chief marketing officer (CMO)	Planning done by supervisory managers
What They Do	1. Define the mission 2. Evaluate the internal and external environment 3. Set organizational or SBU objectives 4. Establish the business portfolio (if applicable) 5. Develop growth strategies	1. Perform a situation analysis 2. Set marketing objectives 3. Develop marketing strategies 4. Implement marketing strategies 5. Monitor and control marketing strategies	1. Develop action plans to implement the marketing plan 2. Use marketing metrics to monitor how the plan is working

Richard Pickering at PaperBackSwap might set an objective to gain 40 percent of a particular market by successfully introducing three new products during the coming year. This objective would be part of a marketing plan. Marketing planning typically includes both a broad 3–5 year plan to support the firm's strategic plan and a detailed annual plan for the coming year.

- Still farther down the planning ladder are the first-line managers. In marketing, these include people such as sales managers, marketing communications managers, brand managers, and marketing research managers. These managers are responsible for planning at a third level we call **operational planning**. This level of planning focuses on the day-to-day execution of the functional plans and includes detailed annual, semiannual, or quarterly plans. Operational plans might show exactly how many units of a product a salesperson needs to sell per month, or how many television commercials the firm will place on certain networks during a season. At the operational planning level, PaperBackSwap may develop plans to promote the service to potential customers through Internet pop-ups, while also developing a quarterly plan for the company's customer service activities. Both of these actions are forms of operational planning.

Large firms like the Walt Disney Company typically operate several self-contained divisions, or strategic business units (SBUs).

operational planning
A decision process that focuses on developing detailed plans for day-to-day activities that carry out an organization's functional plans.

Of course, marketing managers don't just sit in their offices dreaming up plans without any concern for the rest of the organization. Even though we've described each layer separately, *all business planning is an integrated activity*. This means that the organization's strategic, functional, and operational plans must work together for the benefit of the whole. So planners at all levels must consider good principles of accounting, the value of the company to its stockholders, and the requirements for staffing and human resource management—that is, they must keep the "big picture" in mind even as they plan for their corner of the organization's world.

In short, the different functional- and operational-level planners within an organization have to make sure that their plans support the overall organization's mission and objectives and that they work well together. A marketer like Richard Pickering at PaperBackSwap can't go off and develop a successful plan for the marketing side of the firm without fully understanding how what he's doing fits with the overall organization's direction and resources. In the case of PaperBackSwap, this means Richard's plan must fit in with the overall strategic direction of National Book Swap PaperBackSwap's parent company. In the next sections, we'll further explore planning at each of the three levels that we've just introduced.

Richard
Pickering

APPLYING operational planning

Richard understands how what he's planning fits with the overall organization's direction and resources. This means Richard's plan must fit with strategic direction of National Book Swap LLC, Inc., PaperBackSwap's parent company. ➥

3 OBJECTIVE

Describe the steps in marketing planning.
(pp. 43–52)

Strategic Planning: Frame the Picture

Many large firms realize that relying on only one product can be risky, so they have become multiproduct companies with self-contained divisions organized around products or brands. You know that firms such as Disney operate several distinctly different businesses (Disney's theme parks, movie studios, television networks, and cruise line). For National Book Swap LLC, we could consider PaperBackSwap an SBU—other SBUs in its stable include SwapaCD and SwapaDVD.

In firms with multiple SBUs, the first step in strategic planning is for top management to establish a mission for the entire corporation. Top managers then evaluate the internal and external environments of the business and set corporate-level objectives that guide decision making within each individual SBU. In small firms that are not large enough to have separate SBUs, strategic planning simply takes place at the overall firm level. Whether or not a firm has SBUs, the process of strategic planning is basically the same. Let's look at the planning steps in a bit more detail.

Step 1: Define the Mission

Theoretically, top management's first step in the strategic planning stage is to answer questions such as:

- What business are we in?

- What customers should we serve?

- How should we develop the firm's capabilities and focus its efforts?

mission statement
A formal statement in an organization's strategic plan that describes the overall purpose of the organization and what it intends to achieve in terms of its customers, products, and resources.

In many firms, the answers to questions such as these become the lead items in the organization's strategic plan. The answers become part of a **mission statement**—a formal document that describes the organization's overall purpose and what it hopes to achieve in terms of its customers, products, and resources. For example, the mission of Mothers Against Drunk Driving (MADD) is "to stop drunk driving, support the victims of this violent crime, and prevent underage drinking."[6] The mission statement of PaperBackSwap's parent firm National Book Swap is "to become the nation's largest book club and in the process bring a lifetime of reading material to every American."

The ideal mission statement is not too broad, too narrow, or too shortsighted. Note that National Book Swap's mission statement leaves no doubt about the focus of its business. A mission that is too broad will not provide adequate focus for the organization. It doesn't do much good to claim, "We are in the business of making high-quality products" or "Our business is keeping customers happy" as it is hard to find a firm that doesn't make these claims.

Continental Airlines flies 24/7. They asked Xerox to plot a course to create and track maintenance advisories digitally. Result? Paper's eliminated. Uptime's sky high. There's a new way to look at it.

Learn more: www.xerox.com/learn Or call: 1-800-ASK-XEROX ext. LEARN

THE DOCUMENT COMPANY
XEROX

Xerox is working to change the perception that it is a copier-only company.

However, a mission statement that is *too narrow* may inhibit managers' ability to visualize possible growth opportunities. If, for example, a firm sees itself in terms of its product only, consumer trends or technology can make that product obsolete—and the firm is left with no future. Years ago, Xerox was the undisputed king of the photocopier—to the point where many people refer to photocopying generically as "Xeroxing." But in the digital age, if Xerox had continued to define its mission in terms of just producing copy machines instead of providing "document solutions," the shift to electronic documents would have left them in the dust the way the Model T Ford replaced the horse and buggy. Take a look at how today's Xerox defines itself:

Xerox is the world's leading document management technology and services enterprise. A $16 billion company, Xerox provides the document industry's broadest portfolio of offerings. Digital systems include color and black-and-white printing and publishing systems, digital presses and "book factories," multifunction devices, laser and solid ink network printers, copiers and fax machines. Xerox's services expertise is unmatched and includes helping businesses develop on-line document archives, analyzing how employees can most efficiently share documents and knowledge in the office, operating in-house print shops or mailrooms, and building Web-based processes for personalizing direct mail, invoices, brochures, and more. Xerox also offers associated software, support, and supplies such as toner, paper, and ink.[7]

It's also important to remember that the need for a clear mission statement applies to virtually any type of organization, even those like Mothers Against Drunk Driving, whose objective is to serve society rather than to sell goods or services.

Step 2: Evaluate the Internal and External Environment

The second step in strategic planning is to assess the firm's internal and external environments. We refer to this process as a **situation analysis**, *environmental analysis*, or sometimes a *business review*. The analysis includes a discussion of the firm's internal environment, which can identify a firm's strengths and weaknesses, as well as the external environment in which the firm does business so the firm can identify opportunities and threats.

By **internal environment** we mean all the controllable elements inside a firm that influence how well the firm operates. Internal strengths may lie in the firm's technologies. What is the firm able to do well that other firms would find difficult to duplicate? What patents does it hold? A firm's physical facilities can be an important strength or weakness, as can its level of financial stability, its relationships with suppliers, its corporate reputation, its ability to produce consistently high-quality products, and its ownership of strong brands in the marketplace.

Internal strengths and weaknesses often reside in the firm's employees—the firm's *human and intellectual capital*. What skills do the employees have? What kind of training have they had? Are they loyal to the firm? Do they feel a sense of ownership? Has the firm been able to attract top researchers and good decision makers?

Southwest Airlines has always been very focused on hiring and developing employees who reflect the "Southwest Spirit" to customers. Anyone who has flown on Southwest can attest to the fact that the atmosphere is lively and fun, and flight attendants are likely to do most any crazy stunt—bowling in the aisle, serenading the captain and first officer (and passengers) with a favorite tune, or one of the best is a guy who does galloping horse hooves and neighing sounds during takeoff and landing to promote a fun atmosphere. For Southwest, a real strength—one that's hard for the competition to crack—lies in this employee spirit.[8]

The **external environment** consists of elements outside the firm that may affect it either positively or negatively. The external environment for today's businesses is global, so managers/marketers must consider elements such as the economy, competition, technology, law, ethics, and sociocultural trends. Unlike elements of the internal environment that management can control to a large degree, the firm can't directly control these external factors, so management must respond to them through its planning process.

Chapter 3 develops in depth the various elements of the external environment in which marketing takes place, within a context of today's global enterprise. For now, it is important for you to be aware that opportunities and threats can come from any part of the external environment. On the one hand, trends or currently unserved customer needs may provide opportunities for growth. On the other hand, if changing customer needs or buying patterns mean customers are turning away from a firm's products, it's a signal of possible danger or threats down the road.

Even wildly successful firms have to change to keep up with external environmental pressures. Like all airlines, Southwest been affected in recent years by tighter security regulations driven by the federal government through the Transportation Safety Administration. These regulations entail additional costs for

situation analysis
An assessment of a firm's internal and external environments.

internal environment
The controllable elements inside an organization, including its people, its facilities, and how it does things that influence the operations of the organization.

external environment
The uncontrollable elements outside an organization that may affect its performance either positively or negatively.

This brand's emphasis on being organic is in step with a sociocultural trend.

Advancements in technology allow Maxell to eliminate the need for you to touch the adhesive side of a CD label by hand—and gets rid of bubbles and curling too.

Southwest that are not optional and the firm has no choice but to react to this demand from the external environment. Prices of jet fuel have skyrocketed recently; for awhile Southwest reacted by "hedging" against jet fuel futures—that is, speculatively committing to a price in the hope that it will beat the actual future price of fuel. For a long time, the hedging resulted in major cost advantages for Southwest over airlines that were not engaged in hedging, but this is no longer a competitive advantage since most airlines now hedge. Then too, the rise of JetBlue and other new customer-friendly competitors has caused Southwest to rethink its longstanding open seating policy, resulting in a new system to cut down on the infamous A, B, and C lines at the jetway.[9]

What is the outcome of an analysis of a firm's internal and external environments? Managers often synthesize their findings from a situation analysis into a format we call a **SWOT analysis**. This document, a summary of the ideas developed in the situation analysis, allows managers to focus clearly on the meaningful strengths (S) and weaknesses (W) in the firm's internal environment and opportunities (O) and threats (T) coming from outside the firm (the external environment). A SWOT analysis enables a firm to develop strategies that make use of what the firm does best in seizing opportunities for growth, while at the same time avoiding external threats that might hurt the firm's sales and profits. Table 2.2 shows an example of a partial SWOT analysis for McDonald's.

SWOT analysis
An analysis of an organization's strengths and weaknesses and the opportunities and threats in its external environment.

Step 3: Set Organizational or SBU Objectives

After constructing a mission statement, top management translates that mission statement into *organizational* or *SBU objectives*. These goals are a direct outgrowth of the mission statement and broadly identify what the firm hopes to accomplish within the general time

Table 2.2	Example of a Partial SWOT Analysis for McDonald's
Strengths	World-class research and product development. Global franchise system that is second to none. Strong cash position. Consistency of product and service quality across the globe.
Weaknesses	Until recently, slow to react to consumer trends and preferences.
Opportunities	Changing consumer tastes and dining preferences signals opportunity to remake some of the locations into more upscale bistro formats, including the addition of a cool new genre of McDonald's coffee houses to compete directly with Starbucks. Reconnecting with Baby Boomers and Gen X while cultivating Gen Y and Millennials provides opportunity for product innovation and more flexibility by market area. Rising cost of gasoline means more people are seeking dining experiences closer to home.
Threats	The general degeneration of the image of America globally, especially in Europe, may have an impact on sales. Strongly negative media coverage surrounding unhealthy eating has tarnished the brand. Burger King has emerged as an innovator. The rival chain has been hugely successful with off-beat advertising strategies both off-line and on-line that appeal to younger consumers.

frame of the firm's long-range business plan. If the firm is big enough to have separate SBUs, each unit will have its own objectives relevant to its operations.

To be effective, objectives need to be *specific*, *measurable* (so firms can tell whether they've met them or not), *attainable*, and *sustainable*. Attainability is especially important—firms that establish "pie in the sky" objectives they can't realistically obtain can create frustration for their employees (who work hard but get no satisfaction of accomplishment) and other stakeholders in the firm, such as vendors and shareholders who are affected when the firm doesn't meet its objectives. That a firm's objectives are sustainable is also critical—what's the point of investing in attaining an objective for only a very short term? This often happens when a firm underestimates the likelihood a competitor will come to market with a better offering. Without some assurance that an objective is sustainable, the financial return on an investment likely will not be positive.

Competitive pressures are forcing Southwest to rethink its longstanding open seating policy.

Objectives may relate to revenue and sales, profitability, the firm's standing in the market, return on investment, productivity, product development, customer satisfaction, social responsibility, and many other attributes. To ensure measurability, marketers increasingly try to state objectives in numerical terms. For example, a firm might have as an objective a 10 percent increase in profitability. It could reach this objective by increasing productivity, by reducing costs, or by selling off an unprofitable division. Or it might meet this 10 percent objective by developing new products, investing in new technologies, or entering a new market.

For many years, Procter & Gamble (P&G) had an objective of having a number-one brand in every product category in which it competed. This objective was specific and clearly it was attainable, since P&G could boast of market leaders such as Crest in the toothpaste category, Folgers in coffee, Pampers in diapers, and Head & Shoulders in shampoo. It also was measurable in terms of the share of market of P&G's products versus those competitors sold. However, in the long run this objective is very difficult to sustain because of competitive activity and ever-changing consumer tastes.

Sure enough, over time some P&G brands continued to hold a respectable market share, but they dropped from the number-one position. Should P&G not sell in a product category simply because its brand is not number one? Management realized the answer to this question was clearly "no," and the objective morphed from category leadership into one focused on profitability for each brand.

Step 4: Establish the Business Portfolio

For companies with several different SBUs, strategic planning includes making decisions about how to best allocate resources across these businesses to ensure growth for the total organization. As Figure 2.2 illustrates, each SBU has its own focus within the firm's overall strategic plan, and each has its own target market and strategies for reaching its objectives. Just like an independent business, each SBU is a separate *profit center* within the larger corporation—that is,

Competition is fierce in the ongoing battle to sell household products.

Figure 2.2 | SBUs and the Strategic plan

Very large corporations are normally divided into self-contained divisions, or SBUs. SBUs represent different major areas of the overall firm's business. For example, General Electric (GE) has a jet engine division, a lighting division, an appliance division, and numerous other divisions. At GE, as with most corporations, each SBU operates as an independent business with its own mission and objectives—and its own marketing strategy.

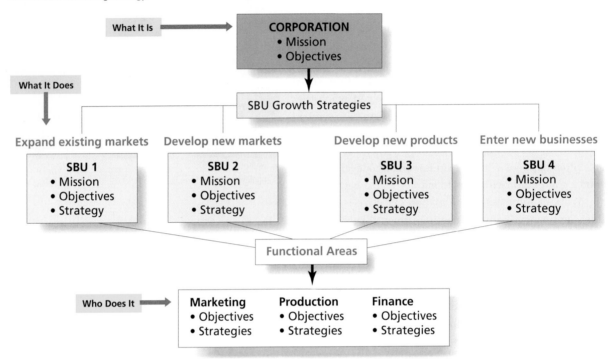

each SBU within the firm is responsible for its own costs, revenues, and profits, and these items can be accounted for separately for that SBU.

Just as we call the collection of different stocks an investor owns a portfolio, the range of different businesses that a large firm operates is its **business portfolio**. As with the GE example in Figure 2.2, these different businesses usually represent very different product lines, each of which operates with its own budget and management. Having a diversified business portfolio reduces the firm's dependence on one product line or one group of customers. For example, if consumers don't travel as much and Disney has a bad year in theme park attendance and cruises, its managers hope that the sales will be made up by stay-at-homers who go to Disney movies and watch Disney's television networks and DVDs.

Portfolio analysis is a tool management uses to assess the potential of a firm's business portfolio. It helps management decide which of its current SBUs should receive more—or less—of the firm's resources, and which of its SBUs are most consistent with the firm's overall mission. There are a host of portfolio models available for use. To exemplify how one works, let's examine the especially popular model the Boston Consulting Group (BCG) developed: the **BCG growth–market share matrix**.

The BCG model focuses on determining the potential of a firm's existing successful SBUs to generate cash that the firm can then use to invest in other businesses. The BCG matrix in Figure 2.3 shows that the vertical axis represents the attractiveness of the market: the *market growth rate*. Even though the figure shows "high" and "low" as measurements, marketers might ask whether the total market for the SBU's products is growing at a rate of 10, 50, 100, or 200 percent annually.

The horizontal axis in Figure 2.3 shows the SBU's current strength in the market through its relative market share. Here, marketers might ask whether the SBU's share is 5, 25, or perhaps 75 percent of the current market. Combining the two axes creates four quadrants

business portfolio
The group of different products or brands owned by an organization and characterized by different income-generating and growth capabilities.

portfolio analysis
A management tool for evaluating a firm's business mix and assessing the potential of an organization's strategic business units.

BCG growth–market share matrix
A portfolio analysis model developed by the Boston Consulting Group that assesses the potential of successful products to generate cash that a firm can then use to invest in new products.

representing four different types of SBUs. Each quadrant of the BCG grid uses a symbol to designate business units that fall within a certain range for market growth rate and market share. Let's take a closer look at each cell in the grid:

- **Stars** are SBUs with products that have a dominant market share in high-growth markets. Because the SBU has a dominant share of the market, stars generate large revenues, but they also require large amounts of funding to keep up with production and promotion demands. Because the market has a large growth potential, managers design strategies to maximize market share in the face of increasing competition. The firm aims at getting the largest share of loyal customers so that the SBU will generate profits that it can reallocate to other parts of the company. For example, in recent years, Disney has viewed its movie brand Walt Disney Pictures as a star, investing heavily in such franchise players as Hannah Montana and Narnia.

- **Cash cows** have a dominant market share in a low-growth-potential market. Because there's not much opportunity for new companies, competitors don't often enter the market. At the same time, the SBU is well established and enjoys a high market share that the firm can sustain with minimal funding. Firms usually milk cash cows of their profits to fund the growth of other SBUs. Of course, if the firm's objective is to increase revenues, having too many cash cows with little or no growth potential can become a liability. For Disney, its theme parks unit fits into the cash cow category in that sales have been very steady or slightly increasing for the past five years.

- **Question marks**—sometimes called "problem children"—are SBUs with low market shares in fast-growth markets. When a business unit is a question mark, it suggests that the firm has failed to compete successfully. Perhaps the SBU's products offer fewer benefits than competing products. Or maybe its prices are too high, its distributors are ineffective, or its advertising is too weak. The firm could pump more money into marketing the product and hope that market share will improve. But the firm may find itself "throwing good money after bad," gaining nothing but a negative cash flow and disappointment. For Disney, its Disney Stores are in the question-mark category, as their performance compared to the overall specialty retail market has lagged in recent years.

- **Dogs** have a small share of a slow-growth market. They are businesses that offer specialized products in limited markets that are not likely to grow quickly. When possible, large firms may sell off their dogs to smaller firms that may be able to nurture them—or they may take the SBU's products off the market. Disney, being a savvy strategic planner, does not appear to have any businesses that are currently in the doghouse (so to speak).

    Like Disney, Richard Pickering at PaperBackSwap may use the BCG matrix to evaluate his product lines in order to make important decisions about where to invest for

Figure 2.3 | BCG Matrix

The Boston Consulting Group's (BCG) growth-market share matrix is one way a firm can examine its portfolio of different products or SBUs. By categorizing SBUs as stars, cash cows, question marks, or dogs, the matrix helps managers make good decisions about how the firm should grow.

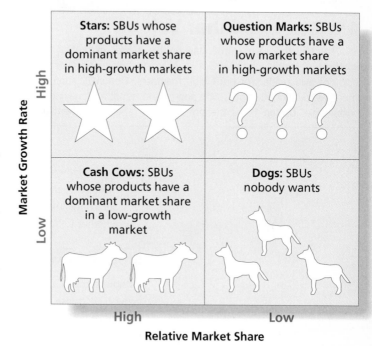

stars
SBUs with products that have a dominant market share in high-growth markets.

cash cows
SBUs with a dominant market share in a low-growth-potential market.

question marks
SBUs with low market shares in fast-growth markets.

dogs
SBUs with a small share of a slow-growth market. They are businesses that offer specialized products in limited markets that are not likely to grow quickly.

Jeep's product development strategy offers vehicles for different needs.

Ann Marie
Vega

a professor at the University of New Hampshire

My Advice for PaperBackSwap would
be to choose

1

Option

real people, **Other Voices**

Strategically, the focus must stay on the target market—young mothers, not very tech savvy. Option 2 targets the expansion of literacy, not avid readers or book club members. Option 3, entertainment, as mentioned, moves with pop culture trends and may not be sustainable. **Option 1** ties the site with the green movement and speaks to the target market. Young mothers are concerned with keeping the earth healthy for their children. The green approach will be appealing to the target market and will create a buzz for the company. The company may want to consider a focus on book club exchange packages. This would allow book clubs who have a set of the same book to exchange with another book club. This option would drive economy of scale into the business much like Box-O-Books, but for a targeted market segment. Book clubs often read recent best sellers and this would provide the site with a continuous flow of best selling materials. Another focus area worth exploring would be Mothers' Clubs. These clubs mirror the target demographics and often share in a viral marketing format. ➤

future growth of his business. He would look across his offerings of PaperbackSwap, SwapaCD, and SwapaDVD to assess the market growth rate and relative market share, determine the degree to which each is a cash generator or a cash user, and decide whether to invest further in these or other business opportunities.

Step 5: Develop Growth Strategies

Although the BCG matrix can help managers decide which SBUs they should invest in for growth, it doesn't tell them much about *how* to make that growth happen. Should the growth of an SBU come from finding new customers, from developing new variations of the product, or from some other growth strategy? Part of the strategic planning at the SBU level entails evaluating growth strategies.

Marketers use the product-market growth matrix Figure 2.4 shows to analyze different growth strategies. The vertical axis in Figure 2.4 represents opportunities for growth, either in existing markets or in new markets. The horizontal axis considers whether the firm would be better off putting its resources into existing products or if it should acquire new products. The matrix provides four fundamental marketing strategies: market penetration, market development, product development, and diversification:

market penetration strategies
Growth strategies designed to increase sales of existing products to current customers, nonusers, and users of competitive brands in served markets.

market development strategies
Growth strategies that introduce existing products to new markets.

- **Market penetration strategies** seek to increase sales of existing products to existing markets such as current users, nonusers, and users of competing brands within a market. For example, both Quaker Oatmeal and General Mills' Cheerios (also an oats product) have been aggressively advertising a new use for their products as products that can help lower total cholesterol and LDL ("bad") cholesterol, and that can help keep arteries clean and healthy. General Mills advertises that a clinical study showed that eating two half-cup servings daily of Cheerios cereal for six weeks reduced bad cholesterol about four percent (when eaten as part of a diet low in saturated fat and cholesterol). Quaker urges users to lower their cholesterol by taking the 30 day Quaker Oatmeal Smart Heart Challenge™. Both approaches aim to increase usage based on important new product claims.[10]

- **Market development strategies** introduce existing products to new markets. This strategy can mean expanding into a new geographic area, or it may mean reaching new customer segments within an existing geographic market. For example, the wildly popular Wii home gaming system by Nintendo has also become popular with older consumers because its active functionality during the game provides an opportunity for a light and fun physical

Figure 2.4 | Product-Market Growth Matrix

Product Emphasis

	Existing **Products**	New **Products**
Existing Markets	**Market penetration strategy** • Seek to increase sales of existing products to existing markets	**Product development strategy** • Create growth by selling new products in existing markets
New Markets	**Market development strategy** • Introduce existing products to new markets	**Diversification strategy** • Emphasize both new products and new markets to achieve growth

Market Emphasis

GREENLAND

ARC

ICELAND

ALASKA

C A N A D A

UNITED STATES
OF AMERICA

PACIFIC
OCEAN

NORTH
ATLANTIC
OCEAN

UNITED
KINGDOM
IRELAND   NETH
                 BEL
                 LUX
                 FRAN

SPAIN
PORTUGAL   ANDOR

MOROCCO

WESTERN
SAHARA   ALGERI

MAURITANIA   MALI

HAWAII

MEXICO

CUBA

JAMAICA

BELIZE
GUATEMALA   HONDURAS
EL SALVADOR   NICARAGUA
   COSTA RICA
      PANAMA

DOMINICAN
REPUBLIC

HAITI   PUERTO
           RICO

TRINIDAD &
TOBAGO

VENEZUELA
GUYANA
         FRENCH
         GUIANA
SURINAME

SENEGAL
GAMBIA   BURKINA
GUINEA-BISSAU GUINEA FASO

SIERRA LEONE   IVORY   GHANA
                COAST   TOGO
        LIBERIA   BENIN

EQUA
GU

GALAPAGOS
ISLANDS

COLOMBIA

ECUADOR

B R A Z I L

SOUTH

ATLANTIC

OCEAN

PERU

BOLIVIA

PARAGUAY

URUGUAY

ARGENTINA

FALKLAND ISLANDS/
MALVINAS

workout. Wii exercise sessions have become especially popular in retirement homes where the activity takes on a strong social and community building flavor. And because the technology part of Wii is so straightforward and user-friendly, even the most technophobic of seniors are not reluctant to join in the Wii events.[11]

Nintendo follows a market development strategy as it finds new markets for its successful Wii.

- **Product development strategies** create growth by selling new products in existing markets. *Product development* may mean extending the firm's product line by developing new variations of the item, or it may mean altering or improving the product to provide enhanced performance.

  Take the humble mattress for example. Lately, business-class hotels like Sheraton, Wyndham, and Marriott are fighting something of a "mattress war"; each one is trying to convince the traveler that its bed is softer, more comfortable, and more inviting than the competition's (and in some cases if you fall in love with the bed you can actually buy it and take it home!). This "sleeper" strategy appears to be effective: Radisson Hotels' research with guests told it that the mere fact that a bed was "upgraded" would allow the chain to charge an additional $10 more per room. These new-age beds carry their own brand names—"Heavenly Bed" at Westin, "The Revive Collection" at Marriott, and "Sweet Sleeper" at Sheraton. Radisson's "Sleep Number" beds even allow each occupant to adjust the firmness of her side with a remote control device.[12] A product development strategy like that is waking up the hotel industry, as the major players (and some smaller luxury hotels) now are scrambling to merchandise other room elements, such as toiletries.

product development strategies
Growth strategies that focus on selling new products in existing markets.

- **Diversification strategies** emphasize both new products and new markets to achieve growth. After a long period of sluggish performance in the fast-food market, McDonald's has reenergized itself over the past several years through successful strategic planning. For example, feeling that it was maxing out in the hamburger business in the late 1990s, McDonald's sought to attract different customers with lines of business to diversify its portfolio of food offerings. Among those are Donatos Pizza, Boston Market, and a controlling interest in Chipotle Mexican Grills. Interestingly, now that their core hamburger and fries business has been back on track for several years, McDonald's has divested these other brands and is shifting from a diversification strategy back to more of a product development strategy around the core McDonald's brand.[13]

diversification strategies
Growth strategies that emphasize both new products and new markets.

For Richard Pickering at PaperBackSwap, using the product-market growth matrix can be a very important way to analyze where his future opportunities lie. Is he primarily focused on growing totally new customers for the paperback book market

---

Ted Wallin
a professor at Syracuse University
My Advice for PaperBackSwap would be to choose

2 Option

real people, **Other** Voices

I would choose **Option 2** because of the nature of the current core consumer base. The typical users (women, over 40, mothers) would likely be most interested in literacy. Education and children are key

concerns to the audience, which believes strongly in reading and is sensitive to human needs. I would be eager to see a connection of participation in the site to the promotion of literacy. The firm could easily undertake a low cost program to support its cause, perhaps having members donate/collect books. The current member likely appreciates the value of reading and is less knowledgeable about environmental issues and less convinced that fun/entertainment is the goal. The firm needs to undertake an effort that nourishes its key market, cultivates a positive additional conviction to link users to its expanded use, promotes itself to other potential members, and offers a low cost, easy way to implement support actions. ➤

(diversification)? Or can he move some existing customers of National Book Swap's other product lines over to become users of PaperBackSwap as well (product development)? To what degree does PaperBackSwap afford him the chance to grow current customers in usage of existing product lines (penetration)? These are fundamental issues in planning for his firm's future growth.

To review what we've learned so far, strategic planning includes developing the mission statement, assessing the internal and external environment (resulting in a SWOT analysis), setting objectives, establishing the business portfolio, and developing growth strategies. In the next section, we'll look at marketers' functional plans—marketing planning.

4 Marketing Planning: Select the Camera Setting

Richard
Pickering

APPLYING Situation Analysis

Richard needs to know:
- what media they connect with
- what messages will make them buy
- how they perfer to communicate about new services and customer care
- what his competitors are marketing. ➥

OBJECTIVE

Explain operational planning.

(pp. 52–58)

Up until now, we have focused on fairly broad strategic plans. This big-picture perspective, however, does not provide details about how to reach the objectives we set. Strategic plans "talk the talk" but put the pressure on lower-level functional-area managers, such as the marketing manager, production manager, and finance manager to "walk the walk" by developing the functional plans—the nuts and bolts—to achieve organizational and SBU objectives. Thus, marketers develop functional plans (that is, marketing plans)—the next step in planning as we showed back in Figure 2.1.

The Four Ps of the marketing mix we discussed in Chapter 1 remind us that successful firms must have viable *products* at *prices* consumers are willing to pay, a way to *promote* the products to the right consumers, and the means to get the products to the *place* where consumers want to buy them.

Making this happen requires a tremendous amount of planning by the marketer. The steps in this marketing planning process are quite similar to the steps at the strategic planning level. An important distinction between strategic planning and marketing planning, however, is that marketing professionals focus much of their planning efforts on issues related to the *marketing mix*—the firm's product, its price, promotional approach, and distribution (place) methods. In the end, as you learned in Chapter 1, marketing focuses on creating, communicating, delivering, and exchanging offerings that have value, and marketing planning plays a central role in making these critical components of marketing successful. Let's look at the steps involved in the marketing planning process in a bit more detail.

Step 1: Perform a Situation Analysis

The first step in developing a marketing plan is for marketing managers to conduct an analysis of the *marketing* environment. To do this, managers build on the company's SWOT analysis by searching out information about the environment that specifically affects the marketing plan. For example, for Richard Pickering at PaperBackSwap to develop an effective marketing communication program, it's not enough for him to have a general understanding of the target market. He needs to know specifically what media potential customers connect with, what messages about the product are most likely to make them buy, and how they prefer to communicate with his firm about new services and customer care issues. Richard also must know how his competitors are marketing to customers so that he can plan effectively.

Seven grams of fat.
Seven gazillion grams of taste.

THE SURPRISING TASTE OF LEAN POCKETS...

LEAN POCKETS

Courtesy of Nestle Foods

Companies develop new products like Lean Pockets in response to consumers' demands for low-fat alternatives.

Step 2: Set Marketing Objectives

Once marketing managers have a thorough understanding of the marketing environment, the next step is to develop specific marketing objectives. How are marketing objectives different from corporate objectives? Generally, marketing objectives are more specific to the firm's brands, sizes, product features, and other marketing mix–related elements. Think of the connection between business objectives and marketing objectives this way: Business objectives guide the entire firm's operations, while marketing objectives state what the marketing function must accomplish if the firm is ultimately to achieve these overall business objectives. So for Richard Pickering at PaperBackSwap, setting marketing objectives means deciding what he wants to accomplish in terms of PaperBackSwap's marketing mix–related elements, such as the development of products, his pricing strategies, or specific marketing communication approaches.

Step 3: Develop Marketing Strategies

In the next stage of the marketing planning process, marketing managers develop their actual marketing strategies—that is, they make decisions about what activities they must accomplish to achieve the marketing objectives. Usually this means deciding which markets to target and actually developing the marketing mix strategies (product, price, promotion, and place [supply chain]) to support how the product is positioned in the market. At this stage, marketers must figure out how they want consumers to think of their product compared to competing products.

California's almond growers have a marketing strategy to increase consumption by promoting the nut's health benefits.

Select a Target Market

As we mentioned in Chapter 1, the target market is the market segment(s) a firm selects because it believes its offerings are most likely to win those customers. The firm assesses the potential demand—the number of consumers it believes are willing and able to pay for its products—and decides if it is able to create a sustainable competitive advantage in the marketplace among target consumers. The mission statement for National Book Swap, PaperBackSwap's parent firm, provides insight about what businesses it is in. From this mission statement, Richard Pickering can rest assured that he is responsible for focusing resources on developing target markets for PaperBackSwap's unique and value-adding service for readers.

Develop Marketing Mix Strategies

Marketing mix decisions identify how marketing will accomplish its objectives in the firm's target markets by using product, price, promotion, and place.

- Because the product is the most fundamental part of the marketing mix—firms simply can't make a profit without something to sell—carefully developed *product strategies* are essential to achieving marketing objectives. Product strategies include decisions such as product design, packaging, branding, support services (such as maintenance), if there will be variations of the product, and what product features will provide the unique benefits targeted customers want. For example, product planners for JetBlue Airways

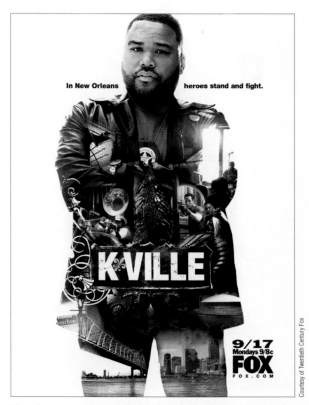

Like other products, TV shows appeal to distinct segments of consumers who tune in specific genres such as action, comedy, or reality.

Changes in consumers' values regarding beef consumption create opportunities for companies that promote beef alternatives.

Nature Valley's target market includes people who look for other benefits in addition to taste when they choose a snack.

decided to include in-seat video games and television as a key product feature during the flight. Their planes get you from point A to point B just as fast (or slow) as the other airlines—that is, the basic product is the same—but the flight seems shorter because there is more to do while you're in the air.

- The *pricing strategy* determines how much a firm charges for a product. Of course, that price has to be one that customers are willing to pay. If not, all the other marketing efforts are futile. In addition to setting prices for the final consumer, pricing strategies usually establish prices the company will charge to wholesalers and retailers. A firm may base its pricing strategies on costs, demand, or the prices of competing products. Southwest Airlines uses a pricing strategy to successfully target customers who could not previously afford air travel. Southwest does not compete solely on price; however, consumers do perceive Southwest as a low-priced airline compared with others, and the airline reinforces this theme regularly in its ads. You may now move about the country.[14]

- A *promotional strategy* is how marketers communicate a product's value proposition to the target market. Marketers use promotion strategies to develop the product's message and the mix of advertising, sales promotion, public relations and publicity, direct marketing, and personal selling that will deliver the message. Many firms use all these elements to communicate their message to consumers. American Airlines strives to portray an image of quality and luxury for the serious business traveler. To do so, it combines television ads focused on that target with sales promotion in the form of the AAdvantage loyalty program, personal selling to companies and conventions to promote usage of American as the "official carrier" for the groups, direct marketing via mail and e-mail providing information to loyal users, and (its managers hope) positive publicity through word-of-mouth about the airline's good service and dependability. The carrier also pays millions of dollars each year for the "naming rights" to two stadiums: the American Airlines Arena in Miami and the American Airlines Center in Dallas.

- *Distribution strategies* outline how, when, and where the firm will make the product available to targeted customers (the *place* component). In developing a distribution strategy, marketers must decide whether to sell the product directly to the final customer or to sell through retailers and wholesalers. And the choice of which retailers should be involved depends on the product, pricing, and promotion decisions. For example, if the firm produces a luxury good it may wish to avoid being seen on the shelves of discount stores for fear that it will cheapen the brand image. In recent years, the airline industry has made major changes in its distribution strategy. For many years, most customers bought their airline tickets through travel agencies or at the ticket counters of the major airlines. Today, most airlines actually penalize customers who don't opt for on-line purchase of "ticketless" flight reservations by charging them a "ticketing fee" of $5 or $10. This strategy has molded the behavior of many consumers to go on-line 24/7 to save money as well as experience the convenience of personally scheduling the flight they want.

Step 4: Implement and Control the Marketing Plan

Once the plan is developed, it's time to get to work and make it successful. In practice, marketers spend much of their time managing the various elements involved in implementing the marketing plan. For PaperBackSwap, once Richard Pickering and his group understand the marketing environment, determine the most appropriate objectives and strategies, and get their ideas organized and on paper in the formal plan, the rubber really hits the road. Like all firms, how PaperBackSwap implements its plan is what will make or break the success of the firm in the marketplace.

During the implementation phase, marketers must have some means to determine to what degree they are actually meeting their stated marketing objectives. Often called **control**, this formal process of monitoring progress entails three steps: (1) measuring actual performance, (2) comparing this performance to the established marketing objectives or strategies, and (3) making adjustments to the objectives or strategies on the basis of this analysis. This issue of making adjustments brings up one of the most important aspects of successful marketing planning: Marketing plans aren't written in stone, and marketers must be flexible enough to make such changes when changes are warranted.

Effective control requires appropriate *marketing metrics*, which, as we discussed in Chapter 1, are concrete measures of various aspects of marketing performance. You will note throughout the book a strong emphasis on metrics within each chapter. Today's CEOs are keen on quantifying just how an investment in marketing has an impact on the firm's success, financially and otherwise. Think of this overall notion as **return on marketing investment (ROMI)**. Considering marketing as an investment rather than an expense is critical, because this distinction drives firms to use marketing more strategically to enhance the business. The ROMI concept heightens the importance of identifying and tracking appropriate marketing metrics.[15]

Just to give you a sense for some of the many available marketing metrics, Table 2.3 provides some examples of metrics that managers apply across an array of marketing planning situations, including all the marketing mix variables. We'll be talking about many of these later on in the book.

Richard Pickering at PaperBackSwap has to establish appropriate metrics related to his marketing objectives and then track those metrics to know how successful his marketing strategy is, as well as whether he needs to make changes in the strategy along the way. For example, what happens if PaperBackSwap sets an objective to increase usage by the 18–25-year-old market by 20 percent in a given

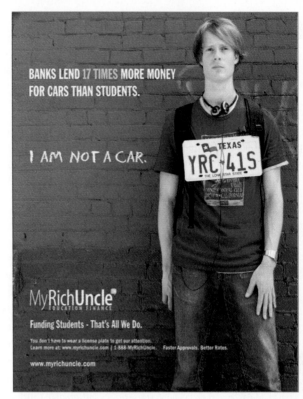

My Rich Uncle uses high-impact promotions to get students' atttention.

Metrics Moment

ROMI—return on marketing investment

—is the *metric du jour* for analyzing many firms' marketing bottom lines. What exactly is ROMI? It is the revenue or profit margin (both are widely used) generated by investment in a specific marketing program divided by the cost of that program (expenditure) at a given risk level (the risk level is determined by management). The key word is *investment*—that is, in the planning process thinking of marketing as an investment rather than an expense keeps managers focused on using marketing dollars to achieve specific goals.

But is ROMI the perfect measure to establish marketing's effectiveness and efficiency? Here are five major objections to relying exclusively on ROMI:

1. In a company's accounting statements, marketing expenditures aren't treated as an investment. This perpetuates the "marketing is an expense" mentality in the firm.
2. ROMI requires the profit to be divided by expenditure, yet all other bottom-line performance measures (like the ones taught in your finance course) consider profit or cash flow *after* deducting expenditures.
3. Calculating ROMI requires knowing what would have happened if the marketing expenditure in question had never taken place. Few marketers have those figures.
4. ROMI has become a fashionable term for marketing productivity in general, yet much evidence exists that firms interpret how to calculate ROMI quite differently. When executives discuss ROMI with different calculations of it in mind, only confusion can result.
5. ROMI, by nature, ignores the effect of marketing assets of the firm (for example, its brands) and tends to lead managers toward a more short-term decision perspective. That is, it typically considers only short-term incremental profits and expenditures without looking at longer-term effects or any change in brand equity.

For ROMI to be used properly a firm must: (a) come to grips with the most appropriate and consistent measure to be applied and (b) combine review of ROMI with other critical marketing metrics (one example is *marketing payback*—how quickly marketing costs are recovered).[16]

Is your fantasy (or one of them) to get free burritos for life? Moe's Southwest Grill is one of the many forward-looking companies that has figured out the value of adding its customers to its marketing team. Customers created the chain's latest ads and burritos are exactly what the winner got (or more specifically, one free burrito per week for 55 years). Moe's knows that consumer-generated advertising generates brand awareness at relatively low cost at the same time that it reinforces consumers' brand loyalty. Moe's collaborates with ViTrue, Inc., and invites consumers to create and submit their homemade ads to the YouTube-like website. The company lets consumers use its logo, backgrounds, sound effects, and music to create the ads. Consumers can visit Moe's website and vote for their favorite even if they did not create their own ad for the contest.

Moving apart from traditional marketing approaches, Moe's new strategy aims at building brand awareness and spreading brand messages on a viral level. By making its customers a part of the marketing team, Moe's obtains a better understanding of its target market, which helps it to develop a positioning strategy. And if nothing else, Moe's knows it has at least <u>one</u> customer for life.

Sources: Gregg Cebrzynski, "Moe's to Consumers: Don't Just Watch Our Ads, Create Them," *Nation's Restaurant News* (August 14, 2006), pp. 4, 89; Margaret Littman, "By the People, For the People," *Chain Leader* (February 2007), pp. 26–27.

control

A process that entails measuring actual performance, comparing this performance to the established marketing objectives, and then making adjustments to the strategies or objectives on the basis of this analysis.

return on marketing investment (ROMI)

Quantifying just how an investment in marketing has an impact on the firm's success, financially and otherwise.—**See** M **METRICS MOMENT on** page 55

action plans

Individual support plans included in a marketing plan that provide the guidance for implementation and control of the various marketing strategies within the plan. Action plans are sometimes referred to as "marketing programs."

year but after the first quarter sales in this market are only even with the last year? The *control process* means that Richard would have to look carefully at why the company isn't meeting its objectives. Is it due to internal factors, external factors, or a combination of both?

Depending on the cause, Richard would then have to either adjust the marketing plan's strategies (such as to implement product alterations, modify the price, or increase or change advertising). Alternatively, he could decide to adjust the marketing objective so that it is more realistic and attainable. This scenario illustrates the important point made earlier in our discussion of strategic planning: Objectives must be specific and measurable, but also *attainable* (and *sustainable*) in the sense that if an objective is not realistic it can become very demotivating for everyone involved in the marketing plan.

Action Plans

How does the implementation and control step actually manifest itself within a marketing plan? One very convenient way is through the inclusion of a series of **action plans** that support the various marketing objectives and strategies within the plan. We sometimes refer to action plans as "marketing programs." The best way to use action plans is by including a separate action plan for each important element involved in implementing the marketing plan. Table 2.4 provides a template for an action plan.

For example, let's consider the use of action plans in the context of supporting Richard's objective at PaperBackSwap to increase usage by the 18–25-year-old market by

Table 2.3	Examples of metrics

- Cost of a prospect
- Value of a prospect
- ROI of a campaign
- Value of telesales
- Conversion rates of users of competitor products
- Long-term value of a customer
- Customer commitment to relationship/partnership
- Referral rate
- Response rates to direct marketing
- Perceived product quality
- Perceived service quality
- Customer loyalty/retention
- Customer turnover

- Customer/segment profitability
- Customer mind set/customer orientation
- Customer satisfaction
- Company/product reputation
- Customer word-of-mouth (buzz) activity
- Salesperson perceived self-efficacy
- Timeliness and accuracy of competitive intelligence
- Usage rates of technology in customer initiatives
- Reach and frequency of advertising
- Recognition and recall of message
- Sales calls per day/week/month
- Order fulfillment efficiency/stock-outs
- Timeliness of sales promotion support

Table 2.4 | Template for an action plan

Title of Action Plan	Give the action plan a relevant name.
Purpose of Action Plan	What do you hope to accomplish by the action plan—that is, what specific marketing objective and strategy within the marketing plan does it support?
Description of Action Plan	Be succinct, but still thorough, in explaining the action plan. What are the steps involved? This is the core of the action plan. It describes what must be done in order to accomplish the intended purpose of the action plan.
Responsibility for the Action Plan	What person(s) or organizational unit(s) are responsible for carrying out the action plan? What external parties are needed to make it happen? Most importantly, who specifically has final "ownership" of the action plan—that is, who is accountable for it?
Time Line for the Action Plan	Provide a specific timetable of events leading to the completion of the plan. If different people are responsible for different elements of the time line, provide that information.
Budget for the Action Plan	How much will implementation of the action plan cost? This may be direct costs only, or may also include indirect costs, depending on the situation. The sum of all the individual action plan budget items will ultimately be aggregated by category to create the overall budget for the marketing plan.
Measurement and Control of the Action Plan	Indicate the appropriate metrics, how and when they will be measured, and who will measure them.

20 percent this year. To accomplish this, the marketing plan would likely include a variety of strategies related to how he will use the marketing mix elements to reach this objective. Important questions will include:

- What are the important needs and wants of this target market?

- How will the product be positioned in relation to this market?

- What will be his product and branding strategies?

- What will be his pricing strategy for this group?

- How will the product be promoted to them?

- What is the best distribution strategy to access the market? Any one of these important strategic issues may require several action plans to implement.

Action plans also help managers when they need to assign responsibilities, time lines, budgets, and measurement and control processes for marketing planning. Notice in Table 2.4 that these four elements are the final items an action plan documents. Sometimes when we view a marketing plan in total it can seem daunting and nearly impossible to actually implement. Like most big projects, implementation of a marketing plan is best done one step at a time, paying attention to maximizing the quality of executing that step. In practice, what happens is that marketers combine the input from these last four elements of each action plan to form the overall implementation and control portion of the marketing plan. Let's examine each element a bit further.

Richard
Pickering

APPLYING Action Plans

Richard would need to know the following about the target market:
- Needs and wants
- How to position the product
- Branding strategies
- Pricing strategies
- How to promote the product
- Best distribution

Assign Responsibility

A marketing plan can't be implemented without people. And not everybody who will be involved in implementing a marketing plan is a marketer. The truth is marketing plans touch most areas of an organization. Upper management and the human resources department will need to deploy the necessary employees to accomplish the plan's objectives. You learned in Chapter 1 that marketing isn't the responsibility only of a marketing department. Nowhere is that idea more vivid than in marketing plan implementation. Sales, production, quality control, shipping, customer service, finance, information technology—the list goes on—all will likely have a part in making the plan successful.

Create a Time Line

Notice that each action plan requires a time line to accomplish the various tasks it requires. This is essential to include in the overall marketing plan. Most marketing plans portray the timing of tasks in flow-chart form so that it is easy to visualize when the pieces of the plan will come together. Marketers often use *Gantt charts* or *PERT charts*, popular in operations management, to portray a plan's time line. These are the same types of tools that a general contractor might use to map out the different elements of building a house from the ground up. Ultimately, managers develop budgets and the financial management of the marketing plan around the time line so they know when cash outlays are required.

Set a Budget

Each action plan carries a *budget item*, assuming there are costs involved in carrying out the plan. Forecasting the needed expenditures related to a marketing plan is difficult, but one way to improve accuracy in the budgeting process overall is to ensure estimates for expenditures for the individual action plans that are as accurate as possible. At the overall marketing plan level, managers create a master budget and track it throughout the market planning process. They report variances from the budget to the parties responsible for each budget item. For example, a firm's vice president of sales might receive a weekly or monthly report showing each sales area's performance against its budget allocation. The VP would note patterns of budget overage and contact affected sales managers to determine what, if any, action they need to take to get the budget back on track. The same approach would be repeated across all the different functional areas of the firm on which the budget has an impact. In such a manner, the budget itself becomes a critical element of control.

Decide on Measurements and Controls

Earlier we described the concept of control as a formal process of monitoring progress through measuring actual performance, comparing the performance to the established marketing objectives or strategies, and making adjustments to the objectives or strategies on the basis of this analysis. The metric(s) a marketer uses to monitor and control individual action plans ultimately forms the overall control process for the marketing plan. It is an unfortunate fact that many marketers do not consistently do a good job of measurement and control, which of course compromises their marketing planning. Pay close attention throughout the remainder of the book to highlights on marketing metrics and how they are used to assess the effectiveness of the different components of marketing. Learning about these metrics will help you make better decisions as a marketer and increase your opportunities to move up the corporate ladder.

OBJECTIVE

Explain the key role of implementation and control in marketing planning.

(pp. 58–60)

Create and Work with a Marketing Plan: Snap the Picture

As we noted earlier, a marketing plan should provide the best possible guide for the firm to successfully market its products. In large firms, top management often requires such a written plan because putting the ideas on paper encourages marketing managers to formulate concrete objectives and strategies. In small entrepreneurial firms, a well-thought-out marketing plan is often the key to attracting investors who will help turn the firm's dreams into reality.

Make Your Life Easier! Use the Marketing Planning Template

Ultimately, the planning process we've described in this section is documented in a formal, written marketing plan. You'll find a tear-out template for a marketing plan in the foldout located at the end of this chapter. The template will come in handy as you make your way through the book, as each chapter will give you information you can use to "fill in the blanks" of a marketing plan. You will note that the template is cross-referenced with the questions you must answer in each section of the plan and that it also provides you with a general road map of the topics covered in each chapter that need to flow into building the marketing plan. By the time you're done, we hope that all these pieces will come together and you'll understand how real marketers make real choices.

Operational Planning: Day-to-Day Execution of Marketing Plans

In the previous section, we discussed marketing planning—the process by which marketers perform a situation analysis; set marketing objectives; and develop, implement, and control marketing strategies. But talk is cheap: The best plan ever written is useless if it's not properly carried out. That's what **operational plans** are for. They put the pedal to the metal by focusing on the day-to-day execution of the marketing plan.

The task falls to the first-line supervisors we discussed earlier, such as sales managers, marketing communications managers, and marketing research managers. Operational plans generally cover a shorter period of time than either strategic plans or marketing plans—perhaps only one or two months—and they include detailed directions for the specific activities to be carried out, who will be responsible for them, and time lines for accomplishing the tasks. In reality, the action plan template we provide in Table 2.4 is most likely applied at the operational level.

Significantly, many of the important marketing metrics managers use to gauge the success of plans actually get used at the operational planning level. For example, sales managers in many firms are charged with the responsibility of tracking a wide range of metrics related to the firm–customer relationship, such as number of new customers, sales calls per month, customer turnover, and customer loyalty. The data are collected at the operational level and then sent to upper management for use in planning at the functional level and above.

operational plans
Plans that focus on the day-to-day execution of the marketing plan. Operational plans include detailed directions for the specific activities to be carried out, who will be responsible for them, and time lines for accomplishing the tasks.

The Value of a Marketing Culture

A central issue for marketers is to gain a good understanding of the environment in which their planning must take place. Earlier in the chapter, we defined the internal environment as the controllable elements inside an organization that influence how well the organization operates. We also mentioned that internal strengths and weaknesses may lie in the firm's technologies, physical facilities, financial stability, reputation, quality of its products and services, and employees. Marketers must analyze and document all these elements in the SWOT analysis part of the marketing plan.

Ultimately, a firm's **corporate culture** determines much of its internal environment—by this we mean the values, norms, and beliefs that influence the behavior of everyone in the organization. Corporate culture dictates whether employees welcome or discourage new ideas, whether they are rewarded for displaying ethical decisions, and even day-to-day behavior such as whether it's permissible to wear flip-flops to work on Casual Fridays.

corporate culture
The set of values, norms, and beliefs that influence the behavior of everyone in the organization.

The way employees dress reflects their organization's corporate culture.

For many years, IBM was known as "the white shirt company" because of its unwritten rule that all employees must wear white shirts to look the part of an "IBMer." Fortunately, corporate cultures do evolve over time, and even radical changes such as blue shirts now are tolerated at "Big Blue." In contrast, Microsoft has always prided itself on having a more casual dress code, reflecting its roots as an entrepreneurial upstart (at least compared to IBM). If you visit Microsoft's headquarters in Redmond, Washington, you will notice everyone's informal attire right away. However, don't make the mistake of equating informal dress with low work productivity. Microsoft hasn't evolved into the corporate giant it is today by hiring slackers.

Some corporate cultures are more inclined to take risks than others. These firms value individuality and creativity; they recognize that by nurturing these characteristics their employees are more likely to create important competitive advantages. A risk-taking culture is especially important to the marketing function because firms must continually improve their products, their distribution channels, and their promotion programs to remain successful in a competitive environment. In firms with more traditional corporate cultures, getting managers to buy into a new way of doing things is like inviting the board of directors to go on a skydiving mission.

If a firm is totally focused on economic profit—increasing revenues and decreasing costs—management attitudes will be profit-centered, often at the expense of employee morale. Firms that harbor a concern for employees, customers, and society, as well as shareholder profits, produce a corporate culture that is much more appealing for employees and other stakeholders in the business. In which corporate culture would *you* rather work?

Fortune magazine publishes an annual list of the best companies to work for based on a variety of criteria, including company philosophy and practices, employee trust in management, pride in work and the company, and camaraderie. In 2007, the number-one employer on *Fortune*'s list was Google. What makes Google so great? For one thing, life for Google employees at the Mountain View, California campus is like college. It feels like the brainiest university imaginable—one in which every kid can afford a sports car (though geeky hybrids are cooler here than hot rods). And, the shabbily dressed engineers always will be the big men and women on campus. "Hard-core geeks are here because there's no place they'd rather be," says Dennis Hwang, a Google Webmaster. The cuisine at Google's 11 cafeterias is not only fabulous, it's free. Another similarity to college is that New Googlers (Nooglers, in Google parlance) tend to pile on the "Google 15" when they're confronted with all the free food.[17]

To summarize what we've discussed in this chapter, business planning—a key element of a firm's success—occurs in several different stages. Strategic planning takes place at both the corporate and the SBU level in large firms and in a single stage in smaller businesses. Marketing planning, one of the functional planning areas, comes next. Operational planning ensures proper implementation and control of the marketing plan. It is critical that firms approach the marketing planning process in a highly ethical manner, mindful of the importance of establishing an organizational code of ethics to eliminate ambiguity about which behaviors by organization members are acceptable and which are not. In the next chapter, we'll continue the dialogue by focusing on how marketing can best help firms thrive in today's global business environment.

Now that you've learned the basics of strategic market planning, read "Real People, Real Choices: How It Worked Out" to see which strategy Richard selected to develop a market for PaperBackSwap.

real people, **Real Choices**

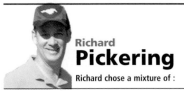

Richard Pickering

Richard chose a mixture of :

 1 & **3**

Option   Option

to one another. Media Mail takes a little longer than First Class postage but is less than half of the cost. As members got caught up in the service and realized how much money they were saving by getting their books this way, they started to promote it to others even more aggressively. As of early 2008 the site had posted over five million books, it had mailed well over two million books, and it receives about 1.1 million hits per day. The site's usage is increasing by over 55% per year with no end in sight. That's a lot of beach reading.

How it Worked Out at PaperBackSwap

Richard chose a mixture of options one and three. He decided that positioning the company as a provider of inexpensive entertainment while doing something positive for the environment would give PaperBackSwap the best chance of getting consumers' attention in a crowded marketplace. The company incorporated the recycling symbol right into its logo to reinforce its green attributes. It encourages members to keep their costs down by using Media Mail to ship their books

How PaperBackSwap Measures Success

The company is trying to collect information about its users without going overboard and violating their privacy. When a new member registers on the website, she is asked how she heard about the service. Other items ask about gender and age range. The company tracks which media outlets send them the most members so they can get feedback about whether they are focusing their marketing efforts correctly.

Trade multiple books without using PaperBackSwap credits, and spend less on postage!

Box-O-Books is very simple: find another member with books you want and trade books with him or her. USPS rates make it less expensive to send books "in bulk".

The more books you send, the more money you save on postage!

The Daily Digest

Browse newly listed books with your morning coffee!

Be the first to know when books you want are added to the PaperBackSwap library: get an updated Daily Digest of new additions to the database delivered to your email inbox each morning, in the genres you preselect. You can request books right from the list.

Organize and Manage Your Personal Library Online

Never forget where you put a book! You can catalog all of your books here, not just those you intend to swap. Book Journal allows you to record comments about books you've read and move books to and from lists in your PaperBackSwap account with just a few clicks. Book Journal is your personal online book-management system.

Community

Meet other book lovers in Live Chat or the Discussion Forums -- we have a forum for every genre and every kind of reader, as well as for homeschoolers and teachers. We even have The Eclectic Pen, a place for writers to share their work with the PaperBackSwap community, and get comments and "reviews" from other members. Aspiring and published writers are equally welcome.

Fine Print: This is where the fine print would go if we had any. But we don't. PaperBackSwap works well because it is simple. Join the club and find out for yourself.

Join our Book Club and get free books!

PaperBackSwap.com

Your source for swapping books online!

PaperBackSwap promotes its service on flyers, bookmarks and posters.

Refer back to **page 37** for Richard's story ➡

Brand **YOU**!

Do you cringe when someone asks you, "What do you want to do when you graduate?" Learn about yourself and what professions might be best for you in Chapter 2 of the *Brand You* supplement. You'll create a personal mission statement, complete a skills inventory, and identify your career objectives. It's never too early to plan your career.

Objective Summary ➡ Key Terms ➡ Apply

1. Objective Summary (pp. 38–41)

Explain the strategic planning process.

Strategic planning is the managerial decision process in which top management defines the firm's purpose and specifies what the firm hopes to achieve over the next five or so years. For large firms that have a number of self-contained business units, the first step in strategic planning is for top management to establish a mission for the entire corporation. Top managers then evaluate the internal and external environment of the business and set corporate-level objectives that guide decision making within each individual SBU. In small firms that are not large enough to have separate SBUs, strategic planning simply takes place at the overall firm level. For companies with several different SBUs, strategic planning also includes: (1) making decisions about how to best allocate resources across these businesses to ensure growth for the total organization and (2) developing growth strategies.

Key Terms

business planning, p. 39

business plan, p. 39

marketing plan, p. 39

business ethics, p. 40 (Ethical Decisions in the Real World, p. 40)

code of ethics, p. 40 (Table 2.2, p. 46)

2. Objective Summary (pp. 42–43)

Understand the three levels of business planning: strategic, functional, and operational.

Planning takes place at three key levels. Strategic planning is the managerial decision process that matches the firm's resources and capabilities to its market opportunities for long-term growth. Functional (or tactical) planning gets its name because the various functional areas of the firm, such as marketing, finance, and human resources get involved. And operational planning focuses on the day-to-day execution of the functional plans and includes detailed annual, semiannual, or quarterly plans.

Key Terms

strategic planning, p. 42 (Figure 2.1, p. 42)

strategic business units (SBUs), p. 42 (Figure 2.2, p. 48)

functional planning, p. 42 (Figure 2.1, p. 42)

operational planning, p. 43 (Figure 2.1, p. 42 and ➡ Applying, p. 43)

3. Objective Summary (pp. 43–52)

Describe the steps in marketing planning.

Marketing planning is one type of functional planning. Marketing planning begins with an evaluation of the internal and external environments. Marketing managers then set marketing objectives usually related to the firm's brands, sizes, product features, and other marketing mix–related elements. Next, marketing managers select the target market(s) for the organization and decide what marketing mix strategies they will use. Product strategies include decisions about products and product characteristics that will appeal to the target market. Pricing strategies state the specific prices to be charged to channel members and final consumers. Promotion strategies include plans for advertising, sales promotion, public relations, publicity, personal selling, and direct marketing used to reach the target market. Distribution (place) strategies outline how the product will be made available to targeted customers when and where they want it. Once the marketing strategies are developed, they must be implemented. Control is the measurement of actual performance and comparison with planned performance. Maintaining control implies the need for concrete measures of marketing performance called "marketing metrics."

Key Terms

mission statement, p. 44

situation analysis, p. 45 (➡ Applying, p. 52)

internal environment, p. 44

external environment, p. 44

SWOT analysis, p. 46 (Table 2.2, p. 46)

business portfolio, p. 48 (Figure 2.2, p. 48)

portfolio analysis, p. 48 (Figure 2.3, p. 49)

BCG growth–market share matrix, p. 48 (Figure 2.3, p. 49)

stars, p. 49 (Figure 2.3, p. 49)

cash cows, p. 49 (Figure 2.3, p. 49)

question marks, p. 49 (Figure 2.3, p. 49)

dogs, p. 49 (Figure 2.3, p. 49)

market penetration strategies, p. 50 (Figure 2.4, p. 50)

market development strategies, p. 50 (Figure 2.4, p. 50)

product development strategies, p. 51 (Figure 2.4, p. 50)

diversification strategies, p. 51 (Figure 2.4, p. 50)

4. Objective Summary (pp. 52–58)

Explain operational planning.

Operational planning is done by first-line supervisors such as sales managers, marketing communication managers, and marketing research managers, and focuses on the day-to-day execution of the marketing plan. Operational plans generally cover a shorter period of time and include detailed directions for the specific activities to be carried out, who will be responsible for them, and time lines for accomplishing the tasks.

Key Terms

control, p. 56

return on marketing investment (ROMI), p. 56 (Metrics Moment, p. 55)

action plans, p. 56 (Table 2.4 & ➡ Applying, p. 57)

5. Objective Summary (pp. 58–60)

Explain the key role of implementation and control in marketing planning.

To ensure effective implementation, a marketing plan must include individual action plans, or programs, that support the plan at the operational level. Each action plan necessitates providing a budget estimate, schedule or time line for its implementation, and appropriate metrics so that the marketer can monitor progress and control for discrepancies or variation from the plan. Sometimes variance from a plan requires shifting or increasing resources to make the plan work; other times, it requires changing the objectives of the plan to recognize changing conditions.

Key Terms

operational plans, p. 59

corporate culture, p. 59

Chapter **Questions** and **Activities**

Concepts: Test Your Knowledge

1. What is strategic, functional, and operational planning? How does strategic planning differ at the corporate and the SBU levels?
2. What is a mission statement? What is a SWOT analysis? What role do these play in the planning process?
3. What is a strategic business unit (SBU)? How do firms use the Boston Consulting Group model for portfolio analysis in planning for their SBUs?
4. Describe the four business growth strategies: market penetration, product development, market development, and diversification.
5. Explain the steps in the marketing planning process.
6. How does operational planning support the marketing plan?
7. What are the elements of a formal marketing plan?
8. What is an action plan? Why are action plans such an important part of marketing planning? Why is it so important for marketers to break the implementation of a marketing plan down into individual elements through action plans?
9. What is return on marketing investment (ROMI)? How does considering marketing as an investment instead of an expense affect a firm?
10. Give several examples of marketing metrics. How might a marketer use each metric to track progress of some important element of a marketing plan?
11. What is corporate culture? What are some ways that the corporate culture of one organization might differ from that of another? How does corporate culture affect marketing decision making?

12. Why is it essential, even in firms with a strong corporate culture, to have a written Code of Ethics? What are some important potential negative consequences of not formalizing a Code of Ethics in written form?

Choices and Ethical Issues: You Decide

1. The Boston Consulting Group matrix identifies products as stars, cash cows, question marks, and dogs. Do you think this is a useful way for organizations to examine their businesses? What are some examples of product lines that fit in each category?
2. In this chapter we talked about how firms do strategic, functional, and operational planning. Yet some firms are successful without formal planning. Do you think planning is essential to a firm's success? Can planning ever hurt an organization?
3. Most planning involves strategies for growth. But is growth always the right direction to pursue? Can you think of some organizations that should have contraction rather than expansion as their objective? Do you know of any organizations that have planned to get smaller rather than larger in order to be successful?
4. When most people think of successful marketing, internal firm culture doesn't immediately come to mind as a contributing factor. What are some reasons a firm's corporate culture is important to the capability of doing good marketing? Give some examples of what you consider to be a good corporate culture for marketing.
5. Most marketers today feel pressure to measure (quantify) their level of success in marketing planning. Is it easy to

measure marketing's success (compared to, say, measuring the success of a firm's financial management or production quality)? Explain your viewpoint.

6. Review the *AMA Code of Ethical Norms and Values for Marketers*, provided in Table 2.1. Which of the areas represented within the document do you anticipate are the most challenging for marketers to consistently follow? What makes these issues particularly troublesome? Do you think marketing in general does a good job adhering to the AMA Code? Provide specific evidence from your knowledge and experience to support your position.

Practice: Apply What You've Learned

1. Assume that you are the marketing director for a small firm that manufactures educational toys for children. Your boss, the company president, has decided to develop a mission statement. He's admitted that he doesn't know much about developing a mission statement and has asked you to help guide him in this process. Write a memo outlining exactly what a mission statement is, why firms develop such statements, how firms use mission statements, and your thoughts on what the firm's mission statement might be.

2. As a marketing student, you know that large firms often organize their operations into a number of strategic business units (SBUs). A university might develop a similar structure in which different academic schools or departments are seen as separate businesses. Working with a group of four to six classmates, consider how your university might divide its total academic units into separate SBUs. What would be the problems with implementing such a plan? What would be the advantages and disadvantages for students and for faculty? Present your analysis of university SBUs to your class.

3. An important part of planning is a SWOT analysis, understanding an organization's strengths, weaknesses, opportunities, and threats. Choose a business in your community with which you are familiar. Develop a brief SWOT analysis for that business.

4. As an employee of a business consulting firm that specializes in helping people who want to start small businesses, you have been assigned a client who is interested in introducing a new concept in health clubs—one that offers its customers both the usual exercise and weight-training opportunities and certain related types of medical assistance such as physical therapy, a weight-loss physician, and diagnostic testing. As you begin thinking about the potential for success for this client, you realize that developing a marketing plan is going to be essential. In a role-playing situation, present your argument to the client as to why she needs to invest in formal marketing planning.

5. Review the Code of Ethics for any three business organizations of your choosing. What elements do you find in common across the three examples? Which Code of Ethics do you think is the most effective overall, and why?

Miniproject: Learn by Doing

The purpose of this miniproject is to gain an understanding of marketing planning through actual experience.

1. Select one of the following for your marketing planning project:
   • Yourself (in your search for a career)
   • Your university
   • A specific department in your university

2. Next, develop the following elements of the marketing planning process:
   • A mission statement
   • A SWOT analysis
   • Objectives
   • A description of the target market(s)
   • A positioning strategy
   • A brief outline of the marketing mix strategies—the product, pricing, distribution, and promotion strategies—that satisfy the objectives and address the target market.

3. Prepare a brief outline of a marketing plan using the template provided at the end of this chapter as a guide.

Real people, **real surfers**: explore the web

Visit the home pages of one or more firms in which you are interested. Follow the links to find out about the company's products, pricing, distribution, and marketing communications strategies. Do a search of the Web for other information about the company. Based on your findings, answer the following questions:

1. What is the organization's business? What is the overall purpose of the organization? What does the organization hope to achieve?

2. What customers does the business want to serve?

3. What elements of the Web page specifically reflect the business of the organization? How is the Web page designed to attract the organization's customers?

4. Do you think the marketing strategies and other activities of the firm are consistent with its mission? Why do you feel this way?

5. Do you find evidence that the firm values ethical practices by its employees? If so, what evidence leads you to conclude the firm is highly ethical?

6. Develop a report based on your findings and conclusions about the firm. Present your report to your class.

Marketing Plan Exercise

The airline industry has experienced a lot of turbulence in recent years that inhibits its ability to plan for the future. Pick your favorite airline and help it plan by doing the following:

1. See if you can locate its mission statement, then develop a few marketing objectives that you believe would support it nicely.
2. Take a look at Figure 2.4, the product–market growth matrix, and the accompanying discussion. How might your chosen airline go about developing some strategies in each of the boxes: penetration, market development, product development, and diversification? (*Hint*: Remember that airlines are in the business of providing a service. Most likely the strategies you come up with will entail adding new or modified services in their targeted markets.)
3. Considering the strategies you identified in question 2, identify some specific marketing metrics that are appropriate for use in control.

Marketing in Action Case

Real **Choices** for the **Apple** iPhone

Time magazine named it the Invention of the Year. Experts and consumers alike called it "revolutionary." Introduced in June 2007, the iPhone is Apple's Internet-enabled multimedia mobile phone. In the first six months after Steve Jobs announced the planned launch of the iPhone at the Macworld Expo in January, 2007, the invention was the subject of 11,000 print articles and 69 million hits on Google.

So why is the iPhone revolutionary? For starters, the iPhone is a quad-band mobile phone that uses GSM standard, thus having international calling capability. It is a portable media player or iPod and an Internet browser, thus accessing owners' e-mail. It does text messaging, visual voice-mail, and has local Wi-Fi connectivity. It's sleek, slim, and is outfitted with a multi-touch screen with virtual keyboard. The multi-touch screen technique means the owner can expand or shrink the screen image by sliding her finger and thumb apart or together. The iPhone offers owners three types of radio: cellular, Wi-Fi, and Bluetooth. As an added benefit, one iPhone battery charge provides 8 hours of calls, 7 hours of video or 24 hours of music.

Indeed the iPhone was the year's most desired gadget. Customers stood in line to be the first to own one. In fact, some more entrepreneurially-minded customers bought more than one, convinced they could sell one at a profit and make enough to pay for the second!

Apple made the iPhone available to U.S. consumers through an alliance that made AT&T the exclusive carrier and under which AT&T subsidized the cost of the iPhone. To use an iPhone, customers had to sign a two-year contract with AT&T for cellular and Internet service. The price of the phone itself was $499 for the four-gigabyte model or $599 for the eight-gig version.

But consumers' love affair with the iPhone soon faced trouble. Just two months after the iPhone introduction, Apple dropped the price from $600 to $399, angering customers who had paid top dollar only two months before. And those customers immediately let Apple know of their dissatisfaction by phone, by e-mail, and on blogs. In response, Steve Jobs admitted that the company had abused its core customers and offered a $100 store credit to early iPhone buyers.

Furthermore, consumers were not happy that they were restricted to AT&T with their iPhones. Soon after introduction, hackers posted directions on the Internet for consumers to unlock the cellular service feature of their phone, allowing them to use the iPhone with any cellular service provider. Even though Apple was quick to warn consumers that unlocking the phone might damage the iPhone software, eventually making downloading with upgraded software impossible, unlocked phones continued to be available.

To make matters worse, various European countries have laws to protect consumers from being forced to buy something as a condition of buying a product, thus creating barriers for the global iPhone business. The courts in both France and Germany have refused to allow Apple to sell the iPhone locked to a long-term contract with a single cellular service supplier.

For Apple, the iPhone is the product of the future with plans for introducing software upgrades and newer versions to stimulate increased world sales. Steve Jobs is betting that the iPhone will enjoy the same success he has had with the iPod and with Apple computers. But for that success to materialize, Apple must carefully consider what long term strategies are necessary to make the iPhone both popular and profitable.

You Make the Call

1. What is the decision facing Apple?
2. What factors are important in understanding this decision situation?
3. What are the alternatives?
4. What decision(s) do you recommend?
5. What are some ways to implement your recommendation?

Based on: Katie Hafner and Brad Stone, "iPhone Owners Crying Foul Over Price Cut," *New York Times*, September 7, 2007, **http://www. nytimes.com/2007/09/07/technology/07apple.html**; Times Topics, iPhone, **http://topics.nytimes.com/top/reference/timestopics/ subjects/i/iphone/index.html?8qa&scp=1-spot&sq=iphone&st=nyt**; The Associated Press, "Altered iPhones at Risk of Failure," *New York Times*, September 25, 2007, **http://www.nytimes.com/2007/09/25/technology/25iphone.html?sq=iphone%20unlocked&st= nyt&scp=6&pagewanted=print**; Victoria Shannon, "iphone Must Be offered Without Contract Restrictions, German Court Rules," *New York Times*, November 21, 2007, **http://www.nytimes.com/2007/11/21/technology/21iphone.html?scp=3&sq=iphone+unlocked&st=nyt**; David Pogue, "The iPhone Matches Most of Its Hype," *New York Times*, June 27, 2007, **http://www.nytimes.com/2007/06/27/technology/ circuits/27pogue.html**.

Thrive in the Marketing Environment: The World *Is* Flat

Robert
Chatwani
Profile ▼

A **Decision Maker** at eBay

Robert Chatwani oversees the marketing, strategic planning, operations, and business development for eBay's marketplace for socially responsible shopping. Formerly a senior manager on eBay's Internet marketing team, Robert helped to manage the company's relationships with Google, Yahoo!, and Microsoft. Robert joined eBay in 2003 as manager of platform strategy, and he helped transform eBay into the world's largest Web Services platform.

Prior to joining eBay, Robert was the Co-founder and COO of MonkeyBin, the leading software company to the global barter and corporate trading industry. Before starting MonkeyBin, Robert worked with McKinsey & Company where he served *Fortune* 500 clients and also helped to start McKinsey's Globalization Practice.

Robert has a bachelor of science degree from DePaul University, has completed graduate work in computer science at the University of Chicago, and holds an MBA from UC Berkeley's Haas School of Business.

real people, **Real Choices**

Decision Time at eBay

A small, entrepreneurial group of eBay employees was developing a new on-line marketplace to help small producers and artisans throughout the world gain improved access to global consumers.

The group was particularly interested in creating a marketplace for products that were ethically sourced, ensuring that the people and organizations that created them could directly benefit from the income generated from sale of the products. The team's research showed that there was an abundance of supply of products such as handcrafted artisan goods and consumables such as coffee, tea, and chocolate. The group referred to these products as "People Positive" goods, meaning that the sale of the products positively impacts the producer and their community.

The group faced a key business question: Should it create a new, separately branded on-line marketplace or should it integrate the concept directly into eBay's existing on-line marketplace?

Robert's role as general manager of the business was to ensure that the team made a decision that could maximize both long-term revenue and social impact. And because eBay Inc. typically added new marketplace businesses to its portfolio through acquisition rather than by developing them internally, there was not much of a precedent for the decision he needed to make.

Robert considered his Options 1·2·3

1 **Option** **Customize the existing eBay shopping experience on eBay.com by adding additional categories to accommodate the supply of artisans' products, and do not create a separate brand.** The listings could be highlighted or marked in some way to indicate that the products were ethically sourced and a benefit to the producer. This would ensure that that all listings would be visible to millions of eBay users who currently shop on eBay.com. In addition, existing eBay users would not have to register on a new site. Custom page designs could be created to highlight inventory, and merchandising and marketing could be easily featured on the eBay homepage that millions of unique users visit each day. And, the availability of socially responsible products on eBay.com, such as fair trade and ethically sourced artisan goods, could help shed positive light on the eBay brand and lend to increased intangible brand value for eBay Inc. The financial risk of this approach was also low due to the quick development and rapid time-to-market for the solution.

On the other hand, this option would position the business primarily as an incremental extension of eBay rather than a whole new business with an independent identity and its own customers. Plus, historically, artisan goods and fair trade products have sold on eBay with only moderate success; simple customization to eBay's current shopping experience might not significantly improve sales volume.

2 **Option** **Create a completely separate, custom branded marketplace.** It would exist as a separate new brand, and offer a unique and highly tailored on-line shopping experience for consumers. There was some precedent for this amongst eBay's competitors. For example, Amazon.com had recently launched a newly branded marketplace for designer shoes and handbags called Endless.com. By developing a new brand identity, the business might attract new users who currently do not shop on eBay Inc. properties. This option also would allow for the creation of new, stand-alone marketing and merchandising campaigns, as opposed to marketing efforts that are simply "tacked on" to current eBay marketing programs. The unit would have the ability to fully customize a shopping experience that is specifically designed around the needs of consumers who shop for People Positive such as home décor, furniture, artwork, paintings, and other handcrafted and fair trade goods and consumables. It would also provide the opportunity to create a custom on-line community that is specifically targeted towards socially conscious consumers who purchase fair trade and ethically sourced handcrafted artisan goods.

But, this option would be very expensive. Developing a new brand and independent marketplace from scratch requires a large investment. It would also be time-consuming because the team would have to recreate many existing eBay functions and features for the marketplace such as a billing infrastructure, a search and browse experience, and checkout flows. And, it was risky because there was little precedent within for creating entirely new marketplaces within the company, and it would be hard to predict how this new business would work.

3 **Option** **Create a hybrid model to take advantage of everything that the core eBay.com platform and brand offered with the flexibility and customization of an independent marketplace with a different brand.** License a brand name that socially responsible consumers were already familiar with, that was reinforced by eBay as the ingredient brand (e.g., XYZ.com by eBay). Sellers' listings would appear on both the newly branded marketplace as well as the core eBay.com marketplace. The new marketplace and its listings would have an entirely distinct visual experience, while the exact same listings on eBay.com would appear just like all other eBay listings. This option might attract a new market of socially conscious consumers who buy ethically sourced goods, but who are not currently active on eBay. The marketplace experience could be customized, but the business unit would avoid the heavy investment that an entirely new platform would need. And, nearly 300 million registered eBay users would automatically be users of the new marketplace because they would retain the same username and password information. On the other hand, the brand licensing option would require the unit to establish a brand alliance with another company to co-brand the marketplace. This would present complexities in terms of a licensing agreement and a need to adhere to certain trademark and brand quality standards of another organization.

Now, put yourself in Robert's shoes: Which option would you choose, and why?

You Choose

Which **Option** would you choose, and **why**?
1. ☐YES ☐NO 2. ☐YES ☐NO 3. ☐YES ☐NO

See what **option** Robert chose and its success on **page 94** ➡

1

Global Marketing:
Play on an International Stage

Around the world, business leaders, government officials, and, yes, university professors all sooner or later visit the topic of the global marketplace. Some argue that the development of free trade will benefit us all, allowing the people of least developed countries to enjoy the same economic benefits as citizens of more developed countries. Others warn of problems such as global warming, and stress the need for international agreements that would force industries and governments to develop and adhere to environmental standards to protect the future of the planet. Still others argue for limits on trade, either to protect domestic industries or because some imported products, produced in countries with inadequate industry regulations and controls, are dangerous.

In his bestselling book, *The World is Flat: A Brief History of the Twenty-first Century*, Thomas Friedman argues that in today's fiercely competitive and global marketplace, the world is indeed flat. Friedman's perspective is that marketers must recognize that national borders are not as important as they once were, or risk disappearing off the face of the earth. Today, businesses—like eBay—must seek new and improved ways to attract customers down the street and around the globe.

The global marketing game is exciting, the stakes are high—and it's easy to lose your shirt. Competition comes from both local and foreign firms, and differences in national laws, customs, and consumer preferences can make your head spin. The successful global business needs to set its sights on far-flung markets around the world, but it needs to act locally by being willing to adapt its business practices to unique conditions in other parts of the globe—and hopefully to provide benefits to the people who live there as well.

Like many American companies that feel they are running out of growth opportunities in the American marketplace, the retail giant Wal-Mart is aggressively expanding its international presence. After successfully conquering the Mexican market in 1991, Wal-Mart de Mexico now controls 60 percent of our southern neighbor's retail market.[1] By January 2010, Wal-Mart projects that over 40 percent of its spending on new stores will be outside the U.S.A.[2]

In China, Wal-Mart more than doubled its presence when it spent $1 billion to acquire Trust-Mart, a Taiwanese-owned chain of more than 100 big-box stores in 20 Chinese provinces.[3] Despite some success internationally, the company learned the hard way the importance of flexibility when addressing the needs of different local markets. Wal-Mart failed to get a foothold in other European and Asian markets, such as Germany and South Korea, where it lost $1 billion because it didn't understand the local culture.[4] With plans to expand its existence in such huge Asian markets as China and India, the company must learn how to adapt its business model to local market needs.

World Trade

World trade refers to the flow of goods and services among different countries—the value of all the exports and imports of the world's nations. World trade activity steadily increases year by year. In 2007, worldwide exports of merchandise totaled $13.6 trillion, up 15 percent from 2006. Similarly, world exports of commercial services totaled $3.3 trillion, up 18 percent.[5]

Of course, not all countries participate equally in the trade flows among nations. Understanding the "big picture" of who does business with whom is important to marketers when they devise global trade strategies. Figure 3.1 shows the amount of merchandise North American countries trade with major partners around the world in 2006.

Having customers in far-reaching places is important, but it requires flexibility because you have to conduct your business differently to adapt to local social and economic conditions. For example, you have to accommodate the needs of trading partners when those foreign firms can't pay cash for the products they want to purchase. Believe it or not, the currency of as many as 70 percent of all countries is not *convertible*; it cannot be spent or exchanged outside the country's borders. In other countries, because sufficient cash or credit is simply not available, trading firms work out elaborate deals in which they trade (or *barter*) their products with each other or even supply goods in return for tax breaks from the local government. This **countertrade** accounts for about 25 percent of all world trade. For instance, the Philippine International Trading Corp. agreed to import 900,000 metric tons of rice from Vietnam in exchange for fertilizer, coconuts, and coconut by-products it produces in the Philippines.[6]

Our ever-increasing access to products from around the world does have a dark side: The growth in world trade in recent years has been accompanied by a glut of unsafe products, many of which have come from China. While most of the thousands of Chinese manufacturers produce quality products, some unscrupulous producers have damaged the reputation of Chinese manufacturers and prompted U.S. and European officials to increase their inspections of Chinese imports. The problems include the following:

- Mattel Inc. recalled millions of Chinese-made toys in 2006. Some contained magnets that might be swallowed by children and others could have contained dangerous levels of lead paint. Later Mattel issued an apology to China, saying that some of the recalled toys were defective because of Mattel's design flaws rather than manufacturing and that the company had recalled more lead-tainted toys than was justified.[7]

- In May 2006, U.S. Food and Drug Administration officials found toothpaste containing a small amount of the poison diethylene glycol in 10 brands of toothpaste imported from

The retail giant Wal-Mart is aggressively expanding its international presence.

world trade
The flow of goods and services among different countries—the value of all the exports and imports of the world's nations.

countertrade
A type of trade in which goods are paid for with other items instead of with cash.

Figure 3.1 | North American Merchandise Trade Flows (in $ Billions)

Knowing who does business with whom is essential for overseas marketing strategies. As this figure shows, North America trades most heavily with Asia, Europe, and Latin America.

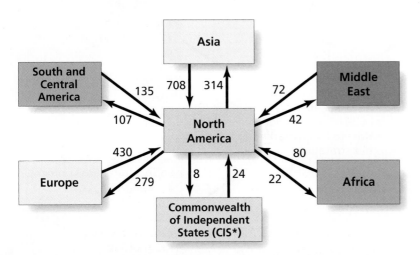

* Armenia, Azerbaijan, Belarus, Kazakhstan, Kyrgistan, Republic of Moldova, Russian Federation, and Ukraine

China. This made the United States the seventh country to discover tainted Chinese toothpaste in local stores.[8] As a result, the FDA announced that it would block Chinese imports of toothpaste until it can test them. Only weeks later, Colgate-Palmolive Co. found counterfeit toothpaste falsely packaged as "Colgate" in several discount stores.[9]

- In June 2006, a U.S. tire distributor found that Chinese-made tires might lack an important safety feature; about 450,000 were recalled.[10]

- In March of 2006, following consumer complaints, Menu Foods Inc. recalled cat and dog food made with tainted wheat gluten imported from China.

- In June 2006, the FDA found 25 percent of farm-raised seafood tested contained illegal antibiotics and chemicals.[11]

- Because Chinese chemical companies are not required to meet even minimal drug-manufacturing standards, some chemical manufacturers are exporting unapproved, adulterated, or counterfeit ingredients that end up in drugs sold in pharmacies in developing countries and on the Internet. Over 200 people died and countless others injured in Haiti and in Panama when two Chinese exporters owned by the Chinese government sold poison, mislabeled as a drug ingredient.[12]

Deciding to Go Global

When firms consider going global, they must make a number of decisions. As you can see in Figure 3.2, the first two crucial decisions are as follows:

1. "Go" or "no go"—Is it in the best interest of the firm to remain in its home market or to go elsewhere where there are good opportunities?

2. If the decision is "go," which global markets are most attractive?

Although the prospect of millions or even billions of consumers salivating for your goods in other countries is very tempting, not all firms can or should go global, and cer-

Figure 3.2 | Decision Model for Entering Foreign Markets

Entering global markets involves a complex decision process. Marketers must fully understand market conditions and environmental factors in order to determine the best strategy for entering the market and to create a successful marketing mix.

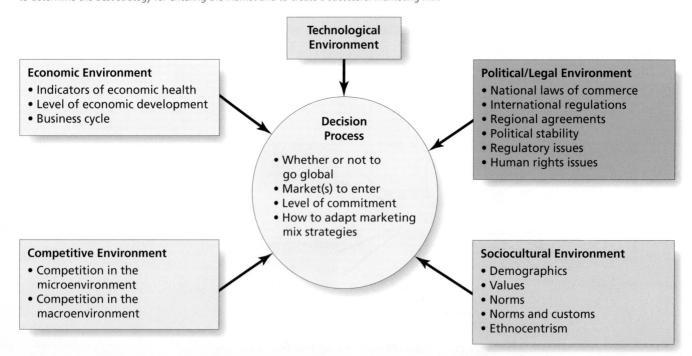

tainly not all global markets are alike. When they make these decisions, firms need to consider a number of factors that may enhance or detract from their possible success abroad. Let's review some big ones now.

One key factor—and it's a fairly broad one—is domestic and foreign market conditions, particularly those that affect a firm's ability to develop a competitive advantage in foreign markets. A second key factor is identifying which global markets are attractive given the firm's unique capabilities. Finally, the company must consider the extent to which opportunities for success may be hampered by regulations or other constraints on trade that local governments or international bodies impose.

Look at Market Conditions

Many times, a firm makes a decision to go global because domestic demand is declining while demand in foreign markets is growing. For example, the market for personal computers has leveled off in the United States, where more sales come from people replacing old or obsolete machines than from those buying a personal computer for the first time. In examining the market potential abroad for computers, however, the demand is much greater in some parts of the world where consumers and businesses are only now beginning to tune into the power of the Web. So, it's no coincidence that in 2005 IBM sold its entire personal computing business to Lenovo, a Chinese company.

Of course, it isn't only Western countries that are going global. Countries such as China that have been a vast market for Western firms to expand into, now are turning the tables as they carve out a larger role in the global marketplace. Dozens of Chinese companies have global ambitions, including government-owned Chery Automobile. Chery, founded in 1997, realizes that growth in its home Chinese market has slowed while competition has increased, and it sees opportunities around the globe. In July 2007, Chery signed an agreement with Chrysler to develop international markets in North American and Europe.[13] The agreement will allow Chery to take advantage of the Chrysler brand while using its experience to develop inexpensive medium- and small-sized cars for the domestic Chinese market. A second agreement with Fiat includes a 50:50 joint venture to produce Chery, Fiat, and Alfa Romeo cars. Chery has overseas plants in Iran, Russia, Ukraine, Indonesia, Egypt, and Uruguay; it plans to expand overseas assembly plants to include Argentina and India. Other Chinese carmakers such as Great Wall and Geely are also hungrily looking to the United States.[14] Watch for a flood of new, low-priced cars from Asia—including one that features a karaoke player in the dashboard!

Identify Competitive Advantage

In Chapter 1, we saw how firms hope to create competitive advantage over rivals. When firms compete in a global marketplace, this challenge is even greater because there are more players involved, and typically some of these local firms have a "home-court advantage." It's kind of like soccer—increasing numbers of Americans play the game, but they are up against an ingrained tradition of soccer fanaticism in Europe and South America where kids start dribbling a soccer ball when they start to walk.

Firms need to capitalize on their home country's assets and avoid competing in areas in which they are at a disadvantage. For example, German firms have trouble keeping production costs down because of the high wages, short workweeks, and long vacations that their skilled factory workers enjoy, so they compete better on high quality than on low price. German automakers have used superb engineering and good marketing to make "Mercs" and "Beamers" status symbols around the globe. In Germany, the car business accounts for one in seven manufacturing jobs.[15] Developing countries typically have a large labor force and low wages but relatively little in the way of highly trained workers or high-tech facilities, so they compete better for handmade crafts and low-cost manufacturing.

Some of the most significant U.S. exports are foods, industrial supplies, and services, including tourism and entertainment—industries in which consumers around the world value American products. The success of these industries shows that a firm's prospects for success depend not only on its own abilities, but also on its home country's competitive advantage. As we'll see next, barriers to trade and memberships in economic communities also affect a firm's success in global markets.

2

OBJECTIVE

Explain the World Trade Organization (WTO), economic communities, and how countries protect local industries by establishing roadblocks to foreign companies.

(pp. 72–74)

Road Blocks at the Borders

Even the best of competitive advantages may not allow a firm to succeed in foreign markets without a level playing field. At the beginning of the chapter, we stated that the world is flat—but in reality there are still some pretty big speed bumps here and there. We like to think of one big, open marketplace where companies from every country are free to compete for business by meeting customers' needs better than the next guy. Although we seem to be moving toward such an ideal of free trade, we're not quite there yet. Often roadblocks (or at least those pesky speed bumps) designed to favor local businesses over outsiders hinder a company's efforts to expand into foreign markets.[16]

Protected Trade: Quotas, Embargoes, and Tariffs

protectionism
A policy adopted by a government to give domestic companies an advantage.

import quotas
Limitations set by a government on the amount of a product allowed to enter or leave a country.

embargo
A quota completely prohibiting specified goods from entering or leaving a country.

tariffs
Taxes on imported goods.

In some cases, a government adopts a policy of **protectionism** in which it enforces rules on foreign firms to give home companies an advantage. Many governments set **import quotas** on foreign goods to reduce competition for their domestic industries. Quotas can make goods more expensive to a country's citizens because the absence of cheaper foreign goods reduces pressure on domestic firms to lower their prices. For example, Russia recently put import quotas on meat products to protect its own meat production industry.[17] An **embargo** is an extreme quota that prohibits specified foreign goods completely. Much to the distress of hard-core cigar smokers in the United States, the U.S. government prohibits the import of Cuban cigars as well as rum and other products because of political differences with its island neighbor.

Governments also use **tariffs**, or taxes on imported goods, to give domestic competitors an advantage in the marketplace by making foreign competitors' goods more expensive than their own products. For example, after the trade deficit with China reached $103 billion in 2002, the U.S. government proposed tariffs against some Chinese textiles and clothing.[18] In November 2005, however, China and the United States signed a textile export agreement that imposed quotas on 34 types of clothing and textiles that began January 1, 2006.[19] In 2007, when the trade deficit with China was expected to approach $300 billion, U.S. government officials claimed that China had purposefully devalued its currency in order to gain a greater trade advantage. They introduced a bill that would levy tariffs of over 25 percent on goods from China if the government did not allow the currency to float on the open market.[20]

Initiatives in International Regulation and Cooperation

General Agreement on Tariffs and Trade (GATT)
International treaty to reduce import tax levels and trade restrictions.

World Trade Organization (WTO)
An organization that replaced GATT, the WTO sets trade rules for its member nations and mediates disputes between nations.

In recent years a number of initiatives have made major changes in how marketers do business in markets around the globe. Established by the United Nations after World War II, the **General Agreement on Tariffs and Trade (GATT)** did a lot to reduce the problems that protectionism creates. This regulatory group is now known as the **World Trade Organization (WTO)**. With nearly 150 members (and around 30 more negotiating membership now), the WTO member nations account for over 97 percent of world trade. The World Trade Organization has made giant strides in creating a single open world market. The objective of the WTO is to "help trade flow smoothly, freely, fairly, and predictably." With over three-fourths of its membership drawn from the world's poorer countries, negotiations in recent years have largely focused on issues concerning economic development.[21]

One important issue that the WTO tackles is protection of copyright and patent rights. This protection will help firms prevent stolen or counterfeit versions of their software, books, and music CDs from being sold in other countries. *Pirating* is a serious problem for U.S. companies because illegal sales significantly erode their profits. According to a senior Microsoft executive based in Asia, "Piracy is clearly our number one competitor, and not only Microsoft's number one competitor but also a big impediment to the growth of the local software industry."[22]

Economic Communities

Groups of countries may also band together to promote trade among themselves and make it easier for member nations to compete elsewhere. These **economic communities** coordinate trade policies and ease restrictions on the flow of products and capital across their borders. Economic communities are important to marketers because they set policies in areas such as product content, package labeling, and advertising regulations that influence strategic decisions when they do business in these areas. Table 3.1 lists the economic communities that are now in place around the world. Each economic community includes a number of countries:

economic communities
Groups of countries that band together to promote trade among themselves and to make it easier for member nations to compete elsewhere.

- South America includes two economic communities: Mercado Comùn del Sur, or Southern Common Market (*MERCOSUR*) includes five countries, and the Andean Community includes four countries.

- Central America has the Central American Free Trade Agreement (*CAFTA*) that includes Costa Rica, the Dominican Republic, El Salvador, Guatemala, Honduras, Nicaragua, and the United States.

Table 3.1 | Major Economic Communities around the World

Community	Member Countries
The Andean Community **www.comunidadandina.org**	Bolivia, Colombia, Ecuador, Peru
APEC: Asia-Pacific Economy Cooperation **www.apecsec.org**	Australia, Brunei Darussalam, Canada, Chile, China, Hong Kong (China), Indonesia, Japan, Malaysia, Mexico, New Zealand, Papua New Guinea, Peru, Philippines, Republic of Korea, Russian Federation, Singapore, Chinese Taipei, Thailand, United States, Vietnam
ASEAN Association of Southeast Asian Nations **www.aseansec.org**	Brunei, Cambodia, Indonesia, Lao PDR, Malaysia, Myanmar, Philippines, Singapore, Thailand, Vietnam
CAFTA Central American Free Trade Agreement	Costa Rica, Dominican Republic, El Salvador, Guatemala, Honduras, Nicaragua, United States
CEFTA Central European Free Trade Agreement	Albania, Bosnia and Herzegovina, Bulgaria, Croatia, Czech Republic, Hungary, Kosovo, Moldova, Montenegro, Poland, Republic of Macedonia, Romania, Serbia, Slovak Republic, Slovenia
COMESA Common Market for Eastern and Southern Africa **www.comesa.int**	Angola, Burundi, Comoros, Democratic Republic of Congo, Djibouti, Egypt, Eritrea, Ethiopia, Kenya, Lybia, Madagascar, Malawi, Mauritius, Namibia, Rwanda, Seychelles, Sudan, Swaziland, Uganda, Zambia, Zimbabwe
EU: European Union **www.Europa.eu.int**	Austria, Belgium, Bulgaria, Cyprus, Czech Republic, Denmark, Estonia, Finland, France, Germany, Greece, Hungary, Ireland, Italy, Latvia, Lithuania, Luxembourg, Malta, Netherlands, Poland, Portugal, Slovakia, Slovenia, Spain, Sweden, United Kingdom
MERCOSUR **www.mercosur.org**	Brazil, Paraguay, Uruguay, Venezuela
NAFTA: North American Free Trade Agreement **www.nafta-sec-alena.org**	Canada, Mexico, United States
SAPTA: South Asian Association for Regional Cooperation **www.south-asia.com**	Afghanistan, Bangladesh, Bhutan, India, Maldives, Nepal, Pakistan, Sri Lanka

- Africa has the Common Market for Eastern and Southern Africa (*COMESA*) that includes 21 African countries.

- Asia has three groups: the Asia-Pacific Economy Cooperation (*APEC*) includes 21 countries, the Association of Southeast Asian Nations (*ASEAN*) includes 10 nations, and the South Asia Association for Regional Cooperation (*SAPTA*) includes 8 countries.

- Europe has two economic communities: the Central European Free Trade Agreement (*CEFTA*) includes 15 countries, and the European Union (*EU*) includes 25 countries. The EU now represents 490 million consumers, 3 million of whom use the Euro as their currency.

- North America has the North American Free Trade Agreement (*NAFTA*), which includes the United States, Canada, and Mexico.

An even larger American free trade zone might be in the making. Although talks stalled in November 2005, there is still hope that the Free Trade Area of the Americas (*FTAA*) will eventually be a reality. If and when the parties reach an agreement, FTAA will include 34 countries in North, Central, and South America, with a combined population of 800 million and a combined output of $11 trillion.[23]

3 Analyze the Global Marketing Environment

OBJECTIVE

Understand how factors in the external business environment influence marketing strategies and outcomes.

(pp. 74–87)

Once a marketer makes initial decisions about whether or not to go global and about what country or countries provide attractive opportunities, he must gain a good understanding of the local conditions in the targeted country or region. As we saw in Chapter 2, successful marketing planning depends on a clear understanding of the environment. In this section, we'll see how economic, competitive, technological, political/legal, and sociocultural factors in a firm's external environment affect marketers' global strategies.

The Economic Environment

Understanding the economy of a country in which a firm does business is vital to the success of marketing plans. Marketers need to understand the state of the economy from two different perspectives: the overall economic health and level of development of a country, and the current stage of its business cycle.

Indicators of Economic Health

Just as a doctor takes your temperature during a medical checkup, companies need to know how "healthy" the economies of different countries are. The most commonly used measure of economic health of a country is the **gross domestic product (GDP)**: the total dollar value of goods and services a country produces within its borders in a year. A similar but less frequently used measure of economic health is the **gross national product (GNP)**, which measures the value of all goods and services a country's individuals or organizations produce, whether located within the country's borders or not. Table 3.2 shows the GDP and other economic and demographic characteristics of a sampling of countries. In addition to total GDP, marketers may also compare countries on the basis of *per capita GDP*: the total GDP divided by the number of people in a country.

Still, these comparisons may not tell the whole story. Per capita GDP can be deceiving because the wealth of a country may be concentrated in the hands of a few. Furthermore, the costs of the same goods and services are much lower in some global markets. For example, goods and services valued at $30,000 in the United States would cost only $4,800 in

gross domestic product (GDP)
The total dollar value of goods and services produced by a nation within its borders in a year.

gross national product (GNP)
The value of all goods and services produced by a country's citizens or organizations, whether located within the country's borders or not.

Table 3.2 | Comparisons of Several Countries on Economic and Demographic Characteristics

	United States	China	Japan	Spain	Hungary	Ecuador
Total GDP	$13.8 trillion	$7.0 trillion	$4.4 trillion	$1.4 trillion	$194.2 billion	$98.3 billion
Per capita GDP	$46,000	$5,300	$33,800	$33,700	$19,500	$7,100
Population below poverty level	12%	8%	NA	19.8%	8.6%	38.3%
Inflation rate	2.7%	4.7%	0%	2.4%	7.8%	3.3%
Unemployment rate	4.6%	4.0%	4.0%	7.6%	7.1%	9.8%
Population	303.8 Million	1.3 trillion	127.3 million	40.5 million	9.9 million	13.9 million
Birth rate per 1,000 population	14.2	13.7	7.9	9.9	9.6	21.5
Population growth rate	0.88%	0.63%	−0.14%	0.10%	−0.25%	0.94%
Population aged 0–14	20.1%	20.1%	13.75%	14.4%	15.2%	32.1%
Population aged 15–64	67.1%	71.9%	64.7%	67.6%	69.3%	62.7%
Population aged 65 and over	12.7%	8.0%	21.6%	17.9%	15.6%	5.2%

Source: Adapted from Central Intelligence Agency, *The 2008 World Factbook*, **https://www.cia.gov/library/publications/the-world-factbook/index.html**.

Uganda.[24] And indeed, in some least developed and developing countries businesses operate on a cash basis without creating a paper trail of transactions. Therefore, the purchase of a house may involve carrying a suitcase of money to the seller. In these cash societies, a proportion of the goods and services sold may never be reported. Thus the actual GDP may be much higher than we estimate.

Of course, GDP alone does not provide the information marketers need to decide if a country's economic environment makes for an attractive market. They also need to consider whether they can conduct "business as usual" in another country. The **economic infrastructure** refers to the quality of a country's distribution, financial, and communications systems. For example, Argentina boasts many modern conveniences, but its antiquated phone system is just starting to work properly after years of neglect by the government.

economic infrastructure
The quality of a country's distribution, financial, and communications systems.

Level of Economic Development

These are just some of the issues marketers must think about when determining whether a country will be a good prospect. However, there are other economic conditions that marketers must understand as well, including the broader economic picture of a country that we call its **level of economic development**.

When marketers scout the world for opportunities, it helps if they consider a country's level of economic development to understand the needs of people who live there and the infrastructure conditions with which they must contend. Economists look past simple facts such as growth in GDP to decide this; they also look at what steps are being taken to reduce poverty, inequality, and unemployment. Analysts also take into account a country's **standard of living**; an indicator of the average quality and quantity of goods and services a country consumes. They describe the following three basic levels of development:

level of economic development
The broader economic picture of a country.

standard of living
An indicator of the average quality and quantity of goods and services consumed in a country.

1. A country at the lowest stage of economic development is a **least developed country (LDC)**. In most cases, its economic base is agricultural. Analysts consider many nations in Africa and South Asia to be LDCs. In least developed countries, the standard of living is low, as are literacy levels. Opportunities to sell many products, especially luxury items, such as diamonds and caviar, are minimal because most people don't have enough spending money. They grow what they need and barter for the rest. These countries are attractive markets for staples and inexpensive items. They may export important raw materials, such as minerals or rubber, to industrial nations.

least developed country (LDC)
A country at the lowest stage of economic development.

The carmaker Chery is one of several Chinese companies that is starting to export its brands to other countries, including the U.S.A.

developing countries
Countries in which the economy is shifting its emphasis from agriculture to industry.

developed country
A country that boasts sophisticated marketing systems, strong private enterprise, and bountiful market potential for many goods and services.

business cycle
The overall patterns of change in the economy—including periods of prosperity, recession, depression, and recovery—that affect consumer and business purchasing power.

2. When an economy shifts its emphasis from agriculture to industry, standards of living, education, and the use of technology rise. These countries are **developing countries**. In such locales, there may be a viable middle class, often largely composed of entrepreneurs working hard to run successful small businesses. Because over three-fourths of the world's population lives in developing countries, the number of potential customers and the presence of a skilled labor force attracts many firms to these areas. Eastern Europe, with its more than 300 million consumers, is an important region that includes a number of developing countries. Similarly, the countries of Latin America are emerging from decades of state control, and their economies are opening to foreign business.[25] Finally, the Pacific Rim countries of China, South Korea, Malaysia, Indonesia, Thailand, Singapore, and Hong Kong are nicknamed the "Tigers of Asia" because of their tremendous economic growth. For example, in China, there are over 300 million cell phone users and demand for phones with MP3 players and cameras is growing fast.[26]

3. A **developed country** boasts sophisticated marketing systems, strong private enterprise, and bountiful market potential for many goods and services. Such countries are economically advanced, and they offer a wide range of opportunities for international marketers. The United States, the United Kingdom, Canada, France, Italy, Germany, Russia, and Japan are the most economically developed countries in the world.

The Business Cycle

The **business cycle** is the overall pattern of changes or fluctuations of an economy. All economies go through cycles of *prosperity* (high levels of demand, employment and income), *recession* (falling demand, employment and income), and *recovery* (gradual improvement in production, lowering unemployment, and increasing income).

A severe recession is a *depression*, a period during which prices fall but there is little demand because few people have money to spend and many are out of work. *Inflation* occurs when prices and the cost of living rise while money loses its purchasing power because the cost of goods escalates. For example, between 1960 and 2004, prices increased over five percent per year so that an item worth $1.00 in 1960 would cost over $6.00 in 2004. During inflationary periods, dollar incomes may increase, but real income—what the dollar will buy—decreases because goods and services cost more.

The business cycle is especially important to marketers because of its effect on customer purchase behavior. During times of prosperity, consumers buy more goods and services. Marketers are busy trying to grow the business and maintain inventory levels and even to develop new products to meet customers' willingness to spend. During periods of recession, consumers simply buy less. We clearly see that pattern in recent years as many people scale back on buying houses, expensive cars and even restaurant dinners. The challenge to most marketers is to maintain their firm's level of sales by convincing the customers who are buying to select the firm's product over the competition's. Of course, even recessions aren't bad for all businesses. Although it may be harder to sell luxury items, firms that make basic necessities are not likely to suffer significant losses.

It is important to note that when firms assess the economic environment, they evaluate all factors that influence consumer and business buying patterns, including the amount of confidence people have in the health of the economy. This "crystal ball" must be a global one because events in one country can have an impact on the economic health of other countries. For instance, the economic impact of the terrorist attacks on the United States in September 2001 affected the fortunes of businesses around the world, as did the meltdown in the American subprime mortgage industry in 2007.

The Competitive Environment

A second important element of a firm's external environment is the competitive environment. For products ranging from toothpaste to sport-utility vehicles, firms must keep abreast of what the competition is doing so they can develop new product features, new pricing schedules, or new advertising to maintain or gain market share.

Analyze the Market and the Competition

Before a firm can begin to develop strategies that will create a competitive advantage in the marketplace, it has to know who its competitors are and what they're doing. Marketing managers size up the competitors according to their strengths and weaknesses, monitor their marketing strategies, and try to predict their moves.

An increasing number of firms around the globe engage in **competitive intelligence (CI)** activities, the process of gathering and analyzing publicly available information about rivals. In fact, many firms have budgets in the millions for CI activities. Banks continually track home loan, auto loan, and certificate of deposit (CD) interest rates of their competitors. Major airlines change hundreds of fares daily as they respond to competitors' fares. Car manufacturers keep abreast of cuts and increases in their rivals' production numbers, sales, and sales incentives (e.g., rebates and low or no interest loan rates) and use the information in their own marketing strategies.

Most of the information that companies need to know about their competitors is available from rather mundane sources, including the news media, the Internet, and publicly available government documents such as building permits and patent grants (or even for some hardball players a rival's garbage if they're into "dumpster diving!"). Successful CI means that a firm learns about a competitor's new products, its manufacturing, or the management styles of its executives. Then the firm uses this information to develop superior marketing strategies (we'll learn more about collecting marketing intelligence in Chapter 4, so stay tuned).

Competition in the Microenvironment

To succeed in a competitive marketplace, marketers must have a clear understanding of exactly who their competition is. Competition in the *microenvironment* means the product alternatives from which members of a target market may choose. We think of these choices at three different levels.

At a broad level, marketers compete for consumers' **discretionary income**: the amount of money people have left after paying for necessities such as housing, utilities, food, and clothing. Few consumers are wealthy enough to buy anything and everything, so each of us is constantly faced with choices: Do we plow "leftover" money into a new MP3 player,

Developed countries like Japan provide rich markets for a variety of products of global companies.

competitive intelligence (CI)
The process of gathering and analyzing publicly available information about rivals.

discretionary income
The portion of income people have left over after paying for necessities such as housing, utilities, food, and clothing.

product competition
When firms offering different products compete to satisfy the same consumer needs and wants.

brand competition
When firms offering similar goods or services compete on the basis of their brand's reputation or perceived benefits.

monopoly
A market situation in which one firm, the only supplier of a particular product, is able to control the price, quality, and supply of that product.

oligopoly
A market structure in which a relatively small number of sellers, each holding a substantial share of the market, compete in a market with many buyers.

Marketers sometimes hire specialized research firms like Asia Insight to help them master the intricacies of foreign markets.

donate it to charity, or turn over a new leaf and lose those extra pounds by investing in a healthy lifestyle? Thus, the first part of understanding who the competition is means understanding all the alternatives consumers consider for their discretionary income—not just the brands against which the firm directly competes within a product category.

A second type of choice is **product competition**, in which competitors offering different products attempt to satisfy the same consumers' needs and wants. So, for example, if a couch potato decides to use some of his discretionary income to get buff, he may join a health club or buy a Soloflex machine and pump iron at home. Starbucks is successfully competing against home favorite tea in England. In a country known as much for its afternoon tea as for Big Ben, there are already close to 500 Starbucks outlets (more in London than in New York) in addition to fast-growing local chains with such names as Caffè Nero and Coffee Republic. Meanwhile, U.K. tea sales have declined 12% in the past five years. Score one for latte.[27]

The third type of choice is **brand competition**, in which competitors offering similar goods or services vie for consumer dollars. So, if our flabby friend decides to join a gym, he still must choose among competitors within this industry, such as between Gold's Gym and the YMCA. And he may forgo the exercise thing altogether and count on the South Beach diet to work its magic by itself—or just buy bigger pants.

Competition in the Macroenvironment

When we talk about examining competition in the *macroenvironment*, we mean that marketers need to understand the big picture—the overall structure of their industry. This structure can range from one firm having total control to numerous firms that compete on an even playing field.

Four structures describe differing amounts of competition. Let's review each structure, beginning with total control by one organization and ending with tons of competitors.

- No, it's not just a board game: A **monopoly** exists when one seller controls a market. Because the seller is "the only game in town," it feels little pressure to keep prices low or to produce quality goods or services. In the old days, the U.S. Postal Service had a monopoly on the delivery of written documents. Now, the days of a snail-mail monopoly are over because the U.S. Postal Service must battle fax machines, e-mail, and couriers such as FedEx for market share.

  In most U.S. industries today, the government attempts to ensure consumers' welfare by limiting monopolies through the prosecution of firms that engage in activities that would limit competition and thus violate antitrust regulations. Of course, these laws may generate controversy as powerful firms argue that they dominate a market simply because they provide a product most people want. This is at the heart of the ongoing controversy about Wal-Mart's domination of the retail business. The world's largest retailer (and getting bigger all the time) generates some amazing statistics. In 2006, Wal-Mart generated $345 billion in sales through its more than 4,000 facilities in the United States and more than 2,800 in Argentina, Brazil, Canada, China, Costa Rica, El Salvador, Guatemala, Honduras, Japan, Mexico, Nicaragua, Puerto Rico, and the United Kingdom. Wal-Mart attracted 180 million shoppers each week to its stores and bought $200 billion in merchandise from 61,000 U.S. suppliers in 2005.[28]

- In an **oligopoly**, there are a relatively small number of sellers, each holding substantial market share, in a market with many buyers. Because there are few sellers, each seller is very conscious of other sellers' actions. Oligopolies most often exist in industries requiring substantial investments in equipment or technology to produce a product—this means only a few competitors have the resources to enter the game. The airline industry is an oligopoly. It is pretty hard for an entrepreneur with little start-up cash to be successful entering the airline industry—that's left to billionaires like Richard Branson, who can afford to launch a new entry like Virgin Airlines. Relatively smaller firms, such as JetBlue and Frontier, succeed by offering something special, such as onboard entertainment, direct routes to smaller cities, or more leg room. Others that just can't compete either on price or amenities (like Mesa, Frontier, or Aloha Airlines) simply fly to that Great Hangar in the Sky.

- In a state of **monopolistic competition**, there are many sellers who compete for buyers in a market. Each firm, however, offers a slightly different product, and each has only a small share of the market. For example, many athletic shoe manufacturers, including Nike, New Balance, Reebok, and a host of others vigorously compete with one another to offer consumers some unique benefit—even though only Adidas (at least for now) offers you a $250 computerized running shoe that senses how hard the ground is where you are running and adapts to it.

monopolistic competition
A market structure in which many firms, each having slightly different products, offer unique consumer benefits.

- Finally, **perfect competition** exists when there are many small sellers, each offering basically the same good or service. In such industries, no single firm has a significant impact on quality, price, or supply. Although true conditions of perfect competition are rare, agricultural markets in which there are many individual farmers where each produces the same corn or jalapeño peppers come the closest. Even in the case of food commodities, though, there are opportunities for marketers to distinguish their offerings. Egg-Land's Best Inc., for example, says it feeds its hens a high-quality, all-vegetarian diet, so the eggs they lay contain less cholesterol and six times more vitamin E than regular eggs.[29] It brands each egg with a red "EB" seal. The company has scrambled the competition by creating an "egg-straordinary" difference where none existed before.

perfect competition
A market structure in which many small sellers, all of whom offer similar products, are unable to have an impact on the quality, price, or supply of a product.

The Technological Environment

Firms today see technology as an investment they can't afford not to make, as technology provides firms with important competitive advantages. The technological environment profoundly affects marketing activities. Toll-free telephone numbers, easy computer access to customer databases, and of course the Internet have made it possible for people to buy virtually anything they want (and even some things they don't want) without ever leaving their homes. And distribution has also improved because of automated inventory control afforded by advancements such as bar codes, RFID (radio frequency identification) chips, and computer light pens.

Changes in technology can dramatically transform an industry, as when transistors revolutionized the field of consumer electronics. Successful marketers continuously scan the external business environment in search of ideas and trends to spark their own research efforts. They also monitor ongoing research projects in government and private organizations. When inventors feel they have come across something exciting, they usually want to protect their exclusive right to produce and sell the invention by applying for a patent. A **patent** is a legal document a country's patent office issues that gives inventors—or individuals and firms—exclusive rights to produce and sell a particular invention in that country. Marketers monitor government patent applications to discover innovative products they can purchase from the inventor.

Robert
Chatwani

APPLYING Technology

Robert knows that as increasing numbers of consumers around the world gain access to the World Wide Web, the global marketplace will continue to expand. This growth works in favor of an online enterprise like eBay. ➡

patent
Legal documentation granting an individual or firm exclusive rights to produce and sell a particular invention.

The Political and Legal Environment

The political and legal environment refers to the local, state, national, and global laws and regulations that affect businesses. Legal and regulatory controls can be prime motivators for many business decisions. While firms who choose to remain at home have to worry about only local regulations, global marketers must understand more complex political issues that can affect how they do business and their potential for success.

High-tech changes everything, even low-tech products like apparel. Fashion brands like H&M (**http://www.hm.com/us/**) now promote and display their upcoming collections in virtual worlds. On-line games like *The SIMS 2* and *Second Life* provide an excellent platform for fashion brands and new product developers to test their new concepts and products. What's more, these on-line runways allow consumers from all over the world to check out the same styles so hard-core *fashionistas* can get the global scoop much easier.

These virtual fashion worlds also empower customers to create and share their designs and concepts with others.

Magazines like *Second Style* provide a channel for budding designers to share and display their designs on-line. Consumers can create their own designs by using simple graphic design tools. Knowledge of garment construction is no longer a prerequisite. And, members of virtual communities from around the world can trade their designs with one another so magazines and store windows no longer determine what's hot and what's not.

Source: Jessica Michault, "Fashion giants are venturing into virtual worlds," *International Herald Tribune*, August 6, 2007, **http://www.iht.com/articles/2007/08/06/style/favatar.php**.

American Laws

Laws in the United States governing business have two purposes. Some such as the Sherman Antitrust Act and the Wheeler–Lea Act make sure that businesses compete fairly with each other. Others, such as the Food and Drug Act and the Consumer Products Safety Commission Act, make sure that businesses don't take advantage of consumers. Although some businesspeople argue that excessive legislation only limits competition, others say that laws ultimately help firms by maintaining a level playing field for businesses and supporting troubled industries.

As world trade increases and problems with imports continue, it is likely that new regulations will be created to address the problems. So far, the United States has signed safety agreements with China that require that Chinese producers must register with the Chinese government, that China will inspect food and feed exports to the United States, and that the two countries will notify each other of public health risks they discover.[30]

Table 3.3 lists some of the major federal laws that protect and preserve the rights of U.S. consumers and businesses. Federal and state governments have created a host of regulatory agencies—government bodies that monitor business activities and enforce laws. Table 3.4 lists some of the agencies whose actions affect marketing activities.

Sometimes firms learn the hard way that government watchdog activities can put a stop to their marketing plans. The Federal Trade Commission (FTC) ruled that KFC Corporation, owner of the Kentucky Fried Chicken restaurant chain, made false claims in a national television advertising campaign about the relative nutritional value and healthiness of its fried chicken.[31] KFC ads claimed that "Two KFC breasts have less fat than a BK Whopper." The FTC said that although two fried chicken breasts have slightly less total fat and saturated fat than a Whopper, they also have more than three times the trans fat and cholesterol, more than twice the sodium, and more calories. The FTC also said the company made false claims that its fried chicken is compatible with certain popular weight-loss programs, and ordered KFC not to run these ads or others making similar claims about the nutritional value, weight-loss benefits, or other health benefits of its chicken products and meals. Fowl play comes back to bite you.

Political Constraints on Trade

Global firms know that the political actions a government takes can drastically affect their business operations. At the extreme, of course, when two countries go to war, the business environment changes dramatically. Often people overseas dislike the actions of another country. This was the case when the United States invaded Afghanistan in 2001 and sent troops to Iraq a few years later, and more recently when a Danish newspaper printed cartoons that highly offended Muslims around the globe. In such times, it's common for symbols of a country's culture, like the Golden Arches, to be the first target of demonstrations, vandalism, and in some cases destruction.

Table 3.3 | Significant U.S.A. Legislation Relevant to Business

Law	Purpose
Sherman Antitrust Act (1890)	Developed to eliminate monopolies and to guarantee free competition. Prohibits exclusive territories (if they restrict competition), price fixing, and predatory pricing.
Food and Drug Act (1906)	Prohibits harmful practices in the production of food and drugs.
Clayton Act (1914)	Prohibits tying contracts that require a dealer to take other products in the seller's line. Prohibits exclusive dealing if it restricts competition.
Federal Trade Commission Act (FTC) (1914)	Created the Federal Trade Commission to monitor unfair practices.
Robinson–Patman Act (1936)	Prohibits price discrimination (offering different prices to competing wholesalers or retailers) unless cost-justified.
Wheeler–Lea Amendment to FTC Act (1938)	Revised the FTC Act. Makes deceptive and misleading advertising illegal.
Lanham Trademark Act (1946)	Protects and regulates brand names and trademarks.
Fair Packaging and Labeling Act (1966)	Ensures that product packages are labeled honestly.
National Traffic and Motor Vehicle Safety Act (1966)	Sets automobile and tire safety standards.
Cigarette Labeling Act (1966)	Requires health warnings on cigarettes.
Child Protection Act (1966)	Bans dangerous products children use.
Child Protection and Toy Safety Act (1969)	Sets standards for child-resistant packaging.
Consumer Credit Protection Act (1968)	Protects consumers by requiring full disclosure of credit and loan terms and rates.
Fair Credit Reporting Act (1970)	Regulates the use of consumer credit reporting.
Consumer Products Safety Commission Act (1972)	Created the Consumer Product Safety Commission to monitor and recall unsafe products. Sets product safety standards.
Magnuson–Moss Consumer Product Warranty Act (1975)	Regulates warranties.
Children's Television Act (1990)	Limits the amount of television commercials aired on children's programs.
Nutrition Labeling and Education Act (1990)	Requires that new food labeling requirements be set by the Food and Drug Administration.
National Do Not Call Registry (2003)	Established by the Federal Trade Commission to allow consumers to limit number of telemarketing calls they receive.

Table 3.4 | U.S. Regulatory Agencies and Responsibilities

Regulatory Agency	Responsibilities
Consumer Product Safety Commission (CPSC)	Protects the public from potentially hazardous products. Through regulation and testing programs, the CPSC helps firms make sure their products won't harm customers.
Environmental Protection Agency (EPA)	Develops and enforces regulations aimed at protecting the environment. Such regulations have a major impact on the materials and processes that manufacturers use in their products and thus on the ability of companies to develop products.
Federal Communications Commission (FCC)	Regulates telephone, radio, and television. FCC regulations directly affect the marketing activities of companies in the communications industries, and they have an indirect effect on all firms that use broadcast media for marketing communications.
Federal Trade Commission (FTC)	Enforces laws against deceptive advertising and product labeling regulations. Marketers must constantly keep abreast of changes in FTC regulations to avoid costly fines.
Food and Drug Administration (FDA)	Enforces laws and regulations on foods, drugs, cosmetics, and veterinary products. Marketers of pharmaceuticals, over-the-counter medicines, and a variety of other products must get FDA approval before they can introduce products to the market.
Interstate Commerce Commission (ICC)	Regulates interstate bus, truck, rail, and water operations. The ability of a firm to efficiently move products to its customers depends on ICC policies and regulation.

Koren
Borges
a professor at the University of North Florida

My Advice for eBay would be to choose   Option

real people, **Other Voices**

I would choose Option 3 because it positions eBay to have the most opportunity for value creation. Option 3 creates a hybrid model that takes advantage of eBay's marketplace and technological strengths while allowing the company to create the new product category to enhance its overall revenue streams. The hybrid model also allows for the creation of a flexible site that can cater to the unique opportunities available in the People Positive area, a new segment for on-line auctions and sales. One example of this might be that buyers in this sector would like substantially more information about the seller, the seller's situation, and the impact on the village from sales of the product than in a typical eBay sale. Additionally, Option 3 helps eBay position itself as a socially responsible citizen of the world. As long as eBay chooses a partner with similar style and goals—for the short term and long term—partner management issues could be manageable. I would not choose Option 1 because the People Positive opportunity will be forced into eBay's current model and likely "get lost" in the rest of the site thereby showing little or no revenue enhancement. I would also not select Option 2 because eBay will need to pay significantly more to build the new brand/company, thereby assuming more risk but without benefit of the eBay name and brand equity. ➤

Short of war, though, a country may impose *economic sanctions* that prohibit trade with another country (as the United States has done with several countries, including Cuba and North Korea), so access to some markets may be cut off. For example, in efforts to stop Iran's alleged efforts to build nuclear weapons, the U.S. government imposed financial and economic sanctions against the country, some as recently as October 2007. These rules prevented any American from engaging in financial transactions with the Revolutionary Guards or any of their many associated businesses and with three state-owned banks.[32]

In some situations, internal pressures may prompt the government to take over the operations of foreign companies that do business within its borders. *Nationalization* is when the domestic government reimburses a foreign company (often not for the full value) for its assets after taking it over. *Expropriation* is when a domestic government seizes a foreign company's assets (and that firm is just out of luck). To keep track of the level of political stability or instability in foreign countries, firms often engage in formal or informal analyses of the potential political risk in various countries.

Regulatory Constraints on Trade

Governments and economic communities impose numerous regulations about what products should be made of, how they should be made, and what can be said about them. For example, sometimes a company has no choice but to alter product content to comply with local laws. Heinz 57 Sauce tastes quite different in Europe simply because of different legal restrictions on preservatives and color additives.[33]

Other regulations are more focused on ensuring that the host country gets a piece of the action. **Local content rules** are a form of protectionism stipulating that a certain proportion of a product must consist of components supplied by industries in the host country or economic community. For example, under NAFTA rules, cars Mercedes-Benz builds in Alabama must have 62.5 percent of their components made in North America to be able to enter Mexico and Canada duty-free.[34] That helps explain why Asian automakers such as Toyota, Hyundai, and Kia have already beefed up their local presence by opening manufacturing plants in the United States and hiring local workers to run them. For example, the U.S. and Canadian content in 2006 models of foreign automakers in North America were as follows: Toyota, 73 percent; Honda, 68 percent; Nissan, 64 percent, and Mercedes 62 percent. [35]

Human Rights Issues

Some governments and companies are vigilant about denying business opportunities to countries that mistreat their citizens. They are concerned about conducting trade with local firms that exploit their workers or that keep costs down by employing children or prisoners for slave

---

local content rules

A form of protectionism stipulating that a certain proportion of a product must consist of components supplied by industries in the host country or economic community.

wages. The **U.S. Generalized System of Preferences (GSP)** is a program established by Congress to promote economic growth in the developing world. GSP regulations allow developing countries to export goods duty-free to the United States. The catch is that each country must constantly demonstrate that it is making progress toward improving the rights of its workers. [36]

On the other side of the coin, the low wages they can pay to local workers often entice U.S. firms looking to expand their operations overseas. Although they provide needed jobs, some companies have been criticized for exploiting workers by paying wages that fall below local poverty levels, for damaging the environment, or for selling poorly made or unsafe items to consumers. For example, in 2004 Gap Inc. conceded that working conditions were far from perfect at many of the 3,000 overseas factories that make its clothing. The company also observed that the situation is even worse in many of the overseas factories that *don't* earn its business—about 90 percent of foreign manufacturers who apply for a Gap contract fail the retailer's initial evaluation. [37] In 2007, Gap again faced disturbing publicity when news reports surfaced that an Indian company had used children as young as 10 working 16 hours a day for no pay to hand-embroider decorations on blouses for GapKids. Gap, embarrassed by the reports, established a grant of $200,000 to improve working conditions, pay back wages, and provide the education the children deserved. The company also announced plans to hold an international conference in 2008 to come up with solutions for child labor issues. [38]

In 2006, Apple was forced to investigate the working conditions in Chinese factories that manufacture its iPod. While Apple did not find evidence of sweatshops or child labor, the company did discover that employees in many cases were working more than 60 hours or 6 days a week and ordered the Chinese factory to enforce Apple's overtime limits. [39] Even retail giant Wal-Mart, which buys about $9 billion in goods from China has been troubled by child labor practices. In December 2007, reports surfaced that documented abuse and labor violations in 15 factories that produce goods for Wal-Mart. [40]

The Sociocultural Environment

Another element of a firm's external environment is the sociocultural environment. This term refers to the characteristics of the society, the people who live in that society, and the culture that reflects the values and beliefs of the society. Whether at home or in global markets, marketers need to understand and adapt to the customs, characteristics, and practices of its citizens. Basic beliefs about cultural priorities, such as the role of family or proper relations between the sexes, affect people's responses to products and promotional messages in any market.

Disney learned the hard way about the importance of being sensitive to local cultures after it opened its Euro Disney Park in 1992. The company got slammed for creating an entertainment venue that recreated its American locations without catering to local customs (such as serving wine with meals). More recently, the company applied the lessons it learned in cultural sensitivity to its new Hong Kong Disneyland. Executives shifted the angle of the front gate by 12 degrees after consulting a *feng shui* specialist, who said the change would ensure prosperity for the park. Disney also put a bend in the walkway from the train station to the gate to make sure the flow of positive energy, or *chi*, did not slip past the entrance and out to the China Sea. Cash registers are close to corners or along walls to increase prosperity. And, since the Chinese consider the number four to be bad luck, you won't find any fourth-floor buttons in hotel elevators. [41] As Disney (eventually) discovered, understanding consumers' attitudes, beliefs, and ways of doing things in different parts of the world is especially important to firms when developing marketing strategy.

Demographics

The first step toward understanding the characteristics of a society is to look at its **demographics**. These are statistics that measure observable aspects of a population, such as size, age, gender, ethnic group, income, education, occupation, and family structure. The

U.S. Generalized System of Preferences (GSP)
A program to promote economic growth in developing countries by allowing duty-free entry of goods into the U.S.

demographics
Statistics that measure observable aspects of a population, including size, age, gender, ethnic group, income, education, occupation, and family structure.

information demographic studies reveal is of great value to marketers in predicting the size of markets for many products, from home mortgages to brooms and can openers. We'll talk more about how demographic factors impact marketing strategies in Chapter 7.

Values

More than 100 million women read 59 editions of *Cosmopolitan* in 34 different languages—even though, because of local norms about modesty, some of them have to hide the magazine from their husbands. Adapting the *Cosmo* credo of "Fun, Fearless Female" in all these places gets a bit tricky. Different cultures emphasize varying belief systems that define what it means to be female, feminine, or appealing—and what is considered appropriate to see in print on these matters. For example, in India and China, *Cosmo* is likely to have articles relating to sex replaced with stories about youthful dedication. Ironically, there isn't much down-and-dirty material in the Swedish edition either—but for the opposite reason; the culture is so open about this topic that it doesn't grab readers' attention the way it would in the United States. [42]

cultural values
A society's deeply held beliefs about right and wrong ways to live.

As this example shows, every society has a set of **cultural values**, or deeply held beliefs about right and wrong ways to live, that it imparts to its members.[43] Those beliefs influence virtually every aspect of our lives, even the way we mark the time we live them. For example, for most Americans *punctuality* is a core value; indeed, business leaders often proclaim that "Time is money." For countries in Latin America and other parts of the world, this is not at all true. If you schedule a business meeting at 10:00, you can be assured most people will not arrive until around 10:30—or later.

collectivist cultures
Cultures in which people subordinate their personal goals to those of a stable community.

individualist cultures
Cultures in which people tend to attach more importance to personal goals than to those of the larger community.

These differences in values often explain why marketing efforts that are a big hit in one country can flop in another. For example, Italian housewives spend about five times as many hours per week than do their American counterparts on household chores. On average they wash their kitchen and bathroom floors at least four times a week, and they typically iron everything they wash, including socks! This dedication (obsession?) should make them perfect customers for cleaning products—but when Unilever launched an all-purpose spray cleaner there, the product flopped. And when Procter & Gamble tested its top-selling Swiffer Wet mop, which eliminates the need for a clunky bucket of water, the product bombed so badly in Italy that P&G took it off the market. These successful consumer-products companies failed to realize that the benefit of labor-saving convenience is a huge turnoff to Italian women who want products that are tough cleaners, not timesavers. Unilever had to make big adjustments in order to clean up in the Italian market—including making the bottles 50 percent bigger because Italians clean so frequently.[44]

One important dimension on which cultures differ is their emphasis on collectivism versus individualism. In **collectivist cultures**, such as those found in Venezuela, Pakistan, Taiwan, Thailand, Turkey, Greece, and Portugal, people tend to subordinate their personal goals to those of a stable community. In contrast, consumers in **individualist cultures**, such as the United States, Australia, Great Britain, Canada, and the Netherlands, tend to

Metrics Moment

For many years, U.S. marketers have benefited from the VALS™ system that segments the consumer marketplace on the basis of personality traits that drive consumer behavior. We'll talk more about VALS™ in Chapter 7. The Original VALS™ system segments the American market into eight types: Innovators, Thinkers, Achievers, Experiencers, Believers, Strivers, Makers, and Survivors.[46] But the VALS™ types represent only U.S. consumers. As more and more companies enter global markets, they need to understand the markets of a variety of countries. Japan-VALS™ allows Japanese marketers to understand the unique Japanese consumer better and develop more targeted strategies and communications.[47]

Japan-VALS™ segments the Japanese marketplace based on 1) life orientation, i.e., what interests and animates a person the most, and 2) attitudes toward social change. The Japan-VALS™ includes these segments:

- **Integrators**: active, inquisitive, trend-leading, informed, and affluent
- **Self Innovators and Self Adapters**: desire personal experience, fashionable display, social activities, daring ideas and exciting entertainment
- **Ryoshiki Innovators and Ryoshiki Adapters**: education, career achievement and professional knowledge are their personal focus, while their major concerns are home, family, and social status.
- **Tradition Innovators and Tradition Adapters**: adhere to traditional religions and customs, prefer long-familiar home furnishing and dress, and hold conservative social opinions.
- **High Pragmatists and Low Pragmatists**: not very active and not well informed, they have few interests and are flexible or uncommitted in their lifestyle choices.
- **Sustainers**: lack money, youth, and high education; dislike innovation and wish to sustain the past.

attach more importance to personal goals, and people are more likely to change memberships when the demands of the group become too costly.[45] This difference can be a big deal to marketers who are appealing to one extreme or the other—try selling a garment that is "sure to make you stand out" to consumers who would much prefer to "fit in."

Norms and Customs

Values are general ideas about good and bad behaviors. From these values flow **norms**, or specific rules dictating what is right or wrong, acceptable or unacceptable. Some specific types of norms include the following: [48]

- A **custom** is a norm handed down from the past that controls basic behaviors, such as division of labor in a household.

- **Mores** are customs with a strong moral overtone. Mores often involve a taboo or forbidden behavior, such as incest or cannibalism. Violation of mores often meets with strong punishment from other members of a society.

- **Conventions** are norms regarding the conduct of everyday life. These rules deal with the subtleties of consumer behavior, including the "correct" way to furnish one's house, wear one's clothes, or host a dinner party.

All three types of norms may determine what behaviors are appropriate in different countries. For example, mores may tell us what kind of food is permissible to eat. A meal of dog may be taboo in the United States, whereas Hindus would shun a steak, and Muslims avoid pork products. A custom dictates the appropriate hour at which the meal should be served—many Europeans, Middle Easterners, and Latin Americans do not begin dinner until around 9:00 or later, and they are amused by American visitors whose stomachs are growling by 7:00. Conventions tell us how to eat the meal, including such details as the utensils, table etiquette, and even the appropriate apparel for dinnertime (no thongs at the dinner table!).

Conflicting customs can be a problem when U.S. marketers try to conduct business in other countries where executives have different ideas about what is proper or expected. These difficulties even include body language; people in Latin countries tend to stand much closer to each other than do Americans, and they will be insulted if their counterpart tries to stand farther away. In many countries, even casual friends greet each other with a kiss (or two) on the cheek. In the United States, one should only kiss a person of the opposite sex, and one kiss only, please. In Spain and other parts of Europe, kissing includes a kiss on each cheek for both people of the same and the opposite sex, while in the Middle East, unless a very special friend, it is unacceptable for a man to kiss a woman or a woman to kiss a man. Instead it is the norm to see two men or two women holding hands or walking down the street with their arms entwined. Understanding customs such as these can spell the difference between a firm's success and failure on the global stage.

norms
Specific rules dictating what is right or wrong, acceptable or unacceptable.

custom
A norm handed down from the past that controls basic behaviors.

mores
Customs with a strong moral overtone.

conventions
Norms regarding the conduct of everyday life.

Michael
Lee
a student at Washington State University
My Advice for eBay would be to choose

Option

real people, **Other Voices**

I would choose option number 3 because of the fact that it has the best of both worlds. Taking an already strong brand name such as eBay and combining it with another partnership to create a new brand can save money (no huge costs to creating a new brand), create more awareness for current eBay users and also draw in new eBay users that consume the "People Positive" goods, and form a long-term relationship between organizations. Granted there may be complications of licensing agreements in the beginning to get the brand name started, after it is all said and done and the partnership comes to an agreement, eBay has formed a long-term relationship with another company that will be beneficial to the future and success of eBay and the other company in the long run. ➤

Language

The language barrier is one obvious problem that confronts marketers who wish to break into foreign markets. Travelers abroad commonly encounter signs in tortured English such as a note to guests at a Tokyo hotel that said, "You are invited to take advantage of the chambermaid," a notice at a hotel in Acapulco that proclaimed "The manager has personally passed all the water served here," or a dry cleaner in Majorca who urged passing customers to "drop your pants here for best results."

These barriers are not just embarrassing, but they can affect product labeling and usage instructions, advertising, and personal selling. It's vital for marketers to work with local people who understand the subtleties of language to avoid confusion. For example, the meaning of a brand name—one of the most important signals a marketer can send about the character and quality of a product—can get mangled as it travels around the world. Local product names often raise eyebrows to visiting Americans who may be surprised to stumble on a Japanese coffee creamer called Creap, a Mexican bread named Bimbo, or even a Scandinavian product that unfreezes car locks called Super Piss.[49]

Ethnocentrism

ethnocentrism
The tendency to prefer products or people of one's own culture.

Even *if* a firm succeeds in getting its products to a foreign market, there's no guarantee that local consumers will be interested. Sometimes a willingness to try products made elsewhere comes slowly. In marketing, we call the tendency to prefer products or people of one's own culture over those from other countries **ethnocentrism**. For example, the French tend to be a bit finicky about their cuisine, and they evaluate food products from other countries critically. However, the upscale British department store Marks & Spencer is making inroads in France by selling English-style sandwiches like egg and watercress on whole wheat bread and ethnic dishes such as chicken tikka masala. Young office workers view these as convenience foods, and they are less expensive than the traditional French loaf split down the middle and lathered with butter and ham or Camembert cheese.

Ethical Issues for Global Business

Whether the organization operates in one's own home market or in a global environment, marketers face ethical dilemmas on an almost daily basis. Thus, understanding the environment where you do business means staying on top of the ethical values and norms of the business culture in the marketplace—often not an easy task. Indeed, there are vast differences in what people consider ethical business behavior around the world.

Business leaders who have experienced a sheltered life in American companies are often shocked to find that they cannot expect the same ethical standards of others in the global community. Westerners, for example, are often painfully honest. If an American business contact cannot meet a deadline or attend a meeting or provide the needed services, he will normally say so. In other cultures the answer, even if untrue, will always be "yes." Westerners see such dishonest answers as unethical but in some areas of the world people just believe saying "no" to any request is extremely rude—even if there's no way the request is happening.

In many least developed and developing countries, salaries for mid-level people are sadly very low; the economy runs on a system we would call blatant bribery. Some of these "payments" are only petty corruption and the "favors" are inconsequential, while others may involve high level government or business officials, and can have devastating

American Krispy Kreme donuts are very popular at Harrods in London despite criticisms that they are contributing to increasing obesity in the United Kingdom.

consequences. If you need to park your car or your delivery truck illegally where there is no parking space, you give a little money to the policeman. If the shopkeeper wants the policeman to watch out for his store, he gives the policeman a shirt from his stock once in a while. If an importer wants to get his merchandise out of customs before it spoils, he pays off the government worker who can hold up his shipment for weeks and perhaps charge him very high customs duties as well. If a company wants to buy a piece of land for a new factory, a company representative may quietly leave a suitcase of cash in the office of the person who is facilitating the sale. And if someone wants the contract to build a new building or wants an unsafe building to pass inspection—well, you get the idea.

Bribery occurs when someone voluntarily offers payment to get an illegal advantage. **Extortion** occurs when someone in authority extracts payment under duress.[50] Some businesspeople give bribes to speed up required work, secure a contract, or avoid having a contract cancelled. Such payments are a way of life in many countries because many people consider them as natural as giving a waiter a tip for good service. The Foreign Corrupt Practices Act of 1977 (FCPA), however, puts U.S. businesses at a disadvantage because it bars them from paying bribes to sell overseas. The FCPA does, however, allow payments for "routine governmental action ... such as obtaining permits, licenses, or other official documents; processing governmental papers, such as visas and work orders; [and] providing police protection." But, FCPA does not permit payment to influence "any decision by a foreign official to award new business or to continue business with a particular party."[51] So, under U.S. rules bribes are out.

Transparency International, an anti-corruption organization, publishes an annual survey, the *Bribe Payers Index*, that measures the propensity of firms from 30 various countries to pay bribes. Table 3.5 provides the results of the 2007 survey and shows that even among developed countries, there is great variation in the frequency of this practice.

bribery
When someone voluntarily offers payment to get an illegal advantage.

extortion
When someone in authority extracts payment under duress.

Table 3.5 | The Transparency International 2006 *Bribe Payers Index*: Some Winners and Some Losers

2006 Country Rank	Country	2006 BPI Score*
1	Switzerland	7.81
2	Sweden	7.62
3	Australia	7.59
4	Austria	7.50
5	Canada	7.46
9	U.S.	7.22
26	Taiwan	5.41
27	Turkey	5.23
28	Russia	5.16
29	China	4.94
30	India	4.62

*(A low score indicates a propensity to pay bribes)

Source: Adapted from Transparency International, "Bribe Payers Index 2006," **http://www.transparency.org/ policy_research/surveys_indices/bpi/bpi_2006**.

Ethical Decisions in the Real World

Executives at a large American tobacco company see the writing on the wall: Smoking rates in the U.S. are dwindling. If the company is going to continue to make money from cigarettes it needs to look overseas. But, tastes regarding tobacco aren't the same everywhere. One way to grow a brand is to develop other versions of it made from local materials. After all, even if they aren't smoking the regular version, at least they're still smoking something—and it's not the competition's brand. On the other hand, this form of aggressive marketing will inevitably increase the number of people who smoke worldwide—and tax the already beleaguered medical resources of developing countries as they scramble to cope with increased health problems related to smoking. What do you do?

Ripped from the Headlines! See what happened in the Real World at **www.mypearsonmarketinglab.com**

ETHICS CHECK: ↖

Find out what other students taking this course **would do** and **why** on **www. mypearsonmarketinglab. com**

Would you market cigarette products to consumers in other countries?

☐ YES ☐ NO

4

OBJECTIVE

Explain the strategies that a firm can use to enter global markets.

(pp. 88–91)

Is The World Flat Or Not? How "Global" Should A Global Marketing Strategy Be?

Going global is not a simple task. Even a popular television show may have to make "adjustments" as it travels across borders. Consider, for example, the incredibly popular show *American Idol*, which isn't really American at all—the concept originated in the United Kingdom. More than 100 million people around the globe tune into over 20 local versions of the *Idol* show, but sometimes the format has to be fine-tuned:[52]

- When a South African contestant was bluntly told to work on her clothes and her appearance, she broke down and told the judges she was too poor to afford nicer things. The station was swamped with calls from angry viewers who offered to donate clothing.

- Because the word "idol" has Hitler-like connotations for Germans, producers there had to change the show's title to *Germany Seeks the Superstar*. Similarly, "idol" is sacrilegious in Arabic countries and can't be used in those markets.

- A riot broke out in Beirut when a Lebanese contestant was voted out in favor of a Jordanian woman—viewers accused the producers of fixing the show for political reasons.

As you can see, understanding all the economic, legal, and cultural differences around the world can be a daunting task—even for astute judges like Randy, Paula, and Simon. But if a firm decides to expand beyond its home country, it must make important decisions about how to structure its business and whether to adapt its product marketing strategy to accommodate local needs. First, the company must decide on the nature of its commitment, including whether the company will partner with another firm or go it alone. Then it must make specific decisions about the marketing mix for a particular product. In this final section, we'll consider issues related to global strategy at these two levels: the company and the product.

Company-Level Decisions: Choose a Market-Entry Strategy

In 2004, General Electric (GE) was named the world's most respected company for the seventh straight year in a worldwide survey of chief executives the *Financial Times* and accounting firm PricewaterhouseCoopers conducted.[53] Much of GE's success has come from its global operations.

GE made the decision to go global, and the company has never looked back. GE's strategy for shifting its "center of gravity" from the industrialized world of the United States to Asia and Latin America made it a local assembler of low-tech goods in some countries and a high-tech manufacturer of appliances and other products for export in others. GE tailors the type and extent of its commitment to local conditions in each market it chooses to enter.

Just like a romantic relationship, a firm deciding to go global must determine the level of commitment it is willing to make to operate in another country. This commitment ranges from a casual involvement to a full-scale "marriage." At one extreme, the firm simply exports its products, while at the other extreme it directly invests in another country by buying a foreign subsidiary or opening its own stores. The decision about the extent of commitment entails a trade-off between *control* and *risk*. Direct involvement gives the firm more control over what happens in the country, but risk also increases if the operation is not successful.

Let's review four strategies representing increased levels of involvement: exporting, contractual arrangements, strategic alliances, and direct investment. Figure 3.3 summarizes these options.

Exporting

If a firm chooses to export, it must decide whether it will attempt to sell its products on its own or rely on intermediaries to represent it in the target country. These specialists called **export merchants** who understand the local market and who can find buyers and negotiate terms.[54] An exporting strategy allows a firm to sell its products in global markets and cushions it against downturns in its domestic market. Because the firm actually makes the products at home, it is able to maintain control over design and production decisions.[55]

Sometimes, exporting is the best way to be successful in a foreign market. Frontier Foods, Ltd., an Australian food-distributing company, has developed a thriving business importing cheese to China where wealthy Chinese consumers are developing an unprecedented taste for it. Because there is so little open farmland in China for large herds of dairy cows, China can't produce enough milk to sustain a domestic cheese industry. Hence, it is easier to import cheese than to make it in China.[56]

Contractual Agreements

The next level of commitment a firm can make to a foreign market is a contractual agreement with a company in that country to conduct some or all of its business there. These agreements can take several forms. Two of the most common are licensing and franchising.

In a **licensing agreement**, a firm (the *licensor*) gives another firm (the *licensee*) the right to produce and market its product in a specific country or region in return for royalties on goods sold. Because the licensee produces the product in its home market, it can avoid many of the barriers-to-entry that the licensor would have encountered. However, the licensor also loses control over how the product is produced and marketed, so if the licensee does a poor job, this may tarnish the company's reputation. Licensors also have to accept the possibility that local licensees will alter its product to suit local tastes. That's what's happened with America's loveable *Sesame Street* characters. The show now is

Robert
Chatwani

APPLYING Exporting

Robert sees huge potential for locally-made goods to find markets around the world. He wants the new eBay service to be an intermediary in this process.

export merchants
Intermediaries a firm uses to represent it in other countries.

licensing agreement
An agreement in which one firm gives another firm the right to produce and market its product in a specific country or region in return for royalties.

Figure 3.3 | Market-Entry Strategies

Choosing a market-entry strategy is a critical decision for companies that want to go global. A decision to operate the new venture versus sharing responsibility with organizations in the local market involves a trade-off between control and risk.

franchising
A form of licensing involving the right to adapt an entire system of doing business.

licensed in many countries, including India, France, Japan, and South Africa with some editorial changes that include new characters with names like Nac, Khokha, and Kami.

Franchising is a form of licensing that gives the franchisee the right to adapt an entire way of doing business in the host country. Again, there is a risk to the parent company if the *franchisee* does not use the same-quality ingredients or procedures, so firms monitor these operations carefully. More than 400 U.S. franchising companies, including 7-Eleven, Century 21, and Starbucks operate about 40,000 outlets internationally. McDonald's, a major franchiser, has over 30,000 restaurants serving 52 million people in 119 countries.[57] In India, where Hindus do not eat beef, all McDonald's have vegetarian and nonvegetarian burger-cooking lines and offer customers vegetarian specialties such as Pizza McPuff and McAloo Tikki (a spiced-potato burger).[58]

Strategic Alliances

strategic alliance
Relationship developed between a firm seeking a deeper commitment to a foreign market and a domestic firm in the target country.

joint venture
A strategic alliance in which a new entity owned by two or more firms allows the partners to pool their resources for common goals.

Firms seeking an even deeper commitment to a foreign market develop a **strategic alliance** with one or more domestic firms in the target country. These relationships often take the form of a **joint venture**: Two or more firms create a new entity to allow the partners to pool their resources for common goals. Strategic alliances also allow companies easy access to new markets, especially because these partnerships often bring with them preferential treatment in the partner's home country. We tend to think of the international automobile industry as fiercely competitive, but in reality many companies actually own pieces of each other. For example, General Motors has alliances with Fiat Auto SpA, Fuji Heavy Industries, Isuzu Motors, and Suzuki Motor Corp., and is now considering a more far-reaching partnership with Renault and Nissan.[59]

Direct Investment

An even deeper level of commitment occurs when a firm expands internationally through ownership, usually by buying a business in the host country outright. Instead of starting from scratch in its quest to become multinational, buying part or all of a domestic firm allows a foreign firm to take advantage of a domestic company's political savvy and market position in the host country. Take for example the Chinese appliance maker Haier, which *Fortune China* named "China's Most Admired Company" in 2006. The firm manufactures over 15,000 different home appliances in 96 categories and it operates in more than 100 countries worldwide. To achieve its goal of being "local" in the U.S. and European markets, Haier has set up manufacturing plants in the U.S., Italy, Pakistan, Jordan, and Nigeria.[60]

born-global firms
Companies that try to sell their products in multiple countries from the moment they're created.

Ownership gives a firm maximum freedom and control, and it also dodges import restrictions. For example, the United States bans the import of so-called Saturday Night Specials (cheap, short-barreled pistols), but it permits their sale. So, the Italian gun manufacturer Beretta got around this restriction by opening a manufacturing plant in Maryland.[61] But direct investment also carries greater risk. Firms that own businesses in foreign countries could suffer losses of their investment if economic conditions deteriorate or if political instability leads to nationalization or expropriation.

Born-Global Firms

The appeal of catering to a global market is so strong that it's even spawning a new breed of start-up companies we call **born-global firms**. These companies

While marketers for some Toyota models are limited to only one or a few countries, Toyota has selected its popular Corolla to be a true "world car" that is sold in all its markets from Egypt to Iceland.

deliberately try to sell their products in multiple countries from the moment they're created rather than taking the usual path of developing business in their local market and then slowly expanding into other countries. For example, Logitech International is a Swiss company that quite possibly made your computer mouse. The company has operational headquarters through its U.S. subsidiary in California and regional headquarters through local subsidiaries in Switzerland, Taiwan, and Hong Kong. The company has manufacturing facilities in Asia and offices in major cities in North America, Europe, and Asia. Logitech currently employs over 4,500 people worldwide. It's truly "born global."

5 Product-Level Decisions: Choose a Marketing Mix Strategy

OBJECTIVE

Understand the arguments for standardization versus localization of marketing mix strategies in global markets.

(pp. 91–94)

In addition to "big picture" decisions about how a company will operate in other countries, managers must decide how to market the product in each country. They may need to modify the famous Four P's—product, price, promotion, and place—to suit local conditions. To what extent will the company need to adapt its marketing communications to the specific styles and tastes of each local market? Will the same product appeal to people there? Will it have to be priced differently? And, of course, how does the company get the product into people's hands? Let's consider each of these questions in turn.

Standardization versus Localization

The executive in charge of giant VF Corporation's overseas operations recently observed that when most American brands decide to branch out to other countries, they "...tend to take every strategy used in their home market—products, pricing, marketing—and apply it in the same way." VF, which owns several fashion brands including Tommy Hilfiger and Nautica, discovered that this doesn't necessarily work very well. It reintroduced its Nautica men's sportswear brand in Europe after finding that Europeans' tastes are different—for example, they tend to like orange coats that American men avoid and prefer a more body-conscious fit.

Similarly, Hilfiger's initial foray into the U.K. fizzled—and it didn't help that Tommy had to contend with a cheap counterfeit brand called Tommy Sport (which VF later acquired to deal with the problem). The European division had to scramble to tweak its offerings to suit local tastes. It booted American underwear packaging that showed beefy, muscular men in briefs and boxer shorts and replaced these images with thinner men and racier photos; now they feature a woman in bra and panties standing seductively behind the male model. The local merchandising team also found that its signature cotton knit sweaters didn't go over well because European men prefer wool sweaters. And they gave American-style baggy jeans the boot in favor of a thinner, more tailored silhouette (the American flag in the logo shrank as well). Today, Hilfiger's European clothes are designed from scratch by a team based in Amsterdam that appeals to a more sophisticated, upscale European consumer.[62]

When top management makes a company-level decision to expand internationally, the firm's marketers have to answer a crucial question: How necessary is it to develop a customized marketing mix for each country? Gillette decided to offer the same products in all its markets—a *standardization strategy*. In contrast, Proctor & Gamble (P&G) adopted a *localization strategy* in Asia, where consumers like to experiment with different brands of shampoo. P&G now packages most of the shampoos it sells in

Verizon hopes to expand its market by launching communications services that span geographic regions.

INDIA
Married

USA
Married

Never underestimate the importance
of local knowledge.

HSBC ◀▶
The world's local bank

Because norms and customs may differ greatly from one country to another, the decision to standardize or localize marketing strategies is not an easy one. This ad shows how HSBC has positioned itself as a global bank that understands and adapts to differences around the globe.

Asia in single-use sachets to encourage people to try different kinds.[63] Offering single-use packages is even more important in poorer countries in Asia and other parts of the world for another reason; consumers simply cannot afford to purchase a bottle of shampoo but still can occasionally purchase and use the sachet-size product.

So, which strategy is right? Advocates of standardization argue that the world has become so small that basic needs and wants are the same everywhere.[64] A focus on the similarities among cultures certainly is appealing. After all, if a firm didn't have to make any changes to its marketing strategy to compete in foreign countries, it would realize large economies of scale because it could spread the costs of product development and promotional materials over many markets. Reebok, realizing this, created a new centralized product development center to develop shoe designs that can easily cross borders.[65] Widespread, consistent exposure also helps create a global brand by forging a strong, unified image all over the world—Coca-Cola signs are visible on billboards in London and on metal roofs deep in the forests of Thailand.

In contrast, those in favor of localization feel that the world is not *that* small; you need to tailor products and promotional messages to local environments. These marketers feel that each culture is unique and that each country has a *national character*—a distinctive set of behavioral and personality characteristics.[66] Snapple failed in Japan because consumers there didn't like the drink's cloudy appearance. Similarly, Frito-Lay Inc. stopped selling Ruffles potato chips (too salty for Japanese tastes) and Cheetos there (the Japanese didn't appreciate having their fingers turn orange after eating a handful).[67]

To P or Not to P: Tweak the Marketing Mix

Once a firm decides whether they will adopt a standardization or a localization strategy, it is time to plan for the four Ps. As in domestic marketing planning, this is where the real action occurs.

Product Decisions   A firm seeking to sell a product in a foreign market has three choices: sell the same product in the new market, modify it for that market, or develop a brand-new product to sell there. Let's take a closer look at each possibility.

straight extension strategy
Product strategy in which a firm offers the same product in both domestic and foreign markets.

A **straight extension strategy** retains the same product for domestic and foreign markets. For generations, proper etiquette in Japan was for girls to bow and never raise their eyes to a man.[68] However, the new generation of Japanese women wants to look straight at you, showing their eyes and eyelashes. Japanese eyelashes are very short, so they have to be curled to show. To meet this need, L'Oréal introduced its Maybelline brand Wonder Curl that dramatically thickens and curls lashes as a woman applies it. The launch was such a success in Japan that local television news showed Japanese customers standing in line to buy the product.

product adaptation strategy
Product strategy in which a firm offers the a similar but modified product in foreign markets.

A **product adaptation strategy** recognizes that in many cases people in different cultures do have strong and different product preferences. Sometimes these differences can be subtle yet important. When Apple sought to introduce its innovative iPhone to European markets, critics warned that the device's Internet connection would be too slow for Europeans used to faster mobile phone networks. To solve the problem, Apple set up agreements with hot-spot providers in the UK and Germany so that iPhone users could use these providers' speedy wireless networks free of charge.[69] Kellogg faced a more low-tech product adaptation problem when it tried to introduce Froot Loops cereal in European markets. Kellogg had to remove the green "loops" from Froot Loops in European markets after research showed that Europeans felt they were too artificial looking. Americans, in contrast, like the green loops just fine.[70]

A **product invention strategy** means a company develops a new product as it expands to foreign markets. For example, firms that wish to market household appliances in Japan, where apartments are very small by Western standards, must design and manufacture smaller products. In some cases, a product invention strategy takes the form of *backward invention*. A firm may find that it needs to offer a less complex product than it sells elsewhere such as a manually operated sewing machine or a hand-powered clothes washer for people without access to a reliable source of electricity.

In some cases, marketers develop a product for an overseas market and then discover it could do well at home too. After tremendous success with its caramelized-milk-flavored dulce de leche ice cream in Buenos Aires, Häagen Dazs was able to duplicate that success among Latino consumers in the United States.

Promotion Decisions   Marketers must also decide whether it's necessary to modify their product promotions for a foreign market. Some firms endorse the idea that the same message will appeal to everyone around the world, while others feel the need to customize it. The 2006 World Cup was broadcast in 189 countries to one of the biggest global television audiences ever. This mega-event illustrates how different marketers make different decisions—even when they're creating ads to be run during the same game. MasterCard ran ads that appeared in 39 countries, so its ad agency came up with a spot called "Fever," in which 100-odd cheering fans from 30 countries appear. There's no dialogue, so it works in any language. At the end, the words, "Football fever. Priceless" appeared under the MasterCard logo. Similarly, Anheuser-Busch's spot that it showed in the United States, United Kingdom, Italy, Spain, and China is a tweaked version of a Super Bowl ad that shows fans in a stadium holding up cards that create an image of Budweiser beer being poured into a glass. Gillette, in contrast, ran an ad in over 20 countries that it digitally altered to reflect local differences. The spot shows cheering fans, wearing the colors and carrying the flags of their national team. But the colors will be changed depending on where the ad is shown. In the United States, for example, actors posing as fans wore red, white, and blue, while in Australia, the same actors wore green and gold.[71]

Price Decisions   Costs stemming from transportation, tariffs, differences in currency exchange rates, and even bribes paid to local officials often make a product more expensive for a company to manufacture for foreign markets than in its home country. For example, Chrysler Corporation had a hard time offering its Jeep Cherokee to Japanese consumers at a competitive price. Chrysler priced the vehicle at about $19,000 when it left the plant in Toledo, Ohio. By the time it was sitting in a Tokyo showroom, the price had mushroomed to over $31,000 Because it didn't build the cars in Japan, Chrysler fell victim to a number of factors, including the currency exchange rate, the cost of adapting the Jeep to comply with Japanese regulations, tariffs, and profits local distributors took.[72] To ease the financial burden of tariffs on companies that import goods, some countries have established free trade zones. These are designated areas where foreign companies can warehouse goods without paying taxes or customs duties until they move the goods into the marketplace.

One danger of pricing too high is that competitors will find ways to offer their product at a lower price, even if they do this illegally. **Gray market goods** are items that are imported without the consent of the trademark holder. While gray market goods are not counterfeits,

product invention strategy
Product strategy in which a firm develops a new product for foreign markets.

gray market goods
Items manufactured outside a country and then imported without the consent of the trademark holder.

Companies like DHL need to adapt their practices to local conditions.

dumping
A company tries to get a toehold in a foreign market by pricing its products lower than it offers them at home.

they may be different from authorized products in warranty coverage and compliance with local regulatory requirements.[73]

Another unethical and often illegal practice is **dumping**, in which a company prices its products lower than they are offered at home—often removing excess supply from home markets and keeping prices up there. In one case, Eastman Kodak accused Japanese rival Fuji Photo Film of selling color photographic paper in the United States for as little as a quarter of what it charges in Japan.[74]

Distribution Decisions Getting the product to consumers in a remote location is half the battle. Thus, it's essential for a firm to establish a reliable distribution system if it's going to succeed in a foreign market. Marketers used to dealing with a handful of large wholesalers or retailers in their domestic market may have to rely instead on thousands of small "mom-and-pop" stores or distributors, some of whom transport goods to remote rural areas on oxcarts or bicycles. In least developed countries, marketers may run into problems finding a way to package, refrigerate, or store goods for long periods.

Even the retailing giant Wal-Mart occasionally stumbles when it expands to new markets. The company recently joined the ranks of multinationals like Nokia, Nestlé, and Google that have failed to adjust to the tastes of South Korean consumers. Wal-Mart (as well as European rival Carrefours) stuck to Western marketing strategies that concentrated on dry goods from electronics to clothing, while their local rivals like E-Mart and Lotte emphasize food and beverages that are more likely to attract South Koreans to large stores. Local customers also didn't take to a relatively sterile environment where products sell by the box; their competitors enticed shoppers with eye-catching displays and clerks who hawked their goods with megaphones and hand-clapping. Wal-Mart bailed out of South Korea entirely in 2006.[75]

Now that you've learned about global marketing, read "Real People, Real Choices: How It Worked Out" to see which strategy Robert Chatwani of eBay selected.

---

real people, **Real Choices**

Robert **Chatwani**
Robert chose:

Option

How it Worked Out at eBay

Robert selected option #3. eBay licensed the brand "WorldofGood.com" from the company World of Good, Inc. This existing company works with wholesale, retail, and on-line companies to create shopping experiences based on information, trust, and social impact—their main business is the import of hand-crafted artisan goods for sale to U.S. retailers. The unit decided that the name of the new marketplace would be WorldofGood.com, an eBay Marketplace.

Robert and his colleagues decided on this option because they felt it presented the greatest opportunity in terms of attracting new consumers and generating a customized marketplace while at the same time minimizing the financial and technology risk because eBay did not have to create an entirely new brand from scratch an independent technology platform to support it. The new entity's mission statement is:

> Our mission is to provide a trusted platform where individuals can create positive change through commerce, as part of a global community. We believe that a growing number of individuals want to understand

how the choices they make impact people and the planet. There is an important need for trusted information, and a need for transparency into how and where products are made. Our goal is to provide our community with the resources needed to make good choices and connect with others who share the same passion.

The team decided to launch the new business in two phases. Phase 1 was the launch of the WorldofGood.com Community (**http://community. worldofgood.com**), and Phase 2 would be the launch of the e-commerce marketplace. The Phase 1 Community launched in February 2008, and was designed to attract consumers interested in engaging on the topic of commerce as a force for social change. Phase 2 launched in late Spring 2008; this integrates both the community and commerce platforms into a single on-line shopping experience. eBay will use several marketing channels to promote the community and the marketplace:

- **Internet Marketing.** Search engine marketing (SEM), including paid search keyword advertising and search engine optimization (SEO), on-line banner advertising, and affiliate marketing.
- **Relationship Marketing.** Direct on-line e-mail marketing to current eBay users, merchandising and marketing to eBay users on eBay.com, and marketing in eBay's quarterly print catalog.
- **On-line Viral Marketing.** Use of social media such as social networking sites, outreach to the blogosphere and other on-line communities, and availability of marketing widgets customizable by users.
- **PR and Event Marketing.** PR to media publications, promotions at industry events that are frequented by socially responsible consumers.

How eBay Measures Success

eBay plans to use several success metrics once the marketplace launches. These include operational performance metrics as well as key marketing metrics.

Operational business metrics:

- Total seller listings
- Successful listings
- Gross Merchandise Volume (total value of all goods sold)
- Revenue
- Total number of registered users
- Number of repeat visits (sessions) from current users

Metrics to determine success of co-branding strategy:

- Number of new sellers (who did not have pre-existing eBay accounts)
- Number of new registered buyers (who did not have pre-existing eBay accounts)
- Increase in buying activity on WorldofGood.com, an eBay Marketplace by users registered on eBay.com
- Brand awareness via quantitative surveys

The new World of Good home page.

Refer back to **page 67** for Robert's story

Brand **YOU**!

Do what you love and love what you do.

It's a mantra for life. Explore what you love to do (and don't love to do) and how that can translate into your career in Chapter 3 of the *Brand You* supplement. You'll be surprised at the choices you have and how easily you'll be able to narrow down the direction that is best for you.

Objective Summary → Key Terms → Apply

CHAPTER 3
Study Map

1. Objective Summary (pp. 68–72)

Understand the big picture of international marketing, including world trade flows and the decision criteria firms use in their decisions to go global.

The increasing amount of world trade—the flow of goods and services among countries—may take place through cash, credit payments, or countertrade. A decision to go global often comes when domestic market opportunities dwindle and the firm perceives a likelihood for success in foreign markets due to a competitive advantage.

Key Terms

world trade, p. 69 (Figure 3.1, p. 69)

countertrade, p. 69

2. Objective Summary (pp. 72–74)

Explain the WTO, economic communities, and how countries protect local industries by establishing roadblocks to foreign companies.

Some governments adopt policies of protectionism with rules designed to give home companies an advantage. Such policies may include trade quotas, embargoes, or tariffs that increase the costs of foreign goods. Countering this, the World Trade Organization with over 150 members works to create a single open world market. In addition, many countries have banded together to form economic communities to promote free trade.

Key Terms

protectionism, p. 72

import quotas, p. 72

embargo, p. 72

tariffs, p. 72

General Agreement on Tariffs and Trade (GATT), p. 72

World Trade Organization (WTO), p. 72

economic communities, p. 73 (Table 3.1, p. 73)

3. Objective Summary (pp. 74–87)

Understand how factors in the external business environment influence marketing strategies and outcomes.

The economic environment refers to the economic health of a country that may be gauged by its gross domestic product and its economic infrastructure, its level of economic development, and its stage in the business cycle. Marketers use competitive intelligence to examine brand, product, and discretionary income competition in the microenvironment and in the structure of the industry within the macroenvironment. A country's political and legal environment includes laws and regulations that affect business. Marketers must understand any local political constraints, that is, the prospects for nationalization or expropriation of foreign holdings, regulations such as local content rules, and labor and human rights regulations. Because technology can affect every aspect of marketing, marketers must be knowledgeable about technological changes, often monitoring government and private research findings. Marketers also examine a country's sociocultural environment including demographics, values, norms and customs, language, and ethnocentricity. The ethical environment in some countries can cause problems for marketers if they do not understand the differences in the ethical perspective of such things like honesty. In many least developed and developing countries, corruption is a major stumbling block for Western businesses. Bribery and extortion present ethical dilemmas for U.S. companies who must abide by the Foreign Corrupt Practices Act of 1977 (FCPA).

Key Terms

gross domestic product (GDP), p. 74

gross national product (GNP), p. 74 (Table 3.2, p. 75)

economic infrastructure, p. 75

level of economic development, p. 75

standard of living, p. 75

least developed country (LDC), p. 75

developing countries, p. 76

developed country, p. 76

business cycle, p. 76

competitive intelligence (CI), p. 77

discretionary income, p. 77

product competition, p. 78

brand competition, p. 78

monopoly, p. 78

oligopoly, p. 78

monopolistic competition, p. 79

perfect competition, p. 79

patent, p. 79

local content rules, p. 82

U.S. Generalized System of Preferences (GSP), p. 83

demographics, p. 83

cultural values, p. 84 (Metrics Moment, p. 84)

collectivist cultures, p. 84

individualist cultures, p. 84

norms, p. 85

custom, p. 85

mores, p. 85

conventions, p. 85

ethnocentrism, p. 86

bribery, p. 87 (Table 3.3, p. 87)

extortion, p. 87

4. Objective Summary (pp. 88–91)

Explain the strategies that a firm can use to enter global markets.

Different foreign-market-entry strategies represent varying levels of commitment for a firm. Exporting of goods entails little commitment but allows little control over how products are sold. Contractual agreements such as licensing or franchising allow greater control. With strategic alliances through joint ventures, commitment increases. Finally, the firm can choose to invest directly by buying an existing company or starting a foreign subsidiary in the host country.

Key Terms

export merchants, p. 89

licensing agreement, p. 89

franchising, p. 90

strategic alliance, p. 90

joint venture, p. 90 (Figure 3.1, p. 69)

born-global firms, p. 90

5. Objective Summary (pp. 91–94)

Understand the arguments for standardization versus localization of marketing mix strategies in global markets.

Firms that operate in two or more countries can choose to standardize their marketing strategies by using the same approach in all countries or choose to localize by adopting different strategies for each market. The firm needs to decide whether to sell an existing product, change an existing product, or develop a new product. In many cases, the promotional strategy must be tailored to fit the needs of consumers in another country. The product may need to be priced differently, especially if income levels are not the same in the new market. Finally, different methods of distribution may be needed, especially in countries lacking a solid infrastructure that provides adequate transportation, communications, and storage facilities.

Key Terms

straight extension strategy, p. 92

product adaptation strategy, p. 92

product invention strategy, p. 93

gray market goods, p. 93

dumping, p. 94

Chapter **Questions** and **Activities**

Concepts: Test Your Knowledge

1. Describe the market conditions that influence a firm's decision to enter foreign markets.
2. Explain what world trade means. What is the role of the WTO and economic communities in encouraging free trade? What is protectionism? Explain import quotas, embargoes, and tariffs.
3. Explain how GDP, the categories of economic development, and the business cycle influence marketers' decisions in entering global markets.
4. Explain the types of competition marketers face: discretionary income competition, product competition, and brand competition.
5. What are a monopoly, an oligopoly, monopolistic competition, and pure competition?
6. What aspects of the political and legal environment influence a firm's decision to enter a foreign market? Why are human rights issues important to firms in their decisions to enter global markets?
7. What do marketers mean when they refer to technological and sociocultural environments? Why do they need to understand these environments in a global marketplace?
8. What are some of the problems countries typically encounter within their ethical environments?
9. What is ethnocentricity? How does it affect a firm that seeks to enter a foreign market?
10. How is a firm's level of commitment related to its level of control in a foreign market? Describe the four levels of involvement that are options for a firm: exporting, contractual agreements, strategic alliances, and direct investment.
11. What are the arguments for standardization of marketing strategies in the global marketplace? What are the arguments for localization? What are some ways a firm can standardize or localize its marketing mix?

Choices and Ethical Issues: You Decide

1. Do you think U.S. firms should be allowed to use bribes to compete in countries where bribery is an accepted and legal form of doing business? Why or why not?

2. Some countries have been critical of the exporting of American culture by U.S. businesses. What about American culture might be objectionable? Can you think of some products that U.S. marketers export that can be objectionable to some foreign markets?
3. The World Trade Organization seeks to eventually remove all barriers to world trade. Do you think this will ever be a reality? What do you think are the positive and negative aspects of a totally free marketplace? Which countries will win and which will lose in such a world?
4. In recent years, terrorism and other types of violent activities around the globe have made the global marketplace seem very unsafe. How concerned should firms with international operations be about such activities? Should these firms consider abandoning some global markets? How should firms weigh their concerns about terrorism against the need to help the economies of developing countries? Would avoiding countries such as those in the Middle East make good sense in terms of economic profit? What about in terms of social profit?
5. In 2006, the National Institutes of Health released the results of a study showing that young people tend to drink more in areas with more alcohol advertising compared to areas with less advertising.[76] Do alcohol companies have an ethical obligation to curtail their advertising in order to decrease drinking rates among young people?
6. Is the world indeed flat, as author Thomas Friedman argues? Why or why not?

Practice: Apply What You've Learned

1. Assume that your firm is interested in the global market potential for a chain of coffee shops in Italy, China, and India. You recognize that an understanding of the external environments in each of these potential markets is essential. First, decide which environmental factors are most important to your business. Then, use your library to gather information about the environments of each of these countries. Finally, tell how the differences among

the environments might affect marketing strategies for coffee shops.

2. Tide laundry detergent, McDonald's food, and Dell computers are very different U.S. products that are marketed globally. Outline the reasons each of these companies might choose to
   a. standardize product strategies or localize product strategies.
   b. standardize promotion strategies or localize promotion strategies.

3. Organize a debate in your class to argue the merits of the standardization perspective versus the localization perspective.

4. Although most large corporations have already made the decision to go global, many small to midsize firms are only now considering such a move. Consider a small firm that manufactures gas barbecue grills:
   a. What type of market-entry strategy (exporting, contractual agreement, strategic alliance, or direct investment) do you feel would be best for the firm? Why?
   b. How would you recommend that the firm implement the strategy? That is, what type of product, price, promotion, and distribution strategies would you suggest? What role can the Internet play?

Miniproject: Learn by Doing

The purpose of this miniproject is to begin to develop an understanding of a culture other than your own and how customer differences lead to changes in the ways marketing strategies and socially responsible decision making can be implemented in that culture.

1. As part of a small group, select a country you would like to know more about and a product you think could be successful in that market. As a first step, gather information about the country. Many campuses have students from different countries. If possible, find a fellow student from the country and talk with him about the country. You will probably also wish to investigate other sources of information, such as books and magazines found in your library, or access information from the Web.

2. Prepare a summary of your findings that includes the following:
   a. An overall description of the country, including facts such as its history, economy, religions, and so on, that might affect marketing of the product you have selected
   b. A description of the cultural values and business ethics dominant in the country
   c. The current status of this product in the country
   d. Your recommendations for a product strategy (product design, packaging, and brand name), and so on
   e. Your recommendations for a pricing strategy
   f. Your recommendations for promotional strategies
   g. A discussion of the ethical and social responsibility issues present in the recommendations you have made

3. Present your findings and recommendations to the class.

Real people, **real surfers**: explore the web

Assume that you are the director of marketing for a firm that manufactures large home appliances, often referred to as "white goods." You are considering entering the market in _____ (the country you have selected). You recognize that businesses must carefully weigh opportunities for global marketing. Use the Internet to gather information that would be useful in your firm's decision. Although there are many governments, not-for-profit organizations, and businesses that have Web sites with information on international markets, the following sites may be useful to you:

- The United States Central Intelligence Agency (CIA) annual *World Factbook* that provides data about nations of the world: **https://www.cia.gov/cia/publications/factbook/index.html**
- I-Trade, a commercial site that also provides much free information of international trading: **www.i-trade.com**
- TradePort, a free site that provides a large number of links to country-specific Web sites: **www.tradeport.org**

Write a report that answers the following questions:

1. What are the physical characteristics of the country (geography, weather, natural resources, and so forth)?
2. Describe the economy of the country. What is the country's investment climate?
3. What trade regulations will your firm face in entering the country?
4. What is the country's political climate? Are there obvious political risks?
5. Based on this information, what overall strategy do you recommend for your firm—exporting, a contractual agreement, a strategic alliance, or direct investment?
6. What are your specific recommendations for implementing the strategy?

As a final part of your report, describe the Internet sites you used to gather this information. Which sites were most useful and why?

Marketing Plan Exercise

What are some important global marketing issues that one must be mindful of when developing a marketing plan? Why do these issues need to be considered separately from a firm's domestic plan?

Marketing in Action Case

Real **Choices** at **Mattel**

In 1945 Mattel's founders, Ruth and Elliott Handler were manufacturing picture frames out of a garage workshop. The couple also ran a side business where they made dollhouse furniture from the frame scraps; this became so successful that they turned to making toys. In 1955, Mattel began advertising its toys through the Mickey Mouse Club TV show and thus revolutionized the way toys are sold. In 1959, Ruth Handler, noting her own daughter Barbara's love for cut-out paper dolls, created the idea of a three-dimensional paper doll. Barbie was born and very quickly propelled Mattel to the forefront of the toy industry. The 1960s saw Mattel grow with such new products as Barbie's boyfriend Ken, See-and-Say toys, and Hot Wheels toy cars. In the 1980s Mattel became a global company with the purchase of Hong Kong-based ARCO industries, Correlle, SA, a maker of collector-quality dolls based in France and a British company, Corgi Toys Ltd., and a joint venture with Japan's largest toy company, Bandai.

Mattel stresses social responsibility. Its Sustainability Mission states "...we regard the thoughtful management of the environment and the health and safety of our employees, customers, and neighbors as among our highest priorities and as key elements of our responsibility to be a sustainable company...." In 2006, Mattel's Children's Foundation donated approximately $4.8 million in cash grants and approximately $10 million in toys to organizations serving children around the world. Over 2,500 Mattel employees volunteered for charitable activities Special Olympics programs in 13 countries.

In 2007 trouble arrived in Toyland. Like many other toy makers, in recent years Mattel commissioned Chinese companies to produce its products. In August, Mattel was forced to recall 1.5 million of its Fisher-Price toys, including such favorites as Elmo and Big Bird, because they were suspected of containing hazardous levels of lead paint. Later in August, Mattel recalled over 19 million more Chinese-made toys because they contained magnets that could be swallowed by children or because they were made with dangerous lead paint.

Following the second recall the company purchased full-page ads in the *New York Times* and the *Wall Street Journal* to assure parents that it understands how they feel. CEO Robert Eckert, a father of four, appeared on an on-line video to state, "I can't change what has happened in the past, but I can change how we work in the future." Mattel pledged to test the paint in every batch of paint delivered to all of its toy producers and to take other safety measures. Consumers, however, were not all convinced. Video clips appeared on YouTube mocking the company's efforts. One video referred to the recall of "Tickle Me Lead-Mo."

The recall dramatically cut into Mattel's revenues. Sales of Dora the Explorer toys fell 34 percent in the United States and 21 percent internationally. Barbie sales fell 19 percent in the United States, and Brazil banned imports of all Mattel products while it evaluated whether or not the company was complying with its safety regulations.

Mattel must work hard to recover from this disaster. Are apologies and claims for new safety regulations enough, or should the company stop producing its toys in China? Perhaps they should move production to another country such as Viet Nam where production costs would be even lower. Or should Mattel return to its roots and produce the millions of Polly Pockets, "Sarge" toy cars, and Barbie playsets in the United States where costs are substantially higher but standards are tougher?

You Make the Call

1. What is the decision facing Mattel?
2. What factors are important in understanding this decision situation?
3. What are the alternatives?
4. What decision(s) do you recommend?
5. What are some ways to implement your recommendation?

Based on: http://www.mattel.com/about_us/history/default.asp; Nicholas Casey and Nicholas Zamiska, "Mattel Does Damage Control After Recall," *The Wall Street Journal*, August 17, 2007, accessed January 16, 2008 at **http://on-line.wsj.com/article/SB118709567221897168. html**; "Key Dates in China Export Scares," *The Wall Street Journal*, October 21, 2007, accessed Jan. 16, 2008, at **http://on-line.wsj.com/article/ SB118606827156686195.html**; Roger Parloff, "Not Exactly Counterfeit," *Fortune*, May 1, 2006, 108–116; "Mattel, Battered by Recalls Posts Quarterly Profit Drop, " *The International Herald Tribune*, October 16, 2007, pg. 19.

Marketing Research:

Gather, Analyze, and Use Information

Cindy
Tungate
Profile ▼

A Decision Maker at Plan-it Marketing

Cindy Tungate is president and cofounder of Plan-it Marketing, a marketing research firm. Plan-it's clients include Bank of America, Dunkin' Donuts, Red Bull, John Hancock, Stop & Shop, and Timberland. Prior to starting the firm in 1997, Cindy worked for nine years at Hill, Holliday Advertising as Director of Marketing Research and Planning, and prior to that she worked for two large, national packaged goods companies—The Gillette Company and Tambrands—as a Brand/Project Manager in Marketing Research. She got her start in the field of marketing at Campbell–Ewald, an advertising agency in Detroit, as an analyst in the marketing research department.

Cindy received a BA in journalism and English from Michigan State University and an MS in advertising from Northwestern University. In her spare time, Cindy enjoys running and playing with her three children. In the past, she has been seen running away from her three children, thus giving her the opportunity to combine her two passions.

Decision Time at Plan-it Marketing

In 1997, entrepreneurs were just starting to realize the potential of the Net to transform the way businesses operate. The travel industry was one of the categories driving these changes; Internet technology could potentially revolutionize how people planned trips and purchased airline tickets and hotel rooms. A new company called Priceline had an idea about how to change the way people booked travel plans. Priceline's business model was unique; it let customers name their own price on air travel they purchased via the Internet. This new approach gave consumers a way to design their own travel plans and control their budget.

The ability to name your own price was novel and unfamiliar to most people, so Priceline didn't know if this concept would fly like a 747 or sink like a lead balloon. Clearly, marketing research would be needed to help Priceline figure out just what features it should include on its Web site and how these should be organized and promoted to attract customers who were unfamiliar with this new way of buying travel services. As a first step, Priceline wanted to understand who the optimal target audience would be for its new concept. Would it be leisure travelers, business travelers, or both?

Things to remember:

Knowledge is valuable—and it's expensive. It will cost the client 40% more to collect both qualitative and quantitative data about Priceline.

It's often most effective to first conduct qualitative research in order to be sure you have clearly identified the important factors behind the issue before you invest in a larger, quantitative study.

Plan-it's task was to assist Priceline in this early planning by assessing the overall viability of this innovative, interactive travel service. The firm's work included determining the critical combination of features that would generate the greatest volume potential for the brand and just what should be included in the service. Some options were offering tickets on major airlines versus less-well-known carriers, the ability to choose a specific time of departure versus a more general time of day, and non-stop versus one or more layovers. The challenge was to try to understand and predict consumer behavior for a service that didn't yet exist. This meant that Plan-it had to design a *viability study* that would inform its client about what would probably work and what wouldn't. As a new company, Priceline was in start-up mode and therefore, its marketing research budget was limited. Part of Plan-it's challenge was to design a marketing research strategy that would maximize results within a reasonable budget.

Cindy considered her Options 1·2·3

1
Option

Conduct an exploratory qualitative study. Run several focus groups among both leisure and business travelers to try to understand the mind-set of these key target audiences toward the travel industry overall, and to test their reactions to Priceline's proposed business model. In addition, the firm could get a handle on people's feelings about working with travel agents and/or with the airlines directly to purchase tickets. Cindy felt that this approach would be a cost-efficient way to probe for the key emotional and rational drivers/barriers related to using Priceline. However, she also knew that the results from focus groups alone would be suggestive only, and because they are not statistically reliable, they couldn't necessarily be projected to the real-world marketplace.

2
Option

Conduct a quantitative survey of 700 + leisure and business travelers. A phone questionnaire administered to a large sample of respondents about their attitudes toward travel would provide statistically reliable results to help determine the size of the potential market for Priceline's new approach. Results from this survey would ultimately shape the client's new business model prior to launch. The research instrument would let Plan-it measure reactions to the proposed features and to rank them in terms of their likely reception in the marketplace. This approach would be more expensive than the qualitative focus group approach because of the large number of interviews necessary to achieve statistical reliability. The majority of the costs connected with a study like this are called *field and tab*, which refers to the process involving writing and programming the questionnaire, paying interviewers to call respondents, entering data, and analyzing the results.

On the other hand, this structured approach to assessing an evolving idea might limit the understanding of consumer perceptions of, interest in, and likelihood of using the service. The way Plan-it presented the concepts and specific offerings to respondents might bias their answers, especially since they could give feedback only about prespecified options rather than suggesting new ideas the company hadn't thought of.

3
Option

Conduct a viability study that included both a qualitative exploratory study and a confirmatory quantitative study. As with Option 1, a qualitative study would provide an initial platform to understand consumer interest and receptivity to the new business model. The results of this study could then help to shape the content of a structured questionnaire so that the second phase would be more likely to include most of the options Priceline should consider. The second study would then confirm (or not) the hunches that Plan-it derived from the first study. As with Option 2, data from the second study would provide a statistically reliable measure of interest in the new product/business model that was projectable to the real-world marketplace. While this option would allow Plan-it to have its research cake and eat it too, a two-phase approach would be much more expensive than doing just a qualitative or just a quantitative study. Cindy estimated that this option would cost the client 40 percent more than running just a qualitative or a quantitative study. Given Priceline's start-up–mode budget, which required the entrepreneurs to gain support from their investors, this substantial cost would be an investment the company would have to justify and therefore "get it right the first time" if it wanted to be the first to go to market with its concept. That was a risky proposition for a new company and for the study designers at Plan-it Marketing.

Now, put yourself in Cindy's shoes: Which option would you choose, and why?

You Choose

Which **Option** would you choose, and **why**?
1. ☐YES ☐NO 2. ☐YES ☐NO 3. ☐YES ☐NO

See what **option** Cindy chose and its success on **page 127** ➡

Objective Outline

1. Explain the role of a marketing information system and marketing decision support system in marketing decision making. (pp. 102–107)

   KNOWLEDGE IS POWER (p. 102)

2. Understand data mining and how marketers can put it to good use. (pp. 107–108)

   SEARCHING FOR GOLD: DATA MINING (p. 107)

3. List and explain the steps and key elements of the marketing research process. (pp. 109–125)

   STEPS IN THE MARKETING RESEARCH PROCESS (p. 109)

4. Appreciate the importance of high ethical standards in marketing research. (pp. 125–126)

   ETHICS IN MARKETING RESEARCH (p. 125)

Check out chapter 4 **Study Map** on page 127

1

OBJECTIVE

Explain the role of a marketing information system and marketing decision support system in marketing decision making. (pp. 102–107)

Knowledge Is Power

In Chapter 1, we talked about how marketing is a decision process in which marketing managers determine the strategies that will help the organization meet its long-term objectives. In Chapter 2, we said that successful planning means that managers make good decisions for guiding the organization. But how do marketers make good decisions? How do they go about developing marketing objectives; selecting a target market; positioning (or repositioning) their product; and developing product, price, promotion, and place strategies?

The answer is *information*. Information is the fuel that runs the marketing engine. To make good decisions, marketers must have information that is accurate, up-to-date, and relevant. As Figure 4.1 shows, we are now in Part 2 of the book: "Understand Consumers' Value Needs." Part of the marketer's role in understanding these needs is to conduct *marketing research* to identify them. In this chapter, we will discuss some of the tools that marketers use to get that information. In the chapters that follow, we will look at consumer behavior, how and why organizations buy, and then how marketers sharpen their focus through target marketing strategies. But first, let's talk about the marketing information system.

The Marketing Information System

One of the ways firms collect information is through a **marketing information system (MIS)**. The MIS is a process that first determines what information marketing managers need. Then it gathers, sorts, analyzes, stores, and distributes relevant and timely marketing information to system users. As you can see in Figure 4.2, the MIS system includes three important components:

- Four types of data

- Computer hardware and software to analyze the data and to create reports

- Information for marketing decision makers

Where exactly do all the data come from? As we mentioned, information to feed the system comes from four major sources: internal company data, marketing intelligence data on competition and other elements in the firm's business environment, information marketing research gathers, and acquired databases.

Computer hardware and software store and access this information. Based on an understanding of managers' needs, MIS personnel generate a series of regular reports for various decision makers. For example, Frito-Lay's MIS generates daily sales data by product line and by region. Its managers then use this information to evaluate the market share of different Frito-Lay products compared to each other and to competing snack foods in each region where the company does business.[1]

Let's take a closer look at each of the four different data sources for the MIS.

1. Internal Company Data

The internal company data system uses information from within the company to produce reports on the results of sales and marketing activities. Internal company data include a firm's internal records of sales—information such as which customers buy which products in what quantities and at what intervals, which items are in stock and which are back-ordered because they are out of stock, when items were shipped to the customer, and which items have been returned because they are defective.

Often, an MIS allows salespeople and sales managers in the field to access internal records through a company intranet. An **intranet** is an internal corporate communications network that uses Internet technology to link company departments, employees, and databases. Intranets are secured so that only authorized employees have access. When the MIS is made available to salespeople and sales managers, they can better serve their customers by having immediate access to information on pricing, inventory levels, production schedules, shipping dates, and the customer's sales history.

But equally important, because salespeople and sales managers are the ones in daily direct contact with customers, the company intranet enters their reports directly into the system. This means the reports can provide an important source of information to upper management on changes in sales patterns or new sales opportunities.

Marketing managers can see daily or weekly sales data by brand or product line from the internal company data system. They also can see monthly sales reports to measure progress toward sales goals and market share objectives. For example, managers and buyers at Target's headquarters in Minneapolis use up-to-the-minute sales information they obtain from store cash registers around the country so they can detect problems with products, promotions, and even the firm's distribution system.

2. Marketing Intelligence

As we saw in Chapter 2, to make good decisions marketers need to have information about the marketing environment. Thus, a second important element of the MIS is the **marketing intelligence system**, a method by which marketers get information about everyday happenings in the marketing environment. Although the name *intelligence* may suggest cloak-and-dagger spy activities, in reality nearly all the information companies need about their environment—including the competitive environment—is available by monitoring everyday sources: newspapers, trade publications, or simple observations of the marketplace. And because salespeople are the ones "in the trenches" every day, talking with customers, distributors, and prospective customers, they too can provide valuable information.

The Web has become a major source of marketing intelligence in recent years. Tremendous amounts of information are available on company Web pages (including those of competitors), through news sources from around the globe, through government reports, and on trade association sites. The ease of accessing and searching the Web and individual sites makes the Internet an attractive source of marketing intelligence.

Sometimes companies engage in specific activities to gain intelligence. For example, retailers often hire "mystery shoppers" to visit their stores and those of their competitors posing as customers to see how people are treated. (Imagine being paid to shop!) Other information may come from speaking with organizational buyers about competing products, attending trade shows, or simply purchasing competitors' products.

Figure 4.1 | Make and Deliver Value

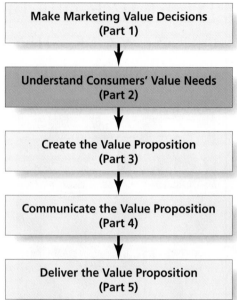

marketing information system (MIS)
A process that first determines what information marketing managers need and then gathers, sorts, analyzes, stores, and distributes relevant and timely marketing information to system users.

intranet
An internal corporate communication network that uses Internet technology to link company departments, employees, and databases.

marketing intelligence system
A method by which marketers get information about everyday happenings in the marketing environment.

Figure 4.2 | The Marketing Information System

A firm's marketing information system (MIS) stores and analyzes data from a variety of sources and turns the data into information for useful marketing decision making.

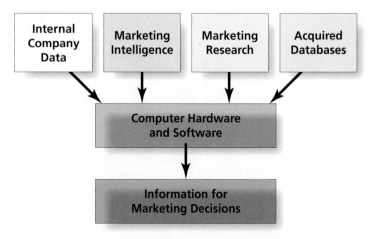

BEFORE OUR DESIGNERS CREATE A CAR THEY TALK TO OUTSIDE *EXPERTS.*

SEVERAL times a year we invite people to come and brainstorm with Ford Motor Company designers and engineers. We talk about cars, sure. But often we talk about NON-CAR THINGS: computers, appliances, music, the environment, quality in very general terms. We know that to design cars and trucks with relevance and appeal, you have to LISTEN to your customers. It's part of the learning process that leads us to quality.

· FORD · FORD TRUCKS · *Ford* · LINCOLN · MERCURY ·

QUALITY IS JOB 1.

Automakers such as Ford conduct extensive market research on consumers' car preferences.

scenario
Possible future situation that futurists use to assess the likely impact of alternative marketing strategies.

marketing research
The process of collecting, analyzing, and interpreting data about customers, competitors, and the business environment in order to improve marketing effectiveness.

syndicated research
Research by firms that collect data on a regular basis and sell the reports to multiple firms.

Marketing managers may use marketing intelligence data to predict fluctuations in sales due to economic conditions, political issues, and events that heighten consumer awareness, or to forecast the future so that they will be on top of developing trends. For example, knowledge of trends in consumer preferences, driven by the younger teen generation, prompted Sprint to become the first cellular provider to offer a plan that for $99.99 per month includes virtually unlimited use of all key cell phone functionalities (including talking, text messaging, Web browsing, GPS navigation, picture messaging—the list goes on and on). Sprint's CEO personally hawked this "Simply Everything Plan" in television ads that made the other cellular providers seem old fashioned by limiting their similar plans to talk only.[2]

Indeed, some marketing researchers known as *futurists* specialize in predicting consumer trends. They try to forecast changes in lifestyles that will affect the wants and needs of customers in the coming years. Futurists try to imagine different **scenarios**— possible future situations that might occur—and assign a level of probability to each.

A number of key outcomes can shape these scenarios. For example, deregulation laws could influence the future of the banking or telecommunications industries. In those cases a futurist might develop different scenarios for different levels of deregulation; she would generate forecasts assuming no deregulation, moderate deregulation, and complete deregulation. Each scenario allows marketers to consider the impact of different marketing strategies and to come up with plans based on which outcomes they consider most likely to happen. No one can predict the future with certainty (if you believe someone can, we've got a bridge to sell you...), but it's better to make an educated guess than no guess at all and be caught totally unprepared. Even something as seemingly straightforward as accurately predicting the price of a gallon of gasoline next year has a great impact on business success.

Of course, collecting marketing intelligence data is just the beginning. An effective MIS must include procedures to ensure that the marketing intelligence data are translated and combined with internal company data and other marketing data to create useful reports for marketing managers.

3. Marketing Research

Marketing research refers to the process of collecting, analyzing, and interpreting data about customers, competitors, and the business environment to improve marketing effectiveness. Although companies collect marketing intelligence data continuously to keep managers abreast of happenings in the marketplace, marketing research also is called for when managers need unique information to help them make specific decisions. Whether their business is selling cool stuff to teens or coolant to factories, firms succeed when they know what customers want, when they want it, where they want it—and what competing firms are doing about it. In other words, the better a firm is at obtaining valid marketing information, the more successful it will be. Therefore, virtually all companies rely on some form of marketing research, though the amount and type of research they conduct vary dramatically. In general, marketing research data available in an MIS include syndicated research reports and custom research reports.

Syndicated research is general research collected by firms on a regular basis, and then sold to other firms. INC/The QScores Company, for instance, reports on consumers' perceptions of over 1,700 celebrity performers for companies that want to feature a performer in their advertising. The company also rates consumer appeal of cartoon characters, sports stars, and even deceased celebrities.[4] Other examples of syndicated research reports include Nielsen's television ratings and Arbitron's radio ratings. Simmons Market Research Bureau and Mediamark Research Inc. are two syndicated research firms that combine information about consumers' buying behavior and their media usage with geographic and demographic characteristics.

As valuable as it may be, syndicated research doesn't provide all the answers to marketing questions because the information it collects typically is broad but shallow; it gives good insights about general trends such as who is watching what television shows or what brand of perfume is hot this year.

In contrast, **custom research** is research a single firm conducts to provide answers to specific questions. This kind of research is especially helpful for firms when they need to know more about why certain trends have surfaced.

Some firms maintain an in-house research department that conducts studies on its behalf. Many firms, however, hire outside research companies, like Plan-it Marketing, that specialize in designing and conducting projects based on the needs of the client. These custom research reports are another kind of information an MIS includes. Marketers may use marketing research to identify opportunities for new products, to promote existing ones, or to provide data about the quality of their products, who uses them, and how.

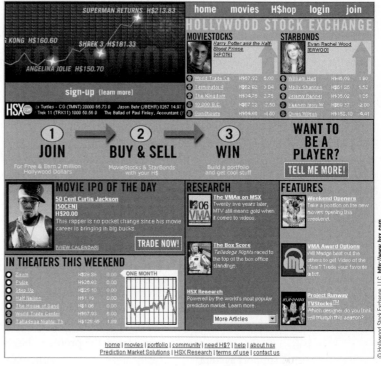

Hollywood executives closely monitor how movies and their stars are faring on the Hollywood Stock Exchange.

custom research
Research conducted for a single firm to provide specific information its managers need.

4. Acquired Databases

A large amount of information that can be useful in marketing decision making is available in the form of external databases. Firms may acquire these databases from any number of sources. For example, some companies are willing to sell their customer database to noncompeting firms. Government databases, including the massive amounts of economic and demographic information the U.S. Census Bureau compiles are available at little or no cost. State and local governments may make information such as automobile license data available for a fee.

In recent years, the use of such databases for marketing purposes has come under increased government scrutiny as some consumer advocates protest against the potential

prediction markets
Approach to forecasting and trend identification that pools opinions from a group of knowledgeable people about a product or service.

By the **People,** for the **People**

A few companies enlist consumers' help to predict the success or failure of different products. Recently, global firms including General Electric, Microsoft, Pfizer, and Google have used so-called **prediction markets** to forecast sales and profits as well as identify trends. These new research tools enlist a group of people who are knowledgeable about a product or service. Participants try to predict the future of these brands; researchers then pool their responses to derive an overall prediction that often turns out to be more accurate than traditional experts' forecasts.

For example, visitors to the Hollywood Stock Exchange (**www.hsx.com**) use virtual dollars to "buy and sell" stocks. In this case though the traders are avid moviegoers who trade soon-to-be released movies and bet on which will be hits or misses. Stocks start trading on the exchange as soon as a studio green lights a project. Every participant starts with two million in virtual currency (H$) and the objective is to increase the value of your portfolio by buying and selling shares of your favorite movies and celebrities. Because some studios find reactions to a movie stock very helpful to predict box office receipts once they release a film, they monitor this "stock market" very closely.[3]

Metrics Moment

Bigelow Teas, makers of Constant Comment and over 50 other tea flavors, was struggling to develop a planning system that would let sales and marketing executives access data about the company's performance in order to make decisions about which products to promote, how to help a retailer with low sales, or to identify just what kinds of consumers were buying which varieties of tea Bigelow sold. The IT (Information Technology) department chose a business intelligence program called BusinessObjects Enterprise 6 to better understand the firm's performance.

This software allows Bigelow Teas to analyze factory sales, forecast sales based on shipment levels, and compare consumer and market trends up to five years old. Metrics such as these help the company determine which products are no longer profitable and where opportunities exist for new tea varieties. One lump or two with your data?

invasion of privacy these may cause. Using the data to analyze consumer trends is one thing—using it for outbound mailings and unsolicited phone calls and e-mails has evoked a backlash resulting in "do-not-call" lists and antispam laws. Maybe you have noticed that when you sign up for a credit card or have other occasion to give a seller your contact information, you receive an invitation to "opt out" of receiving promotional mailings from the company or from others who may acquire your contact information from the organization later. By law, if you decide to opt out, companies cannot use your information for marketing purposes.

The Marketing Decision Support System

As we have seen, a firm's marketing information system generates regular reports for decision makers on what is going on in the internal and external environment. But sometimes these reports are inadequate. Different managers may want different information, and in some cases, the problem they must address is too vague or unusual for the MIS process to easily answer. As a result, many firms beef up their MIS with a **marketing decision support system (MDSS)**. An MDSS includes analysis and interactive software that allows marketing managers, even those who are not computer experts, to access MIS data and conduct their own analyses, often over the company intranet. Figure 4.3 shows the elements of an MDSS.

Typically, an MDSS includes sophisticated statistical and modeling software tools. Statistical software allows managers to examine complex relationships among factors in the marketplace. For example, a marketing manager who wants to know how consumers perceive her company's brand in relation to the competition's brand might use a sophisticated statistical technique called "multidimensional scaling" to create a "perceptual map," or a graphic presentation of the various brands in relationship to each other. You'll see an example of a perceptual map in Chapter 7.

Modeling software allows decision makers to examine possible or preconceived ideas about relationships in the data—to ask "what-if" questions. For example, media modeling software allows marketers to see what would happen if they made certain decisions about where to place their advertising. A manager may be able to use sales data and a model to find out how many consumers stay with her brand and how many switch, thus developing projections of market share over time. Table 4.1 gives some examples of the different marketing questions an MIS and an MDSS might answer.

marketing decision support system (MDSS)

The data, analysis software, and interactive software that allow managers to conduct analyses and find the information they need.

Figure 4.3 | The MDSS

Although an MIS provides many reports managers need for decision making, it doesn't answer all their information needs. The marketing decision support system (MDSS) is an enhancement to the MIS that makes it easy for marketing managers to access the MIS system and find answers to their questions.

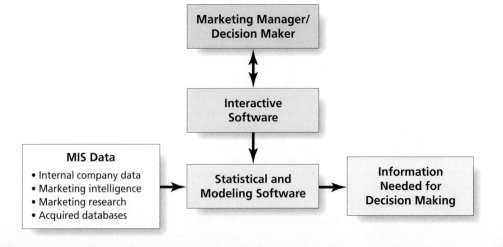

Table 4.1 | Examples of Questions an MIS and an MDSS Might Answer

Questions an MIS Answers	Questions an MDSS Answers
What were our company sales of each product during the past month and the past year?	Has our decline in sales simply reflected changes in overall industry sales, or is there some portion of the decline that industry changes cannot explain?
What changes are happening in sales in our industry, and what are the demographic characteristics of consumers whose purchase patterns are changing the most?	Do we see the same trends in our different product categories? Are the changes in consumer trends very similar among all our products? What are the demographic characteristics of consumers who seem to be the most and the least loyal?
What are the best media for reaching a large proportion of heavy, medium, or light users of our product?	If we change our media schedule by adding or deleting certain media buys, will we reach fewer users of our product?

2

Searching for Gold:
Data Mining

OBJECTIVE

Understand data mining and how marketers can put it to good use.

(pp. 107–109)

As we have explained, most MIS systems include internal customer transaction databases and many include acquired databases. Often these databases are extremely large. To take advantage of the massive amount of data now available, a sophisticated analysis technique called data mining is now a priority for many firms. **Data mining** is a process in which analysts sift through data (often measured in terabytes—much larger than kilobytes or even gigabytes) to identify unique patterns of behavior among different customer groups.

data mining
Sophisticated analysis techniques to take advantage of the massive amount of transaction information now available.

Harrah's Entertainment, for example, uses data mining to create customized services for its hotel and casino patrons. By mining the data, the company identifies customer segments whose preferences indicate that they may respond to different types of promotional offers. If the data show that some of the company's clientele favor one property over another, one form of gaming over another, or even one type of show over another, those customers will receive promotional materials tailored to their specific preferences. Slot players are notified of slot tournaments, fans of magic shows are notified when Lance Burton is scheduled to appear, and so forth. Place your bets!

Data mining uses computers that run sophisticated programs so that analysts can combine different databases to understand relationships among buying decisions, exposure to marketing messages, and in-store promotions. These operations are so complex that often companies need to build a *data warehouse* (sometimes costing more than $10 million) simply to store and process the data.[5] Marketers at both Yahoo! and Facebook are onto data mining big time. Yahoo! collects between 12 and 15 terabytes of data each day, and Facebook has access to valuable information that its over 50 million users post. Both firms want to use the data to facilitate targeted advertising by clients who are willing to pay big bucks to get their on-line ads in front of people who are likely to buy.[6]

Behavioral Targeting

Behavioral targeting is the practice of using data to track a user's on-line travels in order to show (immediately or later on) an ad for a related product. For example, a person might click on Realtor.com and then see ads for mortgages "magically" appear on her screen. This practice is getting to be so widespread that some enterprising businesses make money by helping consumers avoid being a target: Companies like IAC/InterActive offer tools that enable Web surfers to erase their keywords from the Yahoo!'s databases.

behavioral targeting
The practice of using data to track a user's on-line travels in order to show (immediately or later on) an ad for a product to someone who has visited a related Web site.

Ethical Decisions in the Real World

It seemed only a matter of time before marketing would fully intersect with social network Web sites like Facebook, on which users share lots of details with friends—and not only basic information like age, gender, and location, but also all kinds of personal information. Facebook founder Mark Zuckerberg seems set on finding ways to get users to pay more attention to the ads that support the site (MySpace and others have a similar history of low performing ads and thus low ad revenues). The pressure is really on to jack up ad revenues now that Microsoft has a $240 million stake in Facebook, along with strong expectations of increased financial performance.

ETHICS CHECK: ↖
Find out what other students taking this course **would do** and **why** on **www. mypearsonmarketinglab. com**

Zuckerberg opened the door for marketers to create brand pages where Facebook users can view related media, review products or services, add items they like to their personal pages, and become "fans" of the brand. The plan was that every interaction a user has with a brand turns into an advertisement—complete with a user's picture, what she did, and an image of the brand—and feeds directly to that user's Facebook friends via news feeds that update members on friends' recent activities. It's the ultimate in "brand advocacy"—trusted friends continually promoting what they like and have bought to their on-line connections that most likely trust them and value their opinions. Put another way, this is viral marketing at its finest!

Does the move by Facebook into viral marketing violate the spirit of a social network? If you were Zuckerberg would you push for this kind of targeting?

Ripped from the Headlines! See what happened in the Real World at **www.mypearsonmarketinglab.com**

Does Facebook's move into viral marketing violate its users' privacy?

☐YES ☐NO

What Marketers Can Do with Data Mining

Data mining has four important applications for marketers:[7]

1. **Customer acquisition:** Many firms include demographic and other information about customers in their database. For example, a number of supermarkets offer weekly special price discounts for store "members." These stores' membership application forms require that customers indicate their age, family size, address, and so on. With this information, the supermarket determines which of its current customers respond best to specific offers and then sends the same offers to noncustomers who share the same demographic characteristics.

2. **Customer retention and loyalty:** The firm identifies big-spending customers and then targets them for special offers and inducements other customers won't receive. Keeping the most profitable customers coming back is a great way to build business success because keeping good customers is less expensive than constantly finding new ones.[8]

3. **Customer abandonment:** Strange as it may sound, sometimes a firm wants customers to take their business elsewhere because servicing them actually costs the firm too much. Today, this is popularly called "firing a customer." For example, a department store may use data mining to identify unprofitable customers—those who are not spending enough or who return most of what they buy. In recent years, data mining has allowed Sprint to famously identify customers as "the good, the bad, and the ugly."[9]

4. **Market basket analysis** develops focused promotional strategies based on the records of which customers have bought certain products. Hewlett-Packard, for example, carefully analyzes which of its customers recently bought new printers and targets them to receive e-mails about specials on ink cartridges and tips on getting the most out of their machines.

So far, we have looked at the MIS and the MDSS, the overall systems that provide the information marketers need to make good decisions. We've seen how MIS and MDSS data include internal company data, marketing intelligence data gathered by monitoring everyday sources, acquired databases, and information gathered to address specific marketing decisions through the marketing research process. In the rest of the chapter, we'll look at the steps that marketers must take when they conduct marketing research.

3

OBJECTIVE

List and explain the
steps and key elements
of the marketing
research process.

(pp. 109–125)

Steps in the Marketing Research Process

The collection and interpretation of strategic information is hardly a one-shot deal that managers engage in "just out of curiosity." Ideally, marketing research is an ongoing process, a series of steps marketers take repeatedly to learn about the marketplace. Whether a company conducts the research itself or hires another firm to do it, the goal is the same: to help managers make informed marketing decisions. Figure 4.4 shows the steps in the research process, and we'll go over each of these now.

Step 1: Define the Research Problem

The first step in the marketing research process is to clearly understand what information managers need. We refer to this step as defining the research problem. You should note that the word *problem* here does not necessarily refer to "something that is wrong," but instead it refers to the overall questions for which the firm needs answers. Defining the problem has three components:

1. **Specify the research objectives:** What questions will the research attempt to answer?

2. **Identify the consumer population of interest:** What are the characteristics of the consumer group(s) of interest?

3. **Place the problem in an environmental context:** What factors in the firm's internal and external business environment might influence the situation?

Providing the right kind of information for each of these pieces of the problem is not as simple as it seems. For example, suppose a luxury car manufacturer wants to find out why its sales have fallen off dramatically over the past year. The research objective could revolve around any number of possible questions: Is the firm's advertising failing to reach the right consumers? Is the right message being sent? Do the firm's cars have a particular feature (or lack of one) that's turning customers away? Is there a problem with the firm's reputation for providing quality service? Do consumers believe the price is right for the value they get? The particular objective researchers choose depends on a variety of factors, such as the feedback the firm gets from its customers, the information it receives from the marketplace, and sometimes even the intuition of the people who design the research.

Often the focus of a research question comes from marketplace feedback that identifies a possible problem. Mercedes-Benz is a great example of a firm that for years has continually monitored drivers' perceptions of its cars. When the company started to get reports from its dealers in the 1990s that more and more people viewed Mercedes products as "arrogant" and "unapproachable," even to the point at which they were reluctant to sit in showroom models, the company undertook a research project to better understand the reasons for this perception. Likewise, Humana—the big health insurance provider—recently was compelled by bad press and a mounting movement for overall reform in the U.S. health care system to begin (of all things) actually talking to groups of its subscribers to find out what aspects of Humana's service delivery cause problems for patients.[10]

The research objective determines the consumer population the company will study. In the case of Mercedes, the research could have focused on current

Figure 4.4 | Steps in the Marketing Research Process

The marketing research process includes a series of steps that begins with defining the problem or the information needed and that ends with the finished research report for managers.

Define the Research Problem
- Specify the research objectives
- Identify the consumer population of interest
- Place the problem in an environmental context

↓

Determine the Research Design
- Determine whether secondary data are available
- Determine whether primary data are required
  —Exploratory research
  —Descriptive research
  —Causal research

↓

Choose the Method to Collect Primary Data
- Determine which survey methods are most appropriate
  —Mail questionnaires
  —Telephone interviews
  —Face-to-face interviews
  —On-line questionnaires
- Determine which observational methods are most appropriate
  —Personal observation
  —Unobtrusive measures
  —Mechanical observation

↓

Design the Sample
- Choose between probability sampling and nonprobability sampling

↓

Collect the Data
- Translate questionnaires and responses if necessary
- Combine data from multiple sources (if available)

↓

Analyze and Interpret the Data
- Tabulate and cross-tabulate the data
- Interpret or draw conclusions from the results

↓

Prepare the Research Report
- In general, the research report includes the following:
  —An executive summary
  —A description of the research methods
  —A discussion of the results of the study
  —Limitations of the study
  —Conclusions and recommendations

Peter J.
Gordon
a professor at Southeast Missouri State University

My Advice for Plan-it Marketing would be to choose

Option

real people, **Other Voices**

I would choose Option 3. Although it costs 40 percent more than either of the other two options alone, the added information makes it worthwhile. Option 1 seems to be needed as she is investigating a new concept and has no idea how potential customers might respond—or for that matter who exactly the potential customers are most likely to be. Option 1 would provide the information needed to both design a questionnaire and describe the target market(s) that should be included in the sample. Option 2 adds statistically reliable results. However, it would be really difficult to plan a study like Option 2 without the benefit of the input from Option 1. ➤

---

owners to find out what they especially like about the car. Or it could have been directed at non-owners to understand their lifestyles, what they look for in a luxury automobile, or their beliefs about the company itself that keep them from choosing its cars. So what did Mercedes find out? Research showed that although people rated its cars very highly on engineering quality and status, many were too intimidated by the elitist Mercedes image to consider actually buying one. Mercedes dealers reported that a common question from visitors to showrooms was "May I actually sit in the car?" Based on these findings, Mercedes in recent years has worked hard to adjust perceptions by projecting a slightly more down-to-earth image in its advertising, and it ultimately created new downsized classes of vehicles to appeal to consumers who want something a little less ostentatious.[11]

Placing the problem in the context of the firm's environment helps to structure the research, determine the specific types of questions to ask, and identify factors to take into account when measuring results. Environmental conditions also matter. For example, when the economy is tight and sales of luxury cars generally decline, researchers may narrow the population to study to a select group of consumers who are still willing and able to indulge in a luxury vehicle. Today, many consumers are moving away from status-conscious materialism and more toward functionality. In addition, as gasoline prices have skyrocketed in recent years, drivers' sensitivity to miles per gallon translates even to luxury brands and huge sport-utility vehicles like the mighty Hummer. Thus, a research question might be to see how consumers react to different promotional strategies for luxury goods that go beyond simply "snob appeal."

Step 2: Determine the Research Design

research design
A plan that specifies what information marketers will collect and what type of study they will do.

Once marketers isolate specific problems, the second step of the research process is to decide on a "plan of attack." This plan is the **research design**, which specifies exactly what information marketers will collect and what type of study they will do. Figure 4.5 summarizes many of the types of research designs in the researcher's arsenal. As you can see, research designs fall into two broad categories: *secondary research* and *primary research*. All marketing problems do not call for the same research techniques, and marketers solve many problems most effectively with a combination of techniques.

Secondary Research

secondary data
Data that have been collected for some purpose other than the problem at hand.

The first question marketers must ask when they determine their research design is whether the information they require to make a decision already exists. For example, a coffee producer who needs to know the differences in coffee consumption among different demographic and geographic segments of the market may find that the information needed is already available from a study conducted by the National Coffee Association. We call data that have been collected for some purpose other than the problem at hand **secondary data**.

Figure 4.5 | Marketing Research Designs

For some research problems, the secondary research may provide the information needed. At other times, one of the primary research methods may be needed.

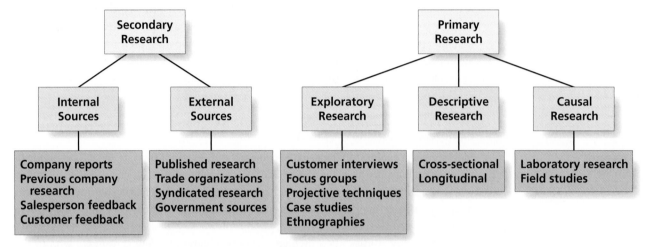

Many marketers thrive on going out and collecting new, "fresh" data from consumers. However, if secondary data are available, it saves the firm time and money because the expense to design and implement a study has already been incurred. Sometimes the data that marketers need may be "hiding" right under the organization's nose in the form of company reports; previous company research studies; feedback received from customers, salespeople, or stores; or even in the memories of longtime employees. More typically, though, researchers need to look elsewhere for secondary data. They may obtain reports published in the popular and business press, studies that private research organizations or government agencies conduct, and published research on the state of the industry from trade organizations.

For example, many companies subscribe to the *Simmons Study of Media & Markets*, a national survey conducted semiannually by Simmons Market Research Bureau, the syndicated research firm we mentioned earlier. Simmons publishes results that it then sells to marketers, advertising agencies, and publishers. This information is based on the self-reports of over 25,000 consumers who complete monthly logs detailing their purchases of products from aspirin to snow tires. Simmons data can give a brand manager a profile of who uses a product, identify heavy users, or even provide data on what magazines a target market reads. Marketers can also turn to the Internet for external information sources. Table 4.2 lists a number of Web sites helpful to marketers when they look for secondary research topics.

Table 4.2 | Helpful Internet Sites for Marketing Research

URL	Description
www.guideline.com	Guideline.com offers numerous industry and trend reports that are useful as secondary data sources.
www.census.gov	The U.S. Census Bureau publishes separate reports on specific industries (such as agriculture, construction, and mining) as well as on housing, population growth and distribution, and retail trade.
www.marketingpower.com	The American Marketing Association provides many resources to its members on a variety of industry topics.
www.dialog.com	Dialog sorts companies by location, size, and industry. The user can request telemarketing reports, preaddressed mailing labels, and company profiles.
www.lexisnexis.com	LexisNexis is a large database featuring information from sources such as Dun & Bradstreet, the *New York Times*, CNN, and National Public Radio transcripts.

primary data

Data from research conducted to help make a specific decision.

exploratory research

A technique that marketers use to generate insights for future, more rigorous studies.

consumer interview

One-on-one discussion between a consumer and a researcher.

Primary Research

Of course, secondary research is not always the answer. When a company needs to make a specific decision, it often needs to collect **primary data**; information it gathers directly from respondents to specifically address the question at hand. Primary data include demographic and psychological information about customers and prospective customers, customers' attitudes and opinions about products and competing products, as well as their awareness or knowledge about a product and their beliefs about the people who use those products. In the next few sections, we'll talk briefly about the various designs options to conduct primary research.

Exploratory (Qualitative) Research

Marketers use **exploratory research** to come up with ideas for new strategies and opportunities or perhaps just to get a better handle on a problem they are currently experiencing with a product. Because the studies are usually small scale and less costly than other techniques, marketers may use exploratory research to test their hunches about what's going on without too much risk.

Exploratory studies often involve in-depth probing of a few consumers who fit the profile of the "typical" customer that's of interest. Researchers may interview consumers, salespeople, or other employees about products, services, ads, or stores. They may simply "hang out" and watch what people do when they choose among competing brands in a store aisle. Or they may locate places where the consumers of interest tend to be and ask questions in these settings. For example, some researchers find that younger people often are too suspicious or skeptical in traditional research settings, so they may interview them while they wait in line to buy concert tickets or in clubs.[12] Some firms like Look-Look (**www.look-look.com**) send young "coolhunters" armed with video cameras to urban areas to interview people about the latest styles and trends.

We refer to most exploratory research as *qualitative*: that is, the results of the research project tend to be nonnumeric and instead might be detailed verbal or visual information about consumers' attitudes, feelings, and buying behaviors in the form of words rather than in numbers. For example, when DuPont wanted to know how women felt about panty hose, marketers asked research participants to collect magazine clippings that expressed their emotions about the product.

Exploratory research can take many forms. **Consumer interviews** are one-on-one discussions in which an individual shares her thoughts in person with a researcher. When Kimberly-Clark, maker of Huggies disposable diapers, was thinking about producing training pants, the company sent researchers into women's homes and asked them to talk about their frustrations with toilet training. Many women expressed feelings of failure and a horror at having to admit to other parents that their child was "still in diapers." Based on the research, Kimberly-Clark caught its competitors with their pants down: It introduced Pull-Ups disposable training pants and sold $400 million worth per year before its rivals caught up.

Intuit, the software company that produces the personal finance software packages Turbo-Tax and Quicken, used personal interviews to better understand consumers' frustrations when they try to install and use its products. When customers told researchers that the software itself should "tell me how to do it,"

LOOK LOOK

Look-Look. The magazine by young photographers, writers, and artists

:HISTORY
:HOW TO CONTRIBUTE
:SUBMISSIONS
:FOUNDATION
:GALLERY EVENTS
:SPONSORS
:GO GET IT
:FAQ'S
:CONTACT

subscribe!

ISSUE 06

LOOK ISSUE 06 2006

TEAM LOOK-LOOK.COM

© look-look.com

Look-Look employs an army of "coolhunters" to report on the latest trends they observe on the streets of major cities.

they took this advice literally and developed software that used computer audio to give verbal instructions. Intuit's probing went one step beyond interviews. Its researchers left respondents microcassette recorders so that whenever they were having problems, they could simply push a button and tell the company of their frustration.

The **focus group** is the technique that marketing researchers use most often for collecting exploratory data. Focus groups typically consist of five to nine consumers who have been recruited because they share certain characteristics (they all play golf at least twice a month, are women in their twenties, and so on). These people sit together to discuss a product, ad, or some other marketing topic a discussion leader introduces. Typically, the leader records (by videotape or audiotape) these group discussions, which may be held at special interviewing facilities that allow for observation by the client who watches from behind a one-way mirror.

In addition to getting insights from what the participants say about a product, a good moderator can sometimes learn by carefully observing body language. While conducting focus groups on bras, an analyst noted that small-chested women typically reacted with hostility when they discussed the subject. The participants would unconsciously cover their chests with their arms as they spoke and complained that the fashion industry ignored them. To meet this overlooked need, the company introduced a line of A-cup bras called "A-OK" that depicted these women in a positive light.[13]

Researchers use **projective techniques** to get at people's underlying feelings, especially when they think that people will be unable or unwilling to express their true reactions. This method asks the participant to respond to some object, often by telling a story about it. For example, Georgia-Pacific, the manufacturer of Brawny paper towels, was locked in a struggle with Scot Towels (made by Kimberly-Clark) for the number two market position behind leading seller Bounty (made by Procter & Gamble). The company decided to reexamine its brand identity, which was personified by a 60-foot character named Brawny who holds an ax. Managers were afraid that Brawny was too old-fashioned or that women were confused about why a man was selling paper towels in the first place. Researchers asked women in the focus groups questions such as "What kind of woman would he go out with?" and "What is his home life like?" Then the researchers asked the women to imagine how he would act in different situations and even to guess what would happen if they were locked in an elevator with him for 20 minutes.

Responses were reassuring; the women saw Brawny as a knight in shining armor who would get them out of the elevator—a good spokesman for a product that's supposed to be reliable and able to get the job done. Brawny kept his job and, in fact, has had two makeovers since he was originally introduced in 1975 to keep his look modern.

The **case study** is a comprehensive examination of a particular firm or organization. In business-to-business marketing research in which the customers are other firms, for example, researchers may try to learn how one particular company makes its purchases. The goal is to identify the key decision makers, to learn what criteria they emphasize when choosing among suppliers, and perhaps to learn something about any conflicts and rivalries among these decision makers that may influence their choices.

An ethnographic study is a different kind of in-depth report. It employs **ethnography**, which is a technique marketers borrow from anthropologists who go to "live with the natives" for months or even years. Some marketing researchers visit people's homes or participate in real-life consumer activities to get a handle on how they really use products. Imagine having a researcher follow you around while you shop and then while you use the products you bought to see what kind of consumer you are.

Of course, unlike anthropologists who live with indigenous tribes, marketing researchers usually don't have months or years to devote to a project. So, they devise shortcuts to get the information they need. For example, when Nissan was preparing for the $60 million launch of its first full-size truck, the Titan, its ad agency (TBWA/Chiat/Day) deployed researchers to the field to understand the psyche of full-size truck owners. Team members hung out for several months at hunting expos, gun shows, Super Cross events,

focus group
A product-oriented discussion among a small group of consumers led by a trained moderator.

projective technique
A test that marketers use to explore people's underlying feelings about a product; especially appropriate when consumers are unable or unwilling to express their true reactions.

case study
A comprehensive examination of a particular firm or organization.

ethnography
An approach to research based on observations of people in their own homes or communities.

and even Montana fishing spots—places where target consumers were likely to show up. Results from the observations, supported by focus groups and interviews, provided strong ammunition for Nissan to communicate its message of what the Titan can do. Ultimately, to portray a rough-and-tumble image, the ads showed dirty Titans in action, sloshing through mud and driving up inclines.[14]

Descriptive (Quantitative) Research

We've seen that marketers have many tools in their arsenal, including focus groups and observational techniques, to help them better define a problem or opportunity. These are usually modest studies of a small number of people, enough to get some indication of what is going on but not enough for the marketer to feel confident about generalizing what she observes to the rest of the population.

descriptive research
A tool that probes more systematically into the problem and bases its conclusions on large numbers of observations.

The next step in marketing research, then, often is to conduct **descriptive research**. This kind of research probes systematically into the marketing problem and bases its conclusions on a large sample of participants. Results typically are expressed in quantitative terms—averages, percentages, or other statistics that result from a large set of measurements. In such quantitative approaches to research, the project can be as simple as counting the number of Listerine bottles sold in a month in different regions of the country or as complex as statistical analyses of responses to a survey mailed to thousands of consumers. In each case, marketers conduct the descriptive research to answer a specific question, in contrast to the "fishing expedition" that may occur in exploratory research.

cross-sectional design
A type of descriptive technique that involves the systematic collection of quantitative information.

Marketing researchers who employ descriptive techniques most often use a **cross-sectional design**. This approach usually involves the systematic collection of responses to a consumer survey instrument, such as a *questionnaire*, from one or more samples of respondents at one point in time. The data may be collected on more than one occasion but generally not from the same pool of respondents.

longitudinal design
A technique that tracks the responses of the same sample of respondents over time.

In contrast to these one-shot studies, a **longitudinal design** tracks the responses of the same sample of respondents over time. Market researchers sometimes create consumer panels to get information; in this case a sample of respondents that are representative of a larger market agrees to provide information about purchases on a weekly or monthly basis. Procter & Gamble, for instance, recruits consumer advisory panels on a market-by-market basis to keep its finger on the pulse of local shoppers. But in the past P&G's market has mainly consisted of female consumers. When the company acquired the Gillette line of razors and blades a few years back for the first time it had to recruit special all-male consumer panels to contribute to the development of new products, such as the Fusion line of razors.[15]

Causal Research

It's a fact that purchases of both diapers and beer peak between 5:00 PM and 7:00 PM. Can we say that purchasing one of these products caused shoppers to purchase the other as well—and, if so, which caused which? Or is the answer simply that this happens to be the time when young fathers stop at the store on their way home from work to pick up some brew and Pampers?[16]

The descriptive techniques we've examined do a good job of providing valuable information about what is happening in the marketplace, but by its very nature descriptive research can only *describe* a marketplace phenomenon—it cannot tell us *why* it occurs. Sometimes marketers need to know if something they've done has brought about some change in behavior. For example, does placing one product next to another in a store mean that people will buy more of each? We can't answer this question through simple observation or description.

Causal research attempts to identify cause-and-effect relationships. Marketers use causal research techniques when they want to know if a change in something (for example, placing cases of beer next to a diaper display) is responsible for a change in something else (for example, a big increase in diaper sales). They call the factors that might cause such a change *independent variables* and the outcomes *dependent variables*. The independent variable(s) cause some change in the dependent variable(s). In our example, then, the beer display is an independent variable, and sales data for the diapers are a dependent variable—that is, the study would investigate whether an increase in diaper sales "depends" on the proximity of beer. Researchers can gather data and test the causal relationship statistically.

To rule out alternative explanations, researchers must carefully design **experiments** that test predicted relationships among variables in a controlled environment. Because this approach tries to eliminate competing explanations for the outcome, researchers may bring respondents to a laboratory so they can control precisely what the participants experience. For example, a study to test whether the placement of diapers in a grocery store influences the likelihood that male shoppers will buy them might bring a group of men into a testing facility and show them a "virtual store" on a computer screen. Researchers would ask the men to fill a grocery cart as they click through the "aisles." The experiment might vary the placement of the diapers—next to shelves of beer in one scenario, near paper goods in a different scenario. The objective is to see which placement gets the guys to put diapers into their carts.

Although a laboratory allows researchers to exert control over what test subjects see and do, marketers don't always have the luxury of conducting this kind of "pure" research. But it is possible to conduct *field studies* in the real world, as long as the researchers still can control the independent variables.

For example, a diaper company might choose two grocery stores that have similar customer bases in terms of age, income, and so on. With the cooperation of the grocery store's management, the company might place its diaper display next to the beer in one store and next to the paper goods in the other and then record diaper purchases men make over a two-week period. If a lot more guys buy diapers in the first store than in the second (and the company was sure that nothing else was different between the two stores, such as a dollar-off coupon for diapers being distributed in one store and not the other), the diaper manufacturer might conclude that the presence of beer in the background does indeed result in increased diaper sales.

Step 3: Choose the Method to Collect Primary Data

When the researcher decides to collect primary data, the next step in the marketing research process is to figure out just how to collect it. We broadly describe primary data-collection methods as either *survey* or *observation*. There are many ways to collect data, and marketers try new ones all the time. Today, a few marketing researchers even turn to sophisticated brain scans to directly measure our brains' reactions to various advertisements or products. These "neuromarketers" hope to be able to tell companies how people will react to their brands by scanning consumers' brains rather than collecting data the old-fashioned way—by asking them.[17] These techniques are still in their infancy, so for now we'll still rely on other methods to collect primary data.

Survey Methods

Survey methods involve some kind of interview or other direct contact with respondents who answer questions. Questionnaires can be administered on the phone, in person, through the mail, or over the Internet. Table 4.3 summarizes the advantages and disadvantages of different methods for collecting data.

causal research
A technique that attempts to understand cause-and-effect relationships.

experiment
A technique that tests prespecified relationships among variables in a controlled environment.

Table 4.3	Advantages and Disadvantages of Data-Collection Methods	

Data-Collection Method	Advantages	Disadvantages
Mail questionnaires	• Respondents feel anonymous • Low cost • Good for ongoing research	• May take a long time for questionnaires to be returned • Low rate of response; many may not return questionnaires • Inflexible questionnaire • Length of questionnaire limited by respondent interest in the topic • Unclear whether respondents understand the questions • Unclear who is responding • No assurance that respondents are being honest
Telephone interviews	• Fast • High flexibility in questioning • Low cost • Limited interviewer follow-up	• Decreasing levels of respondent cooperation • Limited questionnaire length • High likelihood of respondent misunderstanding • Respondents cannot view materials • Cannot survey households without phones • Consumers screen calls with answering machines and caller ID • Do-not-call lists allow many research subjects to opt out of participation
Face-to-face interviews	• Flexibility of questioning • Can use long questionnaires • Can determine whether respondents have trouble understanding questions • Can use visuals or other materials	• High cost • Interviewer bias a problem • Take a lot of time
On-line questionnaires	• Instantaneous data collection and analysis • Questioning very flexible • Low cost • No interviewer bias • No geographic restrictions • Can use visuals or other materials	• Unclear who is responding • No assurance that respondents are being honest • Limited questionnaire length • Unable to determine whether respondent is understanding the question • Self-selected samples

Cindy Tungate

APPLYING **Survey Methods**

Cindy considered the option of conducting a large-scale, structured telephone survey to assess consumers' preferences for Priceline's possible services. This technique would enable her to collect data from a large number of people, but the ability to probe beyond the predetermined questions would be limited.

Questionnaires

Questionnaires differ in their degree of structure. With a totally *unstructured questionnaire*, the researcher loosely determines the items in advance. Questions may evolve from the respondent's answers to previous questions. At the other extreme, the researcher uses a *completely structured questionnaire*. She asks every respondent the exact same questions and each participant responds to the same set of fixed choices. You have probably experienced this kind of questionnaire, where you might have had to respond to a statement by saying if you "strongly agree," "somewhat agree," and so on. *Moderately structured questionnaires* ask each respondent the same questions, but the respondent is allowed to answer the questions in her own words.

Mail questionnaires are easy to administer and offer a high degree of anonymity to respondents. On the downside, because the questionnaire is printed and mailed, researchers have little flexibility in the types of questions they can ask and little control over the circumstances under which the respondent answers them. Mail questionnaires also take a long time to get back to the company and are likely to have a much lower response rate than other types of data-collection methods because people tend to ignore them.

Telephone interviews usually consist of a brief phone conversation in which an interviewer reads a short list of questions to the respondent. There are several problems with using telephone interviews as a data-collection method. One problem with this method is that the growth of **telemarketing**, in which businesses sell directly to consumers over the phone, has eroded consumers' willingness to participate in phone surveys. In addition to aggravating people by barraging them with telephone sales messages (usually during dinnertime!), some unscrupulous telemarketers have "poisoned the well" for legitimate marketing researchers by hiding their pitches behind an illusion of doing research. They contact consumers under the pretense of doing a research study when, in fact, their real intent is to sell the respondent something or to solicit funds for some cause. The respondent also may not feel comfortable speaking directly to an interviewer, especially if the survey is about a sensitive subject. Of course, increasing numbers of people use voice mail and caller ID to screen calls, further reducing the response rate. And, as noted earlier, state and federal *do-not-call lists* allow many would-be research subjects to opt out of participation both in legitimate marketing research and unscrupulous telemarketing.[18]

Using *face-to-face interviews*, a live interviewer asks questions of one respondent at a time. Although in "the old days" researchers often went door-to-door to ask questions, that's much less common today because of fears about security and because the large numbers of two-income families make it less likely to find people at home during the day. Typically, today's face-to-face interviews occur in a **mall-intercept** study in which researchers recruit shoppers in malls or other public areas. You've probably seen this going on in your local mall, where a smiling person holding a clipboard stops shoppers to see if they are willing to answer a few questions.

Mall-intercepts offer good opportunities to get feedback about new package designs, styles, or even reactions to new foods or fragrances. However, because only certain groups of the population frequently shop at malls, a mall-intercept study does not provide the researcher with a representative sample of the population (unless the population of interest is mall shoppers). In addition to being more expensive than mail or phone surveys, respondents may be reluctant to answer questions of a personal nature in a face-to-face context.

On-line questionnaires are growing in popularity, but the use of such questionnaires is not without concerns. Many researchers question the quality of responses they will receive—particularly because (as with mail and phone interviews) no one can be really sure who is typing in the responses on the computer. In addition, it's uncertain whether savvy on-line consumers are truly representative of the general population.[19] However, these concerns are rapidly evaporating as research firms devise new ways to verify identities; present

telemarketing
The use of the telephone to sell directly to consumers and business customers.

mall-intercept
A study in which researchers recruit shoppers in malls or other public areas.

Kathleen
Finlayson
a student at San Diego State University
My Advice for Plan-it Marketing would
be to choose

3 Option

real people, **Other Voices**

I would recommend Option 3 to Cindy Tungate and Plan-it Marketing. Proper market research should be the foundation of any campaign. Without proper research, potentially large amounts of time and money may be wasted on inappropriate or inaccurate marketing strategies. For a new business concept such as Priceline's, research will be critical in determining whether a market even exists for this type of product, and, if so, who should be targeted, what

features should be offered, etc. Qualitative research should never be used individually, as the results cannot be generalized to the whole market. Using quantitative research without first conducting exploratory research could result in useless findings and wasted efforts. The two methods should be used in conjunction, with qualitative research providing the hypothesis and quantitative research providing the confirmation. While Option 3 will cost 40 percent more than Options 1 or 2 individually, spending more up front can save time and money in the future. Plan-it Marketing and Priceline should consider how much it will cost to redo the research or to repair the damage caused by a poor campaign. Getting it "right the first time" should always be the goal, especially for a new company on a start-up budget. Also, conducting thorough market research will increase investors' confidence in both Priceline's management and the company's ability to be first to market. ➤

The "Connection Court" in a Texas shopping mall allows high-tech companies to observe how people work in a wireless environment.

unobtrusive measure

Measuring traces of physical evidence that remain after some action has been taken.

surveys in novel formats, including the use of images, sound, and animation; and recruit more diverse respondents.[20]

Observational Methods

As we said earlier, the second major primary data-collection method is observation. *Observation* is a type of data collection that uses a passive instrument in which the researcher simply records the consumer's behaviors—often without her knowledge. Researchers do this through personal observation, unobtrusive measures, and mechanical observation.

When researchers use *personal observation*, they simply watch consumers in action to understand how they react to marketing activities. A shopping mall in Texas became a laboratory for the workplace of the future when it put a "Connection Court" in the middle of the mall. In an observational project sponsored by the Internet Home Alliance, a group of mostly high-tech companies, including Cisco Systems, Microsoft, and IBM, workers installed chairs and couches; set up desks with laptops, flat-panel monitors, and printers; and hooked up a high-speed wireless Internet network. This space is free for use by people who want to work in a more casual—and public—setting. The motivation is to understand if and how people want to work outside their homes and offices. (Where are you reading this book now?) With the spread of wireless Internet by companies like McDonald's and Starbucks that are setting up networks to let their customers work, these companies are doing observational research to understand just how to structure the physical environment that will let them do that more comfortably.[21]

Researchers use **unobtrusive measures** to record traces of physical evidence that remain after people have consumed something when they suspect that respondents will probably alter their behavior if they know they are being observed. For example, instead of asking a person to report on the alcohol products currently in her home, the researcher might go to the house and perform a "pantry check" by actually counting the bottles in her liquor cabinet. Another option for collecting primary data is to sift through garbage, searching for clues about each family's consumption habits. The "garbologists" can tell, for example, which soft drink accompanied what kind of food. Since people in these studies don't know that researchers are looking through products they've discard, the information is totally objective—although a bit smelly!

Mechanical observation is a primary-data–collection method that relies on nonhuman devices to record behavior. For example, one well-known application of mechanical observation is A.C. Nielsen's famous use of "people meters"—boxes the company attaches to the television sets of selected viewers to record patterns of television watching. The data Nielsen obtains from these devices indicate who is watching which shows. These "television ratings" help Nielsen's network clients determine how much to charge advertisers for commercials and which shows to cancel or renew. Similarly, Arbitron deploys thousands of "portable people meters," or PPMs. PPMs resemble pagers and automatically record the wearer's exposure to any media that has inserted an inaudible code into its promotion (TV ad, shelf display, and so forth). Thus, when the consumer is exposed to a broadcast commercial, cinema ad, Internet banner ad, or other form of commercial the PPM registers, records, and time-stamps the signal. At day's end, a home docking station downloads the media history. Portability ensures that all exposures register; this eliminates obtrusive people meters and written diaries that participants often forget to fill out.[22]

Of course, many research firms are developing techniques to measure which Web sites are being visited and by whom. (Ever heard of "cookies"—the nonedible kind, that is?) As we'll

Garbologists search for clues about consumption activities unobtrusively.

see shortly, there are ways for companies to tell where you've traveled in virtual space, so be careful about the sites you surf!

On-line Research

The growth of the Internet rewrites some of the rules of the marketing research process. As more and more people have access to the Web, many companies find that the Internet is a superior way to collect data—it's fast, it's relatively cheap, and it lends itself well to forms of research from simple questionnaires to on-line focus groups. In fact, some large companies like Procter & Gamble now collect a large portion of their consumer intelligence on-line. Developments in on-line research are happening quickly, so let's take some time now to see where things are headed.

There are two major types of on-line research. One type is information we gather by tracking consumers while they are surfing. The second type is information we gather through questionnaires on Web sites, through e-mail, or from focus groups virtual moderators conduct in chat rooms.

The Internet offers an unprecedented ability to track consumers as they search for information. Marketers can better understand where people look when they want to learn about products—and which advertisements they stop to browse along the way. How can marketers do this? Beware the Cookie Monster! **Cookies** are text files a Web site sponsor inserts into a user's hard drive when the user connects with the site. Cookies remember details of a visit to a Web site, typically tracking which pages the user visits. Some sites request or require that visitors "register" on the site by answering questions about themselves and their likes and dislikes. In such cases, cookies also allow the site to access these details about the customer.

This technology allows Web sites to customize services, such as when Amazon.com recommends new books to users on the basis of what books they have ordered in the past. Most consumers have no idea that cookies allow Web sites to gather and store all this information. You can block cookies or curb them, although this can make life difficult if you are trying to log on to many sites, such as on-line newspapers or travel agencies that require this information to admit you. Facebook has jumped on the bandwagon, using cookies to launch a new shopping service complete with messages like "54 people in your network have already bought Product X." However, the public vetting of members' purchases created a storm of protest from many on Facebook who felt their privacy was betrayed.[23]

This information generated from tracking consumers' on-line journeys has become a product as well—companies sell these consumer data to other companies that want to target prospects. But consumers increasingly are concerned about the sharing of these data. In a study of 10,000 Web users, 84 percent objected to the reselling of their information to other companies. Although Internet users can delete cookie files manually or install anticookie software on their computers, many people feel there is a need for privacy regulation and for cookies to limit potential abuses.

To date, the Federal Trade Commission has relied on the Internet industry to develop and maintain its own standards instead of developing its own extensive privacy regulations, but many would like to see that situation changed. Privacy rights proponents advocate the following:

- Information about a consumer belongs to the consumer.

- Consumers should be made aware of information collection.

- Consumers should know how information about them will be used.

- Consumers should be able to refuse to allow information collection.

- Information about a consumer should never be sold or given to another party without the permission of the consumer.

cookie
Text file inserted by a Web site sponsor into a Web surfer's hard drive that allows the site to track the surfer's moves.

Despite these issues, the Internet offers a faster, less expensive alternative to traditional communication data-collection methods. Here are some ways companies use the Internet to get feedback from consumers:

- **New-product development:** In the 1990s, Procter & Gamble spent more than five years testing products such as Febreze, Dryel, and Fit Fruit & Vegetable Wash the old-fashioned way before it launched them nationally. Using on-line tests, it launched its Crest MultiCare Flex & Clean toothbrush in less than a year. Most automakers now gather on-line consumer reactions to upcoming products. This research allows manufacturers to learn what consumers want in future vehicles.[24]

- **Estimating market response:** A few cutting-edge companies create virtual worlds and use them to test consumers' responses to brands. When they spend "There-bucks," people who sign up to join the virtual community at There.com can "buy" products like Levi's Type I jeans or Nike's high-end Zoom Celar shoes on the site. Companies can then analyze who chose to buy which brands and which activities they engaged in while on the site. (For example, do people who select the Levi's style tend to spend a lot of time socializing in There clubs that are available on the site?) Similarly, sites such as Kaboodle, ShopStyle.com, and ThisNext are a blend of social networking and e-commerce. They offer product recommendations—some from the staff of the sites, some from random users—and let shoppers create wish lists, comment on items and prices, post photos, and make purchases. Marketing executives say the sites are attractive because visitors tend to focus on shopping rather than just browsing.[25]

- **Exploratory research:** On-line focus groups have mushroomed in popularity in recent years. Of course, with on-line groups it is impossible to observe body language, facial expressions, and vocal inflection. But marketers continue to develop new ways to talk to consumers in virtual space, including software that allows participants in on-line focus groups to indicate nonverbal responses. For example, an on-line participant can register an expression of disgust by clicking on the command to "roll eyes."[26]

- **IM:** A few forward-thinking marketers are starting to take advantage of the fact that 75 percent of teens who go on-line use IM (Instant Messaging) and 48 percent trade IM messages at least once a day. These researchers link IM to on-line focus groups: A moderator can conduct a chat with a respondent using IM technology in order to probe her answers more deeply in a separate conversation.[27]

Many marketing research companies are running, not walking, to the Web to conduct studies for clients. Why? For one thing, replacing traditional mail consumer panels with Internet panels allows marketers to collect the same amount of data in a weekend that used to take six to eight weeks. And consumers can complete surveys when it is convenient—even at 3 AM in their pajamas. There are other advantages: Companies can conduct large studies at low cost. International borders are not a problem either, since in many regions (such as Scandinavia) Internet use is very high and it's easy to recruit respondents. Web-based interviews certainly reduce or eliminate interviewer bias and errors in data entry.

However, no data-collection method is perfect, and on-line research is no exception—though many of the criticisms of on-line techniques also apply to off-line techniques. One potential problem is the representativeness of the respondents. Although the number of Internet users continues to grow, many segments of the consumer population, mainly the poor and elderly, do not have equal access to the Internet. In addition, in many studies (just as with mail surveys or mall intercepts) there is a self-selection bias in the sample. That is, because respondents have agreed to receive invitations to take part in on-line studies by definition they tend to be the kind of people who like to participate in surveys. As with other kinds of research such as live focus groups, it's not unusual to encounter "professional respondents"—people who just enjoy taking part in studies (and getting paid for it).

On-line firms such as Harris Interactive, Survey Sampling, and Greenfield Online address this problem by monitoring their participants and regulating how often they are allowed to participate in different studies over a period of time.

There are other disadvantages of on-line research. Hackers can actually try to influence research results. Even more dangerous may be competitors who can learn about a firm's marketing plans, products, advertising, and so forth when they intercept information from these studies (though this can occur in off-line studies just as easily). Despite the potential drawbacks, on-line research has a bright future. This research has the potential to take off even faster as a result of the 2001 terrorist attacks since many people are more hesitant to answer questions from strangers, drive to focus group facilities, or open mail surveys from sources they don't recognize.

Data Quality: Garbage In, Garbage Out

We've seen that a firm can collect data in many ways, including focus groups, ethnographic approaches, observational studies, and controlled experiments. But how much faith should marketing managers place in what they find out from the research?

All too often, marketers who commission a study assume that because the researchers give them a massive report full of impressive-looking numbers and tables, they must be looking at the "truth." Unfortunately, there are times when this "truth" is really just one person's interpretation of the facts. At other times, the data researchers use to generate recommendations are flawed. As the expression goes, "Garbage in, garbage out!"[28] That is, your conclusions can only be as good as the information you use to make them. Typically, three factors influence the quality of research results—validity, reliability, and representativeness.

Validity is the extent to which the research actually measures what it was intended to measure. This was part of the problem underlying the famous New Coke fiasco in the 1980s, in which Coca-Cola underestimated people's loyalty to its flagship soft drink after it replaced "Old Coke" with a new, sweeter formula. In a blind taste test, the company assumed testers' preferences for one anonymous cola over another was a valid measure of consumers' preferences for a cola brand. Coca-Cola found out the hard way that measuring taste only is not the same as measuring people's deep allegiances to their favorite soft drinks. After all, Coke is a brand that elicits strong consumer loyalty and is nothing short of a cultural icon. Tampering with the flavors was like assaulting Mom and apple pie. Sales eventually recovered after the company brought back the old version as "Coca-Cola Classic."[29]

Reliability is the extent to which the research measurement techniques are free of errors. Sometimes, for example, the way a researcher asks a question creates error by biasing people's responses. Imagine that an attractive female interviewer working for Trojans condoms stopped male college students on campus and asked them if they used contraceptive products. Do you think their answers might change if they were asked the same questions on an anonymous survey they received in the mail? Most likely, their answers would be different because people are reluctant to disclose what they actually do when their responses are not anonymous. Researchers try to maximize reliability by thinking of several different ways to ask the same questions, by asking these questions on several occasions, or by using several analysts to interpret the responses. Thus, they can compare responses and look for consistency and stability.

Reliability is a problem when the researchers can't be sure the consumer population they're studying even understands the questions. For example, kids are difficult subjects for market researchers because they tend to be undependable reporters of their own behavior, they have poor recall, and they often do not understand abstract questions. In many cases, the children cannot explain why they prefer one item over another (or they're not willing to share these secrets with grown-ups).[30] For these reasons, researchers have to be especially creative when they design studies involving younger consumers. Figure 4.6 shows part of a completion test a set of researchers used to measure children's preferences for television programming in Japan.

validity
The extent to which research actually measures what it was intended to measure.

reliability
The extent to which research measurement techniques are free of errors.

Figure 4.6 │ Completion Test

It can be especially difficult to get accurate information from children. Researchers often use visuals such as this Japanese completion test to encourage children to express their feelings. The test asked boys to write in the empty balloon what they think the boy in the drawing will answer when the girl asks, "What program do you want to watch next?"

representativeness
The extent to which consumers in a study are similar to a larger group in which the organization has an interest.

sampling
The process of selecting respondents for a study.

probability sample
A sample in which each member of the population has some known chance of being included.

Representativeness is the extent to which consumers in the study are similar to a larger group in which the organization has an interest. This criterion for evaluating research underscores the importance of **sampling**; the process of selecting respondents for a study. The issue then becomes how large the sample should be and how to choose these people. We'll talk more about sampling in the next section.

Step 4: Design the Sample

Once the researcher defines the problem, decides on a research design, and determines how to collect the data, the next step is to decide from whom to obtain the needed information. Of course, she *could* collect data from every single customer or prospective customer, but this would be extremely expensive and time consuming if possible at all. Instead, researchers collect most of their data from a small proportion or sample of the population of interest. Based on the answers from this sample, researchers hope to generalize to the larger population. Whether such inferences are accurate or inaccurate depends on the type and quality of the study sample. There are two main types of samples: probability and nonprobability samples.

Probability Sampling

In a **probability sample**, each member of the population has some known chance of being included. Using a probability sample ensures that the sample represents the population and that inferences we make about the population from what members of the sample say or do are justified. For example, if a larger percentage of males than females in a probability sample say they prefer action movies to "chick flicks," one can infer with confidence that a larger percentage of males than females in the general population also would rather see a character get sliced and diced.

The most basic type of probability sample is a *simple random sample* in which every member of a population has a known and equal chance of being included in the study. For example, if we simply take the names of all 40 students in your class and put them in a hat and draw one out, each member of your class has a one in 40 chance of being included in the sample. In most studies, the population from which the sample will be drawn is too large for a hat, so marketers use a computer program to generate a random sample from a list of members.

Sometimes researchers use a *systematic sampling procedure* to select members of a population; they select the *n*th member of a population after a random start. For example, if we want a sample of 10 members of your class, we might begin with the second person on the roll and select every fourth name after that—the 2nd, the 6th, the 10th, the 14th, and so on. Researchers know that studies that use systematic samples are just as accurate as those that use simple random samples. But unless a list of members of the population of interest is already in a computer data file, it's a lot simpler just to create a simple random sample.

Yet another type of probability sample is a *stratified sample*, in which a researcher divides the population into segments that relate to the study's topic. For example, imagine you want to study what movies most members of a population like. You have learned from previous studies that men and women in the population differ in their attitudes toward different types of movies—men like action flicks and women like romances. To create a stratified sample, you would first divide the population into male and female segments. Then you would randomly select respondents from each of the two segments in proportion to their percentage of the population. In this way, you have created a sample that is proportionate to the population on a characteristic that you know will make a difference in the study results.

Nonprobability Sampling

Sometimes researchers do not believe the time and effort required to develop a probability sample are justified, perhaps because they need an answer quickly or they just want to get a general sense of how people feel about a topic. They may choose a **nonprobability sample**, which entails the use of personal judgment in selecting respondents—in some cases they just ask whomever they can find. With a nonprobability sample, some members of the population have no chance at all of being included. Thus, there is no way to ensure that the sample is representative of the population. Results from nonprobability studies can be generally suggestive of what is going on in the real world but are not necessarily definitive.

A **convenience sample** is a nonprobability sample composed of individuals who just happen to be available when and where the data are being collected. For example, if you simply stand in front of the student union and ask students who walk by to complete your questionnaire, the "guinea pigs" you get to agree to do it would be a convenience sample.

Finally, researchers may also use a *quota sample* that includes the same proportion of individuals with certain characteristics as in the population. For example, if you are studying attitudes of students in your university, you might just go on campus and find freshmen, sophomores, juniors, and seniors in proportion to the number of members of each class in the university. The quota sample is much like the stratified sample except that with a quota sample, the researcher uses her individual judgment to select respondents.

nonprobability sample
A sample in which personal judgment is used to select respondents.

convenience sample
A nonprobability sample composed of individuals who just happen to be available when and where the data are being collected.

Step 5: Collect the Data

At this point, the researcher has determined the nature of the problem she needs to address. She has decided on a research design that will specify how to investigate the problem and what kinds of information (data) she will need. The researcher has also selected the data-collection and sampling methods. Once she has made these decisions, the next task is to actually collect the data.

Garbage (Collector) In, Garbage Out

Although collecting data may seem like a simple process, researchers are well aware of its critical importance to the accuracy of research. When interviewers are involved, researchers know that the quality of research results is only as good as the poorest interviewer who collects the data. Careless interviewers may not read questions exactly as written, or they may not record respondent answers correctly. So marketers must train and supervise interviewers to make sure they follow the research procedures exactly as outlined. In the next section, we'll talk about some of the problems in gathering data and some solutions.

Challenges to Gathering Data in Foreign Countries

Conducting market research around the world is big business for U.S. firms. Among the top 50 U.S. research firms, nearly 50 percent of revenues come from projects outside the United States.[31] However, market conditions and consumer preferences vary worldwide, and there are major differences in the sophistication of market research operations and the amount of data available to global marketers. In Mexico, for instance, because there are still large areas where native tribes speak languages other than Spanish, researchers may end up bypassing these groups in surveys. In Egypt, where the government must sign off on any survey, the approval process can take months or years. And in many developing countries, infrastructure is an impediment to executing phone or mail surveys and lack of on-line connectivity blocks Web-based research.

Here's another example. Estimated expenditures for research by marketing research companies rank China number two in Asia Pacific markets with nearly $500 million, topped only by Japan. In fact, the amount firms spend on marketing research in China is growing faster than in any other country in the world, with growth rates of over 25 percent per year.

The reason for such expenditures is obvious: China is an emerging market of more than 1.3 billion potential consumers. Interestingly, however, there's an erroneous impression among foreign marketers that most of the population lives in large cities. Coupled with real infrastructure and transportation challenges, this demographic misconception has left large portions of the vast Chinese countryside virtually untouched by modern marketing—so far.[32]

For these and other reasons, choosing an appropriate data-collection method is difficult. In some countries, many people may not have phones, or low literacy rates may interfere with mail surveys. *Local customs* can be a problem as well. Offering money for interviews is rude in Latin American countries. Saudi Arabia bans gatherings of four or more people except for family or religious events (so much for focus groups), and it's illegal to stop strangers on the street or knock on the door of someone's house.[33]

Cultural differences also affect responses to survey items. Both Danish and British consumers, for example, agree that it is important to eat breakfast. However, the Danish sample may be thinking of fruit and yogurt while the British sample has toast and tea in mind. Sometimes marketers can overcome these problems by involving local researchers in decisions about the research design.

Another problem with conducting marketing research in global markets is *language*. Sometimes translations just don't come out right. In some cases entire subcultures within a country might be excluded from the research sample. In fact, this issue is becoming more and more prevalent inside the United States as non-English speakers increase as a percentage of the population.

back-translation
The process of translating material to a foreign language and then back to the original language.

To overcome language difficulties, researchers use a process of **back-translation**, which requires two steps. First, a native speaker translates the questionnaire into the language of the targeted respondents. Then they translate this new version back into the original language to ensure that the correct meanings survive the process. Even with precautions such as these, researchers must interpret data they obtain from other cultures with care.

Step 6: Analyze and Interpret the Data

Once marketing researchers collect the data, what's next? It's like a spin on the old "if a tree falls in the woods" question: "If results exist but there's no one to interpret them, do they have a meaning?" Well, let's leave the philosophers out of it and just say that marketers would answer "no." Data need interpretation if the results are going to be useful.

To understand the important role of data analysis, let's take a look at a hypothetical research example. In our example, a company that markets frozen foods wishes to better understand consumers' preferences for varying levels of fat content in their diets. They conducted a descriptive research study where they collected primary data via telephone interviews. Because they know that dietary preferences relate to gender, they used a stratified sample that includes 175 males and 175 females.

Typically, marketers first tabulate the data as Table 4.4 shows —that is, they arrange the data in a table or other summary form so they can get a broad picture of the overall responses. The data in Table 4.4 show that 43 percent of the sample prefers a low-fat meal. In addition, there may be a desire to cross-classify or cross-tabulate the answers to questions by other variables. *Cross-tabulation* means that we examine the data we break down into *subgroups*, in this case males and females separately, to see how results vary between categories. The cross-tabulation in Table 4.4 shows that 59 percent of females versus only 27 percent of males prefer a meal with a low fat content. In addition, researchers may wish to apply additional statistical tests, which you'll probably learn about in subsequent courses (something to look forward to).

Based on the tabulation and cross-tabulations, the researcher interprets the results and makes recommendations. For example, the study results in Table 4.4 may lead to the conclusion that females are more likely than males to be concerned about a low-fat diet. Based on these data, the researcher might then recommend that the firm should target females when it introduces a new line of low-fat foods.

Table 4.4 | Examples of Data Tabulation and Cross-Tabulation Tables

Fat Content Preference (number and percentages of responses)		
Questionnaire Response	Number of Responses	Percentage of Responses
Do you prefer a meal with high fat content, medium fat content, or low fat content?		
High fat	21	6
Medium fat	179	51
Low fat	150	43
Total	350	100

Fat Content Preference by Gender (number and percentages of responses)						
Questionnaire Response	Number of Females	Percentage of Females	Number of Males	Percentage of Males	Total Number	Total Percentage
Do you prefer a meal with high fat content, medium fat content, or low fat content?						
High fat	4	2	17	10	21	6
Medium fat	68	39	111	64	179	51
Low fat	103	59	47	27	150	43
Total	175	100	175	100	350	100

Step 7: Prepare the Research Report

The final step in the marketing research process is to prepare a report of the research results. In general, a research report must clearly and concisely tell the readers—top management, clients, creative departments, and many others—what they need to know in a way that they can easily understand. A typical research report includes the following sections:

- An Executive Summary of the report that covers the high points of the total report

- An understandable description of the research methods

- A complete discussion of the results of the study, including the tabulations, cross-tabulations, and additional statistical analyses

- Limitations of the study (no study is perfect)

- Conclusions drawn from the results and the recommendations for managerial action based on the results

Ethics in Marketing Research

OBJECTIVE

Appreciate the importance of high ethical standards in marketing research.
(pp. 125–126)

A marketer following the steps outlined previously for conducting effective research shouldn't encounter any ethical challenges, right? Well, maybe. In reality, several aspects of marketing research are fraught with the *potential* for ethics breaches. **Marketing research ethics** refers to taking an ethical and above-board approach to conducting marketing research that does no harm to the participant in the process of conducting the research. You've learned that research is serious business for marketers because without accurate and timely information they are unable to make the right decisions about marketing their products. So it stands to reason that if collected data are sullied by unscrupulous or dishonest collection or analyses, the quality of the information for decision making is negatively impacted.

Once data are acquired important issues of privacy and confidentiality come into play. Marketers must be very clear when they work with research respondents about how they will use the data and give them full disclosure on their options for confidentiality and anonymity. It is unethical to collect data under the guise of marketing research when your

marketing research ethics
Taking an ethical and above-board approach to conducting marketing research that does no harm to the participant in the process of conducting the research.

real intent is to develop a database of potential customers for direct marketing. Firms who abuse the trust of respondents in collecting data run a serious risk of damaging their reputation when word gets out that they are engaged in unethical research practices, making it difficult to attract participants in future research projects.

Now that you've learned about marketing research, read "Real People, Real Choices: How It Worked Out" to see which market research strategy Cindy Tungate chose for her client, Priceline.com.

real people, **Real Choices**

Cindy
Tungate
Cindy chose:

3
Option

How It Worked Out at Plan-it Marketing

She proposed to the client that they conduct both qualitative and quantitative research to probe for the viability of Priceline's business model. She argued that a large sample size was necessary to be able to determine the viability (real potential) of the concept with statistical reliability, but that without doing the initial qualitative study to identify the relevant features this study would probably be a case of "garbage in, garbage out." The specific objectives of this two-phase study were to explore the mind-set of leisure and business travelers in terms of the following:

- Behavior and attitudes toward travel-related purchases (e.g., airline, hotel, car rental)
- Key drivers and barriers to purchasing from existing/traditional resources such as travel agents and booking directly with hotels, airlines, and rental car companies
- Reactions to Priceline's novel business model that would allow consumers to name their own price and then identify vendors willing to provide the requested service at that price
- Likelihood of considering Priceline for travel purchases
- Perceptions of the Priceline concept versus existing alternatives, such as travel agents
- Perceived advantages/disadvantages of the Priceline pricing model
- Most motivating messages that would have an impact on the likelihood of using Priceline to purchase travel

Once the concept design was refined with input from the qualitative exploratory study, Plan-it Marketing conducted the quantitative study with a sample of over 700 respondents. This study confirmed the viability of Priceline's product strategy. Leisure travelers were especially interested in the name-your-price concept because they were more flexible in scheduling their travel and also more cost-conscious than business travelers.

To help Priceline determine the optimal and most cost-effective combination of service features, Plan-it Marketing utilized a *TURF* (Total Unduplicated Reach and Frequency) *Analysis*. This is a way to identify the optimal penetration in customers Priceline might achieve by adding different service features to the basic concept, which is *name your own price for travel*. For example, when Plan-it combined this concept description with the service feature *ability to choose to fly with a major airline* carrier, this pair of concepts achieved the highest score (42 percent) for motivating respondents

to do business with Priceline. (Note: the actual data have been disguised; these numbers are examples only.) When it also added the *non-stop vs. layover* feature, this combination yielded an additional 23 percentage points to a total of 65 percent. That means that on a net basis, 65 percent of respondents were motivated to use Priceline when these two service features were offered in conjunction with the ability to name your own price. When the analysis also added the service feature *ability to choose a specific time to fly*, the total combination moved the score another 8 points, to bring the overall motivation score to purchase through Priceline to 73 percent (in other words, 73 percent of respondents said they would use Priceline if it offered this specific set of features). As Plan-it's analysts added still other service features, they got smaller and smaller gains, so they were able to decide that this key set of service features would be what Priceline needed to launch its business model. Priceline.com was launched nationally in April 1998, and it continues to flourish. Over the years it has added other travel services, such as cruises and vacation packages (not to mention quirky ads featuring William Shatner). In 2006, *Forbes* named it a Best Travel Site.

Brand **YOU**!

Or, "Don't Skate to Where the Puck Is; Skate to Where the Puck Will Be"

Learn how to apply this futuristic philosophy to your job search. Find out how to identify the fastest growing companies, the best places to work, the best small businesses, top companies and trends in your target industry in Chapter 4 of the *Brand You* supplement. Don't put it off...the future is now!

Objective Summary ➡ Key Terms ➡ Apply

CHAPTER 4
Study Map

1. Objective Summary (pp. 102–106)

Explain the role of a marketing information system and a marketing decision support system in marketing decision making.

A marketing information system (MIS) is composed of internal data, marketing intelligence, marketing research data, acquired databases, and computer hardware and software. Firms use an MIS to gather, sort, analyze, store, and distribute information needed by managers for marketing decision making. The marketing decision support system (MDSS) allows managers to use analysis software and interactive software to access MIS data and to conduct analyses and find the information they need.

Key Terms

marketing information system (MIS), p. 102 (Figure 4.2, p. 103)

intranet, p. 103

marketing intelligence system, p. 103 (Table 4.1, p. 107)

scenario, p. 104

marketing research, p. 104

syndicated research, p. 104

custom research, p. 105

prediction markets, p. 105

marketing decision support system (MDSS), p. 106 (Table 4.1, p. 107) (Figure 4.5, p. 111)

2. Objective Summary (pp. 107–108)

Understand data mining and how marketers can put it to good use.

When marketers data mine they methodically sift through large datasets using computers that run sophisticated programs to understand relationships, among things like consumer buying decisions, exposure to marketing messages, and

in-store promotions. Data mining leads to the ability to make important decisions about which customers to invest in further and which to abandon.

Key Terms

data mining, p. 107

behavioral targeting, p. 107

3. Objective Summary (pp. 109–125)

List and explain the steps and key elements of the marketing research process.

The research process begins by defining the problem and determining the research design or type of study. Next, researchers choose the data-collection method—that is, whether there are secondary data available or if primary research with a communication study or through observation is necessary. Then researchers determine what type of sample is to be used for the study and then collect the data. The final steps in the research are to analyze and interpret the data and prepare a research report.

Exploratory research typically uses qualitative data collected by individual interviews, focus groups, or observational methods such as ethnography. Descriptive research includes cross-sectional and longitudinal studies. Causal research goes a step further by designing controlled experiments to understand cause-and-effect relationships between independent marketing variables, such as price changes, and dependent variables, such as sales.

Researchers may choose to collect data via survey methods and observation approaches. Survey approaches include mail questionnaires, telephone interviews, face-to-face interviews, and on-line questionnaires. A study may use a probability sample such as a simple random or stratified sample, in which inferences can be made to a population on the basis of sample results. Nonprobability sampling methods include a convenience sample and a quota sample. The researcher tries to ensure that the data are valid, reliable, and representative.

On-line research accounts for a rapidly growing proportion of all marketing research. On-line tracking uses cookies to record where consumers go on a Web site. Consumers have become increasingly concerned about privacy and how this information is used and made available to other Internet companies. The Internet also provides an attractive alternative to traditional communication data-collection methods because of its speed and low cost. Many firms use the Internet to conduct on-line focus groups.

Key Terms

research design, p. 110

secondary data, p. 110 (Table 4.2, p. 111) (Figure 4.5, p. 111)

primary data, p. 112 (Figure 4.5, p. 111)

exploratory research, p. 112 (Figure 4.5, p. 111)

consumer interviews, p. 112

focus group, p. 113

projective techniques, p. 113

case study, p. 113

ethnography, p. 113

descriptive research, p. 114 (Figure 4.5, 111)

cross-sectional design, p. 114

longitudinal design, p. 114

causal research, p. 115 (Figure 4.5, p. 111)

experiments, p. 115

telemarketing, p. 117

mall-intercept, p. 117

unobtrusive measures, p. 118

cookies, p. 119

validity, p. 121

reliability, p. 121

representativeness, p. 122

sampling, p. 122

probability sample, p. 122

nonprobability sample, p. 123

convenience sample, p. 123

back-translation, p. 124

4. Objective Summary (pp. 125–127)

Appreciate the importance of high ethical standards in marketing research.

It is essential that marketers take an ethical and above-board approach to conducting marketing research that does no harm to the participant in the process of conducting the research. If collected data are sullied by unscrupulous or dishonest collection or analyses, the quality of the information for decision making is negatively impacted.

Key Term

marketing research ethics, p. 125 (Ethical Decisions in the Real World, p. 108)

Chapter **Questions** and **Activities**

Concepts: Test Your Knowledge

1. What is a marketing information system (MIS)? What types of information are included in a marketing information system? How does a marketing decision support system (MDSS) allow marketers to easily get the information they need?
2. What is data mining? How is it used by marketers?
3. What are the steps in the marketing research process? Why is defining the problem to be researched so important to ultimate success with the research project?
4. What techniques are used to gather data in exploratory research? How can exploratory research be useful to marketers?
5. What are some advantages and disadvantages of telephone interviews, mail questionnaires, face-to-face interviews, and on-line interviews?
6. When considering data quality, what are the differences among validity, reliability, and representativeness? How do you know data have high levels of these characteristics?

7. How do probability and nonprobability samples differ? What are some types of probability samples? What are some types of nonprobability samples?
8. What is a cross-tabulation? How are cross-tabulations useful in analyzing and interpreting data?
9. What is a cookie? What ethical and privacy issues are related to cookies?
10. What important issues must researchers consider when planning to collect their data on-line?

Choices and Ethical Issues: You Decide

1. Some marketers attempt to disguise themselves as marketing researchers when their real intent is to sell something to the consumer. What is the impact of this practice on legitimate researchers? What do you think might be done about this practice?
2. Do you think marketers should be allowed to conduct market research with young children? Why or why not?

3. Are you willing to divulge personal information to marketing researchers? How much are you willing to tell, or where would you draw the line?

4. What is your overall attitude toward marketing research? Do you think it is a beneficial activity from a consumer's perspective? Or do you think it merely gives marketers new insights on how to convince consumers to buy something they really don't want or need?

5. Sometimes firms use data mining to identify and abandon customers who are not profitable because they don't spend enough to justify the service needed or because they return a large proportion of the items they buy. What do you think of such practices? Is it ethical for firms to prune out these customers?

6. Many consumers are concerned about on-line tracking studies and their privacy. Do consumers have the right to "own" data about themselves? Should governments limit the use of the Internet for data collection?

7. One unobtrusive measure mentioned in this chapter involved going through consumers' or competitors' garbage. Do you think marketers should have the right to do this? Is it ethical?

8. Consider the approach to tracking consumers' exposure to promotions via portable people meters, or PPMs. How would you feel about participating in a study that required you to use a PPM? What would be the advantage of a PPM approach versus keeping a written diary of television shows you watched and ads you saw?

Practice: Apply What You've Learned

1. Your firm is planning to begin marketing a consumer product in several global markets. You have been given the responsibility of developing plans for marketing research to be conducted in South Africa, in Spain, and in China. In a role-playing situation, present the difficulties you expect to encounter, if any, in conducting research in each of these areas.

2. As an account executive with a marketing research firm, you are responsible for deciding on the type of research to be used in various studies conducted for your clients. For each of the following client questions, list your choices of research approaches.
   a. Will television or magazine advertising be more effective for a local bank to use in its marketing communication plan?
   b. Could a new package design for dry cereal do a better job at satisfying the needs of customers and, thus, increase sales?
   c. Are consumers more likely to buy brands that are labeled as environmentally friendly?
   d. How do female consumers determine if a particular perfume is right for them?
   e. What types of people read the local newspaper?
   f. How frequently do consumers switch brands of soft drinks?
   g. How will an increase in the price of a brand of laundry detergent affect sales?
   h. What are the effects of advertising and sales promotion in combination on sales of a brand of shampoo?

3. Your marketing research firm is planning to conduct surveys to gather information for a number of clients. Your boss has asked you and a few other new employees to do some preliminary work. She has asked each of you to choose three of the topics (from among those listed next) that will be included in the project and to prepare an analysis of the advantages and disadvantages of these communication methods of collecting data: mail questionnaires, telephone interviews, face-to-face interviews, and on-line questionnaires.
   a. The amount of sports nutrition drinks consumed in a city
   b. Why a local bank has been losing customers
   c. How heavily the company should invest in manufacturing and marketing home fax machines
   d. The amount of money being spent "over the state line" for lottery tickets
   e. What local doctors would like to see changed in the hospitals in the city
   f. Consumers' attitudes toward several sports celebrities

4. For each of the topics you selected in item 3, how might a more passive (observation) approach be used to support the communication methods employed?

Miniproject: Learn by Doing

The purpose of this miniproject is to familiarize you with marketing research techniques and to help you apply these techniques to managerial decision making.

1. With a group of three other students in your class, select a small retail business or fast-food restaurant to use as a "client" for your project. (Be sure to get the manager's permission before conducting your research.) Then choose a topic from among the following possibilities to develop a study problem:
   • Employee–customer interactions
   • The busiest periods of customer activity
   • Customer perceptions of service
   • Customer likes and dislikes about offerings
   • Customer likes and dislikes about the environment in the place of business
   • The benefits customers perceive to be important
   • The age groups that frequent the place of business
   • The buying habits of a particular age group
   • How customer complaints are handled

2. Develop a plan for the research.
   a. Define the problem as you will study it
   b. Choose the type of research you will use
   c. Select the techniques you will use to gather data
   d. Develop the mode and format for data collection

3. Conduct the research.

4. Write a report (or develop a class presentation) that includes four parts:
   a. Introduction: a brief overview of the business and the problem studied
   b. Methods: the type of research used, the techniques used to gather data (and why they were chosen), the instruments and procedures used, the number of respondents, duration of the study, and other details that would allow someone to replicate your study

c. Results: a compilation of the results (perhaps in table form) and the conclusions drawn

d. Recommendations: a list of recommendations for actions management might take based on the conclusions drawn from the study

---

Real people, **real surfers**: explore the web

As we discussed in this chapter, monitoring changes in demographics and other consumer trends is an important part of the marketing intelligence included in an MIS. Today, much of this information is gathered by government research and is available on the Internet.

The U.S. Census Bureau provides tabled data for cities and counties across the nations at its site, **www.census.gov**. On the home page, click on Statistical Abstract. In addition, most states produce their own statistical abstract publications that are available on the Web. You should be able to locate the statistical abstract for your state by using a search engine such as Google, and entering something like "Florida Statistical Abstract." Using both state data and U.S. Census data,

develop a report on a city or county of your choice that answers these questions:

1. What is the total population of the city or county?
2. Describe the population of the area in terms of age, income, education, ethnic background, marital status, occupation, and housing.
3. How does the city or county compare to the demographic characteristics of the entire U.S. population?
4. What is your opinion of the different Web sites you used? How useful are they to marketers? How easy were they to navigate? Was there information that you wanted that was not available? Was there more or less information from the sites than you anticipated? Explain.

Marketing Plan Exercise

Select a company that produces a product that you use and with which you are familiar. For the company to make decisions about developing new products and attracting new customers, it must rely on marketing research. These decisions feed into the company's marketing plan. For the firm you selected complete the following:

1. Define one specific problem it could address through marketing research.

2. What type of research design do you recommend for addressing that problem, and why?
3. What is the most appropriate way to collect the data? Justify your choice.
4. How will you ensure high validity, reliability, and representativeness of the data?
5. Design an appropriate sampling plan.

Marketing in Action Case

Real **Choices** at **IMMI**

Marketing executives claim, "Half the money I spend on advertising is wasted; I just don't know which half." With more than half of all ad dollars spent on broadcast media like television and radio, advertisers need to have a way to determine the exposure and effectiveness of these media. The people meters and diaries that firms have used to track television and radio audiences for decades provide some estimates, but they do not track the other media (like the Internet) that are also key today.

Integrated Media Measurement Inc. also known as IMMI, uses existing technologies to measure broadcast audiences in a new way. IMMI recruits adults and teens, aged 13 to 54, to carry a special cell phone at all times for two years. The phone captures 10 seconds of audio from its surroundings every 30 seconds, 24 hours a day, seven days a week. The samples are then compressed into small digital files and uploaded to the company's servers where they are compared to samples of the media

being measured using a technology called *acoustic matching*. This allows IMMI to measure the number of people who have been exposed to an advertisement not only on television or radio but also on digital video recorders, game players, cellphones, DVDs, and CDs. Based on the data, IMMI produces real-time reports that get to individual behavior, not just group averages, thus connecting advertising to consumer behavior more accurately than possible with older methodologies. IMMI can answer questions such as the following: How many people are actually watching my network including outside the home and with time-shifting devices? How many people actually see my commercial? What songs cause radio listeners to change stations? What programs cause TV viewers to change channels?

Of course, IMMI's research methodology is not without potential problems. For example, IMMI only tracks audible media—not print or Internet advertising. Furthermore, many people are unwilling to participate in the study because they feel the technology is an invasion of their privacy. IMMI has been able to recruit an initial 3,000 panelists, but it will have to work hard to replenish that group when its two-year participation ends. While the cell phones only tracks broadcast media, many people are concerned that the company will also record their personal phone conversations.

For IMMI and for advertisers, the future is unclear. IMMI founders agree that this is not the last step in the attempt to more accurately understand media usage and advertising effectiveness. Surely better methodologies will follow. IMMI must consider its future and plan now in order to remain on top.

You Make the Call

1. What is the decision facing IMMI?
2. What factors are important in understanding this decision situation?
3. What are the alternatives?
4. What decision(s) do you recommend?
5. What are some ways to implement your recommendation?

Based on: "How It Works," http://immi.com/howItWorks.html; Jason Pontin, "Are Those Commercials Working? Just Listen," *New York Times*, September 9, 2007; http://immi.com;09stream.html (accessed February 28, 2008).

Chapter 5

Part 1 Make Marketing Value Decisions (Chapters 1, 2, 3)
Part 2 Understand Consumers' Value Needs (Chapters 4, 5, 6, 7)
Part 3 Create the Value Proposition (Chapters 8, 9, 10, 11)
Part 4 Communicate the Value Proposition (Chapters 12, 13, 14)
Part 5 Deliver the Value Proposition (Chapters 15, 16)

Consumer Behavior:

How and Why We Buy

Julie
Cordua
Profile ▼

A Decision Maker at (RED)

Julie Cordua is the vice president of marketing at (RED), a new brand created by U2 lead singer Bono and Bobby Shriver to engage business in the fight against AIDS in Africa. (RED) partners with the world's best brands to make uniquely branded products from which up to 50 percent of the profits are directed to the Global Fund to finance African HIV/AIDS programs with a focus on women and children. In her role at (RED), she is responsible for building the (RED) brand through innovative marketing programs including public relations, advertising, events, and co-branding.

Prior to joining (RED), Julie spent the bulk of her career in marketing in the wireless industry. Most recently, she was the senior director of buzz marketing and part of the start-up team at HELIO, a new mobile brand for young, connected consumers. Before HELIO, Julie spent five years at Motorola in the Mobile Devices division in Chicago. At Motorola, she led the global category marketing group and was part of the team that orchestrated the RAZR launch in 2002.

Julie started her career in public relations at Hill & Knowlton in Los Angeles. She holds a BA in communications, with an emphasis in business administration, from UCLA, and an MBA from the Kellogg School at Northwestern University. She currently lives in Manhattan Beach, California with her husband.

real people, **Real Choices**

Decision Time **at (RED)**

(RED) works with the world's best brands to make unique (PRODUCT) RED-branded products and directs up to 50 percent of its gross profits to the Global Fund to invest in African AIDS programs with a focus on the health of women and children. (RED) is not a charity or "campaign." It is an economic initiative that aims to deliver a sustainable flow of private sector money to the Global Fund.

Things to remember:

A sizeable portion of consumers have strong negative attitudes toward big corporations. They don't necessarily want to deal with companies now aligned with (RED) as part of their charitable activities.

Launch product partners included Converse, Gap, Motorola, Emporio Armani, Apple, and American Express (U.K. only). In its first year, (RED) added Hallmark, DELL, and Microsoft as partners. These companies were chosen because they were strong international consumer brands that could drive significant awareness and sell large volumes of products. And, more importantly, they were the few brave companies that were willing to take a risk on the idea of (RED) before it was a proven concept.

By fall 2007, with a successful first year behind it, (RED) was evaluating how to ensure sustained success for the brand. One of the main inputs Julie needed was more consumer insights about how shoppers related to the (RED) concept and how to cause marketing/charity in general. The company had not done this research before launch, so Julie decided it was time to do an extensive consumer research study in the United States.

Specifically, Julie wanted to know what consumers thought about the following (and how their beliefs affected their purchasing/participation actions):

- A corporation's role in solving social issues
- Churches/community organization's roles in solving social issues
- An individual's role in solving social issues (via donation or volunteering)
- Government's role in solving social issues
- Celebrity involvement in solving social issues
- The idea of combining charity with capitalism (buying and contributing at the same time)

The research project included three stages: 1) interviews with a variety of consumers to qualitatively understand major issues on people's minds, how consumers relate to shopping and charity, and what people know about (RED); 2) a nationwide quantitative survey to identify major attitudinal and behavioral trends across the population; and 3) ethnographies where researchers actually spent time with people as they went about their daily lives and that helped bring some of the key learnings from the survey to life.

The research showed that teens were most open to the idea of cause marketing. This finding made sense to Julie; this is a group that has grown up with the idea of "creative capitalism" and doesn't understand why doing good and having what you want would need to be separated. Also, this group looked up to celebrities more than any other age segment; they cited famous people across music, film, TV, and sports as major influences on their opinions and behaviors. However, when describing how they relate to (RED), they often commented that the brands that were current partners were not relevant to them.

A surprisingly large portion of the population rejected the idea of combining charity and capitalism. These "traditionalists" believed that social issues were best taken care of by the government or churches and community organizations. They were highly skeptical of corporations that promoted

an ability to do good by buying a product. These consumers wanted a more traditional way to get involved—through donations, volunteering, or simply through paying taxes and allowing their government to address the issues.

With these insights in hand, Julie and her colleagues, including the head of business development, several outside advisors, and the CEO, had to decide if the (RED) model—partnering with mass market international brands for long-term deals—was the optimal way to generate the most money for the Global Fund.

Julie considered her **Options** 1·2·3

1 Option
Expand the (RED) model based on what the research revealed about the teen market. Complement the bigger deals involving mainstream brands with the introduction of smaller "special edition" deals with younger, more relevant brands. Engage celebrities that specifically appeal to the younger demographic. If young people buy into the concept now this would build loyalty and they would remain long-term fans of the brand. On the down side, this additional investment in smaller brands would require additional resources and divert (RED)'s small staff from its primary task of working with larger companies.

2 Option
Stick with the existing (RED) model. Continue to only partner with large, international brands that make significant marketing and contribution commitments. Use celebrity engagement to draw attention to the brand. This option would let (RED) tap into the growing sentiment toward combining charity and capitalism. It would provide opportunities for significant exposure for (RED) through large scale marketing programs.

On the other hand, this approach might alienate those who prefer more traditional avenues of giving to charity; these people might not give to the Global Fund under these circumstances. And, with such a mass-market approach, (RED) might not maximize engagement with the high-potential teen segment, which may be valuable long-term.

3 Option
Expand the (RED) model to include more traditional non-profit aspects, such as donation and volunteering, in order to appeal to all consumer groups and increase engagement. This would allow (RED) to expand its reach to a much broader audience and potentially drive more revenue for the Global Fund through donations. But such an expansion might create brand confusion since (RED) is all about shopping and doing good at the same time. Julie feared that the company might not be able to be "all things to all people" by appealing to those who endorse the idea of "creative capitalism" and to those who want to contribute via more traditional avenues.

Now, put yourself in Julie's shoes: Which option would you choose, and why?

You Choose

Which **Option** would you choose, and **why**?
1. ☐YES ☐NO 2. ☐YES ☐NO 3. ☐YES ☐NO

See what **option** Julie chose and its success on **page 162** ➡

1

OBJECTIVE

Define *consumer behavior* and explain why consumers buy what they do. (pp. 134–136)

Decisions, Decisions

Compelling new products, clever packaging, and creative advertising surround us, clamoring for our attention—and our money. But consumers don't all respond in the same way. Each of us is unique, with our own reasons for choosing one product over another. Recall that the focus of the marketing concept is to satisfy consumers' wants and needs. To do that, we need to understand what those wants and needs are.

Consumer behavior is the process individuals or groups go through to select, purchase, use, and dispose of goods, services, ideas, or experiences to satisfy their needs and desires. Marketers recognize that consumer decision making is an ongoing process—it's much more than what happens at the moment a consumer forks over the cash and in turn receives a good or service.

Let's look at an example of a consumer purchase—one you probably make on a regular basis: dry cereal. While this may seem like a simple purchase, in reality there are quite a few steps in the process that cereal marketers need to understand. The first decision in the process is where to buy your cereal. If you eat a lot of cereal, you may choose to make a special trip to a warehouse-type retailer that sells super-duper-sized boxes rather than just picking up a box while at the local supermarket. Of course, if you get a craving for cereal in the middle of the night, you may dash to the local convenience store. Then there is the decision of the type of cereal. Do you eat only low-fat, high-fiber bran cereals, or do you go for the sugar-coated varieties with marshmallows? Of course, you may also like to have a variety of cereals available to you.

Marketers also need to know how and when you consume their products. Do you eat cereal only for breakfast, or do you snack on it while sitting in front of the TV at night? Do you eat certain kinds of cereal only at certain times (like sugary "kids' cereals" that serve as comfort food when you're pulling an all-nighter)? What about storing the product (if it lasts that long)? Do you have a kitchen pantry where you can store the supersized box, or is space an issue?

And there's more. Marketers also need to understand the many factors that influence each of these steps in the consumer behavior process—internal factors unique to each of us, situational factors at the time of purchase, and the social influences of people around us. In this chapter, we'll talk about how all these factors influence how and why consumers do what they do. But first we'll look at the types of decisions consumers make and the steps in the decision-making process.

Not All Decisions Are the Same

Traditionally, researchers tried to understand how consumers make decisions by assuming that people carefully collect information about competing products, determine which products possess the characteristics or product attributes important to their needs, weigh the pluses and minuses of each alternative, and arrive at a satisfactory decision. But how accurate is this picture of the decision-making process?

Although it does seem that people take these steps when making an important purchase such as a new car, is it realistic to assume that they do this for everything they buy, like that box of cereal? Researchers now realize that decision makers actually possess a set of approaches ranging from painstaking analysis to pure whim, depending on the importance of what they are buying and how much effort the person wants to put into the decision.[1] Researchers find it convenient to think in terms of an "effort" continuum that is anchored on one end by *habitual decision making*, such as deciding to purchase a box of cereal, and at the other end by *extended problem solving*, such as deciding to purchase a new car.

When consumers make very important decisions—such as buying a new house or a car—they engage in extended problem solving and carefully go through the steps Figure 5.1 outlines: problem recognition, information search, evaluation of alternatives, product choice, and postpurchase evaluation.

When they make habitual decisions, however, consumers make little or no conscious effort. They don't search for information, and they don't compare alternatives. Rather, they make purchases automatically. You may, for example, simply throw the same brand of cereal in your shopping cart week after week without thinking about it. Figure 5.2 provides a summary of the differences between extended problem solving and habitual decision making.

Many decisions fall somewhere in the middle and are characterized by limited problem solving, which means that consumers do some work to make a decision but not a great deal. This is probably how you decide on a new pair of running shoes or a new calculator for math class. We often rely on simple "rules of thumb" instead of painstakingly learning all the ins and outs of every product alternative.

So, just how much effort do we put into our buying decisions? The answer depends on our level of **involvement**—how important we perceive the consequences of the purchase to be. As a rule, we are more involved in the decision-making process for products that we think are risky in some way. **Perceived risk** may be present if the product is expensive or complex and hard to understand, such as a new computer or a sports car.

Perceived risk can also be a factor in product choice if choosing the wrong product results in embarrassment or social rejection. For example, a person who wears a pair of Skechers on a job interview may jeopardize the job if the interviewer doesn't approve of his footwear.

When perceived risk is low, as in buying a box of cereal, the consumer feels low involvement in the decision-making process—he is not overly concerned about which option he chooses because it is not especially important or risky. In *low-involvement* situations, the consumer's decision is often a response to environmental cues, such as when a person decides to try a new type of cereal because the grocery store prominently displays it at the end of the aisle. Under these circumstances, managers must concentrate on how a store displays products at the time of purchase to influence the decision maker. For example, a cereal marketer may decide to spend extra money to be sure its cereal stands out at a store display or to change the packaging so consumers notice it.

For *high-involvement* purchases, such as buying a house or a car, the consumer is likely to carefully process all the available information and to have thought about the decision well before going to buy the item. The consequences of the purchase are important and risky, especially because a bad decision may result in significant financial losses, aggravation, or embarrassment.

consumer behavior
The process involved when individuals or groups select, purchase, use, and dispose of goods, services, ideas, or experiences to satisfy their needs and desires.

involvement
The relative importance of perceived consequences of the purchase to a consumer.

perceived risk
The belief that choice of a product has potentially negative consequences, whether financial, physical, and/or social.

Figure 5.1 | The Consumer Decision-Making Process

The consumer decision-making process involves the series of steps summarized here.

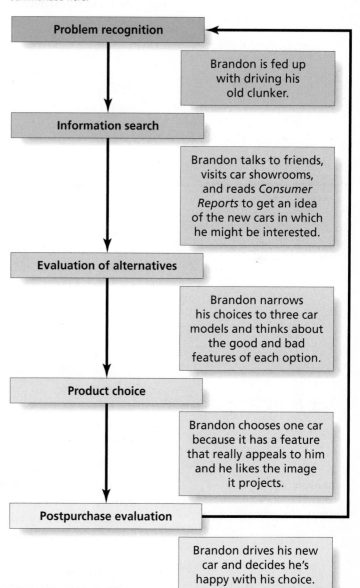

Problem recognition

Brandon is fed up with driving his old clunker.

Information search

Brandon talks to friends, visits car showrooms, and reads *Consumer Reports* to get an idea of the new cars in which he might be interested.

Evaluation of alternatives

Brandon narrows his choices to three car models and thinks about the good and bad features of each option.

Product choice

Brandon chooses one car because it has a feature that really appeals to him and he likes the image it projects.

Postpurchase evaluation

Brandon drives his new car and decides he's happy with his choice.

Figure 5.2 | Extended Problem Solving versus Habitual Decision Making

	Extended Problem Solving	*Habitual Decision Making*
Product	New car	Box of cereal
Level of involvement	High (important decision)	Low (unimportant decision)
Perceived risk	High (expensive, complex product)	Low (simple, low-cost product)
Information processing	Careful processing of information (search advertising, magazines, car dealers, Web sites)	Respond to environmental cues (store signage or displays)
Learning model	Cognitive learning (use insight and creativity to use information found in environment)	Behavioral learning (ad shows product in beautiful setting, creating positive attitude)
Needed marketing actions	Provide information via advertising, salespeople, brochures, Web sites. Educate consumers to product benefits, risks of wrong decisions, etc.	Provide environmental cues at point-of-purchase, such as product display

Most of us would not just walk into a real estate agent's office at lunchtime and casually plunk down a deposit on a new house. For high-involvement products, managers must start to reduce perceived risk by educating the consumer about why their product is the best choice well in advance of the time that the consumer is ready to make a decision.

To understand each of the steps in the decision-making process, in the next section we'll follow the fortunes of a consumer named Brandon, who as Figure 5.1 shows, is in the market for a new ride—a highly-involved purchase decision to say the least.

2

OBJECTIVE

Describe the prepurchase, purchase, and postpurchase activities in which consumers engage when they buy a product or service.
(pp. 136–141)

Step 1: Problem Recognition

Problem recognition occurs whenever a consumer sees a significant difference between his current state of affairs and some desired or ideal state. A woman whose 10-year-old Hyundai lives at the mechanic's shop has a problem, as does the man who thinks he'd have better luck getting dates if he traded his Hyundai for a new sports car. Brandon falls into the latter category—his old clunker runs okay, but he wants to sport some wheels that will get him admiring stares instead of laughs.

Do marketing decisions have a role in consumers' problem recognition? Although most problem recognition occurs spontaneously or when a true need arises, marketers often develop creative advertising messages that stimulate consumers to recognize that their current state (that old car) just doesn't equal their desired state (a shiny, new convertible). Figure 5.3 provides examples of marketers' responses to consumers' problem recognition and the other steps in the consumer decision-making process.

problem recognition
The process that occurs whenever the consumer sees a significant difference between his current state of affairs and some desired or ideal state; this recognition initiates the decision-making process.

Step 2: Information Search

Once Brandon recognizes his problem (that he wants a newer car), he needs adequate information to resolve it. **Information search** is the step of the decision-making process in which the consumer checks his memory and surveys the environment to identify what options are out there that might solve his problem. Advertisements in newspapers, on TV or the radio, in the Yellow Pages, or on the Internet often provide valuable guidance during this step. Brandon might rely on television ads about different cars, recommendations from his friends, and additional information he finds in *Consumer Reports*, at **www.caranddriver.com**, in brochures from car dealerships, or on the manufacturers' Web sites.

information search
The process whereby a consumer searches for appropriate information to make a reasonable decision.

Figure 5.3 | Marketers' Responses to Decision-Process Stages

Stage in the Decision Process	Marketing Strategy	Example
Problem recognition	Encourage consumers to see that existing state does not equal desired state	• Create TV commercials showing the excitement of owning a new car
Information search	Provide information when and where consumers are likely to search	• Target advertising on TV programs with high target-market viewership • Provide sales training that ensures knowledgeable salespeople • Make new-car brochures available in dealer showrooms • Design exciting, easy-to-navigate, and informative Web sites
Evaluation of alternatives	Understand the criteria consumers use in comparing brands and communicate own brand superiority	• Conduct research to identify most important evaluative criteria • Create advertising that includes reliable data on superiority of a brand (e.g., miles per gallon, safety, comfort)
Product choice	Understand choice heuristics used by consumers and provide communication that encourages brand decision	• Advertise "Made in America" (country of origin) • Stress long history of the brand (brand loyalty)
Postpurchase evaluation	Encourage accurate consumer expectations	• Provide honest advertising and sales presentations

The Internet as a Search Tool

Increasingly, consumers use Internet search engines, portals, or "shopping robots" to find information. Search engines, sites such as Google (**www.google.com**) and Excite (**www. excite.com**), help us locate useful information by searching millions of Web pages for key words and returning a list of sites that contain those key words. Shopping portals such as Yahoo! (**www.yahoo.com**) simplify searches by organizing information from many Web sites into topics or categories.

Shopping robots, also called "shopbots" or just "bots," are software programs some Web sites use to find Internet retailers selling a particular product. The programs troll the Web for information and then report it back to the host site. Some of these sites also provide information on competitors' prices and ask customers to rate the retailers that they have listed on their site; this enables consumers to view both positive and negative feedback from other consumers. Increasingly consumers are also searching out other consumers' opinions and experience through networking Web sites such as YouTube and Facebook. We'll talk more about these sites and others similar to them later in the chapter.

By the **People**, For the **People**

Have you ever booked an "ocean view" room at a beach hotel, only to find out when you arrive that this view is only available if you're hovering in a helicopter 1,000 feet above a grungy motel? Consumers tend to put more stock in personal recommendations than in company-sponsored ads—if they can get access to them. New travel Web sites that combine a ton of reliable factual information with personal recommendations from actual travelers let us use input from real people to decide whether to believe the ads we see hyping a resort or a hotel. Sites such as TripAdvisor, IgoUgo, and HotelChatter gather travelers' experiences and recommendations to give us the real scoop on exotic places.

For instance, TripAdvisor collects over 10 million reviews and opinions from real travelers all over the world who give their unvarnished views on more than 200,000 hotels and 200,000 restaurants. Many traveler-feedback Web sites now allow consumers to post comments and opinions about their previous travel experiences. Some of them create forum sections and allow visitors to exchange insights with other travelers and potential travelers. Many travelers even share their travel photos and videos with others. TripAdvisor alone features over one million photos of more than 50,000 top-rated hotels. When the people speak, we're more likely to get an ocean view for real.[2]

Sources: Graham Donoghue, "Content is King and Users are in Control," *Travel Trade Gazette* (20 September 2006), pp. 13; Jennifer Merritt, "Advancing Online with Web 2.0," *TravelAgent* (August 27, 2007), pp. 18-20; Lodging Hospitality, "Embrace the Customer," *Lodging Hospitality* (December 2007), p. 110; *TripAdvisor*, "Fact Sheet," Official Web site of *TripAdvisor* (**http://www.tripadvisor.com/PressCenter-c4-Fact_Sheet.html**).

Behavioral Targeting

behavioral targeting

The practice of using data to track a user's on-line travels in order to show (immediately or later on) an ad for a product to someone who has visited a related Web site.

The role of marketers during the information search step of the consumer decision-making process is to make the information consumers want and need about their product easily accessible. For example, automakers make sure information about their newest models is on the Web; in magazines, radio, and TV; and, of course, available in dealer showrooms. This strategy is getting even more finely-tuned as some marketers start to experiment with **behavioral targeting** techniques. This describes a strategy that presents individuals with advertisements based on their Internet use. In other words, with today's technology it has become fairly easy for marketers to tailor the ads you see to Web sites you've visited. Some critics feel this is a mixed blessing because it implies that big companies are tracking where we go and keeping this information. Here are some pioneers who use this approach to target you:

- Microsoft combines personal data from the 263 million users of its free Hotmail e-mail service—the biggest in the world—with information it gains from monitoring their searches. When you sign up for Hotmail, the service asks you for personal information including your age, occupation, and address (though you're not required to answer). If you use Microsoft's search engine, Live Search, the company keeps a record of the words you search for and the results you click on. Microsoft's behavioral targeting system will allow its advertising clients to send different ads to each person surfing the Web. For instance, if a 25-year-old financial analyst living in a big city is comparing prices of cars on-line, BMW could send him an ad for a Mini Cooper. But it could send a 45-year-old suburban businessman with children who is doing the same search an ad for the X5 SUV.[3]

- Starwood Hotels & Resorts Worldwide Inc. uses a behavioral targeting campaign to promote spas at its hotels. The hospitality company works with an on-line media company to deliver ads to people who have browsed travel articles on the Internet or surfed the Web site of a Starwood-branded hotel, such as Westin or Sheraton. An internal survey showed that the campaign was rated the highest among all of the company's efforts to raise awareness about the spas.

- Blockbuster.com uses software that recommends a video to a customer based on attributes the flick shares with other movies he has already ordered. This results in some suggestions that may not be immediately obvious. For example, someone who watched *Crash* might receive a recommendation for *Little Miss Sunshine* because both involve dysfunctional social groups, dynamic pacing, and an interdependent ensemble cast. Blockbuster says the service has increased its average customer's "to watch list" by almost 50 percent.[4]

- A start-up company called Pudding Media is betting you'll let it eavesdrop on your calls. In late 2007, the firm introduced a service like Skype that provides phone service through the Internet. The difference is that it will use voice recognition software to monitor what you're talking about and push ads to your computer screen based on your conversation. So, as you and your friend debate which movie you want to see this weekend, you might see a movie ad magically appear on your monitor.[5]

Step 3: Evaluation of Alternatives

Once Brandon has identified his options, it's time to decide on a few true contenders. There are two components to this stage of the decision-making process. First, a consumer armed with information identifies a small number of products in which he is interested. Then he narrows down his choices by deciding which of all the possibilities are feasible and by comparing the pros and cons of each remaining option.

Brandon has always wanted a red Ferrari, but after allowing himself to daydream for a few minutes, he returns to reality and reluctantly admits that an Italian sports car is probably not in the cards for him right now. As he looks around, he decides that the cars he likes in his price range are the Scion xB, the Ford Focus, and the Honda Element. He has narrowed down his options by considering only affordable cars that come to mind or that his buddies suggest.

Now it's decision time! Brandon has to look more systematically at each of the three possibilities and identify the important characteristics, or **evaluative criteria**, that he will use to decide among them. The criteria may be power, comfort, price, the style of the car, and even safety. Keep in mind that marketers often play a role in educating consumers about which product characteristics they should use as evaluative criteria—usually they will emphasize the dimensions in which their product excels. To make sure customers like Brandon come to the "right" conclusions in their evaluation of the alternatives, marketers must understand which criteria consumers use, and which are more or less important. With this information, sales and advertising professionals can point out a brand's superiority on the most important criteria as *they* have defined them.

evaluative criteria
The dimensions consumers use to compare competing product alternatives.

Step 4: Product Choice

After Brandon has examined his alternatives and gone on a few test drives, it's time to "put the pedal to the metal." Deciding on one product and acting on this choice is the next step in the decision-making process. After agonizing over his choice, Brandon decides that even though the Element and the Scion have attractive qualities, the Focus has the affordability he needs and its carefree image is the way he wants others to think about him. All this thinking about cars is "driving" him crazy, and he's relieved to make a decision to buy the Focus and get on with his life.

How do consumers decide? Choices such as Brandon's often are complicated because it's hard to juggle all the product characteristics in your head. One car may offer better gas mileage, another is $2,000 cheaper, while another boasts a better safety record. How do we make sense of all these characteristics and arrive at a decision?

Consumers often rely on decision guidelines when weighing the claims that companies make. These **heuristics**, or rules, help simplify the decision-making process. One such heuristic is "price = quality"; many people willingly buy the more expensive brand because they assume that if it costs more, it must be better (even though this isn't always true).

Perhaps the most common heuristic is **brand loyalty**, when people buy from the same company over and over because they believe that the company makes superior products. Consumers who have strong brand loyalty feel that it's not worth the effort to consider competing options. Creating this allegiance is a prized goal for marketers. People form preferences for a favorite brand and then may never change their minds in the course of a lifetime, making it extremely difficult for rivals to persuade them to switch. That explains

heuristics
A mental rule of thumb that leads to a speedy decision by simplifying the process.

brand loyalty
A pattern of repeat product purchases, accompanied by an underlying positive attitude toward the brand, that is based on the belief that the brand makes products superior to those of its competition.

Metrics Moment

Marketers use some or all of a variety of metrics to better understand how consumers make decisions.

- **Awareness** is the percentage of all customers who recognize or know the name of a brand. Unaided brand recognition for toothpaste may be measured by asking consumers to name all the brands of toothpaste that come to mind. Aided recognition is measured by asking consumers questions such as "Have you heard of Tom's of Maine toothpaste?"
- **Top of Mind Awareness (TOMA)** is the first brand that comes to mind when a consumer thinks of a product category. Marketers measure TOMA with questions such as "What brand comes to mind when you think of toothpaste?"
- **Brand Knowledge** is measured by asking consumers if they have specific knowledge about a brand. To measure brand knowledge, marketers may ask consumers if they believe the brand possesses certain attributes or characteristics.
- **Measures of Attitudes** toward a brand may include survey questions about 1) beliefs that the brand possesses certain characteristics, 2) the relative importance of those characteristics to the product category, and 3) the overall measure of how much the consumer likes the brand.
- **Intentions** are consumers' stated willingness to buy or their likelihood of certain behavior. A consumer survey may ask "If you are in the market for a new pair of shoes, what is the likelihood that you would purchase a pair of Nike shoes?"
- **Purchase Habits** measure consumers' self-reported behavior. Marketers ask consumers questions such as "On average, how many times a month do you eat out? Which restaurant did you go to the last time you ate out? How much do you normally spend on a dinner out with your family?"
- **Loyalty** is a measure of consumers' commitment to a specific brand. Marketers measure loyalty by asking such questions as "If on your next trip to the store you plan to purchase hand soap and your favorite brand of hand soap is not available, would you buy another brand or wait until you find your favorite brand to make the purchase?"
- **Customer satisfaction** is generally based on a survey data in which consumers are asked if they are 1) very satisfied, 2) somewhat satisfied, 3) neither satisfied nor dissatisfied, 4) somewhat dissatisfied, or 5) very dissatisfied with a brand.[8]

why many companies work hard to woo consumers early on. For example, it's hard to find an adult in Helsinki, home to the Finnish company Nokia, who doesn't have a cell phone—92 percent of its households have at least one, if not several. But, while the phones have been an accepted part of daily life for grown-ups and teenagers for over a decade, the latest boom in phone use is occurring among children. Many of them get their first phone at age seven or so when they start to engage in activities, like soccer practice, where their parents aren't present. Now, there's an expanding market for accessories like phone covers decorated with pictures of Donald Duck or *Star Wars* characters.[6]

Still another heuristic is based on *country-of-origin*. We assume that a product has certain characteristics if it comes from a certain country. In the car category, many people associate German cars with fine engineering and Swedish cars with safety. Brandon assumed that the Japanese-made Honda would be a bit more reliable than the Ford or Saturn, so he factored that into his decision.

Sometimes a marketer wants to encourage a country association even when none exists. Anheuser-Busch, for example, introduced a new beer brand that it hopes customers will think of as an import—even though it's not. Anheuser World Select comes in a Heineken-style green bottle and a tagline that reads, "Ten Brewmasters. Four Continents. One Beer." The label on the neck of the bottle lists the home countries of the brewmasters involved in the beer's production (Japan, Ireland, Canada, and Spain), but the reality is that the beer is actually made in America.[7]

Step 5: Postpurchase Evaluation

In the last step of the decision-making process, the consumer evaluates just how good a choice he made. Everyone has experienced regret after making a purchase ("what was I *thinking*?"), and (hopefully) we have all been pleased with something we've bought. The evaluation of the product results in a level of **consumer satisfaction/dissatisfaction**, which is determined by the overall feelings, or attitude, a person has about a product after purchasing it.

consumer satisfaction/dissatisfaction
The overall feelings or attitude a person has about a product after purchasing it.

Just how do consumers decide if they're satisfied with their purchases? The obvious answer would be, "That's easy. The product is either wonderful or it isn't." However, it's a little more complicated than that. When we buy a product, we have some *expectations* of product quality. How well a product or service meets or exceeds these expectations determines customer satisfaction. In other words, consumers assess product quality by comparing what they have bought to a performance standard created by a mixture of information from marketing communications, informal information sources such as friends and family, and their own experience with the product category. That's why it's very important that marketers create accurate expectations of their product in advertising and other communications.

Hollyanne
Pronko

a student at Saint Joseph's University

My Advice for (RED) would be to choose

Option

real people, **Other** Voices

I would choose **Option 1**: to shift the focus of (RED) onto the teen market. Since the research showed that teens are open to the ideas of cause marketing, and they are also open to integrating doing good and getting what they want, I think this is an ideal direction for (RED)

to move. Teens spend millions of dollars per year, and will likely hold on to their fondness for the (RED) brand into the future. If (RED) focuses on them now, it will likely be able to keep them coming back into their adult years. Though (RED) would have to divert some of its attention from larger brands, this new direction could prove more successful than originally intended. Teens are highly influenced by their peers; if (RED) can appeal to teen innovators, it may find the (RED) brand becoming increasingly more popular! ➤

Even when a product performs to expectations, consumers may suffer anxiety or regret, something we call **cognitive dissonance**, after making a purchase. When rejected product alternatives have attractive features, a consumer may second-guess his decision after it is made. Brandon, for example, might begin thinking, "Maybe I should have chosen the Honda Element—everyone says Hondas are great cars." To generate satisfied customers and remove dissonance, marketers often seek to reinforce purchases through direct mail or other personalized contacts after the sale.

So, even though Brandon's new Focus is not exactly as powerful as a Ferrari, he's still happy with the car because he never really expected a fun little car to eat up the highway like a high-performance sports car costing 10 times as much. Brandon has "survived" the consumer decision-making process by recognizing a problem, conducting an informational search to resolve it, identifying the (feasible) alternatives available, making a product choice, and then evaluating the quality of his decision.

Apart from understanding the mechanics of the consumer decision-making process, marketers also try to ascertain what influences in consumers' lives affect this process. There are three main categories: internal, situational, and social influences. In Brandon's case, for example, the evaluative criteria he used to compare cars and his feelings about each were influenced by internal factors such as the connection he learned to make between a name like Ford Focus and an image of "slightly hip, yet safe and solid," situational factors such as the way the Ford salesperson treated him, and social influences such as his prediction that his friends would be impressed when they saw him cruising down the road in his new wheels.

Figure 5.4 shows the influences in the decision-making process and emphasizes that all these factors work together to affect the ultimate choice each person makes. Let's consider how each of these three types of influences work, starting with internal factors.

cognitive dissonance
The anxiety or regret a consumer may feel after choosing from among several similar attractive choices.

Internal Influences
- Perception
- Motivation
- Learning
- Attitudes
- Personality
- Age groups
- Lifestyle

Situational Influences
- Physical environment
- Time

Social Influences
- Culture
- Subculture
- Social class
- Group memberships

Decision Process → **PURCHASE**

Figure 5.4 | Influences on Consumer Decision Making

A number of different factors in consumers' lives influence the consumer decision-making process. Marketers need to understand these influences and which ones are important in the purchase process.

3 Internal Influences on Consumers' Decisions

OBJECTIVE

Explain how internal factors influence consumers' decision-making processes.

(pp. 142–149)

Automakers know that one consumer's choice of the ideal car can be quite different from another's. You may think the ideal car is a sporty Ferrari, while your roommate dreams of a pimped-out Escalade and your dad is set on owning a big Mercedes. Much of the cause of such differences can be attributed to the internal influences on consumer behavior—those things that cause each of us to interpret information about the outside world, including which car is the best, differently from one another. Let's see how internal factors relating to the way people absorb and interpret information influence the decision-making process.

Perception

perception
The process by which people select, organize, and interpret information from the outside world.

Perception is the process by which people select, organize, and interpret information from the outside world. We receive information in the form of sensations, the immediate response of our sensory receptors—eyes, ears, nose, mouth, and fingers—to basic stimuli such as light, color, and sound. The physical qualities of products often influence our impressions of them. We try to make sense of the sensations we receive by interpreting them in light of our past experiences.

For example, marketers are exploring how they can use touch in packaging to arouse consumer interest. Some new plastic containers for household beauty items incorporate "soft touch" resins that provide a soft, friction-like resistance when people hold them. Focus-group members who tested one such package for Clairol's Daily Defense shampoo described the sensations as "almost sexy" and were actually reluctant to let go of the containers![9] That's a powerful impact for a piece of plastic.

We are bombarded with information about products—thousands of ads, in-store displays, special offers, our friends' opinions, and on and on. The perception process has important implications for marketers because, as consumers absorb and make sense of the vast quantities of information that compete for their attention, the odds are that any single message will get lost in the clutter. And, if they do notice the message, there's no guarantee that the meaning they give it will be the same one the marketer intended. The issues that marketers need to understand during this process include exposure, attention, and interpretation.

The stimulus must be within range of people's sensory receptors to be noticed; in other words, people must be physically able to see, hear, taste, smell, or feel the stimulus. For example, the lettering on a highway billboard must be big enough for a passing motorist to read easily, or the message will be lost. **Exposure** is the extent to which a person's sensory receptors are capable of registering a stimulus.

exposure
The extent to which a stimulus is capable of being registered by a person's sensory receptors.

subliminal advertising
Supposedly hidden messages in marketers' communications.

Many people believe that even messages they can't see will persuade them to buy advertised products. Claims about **subliminal advertising** of messages hidden in ice cubes (among other places) have been surfacing since the 1950s. A survey of American consumers found that almost two-thirds believe in the existence of subliminal advertising, and over one-half are convinced that this technique can get them to buy things they don't really want.[10]

There is very little evidence to support the argument that this technique actually has any effect at all on our perceptions of products. But still, concerns persist. In 2006, ABC rejected a commercial for KFC that invites viewers to slowly replay the ad to find a secret message, citing the network's long-standing policy against subliminal advertising. The ad (which other networks aired), is a seemingly ordinary pitch for KFC's $.99 Buffalo Snacker chicken sandwich. But if replayed slowly on a digital video recorder or VCR, it reveals a message that viewers can enter on KFC's Web site to receive a coupon for a free sandwich. Ironically, this technique is really the *opposite* of subliminal advertising because instead of secretly placing words or images in the ad, KFC blatantly publicized its campaign by informing viewers that it contains a message and how to find it.[11]

As you drive down the highway, you pass hundreds of other cars. But to how many do you pay attention? Probably only one or two—the bright pink and purple VW Bug and the Honda with the broken taillight that cut you off at the exit ramp. **Attention** is the extent to which we devote mental-processing activity to a particular stimulus. Consumers are more likely to pay attention to messages that speak to their current needs. For example, you're far more likely to notice an ad for a fast-food restaurant when you're hungry, while smokers are more likely than nonsmokers to block out messages about the health hazards of smoking.

Grabbing consumers' attention is becoming harder than ever, because people's attention spans are shorter than ever. Now that we are accustomed to *multitasking*, flitting back and forth between our e-mails, TV, IMs, and so on, advertisers have to be more creative by mixing up the types of messages they send. That's why we're seeing on the one hand long (60-second) commercials that almost feel like miniature movies and short (some as brief as five seconds) messages that are meant to have surprise value: They are usually over before commercial-haters can zap or zip past them. Indeed, brief blurbs that are long enough to tantalize viewers but short enough not to bore them are becoming commonplace. In contrast to the old days when most commercials on television networks were 30-second spots, today more than one-third run for only 15 seconds.[12]

Another cutting-edge strategy to grab attention by increasing the relevance of ads is to actually customize them to the audience that's viewing them. News Corp.'s Fox plans to offer *tweakable ads*—spots it can digitally alter to contain elements relevant to particular viewers at the time they see them. By changing voiceovers, scripts, graphic elements, or other images, for instance, advertisers could make an ad appeal to teens in one instance and seniors in another. As this approach is refined, a cola company could have actors refer to the particular teams in a sporting event. Or a soup company could call viewers' attention to a snowstorm brewing outside to encourage people to stock up on soup. Stay tuned.[13]

Interpretation is the process of assigning meaning to a stimulus based on prior associations a person has with it and assumptions he makes about it. Extra Strength Maalox Whip Antacid flopped, even though a spray can is a pretty effective way to deliver this kind of tummy ache relief. But to consumers, aerosol whips mean dessert toppings, not medication.[14] If we don't interpret the product the way it was intended because of our prior experiences, the best marketing ideas will be "waisted."

Critics of subliminal perception claim that hidden messages lurk in ice cubes and elsewhere. This Pepsi ad borrows from that idea.

attention
The extent to which a person devotes mental processing to a particular stimulus.

interpretation
The process of assigning meaning to a stimulus based on prior associations a person has with it and assumptions he makes about it.

Motivation

Motivation is an internal state that drives us to satisfy needs. Once we activate a need, a state of tension exists that drives the consumer toward some goal that will reduce this tension by eliminating the need.

For example, think about Brandon and his old car. Brandon began to experience a gap between his present state (owning an old car) and a desired state (having a car that gets him noticed and is fun to drive). This activated the need for a new car, which in turn motivated Brandon to test different models, to talk with friends about different makes, and finally to buy a new car.

motivation
An internal state that drives us to satisfy needs by activating goal-oriented behavior.

hierarchy of needs
An approach that categorizes motives according to five levels of importance, the more basic needs being on the bottom of the hierarchy and the higher needs at the top.

Psychologist Abraham Maslow developed an influential approach to motivation.[15] He formulated a **hierarchy of needs** that categorizes motives according to five levels of importance, the more basic needs being on the bottom of the hierarchy and the higher needs at the top. The hierarchy suggests that before a person can meet needs in a given level, he must first meet the lower level's needs—somehow those hot new Seven jeans don't seem as enticing when you don't have enough money to buy food.

As you can see from Figure 5.5, people start at the lowest level, with basic physiological needs for food and sleep, and then progress to higher levels to satisfy more complex needs, such as the need to be accepted by others or to feel a sense of accomplishment. Ultimately, people can reach the highest-level needs, where they will be motivated to attain such goals as self-fulfillment. As the figure shows, if marketers understand the level of needs relevant to consumers in their target market, they can tailor their products and messages to them.

Learning

learning
A relatively permanent change in behavior caused by acquired information or experience.

Learning is a change in behavior caused by information or experience. Learning about products can occur deliberately, as when we set out to gather information about different MP3 players before we buy one brand. We also learn even when we are not trying. Consumers recognize many brand names and can hum many product jingles, for example, even for products they themselves do not use. Psychologists who study learning have advanced several theories to explain the learning process, and these perspectives are important because a major goal for marketers is to "teach" consumers to prefer their products. Let's briefly review the most important perspectives on how people learn.

Behavioral Learning

behavioral learning theories
Theories of learning that focus on how consumer behavior is changed by external events or stimuli.

classical conditioning
The learning that occurs when a stimulus eliciting a response is paired with another stimulus that initially does not elicit a response on its own but will cause a similar response over time because of its association with the first stimulus.

Behavioral learning theories assume that learning takes place as the result of connections that form between events that we perceive. In one type of behavioral learning, **classical conditioning**, a person perceives two stimuli at about the same time. After a while, the person transfers his response from one stimulus to the other. For example, an ad shows a product and a breathtakingly beautiful scene so that (the marketer hopes) you will transfer

Figure 5.5 | Maslow's Hierarchy of Needs and Related Products

Abraham Maslow proposed a hierarchy of needs that categorizes motives. Savvy marketers know they need to understand the level of needs that motivates a consumer to buy a particular product or brand.

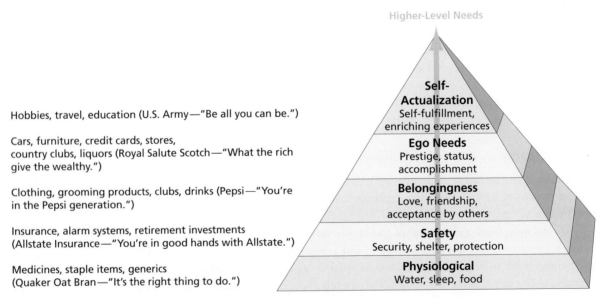

Higher-Level Needs

Hobbies, travel, education (U.S. Army—"Be all you can be.")

Cars, furniture, credit cards, stores, country clubs, liquors (Royal Salute Scotch—"What the rich give the wealthy.")

Clothing, grooming products, clubs, drinks (Pepsi—"You're in the Pepsi generation.")

Insurance, alarm systems, retirement investments (Allstate Insurance—"You're in good hands with Allstate.")

Medicines, staple items, generics (Quaker Oat Bran—"It's the right thing to do.")

Self-Actualization
Self-fulfillment, enriching experiences

Ego Needs
Prestige, status, accomplishment

Belongingness
Love, friendship, acceptance by others

Safety
Security, shelter, protection

Physiological
Water, sleep, food

Lower-Level Needs

the positive feelings you get from looking at the scene to the advertised product. Did you ever notice that car ads often show a new auto on a beautiful beach at sunset or speeding down a mountain road with brightly colored leaves blowing across the pavement?

Another common form of behavioral learning is **operant conditioning**, which occurs when people learn that their actions result in rewards or punishments. This feedback influences how they will respond in similar situations in the future. Just as a rat in a maze learns the route to a piece of cheese, consumers who receive a reward, such as a prize in the bottom of a box of cereal, will be more likely to buy that brand again. We don't like to think that marketers can train us like lab mice, but that kind of feedback does reward us for the behavior. Will that be American or Swiss for you?

These learned associations in classical and operant conditioning also have a tendency to transfer to other similar things in a process of **stimulus generalization**. This means that the good or bad feelings we associate with a product will "rub off" on other products that resemble it. For example, some marketers create *product line extensions* in which new products share the name of an established brand so that people's good feelings about the current product will transfer to the new one. Dole, which people associate with fruit, introduced refrigerated juices and juice bars, while Sun Maid branched out from raisins to raisin bread. More on this in Chapter 9.

Cognitive Learning

In contrast to behavioral theories of learning, **cognitive learning theory** views people as problem solvers who do more than passively react to associations between stimuli. Supporters of this viewpoint stress the role of creativity and insight during the learning process. Cognitive learning occurs when consumers make a connection between ideas or by observing things in their environment.

Observational learning occurs when people watch the actions of others and note what happens to them as a result. They store these observations in memory and at some later point use the information to guide their own behavior. Marketers often use this process to create advertising and other messages that allow consumers to observe the benefits of using their products. Health clubs and manufacturers of exercise equipment feature well-muscled men and women using their products, while mouthwash makers show that fresh breath is the key to romance.

Now we've discussed how the three internal processes of perception, motivation, and learning influence how consumers absorb and interpret information. But the results of these processes—the interpretation the consumer gives to a marketing message—differ depending on unique consumer characteristics. Let's talk next about some of these characteristics: existing consumer attitudes, the personality of the consumer, and consumer age groups.

Attitudes

An **attitude** is a lasting evaluation of a person, object, or issue.[16] Consumers have attitudes toward brands, such as whether McDonald's or Wendy's has the best hamburgers, as well as toward more general consumption-related behaviors, for example, whether high-fat foods, including hamburgers, are a no-no in a healthy diet. A person's attitude has three components: affect, cognition, and behavior.

Affect is the *feeling* component of attitudes. This term refers to the overall emotional response a person has to a product. Affect is usually dominant for expressive products, such as perfume, in which simply whether or not and how much we like the product determines our attitude toward it. Some marketing researchers are trying to understand how consumers' emotional reactions influence how they feel about products. A company called Sensory Logic, for example, studies videotapes of people's facial reactions—to products and commercials—in increments as fleeting as 1/30 of a second. Staffers look for the difference between, say, a true smile (which includes a relaxation of the upper eyelid) and a social smile (which occurs only around the

operant conditioning
Learning that occurs as the result of rewards or punishments.

stimulus generalization
Behavior caused by a reaction to one stimulus occurs in the presence of other similar stimuli.

cognitive learning theory
Theory of learning that stresses the importance of internal mental processes and that views people as problem solvers who actively use information from the world around them to master their environment.

observational learning
Learning that occurs when people watch the actions of others and note what happens to them as a result.

attitude
A learned predisposition to respond favorably or unfavorably to stimuli on the basis of relatively enduring evaluations of people, objects, and issues.

affect
The feeling component of attitudes; refers to the overall emotional response a person has to a product.

PowerBar hopes to influence consumers' beliefs about the evaluative criteria they should use when they choose a snack.

cognition

The knowing component of attitudes; refers to the beliefs or knowledge a person has about a product and its important characteristics.

behavior

The doing component of attitudes; involves a consumer's intention to do something, such as the intention to purchase or use a certain product.

personality

The set of unique psychological characteristics that consistently influences the way a person responds to situations in the environment.

mouth). Whirlpool hired the company to test consumers' emotional reactions to its Duet washers and dryers. Its (perhaps ambitious) goal was to design appliances that would actually make people happy. The research led Whirlpool to change some design options on the Duet products, including geometric patterns and certain color combinations.[17] Smile, it's Laundry Day!

Cognition, the *knowing* component, is the beliefs or knowledge a person has about a product and its important characteristics. You may believe that a Mercedes is built better than most cars, or (like Brandon) that a Ford Focus is slightly hip, yet solid. Cognition is important for complex products, such as computers, for which we may develop beliefs on the basis of technical information.

Behavior, the *doing* component, involves a consumer's intention to do something, such as the intention to purchase or use a certain product. For products such as cereal, consumers act (purchase and try the product) on the basis of limited information and then form an evaluation of the product simply on the basis of how the product tastes or performs.

Depending on the nature of the product, one of these three components—feeling, knowing, or doing—will be the dominant influence in creating an attitude toward a product. Marketers often need to decide which part of an attitude is the most important driver of consumers' preferences. For example, Pepsi's advertising focus changed from its typical emotional emphasis on celebrities, jingles, special effects, and music to emphasizing rational reasons to drink the beverage. Its new campaign portrays the soft drink as the perfect accompaniment to foods and social situations like football games and dates.[18]

Personality

Personality is the set of unique psychological characteristics that consistently influences the way a person responds to situations in the environment. One adventure-seeking consumer may always be on the lookout for new experiences and cutting-edge products, while another is happiest in familiar surroundings using the same brands over and over. Today, popular on-line matchmaking services like match.com, Matchmaker.com, and Tickle.com offer to create your "personality profile" and then hook you up with other members whose profiles are similar.

Personality Traits

For marketers, differences in *personality traits* , such as thrill-seeking, underscore the potential value of considering personality when they craft their marketing strategies. The following are some particularly relevant personality traits for this purpose:

- **Innovativeness**: The degree to which a person likes to try new things. Cutting-edge products, such as radical new fashions, might appeal to innovative women.

- **Materialism**: The amount of emphasis placed on owning products. Materialistic consumers focus on owning products simply for the sake of ownership and "bragging rights."

- **Self-confidence**: The degree to which a person has a positive evaluation of his abilities, including the ability to make good decisions. People who don't have much self-confidence are good candidates for services like image consultants, who help clients select the right outfit for a job interview.

- **Sociability**: The degree to which a person enjoys social interaction. Sociable people might respond to entertainment-related products that claim to bring people together or make parties more fun.

- **Need for cognition**: The degree to which a person likes to think about things and expend the necessary effort to process brand information.[19]

The Self: Are You What You Buy?

It makes sense to assume that consumers buy products that are extensions of their personalities. That's why marketers try to create brand personalities that will appeal to different types of people. For example, consider the different "personalities" fragrance marketers invent: A brand with a "wholesome, girl-next-door" image such as Clinique's Happy would be hard to confuse with the sophisticated image of Christian Dior's Dolce Vita. We'll talk more about this in Chapter 8.

A person's **self-concept** is his attitude toward himself. The self-concept is composed of a mixture of beliefs about one's abilities and observations of one's own behavior and feelings (both positive and negative) about one's personal attributes, such as body type or facial features. The extent to which a person's self-concept is positive or negative can influence the products he buys and even the extent to which he fantasizes about changing his life.

Kenra, a marketer of hair and grooming products, recognized that many African-American women have a poor self-concept because mainstream society tells them that only straight hair is beautiful.[20] A Kenra ad said to these women, "All your life, you've been told there's one kind of beautiful. And you're not it. Haven't we fought too hard for freedom to become slaves to fashion? Wear your hair any way you want." *Self-esteem advertising* attempts to stimulate positive feelings about the self.[21] This technique is also used in ads for Clairol ("You're not getting older, you're getting better"), Budweiser ("For all you do, this Bud's for you"), and L'Oréal ("Because you're worth it").

Age

A person's age is another internal influence on purchasing behavior. Many of us feel we have more in common with those of our own age because we share a common set of experiences and memories about cultural events, whether these involve the Vietnam War or the September 11 terrorist attacks.

Indeed, marketers of products from cookies to cars bank on *nostalgia* to draw in customers, as people are attracted to products that remind them of past experiences. Advertising for Ameriprise Financial services features scenes of young people cavorting in the 1950s and 1960s. As the 1966 rock tune "Gimme Some Lovin'" by the Spencer Davis Group plays in the background, the voiceover proclaims, "A generation as unique as this needs a new generation of personal financial planning."[22] Similarly, Mitchum antiperspirant is trying to appeal to men in their late 20s or early 30s by reminding them of days gone by when they sowed their wild oats. The brand is distributing drink coasters to bars men of this age frequent with sayings like "If you let your buddy have the hot one, you're a Mitchum man" and "If you can see the inner beauty of the girl dancing on the bar, you're a Mitchum man."[23]

Goods and services often appeal to a specific age group. Although there are exceptions, it is safe to assume that most buyers of Lil' Kim's CDs are younger than those who buy Barbra Streisand discs. Thus, many marketing strategies appeal to the needs of different age groups such as children, teenagers, the middle-aged, and the elderly.

Young people are among the most enthusiastic users of the Internet. In fact, teens spend over $1 billion on-line each year, so many firms are working hard to develop Web sites that will capture their interest. What do teens do on-line? Approximately three out of four teens do research, and nearly two out of three

Some marketers believe we choose products that express our personalities. What do you think?

self-concept
An individual's self-image that is composed of a mixture of beliefs, observations, and feelings about personal attributes.

This German ad appeals directly to the self-concept of potential customers who want to shed a few pounds.

Eleanor
isn't into gingham
any more
than her mother is.

ooba
jumpstarting style

This ad targets young mothers who have to make many decisions about baby-related products.

family life cycle

A means of characterizing consumers within a family structure on the basis of different stages through which people pass as they grow older.

lifestyle

The pattern of living that determines how people choose to spend their time, money, and energy and that reflects their values, tastes, and preferences.

use the Internet for e-mail, while far fewer use it for finding or buying products. For marketers, this means that the Internet may be a great way to get information about their goods and services to teens but not so good for sales.

Marketers know that the process of change continues throughout consumers' lives. Interestingly, the purchase of goods and services may depend more on consumers' current position in the **family life cycle**—the stages through which family members pass as they grow older—than on chronological age. Singles (of any age) are more likely to spend money on expensive cars, entertainment, and recreation. Couples with small children purchase baby furniture, insurance, and a larger house, while older couples whose children have "left the nest" are more likely to buy a retirement home in Florida.

Lifestyle

A **lifestyle** is a pattern of living that determines how people choose to spend their time, money, and energy and that reflects their values, tastes, and preferences. We express our lifestyles in our preferences for activities such as sports, interests such as music, and opinions on politics and religion. Consumers often choose goods, services, and activities that they associate with a certain lifestyle. Brandon may drive a Ford Focus, hang out in Internet cafes, and go extreme skiing during spring break because he views these choices as part of a cool college student lifestyle.

Marketers often develop marketing strategies that recognize that people can be grouped into market segments based on similarities in lifestyle preferences.[24] For example, skateboarding has morphed from an activity we associate with the law-breaking daredevils the movie *Dogtown and Z-Boys* depicted to become a full-fledged lifestyle, complete with a full complement of merchandise that boarders need to live the life. For over a dozen years the ESPN X Games that feature extreme action sports have aired on ESPN and ABC. Shows on MTV feature professional skateboarders, and sales of a skateboarding video game, *Tony Hawk* by Activision, are over $ 1 billion.[25] Many kids happily fork over $20 for T-shirts and more than $60 for skate shoes in addition to the hundreds they may spend on the latest boards. In fact, kids spend well over $4 billion a year on skateboard "soft goods," like T-shirts, shorts, and sunglasses, while actual skateboarding equipment "only" sells over $800 million.[26]

If lifestyles are so important, how do marketers identify them so that they can reach consumers who share preferences for products that they associate with a certain lifestyle? *Demographic* characteristics, such as age and income, tell marketers *what* products people buy, but they don't reveal *why*. Two consumers can share the same demographic characteristics yet be totally different people—all 20-year-old male college students are hardly identical to one another. That's why it is often important to further profile consumers in terms of their passions and how they spend their leisure time.

For example, audio equipment manufacturer Pioneer Corp. recently focused on a select group of automobile hobbyists known as "Tuners"—typically single men in their late teens and early 20s with a yen for fast cars. These men come mostly from Latino and Asian communities, and many entered the car lovers' lifestyle by participating in illegal street racing late at night in the New York City and Los Angeles areas. Unlike other hot-rod enthusiasts, Tuners tinker with computer chips as well as carburetors and are always searching for specialized car parts. Pioneer created distinctive ads that ran in lifestyle-oriented media, such as magazines called *Import Tuner* and *Sport Compact Car*.[27] We'll look further at how marketers identify and find these specialized consumer groups in Chapter 7.

To breathe life into demographic analyses, marketers turn to **psychographics**, which groups consumers according to psychological and behavioral similarities. One way to do this is to describe people in terms of their activities, interests, and opinions (*AIOs*). These AIOs are based on preferences for vacation destinations, club memberships, hobbies, political and social attitudes, tastes in food and fashion, and so on. Using data from large samples, marketers create profiles of customers who resemble each other in terms of their activities and patterns of product use.[28]

Marketers at the beginning of the walking shoe craze assumed that all recreational walkers were just burned-out joggers. Subsequent psychographic research that examined the AIOs of these walkers showed that there were actually several psychographic segments within the larger group who engaged in the activity for very different reasons. These different motivations included walking for fun, walking to save money, and walking for exercise. This research resulted in walking shoes for different segments, from Footjoy Walkers to Nike Healthwalkers.

STANDS OUT
BY FITTING IN

Thermador | *An American Icon*

© Thermador

Our choices of clothing, furniture, and other products often reflect our commitment to a consistent lifestyle.

4

OBJECTIVE

Show how situational factors at the time and place of purchase influence consumer behavior.

(pp. 149–150)

Situational Influences on Consumers' Decisions

We've seen that internal factors such as how people perceive marketing messages, their motivation to acquire products, and their unique personalities, age groups, family life cycle and lifestyle influence the decisions they make. In addition, when, where, and how consumers shop—what we call *situational influences*—shape their purchase choices. Some important situational cues are our physical surroundings and time pressures.

psychographics
The use of psychological, sociological, and anthropological factors to construct market segments.

Marketers know that dimensions of the physical environment, including factors such as decor, smells, lighting, music, and even temperature, can significantly influence consumption. If you don't believe this, consider that one study found that pumping certain odors into a Las Vegas casino actually increased the amount of money patrons fed into slot machines.[29] Westin Hotels spray a blend of green tea, geranium, and black cedar into hotel lobbies while Sheraton uses a combination of jasmine, clove, and fig. Sony scents its stores with orange, vanilla, and cedar, and Cadillac puts that "new car" smell into its autos artificially, all to influence the consumer's decision process.[30] Let's see how situational factors influence the consumer decision-making process.

The Physical Environment

It's no secret that physical surroundings strongly influence people's moods and behaviors. Despite all their efforts to presell consumers through advertising, marketers know that the store environment influences many purchases. For example, consumers decide on about two out of every three of their supermarket product purchases in the aisles (so always eat before you go to the supermarket). The messages they receive at the time and their feelings about being in the store influence their decisions.[31]

As consumers are exposed to more and more advertising, advertisers must work harder than ever to get their attention. *Place-based media*, in this case a message strategically put on a bathroom wall, offers a way to reach consumers when they are a "captive audience."

Arousal and Pleasure

Got your attention? Two dimensions, *arousal* and *pleasure*, determine whether a shopper will react positively or negatively to a store environment. In other words, the person's surroundings can be either dull or exciting (arousing) and either pleasant or unpleasant. Just because the environment is arousing doesn't necessarily mean it will be pleasant—we've all been in crowded, loud, hot stores that are anything but. Maintaining an upbeat feeling in a pleasant context is one factor behind the success of theme parks such as Disney World, which tries to provide consistent doses of carefully calculated stimulation to visitors.[32]

The Shopping Experience

The importance of these surroundings explains why many retailers focus on packing as much entertainment as possible into their stores. For example, Bass Pro Shops, a chain of outdoor sports equipment stores, features giant aquariums, waterfalls, trout ponds, archery and rifle ranges, putting greens, and free classes in everything from ice fishing to conservation.[33] Whether entertainment, e-mail, or information, providing surroundings that consumers want increases sales.

In-store displays are a marketing communications tool that attracts attention. Although most displays are just simple racks that dispense the product or related coupons, some marketers use elaborate performances and scenery to display their products. And advertisers also are being more aggressive about hitting consumers with their messages, wherever they may be. A *place-based media strategy* is a growing way to target consumers in nontraditional locations. Today, advertising messages pop up in airports, doctors' offices, college cafeterias, and health clubs. Turner Broadcasting System began a number of place-based media ventures such as Checkout Channel for grocery stores and the Airport Channel you watch while waiting for your flight, and it even tested McDTV for McDonald's restaurants.[34] Although the Checkout Channel and McDTV didn't make it, the Airport Channel entertains bored passengers in many terminals. A company called Privy Promotions and others like it even sell ad space on restroom walls in stadiums. According to the company's president, "It's a decided opportunity for an advertiser to reach a captive audience."[35] Guess so.

Time

In addition to the physical environment, time is another important situational factor. Marketers know that the time of day, the season of the year, and how much time one has to make a purchase affect decision making. Time is one of consumers' most limited resources. We talk about "making time" or "spending time," and we remind one another that "time is money."

Indeed, many consumers believe that they are more pressed for time than ever before.[36] This sense of time poverty makes consumers responsive to marketing innovations that allow them to save time, including services such as one-hour photo processing, drive-through lanes at fast-food restaurants, and ordering products on the Web.[37] A number of Web sites, including Apple's iTunes and even Wal-Mart, now offer consumers the speed and convenience of downloading music. These sites allow consumers to browse through thousands of titles, listen to selections, and order and pay for them—all without setting foot inside a store. This saves the customer time, plus the "store" is always open.

5

OBJECTIVE

Explain how consumers' relationships with other people, including such trends as consumerism and environmentalism, influence their decision-making processes.

(pp. 151–158)

Social Influences on Consumers' Decisions

Our discussion of consumer behavior so far has focused on factors that influence us as individuals, such as the ways we learn about products. Although we are all individuals, we are also members of many groups that influence our buying decisions. Families, friends, and classmates often sway us, as do larger groups with which we identify, such as ethnic groups and political parties. Now let's consider how social influences such as culture, social class, influential friends and acquaintances, and trends within the larger society affect the consumer decision-making process.

Culture

Think of **culture** as a society's personality. It is the values, beliefs, customs, and tastes a group of people produce or practice. Although we often assume that what people in one culture (especially our own) think is desirable or appropriate will be appreciated in other cultures as well, that's far from the truth. Middle Eastern youth may not agree with U.S. politics, but they love Western music and find Arab TV music channels boring. Enter MTV Arabia, a 24-hour free satellite channel. Sure, many U.S. and European videos have to be cleaned up for the Arab audience and many are simply too edgy to air. To meet the values of the Middle Eastern audience, bad language and shots of kissing, revealing outfits or people in bed are blurred or removed and sometimes replaced by more acceptable copy.[38]

culture
The values, beliefs, customs, and tastes a group of people values.

Rituals

Every culture associates specific activities and products with its *rituals*, such as weddings and funerals. Some companies are more than happy to help us link products to cultural events. Consider the popularity of the elaborate weddings Disney stages for couples who want to reenact their own version of a popular fairy tale. At Disney World, the princess bride wears a tiara and rides to the park's lakeside wedding pavilion in a horse-drawn coach, complete with two footmen in gray wigs and gold lamé pants. At the exchange of vows, trumpets blare as Major Domo (he helped the Duke in his quest for Cinderella) walks up the aisle with two wedding bands in a glass slipper on a velvet pillow. Disney stages about 2,000 of these extravaganzas each year.[39]

Even corporations may include myths and legends as a part of their history, and some make a deliberate effort to be sure newcomers to the organization learn these. Nike designates senior executives as "corporate storytellers" who explain the company's heritage to other employees, including the hourly workers at Nike stores. They tell stories about the founders of Nike, including the coach of the Oregon track team who poured rubber into his family waffle iron to make better shoes for his team—the origin of the Nike waffle sole. The stories emphasize the dedication of runners and coaches involved with the company to reinforce the importance of teamwork. Rookies even visit the track where the coach worked to be sure they grasp the importance of the Nike legends.[40]

And, of course, many colleges boast unique rituals—though in recent years some institutions have abolished these due to safety concerns or

Asics appeals to social pressure to create desire for its running shoes.

because some rituals encourage underage drinking. Recent casualties include spring couch burning at the University of Vermont and Princeton's Nude Winter Olympics. The death of 12 people by collapsing logs in 1999 brought to an end the tradition of Texas A&M's bonfire on the eve of the annual football game against the University of Texas (the bonfire has since been revived off campus). Some campus rituals that have survived so far include the following:

- MIT: Each spring students haul a steer into a dorm courtyard, put it on a spit and light a fire under it with a flaming roll of toilet paper lowered from the roof.

- Wesleyan (Connecticut): Students honor the pot-smoking Doonesbury character Zonker Harris each spring with a day of live music, face painting, and plenty of open marijuana use.

- Simon Fraser University (British Columbia): Costumed engineering students throw one another in the reflection pond during February's Polar Plunge.

- Wellesley: Seniors toss the winner of the annual spring hoop roll into chilly Lake Waban. This ritual has changed to keep up with the times—the winner used to be declared the first to marry; now she's proclaimed the most likely to succeed.

- University of California at Santa Barbara: Students run naked through campus on the first rainy day of the year. Princeton and the University of Michigan have banned nude sprints, but at Yale seniors still run naked through two campus libraries at the end of each semester and toss candy at underclassmen cramming for finals.[41]

Values (again)

As we also saw in Chapter 3, cultural values are deeply held beliefs about right and wrong ways to live.[42] Marketers who understand a culture's values can tailor their product offerings accordingly. Consider, for example, that the values for collectivist countries differ greatly from those of individualistic cultures where immediate gratification of one's own needs come before all other loyalties. In collectivist cultures, loyalty to a family or a tribe overrides personal goals. Collectivist cultures put value on self-discipline, accepting one's position in life and honoring parents and elders. Children are dependent on parents, have virtually no freedom or autonomy, and live at home with parents until they get married. Aging parents live at home with their children. Individualist cultures, on the other hand, stress equality, freedom, and personal pleasure. Today, we see the economic growth of some collectivist countries, making many consumers more affluent—and individualistic. For marketers, this means growth opportunities products such as travel, luxury goods, sports activities, and entertainment that satisfy the need for an exciting, varied life.

Subcultures

A **subculture** is a group coexisting with other groups in a larger culture whose members share a distinctive set of beliefs or characteristics. Each of us may belong to many subcultures. These subcultures could be religious groups, ethnic groups, or regional groups as well as those that form around music groups such as the Dave Matthews Band, media creations such as Trekkies (*Star Trek* fans), or leisure activities such as extreme sports. The hip-hop subculture has had enormous influence as many marketers have relied on young trendsetters to help decide what brands were *off the hook* (good) and which were *wack* (bad). Successful hip-hop artists like P. Diddy, Jay-Z, Nelly, and Usher are slowly but surely becoming major players in the marketing world. Nelly branched out into the beverage business by creating Pimp Juice, a hip-hop inspired energy drink, while Trina and Usher have both created their own fragrances, and Gwen Stefani started her own clothing line.[43]

For marketers, some of the most important subcultures are racial and ethnic groups because many consumers identify strongly with their heritage and products that appeal to this aspect of their identities appeal to them. Some racial differences in consumption preferences

Julie
Cordua
APPLYING Values

Julie understands that many of our purchases are driven by our underlying values. She hopes to appeal to consumers' value of compassion to show them that they can buy "stuff" and still help others in need. ➡

subculture
A group within a society whose members share a distinctive set of beliefs, characteristics, or common experiences.

can be subtle but important. When Coffee-Mate discovered that African Americans are more likely than other ethnic groups to drink their coffee with sugar and cream, the company mounted a promotional blitz using black media and in return benefited from double-digit increases in sales volume and market share within this segment.[44]

Emerging Lifestyle Trends: Consumerism and Environmentalism

While in the longer term the culture and subculture of their society influence consumers' decisions, new forces in the form of social movements within a society may also contribute to how we decide what we want and what we don't. One such influence is **consumerism**, the social movement directed toward protecting consumers from harmful business practices. Many consumers are becoming very aware of the social and environmental consequences of their purchases—and making their decisions accordingly.

Organized activities that bring about social and political change are not new to the American scene. Women's right to vote, child labor laws, the minimum wage, equal employment opportunity, and the ban on nuclear weapons testing all have resulted from social movements in which citizens, public and private organizations, and businesses worked to change society.

The modern consumerism movement began in the 1960s, when bestselling books—such as Rachel Carson's *Silent Spring*, which attacked the irresponsible use of pesticides, and Ralph Nader's *Unsafe at Any Speed*, which exposed safety defects in General Motors' Corvair automobiles—put pressure on businesses to mend their ways. Consumers organized to call for safer products and honest information—and they boycotted companies that did not comply with their demands. Consumerism also prompted the establishment of government regulatory agencies and legislation such as the Cigarette Labeling Act of 1966 and the Child Protection and Safety Act of 1969.

One key response to the Consumerism movement was the Consumer Bill of Rights. In his 1961 inaugural speech, President John F. Kennedy outlined this historic endorsement of sound and fair buisness ethics, which includes the following:

- **The right to be safe**: Products should not be dangerous when used as intended. Organizations such as the Consumer Products Safety Board and the *Consumer Reports* magazine regularly announce products they find to be unsafe.

- **The right to be informed**: Businesses should provide consumers with adequate information to make intelligent product choices. This right means that product information provided by advertising, packaging, and salespeople should be honest and complete.

- **The right to be heard**: Consumers should have the means to complain or express their displeasure in order to obtain redress or retribution from companies. Government agencies and industry self-regulatory groups should respond to every customer complaint.

- **The right to choose freely**: Consumers should be able to choose from a variety of products. No one business should be allowed to control the price, quality, or availability of goods and services.

Related to the consumerism movement is **environmentalism**; a social movement coming from the worldwide growing concern for the many ways in which our consumption behaviors impact the physical world in which we live. Environmentalists seek solutions that enable companies to manage resources responsibly.

The **Kyoto Protocol** is an agreement the United Nations Framework Convention on Climate Change (UNFCCC) developed in 1997. The Kyoto Protocol covers 170 countries worldwide. It aims to reduce greenhouse gasses that create climate change. The protocol has been ratified by 175 countries. The United States has not ratified the agreement because of objections that China, as a developing country, is exempt from the emissions requirements of the agreement even though it is the world's second largest emitter of carbon dioxide.

Courtesy of the Beef Checkoff Program.

WE LOVE VEGETARIANS. MORE BEEF FOR US.

The decision to be a vegetarian or a carnivore often reflects a consumer's values.

Julie Cordua

APPLYING Consumerism

(RED) thrives because many people, especially younger ones, are much more in tune with the consumerism movement than they were a decade ago. ➡

consumerism
A social movement that attempts to protect consumers from harmful business practices.

environmentalism
A broad philosophy and social movement that seeks conservation and improvement of the natural environment.

Kyoto Protocol
A global agreement among countries that aims at reducing greenhouse gasses that create climate change.

environmental stewardship
A position taken by an organization to protect or enhance the natural environment as it conducts its business activities.

green marketing
A marketing strategy that supports environmental stewardship by creating a differential benefit in the minds of consumers.

greenwashing
Environmentally-friendly claims that are exaggerated or untrue.

In order to respond to the environmentalists, many firms now have assumed a position of **environmental stewardship** when they make socially responsible business decisions that also protect the environment. A **green marketing** strategy describes efforts to choose packages, product designs, and other aspects of the marketing mix that are earth-friendly but still profitable. One potential red flag in all of this rush to do good is concerns about **greenwashing**. This is what happens when companies claim their products are better for the environment than they really are in order to appeal to consumers' new focus on eco-friendly brands. Although many companies make sincere efforts to clean up their acts, many consumers are skeptical about green claims for this reason.

Still, green marketing practices can indeed result in black ink for a firm's bottom line. As mainstream marketers recognize this change, they are starting to alter their practices to satisfy Americans' desires for healthy and earth-friendly products. Here are some recent examples:

- Wendy's eliminated most artery-clogging trans fats from its menu. The country's third-largest burger chain now sells French fries and chicken sandwiches and strips that either have no trans fats or have only a fraction of what they previously had. Its hamburgers still contain small amounts of the substance, which occur naturally in beef and dairy products.[45]

- Home Depot, the nation's second-largest retailer, introduced an Eco Options label for almost 3,000 products such as fluorescent light bulbs that conserve electricity and natural insect killers that promote energy conservation, sustainable forestry, and clean water. The company expects products it certifies under this program to represent 12 percent of its total sales by 2009.[46]

- H&M is selling clothes made from organic cotton fabrics to fashion-conscious shoppers. Gap introduced an organic cotton T-shirt for men in more than 500 of its stores.[47]

- Procter & Gamble Co. reduced the size of its packaging for its liquid detergent. It's switching to a double concentrate formula to serve its $4 billion North American liquid detergent market. Its competitor Unilever launched its concentrated liquid detergent Small and Mighty in the United States in 2005, which it estimates reduces packaging by more than 40 percent, water usage by about 60 percent, and shipping volumes by 60 percent.[48]

- Scotts' Organic Choice brand is part of the giant gardening company's move toward less dependence on synthetically created chemicals, which include the main components in its distinctive blue Miracle-Gro plant food. The company plans to gradually introduce more gardening soil, fertilizer, and bug killer made with natural ingredients, including animal manure and Sri Lankan coconut husks.[49]

- Airplanes are notorious for their huge carbon footprints (i.e., the pollutants expelled into the atmosphere), but even the aerospace industry is going green. European plane maker Airbus calls its massive A380 superjumbo "the gentle green giant" because, with 550 people onboard, it burns less fuel per passenger than a small car. Its promotional materials show a silhouette of the largest commercial jetliner ever made set against images of dolphins, rain forests, and fishing boats on a misty pond. An Airbus spokesman introduced the behemoth at a 2007 air show with the claim that Airbus is "... saving the planet, one A380 at a time."[50]

The concept of sustainability we discussed in Chapter 1 is a key part of green marketing. For example, a savvy marketer like Interface (**www.interfaceinc.com**) is more aware than ever that long-term profitability depends on making quality products while acting in an ethical and socially responsible manner. Interface, an innovator in the floor coverings industry, has embraced radically new forms of manufacturing that drastically reduce waste while still returning profits. Interface is innovating by converting virtually all of its operations to practices that meet the principle of sustainability by developing processes that preserve the

Ethical Decisions in the Real World

As consumerism has grown more popular, consumers are feeling empowered and demanding their rights; some people call these new activists "consumer vigilantes." Imagine that you are the vice president for marketing for a cable/broadband company that provides television and Internet services to a regional subscriber base of over 5,000,000 customers. One customer complained to the firm's customer service department that his Internet and cable service had been disrupted for the fourth time in two weeks and had not worked for the past three days. When customer service responded that a repair technician could be scheduled to check things out in a week and a half, the customer took things into his own hands. First he set up a YouTube site that bashed the company's customer service activities. Within two days, the site received nearly a million "hits." Eventually, he was able to obtain the company CEO's home phone number and called to complain to him "up close and personal" about the problem.

What would you do to solve this "consumer vigilante" problem?

Ripped from the Headlines! See what happened in the Real World at **www.mypearsonmarketinglab.com**

ETHICS CHECK: ↖
Find out what other students taking this course **would do** and **why** on **www. mypearsonmarketinglab. com**

environment over the long term while still allowing it to operate at a profit. Interface is achieving this goal by eliminating toxic substances from products, vehicles, and facilities and by operating facilities with renewable energy sources—solar, wind, landfill gas, biomass, and low-impact hydroelectric.[51]

Social Class

In 1771, one thousand German aristocrats received a sample from a British potter. The mailing cost £20 per person (a small fortune in those days) but the craftsman quickly recouped the cost.[52] His foresight to identify consumers in terms of social class demonstrates a person's resources and standing in society are an important way to segment consumers. Yes, the rich are different. Just ask Paris Hilton.

Social class is the overall rank of people in a society. People who are within the same class tend to exhibit similarities in occupation, education and income level, and usually share tastes in clothing, decorating styles, and leisure activities. These people may also share many political and religious beliefs as well as ideas regarding valued activities and goals.

Many marketers design their products and stores to appeal to people in a specific social class.[53] Working-class consumers tend to evaluate products in more utilitarian terms, such as sturdiness or comfort, rather than style or fashion. They are less likely to experiment with new products or styles, such as modern furniture or colored appliances, because they tend to prefer predictability to novelty.[54] Marketers need to understand these differences and develop product and communication strategies that appeal to the different groups.

Luxury goods often serve as **status symbols**, visible markers that provide a way for people to flaunt their membership in higher social classes (or at least to make others believe they are members). The desire to accumulate these "badges of achievement" is evident in the popular saying (and occasional bumper sticker), "He who dies with the most toys wins." One of the latest and most unexpected trends is the growing popularity of expensive designer glasses—even for folks who don't need them. From Michael Kors to Carmen Marc Valvo, models walking the designers' runways are wearing bold, big glasses while print ads for Prada and Gucci feature models in retro-looking frames.[55] LensCrafters, once known only for discounts and quick service, now advertises in *Vogue* with supermodels like Heidi Klum while LensCrafters' stores boast chandeliers, fresh flowers, and full-lengh mirrors to let you check out your entire look with your new glasses.

However, it's important to note that over time, the importance of different status symbols rises and falls. For example, when James Dean starred in the movie *Giant*, the Cadillac convertible was the ultimate status symbol car in America. Today, wealthy consumers who want to let the world know of their success are far more likely to choose a Mercedes, a

Should "consumer vigilantes" who are upset about their experience with a company be able to harass the firm's executives?

☐YES ☐NO

social class
The overall rank or social standing of groups of people within a society according to the value assigned to factors such as family background, education, occupation, and income.

status symbols
Visible markers that provide a way for people to flaunt their membership in higher social classes (or at least to make others believe they are members).

This Spanish beer ad makes a statement about social class.

Hummer, or an Escalade. The "in" car five years from now is anyone's guess—perhaps with today's emphasis on the environment the Prius and other hybrids will emerge as the new status symbols?

In addition, traditional status symbols today are available to a much wider range of consumers around the world with rising incomes (not to mention, widely available credit), so this change is fueling demand for mass-consumed products that still offer some degree of panache or style. Think about the success of companies like Nokia, H&M, Zara, ING, Dell Computers, Gap, Nike, EasyJet, or L'Oréal. They cater to a consumer segment that analysts have labeled **mass-class**, the hundreds of millions of global consumers who now enjoy a level of purchasing power that's sufficient to let them afford high-quality products—except for big-ticket items like college educations, housing, or luxury cars. The mass-class market, for example, has spawned several versions of affordable cars: Latin Americans have their Volkswagen Beetles (affectionately called *el huevito*, the little egg); Indian consumers have their Maruti 800s (selling for as little as U.S.D $4,860). The Fiat Palio, the company's "world car," is aimed at emerging countries such as Brazil, Argentina, India, China, and Turkey. Today Fiat markets the Palio in 40 countries.[56]

Group Membership

Anyone who's ever "gone along with the crowd" knows that people act differently in groups than they do on their own. There are several reasons for this phenomenon. With more people in a group, it becomes less likely that any one member will be singled out for attention, and normal restraints on behavior may evaporate (think about the last wild party you attended). In many cases, group members show a greater willingness to consider riskier alternatives than they would if each member made the decision alone.[57]

Since we consume many of the things we buy in the presence of others, group behaviors are very important to marketers. Sometimes group activities create new business opportunities. Consider, for example, the increasing popularity of tailgating during football games. Long a tradition at some college campuses, now many companies are figuring out that there's as much, if not more, money to be made outside the stadium as on the field. Coleman sells grills designed just for tailgating as part of its RoadTrip line. A catalog called American Tailgater features tailgate flags, tailgate tents, and even a gas-powered margarita blender. Ragu offers tailgating training camps that John Madden hosts, and Jack Daniels sponsors parking-lot contests. The National Football League itself says it sells over $100 million per year of tailgating merchandise, including keg-shaped grills.[58]

Reference Groups: We Aim to Please

A **reference group** is a set of people a consumer wants to please or imitate. Consumers "refer to" these groups in evaluating their own behavior—what they wear, where they go, and what brands they buy. Unlike a larger culture, the "group" can be composed of one person, such as your significant other, or someone you've never met, such as a statesman like Martin Luther King Jr., a star like Gwyneth Paltrow, or a sophisticated man of the world like Austin Powers. The group can be small, such as your immediate family, or it could be a large organization, such as People for the Ethical Treatment of Animals (PETA).

Conformity: The Power of the Crowd

Conformity is at work when a person changes his behavior as a reaction to real or imagined group pressure. For example, a student getting dressed to go to a fraternity rush may choose to wear clothing similar to what he knows the brothers will be wearing so that the group accepts him.

mass-class
The hundreds of millions of global consumers who now enjoy a level of purchasing power that's sufficient to let them afford high-quality products—except for big-ticket items like college educations, housing, or luxury cars.

reference group
An actual or imaginary individual or group that has a significant effect on an individual's evaluations, aspirations, or behavior.

Julie
Cordua

APPLYING Reference Groups

Julie understands that a good deal of (RED)'s acceptance will be driven by the celebrities (like Bono) and other admired people who endorse the organization. ➡

conformity
A change in beliefs or actions as a reaction to real or imagined group pressure.

Home shopping parties, capitalize on group pressures to boost sales for Tupperware and other items. A company representative makes a sales presentation to a group of people who have gathered in the home of a friend or acquaintance. Participants *model* the behavior of others who can provide them with information about how to use certain products, especially because a relatively homogeneous group (for example, neighborhood homemakers) is likely to attend the home party. Pressures to conform may be particularly intense and may escalate as more group members begin to "cave in" (we call this process the *bandwagon effect*). Even though Tupperware has moved into new sales venues, including a Web site (**www.tupperware.com**), the Home Shopping Network, and mall kiosks, it hopes the venerable shopping party remains a popular means of generating sales.

Opinion Leaders

If, like Brandon, you are in the market for a new car, is there someone to whom you'd turn for advice? An **opinion leader** is a person who influences others' attitudes or behaviors because they believe that he possesses expertise about the product.[59] Opinion leaders usually exhibit high levels of interest in the product category and may continuously update their knowledge by reading blogs, talking with salespeople, or subscribing to podcasts about the topic. Because of this involvement, opinion leaders are valuable information sources.

Unlike commercial endorsers, who are paid to represent the interests of just one company, opinion leaders have no ax to grind and can impart both positive and negative information about the product. In addition, these knowledgeable consumers often are among the first to buy new products, so they absorb much of the risk, reducing uncertainty for others who are not as courageous.

opinion leader
A person who is frequently able to influence others' attitudes or behaviors by virtue of his active interest and expertise in one or more product categories.

Gender Roles

Some of the strongest pressures to conform come from our **gender roles**, society's expectations regarding the appropriate attitudes, behaviors, and appearance for men and women.[60] For example, men are far less likely than women to see a doctor regularly, and 25 percent say they would delay seeking help as long as possible. Experts suggest that this may be because our culture teaches boys when they play sports to "ignore pain and not ask for help."[61]

gender roles
Society's expectations regarding the appropriate attitudes, behaviors, and appearance for men and women.

Laura
Sutton

a student at Berry College

My Advice for (RED) would be to choose

1

Option

real people, **Other Voices**

I believe that **option 1** will provide (RED) with the means to generate the most money for the global fund. A common characteristic among successful brands is that they are engaged with their consumers. The (RED) brand should take advantage of this because it has benefits that transcend its initial product. Teens want to connect to the (RED) brand so why would you not give them opportunities to do that? As the world continues to change and this generation of teens puts more emphasis on social justice issues, I think it is important that the marketing world adapt with this change. The business model of (RED) is to, "engage businesses and consumer power in the fight against AIDS in Africa." The most effective way to market your brand would be to engage businesses that would tap into the powers of consumers. Using some smaller businesses to specifically target teens would empower the (RED) brand as well as the teen consumer. A brand cannot successfully be all things to all people and in this specific instance I think it is crucial to do everything you can to tap into your teen market. They are your target audience. Teens today have a tremendous impact in today's culture. They not only influence their family's purchasing decisions, but also each other's. They look to celebrities for advice and once it is obtained they cannot wait for the opportunity to tell their friends their new-found information. Isn't this the perfect way to create buzz for a brand? And from what the research suggests, teens have a genuine desire to help others. If you get teens to buy into and believe in (RED) now then they will be much more likely to remember the brand and its cause in the future. This is important because today's minimum wage teens have the opportunity to one day be millionaire business executives.

Option 1 allows (RED) to stand true to its initial business model while shifting its current focus on a particular niche: the teen market. The long term benefits for (RED) from making this decision far outweigh the short term costs. It is not only building a brand, but also, consumers. ➤

Numerous products take on masculine or feminine attributes, and consumers often associate them with one gender or another.[62] Some new parents even make sure they use blue diapers for boys and pink ones for girls! Marketers play a part in teaching us how society expects us to act as men and women. Marketing communications and products promoted to the two groups portray women and men differently. These influences teach us what the "proper" gender roles of women or men should be and which products are appropriate for each gender.

Some of these "sex-typed" products have come under fire from social groups. For example, feminists have criticized the Barbie doll for reinforcing unrealistic ideas about what women's bodies should look like—even though a newer version of the doll isn't quite as skinny and buxom. Other Barbie protests erupted when Mattel introduced a shopping-themed version called Cool Shoppin' Barbie. The doll comes with all the equipment kids need to pretend Barbie is shopping—including a Barbie-size MasterCard. When a child presses the card into the card scanner, the doll proclaims, "Credit approved!" Although Mattel includes a warning about sticking to a budget, some critics fear the doll sends the wrong message to girls about the desirability of shopping.[63]

Sex roles constantly evolve—in a complex society like ours we often encounter contradictory messages about "appropriate" behavior. We can clearly see this in the messages girls have been getting from the media for the last several years: It's cool to be overly provocative. Role models like Paris Hilton, Lindsay Lohan, Britney Spears, and even Bratz dolls convey standards about how far preteens and teens should go in broadcasting their sexuality. Now, as these messages seem to go over the top (at least in the eyes of some concerned parents), we start to see early signs of a backlash. At the Pure Fashion Web site, girls get style tips including skirts and dresses that fall no more than four fingers above the knee and no tank tops without a sweater or jacket over them. Several other sites such as ModestApparelU.S.A.com advocate a return to styles that leave almost everything to the imagination.[64] Is our culture moving from a celebration of "girls gone wild" to "girls gone mild"?

Men's sex roles are changing too. For one, men are concerned as never before with their appearance. Guys spend $7.7 billion on grooming products globally each year. In Europe, 24 percent of men younger than age 30 use skincare products—and 80 percent of young Korean men do.[65] In fact, no doubt one of the biggest marketing buzzwords over the past few years is the **metrosexual**—a straight, urban male who is keenly interested in fashion, home design, gourmet cooking, and personal care. A gay writer named Mark Simpson actually coined the term way back in a 1994 article when he "outed" British (and now American) soccer star and pop icon David Beckham as a metrosexual. Simpson noted that Beckham is "almost as famous for wearing sarongs and pink nail polish and panties belonging to his wife, Victoria (aka Posh from the Spice Girls), as he is for his impressive ball skills."[66]

Hype aside, how widespread is the metrosexual phenomenon? Clearly, our cultural definition of masculinity is evolving as men try to redefine sex roles while they stay in a "safety zone" of acceptable behaviors bounded by danger zones of sloppiness at one extreme and effeminate behavior at the other. For example, a man may decide that it's OK to use a moisturizer but draw the line at an eye cream that he considers too feminine.[67] And, much like the "girls gone milder" trend we just discussed, some cultural observers report the emergence of "retrosexuals"—men who want to emphasize their old-school masculinity by getting plastic surgery to create a more rugged look that includes hairier chests and beards, squarer chins, and more angular jaw lines.[68]

Miller Genuine Draft recently conducted a survey of American men aged 21 to 34 to try to get a handle on these new definitions so that it can position its brand to appeal to them. The company found that, indeed, many "average Joes" are moving on from the days of drinking whatever beer is available and wearing baseball hats backward, but they also don't want to sacrifice their identities as regular guys. They care more about preparing a good meal, meeting friends for a beer, and owning a home than they do about amassing shoes, savoring fine wine, or dining at expensive restaurants. This new man is discerning when it comes to some important everyday and lifestyle decisions but isn't overly concerned about fitting into cultural molds or trends.[69]

metrosexual
A straight, urban male who is keenly interested in fashion, home design, gourmet cooking, and personal care.

6 Consumer-To-Consumer E-Commerce

OBJECTIVE

Show how the Internet offers consumers opportunities to participate in consumer-to-consumer marketing.

(pp. 159–162)

Consumer-to-consumer (C2C) e-commerce refers to on-line communications and purchases that occur among individuals without directly involving the manufacturer or retailer. eBay, the most famous of the consumer-to-consumer sales sites, provides an opportunity for consumers (and an increasing number of small businesses like those we read about in Chapter 3) to sell everything from collectible comic books to a vintage trombone. In 2005, eBay ranked number 14 in *Fortune*'s 100 Fastest-Growing Tech companies list, had outposts in 23 countries, and had 8,000 employees.[70] Today, eBay has nearly 83.9 million active users worldwide who sell $2,040 worth of goods every second. The most expensive item ever sold on eBay was a private jet for $4.9 million.[71]

Much of C2C e-commerce is far less sensational. It's more about groups of "netizens" around the world with similar interests united through the Internet by a shared passion. These virtual communities meet on-line and share their enthusiasm for a product, recording artist, art form, or celebrity.[72] In fact, over 40 million people worldwide participate in such *virtual communities*. How many consumers actually use these sites? Facebook with over 60 million active users and over 1.7 billion photos on the site gets over 250,000 new users a day.[73] Let's review the most popular on-line C2C formats:[74]

consumer-to-consumer (C2C) e-commerce
Communications and purchases that occur among individuals without directly involving the manufacturer or retailer.

On-line Games

The emergence of gaming as an on-line, shared experience opens new vistas to marketers. Before it released the popular Xbox game *Halo 2*, the company put up a Web site to explain the story line. However, there was a catch: The story was written from the point of view of the Covenant (the aliens who are preparing to attack Earth in the game)—and in *their* language. Within 48 hours, avid gamers around the world worked together by sharing information in gaming chat rooms to crack the code and translate the text. More than 1.5 million people preordered the game before its release.

Sony's Online's *EverQuest* is among the most successful of the new breed of *massively multiplayer on-line games* (MMOG) that allow people to live shadow lives. Many thousands of players worldwide belong to "guilds" in a never-ending journey to slay monsters and earn points. (Another MMOG, *World of Warcraft*, boasts over 10 million players!) *EverQuest* combines the stunning graphics of advanced gaming with the social scene of a chat room. Like *The Sims*, players create a character as a virtual alter ego, which may be a wise elf or a backstabbing rogue. Some players sell powerful characters on eBay for $1,000 or more. In fact, the experience is so addicting that many in the gaming community call the game by its nickname: EverCrack.

Chat Rooms, Rings, Lists, and Boards

These include *Internet relay chat (IRC)*, otherwise known as *chat rooms*. *Rings* are organizations of related home pages, and *lists* are groups of people on a single mailing list who share information. The Japanese have embraced chat rooms as a way to express themselves bluntly in a society that avoids face-to-face confrontation. Channel 2 is Japan's largest Internet bulletin board—a place where disgruntled employees leak information about their companies, journalists include tidbits they cannot get into the mainstream news media, and the average company worker (called a *salaryman*) attacks with ferocity and language unacceptable in

Over 10 million people worldwide play the MMOG *World of Warcraft*.

daily life. It is also the place where gays come out in a society in which they mostly remain in the closet. *Ni-channeru*, as the Japanese call it, has become part of Japan's everyday culture. *Boards* are on-line communities organized around interest-specific electronic bulletin boards. Active members read and post messages sorted by date and subject. There are boards devoted to musical groups, movies, wine, cigars, cars, comic strips, even fast-food restaurants.

Social Networks

social network services
On-line applications that use software to build on-line communities of people who share interests and activities.

Checked your Facebook page yet today? Odds are you did before you cracked open this book! **Social network services** like Facebook or MySpace use software to build on-line communities of people who share interests and activities. Most of them offer various ways for users to interact, such as chat, messaging, e-mail, and video-sharing.

Wikipedia lists over 100 "notable" social networking Web sites including those in Table 5.1. The most popular types of social networks contain directories of some categories (such as former classmates of a certain university) and the means to connect with friends. Social networks can create or increase a feeling of group or social identity among members. Many allow members to upload pictures of themselves and share videos with their on-line "friends." The more popular general social networks are free to participants and gain revenues through on-line advertising.

Social networks are fun, useful, and even liberating—but they also can be dangerous. Members need to avoid giving out too much information that may attract sexual predators. There is also the less scary but equally real danger that pictures or videos uploaded by an individual or his "friends" may prove an embarrassment. For example, police, university officials, and prospective employers are increasingly searching sites such as Facebook and MySpace to gather information on individuals of interest. You might want to keep that photo of you from the party last Saturday night in a photo album instead.

As we saw in Chapter 1, social networking is changing the way companies decide what products to offer and how to make them available as new business models emerge from "the power of crowds." Here are some more crowd-based sites to watch:

- At the French CrowdSpirit.com site, participants submit ideas for consumer electronics products and the community votes for the best ones. Those go to the site's R&D partners and investors who then decide which to finance for further development. Community

Table 5.1 | Some Popular Social Networks

Name	Description/Focus	Number of Registered Users
Bebo	General, popular in the U.K., Ireland, New Zealand, and the Pacific Islands	40,000,000
Broadcaster.com	Video sharing and webcam chat	26,000,000
Car Domain	Car enthusiasts	1,600,000
Care2	Green living and social activism	8,123,058
Classmates.com	School, college, work and military	40,000,000
Facebook	General, popular in Canada, U.K., U.S.A., and New Zealand	62,000,000
Flickr	Photo sharing	4,000,000
Flixster	Movies	36,000,000
Friendster	General, popular in Southeast Asia	50,000,000
hi5	General, Latin American, and Asian teens	98,000,000
iLike	Music, video, photos, blogs	25,000,000
MySpace	General, popular worldwide	300,000,000
orkut	Owned by Google, popular in Brazil and India	67,000,000
Windows Live Spaces	Blogging (formerly MSN Spaces)	40,000,000

Source: Adapted from Wikipedia, "List of Social Networking Websites," **http://en.wikipedia.org/wiki/List_of_social_networking_websites** (accessed, 2008).

members test and fine-tune a prototype and then they can buy the products that go to market. The community handles product support and recommends the new products to retailers.[75]

- Sermo.com is a social network for physicians. It has no advertising, job listings, or membership fees. It makes its money (about $500,000 a year so far) by charging institutional investors for the opportunity to listen in as approximately 15,000 doctors chat among themselves. Say, for example, a young patient breaks out in hives after taking a new prescription. A doctor might post whether he thinks this is because of a rare symptom or perhaps the drug's side-effect. If other doctors feel it's the latter, this negative news could affect the drug manufacturer's stock, so their opinions have value to analysts. Doctors who ask or answer a question that paying observers deem especially valuable receive bonuses of $5 to $25 per post.[76]

- How about social networking sites that "create" a concert by persuading an artist to perform in a certain city or country? At Eventful.com, fans can *demand* events and performances in their town and spread the word to make them happen. Or how about actually buying a piece of the bands you like? Go to SellaBand.com where fans ("believers") buy "parts" in a band for $10 per share. Once the band sells 5,000 parts, SellaBand arranges a professional recording, including top studios, A&R (Artists & Repertoire managers, or industry talent scouts), and producers. Believers receive a limited edition CD of the recording. They also get a piece of the profits, so they're likely to promote the band wherever they can.

- Individual consumers gain crowd clout by *shopmobbing* with strangers. So far this is most popular in China where the *tuangou* ("team purchase") phenomenon involves strangers organizing themselves around a specific product or service. Members who meet on-line at sites such as TeamBuy.com, Taobao.com, and Liba.com arrange to meet at a certain date and time in a real-world store and literally mob the unsuspecting retailer—the bargain-hungry crowd negotiates a group discount on the spot.[77]

On-line Brand Communities

A **brand community** is a group of consumers who share a set of social relationships based upon usage or interest in a product. Unlike other kinds of communities, these members typically don't live near each other. The notion of a **consumer tribe** is similar to a brand community; it is a group of people who share a lifestyle and who identify with each other because of a shared allegiance to an activity or a product. Although these tribes are often unstable and short-lived, at least for a time members identify with others through shared emotions, moral beliefs, styles of life, and of course the products they jointly consume as part of their tribal affiliation. Some companies, especially those that are

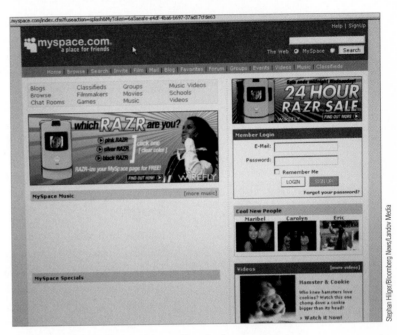

MySpace is one of several key social networking sites for young consumers.

brand community

A group of consumers who share a set of social relationships based upon usage or interest in a product.

At Eventful.com, fans create demand for performances where they live.

consumer tribe
A group of people who share a lifestyle and who can identify with each other because of a shared allegiance to an activity or a product.

more youth-oriented, use a *tribal marketing strategy* that links their product to, say, a group of shredders. However, there also are plenty of tribes with older members, such as car enthusiasts who gather to celebrate such cult products (the Citroën in Europe and the Ford Mustang in the United States), or "foodies" who share their passion for cooking with other Wolfgang Puck wannabees around the world.[78] Pontiac opened a community hub on Yahoo! it calls Pontiac Underground (**www.pontiacunderground.com**), "Where Passion for Pontiac Is Driven By You." The carmaker does no overt marketing on the site; the idea is to let drivers find it and spread the word themselves. Users share photos and videos of cars using Flickr and Yahoo! Video and a Yahoo! Answers zone enables knowledge sharing. Meanwhile, a list of Pontiac clubs in the physical world and on Yahoo! Groups allows users to connect off-line and on-line.[79]

Blogs

blog
On-line personal journals similar to Web pages, but a different technology lets people upload a few sentences without going through the more elaborate process of updating a Web site.

Another form of on-line community is the weblog, or **blog**. These on-line personal journals are building an avid following among Internet users who like to dash off a few random thoughts, post them on a Web site, and read similar musings by others. Although these sites are similar to Web pages offered by Geocities and other free services, blogs use a different technology that lets people upload a few sentences without going through the process of updating a Web site built with conventional home page software. Bloggers can fire off thoughts on a whim, click a button, and quickly have them appear on a site. Weblogs frequently look like on-line diaries, with brief musings about the days' events, and perhaps a link or two of interest. This burgeoning *Blogosphere* (the universe of active Weblogs) is indeed a force to be reckoned with. One survey found that blog readership is increasing dramatically—despite the fact that 62 percent of adult American Internet users still don't know what a blog is, researchers estimate that over 32 million Americans are blog readers.

Now that you've learned about consumer behavior, read "Real People, Real Choices: How It Worked Out" to see which strategy Julie selected to promote the (RED) brand.

---

real people, **Real Choices**

Julie
Cordua

Julie chose:

1

Option

How It Worked Out at (RED)

Julie chose Option #1. (RED) continued to seek out major international brands to partner with, but it is now complementing those partnerships with smaller special editions that appeal to a younger age group. The company decided that this expansion of its business model is necessary to keep (RED) fresh and relevant in the consumer marketplace. Teens are clearly the emerging consumer group that will drive (RED)'s success in the future. One of the first examples of this strategy is the release of a (PRODUCT) RED skateboard in the spring of 2008. (RED) is also looking at adding other action sports products and teen-focused fashion brands to the collection.

How (RED) Measures Success

(RED) implemented a brand-tracking study that will allow the organization to measure awareness, consideration, preference, and brand momentum with its key consumer targets over time. Through this study Julie can determine whether or not (RED)'s investment in key consumer groups via new partnerships and

marketing programs is paying off. Are they more aware of (RED)? Do they prefer (RED) products over non-(RED) products? Are they more likely to choose brands that join (RED)? If (RED) is able to move the needle on these measures, this feedback will give Julie powerful ammunition when she pitches the idea to brands that haven't yet signed up for the program.

(GIRL) RED COLLABORATION, a limited edition skateboard with a portion of profits benefiting the Global Fund.

Refer back to **page 133** for Julies story ➡

Brand **YOU**!

Why are you in college? To get a good job, of course. But how do you know what job is best for you? And how can you increase your chances of getting that perfect job? Think of yourself as the product and prospective employers as customers who might eventually "buy" you. Then you see that you need to understand each customer, how he makes the decision to hire someone, and what criteria he uses to evaluate future employees. So, you have to ask yourself, which customer needs can you satisfy best—where will you find the best fit? Take a look into Chapter 5 of the *Brand You* supplement to learn how to identify what employers want and how to decide which is your top choice.

Objective Summary ➡ Key Terms ➡ Apply

CHAPTER 5
Study Map

1. Objective Summary (pp. 134–136)

Define *consumer behavior* and explain why consumers buy what they do.

Consumer behavior is the process individuals or groups go through to select, purchase, use, and dispose of goods, services, ideas, or experiences to satisfy their needs and desires. Consumer decisions differ greatly, ranging from habitual, repeat (low-involvement) purchases to complex, extended problem-solving activities for important, risky (high-involvement) purchases.

Key Terms

consumer behavior, p. 134 (Figure 5.1, p. 135)
involvement, p. 135 (Figure 5.2, p. 136)
perceived risk, p. 135 (Figure 5.2, p. 136)

2. Objective Summary (pp. 136–141)

Describe the prepurchase, purchase, and postpurchase activities in which consumers engage when they buy a product or service.

When consumers make important purchases, they go through a series of five steps. First, they recognize there is a problem to be solved. Then they search for information to make the best decision. Next they evaluate a set of alternatives and judge them on the basis of various evaluative criteria. At this point, they are ready to make their purchasing decision. Following the purchase, consumers decide whether the product matched their expectations.

Key Terms

problem recognition p. 136, (Figure 5.1, p. 135 & 5.3, p. 137)
information search, p.136 (Figure 5.1, p. 135, & 5.3, p. 137)
behavioral targeting, p. 138
evaluative criteria, p. 139 (Figure 5.1, p. 135, & 5.3, p. 137)
heuristics, p. 139

brand loyalty, p. 139
consumer satisfaction/dissatisfaction, p. 140 (Figure 5.1, p. 135 & 5.3, p. 137)
cognitive dissonance, p. 141

3. Objective Summary (pp. 142–149)

Explain how internal factors influence consumers' decision-making processes.

Several internal factors influence consumer decisions. Perception is how consumers select, organize, and interpret stimuli. Motivation is an internal state that drives consumers to satisfy needs. Learning is a change in behavior that results from information or experience. Behavioral learning results from external events, while cognitive learning refers to internal mental activity. An attitude is a lasting evaluation of a person, object, or issue and includes three components: affect, cognition, and behavior. Personality traits such as innovativeness, materialism, self-confidence, sociability, and the need for cognition may be used to develop market segments. Marketers seek to understand a consumer's self-concept in order to develop product attributes that match some aspect of the consumer's self-concept.

The age of consumers, family life cycle, and their lifestyle also are strongly related to consumption preferences. Marketers may use psychographics to group people according to activities, interests, and opinions that may explain reasons for purchasing products.

Key Terms

perception, p. 142
exposure, p. 142
subliminal advertising, p. 142
attention, p. 143
interpretation, p. 143
motivation, p. 143
hierarchy of needs, p. 144 (Figure 5.5, p. 144)

learning, p. 144

behavioral learning theories, p. 144

classical conditioning, p. 144

operant conditioning, p. 145

stimulus generalization, p. 145

cognitive learning theory, p. 145

observational learning, p. 145

attitude, p. 145

affect, p. 145

cognition, p. 146

behavior, p. 146

personality, p. 146

self-concept, p. 147

family life cycle, p. 148

lifestyle, p. 148

psychographics, p. 149

4. Objective Summary (pp. 149–150)

Show how situational factors at the time and place of purchase influence consumer behavior.

Situational influences include our physical surroundings and time pressures. Dimensions of the physical environment including decor, smells, lighting, music, and even temperature can influence consumption. The time of day, the season of the year, and how much time one has to make a purchase also affect decision making.

5. Objective Summary (pp. 151–158)

Explain how consumers' relationships with other people, including such trends as consumerism and environmentalism, influence their decision-making processes.

Consumers' overall preferences for products are determined by the culture in which they live and their membership in different subcultures. Consumerism is a social movment directed toward protecting consumers from harmful business practices. A response to consumerism was President John F. Kennedy's Consumer Bill of Rights. Environmentalism, another social movement, seeks ways to protect the natural environment. Firms practice environmental stewardship when they make decisions that protect the environment. Green marketing strategies include earth-friendly packaging and product designs. Social class, group memberships, and opinion leaders are other types of social influences that affect consumer choices. A reference group is a set of people a consumer wants to please or imitate, and this affects the consumer's purchasing decisions. Purchases also often result from conformity to

real or imagined group pressures. Another way social influence is felt is in the expectations of society regarding the proper roles for men and women. Such expectations have led to many gender-typed products.

Key Terms

culture, p. 151

subculture, p. 152

consumerism, p. 153 (Ethical Decisions in the Real World, p. 155)

environmentalism, p. 153

Kyoto Protocol, p. 153

environmental stewardship, p. 154

green marketing, p. 154

greenwashing, p. 154

social class, p. 155

status symbols, p. 155

mass-class, p. 156

reference group, p. 156

conformity, p. 156

opinion leader, p. 157

gender roles, p. 157

metrosexual, p. 158

6. Objective Summary (pp. 159–162)

Show how the Internet offers consumers opportunities to participate in consumer-to-consumer marketing.

Consumer-to-consumer (C2C) e-commerce includes on-line marketing communication and purchases between individuals. C2C activities include virtual communities that allow consumers to do things such as share their enthusiasm or dislike for a product or company. Virtual communities and other C2C e-commerce activities provide both a source of information about the market and about competitors for marketers and an opportunity to communicate effectively with consumers. Some of the more popular C2C formats are gaming, chat rooms, rings, lists, boards, social networks on-line brand communities, consumer tribes, and blogs.

Key Terms

consumer-to-consumer (C2C) e-commerce, p. 159

social network services, p. 160 (Table 5.1, p. 160)

brand community, p. 161 (Table 5.1, p. 160)

consumer tribe, p. 161 (Table 5.1, p. 160)

blog, p. 162 (Table 5.1, p. 160)

Chapter **Questions** and **Activities**

Concepts: Test Your Knowledge

1. What is consumer behavior? Why is it important for marketers to understand consumer behavior?

2. Explain habitual decision making, limited problem solving, and extended problem solving. What is the role of perceived risk in the decision process?

3. What are the steps in the consumer decision-making process?

4. What is perception? Explain the three parts of the perception process: exposure, attention, and interpretation. For marketers, what are the implications of each of these components?

5. What is motivation? What is the role of motivation in consumer behavior?

6. What is behavioral learning? What is cognitive learning? How is an understanding of behavioral and cognitive learning useful to marketers?

7. What are the three components of attitudes? What is personality? What are some personality traits that may influence consumer behavior?

8. Explain what lifestyle means. What is the significance of family life cycle and lifestyle in understanding consumer behavior and purchasing decisions?

9. How do culture and subculture influence consumer behavior? What is the significance of social class to marketers?

10. What are reference groups, and how do they influence consumers? What are opinion leaders?

11. What are gender roles? How do metrosexuals differ from other male consumers?

12. What is consumerism? What is environmentalism? How do firms respond to these social movements?

13. What is consumer-to-consumer (C2C) e-commerce? What are social networks, gaming, chat rooms, boards, and blogs and how are they related to consumer behavior? What are on-line brand communities and consumer tribes?

Choices and Ethical Issues: You Decide

1. Demographic or cultural trends are important to marketers. What are some current trends that may affect the marketing of the following products?
   a. Housing
   b. Food
   c. Education
   d. Clothing
   e. Travel and tourism
   f. Automobiles

2. What are the core values of your culture? How do these core values affect your behavior as a consumer? Are they collectivist or individualistic? What are the implications for marketers?

3. Consumers often buy products because they feel pressure from reference groups to conform. Does conformity exert a positive or a negative influence on consumers? With what types of products is conformity more likely to occur?

4. Millions of Americans and consumers around the globe use C2C e-commerce to supplement their incomes or as their primary source of income. What do you think of the future of sites such as eBay? What opportunities does eBay provide for twenty-first-century entrepreneurs?

5. Most university students are members of social networks such as YouTube and Facebook. What are some of the pros and cons of belonging to one of these communities? Should students like yourself be cautious about joining on-line communities?

6. Retailers often place impulse purchase items such as magazines and candy bars near the entrance to the store or near the checkout area. How would you describe the decision process for these products? Why are these locations effective?

7. In different cultures, perceptions about the proper roles for men and women, that is, gender roles, can vary greatly. What are some ways you think gender roles may differ in the following countries, and what are the implications for global marketers?
   a. France
   b. Bahrain
   c. Japan
   d. Canada

8. We noted in this chapter that consumers often use country-of-origin as a heuristic to judge a product. Sometimes this tendency can backfire: While one study found that around the world, "the Golden Arches are now more widely recognized than the Christian cross," the strong link between McDonald's and the United States has been a liability for the food chain in recent years. As antiwar protests in many countries give vent to raw anti-American sentiment, the familiarity of McDonald's has made it a widespread target. In Quito, Ecuador, protesters burned a Ronald McDonald statue. In Paris, demonstrators smashed a McDonald's restaurant window. South Korean activists calling for an end to the war sought attention by

scaling a McDonald's sign. Other McDonald's outlets in Karachi and in Buenos Aires have been ringed with police officers to stave off trouble. Should a company that takes credit for its association with its country-of-origin in good times have to take its lumps in bad times? What steps can marketers take to avoid these problems?[80]

9. Behavioral targeting involves tracking where people go on-line and then feeding them advertising information that's related to what they're looking for. While proponents of this approach argue that it's a very efficient and convenient way for people to conduct information-search, others who are concerned about a potential invasion of privacy aren't so enthusiastic. What's your opinion? Do you mind having marketers know what sites you visit in return for having a better sense of the competing products available while you're searching?

10. The United States has refused to sign the Kyoto Protocol because it says the protocol does not do enough to protect the environment. It specifically objects to the exemption of China as a developing country from the emissions requirements. Do you think the United States is right in not signing the protocol? Explain why you agree or disagree with U.S. policy.

11. Social networks such as Facebook and MySpace provide a means for consumers, especially young people, to communicate with friends and others with similar interests. Still there are concerns about privacy for social network users. Should consumers feel comfortable using social networks? Are there some things they should do or not do to protect themselves when they participate in social networks?

Practice: Apply What You've Learned

1. Assume that you are the vice president of marketing for an automaker. You know that internal factors such as perception, motivation, learning, attitudes, and personality influence consumers' decision making. Develop a report that describes these internal factors, why each is important in the purchase of an automobile, and how you might use these factors in developing marketing strategies for your firm.

2. This chapter indicated that consumers go through a series of steps (from problem recognition to postpurchase evaluation) as they make purchases. Write a detailed report describing what you would do in each of these steps when deciding to purchase one of the following products:
   a. An iPhone or similar device
   b. A university
   c. A fast-food lunch

3. Using one of the products in question 2, what can marketers do to make sure that consumers going through each step in the consumer decision process move toward the purchase of their brand? (*Hint:* Think about product,

place, price, and promotion strategies.)

4. Sometimes advertising or other marketing activities cause problem recognition by showing consumers how much better off they would be with a new product or by pointing out problems with products they already own. For the following product categories, what are some ways marketers might try to stimulate problem recognition?
   a. Life insurance
   b. Mouthwash
   c. A new automobile
   d. A health club membership

5. Assume that you are a marketing manager for a major hotel chain with outlets in major tourism sites around the world. You are concerned about the effects of current consumer trends, including changing ethnic populations, changing roles of men and women, increased concern for time and for the environment, and decreased emphasis on status goods. Others in your firm do not understand or care about these changes. They believe that the firm should continue to do business just as it always has. Develop a role-playing exercise with a classmate to discuss these two different points of view for your class. Each of you should be sure to include the importance of each of these trends to your firm and offer suggestions for marketing strategies to address these trends.

Miniproject: Learn by Doing

The purpose of this miniproject is to increase your understanding of the roles of personal, social, and situational factors in consumer behavior.

1. With several other members of your class, select one of the following product categories (or some other product of your choice):
   • Hairstyling
   • Large appliances, such as refrigerators or washing machines
   • A restaurant
   • Banking
   • Fine jewelry

2. Visit three stores or locations where the product may be purchased. (Try to select three that are very different from each other.) Observe and make notes on all the elements of each retail environment.

3. At each of the three locations, observe people purchasing the product. Make notes about their characteristics (e.g., age, race, gender, and so on), their social class, and their actions in the store in relation to the product.

4. Prepare a report for your class describing the situational variables and individual consumer differences between the three stores and how they relate to the purchase of the product. Present your findings to your class.

Real people, **real surfers**: explore the web

Visit two or three virtual communities such as the ones listed in this chapter's discussion of C2C e-commerce. Based on your experience, answer the following questions for each site you visit:

1. What is the overall reason for the site's existence?

2. What is your overall opinion of the site?
3. What type of consumer do you think would be attracted to the site?
4. How easy or difficult is it to navigate each site?

Marketing Plan Exercise

An important key to success for marketers is understanding consumers and how they go about selecting the products they buy. Pick a product (either a good or a service) that you like and perhaps have purchased in the past. As part of developing a marketing plan for this product, do the following:

1. Make a list of the many things you need to know about consumers of your product and how they make product decisions so you can develop successful marketing strategies.

2. What are some ways you might go about gathering that information?

3. How could you use that information in developing successful marketing strategies?

Marketing in Action Case

Real Choices at Lexus

In 1983 at a top-secret meeting, Toyota chairman Eiji Toyoda suggested that the time was right for Toyota to introduce a true luxury automobile that would challenge the best luxury vehicles in the world. A 6-year development process followed that involved 60 designers and 450 prototypes at a cost of over $1 billion. In 1989 the Lexus was launched. In 1999, Lexus sold its millionth car in the United States and within a little over a decade, Lexus became America's best selling line of luxury vehicles. Following its success in the United States, Toyota introduced the Lexus in markets outside America, and today the luxury cars are available in over 40 different countries. Since its introduction, the Lexus has repeatedly won top awards and accolades for customer satisfaction, dependability, appeal, design, and engineering from the Motoring Press Association, J.D. Power and Associates studies, *The Robb Report*, *Popular Science*, *Car and Driver*, *Popular Mechanics*, *Automobile Magazine*, and *Motor Trend*.

Why has Lexus been such a success? According to North America President and CEO Atsushi Niimi, "Lexus is a success story because there is no compromise in its manufacture, as it always reflects the voice of the customer." Toyota President Ray Tanguay noted that "Manufacturing Lexus demands a deep understanding of what customers want, expect and deserve in a luxury vehicle. We call it the relentless pursuit of perfection."

How did Toyota listen to the voices of its consumers? As early as 1985 while the Lexus was only a concept, Toyota sent a study team to the United States to conduct focus groups with potential customers. More recently, Lexus Great Britain introduced a unique program that helps Lexus consultants better understand customers by giving them a taste of luxury. Staff from Lexus centers are pampered at top-class hotels in order to experience for themselves the kind of quality and service their customers expect. In another program, Lexus GB gets feedback from actual customers. Thousands of U.K. Lexus owners are invited to spend the day at luxury spa hotels to share their opinions on where Lexus is succeeding and where it could be better, all while enjoying the spa facilities.

Such attention to providing the best for luxury car owners has led to Lexus's latest innovation: the Advanced Parking Guidance System. Most consumers find parallel parking a real pain, or worse, they simply avoid parallel parking spaces altogether. Enter the 2007 Lexus LS 460 sedan. The car actually parks itself—or almost. In theory, a driver only need pull up ahead of the empty parking space, make a few minor adjustments on a computer screen, and lift his foot off the brake. As the car backs up, the steering wheel turns as needed and, "voila," the car is in the space, just where you want it to be. Of course the LS isn't perfect. It must have a parking space considerably (about six feet) longer than the car so it isn't useful in those tight city spots. And the system won't work on downward inclines—only on level ground where it can move at a "creeping" speed. As you might expect, the price of the Lexus with the Advanced Parking Guidance System is over $70,000—not a price tag to be taken lightly.

The question many observers ask is whether the parking capability of the Lexus is truly a benefit luxury car owners want and will use—or is it just a gimmick? And, were customers really asking for this feature? Some argue that the Lexus automatic parking capability isn't really useful and that Lexus should have waited to introduce the feature until the company had worked out all the kinks in the system. Has Lexus stepped away from its focus on customer needs and if so, what should the company do now?

You Make the Call

1. What is the decision facing Lexus?
2. What factors are important in understanding this decision situation?
3. What are the alternatives?
4. What decision(s) do you recommend?
5. What are some ways to implement your recommendation?

Based on: "Lexus History," Conceptcarz.com, **http://www.conceptcarz.com/view/makehistory/94,0/Lexus_History.aspx**(accessed March 15, 2008); "Lexus Luxury Lifestyle Training," Carpages, **http://www.carpages.co.uk/lexus/lexus-lifestyle-12-11-05.asp** (accessed March 10, 2008) ; Trevor Hoffman, "First Luxury Lexus Built Outside Japan Rolls off the Line in Cambridge, Ontario," October 1, 2003, Automobile.com, **http://car-reviews.automobile.com/news/worlds-first-lexus-built-outside-of-japan-rolls-off-canadian-line/ 456/** (accessed March 15, 2008); "Lexus," Wikipedia, **http://wikipedia.org/wiki/Lexus**

Business-to-Business Markets: How and Why Organizations Buy

NCR

Brad
Tracy
Profile ▼

A Decision Maker at NCR Corporation

Brad Tracy is VP of Americas Marketing Deployment for NCR Corporation, headquartered in Dayton, Ohio. In this role, Brad has the responsibility for developing and deploying NCR marketing programs for NCR's full portfolio of products throughout the Americas region (that is, North and South America). This includes solutions and best practices for the retail, financial, hospitality, health care, and travel industries. He joined NCR in 1988 as a retail sales representative in Portland, Oregon. His experience includes positions in sales, product management, product marketing, and industry marketing. Prior to his current assignment, he led the Global Marketing team for NCR's retail solutions division, responsible for all aspects of marketing for NCR retail products. Brad holds a bachelor of science degree in business administration from the University of Oregon.

▼ Q & A with Brad Tracy

Q) What I do when I'm not working?
A) I enjoy golf, coaching soccer, and traveling.

Q) First job out of school?
A) NCR sales rep right after college.

Q) My motto to live by?
A) Passion, integrity, and effort.

Q) What drives me?
A) A sense of accomplishment and the belief in what I do and the impact it can have on our customers.

Q) My management style?
A) I am very transparent and direct.

Q) Don't do this when interviewing with me?
A) Come unprepared.

Q) My pet peeve?
A) People who don't assume accountability for their results.

real people, **Real Choices**

Decision Time **at NCR**

NCR had just released a new generation Point of Sale Workstation (POS) that was ahead of the competition by almost a year. The POS workstation is the computer that drives the retail checkout process. It is responsible for accepting input from the scanners and other peripherals, pricing the merchandise, offering discounts, calculating tax, and finalizing the transaction via cash, credit, debit, or other financial instrument. The official launch occurred in January at a major trade show. This launch was to be followed up by other industry shows and events, webinars, and advertising. As Brad and his colleagues planned these events there was a question about NCR's participation in a particular trade show because this would entail a significant amount of resources. The company had sent representatives to the event for many years, and many of its customers regularly participated in the show. While it had traditionally been a great venue for meeting with key clients and marketing NCR's newest solutions, in recent years attendance had been waning and other competing shows had grown in popularity. Suffering from this downturn in attendance and increased competition, the event had decided to combine with another event to boost the number of attendees. This combination involved moving the venue from its traditional location and renaming the combined show.

> **Things to Remember:**
>
> Especially in B2B contexts, trade shows are a major element in a firm's marketing mix. Show attendees gather a lot of information about competing products as they contemplate purchases, but they also use these venues as an opportunity to connect personally with company representatives.

With a superior solution to promote and a legacy of attending the show, the retail division's sales managers made an impassioned case for NCR's continued participation. They felt that this venue would be their last chance to demonstrate the new workstation before the competition responded with its own next-generation product. NCR would miss a golden opportunity to capitalize on its market leadership. In the end, the discussions became quite political as these managers argued their case. The discussion was extremely difficult as a number of key sales leaders were pushing to attend while Brad felt it would be best to skip the show.

Complicating this situation, NCR's retail division (the organization responsible for developing and selling solutions to retailers) had "shared" a booth with another division in prior years. Despite being told of the retail division's concerns, the other division proceeded on the assumption that retail would again participate and fund a significant portion of the event. As the event drew closer, this group pushed hard to force the retail division to continue to fund the event.

Brad considered his Options 1·2·3

1 Option **Attend the show as in past years.** This would allow Brad's division to reinforce the product launch and further solidify its market leadership while the competition again showed an outdated product. But attending the show would consume limited sales and marketing resources. The *cost per touch* (that is, the number of potential clients the team could talk to at the show divided by the total cost of exhibiting at the show) would increase as the number of people attending the show declined.

2 Option **Skip the show this year and reallocate sales and marketing resources to one or more of the other alternatives for marketing the new workstation.** The freed-up budget would allow NCR to attend two smaller but more targeted events in which the company had not previously participated. Because these events are highly targeted and have more of a conference format they tend to be more intimate, and NCR's representatives could spend more quality time with retail clients. However, while costs for these smaller shows would be lower, since NCR hadn't been to these shows before Brad didn't know what kinds of opportunities to interact with customers would actually occur so it was hard to predict the cost per touch.

3 Option **Forego the show this year and find out whether the changes in venue and sponsorship would really diminish the value of the event.** If it turned out that the newly combined show continued to draw enough attendees, NCR could participate the following year. Sitting it out would let the retail division conserve its limited marketing resources. On the other hand, NCR would miss the window to further exploit its market leadership by showcasing its new POS product. And, if Brad decided not to attend, the division would lose its position in the booth selection process. This loss of "seniority" could mean a poor position on the show floor in subsequent years, which would result in decreased foot traffic if NCR's booth was in an out-of-the-way location.

Now, put yourself in Brad's shoes: Which option would you choose, and why?

You Choose

Which **Option** would you choose, and **why**?
1. ☐YES ☐NO   2. ☐YES ☐NO   3. ☐YES ☐NO

See what **option** Brad chose and its success on **page 190** ➡

Check out chapter 6 **Study Map** on page 191

1

OBJECTIVE

Define business-to-business markets.
(pp. 170–171)

Business Markets:
Buying and Selling When Stakes Are High

You might think most marketers spend their days dreaming up the best way to promote cutting-edge Web browsers or funky shoes. This is not so. Many marketers know that the "real action" also lies in point-of-sale products like those NCR sells, or in safety shoes, group medical insurance, meat lockers, or home construction products that other companies sell to businesses and organizations. In fact, some of the most interesting and lucrative jobs for young marketers are in industries you've never heard of because these businesses don't deal directly with consumers.

Like an end consumer, a business buyer makes decisions—but with an important difference: The purchase may be worth millions of dollars, and both the buyer and the seller have a lot at stake (maybe even their jobs). A consumer may decide to buy two or three T-shirts at one time, each emblazoned with a different design. *Fortune* 500 companies such as Exxon, Pepsi-Cola, and FedEx buy hundreds, even thousands, of employee uniforms embroidered with their corporate logos in a single order.

Consider these transactions: Dell makes computer network servers to sell to its business customers. Procter & Gamble contracts with several advertising agencies to promote its brands at home and around the globe. The Metropolitan Opera buys costumes, sets, and programs. Mac's Diner buys a case of canned peas from BJ's Wholesale Club. The U.S. government places an order for 3,000 new HP laser printers.

All the following exchanges have one thing in common: they're part of **business-to-business marketing**. This is the marketing of goods and services that businesses and other organizations buy for purposes other than personal consumption. Some firms resell these goods and services, so they are part of a *channel of distribution*, something we will discuss more in Chapters 15 and 16. Other firms use the goods and services they buy to produce still other goods and services that meet the needs of their customers or to support their own operations. These **business-to-business markets**—also called **organizational markets**—include manufacturers, wholesalers, retailers, and a variety of other organizations, such as hospitals, universities, and governmental agencies.

To put the size and complexity of business markets into perspective, let's consider a single product—a pair of jeans. A consumer may browse through several racks of jeans and ultimately purchase a single pair, but the buyer who works for the store at which the consumer shops had to purchase many pairs of jeans in different sizes, styles, and brands from different manufacturers. Each of these manufacturers purchases fabrics, zippers, buttons, and thread from other manufacturers, which in turn purchase the raw materials to make these components. In addition, all the firms in this chain need to purchase equipment, electricity, labor, computer systems, legal and accounting services, insurance, office supplies, packing materials, and countless other goods and services. So, even a single purchase of a pair of True Religion jeans is the culmination of a series of buying and selling activities among many organizations—many people have been keeping busy while you're out shopping!

In this chapter, we'll look at the big picture of the business marketplace, a world in which the fortunes of business buyers and sellers can hang in the balance of a single transaction. Then we'll examine how marketers categorize businesses and other organizations to develop effective business marketing strategies. We'll look at business buying behavior and the business buying decision process. Finally, we'll talk about the important world of business-to-business e-commerce.

business-to-business marketing
The marketing of goods and services that business and organizational customers need to produce other goods and services for resale or to support their operations.

business-to-business markets
The group of customers that include manufacturers, wholesalers, retailers, and other organizations.

organizational markets
Another name for business-to-business markets.

2

OBJECTIVE

Describe the characteristics that make business-to-business markets different from business-to-consumer markets.

(pp. 171–173)

Factors That Make a Difference in Business Markets

In theory, the same basic marketing principles should hold true in both consumer and business markets—firms identify customer needs and develop a marketing mix to satisfy those needs. For example, take the company that made the desks and chairs in your classroom. Just like a firm that markets consumer goods, the classroom furniture company first must create an important competitive advantage for its target market of universities. Next the firm develops a marketing mix strategy beginning with a product— classroom furniture that will withstand years of use by thousands of students while it provides a level of comfort that a good learning environment requires (and you thought those hardback chairs were intended just to keep you awake during class). The firm must offer the furniture at prices that universities will pay and that will allow the firm to make a reasonable profit. Then the firm must develop a sales force or other marketing communication strategy to make sure your university (and hundreds of others) considers—and hopefully chooses—its products when it furnishes classrooms.

Although marketing to business customers does have a lot in common with consumer marketing, there are differences that make this basic process more complex.[1] Figure 6.1 provides a quick look at some of these differences. Let's review several of them now.

Multiple Buyers

In business markets, products often have to do more than satisfy an individual's needs. They must meet the requirements of everyone involved in the company's purchase decision. If you decide to buy a new chair for your room or apartment, you're the only one who has to be satisfied. For your classroom, the furniture must satisfy not only students but also faculty, administrators, campus planners, and the people at your school who actually do the purchasing. If your school is a state or other governmental institution, the furniture may also have to meet certain government-mandated engineering standards.

TOSHIBA
Don't copy. Lead.

THEY CAN RUN
But they can't hide.

Printers. Everyone has them. But did you know they could be secretly stealing from your bottom line? Toshiba's Encompass™ helps you uncover hidden costs, identifies inefficiencies and gives you the tools and strategies you need to put an end to the stealing. To learn more go to endthestealing.com

© Toshiba America Business Solutions, Inc.

Companies that sell strictly functional products like copiers still can be creative when they advertise to business customers.

Figure 6.1 | Differences between Organizational and Consumer Markets

There are a number of major and minor differences between organizational and consumer markets. To be successful, marketers must understand these differences and develop strategies that can be effective with organizational customers.

Organizational Markets	Consumer Markets
• Purchases made for some purpose other than personal consumption • Purchases made by someone other than the user of the product • Decisions frequently made by several people • Purchases made according to precise technical specifications based on product expertise • Purchases made after careful weighing of alternatives • Purchases based on rational criteria • Purchasers often engage in lengthy decision processes • Interdependencies between buyers and sellers; long-term relationships • Purchases may involve competitive bidding, price negotiations, and complex financial arrangements • Products frequently purchased directly from producer • Purchases frequently involve high risk and high cost • Limited number of large buyers • Buyers often geographically concentrated in certain areas • Products often complex; classified based on how organizational customers use them • Demand derived from demand for other goods and services, generally inelastic in the short run, subject to fluctuations, and may be joined to their demand for other goods and services • Promotion emphasizes personal selling	• Purchases for individual or household consumption • Purchases usually made by ultimate user of the product • Decisions usually made by individuals • Purchases often based on brand reputation or personal recommendations with little or no product expertise • Purchases frequently made on impulse • Purchases based on emotional responses to products or promotions • Individual purchasers often make quick decisions • Buyers engage in limited-term or one-time-only relationships with many different sellers • Most purchases made at "list price" with cash or credit cards • Products usually purchased from someone other than producer of the product • Most purchases are relatively low risk and low cost • Many individual or household customers • Buyers generally dispersed throughout total population • Products: consumer goods and services for individual use • Demand based on consumer needs and preferences, is generally price-elastic, steady over time and independent of demand for other products • Promotion emphasizes advertising

Number of Customers

Organizational customers are few and far between compared to end-user consumers. In the United States, there are about 100 million consumer households but less than half a million businesses and other organizations. When most people think of General Electric the first things that come to mind are light bulbs and home appliances. That's because GE spends millions of dollars advertising those products to the consumer marketplace. But GE's tagline isn't "Imagination at Work" for nothing. The "at work" part has a double meaning, including the fact that, by far, GE targets the vast majority of its products and services to the business marketplace. From jet engines to oilfield equipment to healthcare devices, GE's product line for businesses far exceeds the GE-branded items you see at your local Home Depot. Each of these business markets has far fewer customers than the consumer market for their light bulbs and appliances. And their business marketing strategies must be quite different from consumer marketing strategies. For example, a strong sales force is a far better way to promote GE's business products than the extensive advertising the company does when it wants to talk to consumers.

Size of Purchases

Business-to-business products dwarf consumer purchases both in the quantity of items ordered and how much they cost. A company that rents uniforms to other businesses, for example, buys hundreds of large drums of laundry detergent each year to launder its uniforms. In contrast, even a hard-core soccer mom dealing with piles of dirty socks and shorts only goes through a box of detergent every few weeks. Organizations purchase many products, such as a highly sophisticated piece of manufacturing equipment or computer-based marketing information systems that can cost a million dollars or more. Recognizing such differences in the size of purchases allows marketers to develop effective marketing strategies. Although it makes perfect sense to use mass-media advertising to promote laundry detergent to consumers, selling thousands of dollars' worth of laundry detergent or a million-dollar machine tool is best handled by a strong personal sales force.

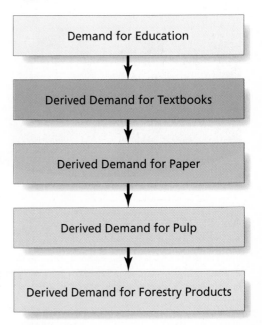

Xerox employs a colorful pitch to sell office products to other companies.

Geographic Concentration

Another difference between business markets and consumer markets is *geographic concentration*, meaning that many business customers are located in a small geographic area rather than being spread out across the country. Whether they live in the heart of New York City or in a small fishing village in Oregon, consumers buy and use toothpaste and televisions. This is not so for business-to-business customers, who may be almost exclusively located in a single region of the country. For years Silicon Valley, a 50-mile-long corridor along the California coast, has been home to thousands of electronics and software companies because of its high concentration of skilled engineers and scientists. For business-to-business marketers who wish to sell to these markets, this means that they can concentrate their sales efforts and perhaps even locate distribution centers in a single geographic area.

3 Business-to-Business Demand

OBJECTIVE

Explain the unique aspects of business-to-business demand.

(pp. 173–174)

Demand in business markets differs from consumer demand. Most demand for business-to-business products is derived, inelastic, fluctuating, and joint. Understanding how these factors influence business-to-business demand is important for marketers when they forecast sales and plan effective marketing strategies. Let's look at each of these concepts in a bit more detail.

Derived Demand

Consumer demand is based on a direct connection between a need and the satisfaction of that need. But business customers don't purchase goods and services to satisfy their own needs. Businesses instead operate on **derived demand**, because a business's demand for goods and services comes either directly or indirectly from consumers' demand for what it produces.

Take a look at Figure 6.2. Demand for forestry products comes from the demand for pulp that paper publishers buy to make the textbooks you use in your classes. The demand for textbooks comes from the demand for education (yes, education is the "product" you're buying—with the occasional party or football game thrown in as a bonus). As a result of derived demand, the success of one company may depend on another company in a different industry. The derived

Figure 6.2 | Derived Demand

Business-to-business demand is derived demand; that is, it is derived directly or indirectly from consumers' demand for another good or service. Some of the demand for forestry products is derived indirectly from the demand for education.

Demand for Education

↓

Derived Demand for Textbooks

↓

Derived Demand for Paper

↓

Derived Demand for Pulp

↓

Derived Demand for Forestry Products

derived demand

Demand for business or organizational products caused by demand for consumer goods or services.

nature of business demand means that marketers must constantly be alert to changes in consumer trends that ultimately will have an effect on business-to-business sales. So if fewer students attend college and fewer books are sold, the forestry industry has to find other sources of demand for its products.

Inelastic Demand

inelastic demand

Demand in which changes in price have little or no effect on the amount demanded.

Inelastic demand means that it usually doesn't matter if the price of a business-to-business product goes up or down—business customers still buy the same quantity. Demand in business-to-business markets is mostly inelastic because what is being sold is often just one of the many parts or materials that go into producing the consumer product. It is not unusual for a large increase in a business product's price to have little effect on the final consumer product's price.

For example, you can buy a Limited Edition Porsche Boxster S "loaded" with options for about $60,000.[2] To produce the car, Porsche purchases thousands of different parts. If the price of tires, batteries, or stereos goes up or down, Porsche will still buy enough to meet consumer demand for its cars. As you might imagine, increasing the price by $30 or $40 or even $100 won't change consumer demand for Boxsters—so demand for parts remains the same. (If you have to ask how much it costs, you can't afford it!)

joint demand

Demand for two or more goods that are used together to create a product.

But business-to-business demand isn't always inelastic. Sometimes a consumer good or service requires only one or a few materials or component parts to produce. If the price of the part increases, demand may become elastic if the manufacturer of the consumer good passes the increase on to the consumer. Currently for example the price of corn is skyrocketing, largely due to the demand for ethanol-based fuel. As a result food products that use corn or corn by-products are much more expensive.

Fluctuating Demand

Business demand also is subject to greater fluctuations than is consumer demand. There are two reasons for this. First, even modest changes in consumer demand can create large increases or decreases in business demand. Take, for example, air travel. A rise in jet fuel prices, causing higher ticket prices and a shift by some consumers from flying to driving vacations, can cause airlines to postpone or cancel orders for new equipment, creating a dramatic decrease in demand for planes from manufacturers such as Boeing and Airbus.

A product's life expectancy is another reason for fluctuating demand. Business customers tend to purchase certain products infrequently. They may only need to replace some types of large machinery every 10 or 20 years. Thus, demand for such products fluctuates—it may be very high one year when a lot of customers' machinery wears out but low the following year because everyone's old machinery is working fine. One solution for keeping production more constant is to use price reductions to encourage companies to order products *before* they actually need them.

Joint Demand

Joint demand occurs when two or more goods are necessary to create a product. For example, Porsche needs tires, batteries, and spark plugs to make that Limited Edition Boxster S that piqued your interest earlier. If the supply of one of these parts decreases, Porsche will be unable to manufacture as many automobiles, and so it will not buy as many of the other items either.

Business-to-business demand is derived demand; manufacturers need to insure that their supplies won't be affected by accidents.

4

OBJECTIVE

Describe how
marketers classify
business-to-business
customers.
(pp. 175–177)

Types of Business-to-Business Customers

As we noted before, many firms buy products in business markets so they can produce other goods. Other business-to-business customers resell, rent, or lease goods and services. Still, other customers, including governments and not-for-profit institutions such as the Red Cross or a local church, serve the public in some way. In this section, we'll look at the three major classes of business-to-business customers that Figure 6.3 shows (producers, resellers, and organizations). Then we'll look at how marketers classify specific industries.

Producers

Producers purchase products for the production of other goods and services that they, in turn, sell to make a profit. For this reason, they are customers for a vast number of products from raw materials to goods that still other producers manufacture. For example, NCR Corporation buys computer components to power its cash registers and Dassault buys engines, high-tech navigation systems, passenger seats, and a host of other component parts to put into its planes. Luxury hotels buy linens, furniture, and food to produce the accommodations and meals their guests expect.

Resellers

Resellers buy finished goods for the purpose of reselling, renting, or leasing to consumers and other businesses. Although resellers do not actually produce goods, they do provide their customers with the time, place, and possession utility we talked about in Chapter 1 by making the goods available to consumers when and where they want them. For example, Wal-Mart buys toothpaste and peanuts and kids shoes and about a gazillion other products to sell in its 3,800-plus stores.

producers
The individuals or organizations that purchase products for use in the production of other goods and services.

resellers
The individuals or organizations that buy finished goods for the purpose of reselling, renting, or leasing to others to make a profit and to maintain their business operations.

government markets
The federal, state, county, and local governments that buy goods and services to carry out public objectives and to support their operations.

Figure 6.3 | The Business Marketplace

The business marketplace consists of three major categories of customers: producers, resellers, and organizations. Business-to-business marketers need to understand the different needs of these customers if they are to build successful relationships.

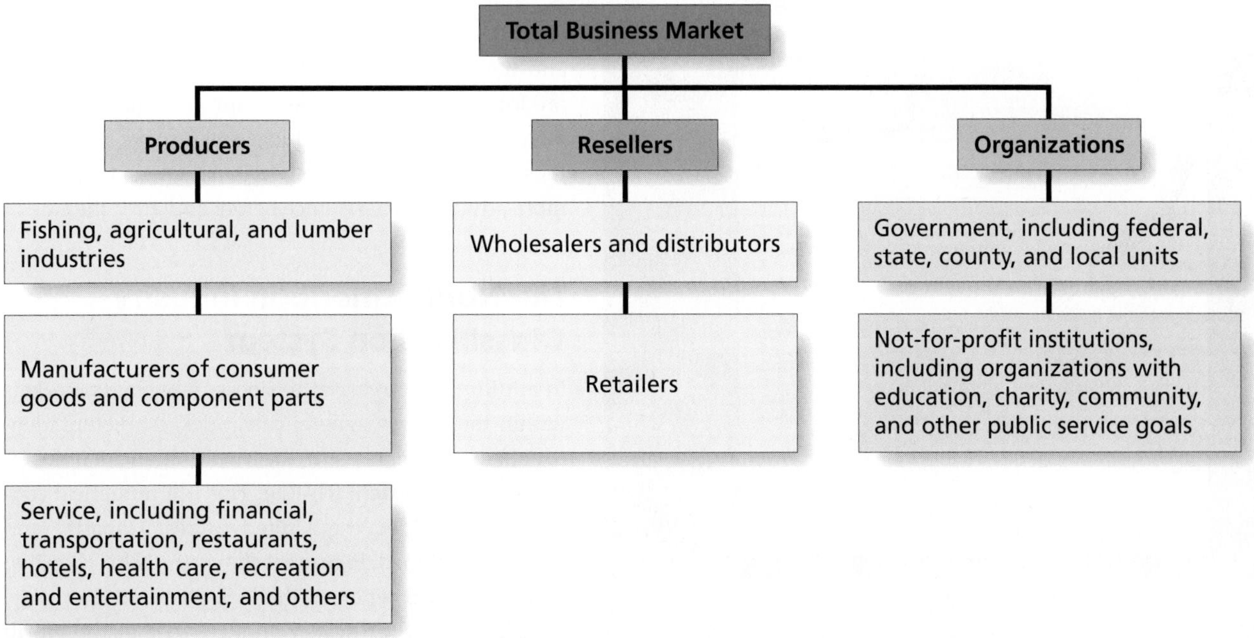

```
                          ┌──────────────────────────┐
                          │  Total Business Market   │
                          └──────────────────────────┘
          ┌──────────────────────────┼──────────────────────────┐
   ┌─────────────┐            ┌─────────────┐            ┌──────────────┐
   │  Producers  │            │  Resellers  │            │ Organizations│
   └─────────────┘            └─────────────┘            └──────────────┘
```

Producers	Resellers	Organizations
Fishing, agricultural, and lumber industries	Wholesalers and distributors	Government, including federal, state, county, and local units
Manufacturers of consumer goods and component parts	Retailers	Not-for-profit institutions, including organizations with education, charity, community, and other public service goals
Service, including financial, transportation, restaurants, hotels, health care, recreation and entertainment, and others		

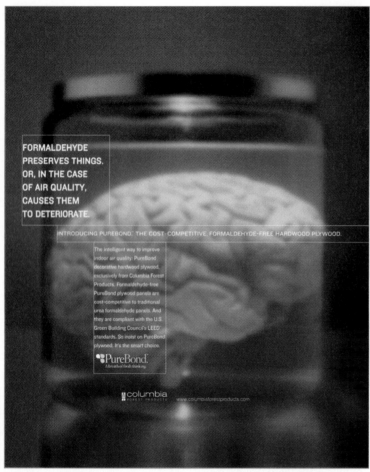

FORMALDEHYDE
PRESERVES THINGS.
OR, IN THE CASE
OF AIR QUALITY,
CAUSES THEM
TO DETERIORATE.

INTRODUCING PUREBOND, THE COST-COMPETITIVE, FORMALDEHYDE-FREE HARDWOOD PLYWOOD.

Companies like Columbia Forest Products that sell building supplies differentiate themselves in the B2B marketplace by using environmentally friendly production processes.

not-for-profit institutions
The organizations with charitable, educational, community, and other public service goals that buy goods and services to support their functions and to attract and serve their members.

The Federal Business Opportunities Web site bills itself as "The U.S. Government's One-Stop Virtual Marketplace."

Government and Not-for-Profit Organizations

Governments and not-for-profit institutions are two other types of organizations in the business marketplace. **Government markets** make up the largest single business and organizational market in the United States. The U.S. government market includes more than 3,000 county governments, 35,000 municipalities and townships, 28,000 special district governments, 50 states and the District of Columbia, plus the federal government. State and local government markets alone account for 15 percent of the U.S. gross national product.[3]

And, of course, there are thousands more government customers around the globe, and many of those governments are just about the only customers for certain products—for example, jet bombers and nuclear power plants. But many government expenditures are for more familiar items. Pens, pencils, and paper for offices; cots, bedding, and toiletries for jails and prisons; and cleaning supplies for routine facilities maintenance are just a few examples of items consumers buy one at a time but that governments purchase in bulk.

To inform possible vendors about purchases they are about to make, governments regularly make information on upcoming purchases available to potential bidders. In the United States, the federal government provides information on business opportunities through its Web site at **www.FBO.gov** (FBO stands for Federal Business Opportunities). This Web site comes with a tag line "The U.S. Government's One-Stop Virtual Marketplace." All federal government buyers can post information directly to FBO.com via the Internet, and vendors can easily search, monitor, and retrieve opportunities at no cost.

Not-for-profit institutions are organizations with educational, community, and other public service goals, such as hospitals, churches, universities, museums, and charitable and cause-related organizations like the Salvation Army and the Red Cross. These institutions tend to operate on low budgets. Because nonprofessional part-time buyers who have other duties often make purchases, these customers may rely on marketers to provide more advice and assistance before and after the sale.

The North American Industry Classification System

In addition to looking at business-to-business markets within these three general categories, marketers identify their customers using the **North American Industry Classification System (NAICS)**. This is a numerical coding of industries the United States, Canada, and Mexico developed. Figure 6.4 shows the NAICS coding system. NAICS replaced the U.S. Standard Industrial Classification (SIC) system in 1997 so that the North

Figure 6.4 | North American Industry Classification System

The North American Industry Classification System (NAICS) identifies industries using a six-digit code that breaks the 20 sectors down into subsectors, industry groups, industries, and specific country industries.

		Frozen Fruit Example		Cellular Telecommunications Example
• Sector (two digits)	31–33	Manufacturing	51	Information
• Subsector (three digits)	311	Food manufacturing	513	Broadcasting and Telecommunications
• Industry group (four digits)	3114	Fruit and vegetable preserving and speciality food manufacturing	5133	Telecommunications
• Industry (five digits)	31141	Frozen food manufacturing	51332	Wireless Telecommunications Carriers (except satellite)
• U.S. Industry (six digits)	311311	Frozen fruit, juice, and vegetable manufacturing	513322	Cellular and Other Wireless Telecommunications

American Free Trade Agreement (NAFTA) countries could compare economic and financial statistics.[4] The NAICS reports the number of firms, the total dollar amount of sales, the number of employees, and the growth rate for industries, all broken down by geographic region. Many firms use the NAICS to assess potential markets and to determine how well they are doing compared to others in their industry group.

Firms may also use the NAICS to find new customers. A marketer might first determine the NAICS industry classifications of her current customers and then evaluate the sales potential of other firms occupying these categories. For example, Brad may find that several of NCR's large customers are in the grocery industry. To find new customers, he could contact other firms in the same industrial group.

North American Industry Classification System (NAICS)
The numerical coding system that the United States, Canada, and Mexico use to classify firms into detailed categories according to their business activities.

5 Business Buying Situations

OBJECTIVE

Identify different business buying situations.
(pp. 177–181)

So far we've talked about how business-to-business markets are different from consumer markets and about the different types of customers that make up business markets. In this section, we'll discuss some of the important characteristics of business buying situations. This is important because just like companies that sell to end consumers, a successful business-to-business marketer needs to understand how her customers make decisions. Armed with this knowledge, the company is able to participate in the buyer's decision process from the start. Take a firm like GE Healthcare that sells a wide range of equipment to hospitals from surgical equipment to molecular imaging machines. Understanding that physicians who practice at the hospital (rather than the employees who actually purchase medical supplies) often initiate new equipment purchases means that GE's salespeople have to be sure that they establish solid relationships with doctors as well as with the hospital's buyers if they expect them to take their products seriously.

The Buyclass Framework

Like end user consumers, business buyers spend more time and effort on some purchases than on others. This usually depends on the complexity of the product and how often they need to make the decision. A **buyclass** framework identifies the degree of effort required of the firm's personnel to collect information and make a purchase decision.

buyclass
One of three classifications of business buying situations that characterizes the degree of time and effort required to make a decision.

These classes, which apply to three different buying situations, are straight rebuys, modified rebuys, and new-task buys.

Straight Rebuy

straight rebuy
A buying situation in which business buyers make routine purchases that require minimal decision making.

A **straight rebuy** refers to the routine purchase of items that a business-to-business customer regularly needs. The buyer has purchased the same items many times before and routinely reorders them when supplies are low, often from the same suppliers. Reordering the items takes little time. Buyers typically maintain a list of approved vendors that have demonstrated their ability to meet the firm's criteria for pricing, quality, service, and delivery. For GE Healthcare, its line of basic surgical scrubs (the clothing and caps doctors and nurses wear in the operating room) is probably purchased very routinely as needed without much evaluation by the buyer.

Because straight rebuys often contribute the "bread and butter" revenue a firm needs to maintain a steady stream of income, many business marketers go to great lengths to cultivate and maintain relationships with customers who submit reorders on a regular basis. Salespeople may regularly call on these customers to personally handle orders and to see if there are additional products the customer needs. The goal is to be sure that the customer doesn't even think twice about just buying the same product every time she is running low. Rebuys keep a supplier's sales volume up and help cover selling costs.

Modified Rebuy

modified rebuy
A buying situation classification used by business buyers to categorize a previously made purchase that involves some change and that requires limited decision making.

Life is sweet for companies whose customers automatically do straight rebuys. Unfortunately, these situations do not last forever. A **modified rebuy** occurs when a firm decides to shop around for suppliers with better prices, quality, or delivery times. This situation also can occur when the organization confronts new needs for products it already buys. A buyer who purchased many laser printers from HP in the past, for example, may have to reevaluate several lines of printers if the firm upgrades its computer system.

new-task buy
A new business-to-business purchase that is complex or risky and that requires extensive decision making.

Modified rebuys require more time and effort than straight rebuys. The buyer generally knows the purchase requirements and she has a few potential suppliers in mind. Marketers know that modified rebuys can mean that some vendors get added to a buyer's approved supplier list while others may be dropped. So even if in the past a company purchased its printers from HP, it doesn't automatically mean it will do so in the future. Now, other firms like Lexmark, Brother, and Oki may gain approved supplier status going forward and the race is on. Astute marketers routinely call on buyers to detect and define problems that can lead to winning or losing in such situations.

New-Task Buy

A first-time purchase is a **new-task buy**. Uncertainty and risk characterize buying decisions in this classification, and they require the most effort because the buyer has no previous experience on which to base a decision.

Your university, for example, may decide (if it hasn't done so already) to go into the "distance learning" business—delivering courses to off-site students. Buying the equipment to set up classrooms with two-way video transmission is an expensive and complex new-task buy for a school. The buyer has to start from scratch to gather information on purchase specifications that may be

We deliver to more countries than any other air express company. Come hell or high water.

Try us to New Orleans.

By offering its customers the capability to send heavier shipments, DHL hopes that its business customers will routinely use the company for all its straight rebuy purchases.

highly technical and complex and require detailed input from others. In new-task buying situations, not only do buyers lack experience with the product, but they also are often unfamiliar with firms that supply the product. Supplier choice is critical, and buyers gather much information about quality, pricing, delivery, and service from several potential suppliers.

A prospective customer's new-task buying situation represents both a challenge and an opportunity. Although a new-task buy can be significant in and of itself, many times the chosen supplier gains the added advantage of becoming an "in" supplier for more routine purchases that will follow. A growing business that needs an advertising agency for the first time, for example, may seek exhaustive information from several firms before selecting one, but then it may continue to use the chosen agency's services for future projects without bothering to explore other alternatives.

Marketers know that to get the order in a new-buy situation, they must develop a close working relationship with the business buyer. And keep in mind that these relationships aren't important just in industries like the ones in which NCR operates. There are, in fact, many situations in which marketers focus on selling their product by wooing people who recommend their products—over and above the end consumers who actually buy them.

To use an example close to home, think about all of the goods and services that make up the higher-education industry. For instance, even though you are the one who shelled out the money for this extremely awesome textbook, your professor was the one who made the exceptionally wise decision to assign it. She made this choice (did we mention it was a really wise choice?) only after carefully considering numerous textbooks and talking to several publishers' sales representatives. Or think about your decision regarding the school you now attend. You probably took into account the suggestions of several people, including (depending on whether you are a recent high school grad or waited awhile to start school) perhaps the recommendation of your high school guidance counselor or friends and coworkers familiar with the school.

Brad
Tracy
APPLYING The Buyclass Framework

How would you categorize the purchase of a new POS workstation for most companies? What does your answer imply about the factors that will influence its purchase? ➡

Professional Buyers and Buying Centers

Just as it is important for marketers of consumer goods and services to understand their customers, it's essential that business-to-business marketers understand who handles the buying for business customers. Trained professional buyers typically carry out buying in business-to-business markets. These people have titles such as *purchasing agents*, *procurement officers*, or *directors of materials management*.

While some consumers like to shop 'til they drop almost every day, most of us spend far less time roaming the aisles. However, professional purchasers do it all day, every day—it's their job and their business to buy! These individuals focus on economic factors beyond the initial price of the product, including transportation and delivery charges, accessory products or supplies, maintenance, and other ongoing costs. They are responsible for selecting quality products and ensuring their timely delivery. They shop as if their jobs depend on it—because they do.

Many times in business buying situations, several people work together to reach a decision. Depending on what they need to purchase, these participants may be production workers, supervisors, engineers, administrative assistants, shipping clerks, or financial officers. In a small organization, everyone may have a voice in the decision. The **buying center** is the group of people in the organization who participate in the decision-making process. Although this term may conjure up an image of "command central" buzzing with purchasing activity, a buying center is not a place at all. Instead, it is a cross-functional team of decision makers. Generally, the members of a buying center have some expertise or interest in the particular decision, and as a group they are able to make the best decision.

Hospitals, for example, frequently make purchase decisions through a large buying center. When they need to purchase disposable protective masks one or more physicians, the director of nursing, and purchasing agents may work together to determine quantities

buying center
The group of people in an organization who participate in a purchasing decision.

Martha
Zenns

a professor at Jamestown Community College

My Advice for NCR Corporation would be to choose

Option

real people, **Other Voices**

I would choose **Option 1**. When it comes to technology, changes come quickly and there are always competitors hoping to take over your share of the market. Given NCR's current competitive advantage, it would

benefit the company to reinforce the product launch and solidify its market leadership. The trade show venue still allows existing and potential clients to have hands-on experience with NCR's POS Workstation. Even though the cost per touch could increase, the company risks losing a good booth position in the future if it does not go this year. It is also not sure of potential customer interaction at the alternative events. Right now, stick with your proven customer base and promotion venue. In the meantime, NCR could send a representative as an observer to the alternative events to determine their potential as a future option. ➤

and select the best products and suppliers. A separate decision regarding the types of pharmaceutical supplies to stock might call for a different cast of characters to advise the purchasing agent, likely including pharmacists and pharmacy technicians. Marketers must continually identify which employees in a firm take part in every purchase decision and develop relationships with them all.

Depending on the complexity of the purchase and the size of the buying center, a participant may assume one, several, or all of the six roles that Figure 6.5 shows. Let's review them now.

- The *user* is the member of the buying center who actually needs the product. The user's role in the buying center varies. For example, an administrative assistant may give her input on the features a new copier should have because she will be chained to it for several hours a day. Marketers need to inform users of their products' benefits, especially if the benefits outweigh those that competitors offer.

- The *initiator* begins the buying process by first recognizing that the firm needs to make a purchase. A production employee, for example, may notice that a piece of equipment is not working properly and notify a supervisor that it is slowing up the production line. At other times, the initiator may suggest purchasing a new product because it will improve the firm's operations. Depending on the initiator's position in the organization and the type of purchase, the initiator may or may not influence the actual purchase decision. For marketers, it's important to make sure that individuals who might initiate a purchase are aware of improved products they offer.

Figure 6.5 | Roles in the Buying Center

A buying center is a group of individuals an organization brings together to make a purchasing decision. Marketers need to understand that the members of the buying center play a variety of roles in the process.

Role	Potential Player	Responsibility
• Initiator	• Production employees, sales manager, almost anyone	• Recognizes that a purchase needs to be made
• User	• Production employees, secretaries, almost anyone	• Individual(s) who will ultimately use the product
• Gatekeeper	• Buyer/purchasing agent	• Controls flow of information to others in the organization
• Influencer	• Engineers, quality control experts, technical specialists, outside consultants	• Affects decision by giving advice and sharing expertise
• Decider	• Purchasing agent, managers, CEO	• Makes the final purchase decision
• Buyer	• Purchasing agent	• Executes the purchase decision

- The *gatekeeper* is the person who controls the flow of information to other members. Typically the gatekeeper is the purchasing agent, who gathers information and materials from salespeople, schedules sales presentations, and controls suppliers' access to other participants in the buying process. For salespeople, developing and maintaining strong personal relationships with gatekeepers is critical to being able to offer their products to the buying center.

- An *influencer* affects the buying decision when she dispenses advice or shares expertise. Highly-trained employees like engineers, quality-control specialists, and other technical experts in the firm generally have a great deal of influence in purchasing equipment, materials, and component parts the company uses in production. The influencers may or may not wind up using the product. Marketers need to identify key influencers in the buying center and persuade them of their product's superiority.

- The *decider* is the member of the buying center who makes the final decision. This person usually has the greatest power within the buying center; she often has power within the organization to authorize spending the company's money. For a routine purchase, the decider may be the purchasing agent. If the purchase is complex, a manager or even the chief executive officer (CEO) may be the decider. Quite obviously, the decider is key to a marketer's success and deserves a lot of attention in the selling process.

- The *buyer* is the person who has responsibility to execute the purchase. Although the buyer often has a role in identifying and evaluating alternative suppliers, this person's primary function is to handle the details of the transaction. The buyer obtains competing bids, negotiates contracts, and arranges delivery dates and payment plans. Once a firm makes the purchase decision, marketers turn their attention to negotiating the details of the purchase with the buyer. Successful marketers are well aware that providing exemplary service in this stage of the purchase can be a critical factor in achieving future sales from this client.

Figure 6.6 | Steps in the Business Buying Process

The steps in the business buying decision process are the same as those in the consumer decision process. But for business purchases, each step may be far more complex and require more attention from marketers.

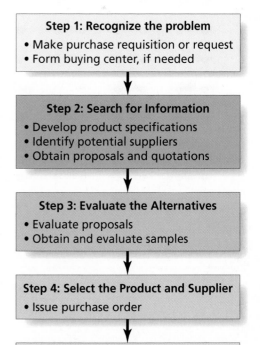

Step 1: Recognize the problem
- Make purchase requisition or request
- Form buying center, if needed

Step 2: Search for Information
- Develop product specifications
- Identify potential suppliers
- Obtain proposals and quotations

Step 3: Evaluate the Alternatives
- Evaluate proposals
- Obtain and evaluate samples

Step 4: Select the Product and Supplier
- Issue purchase order

Step 5: Evaluate Postpurchase
- Survey users
- Document performance

6 The Business Buying Decision Process

OBJECTIVE

Identify and discuss the stages in the business buying decision process.
(pp. 181–186)

We've seen that there are a number of players in the business buying process, beginning with an initiator and ending with a buyer. To make matters even more challenging to marketers, members of the buying team go through several stages in the decision-making process before the marketer gets an order. The *business buying decision process*, as Figure 6.6 shows, is a series of steps similar to those in the consumer decision process. To help understand these steps, let's say you've just started working at the Way Radical Skateboard Company and your boss just assigned you to be in the buying center for the purchase of new software for Web-page design—a new-task buy for your firm.

Step 1: Recognize the Problem

As in consumer buying, the first step in the business buying decision process occurs when someone sees that a purchase can solve a problem. For straight rebuy purchases, this step may result because the firm has run out of paper, pens, or garbage bags. In these cases, the buyer places the order, and the decision-making process ends. Recognition of the need for modified rebuy purchases often comes from wanting to replace outdated existing equipment, from changes in technology, or from an ad, brochure, or some other marketing communication that offers the customer a better product or one at a lower price. Two events may occur in the problem-recognition step. First, a firm makes a request or requisition, usually in writing. Then, depending on the complexity of the purchase, the firm may form a buying center.

The need for new-task purchases often occurs because the firm wants to enhance its operations in some way or when a smart salesperson tells the business customer about a new product that will increase the efficiency of the firm's operations or improve the firm's end products. In the case of Way Radical's new software purchase, your marketing department has previously hired an outside agency to design and maintain its Web page. The company has become dissatisfied with the outside supplier and has decided to move the design function in-house. Now the company needs to select new software to create a truly Way Radical Web site.

Step 2: Search for Information

In the second step of the decision process (for purchases other than straight rebuys) the buying center searches for information about products and suppliers. Members of the buying center may individually or collectively refer to reports in trade magazines and journals, seek advice from outside consultants, and pay close attention to marketing communications from different manufacturers and suppliers. As in consumer marketing, it's the job of marketers to make sure that information is available when and where business customers want it—by placing ads in trade magazines, by mailing brochures and other printed material to prospects, and by having a well-trained sales force regularly calling on customers to build long-term relationships. For Way Radical's purchase, you may try to find out what software your outside supplier uses (if the supplier will tell you), talk to the information technology experts in your firm, or review ads and articles in trade magazines.

There are thousands of specialized publications out there that cater to just about any industry you can think of. Each is bursting with information from competing companies that cater to a specific niche. (Who needs that fluffy romance novel at the beach? Try leafing through the latest issue of *Chemical Processing* or *Meat and Poultry Magazine* instead.)

Of course, sometimes business-to-business marketers try to get the information about their product into the hands of buyers by using less-specialized media. For example, in recent years AFLAC, American Family Life Assurance Company of Columbus—the firm behind the famous duck—has heavily advertised on television even though most of its customers are in the B2B space. In fact, many end-user consumers don't have the foggiest notion what AFLAC sells—but they sure love to "quack up" over the duck's antics. The truth is, AFLAC's primary business is working with businesses (over 400,000 of them in fact) to enhance their employee benefits packages with various types of insurance and other benefits in order to improve recruiting and retention of the firms' people. But their strategy of advertising directly on mass media was brilliant; now when an organizational buyer or HR manager searches for these services, AFLAC's name will surely be at the top of the list. Now there's a duck that's not out of water![5]

Another way business-to-business marketers drive brand awareness and generate buzz is by playing games—

Brad
Tracy

APPLYING the Search for Information

Brad knows that prospective customers need a lot of information about a complex purchase like a POS workstation. He needs to decide upon the best places to make this information available, including which trade shows NCR should attend. ➡

Spot expense policy exceptions as they happen.

When you automate your company's expenses with Concur® Expense Service, you may be surprised by what you learn. Like how easy it is to enforce company policies. Or how powerful your expense data can be when striking a deal with commonly used travel service providers. Instead of guessing on the details, a few clicks can reveal spending patterns all the way down to a specific employee. Which streamlines the process, eliminates paperwork, and most important, saves you a whole lot of money. Call 888.800.4883 or visit www.ExpenseTour.com to take a free Concur Expense Service tour.

concur
TECHNOLOGIES

Many companies sell services—like expense monitoring—to other companies (rather than to end consumers) so that they can operate at peak efficiency.

yes, *games*. Companies like Office Depot, Samsung, and UPS have all introduced viral games in as they appeal to their customers' playful sides. As we'll see in Chapter 12, a viral technique refers to a message that people spread to others (just like catching a cold, but more fun). Using on-line platforms and mimicking simple on-line viral games to promote products like Microsoft's "Flight Simulator," experts contend that business-to-business marketers may also reap rewards if they develop games compelling enough to pass along.[6]

Develop Product Specifications

Business buyers often develop **product specifications**, that is, a written description of the quality, size, weight, color, features, quantity, training, warranty, service terms, and delivery requirements for the purchase. When the product needs are complex or technical, engineers and other experts are the key players who identify specific product characteristics they require and determine whether the organizations can get by with standardized/off-the-shelf items or if it needs to acquire customized/made-to-order goods and services. Although excellent Web-design software is available off-the-shelf, for some computer applications like the ones Way Radical needs, custom-designed software may be necessary.

product specifications
A written description of the quality, size, weight, and so forth required of a product purchase.

Identify Potential Suppliers and Obtain Proposals

Once the product specifications are in hand, the next step is to identify potential suppliers and obtain written or verbal proposals, or *bids*, from one or more of them. For standardized or branded products in which there are few if any differences in the products of different suppliers, this may be as simple as an informal request for pricing information, including discounts, shipping charges, and confirmation of delivery dates. At other times, the potential suppliers receive a formal written *request for proposal* or *request for quotation* that requires detailed information from vendors. For the Way Radical software, which is likely to be a standardized software package, you will probably just ask for general pricing information.

customer reference program
A formalized process by which customers formally share success stories and actively recommend products to other potential clients, usually facilitated through an on-line community.

Step 3: Evaluate the Alternatives

In this stage of the business buying decision process, the buying center assesses the proposals. Total spending for goods and services can have a major impact on the firm's profitability so, all other things being equal, price can be a primary consideration. Pricing evaluations must take into account discount policies for certain quantities, returned-goods policies, the cost of repair and maintenance services, terms of payment, and the cost of financing large purchases. For capital equipment, cost criteria also include the life expectancy of the purchase, the expected resale value, and disposal costs for the old equipment. In some cases, the buying center may negotiate with the preferred supplier to match the lowest bidder.

Although a firm often selects a bidder because it offers the lowest price, there are times when it bases the buying decision on other factors. For example, in its lucrative business-to-business market, American Express wins bids for its travel agency business by offering extra services other agencies don't or can't typically offer such as a corporate credit card, monthly reports that detail the company's total travel expenses, and perks tied to AMEX's customer loyalty program.

The more complex and costly the purchase, the more time buyers spend searching for the best supplier—and the more marketers must do to win the order. In some cases, a company may even ask one or more of its current customers to participate in a **customer reference program**. In these situations customers formally share success stories and actively recommend products to other potential clients, often as part of an on-line

Buyers may need to procure materials that will go into many different products with varying specifications.

Ripped From the **Headlines**

Ethical Decisions in the Real World

Despite all the smooth commercials you see on TV for drugs ranging from Claritin to Cialis, the real battle for supremacy in the high-stakes pharmaceutical industry gets fought at your doctor's office. The physician still is usually the decision maker when it comes to choosing which medications her patients will take. For this reason pharmaceutical companies deploy legions of highly trained sales reps to visit physicians and "detail" them with samples of their products.

But, how do you win the attention (not to mention loyalty) of a busy doctor? For many reps the hardest part is just to get a few minutes of the physician's time to present their arguments for why their solution should be the drug of choice for ailments ranging from arthritis to impotence. How do you stand out from the crowd of other reps that are also beating down the door? And, what criteria do doctors use when they evaluate the competing alternatives? Do they just rely on hard data about the effectiveness of a drug in clinical trials? Sure—but is that the only factor? Doctors are human too (despite what they're taught in medical school!) and they may be swayed by other sales tactics. A dinner at a fancy restaurant? A catered lunch for the staff? A cool premium like a golf cap? A ballpoint pen? Sales managers have to decide what approaches are appropriate—not to mention legal. Should they sell the steak, or focus on the sizzle? What would you do?

Ripped from the Headlines! See what happened in the Real World at **www.mypearsonmarketinglab.com**

ETHICS CHECK: ↖

Find out what other students taking this course **would do** and **why** on **www. mypearsonmarketinglab. com**

Should sales representatives be allowed to give gifts to clients to help them make a sale?

☐ **YES** ☐ **NO**

community composed of people with similar needs. For example, Sun Microsystems offers a very active customer reference program that invites customers to "gain visibility for your business and technology success by participating in reference activities with Sun." Among the popular activities are publication of one-page success story summaries on the Sun Microsystems Web site, cross-branding customer products with the "Powered by Sun" logo, and press releases and other publicity by Sun's PR department related to customer success stories (more on how PR works in Chapter 13).[7]

Marketers often make formal presentations and product demonstrations to the buying center group. In the case of installations and large equipment, they may arrange for buyers to speak with or even visit other customers to examine how the product performs. For less complex products, the buying firm may ask potential suppliers for samples of the products so its people can evaluate them personally. The buying center may ask salespeople from various companies to demonstrate their software for your Way Radical group so that you can all compare the capabilities of different products.

Step 4: Select the Product and Supplier

Once buyers have assessed all proposals, it's time for the rubber to hit the road. The next step in the buying process is the purchase decision—selecting the best product and supplier to meet the firm's needs. Reliability and durability rank especially high for equipment and systems that keep the firm's operations running smoothly without interruption. For some purchases, warranties, repair service, and regular maintenance after the sale are important. For Way Radical, the final decision may be based not only on the capabilities of the software itself but also on the technical support the software company provides. What kind of support is available and at what cost to the customer?

One of the most important decisions a buyer makes is how many suppliers can best serve the firm's needs. Sometimes having one supplier is more beneficial to the organization than having multiple suppliers. **Single sourcing**, in which a buyer and seller work quite closely, is particularly important when a firm needs frequent deliveries or specialized products. Single sourcing also helps assure consistency of quality of materials input into the production process. But reliance on a single source means that the firm is at the mercy of the chosen supplier to deliver the needed goods or services without interruption. If the single source doesn't come through, the firm's relationship with its own end users will very likely be affected.

However, using one or a few suppliers rather than many has its advantages. A firm that buys from a single supplier becomes a large customer with a lot of clout when it comes

single sourcing
The business practice of buying a particular product from only one supplier.

to negotiating prices and contract terms. Having one or a few suppliers also lowers the firm's administrative costs because it has fewer invoices to pay, fewer contracts to negotiate, and fewer salespeople to see than if it uses many sources.

In contrast, **multiple sourcing** means buying a product from several different suppliers. Under this system, suppliers are more likely to remain price-competitive. And if one supplier has problems with delivery, the firm has others to fall back upon. The automotive industry practices this philosophy: A vehicle manufacturer often won't buy a new product from a supplier unless the vendor's rivals also are capable of making the same item! This policy tends to stifle innovation, but it does ensure a steady supply of parts to feed to the assembly line.

multiple sourcing
The business practice of buying a particular product from several different suppliers.

Sometimes supplier selection is based on **reciprocity**, which means that a buyer and seller agree to be each other's customers by saying essentially, "I'll buy from you, and you buy from me." For example, a firm that supplies parts to a company that manufactures trucks would agree to buy trucks from only that firm.

reciprocity
A trading partnership in which two firms agree to buy from one another.

The U.S. government frowns on reciprocal agreements and often determines that such agreements between large firms are illegal because they limit free competition—new suppliers simply don't have a chance against the preferred suppliers. Reciprocity between smaller firms, that is, firms that are not so large as to control a significant proportion of the business in their industry, is legal in the United States if both parties voluntarily agree to it. In other countries, reciprocity is a practice that is common and even expected in business-to-business marketing.

Outsourcing occurs when firms obtain outside vendors to provide goods or services that might otherwise be supplied in-house. For example, Sodexo is the world's largest outsourcer for food and facilities management services with over 6,000 U.S. client sites. Colleges and universities are a major category of clientele for Sodexo, as these educational institutions want to focus on educating students rather than preparing and serving food. (Fortunately your professors don't have to cook as well as teach!)

outsourcing
The business buying process of obtaining outside vendors to provide goods or services that otherwise might be supplied in-house.

Outsourcing is an increasingly popular strategy, but in some cases it can be controversial. Many critics object when American companies contract with companies or individuals in remote places like China or India to perform work that used to be done at home. These tasks range from complicated jobs like writing computer code to fairly simple ones like manning reservations desks, call centers for telephone sales, and even taking drive-through orders at American fast-food restaurants. (Yes, in some cases it's actually more efficient for an operator in India to relay an order from a customer for a #3 Burger Combo to the restaurant's cooks than for an on-site person to take the order!)

Controversy aside, many companies find that it's both cost-efficient and productive to call on outsiders from around the world to solve problems their own scientists can't handle—we call this process **crowdsourcing**. For example, InnoCentive is a network of over 90,000 "solvers" whose member companies like Boeing, DuPont, Procter & Gamble, and Eli Lilly invite to tackle problems they wrestle with internally. InnoCentive's Web site invites you to "join the InnoCentive Open Innovation community to solve some of the toughest

crowdsourcing
Through a formal network, pulling together expertise from around the globe put to work on solving a particular problem for a firm.

Vaidotas
Lukošius
a professor at Tennessee State University

My Advice for NCR Corporation would be to choose

2
Option

real people, **Other Voices**

I choose Option 2. Even if it is a risky approach, it is worth trying for several reasons. One, the new generation Point of Sale Workstation (POS) is likely to be a novelty for the clients. Therefore,

educating the prospective clients about the benefits (for example, offering discounts, calculating tax, etc.) is a very important part, especially in a business to business setting. Two, while claims made by the retail division about "the legacy of attending the show" are important, NCR should venture into the new waters giving POS a chance to succeed with the new audience. Brad should make it clear to the retail division that this year will be different and at the same time ask them to join the new conference. ➤

Sun Microsystems, Inc.

By open-sourcing its core products, companies like Sun Microsystems build up a broad developer community and speed up the innovation process.

reverse marketing

A business practice in which a buyer firm attempts to identify suppliers who will produce products according to the buyer firm's specifications.

problems facing the world today. Win cash awards of up to $1 million for your creative solutions to challenges in business and entrepreneurship, chemistry, engineering and design, life sciences, math and computer science, and physical sciences."[8]

Yet another type of buyer–seller partnership is **reverse marketing**. Instead of sellers trying to identify potential customers and then "pitching" their products, buyers try to find suppliers that can produce specifically needed products and then attempt to "sell" the idea to the suppliers. The seller aims to satisfy the buying firm's needs. Often large poultry producers practice reverse marketing. Perdue supplies baby chickens, chicken food, financing for chicken houses, medications, and everything else necessary for farmers to lay "golden eggs" for the company. This assures the farmer that she will have a buyer, while at the same time it guarantees Perdue's chicken supply.

Step 5: Evaluate Postpurchase

Just as consumers evaluate purchases, an organizational buyer assesses whether the performance of the product and the supplier lives up to expectations. The buyer surveys the users to determine their satisfaction with the product as well as with the installation, delivery, and service the supplier provides. For producers of goods, this may relate to the level of satisfaction of the final consumer of the buying firm's product. Has demand for the producer's product increased, decreased, or stayed the same? By documenting and reviewing supplier performance, a firm decides whether to keep or drop the supplier. Many suppliers recognize the importance of conducting their own performance reviews on a regular basis. Measuring up to a customer's expectations can mean winning or losing a big account. Many a supplier has lost business because of a history of late deliveries or poor equipment repairs and maintenance.

By the **People,** For the **People**

Since 1995, Sun Microsystems has been developing Java, a programming language that many computer applications use—and a key source of revenue for the company. In late 2006, Sun began to make key parts of the program available to outsiders to modify as they wish. The decision to share what were once closely-guarded secrets reflects the shift to the open-source business model that we discussed in Chapter 1. This change is revolutionizing the way businesses connect with one another. By open-sourcing its core products, companies like Sun Microsystems build up a broad developer community and speed up the innovation process. The new strategy helps to ensure that new applications will have the flexibility that business users need because they are allowed to modify the source codes to fit their specific objectives. And now Sun can closely monitor how others adapt its programming so its own engineers can get a better handle on just how people use the software and what needs they should be addressing. Open-source is creating collaborative communities that extend well beyond the traditional buying center—and fundamentally changing the way business-to-business products and services get developed and shared.[9]

7 Business-to-Business E-Commerce

OBJECTIVE

Understand the role of the Internet in business-to-business settings.

(pp. 187–189)

As we saw in our discussion of B2C e-commerce, the Internet has transformed marketing—from the creation of new products to providing more effective and efficient marketing communications to the actual distribution of some products. And this is certainly true in business markets as well. **Business-to-business (B2B) e-commerce** refers to Internet exchanges between two or more businesses or organizations. This includes exchanges of information, goods, services, and payments. It's not as glitzy as consumer e-commerce, but it sure has changed the way businesses operate. Using the Internet for e-commerce allows business marketers to link directly to suppliers, factories, distributors, and their customers, radically reducing the time necessary for order and delivery of goods, tracking sales, and getting feedback from customers. Forrester Research, an Internet research firm, projects that B2B sales growth will approach $3 trillion by the end of the decade with about half of those transactions taking place through auctions, bids, and exchanges.[11]

In the simplest form of B2B e-commerce, the Internet provides an on-line catalog of goods and services that businesses need. Companies find that their Internet site is important to deliver on-line technical support, product information, order status information, and customer service to corporate customers. Many companies, for example, save millions of dollars a year when they replace hard-copy manuals with electronic downloads. And, of course, B2B e-commerce creates some exciting opportunities for brand-new B2B service industries. Companies like RackSpace that host other companies' e-commerce operations provide essential services for successful B2B e-commerce marketers.

business-to-business (B2B) e-commerce

Internet exchanges between two or more businesses or organizations.

extranet

A private, corporate computer network that links company departments, employees, and databases to suppliers, customers, and others outside the organization.

Intranets, Extranets, and Private Exchanges

Although the Internet is the primary means of B2B e-commerce, many companies maintain *intranets*, which provide more secure means of conducting business. As we said in Chapter 4, this term refers to an internal corporate computer network that uses Internet technology to link a company's departments, employees, and databases. Intranets give access only to authorized employees. They allow companies to process internal transactions with greater control and consistency because of stricter security measures than those they can use on the entire Web. Businesses also use intranets to videoconference, distribute internal documents, communicate with geographically dispersed branches, and train employees.

In contrast to an intranet, an **extranet** allows certain suppliers, customers, and others outside the organization to access a company's internal system. A business customer that a company authorizes to use its extranet can place orders on-line. Extranets can be especially useful for companies that need to have secure communications between the company and its dealers, distributors, and/or franchisees.

Metrics Moment

When you think about measuring elements of a customer's experience with a company and its products and brands, we'll bet you automatically think about end-user consumers—like travelers' views of their Marriott hotel stay or the taste of that new Starbucks coffee flavor. Similarly, in the business-to-business world managers pay a lot of attention to the feedback they get about the purchases they've made. Here are some metrics organizational buyers use to measure how well a product or service performs:

Satisfaction—Yes, customer satisfaction is still very relevant in business-to-business and in the buying center; ultimately it is the *user* of the product that should provide this feedback. You can bet that if users are dissatisfied they will quickly relay this information to the rest of the buying center.

Quality—Is the product meeting, exceeding, or falling short of expectations and (for the latter) what can be done to correct the deficiency?

Customer Engagement—It is important to find ways to get and keep customers involved in your business after the sales have been made through customer reference programs or otherwise.

Repurchase Intentions—A common metric is to determine the general budgetary plan a client has for the year ahead, leading to the ability to determine what appropriate sales goals might be going forward.

Problem Resolution Turnaround and Effectiveness—The complexities of the business-to-business market ensure that problems will occur between vendor and client. The true test is how well and how quickly problems are resolved when they do come up.

A final tip: remember that business-to-business customers are busy professionals. They have even less time to fill out lengthy questionnaires than do end-user consumers. Make sure these data are collected efficiently in a manner most comfortable to the client.[10]

Marketers often try to put a human face on business services like data storage.

For several years now, Yum! Brands, parent company of Taco Bell, KFC, and Pizza Hut has relied upon extranets to communicate with franchisees.[12] Taco Bell used to spend hundreds of thousands of dollars per year sending informational update packages—everything from recipes to promotional tie-ins—to its 2,800 independent franchised restaurants around the world. Now thousands of documents are on Taco Bell's extranet, where franchisees can wake up to new information (and perhaps a new meat and cheese concoction) every morning. Yum! runs similar extranet operations for its other restaurant chains as well.

As you can imagine, intranets and extranets are very cost-efficient. Prudential Health Care's extranet allows its corporate customers to enroll new employees and check eligibility and claim status themselves. This saves Prudential money because it can hire fewer customer service personnel, there are no packages of insurance forms to mail back and forth, and Prudential doesn't even have to input policyholder data into the company database.

In addition to saving companies money, extranets allow business partners to collaborate on projects (such as product design) and build relationships. Companies like HP and Procter & Gamble swap marketing plans and review ad campaigns with their advertising agencies through extranets. They can exchange ideas quickly without having to spend money on travel and meetings. GE's extranet, the Trading Process Network, began as a set of purchasing procedures on-line and has morphed into an extensive on-line extranet community that connects GE with large buyers such as Con Edison.

private exchanges
Systems that link an invited group of suppliers and partners over the Web.

Some of the most interesting on-line activity in the B2B world takes place on **private exchanges**. No, these aren't "adult sites"; they are systems that link a specially invited group of suppliers and partners over the Web. A private exchange allows companies to collaborate with suppliers they trust—without sharing sensitive information with others.

Wal-Mart, IBM, and HP are among the giant firms that operate private exchanges. Many other companies are getting on board as well. For example, the director of inventory control for Ace Hardware can click a mouse and instantly receive an up-to-the minute listing of the screwdrivers, hammers, and other products her suppliers have in stock. In addition, suppliers Ace invites to participate in its private exchange (and *only* those suppliers) can submit bids when Ace stores start to run low on hammers. In the "old days" before Ace implemented this process it would take 7 to 10 days to purchase more hammers, and Ace's suppliers could only guess how many they should have on hand to supply the store chain at any given time. The system benefits everyone because Ace keeps tighter controls on its inventories, and its suppliers have a more accurate picture of the store's needs so they can get rid of unneeded inventory and streamline their costs.

The Dark Side of B2B E-Commerce

Doing business the web-enabled way sounds great—perhaps too great. But, there are also security risks because so much information gets passed around in cyberspace. You've no doubt heard all the recent stories about hackers obtaining vast lists of consumers' credit card numbers from retailers and other sources. But companies have even greater worries. When hackers break into company sites, they can destroy company records and steal trade secrets. Both B2C and B2B e-commerce companies worry about *authentication* and ensuring that transactions are secure. This means making sure that only authorized individuals are allowed to access a site and place an order. Maintaining security also requires firms to keep the information transferred as part of a transaction, such as a credit card number, from criminals' hard drives.

Well-meaning employees also can create security problems. They can give out unauthorized access to company computer systems by being careless about keeping their passwords into the system a secret. For example, hackers can guess at obvious passwords—nicknames, birth dates, hobbies, or a spouse's name. To increase security of their Internet sites and transactions, most companies now have safeguards in place—firewalls and encryption devices, to name the two most common methods.

Firewalls

A *firewall* is a combination of hardware and software that ensures that only authorized individuals gain entry into a computer system. The firewall monitors and controls all traffic between the Internet and the intranet to restrict access. Companies may even place additional firewalls within their intranet when they wish only designated employees to have access to certain parts of the system. Although firewalls can be fairly effective (even though none is totally foolproof), they require costly, constant monitoring.

Encryption

Encryption means scrambling a message so that only another individual (or computer) with the right "key" can unscramble it. Otherwise, it looks like gobbledygook. The message is inaccessible without the appropriate encryption software—kind of like a decoder ring you might find in a cereal box. Without encryption, it would be easy for unethical people to get a credit card number by creating a "sniffer" program that intercepts and reads messages. A sniffer finds messages with four blocks of four numbers, copies the data, and voila!—someone else has your credit card number.

Despite firewalls, encryption, and other security measures, Web security for B2B marketers remains a serious problem. The threat to intranet and extranet usage goes beyond competitive espionage. The increasing sophistication of hackers and Internet criminals who create viruses and worms and other approaches to disrupting individual computers and entire company systems mean that all organizations—and consumers—are vulnerable to attacks and must remain vigilant.

Now that you've learned the basics of B2B commerce, read "Real People, Real Choices: How It Worked Out" to see which strategy Brad selected to promote his point of sale products to other businesses.

real people, **Real Choices**

Brad
Tracy
Brad chose:

2

Option

How it Worked Out at NCR

Brad selected Option 2. NCR's retail division passed on the show and reallo-cated its sales and marketing resources to the two smaller events. As it turned out, NCR was only one of a number of large vendors that made this decision. Like a snowball effect, this drop-off in turn decreased the number of retail cus-tomers who chose to attend. Additionally, the change in venue and combina-tion with another trade event failed to generate incremental attendance necessary for continued operation. A few days after the show, the organizers announced they were discontinuing it.

The new events NCR did attend delivered mixed results. One show was sponsored by a national trade association and it drew a solid number of customers and prospects. The number of vendors was limited as only show sponsors (including NCR) participated. Because there was less competition for customers' attention, Brad's staff was able to dramatically increase the quality and length of its interactions with visitors to the booth. However, the second event, sponsored by a trade publication, did not draw the expected number of attendees. Vendor attendees slightly outnumbered retail attendees so the quantity, quality, and duration of NCR's interactions were disappointing.

Moving forward, the division will continue to focus its resources in two areas: 1) large industry leading shows that have sustainable momentum with its tar-geted customers; and 2) small focused conference events that offer the oppor-tunity to have high quality interactions with attendees.

How NCR Measures Success

NCR evaluates its promotional efforts in terms of their value to the company's organizational objectives. This process involves looking closely at expected costs and benefits and comparing these forecasts to what a trade show or other marketing effort actually achieved. But, this equation is a bit more com-plicated, because each event is only one of many touchpoints with a customer that ultimately determines whether the company will win the business. Therefore NCR must use several measures that taken together help its analysts to approximate the impact of a trade show or other initiative. These measures include the following:

- Number of attendees
- Number of interactions (meetings, discussions, or booth tours) with existing customers
- Number of interactions (meetings, discussions, or booth tours) with potential new customers
- Overall cost
- Cost per attendee
- Cost per interaction
- Number of leads captured
- Number of discrete new opportunities (customer projects where NCR has a solution offering that can be proposed)

NCR's trade show exhibit.

Refer back to page 169 for Brad's story ➡

Brand **YOU**!

Inside the business-to-business model.

It's hard to start your job search without knowing how the hiring process works inside companies. What can you expect in the interview process? Who will you meet during interviews? Who makes the hiring deci-sion? How do you know what comes next? Learn the ins and outs of how employers select candidates and how to create a competitive advantage for your brand. Check out Chapter 6 of the *Brand You* supplement and get the inside track.

Objective Summary ➡ Key Terms ➡ Apply

1. Objective Summary (pp. 170–171)

Define business-to-business markets.

Business-to-business markets include business or organizational customers that buy goods and services for purposes other than personal consumption.

Key Terms

business-to-business marketing, p. 170

business-to-business markets, p. 170 (Figure 6.1, p. 172 & Figure 6.3, p. 175)

organizational markets, p. 170

2. Objective Summary (pp. 171–173)

Describe the characteristics that make business-to-business markets different from business-to-consumer markets.

There are a number of major and minor differences between organizational and consumer markets. To be successful, marketers must understand these differences and develop strategies that can be effective with organizational customers. For example, business customers are usually few in number, may be geographically concentrated, and often purchase higher-priced products in larger quantities.

3. Objective Summary (pp. 173–174)

Explain the unique aspects of business-to-business demand.

Business demand derives from the demand for another good or service, is generally not affected by price increases or decreases, is subject to great fluctuations, and may be tied to the demand and availability of some other good.

Key Terms

derived demand, p. 173 (Figure 6.2, p. 173)

inelastic demand, p. 174

joint demand, p. 174

4. Objective Summary (pp. 175–177)

Describe how marketers classify business-to-business customers.

Business customers include producers, resellers, governments, and not-for-profit organizations. Producers purchase materials, parts, and various goods and services needed to produce other goods and services to be sold at a profit. Resellers purchase finished goods to resell at a profit as well as other goods and services to maintain their operations. Governments and other not-for-profit organizations purchase the goods and services necessary to fulfill their objectives. The North American Industry Classification System (NAICS), a numerical coding system developed by NAFTA countries, is a widely used classification system for business and organizational markets.

Key Terms

producers, p. 175

resellers, p. 175

government markets, p. 176

not-for-profit institutions, p. 176

North American Industry Classification System (NAICS), p. 176 (Figure 6.4, p. 177)

5. Objective Summary (pp. 177–181)

Identify different business buying situations.

The buyclass framework identifies the degree and effort required to make a business buying decision. Purchase situations can be straight rebuy, modified rebuy, and new-task buying. A buying center is a group of people who work together to make a buying decision. The roles in the buying center are (1) the initiator, who recognizes the need for a purchase; (2) the user, who will ultimately use the product; (3) the gatekeeper, who controls the flow of information to others; (4) the influencer, who shares advice and expertise; (5) the decider, who makes the final decision; and (6) the buyer, who executes the purchase.

Key Terms

buyclass, p. 177 (➡ Applying, p. 179)

straight rebuy, p. 178

modified rebuy, p. 178

new-task buy, p. 178

buying center, p. 179 (Figure 6.5, p. 180)

6. Objective Summary (pp. 181–186)

Identify and discuss the stages in the business buying decision process.

The stages in the business buying decision process are similar to but more complex than the steps in consumer decision making. These steps include problem recognition; information search, during which buyers, develop product specifications, identify potential suppliers, and obtain proposals from prospective sellers; evaluating the proposals; selecting the product and supplier; and formally evaluating the performance of the product and the supplier. A firm's purchasing options include single or multiple sourcing. In outsourcing, firms obtain outside vendors to provide goods or services that otherwise might be supplied in-house. Other business buying practices are reciprocity and reverse marketing.

Key Terms

product specifications, p. 183

customer reference program, p. 183

single sourcing, p. 184

multiple sourcing, p. 185

reciprocity, p. 185

outsourcing, p. 185

crowdsourcing, p. 185

reverse marketing, p. 186

7. Objective Summary (pp. 187–189)

Understand the role of the Internet in business-to-business settings.

Business-to-business (B2B) e-commerce refers to Internet exchanges of information, goods, services, or payments between two or more businesses or organizations and allows business marketers to link directly to suppliers, factories, distributors, and their customers. An intranet is a secure internal corporate network used to link company departments, employees, and databases. Extranets link a company with authorized suppliers, customers, or others outside the organization. Companies address security issues by using firewalls and encryption.

Key Terms

business-to-business (B2B) e-commerce, p. 187

extranet, p. 187

private exchanges, p. 188

Chapter **Questions** and **Activities**

Concepts: Test Your Knowledge

1. How do business-to-business markets differ from consumer markets? How do these differences affect marketing strategies?
2. Explain what we mean by derived demand, inelastic demand, fluctuating demand, and joint demand.
3. How do we generally classify business-to-business markets? What is the NAICS?
4. Describe new-task buys, modified rebuys, and straight rebuys. What are some different marketing strategies each calls for?
5. What are the characteristics of business buyers?
6. What is a buying center? What are the roles of the various people in a buying center?
7. What are the steps in the business buying decision process? What happens in each step?
8. How are the steps in the business buying decision process similar to the steps in the consumer buying process? How are they different?
9. What is single sourcing? Multiple sourcing? Outsourcing?
10. Explain how reciprocity and reverse marketing operate in business-to-business markets.
11. Explain the role of intranets, extranets, and private exchanges in B2B e-commerce.
12. Describe the security issues firms face in B2B e-commerce. What are some safeguards firms use to reduce their security risks?

Choices and Ethical Issues: You Decide

1. E-commerce is dramatically changing the way business-to-business transactions take place. What are the advantages of B2B e-commerce to companies? To society? Are there any disadvantages of B2B e-commerce?
2. The practice of buying business products based on sealed competitive bids is popular among all types of business buyers. What are the advantages and disadvantages of this practice to buyers? What are the advantages and disadvantages to sellers? Should companies always give the business to the lowest bidder? Why or why not?
3. When firms implement a single sourcing policy in their buying, other possible suppliers do not have an opportunity. Is this ethical? What are the advantages to the company? What are the disadvantages?
4. Many critics say that strict engineering and other manufacturing requirements for products purchased by governments increase prices unreasonably and that taxpayers end up paying too much because of such policies. What are the advantages and disadvantages of such purchase restrictions? Should governments loosen restrictions on their purchases?
5. In the buying center, the gatekeeper controls information flow to others in the center. Thus, the gatekeeper determines which possible sellers are heard and which are not. Does the gatekeeper have too much power? What policies might be implemented to make sure that all possible sellers are treated fairly?
6. In this chapter, we discussed how Sun Microsystems has a reference program in which previous purchasers of products are encouraged to share their experiences with a product with potential new customers. What are the advantages and disadvantages of such a reference program for companies like Sun? For previous customers? For prospective customers? For competitor firms?
7. Some critics complain that outsourcing sends much-needed jobs to competitors overseas (like Airbus) while depriving American workers of these opportunities.

Should a company consider this factor when deciding where to obtain raw materials or brainpower in order to compete efficiently?

Practice: Apply What You've Learned

1. As a director of purchasing for a firm that manufactures motorcycles, you have been notified that the price of an important part used in the manufacture of the bikes has nearly doubled. You see your company having three choices: (1) buying the part and passing the cost on to the customer by increasing your price; (2) buying the part and absorbing the increase in cost, keeping the price of your bikes the same; and (3) buying a lower-priced part that will be of lower quality. Prepare a list of pros and cons for each alternative. Then explain your recommendation and justification for it.

2. Assume that you are the marketing manager for a small securities firm (a firm that sells stocks and bonds) whose customers are primarily businesses and other organizations. Your company has so far not made use of the Internet to provide information and service to its customers. You are considering whether this move is in the best interests of your firm. Write a memo outlining the pros and cons of e-commerce for your firm, the risks your firm would face, and your recommendations.

3. Assume you are a sales manager for a firm that is a distributor of hospital equipment and supplies. Your company offers its customers a wide range of products—everything from disposable rubber gloves to high-tech patient monitors. Thus, purchases made by your customers include straight rebuys, modified rebuys, and new-task purchases. Your job is to explain to your new salesperson the differences among these type of purchases and how to be effective in "getting the business" for all three types of purchases. In a role-playing exercise with another classmate, provide the needed information and advice.

4. As Chief Marketing Officer (CMO) for a four-year-old software firm specializing in applications for use in billing and scheduling systems in medical offices, you are interested in providing a forum for your clients to share their success stories and best practices. You believe that building a community of this type can lead to numerous leads and referrals for new business. What characteristics might a customer reference program have that would best serve you, your firm, and its customers? Be as specific as you can about what this program would be like and how it would work to gain the desired references.

Miniproject: Learn by Doing

The purpose of this miniproject is to gain knowledge about one business-to-business market using the NAICS codes and other government information.

1. Select an industry of interest to you and use the NAICS information you find on the Internet (**http://www.census.gov/naics/2007/index.html**) or in your library.
    a. What are the codes for each of the following classifications?
        NAICS Sector (two digits)
        NAICS Subsector (three digits)
        NAICS Industry Group (four digits)
        NAICS Industry (five digits)
        U.S. Industry (six digits)
    b. What types of products are or are not included in this industry?

2. Locate the *U.S. Industrial Outlook or Standard & Poor's Industry Surveys* in your library to find the answers to the following:
    a. What was the value of industry shipments (sales) for the United States in the latest year reported?
    b. What were worldwide sales for the industry in the most recent year reported?

3. The U.S. Census Bureau publishes a number of economic censuses every five years covering years ending in the digits 2 and 7. These include the following publications: *Census of Retail Trade*, *Census of Wholesale Trade*, *Census of Service Industries*, *Census of Transportation*, *Census of Manufacturers*, *Census of Mineral Industries*, and *Census of Construction Industries*. Use the appropriate publication to determine the value of shipments in your industry for the most recent year reported.

4. *Ward's Business Directory* provides useful industry-specific information. Use it to find the names and addresses of the top four public companies in the industry and their sales revenues.

5. *Compact Disclosure* provides information from company annual reports on CD-ROM (usually available in your school library). Use it or some other similar source to provide the following for the four companies listed in question 4:
    a. Income statements
    b. Net sales, gross profits, and income before tax

6. *The Statistical Abstract of the United States* provides information on the economic, demographic, social, and political structures of the United States. It provides data on the sales of products in consumer markets. Use it to complete the following:
    a. Find a product in the consumer market that is produced by your industry (or is down the value chain from your industry, for example automobiles from the steel industry).
    b. Determine the sales of the consumer product category for the most recent year reported.

Real People, **real surfers**: explore the web

NCR isn't the only company that makes point of sale (POS) workstations (in the "old days" these were called "cash registers"). Visit **www.ncr.com** and then click on Products and Services, then Point of Sale. You will find a wide array of products offered. Also check out the types of Services and Support NCR offers (also under the Products and Services drop-down menu).

Lots of other brands of POS workstations exist including HP, Posiflex, ELO, Ultimate Technology, Partner Tech, Casio, and Epson. Pick any two of these competing brands and peruse their Web sites. Based on this experience, answer the following questions:

1. Among the three providers you reviewed, how do the Web sites compare? Which are easier to navigate, and why? Which are more innovative and attractive, and why?
2. Evaluate each site from the perspective of a retail customer who is interested in upgrading her stores' POS system. What features in each site would be useful in helping make a purchase decision? What information is available that a retailer might need? Overall, which site do you think would be most useful in making the decision? Why?
3. Compare the service and support offered among the three. Which seems to have the best service after the sale? What leads you to that conclusion?

Marketing Plan Exercise

As you have learned, business-to-business marketing, or marketing to organizational markets, is big business. A successful marketing plan—even one focused on products used by end-user consumers—must focus significant attention on getting those products into consumers' hands, usually through a retailer or some other source that involves a business-to-business market.

As an example, pick a product you often buy in the grocery store.

1. What key elements of the organizational market (the grocer) must the product's manufacturer plan for to market it successfully to the grocer?
2. How do the elements Question 1 identifies differ from how it is marketed to you as an end user?
3. In the case of the product you selected, which market is more important (the grocer or you), and why?

Marketing in Action Case

Real **Choices** at **Airbus**

The competitive world of airplane building pits two rivals, Boeing and Airbus, against one another. In the most recent calendar year, Boeing won the battle for total number of orders by just 72 planes with over 1,413 planes sold. However, Airbus delivered 453 new aircraft versus Boeing's 441. Both airlines compete furiously for the increasing demand from China, India, and the Middle East.

Both Boeing and Airbus operate in the business-to-business marketplace as producers of passenger and cargo airplanes. As such, the companies are dependent on other companies, including airlines that fly people around the world and freight haulers, like FedEx and UPS, to purchase their airplanes. The two companies have drastically different views of their airplane-buying customers and the future of air travel. The company that guesses right on the future stands to benefit greatly; industry experts believe that air travel will triple in the next few decades resulting in orders for 40,000 new planes over that time frame. Obviously, the company that provides the majority of those new planes, especially those in the profitable, wide-bodied line of products, stands to reap huge profits. However, before deciding which of the two companies is best positioned to win this competition, it helps to know a little about each one and their views of the marketplace.

Airbus is a company that began in 1970 with funding provided by owners from Germany, Spain, Britain, and France. Airbus is building planes designed to thrive in a *hub-and-spoke system*. In a hub-and-spoke system, commuter airlines associated with the larger carriers transport passengers from smaller airports to large hub airports such as those you find in New York City, Atlanta, Chicago, Dallas, and Denver. From there the larger airlines take the passengers to their final destination, which typically are other large airports. So, someone traveling from Austin, Texas, to New York City would first fly on a smaller plane to Dallas and then change to a larger plane and complete the trip to New York City.

Airbus is betting for most of their future success in the hub-and spoke-system with the A380, a super-jumbo jet that cost Airbus $12 billion to develop. In short, this plane is huge. The A380 is a full double-decker plane with the capacity to carry as many as 850 passengers. It is 240 feet long, has a wingspan of 266 feet, and the top of the tail section stands eight stories off the ground. The plane is so large that airports around the world must make changes to accommodate the A380. Those changes include adding double-decker loading ramps, installing new hallways to accommodate the crowds of arriving and departing passengers, and installing larger luggage carousels in expanded baggage claim areas.

Despite these challenges, and after two years of delays in production, cancelled orders, and financial losses for Airbus, the Airbus A380 super-jumbo, owned and operated by Singapore Airlines, completed its first commercial flight on October 24, 2007. Singapore Airlines plans to use the super-jumbos for offering customers a "new standard for luxury and comfort" by outfitting the A380s with 399 economy seats, 60 business seats, and 12 first class "suites." Each suite includes sliding doors, a leather-upholstered seat, a flat bed, a table, and a 23-inch TV screen plus laptop connections and a range of office software. Two suites can be joined to offer guests a double bed and more intimacy. Some critics see the jet as an environmental concern because the aviation industry is one of the biggest producers of carbon dioxide, which is considered a key factor in global warming.

Boeing, which is headquartered in Chicago, has been in existence for almost 90 years and until recently had been the dominant manufacturer of airplanes in the world. Boeing's view of the future of air travel is different because the company instead endorses the *point-to-point system*. An airline operating in a point-to-point system flies its planes from one city to another with direct flights, often using less crowded airports and without the use of a feeder system provided by smaller commuter airlines. From the previous example, the passenger traveling in a point-to-point system from Austin, Texas, to New York City would get on a smaller airplane in Austin and fly directly to New York City. Boeing's reasoning behind its system is that business people in a hurry do not want to stop in the middle of their trip to change planes. As a result, Boeing's product line is designed to operate in a point-to-point system.

Boeing is betting much of its future on the Dreamliner 787. The Dreamliner is a mid-sized, wide-body twin engine jet that carries between 210 and 350 passengers. Boeing says the Dreamliner will be more fuel efficient and thus more environmentally friendly. But the Dreamliner has also experienced delays and is not scheduled to be in service until early 2009.

Clearly, acceptance of the A380 and the future of Airbus rest on many factors. Even though airlines and freight carriers may already own several Airbus planes, the purchase of an A380 will undoubtedly be a new-task purchase involving many members of the buying center from the CEO down to flight attendants and maintenance personnel. Consequently, Airbus will have to know how to tailor its message to accommodate the needs of each member of the buying center. Another factor is the limited number of airports around the world that may be able or willing to spend the money necessary to handle such a large plane. Finally, what happens to the company if its hub-and-spoke view of the future does not materialize? Boeing's much more flexible product line can operate in a hub-and-spoke system but also can accommodate the point-to-point system. Furthermore, Boeing is winning business from customers because its product line is much more efficient when it comes to fuel usage, which in the world of rising oil prices is a key ingredient to keeping operating costs low. As you can see, this venture by Airbus represents an enormous gamble by a company hoping to capitalize in a market that seems very uncertain. And the winner for correctly predicting the future of airline travel in the world is still very much "up in the air."

You Make the Call

1. What is the decision facing Airbus?
2. What factors are important in understanding this decision situation?
3. What are the alternatives?
4. What decision(s) do you recommend?
5. What are some ways to implement your recommendation?

Based on: Alex Taylor III, "Lord of the Air: What's Left for Airbus after Overtaking Boeing in the Commercial Aircraft Market? Building a Really Big Plane," *Fortune*, November, 10, 2003, pp. 144–152.; Associated Press, "Airbus Reports 117 Plane Orders for First Half, Trailing Boeing," July 10, 2006; "Big Ol' Jet Airliner Readies for Takeoff," October 21, 2007. *CNNMoney.com*, **http://money.cnn.com/2007/10/21/news/companies/bc.apfn.flyingbig.ap/index.htm**(accessed March 16, 2008); "Boeing Beats Airbus on Orders, January 16, 2008, **http://edition.cnn.com/2008/BUSINESS/01/16/airbus.results/index.html**(accessed March 16, 2008); James Thayer, "Flying High: How Boeing Cut Short Airbus's Rule as King of the Skies," the *Weekly Standard*, December 8, 2005, Daily Standard Section; John Gillie, "Airbus' Victory Rings Hollow," the *Tacoma News Tribune*, January 18, 2006, p. D01; "Superjumbo Ends Historic Flight," CNN.com, October 25, 2007, **http://edition.cnn.com/2007/BUSINESS/10/24/airbus.a380/index.html#cnnSTCText** (accessed March 16, 2008).

Chapter 7

Part 1   Make Marketing Value Decisions (Chapters 1, 2, 3)
Part 2   Understand Consumers' Value Needs (Chapters 4, 5, 6, 7)
Part 3   Create the Value Proposition (Chapters 8, 9, 10, 11)
Part 4   Communicate the Value Proposition (Chapters 12, 13, 14)
Part 5   Deliver the Value Proposition (Chapters 15, 16)

Sharpen the Focus:

Target Marketing Strategies and Customer Relationship Management

results not typical

nutrisystem.com/tv

1-800-321-THIN

Thomas F. **Connerty**
Profile ▼

A **Decision Maker** at NutriSystem, Inc.

Thomas Connerty is Chief Marketing Officer and Executive Vice President of Program Development at NutriSystem, Inc. For the past 24 years he has managed thousands of direct marketing campaigns through direct mail, e-commerce, telemarketing, infomercials, home shopping channels, and direct response television. Mr. Connerty has worked for NutriSystem since November 2004 where he oversaw one of the most successful multi-channel direct marketing programs of the decade. In two short years, NutriSystem's revenues have gone from $38 million to over $560 million. Revenues for 2007 exceeded $800 million. Since being at the company NutriSystem has been named by *Forbes*, *BusinessWeek*, and *Fortune* as one of the fastest growing companies in America. Additionally, from a revenue standpoint NutriSystem has replaced Weight Watchers as the most successful weight loss company in the country.

Prior to his stint at NutriSystem, Tom was the vice president of marketing at the Nautilus Group from 2000 where he handled marketing for Bowflex home gyms. Tom saw Nautilus revenues grow from $160 million to over $500 million in just four years. During his tenure the company was rated the number one growth company in the country by *BusinessWeek* and *Brandweek* and Bowflex was named the top fitness equipment brand three years in a row.

Tom also served as the vice president of Global Direct Response Television for The Readers Digest Association. Additionally, he managed all on-air advertising and promotion as vice president of broadcast for the Home Shopping Network. From 1990 to 1993, Tom managed a profit center for Time-Life Video,

---

▼ **Q** & **A** with Thomas F. Connerty

Q) What I do when I'm not working?
A) I like to play tennis, ski, and cook.

Q) First job out of school?
A) I was a telemarketer for the Republican National Committee. It was my first exposure to direct marketing.

Q) Career high?
A) Taking NutriSystem from $38 million in sales in 2004 to nearly $800 million in sales in 2007.

Q) A job-related mistake I wish I hadn't made?
A) I signed a deal with a celebrity endorser who will remain unnamed. The talent was highly unprofessional and awful to work with. Wish I never signed that deal.

Q) Business book I'm reading now?
A) *Scientific Advertising* by Claude Hopkins.

Q) My hero?
A) Winston Churchill.

Q) My motto to live by?
A) What gets measured gets managed.

Q) What drives me?
A) My high school guidance counselor who said I'd never amount to much.

Q) My management style?
A) I try my best to get out of people's way. I believe in George Patton's theory about giving people a lot of responsibility and letting them astound you with their brilliance.

Q) Don't do this when interviewing with me?
A) Try and sell me.

Q) My pet peeve?
A) Ingratitude.

marketing products through direct television advertising. There he launched more than 200 DRTV (direct response television) campaigns. Early in his career he managed all the annual direct mail campaigns for the Republican National Committee's largest membership database. He started out his direct marketing career 24 years ago as a telemarketer.

Tom holds a BA from the Catholic University of America and an MBA from the University of Maryland. In 2007 the Philadelphia Direct Marketing Association named him "Marketer of the Year."

Decision Time at NutriSystem

NutriSystem experienced tremendous growth selling 28-day weight loss programs in 2005. The 28 day program provides dieters with all their breakfasts, lunches, dinners, and desserts. The program is designed to place people on a reduced-calorie program and is low on the Glycemic index—meaning customers could eat "good carbs" while on the program. By extending NutriSystem's media presence beyond an e-commerce only strategy into more traditional media such as direct response television, infomercials, and magazine advertising NutriSystem was able to significantly increase its customer count.

Things to remember:

Only 13% of the dieters who buy NutriSystem's products are male.

The majority of its $212,000,000 sales were to women aged 35–55. Sales to men accounted for 13 percent of revenues. When faced with growth prospects for 2006, NutriSystem's management was concerned that the company couldn't sustain its triple-digit growth rate if the company focused all its marketing activities towards its core group of female customers. The company wanted to expand its market presence so that it would attract significantly more customers. It had developed a program for men that included a higher caloric count and more "hearty meals." But NutriSystem never actively marketed the program. Common experience in this category was that men were highly resistant to going on a diet. Indeed, the company's research indicated that dieting was not a viable option; men would rather reduce their beer consumption or go to a gym if they really wanted to lose weight.

However, the research also suggested that one of the main objections men offered when it came to dieting was that they didn't want to give up the foods they loved. This played right into NutriSystem's core offering. Because NutriSystem's foods are based on portion control and a low rating on the Glycemic Index, the company was able to offer men a diet product that featured pizza, lasagna, burgers, and meatloaf instead of bean sprouts, tofu, and rice cakes. Basically, men who wanted to lose weight but who weren't willing to become sprout eaters could "have their cake and eat it too."

Additionally, NutriSystem's research shows that some of the same drivers that pushed women to go on the program resonated with men. These motivators included vanity, energy, and health concerns. Because these drivers were an intrinsic part of the product's core promise, Tom felt there was a chance the company could grow by targeting male dieters in addition to its core female segment—although chances for success were by no means certain, given the historical resistance of men to diet programs. Also, if the company did enter this market it wasn't clear what the best strategy would be to speak to potential male customers.

Tom considered his Options 1·2·3

1 **Option** Dip a toe into the male market by using testimonials from actual men who had tried the program, and broadcast these spots on cable television stations. Since Tom knew that the odds of successfully appealing to men were pretty low, a more modest effort would be more prudent and perhaps over time the demand might build. A celebrity spokesman might jump-start the campaign and convince men to think about dieting, but on the other hand celebrity endorsers are expensive and they don't always guarantee success.

2 **Option** Stick with what works; don't enter the men's market. Although there is the potential to expand NutriSystem's market significantly, it's by no means clear that enough men will be interested to justify the considerable expense of developing a separate campaign. The company will encounter high entry costs because it will need to convince its channel partners to develop a new suite of products centering around the types of foods men are willing to eat on a diet. And, the chances for failure are high—a big stumble would be embarrassing to the company and also divert management's focus from its core business of appealing to female dieters.

3 **Option** Develop a men's program and launch it with a big splash on national television. To parallel NutriSystem's female campaign, select a well-known male celebrity to serve as spokesman for the new program. This strategy would make use of the company's core organizational competency, since NutriSystem had a proven track record at creating a compelling message and advertising it effectively to a target audience. And, a TV campaign is the fastest way to build brand awareness. On the other hand, this kind of high-profile campaign is very expensive and it could divert resources from the company's core female business. In addition, if the campaign fizzled, its failure would be well-publicized and the credibility of future efforts might be in danger.

Now, put yourself in Tom's shoes: Which option would you choose, and why?

You Choose

Which **Option** would you choose, and **why**?

1. ☐YES ☐NO **2.** ☐YES ☐NO **3.** ☐YES ☐NO

See what **option** Thomas chose and its success on **page 225** ➡

1

OBJECTIVE

Identify the steps in the target marketing process.

(pp. 198–199)

Target Marketing Strategy: Select and Enter a Market

By now, we've heard over and over that the goal of the marketer is to create value, build customer relationships, and satisfy needs. But, in our modern, complex society, it's naive to assume that everyone's needs are the same. Understanding people's needs is an even more complex task today because technological and cultural advances in modern society have created a condition of **market fragmentation**. This condition occurs when people's diverse interests and backgrounds divide them into numerous groups with distinct needs and wants. Because of this diversity, the same good or service will not appeal to everyone.

Consider, for example, the effects of fragmentation in the health-and-fitness industry. Back in the 1960s, dieting was simple. Pritikin was a best-selling weight loss system emphasizing very low fat and high fiber, and health-conscious consumers thought that this combination would surely yield a lean body and good health. Today's consumers, however, have a whole litany of diets from which to choose. There's NutriSystem, Weight Watchers, Jenny Craig, Slim Fast, FitAmerica, the Atkins diet, and dozens of herbal remedies for people with weight problems. Calories, fat, carbs, or all of the above—which to cut?

Marketers must balance the efficiency of mass marketing, serving the same items to everyone, with the effectiveness of offering each individual exactly what she wants. Mass marketing is certainly the most efficient plan. It costs much less to offer one product to everyone because that strategy eliminates the need for separate advertising campaigns and distinctive packages for each item. However, consumers see things differently; from their perspective the best strategy would be to offer the perfect product just for them. Unfortunately, that's often not realistic. Even Burger King's long-time motto, "Have It Your Way," was true only to a point: "Your way" is fine as long as you stay within the confines of familiar condiments such as mustard or ketchup. Don't dream of topping your burger with blue cheese, mango sauce, or some other "exotic" ingredient.

Instead of trying to sell something to everyone, marketers select a **target marketing strategy** in which they divide the total market into different segments based on customer characteristics, select one or more segments, and develop products to meet the needs of those specific segments. Figure 7.1 illustrates the three-step process of segmentation, targeting, and positioning, and it's what we're going to check out in this chapter. Let's start with the first step—segmentation.

Check out chapter 7 **Study Map** on page 226

Figure 7.1 | Steps in the Target Marketing Process

Target marketing strategy consists of three separate steps. Marketers first divide the market into segments based on customer characteristics, then select one or more segments, and finally develop products to meet the needs of those specific segments.

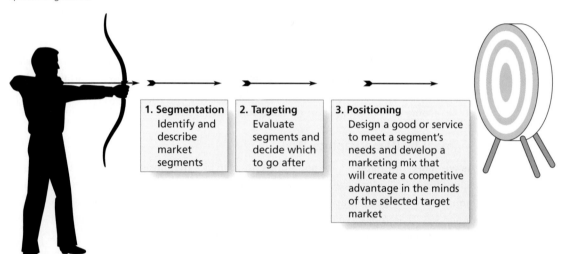

1. Segmentation
Identify and describe market segments

2. Targeting
Evaluate segments and decide which to go after

3. Positioning
Design a good or service to meet a segment's needs and develop a marketing mix that will create a competitive advantage in the minds of the selected target market

2

OBJECTIVE

Understand the need for market segmentation and the approaches available to do it.

(pp. 199–212)

Step 1: Segmentation

Segmentation is the process of dividing a larger market into smaller pieces based on one or more meaningfully shared characteristics. Segmentation is a way of life for marketers. The truth is that you can't please all the people all the time, so you need to take your best shot. Just how do marketers segment a population? How do they divide the whole pie into smaller slices they can "digest"? Segmenting the market is often necessary in both consumer and business-to-business markets. In each case, the marketer must decide on one or more useful **segmentation variables**—that is, dimensions that divide the total market into fairly homogeneous groups, each with different needs and preferences. In this section, we'll take a look at this process, beginning with the types of segmentation variables that marketers use to divide up end consumers.

Segment Consumer Markets

At one time, it was sufficient to divide the sports shoe market into athletes and nonathletes. But take a walk through any sporting goods store today: You'll quickly see that the athlete market has fragmented in many directions, such as shoes designed for jogging, basketball, tennis, cycling, cross training, and even skateboarding beckon us from the aisles.

During the late 1990s Converse began falling well behind its competitors such as Reebok and Nike, who had successfully targeted the younger demographic by tying their shoes to popular athletes who acted as marketing machines for the brands. Converse needed to find a way to appeal to the younger generation as well. More specifically, the marketers at Converse (which Nike acquired in 2003) wanted to target **Generation Y**—people born between 1979 and 1994.[1] They found their stride by reminding these consumers that cultural icons they admired like Kurt Cobain and Jackson Pollack once wore their shoes. These messages appealed to Gen Y "optimistic rebels" who were looking for a "blank canvas for self expression."[2]

We need several segmentation variables if we want to slice up the market for all the shoe variations available today. First, not everyone is willing or able to drop $150 on the latest sneakers, so marketers consider income. Second, men may be more interested in

market fragmentation
The creation of many consumer groups due to a diversity of distinct needs and wants in modern society.

target marketing strategy
Dividing the total market into different segments on the basis of customer characteristics, selecting one or more segments, and developing products to meet the needs of those specific segments.

segmentation
The process of dividing a larger market into smaller pieces based on one or more meaningfully shared characteristics.

segmentation variables
Dimensions that divide the total market into fairly homogeneous groups, each with different needs and preferences.

Generation Y
The group of consumers born between 1979 and 1994.

basketball shoes while women snap up the latest aerobics styles, so marketers also consider gender. Because not all age groups are equally interested in buying specialized athletic shoes, we can slice the larger consumer "pie" into smaller pieces in a number of ways, including demographic, psychological, and behavioral differences.

We'll consider each of these segmentation variables in turn, but first a note of caution. When it comes to marketing to some groups—in particular lower income individuals, the poorly educated, non-native language speakers, and children—it is incumbent on marketers to exercise the utmost care not to take undue advantage of their circumstances. Ethical marketers are sensitive to the different conditions in which people find themselves and proactively work to uphold a high level of honesty and trust with all segments of the public. Doing so is nothing short of marketing's social responsibility.

Segment by Demographics: Age

demographics

Statistics that measure observable aspects of a population, including size, age, gender, ethnic group, income, education, occupation, and family structure.

As we stated in Chapter 3, **demographics** are statistics that measure observable aspects of a population, including size, age, gender, ethnic group, income, education, occupation, and family structure. Demographics are vital to identify the best potential customers for a good or service. These objective characteristics are usually easy to identify, and then it's just a matter of tailoring messages and products to relevant groups.

For over a decade, the U.S. dairy industry trade group has painted milk moustaches onto celebrities who appeal to every conceivable demographic segment, all in the name of making milk a popular drink with all kinds of consumers. Young, old, male, female, black, white—you name the group and "Got Milk?" has had an appealing endorser. The demographic dimensions that marketers usually look at are age, gender, family structure, income and social class, race and ethnicity, and geography (or where people live). Let's take a quick look at how marketers use each of these dimensions to slice up the consumer pie.

generational marketing

Marketing to members of a generation, who tend to share the same outlook and priorities.

Consumers of different age groups have different needs and wants. Members of a generation tend to share the same outlook and priorities. We call such a focus **generational marketing**. During the famous "cola wars" of the 1970s and 1980s, Pepsi managed to convince a generation (the "Pepsi Generation") that its product reflected their core values of youth, idealism, and casting off old ways. By default, Coke became identified as a drink for (ancient) parents, not for the young-at-heart.[3]

Children are an attractive age segment for many marketers. Although kids obviously have a lot to say about purchases of toys and games, they influence other family purchases as well (just watch them at work in the grocery store!). By one estimate, American children aged 4 to 12 have a say in family-related purchases of more than $130 billion a year.[4] The popularity of shows such as Disney's *Hannah Montana* (despite the recent uproar over actress Miley Cyrus' "adult" photo) has successfully translated into a booming toy business including blond wigs, replicas of Hannah's tour van, and even toy musical instruments. The music on the show has spawned several new musical acts—including the Jonas Brothers—and sold millions of CDs and tens-of-millions of downloads. The younger girl market segment loves the idea of being a pop star and the girls live their dream vicariously through Hannah as well as *American Idol* and *High School Musical*.[5]

Teens are also an attractive market segment. The 12 to 17-year-old age group is growing nearly twice as fast as the general population—and teens and *tweens* (kids between the ages of 8 and 14) spend an average of $3,000 per year.[6] Much of this money goes toward "feel-good" products: cosmetics, posters, and fast food—with the occasional nose ring thrown in as well. Because they are so interested in many different products and have the resources to obtain them, many marketers avidly court the teen market.[7] Apple has been a masterful marketer to teens, yet their product line also appeals to other age groups as well. The iPod enables teens to be content creators and empowers them to be masters of their own music world. This satisfies a strong need among this age group for individuality. Teens don't particularly like to be marketed to, which is a great fit for Apple's approach of letting fans and the media do their marketing for them. The iPod itself is iconic as a youth symbol—stylish, nonconforming, and an expression of a clear difference from the past.[8]

And, of course, there are subgroups within the teen market with their own musical idols, distinctive styles, and so on. For example, the *emo* (short for "emotional") youth subculture is a label both for a musical genre and for the youthful adherents to that genre. The common thread uniting emo kids is a strong current of alienation. Emo kids tend to look like they have just shopped at a garage sale. They often sport work jackets, too-small jeans, and old Chuck Taylor sneakers. Their trademark hairstyle is short, slick, dyed-black hair with pronounced bangs.[9]

As we said, Generation Y consists of the consumers born between the years 1979 and 1994. Sometimes labeled the "baby boomlet," Generation Y is made up of the 71 million children of the baby boomers.[10] They are the first generation to grow up online and are more ethnically diverse than earlier generations. Generation Y is an attractive market for a host of consumer products because of its size (approximately 26 percent of the population) and free-spending nature—as a group they spend about $200 billion annually.

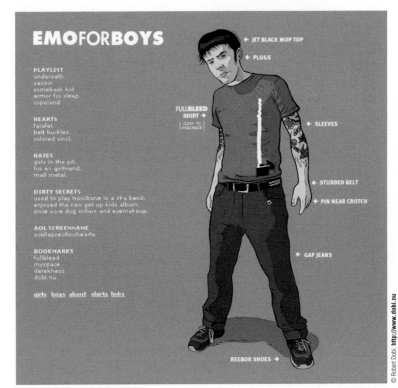

A guide to the Emo subculture.

But Generation Y consumers are also hard to reach because they resist reading and increasingly turn off the TV. When they do watch TV, they tend toward alternative fare such as the late night lineup on Adult Swim, which is consistently the number-one show on basic cable for this age group—outperforming even the *Late Show with David Letterman* with young men.[11] As a result, many marketers have had to develop other ways to reach this generation, including online chat rooms, e-mail promotions, and some of the more unusual guerrilla marketing techniques we'll talk about later in this book.

The group of consumers born between 1965 and 1978 consists of 46 million Americans sometimes known as **Generation X**, slackers, or busters (for the "baby bust" that followed the "baby boom"). Many of these people have a cynical attitude toward marketing—a chapter in a book called *Generation X* is entitled "I am not a target market!"[12] As one 20-year-old Japanese Xer commented, "I don't like to be told what's trendy. I can make up my own mind."[13]

Despite this tough reputation, members of Generation X, the oldest of whom are now entering their early 40s, have mellowed with age. In retrospect, they also have developed an identity for being an entrepreneurial group. One study revealed that Xers are already responsible for 70 percent of new start-up businesses in the United States. An industry expert observed, "Today's Gen Xer is both values-oriented and value-oriented. This generation is really about settling down."[14] Many people in this segment seem to be determined to have stable families after being latchkey children themselves. Seven out of ten regularly save some portion of their income, a rate comparable to that of their parents. Xers tend to view the home as an expression of individuality rather than material success. More than half are involved in home improvement and repair projects.[15] So much for Gen Xers as slackers!

Baby boomers, consumers born between 1946 and 1964 and who are now in their 40s, 50s, and 60s, are an important segment to many marketers—if for no other reason than that there are so many of them who are making a lot of money. Boomers were the result of

Generation X
The group of consumers born between 1965 and 1978.

baby boomers
The segment of people born between 1946 and 1964.

pent-up desires on the part of their parents to start families after World War II interrupted their lives. Back in the 1950s and 1960s, couples started having children younger and had more of them than the previous generation. The resulting glut of kids really changed the infrastructure of the country: more single-family houses, more schools, migration to the suburbs, and so on.

One aspect of boomers for marketers to always remember—they never age. At least, that's the way they look at it. Boomers are willing to invest a ton of money, time, and energy to maintain their youthful image. The show *Nip/Tuck* on FX chronicles the experiences of two cosmetic surgeons in Los Angeles, baby boomers themselves, who crassly market their surgical fountain of youth to a seemingly endless stream of 50-somethings. Other boomer-appealing TV fare includes *Desperate Housewives'* take on middle-aged women acting like college sorority girls but in better living quarters and *Lost's* cosmic-philosophical commentary on life, age, and other ultimate questions of the universe. Time Warner even formed a separate unit to publish magazines, including *Health*, *Parenting*, and *Cooking Light* that specifically address baby boomers' interests in staying young, healthy, and sane.

That helps to explain why boomer women in their 50s are becoming a hot new market for what the auto industry calls "reward cars": sexy and extravagant vehicles. These buyers say that for years they had let the roles of wife and mother restrict them to minivans or stodgy family sedans. As their kids (and perhaps husbands as well?) grow up and leave home, it's reward time. As one woman who bought a snazzy Mercedes convertible for herself stated, "I don't have the disease to please anymore....I'm pleasing me." She's not alone. Vehicle registration records show that the number of women over 45 who purchased cars in the niche known as "mid-sized sporty," which includes two-door models like the Mazda RX-8 and the Chrysler Crossfire, is up 277 percent since 2000. Among women 45 and over earning at least $100,000, smaller luxury cars like the BMW 3 Series and the Audi A4 are up 93 percent.[16]

And what about the men who do stay home? Automakers appeal to them by transforming that stodgy old station wagon into what they call the *manwagon*—station wagons with huge engines, track-ready suspensions, and race-car-style seats. Unlike a sports car, these wagons can fit strollers and coolers in the back. Dodge offers its Magnum wagon with a 425-horsepower SRT8, while Mercedes' version of the manwagon, the 2008 E63 AMG wagon, boasts the 507-horsepower engine that is more powerful than one of the fastest sedans Mercedes has ever built. Likewise, the Audi A4 Avant is an A4 station wagon equipped with the V8 (340 hp) engine from their flagship model; the 2008 BMW M5 Touring is a BMW 5-series wagon with a 500 hp V10 from the M5. Ward and June Cleaver and your "Leave it to Beaver" neighbors—you were born too early![17]

Another important aspect of boomers, in connection with the sociocultural trends we discussed in Chapter 3, is that because there are so many of them they clog the upward mobility pipeline in employment. Generation Xers especially complain that the boomers hold all the power and position, and that the sheer number of boomers in managerial spots impedes promotion opportunities for Xers. This has fueled the entrepreneurial spirit among the generations following boomers. Generation Xers and younger have no expectation of long-term employment with any one firm and even are cynical about their prospects of ever receiving Social Security as a retirement benefit. These generations have had to very much make their own opportunities.

According to 2000 Census Bureau estimates, there are nearly 37 million Americans aged 65 or older—a 13 percent increase in this age segment since 1990.[18] Many *mature consumers* enjoy leisure time and continued good health. Indeed, a key question today is: Just what is a senior citizen? As we will see later in the chapter, perhaps it isn't age but rather lifestyle factors, including mobility, that best define this group. More and more marketers offer products that have strong appeal to active-lifestyle seniors. Even youth-oriented Disney tempts seniors to relive their youth at theme parks and on cruises—with or without their grandchildren.

Segment by Demographics: Gender

Many products, from fragrances to footwear, specifically appeal to men or women. Segmenting by sex starts at a very early age—even diapers come in pink for girls and blue for boys. As proof that consumers take these differences seriously, market researchers report that most parents refuse to put male infants in pink diapers.[19] In some cases, manufacturers develop parallel products to appeal to each sex. For example, male grooming products have traditionally been Gillette's priority since the company's founder King Gillette (yes, his first name was actually King) introduced the safety razor in 1903. Today the company offers the manly five-bladed beast it calls Fusion, and at the same time offers women a soothing shave from the Venus Vibrance system.

Metrosexual is a marketing buzzword you may have heard. The term describes a man who is a straight, urban male who is keenly interested in fashion, home design, gourmet cooking, and personal care. Metrosexuals are usually well-educated urban dwellers that are in touch with their feminine side.[20] This Web posting from *The Urban Dictionary* sums up the metrosexual stereotype.[21]

metrosexual
A straight, urban male who is keenly interested in fashion, home design, gourmet cooking, and personal care.

You might be "metrosexual" if:

1. You just can't walk past a Banana Republic store without making a purchase.
2. You own 20 pairs of shoes, half a dozen pairs of sunglasses, just as many watches, and you carry a man-purse.
3. You see a stylist instead of a barber, because barbers don't do highlights.
4. You can make her lamb shanks and risotto for dinner and Eggs Benedict for breakfast ... all from scratch.
5. You only wear Calvin Klein boxer-briefs.
6. You shave more than just your face. You also exfoliate and moisturize.
7. You would never, ever own a pickup truck.
8. You can't imagine a day without hair styling products.
9. You'd rather drink wine than beer ... but you'll find out what estate and vintage first.
10. Despite being flattered (even proud) that gay guys hit on you, you still find the thought of actually getting intimate with another man truly repulsive.

While many men are reluctant to overtly identify with the metrosexual, there's no denying that a renewed interest in personal care products, fashion accessories, and other "formerly feminine" product categories creates many marketing opportunities. For example, men's jewelry, once considered a fringe market for rockers, rappers, gay men, and gangsters, is inching toward the mainstream. Tiffany quietly expanded its usual watch and cufflink collections to offer a broad range of sporty men's jewelry, including silver pendants, rings, and bracelets mostly priced between $150 and $350. The famous retailer got a boost when it outfitted actor Brad Pitt with a silver pendant and cufflinks for the movie *Ocean's Twelve*. After photos of Mr. Pitt wearing the jewelry appeared in the tabloid *Life and Style*, men showed up at Tiffany's asking for the "Brad Pitt" pieces. Singer Lenny Kravitz and actor Orlando Bloom also have been photographed wearing jewelry on magazine covers. The *LA Times* reports that Jason Schwartzman was spotted at a dinner sponsored by *GQ* magazine sporting "a silver beetle lapel pin with a spot of turquoise that perfectly complemented the shade of his Band of Outsiders suit." For guys—bling is da' thing![22]

Singer Lenny Kravitz exemplifies the "new man."

Segment by Demographics: Family Life Cycle

Because family needs and expenditures change over time, one way to segment consumers is to consider the stage of the *family life cycle* they occupy. (You learned about the family life cycle in Chapter 5.) Not surprisingly, consumers in different life-cycle segments are unlikely to need the same products, or at least they may not need these things in the same quantities. Procter & Gamble introduced Folger's Instant Coffee Singles for people who live alone and don't need to brew a full pot of coffee at a time, while Marriott and other hoteliers actively market vacation ownership (timeshare) opportunities to young couples—because these consumers can tailor these getaways to their changing lifestyles.

But not all attempts at marketing to the family life cycle succeed. Gerber once tried to market single-serving food jars to singles; a quick meal for one person who lives alone. The manufacturer called these containers "Singles." However, Gerber's strong identification with baby food worked against it: The product flopped because people felt that Gerber was trying to sell baby food to adults.[23]

As families age and move into new life stages, different product categories ascend and descend in importance. Young bachelors and newlyweds are the most likely to exercise, go to bars and movies, and consume alcohol (in other words, party while you can). Older couples and bachelors are more likely to use maintenance services. Seniors are a prime market for resort condominiums and golf products. Marketers need to identify the family life-cycle segment of their target consumers by examining purchase data by family life-cycle group.

Segment by Demographics: Income and Social Class

The distribution of wealth is of great interest to marketers because it determines which groups have the greatest *buying power*. It should come as no surprise that many marketers yearn to capture the hearts and wallets of high-income consumers. Perhaps that explains a recent proliferation of ultra-high-end bottled waters such as Voss—which bills itself as extracted from a real Norwegian glacier. To taste this delicacy in gourmet restaurants and mini-bars of top hotels, expect to pay well over $10 a bottle. Tap water anybody?[24] At the same time, other marketers target lower-income consumers (defined as households with annual incomes of $25,000 or less), who make up about 40 percent of the U.S. market. Stores such as Sam's Club and Costco sell generic bottled water in flats of 24 bottles for less than 50 cents per bottle!

In the past, it was popular for marketers to consider *social class segments*, such as upper class, lower class, and the like. However, many consumers buy, not according to where they actually fall in that framework, but rather according to the image they wish to portray. For example, readily available credit facilitates many a sale of a BMW to a consumer whose income doesn't easily support the steep price tag.

This Army recruiting ad speaks to parents who are thinking about options to provide a college education for their children.

Segment by Demographics: Ethnicity

A consumer's national origin is often a strong indicator of his preferences for specific magazines or TV shows, foods, apparel, and leisure activities. Marketers need to be aware of these differences and sensitivities—especially when they invoke outmoded stereotypes to appeal to consumers of diverse races and ethnic groups. An animated show called *Minoriteam* that came and went (but lives on via cult status) on Cartoon Network's edgy "Adult Swim" draws our attention to these assumptions in a humorous way:

- The team's leader, Dr. Wang, is an Asian, wheelchair-bound mathematical genius with a freakishly large brain. He speaks with a heavy Chinese accent and is in the laundry business.

- Non-Stop is the alter ego of Dave Raj, an Indian, former professional skateboarder turned convenience store clerk who is incapable of being killed by firearms. When necessary, his skateboard morphs into a flying carpet.

- Fasto, the world's fastest man, is actually Landon K. Dutton, a black man teaching women's studies at Male University who has an immense appetite for women.

- Richard Escartin, a Mexican oil baron, trades his tailored suits and silk ties for a giant sombrero and a leaf blower when he becomes El Jefe ("The Boss"). This superhero's blower can suck and blow with deadly force and rip holes through time and space. Tequila, not kryptonite, is what his enemies use to weaken him.

- Neil Horvitz is a wimpy mail clerk but his alter ego, Jewcano, is a muscle-bound 62-year-old who wears an XXXL yarmulke and shoots molten lava from his wrists.

This multiethnic crew battles a gang of villains including the sniveling Corporate Ladder (an anthropomorphized ladder with a cape and a pipe), Racist Frankenstein (a bigoted monster), and Standardized Test, whose head is shaped like a No. 2 pencil and whose body resembles a Scantron test (we've all battled this particular villain). White Shadow, the villains' bumbling leader, spews nonsensical corporate-speak, using words like "synergy" and phrases like "Let's all get on the same page."[25]

African Americans, Asian Americans, and Hispanic Americans are the largest ethnic groups in the United States. The Census Bureau projects that by the year 2050, non-Hispanic whites will make up just less than 50 percent of the population (compared to 74 percent in 1995) as these other groups grow. Let's take a closer look at each of these important ethnic segments.

African Americans account for about 12 percent of the U.S. population. This percentage has held steady for 20 years. Reflecting the growing consumer power fueled by the hip-hop and urban scene, magazines such as *The Source* and *Vibe* target this market.[26] Television shows that feature African American heroes and heroines, unheard of until the late 1960s, are commonplace today, and BET is an advertising force to be reckoned with. In many cities, urban-sound radio stations are among the elite few in audience ratings.

These media examples demonstrate the opportunities that await those who develop specialized products to connect with segments of consumers who share an ethnic or racial identity. And what had been the original rap culture has migrated from the inner-city streets to mainstream hip-hop clubs, creating substantial opportunities for marketers to parlay what started out as an urban street trend among the African American community to a broader cultural phenomenon that appeals to young people of many ethnicities.

Though their numbers are still relatively small, *Asian Americans* are the fastest-growing minority group in the United States. The Asian American population is projected to grow from 11.3 million in 2000 to 19.6 million in 2020.[27] The American advertising industry spends between $200 million and $300 million to court these consumers.[28] Ford set up a toll-free consumer hotline that it staffs with operators fluent in three Asian languages, and JCPenney holds one-day sales in stores in Asian communities during certain holidays such as the moon festival.[29] Wonder Bra even launched a special line it sized for the slimmer Asian body.[30]

The *Hispanic American* population is the real sleeping giant, a segment that mainstream marketers largely ignored until recently. Hispanics have overtaken African Americans as the nation's largest minority group. In the United States, Hispanics command well over $400 billion in purchasing power. In addition to its rapid growth, five other factors make the Hispanic segment attractive to marketers:[31]

- Hispanics tend to be brand loyal, especially to products made in their country of origin.

- They tend to be highly concentrated by national origin, which makes it easy to fine-tune the marketing mix to appeal to those who come from the same country. That's why some companies are trying to appeal to Mexican Americans, who make up about 60 percent of Hispanic Americans, by developing promotions celebrating Cinco de Mayo, a minor holiday in Mexico commemorating that country's triumph over France in 1862. McDonald's once added fajitas to its regular menu during the holiday.[32]

- This segment is young (the median age of Hispanic Americans is 23.6, compared with the U.S. average of 32), which is attractive to marketers because it is a great potential market for youth-oriented products such as cosmetics and music.

- The average Hispanic household contains 3.5 people, compared to only 2.7 people for the rest of the United States. For this reason, Hispanic households spend 15 to 20 percent more of their disposable income than the national average on groceries and other household products.

- In general, Hispanic consumers are very receptive to relationship-building approaches to marketing and selling. For this reason there are many opportunities to build loyalty to brands and companies by emphasizing relationship aspects of the customer encounter.[33]

As with any ethnic group, appeals to Hispanic consumers need to take into account cultural differences. For example, the "Got Milk?" campaign was not well received by Hispanics because biting, sarcastic humor is not part of their culture. In addition, the notion of milk deprivation is not funny to a Hispanic mother because running out of milk means she has failed her family. To make matters worse, "Got Milk?" translates as "Are You Lactating?" in Spanish. Thus, new Spanish-language versions were changed to "And you, have you given them enough milk today?" with tender scenes centered on cooking flan (a popular pudding) in the family kitchen.

Latino youth are changing mainstream culture. Many of these consumers are "young biculturals" who bounce back and forth between hip-hop and rock en Español, blend Mexican rice with spaghetti sauce, and spread peanut butter and jelly on tortillas. By the year 2020, the Census Bureau estimates that the number of Hispanic teens will grow by 62 percent, compared with 10 percent growth in teens overall. They seek spirituality, stronger family ties, and more color in their lives—three hallmarks of Latino culture. Music crossovers from the Latin charts to mainstream lead the trend, including pop idols Shakira and Enrique Iglesias, and Reggaeton sensation Daddy Yankee.

One caution about the Hispanic market is that the term *Hispanic* itself is a misnomer. For example, Cuban Americans, Mexican Americans, and Puerto Ricans may share a common language, but their history, politics, and culture have many differences. Marketing to them as though they are a homogeneous segment can be a big mistake.

An important outcome of the increase in multiethnicity in the U.S. is the opportunity for increased cultural diversity in the workplace and elsewhere. **Cultural diversity**, a management practice that actively seeks to include people of different sexes, races, ethnic groups, and religions in an organization's employees, customers, suppliers, and distribution channel partners, is today business as usual rather than an exception. Marketing organizations benefit from employing people of all kinds because they bring different backgrounds, experiences, and points of view that help the firm develop strategies for its brands that will appeal to diverse customer groups.

Segment by Demographics: Place of Residence

Recognizing that people's preferences often vary depending on where they live, many marketers tailor their offerings to *geographic regions*. Pabst Brewing Company sells different brands of beer in different parts of the

cultural diversity
A management practice that actively seeks to include people of different sexes, races, ethnic groups, and religions in an organization's employees, customers, suppliers, and distribution channel partners.

Music crossover Daddy Yankee leads the Reggaeton music trend.

country, so drinkers in Texas buy the company's Lone Star brand, while those in other states buy Old Milwaukee.

When marketers want to segment regional markets even more precisely, they sometimes combine geography with demographics using the technique of **geodemography**. A basic assumption of geodemography is that "birds of a feather flock together"—people who live near one another share similar characteristics. Sophisticated statistical techniques identify geographic areas that share the same preferences for household items, magazines, and other products. This lets marketers construct segments of households with a common pattern of preferences. This way they can hone in on those customers most likely to be interested in its specific offerings, in some cases so precisely that families living on one block will belong to a segment while those on the next block will not.

Companies can even customize Web advertising by **geocoding** so that people who log on in different places will see ad banners for local businesses. For example, the Weather Channel (**www.weather.com**) links localized ads to 1,300 U.S. weather-reporting stations. A surfer can get both the local weather forecast and information about businesses in an area by simply typing a city and state, or an airport code, into the forecast request box.

One widely used geodemographic system is PRIZM, which is a large database developed by Nielsen Claritas. (**www.claritas.com**). This system classifies the U.S. population into 66 segments based on various socio-economic data, such as income, age, race, occupation, education and household composition, as well as lifestyle attributes that are critical to advertisers' marketing strategies, such as where they vacation, what they drive and their favorite brands.

The 66 segments range from the highly affluent "Upper Crust" and "Blue Blood Estates" to the lower income "Big City Blues or "Low Rise Living" neighborhoods. To learn about how the system classifies your ZIP Code, visit **www.mybestsegments.com**.

Here are a few thumbnail sketches of different segments of relatively younger consumers a marketer might want to reach depending on the specific product or service he or she sells:

- *Young Digerati* are tech-savvy and live in fashionable neighborhoods on the urban fringe. Affluent, highly educated, and ethnically mixed, Young Digerati communities are typically filled with trendy apartments and condos, fitness clubs and clothing boutiques, casual restaurants and all types of bars—from juice to coffee to microbrew. They are much more likely than the average American consumer to shop at Banana Republic, order from J.Crew, read *Elle Decor* magazine, watch the Independent Film Channel and drive a Range Rover SUV.

- *Kids & Cul-de-Sacs* are upper-middle class, suburban, married couples with children. With a high rate of Hispanic and Asian Americans, this segment is a refuge for college-educated, white-collar professionals with administrative jobs and upper-middle-class incomes. Their nexus of education, affluence, and children translates into large outlays for child-centered products and services. They are much more likely than the average American consumer to shop at The Disney Store, eat at Chuck E. Cheese, read parenting magazines, watch Nickelodeon, and drive a Nissan Armada SUV.

- *Shotguns & Pickups* scores near the top of all lifestyles for owning hunting rifles and pickup trucks. These Americans tend to be young, working-class couples with large families--more than half have two or more kids—living in small homes and manufactured housing. Nearly a third of residents live in mobile homes, more than anywhere else in the nation. They are much more likely than the average American consumer to own a tent, go to auto races, read *North American Hunter* magazine, watch Country Music TV and drive a Dodge Ram.

Other examples of PRIZM clusters are shown in Table 7.1.

geodemography
A segmentation technique that combines geography with demographics.

geocoding
Customizing Web advertising so that people who log on in different places will see ad banners for local businesses.

Table 7.1 | Examples of PRIZM Clusters

Cluster Name	Demographics	Most Likely To	Neighborhood Examples
Urban Gold Coast	Elite urban singles Age group: 45–64 Professional Average household income: $73,500	Attend the theater Use olive oil Bank on-line Watch *Law and Order: Criminal Intent* Read *Self*	Marina Del Rey, CA Lincoln Park, IL Upper East Side, NY
Starter Families	Young, middle-class families Age group: under 18, 25–34 Blue-collar/service occupations Average household income: $25,300	Belong to a book club Be boxing fans Use caller ID Watch *Nightline* Read *Bride's Magazine*	Woodland, CA Sioux Falls, SD Lowell, MA
Rural Industrial	Low-income, blue-collar families Age group: under 18 Blue-collar/service occupations Average household income: $27,900	Be auto racing fans Belong to a fraternal order Have veterans' life insurance Watch NASCAR and Blue Collar Comedy Tour Read *Field and Stream*	Gas City, IN Wheeler, AR Worthington, KY
Young Literati	Upscale urban singles and couples Age group: 25–44 Professional occupations Average household income: $63,400	Plan for large purchases Take vitamins Use a discount broker Watch Bravo Read *GQ*	Hermosa Beach, CA Diamond Heights, CA Edgewater, NJ
Inner Cities	Inner-city, single-parent families Age group: under 18, 18–34 Blue-collar/service occupations Average household income: $16,500	Buy baby food Buy soul/R&B/black music Pay bills by phone Watch pay-per-view sports Read *National Enquirer*	Detroit, MI Hyde Park, IL Morningside, NY
Hispanic Mix	Urban Hispanic singles and families Age group: under 18, 18–34 Blue-collar/service occupations Average household income: $19,000	Be pro basketball fans Use caller ID Use money orders Watch BET Read *Ebony*	Pico Heights, CA El Paso, TX Bronx, NY
New Ecotopia	Rural white- and blue-collar/farm families Age group: 45+ White-collar/blue-collar/farming occupations Average household income: $39,000	Go cross-country skiing Own a dog Have a Keogh account Watch *Jeopardy* Read *Prevention*	Sutter Creek, CA East Chatham, NY Grafton, VT
Golden Ponds	Retirement town seniors Age group: 65+ White-collar/blue-collar/service occupations Average household income: $28,300	Shop at Wal-Mart Go bowling Eat Grape-Nuts Watch QVC network Read *Golf*	Forest Ranch, CA Dollar Bay, MI Kure Beach, NC *(continues on the next page)*

Norma Rae-Ville	Young families, biracial mill town	Travel by bus	Yazoo City, MS
	Age group: under 18, 18–34	Shop at Payless Shoes	Americus, GA
	Blue-collar/service occupations	Buy Sears tires	Salisbury, NC
	Average household income: $20,500	Watch *Oprah*	
		Read *Seventeen*	
Blue-chip Blues	Upscale blue-collar families	Shop on-line	Redford, MI
	Age group: 35–64	Belong to a religious club	Oakville, CT
	White-collar/blue-collar occupations	Drink Coke	Barrington, NJ
	Average household income: $47,500	Watch *Days of Our Lives*	
		Read *Car Craft*	
Executive Suites	Upscale white-collar couples	Belong to a health club	Irving, CA
	Age group: 45–64	Visit Japan/Asia	Aurora, IL
	Professional occupations	Have an airline travel card	Mount Laurel, NJ
	Average household income: $68,500	Watch *Friends*	
		Read *Entrepreneur*	

Source: Used by permission of Claritas, a Nielsen Company.

Segment by Psychographics

Demographic information is useful, but it does not always provide enough information to divide consumers into meaningful segments. Although we can use demographic variables to discover, for example, that the female college student segment uses perfume, we won't be able to tell whether certain college women prefer perfumes that express an image of, say, sexiness rather than athleticism. As we said in Chapter 5, **psychographics** segments consumers in terms of psychological and behavioral similarities such as shared activities, interests, and opinions, or *AIOs*.[34] For example, most of us are happy driving the speed limit (okay, a few miles over the limit) on the freeway, but some of us crave danger. For this psychographic segment, there is a variety of unique product offerings, including a tour of the sunken *Titanic* at 12,500 feet below the surface of the ocean or getting behind the wheel of a Formula One race car running at 120 miles per hour.[35]

Over the years, Harley-Davidson has done a great job of understanding buyers on the basis of psychographics. A Harley user's profile includes both thrill-seeking and affinity for a countercultural image (at least on weekends). In fact, your doctor, banker, lawyer, or even marketing professor may be a member of HOG (the Harley Owners Group). However, demographics also come into play. Over the past decade, the age of the typical Harley

psychographics
The use of psychological, sociological, and anthropological factors to construct market segments.

Devin
Dadigan
a student at Syracuse University
My Advice for NutriSystem would be to choose

Option

real people, **Other Voices**

I would choose **Option 3** because Thomas Connerty is an established leader and a major player behind NutriSystem's initial success. As evidenced by his outstanding credentials, Connerty knows how to grow a company and I think NutriSystem is the perfect candidate to continue a high growth phase. The company has already shown success segmenting and marketing to women. Since men

and women have different wants and needs when it comes to dieting, it would be unfavorable for NutriSystem to use the same campaign for men as they do for women. Therefore, Connerty should develop a specialized men's program and build a high profile TV campaign around it. In order to be successful, I believe that NutriSystem must develop a new brand, specifically positioned to appeal to men, that is clearly differentiated from the women's dietary product. I think option 3 is the preferable way to market "NutriSystem men." Initially, this strategy will be quite costly. However, when a substantial level of customer awareness is reached, NutriSystem's new male brand will be highly profitable. With a new men's dieting concept that is significantly different than that of the women's program, NutriSystem should be well on its way to success. ➤

buyer has risen to about 46, older than the motorcycle industry average of 38. But because the company knows the psychographics of its target buyers, it isn't lulled into age stereotypes of safety and conservatism. Harley-Davidson knows that in spite of the older age demographic, its buyers are still a thrill-seeking bunch (they may just need a little more time and some aspirin to recover after a long ride).

Although some advertising agencies and manufacturers develop their own psychographic techniques to classify consumers, other agencies subscribe to services that divide the entire U.S. population into segments and then sell pieces of this information to clients for specific strategic applications. The best known of these systems is **VALS2™ (Values and Lifestyles)**. The original VALS™ system was based on social values and lifestyles. Today, VALS2™ is based on psychological traits that correlate with consumer behavior. VALS2™ was developed by SRI Consulting Business Intelligence (**www.sric-bi.com**). You can go to its Web site and click on "VALS™ Survey" to complete a brief questionnaire for free to find out your own VALS™ type (you might be surprised). VALS™ divides U.S. adults into eight groups according to what drives them psychologically as well as by their economic resources.

As Figure 7.2 shows, three primary consumer motivations are key to the system: ideals, achievement, and self-expression. Consumers who are motivated primarily by ideals are guided by knowledge and principles. Consumers who are motivated primarily by achievement look for goods and services that demonstrate success to their peers. And consumers who are motivated primarily by self-expression desire social or physical activity, variety, and risk.

VALS2™ helps match products to particular types of people. For example, VALS2™ survey data show that 12 percent of American adults (many of whom are on the younger side) are Experiencers who tend to be thrill seekers. VALS2™ helped Isuzu market its Rodeo sport-utility vehicle by targeting Experiencers who believe it's fun to break rules. The company and its advertising agency promoted the car as a vehicle that lets a driver break the rules by going off road. One ad showed a kid jumping in mud puddles after his mother went to great lengths to keep him clean. Another ad showed a schoolchild scribbling outside the lines after the teacher made a big deal about coloring carefully within the lines. Isuzu sales increased significantly after this campaign.[36]

As another example of a psychographic segmentation system developed for the luxury car market, German research firm Sigma categorized consumers in a way that inspired BMW's highly publicized product line reinvention and expansion. This system included "upper liberals" (socially conscious, open-minded professionals who prefer the roominess and flexibility of SUVs), "postmoderns" (high-earning innovators like architects, entrepreneurs, and artists who like the individualistic statements made by driving convertibles and roadsters), "upper conservatives" (made up of wealthy, traditional thinkers who like upper-crust, traditional sedans), and "modern mainstream" (family oriented, up-and-comers who want a luxury brand but likely can't afford more than the lowest-end model). Using this segmentation scheme as an anchor, BMW created vehicles for each category and also acquired Rolls Royce and the Mini to serve the

VALS2™ (Values and Lifestyles)
A psychographic system that divides the entire U.S. population into eight segments.

Figure 7.2 | VALS2™

VALS2™ uses psychological characteristics to segment the U.S. market into eight unique consumer groups.
Source: SRI CONSULTING BUSINESS INTELLIGENCE (SRIC-BI); **www.sric-bi.com/VALS**

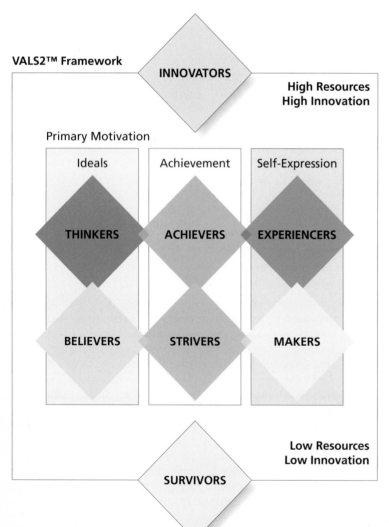

extreme ends—with phenomenal success over the past several years.[37]

Segment by Behavior

People may use the same product for different reasons, on different occasions, and in different amounts. So, in addition to demographics and psychographics, it is useful to study what consumers actually *do* with a product. **Behavioral segmentation** slices consumer segments on the basis of how they act toward, feel about, or use a product. Tropicana Essentials Healthy Heart, for example, targets consumers who want the health benefits of added vitamins and minerals, and no sodium in their OJ.

One way to segment based on behavior is to divide the market into users and nonusers of a product. Then marketers may attempt to reward current users or try to win over new ones. In addition to distinguishing between users and nonusers, marketers can segment current customers further into groups of heavy, moderate, and light users. They often do this according to a rule of thumb we call the **80/20 rule**: 20 percent of purchasers account for 80 percent of the product's sales (the ratio is an approximation, not gospel). This rule means that it often makes more sense to focus on the smaller number of people who are really into a product rather than on the larger number who are just casual users. Kraft Foods began a $30 million campaign to remind its core users not to "skip the zip" after its research showed that indeed 20 percent of U.S. households account for 80 percent of the usage of Miracle Whip. Are you surprised to learn that in this product category "heavy" users consume 17 pounds of Miracle Whip a year?[38]

While the 80/20 rule still holds in the majority of situations, the Internet's ability to offer an unlimited choice of goods to billions of people is changing how marketers think about segmentation. A new approach called the **long tail** is turning traditional thinking about the virtues of selling in high volume on its head. The basic idea is that we need no longer rely solely on big hits (like blockbuster movies or best-selling books) to find profits. Companies can also make money when they sell small amounts of items that only a few people want—if they sell enough different items. For example, Amazon.com maintains an inventory of 3.7 million books compared to the 100,000 or so you'll find in a Barnes & Noble retail store. Most of these will sell only a few thousand copies (if that), but the 3.6 million books that Barnes & Noble *doesn't* carry make up a quarter of Amazon's revenues! Similarly, about a fifth of the videos Netflix delivers to its customers are older or obscure titles rather than the blockbusters you'd find at, well, Blockbuster. Blizzard's *World of Warcraft's* massively multiplayer on-line game is another long tail. Instead of having to constantly release new sequels,

BMW relies on its Mini Cooper line to target a specific lifestyle segment.

The palmOne and other PDAs are lifestyle-oriented products that provide many benefits for today's tech-savvy consumers.

behavioral segmentation
A technique that divides consumers into segments on the basis of how they act toward, feel about, or use a good or service.

80/20 rule
A marketing rule of thumb that 20 percent of purchasers account for 80 percent of a product's sales.

long tail
A new approach to segmentation based on the idea that companies can make money by selling small amounts of items that only a few people want, provided they sell enough different items.

usage occasions
An indicator used in behavioral market segmentation based on when consumers use a product most.

Blizzard only has to release a few updates here and there. The sheer volume of users and the game's open world/do anything environment allows its users to constantly keep it interesting at no additional development costs to Blizzard. Other examples of the long tail include successful microbreweries and TV networks that make money on reruns of old shows on channels like Nick at Night. [39]

Another way to segment a market based on behavior is to look at **usage occasions**, or when consumers use the product most. We associate many products with specific occasions, whether time of day, holidays, business functions, or casual get-togethers. Businesses often divide up their markets according to when and how their offerings are in demand.

For example, consider how the Biltmore Estate in Asheville, North Carolina, increased attendance during its annual Christmas celebration. Set on 8,000 acres and featuring four acres of lavishly decorated floor space under one roof, the Biltmore is the largest private home in America. Although 750,000 people visit the house annually, in the early 1990s attendance was starting to stagnate. Then the estate's marketers mixed things up; they developed four separate strategies to target different types of visitors—heavy users such as those who have made a Christmas pilgrimage an annual family tradition versus light users who have visited only once. Each segment received a different invitation that included a customized package calculated to appeal to that segment. As a result, visits increased by 300 percent in one season, resulting in a Merry Christmas for the Biltmore.

In a similar vein, Google enables its advertising clients to target certain ads to certain segments of search engine users based on data such as Google domain, query entered, IP address, and language preference. This way, companies can have Google automatically sort and send the intended ad to certain market segments. Thus, it is possible for advertisers on Google to tailor their automatically-targeted ads based on seasonality—you will see more TurboTax ads on Google pages during tax season, even if people aren't querying tax software.[40]

Segmenting Business-to-Business Markets

We've reviewed the segmentation variables marketers use to divide up the consumer pie, but how about all those business-to-business marketers out there? Adding to what we learned about business markets in Chapter 6, it's important to know that segmentation also helps them better understand their customers. Though the specific variables may differ, the underlying logic of classifying the larger market into manageable pieces that share relevant characteristics is the same whether the product being sold is pesto or pesticides.

Organizational demographics also help a business-to-business marketer to understand the needs and characteristics of its potential customers. These classification dimensions include the size of the firms either in total sales or number of employees, the number of facilities, whether they are a domestic or a multinational company, purchasing policies, and the type of business they are in. Business-to-business markets may also be segmented on the basis of the production technology they use and whether the customer is a user or a nonuser of the product. General Electric's Aviation Division is one of the world's largest producers of jet engines. GE divides its customers by the types of jets they fly: commercial, corporate, marine, and military, or marine and industrial. The marine category, in fact, doesn't include planes at all but rather large ships and other applications of jet engine technologies.[41]

Many industries use the North American Industry Classification System (NAICS) we discussed in Chapter 6 to obtain information about the size and number of companies operating in a particular industry. Business-to-business marketers often consult information sources on the Web. For example, Hoovers Online (**www.hoovers.com**) provides subscribers with up-to-date information on private and public companies worldwide.

3

Step 2: Targeting

We've seen that the first step in a target marketing strategy is segmentation, in which the firm divides the market into smaller groups that share certain characteristics. The next step is **targeting**, in which marketers evaluate the attractiveness of each potential segment and decide in which of these groups they will invest resources to try to turn them into customers. The customer group or groups they select are the firm's **target market**. In this section, we'll review how marketers assess these customer groups, and we'll discuss selection strategies for effective targeting.

targeting
A strategy in which marketers evaluate the attractiveness of each potential segment and decide in which of these groups they will invest resources to try to turn them into customers.

target market
The market segments on which an organization focuses its marketing plan and toward which it directs its marketing efforts.

Evaluate Market Segments

Just because a marketer identifies a segment does not necessarily mean that it's a useful target. A viable target segment should satisfy the following requirements:

- **Are members of the segment similar to each other in their product needs and wants and, at the same time, different from consumers in other segments?** Without real differences in consumer needs, firms might as well use a mass-marketing strategy. For example, it's a waste of time to develop two separate lines of skin care products for working women and nonworking women if both segments have the same complaints about dry skin.

- **Can marketers measure the segment?** Marketers must know something about the size and purchasing power of a potential segment before they decide if it's worth their efforts.

- **Is the segment large enough to be profitable now and in the future?** For example, a graphic designer who hopes to design Web pages for Barbie-doll collectors must decide whether there are enough hard-core aficionados to make this business worthwhile and whether the trend will continue.

- **Can marketing communications reach the segment?** It is easy to select television programs or magazines that will efficiently reach older consumers, consumers with certain levels of education, or residents of major cities because the media they prefer are easy to identify. It is unlikely, however, that marketing communications can reach only left-handed blondes with tattoos who listen to Jessica Simpson overdubbed in Mandarin Chinese.

- **Can the marketer adequately serve the needs of the segment?** Does the firm have the expertise and resources to satisfy the segment better than the competition? Some years ago, consumer-products manufacturer Warner-Lambert (now a part of Pfizer) made the mistake of trying to enter the pastry business by purchasing Entenmanns's Bakery. Entenmanns's sells high-end boxed cakes, cookies, pastries, and pies in supermarkets. Unfortunately, Warner-Lambert's expertise at selling Listerine mouthwash and Trident gum did not transfer to baked goods, and it soon lost a lot of dough on the deal.

Peter
Hodgson
a student at Arizona State University
My Advice for NutriSystem would be to choose

Option

real people, **Other Voices**

I would choose **Option 3**. If NutriSystem is going to capture the male market, they need to go at it full force. "Dipping their toe" will

alert the competition and reduce NutriSystem's market share. They already understand what the male market is looking for and they know how to deliver that message. Focus on the hearty meals for men 35 to 55 who don't have time to go to the gym and need a supplemental weight-loss program. The female market is becoming saturated. NutriSystem will have to sustain their triple growth by capturing the men as quickly as possible. ➤

Develop Segment Profiles

Once a marketer identifies a set of usable segments, it is helpful to generate a profile of each to really understand segment members' needs and to look for business opportunities. This segment profile is a description of the "typical" customer in that segment. A **segment profile** might, for example, include customer demographics, location, lifestyle information, and a description of how frequently the customer buys the product.

Years ago, when the R.J. Reynolds Company made plans to introduce a new brand of cigarettes called Dakota that it would target to women, it created a segment profile of a possible customer group: The "Virile Female." The profile included these characteristics: Her favorite pastimes are cruising, partying, going to hot-rod shows and tractor pulls with her boyfriend, and watching evening soap operas. Her chief aspiration is to get married in her early 20s.[42] Anyone you know?

In 2003, Puma wanted to target the women athletes market; the company believed this group was largely neglected due to a history of male-dominated marketing in athletics. As a major part of its ad campaign, Puma organized a sporting event it called "4Some" that featured groups of women athletes competing against each other in a series of events. This not only promoted the Puma brand but it also communicated to women consumers that Puma was *serious* about women's sports.

Figure 7.3 | Choose a Target Marketing Strategy

Marketers must decide on a target marketing strategy. Should the company go after one total market, one or several market segments, or even target customers individually?

Undifferentiated Marketing

Differentiated Marketing

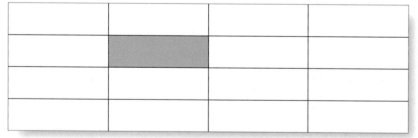

Concentrated Marketing

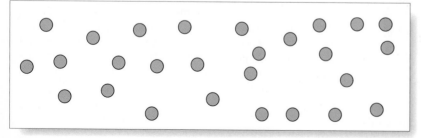

Customized Marketing

Choose a Targeting Strategy

A basic targeting decision revolves around how finely tuned the target should be: Should the company go after one large segment or focus on meeting the needs of one or more smaller segments? Let's look at four targeting strategies, which Figure 7.3 summarizes.

A company like Wal-Mart that selects an **undifferentiated targeting strategy** appeals to a broad spectrum of people. If successful, this type of operation can be very efficient because production, research, and promotion costs benefit from economies of scale—it's cheaper to develop one product or one advertising campaign than to choose several targets and create separate products or messages for each. But the company must be willing to bet that people have similar needs so the same product and message will appeal to many customers.

A company that chooses a **differentiated targeting strategy** develops one or more products for each of several customer groups with different product needs. A differentiated strategy is called for when consumers choose among well-known brands that have distinctive images and the company can identify one or more segments that have distinct needs for different types of products. The cosmetics giant

By the **People,** For the **People**

Behavioral targeting describes the process of tracking your clicking activity on the Internet and then insuring that you see on-line ads that relate to the places you visit. So, for example if you surf to several sites that sell discount contact lenses, you might "coincidentally" find that a pop-up ad for 1-800-CONTACTS magically appears on your screen. As you might imagine, these practices are controversial—advertisers argue they simply make it more likely you'll see content that will interest you, while privacy advocates worry about the idea that companies track what you're doing in cyberspace.

Many users like the idea that they can connect with companies and with other people that share their interests. Social networking sites like Facebook and consumer-generated media like YouTube are creating a consumer revolution in the marketplace; they allow users to call the shots by letting them seek out others who share their interests so they can pool information.

Numerous companies are jumping on the sharing bandwagon. At Dell's "Idea Storm" Web site customers vote for the features and products they want the computer company to take to market. Starbucks launched My Starbucks Ideas where customers vote for improved services or products in each of its stores (e.g., free wireless for frequent customers).

The Hobson and Holtz Report is a podcast that offers UserVoice; this application lets end users create blogs to pool information with others about products and services that interest them. *Across the Sound* is a marketing podcast that allows audiences to suggest their favorite content as well as tell the host what they like and dislike. This site proposes a new advertising strategy—*Advertising on Demand (AOD)*—that allows consumers to "pull" advertising based on their specific needs or moods. As social networking continues to spread, expect to see more examples of consumers segmenting themselves.[46]

L'Oréal follows this philosophy. The company has the resources to offer several product lines at a variety of prices. It targets the luxury market with such brands as Giorgio Armani, Lancôme, and Helena Rubinstein, while it develops less-expensive L'Oréal-branded products for large department stores and discounters, while it also sells Redken and Matrix brands to professional hairstylists.[43]

Likewise, Toyota offers a strong differentiated strategy with distinct product lines that cater to multiple customer groups. Its Lexus product line caters to consumers who want luxury, performance, and the newest technology. The Prius hybrid provides value to drivers who want to save gas money and the environment. And finally, the Scion product line caters to younger drivers who look for a relatively inexpensive car that is highly-customizable and stylish.[44]

Differentiated marketing can also involve connecting one product with different segments by communicating differently to appeal to those segments. Again using the "Got Milk?" ads as an example, Aerosmith's Steven Tyler appeals both to aging boomers who got into the band in the 1970s and Gen Yers who discovered the band in the 1990s due to Run-DMC's remake of "Walk This Way."

When a firm offers one or more products to a single segment, it uses a **concentrated targeting strategy**. Smaller firms that do not have the resources or the desire to be all things to all people often do this. For example, the cosmetics company Hard Candy sells its funky line of nail polish and other products to only 20-something women (or to those who wish they still were). Hard Candy's tagline is "Cosmetics in Cosmic Colors."

Blacksocks.com is a mail order sock company that only makes black dress socks; it targets businessmen who are too busy to go to the store and buy new socks when their old ones wear out. Blacksocks ship 3-packs of black socks once a month to its "sockscribers." The company argues that every guy who wears a business suit wears socks, and most wear black socks. For these busy men, going to the store just to buy socks is boring, time-consuming, and simply unnecessary. Periodically the company wrestles with the dilemma of whether or not to also sell white socks because this expansion will dilute the brand (and force the company to change its name!).[45]

segment profile
A description of the "typical" customer in a segment.

undifferentiated targeting strategy
Appealing to a broad spectrum of people.

differentiated targeting strategy
Developing one or more products for each of several distinct customer groups and making sure these offerings are kept separate in the marketplace.

concentrated targeting strategy
Focusing a firm's efforts on offering one or more products to a single segment.

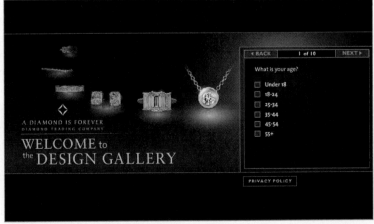

The diamond industry practices mass customization; engaged couples can design their own rings by specifying designs, diamond sizes and shapes, and mounting styles.

Ethical Decisions in the Real World

Targeting is not an exact science. Sometimes, consumers who are not really our targets are attracted to our products for reasons we may not understand. In most cases, this is not a bad thing—to the contrary, it just results in some extra unanticipated sales. But in certain sensitive product categories, like alcoholic beverages, firms often take great care to avoid even a perception of targeting the wrong (read: too young) groups.

Enter beverage giant Diageo, whose brands include Baileys, Guinness, Johnnie Walker, and Smirnoff. For some time, in order to capture the perfectly legal 21–30 Gen Y crowd, Diageo has been operating "virtual bars" through its Web site for promotional purposes. The company can control access to these sites to "card" people who want to enter. But more recently, Diageo setup a similar presence in the virtual world *Second Life*. The company argues that, given the changing face of their consumers who don't watch much TV or read traditional magazines and newspapers, it has to explore new communications channels. But Diageo doesn't want to unwittingly market its drinks to "underage avatars" in the virtual bars in *Second Life*—even though technically you're supposed to certify you're 18 or over to set up an SL account.

Is it appropriate for Diageo to promote its alcohol products in *Second Life*? What would you do?

Ripped from the Headlines! See what happened in the Real World at **www.mypearsonmarketinglab.com**

ETHICS CHECK: ➤

Find out what other students taking this course **would do** and **why** on **www. mypearsonmarketinglab. com**

Should a company that sells alcoholic beverages advertise in online formats that anyone regardless of age can access?

☐**YES** ☐**NO**

custom marketing strategy

An approach that tailors specific products and the messages about them to individual customers.

mass customization

An approach that modifies a basic good or service to meet the needs of an individual.

positioning

Develop a marketing strategy to influence how a particular market segment perceives a good or service in comparison to the competition.

Ideally, marketers should be able to define segments so precisely that they can offer products that exactly meet the unique needs of each individual or firm. This level of concentration does occur (we hope) in the case of personal or professional services we get from doctors, lawyers, and hairstylists. A **custom marketing strategy** also is common in industrial contexts where a manufacturer often works with one or a few large clients and develops products that only these clients will use.

Of course, in most cases this level of segmentation is neither practical nor possible when mass-produced products such as computers or cars enter the picture. However, advances in computer technology, coupled with the new emphasis on building solid relationships with customers, have focused managers' attention on devising new ways to tailor specific products and the messages about them to individual customers. Thus, some forward-looking, consumer-oriented companies are moving toward **mass customization** in which they modify a basic good or service to meet the needs of an individual.[47] Dell does this when it offers customized computer products over the Internet at Dell.com where users configure their own computers—everything from personal computers to networking systems. We'll return to the issue of customization later in this chapter when we introduce the idea of customer relationship management.

4

OBJECTIVE

Understand how marketers develop and implement a positioning strategy.

(pp. 216–219)

Step 3: Positioning

The final stage of developing a target marketing strategy is to provide consumers who belong to a targeted market segment with a good or service that meets their unique needs and expectations. **Positioning** means developing a marketing strategy to influence how a particular market segment perceives a good or service in comparison to the competition. To develop a positioning strategy, the marketers have to clearly understand the criteria target consumers use to evaluate competing products and then convince them that their product will meet those needs. In addition, the organization has to come up with way to communicate this "position" to its target market.

Positioning happens in many ways. Sometimes it's just a matter of making sure that cool people use your product—and that others observe them doing this. After finding out that a close friend was flying to Los Angeles to audition for the film *Any Given Sunday,* the president of the high-performance sportswear company Under Armour sent along with him a bunch of free samples of its athletic wear to give to the film's casting director as a gift. The director liked the quality of the clothes so much he gave them to the wardrobe company the filmmakers hired and they also really liked the clothes. The next thing you know, the movie (starring Al Pacino and Jamie Foxx) featured both the actors wearing Under Armour clothes on screen—and there was even a scene in the film when Jamie Foxx undressed in the locker room with a clear shot of the Under Armour logo on his jock strap. After the movie's release, hits on Under Armour's Web site spiked, and, as they say, the rest is history.[48] Let's take a look at the steps marketers use to decide just how to position their product or service.

BC Ethic positioned its shirts as "cool" by providing popular music groups with custom-designed shirts and then using the groups in its advertising.

1. Analyze Competitors' Positions

The first step is to analyze competitors' positions in the marketplace. To develop an effective positioning strategy, marketers must understand the current lay of the land. What competitors are out there, and how does the target market perceive them? Aside from direct competitors in the product category, are there other goods or services that provide similar benefits?

Sometimes the indirect competition can be more important than the direct, especially if it represents an emerging consumer trend. For years, McDonald's developed positioning strategies based only on its direct competition, which it defined as other large fast-food hamburger chains (translation: Burger King and Wendy's). McDonald's failed to realize that in fact many indirect competitors fulfilled consumers' needs for a quick, tasty, convenient meal—from supermarket delis to frozen microwavable single-serving meals to call-ahead takeout from full-service restaurants like T.G.I. Friday's, Outback, and Chili's. Only recently, McDonald's has begun to understand that it must react to this indirect competition by serving up a wider variety of adult-friendly food and shoring up lagging service.

2. Offer a Good or Service with a Competitive Advantage

The second step is to offer a good or service with a competitive advantage to provide a reason why consumers will perceive the product as better than the competition. If the company offers only a "me-too product," it can induce people to buy for a lower price. Other forms of competitive advantage include offering a superior image (Giorgio Armani), a unique product feature (Levi's 501 button-fly jeans), better service (Cadillac's roadside assistance program), or even better-qualified people (the legendary salespeople at Nordstrom's department stores).

3. Finalize the Marketing Mix

Once they settle on a positioning strategy, the third step for marketers is to finalize the marketing mix by putting all the pieces into place. The elements of the marketing mix must match the selected segment. This means that the good or service must deliver benefits that the segment values, such as convenience or status. Put another way, it must add value and satisfy consumer needs. Furthermore, marketers must price this offering at a level these consumers will pay, make the offering available at places consumers are likely to go, and correctly communicate the offering's benefits in locations where consumers are likely to take notice.

4. Evaluate Responses and Modify as Needed

In the fourth and final step, marketers evaluate the target market's responses so they can modify strategies as needed. Over time, the firm may find that it needs to change which segments it targets or even alter a product's position to respond to marketplace changes. Consider this classic example: Macho Marlboro cigarettes originally were a smoke for women—complete with a red tip to hide lipstick stains!

A change strategy is **repositioning**, and it's fairly common to see a company try to modify its brand image to keep up with changing times. Take as an example Charles Schwab, which used to be pegged primarily as a self-service stock brokerage. Competition in the budget broker business, especially from on-line brokers, prompted Schwab's repositioning to a full-line, full-service financial services firm. Think of it this way: There's not much value Schwab can add as one of a dozen or more on-line providers of stock trades. In that environment, customers simply will view the firm as a commodity (i.e., just a way to buy stocks) with no real differentiation. Schwab still has its no-frills products, but the real growth in sales and profits comes from its expanded product lines and provision of more information—both on-line and through personal selling—hence, its current commercials that encourage customers to "ask Chuck."

Repositioning also occurs when a marketer revises a brand thought to be dead or at least near death. Sometimes these products arise from their deathbeds to ride a wave of nostalgia and return to the marketplace as **retro brands**—venerable brands like Oxydol laundry detergent, Breck Shampoo, Ovaltine cereal, and Tab cola have gotten a new lease on life in recent years.[49]

Bring a Product to Life: The Brand Personality

In a way, brands are like people: We often describe them in terms of personality traits. We may use adjectives such as cheap, elegant, sexy, or cool when we talk about a store, a perfume, or a car. That's why a positioning strategy often tries to create a **brand personality** for a good or service—a distinctive image that captures its character and benefits. An advertisement for *Elle* magazine proclaimed, "She is not a reply card. She is not a category. She is not shrink-wrapped. *Elle* is not a magazine. She is a woman."

Products as people? It seems funny to say, yet marketing researchers find that most consumers have no trouble describing what a product would be like "if it came to life." People often give clear, detailed descriptions, including what color hair the product would have, the type of house it would live in, and even whether it would be thin, overweight, or somewhere in between.[50] If you don't believe us, try doing this yourself.

Part of creating a brand personality is developing an identity for the product that the target market will prefer over competing brands. How do marketers determine where their product actually stands in the minds of consumers? One solution is to ask consumers what characteristics are important and how competing alternatives would rate on these attributes, too. Marketers use this information to construct a **perceptual map**; a vivid way to construct a picture of where products or brands are "located" in consumers' minds.

repositioning
Redoing a product's position to respond to marketplace changes.

retro brand
A once-popular brand that has been revived to experience a popularity comeback, often by riding a wave of nostalgia.

brand personality
A distinctive image that captures a good's or service's character and benefits.

perceptual map
A technique to visually describe where brands are "located" in consumers' minds relative to competing brands.

Brand personalities often are reflected in logos. This clothing ad from Chile pits a shark against the more familiar crocodile—with bloody results.

For example, suppose you wanted to construct a perceptual map of how American women in their 20s perceive magazines to help you develop an idea for a new publication that these readers would like. After you interview a sample of female readers, you might identify two key questions women ask when they select a magazine: (1) Is it "traditional," that is, oriented toward family, home, or personal issues, or is it "fashion-forward," oriented toward personal appearance and fashion? and (2) Is it for "upscale" women who are older and established in their careers or for relatively "downscale" women who are younger and just starting out in their careers?

The perceptual map in Figure 7.4 illustrates how these ratings might look for a set of major women's magazines. The map provides some guidance as to where you might position your new magazine. You might decide to compete directly with either the cluster of "service magazines" in the lower left or the traditional fashion magazines in the upper right. In this case, you would have to determine what benefits your new magazine might offer that these existing magazines do not. Conde Nast, for example, positioned *Allure* to compete against fashion magazines by going into more depth than they do on beauty issues, such as the mental, physical, and emotional dangers of cosmetic surgery.

Figure 7.4 | Perceptual Map

Perceptual mapping allows marketers to identify consumers' perceptions of their brand in relation to the competition.

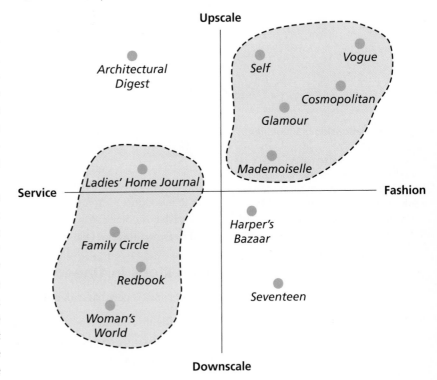

You might try to locate an unserved area in this perceptual map. There may be room for a magazine that targets "cutting-edge" fashion for college-age women. An unserved segment is the "Holy Grail" for marketers: With luck, they can move quickly to capture a segment and define the standards of comparison for the category. This tactic paid off for Chrysler, which first identified the minivan market; JetBlue, which found a spot for low fares and high tech without the poor-boy service attitude of other budget airlines; and Liz Claiborne, which pioneered the concept of comfortable, "user-friendly" clothing for working women. In the magazine category, perhaps *Marie Claire* comes closest to this position.

So, the last step in the target marketing process is to create a positioning strategy. To summarize this sequence of events, look at the positioning strategy the SoBe Beverage Company developed. SoBe is a small drink manufacturer based in Connecticut that offers a line of teas, elixirs, and power drinks. The company first segmented the market in terms of age and psychographic. Then it targeted a segment of 18- to 35-year-olds whose profiles indicated they were into "New Age" beverages that would give them a feeling of energy without unhealthy additives. SoBe created XTC, a drink inspired by "herbal ecstasy" cocktails of extracts and amino acids first made popular at 1990s' "raves" featuring all-night gyrations to techno music. As an industry executive noted, this strategy provides a unique position for the elixir: "People are taking something that provides a four-times-removed high without having to get arrested or wrecking their bodies. It carries the image of being a little further out there without carrying the risk." Today, XTC has given way to SoBe's Adrenaline Rush and No Fear products, which offer the ever-moving and multitasking Gen Yers "sustained energy for non-stop living."[51]

<table>
<tr><td>

5

OBJECTIVE

Explain how marketers increase long-term success and profits by practicing customer relationship management.

(pp. 220–224)

</td><td>

Customer Relationship Management: Toward a Segment of One

</td></tr>
</table>

We've talked about how marketers identify a unique group of consumers and then develop products specifically to meet their needs. And we talked about how marketers today build products to meet the needs of individual consumers by using mass customization techniques. As we discussed in Chapter 1, currently many highly successful marketing firms embrace **customer relationship management (CRM)** programs that involve systematically tracking consumers' preferences and behaviors over time in order to tailor the value proposition as closely as possible to each individual's unique wants and needs. CRM allows firms to talk to individual customers and to adjust elements of their marketing programs in light of how each customer reacts.[52] The CRM trend facilitates *one-to-one marketing*, a term popularized in the writings of Don Peppers and Martha Rogers.[53]

customer relationship management (CRM)

A systematic tracking of consumers' preferences and behaviors over time in order to tailor the value proposition as closely as possible to each individual's unique wants and needs. CRM allows firms to talk to individual customers and to adjust elements of their marketing programs in light of how each customer reacts.

Four Steps in One-to-One Marketing

Peppers and Rogers have identified four steps in one-to-one marketing:[54]

1. Identify customers and get to know them in as much detail as possible.

2. Differentiate among these customers in terms of both their needs and their value to the company.

3. Interact with customers and find ways to improve cost efficiency and the effectiveness of the interaction.

4. Customize some aspect of the goods or services that you offer to each customer. This means treating each customer differently based on what has been learned through customer interactions.

Table 7.2 suggests some activities to implement these four steps. Remember, successful one-to-one marketing depends on CRM. Peppers and Rogers define CRM as "… managing customer relationships. If I'm managing customer relationships, it means I'm treating different customers differently, across all enterprises....The relationship develops a context over time, it drives a change in behavior....[This] means that I have to change my behavior as an enterprise based on a customer."[55] A CRM strategy allows a company to identify its best customers, stay on top of their needs, and increase their satisfaction.

Is CRM for all companies? Should producers of consumer goods that target the entire market adopt CRM strategies? All things equal, CRM makes more sense for firms such as business-to-business companies and consumer products companies that have a limited number of customers. But, as we'll see in the next section, even soft-drink and automobile companies use at least some CRM principles to build customer relationships and enhance brand loyalty.

CRM: A New Perspective on an Old Problem

CRM is about communicating with customers, and about customers being able to communicate with a company "up close and personal." CRM systems are applications that use computers, specialized computer software, databases, and often the Internet to capture information at each **touchpoint**, which is any point of direct interface between customers and a company (online, by phone, or in person).

touchpoint

Any point of direct interface between customers and a company (online, by phone, or in person).

These systems include everything from Web sites that let you check on the status of a bill or package to call centers that solicit your business. When you log on to the Federal

Table 7.2	**Four Steps of One-to-One Marketing**

Step	Suggested Activities
Identify	Collect and enter names and additional information about your customers.
	Verify and update, deleting outdated information.
Differentiate	Identify top customers.
	Determine which customers cost the company money.
	Find higher-value customers who have complained about your product more than once.
	Find customers who buy only one or two products from your company but a lot from other companies.
	Rank customers into A, B, and C categories based on their value to your company.
Interact	Call the top three people in the top five percent of dealers, distributors, and retailers that carry your product and make sure they're happy.
	Call your own company and ask questions; see how hard it is to get through and get answers.
	Call your competitors and compare their customer service with yours.
	Use incoming calls as selling opportunities.
	Initiate more dialogue with valuable customers.
	Improve complaint handling.
Customize	Find out what your customers want.
	Personalize your direct mail.
	Ask customers how and how often they want to hear from you.
	Ask your top 10 customers what you can do differently to improve your product.
	Involve top management in customer relations.

Source: Adapted by permission of *Harvard Business Review* from Don Peppers, Martha Rogers, and Bob Dorf, "Is your Company Ready for One-to-One Marketing?" *Harvard Business Review* (January–February 1999), 151–60. Copyright © 1999 by the Harvard Business School Publishing Corporation. All rights reserved.

Express Web site to track a lost package, that's part of a CRM system. When you get a phone message from the dentist reminding you about your appointment tomorrow to get a root canal, that's CRM (sorry about that). And when you get a call from the car dealer asking how you like your new vehicle, that's also CRM. Remember how in Chapter 4 we said information is the fuel that runs the marketing engine? It is through CRM that companies act upon and manage the information they gather from their customers.

To fully appreciate the value of a CRM strategy, consider the experience of USAA, which began as an insurance company catering to the military market and today is a leading global financial services powerhouse. In 1922, when 25 army officers met in San Antonio and decided to insure each other's vehicles, they could not have imagined that their tiny organization would one day serve 6 million members and become the only fully integrated financial services company in America. Unlike State Farm, Allstate, and other traditional insurance providers, USAA does not provide field agents with an office you can go to, sit down, and shoot the breeze. In fact, USAA's employees conduct business almost

Janice M.
Karlen
a professor at City University of New York—LaGuardia Community College

My Advice for NutriSystem would be to choose

Option

real people, **Other** Voices

I would choose **Option 3** because NutriSystem had an identified core competency and proven track record at creating compelling messages and communicating them effectively to their female target audience. Their marketing research indicated that men were motivated by many

of the same factors as women when faced with a weight loss decision. While men historically preferred not to diet to lose weight, choosing instead to exercise or limit beer intake, a meal plan that allowed men to continue eating their favorite foods and still lose weight was a new alternative for them. The addition of a prominent male celebrity spokesperson to the new campaign would be an effective way of assuring men that this was a product specifically developed to meet their needs and not something that was a woman's product being sold to men. They could eat their favorite foods, lose weight, and be proud to identify with the celebrity associated with NutriSystem. ➤

entirely over the phone. But just ask any USAA member how they feel about the service, and you'll get a glowing report.

The secret to USAA's success is largely due to its state-of-the-art CRM system. No matter where on the globe you are, no matter what time of day or night, a USAA representative will pull up your profile and you'll feel like he knows you. Of course, it takes a good dose of employee training to enable those folks to use the system to its potential. But USAA does a great job of building and maintaining long-term customer relationships, and (more importantly) getting customers to move many or all of their business over to USAA including banking, credit cards, money management, investments, and financial planning. To further build loyalty, USAA even runs an on-line company store that sells all sorts of popular product lines and brands for which members get purchase discounts.[56]

USAA's success helps explain why CRM has become a driving philosophy in many successful firms. A study by the Services & Support Professionals Association (SSPA) estimates that in 2008, organizations with more than $1 billion in revenue spent approximately $565 million on e-service, CRM, contact center, and field service technology. Small and mid-sized businesses spent about $884 million. And, Forrester Research predicts that the CRM market will reach $10.9 billion by 2010.[57]

The airline industry, recently rocked by hyper-escalating fuel prices and resultant financial problems, is especially concerned about maintaining good relationships with its most profitable and loyal customers. Hence, they invest heavily in CRM systems. These systems help fliers by automating crucial information, providing points for advanced contact if flights become disrupted, and (hopefully) reducing phone call volume—and in the process those nasty "holds" to which unfortunately we're all accustomed.[58] CRM also helps identify flying patterns, favored destinations, and loyal users so that airlines can send extra perks (upgrades, tailored special offers, and so on) to their frequent flyers.

Amazon.com is the world champion master of the happy customer approach to CRM. For loyal users, Amazon tracks visits so it can customize advertisements, product promotions, and discounts for each shopper. And, if you happen to have a passion for, say, grunge bands of the 1990s, the Web site is quick to recommend that new retrospective on Pearl Jam the next time you visit.[59]

Perhaps the most important aspect of CRM is that it presents a new way to look at how to effectively compete in the marketplace. For starters, regard your customers as partners. CRM proponents suggest that the traditional relationship between customers and marketers is an adversarial one where marketers try to force their products on their customers—who in turn often try to avoid them.[60] In contrast the customer relationship perspective argues that each party in the transaction needs the other one—and they should work together to make the engagement mutually satisfying. Successful firms compete best when they establish relationships with individual customers on a one-to-one basis through dialogue and feedback. What does *this* customer really want? That's one-to-one marketing.

Metrics Moment

CRM relies almost totally on customer data the firm collects, which it then uses to customize product offerings and marketing communications. All good stuff, right?

Well, not always...at least according to Ian Ayres' book *Super Crunchers: Why Thinking-by-Numbers Is the New Way To Be Smart*. Ayres, an econometrician and law professor at Yale, argues that the proliferation of consumer information available for decision making by marketers forces a shift in marketing from a field that always balanced its decision making between expertise/intuition and with hard data, to one in which data reigns supreme. According to Ayers, those who control and manipulate this data will be the masters of the new economic universe—the "Super Crunchers."

It's hard to argue with his premise. "Marketing metrics" was a phrase unknown to the field a short decade ago. CEOs have gotten the message, and they're demanding all sorts of new analyses from chief marketing officers (CMOs) so they can better "quantify" marketing's contributions to the bottom line. It's not too surprising that a recent *BusinessWeek* survey of the shelf life of the various top-level functional executives revealed that the CMO's average tenure firms is the lowest among the areas—26 months, compared with 44 months for CEOs, 39 months for chief financial officers (CFOs), and 36 months for chief information officers (CIOs). The pressure to provide tangible results is intense.[61]

Metrics let us learn a lot about how we can squeeze the most value from our marketing investments. But, remember what we said in Chapter 4 regarding the need to think carefully about the data we collect—Garbage In, Garbage Out! So, let's not beef up on metrics at the expense of creativity and innovation!

Characteristics of CRM

In addition to having a different mind-set, companies that successfully practice CRM have different goals, use different measures of success, and look at customers in some different ways. Followers of this approach look at their share of the customer, at the lifetime value of a customer, at customer equity, and they focus on high-value customers. Let's have a look at each of these ideas now.

Share of Customer

Historically, marketers measured success in a product category by their share of the market. For example, if people buy 100 million pairs of athletic shoes each year, a firm that sells 10 million of them claims a 10 percent market share. If the shoemaker's marketing objective is to increase market share, it may lower the price of its shoes, increase its advertising, or offer customers a free basketball with every pair of shoes they purchase. Such tactics may increase sales in the short run but, unfortunately, they may not do much for the long-term success of the shoemaker. In fact, such tactics may actually decrease the value of the brand because they cheapen its image with giveaways.

Because it is always easier and less expensive to keep an existing customer than to get a new customer (yes, we've said that already), CRM firms try to increase their **share of customer**, not share of market. Let's say that a consumer buys six pairs of shoes a year—two pairs from each of three different manufacturers. Assume one shoemaker has a CRM system that allows it to send letters to its current customers inviting them to receive a special price discount or a gift if they buy more of the firm's shoes during the year. If the firm can get the consumer to buy three or four or perhaps all six pairs from it, it has increased its share of customer. And that may not be too difficult, because the customer already likes the firm's shoes. Without the CRM system, the shoe company would probably use traditional advertising to increase sales, which would be far more costly than the customer-only direct-mail campaign. So the company can increase sales and profits at a much lower cost than it would spend to get one, two, or three new customers.

share of customer
The percentage of an individual customer's purchase of a product that is a single brand.

Lifetime Value of the Customer

As you'll recall from Chapter 1, the **lifetime value of a customer** is the potential profit a single customer's purchase of a firm's products generates over the customer's lifetime. It just makes sense that a firm's profitability and long-term success are going to be far greater if it develops long-term relationships with its customers so that those customers buy from it again and again. Costs will be far higher and profits lower if each customer's purchase is a first-time sale.

How do marketers calculate the lifetime value of a customer? They first estimate a customer's future purchases across all products from the firm over the next 20 or 30 years. The goal is to try to figure out what profit the company could make from the customer in the future (obviously, this will just be an estimate). For example, an auto dealer might calculate the lifetime value of a single customer by first calculating the total revenue the customer will generate for the company during his life. This figure includes the number of automobiles he will probably buy times their average price, plus the service the dealership would provide over the years, and even possibly the income from auto loan financing. The lifetime value of the customer would be the total profit the revenue stream generates.

lifetime value of a customer
The potential profit a single customer's purchase of a firm's products generates over the customer's lifetime.

Customer Equity

Today an increasing number of companies consider their relationships with customers as financial assets. These firms measure success by calculating the value of their **customer equity**—the financial value of a customer throughout the lifetime of the relationship.[62] To do this, they compare the investments they make to acquire customers and then to retain them to the financial return they'll get on those investments.

customer equity
The financial value of a customer relationship throughout the lifetime of the relationship.

Thomas F.
Connerty
APPLYING CRM

NutriSystem bases its entire marketing strategy on its ability to carefully track its customers and how they respond to its messages over time. ➡

customer experience management (CEM)

The concept of holistically aligning a firm's people, processes, systems, and strategies to maximize the customer's experience with all aspects of your firm and its brands.

Focus on High-Value Customers

Using a CRM approach, the organization prioritizes its customers and customizes its communications to them accordingly. For example, any banker will tell you that not all customers are equal when it comes to profitability. Some generate a lot of revenue because they bank interest on loans or credit cards, while others basically just use the bank as a convenient place to store a small amount of money and take out a little bit each week to buy beer. So banks use CRM systems to generate a profile of each customer based on factors such as value, risk, attrition, and interest in buying new financial products. This automated system helps the bank decide which current or potential customers it will target with certain communications or how much effort it will expend to retain an account—all the while cutting its costs by as much as a third. It just makes sense to use different types of communication contacts based on the value of each individual customer. For example, personal selling (the most expensive form of marketing communication per contact) may constitute 75 percent of all contacts with high-volume customers, while direct mail or telemarketing is more often the best way to talk to low-volume customers.

CEM: The New Kid on the Block

Now, let's take CRM a step further. The concept of holistically aligning a firm's people, processes, systems, and strategies to maximize the customer's experience with all aspects of your firm and its brands has become known as **customer experience management (CEM)**. Firms practicing CEM find that it is an effective bridge between the firm's CRM approach and its leadership, strategies, and operational capabilities. CEM focuses every aspect of the firm on all the *touchpoints* between it and its customers—not just for data collection purposes, but also to enhance the customer's experience. So while CRM tends to be more about building and using customer data for decision making and marketing, CEM is more about aligning internal resources so that all the encounters between the customer and the company are consistently favorable.[63]

And, of course, when we say customers, we don't just mean end-user consumers—CRM (and CEM) strengthen business-to-business relationships as well. To understand the importance of this kind of thinking, consider the experience of SPAR Switzerland, one of the most prominent grocery store chains in Western Europe. Its use of a sophisticated CRM system enabled the organization to create a "virtualized environment" so it could deal with its many suppliers, distributors, and store locations. The system basically works as one big network that maximizes the effectiveness of ordering and distribution processes using variables such as individual store stocking needs, distance to specific stores, and availability of products from suppliers. Through this system, SPAR had its most important channel stakeholders directly in its business—while at the same time it created a sense of trust and community that's hard to put a price tag on.[64]

Real People, **Real Choices**

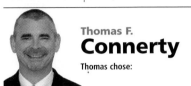

Thomas F.
Connerty

Thomas chose:

Option

How it Worked Out at NutriSystem

Tom chose Option 1. NutriSystem entered the men's market with great trepidation. Based on industry history no one felt that this would be a successful campaign, so the company approached the effort in the most conservative fashion possible. It filmed a bare bones commercial with real customers and an actor (not a celebrity) to convey the benefits of the program. Tom decided not to spend money on a celebrity spokesperson until he could prove that the concept had some life in it.

The company launched the men's program in January 2007 with a "real customer" Direct Response Television campaign. It purchased media on these national cable networks: Bravo, Discovery Channel, FX, National Geographic Channel, Outdoor Life, Spike TV, Sci-Fi Channel, and the Speed Channel Network.

Each commercial had a unique 800 number and URL so that NutriSystem could trace the order back to the placement of the ad. That way the company could determine the value of the media it had purchased. If the acquisition cost exceeded the marginal revenue per customer, Tom would have to renegotiate rates or cancel future placements. If the acquisition cost was lower than the marginal revenue per customer target then he could purchase more time and self-fund the advertising campaign. Such is the nature of direct response media buying.

As it turned out, the acquisition costs were lower than the marginal revenue per customer and the company was able to spend $9 million in media in its initial quarterly launch. Eventually the spend would climb to $14 million, yielding 20,000 new men customers that were traceable to the campaign. During this time the percentage of NutriSystem's customers who are male grew from 13 percent at the beginning of 2006 to nearly 30 percent by the end of the year. Sales to men are on pace to generate more than $225,000,000 in 2007. As a result NutriSystem became the largest weight loss program for men in the United States.

How NutriSystem Measures Success

Tom and his colleagues at NutriSystem live by the adage: "What gets measured, gets managed." As a tried-and-true direct response marketing company, the firm measures and analyzes every creative execution and every media purchase to determine if it made profitable decisions.

NutriSystem relies upon two primary metrics: 1) Media acquisition cost or *Cost per order* (CPO), and 2) Length of stay per customer. Cost per order is the measurement of the effectiveness of the advertisement. Length of stay allows the company to measure a customer's satisfaction with the NutriSystem program. Because NutriSystem's revenue is based upon multiple shipments over time, it's essential that customers continue to renew their monthly orders. That's why a longer length of stay translates into higher revenue per customer.

NutriSystem found during its men's campaign that its CPO's were lower than the revenue per customer number. Thus it was able to continue to buy more media to fuel the campaign. Also the firm found that men stayed on the program approximately seven days longer than its core customer demographic of women aged 35–55 so this greater length of stay allows it to pump even more money into additional media to promote the product line.

NutriSystem's new campaign targets men.

Refer back to **page 197** for Thomas's story

Brand **YOU**!

Great brands are NOT all things to all people.

The best brands target their customers. Learn how to target your brand and work smarter, not harder to land your dream job. Chapter 7 in the *Brand You* supplement helps your job search come into focus.

Objective Summary → Key Terms → Apply | Study Map

1. Objective Summary (pp. 198–199)

Identify the steps in the target marketing process.

Marketers must balance the efficiency of mass marketing, serving the same items to everyone, with the effectiveness of offering each individual exactly what she wants. To accomplish this, instead of trying to sell something to everyone, marketers follow these steps: (1) select a target marketing strategy, in which they divide the total market into different segments based on customer characteristics; (2) select one or more segments; and (3) develop products to meet the needs of those specific segments.

Key Terms

market fragmentation, p. 198

target marketing strategy, p. 198

2. Objective Summary (pp. 199–212)

Understand the need for market segmentation and the approaches available to do it.

Market segmentation is often necessary in today's marketplace because of market fragmentation—that is, the splintering of a mass society into diverse groups due to technological and cultural differences. Most marketers can't realistically do a good job of meeting the needs of everyone, so it is more efficient to divide the larger pie into slices in which members of a segment share some important characteristics and tend to exhibit the same needs and preferences. Marketers frequently find it useful to segment consumer markets on the basis of demographic characteristics, including age, gender, family life cycle, social class, race or ethnic identity, and place of residence. A second dimension, psychographics, uses measures of psychological and social characteristics to identify people with shared preferences or traits. Consumer markets may also be segmented on the basis of how consumers behave toward the product, for example, their brand loyalty, usage rates (heavy, moderate, or light), and usage occasions. Business-to-business markets are often segmented on the basis of industrial demographics, type of business based on the North American Industry Classification (NAICS) codes, and geographic location.

Key Terms

segmentation, p. 199 (Figure 7.1, p. 199)

segmentation variables, p. 199

Generation Y, p. 199

demographics, p. 200

generational marketing, p. 200

Generation X, p. 201

baby boomers, p. 201

metrosexual, p. 203

cultural diversity, p. 206

geodemography, p. 207 (Table 7.1, p. 208–209)

geocoding, p. 207

psychographics, p. 209 (Figure 7.2, p. 210)

VALS2™ (Values and Lifestyles), p. 209 (Figure 7.2, p. 210)

behavioral segmentation, p. 211

80/20 rule, p. 211

long tail, p. 211

usage occasions, p. 212

3. Objective Summary (pp. 213–216)

Explain how marketers evaluate segments and choose a targeting strategy.

To choose one or more segments to target, marketers examine each segment and evaluate its potential for success as a target market. Meaningful segments have wants that are different from those in other segments, can be identified, can be reached with a unique marketing mix, will respond to unique marketing communications, are large enough to be profitable, have future growth potential, and possess needs that the organization can satisfy better than the competition.

After marketers identify the different segments, they estimate the market potential of each. The relative attractiveness of segments also influences the firm's selection of an overall marketing strategy. The firm may choose an undifferentiated, differentiated, concentrated, or custom strategy based on the company's characteristics and the nature of the market.

Key Terms

targeting, p. 213 (Figure 7.1, p. 199)

target market, p. 213

segment profile, p. 214

undifferentiated targeting strategy, p. 214 (Figure 7.3, p. 214)

differentiated targeting strategy, p. 214 (➡ Applying, p. 214) (Figure 7.3, p. 214)

concentrated targeting strategy, p. 215 (Figure 7.3, p. 214)

custom marketing strategy, 216 (Figure 7.3, p. 214)

mass customization, p. 216

4. Objective Summary (pp. 216–219)

Understand how marketers develop and implement a positioning strategy.

After marketers select the target market(s) and the overall strategy, they must determine how they wish customers to perceive the brand relative to the competition—that is, should the brand be positioned like, against, or away from the competition? Through positioning, a brand personality is developed. Marketers can compare brand positions by using such research techniques as perceptual mapping. In developing and implementing the positioning strategy, firms analyze the competitors' positions, determine the competitive advantage offered by their product, tailor the marketing mix in accordance with the positioning strategy, and evaluate responses to the marketing mix selected. Marketers must continually monitor changes in the market that might indicate a need to reposition the product.

Key Terms

positioning, p. 216 (Figure 7.1, p. 199)

repositioning, p. 218

retro brands, p. 218

brand personality, p. 218

perceptual map, p. 218 (Figure 7.4, p. 219)

5. Objective Summary (pp. 220–224)

Explain how marketers increase long-term success and profits by practicing customer relationship management.

Companies using customer relationship management (CRM) programs establish relationships and differentiate their behavior toward individual customers on a one-to-one basis through dialogue and feedback. Success is often measured one customer at a time using the concepts of share of customer, lifetime value of the customer, and customer equity. In CRM strategies, customers are prioritized according to their value to the firm, and communication is customized accordingly.

Key Terms

customer relationship management (CRM) p. 220, ➡ Applying, p. 224

touchpoint, p. 220

share of customer, p. 223

lifetime value of a customer, p. 223

customer equity, p. 223

customer experience management (CEM), p. 224

Chapter **Questions** and **Activities**

Concepts: Test Your Knowledge

1. What is market segmentation, and why is it an important strategy in today's marketplace?
2. List and explain the major demographic characteristics frequently used in segmenting consumer markets.
3. Explain consumer psychographic segmentation.
4. What is behavioral segmentation?
5. What are some of the ways marketers segment industrial markets?
6. List the criteria marketers use to determine whether a segment may be a good candidate for targeting.
7. Explain undifferentiated, differentiated, concentrated, and customized marketing strategies. What is mass customization?
8. What is product positioning? What do marketers mean by creating a brand personality? How do marketers use perceptual maps to help them develop effective positioning strategies?
9. What is CRM? How do firms practice CRM?
10. Explain the concepts of CEM, share of customer, lifetime value of a customer, and customer equity.

Choices and Ethical Issues: You Decide

1. Some critics of marketing have suggested that market segmentation and target marketing lead to an unnecessary proliferation of product choices that wastes valuable resources. These critics suggest that if marketers didn't create so many different product choices, there would be more resources to feed the hungry and house the homeless and provide for the needs of people around the globe. Are the results of segmentation and target marketing harmful or beneficial to society as a whole? Should firms be concerned about these criticisms?

2. One of the criteria for a usable market segment is its size. This chapter suggested that to be usable, a segment must be large enough to be profitable now and in the future and that some very small segments get ignored because they can never be profitable. So how large should a segment be? How do you think a firm should go about determining if a segment is profitable? Have technological advances made it possible for smaller segments to be profitable? Do firms ever have a moral or ethical obligation to develop products for small, unprofitable segments?

3. A few years ago, Anheuser-Busch Inc. created a new division dedicated to marketing to Hispanics and announced it would boost its ad spending in Hispanic media by two-thirds to more than $60 million, while Miller Brewing Co. signed a $100 million, three-year ad package with Spanish-language broadcaster Univision Communications Inc. But Hispanic activists immediately raised public-health concerns about the beer ad blitz on the grounds that it targets a population that skews young and is disproportionately likely to abuse alcohol. Surveys of Hispanic youth are much more likely to drink alcohol, get drunk, and to engage in binge drinking, than their white or black peers. A senior executive at Anheuser-Busch

responded, "We would disagree with anyone who suggests beer billboards increase abuse among Latino or other minority communities. It would be poor business for us in today's world to ignore what is the fastest-growing segment of our population."[65]

Manufacturers of alcohol and tobacco products have been criticized for targeting unwholesome products to certain segments of the market—the aged, ethnic minorities, the disabled, and others. Do you view this as a problem? Should a firm use different criteria in targeting such groups? Should the government oversee and control such marketing activities?

4. Customer relationship management (CRM) focuses on share of customer, lifetime value of the customer, customer equity, and high-value customers. What do you think are some problems with replacing earlier concepts such as share of market with these concepts?

Practice: Apply What You've Learned

1. Assume that a firm has hired you to develop a marketing plan for a small regional beer brewery. In the past, the brewery has simply produced and sold a single beer brand to the entire market—a mass-marketing strategy. As you begin work, you feel that the firm could be more successful if it developed a target marketing strategy. The owner of the firm, however, is not convinced. Write a memo to the owner outlining the following:
   a. The basic reasons for target marketing
   b. The specific advantages of a target marketing strategy for the brewery
2. As the marketing director for a company that is planning to enter the business-to-business market for photocopy machines, you are attempting to develop an overall marketing strategy. You have considered the possibility of using mass marketing, concentrated marketing, differentiated marketing, and custom marketing strategies.
   a. Write a report explaining what each type of strategy would mean for your marketing plan in terms of product, price, promotion, and distribution channel.
   b. Evaluate the desirability of each type of strategy.
   c. What are your final recommendations for the best type of strategy?

3. As an account executive for a marketing consulting firm, your newest client is a university—your university. You have been asked to develop a positioning strategy for the university. With a group of classmates, develop an outline of your ideas, including the following:
   a. Who are your competitors?
   b. What are the competitors' positions?
   c. What target markets are most attractive to the university?
   d. How will you position the university for those segments relative to the competition? Present the results to your class.

4. Assume that a firm hires you as marketing manager for a chain of retail bookstores. You feel that the firm should develop a CRM strategy. Outline the steps you would take in developing that strategy.

Miniproject: Learn by Doing

This miniproject will help you to develop a better understanding of how firms make target marketing decisions. The project focuses on the market for women's beauty-care products.

1. Gather ideas about different dimensions useful for segmenting the women's beauty products market. You may use your own ideas, but you probably will also want to examine advertising and other marketing communications developed by different beauty care brands.
2. Based on the dimensions for market segmentation that you have identified, develop a questionnaire and conduct a survey of consumers. You will have to decide which questions should be asked and which consumers should be surveyed.
3. Analyze the data from your research and identify the different potential segments.
4. Develop segment profiles that describe each potential segment.
5. Generate several ideas for how the marketing strategy might be different for each segment based on the profiles. Develop a presentation (or write a report) outlining your ideas, your research, your findings, and your marketing strategy recommendations.

Real People, **real surfers**: explore the web

In this chapter, we learned about VALS2™, a popular market segmentation system developed by SRI International. Visit the SRI Web site (**www.sric-bi.com**). When you follow the VALS2™ links, you will discover that SRI has also developed at least two other segmentation systems: GeoVALS™ and Japan-VALS™. Follow the links to find out the following:

1. How has VALS2™ been used by various SRI clients?

2. Describe GeoVALS™ and Japan-VALS™. What are some ways these segmentation systems might be used by organizations?

3. What is your opinion of the VALS2™ Web site? Whom do you think SRI is targeting with its site? Do you think the site is an effective way to promote its product to potential customers? What suggestions do you have for improving the Web site? Write a report of your findings.

Marketing Plan Exercise

Check out a Web site for a company that manufactures a product that you like and with which you are familiar. Pay special attention to the company's product lines and how it describes products and product uses. Select one particular product and answer the following questions:

1. What market segmentation approaches do you believe are most relevant for your chosen product given the type of product it is? Why do you recommend these over other possible approaches?

2. Describe the top three target markets for the product you selected. What makes these particular targets so attractive?

3. From your review of the Web site as well as your knowledge of the product, write out a positioning statement for the product. Keep it to a few sentences; start out with "Product X is positioned as...."

4. In what ways could CRM help the company conduct successful target marketing and positioning of the product?

Marketing in Action Case

Real **Choices** at **Mercedes**

When you think of a high-quality luxury car, what name comes to mind? For many, it's Mercedes-Benz. Founded in 1886, Mercedes-Benz is known worldwide for its production of luxury and high performance automobiles, trucks, buses, and engines. The logo, a three-pointed star in a circle, has become a symbol for luxury, excellence, and class.

The Daimler-Benz company was founded in the 1880s in Germany by two men: Gottlieb Daimler and Karl Benz. These two men, unknowingly, each invented an internal combustion engine powered vehicle. Originally competitors of each other, the two companies merged in 1926 to become Daimler-Benz AG.

Mercedes focuses on quality and on innovation when it designs its vehicles. It was the first to introduce fuel injection and anti-locking brakes. It is this focus on innovation which has led Mercedes-Benz to produce what it believes is a superior hybrid automobile. The company developed two hybrids—the S400 BlueHybrid, a so-called mild hybrid, and the ML450, a full hybrid. The mild hybrid uses an internal-combustion engine to provide the main propulsion, while an electric motor assists the engine when extra power is needed. The mild hybrid can provide more fuel efficiency in stop and go traffic and costs significantly less than the full hybrid but it cannot run on battery-power alone. The full hybrid totally integrates the internal combustion engine and battery so that the electric engine operates on its own such as at startup. The full hybrid is able to both generate and use electricity at the same time and is more fuel efficient than mild hybrids.

Both these Mercedes hybrids will be unique in that they will use a newly developed lithium-ion battery, a technology Mercedes plans to use in cars it calls "BlueHybrids." Mercedes also plans to use its new Blue technology for its five-seat GLK compact SUV, which will be a diesel-electric hybrid.

But can and should a luxury car maker compete in the hybrid car market against hybrid leaders Honda and Toyota? Luxury car maker Ferrari says it has no intention to make a smaller, cheaper, more fuel-efficient car. And why should it? Ferrari's two-seater, front-engine 599 GTB Fiorano has a two-year waiting list for buyers.

Mercedes may face a tough sell with its hybrid cars. Will the luxury car market be attracted to a hybrid Mercedes? As one consumer put it, "If you can afford the car, you don't worry about the gas prices." And will Americans, who for years have enjoyed a love affair with big gas-guzzling SUVs, be willing to settle for a small SUV?

To be successful with its hybrids, Mercedes must be careful to select the right target marketing strategy. Positioning Mercedes for the hybrid market without damaging its luxury image is a challenge that Mercedes must consider carefully.

You Make the Call

1. What is the decision facing Mercedes?
2. What factors are important in understanding this decision situation?
3. What are the alternatives?
4. What decision(s) do you recommend?
5. What are some ways to implement your recommendation?

Based on: Joe Benton, "Saab, Mercedes Hybrids on the Way," *Consumeraffairs.com*, March 9, 2007, **http://www.consumeraffairs.com/news04/2007/03/upscale_hybrids.html** (accessed March 15, 2008); Jerry Garrett, "A Power Trip with Green Detours," *The New York Times*, January 13, 2008, Section 10, pg 1; Greg Kable, "Mercedes Maps a Blue Road to a Green World," *Auto Week*, March 10, 2008. pg 08; Gerhard Mauerer and Felix E. Bauer, "Mercedes Now Plans Two Hybrids," *Automobile News German Auto Industry Newsletter*, March 12, 2007, email, accessed March 15, 2008 through LexisNexis; Mercedes-Benz, *Wikipedia*, **http://en.wikipedia.org/wiki/Mercedes-Benz** (accessed March 12 2008); "Mercedes-Benz History," Mercedesforum.com, **http://www.mercedesforum.com/mercedes-benz/history.asp** (accessed March 12 2008);

Create the Product

açai is antioxidants

Palo Hawken Profile ▼

A Decision Maker at Bossa Nova Beverage Company

Palo Hawken is co-founder and vice president of research and innovation at Bossa Nova. His dream from an early age was to become an inventor, which led him to pursue both a degree in physics from UC Santa Cruz and a degree in industrial design from the Rhode Island School of Design. When he completed his degree at RISD in 1996, he was invited to join his mentor and former professor Stephan Copeland to help develop his consulting business. After three years of working at the Copeland studio, primarily in the contract furniture industry for companies like Steelcase, Knoll, and Innovant, Palo moved to New York to start a furniture company. It was not a very successful venture but it eventually led him to Los Angeles where he met Alton Johnson and joined forces to launch Bossa Nova. Palo's specialty is harnessing the underappreciated power of design from formulation, to functionality, to packaging, to maximize any given market opportunity.

real people, **Real Choices**

Decision Time at Bossa Nova

Bossa Nova Beverage Group was born out of the founder Alton Johnson's fascination with the fruits of Brazil. While visiting there on business, he was constantly served platters of local fruits with unrecognizable flavors and names that invariably were accompanied by intriguing stories of health and healing. Because many of these legends seemed too good to be true, he initiated one of the first university studies to analyze them in greater depth. The results were compelling enough to launch a multiyear R&D effort to find the best way to commercialize the two most promising items: the açai and guarana fruits.

In the summer of 2004, Bossa Nova was completing a regional southern California test market of its launch product: a line of premium, guarana flavored carbonated energy drinks. This line had four SKUs: a rainforest refresher and an energy drink in both regular and diet versions. At the same time Bossa Nova was also putting the finishing touches on the crowning achievement of its R&D department—the world's first juice from an unknown Brazilian palm berry called açai. Açai had been overlooked by those outside Brazil for decades as it was notoriously hard to work with—spoiling within hours of picking and containing naturally occurring fats that looked and smelled awful. But it was also rumored to be the world's highest antioxidant fruit (the company's university research partners confirmed this finding). In the fall of 2004, after years of work, Bossa Nova had finally commercialized a method for extracting the bright purple, antioxidant-rich juice from the brownish pulp.

> **Things to Remember:**
> Bossa Nova makes specialty products; people who are looking for healthy beverages aren't likely to be turned off by relatively expensive alternatives because quality is more important to them than price.
>
> A new product needs to have a crisp, clear message that shows consumers how it's different and worth switching to. Most people have never heard of açai juice so Bossa Nova will need to educate them about just what that is and why they should care.

Palo and his partner had succeeded in creating a compelling (and expensive) new ingredient, but he wasn't sure how it fit into the product line Bossa Nova was currently selling. If indeed the company had just created the highest antioxidant juice ingredient in the world, what was the product that best took advantage of this opportunity? Palo's role as head of product development was to make sure the new company could capitalize on this opportunity with the right new product strategy.

Palo considered his Options 1·2·3

Option 1
Add the new açai juice ingredient to one of the three products Bossa Nova was already making to create a carbonated "antioxidant superfruit refresher." This would create a unique health proposition in the carbonated beverage category, not known for substantive health or functional claims. This option lent itself to an easy and rapid product development cycle because Bossa Nova would be leveraging its current product platform rather than having to create a new manufacturing process. It would be fairly easy to stimulate sales because the company would be working with the same buyers making it unnecessary to forge relationships with new retail customers. On the other hand, the powerful health story of açai could get lost in an essentially unhealthy product platform (basically, sugar water). And

the new ingredient would only be included in one of the company's four SKUs, so it wouldn't create the splash Palo hoped for. In addition, the dark açai juice looked murky and intimidating in the cobalt blue bottle that gave Bossa Nova's energy drinks so much life. The company's technical people weren't sure how to change that property of the juice.

Option 2
Go all out: Create a new line of pure açai juices in a new package that would showcase its world-class nutritional features and benefits. Açai would not be an ingredient in an energy drink (as in Option 1); it would be the core ingredient of a whole new product line. At that time the market leader in premium antioxidant juices, POM Wonderful, was pulling in about $20–30 million annually in sales by promoting its antioxidant message, and Palo saw Bossa Nova as a fast follower that could grab a piece of that market. Adding a new product line could diversify the firm's product portfolio, which would also build brand awareness in two places in the store instead of one (on the carbonated, 4-pack dry shelf, and the fresh juice case in the produce department). Bossa Nova could help define the emerging beverage category of premium/functional antioxidant juices.

On the other hand, another product line could overextend Bossa Nova; it would force the company to spread already scarce capital and human resources across two product lines rather than focusing on one. This option would also be risky because the current product line wasn't yet firmly established in the market. Finally, the brand wasn't originally designed to embody the health message of the new açai juice line. It was too playful and needed more science/credibility, which Palo was unclear on how to achieve.

Option 3
Rewrite, re-raise, rebuild. Rewrite the business plan to focus on developing a single product line that could stake the claim to the title of highest antioxidant juice in the world. This option was the riskiest, because it entailed raising a significant amount of capital, selling off the existing carbonated inventory, re-branding the company, and generally moving back to square one. If this option were successful, it would result in a strong seductive product concept with a radical value proposition (both a "world's first..." and a "world's highest..."). The company would also be able to ride the coattails of $5 million of advertising by POM Wonderful designed to educate consumers about the benefits of antioxidants. Of course, this choice would entail huge risk; it would mean a decision to jettison a small but successful product line and remake/rebrand a new company that had already burned through $500,000 in seed capital. And, although the new açai juice ingredient was the world's highest antioxidant juice, it was very expensive to produce and the margins were dangerously low.

Now, put yourself in Palo's shoes: Which option would you pick, and why?

You Choose

Which **Option** would you choose, and **why**?
1. ☐YES ☐NO 2. ☐YES ☐NO 3. ☐YES ☐NO

See what **option** Palo chose and its success on **page 261** ➡

Check out chapter 8 **Study Map** on page 262

1

Build a Better Mousetrap: The Value Proposition

"Build a better mousetrap and the world will beat a path to your door." Although we've all heard that adage, the truth is that just because a product is better, there is no guarantee it will succeed. For decades, the Woodstream Company built Victor brand wooden mousetraps. Then the company decided to build a better one. Woodstream's product-development people researched the eating, crawling, and nesting habits of mice (hey, it's a living....). They built prototypes of different mousetraps to come up with the best possible design and tested them in homes. Then the company unveiled the sleek-looking "Little Champ," a black plastic miniature inverted bathtub with a hole. When the mouse went in and ate the bait a spring snapped upward—and the mouse was history.

Sounds like a great new product (unless you're a mouse), but the Little Champ failed. Woodstream studied mouse habits, *not* consumer preferences. The company later discovered that husbands set the trap at night, but in the morning it was the wives who disposed of the trap holding the dead mouse. Unfortunately, many of them thought the Little Champ looked too expensive to throw away, so they felt they should empty the trap for reuse. This was a task most women weren't willing to do—they wanted a trap they could happily toss into the garbage.[1]

Woodstream's failure in the "rat race" underscores the importance of creating products that provide benefits people seek. It also tells us that any number of products, from low-tech cheese to high-tech traps, potentially deliver these benefits. Despite Victor's claim to be the "World's Leader in Rodent Control Solutions," in this case cheese and a shoe box could snuff out a mouse as well as a high-tech trap.

We need to take a close look at how products successfully trap consumers' dollars. Chapter 1 showed us that the *value proposition* is the consumer's perception of the benefits she will receive if she buys a good or service. So, the marketer's task is twofold: first, to create a better value than what's out there already and second to convince customers that this is true.

As we defined it in Chapter 1, a *product* is a tangible good, service, idea, or some combination of these that satisfies consumer or business customer needs through the exchange process; it is a bundle of attributes including features, functions, benefits, and uses. Products can be physical goods, services, ideas, people, or places. A **good** is a *tangible* product, something that we can see, touch, smell, hear, taste, or possess. It may take the form of a pack of cookies, a digital camera, a house, a fancy new computer, or a pair of stone-washed jeans. In contrast, *intangible* products—services, ideas, people, places—are products that we can't always see, touch, taste, smell, or possess. We'll talk more about intangible products in Chapter 10.

Marketers think of the product as more than just a thing that comes in a package. They view it as a bundle of attributes that includes the packaging, brand name, benefits, and supporting features in addition to a physical good. Figure 8.1 reminds us that we are now in Part 3 of this book, "Create the Value Proposition." The key word here is *create*, and a large part of the marketer's role in creating the value proposition is to develop and market products appropriately. In this chapter, we'll first examine what a product is and see how marketers classify consumer and business-to-business products. Then we'll go on to look at new products, how marketers develop new products, and how markets accept them (or not). In the chapters that follow, we'll look at issues such as managing and pricing goods and services.

Layers of the Product Concept

2

OBJECTIVE

Explain the layers of a product.

(pp. 233–235)

No doubt you've heard someone say, "It's the thought, not the gift that counts." This means that the gift is a sign or symbol that the gift giver has remembered you (or possibly it means that you hate the gift but are being polite!). When we evaluate a gift, we may consider the following: Was it presented with a flourish? Was it wrapped in special paper? Was it obviously a "re-gift"—something the gift giver had received as a gift for herself but wanted to pass on to you? These dimensions are a part of the total gift you receive in addition to the actual goodie sitting in the box.

Like a gift, a product is everything that a customer receives in an exchange. As Figure 8.2 shows, we distinguish among three distinct layers of the product—the core product, the actual product, and the augmented product. When they develop product strategies, marketers need to consider how to satisfy customers' wants and needs at each of these three layers. Let's consider each layer in turn.

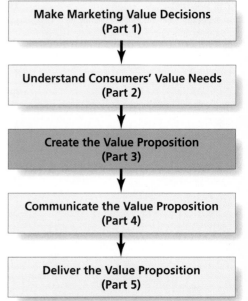

Figure 8.1 │ Make and Deliver Value

Make Marketing Value Decisions (Part 1)

↓

Understand Consumers' Value Needs (Part 2)

↓

Create the Value Proposition (Part 3)

↓

Communicate the Value Proposition (Part 4)

↓

Deliver the Value Proposition (Part 5)

good
A tangible product that we can see, touch, smell, hear, or taste.

Figure 8.2 │ Layers of the Product

A product is everything a customer receives—the basic benefits, the physical product and its packaging, and the "extras" that come with the product.

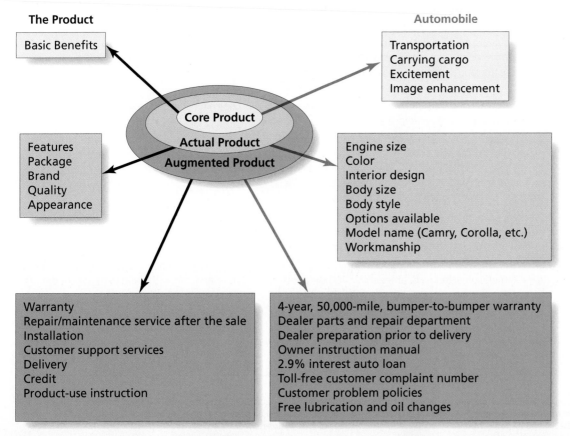

The Core Product

core product
All the benefits the product will provide for consumers or business customers.

The **core product** consists of all the benefits the product will provide for consumers or business customers. As we noted in Chapter 1, a *benefit* is an outcome that the customer receives from owning or using a product. Wise old marketers (and some young ones, too) will tell you, "A marketer may make and sell a half-inch drill bit, but a customer buys a half-inch hole." This tried-and-true saying tells us that people buy the core product, in this case, the ability to make a hole. If a new product, such as a laser, comes along that provides that outcome in a better way or more cheaply, the drill-bit maker has a problem. The moral of this story? *Marketing is about supplying benefits, not products.* Table 8.1 shows how some marketers rigorously test their products "in action" to be sure they deliver the benefits they promise.

Many products actually provide multiple benefits. For example, the primary benefit of a car is transportation—all cars (in good repair) provide the ability to travel from point A to point B. But products also provide customized benefits—benefits customers receive because manufacturers add "bells and whistles" to win customers. Different drivers seek different customized benefits in a car. Some simply want economical transportation; others appreciate an environmentally-friendly hybrid car; and still others want a top-of-the-line, all-terrain vehicle, or perhaps a hot car that will be the envy of their friends.

Table 8.1 | Product Testing

Product	Testing Procedure	Benefit
Louis Vuitton handbags	A mechanical arm lifts a handbag, loaded with an eight-pound weight, 1.5 feet off the floor, and then drops it over and over again, for four days.	An attractive yet durable handbag
BMW	BMW tests the durability of their cars paint jobs by putting them in a room that has extremely powerful ultraviolet lights for extended periods of time. The UV rays are so intense that you would get a nasty sunburn from just being in there for three minutes.	A beautiful, long-lasting exterior finish
Sherwin-Williams paint	40,000 panels, painted with both Sherwin-Williams and competitors' paints, are subjected to the weather for up to 15 years (the length of the warranty on some paint).	A house paint that remains attractive throughout the warranty period
Apple computers	To simulate real-life conditions, computers are drenched with soda, smeared with mayonnaise, and baked in ovens (to mimic the trunk of a car in the summer heat).	Computing power that is impervious to normal wear and tear—and more
Mattel's Barbie	Quality testers yank and pull Barbie's hair and limbs to make sure she can withstand the strong hands and teeth of five-year-olds. They pour sand on her and bake her in simulated sunlight. Only Barbies that pass the tensile strength, UV, heat, and saliva tests are accepted.	A toy that is both fun and safe for children
Shaw Industries carpet products	Workers pace up and down rows of carpet samples eight hours a day. One worker reads three books a week and has lost 40 pounds in three years as a carpet walker.	Carpeting that is attractive and durable after years of wear
Otis elevators	Elevator components are strapped to a vibrating "shaker table," then subjected to heat reaching 400 degrees Fahrenheit and as cold as −150 degrees Fahrenheit.	An elevator that provides a smooth, safe ride and can withstand extreme conditions (such as a lightning strike)
Procter & Gamble hair care products	P&G pays over $1,000 for mannequin heads with realistic hair for testing new hair care products. Each of P&G's 15 "heads" has a name. When the hair begins to get thin, the "head" is retired.	Attractive, healthy hair

Sources: http://paultan.org/archives/2006/06/05/bmw-extreme-testing-technology/, accessed May 6, 2008; Otis Research Center, "Shaking, Baking and Proving Technology," August 27, 2003, http://home.fuse.net/mllwyd/barbie_misc.html: Faye Rice, "Secrets of Product Testing," *Fortune*, November 28, 1994, 166–72; www.utc.com/press/highlights/2003-08-27_tower.htm; and Carol Matlack, "The Vuitton Machine," *BusinessWeek*, March 22, 2004, 98–102.

Donna N.
Yancey
a professor at the University of North Alabama
My Advice for Bossa Nova would
be to choose

Option

real people, **Other Voices**

I would choose **Option 2** because Bossa Nova has achieved a major accomplishment with its extraction of the juice from the highest antioxidant fruit in the world. Why would it risk this extraordinary product's ability to reach a new market that is more in tune with today's quest for nutrition by using it as an ingredient in a sugary drink as Option 1 proposes? Option 3 is a bit too radical and would be too expensive to attempt for such a new company. Bossa Nova can increase its brand name by keeping its other three products as energy drinks, which are sweeping the nation now with the college group, and reach a new target that is a higher socioeconomic market with more focus on nutrition with the açai juice line. This company cannot depend on its brand name reputation because that has not been established yet, so it will be able to achieve higher brand recognition with these two product lines. Positioning the açai

antioxidant juice to a new target market that is upper income should not cannibalize the sales of the company's energy drinks. With labeling laws that require disclosure of juice and sugar water contents, the energy drinks would conceal the value of the antioxidant ingredients in açai juices if Option 1 were followed.

Location of the new line of juices will be critical to the company's success, as well as a unique packaging design to complement the uniqueness of the juices (i.e., a very bright wrapper on its existing bottles). The location should be set apart in the store with its own shelves, highlighting a creative bottle, darker in color, so as to disguise the murky color, and yet, make the product appealing. Perception is everything to this product's success. The bottle should look expensive, be colorful, highlight the antioxidant value, and appeal to the health conscious consumer. Bossa Nova should consider locating this product in gyms and health food stores, as well as the supermarkets. The diversification that the new line of antioxidant fruit juices will offer should more than offset the additional capital and human resources needed to produce it. The açai juice line, if targeted to an upper income group, with a unique designed package, creative nutritional oriented brand name, and front store or end-cap separate shelf location, should become one of the most sought after new products in the marketplace. ➤

The Actual Product

The second layer—the **actual product**—is the physical good or the delivered service that supplies the desired benefit. For example, when you buy a washing machine, the core product is the ability to get clothes clean, but the actual product is a large, square, metal apparatus. When you get a medical exam, the core product is maintaining your health, but the actual product is a lot of annoying poking and prodding. The actual product also includes the unique features of the product, such as its appearance or styling, the package, and the brand name. Sony makes a wide range of televisions from tiny, black and white battery-powered TVs for camping trips, to massive plasma televisions that can display a resolution rivaling reality—but all offer the same core benefit of enabling you to catch the latest episode of *Family Guy*.

actual product
The physical good or the delivered service that supplies the desired benefit.

The Augmented Product

Finally, marketers offer customers an **augmented product**—the actual product plus other supporting features such as a warranty, credit, delivery, installation, and repair service after the sale. Marketers know that adding these supporting features to a product is an effective way for a company to stand out from the crowd.

For example, Apple's iTunes Music Store enables consumers to select from a massive library of music (also TV shows, movies, audiobooks, etc.) and download titles directly to their digital music library. It also saves you the trouble of correctly inserting, labeling, and sorting new music into your library because it does that automatically. Plus, because "everyone" has either an iPod or simply a digital music library, you don't even have to worry about what to do with that pesky CD and its case. Apple's augmented product (convenience, extensive selection, and ease of use) has paid off handsomely for the company in sales and profits, and customers adore the fact that you can do it all without even getting up from your personal computer. You want a song/album, two minutes later you've got it. Are record—rather CD—stores doomed to the fate of the dinosaur?

augmented product
The actual product plus other supporting features such as a warranty, credit, delivery, installation, and repair service after the sale.

3 How Marketers Classify Products

OBJECTIVE

Describe how marketers classify products.

(pp. 236–242)

So far we've learned that a product may be a tangible good or an intangible service or idea and that there are different layers to the product. Now we'll build on that idea by looking at how products differ from one another. Marketers classify products into categories because the categories represent differences in how consumers and business customers feel about products and how they purchase different products. Such an understanding helps marketers develop new products and a marketing mix that satisfies customer needs. Table 8.2 summarizes these categories.

Generally, products are either consumer products or business-to-business products, although sometimes consumers and businesses buy the same products, such as toilet paper, vacuum cleaners, and light bulbs. In these cases, though, businesses tend to buy a lot more of them at once. Of course, as we saw in Chapters 5 and 6, customers differ in how they decide on a purchase, depending on whether the decision maker is a consumer or a business purchaser. Let's first consider differences in consumer products based on how long the product will last and on how the consumer shops for the product. Then we will discuss the general types of business-to-business products.

How Long Does the Product Last?

durable goods
Consumer products that provide benefits over a long period of time, such as cars, furniture, and appliances.

nondurable goods
Consumer products that provide benefits for a short time because they are consumed (such as food) or are no longer useful (such as newspapers).

Marketers classify consumer goods as durable or nondurable depending on how long the product lasts. You expect a refrigerator to last many years, but a gallon of milk will last only a week or so until it turns into a science project. **Durable goods** are consumer products that provide benefits over a period of months, years, or even decades, such as cars, furniture, and appliances. In contrast, we consume **nondurable goods**, such as newspapers and food, in the short term.

We are more likely to purchase durable goods under conditions of *high involvement* (as we saw in Chapter 5), while nondurable goods are more likely to be *low involvement* decisions. When consumers buy a computer or a house, they will spend a lot of time and energy on the decision process. When they offer these products, marketers need to understand consumers' desires for different product benefits and the importance of warranties, service, and customer support. So they must be sure that consumers can find the information they need. One way to do this is by providing a "Frequently Asked Questions" (FAQs) section on a company Web site. Another way is to host a message board or blog to facilitate a sense of community around the product. When a company itself sponsors such forums, odds are the content will be much more favorable and the firm can police peripheral postings. For example, the section of the Microsoft Web site called "Microsoft Technical Communities" allows users to problem-solve by typing in any product (or even an error code that popped up on your computer) and then to track it through a discussion board on that issue.[2]

In contrast, consumers usually don't "sweat the details" so much when they choose among nondurable goods. There is little if any search for information or deliberation. Sometimes this means that consumers buy whatever brand is available and reasonably priced. In other instances, they base their decisions largely on past experience. Because a certain brand has performed satisfactorily before, customers see no reason to consider other brands, and they choose the same one out of habit. For example, even though there are other brands available most consumers buy that familiar red and white can of Campbell's Soup again and again. In such cases, marketers can probably be less concerned with developing new product features to attract customers; they should focus more on pricing and distribution strategies.

Table 8.2	Classification of Products

Consumer Products

Classified by how long they last

Durable: products that provide a benefit over a long period

- Example: Refrigerator

Nondurable: products that provide a benefit over a short time

- Example: Toothpaste

Classified by how consumers buy them

Convenience Products: products that are frequently purchased with little effort

- Examples: Staples (milk)
  Impulse products (candy bars)
  Emergency products (drain opener)

Shopping Products: products that are selected with considerable time and effort

- Examples: Attribute-based (shoes)
  Price-based (water heater)

Specialty Products: products that have unique characteristics to the buyer

- Examples: Favorite restaurant, Rolex watch

Unsought Products: products that consumers have little interest in until need arises

- Example: Retirement plans

Business-to-Business Products

Classified by how organizational customers use them

Equipment

- Examples: Capital equipment (buildings)
  Accessory equipment (computer terminals)

Maintenance, Repair, and Operating (MRO) Products

- Examples: Maintenance products (light bulbs, mops)
  Repair products (nuts, bolts)
  Operating supplies (paper, oil)

Raw Materials

- Example: Iron ore

Processed Materials

- Example: Sheets of steel

Specialized Services

- Example: Legal services

Component Parts

- Example: Car water pump

Marketers classify products to help them understand how consumers make purchase decisions.

How Do Consumers Buy the Product?

Marketers also classify products based on where and how consumers buy the product. We think of both goods and services as convenience products, shopping products, specialty products, or unsought products. Recall that, in Chapter 5, we talked about how consumer decisions differ in terms of effort from habitual decision making to limited

Mohan K.
Menon
a professor at the University of South Alabama
My Advice for Bossa Nova would be to choose

3
Option

real people, **Other Voices**

I would choose **Option 3** because it is possible to build a one-brand/one-product company as POM Wonderful has done. I think that if the açai drink is that good to stand on its own health merits, it deserves the company's complete attention. Given the mass media coverage about healthy products and benefits of antioxidants, in particular, and the resulting increase in consumer appetite for overall well being, I feel that the stand-alone strategy would be perfect. If the claim of having the highest antioxidant juice in the world can be substantiated, then it is powerful, intense, and unique to capture the attention of consumers. Sure it is a risky strategy for Palo, but the other options are riskier. Both Options 1 and 2 are product or product-line extension strategies. From a consumer perspective, it would be incredulous for a company to sell non-healthy carbonated drinks while selling another that claims to be very healthy. This would be a tacit admission on the part of Bossa Nova that the other products it sells are not healthy. Another reason for select Option 3 is the realization by Bossa Nova that the guarana line is not very profitable and is lost in the sea of energy drinks on the market. In the long run, a small company such as Bossa Nova might not be able to compete with giants such as Coca Cola and Pepsi in the same marketspace. ➤

---

problem solving to extended problem solving. Now we can tie this classification of products in terms of how consumers buy them to these differences in consumer decision making. When they understand how consumers buy products, marketers have a clearer vision of the buying process that will help them to develop effective marketing strategies based on the category into which their product falls.

Convenience Products

convenience product
A consumer good or service that is usually low-priced, widely available, and purchased frequently with a minimum of comparison and effort.

A **convenience product** typically is a nondurable good or service that consumers purchase frequently with a minimum of comparison and effort. As the name implies, consumers expect these products to be handy and they will buy whatever brands are easy to obtain. In general, convenience products are low-priced and widely available. You can buy a gallon of milk or a loaf of bread at grocery stores, at convenience stores, and even at many service stations. Consumers generally know all they need or want to know about a convenience product, devote little effort to purchases, and willingly accept alternative brands if their preferred brand is not available in a convenient location. Most convenience product purchases are the results of habitual consumer decision making. What's the most important thing for marketers of convenience products? You guessed it—make sure the product is easily obtainable in all the places where consumers are likely to look for it.

But all convenience product purchases aren't alike. You may stop by a local market on your way home from school or work to pick up that gallon of milk because that's something you always keep in the refrigerator. As long as you're there, why not grab a candy bar for the drive home? Later that night, you dash out to buy something to unclog your kitchen drain—also a convenience product. Marketers classify convenience products as staples, impulse products, and emergency products.

staples
Basic or necessary items that are available almost everywhere.

Staples such as milk, bread, and gasoline are basic or necessary items that are available almost everywhere. Most consumers don't perceive big differences among brands. When selling staples, marketers must offer customers a product that consistently meets their expectations for quality and make sure it is available at a price comparable to the competition's prices.

Consider this situation: You are standing in the checkout line at the supermarket and notice a copy of *US* magazine featuring a photo of Angelina Jolie with a provocative headline. You've got to check out that article! This magazine is an **impulse product**—something people often buy on the spur of the moment. With an impulse product, marketers have two challenges: to create a product or package design that is enticing that "reaches out and grabs the customer," and to make sure their product is highly visible, for example by securing prime end-aisle or checkout-lane space.

impulse product
A product people often buy on the spur of the moment.

As the name suggests, we purchase **emergency products** when we're in dire need; examples include bandages, umbrellas, and something to unclog the bathroom sink. Because we need the product badly and immediately, price and sometimes product quality may be irrelevant to our decision to purchase. If you ever go to Disney World in Florida during the summer months chances are at some point you will get caught in a sudden downpour. When that happens, Disney knows that any umbrella at any price may do and the company stocks its concessions with the product. The company also rolls out the Mickey Mouse ponchos because once the sky opens up everybody's gotta have one.

What are the challenges to marketers of emergency products? As with any other product, emergency products are most successful when they meet customer needs—you won't sell a drain cleaner more than once if it doesn't unclog a drain. And emergency products need to be offered in the sizes customers want. If you cut your finger in the mall, you don't want to buy a box of 100 bandages—you want a box of five or ten. Of course, making emergency products available when and where an emergency is likely to occur is the real key to success.

Recently, it has become trendy to talk about the gamut of convenience products as **fast-moving consumer goods (FMCG)**. An FMCG is any product that exhibits consistently high velocity of sales in the consumer marketplace. Major consumer packaged goods companies such as Procter & Gamble, Colgate Palmolive, Unilever—each of which sells an extensive line of products for various aspects of convenience—refer to the majority of their products as FMCG.

Shopping Products

In contrast to convenience products, **shopping products** are goods or services for which consumers will spend time and effort gathering information on price, product attributes, and product quality. They are likely to compare alternatives before they buy. The purchase of shopping products is typically a limited problem-solving decision. Often consumers have little prior knowledge about these products. Because they gather new information for each purchase occasion, consumers are only moderately brand-loyal and will switch whenever a different brand offers new or better benefits. They may visit several stores and devote considerable effort to comparing products.

Laptop computers are a good example of a shopping product because they offer an ever-expanding array of new features and functions. There are trade-offs and decisions to make about the price, speed, screen size, weight, battery life, and all sorts of features you can bundle. Consumers may ask, "Does it have Bluetooth? What about a Blu-ray drive? Does it have enough power to drive my games?"[3] Designing successful shopping products means making sure they have the attributes that customers want. And it helps to design product packaging that points out the features consumers need to know about to make the right decisions.

Some shopping products have different characteristics. When people shop for *attribute-based shopping products*, such as a new party dress or a pair of designer jeans, they spend time and energy finding the best possible product selection. At other times, when choices available in the marketplace are just about the same, we consider these to be shopping products because of differences in price. For these *price-based shopping products*, determined shoppers will visit numerous stores in hopes of saving an additional $10 or $20.

In business-to-consumer e-commerce, consumers sometimes can shop more efficiently when they use **intelligent agents** or *shopbots*—computer programs that find sites selling a particular product. Some of these programs also provide information on competitors' prices, and they may even ask customers to rate the various e-businesses that they have listed on their site so consumers can learn from other shoppers which sellers are good and which are less than desirable. We should note, however, that some sites do not wish to compete on price and don't give shopbots access to their listings.

emergency products
Products we purchase when we're in dire need.

fast-moving consumer goods (FMCG)
Products that exhibit consistently high velocity of sales in the consumer marketplace.

shopping product
A good or service for which consumers spend considerable time and effort gathering information and comparing alternatives before making a purchase.

intelligent agents
Computer programs that find sites selling a particular product.

Ethical Decisions in the Real World

By definition, specialty products have unique characteristics that are important to buyers at almost any price. Consider, for example, that culinary delicacy *foie gras*—a staple in most fine French restaurants. Serious connoisseurs make decisions about where to dine based on the pâté the establishment serves. But *foie gras* is a product currently mired in controversy due to growing concerns about the treatment of animals in the manufacture of food products.

The problem: *Foie gras* comes from goose livers, and the fatter the liver the better. The process of producing *foie gras*, which dates back to ancient Egypt, involves force-feeding a goose (or duck) until its liver swells to many times its normal size. Like veal production, it's the process behind the product that raises ethical questions. The conundrum, of course, is why does a product so delightful to eat have to be associated with such distasteful (and according to some) immoral treatment of the animal?

Lately there's been a drive by producers toward "ethical" *foie gras* production. They do this by slaughtering the birds only during the time of the year they are preparing to migrate and thus instinctively consume an abnormally large amount of food anyway (of course, these penned birds don't actually migrate anywhere except to your dinner plate).

If you ran a gourmet French restaurant, you would need to decide if you're going to put *foie gras* ("ethically produced" or not) on the menu. What would you do?

Ripped from the Headlines! See what happened in the Real World at **www.mypearsonmarketinglab.com**

ETHICS CHECK: ↘
Find out what other students taking this course **would do** and **why** on **www. mypearsonmarketinglab. com**

If you owned a restaurant would you put a menu item like *foie gras* on the menu if you believe it has possibly been harvested under inhumane conditions?

☐YES ☐NO

specialty product
A good or service that has unique characteristics and is important to the buyer and for which she will devote significant effort to acquire.

Specialty Products

You can buy a mop at Target for well under $10, right? Yet sales are brisk for the $400 Scooba Floor Washing Robot. The iRobot Corporation hawks Scooba as "the first floor washing robot that preps, washes, scrubs, and dries your floor." Consumers can't get enough of this little knee and back saver, and Clorox already has developed a cleaning formula specifically to use with it.[4]

The Scooba is a good example of a **specialty product**, as are Big Bertha golf clubs and Rolex watches. Specialty products have unique characteristics that are important to buyers at almost any price. We can even find specialty products competing in such mundane product categories as drinking water: VOSS water's sleek packaging stands out from other bottled waters. Extracted from an aquifer in Norway that was buried under snow and ice for centuries, VOSS markets its water as the purest in the world (at $10 or more a bottle in chic eateries, it had better be).

Consumers usually know a good deal about specialty products, and they tend to be loyal to specific brands. Generally, a specialty product is an extended problem-solving purchase that requires a lot of effort to choose. That means that firms selling these kinds of products need to create marketing strategies that make their product stand apart from the rest. For example, advertising for a specialty product such as a high definition plasma TV may talk about plasma's unique and superior characteristics and attempt to convince prospective customers that it's worth ponying up extra money for a 1080 resolution screen instead of a measly 760 resolution.

unsought products
Goods or services for which a consumer has little awareness or interest until the product or a need for the product is brought to her attention.

Unsought Products

Unsought products are goods or services (other than convenience products) for which a consumer has little awareness or interest until a need arises. For college graduates with their first "real" jobs, retirement plans and disability insurance are unsought products. It requires a good deal of advertising or personal selling to interest people in these kinds of products—just ask any life insurance salesperson. It's a real challenge to find convincing ways to interest consumers in unsought products. One solution may be to make pricing more attractive; for example, reluctant consumers may be more willing to buy an unsought product for "only pennies a day" than if they have to think about their yearly or lifetime cash outlay.

Business-to-Business Products

Although consumers purchase products for their own use, as we saw in Chapter 6 organizational customers purchase items to use in the production of other goods and services or to facilitate the organization's operation. Marketers classify business-to-business products based on how organizational customers use them. As with consumer products, when marketers know how their business customers use a product, they are better able to design products and craft the entire marketing mix. Let's briefly review the five different types of business-to-business products.

Equipment

Equipment refers to the products an organization uses in its daily operations. *Heavy equipment*, sometimes called *installations* or *capital equipment*, includes items such as buildings and robotics Toyota uses to assemble automobiles. Installations are big-ticket items and last for a number of years. Computers, photocopy machines, and water fountains are examples of *light* or *accessory equipment*; they are portable, cost less, and have a shorter life span than capital equipment. Marketing strategies for equipment usually emphasize personal selling and may mean custom-designing products to meet an industrial customer's specific needs.

MRO Products

Maintenance, repair, and operating (MRO) products are goods that a business customer consumes in a relatively short time. *Maintenance products* include light bulbs, mops, cleaning supplies, and the like. Repair products are items such as nuts, bolts, washers, and small tools. *Operating supplies* include computer paper and oil to keep machinery running smoothly. Although some firms use a sales force to promote MRO products, others rely on catalog sales, the Internet, and telemarketing in order to keep prices as low as possible.

Raw Materials

Raw materials are products of the fishing, lumber, agricultural, and mining industries that organizational customers purchase to use in their finished products. For example, a food company may transform soybeans into tofu, and a steel manufacturer changes iron ore into large sheets of steel used by other firms to build automobiles, washing machines, and lawn mowers. And turning one industry's waste materials into another's raw material is a great business model. Did you know that producers use cotton seeds left over from making textiles to make mayonnaise (check the ingredients on the back for cottonseed oil)?[5]

Processed Materials and Special Services

Firms produce **processed materials** when they transform raw materials from their original state. Organizations purchase processed materials that become a part of the products they make. A builder uses treated lumber to add a deck onto a house, and a company that creates aluminum cans for Red Bull buys aluminum ingots for this purpose.

In addition to tangible materials, some business customers purchase *specialized services* from outside suppliers. Specialized services may be equipment-based, such as repairing a copy machine or fixing an assembly line malfunction, or non-equipment-based, such as market research and legal services. These services are essential to the operation of an organization but are not part of the production of a product.

Component Parts

Component parts are manufactured goods or subassemblies of finished items that organizations need to complete their own products. For example, a computer manufacturer needs silicon chips to make a computer, and an automobile manufacturer needs batteries, tires,

equipment
Expensive goods that an organization uses in its daily operations that last for a long time.

maintenance, repair, and operating (MRO) products
Goods that a business customer consumes in a relatively short time.

raw materials
Products of the fishing, lumber, agricultural, and mining industries that organizational customers purchase to use in their finished products.

processed materials
Products created when firms transform raw materials from their original state.

component parts
Manufactured goods or subassemblies of finished items that organizations need to complete their own products.

and fuel injectors. As with processed materials, marketing strategies for component parts usually involve nurturing relationships with customer firms and on-time delivery of a product that meets the buyer's specifications.

To review, we now understand what a product is. We also know how marketers classify consumer products based on how long they last and how they are purchased, and we've seen how they classify business-to-business products according to how they use them. In the next section we'll learn about the marketing of new products, or *innovations*.

4 "New and Improved!" The Process of Innovation

OBJECTIVE

Understand the importance and types of product innovations.

(pp. 242–246)

"New and improved!" What exactly do we mean when we use the term *new product*? The Federal Trade Commission says that (1) a product must be entirely new or changed significantly to be called new and (2) a product may be called new for only six months.

That definition is fine from a legal perspective. From a marketing standpoint, though, a new product or an **innovation** is *anything* that customers perceive as new and different. An innovation may be a cutting-edge style like the Apple iPhone that is a phone *and* an iPod, or the newest shaving system from Gillette—Fusion—that has, what, about six blades? It can also be an innovative communications approach such as Skype VoIP telephony over the Internet, or a new way to power a vehicle such as hydrogen fuel cell cars like the BMW Hydrogen 7, the Ford Focus FCV, or the Honda FCX. An innovation may be a completely new product that provides benefits never available before, such as personal computers when they were first introduced, or it may simply be an existing product with a new style, in a different color, or with some new feature, like Apple Cinnamon Cheerios.

innovation
A product that consumers perceive to be new and different from existing products.

It's Important to Understand How Innovations Work

If an innovation is successful, it spreads throughout the population. First, it is bought and used by only a few people, and then more and more consumers adopt it. Or (more typically) an innovation can be a flop and it may not be around a year after its introduction.

Firms need to understand the process by which innovations succeed (or not) for at least two reasons. First, technology advances today at a dizzying pace. Companies introduce new products constantly, then these become obsolete more quickly than ever before. In many industries, firms develop another new-and-better product before the last new-and-better one even hits store shelves. Nowhere is this more obvious than with personal computers, for which a steady change in technology makes consumers want smaller and smaller machines that are simultaneously more powerful and faster before the dust even settles on the old model (sometimes even before we finish paying for the one we just bought!). Another reason why understanding new products is important is the high cost of developing new products and the even higher cost of new products that fail. In the pharmaceutical industry, the cost of bringing each new drug to market is over $1.5 billion and rising.[6] Even the most successful firms can't afford many product failures with that kind of price tag.

Video games today, with their amazing level of realism and content, are way more expensive to produce than they used to be, rivaling Hollywood film budgets. It cost Microsoft over $30 million to produce the hit video game *Halo 3*. Compare that to the fact that it cost Namco a mere $100,000 to produce the mega hit *Pac Man* back in 1982.[7]

Marketers must understand what it takes to develop a new product successfully. They must do their homework and learn what it is about existing products consumers find less than satisfactory and exactly what it will take to do a better job to satisfy their (rapidly changing) needs. Savvy marketers know they'll waste a ton of investment money if they don't.

Finally, new products contribute to society. We would never suggest that everything new is good, but many new products like those Table 8.3 lists allow us to live longer, happier lives of better quality than ever before. Although there are some who disagree, most of us feel that our lives are better because of cell phones (if that person next to us blabbing on hers would shut up...), televisions, Smart Phones, iPods, microwave ovens, and laptop computers. And new medical products keep *us* from breaking down: Doctors can replace or assist almost every part of the body with bionic products such as replacement spinal disks, insulin pumps

---

Table 8.3 | Innovations That Have Changed Our Lives

Products that changed how we play

1900	Kodak Brownie camera
1948	Polaroid camera
1976	JVC video recorder
1982	Philips/Sony CD player
1995	DVD player
2001	Apple iPod
2006	Nintendo Wii

Products that changed how we work

1959	Xerox photocopier
1966	Xerox fax machine
1971	Intel microprocessor
1980	3M Post-it Notes
1984	Apple Macintosh
1998	BlackBerry Smart Phone

Products that changed how we travel

1908	Ford Model T
1936	DC-3
1950s	Skateboard
1957	Boeing 707
2001	Segway Human Transporter
2003	Toyota Prius hybrid car
2007	Honda FCX Clarity hydrogen fuel cell car

Products that changed our health and grooming

1921	Johnson & Johnson Band-Aid
1928	Penicillin
1931	Tampax tampon
1960	Searle birth control pill
2003	Crest Whitestrips

Products that changed our homes

1907	Vacuum cleaner
1918	Frigidaire refrigerator
1928	Home air conditioner
1967	Amana microwave oven
2003	TMIO Internet-accessible refrigerated oven
2007	Microsoft Home Server—control all media outlets in a home, accessible anywhere on-line

Products that changed the way we communicate

1921	RCA radio
1935	RCA television
1991	World Wide Web
2003	Treo cell phone/PDA/camera
2007	Apple iPhone

Products that changed our clothing

1913	Zipper
1914	Bra
1939	Nylons
1954	Velcro
1961	Procter & Gamble Pampers
1995	Under Armour microfiber sportswear

Sources: Adapted from Christine Chen and Tim Carvell, "Products of the Century," *Fortune*, November 22, 1999, 133–36; "Best of What's Next," *Popular Science*, November 13, 2003; **http://inventors.about.com/library/inventors/bldvd.htm**; **www.time.com/time/2003/inventions/list.html**; Thomas Hoffman, "Segway's Tech Plans Look Down the Road to Growth," *Computerworld*, January 26, 2004, 4; Louis E. Frenzel, "The BlackBerry Reaps the Fruits of Innovation," *Electronic Design*, March 29, 2004, 41(5); David Stires, "Rx for Investors," *Fortune*, May 3, 2004, 158; and "Procter & Gamble," *Drug Store News*, January 19, 2004, 57; "Apple Presents iPod: Ultra-Portable MP3 Music Player Puts 1,000 Songs in Your Pocket," Apple.com, **http://www.apple.com/pr/library/2001/oct/23ipod.html**; "2007: Definitely the Year of Resurgent Nintendo," WRAL.com, **www.wral.com/business/local_tech_wire/opinion/story/2232671/**; Perry Stern, "Honda Achieves Clarity," MSNautos.com, **http://editorial.autos.msn.com/article.aspx?cp-documentid=442665**; "Exclusive: Windows Home Server in Detail," InsideMicrosoft, **http://microsoft.blognewschannel.com/archives/2007/01/07/exclusive-windows-home-server-in-detail/**; "Apple iPhone Introduced," Yuhreka, January 9, 2007, **http://www.yuhreka.com/archives/2007/01/apple_iphone_in.htm**; "Under Armor...History," GoBros.com, **http://www.gobros.com/under-armour/under-armour-history.php**.

that mimic a natural pancreas in patients with diabetes by automatically testing blood-glucose levels, microdetectors implanted into retinas that allow patients with retinal damage to see light, and bionic ears that allow the deaf to hear.[8] A Scottish man even invented a functional bionic hand that went on the market in 2007. The hand has functional finger and thumb movements with real gripping abilities and it's controlled by a combination of the person's muscles and mind. The hand has been tested by many injured soldiers back from Iraq.[9]

Types of Innovations

Innovations differ in their degree of newness, and this helps to determine how quickly the target market will adopt them. Because innovations that are more novel require us to exert greater effort to figure out how to use them, they are slower to spread throughout a population than new products that are similar to what is already available.

Marketers classify innovations into three categories based on their degree of newness: continuous innovations, dynamically continuous innovations, and discontinuous innovations. However, it is better to think of these three types as ranges along a continuum that goes from a very small change in an existing product to a totally new product. We can then describe the three types of innovations in terms of the amount of disruption or change they bring to people's lives. For example, the first automobiles caused tremendous changes in the lives of people who were used to getting places under "horse power." While a more recent innovation like GPS systems that feed us driving directions by satellite are undoubtedly cool, in a relative sense, we have to make fewer changes in our lives to adapt to them (other than not having to ask a stranger for directions when you're lost). And how about the 2008 Lexus LS 460 that can actually parallel park itself?[10]

Continuous Innovations

continuous innovation
A modification of an existing product that sets one brand apart from its competitors.

A **continuous innovation** is a modification to an existing product, such as when Crocs reinvigorated the market for clogs by offering a version of the comfy shoe with big holes punched in it. This type of modification can set one brand apart from its competitors. For example, people associate Volvo cars with safety, and Volvo comes out with a steady stream of safety-related innovations. Volvo was the first car to offer full front and side air bags, and in some of its 2009 models you can get "Low Speed Collision Avoidance" and "Volvo City Safety." The cars have a radar system that monitors the distance of the car to the car in front of you and if you get too close the car's computer automatically applies the brakes.[11]

The consumer doesn't have to learn anything new to use a continuous innovation. From a marketing perspective, this means that it's usually pretty easy to convince consumers to adopt this kind of new product. For example, the current generation of high-definition plasma flat-screen monitors didn't require computer users to change their behaviors. We all know what a computer monitor is and how it works. The system's continuous innovation simply gives users the added benefits of taking up less space and being easier on the eyes than old style monitors.

How different does a new product have to be from existing products before people think it's *too* different? We've all heard that "imitation is the sincerest form of flattery," but decisions regarding how much (if at all) one's product should resemble those of its competitors often are a centerpiece of marketing strategy. Sometimes marketers feel that the best strategy is to follow the competition. For example, the packaging of "me-too" or look-alike products can create instant market success because consumers assume that similar packaging means similar products. When BMW released its 7-series model with the new "i-Drive" all-in-one control that was supposed to simplify in-car controls, many people and critics hated it because it was way too different from what they were used to. Although it

SHARP

The slimmest, lightest AQUOS® LCD-TV ever.

Presenting the new D64 Series from Sharp–the leading innovator of Liquid Crystal Television. With its stunning picture quality, Full HD 1080p resolution, 10,000:1 dynamic contrast ratio and remarkably thin profile, less is finally more. Visit aquos.com.

AQUOS

The new Sharp Aquos monitor is a continuous innovation.

was an amazing technical achievement, it was too much of a change for drivers to accept.[12]

A **knockoff** is a new product that copies, with slight modification, the design of an original product. Firms deliberately create knockoffs of clothing, jewelry, or other items, often with the intent to sell to a larger or different market. For example, companies may copy the *haute couture* clothing styles of top designers and sell them at lower prices to the mass market. It is difficult to legally protect a design (as opposed to a technological invention) because an imitator can argue that even a very slight change—different buttons or a slightly wider collar on a dress or shirt—means the knockoff is not an exact copy.

Dynamically Continuous Innovations

A **dynamically continuous innovation** is a pronounced modification to an existing product that requires a modest amount of learning or change in behavior to use it. The history of audio equipment is a series of dynamically continuous innovations. For many years, consumers enjoyed listening to their favorite Frank Sinatra songs on record players. Then in the 1960s, that same music became available on a continuous-play eight-track tape (requiring the purchase of an eight-track tape player, of course). Then came cassette tapes (oops, now a cassette player is needed). In the 1980s, consumers could hear Metallica songs digitally mastered on compact discs (that, of course, required the purchase of a new CD player).

Consider this series of innovations: In the 1990s, recording technology moved one more step forward with MP3 technology; it allowed fans to download music from the Internet or to exchange electronic copies of the music with others. Mobile MP3 players hit the scene in 1998, letting music fans download their favorite tunes into a portable player. In November 2001, Apple Computer introduced its first iPod. With the original iPod, music fans could take 1,000 songs with them wherever they went. By 2006, iPods could hold 15,000 songs, 25,000 photos, and 150 hours of video.[13] Music fans go to the Apple iTunes music store or elsewhere to download songs and to get suggestions for new music they might enjoy. Of course, today you can do all this on your Smart phone—you don't even need an iPod to have a portable music player!

Even though each of these changes required us to learn how to operate new equipment, we were willing to buy the new products because of the improvements in music reproduction, the core product benefit. Hopefully the music will continue to improve, too.

Convergence is one of the most talked-about forms of dynamically continuous innovations in the digital world. This term means the coming together of two or more technologies to create new systems that provide greater benefit than the original technologies alone. Originally, the phone, organizer, and camera all came together in the Palm Treo and then the Motorola Q. Cable companies now provide cellular service, land phone lines, and high speed Internet. While we're not quite there yet with full convergence and integration of communication technologies, the dream inches closer to reality every day.[14]

Each of these national brands is standing next to its legal knockoff.

knockoff
A new product that copies, with slight modification, the design of an original product.

dynamically continuous innovation
A change in an existing product that requires a moderate amount of learning or behavior change.

convergence
The coming together of two or more technologies to create a new system with greater benefits than its separate parts.

A service like Netflix offers a new way to access existing products—in this case, movies delivered to the home.

By the **People**, For the **People**

Dreaming of someday writing a great novel? How about today? And by the way, how about doing it with thousands of co-authors? An application of the open-source model we've already discussed makes this dream possible. The publisher Penguin Books created the first wiki-based novel, *A Million Penguins* in 2007 (**www.amillionpenguins.com**). The novel starts with the opening sentence of a classic book: "There was no possibility to taking a walk that day" from *Jane Eyre*, and lets participants take it from there. It has now become a full-length novel with 11 versions and more than 60 characters. Penguin relies on a group of volunteers to monitor the content and remove pornography and obscenities. A dynamically continuous innovation at work.[15]

You too can be an author of the wiki-based novel *A Million Penguins*.

Discontinuous Innovations

discontinuous innovation

A totally new product that creates major changes in the way we live.

A **discontinuous innovation** creates major changes in the way we live. Consumers must learn a great deal to use a discontinuous innovation because no similar product has ever been on the market. Major inventions such as the airplane, the car, and the television radically changed modern lifestyles. Another discontinuous innovation, the personal computer, changed the way we shop and allows more people to work from home or anywhere else. The smart phone has taken this functionality to a whole new level; it lets you do most everything a PC can do but in the palm of your hand. What's the next discontinuous innovation? Is there a product out there already that will gain that distinction? Usually, marketers only know for sure through 20–20 hindsight; in other words, it's tough to plan for the next big one (what the computer industry calls "the killer app").

Why is it important to know just how new an innovation really is? This knowledge helps us develop effective marketing strategies. For example, if marketers know that consumers may resist adopting a new and radically different product, they may offer a free product trial or place heavier emphasis on a personal selling strategy to convince them that the new product offers benefits worth the hassle. When Apple first introduced its Macintosh computers (you've seen those in museums!), the company allowed bewildered customers to take them home and use them for a month for free to see their benefits firsthand. Business-to-business marketers often provide in-service training for employees of their customers who invest in new products.

 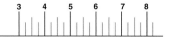

Innovation is a complicated item to try to measure. This is because it involves not only marketing, but the firm's overall culture, leadership, and processes in place that foster innovation. Here's a short list of measures that when taken as a whole can provide a firm's "innovation report card":

Firm Strategy

- How aware are organization members of a firm's goals for innovation?
- How committed is the firm and its leadership to those goals?
- How actively does the firm support innovation among its organization members? Are there rewards and other incentives in place to innovate? Is innovation part of the performance evaluation process?
- To what degree do organization members perceive that resources are available for innovation (money and otherwise)?

Firm Culture

- Does the organization have an appetite for learning and trying new things?
- Do organization members have the freedom and security to try things, fail, and then go forward to try different things?

Outcomes of Innovation

- Number of innovative initiatives (products or otherwise) in process at present, in various stages of development
- Number of innovations launched in the past three years
- Percentage of revenue attributable to launches of innovations during the past three years[16]

5

OBJECTIVE

Show how firms
develop new products.
(pp. 247–253)

New-Product Development

Building on our knowledge of different types of innovations, we'll now turn our attention to how firms actually develop new products. Product development doesn't simply mean creating totally new stuff. Of course a lot of companies do that, but for many other firms product development is a continuous process of looking for ways to make an existing product better or finding just the right shade of purple for this year's new pants styles.

No product category is immune to this process—enterprising companies even constantly improve "boring" products. Consider, for example, the Neorest toilet the Japanese firm Toto introduced in the United States. For a "mere" $5,000, you get a toilet that solves that age-old problem of toilet seat up versus toilet seat down (this could be a marriage-saver for some people). Motion sensors automatically open the lid as you approach and close it as you leave. It also has a heated seat, a temperature-controlled water spray and blow dryer, a catalytic air deodorizer, and even a "white noise" control to mask sounds.[17]

The hit TV show *American Inventor* illustrates the lengths people and companies will go to come up with "the next big thing"—whether screwy or sensible. For several reasons, new-product development is increasingly important to firms. First, as we've already mentioned, technology is changing at an ever-increasing rate so that companies develop products, consumers adopt them, and then companies replace them with better products faster and faster. In addition, competition in our global marketplace makes it essential for firms to continuously offer new choices for consumers if they are to compete with companies all around the world rather than just down the street. Firms need to stay on top of current developments in popular culture, religion, and politics to develop products that are consistent with consumers' mind-sets. Sometimes new hit products are based on careful research, but in many cases being at the right place at the right time doesn't hurt. For example, Hasbro developed a new version of its G.I. Joe toy as a search-and-rescue firefighter prior to the September 11, 2001 attacks; ironically renewed respect for firefighters sparked by that event boosted demand for this gift item that December.[18]

Unfortunately, most new-product introductions need a bit more than good timing to score big in the marketplace. If anything, it's becoming more and more difficult to successfully introduce new products. The costs of research and development often are so huge that firms must limit the number of new products in development. Because products are outdated faster than ever, firms have less time to recover their research-and-development costs. And with so many products competing for limited shelf space, retailers often charge manufacturers exorbitant *slotting fees* to stock a new product, increasing manufacturers' costs even more.[19] Firms must reduce the time it takes to get good products to market and increase the speed of adoption to quickly recover these costs. As Table 8.4 shows, new-product development generally occurs in seven phases.

Phase 1: Idea Generation

In the initial **idea generation** phase of product development, marketers use a variety of sources to come up with great new product ideas that provide customer benefits and that are compatible with the company mission. Sometimes ideas come from customers. Ideas also come from salespeople, service providers, and others who have direct customer contact.

And some companies encourage their designers to "think outside the box" by exposing them to new ideas, people, and places. When Lego decided in 2006 to radically update its Mindstorms programmable robotics kit, the Danish company recruited a panel of outside experts who were well known among Lego fans (and fanatics) for creating complex robots using the firm's older version of the kit. These outsiders worked intensively with Lego's in-house design team for a year to create the next generation of Lego robotics

idea generation
The first step of product development in which marketers brainstorm for products that provide customer benefits and are compatible with the company mission.

Table 8.4 | Phases in New-Product Development

Phases in Development	Outcome
1. Idea generation	Identify product ideas that will provide important customer benefits compatible with company mission.
2. Product concept development and screening	Expand product ideas into more complete product concepts and estimate the potential commercial success of product concepts.
3. Marketing strategy development	Develop preliminary plan for target markets, pricing, distribution, and promotion.
4. Business analysis	Estimate potential for profit. What is the potential demand, what expenditures will be required, and what is the cost to market the product?
5. Technical development	Design the product and the manufacturing-and-production process.
6. Test marketing	Develop evidence of potential success in the real market.
7. Commercialization	Implement full-scale marketing plan.

(Mindstorms NXT) that includes drag-and-drop icons, sophisticated sound sensors, and motors that allow the robots to roam free. It's worth noting that these self-proclaimed "geeks" did all of this work without pay other than being given some Mindstorms prototypes. As one of the panelists observed, "They're going to talk to us about Legos, and they're going to pay us with Legos? They actually want our opinion? It doesn't get much better than that."[20] Now *that's* dedication! Often firms use marketing research activities such as the *focus groups* we discussed in Chapter 4 in their search for new product ideas. For example, a company such as MTV that is interested in developing new channels might hold focus-group discussions across different groups of young people to get ideas for new types of programs.

product concept development and screening
The second step of product development in which marketers test product ideas for technical and commercial success.

Phase 2: Product Concept Development and Screening

The second phase in developing new products is **product concept development and screening**. Although ideas for products initially come from a variety of sources, it is up to marketers to expand these ideas into more-complete product concepts. Product concepts describe what features the product should have and the benefits those features will provide for consumers.

Everyone knows that McDonald's makes the world's best french fries—a fact that has annoyed archrival Burger King for decades. Unfortunately for BK, the chain achieved technical success but not commercial success when the chain invested heavily to out-fry Mickey D's. BK's food engineers came up with a potato stick coated with a layer of starch that makes the fry crunchier and keeps the heat in to stay fresh longer. Burger King created 19 pages of specifications for its new contender, including a requirement that there must be an audible crunch present for seven or more chews. The $70 million rollout of the new product included a "Free Fryday" when BK gave away 15 million orders of fries to customers, placed lavish advertising on the Super Bowl, and engineered official

Lonnie Johnson walked into the slick conference room of the Larami Corporation; smiled mischievously; opened his pink, battered Samsonite suitcase; and took out a gizmo that looked a bit like a phaser gun from Star Trek. Holding this combination of a handheld pump apparatus, PVC tubing, Plexiglas, and plastic soda bottles, Lonnie aimed——and fired! A giant stream of water shot across the room. A year later, the Super Soaker became the most successful water gun in U.S. retail history.

Corbis/SABA Press Photos, Inc.

proclamations by the governors of three states. Unfortunately, the new fry was a "whopper" of a product failure. Burger King blamed the product failure on inconsistent cooking by franchisees and a poor potato crop, but a more likely explanation is that consumers simply did not like the fry as well as those they might find at certain (golden) archrivals. Just because it's new doesn't always make it better.

On the other hand, did you know that Sony was originally working *in conjunction* with Nintendo to create a new video game system? Executives from both sides were happy because Nintendo had the market, the intellectual property, and the know-how to do it and Sony had the financial means. However, Nintendo eventually decided not to move forward with the deal and essentially ditched Sony. The man at Sony who would have been the head guy for the joint project approached the company's president and told him that Sony could enter the market anyway without the big N's help because of the headway it had already made. Sony's CEO reportedly felt dishonored by Nintendo's behavior and approved the project. This rebuff resulted in Sony's highly regarded Playstation, which went on to seriously challenge Nintendo for gaming supremacy.[21]

In new-product development, failures often come as frequently (or more so) than successes. BK's french fry failure illustrates the importance of screening ideas for *both* their technical and their commercial value. When screening, marketers and researchers examine the chances that a new product concept might be successful, while they weed out concepts that have little chance to make it in the market. They estimate *technical success* when they decide whether the new product is technologically feasible—is it possible to actually build this product? Then they estimate *commercial success* when they decide whether anyone is likely to buy the product. The marketing graveyard is piled high with products that sounded interesting but failed to catch on, including jalapeño soda, aerosol mustard, and edible deodorant.[22] Table 8.5 provides other examples of colossal new product failures.

Today, it's not just new functions that companies look for when they devise new product concepts. A product's *appearance* also plays a huge role. In a marketplace loaded with products that seem to do pretty much the same thing, people are attracted to the options that do what they need to do—but look good while doing it. Two young entrepreneurs named Adam Lowry and Eric Ryan discovered that basic truth in the early days of 2000. They quit their day jobs to develop a line of house-cleaning products they called Method.

Cleaning products—what a yawn, right? Think again. For years, companies like Procter & Gamble plodded along, peddling boring boxes of soap powder to generations of housewives. Lowry and Ryan gambled that they could offer an alternative—cleaners in exotic scents like cucumber, lavender, and ylang-ylang that come in aesthetically pleasing bottles. The bet paid off. Within two years the partners were cleaning up, taking in more than $2 million in revenue.

Mass-market consumers thirst for great design, and they're rewarding the companies that give it to them with their enthusiastic patronage and loyalty. To meet this demand, Maytag created a Strategic Initiatives Group to design and introduce a line of mixers, blenders, toasters, and coffee makers under the brand name Jenn-Air Attrezzi (Italian for tools). The product line includes glass bowls and pitchers in colors like cobalt blue and merlot red that can double as serving pieces. Their minimalist bases glow with blue LED displays to reinforce a sleek, forward-looking image.[23]

Even staid P&G is starting to get the idea. Although it's a bit like turning a battleship, Procter & Gamble now recognizes the importance of integrating design into every product initiative. In the "good old days" (that is, a couple of years ago), design was basically an afterthought. Marketing meant appealing to customers in terms of efficiency rather than aesthetics. Now, Chairman-CEO A.G. Lafley wants P&G to focus on what he calls "the first moment of truth"—winning consumers in the store with packaging and displays. As a result, P&G now has a VP of design, strategy, and innovation who reports directly to the CEO. Her philosophy sums it up: "Competitive advantage comes not just from patents, but also from incorporating design into products, much like Apple, Sony, or Dell."[24]

Table 8.5	New Products That Bit the Dust

Product Introduced	Date	Company	Product Description	Why did the product fail?
Wheaties Dunk-A-Balls Cereal	1994	General Mills	Basketball-shaped, sweetened corn and wheat puffs cereal that kids can play with before eating. Advertised as "available for a limited time only."	Parents have never wanted to encourage kids to play with their food and the offering wasn't the slam dunk that General Mills had hoped for.
Hey! There's A Monster In My Room-Spray	1993	OUT! International, Inc.	Get rid of scary creatures from the rooms of children. The spray came in a bubble gum fragrance.	The idea was cute, but the name was not, and set up a fright for the kids.
Premier Cigarettes	1988	R.J. Reynolds (RJR Nabisco Inc.; subsidiary)	A smokeless cigarette.	Premier was priced at a 25% premium to other cigarettes, but cost was not the greatest issue. The problem was that smokeless cigarettes appealed to nonusers—nonsmokers!
Avert Virucidal Tissues	1985	Kimberly-Clark	The tissue contained vitamin C derivatives and was the first tissue scientifically designed to kill cold and flu germs when sneezing, coughing, or blowing your nose into them.	People didn't believe the company's claims and they were frightened by the name.
Look of Buttermilk	1974	Clairol	Shampoo	This product left many consumers asking just what exactly is the "Look of Buttermilk" anyway?
Country People/City People	Early 1980s	Yellow Emperor, Inc.	City People shampoo protects against pollution and exhaust fumes. Country People shampoo protects against the sun and wind.	"Country" didn't sell in the city, and vice versa.
Garlic Cake	1989	Gunderson & Rosario, Inc.	Food to serve as an *hors d'oeuvre* with sweet breads, spreads, and meats.	The company forgot to mention potential usage occasions to consumers. They were left wondering just what is garlic cake and when on earth would a person want to eat it?
Dr. Care	Early 1980s	Dairimetics, Ltd.	Vanilla mint flavored toothpaste in aerosol container advertised as easy to use and sanitary.	Many parents questioned the wisdom of letting their kids loose with an aerosol toothpaste.
Wine & Dine Dinners	Mid-1970s	Heublein	Package of pasta and sauce mix and a mini bottle of salted wine that was intended for creating the sauce.	Consumers assumed the wine was for drinking. The misunderstanding left a bitter taste in the mouths of unforgiving consumers.
Gerber's Singles	1974	Gerber	A variety of fruits, vegetables, and entrees for adults.	Consumers could not relate to adult food products sold in baby food jars.

Source: Courtesy of NewProductWorks. **www.newproductworks.com**

Phase 3: Marketing Strategy Development

The third phase in new-product development is to develop a marketing strategy to introduce the product to the marketplace, a process we began to talk about back in Chapter 2. This means that marketers must identify the target market, estimate its size, and determine how they can effectively position the product to address the target market's needs. And, of course, marketing strategy development includes planning for pricing, distribution, and promotion expenditures both for the introduction of the new product and for the long run. And today, one other element is critically important—the environmental impact of the product. **Green marketing**, the development of marketing strategies that support environmental stewardship by creating an environmentally-

green marketing
The development of marketing strategies that support environmental stewardship by creating an environmentally-founded differential benefit in the minds of consumers.

founded differential benefit in the minds of consumers, is being practiced by most forward-thinking firms today.

Phase 4: Business Analysis

Once a product concept passes the screening stage, the next phase is a **business analysis**. Even though marketers have evidence that there is a market for the product, they still must find out if the product can make a profitable contribution to the organization's product mix. How much potential demand is there for the product? Does the firm have the resources it will need to successfully develop and introduce the product?

Larger firms typically develop new products in-house in their own laboratories, but in some cases they prefer to scout out new ideas from entrepreneurs and just buy the technology. For example, Church and Dwight Company (the Arm & Hammer people) sells the Crest SpinBrush line of battery-powered toothbrushes, which they bill as the "best-selling battery-powered electric toothbrush in the country." Four entrepreneurs originally developed the SpinBrush technology, and then Procter & Gamble bought them out (P&G then divested the product after the P&G/Gillette merger in 2005). Unlike electric toothbrushes that typically sell for upwards of $50, the SpinBrush sells for just slightly more than a decent old-fashioned toothbrush (the kind that requires elbow grease to use).[25]

The business analysis for a new product begins with assessing how the new product will fit into the firm's total product mix. Will the new product increase sales, or will it simply cannibalize sales of existing products? Are there possible synergies between the new product and the company's existing offerings that may improve visibility and the image of both? And what are the marketing costs likely to be?

business analysis
The step in the product development process in which marketers assess a product's commercial viability.

Phase 5: Technical Development

If it survives the scrutiny of a business analysis, a new product concept then undergoes **technical development**, in which a firm's engineers work with marketers to refine the design and production process. For example, when McDonald's recognized the need to bulk up its breakfast menu by adding something sweeter than its Egg McMuffin, the company's executive chef had to scramble to develop a pancake offering that people could eat while they drive. He first considered a pancake shaped like a muffin, but he decided this would be too confusing to customers—and besides, how could he add in the all-important syrup? Fortunately, one of the company's suppliers had just developed a technology that crystallizes syrup—just stir crystals into the batter, and the syrup will seep through the entire pancake once it's heated. McDonald's did a lot of laboratory work to adapt this process so the syrup would melt uniformly and produce what the industry calls the correct "mouth feel." Enter the McGriddle, a breakfast sandwich that can be customized with combinations of sausage, bacon, egg, and cheese. It's served between two "high-tech syrup-infused" pancakes instead of bread and has become a very successful staple on Mickey D's breakfast menu.[26]

The better a firm understands how customers will react to a new product, the better its chances of commercial success. For this reason typically, a company's research-and-development (R&D) department usually develops one or more physical versions or **prototypes** of the product. Prospective customers may evaluate these mockups in focus groups or in field trials at home.

technical development
The step in the product development process in which company engineers refine and perfect a new product.

prototypes
Test versions of a proposed product.

New products often need to be rigorously tested before they are released. This ad from Hong Kong tells us that these jeans have been "tested on humans."

Linda K.
Meyers
a professor at Baker College of Muskegon

My Advice for Bossa Nova would be to choose

Option

real people, **Other** Voices

I would choose **Option 3** because of the old saying "You can't be everything to everyone." The current product line of flavored carbonated energy drinks is in the mature stage of the PLC. The product line hasn't proven itself yet, and may be a question mark for the company. It is in a market with high growth, but the company has low market share. The competition in this market is stiff. To differentiate themselves, they should be a second mover, of sorts. POM Wonderful has already set the stage in the consumers' mind about the benefits of antioxidants. Now Bossa Nova Beverage Group has a chance to solve a consumer problem that no other company has been able to do by creating the world's highest antioxidant juice. This continuous product improvement strategy would give the company a chance to redesign the bottle and create a marketing campaign that could put them on the map. The new product has the potential to keep competitors out of the market because of the technology involved. The company would be better off focusing their efforts on one solid product than trying to stretch themselves thin by having two different product lines. Even though the margins may be dangerously low, you take dollars to the bank not percentages. ➤

Prototypes also are useful for people within the firm. Those involved in the technical development process must determine which parts of a finished good the company will make and which ones it will buy from other suppliers. If it will be manufacturing goods, the company may have to buy new production equipment or modify existing machinery. Someone has to develop work instructions for employees and train them to make the product. When it's a matter of a new service process, technical development includes decisions such as which activities will occur within sight of customers versus in the "backroom," and whether the company can automate parts of the service to make delivery more efficient.

Technical development sometimes requires the company to apply for a patent. Because patents legally prevent competitors from producing or selling the invention, this legal mechanism may reduce or eliminate competition in a market for many years so that a firm gains some "breathing room" to recoup its investments in technical development.

Phase 6: Test Marketing

test marketing

Testing the complete marketing plan in a small geographic area that is similar to the larger market the firm hopes to enter.

The next phase of new-product development is **test marketing**. This means the firm tries out the complete marketing plan—the distribution, advertising, and sales promotion—in a small geographic area that is similar to the larger market it hopes to enter.

There are both pluses and minuses to test marketing. On the negative side, test marketing is extremely expensive. It can cost over a million dollars to conduct a test market even in a single city. A test market also gives the competition a free look at the new product, its introductory price, and the intended promotional strategy—and an opportunity to get to the market first with a competing product. On the positive side, by offering a new product in a limited area of the market, marketers can evaluate and improve the marketing program. Sometimes test marketing uncovers a need to improve the product itself. At other times, test marketing indicates product failure; this advanced warning allows the firm to save millions of dollars by "pulling the plug."

For years, Listerine manufacturer Warner-Lambert (now owned by Pfizer) wanted to introduce a mint-flavored version of the product to compete with Procter & Gamble's Scope (it originally introduced this alternative under the brand Listermint). Unfortunately, every time Warner-Lambert tried to run a test market, P&G found out and poured substantial extra advertising and coupons for Scope into the test market cities. This counterattack reduced the usefulness of the test market results for Warner-Lambert when its market planners were trying to decide whether to introduce Listermint nationwide. Because P&G's aggressive response to Listermint's test marketing actually *increased* Scope's market share in the test cities, there was no way to determine how well Listermint would actually do under normal competitive conditions. Warner-Lambert eventually introduced Listermint nationally, but achieved only marginal success, so the company eventually pulled it from the market. Then, in a "turnabout is fair play" move, in 2006, Pfizer filed suit against P&G for running ads that claimed that more dentists would recommend Crest Pro Health mouth-wash over Listerine.[27]

As we saw in Chapter 4, because of the potential problems and expense of test market-ing marketers instead may use special computer software to conduct simulated tests that imitate the introduction of a product into the marketplace. These simulations allow the company to see the likely impact of price cuts and new packaging—or even to determine where in the store it should try to place the product. The process entails gathering basic research data on consumers' perceptions of the product concept, the physical product, the advertising, and other promotional activity. The test market simulation model uses that information to predict the product's success much less expensively (and more discreetly) than a traditional test market. As this simulated test market technology improves, tradi-tional test markets may become a thing of the past.

Phase 7: Commercialization

The last phase in new-product development is **commercialization**. This means the launch-ing of a new product, and it requires full-scale production, distribution, advertising, sales promotion—the works. For this reason, commercialization of a new product cannot happen overnight. A launch requires planning and careful preparation. Marketers must implement trade promotion plans that offer special incentives to encourage dealers, retailers, or other members of the channel to stock the new product so that customers will find it on store shelves the very first time they look. They must also develop consumer sales promotions such as coupons. Marketers may arrange to have point-of-purchase displays designed, built, and delivered to retail outlets. If the new product is especially complex, customer service employees must receive extensive training and preparation.

As launch time nears, preparations gain a sense of urgency—like countdown to blastoff at NASA. Sales managers explain special incentive programs to salespeople. Soon the media announce to prospective customers why they should buy and where they can find the new product. All elements of the marketing program—ideally—come into play like a carefully planned liftoff of a Delta rocket.

And there is always a huge element of risk in a new product launch—even for prod-ucts that seem like a sure thing. For example, the makers of FluMist, a flu vaccine that is given through a spray in the nose rather than an often painful shot in the arm, predicted they would sell 4 to 6 million doses when the product came on the market—not an unrea-sonable forecast since 60 million to 90 million Americans get a flu shot each year. Despite spending $25 million on advertising to tout the new product, only about 100,000 people bought doses—probably because the product was priced far higher than a flu shot, and the Food and Drug Administration approved the product only for healthy people aged 5 to 49. Unfortunately, the majority of people who most need flu shots are over 50 or have other health problems like asthma or diabetes that make them more likely to die from the flu.[28]

commercialization
The final step in the product development process in which a new product is launched into the market.

6 Adoption and Diffusion of New Products

OBJECTIVE

Explain the process of product adoption and the diffusion of innovations.

(pp. 253–260)

In the previous section, we talked about the steps marketers take to develop new products from generating ideas to launch. Moving on, we'll look at what happens *after* that new product hits the market—how an innovation spreads throughout a population.

A painting is not a work of art until someone views it. A song is not music until someone sings it. In the same way, new products do not satisfy customer wants and needs until the customer uses them. **Product adoption** is the process by which a consumer or business customer begins to buy and use a new good, service, or idea.

product adoption
The process by which a consumer or business customer begins to buy and use a new good, service, or idea.

diffusion
The process by which the use of a product spreads throughout a population.

tipping point
In the context of product diffusion, the point when a product's sales spike from a slow climb to an unprecedented new level, often accompanied by a steep price decline.

The term **diffusion** describes how the use of a product spreads throughout a population. One way to understand how this process works is to think about a new product as if it was a computer virus that spreads from a few computers to infect many machines. A brand like Hush Puppies, for example, might just slog around—sometimes for years and years. At first only a small number of people buy it, but change happens in a hurry when the process reaches the moment of critical mass. This moment of truth is called the **tipping point**.[29] For example, Sharp created the low-price, home/small-office fax market in 1984 and sold about 80,000 in that year. There was a slow climb in the number of users for the next three years. Then, suddenly, in 1987 enough people had faxes that it made sense for everyone to have one—Sharp sold a million units that year as it reached its tipping point. Along with such diffusion almost always come steep price declines—today you can buy a Sharp fax machine at Staples for less than $40 (after mail-in rebate).[30]

After they spend months or even years to develop a new product, the real challenge to firms is to get consumers to buy and use the product and to do so quickly so they can recover the costs of product development and launch. To accomplish this, marketers must understand the product-adoption process. In the next section, we'll discuss the stages in this process. We'll also see how consumers and businesses differ in their eagerness to adopt new products and how the characteristics of a product affect its adoption (or "infection") rate.

Stages in Consumers' Adoption of a New Product

Whether the innovation is better film technology or a better mousetrap, individuals and organizations pass through six stages in the adoption process. Figure 8.3 shows how a person goes from being unaware of an innovation through the stages of awareness, interest, evaluation, trial, adoption, and confirmation. At every stage, people drop out of the process, so the proportion of consumers who wind up using the innovation on a consistent basis is a fraction of those who are exposed to it.

Awareness

Awareness that the innovation exists at all is the first step in the adoption process. To educate consumers about a new product, marketers may conduct a massive advertising campaign: a **media blitz**. For example, to raise awareness of its entry into the electronic-gaming product category Microsoft launched a $500-million media blitz when it introduced the original Xbox; it promoted the new product through in-store merchandising, retailer incentives, events, and sponsorships in addition to traditional advertising.[31] At this point, some consumers will say, "So there's a new gaming console out there. So what?" Many of these, of course, will fall by the wayside and thus drop out of the adoption process. But this strategy works for new products when at least some consumers see a new product as something they want and need and just can't live without.

media blitz
A massive advertising campaign that occurs over a relatively short time frame.

Figure 8.3 | Adoption Pyramid

Consumers pass through six stages in the adoption of a new product—from being unaware of an innovation to becoming loyal adopters. The right marketing strategies at each stage help ensure a successful adoption.

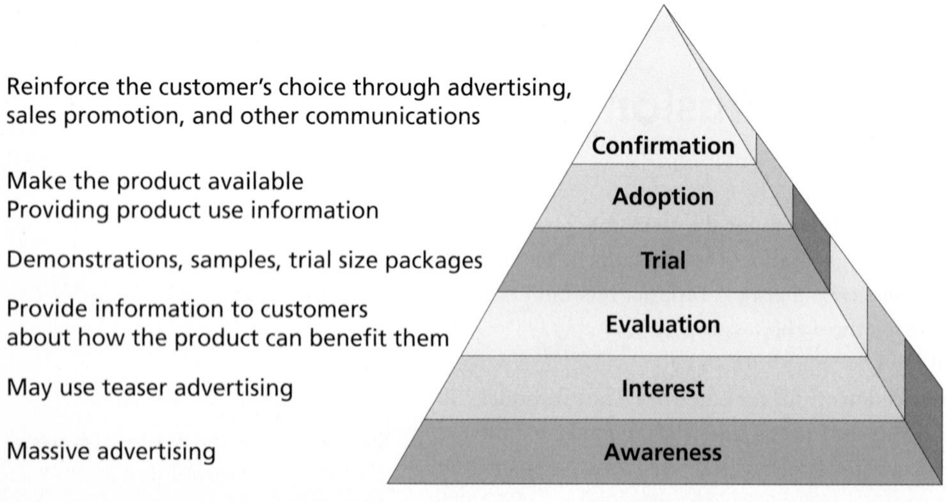

Reinforce the customer's choice through advertising, sales promotion, and other communications

Make the product available
Providing product use information

Demonstrations, samples, trial size packages

Provide information to customers about how the product can benefit them

May use teaser advertising

Massive advertising

Confirmation
Adoption
Trial
Evaluation
Interest
Awareness

Interest

For some of the people who become aware of a new product, a second stage in the adoption process is *interest*. In this stage, a prospective adopter begins to see how a new product might satisfy an existing or newly-realized need. Interest also means that consumers look for and are open to information about the innovation. Volkswagen's Jetta, for instance, developed a certain *panache* with the young 20s crowd around 2000 or so. But, as today's 20- and 30-something car buyers start having families and need bigger cars with more carrying space, they began to lose interest in the Jetta. To get the lucrative young-parent group interested in the product again, Volkswagen reverted to a stronger emphasis on safety and also touts the quality and reliability virtues of German engineering.[32] Marketers often design teaser advertisements that give prospective customers just enough information about the new product to make them curious and to stimulate their interest. Despite marketers' best efforts, however, some more consumers drop out of the process at this point.

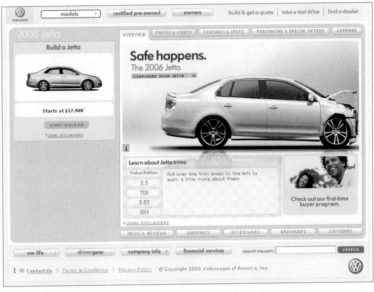

Volkswagen continues to modify its message to retain the interest of its core drivers.

Evaluation

In the *evaluation* stage, we weigh the costs and benefits of the new product. On the one hand, for complex, risky, or expensive products, people think about the innovation a great deal before they will try it. For example, a firm will carefully evaluate spending hundreds of thousands of dollars on manufacturing robotics prior to purchase. Marketers for such products help prospective customers see how such products can benefit them.

But as we've seen in the case of impulse products, sometimes little evaluation may occur before someone decides to buy a good or service. A person may do very little thinking before she makes an **impulse purchase**, like the virtual *Tamagotchi* (Japanese for "cute little egg") pets. For these goods, marketers design the product to be eye-catching and appealing to get consumers to notice the product quickly. Tamagotchis certainly did grab the attention of consumers—40 million of them bought the first generation of them. Toymaker Bandai Co. has since come out with a new generation of Tamagotchis—the current version allows the pet owner to control aspects of the Tamagotchi's life such as career choices and who they eventually become. Bandai's newest tagline for the product is "Start livin' the Tamagotchi life!"—a not too-veiled reference to virtual worlds such as *Second Life*.[33]

impulse purchase
A purchase made without any planning or search effort.

Some potential adopters will evaluate an innovation positively enough to move on to the next stage. Those who do not think the new product will provide adequate benefits drop out at this point.

Trial

Trial is the stage in the adoption process when potential buyers will actually experience or use the product for the first time. Often marketers stimulate trial when they provide opportunities for consumers to sample the product. Travel through any major U.S. airport, for example, and you'll see Dell demonstration kiosks—a major departure from the company's usual focus on on-line direct marketing. That's because there is a drawback to on-line direct marketing: Some consumers just can't stand to buy without first touching, holding, and using a product—in short, conducting a "trial." Interestingly, people are also buying

Marketers often build interest for a good or service by showing how it will benefit customers. This Hong Kong ad for a spa and salon boasts "dramatic transformations daily."

Your body is a temple.
Even if you do let
cupcakes in once in
a while.

Silk soymilk stimulated the adoption process by distributing free samples of its product to American consumers who were not familiar with milk that doesn't come from cows.

Dells right at the kiosks. In retrospect this is not too surprising, given that the passenger demographics tend toward 24 to 49 years of age, most with annual household incomes above $70,000—just the type of people who want the latest computer. Dell also showcases the PC gaming power of its higher-end computers kiosks at Gamestop locations around the country, in part because of its acquisition of Alienware—a long-time champion of high-powered PC gaming. For gamers, it's really important to touch, feel, and experience the product first-hand before they buy.[34]

Even if the trial is satisfactory, however, some prospective buyers still won't actually adopt the new product because it costs too much. Initially, this was the case with onboard navigation systems in cars. Consumers could try out the system in rental cars from Hertz and Avis, but the price (over $2,000) understandably put off most prospective customers. By 2006, with prices having dipped below $500, many more consumers were buying the units for their own cars and ordering them with new vehicles.[35]

Adoption

In the *adoption* stage, a prospect actually buys the product (Hallelujah!). If the product is a consumer or business-to-business good, this means buying the product and learning how to use and maintain it. If the product is an idea, this means that the individual agrees with the concept.

Does this mean that all individuals or organizations that first choose an innovation are permanent customers? That's a mistake many firms make. Marketers need to provide follow-up contacts and communications with adopters to ensure they are satisfied and remain loyal to the new product over time.

Confirmation

After she adopts an innovation, a customer weighs expected versus actual benefits and costs. Favorable experiences make it more likely that she will become a loyal adopter as her initially positive opinions result in *confirmation*. Of course, nothing lasts forever—even a loyal customer may decide that a new product no longer meets her expectations and reject it (sort of like dropping a boyfriend). Some marketers feel that reselling the customer in the confirmation stage is important. They provide advertisements, sales presentations, and other communications to reinforce a customer's choice.

The Diffusion of Innovations

As we saw earlier, *diffusion* describes how the use of a product spreads throughout a population. Of course, marketers prefer their entire target market to immediately adopt a new product, but this is not the case. Consumers and business customers differ in how eager or willing they are to try something new, lengthening the diffusion process by months or even years. Based on adopters' roles in the diffusion process, experts classify them into five categories.

Some people like to try new products. Others are so reluctant you'd think they're afraid of anything new (do you know anyone like that?). As Figure 8.4 shows, there are five categories of adopters: innovators, early adopters, early majority, late majority, and laggards.[36] To understand how the adopter categories differ, we'll focus on the adoption of one specific technology, Wi-Fi (wireless fidelity).

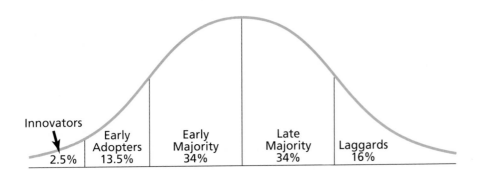

Figure 8.4 | Categories of Adopters

Because consumers differ in how willing they are to buy and try a new product, it often takes months or years for most of the population to adopt an innovation.

Innovators

Innovators make up roughly the first 2.5 percent of adopters. This segment is extremely adventurous and willing to take risks with new products. Innovators are typically well-educated, younger, better off financially than others in the population, and worldly. Innovators who were into new technology knew all about Wi-Fi before other people had heard of it. Because innovators pride themselves on trying new products, they purchased laptops with Wi-Fi cards way back in 1999 when Apple Computer first introduced them in its laptops.

innovators
The first segment (roughly 2.5 percent) of a population to adopt a new product.

Early Adopters

Early adopters, approximately 13.5 percent of adopters, buy product innovations early in the diffusion process but not as early as innovators. Unlike innovators, early adopters are very concerned about social acceptance so they tend to gravitate toward products they believe will make others think they are cutting-edge or fashionable. Typically, they are heavy media users and often are heavy users of the product category. Others in the population often look to early adopters for their opinions on various topics, making early adopters key to a new product's success. For this reason, marketers often target them in their advertising and other communications efforts.

early adopters
Those who adopt an innovation early in the diffusion process, but after the innovators.

Columnists who write about personal technology for popular magazines like *Time* were testing Wi-Fi in mid-2000. They experienced some problems (like PCs crashing when they set up a wireless network at home) but still they touted the benefits of wireless connectivity. Road warriors adopted the technology as Wi-Fi access spread into airports, hotels, city parks, and other public spaces. Intel, maker of the Centrino mobile platform, launched a major campaign with Condé Nast's *Traveler* magazine and offered a location guide to T-Mobile hotspots nationwide.

Early Majority

The **early majority**, roughly 34 percent of adopters, avoid being either first or last to try an innovation. They are typically middle-class consumers and are deliberate and cautious. Early majority consumers have slightly above-average education and income levels. When the early majority adopts a product, we no longer consider it new or different—it is, in essence, already established. By 2002, Wi-Fi access was available in over 500 Starbucks cafés, and monthly subscription prices were dropping rapidly (from $30 to $9.95 per month).

early majority
Those whose adoption of a new product signals a general acceptance of the innovation.

Late Majority

Late majority adopters, about 34 percent of the population, are older, even more conservative, and typically have lower-than-average levels of education and income. The late majority adopters avoid trying a new product until it is no longer risky. By that time, the product has become an economic necessity or there is pressure from peer groups to adopt. By 2004, Wi-Fi capability was being bundled into almost all laptops and you could connect in mainstream venues like McDonald's restaurants and sports stadiums. Cities across the country began considering blanket Wi-Fi coverage throughout the entire town through WiMax technology.

late majority
The adopters who are willing to try new products when there is little or no risk associated with the purchase, when the purchase becomes an economic necessity, or when there is social pressure to purchase.

Laggards

laggards
The last consumers to adopt an innovation.

Laggards, about 16 percent of adopters, are the last in a population to adopt a new product. Laggards are typically lower in social class than other adopter categories and are bound by tradition. By the time laggards adopt a product, it may already be superseded by other innovations. By 2006, it would have seemed strange if Wi-Fi or a similar capability was not part of the standard package in even the lowest-priced laptop computer.[37]

When they understand these adopter categories, marketers can develop strategies that will speed the diffusion or widespread use of their products. For example, early in the diffusion process, marketers may put greater emphasis on advertising in special-interest magazines to attract innovators and early adopters. Later they may lower the product's price or come out with lower-priced models with fewer "bells and whistles" to attract the late majority. We will talk more about strategies for new and existing products in the next chapter.

Product Factors That Affect the Rate of Adoption

Not all products are successful, to say the least. As we saw in Table 8.5, all sorts of products litter the marketing graveyard. Other classic boo-boos include Crystal Pepsi (a product that kept the taste but took out the caramel color), Premier smokeless cigarettes, the Betamax video player, the Ford Edsel automobile, and Snif-T-Panties (women's underwear that smelled like bananas, popcorn, whiskey, or pizza).[38] The reason for such product failures is very simple—consumers did not perceive that the products satisfied a need better than competitive products already on the market.

If you could predict which new products will succeed and which will fail, you'd quickly be in high demand as a marketing consultant by companies worldwide. That's because companies make large investments in new products, but failures are all too frequent. Experts suggest that between one-third and one-half of all new products fail. As you might expect, a lot of people try to develop research techniques that enable them to predict whether a new product will be hot or not.

Researchers identify five characteristics of innovations that affect the rate of adoption: relative advantage, compatibility, complexity, trialability, and observability.[39] The degree to which a new product has each of these characteristics affects the speed of diffusion. It may take years for a market to widely adopt a new product. The five factors in Table 8.6 help to explain both why customers might not adopt a new product during its early years and why adoption could speed up later. Let's take a closer look at the humble microwave oven to understand why each of these five factors is important.

Table 8.6	Adoption-Rate Factors—A Microwave Oven Example		
Product Factors Affecting Rate of Adoption	**Product Rated High on Factor**	**Product Rated Low on Factor**	**Rating of Microwave Oven on the Factors**
Relative advantage	Faster	Slower	Low until consumer lifestyles changed
Compatibility	Faster	Slower	Low—required new types of food products and containers, as well as a different mindset about cooking
Complexity	Slower	Faster	Early instructions and controls were confusing and complex
Trialability	Faster	Slower	Low until retailers facilitated product trial
Observability	Faster	Slower	Once people figured the microwave out, those quickly baked potatoes and cool microwave popcorn were hard not to observe (and taste!)

A variety of product factors cause consumers' adoption of the innovation to be faster or slower. Marketers who understand these factors can develop strategies to encourage people to try a new product.

Relative Advantage

Relative advantage is the degree to which a consumer perceives that a new product provides superior benefits. In the case of the microwave oven, consumers in the 1960s did not feel that the product provided important benefits that would improve their lives. But by the late 1970s, that perception had changed because more women had entered the workforce. The 1960s woman had all day to prepare the evening meal, so she didn't need the microwave. In the 1970s, however, when many women left home for work at 8:00 AM and returned home at 6:00 PM, an appliance that would "magically" defrost a frozen chicken and cook it in 30 minutes provided a genuine advantage.

relative advantage
The degree to which a consumer perceives that a new product provides superior benefits.

Compatibility

Compatibility is the extent to which a new product is consistent with existing cultural values, customs, and practices. Did consumers see the microwave oven as being compatible with existing ways of doing things? Hardly. Cooking on paper plates? If you put a paper plate in a conventional oven, you'll likely get a visit from the fire department. By anticipating compatibility issues early in the new-product development stage, marketing strategies can address such problems in planning communications programs, or there may be opportunities to alter product designs to overcome some consumer objections.

compatibility
The extent to which a new product is consistent with existing cultural values, customs, and practices.

Complexity

Complexity is the degree to which consumers find a new product or its use difficult to understand. Many microwave users today haven't a clue about how a microwave oven cooks food. When appliance manufacturers introduced the first microwaves, they explained that this new technology causes molecules to move and rub together, which creates friction that produces heat. Voilà! Cooked pot roast. But that explanation was too complex and confusing for the homemaker of the Ozzie and Harriet days.

complexity
The degree to which consumers find a new product or its use difficult to understand.

Trialability

Trialability is the ease of sampling a new product and its benefits. Marketers took a very important step in the 1970s to speed up adoption of the microwave oven—product trial. Just about every store that sold microwaves invited shoppers to visit the store and sample an entire meal a microwave cooked.

trialability
The ease of sampling a new product and its benefits.

Observability

Observability refers to how visible a new product and its benefits are to others who might adopt it. The ideal innovation is easy to see. For example, for a generation of kids, scooters like the Razor became the hippest way to get around as soon as one preteen saw her friends flying by. That same generation observed its friends trading Pokémon cards and

observability
How visible a new product and its benefits are to others who might adopt it.

Jeffery A.
Periatt
a professor at Auburn University Montgomery
My Advice for Bossa Nova would be to choose

Option

real people, **Other** Voices

I would choose **Option 2** because the fears associated with overextending scarce capital resources may be overstated. This belief is based on the following assumptions. First, while it's a new manufacturing process, the current selling structure/process will work

because Bossa Nova would be working with the same buyers. Second, the company may still use POM's primary advertising to educate consumers about this product categories' benefits. Finally, while new packaging will have to be designed, the fact that the energy drink's position has not been firmly established in the consumer's mind means there could be brand elements that could transfer to the new product line. Each of these assumptions suggests the strain on resources will be minimal at best. Additionally, adopting this strategy would allow Bossa Nova to finance product and market development with the higher margin energy drink, and if the taste is comparable to POM's, then Bossa Nova's product has a significant relative advantage over current product offerings. ➤

Firms are more likely to accept a new product if they perceive the improvement to be large in relation to the investment they will have to make. The U.S. Army adopted the John Deere Gator to replace some of its more expensive Humvees.

wanted to join in. In the case of the microwave, it wasn't quite so readily observable for its potential adopters—only close friends and acquaintances who visited someone's home would likely see an early adopter using it. But the fruits of the microwave's labors—tasty food dishes—created lots of buzz at office water coolers and social events and its use spread quickly.

How Organizational Differences Affect Adoption

Just as there are differences among consumers in their eagerness to adopt new products, businesses and other organizations are not alike in their willingness to buy and use new industrial products. New or smaller companies may be more nimble and able to jump onto emerging trends. Those that do often are rewarded with higher sales (though, of course, the risks are higher, too). Thus, while Samsung recognized early on that color screens on cell phones were going to be in demand by consumers, some other companies (Nokia, for example) were slower to pick up on a trend that had originated in Samsung's home turf in Asia. While other firms continued to try to market monochrome screens for months longer than they should have, Samsung made strong gains with its more innovative move.

Firms that welcome product innovations are likely to be younger companies in highly technical industries with younger managers and entrepreneurial corporate cultures (think Google). Early adopter firms are likely to be market-share leaders that adopt new innovations and try new ways of doing things to maintain their leadership. Firms that adopt new products only when they recognize they must innovate to keep up are in the early majority. Late majority firms tend to be oriented toward the *status quo* and often have large financial investments in existing production technology. Laggard firms are probably already losing money.

Business-to-business products, like consumer products, also may possess characteristics that will increase their likelihood of adoption. Organizations are likely to adopt an innovation that helps them increase gross margins and profits. It is unlikely that firms would have adopted new products like voice mail unless they provided a way to increase profits by reducing labor costs. Organizational innovations are attractive when they are consistent with a firm's ways of doing business.

Cost is also a factor in the new products firms will adopt. Recall the concept of *value* as we introduced it in Chapter 1. For similar reasons, firms are more likely to accept a new product if they perceive the improvement to be large in relation to the investment they will have to make. This was the case when the U.S. Army adopted the John Deere Gator. At under $10,000, or about an eighth of the price of a Humvee, the Gator is an inexpensive off-road utility vehicle that's just right for rescuing wounded soldiers from foxholes. Although the Gator won't replace the Humvee altogether, the military is able to buy fewer of the expensive Humvees and save taxpayers some big bucks.[40]

Now that you've learned the basics of creating a product, read "Real People, Real Choices: How It Worked Out" to see which strategy Palo Hawken selected for Bossa Nova Beverages.

Palo
Hawken

APPLYING Complexity

Palo and his colleagues realized they were better off with a simple, focused message to make it more likely that consumers would adopt their new Bossa Nova beverage product. ➡

real people, **Real Choices**

Palo
Hawken

Palo chose:

Option

How it Worked Out at Bossa Nova

Bossa Nova clung to Options 1 and 2 for many months, but in the end Palo and his colleagues took the leap and chose Option 3: The company committed to a path of pure focus to pursue what they believed to be the greatest business opportunity in its portfolio of products and ideas. The result of this decision was the creation of Bossa Nova: Açai juice in three flavors—mango, passion fruit, and original (the pure açai experience). At the Natural Product Expo in 2005 in Anaheim, California, Bossa Nova took its first order from Whole Foods Market, the industry's leading retailer. This order and the general show excitement was enough to close Bossa Nova's first round of VC (venture capital) funding in August of 2005, which set it in motion to achieve 300 percent growth annually for the next three years. Bossa Nova's full line of antioxidant juices is now found in every influential retailer in the country, including Kroger, Safeway, Wegmans, HEB, Publix, and many others. The new product's core customer is educated, health-oriented women between the ages of 28 and 55. In 2008, Bossa Nova is expanding from 5 to 15 SKUs and expects its annual triple digit growth to continue.

How Bossa Nova Measures Success

Unlike a marketing decision in a larger organization where incremental changes can be quantified and measured, this fundamental decision pitted two philosophies against one another: 1) the conservative position of building on an existing brand, with modest but measurable sales, versus 2) a more aggressive, intuition-based direction that requires re-imagining and re-writing the business fundamentals, with a strong core product, risky financial assumptions, and a yet to be tested product.

When measured against industry standards of carbonated beverage sales, Bossa Nova's açai juice eclipsed the monthly run-rate in its first month and was at 10 times the carbonated run-rate within 8 months. Palo hopes to develop further metrics as this new product category matures.

Part of Bossa Nova's new product line.

Refer back to **page 231** for Palo's story

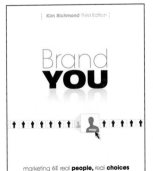

Brand **YOU**!

Companies don't just hire people—they hire people who produce results.

Be one of those people by identifying your features, benefits, and extras in Chapter 8 of the *Brand You* supplement.

1. Objective Summary (pp. 232–233)

Articulate the value proposition.

Products can be physical goods, services, ideas, people, or places. A good is a *tangible* product, something that we can see, touch, smell, hear, taste, or possess In contrast, *intangible* products—services, ideas, people, places—are products that we can't always see, touch, taste, smell, or possess. Marketers think of the product as more than just a thing that comes in a package. They view it as a bundle of attributes that includes the packaging, brand name, benefits, and supporting features in addition to a physical good. The key issue is marketer's role in creating the value proposition in order to develop and market products appropriately.

Key Terms

good, p. 232

2. Objective Summary (pp. 233–235)

Explain the layers of a product.

A product may be anything tangible or intangible that satisfies consumer or business-to-business customer needs. Products include goods, services, ideas, people, and places. The core product is the basic product category benefits and customized benefit(s) the product provides. The actual product is the physical good or delivered service, including the packaging and brand name. The augmented product includes both the actual product and any supplementary services, such as warranty, credit, delivery, installation, and so on.

Key Terms

core product, p. 234 (Figure 8.2, p. 233)

actual product, p. 235 (Figure 8.2, p. 233)

augmented product, p. 235 (Figure 8.2, p. 233)

3. Objective Summary (pp. 236–242)

Describe how marketers classify products.

Marketers generally classify goods and services as either consumer or business-to-business products. They further classify consumer products according to how long they last and by how they are purchased. Durable goods provide benefits for months or years, whereas nondurable goods are used up quickly or are useful for only a short time. Consumers purchase convenience products frequently with little effort. Customers carefully gather information and compare different brands on their attributes and prices before buying shopping products. Specialty products have unique characteristics that are important to the buyer. Customers have little interest in unsought products until a need arises. Business products are for commercial uses by organizations.

Marketers classify business products according to how they are used, for example, equipment; maintenance, repair, and operating (MRO) products; raw and processed materials; component parts; and business services.

Key Terms

durable goods, p. 236

nondurable goods, p. 236

convenience product, p. 238

staples, p. 238

impulse product, p. 238

emergency products, p. 239

fast-moving consumer goods (FMCG), p. 239

shopping products, p. 239

intelligent agents, p. 239

specialty product, p. 240 (Ethical Decisions in the Real World, p. 240)

unsought products, p. 240

equipment, 241

maintenance, repair, and operating (MRO) products, p. 241

raw materials, p. 241

processed materials, p. 241

component parts, p. 241

4. Objective Summary (pp. 242–246)

Understand the importance and types of product innovations.

Innovations are anything consumers perceive to be new. Understanding new products is important to companies because of the fast pace of technological advancement, the high cost to companies for developing new products, and the contributions to society that new products can make. Marketers classify innovations by their degree of newness. A continuous innovation is a modification of an existing product, a dynamically continuous innovation provides a greater change in a product, and a discontinuous innovation is a new product that creates major changes in people's lives.

Key Terms

innovation, p. 242 (Metrics Moment, p. 246)

continuous innovation, p. 244

knockoff, p. 245

dynamically continuous innovation, p. 245

convergence, p. 245

discontinuous innovation, p. 246

5. Objective Summary (pp. 247–253)

Show how firms develop new products.

In new-product development, marketers first generate product ideas from which product concepts are first developed and then screened. Next they develop a marketing strategy and conduct a business analysis to estimate the profitability of the new product. Technical development includes planning how the product will be manufactured and may mean obtaining a patent. Next, the effectiveness of the new product may be assessed in an actual or a simulated test market. Finally, the product is launched, and the entire marketing plan is implemented.

Key Terms

idea generation, p. 247

product concept development and screening, p. 248

green marketing, p. 250

business analysis, p. 251

technical development, p. 251

prototypes, p. 251

test marketing, p. 252

commercialization, p. 253

6. Objective Summary (pp. 253–260)

Explain the process of product adoption and the diffusion of innovations.

Product adoption is the process by which an individual begins to buy and use a new product, whereas the diffusion of innovations is how a new product spreads throughout a population. The stages in the adoption process are awareness, interest, trial, adoption, and confirmation. To better understand the diffusion process, marketers classify consumers—according to their readiness to adopt new products—as innovators, early adopters, early majority, late majority, and laggards.

Five product characteristics that have an important effect on how quickly (or if) a new product will be adopted by consumers are relative advantage, compatibility, product complexity, trialability, and observability. Similar to individual consumers, organizations differ in their readiness to adopt new products based on characteristics of the organization, its management, and characteristics of the innovation.

Key Terms

product adoption, p. 253

diffusion, p. 254

tipping point, p. 254

media blitz, p. 254

impulse purchase, p. 255

innovators, p. 257 (Figure 8.4, p. 257)

early adopters, p. 257 (Figure 8.4, p. 257)

early majority, p. 257 (Figure 8.4, p. 257)

late majority, p. 257 (Figure 8.4, p. 257)

laggards, p. 258 (Figure 8.4, p. 257)

relative advantage, p. 259

compatibility, p. 259

complexity, p. 259

trialability, p. 259

observability, p. 259

Chapter Questions and Activities

Concepts: Test Your Knowledge

1. What is the difference between the core product, the actual product, and the augmented product?
2. What is the difference between a durable good and a nondurable good? What are the main differences among convenience, shopping, and specialty products?
3. What is an unsought product? How do marketers make such products attractive to consumers?
4. What types of products are bought and sold in business-to-business markets?
5. What is a new product? Why is understanding new products so important to marketers? What are the types of innovations?
6. List and explain the steps marketers undergo to develop new products.
7. What is a test market? What are some pros and cons of test markets?
8. Explain the stages a consumer goes through in the adoption of a new product.
9. List and explain the categories of adopters.
10. What product factors affect the rate of adoption of innovations?
11. Explain how organizations may differ in their willingness to buy and use new industrial products.

Choices and Ethical Issues: You Decide

1. Technology is moving at an ever-increasing speed, and this means that new products enter and leave the market faster than ever. What are some products you think technology might be able to develop in the future that you would like? Do you think these products could add to a company's profits?
2. In this chapter, we talked about the core product, the actual product, and the augmented product. Does this mean that marketers are simply trying to make products that are really the same seem different? When marketers understand these three layers of the product and develop products with this concept in mind, what are the benefits to consumers? What are the hazards of this type of thinking?
3. Discontinuous innovations are totally new products—something seldom seen in the marketplace. What are some examples of discontinuous innovations introduced in the past 50 years? Why are there so few discontinuous innovations? What products have companies recently

introduced that you believe will end up being regarded as discontinuous innovations?

4. Consider the differences in marketing to consumer markets versus business markets. Which aspects of the processes of product adoption and diffusion apply to both markets? Which aspects are unique to one or the other? Provide evidence of your findings.

5. In this chapter, we explained that knockoffs are slightly modified copies of original product designs. Should knockoffs be illegal? Who is hurt by knockoffs? Is the marketing of knockoffs good or bad for consumers in the short run? In the long run?

6. It is not necessarily true that all new products benefit consumers or society. What are some new products that have made our lives better? What are some new products that have actually been harmful to consumers or to society? Should there be a way to monitor or "police" new products that are introduced to the marketplace?

Practice: Apply What You've Learned

1. Assume that you are the director of marketing for the company that has developed a smart phone to outdo the iPhone. How would you go about convincing the late majority to go ahead and adopt it—especially since they still haven't quite caught onto the iPhone yet?

2. Assume that you are employed in the marketing department of a firm that is producing a hybrid automobile. In developing this product, you realize that it is important to provide a core product, an actual product, and an augmented product that meets the needs of customers. Develop an outline of how your firm might provide these three product layers in the hybrid car.

3. Firms go to great lengths to develop new product ideas. Sometimes new ideas come from brainstorming, in which groups of individuals get together and try to think of as many different, novel, creative—and hopefully profitable—ideas for a new product as possible. With a group of other students, participate in brainstorming for new product ideas for one of the following (or some other product of your choice):
   - An exercise machine with some desirable new features

   - A combination shampoo and body wash
   - A new type of university

   Then, with your class, screen one or more of the ideas for possible further product development.

4. As a member of a new product team with your company, you are working to develop an electric car jack that would make changing tires for a car easier. You are considering conducting a test market for this new product. Outline the pros and cons for test marketing this product. What are your recommendations?

Miniproject: Learn by Doing

What product characteristics do consumers think are important in a new product? What types of service components do they demand? Most important, how do marketers know how to develop successful new products? This miniproject is designed to let you make some of these decisions.

1. Create (in your mind) a new product item that might be of interest to college students such as yourself. Develop a written description and possibly a drawing of this new product.

2. Show this new product description to a number of your fellow students who might be users of the product. Ask them to tell you what they think of the product. Some of the questions you might ask them are the following:
   - What is your overall opinion of the new product?
   - What basic benefits would you expect to receive from the product?
   - What about the physical characteristics of the product? What do you like? Dislike? What would you add? Delete? Change?
   - What do you like (or would you like) in the way of product packaging?
   - What sort of services would you expect to receive with the product?
   - Do you think you would try the product? How could marketers influence you to buy the product?

   Develop a report based on what you found. Include your recommendations for changes in the product and your feelings about the potential success of the new product.

Real people, **real surfers**: explore the web

Go to the Bossa Nova açai juice Web site (**www.bossausa.com**). Check out the information about the company's products and what açai juice is. Also go to the "In the Media" section and review some of the TV, Web, and print news items about the company and its products.

1. How would you classify Bossa Nova's products (convenience, shopping, or specialty)? What leads you to this conclusion?

2. In your opinion, is Bossa Nova engaged in product innovation? How do you know?

3. How compelling do you find these two product claims to be:
   a. "Packed with more disease-fighting antioxidants than any other fruit on earth."
   b. "Every bottle you buy saves another rainforest tree."

Marketing Plan Exercise

Go to the Procter & Gamble Web site (**www.pg.com**) and click on "Products" at the top of the page. Next, navigate to

the "Oral Care" products section and then click on "Crest." Look over the information about Crest products, then answer these questions that Procter & Gamble must answer when doing marketing planning for the Crest product line:

1. Crest lists several product innovations, including Whitestrips, Night Effects, and others. How would you "classify" each of these products based on the discussion in the chapter? What leads you to classify each as you do?
2. What type of innovation do you consider each of these products? Why?
3. Pick any one of the products and consider the process that Procter & Gamble probably went through when initially developing it. Give an example of how each of the steps in Table 8.4, "Phases in New-Product Development," might have been used for that product.
4. For the same product you selected in item 3, what stage in the adoption process do you believe that product currently occupies with most consumers? What leads you to this conclusion? Why is knowledge of the adoption process important in marketing planning?

Marketing in Action Case

Real Choices at Kodak

What do you do if you're made CEO of a company whose bread and butter product, the one that provided the bulk of its sales and profits over the last 115 years, is massively losing market share to the digital film business. How do you respond when you watch your competitors Agfa and Minolta Konica move away from the traditional film business entirely and "go digital"? Well, if you're Antonio Perez, the new CEO of Eastman Kodak, you do exactly the same. Only, you want to carefully maintain your century-old brand identity and pride in your know-how. You convert the bulk of your giant business from silver-halide film to digital photography and related services. And you hope—no, pray—that the unavoidable crash of traditional film product sales will not happen too quickly and force Kodak to go the way of the dodo bird and become extinct.

For over a century, Kodak operated its business by its 1888 advertising slogan, "you press the button, we do the rest." While Kodak did produce cameras, the company made money from its film business, from processing film and from selling film processing supplies, like paper and the chemicals needed to develop pictures. However, Kodak's business model changed in a big way when digital technology arrived on the scene.

Digital cameras not only provide the core product benefits of taking a picture, but they also offer enhanced actual and augmented product features. With a digital camera, consumers can preview a picture immediately after taking it and, if the picture did not turn out satisfactorily, delete it. This benefit results in cost savings for consumers because they don't have to pay for poor-quality pictures. Furthermore, you can save digital photos on a computer, print them on your home printer, share them with friends and family on your FaceBook page, incorporate them into a slide show that you can later watch on a DVD player, and even modify them to cut out the boy- or girlfriend you no longer have. Consequently, the augmented product benefits digital technology provides go far beyond what Kodak used to offer with its traditional film product.

Under Perez's leadership, Kodak has made several successful replacements in its product line. The old Kodak gained much of its revenue from film; the new Kodak is big in the printer ink market. Kodak's old business model reflected its slogan, "you press the button, we do the rest." True to that slogan, today's Kodak focuses on "turnkey" strategies that emphasize e-commerce and other support solutions that meet customer demand. For example, Kodak created the EasyShare Gallery, the world's largest on-line photo-printing and sharing service that boasted 20 million members in 2005 alone. Still the company faces future challenges—it cannot stand still but must look for more strategic opportunities in the future.

For example, a new market for storage and archiving systems of digital photos and films is just opening up. Any digital camera user knows from experience that billions of the pictures taken around the world are actually never printed. No one, it seems, is really sure just how long digital pictures will survive stored on conventional hard-drives or burned onto CDs. This is why many people believe that a big market is likely to develop for storage and archiving systems, both on-line and off-line. If people want their memories to last long into the future, they may have to buy or subscribe to new products and services.

At the beginning of 2008, Kodak's CEO Perez said, "Kodak is now a company with a broad portfolio of digital businesses with diverse sources of revenue, and earnings powered by an unmatched intellectual property position and a sustainable traditional business model. I am confident that we will continue to achieve success in the digital market."

But to do that, Kodak must continue to develop new products—to find other opportunities to increase its share of the digital photo market. Certainly Kodak will have to continue innovating to remain an option for customers in the future and enhance the company's chances of survival.

You Make the Call

1. What is the decision facing Kodak?
2. What factors are important in understanding this decision situation?
3. What are the alternatives?
4. What decision(s) do you recommend?
5. What are some ways to implement your recommendation?

Based on: "Photography: Down With the Shutters, Competition in Digital Photography Takes Another Turn," *The Economist* print edition, March 23, 2006, **http://www.economist.com/business/displaystory.cfm?story_id=E1_VGGNRPR** (accessed March 5, 2008); "Kodak Poised to Accelerate Profitable Growth," **www.businesswire.com**, February 7, 2008, **http://www.kodak.com/eknec/PageQuerier.jhtml?pq-path=2709&gpcid=0900688a80888a2c&pq-locale=en_US** (accessed April 21, 2008; Eastman Kodak: Another Kodak moment, A photography giant changes boss to survive in the digital age, *The Economist* print edition, May 12, 2005, **http://www.economist.com/business/displaystory.cfm?story_id=E1_PJSQSSN** (accessed March 5, 2008).

Note: Special thanks to Domenica Preysing for her work on this case.

Manage the Product

Tom
Petters
Profile ▼

A **Decision Maker** at Petters Group Worldwide

Tom Petters is chairman and CEO of Petters Group Worldwide. He started this trading company in 1988 with little or no capital. Under his management and guidance, Petters Group Worldwide has grown from a one-man operation into an investment company that employs people across the globe. The core areas of focus for Petters Group are aviation, real estate and hospitality, brand management, media and marketing, and investment capital and learning.

In 2002, Tom was a partner in acquiring and restarting Fingerhut, one of the largest catalog and direct mail companies in the country. The following year he acquired uBid.com, the second largest Internet auction site. His latest acquisition, Sun Country Airlines, was recently voted number one for customer service by the Metrix Media group.

Tom is a contributor to many charitable organizations. He serves on the board of trustees at the College of St. Benedict and Rollins College, and is on the Business Advisory Council and Board of Visitors for Miami University–Ohio.

Real People, Real Choices

Decision Time at Petters Group Worldwide

In 2004 Petters Group started as a licensee of the Polaroid brand for consumer electronics. Polaroid was best known for the instant photo camera that its founder Dr. Land invented many years ago. After a year in this market, the firm found that the brand was very well received by consumers and Petters exceeded its revenue goals. But Polaroid had its challenges: it had just emerged from bankruptcy and was owned by a financial investor, and sales of its signature instant film were in decline as photographers switched to newer digital technology. The current owner was thinking about pulling back the license to split up the company and sell it off. It was at this point that Tom evaluated the brand's long-term possibilities for Polaroid as a company and its future in this market. He had to make a fast decision on whether he could change a very difficult culture, one which had turned away from Dr. Land's entrepreneurial and visionary roots and now had very little forward thinking in the tough consumer electronics industry.

Things to remember:

The brand name Polaroid had a 98% recognition rate among consumers.

Tom considered his Options 1·2·3

1 Option
Offer Polaroid a larger percentage of the company's revenues and continue as a licensee. While this was a safe option, the revenue percentages in consumer electronics are narrow and the firm's ability to grow the line would continue to depend upon Polaroid's approvals.

2 Option
Acquire a new brand to place in the consumer electronics line Petters had created in portable DVD players and LCD television for the Polaroid brand. The difficulty here was brand awareness. Polaroid had 68 years of history with a 98 percent recognition rating. Acquiring or creating a new brand would require millions of dollars in marketing efforts to create a new identity in the electronics market.

3 Option
Buy Polaroid Corporation. Polaroid was a company that was experiencing financial problems, and had recently emerged from bankruptcy. Tom had received indications that management would be open to an acquisition offer. The stumbling block was that Polaroid's instant film division was in the "decline" stage of its product life cycle, so Petters Group would be buying a company that was losing its main product.

Now, put yourself in Tom's shoes: Which option would you choose, and why?

You Choose

Which **Option** would you choose, and **why**?
1. ☐YES ☐NO   2. ☐YES ☐NO   3. ☐YES ☐NO

See what **option** Tom chose and its success on **page 293** ⇒

1

OBJECTIVE

Explain the different product objectives and strategies a firm may choose.
(pp. 268–276)

Product Planning: Use Product Objectives to Decide on a Product Strategy

When Lexus introduced the GS450h in 2006—that's "h" as in hybrid—it was a very big deal. That's because it was the first hybrid ever brought to market on a rear-wheel drive car with an acceleration claim of 0 to 60 mph in 5 1/2 seconds and a base price of $54,900. Today, they've added the LS 600h L Hybrid with all-wheel drive and a starting price of $104,000! Pretty pricey, right? Maybe at those prices you're thinking, "I'll just keep my gas guzzler and pay today's high fuel prices!" But Lexus is banking on reeducating high-end car buyers that they can (and should want to) have their cake and eat it too with fuel economy, comfort, and performance.[1]

At the lower end of the emerging hybrid market, Toyota's Prius has been a sales phenomenon—although several other Prius rivals have posted more disappointing sales. Will the Lexus offering succeed? A lot depends on how the automaker markets and manages this innovative product. What makes one product fail and another succeed? It's worth repeating what we said in Chapter 2: *Firms that plan well succeed*. Product planning plays a big role in the firm's *tactical marketing plans*. Strategies the product plan outlines spell out how the firm expects to develop a value proposition that will meet marketing objectives.

Today, successful product management is more important than ever. As more and more competitors enter the global marketplace and as technology moves forward at an ever-increasing pace, firms create products that grow, mature and then decline at faster and faster speeds. This means that smart product management strategies are more critical than ever. Marketers just don't have the luxury of trying one thing, finding out it doesn't work, and then trying something else.

In Chapter 8, we talked about how marketers think about products—both core and augmented—and about how companies develop and introduce new products. In this chapter, we'll finish the product part of the story by seeing how companies manage products and then we'll examine the steps in product planning as Figure 9.1 outlines. These steps include developing product objectives and the strategies required to successfully market products as they evolve from "new kids on the block" to tried-and-true favorites—and in some cases finding new markets for these favorites. Next, we'll discuss branding and packaging, two of the more important tactical decisions product planners make. Finally, we'll examine how firms organize for effective product management. Let's start by seeing how firms develop product-related objectives.

When marketers develop product strategies, they make decisions about product benefits, features, styling, branding, labeling, and packaging. But what do they want to accomplish? Clearly stated product objectives provide focus and direction. They should support the broader marketing objectives of the business unit in addition to being consistent with the firm's overall mission. For example, the objectives of the firm may focus on return on investment (ROI). Marketing objectives then may concentrate on building market share and/or the unit or dollar sales volume necessary to attain that return on investment. Product objectives need to specify how product decisions will contribute to reaching a desired market share or level of sales.

To be effective, product-related objectives must be measurable, clear, and unambiguous—and feasible. Also, they must indicate a specific time frame. Consider, for example, how a frozen entrée manufacturer might state its product objectives:

- "In the upcoming fiscal year, eliminate the product's trans fat content to satisfy consumers' health concerns."

- "Introduce three new items this quarter to the product line to take advantage of increased consumer interest in Mexican foods."

- "During the coming fiscal year, improve the chicken entrées to the extent that consumers will rate them better tasting than the competition."

Planners must keep in touch with their customers so that their objectives accurately respond to their needs. An up-to-date knowledge of competitive product innovations also is important to develop product objectives. Above all, these objectives should consider the *long-term implications* of product decisions. Planners who sacrifice the long-term health of the firm to reach short-term sales or financial goals choose a risky course. Product planners may focus on one or more individual products at a time, or they may look at a group of product offerings as a whole. In this section, we'll briefly examine both of these approaches. We'll also look at one important product objective: product quality.

Objectives and Strategies for Individual Products

Back to our love affair with cars: How do you launch a new car that's only 142 inches long and makes people laugh when they see it? BMW did it by calling attention to the small size and poking fun at the car itself. The original launch of the MINI Cooper a few years back included bolting the MINI onto the top of a Ford Excursion with a sign "What are you doing for fun this weekend?" BMW also mocked up full-size MINIs to look like coin-operated kiddie rides you find outside grocery stores with a sign proclaiming: "Rides $16,850. Quarters only." The advertising generated buzz in the 20- to 34-year-old target market and today the MINI is no joke.

As a smaller brand, the MINI didn't have a huge advertising budget—in fact, it was the first launch of a new car in modern times that didn't include TV advertising. Instead, the MINI launched with print, outdoor billboards, and Web ads. The aim wasn't a heavy car launch but more of a "discovery process." Ads promoted "motoring" instead of driving, and magazine inserts included MINI-shaped air fresheners and pullout games. *Wired* magazine ran a cardboard foldout of the MINI suggesting readers assemble and drive it around their desks making "putt-putt" noises. *Playboy* came up with the idea of a six-page MINI "centerfold" complete with the car's vital statistics and hobbies. By the end of its first year on the market, the MINI was the second most memorable new product of the year, following the heavily advertised Vanilla Coke.[2]

Some product strategies, for example, the new hybrid Lexus LS600h L or the MINI Cooper, focus on a single new product. (As an interesting sidebar, enough customers have complained about the cramped quarters in the MINI's back seat—it is, after all, a "mini"—that BMW is introducing a larger MINI. Now that's an oxymoron!)[3] Strategies for individual products may be quite

Figure 9.1 | Steps to Manage Products

Effective product strategies come from a series of orderly steps.

Develop Product Objectives
- For individual products
- For product lines and mixes

↓

Design Product Strategies

↓

Make Tactical Product Decisions
- Product branding
- Packaging and labeling design

With a relatively tiny advertising budget for a new car model, the marketers of the MINI Cooper had to be very creative.

© 2009 MINI, a division of BMW of North America, LLC

WE CAN SUM IT UP IN TWO WORDS:
EXCEPTIONAL, EXTRAORDINARY, FANTASTIC, FRESH TASTE.

ADMITTEDLY, WE'RE BAD AT SUMMATION.

There just aren't enough adjectives to describe the
straight-from-the-orange taste of Tropicana Pure Premium.

A product objective can be as simple as reinforcing a basic brand message, such as freshness.

different for new products, for regional products, or for mature products. For new products, not surprisingly, the objectives relate to successful introduction. After a firm experiences success with a product in a local or regional market, it may decide to introduce it nationally. Coors, for example, started out in 1873 as a regional beer you could buy only in Colorado. It didn't move east of the Mississippi until 1981 and took another decade to move into all 50 states.

For mature products like tasty, cheddar Goldfish snack crackers that Campbell's Soup Company manufactures under its Pepperidge Farm label, product objectives may focus on breathing new life into a product while holding on to the traditional brand personality. For Goldfish, "The snack that smiles back," this means introducing a host of spin-offs—peanut butter flavored, giant-sized, multi-colored, and color-changing to name a few. Goldfish has been around since 1962 but continues to stay fresh with 25 varieties it sells in more than 40 countries. In fact, people eat over 75 billion Goldfish per year—if strung together, enough to wrap around the earth 30 times![4]

Objectives and Strategies for Multiple Products

Although a small firm might get away with a focus on one product, a larger firm often sells a set of related products. This means that strategic decisions affect two or more products simultaneously. The firm must think in terms of its entire portfolio of products. As Figure 9.2 shows, product planning means developing *product line* and *product mix* strategies to encompass multiple offerings. Figure 9.3 illustrates how this works for a selection of Procter & Gamble's products.

Figure 9.2 | Objectives for Single and Multiple Products

Product objectives provide focus and direction for product strategies. Objectives can focus on a single product or a group of products.

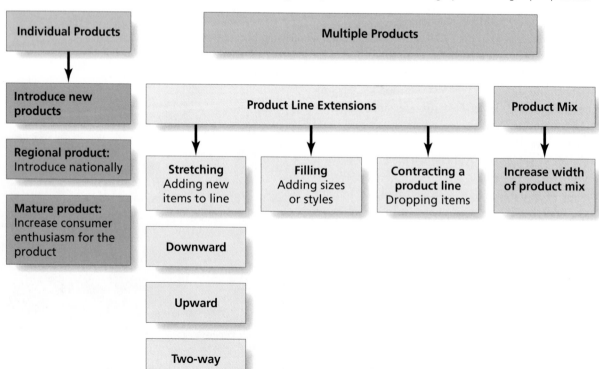

the new product. That may explain why Procter & Gamble met consumer demands for an antibacterial dish liquid by creating new versions of the existing brands Joy and Dawn.

Product Mix Strategies

A firm's **product mix** is its entire range of products. For example, in addition to a deep line of shaving products, Procter & Gamble's 2005 acquisition of Gillette gave P&G Oral B toothbrushes, Braun oral care products, and Duracell batteries.

When they develop a product mix strategy, planners usually consider the *width of the product mix*: the number of different product lines the firm produces. By developing several different product lines, firms reduce the risk of putting all their eggs in one basket. Normally, firms develop a mix of product lines that have some things in common.

Wine and spirits distributor Constellation Brands' entry into the mainstream supermarket wine space through its acquisition of Robert Mondavi is an example of a successful product mix expansion strategy. Americans drink more wine (and hard liquor) of late, and the Mondavi brand gives Constellation the crown jewel in the $3.6+ billion supermarket wine channel (i.e. mass market wines that people buy in large volume where they shop for groceries rather than at specialty wine shops).[9]

Quality as a Product Objective

Product objectives often focus on product quality: the overall ability of the product to satisfy customers' expectations. Quality is tied to how customers *think* a product will perform, and not necessarily to some technological level of perfection. Product quality objectives coincide with marketing objectives for higher sales and market share and to the firm's objectives for increased profits.

In some cases, quality means fanatical attention to detail and also an emphasis on getting extensive input from actual users of a product as it's being developed or refined— marketers refer to this as integrating the *voice of the consumer* into product design. The Japanese take this idea a step further with a practice they call **Kansei engineering**, which is a philosophy that translates customers' feelings into design elements. In one application of this practice, the designers of the Mazda Miata (now called the MX-5) focused on young drivers who saw the car as an extension of their body, a sensation they call "horse and rider as one." After extensive research, they discovered that making the stick shift exactly 9.5 centimeters long conveys the optimal feeling of sportiness and control.[10]

Total Quality Management (TQM)

In 1980, just when the economies of Germany and Japan were finally rebuilt from World War II and were threatening American markets, an NBC documentary on quality titled *If Japan Can Do It, Why Can't We?* demonstrated to the American public—and to American CEOs—the poor quality of American products.[11] So began the TQM revolution in American industry.

As we noted in Chapter 1, many firms with a quality focus have adopted the principles and practices of **total quality management (TQM)**. This philosophy calls for companywide dedication to the development, maintenance, and continuous improvement of all aspects of the company's operations. Indeed, some of the world's most admired, successful companies—top-of-industry firms such as Nordstrom, 3M, Boeing, and Coca-Cola— endorse a total quality focus.

Product quality is one way that marketing adds value to customers. However, TQM as an approach to doing business is far more sophisticated and effective than simply paying attention to product quality. TQM firms promote the attitude among employees that *everybody* working there serves its customers—even employees who never interact with people outside the firm. In such cases, employees' customers are *internal customers*—other employees with whom they interact. In this way, TQM maximizes customer satisfaction by

product mix
The total set of all products a firm offers for sale.

Kansei engineering
A Japanese philosophy that translates customers' feelings into design elements.

total quality management (TQM)
A management philosophy that focuses on satisfying customers through empowering employees to be an active part of continuous quality improvement.

involving all employees, regardless of their function, in efforts to continually improve quality. For example, TQM firms encourage all employees, even the lowest-paid factory workers, to suggest ways to improve products—and then reward them when they come up with good ideas.

But how do you know when you've attained your goal of quality? Other than increased sales and profits, a few key award programs recognize firms that do the job well. For example, in 1987, the U.S. Congress established the Malcolm Baldrige National Quality Award to recognize excellence in U.S. firms. Major goals for the award are "...helping to stimulate American companies to improve quality and productivity for the pride of recognition while obtaining a competitive edge through increased profits" and "...recognizing the achievements of those companies that improve the quality of their goods and services."[12] Table 9.1 lists recent winners of the Baldrige Award.

Around the world, many companies look to the uniform standards of the International Organization for Standardization (ISO) for quality guidelines. This Geneva-based organization developed a set of criteria in 1987 to improve and standardize product quality in Europe. The **ISO 9000** is a broad set of guidelines that establishes voluntary standards for quality management. These guidelines insure that an organization's products conform to the customer's requirements. In 1996, the ISO developed **ISO 14000** standards, which concentrate on "environmental management." This means the organization works to minimize any harmful effects it may have on the environment. Because members of the European Union and other European countries prefer suppliers with ISO 9000 and ISO 14000 certification, U.S. companies must comply with these standards to be competitive there.[13]

One way that companies can improve quality is to use the **Six Sigma** method. The term *Six Sigma* comes from the statistical term *sigma*, which is a standard deviation from the mean. Six Sigma refers to six standard deviations from a normal distribution curve. In practical terms, that translates to no more than 3.4 defects per million—getting it right 99.9997 percent of the time. As you can imagine, achieving that level of quality requires a very rigorous approach (try it on your term papers—even when you use spell-check!), and that's what Six Sigma offers. The method involves a five-step process called "DMAIC" (*define, measure, analyze, improve,* and *control*). The company trains its employees in the method, and as in karate they progress toward "black belt" status when they successfully complete all the levels of training. Employees can use Six Sigma processes to remove defects from services, not just products. In these cases a "defect" means failing to meet customer expectations. For example, hospitals use Six Sigma processes to reduce medical errors, and airlines use the system to improve flight scheduling.

ISO 9000

Criteria developed by the International Organization for Standardization to regulate product quality in Europe.

ISO 14000

Standards of the International Organization for Standardization concerned with "environmental management" aimed at minimizing harmful effects on the environment.

Six Sigma

A process whereby firms work to limit product defects to 3.4 per million or fewer.

Table 9.1	2007 Malcolm Baldrige Award Winners

Award Category	Company
Small business	PRO-TEC Coating, Leipsic, OH
Health care	Mercy Health System, Janesville, WI
Health care	Sharp HealthCare, San Diego, CA
Nonprofit	City of Coral Springs, Coral Springs, FL
Nonprofit	U.S. Army Armament Research, Development, and Engineering Center (ARDEC), Picatinny Arsenal, NJ

To receive the prestigious Malcolm Baldrige National Quality Award, companies must demonstrate excellence in seven areas: strategic planning, leadership, information and analysis, customer and market focus, human resources focus, process management, and business results. Winners come from five general categories: service, manufacturing, education, health care, and small business. To read why these companies won, visit the National Institute of Standards and Technology's Web site at **www.nist.gov/public_affairs/ releases/2007baldrigerecipients.htm**.

Adding a Dose of Quality to the Marketing Mix

The price-versus-quality decision is a major issue when companies figure out how to provide value to consumers. Marketing also has to inform consumers about product quality through its marketing communications.

But keeping on top of what customers want is just the beginning. Firms also have to deliver a product consumers perceive to be of high quality at the right place and at the right price. Instead of being satisfied with doing things the same way year after year, marketers must continually seek ways to improve product, place, price, and promotion. Let's see how quality concerns affect the marketing mix.

- **Product:** One way firms offer quality to their customers is to improve their customer service support. For example, Whirlpool steadily improves the repair services it offers on its appliances. In the past, if your washing machine broke down, you'd call Whirlpool, they'd refer you to a service center, and you'd call the service center and try to schedule a repair time. Today, technology lets Whirlpool's customer service reps view the schedules of all its repair technicians in your area and then schedule a repair time that suits your schedule—all during the first phone call. Whirlpool also offers an on-line service that lets customers schedule service themselves, without even talking to a rep. The easier it is for customers to interact with the company and get results, the more satisfied they will be. And Whirlpool's acquisition of Maytag gave the company the opportunity to expand this quality emphasis to include customers of the already quality-focused Maytag product line.[14]

  Another interesting customer service example is Toshiba, which has begun to outsource the entire process of its laptop service and repair to UPS. When someone's laptop needs to be fixed, UPS picks it up, transports it to Memphis where Toshiba-trained UPS employees fix it, and then UPS ships it directly back to the customer. Thus, the company shaves the repair cycle time to only a few days.[15]

- **Place:** TorPharm, the largest generic pharmaceutical manufacturer in Canada, involves its suppliers in its efforts to improve on-time delivery to customers. First, TorPharm developed purchasing and delivery strategies to ensure that more than 99 percent of the time the right quantities of raw materials arrived from suppliers when expected. Then TorPharm worked with its pharmacy customers to improve its on-time delivery rate of products from as low as 60 to 95 percent or better.[16]

- **Price:** Hewlett-Packard (HP) lowers costs and improves service to customers at the same time. HP developed a "sure supply" technology that it embeds into its printer cartridges. A sensor detects when the ink supply is low, and the networked printer automatically orders a new cartridge. By building an automated cartridges-supply service into the printer, HP also reduces its own costs related to processing a customer's phone order.[17]

- **Promotion:** Today's marketing firms realize that customers want information when they need it, not when it's convenient for the marketer. Gap exemplifies this philosophy. At Gap's Old Navy stores, salespeople wear headsets so they can quickly get information to answer customers' questions. At Walt Disney World Resort, all of the merchandise locations on the property are connected via a sophisticated network that tracks inventory levels. So, even if a guest is at the Magic Kingdom and wants to buy something that is out of stock there, if a store at Downtown Disney has the item a merchandise manager will have it waiting for the guest at the gate when he exits the park.

Dimensions of Product Quality

It's fine to talk about quality, but what exactly is it? Figure 9.4 summarizes the many meanings of quality. In some cases, product quality means durability. For example, athletic shoes shouldn't develop holes after their owner shoots hoops for a few weeks. Reliability also is

Figure 9.4 | Product Quality

Some product objectives focus on quality or the ability of a product to satisfy customer expectations—no matter what those expectations are.

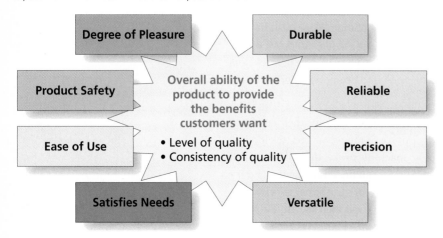

an important aspect of product quality—just ask Maytag and the "lonely repairman" it featured in its commercials for years. For many customers, a product's versatility and its ability to satisfy their needs are central to product quality.

For other products, quality means a high degree of precision. For example, purists compare HD TVs in terms of the number of pixels and their refresh rate. Quality, especially in business-to-business products, also relates to ease of use, maintenance, and repair. Yet another crucial dimension of quality is product safety. Finally, the quality of products such as a painting, a movie, or even a wedding gown relates to the degree of aesthetic pleasure they provide. Of course, evaluations of aesthetic quality differ dramatically among people: To one person, quality TV may mean PBS's *Masterpiece Theater*, while to another it's Adult Swim's *Aqua Teen Hunger Force* or *The Venture Brothers*.

Marketing planners often focus product objectives on one or both of two key aspects of quality: level and consistency. Customers often determine the *level of quality* of a product when they compare it with other brands in the same product category. A handcrafted Rolls-Royce boasts higher quality than an assembly-line Ford Mustang, but this may be irrelevant to a Mustang buyer inclined to compare his sports car to a Mitsubishi Eclipse Spyder and not to an elite luxury car.

Consistency of quality means that customers experience the same level of quality in a product time after time, bringing repeat business and free word-of-mouth advertising, or *buzz* (more on this in Chapter 12). Consistent quality is also one of the major benefits of adopting TQM practices. Consumer perceptions can change overnight when quality is lacking. Ask anybody who's ever bought a new car that turned out to be a lemon.

How E-Commerce Affects Product Quality

The Internet has made product quality even more of a crucial strategic focus. One of the most exciting aspects of the digital world is that consumers interact directly with other people—around the block or around the world. But this form of communication cuts both ways; it lets people praise what they like and slam what they don't to an audience of thousands or perhaps even millions. Numerous Web sites like Planet Feedback (**www.planetfeedback.com**) let consumers "vent" about bad experiences they have with products.

product life cycle
A concept that explains how products go through four distinct stages from birth to death: introduction, growth, maturity, and decline.

2

OBJECTIVE

Explain how firms manage products throughout the product life cycle.
(pp. 276–280)

Marketing Throughout the Product Life Cycle

Many products have very long lives, while others are "here today, gone tomorrow." The **product life cycle (PLC)** is a useful way to explain how the market's response to a product and marketing activities change over the life of a product. In Chapter 8, we talked about how marketers go about introducing new products, but the launch is only the beginning. Product marketing strategies must evolve and change as they continue through the product life cycle.

Alas, some brands don't have long to live. Who remembers the Nash car or Evening in Paris perfume? In contrast, other brands seem almost immortal. For example, Coca-Cola has been the number one cola brand for more than 120 years, General Electric has been the number one light bulb brand for over a century, and Kleenex has been the number one tissue brand for over 80 years.[18] Let's take a look at the stages of the PLC.

The Introduction Stage

Like people, products are born, they "grow up" (well, most people grow up anyway), and eventually they die. We divide the life of a product into four separate stages. The first stage we see in Figure 9.5 is the **introduction stage**. Here customers get the first chance to purchase the good or service. During this early stage, a single company usually produces the product. If it clicks and is profitable, competitors usually follow with their own versions.

During the introduction stage, the goal is to get first-time buyers to try the product. Sales (hopefully) increase at a steady but slow pace. As is also evident in Figure 9.5, the company usually does not make a profit during this stage. Why? Research-and-development (R&D) costs and heavy spending for advertising and promotional efforts cut into revenue.

As Figure 9.6 illustrates, during the introduction stage pricing may be high to recover the R&D costs (demand permitting) or low to attract a large numbers of consumers. For example, the introductory base price of the Lexus GS450h we described at the beginning of this chapter was $54,900, nearly the same as the BMW 550i's base price of $57,400 at the time. Lexus intended the price to appeal to consumers who are willing to pay for the GS450h's unique combination of comfort, great gas mileage, and superb performance. The high price is also necessary so that Lexus can recover its R&D costs for this revolutionary new engineering design, and ultimately develop more hybrid products like the LS 600h L, which hit the market at $104,000.

How long does the introduction stage last? As we saw in Chapter 8's microwave oven example, it can be quite long. A number of factors come into play, including marketplace acceptance and the producer's willingness to support its product during start-up. Sales for hybrid cars started out pretty slowly except for the Prius, but now with gas prices at astronomical levels and sales reaching new heights, hybrids are well past the introduction stage.

It is important to note that many products never make it past the introduction stage. For a new product to succeed, consumers must first know about it. Then they must believe that it is something they want or need. Marketing during this stage often focuses on informing consumers about the product, how to use it, and its promised benefits. However, this isn't nearly as easy as it sounds: Nearly 40 percent of all new products fail![19]

The Growth Stage

In the **growth stage**, sales increase rapidly while profits increase and peak. Marketing's goal here is to encourage brand loyalty by convincing the market that this brand is superior to others. In this stage, marketing strategies may include the introduction of product variations to attract market segments and increase market share. The cell phone is an example of a product

**Tom
Petters**

APPLYING The Product Life Cycle

In what stage of the PLC is the Polaroid camera? How should your answer influence the strategy a marketer should choose to manage this brand? ➥

introduction stage
The first stage of the product life cycle in which slow growth follows the introduction of a new product in the marketplace.

growth stage
The second stage in the product life cycle, during which consumers accept the product and sales rapidly increase.

Figure 9.5 | The Product Life Cycle

The product life cycle helps marketers understand how a product changes over its lifetime and suggests how to modify their strategies accordingly.

$ Sales and Profits	Introduction Stage	Growth Stage	Maturity Stage	Decline Stage
	No profits because the company is recovering R&D costs	Profits increase and peak	Sales peak	Market shrinks: Sales fall
			Profit margins narrow	Profits fall

Sales

Profits

0

Time

Figure 9.6 | Marketing Mix Strategies through the Product Life Cycle

Marketing mix strategies—the Four Ps—change as a product moves through the life cycle.

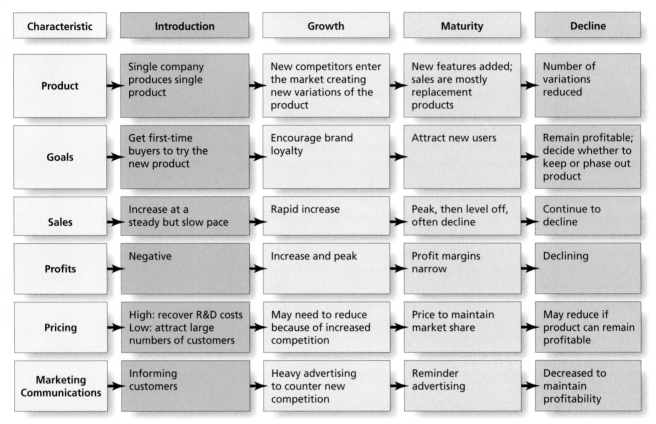

Characteristic	Introduction	Growth	Maturity	Decline
Product	Single company produces single product	New competitors enter the market creating new variations of the product	New features added; sales are mostly replacement products	Number of variations reduced
Goals	Get first-time buyers to try the new product	Encourage brand loyalty	Attract new users	Remain profitable; decide whether to keep or phase out product
Sales	Increase at a steady but slow pace	Rapid increase	Peak, then level off, often decline	Continue to decline
Profits	Negative	Increase and peak	Profit margins narrow	Declining
Pricing	High: recover R&D costs Low: attract large numbers of customers	May need to reduce because of increased competition	Price to maintain market share	May reduce if product can remain profitable
Marketing Communications	Informing customers	Heavy advertising to counter new competition	Reminder advertising	Decreased to maintain profitability

that is still in its growth stage, as worldwide sales continue to increase. A big part of its continued growth is due to relentless product innovation as manufacturers continue to build in more and more communication features.

When competitors appear on the scene, marketers must advertise heavily and also rely on other forms of promotion we'll discuss in Chapter 12. Price competition may develop, which drives profits down. Some firms may seek to capture a particular segment of the market by positioning their product to appeal to a certain group. And, if it initially set the price high, the firm may now reduce it to meet increasing competition.

The Maturity Stage

maturity stage
The third and longest stage in the product life cycle, during which sales peak and profit margins narrow.

The **maturity stage** of the product life cycle is usually the longest. Sales peak and then begin to level off and even decline while profit margins narrow. Competition gets intense when remaining competitors fight for their share of a shrinking pie. Firms may resort to price reductions and reminder advertising ("did you brush your teeth today?") to maintain market share. Because most customers have already accepted the product, they tend to buy to replace a "worn-out" item or to take advantage of product improvements. For example, almost everyone in the United States owns a TV, which means most people who buy a new set replace an older one—especially when television stations nationwide stopped using analog signals and began to broadcast exclusively in a digital format in February 2009. During the maturity stage, firms try to sell their product through as many outlets as possible because availability is crucial in a competitive market. Consumers will not go far to find one particular brand if satisfactory alternatives are close at hand.

To remain competitive and maintain market share during the maturity stage, firms may tinker with the marketing mix. Competitors may add new "bells and whistles," as when producers of potato chips and other snack foods modify their products. When consumers became concerned about carbohydrates and turned to diets such as Atkins and South Beach, Frito-Lay introduced new lines of low-carb chips like the Tostitos Edge low-carb tortilla chips. Unilever likewise rolled out 18 new low-carb products to rejuvenate venerable brands like Ragu spaghetti sauce and Wishbone salad dressing.[20] Now the focus is on trans fat, and Unilever introduced Promise Healthy Heart spread as a substitute for traditional margarine and butter. Promise features no trans fat, is non-hydrogenated, and has high levels of heart friendly omega-3 and omega-6.[21]

Marketers may also try to attract new users of the product when it enters its maturity stage. As you learned in Chapter 2, *market development* means introducing an existing product to a market that doesn't currently use it. Many U.S. firms find new markets in developing countries such as China for products when their domestic sales are stagnant. For example, Emerson Electric, a venerable brand in the United States for over 125 years, developed an aggressive strategy to offset stagnated domestic sales with aggressive investment in growth in China—over 25 percent per year that resulted in sales of over $1 billion there.[22]

The Decline Stage

We characterize the **decline stage** of the product life cycle by a decrease in product category sales. The reason may be obsolescence forced by new technology—where (other than in a museum) do you see a typewriter today? Although a single firm may still be profitable, the market as a whole begins to shrink, profits decline, there are fewer variations of the product, and suppliers pull out. In this stage there are usually many competitors but none has a distinct advantage.

Just as Tom Petters grappled with what to do about Polaroid and its decline stage film product, a firm's major product decision in the decline stage is whether to keep the product at all. An unprofitable product drains resources that it could use to develop newer products. If the firm decides to keep the product, it may decrease advertising and other marketing communications to cut costs, and reduce prices if the product can still remain profitable. If the firm decides to drop the product, it can eliminate it in two ways: 1) phase it out by cutting production in stages and letting existing stocks run out, or 2) simply dump the product immediately. If the established market leader anticipates that there will be some residual demand for the product for a long time, it may make sense to keep the product on the market. The idea is to sell a limited quantity of the product with little or no support from sales, merchandising, advertising, and distribution and just let it "wither on the vine."

In the Internet era, some products that otherwise would have died a natural death in stores continue to sell on-line to a cadre of fans, backed by zero marketing support. On-line purveyors such as candydirect.com sell Beeman's gum direct to consumers. In the "old days" (that is, before the Internet), a brand like Beeman's would have been doomed by aggressive marketing budgets for all the crazy new product introductions in the category by behemoth gum competitors Wrigley and American Chicle. eBay has certainly helped proliferate the life cycle of many products—yes, you can buy Beeman's there too (as well as occasionally Clove and Blackjack gum too), hopefully with current expiration dates for freshness!

Oil of Olay is a great example of a product that, like a cat, has had multiple lives through the product life cycle. Britain's Royal Air Force first developed the pink moisturizer during World War II as a lotion to treat burns. In 1962, another company bought it and started to market it as a "beauty fluid." Procter & Gamble acquired that company in 1985 and reinvigorated it by pumping in a lot of advertising dollars. In the early 1990s, P&G

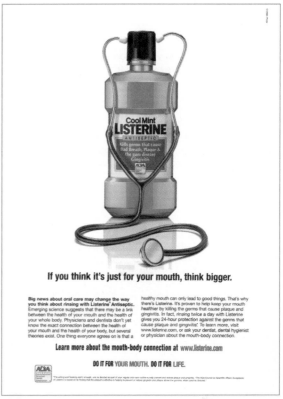

Products in the mature stage need to keep giving consumers new reasons to buy their products.

decline stage
The final stage in the product life cycle, during which sales decrease as customer needs change.

could be used in the negotiation process to broker a great deal for
an ailing business with potential to be reenergized. In order to
accomplish the repositioning of the brand that is necessary, total
control over the brand is needed vs. licensing with the need for
Polaroid approval. Obviously, Polaroid on its own has not been able
to accomplish the task at hand. Therefore, the need is imminent to
take control over the enterprise to move it in new directions. ➤

---

launched line extensions built around the Oil of Olay name. The company also began
revamping the product's image to make it more appealing to women. P&G figured out that
women were grossed-out by the word "oil" because they equated it with grease. Now the
$500 million line of skin-care products and cosmetics is known simply as Olay. The reborn
product targets women who want "personalized skin care," which can include a consult
with a skin expert to determine which blend of Olay products is right for them. The Olay
line includes over a dozen brand extensions such as Total Effects (to diminish Baby
Boomers' fine lines and wrinkles), Complete (an all-day moisturizer with UV protection),
and Ribbons body wash (with your choice of aloe extract, almond oil, or jojoba butter).
Olay's an example of a product with life cycle staying power![23]

3 Create Product Identity:
Branding Decisions

OBJECTIVE

Discuss how branding
strategies create
product identity.
(pp. 280–288)

brand
A name, a term, a symbol, or any other unique
element of a product that identifies one firm's
product(s) and sets it apart from the
competition.

Successful marketers keep close tabs on their products' life cycle status, and they plan accordingly. Equally important, though, is to give
that product an *identity* like Skippy Peanut Butter did with its Skippy
Snack Bars. These scrumptious delights are made of layers of peanut
butter and granola combined with kid-pleasing ingredients such as
marshmallows and fudge. That's where branding comes in. Here, the
brand personality connotes pure, unadulterated fun, and the launch of the new
snack bars featured TV commercials with the animated Nutshells, a band of
musical elephants. How important is branding? Well, of the more than 17,000
new products or line extensions companies introduce each year, 25 percent are
new brands. Marketers spend about $127.5 billion per year to introduce these
new brands—that's $7.5 million per brand, on average.

We said earlier that nearly 40 percent of all new products fail, but for *new
brands* the failure rate is even higher—up to 80 to 90 percent.[24] Branding is an
extremely important (and expensive) element of product strategies. In this section,
we'll examine what a brand is and how certain laws protect brands. Then we'll
discuss the importance of branding and how firms make branding decisions.

What's in a Name (or a Symbol)?

How do you identify your favorite brand? By its name? By the logo (how the
name appears)? By the packaging? By some graphic image or symbol, such as
Nike's swoosh? A **brand** is a name, a term, a symbol, or any other unique element of a product that identifies one firm's product(s) and sets it apart from the
competition. Consumers easily recognize the Coca-Cola logo, the Jolly Green
Giant (a *trade character*), and the triangular red Nabisco logo (a *brand mark*) in
the corner of the box. Branding provides the recognition factor products need
to succeed in regional, national, and international markets.

It's time to fight back.

The Michelin Man is one of the oldest trade characters.

There are several important considerations when an organization selects a brand name, brand mark, or trade character. First, it must have a positive connotation and be memorable. Consider Toro's experience when it introduced a lightweight snow thrower it called the "Snow Pup." Sales were disappointing because "pup" conveyed a small, cuddly animal—not a desirable image for a snow thrower. When Toro renamed the product with the more rugged "Snow Master" and later the "Snow Commander," the move generated a blizzard of sales.[25]

A brand name is probably the most used and most recognized form of branding. Kool-Aid and Jell-O are two of the first words kids learn. Smart marketers use brand names to maintain relationships with consumers "from the cradle to the grave." For example, Jell-O now markets low-carb versions of its gelatin dessert to appeal to carb-counting adults.[26]

A good brand name may position a product because it conveys a certain image or personality (Ford Mustang) or by describing how it works (Drano). Brand names such as Caress and Shield help position these different brands of bath soap by saying different things about the benefits they promise. Irish Spring soap provides an unerring image of freshness (can't you just smell it now?). The Nissan Xterra combines the word *terrain* with the letter *X*, which many young people associate with extreme sports, to give the brand name a cutting-edge, off-road feel. Apple's use of "i-everything" is a brilliant branding strategy, as it conveys individuality and personalization—characteristics that Gen Y buyers prize.

How does a firm select a good brand name? Good brand designers say there are four "easy" tests: *easy to say, easy to spell, easy to read, and easy to remember*—like P&G's Tide, Cheer, Dash, Bold, Gain, Downy, and Ivory Snow. And the name should also "fit" four ways:

1. *fit the target market,*
2. *fit the product's benefits,*
3. *fit the customer's culture,* and
4. *fit legal requirements.*

When it comes to graphics for a brand symbol, name, or logo, the rule is that it must be recognizable and memorable. No matter how small or large, the triangular Nabisco logo in the corner of the box is a familiar sight. And it should have visual impact. That means that from across a store or when you quickly flip the pages in a magazine, the brand will catch your attention. Some successful marketers enhance brand recognition when they create a trade character such as the Pillsbury Dough Boy or the Playboy Bunny.

A **trademark** is the legal term for a brand name, brand mark, or trade character. The symbol for legal registration in the United States is a capital "R" in a circle ®. Marketers register trademarks to make their use by competitors illegal. Because trademark protection applies only in individual countries where the owner registers the brand, unauthorized use of marks on counterfeit products is a huge headache for many companies.

A firm can claim protection for a brand even if it has not legally registered it. In the United States, *common-law protection* exists if the firm has used the name and established it over a period of time (sort of like a common-law marriage). Although a registered trademark prevents others from using it on a similar product, it may not bar its use for a product in a completely different type of business. Consider the range of "Quaker" brands: Quaker Oats (cereals), Quaker Funds (mutual funds), Quaker State (motor oil), Quaker Bonnet (gift food baskets), and Quaker Safety Products Corporation (firemen's clothing). A court applied this principle when Apple Corp., the Beatles' music company, sued Apple Computers in 2006 over its use of the Apple logo. The plaintiff wanted to win an injunction to prevent Apple Computer from using the Apple logo in connection with its iPod and iTunes products; it argued that the application to music-related products came too close to the Beatles' musical products. The

A brand name should be memorable. Nobody is likely to confuse this product with another brand of glue.

Courtesy of The Gorilla Glue Company, Inc.

trademark

The legal term for a brand name, brand mark, or trade character; trademarks legally registered by a government obtain protection for exclusive use in that country.

A good brand name communicates a clear and desirable image.

Courtesy of Colgate-Palmolive Company.

brand equity
The value of a brand to an organization.

brand extensions
A new product sold with the same brand name as a strong existing brand.

judge didn't agree; he ruled that Apple Computer clearly used the logo to refer to the download service, not to the music itself.[27]

Why Brands Matter

A brand is *a lot* more than just the product it represents—the best brands build an emotional connection with their customers. Think about the most popular diapers—they're branded Pampers and Luvs, not some functionally descriptive name like Absorbancy Master. The point is that Pampers and Luvs evoke the joys of parenting, not the utility of the diaper.

Marketers spend huge amounts of money on new-product development, advertising, and promotion to develop strong brands. When they succeed, this investment creates **brand equity**. This term describes a brand's value over and above the value of the generic version of the product. For example, how much extra will you pay for a golf shirt with a Ralph Lauren logo on it than for the same shirt with no logo? The difference reflects the polo player's brand equity in your mind.

We identify different levels of loyalty, or lack thereof, by observing how customers feel about the product. At the lowest level, customers really have no loyalty to a brand and they will change brands for any reason—often they will jump ship if they find something else at a lower price. At the other extreme, some brands command fierce devotion, and loyal users will go without rather than buy a competing brand.

Figure 9.7 shows one way to think about these escalating levels of attachment to a brand. At the lowest level of the "brand equity pyramid," consumers become aware of a brand's existence. Moving up the pyramid, they might look at the brand in terms of what it literally does for them or how it performs relative to competitors. Going up still farther, they may think more deeply about the product and form beliefs and emotional reactions to it. The truly successful brands, however, are those that make the long climb to the top of the pyramid—they "bond" with their customers so that people feel they have a real relationship with the product. Here are some of the types of relationships a person might have with a product:

- **Self-concept attachment:** The product helps establish the user's identity. (For example, do you feel better in Ralph Lauren or Sean John clothing?)

- **Nostalgic attachment:** The product serves as a link with a past self. (Does eating the inside of an Oreo cookie remind you of childhood? How about a vintage T-shirt with a picture of Strawberry Shortcake or Mayor McCheese—both recent fashion hits?)[29]

- **Interdependence:** The product is a part of the user's daily routine. (Could you get through the day without a Starbucks coffee?)

- **Love:** The product elicits emotional bonds of warmth, passion, or other strong emotion. (Hershey's Kiss, anyone?)[30]

As the pyramid in Figure 9.7 shows us, the way to build strong brands is to forge strong bonds with customers—bonds based on *brand meaning*. This concept encompasses the beliefs and associations that a consumer has about the brand. In many ways, the practice of brand management revolves around the management of meanings. Brand managers, advertising agencies, package designers, name consultants, logo developers, and public relations firms are just some of the collaborators in a global industry devoted to the task of *meaning management*. Table 9.2 shows some of the dimensions of brand meaning.

Brand equity means that a brand enjoys customer loyalty because people believe it is superior to the competition. For a firm, brand equity provides a competitive advantage because it gives the brand the power to capture and hold on to a larger share of the

Ethical Decisions in the Real World

Because of the power of branding, marketers constantly are on the lookout for new trends and ways they can connect to those trends through their branding. One of the hottest consumer trends now is "organic" food, as in organically grown agricultural products. A lot of stores and products use the word "organic" in their branding. Unfortunately for consumers there is no precise definition of "organic" so a lot of food products that carry this label may really be stretching it. Recently, the U.S. Department of Agriculture (USDA) has begun to take on this controversial topic as it tries to categorize ingredients as organic or not organic.

Also, unfortunately for consumers, the big food companies are pressuring the USDA to add a whole bunch of ingredients to the organic list; these include 38 nonorganic ingredients they want to use in products that qualify to bear the "USDA Organic" seal. Remarkably, some of these are artificial food colorings that will ensure your organic food has pleasing eye appeal.

Assume you are a retailer like Whole Foods whose business (and reputation) is built around giving consumers true healthy choices. You have to decide whether to feature the "USDA Organic" designation as part of your branding. Under the circumstances, what would you do?

Ripped from the Headlines! See what happened in the Real World at **www.mypearsonmarketinglab.com**

ETHICS CHECK: ↖

Find out what other students taking this course **would do** and **why** on **www.mypearsonmarketinglab.com**

Would you describe products labeled USDA Organic as organic to your customers even if they may contain nonorganic ingredients?

☐YES ☐NO

market and to sell at prices with higher profit margins. For example, among pianos, the Steinway name has such powerful brand equity that its market share among concert pianists is 95 percent.[31]

What makes a brand successful? Here is a list of 10 characteristics of the world's top brands:[32]

1. The brand excels at delivering the benefits customers truly desire.
2. The brand stays relevant.
3. The pricing strategy is based on consumers' perceptions of value.
4. The brand is properly positioned.
5. The brand is consistent.
6. The brand portfolio and hierarchy make sense.
7. The brand makes use of and coordinates a full repertoire of marketing activities to build equity.
8. The brand's managers understand what the brand means to consumers.
9. The brand is given proper support, and that support is sustained over the long run.
10. The company monitors sources of brand equity.

Products with strong brand equity provide enticing opportunities. A firm may leverage a brand's equity with **brand extensions**—new products it sells with the same brand name. For example, premium ice cream maker Häagen-Dazs decided to get into the growing low-fat ice cream market (keep in mind, in this context "low" fat is a relative concept). Its choices were to create a new brand or modify the existing one. The result was Häagen-Dazs Light, which it proclaimed to have "all the taste and texture of original Häagen-Dazs with only half the fat." The brand extension was an immediate success, and the company now offers 14 flavors under the Light banner, many of which are available only in a Light version. More generally, this success highlights the potential value of a strong brand name: Although many people assume that the European-sounding name ensures high quality, in reality the name is made up. Häagen-Dazs started in the Bronx, New York, and today Pillsbury owns it![33]

Well-established brands constantly jockey for position to win consumers' loyalty.

The toothpaste that never sleeps.

Fights germs for 12 hours day & night.

Colgate Total

www.colgatetotal.com   #1 Recommended by Dentists.

Hershey's is a well-established brand that elicits warm emotional reactions from chocolate lovers; the company counts on these feelings to transfer to the new version as well.

Have you ever thought it would be cool to see your own name on a piece of candy? M&M's makes this idea a reality. One way to strengthen the bond with a consumer is to personalize the product—it's hard not to be loyal to "your" brand! In this spirit M&M's, a unit of Mars, customizes chocolate packages for consumers who are willing to pay for the privilege. Each M&M candy can carry a personalized message up to eight characters per line (maximum two lines). Consumers can pick the color of the chocolate (it's available in 22 colors) and even to select multiple colors to mesh with a theme—you can serve your college's colors at your next tailgating party. The company expects that the new strategy will generate $100 million annually in a few years.[28] New printing technologies make it possible to personalize almost anything these days—from rose petals to ice cream boxes. Make yourself a big star—"bond" with something fattening.

Figure 9.7 | The Brand Equity Pyramid

The brand equity pyramid shows one way to think about escalating levels of attachment to a brand.

Source: Kevin Lane Keller, p.7 from *Building Customer-Based Brand Equity: A Blueprint for Creating Strong Brands*, Working Paper Series, Report 01-107 Copyright © 2001 Marketing Science Institute. Reprinted by permission.

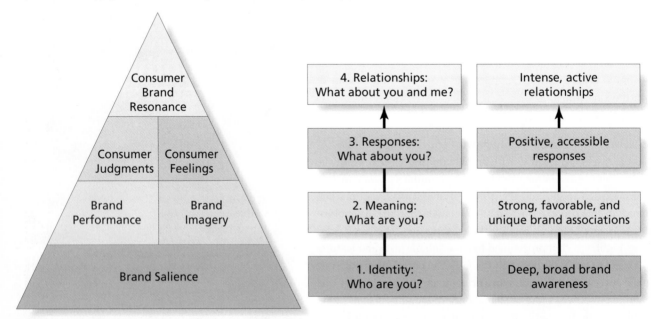

Table 9.2	Dimensions of Brand Meaning

Dimension	Example
Brand identification markers	Coca-Cola's red and white colors, the Nike swoosh logo, Harley-Davidson's characteristic sound
Product attribute and benefit	Starbucks as good coffee; BMW as "The Ultimate Driving Machine"
Gender	NASCAR, Harley-Davidson, Marlboro and masculinity; Laura Ashley and femininity
Social class	Mercedes and the old-guard elite; Jell-O and the lower-middle class
Age	Facebook, MySpace, Skechers, iPod, Adult Swim
Reference group	Dockers and the casual workforce; Williams-Sonoma and the serious cook
Life stage	Dewar's and the coming of age; Parent's Soup and new mothers
Lifestyles and taste subcultures	BMW and the yuppie; Red Bull and the club culture
Place	Coke and America; Ben & Jerry's and rural Vermont
Time and decade	Betty Crocker and the 1950s; VW and the 1960s countercultural revolution
Trends	Pottery Barn and cocooning; Starbucks and small indulgences
Traditions and rituals	Häagen-Dazs ice cream and the pampering of self

Source: Parts of the table are adapted from Fournier, Susan G., Michael R. Solomon, and Basil G. Englis, "Brand Resonance," in ed. Bernd Schmitt, *Handbook on Brand and Experience Management*, Elgar Publishing, 2009.

Because of the existing brand equity, a firm is able to sell its brand extension at a higher price than if it had given it a new brand, and the brand extension will attract new customers immediately. Of course, if the brand extension does not live up to the quality or attractiveness of its namesake brand equity will suffer, as will brand loyalty and sales.

Sometimes a brand's meaning simply becomes so entrenched with a particular consumer group that it can be tough to find ways to branch out and achieve new users through extensions. Take for example Quiksilver, whose original line of wetsuits and swimwear was aimed squarely at teenage boys who identified with the surf and skate cultures. But now, Quiksilver hopes to appeal to women who may have never hit the waves with items from sweaters to jeans. The new line is in Quiksilver's 650+ stores as well as Nordstrom and other high-end retail outlets. The competition will be fierce, though—Urban Outfitters' Anthropologie and Liz Claiborne's Lucky Brand Jeans are formidable in the 20-something female market and are aimed at the same genre of retailer as Quiksilver uses for its new line.[34]

Branding Strategies

Because brands are key to a marketing program's success, a major part of product planning is to develop and execute branding strategies. Marketers have to determine whether to create individual or family brands, national or store brands, or co-brands—not always easy or obvious decisions.

Henry H.
Rodkin
a professor at DePaul University

My Advice for Tom Petters and Polaroid would be to choose

Option

real people, **Other Voices**

I would choose Option 2 because it is axiomatic in the decline phase of a product life cycle to "harvest" or "divest." In the case of options with Polaroid, category technology and even internal hubris produced a brand and a firm with little forward growth. Further, the brand came into the marketplace well before the global economy, myriad new brands, and rapidly advancing technology took hold...all factors to inhibit Polaroid brand equity and value. In this exciting new world of continuous innovation, Petters can certainly afford to "divest" and "invest" in some of the new brands entering with newer technology. ➤

Metrics Moment

Brand equity represents the value of a product with a particular brand name compared to what the value of the product would be without that brand name (think Coca-Cola versus generic supermarket soda). Companies, marketing research firms, and creative agencies create measures of brand equity because this is an important way to assess whether a branding strategy has been successful. For example, Harris Interactive conducts its EquiTrend® study twice a year to measure the brand equity of over 1,000 brands. The company interviews over 25,000 consumers to determine how they feel about competing brands.[36] Each year, *BusinessWeek* applies its brand equity formulas to come up with a list of its top 100 global brands. In 2007, the top in order of brand value were Coca-Cola, Microsoft, IBM, GE, Nokia, Toyota, Intel, McDonald's, Disney, and Mercedes-Benz.[37]

If consumers have strong, positive feelings about a brand and are willing to pay extra to choose it over others, you are in marketing heaven. Each of the following approaches to measuring brand equity has some good points and some bad points:

1. *Customer mind-set metrics* focus on consumer awareness, attitudes, and loyalty toward a brand. However, these metrics are based on consumer surveys and don't usually provide a single objective measure that a marketer can use to assign a financial value to the brand.

2. *Product-market outcomes metrics* focus on the ability of a brand to charge a higher price than the one an unbranded equivalent charges. This usually involves asking consumers how much more they would be willing to pay for a certain brand compared to others. These measures often rely on hypothetical judgments and can be complicated to use.

3. *Financial market metrics* consider the purchase price of a brand if it is sold or acquired. They may also include subjective judgments about the future stock price of the brand.

4. A team of marketing professors proposed a simpler measure that they claim reliably tracks the value of a brand over time. Their *revenue premium* metric compares the revenue a brand generates with the revenue generated by a similar private-label product (that doesn't have any brand identification). In this case, brand equity is just the difference in revenue (net price times volume) between a branded good and a corresponding private label.[38]

Individual Brands versus Family Brands

Part of developing a branding strategy is to decide whether to use a separate, unique brand for each product item—an *individual brand strategy*—or to market multiple items under the same brand name—a **family brand** or *umbrella brand* strategy. Individual brands may do a better job of communicating clearly and concisely what the consumer can expect from the product, while a well-known company like Apple may find that its high brand equity in other categories (like computers) can sometimes "rub off" on a new brand (like the iPod). The decision often depends on characteristics of the product and whether the company's overall product strategy calls for introduction of a single, unique product or for the development of a group of similar products. For example, Microsoft serves as a strong umbrella brand for a host of diverse individually branded products like Office, Internet Explorer, Xbox 360, and Microsoft Live or Live Search, while Procter & Gamble prefers to brand each of its household products separately.

But there's a potential dark side to having too many brands, particularly when they become undifferentiated in the eyes of the consumer due to poor positioning. Recently, venerable General Motors suffered from muddy differentiation among the eight brands in its portfolio—namely, Chevrolet, GMC, Pontiac, Saturn, Cadillac, Buick, Hummer, and Saab. The brands often compete with each other—both for customers and a slice of GM's marketing budget. For example, GM has four mainstream midsize sedans. It backs its top selling Chevy Malibu with an aggressive ad campaign, while the Buick LaCrosse, Pontiac G6, and Saturn Aura struggle to build the awareness and recognition these lines need to compete. To put things into perspective, Toyota has but one midsize sedan—the Camry—and in 2007, it alone outsold GM's four models 473,308 to 386,024![35]

National and Store Brands

Retailers today often are in the driver's seat when it comes to deciding what brands to stock and push. In addition to choosing from producers' brands, called **national or manufacturer brands**, retailers decide whether to offer their own versions. **Private-label brands**, also called *store brands*, are the retail store's or chain's exclusive trade name. Wal-Mart, for example, sells store brand Sam's Cola and Sam's cookies along with national brands such as Coke and Oreos. Store brands are gaining in popularity for many value-conscious shoppers. Retailers continue to develop new ones, and some add services to the mix: Target and others now offer walk-in medical care in select locations, staffed by a nurse practitioner or physician's assistant. And Wal-Mart has set the pharmacy business on end by offering some types of generic prescriptions, such as basic antibiotics, for $4.00.[39]

Retailers may prefer a private-label branding strategy because they generally make more profit on these than on national brands. Even midrange retailers such as JCPenney now offer private-label clothing to lure millions of customers away from more upscale department stores as well as lower-end discounters. Penney's Stafford and St. John's Bay

family brand
A brand that a group of individual products or individual brands share.

national or manufacturer brands
Brands that the product manufacturer owns.

private-label brands
Brands that a certain retailer or distributor owns and sells.

brands for men have become a significant competitive force against national brands like Dockers, Haggar, and Levi's. In addition, it recently added a new American Living line that the company bills as "a new tradition in American style for your family and home."

In addition, if you stock a unique brand that consumers can't find in other stores, it's much harder for shoppers to compare "apples to apples" across stores and simply buy the brand where they find it sold for the lowest price. Loblaws, Canada's largest supermarket chain, sells over 4,000 food items under the "premium quality" President's Choice label, from cookies to beef, olive oil, curtains, and kitchen utensils. Sales of President Choice items run from 30 to 40 percent of total store volumes. Under the private label, Loblaws can introduce new products at high quality but for lower prices than brand names. It can also keep entire categories profitable by its mix of pricing options. Competitors that sell only national brands can cut prices on those brands, but that hurts their overall profitability. Loblaws can bring prices down on national brands but still make money on its private-label products.[40]

Generic Brands

An alternative to either national or store branding is **generic branding**, which is basically no branding at all. Generic branded products are typically packaged in white with black lettering that names only the product itself (for example, "Green Beans"). Generic branding is one strategy to meet customers' demand for the lowest prices on standard products such as dog food or paper towels. Generic brands first became popular during the inflationary period of the 1980s when consumers became especially price conscious because of rising prices. However, today generic brands account for very little of consumer spending.

generic branding
A strategy in which products are not branded and are sold at the lowest price possible.

Licensing

Some firms choose to use a **licensing** strategy to brand their products. This means that one firm sells another firm the right to use a legally protected brand name for a specific purpose and for a specific period of time. Why should an organization sell its name? Licensing can provide instant recognition and consumer interest in a new product, and this strategy can quickly position a product for a certain target market as it trades on the high recognition of the licensed brand among consumers in that segment. For example, distiller Brown-Forman licensed its famous Jack Daniel's bourbon name to T.G.I. Friday's to use on all sorts of menu items from shrimp to steak to chicken. In addition to this "Jack Daniel's Grill," Friday's features menu items inspired by the popular Food Network reality show *Ultimate Recipe Showdown*.[41]

A familiar form of licensing occurs when movie producers license their properties to manufacturers of a seemingly infinite number of products. Each time a blockbuster Harry Potter movie hits the screens, a plethora of Potter products packs the stores. In addition to toys and games, you can buy Harry Potter candy, clothing, all manner of back-to-school items, home items, and even wands and cauldrons.[42]

licensing
An agreement in which one firm sells another firm the right to use a brand name for a specific purpose and for a specific period of time.

cobranding
An agreement between two brands to work together to market a new product.

Cobranding

Frito-Lay sells K.C. Masterpiece–flavored potato chips, and Post sells Oreo O's cereal. Strange marriages? No, these are examples of **cobranding**, as are the Jack Daniel's and Food Network combinations with T.G.I. Friday's that we already mentioned. This branding strategy benefits both partners when combining the two brands provides more recognition power than either

The phenomenal success of the Harry Potter books and movies have made it a hot property. Characters popped up all over in numerous licensed products.

National Pictures/Topham/The Image Works

enjoys alone. For example, Panasonic markets a line of digital cameras that use Leica lenses, which are legendary for their superb image quality. Panasonic is known for its consumer electronics. Combining the best in traditional camera optics with a household name in consumer electronics helps both brands.

A new and fast-growing variation on cobranding is **ingredient branding**, in which branded materials become "component parts" of other branded products.[43] This was the strategy behind the classic "Intel inside" campaign that convinced millions of consumers to ask by name for a highly technical computer part (a processor) that they wouldn't otherwise recognize if they fell over it.[44] Today, consumers can buy Breyer's Ice Cream with Reese's Peanut Butter Cups or M&M's candies, Twix cookies or Snickers bars. Van De Camp's Fish & Dips come with Heinz ketchup dipping cups. The ultimate cobranding deal may be an Oscar Meyer Lunchables Mega Pack, which includes up to five brands in a single package. Its Pizza Stix pack, for example, comes with Tombstone pizza sauce, Kraft cheese, a Capri Sun Splash Cooler, and a 3 Musketeers bar. Brand heaven!

The practice of ingredient branding has two main benefits. First, it attracts customers to the host brand because the ingredient brand is familiar and has a strong brand reputation for quality. Second, the ingredient brand's firm can sell more of its product, not to mention the additional revenues it gets from the licensing arrangement.[45]

ingredient branding
A form of cobranding that uses branded materials as ingredients or component parts in other branded products.

4 Create Product Identity: The Package and Label

OBJECTIVE
Explain how packaging and labeling contribute to product identity.
(pp. 288–291)

How do you know if the soda you are drinking is "regular" or "caffeine-free"? How do you keep your low-fat grated cheese fresh after you have used some of it? Why do you always leave your bottle of Glow by JLO perfume out on your dresser so everyone can see it? The answer to all these questions is effective packaging and labeling. So far, we've talked about how marketers create product identity with branding. In this section, we'll learn that packaging and labeling decisions also help to create product identity. We'll also talk about the strategic functions of packaging and some of the legal issues that relate to package labeling.

Packaging Functions

A **package** is the covering or container for a product, but it's also a way to create a competitive advantage. So, the important functional value of a package is that it protects the product. For example, packaging for computers, TV sets, and stereos protects the units from damage during shipping, and warehousing. Cereal, potato chips, or packs of grated cheese wouldn't be edible for long if packaging didn't provide protection from moisture, dust, odors, and insects. The multilayered, soft box you see in Figure 9.8 prevents the chicken broth inside from spoiling. In addition to protecting the product, effective packaging makes it easy for consumers to handle and store the product. Figure 9.8 shows how packaging serves a number of different functions.

Over and above these utilitarian functions, however, the package communicates brand personality. Effective product packaging uses colors, words, shapes, designs, and pictures to provide brand and name identification for the product. In addition, packaging provides product facts including flavor, fragrance, directions for use, suggestions for alternative uses (for example, recipes), safety warnings, and ingredients. Packaging may also include warranty information and a toll-free telephone number for customer service.

We've already talked about Häagen-Dazs; now let's see how rival Ben & Jerry's Ice Cream redesigned its package in the late 1990s to make its products more user-friendly.[46] Because the top of the carton is the first thing customers see in a coffin-type freezer, the

package
The covering or container for a product that provides product protection, facilitates product use and storage, and supplies important marketing communication.

Figure 9.8 | Functions of Packaging

Great packaging provides a covering for a product, and it also creates a competitive advantage for the brand.

company replaced the photo of Ben and Jerry that used to appear on the top lid with text to identify the flavor. Other changes included a more upscale look of a black-on-gold color scheme and enticing realistic watercolors of the product's ingredients. These made it easier for consumers to find the flavors they wanted.

A final communication element is the **Universal Product Code (UPC)**, which is the set of black bars or lines printed on the side or bottom of most items sold in grocery stores and other mass-merchandising outlets. The UPC is a national system of product identification. It assigns each product a unique 10-digit number. These numbers supply specific information about the type of item (grocery item, meat, produce, drugs, or a discount coupon), the manufacturer (a five-digit code), and the specific product (another five-digit code). At checkout counters, electronic scanners read the UPC bars and automatically transmit data to a computer in the cash register so that retailers can easily track sales and control inventory.

Design Effective Packaging

Should the package have a zip-lock, feature an easy-to-pour spout, be compact for easy storage, be short and fat so it won't fall over, or be tall and skinny so it won't take up much shelf space? Effective package design involves a multitude of decisions.

Planners must consider the packaging of other brands in the same product category. For example, when Procter & Gamble introduced Pringles potato chips, it packaged them in a cylindrical can instead of in bags like Lay's and others. This was largely out of necessity, since P&G doesn't have all the local trucks to deliver to stores that Frito-Lay does, and the cans keep the chips fresher much longer. However, P&G discovered that not all customers will accept a radical change in packaging, and retailers may be reluctant to adjust their shelf space

Universal Product Code (UPC)
The set of black bars or lines printed on the side or bottom of most items sold in grocery stores and other mass-merchandising outlets. The UPC, readable by scanners, creates a national system of product identification.

to accommodate such packages. To partly answer the concern, Pringles now comes in bags of Pringles Minis, in bags of Pringles Select Bold Crunch with several flavors, in Pringles Stix, and in Pringles 100 Calorie Packs apportioned for those who want a snack while they also watch their weight.[47]

In addition to functional benefits, the choice of packaging material can make an aesthetic statement. Enclosing a fine liqueur in a velvet or silk bag may enhance its image. A fine perfume packaged in a beautifully designed glass bottle means consumers buy not only the fragrance but an attractive dressing table accessory as well. Who says people don't judge a book by its cover? NXT, a new brand of shaving gel targeted at younger men, makes a glitzy statement on the shelf. It's sold in an arresting triangular container that lights up from the bottom to illuminate air bubbles suspended in the clear gel. The plastic is tinted blue, and when its base lights up (yes, this package requires batteries!), the whole thing looks like a miniature lava lamp or tiny fishless aquarium. How does NXT afford such a fancy container? It doesn't spend a dime on traditional advertising—the brand counts on its innovative package to sell the gel in the grocery aisle.[48]

Firms that wish to act in a socially responsible manner must also consider the environmental impact of packaging. Shiny gold or silver packaging transmits an image of quality and opulence, but certain metallic inks are not biodegradable. Some firms are developing innovative *green packaging* that is less harmful to the environment than other materials. Of course, there is no guarantee that consumers will accept such packaging. They didn't take to plastic pouch refills for certain spray bottle products even though the pouches may take up less space in landfills than the bottles do. They didn't like pouring the refill into their old spray bottles. Still, customers have accepted smaller packages of concentrated products such as laundry detergent, dishwashing liquid, and fabric softener.

What about the shape: Square? Round? Triangular? Hourglass? How about an old-fashioned apothecary jar that consumers can reuse as an attractive storage container? What color should it be? White to communicate purity? Yellow because it reminds people of lemon freshness? Brown because the flavor is chocolate? Sometimes we can trace these decisions back to personal preferences. The familiar Campbell's Soup label is red and white because a company executive many years ago liked the football uniforms at Cornell University!

Finally, what graphic information should the package show? Should there be a picture of the product on the package? Should cans of green beans always show a picture of green beans? Should there be a picture that demonstrates the results of using the product, such as beautiful hair? Should there be a picture of the product in use, perhaps a box of crackers that shows them with delicious-looking toppings arranged on a silver tray? Should there be a recipe or coupon on the back? Of course, all these decisions rest on a marketer's understanding of consumers, ingenuity, and perhaps a little creative luck.

Labeling Regulations

The Federal Fair Packaging and Labeling Act of 1966 controls package communications and labeling in the United States. This law aims to make labels more

In many cases, the package is part of the product's story.

Cheers!
There's big news for big and little sippers.

Great new designs. Great new colors. They're the new Playtex® Sipster™ Cups. Available in your choice of spouts – one designed for littler sippers. One for bigger ones. And each our break-proof, spill-proof best. Now that's something to cheer about.

Trademarks of Playtex Products, Inc.
©2004

Playtex

FIRST SIPSTER • **SIPSTER** • SPARKLIN' SIPSTER • INSULATOR • BIG SIPSTER helpful to consumers by providing useful information. More recently, the requirements of the Nutrition Labeling and Education Act of 1990 forced food marketers to make sweeping changes in how they label products. Since August 18, 1994, the U.S. Food and Drug Administration (FDA) requires most foods sold in the United States to have labels telling, among other things, how much fat, saturated fat, cholesterol, calories, carbohydrates, protein, and vitamins are in each serving of the product. These regulations force marketers to be more accurate when they describe the contents of their products. Juice makers, for example, must state how much of their product is real juice rather than sugar and water.

As of January 1, 2006, the FDA also requires that all food labels list the amount of trans fats in the food, directly under the line for saturated fat content. The new labeling reflects scientific evidence showing that consumption of trans fat, saturated fat, and dietary cholesterol raises "bad" cholesterol levels, which increase the risk of coronary heart disease. The new information is the first significant change on the Nutrition Facts panel since it was established.[49]

5 Organize for Effective Product Management

OBJECTIVE

Describe how marketers structure organizations for new and existing product management.
(pp. 291–292)

Of course, firms don't create great packaging, brands, or products—people do. Like all elements of the marketing mix, product strategies are only as effective as their managers make them and carry them out. In this section, we'll talk about how firms organize to manage existing products and to develop new products.

Manage Existing Products

In small firms, a single marketing manager usually handles the marketing function. He is responsible for new-product planning, advertising, working with the company's few sales representatives, marketing research, and just about everything else. But in larger firms, there are a number of managers who are responsible for different brands, product categories, or markets. Depending on the organization, product management may include brand managers, product category managers, and market managers. Let's take a look at how each operates.

Brand Managers

Sometimes, a firm sells several or even many different brands within a single product category. Take the laundry soap aisle in the supermarket for example. Before you read this chapter and reviewed Figure 9.3, could you have ever guessed that Procter & Gamble manufactures and markets all these brands: Bounce, Cheer, Downy, Dreft, Era, Febreze, Gain, Ivory, and Tide? In such cases, each brand may have its own **brand manager** who coordinates all marketing activities for a brand; these duties include positioning, identifying target markets, research, distribution, sales promotion, packaging, and evaluating the success of these decisions.

While this assignment is still common, some big firms are changing the way they allocate responsibilities. For example, today P&G's brand managers function more like internal consultants to cross-functional teams located in the field that have responsibility for managing the complete business of key retail clients across all product lines. Brand managers still are responsible for positioning of brands and developing brand equity, but they also work heavily with folks from sales, finance, logistics, and others to serve the needs of the major retailers that comprise the majority of P&G's business.

By its very nature, the brand management system is not without potential problems. Acting independently and sometimes competitively against each other, brand managers may fight for increases in short-term sales for their own brand. They may push too hard

brand manager
An individual who is responsible for developing and implementing the marketing plan for a single brand.

with coupons, cents-off packages, or other price incentives to a point at which customers will refuse to buy the product when it's not "on deal." Such behavior can hurt long-term profitability and damage brand equity.

Product Category Managers

Some larger firms have such diverse product offerings that they need more extensive coordination. Take IBM, for example. Originally known as a computer manufacturer, IBM now generates much of its revenue from a wide range of consulting and related client services across the spectrum of IT applications (and the company doesn't even sell personal computers anymore!). In cases such as IBM, organizing for product management may include **product category managers**, who coordinate the mix of product lines within the more general product category and who consider the addition of new-product lines based on client needs.

Market Managers

Some firms have developed a **market manager** structure in which different managers focus on specific customer groups rather than on the products the company makes. This type of organization can be useful when firms offer a variety of products that serve the needs of a wide range of customers. For example, Raytheon, a company that specializes in consumer electronics products, special-mission aircraft, and business aviation, sells some products directly to consumer markets, others to manufacturers, and still others to the government. Its serves its customers best when it focuses separately on each of these very different markets.

Organize for New-Product Development

Because launching new products is so important, the management of this process is a serious matter. In some instances, one person handles new-product development, but within larger organizations new-product development almost always requires many people. Often especially creative people with entrepreneurial skills get this assignment.

The challenge in large companies is to enlist specialists in different areas to work together in **venture teams**. These teams focus exclusively on the new-product development effort. Sometimes the venture team is located away from traditional company offices in a remote location called a "skunk works." This colorful term originated with the Skonk Works, an illicit distillery in the comic strip *Li'l Abner*. Because illicit distilleries were bootleg operations, typically located in an isolated area with minimal formal oversight, organizations have adopted the colorful description "skunk works" to refer to a small and often isolated department or facility that functions with minimal supervision (not because of its odor).[50]

Now that you've learned about product management and branding, read "Real People, Real Choices: How It Worked Out" to see which strategy Tom selected for Polaroid.

product category managers
Individuals who are responsible for developing and implementing the marketing plan for all the brands and products within a product category.

market manager
An individual who is responsible for developing and implementing the marketing plans for products sold to a particular customer group.

venture teams
Groups of people within an organization who work together to focus exclusively on the development of a new product.

Tom
Petters
APPLYING Product Mix Strategies

Tom and his team knew the Polaroid name had value even though its hallmark product (the Land camera) had run its course. The Petters Group retained the Polaroid brand but tweaked the company's product mix to focus on the realities of today's marketplace.

real people, **Real Choices**

Tom
Petters

Tom chose:

Option

How it Worked Out at Petters Group Worldwide

Tom chose Option 3, and after extensive negotiations Petters Group purchased Polaroid for $426 million. At the time of the purchase there were three key product areas for Polaroid: instant film, commercial, and consumer electronics. The instant film division had entered into its wind-down stage because of the cost of the chemicals to produce the film and the decreasing market demand—although in its last few years this division was very profitable because it dramatically streamlined some of its production processes.

Still, in 2008 Polaroid stopped production of its instant film products. The limited access to the chemicals needed to make the film and the decreasing demand for the product indicated to Tom that this product line simply didn't have a future. The commercial division focused on security and other licensed uses of technology. At the time of the purchase portable DVD players and LCD televisions were Polaroid's main consumer electronics lines. The new owners added digital cameras and digital frame lines to the assortment and it also expanded into new technologies including adding Zink™ technology (which doesn't use any ink) to its hand-held instant printer. This will most likely be one of the most disruptive technologies of our time; as the industry introduces new, larger printers, ink will become a commodity that won't be needed, and, in fact, the billion dollar ink industry could be in its decline stage now. At the 2008 Consumer Electronics Show in Las Vegas, Polaroid received the Innovator Award for this product, returning the company to the rich heritage Dr. Edwin Land established when he founded Polaroid. By moving into a production-on-demand model Petters Group minimized its inventory costs and increased efficiency for product production. These changes have transformed Polaroid by providing a lower cost infrastructure while bringing back its entrepreneurial spirit to explore new innovative product opportunities.

The Petters Group is breathing new life into the Polaroid brand.

Refer back to **page 267** for Toms story

Brand **YOU**!

What makes you special? What makes your brand unique? For example, do you describe yourself as "good with people" or do you make the description into a compelling advantage by saying you are a "collaborative problem solver"? Turn your features into benefits that a company wants by creating your personal brand value proposition. Chapter 9 in the *Brand You* supplement takes you through this important process, which creates the framework for your resumé.

Objective Summary ➡ Key Terms ➡ Apply

1. Objective Summary (pp. 268–276)

Explain the different product objectives and strategies a firm may choose.

Objectives for individual products may be related to introducing a new product, expanding the market of a regional product, or rejuvenating a mature product. For multiple products, firms may decide on a full- or a limited-line strategy. Often companies decide to extend their product line with an upward, downward, two-way stretch or with a filling-out strategy, or they may decide to contract a product line. Firms that have multiple product lines may choose a wide product mix with many different lines or a narrow one with few. Product quality objectives refer to the durability, reliability, degree of precision, ease of use and repair, or degree of aesthetic pleasure.

Key Terms

product line, p. 271 (Figure 9.2, p. 270 & Figure 9.3, p. 271)

cannibalization, p. 272

product mix, p. 273 (➡ Applying, p. 277) (Figure 9.2, p. 270 & Figure 9.3, p. 271)

Kansei engineering, p. 273

total quality management (TQM), p. 273 (Table 9.1, p. 274)

ISO 9000, p. 274

ISO 14000, p. 274

Six Sigma, p. 274

2. Objective Summary (pp. 276–280)

Explain how firms manage products throughout the product life cycle.

The product life cycle explains how products go through four stages from birth to death. During the introduction stage, marketers seek to get buyers to try the product and may use high prices to recover research and development costs. During the growth stage, characterized by rapidly increasing sales, marketers may introduce new-product variations. In the maturity stage, sales peak and level off. Marketers respond by adding desirable new-product features or market-development strategies. During the decline stage, firms must decide whether to phase a product out slowly, to drop it immediately, or, if there is residual demand, to keep the product.

Key Terms

product life cycle (PLC), p. 276 (➡ Applying, p. 277) (Figure 9.5, p. 277 & Figure 9.6, p. 278)

introduction stage, p. 277 (Figure 9.5, p. 277 & Figure 9.6, p. 278)

growth stage, p. 277 (Figure 9.5, p. 277 & Figure 9.6, p. 278)

maturity stage, p. 278 (Figure 9.5, p. 277 & Figure 9.6, p. 278)

decline stage, p. 279 (Figure 9.5, p. 277 & Figure 9.6, p. 278)

3. Objective Summary (pp. 280–288)

Discuss how branding strategies create product identity.

A brand is a name, term, symbol, or other unique element of a product used to identify a firm's product. A brand should be selected that has a positive connotation and is recognizable and memorable. Brand names need to be easy to say, spell, read, and remember, and should fit the target market, the product's benefits, the customer's culture, and legal requirements. To protect a brand legally, marketers obtain trademark protection. Brands are important because they help maintain customer loyalty and because brand equity or value means a firm is able to attract new customers. Firms may develop individual brand strategies or market multiple items with a family or umbrella brand strategy. National or manufacturer brands are owned and sold by producers, whereas private-label or store brands carry the retail or chain store's trade name. Licensing means a firm sells another firm the right to use its brand name. In cobranding strategies, two brands form a partnership in marketing a new product.

Key Terms

brand, p. 280

trademark, p. 281

brand equity, p. 282 (Metrics Moment, p. 286)

brand extensions, p. 283

family brand, p. 286

national or manufacturer brands, p. 286

private-label brands, p. 286

generic branding, p. 287

licensing, p. 287

cobranding, p. 287

ingredient branding, p. 288

4. Objective Summary (pp. 288–291)

Explain how packaging and labeling contribute to product identity.

Packaging is the covering or container for a product and serves to protect a product and to allow for easy use and storage of the product. The colors, words, shapes, designs, pictures, and materials used in package design communicate a product's identity, benefits, and other important product information. Package designers must consider cost, product protection, and communication in creating a package that is functional, aesthetically pleasing, and not harmful to the environment. Product labeling in the United States is controlled by a number of federal laws aimed at making package labels more helpful to consumers.

Key Terms

package, p. 288 (Figure 9.8, p. 289)

Universal Product Code (UPC), p. 289

5. Objective Summary (pp. 291–292)

Describe how marketers structure organizations for new and existing product management.

To successfully manage existing products, the marketing organization may include brand managers, product category managers, and market managers. Large firms, however, often give new-product responsibilities to new-product managers or to venture teams, groups of specialists from different areas who work together for a single new product.

Key Terms

brand manager, p. 291

product category managers, p. 292

market manager, p. 292

venture teams, p. 292

Chapter **Questions** and **Activities**

Concepts: Test Your Knowledge

1. What are some reasons a firm might determine it should expand a product line? What are some reasons for contracting a product line? Why do many firms have a product mix strategy?
2. Why is quality such an important product strategy objective? What are the dimensions of product quality? How has e-commerce affected the need for quality product objectives?
3. Explain the product life cycle concept. What are the stages of the product life cycle?
4. How are products managed during the different stages of the product life cycle?
5. What is a brand? What are the characteristics of a good brand name? How do firms protect their brands?
6. What is a national brand? A store brand? Individual and family brands?
7. What does it mean to license a brand? What is cobranding?
8. What are the functions of packaging? What are some important elements of effective package design?
9. What should marketers know about package labeling?
10. Describe some of the ways firms organize the marketing function to manage existing products. What are the ways firms organize for the development of new products?

Choices and Ethical Issues: You Decide

1. Brand equity means that a brand enjoys customer loyalty, perceived quality, and brand name awareness. To what brands are you personally loyal? What is it about the product that creates brand loyalty and, thus, brand equity?
2. Quality is an important product objective, but quality can mean different things for different products, such as durability, precision, aesthetic appeal, and so on. What does quality mean for the following products?
   a. Automobile
   b. Pizza
   c. Running shoes
   d. Hair dryer
   e. Deodorant
   f. College education

3. Many times firms take advantage of their popular, well-known brands by developing brand extensions because they know that the brand equity of the original or parent brand will be transferred to the new product. If a new product is of poor quality, it can damage the reputation of the parent brand, while a new product that is of superior quality can enhance the parent brand's reputation. What are some examples of brand extensions that have damaged and that have enhanced the parent brand equity?
4. Sometimes marketers seem to stick with the same packaging ideas year after year regardless of whether they are the best possible design. Following is a list of products. For each one, discuss what, if any, problems you have with the package of the brand you use. Then think of ways the package could be improved. Why do you think marketers don't change the old packaging? What would be the results if they adopted your package ideas?
   a. Dry cereal
   b. Laundry detergent
   c. Frozen orange juice
   d. Gallon of milk
   e. Potato chips
   f. Loaf of bread
5. You learned in this chapter that it's hard to *legally* protect brand names across product categories—Quaker and Apple, for example, and also Delta—which is an airline and a faucet. But what about the *ethics* of borrowing a name and applying it to some unrelated products? Think of some new business you might like to start up. Now consider some possible names for the business that are already in use as brands in other unrelated categories. Do you think it would be ethical to borrow one of those names? Why or why not?

Practice: Apply What You've Learned

1. The Internet allows consumers to interact directly through blogs and other means with other people so they can praise products they like and slam those they don't. With several of your classmates, conduct a brief survey of students and of older consumers. Find out if consumers

complain to each other about poor product quality. Have they ever used a Web site to express their displeasure over product quality? Make a report to your class.

2. You may think of your college or university as an organization that offers a line of different educational products. Assume that you have been hired as a marketing consultant by your university to examine and make recommendations for extending its product line. Develop alternatives that the university might consider:
   a. Upward line stretch
   b. Downward line stretch
   c. Two-way stretch
   d. Filling-out strategy
   Describe how each might be accomplished. Evaluate each alternative.

3. Assume that you are the vice president of marketing for a firm that markets a large number of specialty food items (gourmet sauces, marinades, relishes, and so on). Your firm is interested in improving its marketing management structure. You are considering several alternatives: using a brand manager structure, having product category managers, or focusing on market managers. Outline the advantages and disadvantages of each type of organization. What is your recommendation?

4. Assume that you are working in the marketing department of a major manufacturer of athletic shoes. Your firm is introducing a new product, a line of disposable sports clothing. That's right—wear it once and toss it! You wonder if it would be better to market the line of clothing with a new brand name or use the family brand name that has already gained popularity with your existing products. Make a list of the advantages and disadvantages of each strategy. Develop your recommendation.

5. Assume that you have been recently hired by Kellogg, the cereal manufacturer. You have been asked to work on a plan for redesigning the packaging for Kellogg's cereals.

In a role-playing situation, present the following report to your marketing superior:
   a. Discussion of the problems or complaints customers have with current packaging
   b. Several different package alternatives
   c. Your recommendations for changing packaging or for keeping the packaging the same

Miniproject: Learn by Doing

In any supermarket in any town, you will surely find examples of all the different types of brands discussed in this chapter: individual brands, family brands, national brands, store brands, and cobranded and licensed products. This miniproject is designed to give you a better understanding of branding as it exists in the marketplace.

1. Go to a typical supermarket in your community.
2. Select two product categories of interest to you: ice cream, cereal, laundry detergent, soup, paper products, and so on.
3. Make a list of the brands available in each product category. Identify what type of brand each is. Count the number of shelf facings (the number of product items at the front of each shelf) for each brand.
4. Arrange to talk with the store manager at a time that is convenient with him. Ask the manager to discuss the following:
   a. How the store decides which brands to carry
   b. Whether the store is more likely to carry a new brand that is an individual brand versus a family brand
   c. What causes a store to drop a brand
   d. The profitability of store brands versus national brands
   e. Other aspects of branding that the store manager sees as important from a retail perspective
5. Present a report to your class on what you learned about the brands in your two product categories.

Real People, **real surfers**: explore the web

As we discussed in this chapter and in Chapter 8, companies protect their products by obtaining patents and legal protection for their brands with trademarks. The U.S. Patent and Trademark Office issues both of these forms of protection. Visit the Patent Office Web site at **www.uspto.gov**. Use the Internet site to answer the following questions.

1. What is a patent? What can be patented?
2. Who may apply for a patent? Can foreign individuals or companies obtain a U.S. patent? Explain.
3. What happens if someone infringes on a patent?
4. What does the term *patent pending* mean?

5. What is a trademark? What is a service mark?
6. Who may file a trademark application? Do firms have to register a trademark? Explain.
7. What do the symbols TM, SM, and ® mean?
8. What are the benefits of federal trademark registration?
9. What are common-law rights regarding trademarks?
10. How long does a trademark registration last? How long does a patent last?
11. How would you evaluate the Patent and Trademark Office Web site? Was it easy to navigate? Was it useful? What recommendations do you have for improving the Web site?

Marketing Plan Exercise

Dr. Pepper is an interesting brand with a long history (the history is worth reading—go to **www.drpepper.com**, then click on "About Us" and then "Our Story"). Suffice it to say, it is the oldest soft-drink brand in the United States. Assume for a

moment that Cadbury Schweppes, the London-based firm that owns Dr. Pepper, is doing some marketing planning involving this brand.

1. What are some product line strategies you might suggest that Dr. Pepper consider?
2. How important is TQM and product quality in general to a brand like Dr. Pepper? How do these issues play into its marketing plan?
3. Take a look at the different Dr. Pepper products portrayed on its Web site. Where does each fall on the product life cycle? What leads you to conclude this?

4. What realistic opportunities do you believe exist for brand extensions for Dr. Pepper? Explain how the company might go about introducing each to the market.
5. Does Dr. Pepper have high brand equity? What evidence do you have for your answer? What can Dr. Pepper do to enhance its brand equity, given the 800-pound gorillas it competes against (Coke and Pepsi)?

Marketing in Action Case

Real **Choices** at **Sony**

Founded in 1946, Sony Corporation is a global giant in the manufacture of electronics, games, music, and movies with annual sales of over $70 billion. The Sony name is synonymous with innovative products including the popular brands Walkman, Trinitron television, and PlayStation. The Sony brand name is repeatedly ranked number one among world brands. For example, the Bravia line of liquid-crystal-display TV sets the company introduced in 2005 remains the market leader. Sony's brand equity is the result of the quality, trust, and reliability its brands communicate to customers.

Yet, managing Sony's vast array of products is not easy. After faltering sales during the early years of the decade, in 2006 Sony set upon a revitalization program. Starring in that revitalization was Sony's PlayStation 3 (PS3). The PS3 is Sony's latest upgrade to this highly successful product. Sony's objectives for the PS3 were to use the new product to help establish global industry standards for high-definition video projection and consumer data storage needs and to serve as a platform for multiple Sony products to seamlessly share music, video, and data. Lofty goals for just one product to achieve, right?

Unfortunately, the PS3 has not met all of Sony's expectations. Due to quality control issues, the PS3 launch was delayed nearly a year. This hiccup bought archrival Microsoft's Xbox 360 additional time as the most advanced game system on the market—Microsoft sold nearly 10 million Xbox 360s by the time the PS3 hit store shelves. And more than a year after introduction, sales of the higher priced PS3 at $500 lagged behind market leader Nintendo's Wii with a price tag of only $250. But price wasn't the only issue. Owners complained that the PS3 was clunky to use and didn't provide many basic functions that users have come to expect, especially on-line, and that it was far more difficult to use than the market leader Wii.

In addition to "fixing" what consumers found wrong with the PS3, Sony faces other challenges with its gaming product. The future of the gaming industry is in on-line communities. Today games are migrating to social-networking sites where players challenge new friends to games and taunt each other

with their high scores. To meet this opportunity, Sony already has the PlayStation Network that allows its more than seven million users to download games and play a handful of games with opponents on-line.

But, to compete successfully with Nintendo's Wii and Microsoft's Xbox, Sony plans to release a 3D virtual world similar to *Second Life* for the PlayStation 3. The *Home* service will allow users to create and dress avatar characters, decorate homes, and interact with other users in a virtual world. *Home* will include casual games embedded in-world, voice chat, and the ability to invite any user to play a PlayStation game against you. Users will also be able to share music and videos from their libraries with other "residents" of the world. In the long term, Sony hopes to turn *Home* into a service that will let users watch movies through virtual movie theatres or play games with friends at a virtual arcade.

Still there will be obstacles for Sony. Will consumers want and be willing to pay for the services of *Home* in large enough numbers? And what about the competition? In such an innovative industry, Sony must stay ahead of the pack or lose out. More importantly, how can Sony adapt the *Home* site to meet its corporate goal of seamlessly sharing the products of its various divisions—music, video, and data? And finally, what should the company do if its virtual world is not as successful as it hopes?

You Make the Call

1. What is the decision facing Sony?
2. What factors are important in understanding this decision situation?
3. What are the alternatives?
4. What decision(s) do you recommend?
5. What are some ways to implement your recommendation?

Based on: Se Young Lee and Jay Alabaster, "Sony's PS3 Gets Boost From Its Blu-ray Drive," the *Wall Street Journal*, March 12, 2008, Page D7; Seth Schiesel, "A Weekend Full of Quality Time With PlayStation 3," the *New York Times*, November 20, 2006, Accessed August 16 at **http://www.nytimes.com/2006/11/20/arts/20game.html**; Yukari Iwatani Kane, "Nintendo Is Ahead of the Game, But Sustaining May Be Hard," the *Wall Street Journal*, April 15, 2008; Page C3; Yukari Iwatani Kane, "Sony Again Delays PS3 Virtual Community," the *Wall Street Journal*, April 23, 2008, Page B12.

Chapter 10

Part 1   Make Marketing Value Decisions (Chapters 1, 2, 3)
Part 2   Understand Consumers' Value Needs (Chapters 4, 5, 6, 7)
Part 3   Create the Value Proposition (Chapters 8, 9, 10, 11)
Part 4   Communicate the Value Proposition (Chapters 12, 13, 14)
Part 5   Deliver the Value Proposition (Chapters 15, 16)

Services and Other Intangibles: Marketing the Product

That Isn't There

Lara L. **Price** Profile ▼

A **Decision Maker** at the Philadelphia 76ers

Lara Price is Senior Vice President of Business Operations for the Philadelphia 76ers professional basketball team. When Lara was elevated to Vice President of Marketing in August of 1998, she became one of only 18 female vice presidents in the NBA (National Basketball Association). After being named the team's Senior Vice President in August 2001, Price was promoted to her current position in June of 2003 and continues to oversee the day-to-day activities of the 76ers business operation. She is responsible for the team's sales and marketing along with the communications department, which includes public relations, community relations and new media, as well as game entertainment. She also oversees the Sixers television and radio broadcasts.

The recipient of several awards for excellence in advertising and public relations, Price joined the 76ers in 1996 as Director of Marketing after serving as Manager of Team Services for the NBA. She also served as Director of Team Services for the Continental Basketball Association. A native of Boulder, Colorado, Price is a graduate of Colorado State University, where she was also a member of the women's basketball team.

real people, **Real Choices**

Decision Time **at the Philadelphia 76ers**

To better serve its fans (customers), the 76ers needed to compile more detailed information about its customer base. The team's management had access to several data sources; these included some surveys, notes from customer service representatives that recorded highlights of conversations with fans, and a ticketing system (which showed past purchases)—but this system only recorded a ticket buyer's name, address, length of being a season ticket holder, and any miscellaneous notes that customer service representatives added to the account. Lara knew that she needed a better system to compile buying habit information to predict what Sixers fans wanted, as opposed to the poorly organized "spray and pray" strategy the team was currently using.

Things to Remember:

The Philadelphia 76ers didn't have a rigorous system in place to measure their fans' experiences. The team needed to do a better job of tracking the specific aspects of its service that either attracted or turned off potential ticket buyers.

Sports have been a little bit slower than other industries to jump on board with CRM techniques (customer relationship management, see Chapter 7). Many professional teams don't have the resources or type of internal culture that encourage a lot of rigorous analysis of what fans want and do, but Lara recognized the value of systematically tracking this information to fine-tune her marketing strategies. Still, she acknowledged that you can't run before you can walk: The company (not just the 76ers but the team's parent company Comcast Spectacor, which owns the Flyers, 76ers, Phantoms, the Wachovia Center/Spectrum, and Comcast SportsNet) needed to find a workable CRM solution. This solution had to grow with Comcast's business needs; it wouldn't work to put an overly sophisticated system in place that was too complicated to use and would be rejected before it had a chance to show why it was superior to the way the team tracked customers' buying habits now.

Lara considered her Options 1·2·3

1 Option **Phase in a CRM database approach.** This would allow Lara to obtain a full view of her customers and segment her base according to relevant drivers, such as purchasing behaviors, website viewing habits (even which specific pages customers were going to on the site), which e-mails people are opening, who responds to direct mail/letters, text messages, etc. This system is more efficient in the long run because it tracks behaviors (purchasing) and requires minimal human input. However, to adopt such a system would require buy-in from the company at all levels (including senior management) and it wasn't clear that her colleagues would be receptive to this more analytical approach to monitoring fans' behavior as opposed to a more traditional "hands-on" perspective. And, depending upon the CRM system the company adopted, this could be a pricey option, ranging from six figures to more than $2 million.

2 Option **Send out several surveys to season ticket holders each year.** These would request feedback about many topics including game operations, payment options, broadcast preferences, and the general direction of the team. Although this is a proven (and relatively inexpensive) method to get feedback from customers, mail surveys might not capture rapid changes in preferences. In addition, it's risky to base business decisions on customers' opinions rather than taking into account their actual behaviors.

3 Option **Analyze the lifetime value of customers by projecting how their spending habits over time will provide revenue to the organization.** This technique would allow Lara to identify her most profitable customers to be sure she was allocating her marketing dollars toward satisfying their needs. The Sixers' full season ticket holders are the lifeblood of the team's business, but other segments such as partial plan holders, individual game purchasers, and broadcast viewers are very important as well. This approach would let Lara's staff identify which types of customers provide the largest revenue to the company over time and tailor its promotions accordingly. A lifetime value analysis is useful because it's based on actual behavior rather than on what fans say they will do in the future. On the other hand, these behaviors don't tell the whole story: It's still important to know about customers' demographics and psychographics (see Chapter 5) to enable the team to market one-to-one. For example, a lifetime value analysis doesn't indicate if a customer wants her Sixers information delivered via the Web, phone, or mail.

Now, put yourself in Lara's shoes: Which option would you choose, and why?

You Choose

Which **Option** would you choose, and **why**?
1. ☐YES ☐NO **2.** ☐YES ☐NO **3.** ☐YES ☐NO

See what **option** Lara chose and its success on **page 323** ➥

Check out chapter 10 **Study Map** on page 324

1

OBJECTIVE
Describe the characteristics of services and the ways marketers classify services.
(pp. 300–313)

Marketing What Isn't There

Instead of something tangible like toothpaste or a new car, the product that the Philadelphia 76ers sell is an experience (hopefully a winning one). Lara Price understands the challenges of marketing what people can't touch. She realizes that a fan's decision to go to a basketball game—instead of just watching it at home—is based on a number of different considerations. And if the experience isn't a good one, future sales just won't happen. That's why it's important to successfully meet challenges the first time.

These same challenges apply to other types of consumer experiences. For example, what do an Akon concert, a college education, and a visit to Disney World have in common? Like a Sixers game, each is a product that combines experiences with physical goods to create an event that the buyer consumes. You can't have a concert without musical instruments, a college education without textbooks (Thursday night parties don't count), or a Disney experience without the mouse ears. But these tangibles are secondary to the primary product, which is some act that, in these cases, produces enjoyment, knowledge, or excitement.

In this chapter we'll consider some of the challenges and opportunities that face marketers like Lara Price whose primary offerings are **intangibles**: services and other experience-based products that we can't touch. The marketer whose job is to build and sell a better football, automobile, or smartphone—all tangibles—deals with different issues than the one who wants to sell tickets to a basketball game, limousine service to the airport, or allegiance to a hot new rock star. In the first part of this chapter, we'll discuss services, a type of intangible that also happens to be the fastest-growing sector in our economy. As we'll see, all services are intangible, but not all intangibles are services. Then we'll look at other types of intangibles as well.

Does Marketing Work for Intangibles?

Does marketing work only for companies that sell laundry detergent and automobiles—or does it apply to many types of "products," including politicians, the arts, and the places we live and visit? We might look to the Boston Symphony Orchestra (BSO) for an answer. In the 1990s, the BSO saw a steady decline in ticket sales. Beginning in 1998, the orchestra began an integrated marketing program designed to attract younger audiences.[1] Marketing research found that whereas older audiences were avid readers of magazines and books, younger audiences preferred the Internet and electronic media (surprise!). BSO's new marketing campaign included broadcast commercials, taxi-top ads (to promote a specific concert date or performance), customized Internet infomercials, and e-mail. The result? The BSO increased ticket sales nearly 25 percent—and other major orchestras took notice. Similarly, the Colorado Symphony has done a great job of targeting and attracting baby boomers by partnering with top musical acts of their youth such as the Moody Blues, Three Dog Night, and Randy Newman to add full orchestra to the rockers' performances. Some of the summer shows play in the gorgeous Red Rocks out-door venue. The organization has also started a series called "CSO Rocks" with evenings devoted to play-ing the music of the Eagles, the Beatles' *Abbey Road* album, and "California Dreamin'" tunes.[2] Yes, mar-keting does work for intangibles.

Even an intangible such as electric power (not a product we usually associate with "electric" marketing opportunities) now is commonly branded and mar-keted directly to consumers. In an increasing number of states, customers can pick an electricity supplier from several competitors due to deregulation of the industry. UtiliCorp United introduced EnergyOne, the first national energy brand back in 1995, and by now most other utility companies have climbed on the bandwagon. Cinergy Corp. of Cincinnati paid $6 mil-lion to gain brand exposure when it renamed the city's Riverfront Stadium to Cinergy Field.[3] And the Orlando Utility Commission (OUC), whose tagline is "The Reliable One," proved after Hurricane Charlie deci-mated its power system in August 2004 that reliability is much more than just a catch phrase. OUC got strong kudos after the storm for its broad-based community initiatives to heal Charlie's scars, and the goodwill among customers its actions generated continues today.[4]

Sound marketing concepts don't apply only to companies looking to make a buck or two. Indeed, not-for-profit organizations including charities, social wel-fare organizations, zoos, museums, and religious congregations increasingly think about branding and image building. The not-for-profit sector is no minor piece of the U.S. economy—it consists of over a million organizations with over 10 million employees and millions more volunteers—so competition for both customers and donors is fierce. These organizations have to come up with new marketing strategies all the time.[5] Even the venerable Salvation Army, which received high praise in the media for its quick and steady-handed approach to aiding Hurricane Katrina victims, operates a state-of-the-art Web site complete with an on-line "media room."[6]

And what about the government? Should it engage in marketing? Lydia Gardner, the Clerk of the Court of Orange County, Florida (Orlando area), thinks so. She became famous for spearheading an effort that revamped the way the courthouse and county services looked at and treated their customers. (Wow—imagine the government regarding you as its "customer"!) She encouraged county employees to look at residents who needed to pay a fine or a fee for filing something as "customers" just like in any other service-oriented business. She even was responsible for launching the Orange County Clerk of Courts (**www.myorangeclerk.com**) Web site that enabled people to pay simple fines such as speeding violations on-line after she discovered the vast majority of people who drive to the courthouse to take care of these simple tasks come from far away.[7]

Still, some producers of intangibles have been slow to accept the idea that what they do *should* be marketed. Sometimes, people who work in health care, the legal profession, or the arts resist the notion that the same market forces that drive the fortunes of paper pro-ducers, food canners, or even power utilities affect the quality of what they produce and the demand for their services. Do you agree?

Many not-for-profit organizations, including charities, know that marketing is key to their success.

intangibles
Experience-based products.

Let's take a quick look at how some basic marketing concepts apply to an artistic product. Suppose a local theater company wanted to increase attendance at its performances. Remembering the basics of developing a marketing plan (Chapter 2), here are some marketing actions the organization might take to realize its goals:

- The organization could develop a *mission statement*, such as "We seek to be the premier provider of quality theater in the region."

- A *SWOT analysis* could include an assessment of the organization's strengths and weaknesses and the environmental threats and opportunities. The arts marketer after all, competes for the consumer's discretionary dollar against other theater groups. The marketer also has to confront other forms of entertainment the consumer might choose instead of going to a play, from attending a Blue Man Group performance to a Will Ferrell movie to an Ultimate Fighting Championship match. The theater company should use information it obtains in the SWOT analysis to develop a number of concrete measurable *objectives*, such as to "increase the number of season ticket holders by 20 percent over the next two years."

- Next, the organization must develop marketing strategies. For example, it must consider which *target markets* it wishes to attract. If audience levels for its plays have been fairly stable for several years, it might try to develop new markets for its performances. This might lead to product modifications, as some opera companies do when they project English translations above the stage to draw new patrons who are unfamiliar with opera's foreign tongues.

What Is a Service?

As we've said, marketing can help to promote all kinds of intangibles, from theater performances to ideas about birth control. But first, let's take a look at services, a very important type of intangible.

Services are acts, efforts, or performances exchanged from producer to user without ownership rights. Like other intangibles, a service satisfies needs by providing pleasure, information, or convenience. In 2008, service industry jobs accounted for over 75 percent of all employment in the United States and over two-thirds of the gross domestic product (GDP).[8] If you pursue a marketing career, it's highly likely that you will work somewhere in the services sector of the economy. Got your interest?

Of course, the service industry includes many consumer-oriented services, ranging from dry cleaning to body piercing. But it also includes a vast number of services directed toward organizations. Some of the more common business services include vehicle leasing, information technology services, insurance, security, Internet transaction services (Amazon.com, Google, on-line banking, etc.), legal advice, food services, consulting, cleaning, and maintenance. In addition, businesses also purchase some of the same services as consumers, such as electricity, telephone service, and gas (although as we saw in Chapter 6 these purchases tend to be in much higher quantities).

The market for business services has grown rapidly because it is often more cost effective for organizations to hire outside firms that specialize in these services than to hire a workforce and handle the tasks themselves. This *outsourcing* is commonly implemented to call centers outside the United States. Most of us have encountered a customer service rep for a U.S. firm, such as Dell or Delta Airlines, who works at one of the many call centers that have sprung up in India and elsewhere. In other instances, firms buy business services because they do not have the expertise necessary to provide the service. Even the marketing function itself often gets outsourced by organizations—it's not unusual for

services
Intangible products that are exchanged directly from the producer to the customer.

companies to hand over their advertising and public relations functions to outside agencies.

Characteristics of Services

Services come in many forms, from those done to you, such as a massage or a teeth cleaning, to those done to something you own, such as having your HD TV repaired or getting a new paint job on your classic 1965 Mustang. Regardless of whether they affect our bodies or our possessions, all services share four characteristics: intangibility, perishability, inseparability, and variability. Table 10.1 shows how marketers can address the unique issues related to these characteristics of services that don't pop up when they deal with tangible goods.

Intangibility

Intangibility means customers can't see, touch, or smell good service. Unlike the purchase of a tangible good, we can't inspect or handle services before we buy them. This makes it much more difficult for consumers to evaluate many services. Although it may be easy to evaluate your new haircut, it is far less easy to determine whether the dental hygienist did a great job cleaning your teeth.

Because they're buying something that isn't there, customers look for reassuring signs before they purchase so marketers must ensure that these signs are readily available. That's why they try to overcome the problem of intangibility by providing physical cues to reassure the buyer. These cues might be the "look" of the facility, its furnishings, logo, stationery, business cards, the appearance of its employees, or well-designed advertising and Web sites.

Toshiba reminds us that tangible products like office copiers often include a service component as well.

intangibility
The characteristic of a service that means customers can't see, touch, or smell good service.

Table 10.1	Marketing Strategies for Different Service Characteristics
Characteristic	**Marketing Response**
Intangibility	Provide tangibility through physical appearance of the facility
	Furnishings
	Employee uniforms
	Logo
	Web sites
	Advertising
Perishability	Adjust pricing to influence demand
	Adjust services to match demand (*capacity management*)
Variability	Institute total quality management programs
	Offer service guarantees
	Conduct gap analysis to identify gaps in quality
Inseparability	Train employees about successful service encounters
	Explore means for disintermediation

YOU CAN'T RIDE OFF INTO THE SUNSET IF YOUR NEST EGG WON'T CARRY YOU. We're big believers in a long-term retirement strategy based on objective financial advice. And in having a financial consultant who can help you every step of the way. To see if your nest egg could benefit from a little Midwestern horse sense, visit agedwards.com or call 866-379-4243.

A.G. EDWARDS.
FULLY INVESTED IN OUR CLIENTS.

Financial services are highly intangible, so investment firms need to use vivid imagery to communicate their benefits.

Lara L.
Price

APPLYING Perishability

A 76ers basketball game like any other sports event is perishable—while die-hard fans might record a game and watch it over and over for most of us once it's over, it's over. ➡

perishability
The characteristic of a service that makes it impossible to store for later sale or consumption.

capacity management
The process by which organizations adjust their offerings in an attempt to match demand.

variability
The characteristic of a service that means that even the same service performed by the same individual for the same customer can vary.

Perishability

Perishability refers to the characteristic of a service that makes it impossible to store for later sale or consumption—it's a case of use it or lose it. When rooms go unoccupied at a ski resort, there is no way to make up for the lost opportunity to rent them for the weekend. Marketers try to avoid these problems when they use the marketing mix to encourage demand for the service during slack times. One option is to reduce prices to increase demand for otherwise unsold services. Airlines do this when they offer more lower-priced seats in the final days before a flight. In a last-ditch effort to fill their ships to the highest possible capacity, Disney Cruise Lines offers Walt Disney World Resort employees discounts in excess of 50 percent off starting about a week before the ship sets sail. We'll talk more about these pricing tactics in Chapter 11.

Capacity management is the process by which organizations adjust their services in an attempt to match supply with demand. This strategy may mean adjusting the product, or it may mean adjusting the price. In the summer, for example, the Winter Park Ski Resort in Colorado combats its perishability problem by opening its lifts to mountain bikers who tear down the sunny slopes. Rental car companies offer discounts on days of the week when business travel is light, and many hotels offer special weekend packages to increase weekend occupancy rates.

Even movie theaters are starting to catch on to the idea of encouraging greater usage of their facilities during weeknights when they often show films to a few people at a time: When Prince started his "Musicology" tour, the cheapest concert ticket was $49.50. But fans who wanted a version of "Prince Lite" could attend the concert as it was simulcast in a chain of movie theaters where tickets went for $15.00. Similarly, Garth Brooks did a simulcast concert in November 2007 with a ticket price of $10.00.[9]

Variability

An NFL quarterback may be hot one Sunday and ice cold the next, and the same is true for most services. **Variability** means that over time even the same service the same individual performs for the same customer changes—even only in minor ways. It's rare when you get exactly the same cut from a hairstylist each time you visit her.

It's difficult to standardize services because service providers and customers vary. Think about your experiences in your college classes. A school can standardize its offerings to some degree—course catalogs, course content, and classrooms are fairly controllable. Professors, however, vary in their training, life experiences, and personalities, so there is little hope of being able to make teaching uniform (not that this would necessarily be desirable anyway). And because students with different backgrounds and interests vary in their needs, the lecture that you find fascinating might put your friend to sleep (trust us on this). The same is true for customers of organizational services. Differences in the quality of individual security guards or cleaning personnel mean variability in how organizations deliver these services.

In fact, we don't necessarily *want* standardization when we purchase a service. Most of us desire a hairstyle that fits our face and personality, and a personal trainer who will address our unique physical training needs. Businesses like McDonald's, Wendy's, and Burger King want unique advertising campaigns, not cookie-cutter messages. Because of the nature of the tasks service providers perform, customers often appreciate the one that customizes its service for each individual.

One solution to the problem of variability is to institute *total quality management (TQM) programs* for continuous improvement of service quality. As you learned in Chapter 9, TQM

David J.
Urban

a professor at Virginia Commonwealth University

My Advice for the Philadelphia 76ers would be to choose

Option

real people, **Other Voices**

I would choose **Option 2** first, followed by Option 3, because Option 1 is a long-term solution that will require a considerable financial investment and a substantial amount of internal selling effort on Lara's part. The scenario leads one to think that Option 3 is an obvious choice, and there are several good reasons given for conducting a lifetime value analysis. However, any such analysis is constrained by the quality of the data that are input to the analysis. Therefore, the lifetime value analysis must be accompanied by a better means of collecting information from *all* the team's constituent groups—not just season ticket holders. That's where Option 2 comes in with a caveat: mail surveys are slow and inefficient compared to Web-based surveys. The team should use every touchpoint it has with its customers to gather e-mail addresses that can be entered into a Web survey engine. Using the Web will allow the team's management to do faster, cheaper, and more frequent surveys of customers. The survey data can supplement the other data sources already on hand by providing customer demographics and psychographics, and the enhanced data can fuel Option 3, the lifetime value analysis. The improvement in decision making provided by the lifetime value analysis will then give Lara a platform for phasing in Option 1 over the long term. ➤

---

is a management effort to involve all employees from the assembly line onward in continuous product quality improvement. In addition to instituting TQM programs, offering service guarantees ensures consumers that if service quality fails, they will be compensated. We'll talk later in the chapter about how service marketers can provide greater quality and consistency in service delivery through gap analysis and employee empowerment.

Inseparability

In services, **inseparability** means that it is impossible to separate the production of a service from the consumption of that service. Think of the concept of inseparability this way: A firm can manufacture goods at one point in time, distribute them, and then sell them later (likely at a different location from the manufacturing facility). In contrast, by its nature a service can take place only at the time the actual service provider performs an act on either the customer or the customer's possession. Nobody wants to eat a meal at a restaurant that was prepared yesterday at another location—that's inseparability. And you can't bulk up haircuts or empty seats on airplanes as inventory for future use!

Still, it's difficult if not impossible to detach the expertise, skill, and personality of a provider or the quality of a firm's employees, facilities, and equipment from the offering itself. The central role employees play in making or breaking a service underscores the importance of the **service encounter**, or the interaction between the customer and the service provider.[10] The most expertly cooked meal is just plain mush if a surly or incompetent waiter brings it to the table. We'll talk more about the importance of service providers later in this chapter.

To minimize the potentially negative effects of bad service encounters and to save on labor costs, some service businesses turn to **disintermediation**, which means removing the "middleman" and thus eliminating the need for customers to interact with people at all. Examples include self-service gas pumps and bank ATMs. Even salad and dessert bars reduce reliance on a waitperson. Although some consumers resist dealing with machines, pumping their own gas, or fixing their own salad, most prefer the speed and efficiency disintermediation provides. The remaining consumers who want a Caesar salad prepared table-side or a fill-up that includes an oil check and a clean windshield provide marketing opportunities for full-service restaurants and the few gas stations that still provide these higher levels of service—usually at a higher price.

inseparability
The characteristic of a service that means that it is impossible to separate the production of a service from the consumption of that service.

service encounter
The actual interaction between the customer and the service provider.

disintermediation
Eliminating the interaction between customers and salespeople so as to minimize negative service encounters and reduce costs.

Metrics Moment

Harrah's, the casino operator, focuses on four key customer-centric metrics: customer gaming dollars, percentage of revenue from customers who play at more than one Harrah's casino, customer satisfaction across Harrah's casinos, and the percentage of customers in its loyalty program who advance to a higher status as a result of the company's higher expenditures. Ultimately, Harrah's realizes that the individual value of each customer is critical to its success. While some high-rolling customers appear on the surface to be profitable, they actually require too many special services and pampering. For this reason it turns out that lower-volume customers may actually be more profitable. Harrah's uses the results from its four metrics to help it identify which customers really are worth the royal Vegas treatment.[11]

The Internet provides many opportunities for disintermediation, especially in the financial services area. Banking customers can access their accounts, transfer funds from one account to another, and pay their bills with the click of a mouse. Many busy consumers can check out mortgage interest rates and even apply for a loan at their convenience—a much better option than taking an afternoon off from work to sit in a mortgage company office. On-line brokerage services are increasingly popular, as many consumers seek to handle their investments themselves so they can avoid the commission a full-service brokerage firm charges. Insurance companies like GEICO and Progressive aggressively lead consumers to the Web instead of to an agent's office to get rate quotes.

Classify Services

When they understand the characteristics of different types of services, marketers can develop strategies to ramp up customer satisfaction. As Figure 10.1 shows, we classify services in terms of whether the service is performed directly on the customer or on something the customer owns, and whether the service consists of tangible or intangible actions. Customers themselves receive tangible services to their bodies—a haircut or a heart transplant. The education (we hope!) you are receiving in this course is an intangible service directed at the consumer. A customer's possessions are the recipient of tangible services such as the repair of a favorite carpet. Intangible services directed at a consumer's possessions include insurance and home security.

The Service Continuum

In reality, most products are a combination of goods and services. The purchase of a "pure good" like a Cadillac Escalade still has service components, such as bringing it to the dealer for maintenance work or using its OnStar service to figure out how to find the dealer at all. The purchase of a "pure service" like a makeover at a department store has product components, for example, lotions, powders, and lipsticks the cosmetologist uses to create the "new you."

The service continuum in Figure 10.2 shows that either tangible or intangible elements dominate some products, such as salt versus teaching, whereas others such as a commercial airline flight tend to include a mixture of goods and services. A product's placement on this continuum gives some guidance as to which marketing issues are most likely to be relevant. As the product approaches the tangible pole of this continuum, there is fairly little emphasis on service. The physical product itself is the focal point, and we choose one option over others because of the product's function or image.

But, as the product gets near the intangible pole, the issues we've discussed, such as intangibility and inseparability, play a key role in shaping the service experience. In the middle of the continuum, both goods and services contribute substantially to the quality of

Figure 10.1 | Classification of Services by Inputs and Tangibility

Marketers classify services according to whether the customer or his possessions are the recipient of the service and whether the service itself consists of tangible or intangible elements.

	Tangible Services	*Intangible Services*
Customer	Haircut	College education
	Plastic surgery	A religious service
	Manicure	A TV program
	Personal trainer	A flower-arranging course
		Marriage counseling
Possessions	Dry cleaning	Banking
	Auto repair	Accounting services
	Housecleaning	Insurance
	Package delivery	Home security service

Figure 10.2 | The Service Continuum

Products vary in their level of tangibility. Salt is a tangible product, teaching is an intangible product, and the products fast-food restaurants offer include both tangible and intangible elements.

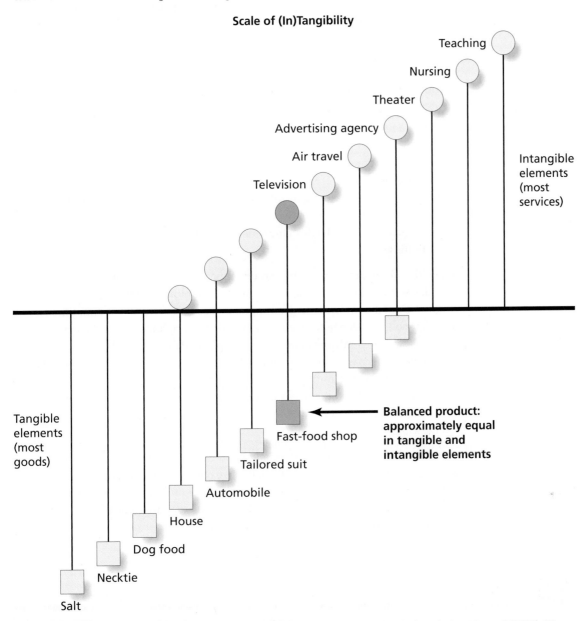

Scale of (In)Tangibility

Teaching

Nursing

Theater

Advertising agency

Air travel

Television

Intangible elements (most services)

Tangible elements (most goods)

Balanced product: approximately equal in tangible and intangible elements

Fast-food shop

Tailored suit

Automobile

House

Dog food

Necktie

Salt

Source: Adapted from G. Lynn Shostack, "How to Design a Service," *European Journal of Marketing* 16, no. 1 (1982): 52.

the product because these products rely on people to satisfactorily operate equipment that will in turn deliver quality service. As you move across the service continuum from tangibles to intangibles, it's useful to consider the various products within the context of three categories: goods-dominated products, equipment- or facility-based services, and people-based services.

Goods-Dominated Products

Even if this means only that the company maintains a toll-free telephone line for questions or provides a 30-day warranty against defects, companies that sell tangible products still must provide support services. Automobile, home appliance, and electronics firms can realize a major competitive advantage when they provide customers with this support better than the competition. Services may be even more important for marketers of business-to-business tangibles. Business customers often will not even consider buying from manufacturers who don't provide services like employee training and equipment maintenance. For example, hospitals that buy lifesaving patient care and monitoring equipment costing hundreds of thousands of dollars demand not only in-service training for their nursing and technician personnel, but also quick response to breakdowns and regular maintenance of the equipment.

Equipment- or Facility-Based Services

As we see in Figure 10.2, some products include a mixture of tangible and intangible elements. While a restaurant is a balanced product because it includes the preparation and delivery of the food to your table plus the food itself, the tangible elements of the service are less evident for other products. Many hospitals and hotels fall in the middle of the continuum not because customers take a tangible good away from the service encounter, but because these organizations rely on expensive equipment or facilities to deliver a product. Other services such as automatic car washes, amusement parks, museums, movie theaters, health clubs, tanning salons, and zoos, also must be concerned with these factors:[12]

- **Operational factors:** Clear signs and other guidelines must show customers how to use the service. In particular, firms need to minimize waiting times. Marketers employ a number of tricks to give impatient customers the illusion that they aren't waiting too long. One hotel chain, responding to complaints about the long wait for elevators, installed mirrors in the lobby: People tended to check themselves out until the elevators arrived, and lo and behold, protests decreased.[13] Burger King's research showed that multiple lines create stress in customers—especially if one moves faster than the others—so it shifted to single lines in which customers at the head of the line order at the next available register. Now if supermarkets would only do the same!

- **Locational factors:** These are especially important for frequently purchased services, such as dry cleaning or retail banking, that we obtain at a fixed spot. When you select a bank, a restaurant, or a health club, its location often factors into your decision. Marketers of these services make sure their service sites are convenient and in neighborhoods that are attractive to prospective customers.

By the **People**, For the **People**

Carpooling is not a new practice, but rocketing gas prices and clogged roadways make it more desirable today than ever before. Americans take well over one billion car trips a day—and over three-quarters of these are solo! Can the simple act of sharing a ride turn into a profitable service business? Some frustrated commuters are taking the wheel as they organize pools, often on-line. When your organization joins nuride (**www.nuride.com**) you match up with others who share your route (and without the danger of riding with weird strangers since every participant registers through her employer). After your trip is over, you earn points that you can redeem for restaurant meals or other goodies from local retailers.[14]

Nuride is a new service that matches commuters with others who share their route.

- **Environmental factors:** Service managers who operate a storefront service that requires people to come to their location realize they must create an attractive environment to lure customers. That's why NFL stadiums upgrade their facilities by offering plush "sky boxes" to well-heeled patrons and a better assortment of food and merchandise to the rest of us. One trend is for such services to adopt a more retail-like philosophy, borrowing techniques from clothing stores or restaurants to create a pleasant environment as part of their marketing strategy. Banks, for example, increasingly create signature looks for their branches through the careful use of lighting, color, and art.

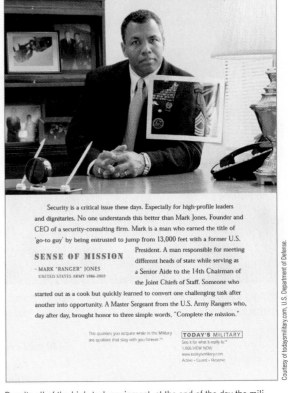

Despite all of the high-tech equipment, at the end of the day the military is a people-based service that depends on well-trained soldiers to carry out its objectives.

People-Based Services

At the intangible end of the continuum are people-based services. Take for example the ultimate father–son bonding experience through good grooming—a trip to Big League Haircuts for Men. Big League only cuts the hair of boys of all ages. And it loves to boast that its stores have "no perms, color, or smelly chemical services" to detract from the macho experience. There's a big screen TV in the waiting area, box seats from sports stadiums, and sports memorabilia scattered throughout the store. During the haircut you can watch the game on a personal TV while you're clipped by a stylist who is specially trained in customer service for guys. Big League Haircuts for Men creates a competitive advantage because it provides unique benefits male consumers want and other shops can't deliver.[15]

Because people have less and less time to get things done, the importance of people-based services is increasing. Self-improvement services such as those wardrobe consultants and personal trainers offer are increasingly popular, and in some cities even professional dog walkers and mobile pet washing trucks do a brisk business. Many of us hire someone to do our legal work, repair our cars and appliances, or do our tax returns.

Core and Augmented Services

When we buy a service, we may actually purchase a *set* of services. The **core service** is a benefit that a customer gets from the service. For example, when your car breaks down, repairing the problem is a core service you seek from an auto dealer or a garage. In most cases though, the core service alone just isn't enough. To attract customers, a service firm often tries to offer **augmented services**—additional service offerings that differentiate the firm from the competition. When the auto dealership provides pickup and delivery of your car, a free car wash, or a customer lounge with donuts and coffee, it gains your loyalty as a customer.

Think about the core service you buy with an airline ticket: transportation. Yet airlines rarely stress the basic benefit of arriving safely at your destination. Instead, they emphasize augmented services such as frequent-flyer miles, speedy check-in, laptop connections, and in-flight entertainment. In addition, augmented services may be necessary to deliver the core service. In the case of air travel, airports often add attractions to encourage travelers to fly to one site rather than another.[16] Here are some augmented services now available at airports around the world:

- Dallas-Fort Worth's New International Terminal D: laptop rental, massage chairs, children's' playground, four airline lounges and a luxury VIP lounge called The Club at

Lara L.
Price

APPLYING Core and Augmented Services

When you go to a professional basketball game, the core service you buy is the chance to watch the players show their moves. What are some augmented services you look for as well? ➡

core service
The basic benefit of having a service performed.

augmented services
The core service plus additional services provided to enhance value.

A college's core service may be education, but students often are attracted by augmented services, including recreation facilities like those offered at the University of Houston.

DFW, upscale shopping (Mont Blanc, Fossil, Brooks Brothers, PGA Tour Shop, and more), and an assortment of truly local food fare

- Amsterdam Schiphol: casino, airport television station, sauna, dry cleaner, grocery store

- Frankfurt International: supermarket and disco

- Singapore Changi: fitness center, karaoke lounge, putting green

And what about your college education? With increased competition for students, universities find that their augmented products must provide a variety of amenities like the University of Houston's $53 million wellness center that features a five-story climbing wall, hot tubs, waterfalls, and pool slides. At the University of Wisconsin, Oshkosh, students get massages, pedicures, and manicures, while Washington State University boasts the largest jacuzzi on the West Coast—it holds 53 people. And Ohio State University just spent over $140 million to build a 657,000-square-foot complex featuring kayaks and canoes, indoor batting cages, rope courses, and a climbing wall that 50 students can scale simultaneously.[17] Hopefully in their spare moments students even squeeze in a few classes!

Services on the Internet

From DVD rentals to fine restaurant cuisine, almost anything an organization delivers it can sell on the Web. In some cities, Web site companies arrange to pick up your dry cleaning, develop your family photos, or repair your shoes. Here are some of the newest and most popular Web services:

- **Banking and brokerages:** Cyberbanking is not new, but today all the big global banks heavily promote the fact that customers can check their statements, pay bills, transfer money, and balance their accounts 24/7, whether they're at home or traveling around the globe. As an incentive not to drive to the branch, some banks offer on-line customers higher interest rates on deposits, lower rates on loans, and free electronic bill payment. On-line discount brokerage houses such as E*trade.com offer lower fees for stock purchases, and some sites allow traders to track their portfolios on-line.

- **Software:** Oracle and Salesforce.com, market leaders in CRM software, are spearheading an industry shift toward Internet-accessed software they sell or rent to user companies that pay for these services on a monthly basis.[19] And companies like IBM and Microsoft are starting to invest heavily in *cloud computing*. This new approach involves using supercomputers with insane processing power that your PC at home can access so that you can store all your important files "in the cloud" for access from anywhere there is an Internet connection (wireless is getting better all the time). In addition you can

 **etrics Moment**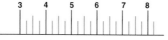

Disney Company marketing executives decided to improve profitability by measuring how much families spent on vacations and the percentage that they spent at Disney properties. The company found that even though its theme parks were the primary destination for travelers to Orlando, Florida, in fact Disney captured only approximately 25 cents out of every dollar people spent once they arrived.

Acting on these findings, Disney teamed up with airlines to offer travel packages to vacationers and invested a great deal of money to build Disney hotels and Disney stores. Its goal was to pick families up at the airport in Disney's Magical Express shuttle and bring them directly to a Disney hotel where they watch Disney TV and eat in Disney restaurants. This metric has paid off big-time: The company now finds that vacationing families "donate" approximately 75 percent of their money to the Disney cause.[18]

capitalize on the immense processing power of other computers to run programs and process data—and possibly even make personal computer hardware upgrades a thing of the past. Imagine being able to access your work files or your iTunes library anywhere you want in an instant![20]

- **Music:** After years of struggling with illegal downloading, personified by the now (in)famous Napster introduction, music merchants including Apple, Dell, Sony, Wal-Mart, Target, and a new and improved Napster sell legal tracks via the Internet. These on-line music firms have introduced a number of innovations, including cheaper downloads, better-quality files, hardware to handle more tunes and larger files, and the opportunity for consumers to share songs and listen to them before paying.[21]

- **Travel:** Internet airline, travel, and tourism sites now command a large portion of the travel business for both business customers and individual consumers. Priceline.com pitchman William Shatner of *Star Trek* and *Boston Legal* exhorts consumers to place bids for the price they want to pay for airline tickets, hotel rooms, and other travel products. Traditional travel agencies now tend to focus on specialized markets such as outsourcing a firm's business travel function or booking unique packaged travel deals for consumers.

- **Dating sites:** Dating services are big on the Internet. eHarmony. com heavily advertises and holds a patent for its system that identifies partners likely to have a successful relationship. eHarmony develops personality profiles from clients' answers to more than 430 on-line questions. The service pairs couples only when eHarmony's "marital satisfaction index" indicates 95 percent confidence that they are compatible.[22] The company is so wildly popular that it is beginning to suffer from its success. The system "rejects" many people—an issue rival Chemistry. com constantly emphasizes in its advertising.[23]

- **Career-related sites:** Employment agencies and recruiting firms such as Monster.com and CareerBuilder.com provide important job services and a less expensive way for applicants and employers to advertise their availability.

- **Medical care:** An increasing number of physicians are available to patients in one way or another through the Internet and e-mail. For example, AskPhysicians.com promises that if you post an inquiry on its bulletin board a qualified physician will post a response within two to three days.[24] WebMD.com does pretty much the same thing, but it's more of a database than an interactive bulletin board.[25]

To stay in the game, other marketers of such services need to think seriously about developing an Internet presence. Effective Internet sites not only allow customers to access the services on-line, but they also provide information for those customers who still want personal contact. Because customers seek access to Internet-based services for *convenience*, marketers must make sure Internet sites are fast, simple, continuously updated, and easy to navigate.

Financial services complete fiercely both off-line and on-line to help consumers fund their dreams.

Music downloading, both the illegal kind and the legal version offered by the reincarnated Napster, is one of the most popular Internet services.

Ripped from the **Headlines**

Ethical Decisions in the Real World

Ever heard of "on-line reputation management services"? It's the latest service craze in the already pretty crazy Internet services world. Providers in the on-line reputation management industry promise to remove unfavorable information about your company from searches that popular Internet search engines (including Google and Yahoo!) turn up.

Let's suppose you Googled your company's name and—oops—you find an unfavorable review or a news article that shines a negative light on your firm. You can have these service providers make sure that consumers won't find that information when they search your company, or even from more general searches related to your industry or its products.

Assume you work for a firm that strives to maintain a pristine reputation in the marketplace. Given that consumers have become so heavily reliant on the use of search engines to do research about potential purchases, is it ethical for you to pay to have your reputation "scrubbed" by a reputation management firm? What would you do?

Ripped from the Headlines! See what happened in the Real World at **www.mypearsonmarketinglab.com**

ETHICS CHECK: ➤

Find out what otherstudents taking this course **would do** and **why** on **www.mypearsonmarketinglab.com**

Would you hire a reputation management firm to "scrub" your on-line entries?

☐YES ☐NO

The Service Encounter

Earlier we said that a service encounter occurs when the customer comes into contact with the organization—which usually means she interacts with one or more employees who represent that organization. The *service encounter* has several dimensions that are important to marketers.[26] First, there is the social contact dimension—one person interacting with another person. The physical dimension is also important—customers often pay close attention to the environment where they receive the service.

Despite all the attention (and money) firms pay to create an attractive facility and deliver a quality product, this contact is "the moment of truth"—the employee often determines whether the customer will come away with a positive or a negative impression of the service. Our interactions with service providers can range from the most superficial, such as when we buy a movie ticket, to telling a psychiatrist (or bartender) our most intimate secrets. In each case, though, the quality of the service encounter exerts a big impact on how we feel about the service we receive.

Social Elements of the Service Encounter: Employees and Customers

Because services are intimately tied to company employees who deliver the service, *the quality of a service is only as good as its worst employee*. The employee represents the organization; her actions, words, physical appearance, courtesy, and professionalism—reflect its values. Customers entrust themselves and/or their possessions to the care of the employee, so it is important that employees look at the encounter from the customer's perspective.

However, the customer also plays a part the type of experience that results from a service encounter. When you visit a doctor, the quality of the health care you receive depends not only on the physician's competence. It's also influenced by your ability to accurately and clearly communicate the symptoms you experience and how well you follow the regimen she prescribes to treat you. The business customer must provide accurate information to her accounting firm. And even the best personal trainer is not going to make the desired improvements in a client's physique if the client refuses to do the workout designed for her.

At times, being a good customer means controlling your temper when the encounter is worse than expected. Companies increasingly report incidents of "customer rage" including the following:

- **Checkout counter rage:** A woman who barged into the express lane with more than 12 items had half her nose bitten off by a fellow shopper.

- **Pub rage:** A man who was refused service at closing time repeatedly smashed his tractor into a bar.

- **ATM rage:** When a bank machine ate a man's ATM card, he stuck it with a utility knife and threw a second knife at a cashier.[27]

Physical Elements of the Service Encounter: Servicescapes and Other Tangibles

As we noted earlier in the chapter, because services are intangible marketers have to be mindful of the *physical evidence* that goes along with them. An important part of this physical evidence is the **servicescape**: the environment in which the service is delivered and where the firm and the customer interact. Servicescapes include facility exteriors—elements such as building's architecture, the signage, parking, and even the landscaping. They also include interior elements, such as the design of the office or store, equipment, colors, air quality, temperature, and smells. For hotels, restaurants, banks, airlines, and even schools, the servicescape is quite elaborate. For other services, such as an express mail drop-off, a dry cleaner, or an ATM, the servicescape can be very simple.

Marketers know that carefully designed servicescapes can have a positive influence on customers' purchase decisions, their evaluations of service quality, and their ultimate satisfaction with the service. Thus, for a service such as a pro basketball game that Lara Price sells, much planning goes into designing not only the actual court, but also the exterior design and entrances of the stadium, landscaping, seating, restrooms, concession stands, and ticketing area. Similarly, marketers pay close attention to the design of other tangibles that facilitate the performance of the service or provide communications. For the basketball fan, these include the signs that direct people to the stadium, the game tickets, the programs, the team's uniforms, and the hundreds of employees who help to deliver the service.

Nowadays, for many consumers the first tangible evidence of a business (service or otherwise) is its Web site. Web sites send a strong cue to customers about you, and sites that are unattractive or frustratingly dysfunctional provide a horrible first impression of the company and its service. Searchability is important, as is paying attention to **search engine optimization (SEO)**: a systematic process of ensuring that your firm comes up at or near the top of lists of typical search phrases related to your business. SEO is critical, because if your organization's name doesn't come up when someone Googles she'll just click on one of the competitors that does appear on the list.

Overall, investments by service firms in user-friendly Web sites pay back through increased business and higher customer satisfaction and loyalty. Consider the FedEx Web site (**www.fedex.com**) for example: Users can use alternative rate plans to price the shipment, find the nearest drop-off location, and then track progress in real-time toward delivery of the package. This functionality not only makes customers happy, but it also saves FedEx money because it reduces the number of phone inquiries its customer service representatives need to handle.[28]

servicescape
The actual physical facility where the service is performed, delivered, and consumed.

search engine optimization (SEO)
A systematic process of ensuring that your firm comes up at or near the top of lists of typical search phrases related to your business.

2

OBJECTIVE

Appreciate the importance of service quality to marketers.
(pp. 313–319)

Provide Quality Service

If a service experience isn't positive, it can turn into a *disservice* with nasty consequences. Quality service ensures that customers are satisfied with what they have paid for. However, satisfaction is relative because the service recipient compares the current experience to some prior set of expectations. That's what makes delivering quality service tricky. What may seem like excellent service to one customer may be mediocre to another person who has been "spoiled" by earlier encounters with an exceptional service provider. So, marketers must identify customer expectations and then work hard to exceed them. That's just what JetBlue has done with how its passengers define a low-fare airline. JetBlue gives customers a friendly cabin crew, roomy overhead bins, live satellite TV at every leather seat, and even pay-per-view movies.[29]

At any one moment   there are a million reasons to get away with the girls.

Call your travel agent • 1-800-CARNIVAL • carnival.com

Carnival.
The Fun Ships.

Passengers evaluate the quality of a hospitality-related service like a cruise in light of their prior expectations.

At the new Kowloon Shangri-La much has changed,
but the important things remain the same.

Kowloon Shangri-La

Upscale hotels like the Kowloon Hong Kong feature elaborate servicescapes to underscore their claims to luxury and careful attention to guests' needs.

Compare this to a more typical airline, and you'll see why JetBlue's extras exceed customer expectations. Of course, JetBlue is far from perfect—in February 2007 for example it left hundreds of passengers stranded in planes at JFK airport during a snowstorm in what the company described as an "operational meltdown." Still, the carrier's long-term commitment to service quality in an industry that generally fails in this area resulted in a #2 ranking in the *2008 Airline Quality Ratings* study, topped only by fellow low-price airline AirTran.[30]

Of course, it's not always so easy to meet or exceed customer expectations. The stories we hear from friends and acquaintances may influence our standards, and these may not always be realistic in the first place.[31] In some cases, there is little marketers can do to soothe ruffled feathers. Exaggerated customer expectations, such as providing a level of personal service impossible for a large company to accomplish, account for about 75 percent of the complaints service businesses report. However, providing customers with logical explanations for service failures and compensating them in some way can substantially reduce dissatisfaction.

Service Quality Attributes

Because services are inseparable in that an organization doesn't produce one until the time a customer consumes it, it is difficult to estimate how good a service will be until you buy it. Most service businesses cannot offer a free trial. Because services are variable, it is hard to predict consistency of quality and there is little or no opportunity for comparison shopping. The selection process for services is somewhat different than for goods, especially for services that are highly intangible—such as those on the right end of the continuum in Figure 10.2. Service marketers have to come up with creative ways to illustrate the benefits their service will provide.

Search qualities are product attributes that the consumer can examine prior to purchase. These include color, style, price, fit, smell, and texture. Tangible goods, of course, are more likely to have these characteristics, so services need to build them in by paying attention to details such as the style of flight attendants' uniforms or the decor of a hotel room. The "Service Experience Blueprint™" in Figure 10.3 illustrates how one design firm tried to build in such cues for a grocery chain. The company planned an upgraded, freshly painted parking lot that included a special preferred parking space for expectant mothers (complete with a stork logo) to signal that the company cares.[32] Attention to detail makes a difference.

Experience qualities are product attributes that customers identify during or after consumption. For example, we can't really predict how good a vacation will be until we have it, so marketers need to reassure customers *before* the fact that they are in for a positive experience. A travel agency may invest in a slick presentation complete with alluring images of a tropical resort and perhaps even supply enthusiastic recommendations from other clients who had a positive experience at the same location. On the other hand, the last thing a marketer wants to do is overpromise and then fall short in the actual delivery—so conveniently cropping out that construction site that's located right next to the resort may not be a great idea.

Credence qualities are product attributes we find difficult to evaluate even *after* we've experienced them. For example, most of us don't

Figure 10.3 | Service Experience Blueprint

Firms often build in cues their customers can easily see because service quality is often difficult to determine. Grocery stores such as this one often use a variety of cues to convince consumers of superior quality.

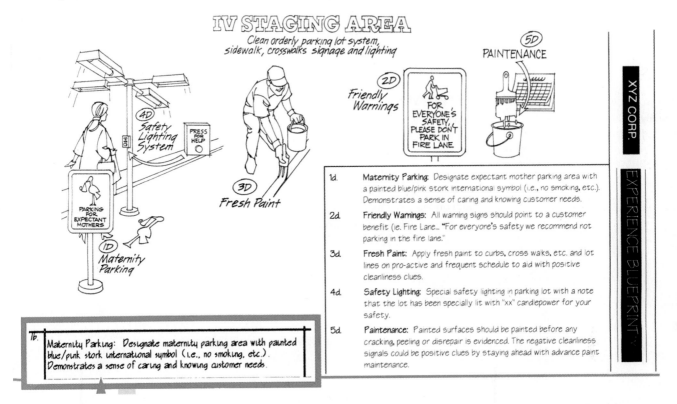

Source: Lewis P. Carbone and Stephan H. Haeckel, "Engineering Customer Experiences," *Marketing Management* 3 (Winter 1994), Exhibit 4.

have the expertise to know if our doctor's diagnosis is correct.[33] To a great extent the client must trust the service provider. That is why tangible clues of professionalism, such as diplomas, an organized office, or even the professional's attire (for example, a physician in a lab coat instead of blue jeans) count toward purchase satisfaction.

Measure Service Quality

Because the customer's experience of a service determines if she will return to the provider in the future, service marketers feel that measuring positive and negative service experiences is the "Holy Grail" for the services industry. Marketers gather consumer responses in a variety of ways (see Chapter 4). For example, some companies hire "mystery shoppers" to check on hotels and airlines and report back. These shoppers usually work for a research firm, although some airlines reportedly recruit "spies" from the ranks of their most frequent flyers. Some firms also locate "lost customers" (former patrons) so they can find out what turned them off and correct the problem.

SERVQUAL

The **SERVQUAL** scale is one popular instrument to measure consumers' perceptions of service quality. SERVQUAL identifies five dimensions, or components, of service quality:

- *Tangibles:* the physical facilities and equipment and the professional appearance of personnel

- *Reliability:* the ability to provide dependably and accurately what was promised

- *Responsiveness:* the willingness to help customers and provide prompt service

search qualities
Product characteristics that the consumer can examine prior to purchase.

experience qualities
Product characteristics that customers can determine during or after consumption.

credence qualities
Product characteristics that are difficult to evaluate even after they have been experienced.

SERVQUAL
A multiple-item scale used to measure service quality across dimensions of tangibles, reliability, responsiveness, assurance, and empathy.

- *Assurance:* the knowledge and courtesy of employees, and the ability to convey trust and confidence

- *Empathy:* the degree of caring and individual attention customers receive[34]

Thousands of service businesses apply the SERVQUAL scale. They usually administer it in a survey format through a written, on-line, or phone questionnaire. Firms often track SERVQUAL scores over time to understand how their service quality is (hopefully) improving. They also can use this measure to apply the gap analysis approach we describe next.

Gap Analysis

gap analysis
A marketing research method that measures the difference between a customer's expectation of a service quality and what actually occurred.

Gap analysis (no, nothing to do with a Gap clothing store) is a measurement approach that gauges the difference between a customer's expectation of service quality and what actually occurs. By identifying specific places in the service system where there is a wide gap between what customers expect and what they receive, services marketers can get a handle on what needs improvement. Figure 10.4 illustrates where the gaps can occur in service, both on the consumer's side (often referred to as "in front of the curtain") and on the marketer's side ("behind the curtain"). Some major gaps include the following:[35]

Figure 10.4 | The Gap Model of Service Delivery

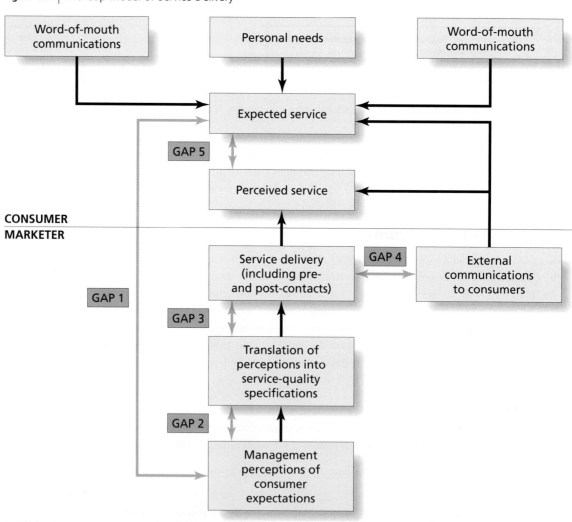

Source: A. Parasuraman, Valarie A. Zeithaml, and Leonard L. Berry, "A Conceptual Model of Service Quality and its Implications for Future Research," *Journal of Marketing* (Fall 1985), pp. 41–50.

- **Gap between consumers' expectations and management's perceptions:** A major quality gap occurs when the firm's managers don't understand what its customers' expectations are in the first place. Many service organizations have an *operations orientation* rather than a *customer orientation*. For example, banks often used to close branches at midday to balance transactions because that's more efficient for them, even though it's not convenient for customers who want to do their banking during their lunch hour. Today more and more banks are open late and on weekends.

- **Gap between management's perception and quality standards the firm sets:** Quality suffers when a firm fails to establish a quality-control program. Successful service firms, such as American Express and McDonald's, develop written quality goals. American Express found that customers complained most about its responsiveness, accuracy, and timeliness. The company established 180 specific goals to correct these problems, and it now monitors how fast employees answer phones in an effort to be more responsive.

- **Gap between established quality standards and service delivery:** One of the biggest threats to service quality is poor employee performance. When employees do not deliver the service at the level the company specifies, quality suffers. Teamwork is crucial to service success. Unfortunately, many companies don't clearly specify what they expect of employees. Merrill Lynch addressed this problem when the brokerage firm assembled its operations personnel into quality groups of 8 to 15 employees each to clarify its expectations for how its personnel should interact with clients.

   Disney Parks and Resorts is a real champion of consistency between standards and delivery. Disney makes all employees, or "Cast Members" (whether they sell ice cream on Main Street USA or they come in from another company to fill an executive role), go through "Traditions" training, as well as many other training programs to help ensure that *all* Disney cast members know how they should interact with guests. They follow up frequently with refresher seminars and meetings to remind everyone of the company's history and traditions.

- **Gap between service quality standards and consumers' expectations:** Sometimes a firm makes exaggerated promises or does not accurately describe its service to customers. When the Holiday Inn hotel chain developed an advertising campaign based on the promise that guests would receive "No Surprises," many operations personnel opposed the idea. The personnel pointed out that no service organization, no matter how good, can anticipate every single thing that can go wrong. Sure enough, the campaign was unsuccessful. A services firm is better off when it communicates exactly what the customer can expect and how the company will make it right if it doesn't deliver on its promises.

- **Gap between expected service and actual service:** Sometimes consumers misperceive the quality of the service. Thus, even when communications accurately describe what service quality the firm provides and what customers can expect, buyers are less than satisfied. Some diners at fine restaurants are so demanding that even their own mothers couldn't anticipate their every desire (that's probably why they're eating out in the first place).

The Critical Incident Technique

The **critical incident technique** is another way to measure service quality.[36] Using this approach, the company collects and closely analyzes very specific customer complaints. It can then identify *critical incidents*—specific contacts between consumers and service providers that are most likely to result in dissatisfaction.

Some critical incidents happen when the service organization simply can't meet a customer's expectations. For example, it is impossible to satisfy a passenger who says to a flight attendant, "Come sit with me. I don't like to fly alone." In other cases though, the firm is capable of meeting these expectations but fails to do so. For example, the customer

critical incident technique
A method for measuring service quality in which marketers use customer complaints to identify critical incidents—specific face-to-face contacts between consumer and service providers that cause problems and lead to dissatisfaction.

Metrics Moment

The consulting firm Market Metrix developed a metric it calls the *Marketing Metrix Hospitality Index* (MMHI) to measure customer satisfaction with hotel, airline, and car rental companies that it bases on 35,000 in-depth consumer interviews. The MMHI includes over 250 hotel brands, 25 airlines, and 11 car rental companies—each rated on over 50 different dimensions. Subscribers to the quarterly report can measure their company's stand-alone performance and also benchmark its ratings against those of competitors and highly ranked companies within and across the other hospitality industries. In 2007, the top-rated hospitality services were Kimpton Hotels, Sun Country Airlines, and Enterprise Rent-A-Car. Also, the metric includes measures of customer satisfaction with Web sites that offer on-line hotel reservations—Hotwire.com placed first.[38]

might complain to a flight attendant, "My seat won't recline."[37] A service provider can turn a potentially dissatisfied customer into a happy one if it addresses the problem or perhaps even tells the customer why the problem can't be solved at this time. Customers tend to be fairly forgiving if the organizations gives them a reasonable explanation for the problem.

Strategic Issues in Service Quality

We've seen that delivering quality is the goal of every successful service organization. What can the firm do to maximize the likelihood that a customer will choose its service and become a loyal customer? Because services differ from goods in so many ways, decision makers struggle to market something that isn't there. But, just as in goods marketing the first step is to develop effective marketing strategies. Table 10.2 illustrates how three different types of service organizations might devise effective marketing strategies.

Of course, no one (not even your marketing professor) is perfect, and mistakes happen. Some failures, such as when your dry cleaner places glaring red spots on your new white sweater, are easy to see at the time the firm performs the service. Others, such as when the dry cleaner shrinks your sweater, are less obvious and you recognize them only at a later time when you're running late and get a "surprise." But no matter when or how you discover the failure, the important thing is that the firm takes fast action to resolve the problem. A timely and appropriate response means that the problem won't occur again

Table 10.2 | Marketing Strategies for Service Organizations

	Dry Cleaner	City Opera Company	A State University
Marketing objective	Increase total revenues by 20 percent within one year by increasing business of existing customers and obtaining new customers	Increase to 1,000 the number of season memberships to opera productions within two years	Increase applications to undergraduate and graduate programs by 10 percent for the coming academic year
Target markets	Young and middle-aged professionals living within a five-mile radius of the business	Clients who attend single performances but do not purchase season memberships	Primary market: prospective undergraduate and graduate students who are residents of the state
		Other local residents who enjoy opera but do not normally attend local opera performances	Secondary market: prospective undergraduate and graduate students living in other states and in foreign countries
Benefits offered	Excellent and safe cleaning of clothes in 24 hours or fewer	Experiencing professional-quality opera performances while helping ensure the future of the local opera company	High-quality education in a student-centered campus environment
Strategy	Provide an incentive offer to existing customers such as one suit cleaned for free after 10 suits cleaned at regular price	Write letters to former membership holders and patrons of single performances encouraging them to purchase new season memberships	Increase number of recruiting visits to local high schools; arrange a special day of events for high-school counselors to visit campus
	Use newspaper advertising to communicate a limited-time discount offer to all customers	Arrange for opera company personnel and performers to be guests for local television and radio talk shows	Send letters to alumni encouraging them to recommend the university to prospective students they know

Wendy
Wysocki
a professor at Monroe County Community College
My Advice for the Philadelphia 76ers would
be to choose

Option

real people, **Other Voices**

I would choose **Option 3** because Lara knows that she needs to develop a better system to gather, compile, and analyze customer data as well as predict future customer behaviors. Both Options 1 and 3 utilize customer relationship management (CRM) approaches that will accomplish those goals. However, Option 3

provides the opportunity to gradually integrate CRM components into the Comcast Spectacor organization without the price tag of Option 1. Developing customer relationship management systems will be a change in philosophy for the Comcast Spectacor Company and should be approached gradually in order to allow for the members of the internal organization to recognize and eventually embrace the benefits of this new philosophy. Analyzing the lifetime value of the 76er's full season ticket holders is an excellent place to begin since they are vital to the long-term profitability of the organization. This approach would be a good place to begin building long-term relationships and integrating CRM strategies and then progress to Option 1 to integrate a more comprehensive CRM database approach in the future. ➤

(hopefully) and that the customer's complaint will be satisfactorily resolved. The key is speed; research shows that customers whose complaints are resolved quickly are far more likely to buy from the same company again than from those that take longer to resolve complaints.[39]

To make sure that they keep service failures to a minimum and that when they do blow it they can recover quickly, managers should first understand the service and the potential points at which failures are most likely to occur so they can plan how to recover ahead of time.[40] That's why it's so important to identify critical incidents. In addition, employees should be trained to listen for complaints and be empowered to take appropriate actions immediately. For example, Marriott allows employees to spend up to $2,500 to compensate guests for certain inconveniences.[41]

3

OBJECTIVE

Explain the marketing of people, places, and ideas.

(pp. 319–323)

The Future of Services

As we look into the future, we recognize that service industries will continue to play a key role in the growth of both the United States and the global economy. In fact, in recent years the accelerating impact of service as an integral part of any firm's value proposition has led some analysts to argue that there is now a **new dominant logic for marketing**. This means that we need to rethink our traditional distinction between services and goods. Instead, we need to recognize that a service is the central (core) deliverable in *every* exchange; any physical products involved are relatively minor in terms of their contribution to the value proposition.[42] Let's consider several important trends that will provide both opportunities and challenges for the marketers of services down the road (that means you). In the future, we can expect services we can't even imagine yet. Of course, they will also provide many new and exciting job opportunities for future marketers.

new dominant logic for marketing
A reconceptualization of traditional marketing to redefine service as the central (core) deliverable and the actual physical products purveyed as comparatively incidental to the value proposition.

- **Changing demographics:** As the population ages, service industries that meet the needs of older consumers will see dramatic growth. Companies that offer recreational opportunities, health care, and living assistance for seniors will be in demand.

- **Globalization:** The globalization of business will increase the need for logistics and distribution services to move goods around the world (we'll talk more about these in Chapter 15) and for accounting and legal services that facilitate these global exchanges. In addition, global deregulation will affect the delivery of services by banks, brokerages, insurance, and other financial service industries because globalization means greater competition. For example, many "medical tourists" now journey to countries like Thailand and India to obtain common surgical procedures that may cost less than half what they would in the United States. Meanwhile, hospitals back home often look more like luxury spas as

You love your pet. You want her to get the best care when she gets sick or hurt. With VPI Pet Insurance, you can be sure of it. As the nation's largest and oldest provider of health insurance for pets, VPI offers affordable coverage for emergency and major medical care, plus routine procedures like spaying/neutering and vaccinations. We even help cover prescriptions and lab fees. What's more, you can go to the veterinarian of your choice. Which leads us to the biggest benefit of all: peace of mind. For an instant quote, visit petinsurance.com or call 800-USA-PETS (800-872-7387).

The health insurance is

FOR HER

Many of the benefits are

FOR YOU

Enroll Today
it's Easy and Affordable
petinsurance.com
800-USA-PETS

VPI PET
insurance

Services such as health insurance for pets that were once unimaginable are now a very real—and fast-growing—part of our culture as companion pets increasingly become thought of as family members and veterinary care has become both more sophisticated and costly.

they offer amenities such as adjoining quarters for family members, choice of different ethnic cuisines, and in-room Internet access.[43] In the hotel industry, demand for luxury properties is growing around the world. Hyatt International is expanding aggressively in China with fourteen luxury properties either open or scheduled to open. Hyatt expects to have as many as 24 properties there within a decade.[44]

- **Technological advances:** Changing technology provides opportunities for growth and innovation in global service industries such as telecommunications, health care, banking, and Internet services. And we can also expect technological advances to provide opportunities for services that we haven't even thought of yet but that will dramatically change and improve the lives of consumers. Best Buy's Geek Squad makes the company a ton of money by showing people how to set up and use their home computers—with new advances there will always be "clueless" customers who need help to keep up with progress! Meanwhile, the Internet, and especially blogs, are now an important way to market all kinds of intangibles. In the U.S. presidential campaign of 2008, handlers for both parties' candidates invested heavily to support these "real-time" methods of communicating with tech-savvy voters about their candidate's ideas and position on the issues *du jour*.

- **Shift to flow of information:** In many ways, we have become an information society. The availability of, flow of, and access to information are critical to the success of organizations. These changes will provide greater opportunities for database services, artificial intelligence systems, communications systems, and other services that facilitate the storage and transfer of knowledge.

Marketing People, Places, and Ideas

By now, you understand that services are intangibles that marketers work hard to sell. But as we said earlier, services are not the only intangibles that organizations need to market. Intangibles such as people, places, and ideas often need to be "sold" by someone and "bought" by someone else. Let's consider how marketing is relevant to each of these.

Marketing People

As we saw in Chapter 1, people are products, too. If you don't believe that, you've never been on a job interview or spent a Saturday night in a singles bar! Many of us find it distasteful to equate people with products. In reality though, a sizable number of people hire personal image consultants to devise a marketing strategy for them, and others undergo plastic surgery, physical conditioning, or cosmetic makeovers to improve their "market position" or "sell" themselves to potential employers, friends, or lovers.[45] Let's briefly touch on a few prominent categories of people marketing.

Sophisticated consultants create and market politicians by "packaging" candidates (clients) who then compete for "market share" of votes. We trace this perspective all the way back to the 1952 and 1956 presidential campaigns of Dwight Eisenhower, when advertising executive Rosser Reeves repackaged the bland but amiable army general as he invented jingles and slogans such as "I like Ike" and contrived man-on-the-street interviews to improve the candidate's market position.[46] For better or worse, Reeves's strategies revolutionized the political landscape as people realized they could harness the tactics they use to sell soap to sell candidates for public office. Today, the basic idea remains the same, even though the techniques are more sophisticated.

In the age of electronic everything, marketing politics gets a little wackier. For example, comedian Stephen Colbert announced on his show that he was running for president in the 2008 election as "both a Democrat and a Republican." After his announcement, an on-line group was set up, and through links with social networking sites such as Facebook, he managed to acquire one million supporters! In fact, his fans' responses inspired the creation of the "1,000,000 Strong for Stephen T. Colbert" Facebook group, which modeled itself after a similarly-named group set up for Democratic candidate Barak Obama's campaign. It took more than eight months for Obama to gain 380,000 supporters, while it took less than two weeks for Colbert's group to become one of the largest political groups on Facebook.[47]

From actors and musicians to athletes and supermodels, the famous and near-famous jockey for market position in popular culture. Agents carefully package celebrities as they connive to get their clients exposure on TV, starring roles in movies, recording contracts, or product endorsements.[48] Like other products, celebrities even rename themselves to craft a "brand identity." They use the same strategies marketers use to ensure that their products make an impression on consumers, including memorability (Evel Knievel), suitability (fashion designer Oscar Renta reverted to his old family name of de la Renta because it sounded more elegant), and distinctiveness (Steveland Morris Hardaway became Stevie Wonder).

In addition to these branding efforts, there are other strategies marketers use to "sell" a celebrity as Figure 10.5 shows. These include the following:

1. The *pure selling approach*: An agent presents a client's qualifications to potential "buyers" until she finds one who is willing to act as an intermediary.

Superstar Beyoncé is one of the latest celebrities to extend her "brand identity" by branching out to other areas. In addition to her singing career, she has starred in films and is a spokeswoman for various products, including Pepsi and the Tommy Hilfiger perfume True.

Globe Photos, Inc.

Figure 10.5 | Strategies to Sell a Celebrity

There is more than one approach to selling an intangible—even a celebrity.

Marketing Approach	Implementation
Pure Selling Approach	*Agent presents a client* – to record companies – to movie studios – to TV production companies – to talk show hosts – to advertising agencies – to talent scouts
Product Improvement Approach	*Client is modified* – New name – New image – Voice lessons – Dancing lessons – Plastic surgery – New back-up band – New music genre
Market Fulfillment Approach	*Agent looks for market opening* – Identify unmet need – Develop a new product (band, singer) to the specifications of consumer wants

Many cities, states, and countries recognize that by using effective marketing strategies, they can increase vital tourism revenues and attract business investment needed for growth.

Many religious organizations use a variety of marketing strategies to grow their organizations.

2. The *product improvement approach*: An agent works with the client to modify certain characteristics that will increase her market value.

3. The *market fulfillment approach*: An agent scans the market to identify unmet needs. After identifying a need, the agent then finds a person or a group that meets a set of minimum qualifications and develops a new "product."

Marketing Places

Place marketing strategies regard a city, state, country, or other locale as a brand. Marketers use the marketing mix to create a suitable identity so that consumers choose this brand over competing destinations when they plan their travel. Because of the huge amount of money tourism generates, the competition to attract visitors is fierce. There are about 1,600 visitors' bureaus in the United States alone that try to brand their locations. In addition, almost every town or city has an economic development office charged with luring new businesses or residents. For example, after the 2001 attack on the World Trade Center, New York City unveiled a new tourism advertising campaign that November with the slogan "The New York Miracle: Be a Part of It." The campaign included six 30-second TV commercials and some of New York's biggest celebrities such as Woody Allen and Robert DeNiro.[49] Since then, NYC & Company, the city's official tourism marketer, reports that both the domestic and overseas visitor counts are returning to pre-9/11 levels.[50]

Marketing Ideas

You can see people. You can stand in a city. So how do you market something you can't see, smell, or feel? **Idea marketing** is about gaining market share for a concept, philosophy, belief, or issue. Even religious organizations market ideas about faith and desirable behavior when they adopt secular marketing techniques to attract young people. Some evangelists use the power of television to convey their messages. So-called *megachurches* are huge steel and glass structures, with acres of parking and slickly produced services complete with live bands and professional dancers that draw huge audiences. Some even offer aerobics, bowling alleys, and multimedia Bible classes inspired by MTV to attract "customers" turned off by traditional approaches to religion.[51]

Founders of the upscale ice cream maker Ben & Jerry's care deeply about global warming, an idea brought to the public forefront again by the 2006 release and subsequent wide distribution of Al Gore's documentary *An Inconvenient Truth*. In support of the overall cause-related marketing program, Ben & Jerry's launched Dave Matthews Band Magic Brownies (no, these are not Alice B. Toklas brownies), packaged in a container that makes it clear that Ben and Jerry's supports the band's efforts to combat global warming. They've also launched a Web site, found at **www.lickglobalwarming.com**, that provides energy conservation tips, and they ran a nationwide search for an "Enviro-Roadie" to go on tour with the band to mobilize the public into action for the cause.[52]

The marketing of ideas, however, can be even more difficult than marketing goods and services. Consumers often do not perceive that the *value* they receive when they wear seat belts or recycle garbage or designate a driver or even when they conserve to reduce global warming is worth the *cost*—the extra effort necessary to realize these goals. Governments and other organizations use marketing strategies, often with only limited success, to sell ideas that will save the lives of millions of unwilling consumers or that will save our planet.

place marketing
Marketing activities that seek to attract new businesses, residents, or visitors to a town, state, country, or some other site.

idea marketing
Marketing activities that seek to gain market share for a concept, philosophy, belief, or issue by using elements of the marketing mix to create or change a target market's attitude or behavior.

real people, **Real Choices**

Lara L.
Price

Lara chose:

Option

How it Worked out at the Philadelphia 76ers

Lara selected Option 1. The Sixers hired a web-based company that provided a data warehouse, and the vendor also developed software to help the Sixers track its customer base. The team realized a 150 to 1 return on its investment due to the money it saved in advertising spending (TV, print, and radio). In fact, one quick, targeted e-mail campaign based on the system paid for it due to the great response the organization received. The CRM approach has proven to be so successful that the company is in the process of developing more sophisticated systems. For example, when the systems are in place and you purchase an individual ticket to a family show at the Wachovia Center, you would automatically be sent an offer the next day for a Sixers Family Pack (or vice versa). If you purchased a ticket to the Celtics game, you would be sent an e-mail a week prior to the next Celtics game. If you purchased a 5-game plan and all the games had expired, you would receive a new e-mail or direct mail piece and an automated flag will appear on a salesperson's in-box to follow up with you.

How the Philadelphia 76ers Measure Success

The Sixers use metrics based upon the size of the team's new customer database and the percentage of e-mails the system sends that people open and click-through. For example, the CRM system allows Lara to easily utilize *A/B testing*, where she sends the same e-mail offer with different subject lines so that she can measure which subject lines yield a better response to the offer. Lara compares these percentages to industry standards to gauge the success of

her e-mail campaigns. Entertainment industry standards are close to 28 percent for open rates and 5 percent for click-through rates. Maximizing your *conversion rate* (i.e., ensuring that recipients actually open your marketing message) is the biggest challenge in e-mail marketing. Moving the needle just a few percentage points on this metric translates into thousands of dollars in revenue.

The 76ers' Sixth Man Club enrolls fans so the team's database can track them and provide offers to meet their needs.

Refer back to **page 299** for Lara's story ➥

Brand **YOU**!

Corporate life is not for everyone.

You can blaze a trail to success in many different ways. Learn about the myths and realities of the job market and how you can explore different options for your career including being a contract employee with flexible hours, a free agent with many clients and projects or even pursue your personal passion while you are working. Consider your options in Chapter 10 of the *Brand You* supplement.

1. Objective Summary (pp. 300–313)

Describe the characteristics of services and the ways marketers classify services.

Services are products that are intangible and that are exchanged directly from producer to customer without ownership rights. Generally, services are acts that accomplish some goal and may be directed either toward people or toward an object. Both consumer services and business-to-business services are important parts of the economy. Important service characteristics include the following: (1) intangibility (they cannot be seen, touched, or smelled), (2) perishability (they cannot be stored), (3) variability (they are never exactly the same from one time to the next), and (4) inseparability from the producer (most services are produced, sold, and consumed at the same time).

In reality, most products are a combination of goods and services. Some services are goods-dominant (i.e., tangible products are marketed with supporting services). Some are equipment- or facility-based (i.e., the creation of the service requires elaborate equipment or facilities). Other services are people-based (i.e., people are actually a part of the service marketed).

Like goods, services include both a core service, or the basic benefit received, and augmented services, including innovative features and convenience of service delivery. Banking and brokerages, computer software, music, travel, dating services, career services, distance learning, and medical care are among some of the services available on the Internet. Marketers know that both the social elements of the service encounter (i.e., the employee and the customer) and the physical evidence including the servicescape are important to a positive service experience.

Key Terms

intangibles, p. 300 (Figure 10.1, p. 306)

services, p. 302

intangibility, p. 303 (Figure 10.2, p. 307)

perishability, p. 304 (➡ Applying, p. 304)

capacity management, p. 304

variability, p. 304

inseparability, p. 305

service encounter, p. 305

disintermediation, p. 305

core service, 309 (➡ Applying, p. 309)

augmented services, 309 (➡ Applying, p. 309)

2. Objective Summary (pp. 313–319)

Appreciate the importance of service quality to marketers.

The customer's perception of service quality is related to prior expectations. Because services are intangible, evaluation of service quality is more difficult, and customers often look for cues to help them decide whether they have received satisfactory service. Marketers improve customers' perceptions of services by designing important search qualities, experience qualities, and credence qualities.

SERVQUAL is a multiple-item scale used to measure consumer perceptions of service quality across dimensions of tangibles, reliability, responsiveness, assurance, and empathy. Gap analysis measures the difference between customer expectations of service quality and what actually occurred. Using the critical incident technique, service firms can identify the specific contacts between customers and service providers that create dissatisfaction. When service quality does fail, marketers must understand the points at which failures occur and take fast action.

Key Terms

servicescape, p. 313

search engine optimization (SEO), p. 313

search qualities, p. 314 (Figure 10.3, p. 315)

experience qualities, p. 314

credence qualities, p. 314

SERVQUAL, p. 315

gap analysis, p. 316 (Figure 10.4, p. 316)

critical incident technique, p. 317

3. Objective Summary (pp. 319–323)

Explain the marketing of people, places, and ideas.

Managers follow the steps for marketing planning when marketing other intangibles as well. People, especially politicians and celebrities, are often packaged and promoted. Place marketing aims to create or change the market position of a particular locale, whether a city, state, country, resort, or institution. Idea marketing (gaining market share for a concept, philosophy, belief, or issue) seeks to create or change a target market's attitude or behavior. Marketing is used by religious organizations and to promote important causes. Marketing of ideas may be especially difficult, as consumers may not consider the value to be worth the cost.

Key Terms

new dominant logic for marketing, p. 319

place marketing, p. 322

idea marketing, p. 322

Chapter **Questions** and **Activities**

Concepts: Test Your Knowledge

1. What are intangibles? How do basic marketing concepts apply to the marketing of intangibles?
2. What is a service? What are the important characteristics of services that make them different from goods?
3. What is the service continuum? What are goods-dominated services, equipment- or facility-based services, and people-based services?
4. What are core and augmented services? How do marketers increase market share with augmented services?
5. What are the physical and social elements of the service encounter?
6. Describe how the Internet is used to market services.
7. What dimensions do consumers and business customers use to evaluate service quality? How do marketers measure service quality?
8. How should marketers respond to failures in service quality?
9. What is the so-called "new dominant logic for marketing"? Why is it especially relevant to someone just starting a career in business (either in marketing or otherwise)?
10. What do we mean by marketing people? Marketing places? Marketing ideas?

Choices and Ethical Issues: You Decide

1. Why are first impressions we form about a service through the Internet so important? What can a service firm do to ensure a favorable first impression on-line? (*Hint:* Consider issues beyond the Web site itself.)
2. Sometimes service quality may not meet customers' expectations. What problems have you experienced with quality in the delivery of the following services?
   a. A restaurant meal
   b. An airline flight
   c. Automobile repairs
   d. Your college education
   What do you think is the reason for the poor quality?
3. Internet dating services, while becoming very popular, may present some dangers for those who use their services. Who do you think uses Internet dating services? What, if anything, should dating services do to protect their clients?
4. What "service" do providers such as MySpace convey? What core and augmented services do they offer? How should we evaluate MySpace's service quality?
5. There has been a lot of criticism about the way politicians have been marketed in recent years. What are some of the ways marketing has helped our political process? What are some ways the marketing of politicians might have an adverse effect on our government?
6. Many not-for-profit and religious organizations have found that they can be more successful by marketing their ideas. What are some ways that these organizations market themselves that are similar to and different from the marketing by for-profit businesses? Is it *ethical* for churches and religious organizations to spend money on marketing? Why or why not?

7. In the chapter we learned of Ben & Jerry's promotion of the cause against global warming. Is there a danger that cause-related marketing might turn some potential customers off to a firm's core product? Evaluate the pros and cons of cause-related marketing by for-profit organizations.
8. Many developed countries, including the United States, have in recent decades become primarily service economies; that is, there is relatively little manufacturing of goods, and most people in the economy are employed by service industries. Why do you think this has occurred? In what ways is this trend a good and/or a bad thing for a country? Do you think this trend will continue?

Practice: Apply What You've Learned

1. Because of increased competition in its community, you have been hired as a marketing consultant by a local bank. You know that the characteristics of services (intangibility, perishability, variability, and inseparability) create unique marketing challenges. You also know that these challenges can be met with creative marketing strategies. Outline the challenges for marketing the bank created by each of the four characteristics of services. List your ideas for what might be done to meet each of these challenges.
2. Assume that you are a physician. You are opening a new family practice clinic in your community. You feel that you have the best chance of being successful if you can create a product that is superior to that offered by competing businesses. Put together a list of ways in which you can augment the basic service offering to develop a better product. List the advantages and disadvantages of each.
3. You are currently a customer for a college education, a very expensive service product. You know that a service organization can create a competitive advantage by focusing on how the service is delivered after it has been purchased—making sure the service is efficiently and comfortably delivered to the customer. Develop a list of recommendations for your school for improving the delivery of its service. Consider both classroom and nonclassroom aspects of the educational product.
4. Assume that you work for a marketing firm that has been asked to develop a marketing plan for an up-and-coming rock band called Stalagmite and its new CD "Slow Drip." Prepare an outline for your marketing plan. First, list the special problems and challenges associated with marketing people rather than a physical product. Then outline your ideas for product, price, and promotion strategies.
5. Address the same issues in question #4 for a marketing plan for your hometown.
6. Assume that you have been recently hired by your city government to head up a program to create 100 percent compliance with recycling regulations. Develop a presentation for the city council in which you will outline the problems in "selling" recycling. Develop an outline for the presentation. Be sure to focus on each of the *Four Ps.*

Miniproject: Learn by Doing

1. Select a service that you, as a consumer, will purchase in the next week or so.
2. As you experience the service, record the details of every aspect, including the following:
   a. People
   b. Physical facilities
   c. Location
   d. Waiting time
   e. Hours
   f. Transaction
   g. Other customers
   h. Tangible aspects
   i. Search qualities
   j. Credence qualities
3. Recommend improvements for this service encounter.

Real people, **real surfers**: explore the web

Theme and entertainment parks like Universal Studios fall in the middle of the goods/services continuum—half goods and half services. To be successful in this highly competitive market, these parks must carefully develop targeting and positioning strategies. Visit the Web sites of the four top theme park organizations: Walt Disney World (**www.disneyworld.com**), Six Flags parks (**www.sixflags.com**), Universal's Orlando® Theme Park (**www.universalstudios.com**), and Busch Gardens (**www.buschgardens.com**). Thoroughly investigate each site.

1. How is the Web site designed to appeal to each theme park organization's target market?
2. How does each park position its product? How is this positioning communicated through the Web site?
3. What changes or improvements would you recommend for each Web site?

Marketing Plan Exercise

Organizations that market services face special challenges because services are intangible. One way they address the challenges created by intangibility is by designing an effective *servicescape*—that is, the environment in which the service is delivered and in which the firm and the customer interact.

1. Select a service that you are familiar with, such as a bank, an airline, or even your university.
2. Describe the weaknesses that might be in a SWOT analysis for the business that occur because of the intangibility of the service.
3. Develop strategies for creating a servicescape that will be a positive influence on customers' purchase decision, their evaluations of the service quality, and their ultimate satisfaction with the service.

Marketing in Action Case

Real **Choices** at **Clear & SIMPLE™**

Want to know how to fit your very complicated life into your very small apartment? How to organize your clothes so you can find that great pink sweater on Friday night? What to do with those very valuable high school football trophies? Like many people, you may be faced with a seemingly insurmountable problem of clutter.

As evidenced by the increasing popularity of TV programs like *Clean Sweep* (TLC), *Clean House* (Style Network), and *Mission: Organization* (HGTV), many consumers recognize that they suffer from home chaos. For some of us, the clutter comes from excessive buying or an attachment to things, while for others the problem is simply a lack of organizational skills. A disorganized home or office not only lowers our efficiency but also create stress and interrupts the harmony of the space. Fortunately, there is help.

Clear & SIMPLE™, founded in 1999, is one of a number of professional organizing companies that meets the growing need for home and office organization skills. Because many of us seem to be missing a gene for good organizational skills, professional organizers like Clear & SIMPLE™ help clients to build a harmonized life and restore order to their homes and workplaces.

Clear & SIMPLE™ owners Marla Dee and Lisa Parsons try to convince home owners and businesses that "Getting Organized can be Fun, Simple, and Freeing!" The company offers clutter-afflicted consumers a variety of services. Their two major systems, SEE IT • MAP IT • DO IT and S.T.A.C.K.S.™ aim to train clients how to identity their problems with clutter and chaos and then show them how to better organize their space.

Most of the objects we accumulate relate to our memories; we're afraid to throw away and/or give away these things because it means losing part of our past. Thus, a major part of the training is learning how to separate meaningful things that are also useful from those that no longer are very meaningful. In addition to its training programs, Clear & SIMPLE™ products include workshops, individual consultation and needs assessment, plus a variety of organizational skills books, kits, and self-study courses. Clear & SIMPLE™ also introduced a certificate program to train more professional organizers to meet the growing demand in the market.

Despite its current success, Clear & SIMPLE™ faces a number of challenges. The increasing number of competitors in the industry and the growing number of Internet Web sites on delivering organizing skills can have a direct impact on Clear & SIMPLE's™ future success. While we wouldn't classify Clear & SIMPLE™ as a luxury product, consumers may question if help in organizing their space is a necessary expense in times of economic recession. How can Clear & SIMPLE™ build on its current success for a sustainable future that will endure economic ups and downs? Even more important, what should Marla and her colleagues do to make their brand stand out among their other "neat" competitors?

You Make the Call

1. What is the decision facing Clear & SIMPLE™?
2. What factors are important in understanding this decision situation?
3. What are the alternatives?
4. What decision(s) do you recommend?
5. What are some ways to implement your recommendation?

Based on: Russell W. Belk, Joon Yong Seo, and Eric Li, "Dirty Little Secret: Home Chaos and Professional Organizers," *Consumption, Markets and Culture*, Volume 10, Number 2, June 2007, pp. 133–40; Clear & SIMPLE™ Official Website, "About Us," Clear & SIMPLE™ Official Website (Website: **http://www.clearsimple.com/aboutus.html**).

Price the Product

Danielle **Blugrind**
Profile ▼

A Former Decision Maker at Taco Bell

Danielle Blugrind was Director of Consumer and Brand Insights for Taco Bell Corporation. After she received her BA from the University of California, Irvine, in 1989, she earned an MBA in marketing at Claremont Graduate School. Her first job out of the MBA program was as an analyst in the Consumer Research department of Mattel Toys. At first, she worked on research for sports toys, activity toys, and action figures. Then she was promoted to senior analyst working on the Barbie brand, and she spent the next six years on Barbie for girls and Barbie Collectibles before working her way up to senior manager. At Taco Bell, Danielle oversaw all research related to overall brand and advertising strategy, value products, late night, beverages, promotions, and combos. She left the company in 2008 to open her own consulting practice.

▼ Q & A with Danielle Blugrind

Q) What I do when I'm not working?
A) I'm a mom to a wonderful daughter! And I can't get enough of reading.

Q) Career high?
A) Every day is a new one! There is always something to look forward to.

Q) Business book I'm reading now?
A) *The Sweet Spot* by Lisa Fortini Campbell.

Q) Don't do this when interviewing with me?
A) Never act nervous! Don't try to sell me on what a big Taco Bell fan you are. And don't try to tell me you don't have a single question about the job or the company.

Q) My management style?
A) Too hands-on, at times! Let's say it is evolving into a better demonstration of my belief in people and their abilities.

Q) My motto to live by?
A) There is always a bright side.

Decision Time **at Taco Bell**

Back in the 1990s, Taco Bell realized that a major barrier to broadening its reach and sales was the fact that many consumers found its food too expensive. To combat this problem, the company developed a 59–79–99¢ Value Menu. Taco Bell's sales shot through the roof as consumers responded positively to the price-based approach. However, after several years, the competition began to offer similar alternatives (such as the McDonald's Value Meals), so Taco Bell no longer "owned" a value position in the industry as it had in the mid-1990s. In response, the company tried to refocus its strategy and move away from a value emphasis—a decision that wound up hurting the company.

Fast-forward to the year 2000. Taco Bell knew that value was here to stay in the fast-food industry, but it had abandoned its 59–79–99¢ menu and needed a new direction. The firm test-marketed several value menus and ideas, but nothing really generated a much-needed boost in sales. Danielle and her colleagues were forced to step back and think hard about what value means to their customers and how the chain could deliver the food people wanted at the price they wanted. Danielle knew that as competitors began to claim they were providing greater value, Taco Bell needed to break through the cluttered value landscape that is fast food and "think outside the bun."

The company looked at numerous alternatives, including new products, new ways to price its menu, and new product combinations. A pricing strategy began to take shape. Many of Taco Bell's competitors continued to focus on the $.99 price point, which is virtually synonymous with value in the fast-food world. Although it was tempting for Taco Bell to follow suit by adding items to the menu for $.99, most of the company's products could not feasibly be offered at such a low price. And Taco Bell wanted to show that it was different from other fast-food restaurants—this wouldn't happen if it used the same pricing strategy as everyone else.

Danielle and her team began to test other pricing options, including the idea of pricing all menu items the same. She knew from other research that the "value threshold" for Taco Bell's menu items was $1.29; this represents the highest possible price that consumers might still consider to be a value for some items. In total, the company tested eight different price configurations that it determined would make financial sense; these

> **Things to remember:**
>
> Danelle knew that Taco Bell couldn't afford to get into a price war with its fast food competitors. The major chains had already responded to the company's value prices by offering their own versions so she needed to do something else to grab the attention of hungry, but price-conscious, customers.

included four options in which each menu item was priced the same and would cost $.99, $1.09, $1.19, or $1.29 as well as four other mixed price options. These are the eight combinations they tested:

	$.99 Menu	$1.09 Menu	$1.19 Menu	$1.29 Menu	Mixed Price #1	Mixed Price #2	Mixed Price #3	Mixed Price #4
Burrito #1	$.99	$1.09	$1.19	$1.29	$1.29	$1.29	$ .99	$1.29
Burrito #2	$.99	$1.09	$1.19	$1.29	$1.19	$1.19	$1.29	$1.29
Burrito #3	$.99	$1.09	$1.19	$1.29	$1.29	$1.29	$1.29	$1.29
Taco #1	$.99	$1.09	$1.19	$1.29	$.99	$1.09	$.99	$.99
Taco #2	$.99	$1.09	$1.19	$1.29	$.99	$.99	$.99	$.99
Nachos	$.99	$1.09	$1.19	$1.29	$.99	$.99	$1.19	$.99
Specialty item	$.99	$1.09	$1.19	$1.29	$1.19	$1.19	$1.29	$1.29

Danielle considered her **Options** 1·2·3

Based on the results from the concept testing of the eight different menus, Danielle identified three possible ways to proceed:

1 **Option** **Price the entire menu at $1.29.** This would make things simple for the company, and it would be easy for consumers to understand. This option would also offer the most potential profit per item. But the challenge would be to convince people that these $1.29 items were *all* truly a "value" in a world where competitors offered many items for $.99. This problem surfaced in Taco Bell's research; consumers rated the $1.29 menu the lowest of the eight menus it tested.

2 **Option** **Price items at $.99 and $1.29 (Mixed Price Menu #4).** Purchase intent and overall liking were much stronger than for the $1.29 menu. The pricing structure was still pretty simple since any item would cost either $.99 or $1.29. Not surprisingly, though, consumers didn't rate a menu that included some $1.29 items as high as one that included only $.99 items.

3 **Option** **Price items at $.99, $1.19, and $1.29 (Mixed Price Menu #1).** Danielle's research showed that purchase intent, overall liking, and ratings of uniqueness were all strong for this menu. On the downside, the pricing structure was more complex. If customers were to accept it, they would have to be made to understand why there are three price points on a value menu and why certain items cost more than others.

Now, put yourself in Danielle's shoes: Which option would you choose, and why?

You Choose

Which **Option** would you choose, and **why**?
1. ☐YES ☐NO 2. ☐YES ☐NO 3. ☐YES ☐NO

See what **option** Danielle chose and its success on **page 359** ➡

1

"Yes, but What Does It Cost?" How Marketers Price What They Sell

As Danielle Blugrind discovered, the question of what to charge for a product is a central part of marketing decision making. In this chapter, we'll tackle the basic question—what is price? We'll also see how marketers begin to determine pricing strategies when they develop pricing objectives and we'll look at the roles demand, costs, revenues, and the environment play in the pricing decision process. Then we'll explore how the pricing decision process leads to specific pricing strategies and tactics. Next, we'll look at the dynamic world of pricing on the Internet and at some psychological, legal, and ethical aspects of pricing.

"If you have to ask how much it is, you can't afford it!" We've all heard that, but how often do you buy something without asking the price? If price weren't an issue, we'd all drive dream cars, take trips to exotic places, and live like royalty. In the real world, though, most of us need to at least consider a product's price before we buy it.

As we said in Chapter 1, **price** is the assignment of value, or the amount the consumer must exchange to receive the offering or product. Payment may be in the form of money, goods, services, favors, votes, or anything else that has *value* to the other party. As we also explained in Chapter 1, marketing is the process that creates exchanges of things of value. We usually think of this exchange as people trading money for a good or a service. But in some marketplace practices, price can mean exchanges of nonmonetary value as well. Long before societies minted coins, people exchanged one good or service for another. This practice still occurs today. For example, someone who owns a home at a mountain ski resort may exchange a weekend stay for car repair or dental work. No money changes hands, but there still is an exchange of value (just ask the IRS).

Other nonmonetary costs often are important to marketers. What is the cost of wearing seat belts? What is it worth to people to camp out in a clean national park? It is also important to consider an *opportunity cost*, or the value of something we give up to obtain something else. For example, the cost of going to college includes more than tuition—it also includes the income that the student could have earned by working instead of going to classes (no, we're not trying to make you feel guilty). And what about a public service campaign designed to reduce alcohol-related accidents? The cost to the individual is either agreeing to abstain and be a designated driver or shell out for taxi fare. The value is reducing the risk of having a serious or possibly fatal accident. Unfortunately, too many people feel the chance of having an accident is so slim that the cost of abstaining from drinking is too high.

How important are good pricing decisions? Even during the best of economic times, most consumers rank "reasonable price"—a price that makes the product affordable and that appears to be fair—as the most important consideration in a purchase and one that counts the most when they decide where to shop.[1] The plight of U.S. airlines is a good example of how bad pricing decisions can hurt an entire industry. From about 1982 to

1992, the airline industry engaged in a fierce price war, lowering the per-mile fare nearly 25 percent (accounting for inflation of the dollar) while costs such as labor and fuel more than doubled.[2] As a result, from 1990 to 1992, the airlines lost over $10 billion—more than they had earned since the start of commercial air travel. Of course, things haven't gotten much better for airlines today. In 2005, the U.S. airline industry lost $10.8 billion, adding to the $36 billion in losses suffered between 2001 and 2004. Then, in the latter part of 2007, after a period of profitability, rising fuel prices caused most airlines to again lose millions.[3] As Figure 11.1 shows, there are six steps in price planning. In this chapter we will talk about how marketers go through these steps for successful price planning.

A message from the Reader's Digest Foundation   MADD, Mothers Against Drunk Driving

Selling sobriety behind the wheel: Sometimes intangible costs are too high.

2

OBJECTIVE

Understand the pricing objectives that marketers typically set when they plan pricing strategies.

(pp. 331–333)

Step 1: Develop Pricing Objectives

The first crucial step in price planning is to develop pricing objectives. These must support the broader objectives of the firm, such as maximizing shareholder value, as well as its overall marketing objectives, such as increasing market share. Table 11.1 provides examples of different types of pricing objectives. Let's take a closer look at these.

Sales or Market Share Objectives

Often the objective of a pricing strategy is to maximize sales (either in dollars or in units) or to increase market share. Does setting a price intended to increase unit sales or market share, one that focuses on sales objectives, simply mean pricing the product lower than the competition? Sometimes this is the case. Providers of cellular phone services such as Verizon, Sprint/Nextel, AT&T/Cingular, or T-Mobile relentlessly offer consumers better deals that include more minutes for a standard fee, free nighttime and weekend minutes, rollover minutes, and low or no-cost phones to keep them ahead in the "mobile wars." Service providers pay for numerous television and radio commercials to promote these changes. But lowering prices is not always necessary to increase market share. If a company's product has a competitive advantage, keeping the price at the same level as other firms may satisfy sales objectives.

price
The assignment of value, or the amount the consumer must exchange to receive the offering.

Figure 11.1 | Steps in Price Planning

Successful price planning includes a series of orderly steps beginning with setting pricing objectives.

1. Develop Pricing Objectives
2. Estimate Demand
3. Determine Costs
4. Evaluate the Pricing Environment
5. Choose a Pricing Strategy
6. Develop Pricing Tactics

Profit Objectives

As we discussed in Chapter 2, often a firm's overall objectives relate to a certain level of profit it hopes to realize. When pricing strategies are determined by profit objectives, the focus is on a target level of profit growth or a desired net profit margin. A profit objective is important to firms that believe profit is what motivates shareholders and bankers to invest in a company.

Although profits are an important consideration in the pricing of all goods and services, they are critical when the product is a *fad*. Fad products, from pet rocks to Beanie Babies, have a short market life, making a profit objective essential to allow the firm to recover its investment in a short time. In such cases, the firm must harvest profits before customers lose interest and move on to the next pet rock or hula hoop. Think about the Teen Buzz fad (aka Mosquito Ringtone) for example. This high-pitched, annoying tone that only younger people can detect (before their hearing deteriorates as they reach middle age) was originally intended to keep them from loitering near convenience stores in the United Kingdom. Kids adapted this weapon to their own advantage; they use the Teen Buzz in classrooms to alert them to incoming text messages on their mobile phones without their (old and decrepit) teachers' knowledge.[4] A company

	Table 11.1	Pricing Objectives

Type of Objective	Example
Sales or market share	Institute pricing strategy changes to support a 5 percent increase in sales.
Profit	During the first six months, set a price to yield a target profit of $200,000.
	or
	Set prices to allow for an 8 percent profit margin on all goods sold.
Competitive effect	Alter pricing strategy during first quarter of the year to increase sales during competitor's introduction of a new product.
	or
	Maintain low-end pricing policies to discourage new competitors from entering the market.
Customer satisfaction	Simplify pricing structure to simplify decision process for customers.
	or
	Alter price levels to match customer expectations.
Image enhancement	Alter pricing policies to reflect the increased emphasis on the product's quality image.

prestige products
Products that have a high price and that appeal to status-conscious consumers.

that hawks a tone like this has to move quickly to unload its "inventory" before the next cool idea replaces it.

Competitive Effect Objectives

Competitive effect objectives mean that the pricing plan is intended to have a certain effect on the competition's marketing efforts. Sometimes a firm may deliberately try to preempt or reduce the effectiveness of one or more competitors. That's what happened when new low-fare airline JetBlue entered Delta's hub Atlanta market with flights from Atlanta to Los Angeles. Delta slashed its fares in response, forcing JetBlue to abandon the Atlanta market.[5] Southwest Airlines has now entered the Denver market—you can bet United isn't happy about that!

Customer Satisfaction Objectives

Many quality-focused firms believe that profits result from making customer satisfaction the primary objective. These firms believe that if it focuses solely on short-term profits, a company loses sight of keeping customers for the long term. Recognizing that many people hate to buy new cars because they feel the dealers are untrustworthy hucksters, Saturn started a trend with its value pricing strategy, in which customers get one price and one price only—no haggling, no negotiation, and no "deals." Customers can even go to Saturn's Web site to get detailed price information without needing a salesperson. This objective is not only satisfying customers but also is generating a new breed of car salespeople who use low-pressure sales tactics and promise customer satisfaction and long-term service.

Image Enhancement Objectives

Consumers often use price to make inferences about the quality of a product. In fact, marketers know that price is often an important means of communicating not only quality but also image to prospective customers. The image enhancement function of pricing is particularly important with **prestige products** (or luxury products) that have a high price and appeal to status-conscious consumers. Most of us would agree that the high price tag on a Rolex watch, a Louis Vuitton handbag, or a Rolls-Royce car,

Burger King hopes to increase market share by aggressively pricing its new sandwich.

although representing the higher costs of producing the product, is vital to shaping an image of an extraordinary product that only the wealthy can afford.

People often are willing to pay a premium price for a luxury product like a watch because they believe (rightly or wrongly) that it makes a statement about their own worth.

3

OBJECTIVE

Describe how marketers use costs, demands, and revenue to make pricing decisions.
(pp. 333–342)

Step 2: Estimate Demand

The second step in price planning is to estimate demand. *Demand* refers to customers' desires for a product: How much of a product are they willing to buy as the price of the product goes up or down? Obviously, marketers should know the answer to this question before setting prices. Therefore, one of the earliest steps marketers take in price planning is to estimate demand for their products.

Demand Curves

Economists use a graph that represents a *demand curve* to illustrate the effect of price on the quantity demanded of a product. The demand curve, which can be a curved or straight line, shows the quantity of a product that customers will buy in a market during a period of time at various prices if all other factors remain the same.

Figure 11.2 shows demand curves for normal and prestige products. The vertical axis for the demand curve represents the different prices that a firm might charge for a product (P). The horizontal axis shows the number of units or quantity (Q) of the product demanded. The demand curve for most goods (that we show on the left side of Figure 11.2) slopes downward and to the right. As the price of the product goes up (P_1 to P_2), the number of units that customers are willing to buy goes down (Q_1 to Q_2). If prices decrease, customers will buy more. This is the *law of demand*. For example, if the price of bananas goes up, customers will probably buy fewer of them. And if the price gets really high, customers will eat their cereal without bananas.

There are, however, exceptions to this typical price–quantity relationship. In fact, there are situations in which (otherwise sane) people desire a product more as it *increases* in price. For prestige products such as luxury cars or jewelry, price hike may actually result in an *increase* in the quantity consumers demand because they see the product as more valuable. In such

Danielle
Blugrind

APPLYING Demand Curves

Danielle knew that $1.29 was a value threshold for her customers; if Taco Bell charged more than this amount for some items demand would drop off. ➡

Figure 11.2 | Demand Curves for Normal and Prestige Products

There is an inverse relationship between price and demand for normal products. For prestige products, demand will increase—to a point—as price increases or will decrease as price decreases.

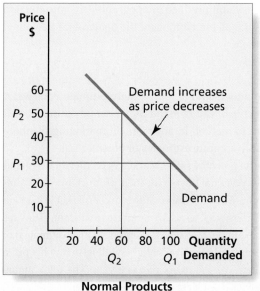

Normal Products

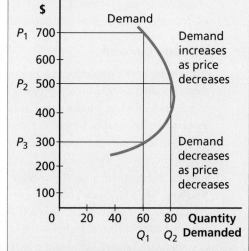

Prestige Products

Figure 11.3 | Shift in Demand Curve

Changes in the environment or in company efforts can cause a shift in the demand curve. A great advertising campaign, for example, can shift the demand curve upward.

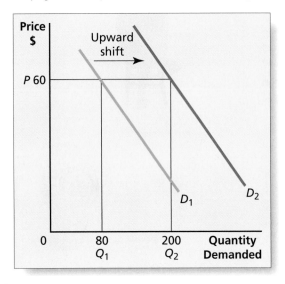

cases, the demand curve slopes upward. The right-hand side of Figure 11.2 shows the "backward-bending" demand curve we associate with prestige products. If the price decreases, consumers perceive the product to be less desirable, and demand may decrease. This is what happens when the price goes from P_2 to P_3; quantity decreases from Q_2 to Q_1. Still, the higher-price/higher-demand relationship has its limits. If the firm increases the price too much, (say from P_2 to P_1) making the product unaffordable for all but a few buyers, demand will begin to decrease. The direction the backward-bending curve takes shows this.

Shifts in Demand

The demand curves we've shown assume that all factors other than price stay the same. But what if they don't? What if the company improves the product? What happens when there is a glitzy new advertising campaign that turns a product into a "must-have" for a lot of people? What if stealthy *paparazzi* catch Brad Pitt using the product at home? Any of these things could cause an *upward shift* of the demand curve. An upward shift in the demand curve means that at any given price, demand is greater than before the shift occurs. And the demand shift would no doubt be even more precipitous if toddler Shiloh Nouvel Jolie-Pitt were also to make an appearance in the pic!

Figure 11.3 shows the upward shift of the demand curve as it moves from D_1 to D_2. At D_1, before the shift occurs, customers will be willing to purchase the quantity Q_1 (or 80 units in Figure 11.3) at the given price, P (or $60 in Figure 11.3). For example, customers at a particular store may buy 80 barbecue grills at $60 a grill. But then the store runs a huge advertising campaign, featuring Queen Latifah on her patio using the barbecue grill. The demand curve shifts from D_1 to D_2. (The store keeps the price at $60.) Take a look at how the quantity demanded has changed to Q_2. In our example, the store is now selling 200 barbecue grills at $60 per grill. From a marketing standpoint, this shift is the best of all worlds. Without lowering prices, the company can sell more of its product. As a result, total revenues go up and so do profits, unless of course the new promotion costs as much as those potential additional profits.

Demand curves may also shift downward. That's what happens, for example, when there is a beef recall. Sales of beef decline at any given price as risk-averse consumers seek out alternative meats.

In the real world, factors other than the price and marketing activities influence demand. If it rains, the demand for umbrellas increases and the demand for tee times on a golf course is a wash. The development of new products may influence demand for old ones. Even though a precious few firms may still produce phonographs, the introduction of cassette tapes, and then CDs and iPods has all but eliminated the demand for new vinyl records and turntables on which to play them.

Estimate Demand

It's extremely important for marketers to understand and accurately estimate demand. A firm's production scheduling is based on anticipated demand that must be estimated well in advance of when products are brought to market. In addition, all marketing planning and budgeting must be based on reasonably accurate estimates of potential sales.

So how do marketers reasonably estimate potential sales? Marketers predict total demand first by identifying the number of buyers or potential buyers for their product and then multiplying that estimate times the average amount each member of the target market is likely to purchase. Table 11.2 shows how a small business, such as a start-up pizza restaurant, estimates demand in markets it expects to reach. For example, the pizza entrepreneur may estimate that there are 180,000 consumer households in his market who would be willing to buy his pizza and that each household would purchase an average of six pizzas a year. The total annual demand is 1,080,000 pizzas (hold the anchovies on at least one of those, please).

Table 11.2 | Estimating Demand for Pizza

Number of families in market	180,000
Average number of pizzas per family per year	6
Total annual market demand	1,080,000
Company's predicted share of the total market	3%
Estimated annual company demand	32,400 pizzas
Estimated monthly company demand	2,700
Estimated weekly company demand	675

Once the marketer estimates total demand, the next step is to predict what the company's market share is likely to be. The company's estimated demand is then its share of the whole (estimated) pie. In our pizza example, the entrepreneur may feel that he can gain 3 percent of this market, or about 2,700 pizzas per month—not bad for a new start-up business. Of course, such projections need to take into consideration other factors that might affect demand, such as new competitors entering the market, the state of the economy, and changing consumer tastes like a sudden demand for low-carb take-out food.

Price Elasticity of Demand

In addition to understanding the relationship between price and demand, marketers also need to know how sensitive customers are to changes in price. In particular, it is critical to understand whether a change in price will have a large or a small impact on demand. How much can a firm increase or decrease its price before seeing a marked change in sales? If the price of a pizza goes up one dollar, will people switch to subs and burgers? What would happen if the pizza went up two dollars? Or even five dollars?

Price elasticity of demand is a measure of the sensitivity of customers to changes in price: If the price changes by 10 percent, what will be the percentage change in demand for the product? The word *elasticity* indicates that changes in price usually cause demand to stretch or retract like a rubber band. We calculate price elasticity of demand as follows:

price elasticity of demand
The percentage change in unit sales that results from a percentage change in price.

$$\text{Price elasticity of demand} = \frac{\text{percentage change in quantity demanded}}{\text{percentage change in price}}$$

Sometimes customers are very sensitive to changes in prices and a change in price results in a substantial change in the quantity they demand. In such instances, we have a case of **elastic demand**. In other situations, a change in price has little or no effect on the quantity consumers are willing to buy. We describe this as **inelastic demand**.

Let's use the formula in this example: Suppose the pizza maker finds (from experience or from marketing research) that lowering the price of his pizza 10 percent (from $10 per pizza to $9) will cause a 15 percent increase in demand. He would calculate the price elasticity of demand as 15 divided by 10. The price elasticity of demand would be 1.5. If the price elasticity of demand is greater than one, demand is elastic; that is, consumers respond to the price decrease by demanding more. Or, if the price increases, consumers will demand less. Figure 11.4 shows these calculations.

As Figure 11.5 illustrates, when demand is elastic, changes in price and in total revenues (total sales) work in opposite directions. If the price is increased, revenues decrease. If the price is decreased, total revenues increase. With elastic demand, the demand curve shown in Figure 11.5 is more horizontal. With an elasticity of demand of 1.5, a decrease in price will increase the pizza maker's total sales.

We saw earlier that in some instances demand is *inelastic* so that a change in price results in little or no change in demand. For example, if the 10 percent decrease in the price of pizza resulted in only a 5 percent increase in pizza sales, then the price elasticity of

elastic demand
Demand in which changes in price have large effects on the amount demanded.

inelastic demand
Demand in which changes in price have little or no effect on the amount demanded.

Figure 11.4 │ Price Elasticity of Demand

Elastic demand

Price changes from $10 to $9.

$10 – 9 = $1

1/10 = 10% change in price

Demand changes from 2,700 per month to 3,100 per month

$$
\begin{array}{r}
3,100 \\
- 2,700 \\
\hline
\end{array}
$$

Increase   400 pizzas

Percentage increase   400/2,700 = .148 ~ 15% change in demand

$$
\text{Price elasticity of demand} = \frac{\text{percentage change in quantity demanded}}{\text{percentage change in price}}
$$

$$
\text{Price elasticity of demand} = \frac{15\%}{10\%} = 1.5
$$

Inelastic demand

Price changes from $10 to $9.

$10 – 9 = $1

1/10 = 10% change in price

Demand changes from 2,700 per month to 2,835 per month

$$
\begin{array}{r}
2,835 \\
- 2,700 \\
\hline
\end{array}
$$

Increase   135 pizzas

Percentage increase   135/2,700 = 0.05 ~ 5% change in demand

$$
\text{Price elasticity of demand} = \frac{\text{percentage change in quantity demanded}}{\text{percentage change in price}}
$$

$$
\text{Price elasticity of demand} = \frac{5\%}{10\%} = 0.5
$$

Figure 11.5 │ Price Elastic and Inelastic Demand Curves

Price elasticity of demand represents how demand responds to changes in prices. If there is little change in demand, then demand is said to be price inelastic. If there is a large change in demand, demand is price elastic.

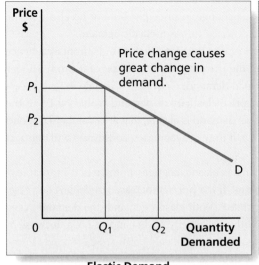

Elastic Demand

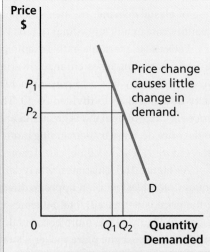

Inelastic Demand

demand calculated would be 5 divided by 10, which is 0.5 (less than one), and our pizza maker faces inelastic demand. When demand is inelastic, price and revenue changes are in the same direction; that is, increases in price result in increases in total revenue, while decreases in price result in decreases in total revenue. With inelastic demand, the demand curve in Figure 11.5 becomes more vertical. Generally, the demand for necessities, such as food and electricity, is inelastic. Even large price increases do not cause us to buy less food or to give up our lights and hot water (though we may take fewer bubble baths).

If demand is price inelastic, can marketers keep raising prices so that revenues and profits will grow larger and larger? And what if demand is elastic? Does it mean that marketers can never raise prices? The answer to these questions is no (surprise!). Elasticity of demand for a product often differs for different price levels and with different percentages of change.

As a general rule, pizza makers and other companies can determine the *actual* price elasticity only after they have tested a pricing decision and calculated the resulting demand (as Taco Bell did with its value menu). Only then will they know whether a specific price change will increase or decrease revenues.

To estimate what demand is likely to be at different prices for new or existing products, marketers often do research. One approach is to conduct a study in which consumers tell marketers how much of a product they would be willing to buy at different prices. For example, researchers might ask participants if they would download fewer iTunes songs if the price per track goes from $.99 to $1.50 or how many bags of their favorite chocolate chip cookies they would buy at $3, $4, or $5. At other times, researchers conduct *field studies* in which they vary the price of a product in different stores and measure how much is actually purchased at the different price levels.

Other factors can affect price elasticity and sales. Consider the availability of *substitute* goods or services. If a product has a close substitute, its demand will be elastic; that is, a change in price will result in a change in demand, as consumers move to buy the substitute product. For example, all but the most die-hard cola fans might consider Coke and Pepsi close substitutes. If the price of Pepsi goes up, many people will buy Coke instead. Marketers of products with close substitutes are less likely to compete on price, recognizing that doing so could result in less profit as consumers switch from one brand to another. And many consumers find that the cost of mobile phone service is so reasonable that they give up their land lines to have totally cellular households.

Changes in prices of other products also affect the demand for an item, a phenomenon called **cross-elasticity of demand**. When products are substitutes for each other, an increase in the price of one will increase the demand for the other. For example, if the price of bananas goes up, consumers may instead buy more strawberries, blueberries, or apples. However, when products are *complements*—that is, when one product is essential to the use of a second—an increase in the price of one decreases the demand for the second. For example, if the price of gasoline goes up, consumers may drive less, carpool or take public transportation, and thus demand for tires (as well as gasoline) will decrease.

cross-elasticity of demand
When changes in the price of one product affect the demand for another item.

Deborah Boyce
a professor at the State University of New York Institute of Technology, Utica, New York
My Advice for Taco Bell would be to choose **Option 3**

real people, **Other Voices**

Price competition is the number-one problem facing the fast-food industry. Taco Bell developed a market offering that has positioned itself in the minds of the target consumers as a higher-quality, higher-prices, quick-serve restaurant. Consumers tend to equate higher prices with higher quality, and are therefore willing to pay a little more for what they perceive as a better value. Option 3 (Mixed Price Menu #1) provides menu choices and a pricing structure that allow the consumer to discriminate. Nachos and tacos prices at $.99 are positioned as offering the best values. Taco Bell can benefit from this three-tiered pricing structure if they take advantage of "the unique-value effect." Buyers are less sensitive to price when the more expensive product is also more distinctive. It should be apparent to consumers that the higher-priced burritos and specialty items are indeed of higher quality. This can be achieved through visual display of the food items on the in-store menu as well as advertising media and presentation of the item at the time of service that should include a distinctive, more expensive wrapping. ➤

Step 3: Determine Costs

Estimating demand helps marketers determine possible prices to charge for a product. It tells them how much of the product they think they'll be able to sell at different prices. Knowing this brings them to the third step in determining a product's price: making sure the price will cover costs. Before marketers can determine price, they must understand the relationship of cost, demand, and revenue for their product. In this next section, we'll talk about different types of costs that marketers must consider in pricing. Then we'll show two types of analyses that marketers use in making pricing decisions.

Variable and Fixed Costs

It's obvious that the cost of producing a product plays a big role when firms decide what to charge for it. If an item's selling price is lower than the cost to produce it, it doesn't take a rocket scientist to figure out that the firm will lose money. Before looking at how costs influence pricing decisions, we need to understand the different types of costs that firms incur.

variable costs

The costs of production (raw and processed materials, parts, and labor) that are tied to and vary depending on the number of units produced.

First, a firm incurs **variable costs**—the per-unit costs of production that will fluctuate depending on how many units or individual products a firm produces. For example, if it takes 25¢ worth of nails—a variable cost—to build one bookcase, it will take 50¢ worth for two, 75¢ worth for three, and so on. Make cents? For the production of bookcases, variable costs would also include the cost of lumber and paint as well as the wages the firm would pay factory workers.

Figure 11.6 shows some examples of the variable cost per unit or average variable cost and the total variable costs at different levels of production (for producing 100, 200, and 500 bookcases). If the firm produces 100 bookcases, the average variable cost per unit is $50, and the total variable cost is $5,000 ($50 × 100). If it doubles production to 200 units, the total variable cost now is $10,000 ($50 × 200).

In reality, calculating variable costs is usually more complex than what we've shown here. As the number of bookcases the factory produces increases or decreases, average variable costs may change. For example, if the company buys just enough lumber for one bookcase, the lumberyard will charge top dollar. If it buys enough for 100 bookcases, the guys at the lumberyard will probably offer a better deal. And if it buys enough for thousands of bookcases, the company may cut variable costs even more. Even the cost of labor goes down with increased production as manufacturers are likely to invest in laborsaving equipment that allows workers to produce bookcases faster. Figure 11.6 shows this is the case. By purchasing wood, nails, and paint at a lower price (because of a volume discount) and by

Figure 11.6 | Variable Costs at Different Levels of Production

Variable Costs to Produce 100 Bookcases		Variable Costs to Produce 200 Bookcases		Variable Costs to Produce 500 Bookcases	
Wood	$13.25	Wood	$13.25	Wood	$9.40
Nails	0.25	Nails	0.25	Nails	0.20
Paint	0.50	Paint	0.50	Paint	0.40
Labor (3 hours × $12.00 per hr)	$36.00	Labor (3 hours × $12.00 per hr)	$36.00	Labor (2½ hours × $12.00 per hr)	$30.00
Cost per unit	$50.00	Cost per unit	$50.00	Cost per unit	$40.00
Multiply by number of units	100	Multiply by number of units	200	Multiply by number of units	500
Cost for 100 units	$5,000	Cost for 200 units	$10,000	Cost for 500 units	$20,000

One bookcase = one unit.

providing a means for workers to build bookcases more quickly, the company reduces the cost per unit of producing 500 bookcases to $40 each.

Of course, variable costs don't always go down with higher levels of production. Using the bookcase example, at some point the demand for the labor, lumber, or nails required to produce the bookcases may exceed the supply: The bookcase manufacturer may have to pay employees higher overtime wages to keep up with production. The manufacturer may have to buy additional lumber from a distant supplier that will charge more to cover the costs of shipping. The cost per bookcase rises. You get the picture.

Fixed costs are costs that *do not* vary with the number of units produced—the costs that remain the same whether the firm produces 1,000 bookcases this month or only 10. Fixed costs include rent or the cost of owning and maintaining the factory, utilities to heat or cool the factory, and the costs of equipment such as hammers, saws, and paint sprayers used in the production of the product. While the cost of factory workers to build the bookcases is part of a firm's variable costs, the salaries of a firm's executives, accountants, human resources specialists, marketing managers, and other personnel not involved in the production of the product are fixed costs. So too are other costs such as advertising and other marketing activities, at least in the short term. All these costs are constant no matter how many items the factory manufactures.

Average fixed cost is the fixed cost per unit, the total fixed costs divided by the number of units (bookcases) produced. Although total fixed costs remain the same no matter how many units are produced, the average fixed cost will decrease as the number of units produced increases. Say, for example, that a firm's total fixed costs of production are $300,000. If the firm produces one unit, it applies the total of $300,000 to the one unit. If it produces two units, it applies $150,000, or half of the fixed costs, to each unit and so on. As we produce more and more units, average fixed costs go down, and so does the price we must charge to cover fixed costs.

Of course, like variable costs, in the long term, total fixed costs may change. The firm may find that it can sell more of a product than it has manufacturing capacity to produce, so it builds a new factory, its executives' salaries go up, and more money goes into purchasing manufacturing equipment.

Combining variable costs and fixed costs yields **total costs** for a given level of production. As a company produces more and more of a product, both average fixed costs and average variable costs may decrease. Average total costs may decrease, too, up to a point. As we said, as output continues to increase, average variable costs may start to increase. These variable costs ultimately rise faster than average fixed costs decline, resulting in an increase to average total costs. As total costs fluctuate with differing levels of production, the price that producers have to charge to cover those costs changes accordingly. Therefore, marketers need to calculate the minimum price necessary to cover all costs—the *break-even price*.

Break-Even Analysis

Break-even analysis is a technique marketers use to examine the relationship between costs and price. This methods lets them determine what sales volume must be reached at a given price before the company will completely cover its total costs and past which it will begin making a profit. Simply put, the **break-even point** is the point at which the company doesn't lose any money and doesn't make any profit. All costs are covered, but there isn't a penny extra. A break-even analysis allows marketers to identify how many units of a product they will have to sell at a given price to exceed the break-even point and be profitable.

Figure 11.7 uses our bookcase manufacturing example to demonstrate break-even analysis assuming a price of $100 per unit is charged. The vertical axis represents the amount of costs and revenue in dollars and the horizontal axis shows the quantity of goods the manufacturer produced and sold. In this break-even model, we assume that there is a given total fixed cost and that variable costs do not change with the quantity produced.

fixed costs
Costs of production that do not change with the number of units produced.

average fixed cost
The fixed cost per unit produced.

total costs
The total of the fixed costs and the variable costs for a set number of units produced.

break-even analysis
A method for determining the number of units that a firm must produce and sell at a given price to cover all its costs.

break-even point
The point at which the total revenue and total costs are equal and beyond which the company makes a profit; below that point, the firm will suffer a loss.

Figure 11.7 | Break-Even Analysis Assuming a Price of $100

Using break-even analysis, marketers can determine what sales volume must be reached before the company makes a profit. This company needs to sell 4,000 bookcases at $100 each to break even.

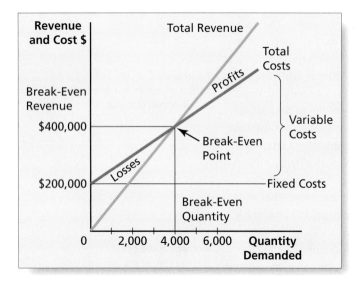

In this example, let's say that the total fixed costs (the costs for the factory, the equipment, and electricity) are $200,000 and that the average variable costs (for materials and labor) are constant. The figure shows the total costs (variable costs plus fixed costs) and total revenues if varying quantities are produced and sold. The point at which the total revenue and total costs lines intersect is the break-even point. If sales are above the break-even point, the company makes a profit. Below that point, the firm will suffer losses.

To determine the break-even point, the firm first needs to calculate the **contribution per unit**, or the difference between the price the firm charges for a product (the revenue per unit) and the variable costs. This figure is the amount the firm has after paying for the wood, nails, paint, and labor to contribute to meeting the fixed costs of production. For our example, we will assume that the firm sells its bookcases for $100 each. Using the variable costs of $50 per unit that we had before, contribution per unit is $100 − $50 = $50. Using the fixed cost for the bookcase manufacturing of $200,000, we can now calculate the firm's break-even point in units of the product:

contribution per unit
The difference between the price the firm charges for a product and the variable costs.

$$\text{Break-even point (in units)} = \frac{\text{total fixed costs}}{\text{contribution per unit to fixed costs}}$$

$$\text{Break-even point (in units)} = \frac{\$200,000}{\$50} = 4,000 \text{ units}$$

We see that the firm must sell 4,000 bookcases at $100 each to meet its fixed costs and to break even. We can also calculate the break-even point in dollars. This shows us that to break even the company must sell $400,000 worth of bookcases:

$$\text{Break-even point (in dollars)} = \frac{\text{total fixed costs}}{1 - \dfrac{\text{variable cost per unit}}{\text{price}}}$$

$$\text{Break-even point (in dollars)} = \frac{\$200,000}{1 - \dfrac{\$50}{\$100}} = \frac{\$200,000}{1 - 0.5} = \frac{\$200,000}{0.5} = \$400,000$$

After the firm's sales have met and passed the break-even point, it begins to make a profit. How much profit? If the firm sells 4,001 bookcases, it will make a profit of $50. If it sells 5,000 bookcases, we calculate the profit as follows:

$$\begin{aligned} \text{Profit} &= \text{quantity above break-even point} \times \text{contribution margin} \\ &= \$1,000 \times 50 \\ &= \$50,000 \end{aligned}$$

Often a firm will set a *profit goal*; the dollar profit figure it wants to earn. Its managers may calculate the break-even point dollar goal in mind. In this case, it is not really a "break-even" point we are calculating because we're seeking profits. It's more of a "target amount." If our bookcase manufacturer thinks it is necessary to realize a profit of $50,000, his calculations look like this:

$$\text{Break-even point (in units) with target profit included} = \frac{\text{total fixed costs} + \text{target profit}}{\text{contribution per unit to fixed costs}}$$

$$\text{Break-even point (in units)} = \frac{\$200,000 + 50,000}{\$50} = 5,000 \text{ units}$$

Sometimes we express the target return or profit goal as a *percentage of sales*. For example, a firm may say that it wants to make a profit of at least 10 percent on sales. In such cases, it adds this profit to the variable cost when it calculates break-even point. In our example, the company wants to earn 10 percent of the selling price of the bookcase, or $10\% \times \$100 = \$10$ per unit. We would simply add this $10 to the variable costs of $50 and calculate the new target amount as we calculated the break-even point before. The contribution per unit becomes:

$$\text{Contribution per unit} = \text{selling price} - (\text{variable costs} + \text{target profit})$$

$$= \$100 - (\$50 + \$10) = \$40$$

$$\text{Break-even point (in units)} = \frac{\text{total fixed costs}}{\text{contribution per unit to fixed costs}}$$

$$\text{Break-even point (in units)} = \frac{\$200,000}{\$40} = 5,000 \text{ units}$$

Break-even analysis does not provide an easy answer for pricing decisions. Yes, it provides answers about how many units the firm must sell to break even and to make a profit—but without knowing whether demand will equal that quantity at that price, companies can make big mistakes. It is, therefore, useful for marketers to estimate the demand for their product and then perform a marginal analysis. Now let's see how to do that.

Marginal Analysis

Marginal analysis provides a way for marketers to look at cost and demand at the same time and to identify the output and the price that will generate the maximum profit. Figure 11.8 shows the various cost and revenue elements we consider in marginal analysis. Like Figure 11.7, the vertical axis in Figure 11.8 represents the cost and revenues in dollars, and the horizontal axis shows the quantity produced and sold. Figure 11.8 shows the average revenue, average cost, marginal revenue, and marginal cost curves.

When they do a marginal analysis, marketers examine the relationship of **marginal cost** (the increase in total costs from producing one additional unit of a product) to **marginal revenue** (the increase in total income or revenue that results from selling one additional unit of a product). Average revenue is also the demand curve and thus represents the amount customers will buy at different prices—people buy more only if price, and thus revenue, decrease. Thus, both average revenue and marginal revenue decrease with each additional unit sold.

If the manufacturer produces only one bookcase, the average total cost per unit is the same as the marginal cost per unit. After the first unit, the cost of *producing each additional unit* (marginal cost) and the average cost at first decrease. Eventually, however, both marginal costs and average costs begin to increase since, as we discussed earlier, both average fixed costs and average variable costs may increase in the long term.

Profit is maximized at the point at which marginal cost is *exactly* equal to marginal revenue. At that point, the cost of producing one unit is exactly equal to the revenue to be realized from selling that one unit. If, however, the company produces one additional unit the

marginal analysis
A method that uses cost and demand to identify the price that will maximize profits.

marginal cost
The increase in total cost that results from producing one additional unit of a product.

marginal revenue
The increase in total income or revenue that results from selling one additional unit of a product.

Figure 11.8 │ Marginal Analysis

Marginal analysis allows marketers to consider both costs and demand in calculating a price that maximizes profits.

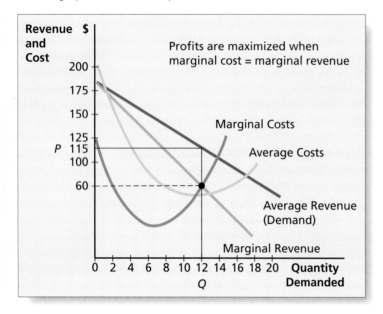

cost of producing that unit is *greater than* the revenue from the sale of the unit, and total profit actually begins to decrease. So it's a no-brainer that firms should maintain production and sales at the point of maximum profit.

One word of caution when you use marginal analysis: Although in theory the procedure is straightforward, in the real world things seldom are. Production costs may vary unexpectedly because of shortages, inclement weather, unexpected equipment repairs, and so on. Revenues may also unexpectedly move up and down because of the economy, what the competition is doing, or a host of other reasons. Predicting demand, an important factor in marginal analysis, is never an exact science. This makes marginal analysis a less-than-perfect way to determine the best price for a product. Indeed, it is theoretically sounder than break-even analysis, but most firms find the break-even approach more useful on a day-to-day basis.

4

OBJECTIVE

Understand some of the environmental factors that affect pricing strategies.

(pp. 342–343)

Step 4: Evaluate the Pricing Environment

In addition to demand and costs, marketers look at factors in the firm's external environment when they make pricing decisions. Thus, the fourth step in developing pricing strategies is to examine and evaluate the pricing environment. Only then can marketers set a price that not only covers costs but also provides a *competitive advantage*—a price that meets the needs of customers better than the competition. This section will discuss some important external influences on pricing strategies—the economic environment, competition, and consumer trends.

The Economy

Broad economic trends, like those we discussed in Chapter 3, tend to direct pricing strategies. The business cycle, inflation, economic growth, and consumer confidence all help to determine whether one pricing strategy or another will succeed. But the upswings and downturns in a national economy do not affect all product categories or all regions equally. Marketers need to understand how economic trends will affect their particular business.

During *recessions* like the one we began to experience in 2008, consumers grow more price-sensitive. They switch brands to get a better price and patronize discount stores and warehouse outlets. Unfortunately many consumers were affected by the subprime mortgage crisis and discovered that they could no longer spend as freely as they had become accustomed to doing.

Some companies actually found ways to profit from the credit crunch. For example, several firms including Sekurus created a product that used car dealers install in vehicles they sell to poor credit risks: It's a box underneath the dashboard that flashes a light when a payment is due. If the buyer doesn't make the payment and punch in a code when the dealer receives it the car won't start and the repo man pays a visit.[6] Even wealthy households, relatively unaffected by the recession, tend to cut back on their consumption. As a result, to keep factories in operation during periods of recession, many firms find it necessary to cut prices to levels at which they cover their costs but don't make a profit.

There are also some economic trends that allow firms to increase prices, altering what consumers see as an acceptable or unacceptable price range for a product. *Inflation* may give marketers causes to either increase or decrease prices. First, inflation gets customers accustomed to price increases. Customers may remain insensitive to price increases, even when inflation goes away, allowing marketers to make real price increases, not just those that adjust for the inflation. Of course, during periods of inflation, consumers may grow fearful of the future and worry about whether they will have enough money to meet basic needs. In such a case, they may cut back on purchases. Then, as in periods of recession, inflation may cause marketers to lower prices and temporarily sacrifice profits to maintain sales levels.

The Competition

Marketers try to anticipate how the competition will respond to their pricing actions. They know that consumers' expectations of what constitutes a fair price largely depend on what the competition is charging. However, it's not always a good idea to fight the competition with lower and lower prices. Pricing wars such as those in the fast-food industry can change consumers' perceptions of what is a "fair" price, leaving them unwilling to buy at previous price levels.

Most industries, such as the airline, restaurant, and wheat farm industries, consist of a number of firms. As we discussed in Chapter 3, these industries can belong to one of three industry structures—an oligopoly, monopolistic competition, or pure competition. The industry structure a firm belongs to will influence price decisions. In general, firms like Delta Airlines that do business in an oligopoly, in which the market has few sellers and many buyers, are more likely to adopt *status quo* pricing objectives in which the pricing of all competitors is similar. Such objectives are attractive to oligopolistic firms because avoiding price competition allows all players in the industry to remain profitable. In a business like the restaurant industry, which is characterized by monopolistic competition in which there are a lot of sellers each offering a slightly different product, it is more possible for firms to differentiate products and to focus on nonprice competition. Then each firm prices its product on the basis of its cost without much concern for matching the exact price of competitors' products. People don't tend to "comparison shop" between the price of a burger at Applebee's versus one at Chili's before deciding which chain to patronize. Of course, this doesn't mean that firms in an oligopoly can just ignore pricing by the competition. As we saw, Taco Bell's pricing decisions do consider the pricing by competing food chains such as McDonald's.

Organizations like wheat farmers that function in a purely competitive market have little opportunity to raise or lower prices. Rather, the price of wheat, soybeans, corn, or fresh peaches is directly influenced by supply and demand. When bad weather decreases the supply of crops, prices go up. And prices for almost any kind of fish have increased dramatically since health-conscious consumers began turning away from red meat.

Consumer Trends

Consumer trends also can strongly influence prices. Culture and demographics determine how consumers think and behave and so these factors have a large impact on all marketing decisions. Take, for example, the buying habits of the women who opted for a career in their twenties but who are hearing the ticking of their biological clocks as they enter their late thirties and forties. Couples having babies later in their lives are often better off financially than younger parents, and on average they will have fewer children to spoil, so they are more willing to spend whatever it costs to give their babies the best.

Another important trend is that even well-off people no longer consider it shameful to hunt for bargains—in fact, it's becoming fashionable to boast that you found one. As a marketing executive for a chain of shopping malls observed, "Everybody loves to save money. It's a badge of honor today." Luxury consumers are looking for prestigious brands at low prices, though they're still willing to splurge for some high-ticket items. Industry analysts have called this new interest in hunting for sales "strategic shopping."[7]

5

OBJECTIVE

Understand key pricing strategies.

(pp. 344–348)

Step 5: Choose a Pricing Strategy

An old Russian proverb says, "There are two kinds of fools in any market. One doesn't charge enough. The other charges too much."[8] In modern business, there seldom is any one-and-only, now-and-forever, best pricing strategy. Like playing a chess game, making pricing moves and countermoves requires thinking two and three moves ahead.

The next step in price planning is therefore to choose a pricing strategy. Some strategies work for certain products, with certain customer groups, in certain competitive markets. When is it best for the firm to undercut the competition and when to just meet the competition's prices? When is the best pricing strategy one that covers costs only and when is it best to use one based on demand?

cost-plus pricing
A method of setting prices in which the seller totals all the costs for the product and then adds an amount to arrive at the selling price.

demand-based pricing
A price-setting method based on estimates of demand at different prices.

target costing
A process in which firms identify the quality and functionality needed to satisfy customers and what price they are willing to pay before the product is designed; the product is manufactured only if the firm can control costs to meet the required price.

yield management pricing
A practice of charging different prices to different customers in order to manage capacity while maximizing revenues.

Pricing Strategies Based on Cost

Marketing planners often choose cost-based strategies because they are simple to calculate and are relatively risk free. They promise that the price will at least cover the costs the company incurs in producing and marketing the product.

Cost-based pricing methods have drawbacks, however. They do not consider factors such as the nature of the target market, demand, competition, the product life cycle, and the product's image. Moreover, although the calculations for setting the price may be simple and straightforward, accurate cost estimating may prove difficult.

Think about firms such as 3M, General Electric, and Nabisco, all of which produce many products. How does cost analysis allocate the costs for the plant, research and development, equipment, design engineers, maintenance, and marketing personnel so that the pricing plan accurately reflects the cost of producing any one product? For example, how do you allocate the salary of a marketing executive who oversees many different products? Should the cost be divided equally among all products? Should costs be based on the actual number of hours spent working on each product? Or should costs be assigned based on the revenues generated by each product? There is no one right answer. Even with these limitations, though, cost-based pricing strategies often are a marketer's best choice.

The most common cost-based approach to pricing a product is **cost-plus pricing**, in which the marketer totals all the costs for the product and then adds an amount (or marks up the cost of the item) to arrive at the selling price. Many marketers, especially retailers and wholesalers, use cost-plus pricing because of its simplicity—users need only estimate the unit cost and add the markup. To calculate cost-plus pricing, marketers usually calculate either a markup on cost or a markup on selling price. With both methods, you calculate the price by adding a predetermined percentage to the cost, but as the names of the methods imply, for one the calculation uses a percentage of the costs and for the other a percentage of the selling price. Which of the two methods is used seems often to be little more than a matter of the "the way our company has always done it." You'll find more information about cost-plus pricing and how to calculate markup on cost and markup on selling price in Appendix B—Marketing Math—at the end of this book.

Our notion of what is a "fair price" very much depends on what we're buying and what we're used to paying for it.

Pricing Strategies Based on Demand

Demand-based pricing means that the firm bases the selling price on an estimate of volume or quantity that it can sell in different markets at different prices. To use any of the pricing strategies based on demand, firms must determine how much product they can sell in each market and at what price. As we noted earlier, marketers often use customer surveys, in which consumers indicate whether they would buy a certain product and how much of it they would buy at various prices. They may obtain more accurate estimates by conducting a *field experiment*. For example, a firm might actually offer the product at different price levels in different test markets and gauge the reaction. Two specific demand-based pricing strategies are target costing and yield management pricing. Let's take a quick look at each approach.

Today, firms are finding that they can be more successful if they match price with demand using a **target costing** process.[9] A firm first determines the price at which customers would be willing to buy the product and then works backward to design the product in such a way that it can produce and sell the product at a profit.

With target costing, firms first use marketing research to identify the quality and functionality needed to satisfy attractive market segments and what price they are willing to pay *before the product is designed*. As Figure 11.9 shows, the next step is to determine what margins retailers and dealers require as well as the profit margin the company requires. On the basis of this information, managers can calculate the target cost—the maximum it can cost the firm to manufacture the product. If the firm can meet customer quality and functionality requirements and control costs to meet the required price, it will manufacture the product. If not, it abandons the product.

Yield management pricing is another type of demand-based pricing strategy that hospitality companies like airlines, hotels, and cruise lines use. These businesses charge different prices to different customers in order to manage capacity while maximizing revenues. Many service firms practice yield management pricing because they recognize that different customers have different sensitivities to price—some customers will pay top dollar for an airline ticket, while others will travel only if there is a discount fare. The goal of yield management pricing is to accurately predict the proportion of customers who fall into each category and allocate the percentages of the airline's or hotel's capacity accordingly so that no product goes unsold.

For example, an airline may charge two prices for the same seat: the full fare ($899) and the discount fare ($299). The airline must predict how many seats it can fill at full fare and how many it can sell only at the discounted fare. The airline begins months ahead of the date of the flight with a basic allocation of seats—perhaps it will place 25 percent in the full-fare "bucket" and 75 percent in the discount-fare "bucket." While it can't sell the seats in the full-fare bucket at the discounted price, the airline may sell the seats it allocated at the discounted price for the full fare if it's lucky (and the passenger isn't).

As flight time gets closer, the airline might make a series of adjustments to the allocation of seats in the hope of selling every seat on the plane at the highest price possible. If the New York Mets need to book the flight, chances are the airline will be able to sell some of the discount seats at full fare, which in turn decreases the number available at the discounted price. If, as the flight date nears, the number of full-fare ticket sales falls below the forecast, the airline will move some of those seats over to the discount bucket. Then, the suspense builds! The pricing game continues until the day of the flight as the airline attempts to fill every seat by the time the plane takes off. This is why you may be able to get a fantastic price on an airline ticket through an Internet auction site such as Priceline.com if you wait until the last minute to buy your ticket. It also tells you why you often see the ticket agents frantically looking for "volunteers" who are willing to give up their seats because the airline sold more seats than actually fit in the plane.

Dell competes on price by allowing its customers to customize their computer systems to match their budgets.

Figure 11.9 | Target Costing Using a Jeans Example

With target costing, a firm first determines the price at which customers would be willing to buy the product and then works backward to design the product in such a way that it can produce and sell the product at a profit.

Step 1: Determine the price customers are willing to pay for the jeans
  $79.99

Step 2: Determine the markup required by the retailer
  40% (.40)

Step 3: Calculate the maximum price the retailer will pay, the price customers are willing to pay minus the markup amount

  Formula: Price to the retailer = Selling price × (1.00 − markup percentage)
  Price to the retailer = $79.99 × (1.00 − .40)
  = $79.99 × 0.60 = **$47.99**

Step 4: Determine the profit required by the firm
  15% (.15)

Step 5: Calculate the target cost, the maximum cost of producing the jeans
  Formula: Target cost = Price to the retailer × (1.00 − profit percentage)
  Target cost = $47.99 × 0.85 = **$40.79**

Pricing Strategies Based on the Competition

Sometimes a firm's pricing strategy involves pricing its wares near, at, above, or below the competition's prices. In the "good old days," when U.S. automakers had the American market to themselves, pricing decisions were straightforward: Industry giant General Motors would announce its new car prices, and Ford, Chrysler, Packard, Studebaker, Hudson, and the others got in line or dropped out. A **price leadership** strategy, which usually is the rule in an oligopolistic industry that a few firms dominate, may be in the best interest of all players because it minimizes price competition. Price leadership strategies are popular because they provide an acceptable and legal way for firms to agree on prices without ever actually coordinating these rates with each other—that's called *collusion* and it's illegal in most cases.

price leadership
A pricing strategy in which one firm first sets its price and other firms in the industry follow with the same or very similar prices.

value pricing or **everyday low pricing (EDLP)**
A pricing strategy in which a firm sets prices that provide ultimate value to customers.

Pricing Strategies Based on Customers' Needs

When firms develop pricing strategies that cater to customers, they are less concerned with short-term results than with keeping customers for the long term. U.S. Cellular refines its pricing strategies by talking to customers to determine the best blend of minutes, plan features, and price.[10] The firm even designed its FarmFlex Plan to offer farmers one rate during the planting season and a lower rate in the off-season.

Firms that practice **value pricing**, or **everyday low pricing (EDLP)**, develop a pricing strategy that promises ultimate value to consumers. What this really means is that, in the customers' eyes, the price is justified by what they receive.[11] At Wal-Mart Stores, Inc., the world's largest company, EDLP is a fundamental part of the company's success. Wal-Mart demands tens of billions of dollars in cost efficiencies from its retail supply chain and passes these savings on to its customers.

BEATING DOWN SUPPLIERS ON PRICE UNTIL THEY CAN'T GET UP?

THIS IS NOT SPEND MANAGEMENT.

Business purchasers often try to get the supplies they need at the lowest possible price so that they can keep their costs down—sometimes at the expense of quality.

To compete, other retailers must reduce their prices. For example, in markets where Wal-Mart sells food products, grocery prices are on the average 14 percent lower. Industry analysts estimate that Wal-Mart saves its U.S. customers at least $20 billion per year on their food bills.[12]

When firms base price strategies solely or mainly on cost, they are operating under the old production orientation we discussed in Chapter 1 rather than under a customer orientation. Value-based pricing begins with customers, then considers the competition, and then determines the best pricing strategy. Changing pricing strategies at Procter & Gamble (P&G) in recent years illustrate value pricing in action. Until about a decade ago, P&G watched as sales dollar volume dropped for its Charmin toilet tissue, Dawn dishwashing liquid, Pringles potato chips, and many other well-established brands. More and more shoppers were buying whatever brand was on sale or had a special promotion offer. To rebuild loyalty, P&G switched to an EDLP pricing strategy. The company reduced everyday prices 12 to 24 percent on nearly all U.S. brands by cutting the amount it spent on trade promotions. P&G said, in effect, "This really *is* our best price, and it's a good value for the money. Buy now. There will be no sale next week. We won't do business that way."

In order to compete more effectively with Wal-Mart, warehouse clubs and other low-price retailers, some retail chains have adopted a "hybrid EDLP" strategy that combines lower prices on hundreds or thousands of items with programs designed to offer consumers additional value in the form of a more fun shopping experience. For supermarket chains, the hybrid EDLP strategies mean abandoning short-term price promotions such as coupon wars and "buy-one-get-one-free" offers in favor of long-term price reductions combined other incentives to keep the shopper coming back. One supermarket provides customers with a customized ad flier each week based on products that are of interest to them. Another replaced its weekly sale advertising with newsletter type fliers that offer recipes and "fun facts" while still another competitor allows frequent shoppers to receive 20 personalized offers each week when they use a biometric finger-scan identification system.[13]

Metrics Moment

Managers often want to know how the price of their product compares to their competitors. One measure they often compute is the *Price Premium*. This metric is the percentage difference between a product's selling price and a *benchmark price*. The latter is either one particular competitor's price, or it may be the average price of all brands in the category. A Price Premium can be either positive or negative although it is normally expressed in the positive mode, e.g., the competition has a price premium of six percent. Here's how we calculate the Price Premium:

$$\text{Price Premium} = \underline{\text{Brand's Price} - \text{Benchmark Price}}$$

Assume that Pizzarama charges $12.00 for a small plain pizza. If the major competitor, Sal's World of Pizza down the street, charges $10.00 for the same pizza, Pizzarama's manager would calculate the price premium as:

$$\text{Price Premium} = \frac{\$12 - \$10}{\$10} = \frac{\$2}{\$10} = .20 = 20\%$$

In this case, Pizzarama has a price premium of 20% relative to its competitor. With that whopping difference, its pies had better be really *fabuloso*!

New-Product Pricing

As we discussed in Chapter 8, new products are vital to the growth and profits of a firm—but they also present unique pricing challenges. When a product is new to the market or when there is no established industry price norm, marketers may use a skimming price strategy, a penetration pricing strategy, or trial pricing when they first introduce the item to the market. Let's take a closer look at each approach.

Setting a **skimming price** means that the firm charges a high, premium price for its new product with the intention of reducing it in the future in response to market pressures. For example, when Top-Flite introduced its new Strata golf balls with a new dimple design and more solid core for better flight with metal clubs, the price was three times that of regular balls. Pro shops still couldn't keep them in stock.[14]

If a product is highly desirable and it offers unique benefits, demand is price inelastic during the introductory stage of the product life cycle, allowing a company to recover research-and-development and promotion costs. When rival products enter the market, the

skimming price
A very high, premium price that a firm charges for its new, highly desirable product.

firm lowers the price to remain competitive. Firms that focus on profit objectives when they develop their pricing strategies often set skimming prices for new products.

A skimming price is more likely to succeed if the product provides some important benefits to the target market that make customers feel they must have it no matter what the cost—like that dimpled golf ball. Handheld calculators were such a product when they entered the market in the late 1960s. To the total astonishment of consumers at that time, these magic little devices could add, subtract, multiply, and divide with just the push of a button. It's equally hard for consumers today to believe that back then these gizmos sold for as much as $200. Today Hewlett-Packard's HP 17bII+ financial calculator features over 250 functions and allows owners to calculate loan payments, interest rates, standard deviations, and NPV—all for under $100.[15]

Second, for skimming pricing to be successful, there should be little chance that competitors can get into the market quickly. With highly complex, technical products, it may be quite a while before competitors can put a rival product into production. Finally, a skimming pricing strategy is most successful when the market consists of several customer segments with different levels of price sensitivity. There must be a substantial number of initial product customers who have very low price sensitivity. After a period of time, the price can go down, and a second segment of the market with a slightly higher level of price sensitivity will purchase and so on.

penetration pricing
A pricing strategy in which a firm introduces a new product at a very low price to encourage more customers to purchase it.

Penetration pricing is the opposite of skimming pricing. In this situation, the company prices a new product very low to sell more in a short time and gain market share early on. One reason marketers use penetration pricing is to discourage competitors from entering the market. The firm first out with a new product has an important advantage. Experience shows that a pioneering brand often is able to maintain dominant market share for long periods. Penetration pricing may act as a *barrier-to-entry* for competitors if the prices the market will bear are so low that the company will not be able to recover development and manufacturing costs. Bayer aspirin and Hoover vacuum cleaners are examples of brands that were first-to-market decades ago and still dominate their industries today.

trial pricing
Pricing a new product low for a limited period of time in order to lower the risk for a customer.

Trial pricing means that a new product carries a low price for a limited time to generate a high level of customer interest. Unlike penetration pricing, in which the company maintains the low price, in this case it increases the trial price after the introductory period. The idea is to win customer acceptance first and make profits later, as when a new health club offers an introductory membership to start pulling people in. When Microsoft first introduced the Access database program, it hit the market at the short-term promotional price of $99 (the suggested retail price was a whopping $495). Microsoft hoped to lure people to try the product at the lower price; it was banking on the idea that they would be so impressed with the program that they would persuade others to buy it at the full price.

Merv
Yeagle
a professor at the University of Maryland at College Park
My Advice for Taco Bell would be to choose

Option

real people, **Other Voices**

I would choose option 3. Consumers need the ability to purchase nutritional items at various prices. This option is also desirable since the purchase intent, overall liking, and uniqueness were all strong for this menu. Taco Bell needs to explain to the consumers why there are three price points on the value menu. Taco Bell must be able to differentiate its fast foods from its competitors, justifying the higher prices. Otherwise, some consumers may not be willing to pay premium prices for fast food. They will go to McDonald's and Burger King. ➤

OBJECTIVE

Explain pricing tactics for single and multiple products.

(pp. 349–351)

Step 6: Develop Pricing Tactics

Once marketers have developed pricing strategies, the last step in price planning is to implement them. The methods companies use to set their strategies in motion are their *pricing tactics*.

Pricing for Individual Products

Once marketers have settled on a product's price, the way they present it to the market can make a big difference. Here are two different tactics with examples of each:

- *Two-part pricing* requires two separate types of payments to purchase the product. For example, golf and tennis clubs charge yearly or monthly fees plus fees for each round of golf or tennis. Likewise, many cellular phone service providers offer customers a set number of minutes for a monthly fee plus a per-minute rate for extra usage.

- *Payment pricing* makes the consumer think the price is "do-able" by breaking up the total price into smaller amounts payable over time. For example, many customers now opt to lease rather than buy a car. The monthly lease amount is an example of payment pricing, which tends to make people less sensitive to the total price of the car (we call a negative reaction to the total retail price *sticker shock*).[16]

Pricing for Multiple Products

A firm may sell several products that consumers typically buy at one time. As fast-food restaurants like Taco Bell know, a customer who buys a taco for lunch usually goes for a soft drink and maybe even a burrito as well. The sale of a paper-cup dispenser usually means a package of cups is not far behind. The two most common tactics for pricing multiple products are price bundling and captive pricing.

Price bundling means selling two or more goods or services as a single package for one price—a price that is often less than the total price of the items if bought individually. A music buff can buy tickets to an entire concert series for a single price. A PC typically comes bundled with a monitor, a keyboard, and software. Even an all-you-can-eat special at the local diner is an example of price bundling. Traditional cable television providers like Cox, Comcast, and Time Warner have gotten into the price bundling act as they entice their customers to sign on for a package of cable, local phone service, high-speed Internet, and (in some cases) cellular phone service.

From a marketing standpoint, price bundling makes sense. If we price products separately, it's more likely that customers will buy some but not all the items. They might choose to put off some purchases until later, or they might buy from a competitor. Whatever revenue a seller loses from the reduced prices for the total package it often makes up in increased total purchases.

Captive pricing is a pricing tactic a firm uses when it has two products that work only when used together. The firm sells one item at a very low price and then makes its profit on the second high-margin item. This tactic is commonly used to sell shaving products where the razor is relatively cheap but the blades are not. Similarly, companies such as HP and Canon offer consumers a desktop printer that also serves as a FAX, copier, and scanner for under $100 in order to keep selling ink cartridges.

price bundling
Selling two or more goods or services as a single package for one price.

captive pricing
A pricing tactic for two items that must be used together; one item is priced very low, and the firm makes its profit on another, high-margin item essential to the operation of the first item.

Distribution-Based Pricing

Distribution-based pricing is a pricing tactic that establishes how firms handle the cost of shipping products to customers near, far, and wide. Characteristics of the product, the customers, and the competition figure in the decision to charge all customers the same price or to vary according to shipping cost.

Often a company states a price as *F.O.B. factory* or *F.O.B. delivered*. F.O.B. stands for "free on board," which means the supplier pays to have the product loaded onto a truck or some other carrier. Also—and this is important—*title passes to the buyer* at the F.O.B. location. F.O.B. factory or **F.O.B. origin pricing** means that the cost of transporting the product from the factory to the customer's location is the responsibility of the customer. **F.O.B. delivered pricing** means that the seller pays both the cost of loading and the cost of transporting to the customer, amounts which are included in the selling price.

Delivery terms for pricing of products sold in international markets are especially important. Some of the more common terms are the following—get ready for a bunch of initials![17]

- *CIF* (cost, insurance, freight) is the term used for ocean shipments and means the seller quotes a price for the goods (including insurance), all transportation, and miscellaneous charges to the point of debarkation from the vessel.

- *CFR* (cost and freight) means the quoted price covers the goods and the cost of transportation to the named point of debarkation but the buyer must pay the cost of insurance. The CFR term is also used for ocean shipments.

- *CIP* (carriage and insurance paid to) and *CPT* (carriage paid to) include the same provisions as CIF and CFR but are used for shipment by modes other than water.

Another distribution-based pricing tactic, **basing-point pricing**, means marketers choose one or more locations to serve as basing points. Customers pay shipping charges from these basing points to their delivery destinations, whether the goods are actually shipped from these points or not. For example, a customer in Los Angeles may order a product from a company in San Diego. The product ships to Los Angeles from the San Diego warehouse. However, if the designated basing point is Dallas, the customer pays shipping charges from Dallas to Los Angeles, charges that the seller never incurred.

When a firm uses **uniform delivered pricing**, it adds an average shipping cost to the price, no matter what the distance from the manufacturer's plant—within reason. For example, when you order a CD from a music supplier, you may pay the cost of the CD plus $2.99 shipping and handling, no matter what the actual cost of the shipping to your particular location. Internet sales, catalog sales, home television shopping, and other types of nonstore retail sales usually use uniform delivered pricing.

Freight absorption pricing means the seller takes on part or all of the cost of shipping. This policy works well for high-ticket items, for which the cost of shipping is a negligible part of the sales price and the profit margin. Marketers are most likely to use freight absorption pricing in highly competitive markets or when such pricing allows them to enter new markets.

Discounting for Channel Members

So far we've talked about pricing tactics used to sell to end customers. Now we'll talk about tactics firms use to price to members of their *distribution channels*.

Whether a firm sells to businesses or directly to consumers, it builds most pricing structures around list prices. A **list price**, that we also refer to as a *suggested retail price*, is the price that the manufacturer sets as the appropriate price for the end consumer to pay. In pricing for members of the channel, marketers recognize that retailers and wholesalers have costs to cover and profit targets to reach as well. Thus, they often begin with the list price and then use a number of discounting tactics to implement pricing to members of the channel of distribution—wholesalers, distributors, and retailers. These tactics include the following:

- **Trade or functional discounts:** Because the channel members perform selling, credit, storage, and transportation services that the manufacturer would otherwise have to provide, manufacturers often offer **trade or functional discounts**, usually set percentage discounts off list price for each channel level.

F.O.B. origin pricing
A pricing tactic in which the cost of transporting the product from the factory to the customer's location is the responsibility of the customer.

F.O.B. delivered pricing
A pricing tactic in which the cost of loading and transporting the product to the customer is included in the selling price and is paid by the manufacturer.

basing-point pricing
A pricing tactic in which customers pay shipping charges from set basing-point locations, whether the goods are actually shipped from these points or not.

uniform delivered pricing
A pricing tactic in which a firm adds a standard shipping charge to the price for all customers regardless of location.

freight absorption pricing
A pricing tactic in which the seller absorbs the total cost of transportation.

list price
The price the end customer is expected to pay as determined by the manufacturer; also referred to as the suggested retail price.

trade or functional discounts
Discounts off list price of products to members of the channel of distribution who perform various marketing functions.

- **Quantity discounts:** To encourage larger purchases from distribution channel partners or from large organizational customers, marketers may offer **quantity discounts**, or reduced prices for purchases of larger quantities. *Cumulative quantity discounts* are based on a total quantity bought within a specified time period, often a year, and encourage a buyer to stick with a single seller instead of moving from one supplier to another. Cumulative quantity discounts may take the form of *rebates*, in which case the firm sends the buyer a rebate check at the end of the discount period or, alternatively, gives the buyer credit against future orders. *Noncumulative quantity discounts* are based only on the quantity purchased with each individual order and encourage larger single orders but do little to tie the buyer and the seller together.

- **Cash discounts:** Many firms try to entice their customers to pay their bills quickly by offering cash discounts. For example, a firm selling to a retailer may state that the terms of the sale are "2 percent 10 days, net 30 days," meaning that if the retailer pays the producer for the goods within 10 days, the amount due is cut by 2 percent. The total amount is due within 30 days, and after 30 days the payment is late.

- **Seasonal discounts:** *Seasonal discounts* are price reductions offered only during certain times of the year. For seasonal products such as snow blowers, lawn mowers, and water-skiing equipment, marketers use seasonal discounts to entice retailers and wholesalers to buy off-season and either store the product at their locations until the right time of the year or pass the discount along to consumers with off-season sales programs. Alternatively, they may offer discounts when products are in-season to create a competitive advantage during periods of high demand.

7 Pricing and Electronic Commerce

OBJECTIVE

Understand the opportunities for Internet pricing strategies.

(pp. 351–354)

As we have seen, price planning is a complex process in any firm. But if you are operating in the "wired world," get ready for even more pricing options! Remember *Project Entropia*, one of the cyberworlds we mentioned back in Chapter 1 that lets members buy and sell on-line properties? Guess what: They even offer ATM cards for quick access to cash assets its residents own in their alternate reality!

Because sellers are connected to buyers around the globe as never before through the Internet, corporate networks, and wireless setups, marketers can offer deals they tailor to a single person at a single moment.[18] On the other hand, they're also a lot more vulnerable to smart consumers, who can easily check out competing prices with the click of a mouse.

Many experts suggest that technology is creating a pricing revolution that might change pricing forever—and perhaps create the most efficient market ever. For example, the Internet is creating major changes in the music industry. Music lovers from around the globe purchase and download billions of songs from numerous Internet sites including the iTunes Music Store.[19] And mobile music is just beginning — 43 percent of mobile users across the globe access music through their phones. In the U.S., consumers spent $1.1 billion on recorded music for their phones in 2007. This figure is about 12 percent of the $9 billion people spent globally on mobile music; analysts expect the total to jump to $17.5 billion by 2012.[20] And many of the sellers find that it is easy to compete on price. While most firms sell single songs for $.99 and albums for $9.99, Wal-Mart Stores, Inc., has tested $.88 downloads, while other firms have experimented with prices as low as $.50 per song and $5 per album.[21]

The Internet also enables firms that sell to other businesses (B2B firms) to change their prices rapidly as they adapt to changing costs. For consumers who have lots of stuff in the

quantity discounts
A pricing tactic of charging reduced prices for purchases of larger quantities of a product.

attic they need to put in someone else's attic (we discussed C2C e-commerce in Chapter 5), the Internet means an opportunity for consumers to find ready buyers. And for B2C firms, firms that sell to consumers, the Internet offers other opportunities. In this section, we will discuss some of the more popular Internet pricing strategies.

Dynamic Pricing Strategies

dynamic pricing
A pricing strategy in which the price can easily be adjusted to meet changes in the marketplace.

One of the most important opportunities the Internet offers is **dynamic pricing**, in which the seller can easily adjust the price to meet changes in the marketplace. If a bricks-and-mortar retail store wants to change prices, employees/workers must place new price tags on items, create and display new store display signage and media advertising, and input new prices into the store's computer system. For business-to-business marketers, employees/workers must print catalogs and price lists and distribute to salespeople and customers. These activities can be very costly to a firm, so they simply don't change their prices very often.

Because the cost of changing prices on the Internet is practically zero, firms are able to respond quickly and, if necessary, frequently to changes in costs, changes in supply, and/or changes in demand. For example, Tickets.com periodically adjusts concert ticket prices on the basis of supply and demand so that a sweet seat to see Outkast might cost more or less depending on which day you log on to buy it. As a result, the company reports it has been able to increase revenue as much as 45 percent.[22]

on-line auctions
E-commerce that allows shoppers to purchase products through on-line bidding.

Hundreds of Internet **on-line auctions** allow shoppers to bid on everything from bobbleheads to health-and-fitness equipment to a Sammy Sosa home-run ball. Auctions provide a second Internet pricing strategy. Perhaps the most popular auctions are the C2C auctions such as those on eBay. The eBay auction is an *open auction*, meaning that all the buyers know the highest price bid at any point in time. On many Internet auction sites, the seller can set a *reserve price*, a price below which the item will not be sold.

A *reverse auction* is a tool used by firms to manage their costs in business-to-business buying. While in a typical auction, buyers compete to purchase a product, in reverse auctions, sellers compete for the right to provide a product at, hopefully, a low price.

Pricing Advantages for On-line Shoppers

The Internet also creates unique pricing challenges for marketers because consumers and business customers are gaining more control over the buying process. With the availability of search engines and "shopbots," they no longer are at the mercy of firms that dictate a price they must accept. The result is that customers have become more price-sensitive. For example, many computer-savvy computer shoppers are finding that shopbots provide them with the best price of both hardware and software. As one illustration, a comparison study found that the same Western Digital 160G USB external hard drive was priced $149.99 at Best Buy, $99.99 at CompUSA, and $79.99 at Beach Camera. Many shopbots also provide buyer reviews of products and ratings of the various sellers, helping consumers make a good, and hopefully safe, purchase choice.

Detailed information about what products actually cost manufacturers, available from sites such as Consumerreports.org, can give consumers more negotiating power when shopping for new cars and other big-ticket items. Finally, e-commerce potentially can lower consumers' costs because of the gasoline, time, and aggravation they save when they avoid a trip to the mall.

Freenomics: What If We Just Give It Away?

It turns out that one of the most exciting revolutions in e-commerce is happening in the area of pricing. Yes folks, once again the Internet is changing the way we look at doing business.[23] In this case this is because the net makes it possible to give products away FOR FREE.

No, you're not hallucinating—we said for free. You're probably thinking this is the dumbest idea you've ever heard of—but it turns out that a new business model based on pricing goods at zero or close to zero actually makes dollars and sense. For example, music groups like Radiohead, Trent Reznor of Nine Inch Nails, and R.E.M. understand that when they make their music freely available on-line they build a fan base that flocks to their concerts and buys their merchandise. Many on-line video games are free to players because they are ad-supported, and almost everything Google "sells" such as unlimited search, Gmail and Picasa is actually free to consumers.

This new business model of **freenomics** is based on the idea that economists call *externalities*; this means that the more people you get to participate in a market, the more profitable it is. So, for example, the more people Google convinces to use its Gmail e-mail service the more eyeballs it attracts which in turn boosts the rates advertisers are willing to pay to talk to those people. Here are a few examples of how freenomics is changing the way at least some savvy marketers think about pricing

- The hugely successful European discount airline Ryanair currently flies passengers from London to Barcelona for about $20. The company's CEO says he hopes eventually to turn all of his flights into a free ride. Don't lose any sleep over the airline's profitability—it makes money when it sells ancillary services *a la carte* such as food, beverages, extra fees for preboarding, checked baggage, and flying with an infant. Ryanair charges extra for credit card transactions, sells in-flight advertising, and the plan is to introduce gambling so that passengers who are riding for free will drop a bundle while en route to their destinations.

- The singer Prince launched his new *Planet Earth* album by putting a free copy of the CD—normally worth about $19—into 2.8 million copies of London's *Daily Mail* newspaper. The Purple One lost a bundle doing that—and then more than made it up by posting record ticket sales to the 21 shows he proceeded to sell out at London's O$_2$ Arena.

- Cable giant Comcast has given about nine million subscribers free set-top digital video recorders. How do you make money by giving away DVRs? Try adding installation fees to put the boxes in and charge customers a monthly fee to use the box. Comcast

freenomics
A business model that encourages giving products away for free because of the increase in profits that can be achieved by getting more people to participate in a market.

By the **People**, For the **People**

When Radiohead released their new album *In Rainbow* on the Internet, the group made pricing history: They let fans decide how much (if anything) they wanted to pay to download it. Based on an unofficial survey, the band "sold" 1.2 million copies of the album in the first two days and two-third of the downloaders did in fact pay for it. The band made around ten dollars on each album. This controversial offer resulted in a barrage of positive free publicity for Radiohead; it was an innovative response to the illegal downloading of music that still allowed the band to distribute new music on legal channels. The experiment showed that a band can still make money when it sells its music—even when listeners have the option to get it for free. And, the group is looking for add-on sales by creating even more interest among its fans: It now offers a boxed set (suggested price: $80.00) for sale that includes an enhanced CD, artwork, a hardcover book, and other extras).

Getty Images

Based on: Anthony Bruno, "The Radiohead Effect," *Billboard*, Vol. 120, Issue 1 (January 5, 2008), pp. 16; Dan Costa "The Music Wants to Be Free," *PC Magazine* (December 4, 2007), pp. 81; NME News, "Radiohead new album: What YOU are paying for the record," NME.com, **http://www.nme.com/news/radiohead/31506**.

also hopes to lure new customers with the offer, and then sell them other services like high-speed internet. All told, Comcast earns back the cost of its free DVR in 18 months, and then the company goes into the black.

The next time someone tells you there's no such thing as a free lunch, point them to the Web for a mouse sandwich.

8 Psychological Issues in Setting Prices

OBJECTIVE

Describe the psychological, legal, and ethical aspects of pricing.
(pp. 354–359)

Much of what we've said about pricing depends on economists' notion of a customer who evaluates price in a logical, rational manner. For example, we express the concept of demand by a smooth curve, which assumes that if a firm lowers a product's price from $10.00 to $9.50 and then from $9.50 to $9.00 and so on, then customers will simply buy more and more. In the real world, though, it doesn't always work that way—consumers aren't nearly as rational as that! Let's look at some psychological factors that keep economists up at night.

Buyers' Pricing Expectations

Often consumers base their perceptions of price on what they perceive to be the customary or *fair price*. For example, for many years a candy bar or a pack of gum was priced at five cents (yes, five). Consumers would have perceived any other price as too high or low. It was a nickel candy bar—period. So when costs went up or inflation kicked in, some candy makers tried to shrink the size of the bar instead of changing the price. Eventually, inflation prevailed, consumers' salaries rose, and that candy bar goes for 10 to 12 times one nickel today—a price that consumers would have found unacceptable a few decades ago.

When the price of a product is above or even sometimes when it's below what consumers expect, they are less willing to purchase the product. If the price is above their expectations, they may think it is a rip-off. If it is below expectations, consumers may think quality is below par. By understanding the pricing expectations of their customers, marketers are better able to develop viable pricing strategies. These expectations can differ across cultures and countries. For example, in one study researchers did in southern California, they found that Chinese supermarkets charge significantly lower prices (only half as much for meat and seafood) than mainstream American supermarkets in the same areas.[24]

Internal Reference Prices

internal reference price
A set price or a price range in consumers' minds that they refer to in evaluating a product's price.

Sometimes consumers' perceptions of the customary price of a product depend on their **internal reference price**. That is, based on past experience, consumers have a set price or a price range in mind that they refer to in evaluating a product's cost. The reference price may be the last price paid, or it may be the average of all the prices they know of for similar products. No matter what the brand, the normal price for a loaf of sandwich bread is about $2.99. In some stores it may be $2.79, and in others it is $3.19, but the average is $2.99. If consumers find a comparable loaf of bread priced much higher than this—say, $4.99—they will feel it is overpriced and grab a competing brand. If they find bread priced significantly lower—say, at $.99 or $1.29 a loaf—they may shy away from the purchase, wondering "what's wrong" with the bread.

In some cases, marketers try to influence consumers' expectations of what a product should cost when they use reference pricing strategies. For example, manufacturers may compare their price to competitors' prices when they advertise. Similarly, a retailer may display a product next to a higher-priced version of the same or a different brand. The consumer must choose between the two products with different prices.

Danielle
Blugrind

APPLYING Internal Reference Price

In the fast food industry, $.99 is a reference price for value.

Two results are likely: On the one hand, if the prices (and other characteristics) of the two products are fairly close, the consumer will probably feel the product quality is similar. This is an *assimilation effect*. The customer might think, "The price is about the same, they must be alike. I'll be smart and save a few dollars." And so the customer chooses the lower-price item because the low price makes it look attractive next to the higher-priced alternative. This is why store brands of deodorant, vitamins, pain relievers, and shampoo sit beside national brands, often accompanied by a shelf talker pointing out how much shoppers can save if they purchase the store brands. On the other hand, if the prices of the two products are too far apart, a *contrast effect* may result, in which the customer equates the gap with a big difference in quality: "Gee, this lower-priced one is probably not as good as the higher-priced one. I'll splurge on the more expensive one." Using this strategy, an appliance store may place an advertised $300 refrigerator next to a $699 model to convince a customer that the bottom-of-the-line model just won't do.

Price–Quality Inferences

Imagine that you go to a shoe store to check out running shoes. You notice one pair that costs $89.99. On another table you see a second pair that looks almost identical to the first pair – but it's price is only $24.95. Which pair do you want? Which pair do you think is the better quality? Many of us will pay the higher price because we believe the bargain-basement shoes aren't worth the risk at any price.

Consumers make *price–quality inferences* about a product when they use price as a cue or an indicator of quality. (An inference means we believe something to be true without any direct evidence.) If consumers are unable to judge the quality of a product through examination or prior experience, they usually assume that the higher-priced product is the higher-quality product.

In fact, new research on how the brain works even suggests that the price we pay can subtly influence how much pleasure we get from the product. Brain scans show that— contrary to conventional wisdom—consumers who buy something at a discount experience less satisfaction than people who pay full price for the very same thing. For example, in one recent study volunteers who drank wine that they were told cost $90 a bottle actually registered more brain activity in pleasure centers than did those who drank the very same wine but who were told it only cost $10 a bottle. Researchers call this the *price-placebo effect*. This is similar to the placebo effect in medicine where people who think they are getting the real thing but who are actually taking sugar pills still experience the effects of the real drug.[25]

Our notion of what is a "fair price" very much depends on what we're buying and what we're used to paying for it.

Psychological Pricing Strategies

Setting a price is part science, part art. Marketers must understand psychological aspects of pricing when they decide what to charge for their products or services.

Odd–Even Pricing

In the U.S. market, we usually see prices in dollars and cents—$1.99, $5.98, $23.67, or even $599.95. We see prices in even dollar amounts—$2.00, $10.00, or $600.00—far less often. The reason? Marketers assume that there is a psychological response to odd prices that differs from the response to even prices. Habit might also play a role here. Whatever the reason, research on the difference in perceptions of odd versus even prices indeed supports the argument that prices ending in 99 rather than 00 lead to increased sales.[26]

But, there are some instances in which even prices are the norm or perhaps a necessity. Theater and concert tickets, admission to sporting events, and lottery tickets tend to

CAFÉ DE QUALITÉ À UN PRIX BIEN SERRÉ.

CHAT NOIR
Dessert

Consumers often associate higher prices with higher quality. This Belgian ad for Chat Noir (Black Cat) coffee tries to convince them otherwise. It reads, "Quality coffee. But we've really squeezed the price."

price lining
The practice of setting a limited number of different specific prices, called price points, for items in a product line.

be priced in even amounts. Professionals normally quote their fees in even dollars. If a doctor or dentist charged $39.99 for a visit, the patient might think the quality of medical care was less than satisfactory. Many luxury items such as jewelry, golf course fees, and resort accommodations use even dollar prices to set them apart.

Price Lining

Marketers often apply their understanding of the psychological aspects of pricing in a practice they call **price lining**, whereby items in a product line sell at different prices, or *price points*. If you want to buy a new digital camera, you will find that most manufacturers have one "stripped-down" model for $100 or less. A better-quality but still moderately priced model likely will be around $200, while a professional quality camera with multiple lenses might set you back $1,000 or more. Price lining provides the different ranges necessary to satisfy each segment of the market.

Why is price lining a good practice? From the marketer's standpoint, it's a way to maximize profits. In theory, a firm would charge each individual customer the highest price that customer was willing to pay. If the maximum one particular person would be willing to pay for a digital camera is $150, then that would be the price. If another person would be willing to pay $300, that would be his price. But charging each consumer a different price is really not possible. Having a limited number of prices that generally fall at the top of the different price ranges customers find acceptable is a more workable alternative.

Prestige Pricing

Finally, although a "rational" consumer should be more likely to buy a product or service as the price goes down, in the real world sometimes this assumption gets turned on its head. Remember that earlier in the chapter we talked about situations where we want to meet an image enhancement objective to appeal to status conscious consumers. For this reason, sometimes luxury goods marketers use a *prestige pricing strategy* that turns the typical assumption about price-demand relationships on its head: Contrary to the "rational" assumption that we value a product or service more as the price goes down, in these cases, believe it or not, people tend to buy more as the price goes up!

Legal and Ethical Considerations in Pricing

The free enterprise system is founded on the idea that the marketplace will regulate itself. Prices will rise or fall according to demand. Firms and individuals will supply goods and services at fair prices if there is an adequate profit incentive.

Unfortunately, the business world includes the greedy and the unscrupulous. Federal, state, and local governments find it necessary to enact legislation to protect consumers and to protect businesses from predatory rivals. For example, under current laws in Europe, car companies are allowed to charge wildly different prices for the same vehicle in different countries—prices can vary by as much as 30 percent. New regulations are now being proposed to create a more level playing field among countries that belong to the European Union—despite fierce opposition by some car manufacturers that want to retain control over their pricing decisions.[27] In this section, we'll talk about deceptive prices, unfair prices, discriminatory prices, and price-fixing, and some regulations to combat them.

Deceptive Pricing Practices

Unscrupulous businesses may advertise or promote prices in a deceptive way. The Federal Trade Commission (FTC), state lawmakers, and private bodies such as the Better Business Bureau have developed pricing rules and guidelines to meet the challenge. They say retailers (or other suppliers) must not claim that their prices are lower than a competitor's unless that claim is true. A going-out-of-business sale should be the last sale before going out of business. A fire sale should be held only when there really was a fire.

Another deceptive pricing practice is the **bait-and-switch** tactic, whereby a retailer will advertise an item at a very low price—the *bait*—to lure customers into the store. An example might be a budget model appliance, such as a washing machine or television that has been stripped of all but the most basic features. But it is almost impossible to buy the advertised item—salespeople like to say (privately) that the item is "nailed to the floor." The salespeople do everything possible to get the unsuspecting customers to buy a different, more expensive, item—the *switch*. They might tell the customer "confidentially" that "the advertised item is really poor quality, lacking important features, and full of problems." It's complicated to enforce laws against bait-and-switch tactics because these practices are similar to the legal sales technique of "trading up." Simply encouraging consumers to purchase a higher-priced item is acceptable, but it is illegal to advertise a lower-priced item when it's not a legitimate, *bona fide* offer that is available if the customer demands it. The FTC may determine if an ad is a bait-and-switch scheme or a legitimate offer by checking to see if a firm refuses to show, demonstrate, or sell the advertised product; disparages it; or penalizes salespeople who do sell it.

bait-and-switch
An illegal marketing practice in which an advertised price special is used as bait to get customers into the store with the intention of switching them to a higher-priced item.

Unfair Sales Acts

Not every advertised bargain is a bait-and-switch. Some retailers advertise items at very low prices or even below cost and are glad to sell them at that price because they know that once in the store, customers may buy other items at regular prices. Marketers call this **loss leader pricing**; they do it to build store traffic and sales volume.

Some states frown on loss leader practices so they have passed legislation called **unfair sales acts** (also called *unfair trade practices acts*). These laws or regulations prohibit wholesalers and retailers from selling products below cost. These laws aim to protect small wholesalers and retailers from larger competitors because the "big fish" have the financial resources that allow them to offer loss leaders or products at very low prices—they know that the smaller firms can't match these bargain prices.

loss leader pricing
The pricing policy of setting prices very low or even below cost to attract customers into a store.

unfair sales acts
State laws that prohibit suppliers from selling products below cost to protect small businesses from larger competitors.

Illegal Business-to-Business Price Discrimination

The *Robinson–Patman Act* includes regulations against price discrimination in interstate commerce. Price discrimination regulations prevent firms from selling the same product to different retailers and wholesalers at different prices if such practices lessen competition. In addition to regulating the price companies charge, the Robinson–Patman Act specifically prohibits offering such "extras" as discounts, rebates, premiums, coupons, guarantees, and free delivery to some but not all customers.

There are exceptions, however:

- The Robinson–Patman Act does not apply to consumers—only resellers.

- A discount to a large channel customer is legal if it is based on the quantity of the order and the resulting efficiencies, such as transportation savings.

- The Act allows price differences if there are physical differences in the product, such as different features. A name-brand appliance may be available through a large national retail chain at a lower price than an almost identical item a higher-priced retailer sells because only the chain sells that specific model.

Ethical Decisions in the Real World

Franchisees—those local folks who own a Pizza Hut, a McDonald's, or a Subway—are often required by their franchise agreement to follow the franchise issuer's guidelines. The company's central management often dictates the menu, the food, the location, the décor, and even the special offers.

So what happens when the pizza franchise home office says that on Super Bowl Sunday, they will offer customers up to three pizzas with "unlimited" toppings?

ETHICS CHECK: ↖

Find out what other students taking this course **would do** and **why** on **www.mypearsonmarketinglab.com**

Should unlimited toppings really mean "unlimited"? With very low margins, can the franchise owner afford to give away five, ten, or fifteen extra toppings on pizzas? On the other hand, if the local owner places a limit on the offer, say no more than five toppings per pizza, customers might accuse him of using a "bait and switch" tactic. If you are one of these franchise owners, what would you do?

Ripped from the Headlines! See what happened in the Real World at **www.mypearsonmarketinglab.com**

If you owned a franchise store would you always follow the directions of the parent company even if you didn't agree with it?

☐YES ☐NO

price-fixing
The collaboration of two or more firms in setting prices, usually to keep prices high.

Price-Fixing

Price-fixing occurs when two or more companies conspire to keep prices at a certain level. For example, General Electric Co. and De Beers Centenary AG were charged with fixing the prices in the $600-million-per-year world market for industrial diamonds used in cutting tools. This type of illicit agreement can take two forms: horizontal and vertical.

In 2003, a number of top fashion-modeling agencies were charged with conspiring to fix the commissions they earn when they book models. Because such practices mean higher prices for customers, in this case the models who were buying the services of the agencies, such practices are against the regulations of the Sherman Antitrust Act we discussed in Chapter 3.[28] *Horizontal price-fixing* occurs when competitors making the same product jointly determine what price they each will charge. In industries in which there are few sellers, there may be no specific price-fixing agreement, but sellers will still charge the same price to "meet the competition." Such parallel pricing is not in-and-of-itself considered price-fixing. There must be an exchange of pricing information between sellers to indicate illegal price-fixing actions.

Sometimes manufacturers or wholesalers attempt to force retailers to charge a certain price for their product. When *vertical price-fixing* occurs, the retailer that wants to carry the product has to charge the "suggested" retail price. The *Consumer Goods Pricing Act* of 1976 limited this practice, leaving retail stores free to set whatever price they choose without interference by the manufacturer or wholesaler. Today, retailers don't need to adhere to "suggested" prices.

Predatory Pricing

Predatory pricing means that a company sets a very low price for the purpose of driving competitors out of business. Later, when they have a monopoly, they turn around and increase prices. The Sherman Act and the Robinson–Patman Act prohibit predatory pricing. For example, in 1999 the Justice Department accused American Airlines of predatory pricing at its Dallas–Ft. Worth hub.[30] In the mid-1990s, three small rivals started flying into the airport. American responded by lowering the prices of its flights on four routes. The Justice Department claimed that the airline planned to scare the three carriers away and monopolize the routes. While American was exonerated in court, the case did send a message to airlines that

A chocolately rip-off? Recently, government officials in Germany, Canada, and the United States began investigating the chocolate industry's pricing practices. German officials raided the offices of seven leading chocolate companies including Mars, Kraft Foods, and Nestle looking for evidence, while Canadian informants provided officials documents showing how the companies exchanged confidential pricing information by e-mail, phone, and meetings. In the United States a number of American lawsuits accused the world's biggest chocolate companies of violating U.S. antitrust laws. As of the writing of this book, none of the governments has reach conclusions of wrongdoing and the companies are still under investigation.[29] But just in case, you might want to stock up on your candy bar stash.

David Young-Wolff/PhotoEdut Inc.

they must be careful when they set prices. Of course that doesn't mean that predatory pricing doesn't happen in the airline industry. In March 2008, Aloha Airlines filed for bankruptcy; it claimed that it was unable to generate sufficient revenue due to "predatory pricing" by Mesa Air Group's *go!* Airline.[31]

Now that you've learned about product pricing, read "Real People, Real Choices: How It Worked Out" to see which strategy Danielle Blugrind of Taco Bell selected for the chain's value menu.

predatory pricing
Illegal pricing strategy in which a company sets a very low price for the purpose of driving competitors out of business.

---

real people, **Real Choices**

Danielle
Blugrind
Danielle chose:

3
Option

How It Worked Out at Taco Bell

Danielle chose Option 3, Mixed Price Menu #1. This configuration features a strategy that uses both the $.99 and $1.29 price points, but that also has some items priced at $1.19 to close the relatively large $.30 gap between the highest and lowest price points.

So far, consumers have responded very well to the Big Bell Value Menu. They seem to understand that items such as burritos, especially those carrying the "half-pound" moniker, are naturally going to be more expensive than some other items such as tacos. Consumers are telling Taco Bell that they like the $1.19 price point because it helps make the menu feel less disjointed; more like a collection of products rather than two separate sets of higher-priced and lower-priced items. The middle price point also allows for some premium pricing where necessary (for example, on chicken) without resorting to the highest price point of $1.29. By carefully crafting its pricing strategy, Taco Bell is successfully reclaiming its position of offering fast-food value for the money.

Marketing Metrics: How Taco Bell Measures Success

Danielle and her colleagues evaluate the performance of the Big Bell Value Menu in three key categories: consumer, operations, and financials. From a consumer perspective, they examine the menu's performance in terms of awareness, trial and usage patterns, repeat purchase intent, and menu mix. When they analyze the menu mix, they look at all of the items purchased by all consumers and their value, and determine what percentage of dollars they spend on the Big Bell Value Menu items in total. They also measure impact on the brand through a tracking study that measures consumers' ratings of Taco Bell's performance on key attributes such as value for the money, everyday low prices, and amount of food for the money relative to the competition.

From an operational perspective, they ensure that the menu is easy to execute, that there has been no negative impact on measures such as speed of

service and order accuracy, and that products are being prepared to specifications. Finally, from a financial perspective they review these detailed metrics:

- Sales lift: How much higher are the company's sales overall because it has the Big Bell Value Menu?
- Occasion-based analysis of purchases: Taco Bell segments its value-driven customers so it can look at the appeal of the Big Bell Value Menu to different segments on different occasions, such as drive-thru, eat in, or carry out.
- Performance relative to the break-even point to ensure that the program remains financially viable.

Taco Bell menu.

Refer back to page 329 for Danielle's story ➡

Brand **YOU**!

Do you know how much you are worth?

The first step to getting the salary you want is knowing how much you are worth. Find out the latest in salary trends, how and when to negotiate your offer and what else you can ask for as part of your compensation in Chapter 11 in the *Brand You* supplement.

CHAPTER 11

Objective Summary ➡ Key Terms ➡ Apply   Study Map

1. Objective Summary (pp. 330–331)

Explain the importance of pricing and how prices can take both monetary and nonmonetary forms.

Pricing is important to firms because it creates profits and influences customers to purchase or not. Prices may be monetary or nonmonetary, as when consumers or businesses exchange one product for another.

Key Term

price, p. 330

2. Objective Summary (pp. 331–333)

Understand the pricing objectives that marketers typically set when they plan pricing strategies.

Effective pricing objectives are designed to support corporate and marketing objectives and are flexible. Pricing objectives often focus on sales (to maximize sales or to increase market share), on a desired level of profit growth or profit margin, on competing effectively, on increasing customer satisfaction, or on communicating a certain image.

Key Term

prestige products, p. 332 (Figure 11.2, p. 333)

3. Objective Summary (pp. 334–342)

Describe how marketers use costs, demand, and revenue to make pricing decisions.

In developing prices, marketers must estimate demand and determine costs. Marketers often use break-even analysis and marginal analysis to help in deciding on the price for a

product. Break-even analysis uses fixed and variable costs to identify how many units must be sold at a certain price in order to begin making a profit. Marginal analysis uses both costs and estimates of product demand to identify the price that will maximize profits. In marginal analysis, profits are maximized at the point at which the revenue from selling one additional unit of a product equals the costs of producing the additional unit.

Key Terms

price elasticity of demand, p. 335 (Figure 11.4, p. 336)

elastic demand, p. 335 (Figure 11.4, p. 336)

inelastic demand, p. 335 (Figure 11.4, p. 336)

cross-elasticity of demand, p. 337

variable costs, p. 338 (Figure 11.6, p. 338 & Figure 11.7, p. 340)

fixed costs, p. 339 (Figure 11.7, p. 340)

average fixed cost, p. 339

total costs, p. 339 (Figure 11.7, p. 340)

break-even analysis, p. 339 (Figure 11.7, p. 340)

break-even point, p. 339 (Figure 11.7, p. 340)

contribution per unit, p. 340

marginal analysis, p. 341 (Figure 11.8, p. 342)

marginal cost, p. 341 (Figure 11.8, p. 342)

marginal revenue, p. 341 (Figure 11.8, p. 342)

4. Objective Summary (pp. 342–343)

Understand some of the environmental factors that affect pricing strategies.

Like other elements of the marketing mix, pricing is influenced by a variety of external environmental factors. This includes economic trends such as inflation and recession and the firm's competitive environment—that is, whether the firm does business in an oligopoly, a monopoly, or a more competitive environment. Pricing may also be influenced by changing consumer trends.

5. Objective Summary (pp. 344–348)

Understand key pricing strategies.

Though easy to calculate and "safe," frequently used cost-based strategies do not consider demand, the competition, the stage in the product life cycle, plant capacity, or product image. The most common cost-based strategy is cost-plus pricing.

Pricing strategies based on demand, such as target costing and yield management pricing can require that marketers estimate demand at different prices in order to be certain they can sell what they produce. Strategies based on the competition may represent industry wisdom but can be tricky to apply. A price leadership strategy is often used in an oligopoly.

Firms that focus on customer needs may consider everyday low price or value pricing strategies. New products may be priced using a high skimming price to recover research, development, and promotional costs, or a penetration price to encourage more customers and discourage competitors from entering the market. Trial pricing means setting a low price for a limited time.

Key Terms

cost-plus pricing, p. 344

demand-based pricing, p. 344

target costing, p. 345 (Figure 11.9, p. 346)

yield management pricing, p. 345

price leadership, p. 346

value pricing, p. 346

everyday low pricing (EDLP), p. 346

skimming price, p. 347

penetration pricing, p. 348

trial pricing, p. 348

6. Objective Summary (pp. 349–351)

Explain pricing tactics for single and multiple products.

To implement pricing strategies with individual products, marketers may use two-part pricing or payment pricing tactics. For multiple products, marketers may use price bundling, wherein two or more products are sold and priced as a single package. Captive pricing is often chosen when two items must be used together; one item is sold at a very low price and the other at a high, profitable price.

Distribution-based pricing tactics, including F.O.B., basing-point, and uniform delivered pricing, address differences in how far products must be shipped. Similar pricing tactics are used for products sold internationally.

Pricing for members of the channel may include trade or functional discounts, cumulative or noncumulative quantity

discounts to encourage larger purchases, cash discounts to encourage fast payment, and seasonal discounts to spread purchases throughout the year or to increase off-season or in-season sales.

Key Terms

price bundling, p. 349

captive pricing, p. 349

F.O.B. origin pricing, p. 350

F.O.B. delivered pricing, p. 350

basing-point pricing, p. 350

uniform delivered pricing, p. 350

freight absorption pricing, p. 350

list price, p. 350

trade or functional discounts, p. 350

quantity discounts, p. 351

7. Objective Summary (pp. 351–354)

Understand the opportunities for Internet pricing strategies.

E-commerce may offer firms an opportunity to initiate dynamic pricing—meaning prices can be changed frequently with little or no cost. Auctions offer opportunities for customers to bid on items in C2C, B2C, and B2B e-commerce. The Internet allows buyers to compare products and prices, gives consumers more control over the price they pay for items, and has made customers more price sensitive.

Key Terms

dynamic pricing, p. 352

on-line auctions, p. 352

freenomics, p. 353

8. Objective Summary (pp. 354–359)

Describe the psychological, legal, and ethical aspects of pricing.

Consumers may express emotional or psychological responses to prices. Customers may use an idea of a customary or fair price as an internal reference price in evaluating products. Sometimes marketers use reference pricing strategies by displaying products with different prices next to each other. A price–quality inference means that consumers use price as a cue for quality. Customers respond to odd prices differently than to even-dollar prices. Marketers may practice price lining strategies in which they set a limited number of different price ranges for a product line. With luxury products, marketers may use a prestige pricing strategy assuming that people will buy more if the price is higher.

Most marketers try to avoid unethical or illegal pricing practices. One deceptive pricing practice is the illegal bait-and-switch tactic. Many states have unfair sales acts, which are laws against loss leader pricing that make it illegal to sell products below cost. Federal regulations prohibit predatory pricing, price discrimination, and horizontal or vertical price-fixing.

Key Terms

internal reference price, p. 354

price lining, p. 356

bait-and-switch, p. 357 (Ethical Decisions in the Real World, p. 358)

loss leader pricing, p. 357

unfair sales acts, p. 357

price-fixing, p. 358

predatory pricing, p. 358

Chapter **Questions** and **Activities**

Concepts: Test Your Knowledge

1. What is price, and why is it important to a firm? What are some examples of monetary and nonmonetary prices?

2. Describe and give examples of some of the following types of pricing objectives: market share, profit, competitive effect, customer satisfaction, and image enhancement.

3. Explain how the demand curves for normal products and for prestige products differ. What are demand shifts and why are they important to marketers? How do firms go about estimating demand? How can marketers estimate the elasticity of demand?

4. Explain variable costs, fixed costs, average variable costs, average fixed costs, and average total costs.

5. What is break-even analysis? What is marginal analysis? What are the comparative advantages of break-even analysis and marginal analysis for marketers?

6. How does recession affect consumers' perceptions of prices? How does inflation influence perceptions of prices? Why do firms in some industries adopt status quo pricing objectives?

7. Explain cost-plus pricing, target costing, and yield management pricing. Explain how a price leadership strategy works.

8. For new products, when is skimming pricing more appropriate, and when is penetration pricing the best strategy? When would trial pricing be an effective pricing strategy?

9. Explain two-part pricing, payment pricing, price bundling, captive pricing, and distribution-based pricing tactics. Give an example of when each would be a good pricing tactic for marketers to use.

10. Why do marketers use trade or functional discounts, quantity discounts, cash discounts, and seasonal discounts in pricing to members of the channel? What is dynamic pricing? Why does the Internet encourage the use of dynamic pricing?

11. Explain these psychological aspects of pricing: price–quality inferences, odd–even pricing, internal reference price, price lining, and prestige pricing.

12. Explain how unethical marketers might use bait-and-switch tactics, price-fixing, and predatory pricing.

Choices and Ethical Issues: You Decide

1. Governments sometimes provide price subsidies to specific industries; that is, they reduce a domestic firm's costs so that it can sell products on the international market at a lower price. What reasons do governments (and politicians) use for these government subsidies? What are the benefits and disadvantages to domestic industries in the long run? To international customers? Who would benefit and who would lose if all price subsidies were eliminated?

2. In many oligopolistic industries, firms follow a price leadership strategy, in which an accepted industry leader sets, raises, or lowers prices and the other firms follow. Why is this good policy for the industry? In what ways is this good or bad for consumers? What is the difference between price leadership and price fixing? Should governments allow industries to use price leadership strategies?

3. Many very successful retailers use a loss leader pricing strategy, in which they advertise an item at a price below their cost and sell the item at that price to get customers into their store. They feel that these customers will continue to shop with their company and that they will make a profit in the long run. Do you consider this an unethical practice? Who benefits and who is hurt by such practices? Do you think the practice should be made illegal, as some states have done? How is this different from "bait-and-switch" pricing?

4. Consumers often make price–quality inferences about products. What does this mean? What are some products for which you are likely to make price–quality inferences? Do such inferences make sense?

5. In pricing new products, marketers may choose a skimming or a penetration pricing strategy. While it's easy to see the benefits of these practices for the firm, what are the advantages and/or disadvantages of the practice for consumers? For an industry as a whole?

Practice: Apply What You've Learned

1. Assume that you are the director of marketing for a firm that manufactures candy bars. You feel the time is right for your company to increase the price of its candy, but you are concerned that increasing the price might not be profitable. You feel you should examine the elasticity of demand. How would you go about doing this? What findings would lead you to increase the price? What findings would cause you to rethink the decision to increase prices?

2. Assume that you and your friend have decided to go into business together manufacturing your personally designed women's handbags. You know that your fixed costs (rent on a building, equipment, and so on) will be $250,000 a year. You expect your variable costs to be $35 per handbag.
   a. If you plan on selling the handbags to retail stores for $48, how many must you sell to break even; that is, what is your break-even quantity?
   b. Assume that you and your partner feel that you must set a goal of achieving a $75,000 profit with your business this year. How many units would you have to sell to make that amount of profit?
   c. What if you feel that you will be able to sell no more than 10,000 handbags? What price will you have to charge to break even? To make $75,000 in profit?

3. You are a marketing consultant, and your new client is the owner of a small chain of ice cream stores. The client has sold his ice cream at the same price since opening the stores seven years ago. Over the years, the costs of operating the stores have increased, cutting profits. The client feels he needs to increase his prices but is concerned that increasing prices may not be a good decision. Design a plan to measure price elasticity and thus determine if increasing prices will be good or bad for your client's profit. In a role-playing situation, explain to the client what you recommend.

4. Assume that you have been hired as the assistant manager of a local store that sells fresh fruits and vegetables. As you look over the store, you notice that there are two different displays of tomatoes. In one display the tomatoes are priced at $1.39 per pound, and in the other the tomatoes are priced at $.89 per pound. The tomatoes look very much alike. You notice that many people are buying the $1.39 tomatoes. Write a report explaining what is happening and give your recommendations for the store's pricing strategy.

5. As the vice president for marketing for a firm that markets computer software, you must regularly develop pricing strategies for new software products. Your latest product is a software package that automatically translates any foreign language e-mail messages to the user's preferred language. You are trying to decide on the pricing for this new product. Should you use a skimming price, a penetration price, or something in between? With a classmate taking the role of another marketing professional with your firm, argue in front of your class the pros and cons for each alternative.

Miniproject: Learn by Doing

The purpose of this miniproject is to help you become familiar with how consumers respond to different prices by conducting a series of pricing experiments.

For this project, you should first select a product category that students such as yourself normally purchase. It should be a moderately expensive purchase such as athletic shoes, a bookcase, or a piece of luggage. You should next obtain two photographs of items in this product category or, if possible, two actual items. The two items should not appear to be substantially different in quality or in price.

Note: You will need to recruit separate research participants for each of the activities listed in the next section.

- **Experiment 1: Reference Pricing**
  a. Place the two products together. Place a sign on one with a low price. Place a sign on the other with a high price (about 50 percent higher will do). Ask your research participants to evaluate the quality of each of the items and to tell which one they would probably purchase.
  b. Reverse the signs and ask other research participants to evaluate the quality of each of the items and to tell which one they would probably purchase.
  c. Place the two products together again. This time place a sign on one with a moderate price. Place a sign on the other that is only a little higher (less than 10 percent higher). Again, ask research participants to evaluate the quality of each of the items and to tell which one they would probably purchase.
  d. Reverse the signs and ask other research participants to evaluate the quality of each of the items and to tell which one they would probably purchase.
- **Experiment 2: Odd–Even Pricing.** For this experiment, you will only need one of the items from experiment 1.
  a. Place a sign on the item that ends in $.99 (for example, $62.99). Ask research participants to tell you if they think the price for the item is very low, slightly low, moderate, slightly high, or very high. Also ask them to evaluate the quality of the item and to tell you how likely they would be to purchase the item.
  b. This time place a sign on the item that is slightly lower but that ends in $.00 (for example, $60.00). Ask different research participants to tell you if they think the price for the item is very low, slightly low, moderate, slightly high, or very high. Also ask them to evaluate the quality of the item and to tell you how likely they would be to purchase the item.

Develop a presentation for your class in which you discuss the results of your experiments and what they tell you about how consumers view prices.

Real People, **real surfers**: explore the web

Barter exchanges are organizations that facilitate barter transactions between buyers and sellers. Many of these exchanges are members of the National Association of Trade Exchanges (NATE).

First, visit the NATE Web page at **www.nate.org**. Using links on that page to NATE member exchanges or an Internet search engine locate and explore several barter exchange Web pages. Based on your Internet experience, answer the following questions:

1. What is NATE?
2. What are the benefits to a business of joining a barter exchange?

3. What types of products are bartered?
4. How does a trade actually work with a barter exchange?
5. How does the exchange make its money? Who pays the exchange and how much is charged?
6. Assuming that the goal of barter exchange Web sites is to attract new members, evaluate the different Web sites you visited. Which Web site do you think was best? What features of the site would make you want to join if you were the owner of a small business? What features of the other sites made them less appealing than this one?

Marketing Plan Exercise

For many service organizations such as restaurants, hotels, airlines, and resorts, pricing strategies are particularly important because of the perishability of services (that is, services can't be stored). Pricing is a vital part of effective marketing strategies that ensure that a maximum number of seats of the plane or rooms in the hotel are purchased—every day.

Think about a new seaside resort complex that offers vacationers luxury villas available for rent for a few days, a week, or longer. Consider possible pricing strategies such as cost-plus, yield management, everyday low pricing, skimming, and penetration and trial pricing.

1. What pricing strategy do you recommend for the resort complex that would maximize its occupancy?
2. What recommendations for pricing tactics or how to implement the strategy do you have?

Marketing in Action Case

Real **Choices** at **True Religion Jeans**

Would you pay $265 for a pair of jeans? Megan Molitor, a columnist for the Kansas State University newspaper, the *Collegian*, did: "I'm ashamed to admit I have blown my entire paycheck on a single item of clothing. Not just any item of clothing, mind you, but a pair of True Religion Brand Jeans ...." Megan's "entire paycheck" is from two weeks of work at a fast-food restaurant, a job she took specifically to earn the money to buy the jeans. She quit after she bought them. True Religion truly exemplifies the power of premium high-fashion clothing and, specifically, the demand for stylish jeans at any price.

True Religion Apparel, Inc. opened in 2001 to sell high-fashion jeans it prices from $265 per pair to a whopping $650 or more per pair. Since then, the company has racked up some very impressive growth, with sales now topping $170 million annually. Clearly, selling jeans at $265 and up is a very lucrative business.

To understand the meteoric success of True Religion Brand Jeans, start by considering its marketing strategy. First, True Religion Apparel targets people willing to pay a premium price for the *prestige factor* inherent in its brand. The prestige comes largely from celebrities who wear the

jeans—something like "prestige by association." You can spot True Religion on the backsides of stars such as Jessica Simpson, Eva Longoria, Jessica Alba, and Katie Holmes. While the demand for blue jeans in general is price elastic, the primo publicity True Religion Jeans gets from top movie or television stars reduces price elasticity and inspires people like Megan Molitor to go to extreme lengths to buy a pair. That's why the company describes itself as a "design-based premium aspirational brand."

For the brand's first-ever advertising campaign in 2008, True Religion selected supermodel and *Sports Illustrated Swimsuit Edition* cover girl Marisa Miller to represent its hippie-bohemian-chic spirit. Through licensing agreements, True Religion now offers trend-conscious consumers its own line of handbags, knits, sportswear, footwear, swimwear, perfume, and accessories in addition to premium denim products. These pricey products are available in premium department stores and boutiques in 50 countries around the world and in a growing number of company-owned full-price and outlet stores.

Despite the early success of True Religion Jeans you have to wonder just how long the roller coaster ride can last. The market for high-fashion jeans and other apparel at a premium price is fairly limited. How many people out there are willing to do something as drastic as get a part-time job just to snag a pair of jeans? Instead, the company will probably have to rely on high-income consumers as its primary market. This strategy is risky because these consumers tend to be far more fashion conscious than they are brand loyal. Eventually the stars who wear these jeans will move on to some other fashion statement, taking with them much of True Religion's fickle consumer base. Perhaps a different item of clothing or designer will usurp True Religion's popularity in the near future. Currently, other stars like Angelina Jolie and Lindsay Lohan make J Brand pants the "in" pair to wear, too. If this continues, will the company's frenzied followers lose their religion?

You Make the Call

1. What is the decision facing True Religion?
2. What factors are important in understanding this decision situation?
3. What are the alternatives?
4. What decision(s) do you recommend?
5. What are some ways to implement your recommendation?

Based on: Lisa Schmeiser, "How True Religion Got to Blue Jeans Heaven; Upscale Jeans Maker Focuses on Quality and Savvy Salesmanship," *Investors Business Daily*, December 12, 2005, A10; Megan Molitor, "Label Hunting," *Kansas State Collegian*, January 20, 2006; Stephanie McGrath, "True Blue: The Jean Craze Has Infected Everybody, From Celeb 'It Girls' to Your Average Janes," the *Toronto Sun*, February 26, 2006, S10; "True Religion Apparel Announces Preliminary 2007 New Sales Results and Outlook for 2008," True Religion news release, **http://phx.corporate-ir.net/phoenix.zhtml?c=140884&p=irol-newsArticle&ID=1097382&highlight=** (accessed March 25, 2008); "True Religion Launches National Consumer Advertising Campaign," True Religion news release, **http://phx.corporate-ir.net/phoenix.zhtml?c=140884&p=irol-newsArticle&ID=1121880&highlight=** (accessed March 25, 2008)

Catch the Buzz:
Promotional Strategy and Integrated Marketing Communication

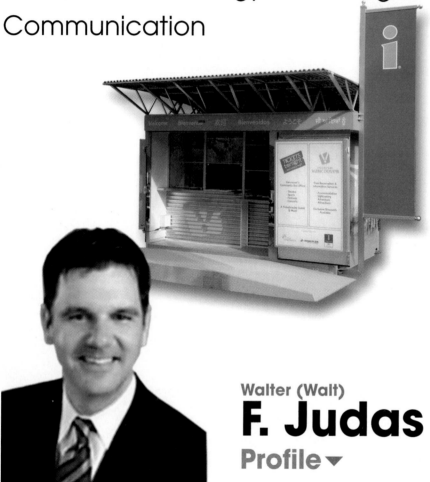

Walter (Walt)
F. Judas
Profile ▼

A **Decision Maker** at Tourism Vancouver

Walt Judas is Vice President of Marketing Communications & 2010 Strategies at Tourism Vancouver. As a member of the senior management team, Walt is responsible for corporate communications and manages the departments of Travel & Trade Media Relations, Marketing Services, and Corporate Sponsorships. Walt has a combined 25 years experience in marketing and communications. Prior to joining Tourism Vancouver, he was a communications consultant for the PACE Group and Shandwick Canada. He also managed communications programs for the Vancouver Port Authority and BC Pavilion Corporation. Walt began his career as a broadcaster for CISL Radio in Richmond, and has also worked in print, video, and television.

He is a member of the International Association of Convention & Visitor Bureaus, the Western Association of Convention & Visitor Bureaus, and the BC Chapter of the Canadian Public Relations Society. His board positions have included president of the BC Chapter of the American Marketing Association, Advisory Board of the Business School of Royal Roads University in Victoria, and board member of the Vancouver Community College (VCC) Foundation. In 2006, Walt was elected to the board of go2—the HR resource for people in Tourism—and in 2007, was named to the VCC School of Hospitality Advisory Board. Walt has a diploma in broadcast journalism, and a management certificate in marketing communications from the British Columbia Institute of Technology.

▼ **Q & A** with Walter (Walt) F. Judas

Q) What I do when I'm not working?
A) In summer, motorcycling, waterskiing; in winter, snowboarding & hockey.

Q) First job out of school?
A) Sportscaster.

Q) Career high?
A) Assuming my present portfolio at Tourism Vancouver.

Q) A job-related mistake I wish I hadn't made?
A) Staying too long in the broadcast industry.

Q) Business book I'm reading now?
A) *The Power of Tact* by Peter Legge.

Q) My motto to live by?
A) Life is short so make the most of every minute of every day.

Q) What drives me?
A) I am very competitive so I strive to get better at whatever task I take on.

Q) My management style?
A) Hire people smarter than me and empower them to do their jobs.

Q) Don't do this when interviewing with me?
A) Take a long time to make a point or ask a question.

Q) My pet peeve:
A) People who think the world revolves around them.

Decision Time at Tourism Vancouver

Tourism Vancouver is a not-for-profit business association with 1,000 members that represents the tourism industry in Vancouver. The organization launched the original bid to host the Vancouver 2010 Olympic & Paralympic Winter Games to benefit the city's tourism industry. Walt's challenge was to identify how the organization would continue to play a lead role to ensure its members realize actual benefits by collectively leveraging the unique opportunity the Games will provide to showcase the Vancouver experience to the world.

> ### Things to remember:
>
> Tourism Vancouver is only one of several agencies trying to promote Vancouver and the 2010 Olympics. Some of these agencies have overlapping responsibilities (and larger budgets), but they don't necessarily share the same marketing objectives.

The Vancouver Organizing Committee for the Olympic Games (VANOC) stated from the outset that the 2010 Olympics is Canada's Games, not merely Vancouver's or the Province of British Columbia's. Similarly, other key tourism agencies, including the Canadian Tourism Commission and Tourism British Columbia, also have a mandate to leverage the Games for the benefit of the region and country. So, other challenges Walt faced were how to work together with these organizations to accomplish everyone's objectives, how to establish marketing priorities, determine who takes the lead for various initiatives, decide what incremental dollars will be required to execute the plans, and how to ensure that the groups appease their stakeholders including members, politicians, and other DMOs (Destination Marketing Organizations). In addition, how does Vancouver itself ensure it derives the tourism benefits from the Games rather than being overshadowed by tourism government marketing agencies with larger budgets and political clout?

As a city Destination Marketing Organization (DMO), Tourism Vancouver's budget is both limited (approximately $12 million CAD annually, which is also roughly $12 million in USD) and committed to annual initiatives that require ongoing investment. Therefore, Walt needed to identify what incremental funds would be required to meet its 2010 obligations to partners and to execute on Tourism Vancouver's own strategies. The organization identified six possible ways to focus its efforts:

1. Help spectators find accommodation during the Games period
2. Provide story ideas and information to Olympic media and travel writers to promote Vancouver, Whistler, British Columbia, and Canada internationally
3. Train volunteers to assist during the Games
4. Set up information booths around Vancouver and Whistler to provide local and Olympic information in multiple languages, as well as sell tickets to local events and activities
5. Promote Vancouver around the world
6. Promote British Columbia and Canada around the world and to visitors during the Games period

Walt considered his Options 1·2·3

Option 1
Be the first agency to put a stake in the ground and declare its intentions to lead a specific initiative (Visitor Services kiosks throughout the city) in advance of and during the Games. This option would provide benefits to members, the community, VANOC, and especially to visitors; affirm Tourism Vancouver's lead role in visitor services in the city; and demonstrate leadership within the industry and to DMO colleagues. This would involve taking the lead on the kiosk initiative while still welcoming the investment and participation of the other tourism agencies. But, building and operating these kiosks would be expensive, and ROI would be very difficult to demonstrate because an Olympic visitor is different from the fully independent traveler. Olympic visitors do not tend to visit major attractions or do a lot of local sightseeing. Therefore, measuring ROI based on gross sales of member products is not necessarily an accurate reflection of the success of the kiosks, which will be used largely for dispensing destination and Olympic information. The visitor services or kiosk program will add to the visitor experience, which is not really quantifiable.

Option 2
Form a tourism steering committee that includes the lead agencies at the local, provincial, and federal levels (tourism consortium) responsible for drafting and implementing a comprehensive, joint 2010 tourism strategy. This plan would allow Tourism Vancouver to leverage its scarce resources. In addition, a coordinated strategy would result in one voice for the tourism strategy, especially to government and VANOC. In other words, all the agencies would work collaboratively on the various tourism strategies rather than executing separate or competitive initiatives or agreements with VANOC. Similarly, the organizing committee would recognize that in communicating with individual DMOs, it is in effect communicating with the consortium; each DMO would share information and cooperate to execute strategies with other consortium members. But, it would be difficult to work with so many different organizations that have different stakeholders or objectives. It would also be hard to demonstrate the value of this effort to Tourism Vancouver's own members, who would like to be able to point to some tangible effort they could squarely identify with the organization.

Option 3
Take action independent of the consortium's joint tourism strategy. Select one of the six options Tourism Vancouver's own 2010 strategy had already identified and implement it. This option would allow Tourism Vancouver to continue with existing investments that provide both short- and long-term results, identify the specific role that the organization plays vis-à-vis 2010, and identify core 2010 activities and budget requirements over a three-year period. On the other hand, Tourism Vancouver would risk alienating the other tourism agencies and it might miss out on other Games-related opportunities.

Now, put yourself in Walt's shoes: Which option would you choose, and why?

You Choose

Which **Option** would you choose, and **why**?
1. ☐YES ☐NO   2. ☐YES ☐NO   3. ☐YES ☐NO

See what **option** Walter chose and its success on **page 391** ➡

367

1

Talk to Your Customers!

Test your advertising memory:

1. Name the tiger that boasts, "They're grrrrrreat!"
2. Name one or more products for which Tiger Woods is a spokesperson.
3. What character do Energizer battery ads feature?
4. At Burger King, you can have it "_____," whereas at Hardee's the burgers are "_____" broiled.
5. Which paper towel brand is "The Quicker Picker-Upper?"*

Did you get them all right? You owe your knowledge about these and a thousand other trivia questions to the efforts of people who specialize in marketing communication. As we said in Chapter 1, **promotion** is the coordination of marketing communication efforts to influence attitudes or behavior. This function is one of the famous *Four Ps* of the marketing mix and it plays a vital role—whether the goal is to sell hamburgers, insurance, ringtones, or healthy diets. Of course, keep in mind that marketers use *all* the elements of the marketing mix to communicate with customers. The package in which the product comes, the price of the product, and the type of retail outlet where the product is available all are part of effective marketing communication because they make statements about the nature of the product and the image it intends to convey.

Marketing communication takes many forms: quirky television commercials, sophisticated magazine ads, Web banner ads that boast the latest Java-language applications, funky T-shirts, and blimps blinking messages over football stadiums—even do-it-yourself, customer-made advertising. Some marketing communications push specific products, whereas others try to create or reinforce a corporate image:

- Marketing communication *informs* consumers about new goods and services and where they can purchase them.[1]

- Marketing communication *reminds* consumers to continue using certain brands.

- Marketing communication *persuades* consumers to choose one brand over others.

- Marketing communication *builds* relationships with customers.

The traditional forms of marketing communication are *advertising*, including traditional mass media, out of home, and Internet advertising; *sales promotion* such as coupons, samples, rebates, or contests; press releases and special events that *public relations* professionals organize; *sales presentations*; and a variety of *direct marketing* activities ranging from telemarketing to home shopping. Today's marketers add newer types of communication tactics, such as *buzz marketing*, *viral marketing*, *guerrilla marketing*, *experiential marketing* and *consumer-generated media (CGM)* to their bag of tricks.

*ANSWERS: 1) Tony the Tiger, brand character for Kellogg's Frosted Flakes, 2) Tiger Woods has been a spokesperson for a number of products including Apple computers, Buick, Accenture, American Express, Gatorade, Gillette, and TLC Laser Eye Centers; 3) the Energizer Bunny; 4) "your way," "char"; 5) Bounty paper towels.

Many marketing experts now believe a successful promotional strategy should integrate several diverse forms of marketing communication. **Integrated marketing communication (IMC)** is the process that marketers use to plan, develop, execute, and evaluate coordinated, measurable, persuasive brand communication programs over time to targeted audiences. As we'll discuss later in this chapter, the IMC approach argues that consumers see the variety of messages they receive from a firm—a TV commercial, a coupon, an opportunity to win a sweepstakes, and a display in a store—as a whole, as a single company speaking to them but in different places and different ways. IMC marketers understand that to achieve their marketing communication goals, they must selectively use some or all of these touchpoints to speak to their customers.

That's a lot different from most traditional marketing communication programs that make little effort to coordinate the varying messages consumers receive. An advertising campaign typically runs independently of a sweepstakes, which in turn has no relation to a NASCAR racing sponsorship. These disjointed efforts can send conflicting messages that leave the consumer confused and unsure of the brand's identity. Just as customer needs are the focus of the marketing concept and of total quality management programs, the customer is also the focus for companies that adopt an IMC perspective. With IMC, marketers seek to understand what information consumers want as well as how, when, and where they want it—and then to deliver information about the product using the best combination of communication methods available to them.

As you'll see in Figure 12.1, we are now in Part 4 of this book, "Communicate the Value Proposition." In today's competitive marketplace, the role of the successful marketer in communicating the value proposition means adopting an IMC perspective. In this chapter, we'll first review the communication process. Next, we'll discuss both the traditional elements of the promotion mix and some of the new tricks marketers use to communicate with us. Finally, we'll describe the characteristics of IMC and the communication planning process.

Figure 12.1 | Make and Deliver Value

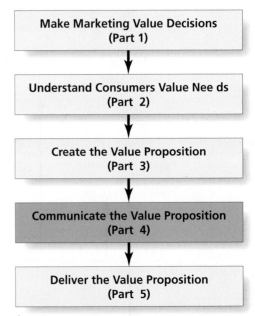

Make Marketing Value Decisions (Part 1)

↓

Understand Consumers Value Needs (Part 2)

↓

Create the Value Proposition (Part 3)

↓

Communicate the Value Proposition (Part 4)

↓

Deliver the Value Proposition (Part 5)

promotion
The coordination of a marketer's communication efforts to influence attitudes or behavior.

integrated marketing communication (IMC)
A strategic business process that marketers use to plan, develop, execute, and evaluate coordinated, measurable, persuasive brand communication programs over time to targeted audiences.

2 The Communication Model

OBJECTIVE

Understand the communication model.

(pp. 369–372)

A good way to understand what marketing communication is all about is to examine the **communication model** in Figure 12.2. In this model, a source transmits a message through some medium to a receiver who (we hope) is listening and understands the message. *Any* way that marketers reach out to consumers, from a simple highway billboard to a customized e-mail message, is part of the basic communication process.

The communication model specifies the elements necessary for effective communication to occur: a source, a message, a medium, and a receiver. Regardless of how a marketer sends messages—whether by a hat with a Caterpillar tractor logo on it, a door-to-door sales pitch from a Mary Kay representative, or a televised fashion show with supermodels strutting their stuff for Victoria's Secret—her objective is to capture receivers' attention and relate to their needs.

communication model
The process whereby meaning is transferred from a source to a receiver.

Marketing communications can take many forms. A company called Beach 'N Billboard will even imprint your ad or logo directly into the sand, and then come back to redo it tomorrow.

Figure 12.2 | Communication Model

The communication model explains how organizations create and transmit messages from the marketer (the source) to the consumer (the receiver) who (we hope) understands what the marketer intends to say.

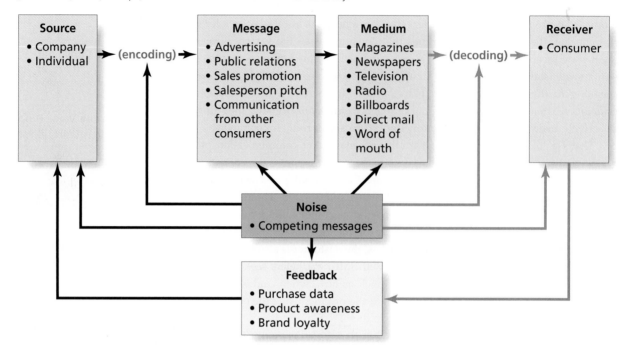

Encoding by the Source (the Marketer)

encoding

The process of translating an idea into a form of communication that will convey meaning.

source

An organization or individual that sends a message.

Encoding is the process by which a source translates an idea into a form of communication that conveys the desired meaning. The **source** is the organization or individual that sends the message. It's one thing for marketers to form an idea about a product in their own minds, but it's not quite as simple to express the idea to their customers. To make their messages more believable or more attractive to consumers, marketers sometimes choose a real person (golf pro Tiger Woods for Nike or cyclist Lance Armstrong for Saturn), hire an actor or a model (Angelina Jolie earned $12 million as spokesperson for St. John Knits, Inc.), or create a character (Tony the Tiger for Kellogg's Frosted Flakes) to represent the source.[2]

In other cases actual customers are the source. In one recent ad campaign Mercedes featured photos of real owners sent in along with short vignettes of the drivers. These testimonials can be a very convincing source of communication for prospective Mercedes buyers.[3] Oil filter-maker Fram involved product users when it combined its Internet marketing activities with traditional advertising. The company featured 13 contest winners who won a new Fram product on its Web site in TV commercials; they told other consumers of their experience with their prizes. Later, when Fram found that winners accessed the Internet to blog about their experience, they contacted the winners to ask if they would post the commercials on sites they frequented.[4]

The Message

message

The communication in physical form that goes from a sender to a receiver.

The **message** is the actual communication that goes from the source to a receiver. It includes information necessary to persuade, inform, remind, or build a relationship. Advertising messages may include both verbal and nonverbal elements, such as beautiful background scenery or funky music. The marketer must select the ad elements carefully so that the message connects with end consumers or business customers in its target market. Otherwise effective communication simply does not occur and the organization just wastes the money it spent to advertise. In contrast to ads and other forms of mass-media communications, a salesperson can deliver a message she carefully tailors for each individual customer, and she can respond to questions or objections.

The Medium

No matter how the source encodes the message, it must then transmit it via a **medium**, a communication vehicle that reaches members of a target audience. This vehicle can be television, radio, a magazine, a company Web site, an Internet blog, a personal contact, a billboard, or even a coffee mug displaying a product logo. When marketers select a medium, they have two major challenges. First, they must make sure the target market will be exposed to the medium—that the intended receivers actually read the magazine or watch the TV show where ads appear. Second, the attributes of the advertised product should match those of the medium. For example, magazines with high prestige are more effective to communicate messages about overall product image and quality, whereas specialized magazines do a better job when they convey factual information.[5]

Decoding by the Receiver

If a tree falls in the forest and no one hears it, did it make a sound? Zen mysteries aside, communication cannot occur unless a **receiver** is there to get the message. The receiver is any individual or organization that intercepts and interprets the message. Assuming that the customer is even paying attention (a big assumption in our overloaded, media-saturated society), she interprets the message in light of her unique experiences. **Decoding** is the process whereby a receiver assigns meaning to a message; that is, she translates the message she sees or hears back into an idea that makes sense to her.

Marketers hope that the target consumer will decode the message the way they intended, but effective communication occurs only when the source and the receiver share a mutual frame of reference. For example, when American rock and folk icon Bob Dylan showed up in a television ad for Victoria's Secret's "Angels" line while models cavorted to a remixed version of his song "Love Sick," not everyone who saw the commercial interpreted it quite the same way. To die-hard fans who remember the "old Dylan" who wrote song lyrics like "Advertising signs that con you/Into thinking you're the one/That can do what's never been done/That can win what's never been won/Meantime life outside goes on/All around you" in his 1965 song "It's Alright Ma (I'm Only Bleeding)," this wasn't business as usual. One disappointed consumer who is also curator of a collection of Dylan material lamented, "I'm going to have to go blow my brains out."[6] Clearly, Victoria's Secret hoped most of the women watching the commercial had a different reaction. Too often sources and receivers aren't on the same page and the results can range from mildly embarrassing to downright disastrous.

Noise

The communication model also acknowledges that **noise**—anything that interferes with effective communication—can block messages. As the many arrows between noise and the other elements of the communication model in Figure 12.2 indicate, noise can occur at any stage of communication. It can pop up at the encoding stage if the source uses words or symbols that the receiver will not understand. Or the receiver may be distracted from receiving the message by a nearby conversation. There may be a problem with transmission of the message through the medium—especially if it's drowned out by the chorus of other marketers clamoring for us to look at *their* messages instead. Marketers try to minimize noise by placing their messages where there is less likely to be distractions or competition for consumers' attention. Calvin Klein, for example, will often buy a block of advertising pages in a magazine so that the reader sees only pictures of its clothing.

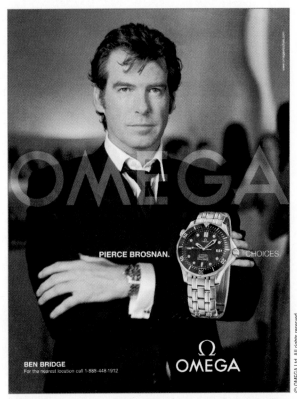

Marketers often hire celebrities as spokespersons for their products, thus adding excitement to the "source" of the message.

medium
A communication vehicle through which a message is transmitted to a target audience.

receiver
The organization or individual that intercepts and interprets the message.

decoding
The process by which a receiver assigns meaning to the message.

noise
Anything that interferes with effective communication.

Feedback

feedback
Receivers' reactions to the message.

To complete the communication loop, the source gets **feedback** from receivers. Feedback is a reaction to the message that helps marketers gauge the effectiveness of the message so they can fine-tune it. Sometimes consumers are assertive in providing feedback, calling a toll-free number or communicating on-line about a product problem. More often, marketers must actively seek their customers' feedback. The need for this "reality check" reminds us of the importance of conducting marketing research (as we discussed in Chapter 4) to verify that a firm's strategies are working.

3

Marketing Communication Strategy and the Promotion Mix

OBJECTIVE

List and describe the traditional elements of the promotion mix.
(pp. 372–375)

As we said earlier, promotion, or marketing communication, is one of the Four Ps. But virtually *everything* an organization says and does is a form of marketing communication. The ads it creates, the packages it designs, the uniforms its employees wear and what other consumers say about their experiences with the firm contribute to the impression people have of the company and its products. In fact, savvy marketers should consider that *every element of the marketing mix is actually a form of communication.* After all, the price of a product, where it is sold, and even the nature of the product itself contribute to the impression we form of it.

Within the marketing mix, we call the communication elements that the marketer controls the **promotion mix**. These elements include the following:

promotion mix
The major elements of marketer-controlled communication, including advertising, sales promotion, public relations, personal selling, and direct marketing.

- Advertising
- Sales promotion
- Public relations
- Personal selling
- Direct marketing

Just as a DJ combines different songs or phrases to create an entertainment experience, the term *mix* implies that a company's promotion strategy focuses on more than one element, so the challenge is to integrate these different communication tools in an effective way.

Another challenge is to be sure that the promotion mix works in harmony with the overall marketing mix, thereby combining elements of promotion with place, price, and product to position the firm's offering in people's minds. For example, marketers must design ads for luxury products such as Rolex watches or Jaguar automobiles to communicate that same luxury character of the product and they should appear in places that reinforce that upscale image. A chic ad that appears before a showing of the latest *Jackass* movie just won't cut it.

By the **People**, For the **People**

Proctor & Gamble is the company behind Tremor, a word of mouth marketing service. Tremor is a teen-oriented program to build word of mouth advocacy among young consumers for P&G brands. Its strategy is to identify and enlist youthful "connectors" (or "trend spreaders") who influence opinions among their peers and get them to spread the word to their friends.

Tremor defines connectors as those who have "...social networks like you would not believe"; only 10 percent of the teen population qualifies. These trendsetters are more open to new ideas and they love to talk to their friends (and perhaps anyone who will listen) about cool new products they've found. As of now there are about 250,000 teens participating in the Tremor community (anyone you know?). Members share information and stories with each other within the community and help brand marketers refine their advertising messages and product concepts. The program was a big success, so P&G launched a second buzz program it calls Vocalpoint that aims to do the same with a network of mothers. Again, participants share their stories and ideas (this time about motherhood issues rather than dating and bad hair days) on a Web site.[7]

Figure 12.3 | Control Continuum

The messages that consumers receive about companies and products differ in the amount of control the marketer has over the message she delivers to the consumer.

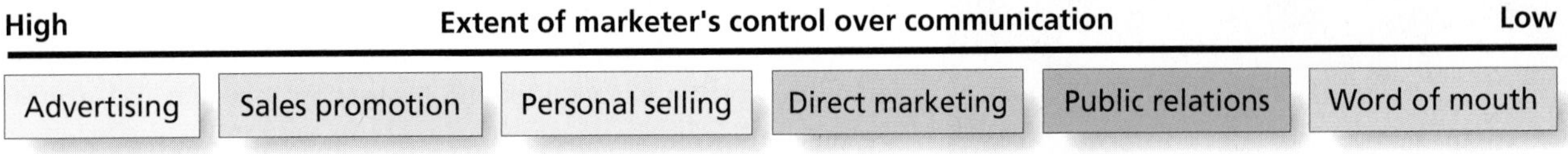

High	Extent of marketer's control over communication				Low
Advertising	Sales promotion	Personal selling	Direct marketing	Public relations	Word of mouth

Marketers have a lot more control over some kinds of marketing communication messages than they do others. As Figure 12.3 shows, *mass-media advertising* and *sales promotion* are at one end of the continuum, where the marketer has total control over the message she delivers. At the other end is *word of mouth (WOM) communication*, where everyday people rather than the company run the show. WOM is a vitally important component of the brand attitudes consumers form—and of their decisions about what and what not to buy.

As we'll discuss later in this chapter, marketers today try to gain some control over what consumers hear from one another through buzz marketing activities where they deliberately provide information or create events to get people to talk to their friends about what's going on. Between the ends we find *personal selling* and *direct marketing*, where marketers have some but not total control over the message they deliver, and *public relations*, where marketers have less control. Table 12.1 presents some of the pros and cons of each element of the promotion mix, which we discuss next.

Table 12.1 | A Comparison of Elements of the Promotion Mix

Promotional Element	Pros	Cons
Advertising	• The marketer has control over what the message will say, when it will appear, and who is likely to see it.	• Often expensive to produce and distribute. • May have low credibility and/or be ignored by audience.
Sales promotion	• Provides incentives to retailers to support one's products. • Builds excitement for retailers and consumers. • Encourages immediate purchase and trial of new products. • Price-oriented promotions cater to price-sensitive consumers.	• Short-term emphasis on immediate sales rather than a focus on building brand loyalty. • The number of competing promotions may make it hard to break through the promotional clutter.
Public relations	• Relatively low cost • High credibility	• Lack of control over the message that is eventually transmitted and no guarantee that the message will ever reach the target. • Hard to track the results of publicity efforts.
Personal selling	• Direct contact with the customer gives the salesperson the opportunity to be flexible and modify the sales message to coincide with the customer's needs. • The salesperson can get immediate feedback from the customer.	• High cost per contact with customer. • Difficult to ensure consistency of message when it is delivered by many different company representatives. • The credibility of salespeople often depends on the quality of their company's image, which has been created by other promotional strategies.
Direct marketing	• Can target specific groups of potential customers with different offers. • Marketers can easily measure the results. • Can provide extensive product information and multiple offers within a single appeal. • Provides a means for collecting information for company marketing databases.	• Consumers may have a negative opinion of some types of direct marketing. • Costs more per contact than mass appeals.

Marketers have a wide range of communication tools from which to choose, ranging from glitzy TV commercials to neon signs.

Mass Appeals

Some elements of the promotion mix include messages intended to reach many prospective customers at the same time. Whether a company offers customers a coupon for 50 cents off or airs a television commercial to millions, it is promoting itself to a mass audience. The following are the elements of the promotion mix that use a mass appeal strategy:

- **Advertising:** Advertising is, for many, the most familiar and visible element of the promotion mix. It is nonpersonal communication from an identified sponsor using the mass media. Because it can convey rich and dynamic images, advertising can establish and reinforce a distinctive brand identity. This helps marketers bond with customers and boost sales. Advertising also is useful in communicating factual information about the product or reminding consumers to buy their favorite brand. However, advertising sometimes suffers from a credibility problem because cynical consumers tune out messages they think are biased or are intended to sell them something they don't need. Advertising can also be very expensive, so firms must ensure that their messages are effective.

- **Sales promotion:** Sales promotion includes programs such as contests, coupons, or other incentives that marketers design to build interest in or encourage purchase of a product during a specified period. Unlike other forms of promotion, sales promotion intends to stimulate immediate action (often in the form of a purchase) rather than build long-term loyalty. More to come on this in Chapter 13.

- **Public relations:** Public relations describes a variety of communication activities that seek to create and maintain a positive image of an organization and its products among various *publics*, including customers, government officials, and shareholders. As we'll see in Chapter 13, public relations activities include writing press releases about product- and company-related issues, dealing with the news media, and organizing special events. Public relations programs also include efforts to present negative company news in the most positive way so that this information will have less damaging consequences. In contrast to sales promotion, public relations components of the promotion mix usually do not seek a short-term increase in sales. Instead, they try to influence feelings, opinions, or beliefs for the long term.

Personal Appeals

Sometimes marketers want to communicate with consumers on a personal, one-on-one level. The most immediate way for a marketer to make contact with customers is simply to tell them how wonderful the product is. This is part of the *personal selling* element of the promotion mix we mentioned previously. It is the direct interaction between a company representative and a customer that can occur in person, by phone, or even over an interactive computer link.

Salespeople are a valuable source of communication because customers can ask questions and the salesperson can immediately address objections and describe product benefits. Personal selling can be tremendously effective, especially for big-ticket consumer items and for industrial products for which the "human touch" is essential.

Keith
Starcher

a professor at Indiana Wesleyan University

My Advice for Tourism Vancouver would
be to choose

Option

real people, **Other Voices**

I dismiss Option #1 because of the limited budget and also Option #2 because of the inability to prove a return on investment. Option #3 allows Tourism Vancouver to fully utilize the creativity

and innovative thinking of its membership to get involved in meeting the above objectives subject to the above constraints. Who knows, there may be a combination of the six options that provides an optimum solution—or even another option not yet considered. Marketing is all about strategy and analysis. Use the collective wisdom of your 1,000 members. None of us is as smart as all of us. ➤

In fact, personal selling can be so effective that some marketers, if given a choice, might neglect other forms of promotion. On the down side, however, this approach can get very expensive and it's more difficult to get the word out to large numbers of people. We'll learn more about the personal selling process in Chapter 14.

Marketers also use direct mail, telemarketing, and other *direct marketing* activities to create personal appeals. Like personal selling, direct marketing provides direct communication with a consumer or business customer. Because direct marketing activities seek to gain a direct response from individual consumers, as we saw in Chapter 7 the source can target a communication to market segments of a few or—with today's technology—even segments of one. Unfortunately, for many products, especially consumer goods—a bottle of shampoo or a pair of running shoes—it's often too expensive to connect with each and every customer personally, so marketers need to use other forms of promotion as well.

4 Buzz Appeals

OBJECTIVE

Explain how word of mouth marketing, buzz marketing, viral marketing, guerrilla marketing, experiential marketing, and consumer-generated media provide exciting alternatives to traditional forms of promotion.
(pp. 375–380)

In addition to these tried-and-true methods, many marketers are starting to figure out that they must find alternatives to traditional advertising—especially when they want to talk to young consumers who are cynical about the efforts of big corporations to buy their allegiance. In addition, traditional advertising media are so saturated that marketers are scrambling to find new, unexpected places to place their messages.

Pepsi's campaign for Tava, its new line of no-calorie, carbonated beverages, bypassed traditional advertising media in favor of its own Web site, banner ads, promotions, product sampling at events such as the Sundance Film Festival, and deliveries of gift bottles of the drink to employees of prominent companies like Apple, Bliss Spa, Google, and MTV. Tava's target market is men and women aged 35–49 who spend tons of time on-line exploring the Web. To capture their attention, the Tava Web site includes downloadable songs from new musicians such as Deccatree, and provides information on arts events such as the Boston Arts Festival and Shakespeare in the Park in Manhattan. Pepsi's goal is to create emotional connections with target consumers and to get them to tell other people about their experiences.[8]

These cutting-edge techniques come under a variety of names including word of mouth marketing, viral marketing, buzz marketing, guerrilla marketing, experiential

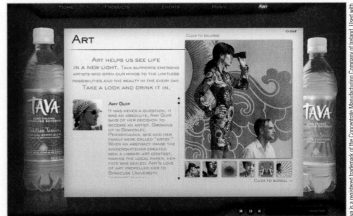

Pepsi harnesses new media and encourages buzz to promote its new line of Tava beverages.

Tava is a registered trademark of the Concentrate Manufacturing Company of Ireland. Used with permission.

marketing, and consumer-generated media. Let's take a closer look at these radical alternatives to traditional methods of promotion.

Buzz, Word of Mouth, and Viral Marketing

Everywhere you turn today, it seems someone is talking about "buzz." In fact, we hear so much buzz about buzz and its counterparts, viral marketing and word of mouth marketing, that it's hard to know exactly what all the terms mean. The Word of Mouth Marketing Association (WOMMA) provides the following definitions:[9]

word of mouth (WOM)
When consumers provide information about products to other consumers.

word of mouth marketing
Giving people a reason to talk about your products and making it easier for that conversation to take place.

buzz marketing
Using high-profile entertainment or news to get people to talk about your brand.

viral marketing
Creating entertaining or informative messages that are designed to be passed along in an exponential fashion, often electronically or by e-mail.

buzz
Word of mouth communication that customers view as authentic.

- **Word of mouth (WOM):** The act of a consumer creating and/or distributing marketing-relevant information to another consumer

- **Word of mouth marketing:** An effort by an organization to affect how consumers create and/or distribute marketing-relevant information to another consumer

- **Buzz marketing:** Using high-profile entertainment or news to get people to talk about your brand

- **Viral marketing:** Creating entertaining or informative messages designed to be passed along in an exponential fashion, often electronically or by e-mail

In more general terms, marketers think of **buzz** as everyday people helping their marketing efforts by talking about a product or a company to their friends and neighbors.[10] As the examples in Table 12.2 illustrate, companies today spend millions to create consumer buzz. Firms like Dell have named word of mouth (WOM) marketing managers, and the WOMMA membership roster includes most of the top consumer brand companies.[11]

Table 12.2 | How Some Marketers Create Buzz

Company	Buzz Marketing Tactic
General Mills	In the 1930s General Mills created the Betty Crocker character. When the Betty Crocker weekly radio show was aired, consumers spread the word. Betty Crocker still gets letters every day.[13]
Burger King	At BK's Web site **www.subservientchicken.com**, consumers could have fun typing in orders for a man in a chicken suit to follow. The site attracted 418 million visitors who stayed on an average of 6 minutes.[14] Result: Young people saw Burger King as a more empathetic and relevant company.
Nike	Nike was supposedly the "brains" behind a cool, illegal warehouse club in Berlin.[15]
Hasbro	Consumers were encouraged to play Monopoly on the streets of London.[16] The fines and clean-up fees Hasbro paid to the city were far less than the advertising costs the company would have incurred in a traditional campaign.
Puma	The company encouraged consumers to stencil its cat logo all over Paris.
Audi	For introduction of its A3 model, Audi staged a fake car heist at the New York Auto Show. Posters placed near the heist appealed to consumers for help and sent them to a Web site where they could participate in an alternate reality game (ARG) and find hidden clues to solve the mystery.[17]
Kellogg's	The company gave a video of never-before-seen ads for Pop-Tarts to 12,000 "tween" girl influencers.[18]
America's Next Top Model (television series)	To promote the launch of its fourth season, the series used alloy.com, a Web site aimed at teen girls, to find 500 "insider" girls who could generate buzz about the show. Alloy.com monitors the chat on its site and identified 7,000 girls who had shown an interest in the show in their "chats." From the initial 7,000, the Web site identified 500 who were the most popular on instant messaging buddy lists. It gave these 500 girls party kits and asked them to invite four friends to their homes for gatherings themed around *America's Next Top Model*.[19]
Procter & Gamble	P&G sent product and information to 250,000 teens who were not paid but were free to form their own opinions and talk about the products.[20]
Microsoft	When it introduced its new *Halo 2* videogame, Microsoft gave gamers it had identified as influencers bits of information about the game before its release so they could talk about the product with other avid gamers who conveniently are also heavy users of chat rooms and videogame message boards.[21]

According to advertising agency JWT Worldwide, over 85 percent of top 1,000 marketing firms now use word of mouth tactics.[12]

Of course, buzz isn't *really* new. Many refer to the *Mona Lisa* as one of the first examples of buzz marketing. In 1911 the famous painting was stolen from the Louvre and became the topic of consumer talk around the globe, giving the previously little recognized painting fame that exists until today. When you think of the effect of consumers talking one-on-one nearly a century ago, imagine the exponential increase in influence of the individual consumer "connectors" or "e-fluentials" who use blogs and other computer-generated media to increase their reach.[22] Compared to traditional advertising and public relations activities, these endorsements are far more credible and thus more valuable to the brand.

Buzz can be especially successful for smaller businesses where customers feel they have more of a personal relationship than with a large corporation. LaRosa's Pizza with 59 restaurants in Kentucky, Indiana, and Ohio attracted more than 4,900 new customers in one month when it combined buzz with viral marketing in an e-mail newsletter containing a game and a "forward-to-a-friend" button.[23]

A word of warning before you decide that a buzz is always good: These campaigns also can backfire big time. For example, McDonald's launched a "Lincoln Fry" buzz campaign. The company used its blog to spread the word about a couple who found a McDonald's fry that looked like Abraham Lincoln. When consumers learned that the blog and the couple were bogus, the buzz turned negative and the chain's rep went from the fryer into the fire.[24]

Of course, marketers don't necessarily create the buzz around their product anyway—sometimes they just catch a wave that's building among consumers and ride it home. WOMMA refers to buzz that comes from deliberate buzz marketing campaigns as "amplified WOM" while it calls buzz that occurs naturally "organic WOM." Organic buzz allowed Procter & Gamble to discover that its Home Café coffee maker had a tendency to start fires after 3,000 buzz agents complained.[25] Naturally occurring buzz also can create negative publicity, as when ex-journalist Jeff Jarvis detailed on a blog his problem getting a $1,600 PC fixed due to poor service from Dell.[26] To create positive organic buzz, companies still need to have a total customer focus; just like the old (pre-buzz) days, they need to do a better job of satisfying customers and then rely on their legions of happy campers to spread the word for them.

Guerrilla Marketing

As the saying goes, "necessity is the mother of invention." A few years back, companies with tiny advertising budgets developed innovative and cheaper ways to capture consumers' attention. These activities—from putting advertising stickers on apples and heads of lettuce to placing product-related messages on the backs of theater tickets and flags on golf courses—became known as **guerrilla marketing**. No, this term doesn't refer to marketers making monkeys out of themselves (that's "gorilla marketing"). A guerrilla marketing strategy involves "ambushing" consumers with promotional content in places where they are not expecting to encounter this kind of activity.[27]

Today, big companies are buying into guerrilla marketing strategies big time. Burger King recently began a guerrilla marketing campaign to increase sales in its Asia-Pacific stores by 25 percent.[28] The company sent CDs with quirky marketing suggestions to local restaurant managers. These included putting "I♥BK" on T-shirts and placing the shirts on Ronald McDonald, placing large footprints from McDonald's stores to Burger King outlets, placing signs on empty benches saying "gone to BK—Ronald," and placing large signs at BK locations that are near KFC locations that read, "It's why the chicken crossed the road."

Companies can use guerrilla marketing to promote new drinks, cars, clothing styles, or even computer systems. Much to the annoyance of city officials in San Francisco and Chicago, IBM painted hundreds of "Peace Love Linux" logos on sidewalks to publicize the company's adoption of the Linux operating system. Even though the company got hit with

guerrilla marketing
Marketing activity in which a firm "ambushes" consumers with promotional content in places they are not expecting to encounter this kind of activity.

a hefty bill to pay for cleaning up the "corporate graffiti," one marketing journalist noted that they "got the publicity they were looking for."[29] Given the success of many of these campaigns that operate on a shoestring budget, expect to see even more of this kind of tactic as other companies climb on the guerrilla bandwagon.

Experiential Marketing

experiential marketing
Marketing activities that attempt to give customers an opportunity to actually interact with brands, thus enabling them to make more intelligent and informed purchase decisions.

Experiential marketing attempts to connect consumers with brands in personally relevant ways by giving customers an opportunity to actually interact with brands, thus enabling them to make more intelligent and informed purchase decisions. Ford Motor Company, Fila, Volkswagen, and Wells Fargo are only a few of the companies that have appointed *experiential marketing managers* so that they can focus on creating positive encounters between their brands and their customers. Compared with traditional marketing where marketers only tell consumers about the features of a brand, "experiential marketing" allows the customer to actually experience benefits of the brand for themselves.

Many marketers believe that if experiential marketing is done right, it can be the most powerful tool possible for creating brand loyalty. Rather than just assure young adult customers that they are a bank that cares, Wells Fargo created an experiential campaign they can access on a Web site they call Stagecoach Island (**http://blog.wellsfargo.com/ StagecoachIsland**). On the "island," visitors can build dream homes, meet new friends, get a virtual job, race a motorbike, snowboard, or skydive. And landing in a virtual tree doesn't hurt nearly as much![30] Other companies including Avon, Campbell Soup, Hershey, Kraft, and Ford sponsor house parties where they invite owners to hang out and swap stories about their experiences with the products.[31]

Consumer-Generated Media

consumer-generated media (CGM)
The on-line consumer-generated comments, opinions, and product-related stories available to other consumers through digital technology.

The latest promotional craze is to let your customers actually create your advertising for you. **Consumer-generated media (CGM)** includes the millions of on-line consumer comments, opinions, and product-related stories available to other consumers through digital technology. CGM includes opinions, advice, consumer-to-consumer discussions, reviews, shared personal experiences, photos, images, videos, even podcasts and webcasts. Marketers that embrace this strategy understand that it's OK to let people have fun with their products. For example, join the millions of others who checked out the infamous YouTube videos where "mad scientists" mix Mentos candies with Diet Coke for explosive results (such as **http://www.youtube. com/watch?v=hKoB0MHVBvM**).

Marketers need to monitor (and sometimes encourage) CGM for two reasons. First, consumers are more likely to trust messages from fellow consumers than what companies tell them. In fact, they're more likely to say they "trust completely" product information they receive from other consumers than from any other source.[32] Second, with the dramatic proliferation of on-line usage, when someone searches on-line for a company or product name, they are certain to access any number of blogs, forums, homegrown commercials, or on-line complaint sites. Some companies resist this trend by restricting access to their material or even suing

M etrics Moment

As on-line content available through consumer-generated media (CGM) grows in importance, marketers need to measure content and learn more about how consumers talk about issues and products and spread information. BuzzMetrics, a subsidiary of the Nielsen Company, offers marketers research services to help them understand how CGM affects their brands. Neilsen's BuzzMetrics search engines identify on-line word of mouth commentary and conversations to closely examine phrases, opinions, keywords, sentences, and images people use when they talk about a client's products. The company's processing programs then analyze vocabulary, language patterns, and phrasing to determine whether the comments are positive or negative, and whether the authors are men or women, young or old in order to more accurately measure buzz. BuzzMetrics' BrandPulse and BrandPulse Insight reports can provide marketers with answers to questions such as the following:

- How do consumers feel about a brand?
- How many consumers are talking on-line, and how many other consumers are influenced by the conversation?
- What specific issues are they discussing? What issues are coming around the corner? What events, trends, and specific issues are influencing your marketplace and your brand?
- Who's talking and where, and are they consumers who are influential?
- Did your marketing initiatives engage, resonate, echo, or backfire with consumers?
- Are customer service and other business processes helping or hurting buzz?
- Can you influence, control, or manage word of mouth? Should your brand start blogging, put a friendly front door on the Web site, or embark upon a "conversation" with consumers?[33]

Ethical Decisions in the Real World

You go to a Fourth of July barbecue at a friend's house. Gwen, a friend and neighbor, arrives with a plate of chicken sausage, telling everyone that it tastes just like pork and is low in fat. When the guests at the party rave about the sausage, Gwen tells everyone that the sausage comes in six flavors and lists which supermarkets carry the brand. Later on you ask Gwen, "What gives with the sausage?" She then explains that she actually was hired by a firm to talk it up. In addition to this party, she has talked to other friends about how the sausage would be great for breakfast and gave a local priest who loves Italian food a recipe for Tuscan white-bean soup using the sausage. While she doesn't actually get paid, she does receive coupons for product discounts. "Why don't you join the firm with me?" she asks.

What would you do?

Ripped from the Headlines! See what happened in the Real World at **www.mypearsonmarketinglab.com**

ETHICS CHECK: ↖

Find out what other students taking this course **would do** and **why** on **www. mypearsonmarketinglab. com**

Would you promote a buzz marketing firm's clients to your friends?

☐YES ☐NO

consumers who talk about them because they fear losing control over their brand messages. They really need to get over it and recognize that in our digital world their messages (like your Facebook page) are almost impossible to control. In Web 2.0, you're either on the train or under it!

Ethical Problems in Buzz Marketing

Just as firms are discovering there are a myriad of opportunities for buzz marketing, there are equally large opportunities for unethical or at least questionable marketing behavior. Some of these are as follows:

- *Activities designed to deceive consumers.* Buzz works best when companies put unpaid consumers in charge of creating their own messages. As Table 12.3 shows, WOMMA considers hiring actors to create buzz deceptive and unethical. This is just what Sony Ericsson Mobile Communications did when the company hired 60 actors to go to tourist attractions. Their role was to act like tourists and get unsuspecting passersby to take their photos using the new Sony Ericsson camera phone, and then hype the phone. WOMMA now has rules that state that anyone talking up products should identify the client for whom they work.[34]

- *Directing buzz marketing at children or teens.* Some critics say buzz marketing should never do this, as these consumers are more impressionable and easier to deceive than adults.[35]

- *Buzz marketing activities that damage property.* Puma encouraged consumers to stencil its cat logo all over Paris. Such activities lead to damage or vandalism which the company will ultimately have to pay for. In addition, individual consumers could find themselves in trouble with the law, a problem which could ultimately backfire and damage the company image.

- *Stealth marketing activities that deliberately deceive or lie on behalf of clients.* WOMMA considers such activities—whether authoring a positive product review on a shopbot, pretending to read a new novel on the subway, or calling a supermarket to ask the manager why she is not stocking a certain product—to be unethical.

Table 12.3 | Positive and Unethical Word of Mouth Marketing Strategies

Positive Word of Mouth Marketing Strategies	Unethical Word of Mouth Marketing Strategies
1. Encourage communication Develop tools to make telling a friend easier Create forums and feedback tools Work with social networks	**1. Stealth Marketing** Any practice designed to deceive people about the involvement of marketers in a communication
2. Giving people something to talk about Information that can be shared or forwarded Advertising, stunts, and other publicity that encourages conversation Working with product development to build WOM elements into products	**2. Shilling** Pay people to talk about (or promote) a product without disclosing that they are working for the company; impersonate a customer
3. Create communities and connect people Create user groups and fan clubs Support independent groups that form around your product Host discussions and message boards about your products Enable grassroots organizations such as local meetings and other real-world participation	**3. Infiltration** Use fake identities in an on-line discussion to promote a product; take over a Web site, conversation, or live event against the wishes or rules set by the proprietor
4. Work with influential communities Find people who are likely to respond to your message Identify people who are able to influence your target customers Inform these individuals about what you do and encourage them to spread the word Good-faith efforts to support issues and causes that are important to these individuals	**4. Comment Spam** Use automated software ("bots") to post unrelated or inappropriate comments to blogs or other on-line communities
5. Create evangelist or advocate programs Provide recognition and tools to active advocates Recruit new advocates, teach them about the benefits of your products, and encourage them to talk about them	**5. Defacement** Vandalize or damage property to promote a product
6. Research and listen to customer feedback Track on-line and off-line conversations by supporters, detractors, and neutrals Listen and respond to both positive and negative conversations	**6. Spam** Send bulk or unsolicited e-mail or other messages without clear, voluntary permission
7. Engage in transparent conversation Encourage two-way conversations with interested parties Create blogs and other tools to share information Participate openly on on-line blogs and discussions	**7. Falsification** Knowingly disseminate false or misleading information
8. Co-creation and information sharing Involve consumers in marketing and creative (feedback on creative campaigns, allow them to create commercials, etc.) Let customers "behind the curtain" to obtain first access to information and content	

Adapted from: "Word of Mouth 101: An Introduction to Word of Mouth Marketing" WOMMA, **www.womma.org/wom101.htm** (accessed March 12, 2008). © WOMMA, 2008.

5

OBJECTIVE

Describe integrated
marketing
communication (IMC)
and its characteristics.

(pp. 381–383)

Integrated Marketing Communication

Marketers have used the elements of the promotion mix for many years, but the concept of integrated marketing communication (IMC) is relatively new. While not all big firms have adopted IMC, many marketing experts believe that IMC provides a competitive advantage in the twenty-first century.

Utilizing an IMC approach, marketers plan and then execute marketing communication programs that create and maintain long-term relationships with customers by satisfying customer needs. This means that they use promotion tools to build ongoing loyal relationships with customers or other stakeholders, rather than simply causing a one-time product purchase or short-term change in behavior.[37] With IMC, marketers like Walt Judas at Tourism Vancouver look at communication the way customers see it—as a flow of information from a single source. Thus, marketers who understand the power of IMC seek to "unify all marketing communication tools—from advertising to packaging—to send target audiences a consistent, persuasive message that promotes company goals."[37]

So why is IMC so important today? A few years ago, marketers could effectively communicate with consumers by placing a few ads on major television networks and perhaps in a few popular magazines. Today, with increased global competition, customers are bombarded with more and more marketing messages. Exactly how many advertising messages is unclear, but estimates range from 500 to over 3,000 per day! And the sheer number of media outlets also is mushrooming. Marketers can choose from literally hundreds of cable and satellite stations, each of which can deliver its messages to a selected portion of the television viewing audience. All this means that consumers are less likely to be influenced by any single marketer-generated message. At the same time, technology now enables even small firms to develop and effectively use customer databases, giving firms greater opportunities for understanding customers and for developing one-to-one communication programs. And technology gives customers the ability to communicate among themselves about products and companies and even to view ads on the Internet and TV at their leisure.[38]

Characteristics of IMC

To fully understand what IMC is all about and before a firm can begin to implement an IMC program, it is essential that managers understand some important characteristics of IMC.

IMC Begins with the Customer

The customer is the primary focus of the communication, *not* the company's goals nor the creative genius of the communication specialists. In today's global marketplace, customer-focused (or *customer-centric*) firms succeed because they recognize that customers are the only group that provides income to the firm. As we noted in Chapter 7, many firms consider their customers financial assets. The goal of IMC in a customer-centric organization, first and foremost, is to provide the information customers want when they want it, where they want it, and in the amount they need. Sometimes that's as simple as letting consumers "vote" on the shows or products they want to see, as when fans of the hit TV comedy *Friends* were allowed to choose their six favorite episodes at a Web site when the producers decided to end the series.[39]

Jordan
Buck
a student at Jamestown Community College
My Advice for Tourism Vancouver would be to choose

Option

real people, **Other Voices**

I would choose option number 2 and form a collaborative committee of all the agencies and associations participating in the event. This option allows all the organizations involved the ability to pool both their funds and ideas together to have a successful event that showcases the area and the agencies participating. The Vancouver Organizing Committee for the Olympic Games emphasized the 2010 Olympics are Canada's Games and not individual agencies. This choice may cause disagreements due to conflicting agendas but it is important to remember the 2010 Olympics is a joint effort to give the visitors a wonderful experience and hopefully bring them back again. This option is particularly satisfying to Vancouver Tourism because of its limited resources. By teaming up with the other organizations, it will bring the focus more on the event, rather than specific agencies competing and taking on different projects. ➤

IMC Creates a Single Unified Voice

Perhaps the most important characteristic of IMC is that it creates a single unified voice for a firm. If we examine the traditional communication program of a typical consumer goods firm—say, a frozen foods manufacturer—we see that it often develops communication tactics in isolation. If a company decides it needs to advertise, what does it do? It hires an ad agency. Or, it may even hire several different ad agencies to develop messages for a range of target markets. It also may realize it needs public relations activities, so now it hires a separate public relations firm. Then some other genius down the hall decides to sponsor a sweepstakes and hires a sales promotion firm to do this. The sales department hires a different firm to develop trade show materials, and someone in the corporate communication department hires a sports-marketing firm to help it sponsor a golf tournament.

Each of these firms may do a good job, but each may also be sending out a different message. The customer can't help but be confused. What is the product? What is the brand image? Whose needs will this product satisfy? IMC strategies present a *unified selling proposition* in the marketplace because they eliminate duplication and conflicting messages. When an organization develops an IMC program, it focuses on *all* communication elements—advertising, public relations, sales promotion, and so forth—to speak with one voice and create a single and powerful brand personality like those we discussed in Chapter 9.

Having a single brand message, however, doesn't mean that marketers don't communicate to different segments of the market or to different stakeholder groups with different tactics. They can communicate the same brand message to employees with a story in the company newsletter about how local workers have helped flood victims, to loyal customers via direct mail that explains how to make their home safe for toddlers, and to prospective customers through mass media and Internet advertising.

The one-voice/one-message focus of IMC also considers other less obvious forms of communication. For example, a firm's communication with customers includes the letters it sends to customers, the way company personnel talk on the phone with clients or customers, the uniforms delivery people or other employees wear, signage, and other policies and procedures that may have an unintended effect on consumers' perceptions of the firm (even the stationery the company uses to correspond with vendors and customers).

IMC Develops Relationships with Customers

As mass-marketing activities have become less effective, many marketers are finding that the road to success is through one-to-one marketing in which the focus is on building and maintaining a long-term relationship with each individual customer. To achieve this, marketers must continuously communicate with each individual or company, or risk losing their business to the competition.

What we said earlier bears repeating—*it is easier and less expensive to keep an existing customer than to attract a new one*. Thus, IMC firms also measure their success by share of customer not share of market, and by the lifetime value of a customer. This means prioritizing customers so that greater resources go to communicating with high-value buyers or clients. Share of customer refers to the proportion of a consumer's purchases that include your brand. For example, if you have ten pairs of athletic shoes in your closet and eight of them are Nikes, the swoosh guys have 80 percent share of <u>you</u> for this category.

Because IMC also is about building and maintaining relationships with customers, IMC strategies often rely on CRM programs and practices we talked about in Chapter 7. With these tools, marketers have the information they need to better understand customers and to deliver unique messages to each consumer—messages that meet the needs of each consumer and build relationships.

IMC Involves Two-Way Communication

Traditional communication programs were built on one-way communication activities. Television, magazine, newspaper, and outdoor advertising spouted clever messages at the consumer, but there was little, if any, way for the consumer to talk back. Today, we know that one-way, impersonal communication is highly ineffective at building long-term relationships with customers. Instead, marketers seek first to learn what information customers have and what additional information they want and then develop communication tactics that let them share information with their customers.

Walter (Walt)
F. Judas

APPLYING **IMC's Focus on Stakeholders**

Walt understands that tourists are only one group of stakeholders he has to please. Tourism Vancouver also has to satisfy the needs of government officials, other tourism specialists, and the local businesses that support the organization's efforts to promote the city and region. ➡

IMC Focuses on Stakeholders, Not Just Customers

As we discussed way back in Chapter 1, stakeholders are any individuals or organizations that are important to the long-term health of an organization. Some of these stakeholders include employees, suppliers, stockholders, the media, trade associations, regulators, and even neighbors. One reason these other stakeholders are so important is that customers and prospective customers don't learn about a company and its products just from the firm. Their attitudes, positive or negative, are also heavily influenced by the mass media, government regulatory bodies, or even their local neighbor who happens to work for the company. Thus, while the primary stakeholder is usually the customer, many other groups or individuals significantly influence customers' attitudes and behaviors.

IMC Generates a Continuous Stream of Communication

A major characteristic of an IMC strategy is that a promotional plan uses many different elements of the communication program—such as advertising, publicity, personal selling, sales promotion, and customer testimonials. As a result, IMC strategies provide a continuous stream of communication. Instead of bombarding consumers with messages from various sources for a week or two and then going underground for months, IMC planning ensures that consumers receive information on a regular basis and in the right amount.

IMC Focuses on Changing Behavior

A final characteristic of IMC is that the ultimate goal of marketing communication is to affect customers' behavior. This means that objectives of marketing communications might include acquiring new customers, retaining present customers, increasing sales among existing customers, or increasing the shares of each customer. It is this focus on behavior that leads IMC boosters to suggest that the only adequate measure of a promotional campaign's effectiveness is to evaluate the return on investment on communication dollars (earlier we referred to this as "marketing ROI"). This means that if a firm spends $1 million on advertising, it should be able to determine what dollar amount of revenue the firm receives as a result of that expenditure. While this type of relationship between promotion dollars and revenues may be difficult to measure exactly because of the long-term effects of advertising and other marketing communications, most firms look for measures of accountability for their communication budgets and demand results. That's why we've made such a big deal of *marketing metrics* in this book.

database marketing
The creation of an ongoing relationship with a set of customers who have an identifiable interest in a good or service and whose responses to promotional efforts become part of future communication attempts.

OBJECTIVE

Explain the important role of database marketing in integrated marketing communication.
(pp. 384–385)

IMC often Relies on a Customer Database

Some companies have maintained a customer database for years, but until recently most did not link the database with their marketing communication activities. **Database marketing** means creating an ongoing relationship with a set of customers with an identifiable interest in a good or service and tracking their responses to promotional messages over time.

If a database marketing programs works well, the firm can use its records of customers' responses to gain insights about which messages work and which flopped. And, it can carefully map customer touchpoints so its marketers know the best times and places to talk to them.

Let's look at an example of how even a small business might make effective use of database marketing. Say you ordered a dozen roses from a local florist to deliver to a friend for her birthday last year. You (and your friend) have become a part of the florist's database. How can the store use this simple piece of information? First, the database is a gold mine of information. By examining (the *data mining* we discussed in Chapter 4) the records of thousands of customers, including you, the florist can find out which customers order flowers frequently (heavy users) and which order only occasionally (light users). They can identify customers who order flowers for themselves, usually when they entertain. They know which customers order flowers only for funerals, and which send flowers to their sweethearts (or ex-sweethearts if you forget). And they can determine what type of customer accounts for their greatest sales and their greatest profits. This helps them to develop a better understanding of their target markets. Table 12.4 provides a list of what database marketing can do and the benefits to the firm.

Table 12.4	What Database Marketing Can Do	
What Database Marketing Can do	**Benefit to Firm**	**Example**
Database marketing is interactive; it elicits a response from consumers	Develops a dialogue with the customer and can create add-on sales	Female cat owners who completed a direct mail survey by H.J. Heinz about cat food preferences received a thank-you note and other direct mail that mentioned the cat by name[40]
Database marketing builds relationships	Builds long-term communication programs by modifying messages based upon previous customer responses.	Amazon.com makes suggestions for books, CDs, and other products based on previous purchases
Database marketing locates new customers	Directs communications to prospects with characteristics similar to those of existing customers.	Web sites such as Cooking.com sends offers for gourmet cooking utensils and cookbooks to subscribers of cooking magazines such as *Bon Appetit*.
Database marketing stimulates cross-selling	Allows firms to offer related products to their customers	Subscribers to magazines such as *Fortune* or *Money* may receive offers to subscribe to the publisher's other magazines at a reduced price.
Database marketing is measurable	Marketers can pinpoint the impact of a specific promotion on the target market	Banks and other financial institutions can measure the response to direct mail to various customer groups such as college students.
Responses are trackable	By measuring the responses to different messages, marketers can assess the effectiveness of different messages, and the responsiveness of different customer groups.	John Deere sent four mailings spaced over eight weeks to 20,000 farmers who were loyal to other brands, each with an inexpensive gift such as a stopwatch that was related to the theme of saving time and money by replacing existing equipment. Nearly 700 bought new equipment, resulting in more than $40 million in new business.[41]

Of course, tapping the information in the database to understand your market is only the beginning. Even more important is how firms, such as our florist, use the database to create that one-to-one communication with their target markets. So you, our florist's customer, may get a call or an e-mail next year to remind you of your friend's birthday and ask if you want the same dozen roses (well, actually, fresh ones of the same type) sent again this year. The customer who entertains frequently may receive a brochure before the New Year's holiday season that offers ideas for table arrangements. Heavy users might receive a special thank-you for their business and an offer to receive a free arrangement after they purchase 12 bouquets. And by the way, what about your friend who received flowers but who has never purchased from our florist? Since we may assume that a consumer who likes to receive flowers will sooner or later want to purchase them as well, she becomes part of the florist's prospective customer database. As such, she may receive a catalog of the most popular arrangements or perhaps a coupon for a discount on her first order.

7

OBJECTIVE

Explain the stages in developing an IMC plan.

(pp. 385–391)

Develop the IMC Plan

Now that we've talked about the characteristics of an IMC strategy, we need to see how to make it happen. How do we go about the complex task of developing an IMC plan—one that delivers just the right message to a number of different target audiences when and where they want it in the most effective and cost-efficient way? Just as with any other strategic decision-making process, the development of this plan includes several steps, as Figure 12.4 shows. Let's review each step.

Walter (Walt) F. Judas

APPLYING **Communication Objectives**

Walt needs to identify specifically what Tourism Vancouver wants to communicate to visitors before he can decide what media he will use to reach these objectives. ➥

Step 1: Identify the Target Audiences

An important part of overall marketing planning is to identify the target audience(s). Remember, IMC marketers recognize that we must communicate with a variety of stakeholders who influence the target market. (Of course, the target market is the most important target audience and the one that we'll focus on here.) With a well-designed database, marketers can know who their target market is as well as the buying behavior of different segments within the total market. This means they can develop targeted messages for each customer.

Step 2: Establish the Communication Objectives

The whole point of communicating with customers and prospective customers is to let them know that the organization has a product to meet their needs in a timely and affordable way. It's bad enough when a product comes along that people don't want or need. An even bigger marketing sin is to have a product that they *do* want—but you fail to let them know about it. Of course, seldom can we deliver a single message to a consumer that magically transforms her into a loyal customer. In most cases, it takes a series of messages that moves the consumer through several stages.

We view this process as an uphill climb, such as the one Figure 12.5 depicts. The marketer "pushes" the consumer through a series of steps, or a **hierarchy of effects**, from initial awareness of a product to brand loyalty. The

hierarchy of effects
A series of steps prospective customers move through, from initial awareness of a product to brand loyalty.

Figure 12.4 | Steps to Develop the IMC Plan

Step 1: Identify the Target Audiences

Step 2: Establish the Communication Objectives

Step 3: Determine and Allocate the Marketing Communication Budget
- Determine the Total Promotion Budget
- Decide on a Push or a Pull Strategy
- Allocate the Budget to a Specific Promotion Mix

Step 4: Design the Promotion Mix

Step 5: Evaluate the Effectiveness of the Communication Program

Figure 12.5 | The Hierarchy of Effects

Communication objectives seek to move consumers through the hierarchy of effects.

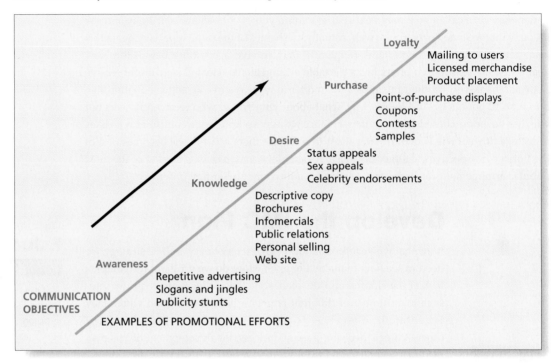

task of moving the consumer up the hierarchy becomes more difficult at each step. Many potential buyers may drop out along the way, leaving less of the target group inclined to go the distance and become loyal customers. Each part of this path entails different communication objectives to "push" people to the next level.

To understand how this process works, consider how a firm would have to adjust its communication objectives as it tries to establish a presence in the market for Hunk, a new men's cologne. Let's say that the primary target market for the cologne is single men aged 18- to 24 who care about their appearance and who are into health, fitness, working out, and looking ripped. The company would want to focus more on some promotion methods (such as advertising) and less on others (such as personal selling). Here are some communication objectives the company might develop for its Hunk promotion.

Create awareness

The first step is to make members of the target market aware that there's a new brand of cologne on the market. The fragrance's marketers could accomplish this by placing simple, repetitive advertising in magazines, on television, and on the radio that push the brand name. The company might even consider creating a "teaser" campaign, in which ads heighten interest because they don't reveal the exact nature of the product (for example, newspaper ads that simply proclaim, "Hunk is coming!"). The promotion objective might be to create an 80 percent awareness of Hunk cologne among 18- to 24-year-old men in the first two months.

Inform the Market

The next step is to provide prospective users with knowledge about the benefits the new product has to offer—to *position* it relative other colognes (see Chapter 7). Perhaps the cologne has a light, slightly mentholated scent with a hint of a liniment smell to remind wearers of how they feel after a good workout. Promotion would focus on communications that emphasize this position. The objective at this point might be to communicate the connection between Hunk and muscle building so that 70 percent of the target market develops some interest in the product.

Create Desire

The next task is to create favorable feelings toward the product and to convince at least some portion of this group that it'd rather splash on some Hunk instead of other colognes. Communications at this stage might consist of splashy advertising spreads in magazines, perhaps with an endorsement by a well-known celebrity "hunk" such as the Rock. The specific objective might be to create positive attitudes toward Hunk cologne among 50 percent of the target market and brand preference among 30 percent of the target market.

Encourage Purchase and Trial

As the expression goes, "How do ya know 'til ya try it?" The company now needs to get some of the men who have become interested in the cologne to try it. A promotion plan might encourage trial by mailing samples of Hunk to members of the target market, inserting "scratch-and-sniff" samples in bodybuilding magazines, placing elaborate displays in stores that dispense money-saving coupons, or even sponsoring a contest in which the winner gets to have the Rock as his personal trainer for a day. The specific objective now might be to encourage trial of Hunk among 25 percent of 18- to 24-year-old men in the first two months.

Build Loyalty

Of course, the real test is loyalty: convincing customers to stay with Hunk after they've gone through the first bottle. Promotion efforts must maintain ongoing communication with current users to reinforce the bond they feel with the product. As before, they will accomplish this with some mix of strategies, perhaps including direct-mail advertising to current users, product placements in popular television programs or movies, and maybe even the development of a workout clothing line bearing a Hunk logo. The objective might be to develop and maintain regular usage of Hunk cologne among 10 percent of men from 18- to 24-years old.

Step 3: Determine and Allocate the Marketing Communication Budget

While setting a budget for marketing communication might seem easy—you just calculate how much you need to accomplish your objectives—in reality it's not that simple. Determining and allocating communication budgets includes three distinct decisions: determining the total communication budget, deciding whether to use a push strategy or a pull strategy, and allocating how much to spend on specific promotion activities.

Determine the Total Promotion Budget

In the real world, firms often view communication costs as an expense rather than as an investment leading to greater profits. When sales are declining or the company is operating in a difficult economic environment, it is often tempting to cut costs by reducing spending on advertising, promotion, and other "soft" activities whose contributions to the bottom line are hard to quantify. When this is the case, marketers must work harder to justify these expenses.

Economic approaches to budgeting rely on *marginal analysis* (we discussed these in Chapter 11), in which the organization spends money on promotion as long as the revenues it realizes through these efforts continue to exceed the costs of the promotions themselves. This perspective assumes that a company always intends promotions solely to increase sales, when in fact these activities may have other objectives such as enhancing a firm's image.

Also, the effects of marketing communication often lag over time. For example, a firm may have to spend a lot on advertising when it first launches a product without seeing any immediate return. Because of these limitations, most firms rely on two budgeting techniques: top-down and bottom-up.

top-down budgeting techniques
Allocation of the promotion budget based on management's determination of the total amount to be devoted to marketing communication.

percentage-of-sales method
A method for promotion budgeting that is based on a certain percentage of either last year's sales or on estimates for the present year's sales.

competitive-parity method
A promotion budgeting method in which an organization matches whatever competitors are spending.

bottom-up budgeting techniques
Allocation of the promotion budget based on identifying promotion goals and allocating enough money to accomplish them.

objective-task method
A promotion budgeting method in which an organization first defines the specific communication goals it hopes to achieve and then tries to calculate what kind of promotional efforts it will take to meet these goals.

push strategy
The company tries to move its products through the channel by convincing channel members to offer them.

pull strategy
The company tries to move its products through the channel by building desire for the products among consumers, thus convincing retailers to respond to this demand by stocking these items.

Top-down budgeting techniques require top management to establish the overall amount that the organization allocates for promotion activities.

The most common top-down technique is the **percentage-of-sales method** in which the promotion budget is based on last year's sales or on estimates for the present year's sales. The percentage may be an industry average provided by trade associations that collect objective information on behalf of member companies. The advantage of this method is that it ties spending on promotion to sales and profits. Unfortunately, this method can imply that sales cause promotional outlays rather than viewing sales as the *outcome* of promotional efforts.

The **competitive-parity method** is a fancy way of saying "keep up with the Joneses." In other words, match whatever competitors are spending. Some marketers think this approach simply mirrors the best thinking of others in the business. However, this method often sees each player maintaining the same market share year after year. This method also assumes that the same dollars spent on promotion by two different firms will yield the same results, but spending a lot of money doesn't guarantee a successful promotion. Firms certainly need to monitor their competitors' promotion activities, but they must combine this information with their own objectives and capacities.

The problem with top-down techniques is that budget decisions are based more on established practices than on promotion objectives. Another approach is to begin at the beginning: identify promotion goals and allocate enough money to accomplish them. That is what **bottom-up budgeting techniques** attempt.

This bottom-up logic is at the heart of the **objective-task method**, which is gaining in popularity. Using this approach, the firm first defines the specific communication goals it hopes to achieve, such as increasing by 20 percent the number of consumers who are aware of the brand. It then tries to figure out what kind of promotional efforts it will take to meet that goal. Although this is the most rational approach, it is hard to implement because it obliges managers to specify their objectives and attach dollar amounts to them. This method requires careful analysis—and a bit of lucky "guesstimating."

Decide on a Push or a Pull Strategy

One crucial issue in determining the promotion mix is whether the company relies on a push strategy or a pull strategy. A **push strategy** means that the company wants to move its products by convincing channel members to offer them and entice their customers to select these items. A push strategy assumes that if consumers see the product on store shelves, they will be enticed to make a trial purchase. In this case, promotion efforts will "push" the products from producer to consumers by focusing on personal selling, trade advertising, and sales promotion activities such as exhibits at trade shows.

In contrast, a company that relies on a **pull strategy** is counting on consumers to first desire its products. This demand will then convince retailers to respond by stocking them. In this case, efforts focus on media advertising and consumer sales promotion to stimulate interest among end consumers who will "pull" the product onto store shelves and then into their shopping carts.

Whether we use a push or a pull strategy and how the promotion mix for a product is designed must vary over time because some elements work better at different points in the product life cycle than others. As an example, we might think about the state of electronics in today's market and the relative positions in the product life cycle.

In the *introduction phase*, the objective is to build awareness of and encourage trial of the product among consumers, often by relying on a push strategy. That's the situation today with 3G (third generation) mobile telephone technology that allows voice and data transmission at incredible speeds. With 3G technology you can watch television, have video conversations with your friends, log into your bank account to pay your bills, view video clips of local tourist attractions, and manage your inventory of items that need restocking from your home's "smart" refrigerator—all from your new 3G mobile phone. Advertising is the primary promotion tool for creating awareness, and a publicity campaign to generate news reports about the new product may help as well. A company may use sales promotion to encourage trial. Business-to-business marketing that emphasizes personal selling—the marketing that a manufacturer does to retailers and other business customers—is important in this phase in order to get channel members to carry the product. For consumer goods that retailers sell, trade sales promotion may be necessary to encourage retailers to stock the product.

In the *growth phase*, promotions must now start stressing product benefits. For products such as MP3 players, advertising increases, while sales promotion that encourages trial usually declines because people are more willing to try the product without being offered an incentive.

The opposite pattern often occurs with products now in their *maturity phase* such as DVD players. In these situations many people have already tried the product. The strategy now shifts to encouraging people to switch from competitors' brands as sales stabilize. This can be tough if consumers don't see enough differences among the options to bother. Usually, sales promotion activities, particularly coupons and special price deals, have greater chances of success than advertising. In some cases an industry revamps a widely used technology when it introduces one or more new versions or formats that force consumers to convert (sometimes kicking and screaming), thus transforming a mature category back to a new one. That's what's happening now in the "DVD format wars," a high-stakes showdown between the HD DVD and Blu-ray disk formats that Blu-ray recently won after it gained the backing of a large number of consumer electronics and entertainment companies.[42]

All bets are off for VCR players, now in their *decline phase*. As sales plummet, the company dramatically reduces spending on all elements of the promotion mix. Sales will be driven by the continued loyalty of a small group of users who keep the product alive until it is sold to another company or discontinued.

Allocate the Budget to a Specific Promotion Mix

Once the organization decides how much to spend on promotion and whether to use a push or a pull strategy, it must divide its budget among the elements in the promotion mix. Although advertising used to get the lion's share of the promotion budget, as we've already seen, today sales promotion and buzz marketing (especially on-line campaigns) are playing a bigger role in marketing strategies. General Motors, for example, spurred its car sales in 2005 by offering consumers the same discounted prices as its employees receive. In 2006, when prices at the pump escalated, GM gave consumers a different offer—a guaranteed fuel price ceiling.[43] Procter & Gamble reduced consumer sales promotion spending in the early 1990s when it adopted its "value pricing" strategy. Today, P&G is revamping its $2 billion-plus annual trade promotion budget to focus more on activities such as in-store merchandising, temporary price reductions, and end-aisle displays.[44]

Several factors influence how companies divide up the promotional pie. For example, the characteristics of the organization itself may influence budget allocation; managers may simply have a preference for advertising versus sales promotion or other elements of the promotion mix. Also, consumers vary widely in the likelihood that they will respond to various communication elements. Some thrifty consumers like to clip coupons or stock up with two-for-one offers while others throw away those Sunday newspaper coupons without a glance. College students are notorious for not reading newspapers (except perhaps for campus papers they browse during lectures), but they do spend a huge amount of time on-line. The size and makeup of a geographic market also influence promotion decisions. In larger markets, the cost of buying media, such as local TV, can be quite high. If only a small percentage of the total market includes potential customers, then mass media advertising can be a very inefficient use of a promotion budget.

For many products, factual information is essential. Magazine advertising provides an opportunity to deliver the desired information.

AIDA model

The communication goals of attention, interest, desire, and action.

Step 4: Design the Promotion Mix

Designing the promotion mix is the most complicated step in marketing communication planning. It includes determining the specific communication tools to use, what message to communicate, and the communication channel(s) on which to send the message. Planners must ask how they can use advertising, sales promotion, personal selling, and public relations most effectively to communicate with different target audiences. Each element of the promotion mix has benefits and shortcomings, so—as we've seen—often a combination of a few techniques works the best.

The message ideally should accomplish four objectives (though a single message can rarely do all of these): It should get attention, hold interest, create desire, and produce action. We call these communication goals the **AIDA model**. Here we'll review some different forms the message can take as well as how we might structure the message.

Type of Appeal

There are many ways to say the same thing, and marketers must take care in choosing what type of appeal, or message strategy, they use when they encode the message. To illustrate, consider two strategies rival car companies used to promote similar automobiles: A few years ago, both Toyota and Nissan introduced large luxury cars. Toyota's advertising for its Lexus model used a rational appeal that focused on the technical advancements in the car's design. This approach is often effective for promoting products that are technically complex and require a substantial investment. Nissan, in contrast, focused on the spiritual fulfillment a driver might feel tooling down the road in a fine machine. Much like Nissan, Volkswagen recently launched an international advertising campaign based on love poems linked to vehicles in an attempt to reach the strong emotions that underlie consumers' preferences for cars. In Germany, double-page newspaper and magazine ads feature a love poem with a paragraph explaining the feelings one of Volkswagen's cars represents.[45]

Structure of the Appeal

Many marketing messages are similar to debates or courtroom trials in which someone presents arguments and tries to convince the receivers to shift their opinions. The way the source presents the argument is important. Most messages merely tout one or more positive attributes of the product or reasons to buy it. These are known as *supportive arguments* or *one-sided messages*. An alternative is to use a *two-sided message*, with both positive and negative information. Two-sided ads can be quite effective, but in reality marketers seldom use them.[46]

A related issue is whether the argument should draw conclusions. Should the ad say only "our brand is superior," or should it explicitly tell the consumer to buy it? The answer depends on the degree of a consumer's motivation to think about the ad and the complexity of the arguments. If the message is personally relevant, people will pay attention to it and draw their own conclusions. But if the arguments are hard to follow or the person's motivation to follow them is lacking, it is best to make these conclusions explicit.

Communication Channel

Even the best message is wasted if it is not placed in communication channels that will effectively reach the target audience. Communication channels include the mass media: newspapers, television, radio, magazines, and direct mail. Other media include outdoor display signs and boards and electronic media, the most important of which is the Internet. Sponsorships provide another channel for communication. In Vermont, skiers can take an Altaics gondola car to the top of Stratton Mountain, while employees at the Whistler ski resort in Canada wear Evian jackets.[47]

The Internet provides a unique environment for promotional messages because it can include text, audio, video, hyperlinking, and personalization, not to mention opportunities for interaction with customers and other stakeholders. Web sites can come alive with the right mix of technical wizardry and good design. One advantage of the Web is that companies can give customers a "feel" for their goods or services before they buy. Even nightclubs are going to the Web to draw virtual crowds.[48] Sites like **http://thewomb.com** feature real-time footage of what's happening in the clubs. No more big, beefy bouncers to worry about!

Step 5: Evaluate the Effectiveness of the Communication Program

The final step in managing marketing communication is to decide whether the plan is working. It would be nice if a marketing manager could simply report, "The $3 million campaign for our revolutionary glow-in-the-dark surfboards brought in $15 million in new sales!" It's not so easy. There are many random factors in the marketing environment: a rival's manufacturing problem, a coincidental photograph of a movie star toting one of the boards, or perhaps a surge of renewed interest in surfing sparked by a cult movie hit like *Blue Crush*.

Still, there are ways to monitor and evaluate the company's communication efforts. The catch is that it's easier to determine the effectiveness of some forms of communication than others. As a rule, various types of sales promotion are the easiest to evaluate because they occur over a fixed, usually short period, making it easier to link to sales volume. Advertising researchers measure brand awareness, recall of product benefits communicated through advertising, and even the image of the brand before and after an advertising campaign. The firm can analyze and compare the performance of salespeople in different territories, although again it is difficult to rule out other factors that make one salesperson more effective than another. Public relations activities are more difficult to assess because their objectives relate more often to image building than sales volume.

Now that you've learned about integrated marketing communication and interactive marketing read "Real People, Real Choices: How It Worked Out" to see which strategy Walt Judas selected to promote the 2010 Olympics.

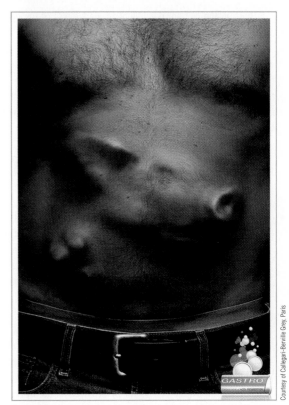

This French ad for an antacid relies on a novel visual approach to get its message across.

real people, **Real Choices**

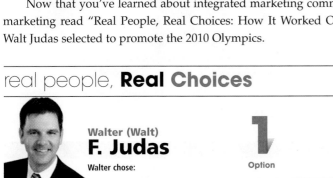

Walter (Walt)
F. Judas
Walter chose:

1 Option

How it Worked Out at Tourism Vancouver

Walt selected Option #1. The organization moved ahead with plans to operate kiosks throughout Vancouver that would provide a variety of services to visitors during the Olympics.

A major component of visitor servicing is to help deliver a positive experience for all guests during the Games and as they prepare for their trip to Vancouver. In

this context, the Visitors Services plan coordinates several communications elements to provide a consistent and satisfying 2010 visitor experience.

Tourism Vancouver currently provides an unparalleled level of travel counseling service to over 350,000 visitor parties at its flagship center downtown, and through other satellite centers. Through these centers, Tourism Vancouver fulfills its core mandate of maximizing the economic impact of visitors to Greater Vancouver by influencing travel patterns and referring visitors to member businesses. There is a need to incorporate into this service information about all aspects of the Games. Tourism Vancouver is perfectly positioned to fill the role of a key service provider and distribution channel.

In the words of a Park City, Utah colleague who was involved with the 2004 Winter Olympics, "The Olympic Games are defined by the atmosphere on the street versus what happens in the field of play. The look, feel and experience people have in the city are paramount to the success of the event." Ideally, Tourism Vancouver will provide customers with a singular point of contact for all information on both the destination and the 2010 Olympic & Paralympic Winter Games. This may include but is not limited to information on accommodation, transportation, tickets, venues, event schedules, cultural and special events, etc. Consumers planning their trips will rely on Tourism Vancouver to make the information easily accessible, readily available, comprehensive, and current. Strategies include the following:

- Tourism Vancouver will secure a Memorandum of Understanding (MOU) with the City of Vancouver that will maintain and promote the organization as the City of Vancouver's official visitor services agency to ensure guests receive credible information and impeccable service before and during their visit.
- Tourism Vancouver will expand its volunteer visitor services program into the community, ideally from point of arrival to point of departure to meet guests' expectations. This will include temporary information kiosks throughout the downtown core and within select 2010 competition venues. The kiosks will be staffed for up to 16 hours per day to ensure the highest level of visitor servicing possible.
- Tourism Vancouver will enhance its point of sale tools to reflect the customer needs for information anytime, anywhere, and any place using multiple types of devices. In areas where it has no physical access, the organization will use self serve or syndication as a means of reaching more visitors with relevant and timely information. Portable, hand-held, wireless point-of-sale devices will be deployed for use by roving information counselors to sell tourism experiences such as tickets to attractions.
- Tourism Vancouver will establish a recruitment, hiring, and training program to fulfill requirements for additional staffing surrounding peak visitation months. This will include formal relationships with community colleges to develop students' skills to complement the current visitor servicing structure. Additionally, training will also be offered to VANOC volunteers vis-à-vis destination specific information.
- Tourism Vancouver will work with the City of Vancouver on a local ambassador campaign to enlist and educate residents and businesses, and provide them with the tools necessary, to welcome the world and be WorldHosts in 2010. Minimum acceptable standards will be developed to ensure that all stakeholders deliver on the brand promise tenets.
- Tourism Vancouver will develop initiatives around the "welcoming" aspect of the Vancouver brand for implementation in 2008. This will include training volunteers and residents of Vancouver on how to deal with visitors from all over the world, and to be "good hosts."
- Additionally, businesses will be encouraged to participate in World Host (customer service) training, as well as to upgrade their facilities to accommodate people with mobility, sight, and hearing disabilities. Information will be made available in a multitude of languages and in various formats (print, digital). Additionally, staff will be either hired or trained in languages other than English to assist visitors during Games time.

- A special edition of the *Official Visitors Guide* will be produced for the Games period, along with the tear-off map used extensively in visitor counseling. These guides will contain extensive 2010 and destination information to be used by all visitors in advance of or during the Games. Additionally, the guide will be available on-line, and will be produced, all or in-part, in select languages.
- Tourism Vancouver will deliver digitized content in a format that can be accessed by all kinds of digital devices including mobile phone, PDA, LCD, and large screen plasma displays.

How Tourism Vancouver Measures Success

Tourism Vancouver is in the process of identifying exactly how it will measure the impact of its actions. The organization has set specific objectives and it will assess its performance when the Games have concluded according to how well it accomplishes the following goals:

- Service one million visitor parties the year of the Games compared with 500,000 at present. These are visitors who use the services of the visitor kiosks for information, buying tickets, etc.
- Generate $20 million in tourism product sales versus $7 million at present.
- Conduct intercept surveys of visitors to gauge the level of customer service provided and opinions on their destination experience.
- Count total distribution of destination information produced such as maps and visitor guides.
- Attract sponsorship investment in the visitor services/kiosk program (one or more sponsors such as Visa or Panasonic) to help offset capital and operating costs.
- Track sponsor sales volume & ROI (e.g., Visa cardholder spend) at the kiosks.
- Insure placement of the kiosks in strategic locations such as within the Games venues.

A kiosk that Tourism Vancouver created.

Refer back to **page 367** for Walt's story

Brand **YOU**!

Get the word out about your brand...to all the right people.

Create an integrated marketing communication plan for your personal brand. It's easy to increase your chances of getting interviews when you use all the available "media" to get your cover letter and resumé to your target audiences. Plan your personal brand IMC plan in Chapter 12 of the *Brand You* supplement.

Objective Summary ➡ Key Terms ➡ Apply

CHAPTER 12
Study Map

---

1. Objective Summary (pp. 368–369)

Understand the role of marketing communication.

Firms use promotion and other forms of marketing communication to influence attitudes and behavior. Through marketing communication, marketers inform consumers about new products, remind them of familiar products, persuade them to choose one alternative over another, and build strong customer relationships. Today, firms believe that the integration of marketing communications, in which firms look at the communication needs of customers, is essential for successful marketing communication programs.

Key Terms

promotion, p. 368

integrated marketing communication (IMC), p. 369

2. Objective Summary (pp. 369–372)

Understand the communication model.

The traditional communication model includes a message source that creates an idea, encodes the idea into a message, and transmits the message through some medium. The message is delivered to the receiver, who decodes the message and may provide feedback to the source. Anything that interferes with the communication is called "noise."

Key Terms

communication model, p. 369 (Figure 1.2, p. 23)

encoding, p. 370 (Figure 1.2, p. 23)

source, p. 370 (Figure 1.2, p. 23)

message, p. 370 (Figure 1.2, p. 23)

medium, p. 371 (Figure 1.2, p. 23)

receiver, p. 371 (Figure 1.2, p. 23)

decoding, p. 371 (Figure 1.2, p. 23)

noise, p. 371 (Figure 1.2, p. 23)

feedback, p. 372 (Figure 1.2, p. 23)

3. Objective Summary (pp. 372–375)

List and describe the traditional elements of the promotion mix.

The four major elements of marketing communication are known as the promotion mix. Personal selling provides direct contact between a company representative and a customer. Direct marketing provides direct communication with a consumer or business customer and seeks to gain a direct response from the individual or organization. Advertising is nonpersonal communication from an identified sponsor using mass media. Sales promotion stimulates immediate sales by providing incentives to the trade or to consumers. Public relations activities seek to influence the attitudes of various publics.

Key Term

promotion mix, p. 372 (Table 12.1, p. 373)

4. Objective Summary (pp. 375–380)

Explain how word of mouth marketing, buzz marketing, viral marketing, guerrilla marketing, experiential marketing, and consumer-generated media provide exciting alternatives to traditional communication techniques.

Marketers have developed several new alternatives to traditional marketing communications in order to reach "hard-to-get" consumers. Viral marketing means firms create messages designed to be passed in an exponential fashion, often electronically. With buzz marketing, marketers use entertainment or news to stimulate consumers to talk about a product or a company to friends and neighbors. These word of mouth (WOM) marketing messages are more credible and thus more valuable, especially when unpaid consumers create their own messages. Guerrilla marketing includes promotional strategies that "ambush" consumers in places they are not expecting it. With experiential marketing, consumer aren't just told about the benefits of the product but they can experience them. Consumer-generated media include comments, opinions, and stories about products that people share with other consumers via digital technology.

Key Terms

word of mouth (WOM), p. 376

word of mouth marketing, p. 376 (Table 12.3, p. 380)

buzz marketing, p. 376 (Table 12.2, p. 376)

viral marketing, p. 376

buzz, p. 376 (Table 12.2, p. 376)

guerrilla marketing, p. 377

experiential marketing, p. 378

consumer-generated media (CGM), p. 378

5. Objective Summary (pp. 381–383)

Describe integrated marketing communication and its characteristics.

Integrated marketing communication (IMC) includes the planning, development, execution, and evaluation of coordinated, measurable persuasive brand communications. IMC programs mean a firm's marketing communication begins with the consumer, includes a single unified voice, seeks to develop relationships with customers, uses two-way communication, focuses on all stakeholders rather than customers only, generates a continuous stream of communication, and focuses on affecting behavior.

6. Objective Summary (pp. 384–385)

Explain the important role of database marketing in integrated marketing communication (IMC).

The effective use of databases is key to an IMC strategy, allows organizations to learn about its customers, fine-tune its offerings, and build an ongoing relationship with its

market. Database marketing is interactive, builds relationships, provides a way to locate new customers, and is measurable and trackable.

Key Term

database marketing, p. 384 (Table 12.4, p. 384)

7. Objective Summary (pp. 385–391)

Explain the stages in developing an IMC plan.

An IMC plan begins with communication objectives, usually stated in terms of communication tasks such as creating awareness, knowledge, desire, product trial, and brand loyalty. Which promotion mix elements will be used depends on the overall strategy (that is, a push versus a pull strategy, the type of product, and the stage of the product life cycle).

Marketers often develop promotion budgets from rules of thumb such as the percentage-of-sales method, the competitive-parity method, and the objective-task method. They then decide on a push or a pull strategy and allocate monies from the total budget to various elements of the promotion mix. Designing the promotion mix includes determining what communication tools the marketer will use and the message the source will deliver.

Marketing messages use a variety of different appeals, including those that are rational and others that are emotional in nature. The message may provide one or two-sided arguments and may or may not draw conclusions. Communication channels must be selected. The Internet provides both challenges and opportunities for communication. Finally, marketers monitor and evaluate the promotion efforts to determine if the objectives are being reached.

Key Terms

hierarchy of effects, p. 385 (Figure 12.5, p. 386)

top-down budgeting techniques, p. 388

percentage-of-sales method, p. 388

competitive-parity method, p. 388

bottom-up budgeting techniques, p. 388

objective-task method, p. 388

push strategy, p. 388 (Figure 12.4, p. 385)

pull strategy, p. 388 (Figure 12.4, p. 385)

AIDA model, p. 390

Chapter **Questions** and **Activities**

Concepts: Test Your Knowledge

1. How is IMC different from traditional promotion strategies?
2. Describe the traditional communication model.

3. List the elements of the promotion mix and describe how they are used to deliver personal and mass appeals.
4. What are word of mouth marketing, buzz marketing, viral marketing, experiential marketing, consumer-generated media, and guerilla marketing? Why are such activities gaining in popularity?

5. What is IMC? Explain the characteristics of IMC.
6. What is database marketing? How do marketers use databases to better meet the needs of their customers?
7. List the stages in developing an IMC strategy.
8. Explain the hierarchy of effects and how it is used in communication objectives.
9. Describe the major ways in which firms develop marketing communication budgets.
10. How does the promotion mix vary in push versus pull strategies?
11. What do we mean by type and structure of the appeal?
12. How do marketers evaluate the effectiveness of their communication programs?

Choices and Ethical Issues: You Decide

1. Some people argue that there is really nothing new about IMC. What do you think?
2. More and more companies are developing word of mouth or buzz marketing campaigns. Is buzz marketing just a craze that will fade in a year or two or is it here to stay? Do you think buzz is effective? Why do you feel that way?
3. Some buzz marketing activities engage buzz "agents" to tell their friends about a product, ask store managers to stock the product, and in other ways purposefully create word of mouth. Are these activities ethical?
4. With an IMC program, firms need to coordinate all of the marketing communication activities. What do you see as the problems inherent in implementing this?
5. Consumers are becoming concerned that the proliferation of databases is an invasion of an individual's privacy. Do you feel this is a valid concern? How can marketers use databases effectively and, at the same time, protect the rights of individuals?

Practice: Apply What You've Learned

1. As a marketing consultant, you are frequently asked by clients to develop recommendations for marketing communication strategies. The traditional elements used include advertising, sales promotion, public relations, and personal selling. Which of these do you feel would be most effective for each of the following clients?
   a. A company that provides cellular phone service
   b. A hotel
   c. A university
   d. A new soft drink
2. Again, assume that you are a marketing consultant for one of the clients in question 1. You believe that the client would benefit from non-traditional marketing. Develop several ideas for guerrilla, viral, and experiential marketing tactics that you feel would be successful for the client.
3. As the director of marketing for a small firm that markets environmentally friendly household cleaning supplies, you

are developing a marketing communication plan. With one or more of your classmates, provide suggestions for each of the following items. Then, in a role-playing situation, present your recommendations to the client.
   a. Marketing communication objectives
   b. A method for determining the communication budget
   c. The use of a push strategy or a pull strategy
   d. Elements of the promotion mix you will use
4. Assume that you are the word of mouth marketing manager for a sports equipment company such as Spalding. Develop ideas on how to create buzz for your company's products.
5. As the marketing manager for a chain of bookstores, you are interested in developing a database marketing plan. Give your recommendations for the following:
   a. How to generate a customer database
   b. How to use the database to better understand your customers
   c. How to increase sales from your existing customers using your database
   d. How to get new customers using your database
6. As a member of the marketing department for a manufacturer of handheld power tools for home improvement, you have been directed to select a new agency to do the promotion for your firm. Of two agencies solicited, one recommends an IMC plan, and the other has developed recommendations for a traditional advertising plan. Write a memo to your boss explaining each of the following:
   a. What is different about an IMC plan?
   b. Why is the IMC plan superior to conventional advertising?

Miniproject: Apply What You've Learned

This miniproject is designed to help you understand how important word of mouth marketing is to consumers like yourself.

1. Ask several of your classmates to participate in a focus-group discussion about how they communication with others about products. Some questions you might ask are the following:
   a. What products that you buy do you discuss with others at least from time to time?
   b. What experiences have you had discussing products or reading comments of others about products on blogs, social networks, or other Internet sites?
   c. What are your experiences with product-related Web sites? Do you participate in games and entertainment opportunities on product-related Web sites?
   d. How do you think firms could improve their Web sites to provide more information for you?
2. Make a presentation of your findings and to your class.

Real People, **real surfers**: explore the web

A vast majority of traditional media (television stations, newspapers, magazines, and radio stations) are now using the Internet to build relationships with readers and viewers. For the media, the Internet provides an excellent way to build a database and to communicate one-on-one with customers.

Although individual sites change frequently, some media sites that have provided opportunities for interactive communication with customers and for building a database are the following:

BusinessWeek (**www.businessweek.com**)
New York Times (**www.nytimes.com**)
Advertising Age (**www.advertisingage.com**)
Newsweek (**www.newsweek.com**)
Explore these or other sites that provide opportunities for consumers to register, answer questionnaires, or in some other

way use the Internet to build a database. After completing your exploration of each site, answer the following questions:

1. In what ways does each Web site facilitate interactive communication between the firm and customers?
2. How does each firm use the Internet to gather information on customers? What information is gathered? Which site does a superior job of gathering information, and why?
3. How do you think the firm might use the information it gathers through the Internet in database marketing activities? How can the information be used to build relationships with customers and prospective customers?
4. What recommendations do you have for each company to improve the interactive opportunities on its Web site?

Marketing in Action Case

Real **Choices** at **American Express**

What do Robert DeNiro, Ellen DeGeneres, Tiger Woods, Kate Winslet, and Laird Hamilton have in common? Let's see, Robert DeNiro is one of the greatest living actors; Ellen DeGeneres is a famous comedienne; Tiger Woods is arguably the best golfer ever; Kate Winslet is a multiple Academy Award nominee; and Laird Hamilton is perhaps the greatest surfer who ever lived. However, being famous and best in their fields are not the only things these folks have in common. They also all carry the American Express credit card and have appeared in television or print commercials to promote the card in the company's "My Life, My Card" campaign.

The fast pace of today's busy lifestyles and the rapid changes in information technology mean that, more than ever, companies like American Express have to rely on the familiar faces of celebrities to get its messages across. In late 2004, American Express started to feature famous and recognizable people as attractive spokespersons in the "My Life, My Card" advertising campaign in an attempt to capture the attention of current and potential consumers. Each of the AMEX ads included brief biographical information on the celebrity such as where they live, profession, greatest triumphs or greatest disappointments, and basic philosophy on life. The final point of each ad showed how the American Express card helps enable individuals to pursue what is important to them. American Express sought to communicate to its current and potential customers that they are just like these celebrities—simply trying to live life at its best. So, the slogan of "My Life, My Card" was perfect for the ad campaign. Consumers loved the ads.

Unfortunately for American Express, its "My Life, My Card" advertising campaign had some serious competition. Visa had been running ads for some time with the slogan of "Life takes Visa," which is a clever variation on Amex's campaign theme. American Express's other main competitor, MasterCard, was using its "Priceless" theme commercials that are aimed at encouraging customers to use the card to create priceless moments.

In the end, however, the "My Life, My Card" campaign, while well-liked, really wasn't working. Measures of customer loyalty showed that American Express was first in its product category in 1997, but by 2007, the American Express card was fifth, trailing Discover, Capital One, Visa, and MasterCard.

So in 2007, American Express replaced its "My Life, My Card" ads with a campaign that that presented a product-oriented approach rather than the general image-oriented approach. New ads asked consumers the question, "Are you a cardmember?"

Historically, American Express has not switched campaigns quickly. The "Do you know me?" campaign ran from 1974 to 1987 and is still a well-known advertising saying. "Membership has its privileges" was used from 1987 to 1996, and the "Do More" campaign ran from 1996 to 2004. With only three campaigns in thirty years, how could consumers respond to this quick change of focus? Was American Express risking confusing consumers about American Express's positioning? And what if the new "Are you a cardmember?" campaign didn't improve loyalty ratings. Should American Express move quickly to develop still another new campaign or stick with this one?

You Make the Call

1. What is the decision facing American Express?
2. What factors are important in understanding this decision situation?
3. What are the alternatives?
4. What decision(s) do you recommend?
5. What are some ways to implement your recommendation?

Based on: Brian Steinberg, "Now Showing: Clustered Ad Spots on Television," *Wall Street Journal*, February 15, 2006, B3; Business Wire Inc., "American Express Launches the Restaurant Partnership Program with Savings, Access and Information," *Business Wire*, June 8, 2006; Centaur Communications Ltd., "Amex Expands Tourist Podcast After Turin Olympics Success," *New Media Age*, March 2, 2006, 2; Dan Sewell, "Companies Use Online Magazines to Woo Customers," *Associated Press Financial Wire*, January 2, 2006; Sentido Comun, "American Express Launches New Promotion Campaign in Mexico," *Latin American News Digest*, February 14, 2006; Stuart Elliott, "American Express Gets Specific and Asks, 'Are You a Cardmember?'" *New York Times*, April 6, 2007, **http://www.nytimes.com/2007/04/06/business/media/06adco.html?scp=7&sq=american+express+marketing&st=nyt** (accessed on April 14).

Advertising, Sales Promotion, and Public Relations

BzzAgent™

Joe
Chernov
Profile ▼

A **Decision Maker** at BzzAgent

Joe Chernov is VP of communications for BzzAgent, Inc., a word-of-mouth marketing and media firm based in Boston. He secures press coverage for BzzAgent in media outlets such as the *Wall Street Journal*, National Public Radio, and television news programs. BzzAgent works by providing samples of new products along with educational materials to its community of trained consumer volunteers, who share their honest opinions with their social networks.

Joe previously founded Upper Right PR, a boutique public relations firm that pioneered insourced communications support to manufacturing, technology, and marketing companies. The Upper Right business model provided clients with on-site PR support, effectively supplying an "acting" director of public relations for emerging companies.

Prior to establishing his own agency, Joe co-directed a global industry analyst relations practice for the world's largest public relations firm. He previously served as director of corporate communications for CMGI's MyWay.com, where he spearheaded the company's high-profile public launch. He lectures regularly at colleges and universities and is quoted frequently by the media on the topic of nontraditional marketing. He is the author of *77½ PR Tips*, an e-book written as a public relations primer for companies in their early stages. He graduated *magna cum laude* from Westfield State College with a BA in Spanish and a BS in criminal justice.

▼ Q & A with Joe Chernov

Q) What I do when I'm not working?
A) Ski with my wife; play fantasy sports; struggle to train an incorrigible cat.

Q) First job out of school?
A) Victim/Witness Advocate for the Massachusetts Parole Board.

Q) Career high?
A) Every time the CEO says, "I defer to you."

Q) A job-related mistake I wish I hadn't made?
A) Being impatient during my first few jobs. I would have been better served to focus more on learning my craft than angling for promotions. In the end, I've discovered that experience does matter.

Q) My motto to live by?
A) "Originality is the art of concealing your sources." (Ben Franklin)

Q) Don't do this when interviewing with me?
A) Don't say "like" or "ya know."

Decision Time at BzzAgent

By late 2005 BzzAgent had established itself as the most widely recognized company in the white hot "word of mouth" marketing sector. This cutting-edge strategy involves inviting unpaid consumers to experience products and share their honest opinions with their friends and family. The company had earned a cover story in the *Sunday New York Times* magazine: its founder was preparing to release a compelling business book, its client roster read as a virtual "who's who" list of *Fortune* 500 companies, and it was approaching the final stages of closing a major round of institutional financing.

Then, on October 18, 2005, a watchdog group named Commercial Alert made public a letter it sent to the Federal Trade Commission calling for an investigation of various types of nontraditional marketing firms, including word of mouth companies. The group, which was launched by consumer advocate Ralph Nader, accused these companies of "perpetrating large scale deception upon consumers by deploying buzz marketers who fail to disclose that they have been enlisted to promote products." The letter cited BzzAgent by name.

> **Things to remember:**
>
> The Commercial Alert organization has a lot of power to sway consumers' opinions, especially because its founder Ralph Nader is a very well-known public figure (and former presidential candidate).

The tone of the articles about BzzAgent changed immediately. No longer describing BzzAgent as the promising future of marketing, articles began to question the company's policies concerning "disclosure" in word of mouth marketing campaigns. A year prior to this controversy, BzzAgent became the first company to explicitly require its word of mouth volunteers to reveal their affiliation with the marketing campaign when "buzzing" others. The company's founder and CEO, Dave Balter, also co-authored the Code of Ethics for the Word of Mouth Marketing Association. However, these facts were consistently left out of published articles and blog postings in the wake of the Commercial Alert letter. As one on-line news site noted, "Public watchdogs just won't leave the buzz marketers alone.... [T]his growing marketing subset may be in for another PR headache."[1]

The company's initial communication strategy was to respond to all reporters' inquiries, but not to conduct proactive outreach to the media. BzzAgent used this technique because it enabled the firm to defend its position without being perceived as defensive. However, the negative articles continued to proliferate, causing BzzAgent to rethink its public relations strategy.

Joe considered his Options 1·2·3

1 **Option**
Take charge of the discussion. Build an aggressive, outbound communication program around BzzAgent's benchmark-setting disclosure policy. Modify internal practices to further strengthen the company's Code of Conduct by requiring all participants to disclose that they were participants in a word of mouth campaign— and bar anyone who didn't follow this policy from participating in future campaigns. As the number of articles on disclosure increases, this volume creates more of an opportunity for BzzAgent to get out the message that the company is not violating ethical principles within the marketing arena. On the other hand, this more aggressive strategy could create the misconception that BzzAgent had bowed to public pressure and that strengthening its disclosure policy in response to Commercial Alert's allegations essentially was admitting wrongdoing. It was also possible that increasing awareness of the debate during the "due diligence" phase of financing could stall or threaten investment, or that sustaining the controversy could discourage publicity-shy potential clients from signing on with BzzAgent.

2 **Option**
Defend without being defensive. Demonstrate confidence by responding to all disclosure-related questions asked by reporters, but do not contribute to the negative exposure by pitching stories that elaborate on BzzAgent's ethical policies. This strategy would get BzzAgent's message out to the public and avoid "no comment" statements that people typically associate with guilt. But a reactive rather than a proactive position limits message control; journalists' opinions tend to be formed prior to contacting BzzAgent, putting the company at a disadvantage. It was also possible that this defensive posture would continue to focus media criticism on BzzAgent rather than on other companies.

3 **Option**
Go quiet. Another company mentioned in the Commercial Alert letter refused to speak to the media. Despite having no overt disclosure policy, this company was cited in articles far less frequently than BzzAgent. By saying nothing to the media, BzzAgent would increase the likelihood that the journalists would direct their criticism to other companies. This silent strategy would ensure that the company would not be misquoted in a damaging manner and perhaps redirect criticism to competitors. It would also lower the volume of debate in the crucial "due diligence" period, during which potential investors were trying to decide whether to back BzzAgent. On the other hand, silence would prevent the company from taking a strong stand as the leader in word of mouth ethics. And this refusal to speak to the media could damage BzzAgent's long-term relationships with journalists.

Now, put yourself in Joe's shoes: Which option would you choose, and why?

> **You Choose**
>
> Which **Option** would you choose, and **why**?
>
> 1. ☐YES ☐NO 2. ☐YES ☐NO 3. ☐YES ☐NO

See what **option** Joe chose and its success on **page 432** ➡

1

OBJECTIVE
Tell what advertising is, describe the major types of advertising, and discuss some of the criticisms of advertising.
(pp. 400–405)

Advertising: The Image of Marketing

Advertising is so much a part of marketing that many people think of the two as the same thing. Remember, product, price, and distribution strategies are just as important as marketing communications. And, as we saw in Chapter 12 there are many ways to get a message out to a target audience in addition to advertising. Advertising is still very important—in 2006 alone, U.S. marketers spent over $285 billion to do it.[2]

However, in today's competitive environment even the big guys like Procter & Gamble and General Motors are rethinking how much they want to invest in pricey ad campaigns as they search for alternative ways to get their messages out there. Indeed while total ad spending increased only five percent over the previous year, spending on alternative media (e.g., on-line, mobile, entertainment and digital out-of-home media) increased a whopping $73.43 billion or 22 percent.[3]

This trend is likely to continue as the number of media outlets mushrooms along with the number of TV viewers who use their trusty remote control or perhaps TiVo to skip over ads. Digital video recorders (DVRs) that let viewers skip through commercials are now in 19 million or 17 percent of the 110 million U.S. television households. In addition, 38 percent of all Americans and 50 percent of those aged 18 to 39 say they use an iPod, video on demand (VOD), DVR, or a computer to watch a TV show each month.[4] One alternative marketers are choosing is paid **product/brand placements**. With product placements, companies pay to have their products embedded in movies, TV shows, and other entertainment vehicles. Today, firms are placing their products not only in traditional movies and television, but also in new platforms including iPods, cell phones, concerts, events, and downloadable Web-based films (no, it's no accident that the logos are so visible).[5] We'll talk more about product placements later in this chapter.

- The hit drama *24* on the FOX Network prominently features Ford vehicles.

- Coca-Cola cups sit on the judges' table during performances of *American Idol*.

- Winners of the reward challenge on *Survivor Micronesia* receive Herbal Essence shampoo to use at the "Great Escape Spa."

- Microsoft Corp.'s Xbox game machine made it onto CBS's *Two and a Half Men*.

Meanwhile, other marketers take their messages to the streets as they rely on publicly sponsored events in addition to traditional advertising. For example, Coca-Cola opened lounges for teens at malls, while the Campbell Soup Company unveiled "Soup Sanctuaries" that offer weary shoppers a chance to relax while they enjoy free soup. BMW scored big points with its series of short films from famous directors that appeared on its Web site (**www.bmw.com**).[6] There are many ways to communicate with a mass audience. In this chapter, we'll learn about some of the major approaches, beginning with advertising.

Wherever we turn, advertising bombards us. Television commercials, radio spots, banner ads, and huge billboards scream, "Buy me!" **Advertising** is nonpersonal communication an identified sponsor pays for that uses mass media to persuade or inform an audience.[7] Advertising can be fun, glamorous, annoying, informative—and hopefully—an effective way to let consumers know what they're selling and why people should run out and buy it *today*.

A long-running Virginia Slims cigarettes advertising campaign proclaimed, "You've come a long way, baby!" We can say the same about advertising itself. Advertising has been with us a long time. In ancient Greece and Rome, advertisements appeared on walls, were etched on stone tablets, or were shouted by criers, interspersed among announcements of successful military battles or government proclamations. Would the ancients have believed that today we get messages about products almost wherever we are, whether cruising down the road or around the Web? Some of us even get advertising messages on our mobile phones or in public rest rooms. It's hard to find a place where ads don't try to reach us.

Advertising is also a potent force that creates desire for products; it transports us to imaginary worlds where the people are happy, beautiful, or rich. In this way, advertising allows the organization to communicate its message in a favorable way and to repeat the message as often as it deems necessary to have an impact on receivers.

Types of Advertising

Although almost every business advertises, some industries are bigger spenders than others. The automotive industry is the top spender on measured advertising (magazines, newspapers, radio, television, and internet) in the United States, with expenditures of nearly $20 billion per year. Annual retail ad spending is just over $19 billion, the telecommunications industry spends nearly $11 billion, and spending for medicines and remedies is around $9.2 billion.[8] Because they spend so much on advertising, marketers must decide which type of ad will work best given their organizational and marketing goals. The advertisements an organization runs can take many forms, so let's review the most common kinds.

Product Advertising

When people give examples of advertising, they are likely to recall the provocative poses in Victoria's Secret ads or the cheeky reminders from the Geico gecko. These are examples of **product advertising**, where the message focuses on a specific good or service. While not all advertising features a product or a brand, most of the advertising we see and hear is indeed product advertising.

Institutional Advertising

Rather than focusing on a specific brand, **institutional advertising** promotes the activities, personality, or point of view of an organization or company. Some institutional messages state an organization's position on an issue to sway public opinion, a strategy we call **advocacy advertising**. For example, U.S. governors joined together in a campaign to get Congress to pass climate change legislation. The campaign included a 30-second TV commercial starring three governors, including California governor and *Terminator* movie star Arnold Schwarzenegger.[9]

Other messages take the form of **public service advertisements (PSAs)** that the media run free of charge. These messages promote not-for-profit organizations that serve society in some way, or they champion an issue such as increasing literacy or discouraging drunk driving. Advertising agencies often take on one or more public service campaigns on a *pro bono* (for free, not the U2 singer) basis. Little League baseball recently aired a 15-second PSA on ESPN that featured a 10-year old at the plate. In the stands the father yells, "Come on, son.

---

product/brand placement
Marketing communication activity in which companies have their products embedded in movies, TV shows, and other entertainment vehicles.

advertising
Nonpersonal communication an identified sponsor pays for that uses mass media to persuade or inform an audience.

product advertising
An advertising message that focuses on a specific good or service.

institutional advertising
An advertising message that promotes the activities, personality, or point of view of an organization or company.

advocacy advertising
A type of public service advertising an organization provides that seeks to influence public opinion on an issue because it has some stake in the outcome.

public service advertisements (PSAs)
Advertising run by the media without charge for not-for-profit organizations or to champion a particular cause.

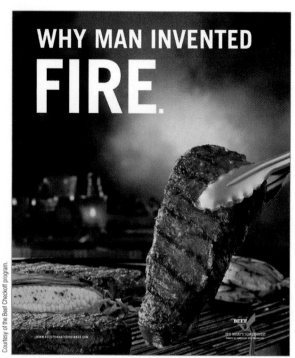

WHY MAN INVENTED FIRE.

Courtesy of the Beef Checkoff program.

This ad intends to stimulate primary demand for beef.

Hit the ball." The boy rolls his eyes, turns around to face his dad and yells back, "DAD, IS THAT THE BEST YOU CAN DO?! THAT'S PATHETIC. I DON'T EVEN KNOW WHY YOU BOTHER SHOWING UP! WHY CAN'T YOU BE MORE LIKE JIMMY'S DAD?! ALL THE OTHER PARENTS ARE GOING TO LAUGH AT YOU! YOU MAKE ME SICK!" The ad ends with a supertitle, "Now you know how it feels. Just let them play."[10]

Retail and Local Advertising

Both major retailers and small, local businesses advertise to encourage customers to shop at a specific store or use a local service. Local advertising informs us about store hours, location, and products that are available or on sale.

Do-it-Yourself Advertising

Today, in what has been referred to as the "Generation C" phenomenon, consumer-generated content including many thousands of blogs abounds on the Web. To take advantage of this blog craze, some marketers encourage consumers to contribute their own ads. In its recent "Priceless" campaign, MasterCard introduced its **www.priceless.com** Web site, where consumers could write their own ad copy for two filmed commercials—all of which must end with the word "Priceless." Converse allowed customers to send in homemade commercials to its Web site, then ran several of them on television.[11] Other companies that have experimented with do it yourself (DIY) advertising are L'Oréal ("You Make the Commercial"), JetBlue ("Travel Stories"), and McDonald's ("Global Casting").[12] GM's consumer-generated ad aired at the 2007 Super Bowl makes fun of sexual stereotypes of men and the use of semi-nude bodies in ads. Guys run up to a car, touch it, tear off their clothes and dance as Nelly's "Hot in Here" plays.[13]

For advertisers there are several benefits of do-it-yourself advertising. First, consumer-generated spots cost only one-third to one-quarter as much as professional TV and Internet ads—about $60,000 compared to the $350,000 or more to produce a traditional 30-second spot. This can be especially important for smaller businesses and emerging brands. Equally important, even to large companies with deep pockets, is the feedback on how consumers see the brand and the chance to gather more creative ideas to tell the brand's story.[14] A recent television commercial for Apple's iTouch was based on a commercial created and posted on YouTube by an 18-year old freshman college student, Nick Haley, from Britain. After Apple's marketers saw the ad on YouTube, they flew Haley to Los Angeles where he worked with the TBWA/Chiat/Day ad agency on the professional production of the ad. Yes, Haley was paid. Apple provided a significant contribution to his education—and a MacBook Pro laptop.[15]

As we saw in Chapter 1, though, putting content in the hands of consumers can be risky. During a commercial on the TV show *The Apprentice*, Chevrolet directed viewers to a Web site (**http://www.chevyapprentice.com/**) to create their own ads for the Chevy Tahoe,

By the **People**, For the **People**

With the increasing popularity of home-made videos, thousands of wannabe directors are getting a chance to strut their stuff before huge audiences. Many consumer brands such as Sony and Dove use consumer-generated ads as part of their promotional mix.

The ad agency Goodby, Silverstein & Partners aired a consumer-generated ad for its client Doritos during the Super Bowl in 2007. Consumers submitted homemade videos for a contest; the ad agency posted the five finalists to Yahoo! Video

and allowed the public to vote for its favorite. The winner was a group of five amateurs from North Carolina that produced its entry for the grand total of $12! This new advertising strategy shifted the responsibility of creating ads from a small advertising team to a large group of consumers. It develops a platform for consumers to publicize their voices and creativity and develop a more coherent relationship with the brand—and to get exposure for some "cheesy" videos.[16]

a popular SUV. As Chevy expected, not all the submissions were complimentary (or suitable for airing on network TV). In one video, a shiny SUV motors down a country road lined with sunflower fields, while jaunty music plays in the background. But then, white lettering appears on the screen: "$70 to fill up the tank, which will last less than 400 miles. Chevy Tahoe." Another submission asked, "Like this snowy wilderness? Better get your fill of it now. Then say hello to global warming." A spokeswoman for Chevrolet observed, "We anticipated that there would be critical submissions. You do turn over your brand to the public, and we knew that we were going to get some bad with the good. But it's part of playing in this space."[17]

Who Creates Advertising?

Although the latest trend toward DIY advertising illustrates how high-tech software like Photoshop and Final Cut Pro can help almost anyone to become a director, most advertising is far more complicated because the messages are part of a broader strategy. An **advertising campaign** is a coordinated, comprehensive plan that carries out promotion objectives and results in a series of advertisements placed in various media over a period of time. Although a campaign may be based around a single ad idea, most use multiple messages with all ads in the campaign having the same look and feel. Take for example, the recent LG mobile phone campaign featuring comic-book superhero Iron Man. LG phones were featured in the movie—Iron Man's alter ego, industrialist Tony Stark, uses his LG 9400 phone to save the day. The campaign includes TV spots, versions of the same spots in cinemas, print, on-line, out-of-home, and retail ads.[18] In addition, LG opened a tie-in internet site for the movie (**www.InsidetheSuit.com**) where fans could win one of 20 LG Iron Man phones dipped in gold.[19]

Although some firms create their own advertising in-house, in many cases several specialized companies work together to develop an advertising campaign. Typically the firm retains one or more outside *advertising agencies* to oversee this process. A **limited-service agency** provides one or more specialized services, such as media buying or creative development. In contrast, a **full-service agency** supplies most or all of the services a campaign requires, including research, creation of ad copy and art, media selection, and production of the final messages. The largest global agencies are Dentsu, BBDO Worldwide, McCann-Erickson Worldwide, and the J. Walter Thompson Co.[20]

A campaign requires the services of many different people. Big or small, an advertising agency hires a range of specialists to craft a message and make the communication concept a reality:

- **Account management:** The *account executive*, or account manager, is the "soul" of the operation. This person develops the campaign's strategy for the client, supervises the day-to-day activities on the account, and is the primary liaison between the agency and the client. The account executive has to ensure that the client is happy while he verifies that people within the agency execute the desired strategy.

- **Creative services:** *Creatives* are the "heart" of the communication effort. These are the people who actually dream up and produce the ads. They include the agency's creative director, copywriters, and art director. Creatives are the artists who breathe life into marketing objectives and craft messages that (hopefully) will interest consumers.

- **Research and marketing services:** *Researchers* are the "brains" of the campaign. They collect and analyze information that will help account executives develop a sensible strategy. They assist creatives in getting consumer reactions to different versions of ads or by providing copywriters with details on the target group.

- **Media planning:** The *media planner* is the "legs" of the campaign. He helps to determine which communication vehicles are the most effective, and recommends the most

advertising campaign
A coordinated, comprehensive plan that carries out promotion objectives and results in a series of advertisements placed in media over a period of time.

limited-service agency
An agency that provides one or more specialized services, such as media buying or creative development.

full-service agency
An agency that provides most or all of the services needed to mount a campaign, including research, creation of ad copy and art, media selection, and production of the final messages.

Mona wanted to be sure *everything* matched her magnificent new bag.

THE
SAK

THESAK.COM Artwork by Sloane Tanen

© The Sak

Advertisers often include unusual imagery to capture the attention of their audiences.

efficient means to deliver the ad by deciding where, when, and how often it will appear.

As we saw in Chapter 12, more and more agencies practice *integrated marketing communication (IMC)*, in which advertising is only one element of a total communication plan. Because IMC includes more than just advertising, client teams composed of people from account services, creative services, media planning, research, public relations, sales promotion, and direct marketing may work together to develop a plan that best meets the communication needs of each client.

Ethical Issues in Advertising

Advertising, more than any other part of marketing, has been sharply criticized for decades. Such criticism certainly may be based less on reality than on the high visibility of advertising and the negative attitudes of consumers who find ads an intrusion in their lives. The objections to advertising are similar to those some people have to marketing in general as we discussed in Chapter 1. Here are the main ones:

- **Advertising is manipulative:** Advertising causes people to behave like robots and do things against their will—to make purchases they would not otherwise do were it not for the ads. However, consumers are not robots. Since they are consciously aware of appeals made in advertising, they are free to choose whether to respond to an ad or not. Of course, consumers can and often do make bad decisions that advertising may influence, but that is not the same as manipulation.

- **Advertising is deceptive and untruthful:** Deceptive advertising means that an ad falsely represents the product and that consumers believe the false information and act on it. Indeed, there is some false or deceptive advertising, but as a whole advertisers try to present their brands in the best possible light while being truthful. In the United States, both government regulation and the industry itself strongly encourage honesty.

To protect consumers from being misled, the Federal Trade Commission (FTC) has specific rules regarding unfair or deceptive advertising. Some deceptive ads make statements that can be proven false. For example, the FTC fined Volvo and its ad agency $150,000 each for an ad containing a "rigged" demonstration. The Volvo "Bear Food" ad campaign showed a monster truck running over a row of cars and crushing all but the Volvo station wagon. The Volvos, however, had been structurally reinforced, while the structural supports in some of the other cars had been cut.[21]

In addition to fining firms for deceptive advertising, the FTC also has the power to require firms to run **corrective advertising**, messages that clarify or qualify previous claims. An FTC ruling required Novartis AG to spend $8 million to change packaging and advertising information about its Doan's Pills back medication saying "Although Doan's is an effective pain reliever, there is no evidence that Doan's is more effective than other pain relievers for back pain."[22]

Other ads, although not illegal, may create a biased impression of products with the use of **puffery**—claims of superiority that neither sponsors nor critics of the ads can prove are true or untrue. For example, Nivea bills itself as "the world's number 1 name in skin care," Neutrogena claims that its cream cleanser produces "the deepest feeling clean," and DuPont says that its Stainmaster Carpet is "a creation so remarkable, it's practically a miracle."

corrective advertising
Advertising that clarifies or qualifies previous deceptive advertising claims.

puffery
Claims made in advertising of product superiority that cannot be proven true or untrue.

Ethical Decisions in the Real World

The battle for leadership in the toothpaste market is intense. The leading producers, Colgate-Palmolive Co. and Procter & Gamble that markets the leading Crest brand vie fiercely for market share. Advertising is an important part of both companies' marketing strategies. In order to convince consumers that a brand is important to fight tooth decay and other tooth maladies, companies often rely on messages that provide data or at least imply that dentists approve of the brand. Some campaigns may include an endorsement by a professional organization or by individual dentists who give testimonials about the toothpaste. But, other ad messages may instead feature an actor who plays the role of a dentist—perhaps a commercial shot on a stage set that looks like a dentist's office. In these cases the ad may provide a *disclaimer* that states this is just a simulation ("I'm not a doctor, but I play one on TV"). Even with a disclaimer (that some viewers may ignore or not notice), is this ethical? Can marketers imply approval of their brand by health professionals without being able to substantiate their claims? If you're a marketer looking to advertise toothpaste, does this idea make sense? Would you try this? Why or why not?

Ripped from the Headlines! See what happened in the Real World at **www. mypersonmarketinglab.com**

ETHICS CHECK: ↖
Find out what other students taking this course **would do** and **why** on **www. mypearsonmarketinglab. com**

If you worked for an advertising agency, would you approve an ad that implies a product has been endorsed by medical professionals without actually making the claim outright?

☐**YES** ☐**NO**

Does this mean that puffery is an unethical marketing practice? Not really. In fact, both advertisers and consumers generally accept puffery as a normal part of the advertising game. Although a little exaggeration may be reasonable, for New Era firms the goal is to create marketing communications that are both honest and that present their products in the most positive way possible. This approach works to the firm's advantage in the long run since it prevents consumers from becoming overly cynical about the claims it makes.

In general, advertisers are motivated to play by the rules. It doesn't benefit them or the client if they make false claims that come to light later.

- **Advertising is offensive and in bad taste:** To respond to this criticism, one must first recognize that what is offensive or in bad taste to one person may not be to another. Yes, some TV commercials are offensive to some people, but then news and program content in the media can be and often is even more explicit or in poor taste. While advertisers seek to go the distance using humor, sex appeals, or fear appeals to get audiences' attention, most shy away from presenting messages that offend the very audience they want to buy their products.

- **Advertising creates and perpetuates stereotypes:** Some advertising critics assert that advertising portrays certain groups of consumers in negative ways. For example, advertising has portrayed women more often as homemakers than as industry leaders. While there is evidence that advertising (and media program content) is guilty of perpetuating stereotypes, it is important to recognize that these stereotypes already exist in the culture. Advertising doesn't create them so much as it reflects them.

- **Advertising causes people to buy things they don't really need:** The truth of this criticism depends on how you define a "need." If we believe that all consumers need is the basic functional benefits of products—the transportation a car provides, the nutrition we get from food, and the clean hair from a shampoo—then advertising may be guilty as charged. If, on the other hand, you think you need a car that projects a cool image, food that tastes fantastic, and a shampoo that makes your hair shine and smell ever-so-nice, then advertising is just a vehicle that communicates those more intangible benefits.

Figure 13.1 | Steps to Develop an Advertising Campaign

Developing an advertising campaign includes a series of steps that will ensure that the advertising meets communication objectives.

Step 1: Understand the Target Audience

Step 2: Establish Message and Budget Objectives

Step 3: Create the Ads

Step 4: Pretest What the Ads Will Say

Step 5: Choose the Media Type(s) and Media Schedule

Step 6: Evaluate the Advertising

Cabo Uno tequila keeps its message simple.

2

Develop the Advertising Campaign

The advertising campaign is about much more than creating a cool ad and hoping people notice it. The campaign should be intimately related to the organization's overall communication goals. That means the firm (and its outside agency if it uses one) must have a good idea of whom it wants to reach, what it will take to appeal to this market, and where and when it should place its messages. Let's examine the steps required to do this, as Figure 13.1 shows.

Step 1: Understand the Target Audience

The best way to communicate with an audience is to understand as much as possible about them and what turns them on and off. An ad that uses the latest "hip-hop" slang may relate to teenagers but not to their parents—and this strategy may backfire if the ad copy reads like an "ancient" 40-year-old trying to sound like a 20-year-old.

Most advertising is directed toward customers, whether the target audience includes college students or industry executives. As we discussed in Chapter 7, marketers often identify the target audience for an advertising campaign from research related to a segmentation strategy. Researchers try to get inside the customer's head to understand just how to create a message that he will understand and to which he will respond. For example, an account executive working on a campaign for Pioneer Stereo was assigned to hang out with guys who were likely prospects to buy car stereos. His observations resulted in an advertising campaign that incorporated the phrases they actually use to describe their cars: "My car is my holy temple, my love shack, my drag racer of doom."[23]

Step 2: Establish Message and Budget Objectives

Advertising objectives should be consistent with the overall communication plan. That means that both the underlying message and its costs need to relate to what the marketer is trying to say about the product and what the marketer is willing or able to spend. Thus, advertising objectives generally will include objectives for both the message and the budget.

Set Message Objectives

As we noted earlier, because advertising is the most visible part of marketing, many people assume that marketing *is* advertising. In truth, advertising alone is quite limited in what it can achieve. What advertising *can* do is inform, persuade, and remind. Accordingly, some advertisements are informational—they aim to make the customer knowledgeable about features of the product or how to use it. At other times, advertising seeks to persuade consumers to like a brand or to prefer one brand over the competition. But many, many ads simply aim to keep the name of the brand in front of the consumer—reminding consumers that this brand is the one to choose when they look for a soft drink or a laundry detergent.

Set Budget Objectives

Advertising is expensive. Procter & Gamble, which leads all U.S. companies in advertising expenditures, spends almost $5 billion per year while second- and third-place ad spenders, AT&T and General Motors, each spend well over $3 billion each.[24]

An objective of many firms is to allocate a percentage of its overall communication budget to advertising, depending on how much and what type of advertising the company can afford. Major corporations like General Motors advertise heavily, using expensive media such as television to promote multiple products throughout the year. Other companies may be more selective, and smaller firms may want to put their advertising dollars into cheaper media outlets such as direct mail or trade publications. As we noted earlier, firms today are reducing their expenditures on traditional media and spending more on alternative media.

The major approaches and techniques to setting overall promotional budgets, such as the percentage-of-sales and objective-task methods we discussed in Chapter 12, also set advertising budgets.

Creative strategy is the process that turns a concept into an advertisement.

Step 3: Create the Ads

Creative strategy is the process that turns a concept into an advertisement. It's one thing to know *what* a company wants to say about itself and its products, and another to figure out *how* to say it. Some marketers like to think of the creative process for an advertising campaign as the "spark between objective and execution."

The goal of an advertising campaign is to present a series of messages and repeat it to a sufficient degree to meet the desired objectives. To do this, advertising creatives—art directors, copywriters, photographers, and others—must develop a "big idea," a concept that expresses aspects of the good, service, or organization in a tangible, attention-getting, memorable manner.

An **advertising appeal** is the central idea of the ad. Some advertisers use an emotional appeal with dramatic color or powerful images, while others bombard the audience with facts. Some feature sexy people or stern-looking experts—even professors from time to time. Different appeals can work for the same product, from a bland "talking head" to a montage of animated special effects. An attention-getting way to say something profound about cat food or laundry detergent is more art than science, but we can describe some common appeals:

- **Reasons why—the USP:** A **unique selling proposition (USP)** gives consumers a single, clear reason why one product is better to solve a problem. The format focuses on a need and points out how the product can satisfy it. For example, "M&Ms melt in your mouth, not in your hands" is a USP. In general, a USP strategy is effective if there is some clear product advantage that consumers can readily identify and that is important to them.

- **Comparative advertising:** A comparative advertisement explicitly names one or more competitors. Pizza Hut's recent "America's Favorite Pizza" spots claimed that consumers preferred its hand-tossed pizzas 2 to 1 over both number two Domino's and number three Papa John's. Ads showed rival pizza delivery drivers eating Pizza Hut pizza at the Pizza Hut driver's home. Papa John's countered with claims that its crust was made fresh while Pizza Hut's was frozen.[25]

Joe Chernov

Younger consumers in particular tend to be skeptical about traditional advertising methods. BzzAgent's word-of-mouth approach can be especially effective for youth-oriented products because members of this target audience prefer to base their choices on what their peers recommend.

This ad vividly demonstrates a concrete product benefit.

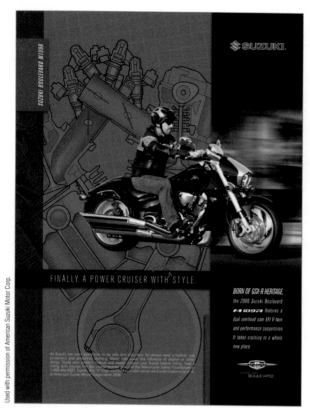

This ad promises an end benefit of power and provides specific details about how the benefit will be delivered to riders.

creative strategy
The process that turns a concept into an advertisement.

advertising appeal
The central idea or theme of an advertising message.

unique selling proposition (USP)
An advertising appeal that focuses on one clear reason why a particular product is superior.

Comparative ads can be very effective, but there is a risk of turning off consumers who don't like the negative tone. While in many countries comparative advertising is illegal, it's a widely used tactic in the United States. Comparative advertising is best for brands that have a smaller share of the market and for firms that can focus on a specific feature that makes them superior to a major brand. When market leaders use comparative advertising, there is the risk consumers will feel they are "picking on the little guy."

- **Demonstration:** The ad shows a product "in action" to prove that it performs as claimed: "It slices, it dices!" Demonstration advertising is most useful when consumers are unable to identify important benefits except by seeing the product in use. In China, however, P&G found that demonstrations of how its shampoo works were not effective. As a result P&G abandoned demonstration advertising in favor of more emotional appeals. One ad shows a woman emerging from an animated cocoon and turning into a butterfly, symbolizing how the shampoo creates a "new life for hair."[26]

- **Testimonial:** A celebrity, an expert, or a "man in the street" states the product's effectiveness. The use of *celebrity endorsers* is a common but expensive strategy. As we saw with NutriSystem's experience in Chapter 7, the weight-loss industry often relies upon celebrity endorsers. Football legends Dan Marino and Don Shula show how many inches they've dropped from their waists since they switched to the company's food products. Jenny Craig spokeswoman Queen Latifah doesn't just talk about weight loss but promotes a "Healthy Curves" approach to weight loss. Consumers can also watch Queen Latifah and Valerie Bertinelli commercials and access a variety of e-tools to track weight and measure progress on the Jenny Craig Web site.[27]

- **Slice of life:** A *slice-of-life* format presents a (dramatized) scene from everyday life. Slice-of-life advertising can be effective for everyday products such as peanut butter and headache remedies that consumers may feel good about if they see "real" people buy and use them.

- **Lifestyle:** A *lifestyle* format shows a person or persons attractive to the target market in an appealing setting. The advertised product is "part of the scene," implying that the person who buys it will attain the lifestyle. For example, a commercial on MTV might depict a group of "cool" California skateboarders who take a break for a gulp of milk and say, "It does a body good."

- **Fear appeals:** This tactic highlights the negative consequences of *not* using a product. Some *fear appeal* ads focus on physical harm, while others try to create concern for social harm or disapproval. Mouthwash, deodorant, and dandruff shampoo makers and life insurance companies successfully use fear appeals. So do ads aimed at changing behaviors, such as messages discouraging drug use or encouraging safe sex. In general, fear appeals can be successful if the audience perceives there to be an

This Chinese ad is for Panadol, a pain reliever.

FreddySu Jin
Lee
a professor at California State University at Los Angeles

My Advice for BzzAgent would be to choose

Option

real people, **Other** Voices

I would choose **Option 2** because, as a public relations firm, keeping silent is definitely not the way out. However, choosing Option 1 would mean that whenever there is another complaint from another consumer group, the business model would change again. In principle, there is nothing wrong with satisfied customers spreading positive word of mouth. On the contrary, the company's defense can be framed to include the negative word of mouth too should the tried and tested products fall below expectations. As the company engages volunteers to increase product publicity through word of mouth, definitely the products have to have certain positive qualities or else it would do more harm than good. The trial itself should mean BzzAgent stands behind good-quality products and the ultimate beneficiary is the consumer. ➤

---

appropriate level of intensity in the fear appeal. For example, horrible photos of teens lying on the highway following an auto accident can be quite effective in PSAs designed to persuade teens not to drink and drive, but they are likely to backfire if an insurance company tries to "scare" people into buying life insurance.

- **Sex appeals:** Some ads appear to sell sex rather than products. In a Guess jeans ad, a shirtless man lies near an almost shirtless woman. Ads such as these rely on sexuality to get consumers' attention. *Sex appeal* ads are more likely to be effective when there is a connection between the product and sex (or at least romance). For example, sex appeals will work well with a perfume but are less likely to be effective when you're trying to sell a lawn mower.

- **Humorous appeals:** Humorous ads can be an effective way to break through advertising clutter. But humor can be tricky, because what is funny to one person may be offensive or stupid to another. Different cultures also have different senses of humor. A recent Reebok commercial showed women at a basketball game checking out the all-male cheerleading squad—people from countries who don't have cheerleaders (you don't find too many pom-poms at soccer matches) might not "get it."

  Perhaps the major benefit of humorous advertising is that it attracts consumers' attention and leaves them with a pleasant feeling. Of course, humor in advertising can backfire. In the United Kingdom, a Renault Megane 225 ad featuring people in everyday situations shaking uncontrollably as the car passed by was banned by the government's Office of Communications: Viewers complained that the ad mocked people with illnesses such as Parkinson's disease.[28]

- **Slogans, jingles, and music:** *Slogans* link the brand to a simple linguistic device that is memorable. *Jingles* do the same but set the slogan to music. We usually have no trouble reciting successful slogans (sometimes years after the campaign has ended); think of such die-hards as "Please don't squeeze the Charmin," "Double your pleasure, double your fun," and "Even a caveman can do it." Firms such as Clorox, Allstate, and Procter & Gamble find that the songs they use in their commercials can become popular on their own; now they offer consumers the opportunity to purchase full-length versions of the music.[29]

Step 4: Pretest What the Ads Will Say

Now that the creatives have worked their magic, how does the agency know if the campaign ideas will work? Advertisers try to minimize mistakes by getting reactions to ad messages before they actually place them. Much of this **pretesting**, the research that goes on in the early stages of a campaign, centers on gathering basic information that will help planners be sure they've accurately defined the product's market, consumers, and competitors. As we saw in Chapter 4, this information comes from quantitative sources, such as surveys, and qualitative sources, such as focus groups.

pretesting
A research method that seeks to minimize mistakes by getting consumer reactions to ad messages before they appear in the media.

As the campaign takes shape, the players need to predict how well the advertising concepts will perform. They will often perform additional pretesting to measure an ad's effectiveness. This process determines whether consumers receive, comprehend, and respond to the ad according to plan.

Step 5: Choose the Media Type(s) and Media Schedule

media planning
The process of developing media objectives, strategies, and tactics for use in an advertising campaign.

aperture
The best place and time to reach a person in the target market group.

Media planning is a problem-solving process for getting a message to a target audience in the most effective way. Planning decisions include audience selection and where, when, and how frequent the exposure should be. Thus, the first task for a media planner is to find out when and where people in the target market are most likely to be exposed to the communication. This is the **aperture**, the best "window" to reach the target market. Many college students read the campus newspaper in the morning (believe it or not, sometimes even during class!), so their aperture would include this medium at this time.

There is no such thing as one perfect medium for advertising. The choice depends on the specific target audience, the objective of the message, and, of course, the budget. For the advertising campaign to be effective, the media planner must match up the profile of the target market with specific media vehicles. For example many Hispanic-American consumers, even those who speak English, are avid users of Spanish-language media. Marketers that wish to reach this segment might allocate a relatively large share of their advertising budget to buying Spanish-language newspapers, magazines, TV, and Spanish Webcasts available to broadband Internet users.

The choice of the right media mix is no simple matter, especially as new options including videos and DVDs, video games, personal computers, the Internet, MP3 players, hundreds of new TV channels, and even satellite radio now vie for our attention. Consider that in 1965, advertisers could reach 80 percent of 18- to 49-year-olds in the United States with three 60-second TV spots. In 2002, it required 117 prime-time commercials to produce the same result. While viewing of traditional broadcast TV is down dramatically in recent years, people spend a lot more time watching cable and satellite channels. This explains why the companies that own broadcast networks are buying up major cable channels—General Electric's NBC owns MSNBC, CNBC, Bravo, SciFi, and USA TV channels; Walt Disney Co., which owns ABC, also owns ESPN and ABC Family and also is a partial owner for Lifetime, A&E, and E! cable channels; and Viacom Inc. owns MTV, VH1, Comedy Central, Showtime, The Movie Channel, and Nickelodeon along with CBS.[30] Figure 13.2 highlights some of the dramatic changes in media usage.

Where to Say It: Traditional Mass Media

What does a 50-inch plasma TV with Dolby Surround Sound have in common with a matchbook? Each is a media vehicle that permits an advertiser to communicate with a potential customer. Depending on the intended message, each medium has its advantages and disadvantages. In this section we'll take a look at the major categories of traditional mass media, then we'll look at Internet advertising and some less-traditional indirect forms of advertising. Table 13.1 summarizes some of the pros and cons of each type.

Figure 13.2 | Changes in Media Usage

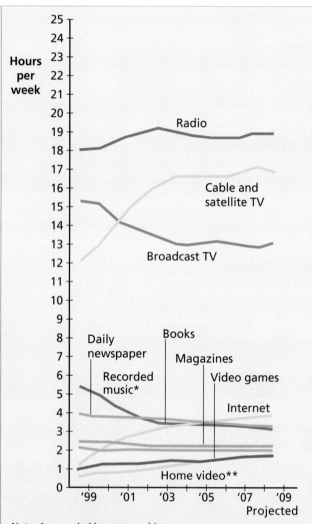

Note: Ages varied by survey subject.

*Excludes Internet-related use of traditional media including MP3s and Internet downloading.

** Playback of prerecorded VHS cassettes and DVDs only.

Based on: Veronis Suhler Stevenson Communications Industry Forecast, 2005 Edition. Copyright © 2005. Used with permission.

Table 13.1 | Pros and Cons of Media Vehicles

Vehicle	Pros	Cons
Television	• Extremely creative and flexible • Network TV is the most cost-effective way to reach a mass audience. • Cable and sattelite TV allow the advertiser to reach a selected group at relatively low cost. • A prestigious way to advertise • Can demonstrate product in use • Can provide entertainment and generate excitement • Messages have high impact because of the use of sight and sound.	• The message is quickly forgotten unless it is repeated often. • The audience is increasingly fragmented. • Although the relative cost of reaching the audience is low, prices are still high on an absolute basis—often too high for smaller companies. A 30-second spot on a prime-time TV sitcom costs well over $250,000. • Fewer people viewing network television • People switch from station to station zapping commercials. • Rising costs have led to more and shorter ads, causing more clutter.
Radio	• Good for selectively targeting an audience • Is heard out of the home • Can reach customers on a personal and intimate level • Can use local personalities • Relatively low cost, both for producing a spot and for running it repeatedly • Because of short lead time, radio ads can be modified quickly to reflect changes in the marketplace. • Use of sound effects and music allows listeners to use their imagination to create a vivid scene.	• Listeners often don't pay full attention to what they hear. • Difficulty in buying radio time, especially for national advertisers • Not appropriate for products that must be seen or demonstrated to be appreciated • The small audience of individual stations means ads must be placed with many different stations and must be repeated frequently.
Newspapers	• Wide exposure provides extensive market coverage. • Flexible format permits the use of color, different sizes, and targeted editions. • Ability to use detailed copy • Allows local retailers to tie in with national advertisers • People in the right mental frame to process advertisements about new products, sales, etc. • Timeliness, i.e., short lead time between placing ad and having it run	• Most people don't spend much time reading the newspaper. • Readership is especially low among teens and young adults. • Short life span—people rarely look at a newspaper more than once. • Very cluttered ad environment • The reproduction quality of images is relatively poor. • Not effective to reach specific audiences
Magazines	• Audiences can be narrowly targeted by specialized magazines. • High credibility and interest level provide a good environment for ads. • Advertising has a long life and is often passed along to other readers. • Visual quality is excellent. • Can provide detailed product information with a sense of authority	• With the exception of direct mail, it is the most expensive form of advertising. The cost of a full-page, four-color ad in a general-audience magazine typically exceeds $100,000. • Long deadlines reduce flexibility. • The advertiser must generally use several magazines to reach the majority of a target market. • Clutter
Directories	• Customers actively seek exposure to advertisements. • Advertisers determine the quality of the ad placement because larger ads get preferential placement.	• Limited creative options • May be a lack of color • Ads are generally purchased for a full year and cannot be changed.

Out-of-home media	• Most of the population can be reached at low cost. • Good for supplementing other media • High frequency when signs are located in heavy traffic areas • Effective for reaching virtually all segments of the population • Geographic flexibility	• Hard to communicate complex messages because of short exposure time • Difficult to measure advertisement's audience • Controversial and disliked in many communities • Cannot pinpoint specific market segments
Internet	• Can target specific audiences and individualize messages • Web user registration and cookies allow marketers to track user preferences and Web site activity. • Is interactive—consumers can participate in the ad campaign; can create do-it-yourself ads. • An entertainment medium allowing consumers to play games, download music, etc. • Consumers are active participants in the communication process, controlling what information and the amount and rate of information they receive. • Web sites can facilitate both marketing communication and transactions. • Consumers visit Web sites with mindset of obtaining information. • Banners can achieve top of mind awareness (TOMA), even without click-throughs.	• Limited to internet users only • Banners, pop-ups, unsolicited e-mail, etc. can be unwanted and annoying. • Declining click-through rates for banners—currently less than 0.03 % • If Web pages take long to load consumers will abandon the site. • *Phishing* is e-mail sent by criminals to get consumers to go to phony Web sites that will seek to gain personal information such as credit card numbers from the consumer. • Because advertisers' costs are normally based on the number of click-throughs, competitors may engage in click fraud by clicking on a sponsored link. • Difficult to measure effectiveness
Place-based media	• Effective for certain markets such a pharmaceutical companies to reach their target audience • In retail locations it can reach customers immediately before purchase providing a last opportunity to influence the purchase decision. • In locations such as airports, it receives a high level of attention because of lack of viewer options.	• Limited audience • Difficult to measure effectiveness
Branded entertainment	• Brand presented in a positive context • Brand message presented in a covert fashion • Less intrusive and thus less likely to be avoided • Connection with a popular movie plot or TV program and with entertaining characters can help a brand's image. • Can build emotional connection with the audience • Can create a memorable association that serves to enhance brand recall	• Little control of how the brand is positioned—is in the hands of the director • Difficult to measure effectiveness • Costs of placement can be very high
Advergaming	• Companies can customize their own games or incorporate brands into existing popular games. • Some game producers now actively pursue tie-ins with brands. • Millions of gamers play an average of 40 hours per game before tiring of it.	• Audience limited to gamers

Based on: Adapted from J. Thomas Russell and Ron Lane, Kleppner's *Advertising Procedure*, 15th ed. (Upper Saddle River, N.J.: Prentice Hall, 2002); Terence A. Shimp, *Advertising, Promotion and Supplemental Aspects of Integrated Marketing Communications*, 7th ed. (Australia: Thomson Southwestern, 2007); and William Wells, John Burnett, and Sandra Moriarty, *Advertising: Principles and Practice*, 6th ed. (Upper Saddle River, N.J.: Prentice Hall, 2003).

- **Television:** Because of television's ability to reach so many people at once, it's often the medium of choice for regional and national companies. Today there are literally hundreds of television choices available to advertisers. However, advertising on a television network can be very expensive. The cost to air a 30-second ad on a popular prime-time network TV show one time normally ranges between $200,000 and $750,000 or more depending on the size of the show's audience. In 2008, ads for a near-finale episode of *American Idol*, the number one TV show for four years, went for $1 million or more.[31] Advertisers may prefer to buy cable, satellite, or local television time rather than network time because it's cheaper or because they want to reach a more targeted market, such as "foodies," who are into cooking. Nevertheless, 78 percent of advertisers say TV advertising has become less effective as DVRs and video-on-demand grow in popularity.[32]

- **Radio:** Radio as an advertising medium dates back to 1922, when a New York City apartment manager went on the air to advertise properties for rent. One advantage of radio advertising is flexibility. Marketers can change commercials quickly, often on the spot by an announcer and a recording engineer.[33]

- **Newspapers:** The newspaper is one of the oldest communication platforms. Retailers in particular have relied on newspaper ads since before the turn of the 20th century to inform readers about sales and deliveries of new merchandise. While most newspapers are local, *USA Today*, the *Wall Street Journal*, and the *New York Times* have national circulations and provide readerships in the millions. Newspapers are an excellent medium for local advertising and for events (such as store sales) that require a quick response. Today, most newspapers also offer on-line versions of their papers to expand their exposure. Some, such as the *New York Times*, offer on-line subscribers downloads of the actual newspaper including all the ads at a much lower cost than the paper version. Rates for newspapers vary depending on the circulation of the paper. Most newspapers help advertisers in putting their ads together, a real advantage to the small business.

- **Magazines:** Today, in addition to general audience magazines such as *Readers Digest*, there are literally thousands of special-interest magazines. Approximately 92 percent of adults look through at least one magazine per month. New technology such as *selective binding* allows publishers to personalize their editions so that they can include advertisements for local businesses in issues they mail to specific locations. For advertisers, magazines also offer the opportunity for multi-page spreads as well as the ability to include special inserts so they can deliver samples of products such as perfumes and other "scratch-and-sniff" treats. Kimberly Clark's Viva brand paper towels, for example, included samples of the product stitched into copies of *Readers Digest* as part of a six-page spread.[34]

Where to Say it: Internet Advertising

The Web gives marketers the ability to reach customers in new and exciting ways. On-line advertising has grown to over $21 billion a year. Major firms like General Mills, Inc. and Kraft Foods are boosting their spending and the number of brands they promote on-line.[35] The reason? Fifteen percent of the time U.S. consumers spend with all media is now on-line—and of course for some segments such as college students that figure is much higher.[36]

On-line advertising offers several advantages. First, the Internet provides new ways to finely target customers. Web user registrations and *cookies* allow sites to track user preferences and deliver ads based on previous Internet behavior. In addition, because the Web site can track how many times an ad is "clicked," advertisers can measure how people are responding to on-line messages. Alaska Airlines has developed a system to create unique ads for individual Web surfers based on their geographic location, the number of times that person has seen an Alaska Airlines ad, the consumer's purchase history with the airline, and his experience with lost bags, delays, and flight cancellations. The program can offer different prices to different customers, even prices below the lowest published fares.[37]

Finally, on-line advertising can be interactive—it lets consumers participate in the advertising campaign, and in some cases they can even become part of the action. Viewers who logged on to a special Web site were able to "direct" TV commercials for the Ford Probe by picking the cast and plotlines that Ford's ad agency then used to create actual spots. Similarly, during its "whatever.com" campaign, Nike sent consumers to the Web to pick the endings of three cliffhanger TV spots.[38]

Specific forms of Internet advertising include banners, buttons, pop-up ads, search engines and directories, and e-mail:

banners
Internet advertising in the form of rectangular graphics at the top or bottom of Web pages.

- **Banners: Banners**, rectangular graphics at the top or bottom of Web pages, were the first form of Web advertising. Although the effectiveness of banners remains in question (banners now get less than a one percent click-through rate which means that fewer than 1 out of 100 of these ads elicits a response from viewers), they still remain the most popular form of Web advertising.

buttons
Small banner-type advertisements that can be placed anywhere on a Web page.

- **Buttons: Buttons** are small banner-type advertisements that a company can place anywhere on a page. Early in the life of the Internet, buttons encouraging surfers to "Download Netscape Now" became a standard on many Web sites and were responsible for much of Netscape's early success.

- **Pop-up ads:** A pop-up ad is an advertisement that appears on the screen while a Web page loads or after it has loaded. Because pop-up ads take up the center of the screen while surfers wait for the desired page to load, they are difficult to ignore. Many surfers find pop-ups a nuisance, so most Internet access software provides an option that blocks all pop-ups. Web advertisers are typically charged only if people actually click through to the ad.

- **Search engine and directory listings:** Just as the *Yellow Pages* and other directories are advertising media, so too are search engines and on-line directory listings. Increasingly, firms are paying search engines for more visible or higher placement on results lists. Who have you Googled today?

- **E-mail:** For advertising, e-mail is becoming as pervasive as radio and television. It is one of the easiest ways to communicate with consumers because marketers can send unsolicited e-mail advertising messages to thousands of users by *spamming*. The industry defines this practice as sending unsolicited e-mail to five or more people not personally known to the sender. Many Web sites that offer e-mail give surfers the opportunity to refuse unsolicited e-mail via junk e-mail blockers. This **permission marketing** gives the consumer the power to opt in or out. Marketers in the United States send about 200 billion e-mails to consumers every year, so they hope that a good portion of these will be opened and read rather than being sent straight to the recycle bin.[39]

permission marketing
E-mail advertising in which on-line consumers have the opportunity to accept or refuse the unsolicited e-mail.

Where to Say It: Indirect Forms of Advertising

While marketers (and consumers) normally think of advertising as messages delivered by the mass media, in reality many ads today are delivered in our homes, our workplaces, and in public venues such as on a restroom wall or on signs that trail behind airplanes or as product placement in movies and television programs. Here we'll look at some of the more important *indirect* forms of advertising.

- **Directories:** Directory advertising is the most "down-to-earth," information-focused advertising medium. In 1883, a printer in Wyoming ran out of white paper while printing part of a telephone book, so he substituted yellow paper instead. Today, the Yellow Pages, including on-line Yellow Pages, posts revenues of more than $16 billion in the United States and over $45 billion globally.[40] Often consumers look through directories just before they are ready to buy.

Out-of-home media provide an excellent way to reach consumers on the go. Billboards such as this one certainly grab our attention.

- **Out-of-home media: Out-of-home media**, such as blimps, transit ads, and billboards, reach people in public places. This medium works best when it tells a simple, straightforward story.[41] For example, four Houston men rented a billboard with the message "4 Middle Class White Males, 32–39, Seek Wives." These "advertisers" got responses from almost 800 women.[42] In the Netherlands Hotels.nl, an on-line reservation company, advertises with low-tech billboards—it fitted 144 sheep with logo-emblazoned blankets. The advertising agency that created the "sheep boards" plans to offer blankets for horses and cows in the future.[43]

- **Place-based media:** Marketers constantly search for new ways to get their messages out to busy people. **Place-based media** like "The Airport Channel" transmit messages to "captive audiences" in public places, such as doctors' offices and airport waiting areas. Place-based video screens are now in thousands of shops, offices, and health clubs across the country including stores like CompUSA, Best Buy, Borders, Foot Locker, and Target. The Wal-Mart TV Network has more than 125,000 screens in 2,850 Wal-Mart stores, and patients who wait in over 10,800 doctors' offices watch medical programming and ads. NBC Universal has its shows on screens installed in office building elevators and on United Airline flights.[44]

  And now, some retailers can even follow you around the store to deliver more up-close and personal messages: A new technology called *RFID* (radio frequency identification) tracks customers as they make their way through the aisles. So a shopper might receive a beep to remind him that he just passed his family's favorite peanut butter.[45] You're not paranoid; they really *are* watching you!

- **Branded Entertainment:** As we noted earlier in this chapter, more and more marketers use paid *product placements*, one form of **branded entertainment**, to grab the attention of consumers who are tuning out traditional advertisements as fast as they see them. Branded entertainment means marketers integrate products into entertainment venues including movies, television shows, or even videogames and novels. In the first half of 2007, there were over 110,000 instances of product placements in just the top 20 shows on cable and broadcast networks. "American Idol" was the show with the most instances of product placements (4,349 brand plugs) while Coca-Cola was the brand most likely to pop up in a show (3,054 times to be exact). And, we're just at the tip of the iceberg in terms of this alternative to isolated ads because advertisers are desperate to break through the clutter and reach consumers where they live. Industry analysts expect that by 2012 advertisers will spend more than $40 billion on branded entertainment.[46]

  Is branded entertainment a solid strategy? When consumers see a popular celebrity using a specific brand in their favorite movie or TV program, they might develop a more positive attitude toward that brand. Successful brand placements include the BMW Z3 James Bond drove, the Nike shoes Forrest Gump wore, and the Ray-Ban sunglasses Tom Cruise sported in *Risky Business*. Audi recently promoted its R8 sports car in the movie *Iron Man*: Superhero Tony Stark drives the car, while Gwyneth Paltrow as Virginia "Pepper" Potts drives the Audi S5 sports sedan.[47]

out-of-home media
A communication medium that reaches people in public places.

place-based media
Advertising media that transmit messages in public places, such as doctors' offices and airports, where certain types of people congregate.

branded entertainment
A form of advertising in which marketers integrate products into entertainment venues.

But placing a Pepsi can in a TV show is only one form of branded entertainment. Today advertisers also take a more active role in developing new television programs to showcase their products. For example, TNT and Dodge paired up to produce "Lucky Chance," a branded miniseries about an undercover Drug Enforcement Agency agent who drives a 2009 Dodge Challenger to transport money to a mob boss.[48]

Beyond movies and television shows, what better way to promote to the video generation than through brand placements in video games? The industry calls this technique **advergaming**. If you are a video game hound, watch for placements of real-life brands such as Ford, Radio Shack, General Motors, Toyota, and Sony embedded in the action of your game. Quiksilver, a clothing manufacturer for extreme-sport participants, now puts its shirts and shorts into video games such as Tony Hawk's *Pro Skater 3*.

advergaming
Brand placements in video games.

Media Scheduling: When to Say It

After choosing the advertising media, the planner then creates a **media schedule** that specifies the exact media to use for the campaign as well as when and how often the message should appear. Figure 13.3 shows a hypothetical media schedule for the promotion of a new video game. Note that much of the advertising reaches its target audience in the months just before Christmas, and that much of the expensive television budget focuses on advertising during specials just prior to the holiday season.

media schedule
The plan that specifies the exact media to use and when to use it.

The media schedule outlines the planner's best estimate of which media will be most effective in attaining the advertising objective(s) and which specific media vehicles will do the most effective job. The media planner considers factors such as the match between the demographic and psychographic profile of a target audience and the people reached by a media vehicle, the advertising patterns of competitors, and the capability of a medium to adequately convey the desired information. The planner must also consider factors such as the compatibility of the product with editorial content. For example, viewers might not respond well to a lighthearted ad for a new snack food during a somber documentary on world hunger.

advertising exposure
The degree to which the target market will see an advertising message placed in a specific vehicle.

When analyzing media, the planner assesses **advertising exposure**, the degree to which the target market will see an advertising message in a specific medium. Media planners speak in terms of **impressions**, the number of people who will be exposed to a message that appears in one or more media vehicles. For example, if five million people watch *The Hills* on MTV, then each time an advertiser runs an ad during that program it gets five million impressions. If the advertiser's spot runs four times during the program, the impression count would be 20 million (even though some of these impressions would represent repeated exposure to the same viewers).

impressions
The number of people who will be exposed to a message placed in one or more media vehicles.

reach
The percentage of the target market that will be exposed to the media vehicle.

To calculate the exposure a message will have if it's placed in a certain media vehicle, planners consider two factors: reach and frequency. **Reach** is the percentage of the target market that will be exposed to the media vehicle at least once. This measure is particularly important for widely used products when the message needs to get to as many consumers as possible. **Frequency** is the average number of times that these members of the target market will be exposed to the message. This measure is important for products that are complex or those that are targeted to relatively small markets for which multiple exposures to the message are necessary to make an impact.

frequency
The average number of times a person in the target group will be exposed to the message.

Say that a media planner wants to be sure his advertising for Club Med effectively reaches college students. He learns that

Figure 13.3 │ Media Schedule for a Video Game PU

Media planning includes decisions on where, when, and how much advertising to do. A media schedule such as this one for a video game shows the plan visually.

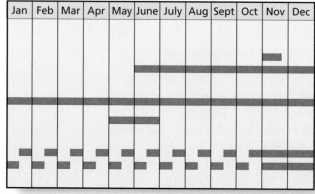

Medium	Jan	Feb	Mar	Apr	May	June	July	Aug	Sept	Oct	Nov	Dec
Television												
Specials											▬	
Saturday cartoons						▬	▬	▬	▬	▬	▬	▬
Newspaper												
Co-op advertising	▬	▬	▬	▬	▬	▬	▬	▬	▬	▬	▬	▬
Direct Mail					▬							
Magazines												
Mag 1		▬	▬	▬		▬		▬		▬	▬	
Mag 2	▬	▬	▬	▬		▬		▬		▬	▬	

25 percent of the target market reads at least a few issues of *Rolling Stone* each year (that's *reach*). He may also determine that these students on average are likely to see three of the 12 monthly ads that Club Med will run in *Rolling Stone* during the year (that's *frequency*). Now, he calculates the magazine's **gross rating points (GRPs)** by multiplying reach times frequency, which in this case allows him to compare the effectiveness of *Rolling Stone* to that of alternative media vehicles. By using this same formula, the planner could then compare this GRP number to that of another magazine or to the GRP of placing an ad on television or on a bus or any other advertising medium.

Although some media vehicles deliver superior exposure, they may not be cost-efficient. More people will see a commercial aired during the Super Bowl than during a 3:00 AM rerun of a Tarzan movie. But the advertiser could run late-night commercials every night for a year for the cost of one 30-second Super Bowl spot. To compare the relative cost-effectiveness of different media and of spots run on different vehicles in the same medium, media planners use a measure they call **cost per thousand (CPM)**. This figure reflects the cost to deliver a message to 1,000 people. CPM allows advertisers to compare the relative cost-effectiveness of different media vehicles that have different exposure rates.

A media vehicle's popularity with consumers determines how much advertisers must pay to put their message there. Television networks are concerned about the size of their audiences because their advertising rates are determined by how many viewers their programming attracts. Similarly, magazines and newspapers try to boost circulation (that explains all the free issues you get) so they can charge higher rates to their advertising clients.

To compare the efficiency of the different media "buys," the media planner will compare the cost per thousand (CPM). Assume that the cost of each 30-second commercial on *American Idol* is $600,000 but the number of target audience members the show reaches is 20 million or $20,000 \times 1,000$ thousand. The CPM of *American Idol* is $600,000/20,000 = $30 CPM. Compare this to the cost of advertising in *Fortune* magazine: A full page 4-color ad costs approximately $115,000,000 and the readership includes approximately 2 million members of our target audience. The cost per thousand for *Fortune* is $115,000/2000 = $57.50. Thus, *American Idol*, while having a much higher total cost, actually is a more efficient buy.

Metrics Moment

When they develop media schedules, media planners set an objective to achieve a certain level of *gross rating points (GRPs)*. Gross rating points measure the quantity of media purchased. Just like we buy so many gallons of gasoline or so many pounds of chocolate, media planners buy a desired number of GRPs of advertising. For example, the objective might be to buy approximately 1600 GRPS of the target audience during a certain time period. Table 13.2 shows what the resulting media schedule might look like.

gross rating points (GRPs)
A measure used for comparing the effectiveness of different media vehicles: average reach × frequency.

cost per thousand (CPM)
A measure used to compare the relative cost-effectiveness of different media vehicles that have different exposure rates; the cost to deliver a message to 1,000 people or homes.

Table 13.2 | A (Hypothetical) Media Schedule

Media vehicle	Rating (Percentage of target audience reached)	Number of ad insertions during the period	GRPs (Rating × Number of Insertions)
American Idol TV show	30	8 (2 ads on each week's show for 4 weeks)	240 GRPs
NBC Nightly News	10	40 (2 ads each week night for 4 weeks)	400
The Today Show	20	40 (2 ads each weekday morning for 4 weeks)	800
Newsweek magazine	20	4 (1 ad in each of 4 editions during the 4-week period)	80
Fortune magazine	12	2 (1 ad in each of the 2 editions each month)	24
USA Today newspaper	7	8 (1 ad each Monday and Thursday during the 4-week period)	56
Total GRPs			1600

Media Scheduling: How Often to Say It

After deciding where and when to advertise, the planner must decide how often. What time of day? And what overall pattern will the advertising follow?

A *continuous schedule* maintains a steady stream of advertising throughout the year. This is most appropriate for products that we buy on a regular basis, such as shampoo or bread. The American Association of Advertising Agencies, an industry trade group, maintains that continuous advertising sustains market leadership even if total industry sales fall.[49] On the downside, some messages can suffer from *advertising wear-out* because people tune out the same old ad messages.

A *pulsing schedule* varies the amount of advertising throughout the year based on when the product is likely to be in demand. A suntan lotion might advertise year-round but more heavily during the summer months. *Flighting* is an extreme form of pulsing, in which advertising appears in short, intense bursts alternating with periods of little to no activity. It can produce as much brand awareness as a steady dose of advertising at a much lower cost if consumers noticed the messages from the previous flight and these made an impact.

Step 6: Evaluate the Advertising

John Wanamaker, a famous Philadelphia retailer, once complained, "I am certain that half the money I spend on advertising is completely wasted. The trouble is, I don't know which half."[50] Now that we've seen how advertising is created and executed, let's step back and see how we decide if it's working.

There's no doubt that a lot of advertising is ineffective. Ironically, as marketers try harder and harder to reach their customers, these efforts can backfire. Many consumers have a love–hate relationship with advertising. Over half the respondents in a recent major survey said they "...avoid buying products that overwhelm them with advertising and marketing," and 60 percent said their opinion of advertising "...is much more negative than just a few years ago."[51] With so many messages competing for the attention of frazzled customers, it's especially important for firms to evaluate their efforts to increase the impact of their messages. How can they do that? Often advertisers do this by posttesting their advertising campaigns.

posttesting
Research conducted on consumers' responses to actual advertising messages they have seen or heard.

Posttesting means conducting research on consumers' responses to advertising messages they have seen or heard (as opposed to *pretesting*, which as we've seen collects reactions to messages *before* they're actually placed in "the real world"). Ironically, many creative ads that are quirky or even bizarre make an advertising agency look good within the industry (and on the resumé of the art director), but are ultimately unsuccessful because they don't communicate what the company needs to say about the product itself.

In some cases, the ads are popular, but they send the wrong message to consumers. A lot of people remember Joe Isuzu, the lying car salesman whose television commercials were very popular for two years but that were no help to Isuzu's car sales during that time.[52] As one advertising executive explained, "The humor got in the way. All you remembered was that car salesmen are dishonest, and the car salesman you remembered most was from Isuzu."[53]

Three ways to measure the impact of an advertisement are *unaided recall, aided recall,* and *attitudinal measures*:

unaided recall
A research technique conducted by telephone survey or personal interview that asks whether a person remembers seeing an ad during a specified period without giving the person the name of the brand.

1. **Unaided recall** tests by telephone survey or personal interview whether a person remembers seeing an ad during a specified period without giving the person the name of the brand.

aided recall
A research technique that uses clues to prompt answers from people about advertisements they might have seen.

2. An **aided recall** test uses the name of the brand and sometimes other clues to prompt answers. For example, a researcher might show a group of consumers a list of brands and ask them to choose which items they have seen advertised within the past week.

3. **Attitudinal measures** probe a bit more deeply by testing consumers' beliefs or feelings about a product before and after they are exposed to messages about it. If, for example, Pepsi's messages about "freshness-dating" make enough consumers believe that the freshness of soft drinks is important, marketers can consider the advertising campaign successful.

attitudinal measures
A research technique that probes a consumer's beliefs or feelings about a product before and after being exposed to messages about it.

3 Sales Promotion

OBJECTIVE

Explain what sales promotion is, and describe the different types of trade and consumer sales promotion activities.
(pp. 419–425)

Sometimes when you walk through your student union on campus you might get assaulted by a parade of people eager for you to enter a contest, taste a new candy bar, or take home a free T-shirt with a local bank's name on it. These are examples of **sales promotion**; programs that marketers design to build interest in or encourage purchase of a good or service during a specified period.[54] Marketers place an increasing amount of their total marketing communication budget into sales promotion for one simple reason—these strategies deliver short-term sales results.

sales promotion
Programs designed to build interest in or encourage purchase of a product during a specified period.

Sales promotion sometimes can be elaborate and high profile. For example, a successful effort by Burger King called "Spidey Sense" capitalized on the enormous popularity of the movie *Spider Man 2*. During the Spidey Sense promotion, customers obtained game pieces at Burger King restaurants and used their "Spidey Sense" to scratch off the right spider web that would let them win one of several possible prizes ranging from sodas at Burger King to $50,000 in cash.

How does sales promotion differ from advertising? Both are paid messages from identifiable sponsors to change consumer behavior or attitudes. In some cases, a traditional advertising medium actually publicizes the sales promotion, such as the Burger King Spidey Sense game commercials that aired when the movie appeared in theaters. But while marketers carefully craft advertising campaigns to create long-term positive feelings about a brand, company, or store, sales promotion tends to focus on short-term objectives, such as an immediate boost in sales or the introduction of a new product.

A sales promotion is very useful if the firm has an *immediate* objective, such as bolstering sales for a brand quickly or encouraging consumers to try a new product. The objective of a promotion may be to generate enthusiasm among retailers to take a chance on a new product or provide more shelf space for an item they already carry. Thus, like advertising, sales promotion can target channel partners (the "trade") or the firm's own employees, as well as end consumers.

As you learned in Chapter 12, sales promotion is but one part of a firm's integrated marketing communication program and thus it must coordinate with other promotion activities. For example, if a brand's marketing communication tries to position the product as an expensive luxury item (think BMW), a sales promotion activity that reduces the price or involves giving away free fried chicken and lemonade at the BMW dealer served by a guy dressed in a clown suit will undoubtedly send conflicting messages to the customer about the BMW brand. And, marketers rarely if ever use sales promotion by itself as their sole form of marketing communication. More typically, they rely on this to support more extensive advertising, direct marketing, public relations, and/or personal selling initiatives.

Table 13.3 summarizes key sales promotion techniques. Sales promotion is directed to two key groups: trade and consumers. Let's start with trade promotions and then learn about consumer promotions.

Table 13.3 | Sales Promotion Techniques: A Sampler

Technique	Primary Target	Description	Example
Allowances, discounts, and deals	Trade	Retailers or other organizational customers receive discounts for quantity purchases or for providing special merchandising assistance.	Retailers get a discount for using a special Thanksgiving display unit for Pepperidge Farm Stuffing Mix.
Co-op Advertising	Trade and consumers	Manufacturers pay part of the cost of advertising by retailers who feature the manufacturer's product in their ads.	Toro pays half of the cost of Brad's Hardware Store newspaper advertising featuring Toro lawn mowers.
Trade shows	Trade	Many manufacturers showcase their products to show attendees.	The National Kitchen and Bath Association trade shows allow manufacturers to display their latest wares to owners of kitchen and bath remodeling stores.
Promotional products	Trade and consumers	A company builds awareness and reinforces its image by giving out items with its name on them.	Coors distributors provide bar owners with highly sought-after "Coors Light" neon signs. Caterpillar gives customers caps with the Caterpillar logo.
Point of purchase (POP) displays	Trade and consumers	In-store exhibits attract consumers' attention. Many POP displays also serve a merchandising function.	The Behr's paint display in Home Depot stores allow consumers to select from over 1,600 colors including 160 Disney colors.
Incentive programs	Trade	A prize is offered to employees who meet a prespecified sales goal or who are top performers during a given period.	Mary Kay cosmetics awards distinctive pink cars to its top-selling representatives.
Push money	Trade	Salespeople are given a bonus for selling a specific manufacturer's product.	A retail salesperson at a cosmetics counter gets $5 every time she sells a bottle of Glow perfume by JLo.
Coupons (newspaper, magazine, in-the-mail, on product packages, in-store, and on the Internet)	Consumers	Certificates for money off on selected products, often with an expiration date, are used to encourage product trial.	Crest offers $5 off its WhiteStrips.
Price-off packs	Consumers	Specially marked packages offer a product at a discounted price.	Tide laundry detergent is offered in a specially marked box for 50 cents off.
Rebates/refunds	Consumers	Purchasers receive a cash reimbursement when they submit proofs of purchase.	Uniroyal offers a $40 mail-in rebate for purchasers of four new Tiger Paw tires.
Continuity/loyalty programs	Consumers	Consumers are rewarded for repeat purchases through points that lead to reduced price or free merchandise.	Airlines offer frequent fliers free flights for accumulated points; a carwash offers consumers a half-price wash after purchasing 10 washes.
Special/bonus packs	Consumers	Additional amount of the product is given away with purchase; it rewards users.	Maxell provides 10 free blank CDs with purchase of a pack of 50.
Contests/sweepstakes	Consumers	Offer consumers the chance to win cash or merchandise. Sweepstakes winners are determined strictly by chance. Contests require some competitive activity such as a game of skill.	Publisher's Clearing House announces its zillionth sweepstakes.

| Premiums: Free premiums include in-pack, on-pack, near pack, or in the mail premiums; consumers pay for self-liquidating premiums | Consumers | A consumer gets a free gift or low-cost item when a product is bought; reinforces product image and rewards users. | A free makeup kit comes with the purchase of $20 worth of Clinique products. |
| Samples (delivered by direct mail, in newspapers and magazines door-to-door, on or in product packages, and in-store) | Consumers | Delivering an actual or trial-sized product to consumers in order to generate trial usage of a new product. | A free small bottle of Clairol Herbal Essences shampoo arrives in the mail. |

Sales Promotion Directed toward the Trade

Trade promotions focus on members of the trade, which include distribution channel members, such as retail salespeople or wholesale distributors with whom a firm must work to sell its products. (We'll discuss these and other distribution channel members in more detail in Chapters 15 and 16.)

Trade promotions take one of two forms: (1) discounts and deals and (2) increasing industry visibility. *Discount promotions* (deals) reduce the cost of the product to the distributor or retailer or help defray its advertising expenses. Firms design these promotions to encourage stores to stock the item and be sure it gets a lot of attention. Trade promotions that focus on increasing awareness and sales (increasing industry visibility) do so by creating enthusiasm among salespeople and customers. Let's take a look at both types of trade promotions in more detail.

Allowances, Discounts, and Deals

One form of trade promotion is a short-term *price break*. A manufacturer can reduce a channel partner's costs with a sales promotion that discounts its products. For example, a manufacturer can offer a **merchandising allowance** to reimburse the retailer for in-store support of a product, such as when a store features an off-shelf display for a brand. Another way in which a manufacturer can reduce a channel partner's cost is a **case allowance** that provides a discount to the retailer or wholesaler during a set period based on the sales volume of a product it orders from the manufacturer.

However, allowances and deals have a downside. As with all sales promotion activities, the manufacturer expects these to be of limited duration, after which the distribution channel partner will again pay full price for the items. Unfortunately, some channel members engage in a practice the industry calls *forward buying*, in which they purchase large quantities of the product during a discount period, warehouse them, and don't buy them again until the manufacturer offers another discount. Some large retailers and wholesalers take this to an extreme by engaging in *diverting*. This describes an ethically questionable practice where the retailer buys the product at the discounted promotional price and warehouses it. Then, after the promotion has expired, the retailer sells the hoarded inventory to other retailers at a price that is lower than the manufacturer's nondiscounted price but high enough to turn a profit. Obviously, both forward buying and diverting go against the manufacturer's intent in offering the sales promotion.

Another type of trade allowance is **co-op advertising**. These programs offer to pay the retailer a portion, usually 50 percent, of the cost of any advertising that features the manufacturer's product. Co-op advertising is a win–win situation for manufacturers because most local media vehicles offer lower rates to local businesses than to national advertisers. Both the retailer and the manufacturer pay for only part (normally half) of the advertising plus the manufacturer gets the lower rate. Normally the amount available to a retailer for co-op advertising is limited to a percentage of the purchases he makes during a year from the manufacturer.

trade promotions
Promotions that focus on members of the "trade," which include distribution channel members, such as retail salespeople or wholesale distributors, that a firm must work with in order to sell its products.

merchandising allowance
Reimburses the retailer for in-store support of the product.

case allowance
A discount to the retailer or wholesaler based on the volume of product ordered.

co-op advertising
A sales promotion where the manufacturer and the retailer share the cost

Increase Industry Visibility

Other types of trade sales promotions increase the visibility of a manufacturer's products to channel partners within the industry. Whether it is an elaborate exhibit at a trade show or a coffee mug with the firm's logo it gives away to channel partners, these aim to keep the company's name topmost when distributors and retailers decide which products to stock and push. These forms of sales promotion include the following:

trade shows
Events at which many companies set up elaborate exhibits to show their products, give away samples, distribute product literature, and troll for new business contacts.

- **Trade shows:** The thousands of industry **trade shows** in the United States and around the world each year are major vehicles for manufacturers to show off their product lines to wholesalers and retailers. Usually large trade shows are held in big convention centers where many companies set up elaborate exhibits to show their products, give away samples, distribute product literature, and troll for new business contacts. Today we also see more and more on-line trade shows that allow potential customers to preview a manufacturer's products remotely. This idea is growing in popularity, though many industry people find it a challenge to "schmooze" in cyberspace (it's also a little harder to collect all the great *swag* [promotional products] they give out at real-life shows!). As we learned through NCR's experience in Chapter 6, an important benefit of traditional trade shows is the opportunity to develop customer leads that the company then forwards to its sales force for follow-up.

promotional products
Goodies such as coffee mugs, T-shirts, and magnets given away to build awareness for a sponsor. Some freebies are distributed directly to consumers and business customers; others are intended for channel partners such as retailers and vendors.

- **Promotional products:** We have all seen them: coffee mugs, visors, T-shirts, ball caps, key chains, refrigerator magnets, and countless other doodads emblazoned with a company's logo. They are examples of **promotional products**. Unlike licensed merchandise we buy in stores, sponsors give away these goodies to build awareness for their organization or specific brands. In many industries, companies vie for the most impressive promotional products and offer business customers and channel partners upscale items such as watches, polar fleece jackets, and expensive leather desk accessories.

point of purchase (POP) displays
In-store displays and signs.

- **Point of purchase (POP) displays:** Point of purchase materials include signs, mobiles, banners, shelf ads, floor ads, lights, plastic reproductions of products, permanent and temporary merchandising displays, in-store television, and shopping card advertisements. Manufacturers spend over $17 billion annually on POP displays because it keeps the name of the brand in front of the consumer, reinforces mass-media advertising, calls attention to other sales promotion offers, and stimulates impulse purchasing. Generally, manufacturers must give retailers a promotion allowance for use of POP materials. For retailers, the POP displays are useful if they encourage sales and increase revenues for the brand.

  It's a challenge for marketers to come up with new and innovative POP displays that will grab attention, such as the promotion Bausch & Lomb ran in Spain. The company wanted to encourage consumers with good vision to buy contact lenses that changed their eye color. By letting shoppers upload their pictures to a computer in the store and digitally altering the photos, the promotion allowed people to see how they would look with five different eye colors without actually inserting the contacts.[55]

push money
A bonus paid by a manufacturer to a salesperson, customer, or distributor for selling its product.

- **Incentive programs:** Mary Kay cosmetics is famous for giving its more productive distributors pink cars to reward their efforts. In addition to motivating distributors and customers, some promotions light a fire under the firm's own sales force. These incentives, or **push money**, may come in the form of cash bonuses, trips, or other prizes. Recently, Starbucks got into the incentive program business by offering gift cards that companies can purchase and provide for their salespeople to give clients as a small "thank you" for closing a sale.

Sales Promotion Directed toward Consumers

Some sales promotions directed toward consumers create a buzz in the form of a contest or a special event. Red Bull, the high-octane energy drink (and popular mixer), became famous for this approach by making its conspicuous Red Bull vans available at rave and hip-hop clubs to raise the party atmosphere profile for the venue. Red Bull's consistent efforts at consumer sales promotion became the signature aspect of its marketing communication to consumers, and for the early stages of Red Bull's product life cycle the company did very little traditional consumer advertising. The buzz these special events created added to the mystique of the brand; this fueled its popularity in its young target market much more effectively than would traditional advertising. Let's take a closer look at several popular forms of consumer-targeted sales promotion.

Price-Based Consumer Sales Promotion

Many sales promotions target consumers where they live—their wallets. They emphasize *short-term price reductions* or *rebates* that encourage people to choose a brand—at least during the deal period. Price-based consumer promotions, however, have a downside similar to trade promotions that involve a price break. If a company uses them too frequently, this "trains" its customers to purchase the product at only the lower promotional price. Price-based consumer sales promotion includes the following:

- **Coupons:** Try to pick up any Sunday newspaper without spilling some coupons. These certificates, redeemable for money off a purchase, are the most common price promotion. Indeed, they are the most popular form of sales promotion overall. Companies distribute billions of them annually in newspapers, magazines, in the mail, in stores, by e-mail, and through the Internet. One company, Val-Pak, has created an entire business around coupons. You've probably received a Val-Pak envelope in the mail—it's the one with dozens of coupons and other offers inside. Even industries such as pharmaceuticals that never tried this approach before now use it in a big way. This industry mails coupons that customers can redeem for free initial supplies of drugs. Coupons are also available through sites such as Viagra.com and Purplepill.com. Companies use the coupons to prompt patients to ask their physician for the specific brand instead of a competing brand or a more economical generic version.[56]

Today, many firms simply send consumers to their Web site for coupons. Wolf Camera (also branded as Ritz Camera) has been a leader in on-line couponing in the film-processing arena as it provides coupon promotions for a variety of products and film processing options on its Web site. The on-line couponing trend has sparked a cottage industry of on-line *coupon consolidators*. SmartSource.com, for example, has users register with the site, including details about family members' ages, gender, and pets along with the names of stores where they shop. After that, users have free access to 30 to 35 coupons on a given day, worth about $14. Manufacturers pay SmartSource a fee each time a consumer redeems a coupon he accesses through its Web site. The average savings for an on-line coupon is about 97 cents, compared with 81 cents for newspaper coupons.[57]

- **Price deals, refunds, and rebates:** In addition to coupons, manufacturers often offer a temporary price reduction to stimulate sales. This price deal

Smart Source is a Web site that provides on-line coupons for many different products.

rebates

Sales promotions that allow the customer to recover part of the product's cost from the manufacturer.

frequency programs

Consumer sales promotion programs that offer a discount or free product for multiple purchases over time; also referred to as loyalty or continuity programs.

may be printed on the package itself, or it may be a price-off flag or banner on the store shelf. Alternatively, companies may offer **rebates** that allow the consumer to recover part of the purchase price via mail-ins to the manufacturer. Today, many retailers, such as Best Buy and Circuit City, print the rebate form for you along with your sales receipt. After you mail in the rebate form, you can track whether the check has been sent to you by visiting the retailer's Web site.

- **Frequency (loyalty/continuity) programs: Frequency programs**, also called *loyalty* or *continuity programs*, offer a consumer a discount or a free product for multiple purchases over time. Mike Gunn, former vice president of marketing at American Airlines, is widely credited with developing this concept in the early 1980s when he coined the phrase "frequent flyer" miles. Of course, all the other airlines were quick to follow suit, as were a host of other firms, including retailers, auto rental companies, hotels, restaurants—you name it, and they have a customer loyalty program. Virgin Atlantic has gone one step farther with its frequent flyer program, which allows Virgin Atlantic Flying Club members the chance to redeem miles for a trip to outer space—only 2 million miles required.[58] More "down to earth" is Six Flags theme park's Carrothead Club, which offers kids ages 6 to 10 who attend "Brunch with Bugs" a club hat, a monthly newsletter, and insider information about the park.[59]

- **Special/bonus packs:** Another form of price promotion involves giving the shopper more product instead of lowering the price.[60] How nice to go to Walgreen's and find an 8-ounce bottle of Nivea lotion packaged with another 4 ounces free! A special pack also can be in the form of a unique package such as a reusable decorator dispenser for hand soap.

Attention-Getting Consumer Sales Promotions

Attention-getting consumer promotions stimulate interest in a company's products. Some typical types of attention-getting promotions include the following:

- **Contests and sweepstakes:** According to their legal definitions, a contest is a test of skill, while a sweepstakes is based on chance.

  - Ben & Jerry's, famous for ice cream flavors such as Chunky Monkey and Phish Food, launched a contest for consumers to create an original flavor ice cream. Consumers enter the "Do Us a Flavor" contest by submitting their flavor name and description through Ben & Jerry's Web site.[61]

  - As part of the kickoff of Disney's global marketing campaign themed "Where Dreams Come True," Disney offered consumers an on-line Keys to the Magic Kingdom sweepstakes. The winning family received a trip to Walt Disney World Resort and a day at the Magic Kingdom.[62]

  - Oreo included consumers as not only the contestants, but also the judges in its Oreo & Milk Jingle Contest. The top five contestants' renditions of the Oreo song were posted on the Oreo.com Web site. Consumers entered part of an Oreo package UPC to vote for their favorite; the winner received $10,000 and a recording session for an Oreo radio spot and a trip to Los Angeles to visit with *American Idol* judge Randy Jackson.[63]

premiums

Items offered free to people who have purchased a product.

- **Premiums: Premiums** are items you get for free when you buy a product. The prize in the bottom of the box of cereal—the reason many college students open the box from the bottom—is a premium. Prepaid phone cards have become highly popular premiums. Companies that jump on the phone card bandwagon offer cards emblazoned with pictures of sports heroes, products, and rock bands. Phone cards make ideal premiums because they are compact, they can display brand logos or attractive graphics, and they provide opportunities for repeat exposure. And an important benefit for the marketer is the ability to build databases by tracking card usage.[64] Your "good neighbor" State Farm agent used to send you a calendar on your birthday—now you're likely to get a phone card with 30 long-distance minutes on it, adorned with a reminder of your agent's phone number to be sure you won't forget who sent it to you.

- **Sampling:** How many starving college students at one time or another have managed to scrape together an entire meal by scooping up free food samples at their local grocery store? Some stores, like Publix and Sam's Club, actually promote Saturdays as sampling day in their advertising. **Product sampling** encourages people to try a product by distributing trial-size and sometimes regular-size versions in stores, in public places such as student unions, or through the mail. In an effort to boost sagging sales, coffee retail giant Starbucks invited consumers to stop by any Starbuck's store between 9 and 9:30 AM PST on August 7, 2008, to try a free cup of a new blend. For consumers who couldn't make it to a local Starbuck's at that time, the company distributed coupons for a free cup of coffee through the media such as *USA Today* and the *Washington Post*.[65] Many marketers now distribute free samples through sites on the Internet.[66] Companies like Procter & Gamble, Unilever, S.C. Johnson, and GlaxoSmithKline are readily taking advantage of Web sites such as **www.freesamples.com** and **www.startsampling.com** that distribute the firms' samples and then follow up with consumer-satisfaction surveys.

Cooking contests (such as the "Bourboncuing" contest sponsored by Jim Beam) are a popular way to let consumers "strut their stuff" and create a buzz about the company's products.

product sampling
Distributing free trial-size versions of a product to consumers.

4

OBJECTIVE

Explain the role of public relations and the steps in developing a public relations campaign.
(pp. 425–431)

Public Relations

Public relations (PR) is the communication function that seeks to build good relationships with an organization's *publics*; these include consumers, stockholders, legislators, and other stakeholders in the organization. Today marketers use PR activities to influence the attitudes and perceptions of various groups not only toward companies and brands but also toward politicians, celebrities, and not-for-profit organizations.

The basic rule of good PR is, *Do something good, and then talk about it*. A company's efforts to get in the limelight—and stay there—can range from humanitarian acts to sponsoring band tours. The big advantage of this kind of communication is that when PR messages are placed successfully they are more credible than if the same information appeared in a paid advertisement. As one marketing executive observed, "There's a big difference between hearing about a product from a pitchman and from your trusted local anchorman."[67] The value of publicity was clearly demonstrated by the huge success of Mel Gibson's controversial film *The Passion of the Christ*. Frequent news stories, TV appearances by Mr. Gibson, radio debates, and even a *Newsweek* cover that asked "Who Really Killed Jesus?" built momentum. Even before the movie opened, 81 percent of moviegoers were aware of it. This high level of interest didn't just "happen"—a year before the movie's release, Gibson toured churches with a rough cut of his movie, giving speeches and charming pastors. His production company, Icon, signed

public relations (PR)
Communication function that seeks to build good relationships with an organization's publics, including consumers, stockholders, and legislators.

publicity
Unpaid communication about an organization that appears in the mass media.

Joe
Chernov

APPLYING **A Crisis Management Plan**

Joe developed a plan to combat the negative publicity about buzz marketing firms that might taint BzzAgent's image and ability to attract new clients. He chose a proactive strategy that acknowledged the seriousness of the issue and clearly explained why BzzAgent's disclosure policy prevented deception from occurring.

up consultants to advise pastors on how best to use the movie to promote the church and recruit new members.[68]

Public relations strategies are crucial to an organization's ability to establish and maintain a favorable image. *Proactive PR* activities stem from the company's marketing objectives. For example, marketers create and manage **publicity**, unpaid communication about an organization that gets media exposure. Publicity often takes the form of a product release, either a written release for print or a video release. Product releases can effectively announce new products and provide consumers with information about the product's benefits, features, etc. Similarly, PR writers may develop newsworthy feature articles about new product technology or industry events. Although some publicity happens naturally, more typically a firm's publicists need to create a "buzz" (which is what BzzAgent does).

Public relations may be even more important when the company's image is at risk because of negative publicity due to product tampering, an industrial accident like the infamous Exxon Valdez oil spill, or perhaps a scandal involving company executives.[69] In such cases, firms engage in *reactive PR*. The goal here is to manage the flow of information to address concerns so that consumers don't panic and distributors don't abandon the product. For example, a few years ago PepsiCo was rocked by claims that consumers had found hypodermic needles in Diet Pepsi cans. The company assembled a crisis team to map out a response and supplied video footage of its bottling process to show that it was impossible for foreign objects to find their way into cans before they were sealed at the factory. The claims proved false, and PepsiCo ran follow-up ads reinforcing the findings. Pepsi's calm, coordinated response averted a PR disaster.

More recently, Wendy's was faced with a similar public image disaster when a customer said she found a finger in a bowl of its chili.[70] The woman and her husband were both sent to prison after investigators discovered that he had actually obtained the finger from a co-worker who had lost it in a workplace accident. While the claim proved false, it still cost the company $2.5 million in lost sales.[71] In another incident, a man stuffed a dead mouse in a Taco Bell burrito in an attempt to extort money from the fast-food chain.[72] Supersize that!

Even a single negative event can cause permanent damage to a company, the success of its products, and its stockholder equity. Public relations professionals know that when a firm handles a crisis well, it can minimize damage and help the company make things right. Thus, a vitally important role of PR is to prepare a *crisis-management plan*. This is a document that details what an organization will do *if* a crisis occurs—who will be the spokesperson for the organization, how the organization will deal with the press, and what sort of messages it will deliver to the press and the public.

The Internet has expanded the capabilities of the traditional PR function.[73] Corporate Web sites post testimonials from customers, make new product announcements, and respond quickly to important events. The Internet can also be very effective medium to handle a crisis. Companies can respond on-line in far less time than through other forms of communication such as news releases or press conferences.[74]

Objectives of Public Relations

Companies that practice IMC know that PR strategies are best used in concert with advertising, sales promotion, and personal selling to send a consistent message to customers and other stakeholders. As part of the total IMC plan, they often rely on PR to accomplish the following objectives:

- **Introduce new products to manufacturers:** When Weyerhaeuser Co. introduced Cellulon, a new biotechnology product, it distributed information kits that clearly explained the technical product and its applications in each of 12 markets to ensure that the trade press properly covered the introduction.[75]

- **Introduce new products to consumers:** When Chrysler Corp. rolled out its trio of LH sedans, the market was already anticipating their arrival. Working months ahead of time, Chrysler's PR teams exposed journalists to the LH project through factory and laboratory tours as well as discussions with designers. These efforts were successful in garnering favorable reviews in automotive magazines.[76]

- **Influence government legislation:** Airplane maker Boeing spent over a decade in public relations activities to persuade regulators that jetliners with two engines are as safe as those with three or four engines even for nonstop international flights, some as long as 16 hours.[77]

- **Enhance the image of an organization:** The Ladies Professional Golf Association (LPGA) used a variety of public relations and other promotion activities—from product endorsements to player blogs to sexy calendars—in its "These Girls Rock" campaign. The program to change the image of ladies' golf to a hip sport seems to be working, as both tournament attendance and television audiences have increased.[78]

- **Enhance the image of a city, region, or country:** Faced with international criticism about possible human rights abuses and restriction of trade, the Chinese government established an office in charge of "overseas propaganda" to present a more favorable image of China to the rest of the world.[79] Prior to the 2008 Summer Olympics in Beijing, the Chinese government's crackdown on demonstrations in Tibet threatened to not only damage the image of China again, but also to destroy any chance of success for the Games. This clearly demonstrates that even the best of public relations programs cannot succeed unless it has a good story to tell.

- **Call attention to a firm's involvement with the community:** In 2007, U.S. marketers spent nearly $15 billion to sponsor sporting events, rock concerts, museum exhibits, and the ballet.[80] PR specialists work behind the scenes to ensure that sponsored events receive ample press coverage and exposure. We'll talk more about sponsorships later in this section.

Gloria
Cockerell

a professor at Collin County Community College

My Advice for BzzAgent would be to choose

Option

real people, **Other** Voices

I recommend **Option 1.** The best course of action would have been immediately to invite both the media and Commercial Alert (CA) to a press conference in which Chernov could explain the policy of disclosure that BzzAgent has had in place for at least a year. At such a press conference he could distribute copies of actual internal information proving that BzzAgent has been instructing its volunteers to reveal their affiliation with marketing campaigns when "buzzing" others for more than a year. Rather than seeing this media problem as a threat, he should have seen it as another promotion opportunity—as material to use to show how BzzAgent differed from other word-of-mouth marketing organizations in the areas of corporate responsibility and ethics. Although we do not know how long BzzAgent has continued to respond but not to reach out to the media, we do know that such a strategy has not worked. The articles reported in the media are using the same channels with which BzzAgent is already familiar, and, therefore, Chernov knows how to work within those channels. Now is the time for him to call the press conference that he should have called in the first place, but because he is no longer at the very beginning of the problem and because many people are aware of the accusations, he will have to address the problem a bit differently. He should take charge of the discussion, but he should be very careful about both being aggressive and making modifications to internal practices. BzzAgent is already protecting consumers with its disclosure policy, so making changes now will appear to outsiders to be an attempt to enforce something that has been policy but not enforced until public opinion pressured the company to act. Chernov should capitalize on the fact that BzzAgent agrees with Commercial Alert and was even ahead of the consumer protection group by initiating its policies before CA made its complaints. BzzAgent can gradually increase the policing of the policy, making sure that no volunteer who has not "disclosed" to consumers is allowed to volunteer for the company again. He should not stop there, though. He should also include in the company's promotions the fact that BzzAgent is already practicing corporate responsibility. There is no reason to mention other word of mouth marketing companies, but there is reason to make sure that the media, the consumers, and the investors know that BzzAgent is in the vanguard when it comes to practicing corporate responsibility. Promotion pieces can include, as appropriate, information noting that BzzAgent's CEO actually co-authored the Code of Ethics for the Word of Mouth Marketing Association. ➤

Planning a Public Relations Campaign

public relations campaign
A coordinated effort to communicate with one or more of the firm's publics.

A **public relations campaign** is a coordinated effort to communicate with one or more of the firm's publics. This is a three-step process that develops, executes, and evaluates objectives. Let's review each step.

Like an advertising campaign, the organization must first develop clear objectives for the PR program that define the message it wants people to hear. Next, the PR specialists must develop a campaign strategy that includes the following:

- A situation analysis

- A statement of objectives

- Specification of target audiences (publics), messages to be communicated, and specific program elements to be used

- A timetable and budget

- Discussion of how to evaluate the program

For example the International Apple Institute, a trade group devoted to increasing the consumption of apples, had to decide if a campaign should focus on getting consumers to cook more with apples, drink more apple juice, or simply to buy more fresh fruit. Because fresh apples brought a substantially higher price per pound to growers than apples used for applesauce or apple juice, the group decided to push the fresh fruit angle. It used the theme "An apple a day..." (sound familiar?) and mounted a focused campaign to encourage people to eat more apples by placing articles in consumer media extolling the fruit's health benefits.

Execution of the campaign means deciding precisely how the message should be communicated to the targeted public(s). An organization can get out its positive messages in many ways: news conferences, sponsorship of charity events, and other attention-getting promotions.

One of the barriers to greater reliance on PR campaigns is the difficulty of devising metrics to gauge their effectiveness. Who can say precisely what impact appearances by company executives on talk shows or sponsoring charity events has on sales? It is possible to tell if a PR campaign is getting media exposure, though compared to advertising it's much more difficult to assess bottom-line impact. Table 13.4 describes some of the most common measurement techniques.

Public Relations Activities

Public relations professionals engage in a wide variety of activities. While some of these may seem more related to marketing and to marketing communication than others, they all lead to the same goal—to create and maintain the positive image the organization needs. Some of these efforts include the following:

press release
Information that an organization distributes to the media intended to win publicity.

- **Press releases:** The most common way for PR specialists to communicate is by a **press release**. This is a report of some event or activity that an organization writes and sends to the media in the hope that it will be published for free. A newer version of this idea is a *video news release* (*VNR*) that tells the story in a film format instead. Some of the most common types of press releases include the following:

    ○ *Timely topics* deal with topics in the news, such as Levi Strauss's efforts to promote "Casual Fridays" to boost sales of its Dockers and Slates casual dress pants by highlighting how different corporations around the country are adopting a relaxed dress code.

Table13.4 | Measuring the Effectiveness of Public Relations (PR) Efforts

Method	Description	Example	Pros	Cons
Personal (subjective) evaluation of PR activities	Evaluation of PR activities by superiors may occur at all levels of the organization.	Items in employee annual reviews relate to the successful fulfillment of PR role.	Simple and inexpensive to complete; assures an annual assessment will be completed	Subjective nature of the evaluation may result in biased appraisal. Employees may focus on the annual review to the exclusion of some important PR goals.
Matching of PR activity accomplishments with activity objectives	Simple counts of actual PR activities accomplished compares with activity goals set for the period.	Goal: to obtain publication of three feature articles in major newspapers in the first quarter of the year Result: four articles published	Focuses attention on the need for quantitative goals for PR activities and achievements Easy and inexpensive to measure	Focuses on activity goals rather than image or communication goals Ignores image perception or attitudes of the firm's publics
Evaluation of communication objectives through opinion surveys among the firm's publics	Surveys are used to determine if image/communication goals are met within key groups.	Goal: to achieve an improved image of the organization among at least 30 percent of financial community stakeholders	Causes PR professionals to focus on actual communication results of activities	May be difficult to measure changes in perceptions among the firm's publics Factors not under the control of PR practitioners may influence public perceptions. It is relatively expensive. Results may take many months, thus, preventing corrective actions in PR activities
Measurement of coverage in print and broadcast media, especially those generated by PR activities	Systematic measurement of coverage achieved in print media (column inches/pages) and broadcast media (minutes of air time)	Total number of column inches of newspaper articles resulting from PR releases Total number of articles including those not from PR releases Total amount of positive print and broadcast coverage Total amount of negative print and broadcast coverage Ratio of negative to positive print and broadcast coverage	Very objective measurements with little opportunity for bias Relatively inexpensive	Does not address perceptions, attitudes, or image issues of the organization
Impression measurement	Measure the size of the audience for all print and broadcast coverage Often assessment includes comparisons in terms of advertising costs for same number of impressions	Network news coverage during the time period equaled over 15 million gross impressions. This number of impressions through advertising would have cost $4,500,000.	Objective, without any potential bias in measurement; provides a monetary measure to justify the expenditures of the PR office or consultant Relatively inexpensive	Does not differentiate between negative and positive news coverage Does not consider responses of publics to the coverage Assumes advertising and PR communication activities are equal

To promote its sponsorship of the New York City Marathon, Tylenol hired flesh-and-blood people to run on treadmills on a billboard above Times Square.

lobbying
talking with and providing information to government officials in order to influence their activities relating to an organization.

sponsorships
PR activities through which companies provide financial support to help fund an event in return for publicized recognition of the company's contribution.

Many company Web sites allow surfers to access recent press releases.

○ *Research project stories* are published by universities to highlight breakthroughs by faculty researchers.

○ *Consumer information releases* provide information to help consumers make product decisions, such as helpful tips from Butterball about how to prepare dishes for Thanksgiving dinner.

- **Internal PR:** These activities aimed at employees often include company newsletters and closed-circuit television. Internal PR activities help keep employees informed about company objectives, successes, or even plans to "downsize" the workforce. Often company newsletters also are distributed outside the firm to suppliers or other important publics.

- **Investor relations:** Investors are a vitally important public, as their financial support is critical especially for publicly-held companies. It is the responsibility of the PR department to develop and distribute annual and quarterly reports and to provide other essential communications with individual and corporate stockholders, with investment firms and with capital market organizations.

- **Lobbying: Lobbying** means talking with and providing information to government officials to persuade them to vote a certain way on pending legislation or even to initiate legislation or regulations that would benefit the organization.

- **Speech writing:** An important job of a firm's PR department is to write speeches on a topic for a company executive to deliver. While some executives do actually write their own speeches, it is more common for a speechwriter on the PR staff to develop an initial draft of a speech to which the executive might add his own input.

- **Corporate identity:** PR specialists may provide input on corporate-identity materials, such as logos, brochures, building design, and even stationery that communicates a positive image for the firm.

- **Media relations:** One of the tasks of the PR professional is to develop close relationships with the media. Of course, this is important if the company is going to receive the best media exposure possible for positive news, such as publicizing the achievements of an employee who has done some notable charity work or for a product it developed that saved someone's life. For example, the Canadian pharmaceutical firm Boehringer Ingelheim Ltd. sent large dolls wearing respirator masks to Canadian pediatricians. The idea was to help doctors ease the fears of their young patients about putting a mask over their mouths and noses. Boehringer won considerably favorable publicity when many Canadian newspapers featured the campaign. And, as we've seen, good media relations can be even more important when things go wrong. News editors are less inclined to present a story of a crisis in its most negative way if they have a good relationship with PR people in the organization.

- **Sponsorships: Sponsorships** are PR activities through which companies provide financial support to help fund an event in return for publicized recognition of the company's contribution. Many companies today find that their promotion dollars are well-spent to sponsor a golf tournament, a NASCAR driver, a symphony concert, or global events such as the Olympics or World Cup soccer competition. These sponsorships are particularly effective because they allow marketers to reach customers in their life-style and when they're relaxed. Consumers often connect their enjoyment of the event with the sponsor, which in turn creates brand loyalty. In addition, sponsorships may enhance the effectiveness of advertising if ads remind consumers that the brand is sponsoring a favorite event. McDonald's, a sponsor of the FIFA World Cup since 1994, has built on its sponsorship to create promotions in its restaurants around the world. McDonald's global Player Escort Program sent 1,408 children ages 6 to 10 to the World Cup in Germany where they escorted players onto the field for all 64 FIFA matches. In Brazil, McDonald's restaurants offered customers sandwiches with flavors from countries competing in the World Cup. World Cup beverage cups were available for customers in some countries, including China and the United States, and some locations in Europe offered consumers a World Cup burger, which was 40 percent larger than McDonald's Big Mac.[81]

Oscar Mayer created an eye-catching promotion with its Wienermobile—guaranteed to draw attention from hot dog lovers.

- **Special events:** Another job of a PR department is to plan and implement special events. Whether it is the visit of a group of foreign investors to a firm's manufacturing facilities, a Fourth of July picnic for company employees, or a hospitality booth set up during a motorcycle race for which the company is a sponsor, the PR staff's job is to make sure the event happens without a glitch and that people go home happy. For New York City shoppers, Unilever created its "All Small & Mighty Clothes Bus," a 40-foot bus it covered in all the shirts, shorts, and socks that one bottle of super-concentrated All laundry detergent can wash. Consumers who spotted the bus during its 12-day campaign could "clean up" if by entering a sweepstakes to win a $5,000 shopping spree or $200 gift cards.[82]

- **Advice and counsel:** When a firm fully understands and appreciates the importance of the PR function, top management recognizes that PR professionals have much more to offer than just planning parties and writing news releases. Because of their expertise and understanding of the effects of communication on public opinion, PR professionals also play the role of consultants to top management. So when a firm needs to shut down a plant or to build a new one, to discontinue a product or add to the product line, to fire a vice president, or to give an award to an employee who spends hundreds of hours a year doing volunteer work in his community, it needs the advice of its PR staff. What is the best way to handle the situation? How should the announcement be made? Who should be told first? What is to be said and how?

Now that you've learned about advertising, sales promotions, and public relations, read "Real People, Real Choices: How It Worked Out" to see which strategy Joe of BzzAgent selected to deal with his PR problem.

real people, **Real Choices**

Joe
Chernov
Joe chose:

1
Option

How it Worked Out at BzzAgent

Joe selected Option 1 and BzzAgent proceeded to take charge of the discussion. Prior to making its final strategic decision, BzzAgent consulted with its investors to prepare them for the possibility of increased public attention to the disclosure debate. The investors recognized the risk, but agreed with BzzAgent that the reward associated with establishing itself as the most responsible player in the word of mouth marketing industry was worth a short-term surge in controversial publicity.

BzzAgent's executive team refined the company's disclosure policy. The enhanced policy not only instructed participants to disclose that they were part of a word of mouth campaign, but also required that they clearly state that they complied with the policy when they submit reports on their word of mouth activities. BzzAgent implemented a program in which any volunteers who failed to disclose their participation would be blocked from future campaigns until they completed an on-line training course related to disclosure.

The company also analyzed thousands of word of mouth reports to determine if disclosure had a discernible impact on campaign performance. After identifying a positive correlation between disclosure and campaign performance, it authored and published a white paper, titled "The Practical Value of Disclosure." To distance disclosure from discussions on ethics, the paper emphasized how the practice of revealing one's affiliation with a campaign enhanced the individual's credibility, thereby improving campaign performance. The company made the white paper available free on its Web site and placed no technical impediments (for example, requiring registration) to slow its dissemination.

BzzAgent issued a press release announcing that it had enhanced its disclosure policy to become the first company to enforce compliance with disclosure policies. The announcement signaled that BzzAgent was listening to the voice of the consumer, and would continue to adjust its policy according to the needs and interests of its clients and participating volunteers. To preempt charges of bowing to external pressures, the announcement tied the policy upgrade to performance-related discoveries articulated in the white paper. To ensure consistent articulation of unambiguous messages, the company limited spokespeople to two: the CEO and the director of public relations. Both executives were supplied with a list of identical messages, each emphasizing the company's "firsts" (first to require disclosure, first to study disclosure, first to police disclosure).

As a follow-up to this paper, BzzAgent teamed with a leading academic to publish a second, more comprehensive report. This report analyzed the impact of disclosure on the reach of word of mouth marketing from a statistical standpoint. Titled "To Tell or Not to Tell," the study was released at the industry's largest event to great fanfare.

Rather than being quoted defensively, as he had been in the past, BzzAgent CEO Dave Balter was represented as taking the lead in this important area. Articles quoted Balter as saying, "Requiring disclosure is not just the proper decision from an ethical standpoint, but it is also the smart policy to drive optimal campaign performance."

Such statements effectively distanced BzzAgent from the ethical debate by positioning that issue as a foregone conclusion. In other words, BzzAgent had moved beyond ethical concerns and instead focused on servicing its clients. Perhaps most importantly, the disclosure debate interfered with neither the company's financing (BzzAgent closed a $13.75 million round of financing on schedule) nor client relationships (it did not fail to close any deals as a result of the increased coverage of the disclosure debate).

BzzAgent, Inc.

Refer back to **page 399** for Joes story ➡

Brand **YOU**!

Create an award-winning advertising campaign for your personal brand.

The award is landing the job you want. Think of your cover letter and resumé as your advertising. Learn simple tips that can make your cover letter and resumé more powerful and stand out in the crowd. Check out the cover letter and resumé examples in Chapter 13 of the *Brand You* supplement.

Objective Summary ➡ Key Terms ➡ Apply

1. Objective Summary (pp. 400–405)

Tell what advertising is, describe the major types of advertising, and discuss some of the criticisms of advertising.

Advertising is nonpersonal communication from an identified sponsor using mass media to persuade or influence an audience. Advertising informs and reminds consumers and creates consumer desire. Product advertising is used to persuade consumers to choose a specific product or brand. Institutional advertising is used to develop an image for an organization or company, to express opinions (advocacy advertising), or to support a cause (public service advertising), and retail advertising informs customers about where to shop. Some advertisers now encourage consumers to participate in do-it-yourself advertising. However, most companies rely on the services of advertising agencies to create successful advertising campaigns. Full-service agencies include account management, creative services, research and marketing services, and media planning, while limited-service agencies provide only one or a few services. Advertising has been criticized for being manipulative, for being deceitful and untruthful, for being offensive and in bad taste, for creating and perpetuating stereotypes, and for causing people to buy things they don't really need. While some advertising may justify some of these criticisms, most advertisers seek to provide honest ads that don't offend the markets they seek to attract.

Key Terms

product/brand placement, p. 400

advertising, p. 401

product advertising, p. 401

institutional advertising, p. 401

advocacy advertising, p. 401

public service advertisements (PSAs), p. 401

advertising campaign, p. 403

limited-service agency, p. 403

full-service agency, p. 403

corrective advertising, p. 404

puffery, p. 404

2. Objective Summary (pp. 406–419)

Describe the process of developing an advertising campaign.

Development of an advertising campaign begins with understanding the target audiences and developing objectives for the message and the ad budget. Next, advertisers create the advertising by choosing an effective type of advertising appeal. Pretesting advertising before placing it in the media prevents costly mistakes. A media plan determines where and when advertising will appear. Media options include traditional media (television, radio, newspapers, and magazines), Internet advertising (banners, buttons, pop-up ads, search engine and directory listings, and email advertising), and indirect forms of advertising (directories, out-of-home media, placed-based media, branded entertainment and advergaming) A media schedule specifies when and how often the advertising will be seen or heard. The final step in any advertising campaign is to evaluate its effectiveness. Marketers evaluate advertising through posttesting. Posttesting research may include aided or unaided recall tests that examine whether the message had an influence on the target market.

Key Terms

creative strategy, p. 407

advertising appeal, p. 407

unique selling proposition (USP), p. 407

pretesting, p. 409

media planning, p. 410

aperture, p. 410

banners, p. 414 (Table 13.1, p. 411)

buttons, p. 414

permission marketing, p. 414

out-of-home media, p. 415 (Table 13.1, p. 411)

place-based media, p. 415 (Table 13.1, p. 411)

branded entertainment, p. 415

advergaming, p. 416 (Table 13.1, p. 411)

media schedule, p. 416 (Figure 13.3, p. 416) (Table 13.2, p. 417)

advertising exposure, p. 416

impressions, p. 416

reach, p. 416 (Table 13.2, p. 417)

frequency, p. 416

gross rating points (GRPs), p. 417 (Table 13.2, p. 417)

cost per thousand (CPM), p. 417 (Table 13.2, p. 417)

posttesting, p. 418

unaided recall, p. 418

aided recall, p. 418

attitudinal measures, p. 419

3. Objective Summary (pp. 419–425)

Explain what sales promotion is, and describe some of the different types of trade and consumer sales promotion activities.

A sales promotion is a short-term program designed to build interest in or encourage purchase of a product. Trade sales promotions include merchandising, case and co-op advertising allowances, trade shows, promotional products, point of purchase (POP) materials, and incentive programs such as push money among others. Consumer sales promotions include coupons, price deals, refunds, rebates, frequency or loyalty programs, bonus packs, contests/sweepstakes, premiums, and sampling.

Key Terms

sales promotion, p. 419 (Table 13.3, p. 420)

trade promotions, p. 421 (Table 13.3, p. 420)

merchandising allowance, p. 421 (Table 13.3, p. 420)

case allowance, p. 421 (Table 13.3, p. 420)

co-op advertising, p. 421 (Table 13.3, p. 420)

trade shows, p. 422 (Table 13.3, p. 420)

promotional products, p. 422 (Table 13.3, p. 420)

point of purchase (POP) displays, p. 422 (Table 13.3, p. 420)

push money, p. 422 (Table 13.3, p. 420)

rebates, p. 424 (Table 13.3, p. 420)

frequency programs, p. 424 (Table 13.3, p. 420)

premiums, p. 424 (Table 13.3, p. 420)

product sampling, p. 425 (Table 13.3, p. 420)

4. Objective Summary (pp. 425–431)

Explain the role of public relations and the steps in developing a public relations campaign.

The purpose of PR is to build good relationships between an organization and its various publics and to establish and maintain a favorable image. Public relations is useful in introducing new products; influencing legislation; enhancing the image of a city, region, or country; enhancing the image of an organization; and calling attention to a firm's community involvement.

The steps in a PR campaign begin with setting objectives, creating and executing a campaign strategy, and planning how the PR program will be evaluated. PR specialists often use print or video news releases to communicate timely topics, research stories, and consumer information. Internal communications with employees include company newsletters and internal TV programs. Other PR activities include investor relations, lobbying, speechwriting, developing corporate identity materials, media relations, arranging sponsorships and special events, and providing advice and counsel for management.

Key Terms

public relations (PR), p. 425

publicity, p. 426

public relations campaign, p. 428

press release, p. 428

lobbying, p. 430

sponsorships, p. 430

Chapter **Questions** and **Activities**

Concepts: Test Your Knowledge

1. What is advertising, and what is its role in marketing?
2. What types of advertising do marketers use most often?
3. What are some of the major criticisms of advertising? What is corrective advertising? What is puffery?
4. How do advertising agencies create campaigns for their clients? Describe the steps in developing an advertising campaign.
5. Describe some of the advertising appeals campaigns use.
6. What are the strengths and weaknesses of television, radio, newspapers, magazines, the Internet, directories, out-of-home media, place-based media, branded entertainment, and advergaming for advertising?
6. Describe the media planning process. How do marketers pretest their ads? How do they posttest ads?
7. What is sales promotion? Explain some of the different types of trade and consumer sales promotions marketers frequently use.
8. What is the purpose of public relations? What is proactive PR? What is a crisis-management plan?
9. What are the steps in planning a PR campaign?
10. Describe some of the activities that are a part of PR.

Choices and Ethical Issues: You Decide

1. Some people are turned off by advertising because they say it is deceptive or offensive, that it creates stereotypes and causes people to buy things they don't need. Others argue that advertising is beneficial and actually provides value for consumers. What are some arguments on each side? How do you feel?
2. Technology in the form of television remotes, DVD players, computers, and cable television is giving today's consumers more and more control over the advertising images they see. How has this affected the advertising industry so far, and do you think this will affect it in the future? What are some ways that advertising has so far responded to this? What ideas do you have for how they can respond in the future?
3. Do-it-yourself (DIY) advertising programs encourage consumers to create their own advertisements. Chevy

found that this can sometimes backfire, as when consumers created anti-SUV TV commercials. Should companies avoid DIY campaigns? What are the benefits of DIY advertising?

4. Companies sometimes teach consumers a "bad lesson" with the overuse of sales promotion. As a result, consumers expect the product always to be "on deal" or have a rebate available. What are some examples of products for which this has occurred? How do you think companies can prevent this?

5. Some critics denounce PR specialists, calling them "flacks" or "spin doctors," whose job is to hide the truth about a company's problems. What is the proper role of PR within an organization? Should PR specialists try to put a good face on bad news?

6. When Internet travel company Hotels.nl began using blankets on sheep for advertising, one town began fining the company for ignoring the town's ban on advertising along the highways. What are the positive and negative aspects of using sheep or even horses and cows to advertise products for companies? For consumers? Can advertising get out of hand?

Practice: Apply What You've Learned

1. As an account executive for an advertising agency, you have been assigned to a new client, a company that has developed a new energy soft drink. As you begin development of the creative strategy, you are considering different types of appeals:
   a. USP
   b. Comparative advertising
   c. A fear appeal
   d. A celebrity endorsement
   e. A slice-of-life ad
   f. Sex appeal
   g. Humor
   Outline the strengths and weaknesses of using each of these appeals for advertising the new soft drink.

2. More and more advertisers are replacing traditional advertising with branded entertainment activities. Some believe that this practice dupes consumers and should not be allowed. Others say that audiences should be informed about the specific product placements in TV shows and movies. What do you think about branded entertainment? Should it be regulated?

3. Look through some magazines to find an ad that fits each of the following categories:
   a. USP strategy
   b. Demonstration

   c. Testimonial
   d. Slice-of-life
   e. Sex appeal
   f. Humor appeal
   Critique each ad. Tell who the target market appears to be. Describe how the appeal is executed. Discuss what is good and bad about the ad. Do you think the ad will be effective? Why or why not?

4. Assume that you are a member of the marketing department for a firm that produces several brands of household cleaning products. Your assignment is to develop recommendations for trade and consumer sales promotion activities for a new laundry detergent. Develop an outline of your recommendations for these sales promotions. In a role-playing situation, present and defend your recommendations to your boss.

5. Timing is an important part of a sales promotion plan. Marketers must decide when the best time is to mail out samples, to offer trade discounts, or to sponsor a sweepstakes. Assume that the introduction of the new laundry detergent in question 4 is planned for April 1. Place the activities you recommended in question 3 on a 12-month calendar. In a role-playing situation, present your plan to your supervisor. Be sure to explain why you have included certain types of promotions and the reasons for your timing of each sales promotion activity.

6. Assume that you are the head of PR for a regional fast-food chain that specializes in fried chicken and fish. A customer has claimed that he became sick when he ate a fried roach that was in his meal along with the chicken. As the director of PR, what recommendations do you have for how the firm might handle this crisis?

Miniproject: Learn by Doing

The purpose of this miniproject is to give you an opportunity to experience the advertising creative process.

1. With one or more classmates, create (imagine) a new brand of an existing product (such as a laundry detergent, toothpaste, perfume, or soft drink).

2. Decide on an advertising appeal for your new product.

3. Create a series of at least three magazine ads for your product, using the appeal you selected. Your ads should have a headline, a visual, and copy to explain your product and to persuade customers to purchase your brand.

4. Present your ads to your class. Discuss the advertising appeal you selected and explain your ad executions.

Real people, **real surfers**: explore the web

Much of the advertising you see every day on television and in magazines is created by a small number of large advertising agencies. To make their agency stand out from the others, the different agencies develop unique personalities or corporate philosophies. Visit the Web sites of several advertising agencies:

Leo Burnett (**www.leoburnett.com**)

BBDO (**www.bbdo.com**)

The Martin Agency (**www.martinagency.com**)

Fallon Worldwide (**www.fallon.com**)

J. Walter Thompson (**www.jwt.com**)

Explore the Web sites to see how they differ. Then answer the following questions:

1. What is the mission of each agency? How does each agency attempt to position itself compared to other agencies?
2. Who are some of the major clients of the agency?
3. How does the site demonstrate the creative ability of the agency? Does the site do a good job of communicating the mission of the agency? Explain.
4. If available, tell a little about the history of the agency.
5. Of the agencies you visited, which would you most like to work for? Why?

Marketing Plan Exercise

An advertising campaign consists of a series of advertisements placed in media over time. While ads may be placed in different media, all will have the same look, feel, and message. Think about one of the following products:

1. A new brand of toothpaste
2. Your local city or state
3. Your university

Assume that you are developing an advertising campaign for the product. Outline how you would develop the campaign. Be sure to discuss the following:

1. The type of appeal you would use
2. The main message you will seek to communicate
3. The media you would use (be sure to include at least one print and one broadcast medium)
4. How you will develop the ads so that they have the same look and feel

---

Marketing in Action Case

Real **Choices** at **Jet Blue**

When low-cost carrier JetBlue Airways began operations in 1999, it promised customers cheap fares combined with exceptional service. JetBlue planes offer more leg room and all seats on JetBlue planes offer passengers 36-channel DIRECTTV® service on seat-back screens.

For seven years, JetBlue, with a few exceptions, kept its promise to passengers and shot to the top of customer satisfaction surveys J.D. Powers and Associates conducted. On Valentine's Day, 2007, however, the airline suffered the worst crisis in its history. Due to an unexpected New York ice storm, nine JetBlue planes full of passengers were stranded on the tarmac for over 6 hours—one plane and its 130 passengers sat on the tarmac for 10 hours. The planes left the gate and then found they couldn't take off but the airlines, feeling that the storm would let up by midmorning, did not allow the planes to return to the gate. In the end, the wheels of the planes were frozen in the slush, unable to move.

In the next few days things got even worse for JetBlue as a snowball effect (pardon the pun) from the storm caused hundreds of flights to be cancelled—JetBlue's flight attendants and pilots were not where they were needed and the company's communication system staff people were not trained to tell them what to do. At some airports, police had to be called in to help calm down the irate customers.

While the airline was far less than satisfactory in its response to the Valentine's Day ice storm, its response to the crisis was a model of excellent PR. Seeking to quickly respond to the crisis and appease angry customers, CEO David Neeleman quickly apologized to customers and explained what went wrong. He said he felt "mortified" and "humiliated." To get his message across, he appeared on CNN's *American Morning*, *Today*, *Fox and Friends*, and *Squawk Box* early the next day. But JetBlue did more than just apologize to consumers. The airline offered passengers who were stranded on JetBlue planes for three hours or more a full refund plus a free round-trip ticket to any JetBlue destination. In all, the airline spent $30 million on vouchers for passengers of the 1,102 cancelled flights.

In addition to its immediate response to the February cancellations, JetBlue cited its dedication to "bringing humanity back to air travel" and established a Customer Bill of Rights retroactive to February 14. The Bill of Rights out-lines what JetBlue will provide to its customers in cases of flight cancellations, departure delays, overbookings (cus-tomers who are denied boarding will receive $1000), and even when the DIRECTV® is inoperable.

But will these changes satisfy customers? Most customers reacted with caution, saying that they would be watching the air-line to see if it lived up to its promise. Other stranded passengers were less positive and some vowed never to fly JetBlue again.

Will the Bill of Rights allow JetBlue to gain the level of cus-tomer loyalty it enjoyed before the crisis? While most customers of delayed flights may be satisfied, others may not. What about customers whose delays fall 10 minutes short of receiving a full-price trip voucher? And what will happen when another crisis occurs? JetBlue must continue to develop customer service and PR programs if it is to stay in the air for the long haul.

You Make the Call

1. What is the decision facing JetBlue?
2. What factors are important in understanding this deci-sion situation?
3. What are the alternatives?
4. What decision(s) do you recommend?
5. What are some ways to implement your recommendation?

Based on: Bloomberg News, "Airlines' Proposals on Long Runway Delays," *New York Times,* February 23, 2007, **http://www.nytimes.com/2007/02/23/business/23air.html?scp=162&sq=jetblue&st=nyt** (accessed April 21, 2008); Jeff Bailey, "JetBlue Cancels More Flights in Storm's Wake," *New York Times,* February 18, 2007, **http://www.nytimes.com/2007/02/18/business/18jetblue.html?scp=173&sq=jetblue&st=nyt** (accessed April 21, 2008); Jeff Bailey, "JetBlue's C.E.O. Is 'Mortified' After Fliers Are Stranded," *New York Times,* February 19, 2007, **http://www.nytimes.com/2007/02/19jetblue.html?scp=170&sq=jetblue&st=nyt** (accessed April 21, 2008);Jeff Bailey, "Long Delays Hurt Image of JetBlue," *New York Times,* February 17, 2007, **http://www.nytimes.com/2007/02/17/business/17air.html?scp=174&sq=jetblue&st=nyt** (accessed April 21, 2008); "JetBlue's Customer Bill of Rights," **http://www.jetblue.com/about/ourcompany/promise/index.html** (accessed April 21, 2008).

Personal Selling, Sales Management, and Direct Marketing

A typical modern trading room.

Jeffrey
Brechman
Profile ▼

▼ **Q & A** with Jeffrey Brechman

Q) What I do when I'm not working?
A) Spend time with my family and play golf.

Q) First job out of school?
A) Telemarketer for American Automobile Association.

Q) Career high?
A) Telling my family about the first deal I won, not the actual win itself.

Q) Business book I'm reading now?
A) *Secrets of the Millionaire Mind: Mastering the Inner Game of Wealth* by T. Harv Eker.

Q) My hero?
A) My grandfather.

Q) My motto to live by?
A) Treat everyone as an equal.

Q) What drives me?
A) To be able to provide not only for my family but the employees that work for me.

Q) My management style?
A) I let the situation drive my style...stern when needed.

A Decision Maker at Woodtronics

Jeffrey Brechman is a principal at Woodtronics Inc., a company that designs and builds trading room furniture and command centers and network operation control centers for financial institutions, the military, police and fire departments. Jeffrey moved into his career in an unconventional way. After a short stint in college, he started a painting business and wasn't thrilled about what he was doing. He got into a conversation about his career aspirations with a woman whose house he was painting. She, in turn, set up a meeting with her husband, who happened to be president of a company that manufactured and sold trading room console furniture. Trading room furniture is a very specialized niche business. It needs to accommodate a lot of electronic equipment to let brokers monitor the market, but also to take up a minimum amount of space so that brokerage houses can fit as many brokers as is comfortably possible in expensive floor space.

Jeffrey landed his first job as a sales executive in New York after that meeting. He worked hard to prove himself to this firm and he became its top salesperson in his very first year. He worked at that first company for four years, but then a competing company approached him to revitalize its business in the New York metropolitan area. This new company was losing money and was not a major competitor in the industry because it was not managed properly and it wasn't making sales it should have been winning. Jeffrey believed he could turn the company around, so he swallowed hard and moved to the competitor—Woodtronics. Within two years the company's sales have tripled and it's now one of the leading manufacturers in the trading desk furniture industry. The turnaround came by carefully examining each area of the business and building on employees' strengths as well as improving products and customer service. In 2006, Woodtronics also opened an office in London to allow the growing company to expand its business overseas.

Decision Time at Woodtronics

An architect had a client in Chicago who was using one of Woodtronics' best-selling trading desk products. The architect liked the product so much that he recommended it to another important client in Jersey City who would also be installing trading desks. Of course, Jeffrey was thrilled with the referral; this new client represented a major sale for Woodtronics. However, in the meantime the company had developed a prototype of a new model it called Evolution that Jeffrey believed would provide an even better solution for this new client. The Evolution technology platform is specifically designed for high-density technology trading environments; it maximizes work-surface area, allows for easier integration of new flat screen technology into the furniture, features a high-volume integrated heat removal system to increase the comfort for users and also offers innovative designs to hide cumbersome computer cables, yet still provides access to them when needed.

Woodtronics really preferred to sell this new product but the architect was hesitant to recommend it because he had used the older product in a prior project and it worked out well for him. And this project would be the first large-scale installation so he was afraid that his client would be a "guinea pig" by taking a chance on a product without a proven track record. To complicate the issue, the Jersey City client had shown a lack of enthusiasm for the original product because it didn't exactly meet his project's needs.

As a principal of the company, Jeffrey is personally involved in every one of its major sales. He had described the new product to the Jersey City client and he was interested in learning more—but the architect was still resisting. Jeffrey had to make a critical sales decision or risk losing out completely on this large sale. Which product should he try to sell?

Jeffrey considered his Options 1·2·3

1 **Option**
Push the original product even though this was not the best solution for the client. This approach would maintain the important relationship Jeffrey already had with the architect. But the new client wasn't satisfied with the current product so the company's reputation was at risk if it offered a product it knew was not completely in line with the client's needs.

2 **Option**
Sell the client using the prototype of the Evolution platform, arguing that this alternative would better meet his needs in terms of both price and functionality. This option would let Jeffrey lead with his best, state-of-the-art product. But, he would risk alienating the architect who had been so helpful in bringing new business to Woodtronics.

3 **Option**
Concentrate on raising the architect's comfort level with the new Evolution product and hope that he would be persuaded to recommend it to the new client instead. This option would deliver the right solution to the client and of course deliver a major sale to Woodtronics. If it succeeded, Jeffrey might even further boost the architect's confidence in Woodtronics to deliver the best solutions for his other clients down the road. But, the architect was set on using the tried-and-true product; there was a real risk he would walk away from Woodtronics and find a competitor that didn't want to "field-test" a new product on one of his clients.

Now, put yourself in Jeffrey's shoes: Which option would you choose, and why?

You Choose

Which **Option** would you choose, and **why**?
1. ☐YES ☐NO   2. ☐YES ☐NO   3. ☐YES ☐NO

See what **option** Jeffrey chose and its success on **page 457**

Things to remember:

Woodtronics operates solely in business-to-business contexts, so the company relies primarily on personal selling to get and retain clients.

Jeffrey has both an ethical and a financial responsibility to do what's best for the client. He needs to recommend the Woodtronics product solution that will be most likely to meet the client's needs rather than just generating more business down the road with other clients.

Check out chapter 14 **Study Map** on page 458

1

OBJECTIVE

Understand the important role of personal selling and how it fits into the promotion mix.

(pp. 440–442)

Personal Selling: Advertising Is Not the Only Game in Town!

Jeffrey Brechman's dilemma is to find the best way for Woodtronics to service its clients' needs. Similarly, when it comes to promoting a product, there's more than one way to skin a cat—or, in one case, a goose: A liquor company once sent attractive models into trendy cigar bars to push the pricey French vodka Grey Goose it was introducing to the U.S. market. To get customers to try it, the women dropped a cherry soaked with the liquor into people's martinis and then gave surprised barflies a sales pitch about the vodka. When word of this "guerrilla marketing" hit the newspapers, the company got some free publicity for its efforts. Unlike Agent 007, who always asks for his Martinis "shaken, not stirred," in this case the company apparently hopes potential customers will be stirred, not shaken![1]

We saw in Chapter 13 that companies increasingly supplement traditional advertising with other communication methods, such as public relations campaigns and various forms of sales promotion as they work harder and harder to cut through the clutter. In this chapter, we'll look at other forms of promotion—personal selling and direct marketing—that marketers commonly use in addition to advertising, public relations, and sales promotion to round out their overall promotion mix.

The Lowdown on Personal Selling

Personal selling occurs when a company representative interacts directly with a customer or prospective customer to communicate about a good or service. This form of promotion is a far more intimate way to talk to the market. Many organizations rely heavily on personal selling because at times the "personal touch" carries more weight than mass-media material. For a business-to-business market situation, such as the one Jeffrey Brechman faces at Woodtronics, the personal touch translates into developing crucial relationships with clients. Also, many industrial goods and services (like trading desks) are too complex or expensive to market effectively in impersonal ways (such as through mass advertising). An axiom in marketing is *the more complex, technical, and intangible the product, the more heavily firms tend to rely on personal selling to promote it.*

Another advantage of personal selling is that salespeople are the firm's eyes and ears in the marketplace. They learn which competitors talk to customers, what they offer, and what new rival goods and services are on the way—all valuable competitive intelligence. As such, salespeople perform a vital role in the success of a firm's CRM system we discussed in Chapter 7—they provide a source of timely and accurate informational input about customers and the market.

Personal selling has special importance for students (that's you) because many graduates with a marketing background will enter professional sales jobs. The U.S. Bureau of Labor Statistics estimates job growth of 9 percent for sales representatives in manufacturing and wholesaling between 2006 and 2016. For technical and scientific products, the growth projection rises to 10 percent. Overall, sales job growth ranks high among all occupations surveyed.[2] Jobs in selling and sales management often provide high upward mobility if you are successful, because firms value employees who understand customers and who can communicate well with them. The old business adage "nothing happens until something is sold" translates into many firms placing quite a bit of emphasis on personal selling in their promotion mixes.

Sold on selling? All right then, let's take a close look at how personal selling works and how professional salespeople develop long-term relationships with customers.

The Role of Personal Selling in the Marketing Mix

When a woman calls Apple's 800 number to order a new computer configured with the Garage Band application so her teenage son and his friends can record their band's music, she deals with a salesperson. When she sits in on a presentation at work by a Web site renewal consultant who proposes a new Content Management System for her firm's Web site, she deals with a salesperson. And when that same woman agrees over lunch at a swanky restaurant to invest some of her savings with a financial manager's recommended mutual fund, she also deals with a salesperson.

For many firms, some element of personal selling is essential to land a commitment to purchase or a contract, so this type of marketing communication is key to their marketing plans. To put the use of personal selling into perspective, Table 14.1 summarizes some of the factors that make it a more or less important element in an organization's promotion mix.

In general, a personal selling emphasis is more important when a firm engages in a *push strategy*, in which the goal is to "push" the product through the channel of distribution so that it is available to consumers. As a vice president at Hallmark Cards observed, "We're not selling *to* the retailer, we're selling *through* the retailer. We look at the retailer as a pipeline to the hands of consumers."[3]

Personal selling also is likely to be crucial in business-to-business contexts where the firm must interact directly with a client's management to clinch a big deal—and often when intense negotiations about price and other factors will occur before the customer signs on the dotted line. In consumer contexts, inexperienced customers may need the hands-on assistance that a professional salesperson provides. Firms that sell goods and services consumers buy infrequently—houses, cars, computers, lawn mowers, even college educations—often rely heavily on personal selling. (*Hint:* Your school didn't pick just any student at random to conduct campus tours for prospective attendees.) Likewise, firms whose goods or services are complex or very expensive often need a salesperson to explain, justify, and sell them—in both business and consumer markets.

If personal selling is so useful, why don't firms just scrap their advertising and sales promotion budgets and hire more salespeople? There are some drawbacks that limit the role personal selling plays in the marketing communication mix. First, when the dollar amount

personal selling
Marketing communication by which a company representative interacts directly with a customer or prospective customer to communicate about a good or service.

Table 14.1 | Factors that Influence a Firm's Emphasis on Personal Selling

Factors that Increase Emphasis on Personal Selling	Factors that Limit Emphasis on Personal Selling
• If a push strategy is used	• If the dollar amount of individual orders will be small
• If the decision maker has higher status within the organization	• If there are many small customers
• If the purchase is a "new task" for the customer	• If the image of the salesperson is poor
• If the product is highly technical or complex	
• If the customer is very large	
• If the product is expensive	
• If the product is a custom good or personalized service	
• If there are trade-in products	
• If negotiation is required	

of individual purchases is low, it doesn't make sense to use personal selling—the cost per contact with each customer is very high compared to other forms of promotion. Analysts estimate that in 2010 the average total cost for a sales call with a *consultative* (problem-solving) approach to selling will be about $350, and this cost increases at a rate of 5 percent per year. And, of course this figure is an average—depending on the industry, some sales calls are much more expensive to make. The per-contact cost of a national television commercial is minuscule by comparison. A 30-second prime-time commercial may run $300,000 to $500,000 (or even around $3 million during the Super Bowl), but with millions of viewers, the cost per contact may be only $10 or $15 per 1,000 viewers.[4] For low-priced consumer goods, personal selling to end users simply doesn't make good financial sense.

Salespeople—even the *really* energetic types—can make only so many calls a day. Thus, reliance on personal selling is effective only when the success ratio is high. Telemarketing, sometimes called *teleselling*, involves person-to-person communication that takes place on the phone. Because the cost of field salespeople is so high, telemarketing continues to grow in popularity (much to the dismay of many prospects when calls interrupt their dinner). Of course, no-call legislation and do-not-call lists at the state and federal levels have given consumers a powerful weapon to ward off unwanted telephone selling. We will talk about this later in the chapter in the context of direct marketing.

Ironically, consumer resistance to telemarketing gives a powerful boost to a form of selling that has been around for a long time: direct selling. *Direct selling is not the same thing as direct marketing*. Direct sellers bypass channel intermediaries and sell directly from manufacturer to consumer through personal, one-to-one contact. Typically, independent sales representatives sell in person in a customer's home or place of business. Tupperware, Avon, Mary Kay, and the Pampered Chef are some well-known examples. Many direct selling firms use a *party plan* approach where salespeople demonstrate products in front of groups of neighbors or friends. Direct selling is on a big upswing, with domestic sales volume doubling in the past 10 years to over $30 billion annually. We'll discuss direct selling in more detail in Chapter 16.[5]

2 Technology and Personal Selling

OBJECTIVE

Explain how technology enhances the personal selling effort.

(pp. 442–443)

Personal selling is supposed to be, well, "personal." By definition, a company uses personal selling for marketing communications in situations when one person (the salesperson) interacts directly with another person (the customer or prospective customer) to communicate about a good or service. All sorts of technologies can enhance the personal selling process. However, as anyone making sales calls knows, technology cannot and should not *replace* personal selling. As we'll discuss later in this chapter, today a key role of personal selling is to manage customer *relationships*—and remember relationships occur between people, not between computers (as much as you love your Facebook and MySpace accounts).

However, there's no doubt that a bevy of technological advancements makes it easier for salespeople to do their jobs more effectively. One such technological advance is *customer relationship management (CRM) software*. For years now, *account management software* such as ACT and GoldMine has helped salespeople. These programs are inexpensive, easy to navigate, and they allow salespeople to track all aspects of customer interaction. Currently, many firms turn to "on demand" on-line CRM applications, which are more customizable and integrative than ACT or GoldMine, yet are less expensive than major companywide CRM installations. These widely used on-line CRM products include SalesForce.com and SalesNet, both of which are user-friendly for salespeople. A key benefit of on-line CRM systems is that firms "rent" them for a flat fee per month (at SalesForce.com, monthly prices are as low as $20 per user) so they avoid major capital outlays.[6] Recently, some sales organizations have turned to a new-generation system called *partner relationship management (PRM)* that links information between selling and buying firms. PRM differs from CRM in that both supplier and buyer firms share at least some of their databases and systems to maximize the usefulness of the data for decision-making purposes. Firms that share information are more likely to work together toward win-win solutions.

Beyond CRM and PRM, numerous other technology applications enhance personal selling, including teleconferencing, videoconferencing, and improved corporate Web sites that offer FAQ (frequently asked questions) pages to answer customers' queries. Many firms also use intranets and blogs to facilitate access to internal and external communication.

Voice-over Internet protocol (VoIP)—systems that rely upon a data network to carry voice calls—are beginning to get a lot of use in day-to-day correspondence between salespeople and customers. With VoIP, the salesperson on the road can just plug into a fast Internet connection and then start to make and receive calls just as if she is in the office. Unlike cell phones, there are no bad reception areas, and unlike hotel phones there are no hidden charges. One popular VoIP product is Skype, whose tagline is "The whole world can talk for free." According to its Web site, Skype "is a little piece of software that allows you to make free calls to other Skype users and really cheap calls to ordinary phones." Skype even offers bargain rates to fixed lines and cell phones outside the United States.[7]

Cellular providers such as T-Mobile now essentially let you use VoIP on your cell phone. You can buy a BlackBerry from T-Mobile with a built-in wireless internet card that allows you to make VoIP calls from anywhere you can access the T-Mobile network. The T-Mobile Hotspot service requires a monthly upcharge of about $20; this fee gives you unlimited phone calls over the wireless network on your BlackBerry (and some other phone models) at no additional charge.[8]

Of course, in general, salespeople use wireless technology more and more to ensure seamless communication with clients. BlackBerry has been around for a while, but experts predict that as wireless becomes predominant the various devices salespeople use to communicate (cell phone, fax, laptop, and so on) will become more integrated.[9] Anyone for a software-packed personal digital assistant (PDA) with cell-phone capabilities, Internet access, and a global positioning system to help you find your way around? And can it also make a decent cup of coffee? (Actually the coffee part isn't so far-fetched, as T-Mobile claims that all Starbucks are supported by their T-Mobile Hotspot wireless network!)[10]

CRM systems such as GoldMine are very popular because they help the sales force organize and utilize information about their customers, thus making salespeople better prepared to make the sales presentation.

Metrics Moment

In its quest to remain competitive with the ever-growing number of insurance offerings, Nationwide Insurance began an initiative to analyze and measure Web site usage and performance. While some insurance firms offer on-line services that provide quotes to all visitors, others have been very reluctant to offer quotes to people who live in states where they sell few or no policies. And, while on-line quoting was designed to facilitate purchases on a more cost-effective channel (the Internet), for the most part it has not boosted on-line sales.

Nationwide formed a team to analyze data reports and identify trends that could aid the company's strategic decisions related to on-line quoting and sales. By measuring data across channels, Nationwide developed a competitive on-line conversion rate that now allows the company to generate the amount of business a medium- to large-sized established agency produces. Its on-line analysis also helped Nationwide better understand consumers' information searches and the time frame consumers use when they purchase policies. The company discovered that the on-line quoting process was a key to establishing a competitive advantage with insurance shoppers, but the metrics also showed that most customers only wanted an estimate before they take their business off-line. This is a good reminder that the "personal touch" isn't obsolete quite yet.[11]

3 Types of Sales Jobs

OBJECTIVE
Identify the different types of sales jobs.
(pp. 444)

Given what you've read about personal selling so far, you can begin to see why professional salespeople have very dynamic career opportunities. And there are several different types of sales jobs from which you can choose, each with its own unique characteristics. Maybe you aspire to work in sales someday, or perhaps you've already held a sales job at some point. Let's look more closely at some of the different types of sales positions.

As you might imagine, sales jobs vary considerably. The person who processes an a Dell computer purchase over the phone is primarily an **order taker**—a salesperson who processes transactions the customer initiates. Many retail salespeople are order takers, but often wholesalers, dealers, and distributors also employ salespeople to assist their business customers. Because little creative selling is involved in order taking, this type of sales job typically is the lowest-paid sales position.

In contrast, a **technical specialist** contributes considerable expertise in the form of product demonstrations, recommendations for complex equipment, and setup of machinery. The technical specialist provides *sales support* rather than actually closing the sale. She promotes the firm and tries to stimulate demand for a product to make it easier for colleagues to actually seal the deal.

Then there is the **missionary salesperson** whose job is to stimulate clients to buy. Like technical specialists, missionary salespeople promote the firm and encourage demand for its goods and services but don't actually take orders.[12] Pfizer salespeople do missionary sales work when they call on physicians to influence them to prescribe the latest and greatest Pfizer medications instead of competing drugs. However, no sale actually gets made until doctors call prescriptions into pharmacies, which then place orders for the drug through their wholesalers.

The **new-business salesperson** is responsible for finding new customers and calls on them to present the company's products. As you might imagine, gaining the business of a new customer usually means that the customer stops doing business with one of the firm's competitors (and they won't give up without a fight). New-business selling requires a high degree of creativity and professionalism, so this type of salesperson is usually very well-paid. Once a new-business salesperson establishes a relationship with a client, she often continues to service that client as the primary contact as long as the client continues to buy from the company. In that long-term-relationship-building role, this type of salesperson is an **order getter**. Order getters are usually the people most directly responsible for a particular client's business; they may also hold the title of "account manager."[13]

More and more, firms find that the selling function works best via **team selling**. A selling team may consist of a salesperson, a technical specialist, someone from engineering and design, and other players who work together to develop products and programs that satisfy the customer's needs. When the company includes people from a range of areas it often calls this group a *cross-functional team*.

order taker
A salesperson whose primary function is to facilitate transactions that the customer initiates.

technical specialist
A sales support person with a high level of technical expertise who assists in product demonstrations.

missionary salesperson
A salesperson who promotes the firm and tries to stimulate demand for a product but does not actually complete a sale.

new-business salesperson
The person responsible for finding new customers and calling on them to present the company's products.

order getter
A salesperson who works to develop long-term relationships with particular customers or to generate new sales.

team selling
The sales function when handled by a team that may consist of a salesperson, a technical specialist, and others.

4 Two Approaches to Personal Selling

OBJECTIVE
Describe the two approaches to personal selling.
(pp. 444–445)

Personal selling is one of the oldest forms of marketing communication. Unfortunately, over the years smooth-talking pitchmen who say anything to make a sale have tarnished its image. Pulitzer Prize–winning playwright Arthur Miller's famous character Willie Loman in *Death of a Salesman*—a must-read for generations of middle- and high-school students—didn't help. Willie Loman (as in "low man" on the totem pole—get it?) is a pathetic, burned-out peddler who leaves home for the road on Monday morning and returns late Friday evening selling "on a smile and a shoeshine." His personal life is in shambles with two dysfunctional sons and a disaffected wife who hardly knows him. Great public relations for selling as a career, right?

Fortunately, personal selling today is nothing like Miller's harsh portrayal. Selling has moved from a transactional, hard-sell approach to an approach based on relationships with customers. Let's see how.

Transactional Selling: Putting on the Hard Sell

Willy Loman practiced a high-pressure, hard-sell approach. We've all been exposed to the pushy electronics salesperson that puts down the competition when she tells shoppers that if they buy elsewhere they will be stuck with an inferior home theater system that will fall apart in six months. Or how about the crafty used car salesman who plays the good cop/bad cop game: She gives you an awesome price but then sadly informs you her boss the sales manager won't go for such a sweet deal? These hard-sell tactics reflect **transactional selling**, an approach that focuses on making an immediate sale with little concern for developing a long-term relationship with the customer.

As customers, the hard sell makes us feel manipulated, resentful, and it diminishes our satisfaction and loyalty. It's a very short-sighted approach to selling. As we said earlier in the book, constantly finding new customers is much more expensive than getting repeat business from the customers you already have. And the behaviors transactional selling promotes (that is, doing anything to get the order) contribute to the negative image many of us have of salespeople as obnoxious and untrustworthy. Such salespeople engage in these behaviors because they don't care if they ever have the chance to sell to you again. This is really bad business!

Relationship Selling: Building Long-Term Customers

Relationship selling is the process by which a salesperson secures, develops, and maintains long-term relationships with profitable customers.[14] Today's professional salesperson is more likely to practice relationship selling than transactional selling. This means that the salesperson tries to develop a mutually satisfying, win-win relationship with the customer. Securing a customer relationship means converting an interested prospect into someone who is convinced that the good or service holds value for her. Developing a customer relationship means ensuring that you and the customer work together to find more ways to add value to the transaction. Maintaining a customer relationship means building customer satisfaction and loyalty—thus, you can count on the customer to provide future business and stick with you for the long haul. And if doing business with the customer isn't profitable to you, unless you're a charitable organization you would probably like to see that customer go somewhere else.

transactional selling
A form of personal selling that focuses on making an immediate sale with little or no attempt to develop a relationship with the customer.

relationship selling
A form of personal selling that involves securing, developing, and maintaining long-term relationships with profitable customers.

Rosemary
Ramsey
a professor at Wright State University

My Advice for Woodtronics would be to choose

2 Option

real people, Other Voices

I choose **Option 2**. The decision hinges on whether or not Jeffrey truly believes the new product is the best solution for the client. If so, then everyone wins. Apparently, the architect feels that Jeffrey

is capable or he would not have allowed Jeffrey to work directly with the client. The new product is the best solution for the client, and ultimately the architect will reap the reward of a great sale. Jeffrey needs to continue to discuss this situation with the architect and gain his acceptance. If Jeffrey is a capable salesperson, which it seems he is, then convincing the architect as well as the client should not be a problem. ➤

5 The Creative Selling Process

OBJECTIVE

List the steps in the creative selling process.

(pp. 446–449)

Many people find selling to be a great profession, partly because something different is always going on. Every customer, every sales call, and every salesperson is unique. Some salespeople are successful primarily because they know so much about what they sell. Others are successful because they've built strong relationships with customers so that they're able to add value to both the customer and their own firm—a win-win approach to selling. Successful salespeople understand and engage in a series of activities to make the sales encounter mutually beneficial.

A salesperson's chances of success increase when she undergoes a systematic series of steps we call the **creative selling process**. These steps require the salesperson to seek out potential customers, analyze their needs, determine how product attributes provide benefits, and then decide how best to communicate this to prospects. As Figure 14.1 shows, there are seven steps in the process. Let's take a look at each.

Step 1: Prospect and Qualify

Prospecting is the process by which a salesperson identifies and develops a list of *prospects* or *sales leads* (potential customers). Leads come from existing customer lists, telephone directories, commercially available databases, and of course through diligent use of Web search engines like Google. The local library usually owns directories of businesses (including those state and federal agencies publish) and directories of association memberships. Sometimes companies generate sales leads through their advertising or sales promotion when they encourage customers to request more information.

As you learned in Chapter 13, trade shows also are an important source of sales leads, as are visits to your company's Web site by potential customers. Accela Communications is one company that tracks these responses for its clients in order to generate leads. Sales organizations turn to Accela to monitor, analyze, and summarize visitors to a company's Web site—in essence, to develop prospect lists. Accela then turns these lists over to salespeople for follow-up by phone or in person.[15]

Salespeople also need to consider on-line *social networks* as a prospecting tool. These are not "friendship" social networks, such as MySpace and Facebook, but rather business networks, such as LinkedIn, Plaxo, Ryze, and Spoke. These sites enable salespeople to create profiles, upload their personal address books to the site, and invite business colleagues to join the network. Business-oriented social networks are growing fast. For example LinkedIn, whose tagline is "Relationships Matter," bills itself as a networking tool that helps you discover inside connections to recommended job candidates, industry experts, and business practices. The site boasts membership of over 20 million experienced professionals from all over the world who represent over 150 industries.[16]

Another way to generate leads is through *cold calling*, in which the salesperson simply contacts prospects "cold," without prior introduction or arrangement. It always helps to know the prospect, so salespeople might rely instead on *referrals*. Current clients who are satisfied with their purchase often recommend a salesperson to others—yet another reason to maintain good customer relationships.

However, the mere fact that someone is willing to talk to a salesperson doesn't guarantee a sale. After they identify potential customers, salespeople need to *qualify* these prospects to determine how likely they are to become customers. To do this they ask questions such as the following:

- Are the prospects likely to be interested in what I'm selling?
- Are they likely to switch their allegiance from another supplier or product?

creative selling process
The process of seeking out potential customers, analyzing needs, determining how product attributes might provide benefits for the customer, and then communicating that information.

prospecting
A part of the selling process that includes identifying and developing a list of potential or prospective customers.

Figure 14.1 | Steps in the Creative Selling Process

In the creative selling process, salespeople follow a series of steps to ensure successful long-term relationships with customers.

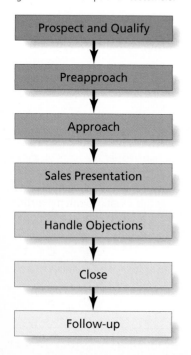

- Is the potential sales volume large enough to make a relationship profitable?
- Can they afford the purchase?
- If they must borrow money to buy the product, what is their credit history?

Step 2: Preapproach

In the **preapproach** stage, you compile background information about prospective customers and plan the sales interview. Firms don't make important purchases lightly, and it's often difficult even to get an appointment to see a prospect. It's foolish for a salesperson to blindly call on a qualified prospect and risk losing the sale because of a lack of preparation. Salespeople try to learn as much as possible about qualified prospects early on. They may probe a prospect's prior purchase history, current needs, or, in some cases, even try to learn about their personal interests.

Salespeople can draw information about a prospect from a variety of sources. In the case of larger companies, they can find financial data, names of top executives, and other information about a business in publications such as *Standard & Poor's 500 Directory* or Dun & Bradstreet's *Million Dollar Directory*. They can also find a great deal of information for the preapproach on customers' Web sites. And, the inside scoop on a prospect often comes from informal sources such as noncompeting salespeople who have dealt with the prospect before.

Of course, if the salesperson's firm has a CRM system she can use it to see whether the database includes information about the prospect. Say for example a salesperson at Mike's Bikes plans to call on a buyer at Greg's Vacation Rentals to see about selling some new bikes for guests to use at Greg's various resort properties. If Mike's has had a CRM system in place for some time, any contacts with customers and potential customers (prospects) are recorded in the database. The salesperson can simply run an inquiry about Greg's Vacation Rentals and with luck, the CRM database will deliver information on the company, prior purchases from Mike's, when and why customers stopped buying from the company, and perhaps even the preferences of the particular buyer.

Today, many leads come from visits to a company's Web site. Companies like Accela Communications work with sales organizations to put in place Web response programs to effectively develop these leads and hopefully turn them into customers.

preapproach
A part of the selling process that includes developing information about prospective customers and planning the sales interview.

Step 3: Approach

After the salesperson lays the groundwork with the preapproach it's time to **approach**, or contact, the prospect. During these important first minutes several key events occur. The salesperson tries to learn even more about the prospect's needs, create a good impression, and build rapport. If the salesperson found the prospect through a referral, she will probably say so up front: "Melissa Sabella with Prentice Industries suggested I call on you."

During the approach, the customer decides whether the salesperson has something to offer that is of potential value. The old saying "You never get a second chance to make a good first impression" rings true here. A professional appearance tells the prospect that the salesperson means business and is competent to handle the sale. A good salesperson is well-groomed and wears appropriate business dress. She doesn't chew gum, use poor grammar or inappropriate language, mispronounce the customer's name, or seem uninterested in the call.

approach
The first step of the actual sales presentation in which the salesperson tries to learn more about the customer's needs, create a good impression, and build rapport.

Preparing demonstrations and video presentations for use in sales calls has been made much more user-friendly by new software such as Visual Communicator, produced by Serious Magic.

Step 4: Sales Presentation

Many sales calls involve a formal **sales presentation**, which lays out the benefits of the product and its advantages over the competition. When possible and appropriate, salespeople should incorporate a great PowerPoint presentation integrated with some sound and media into their sales presentations to jazz things up. The focus of the sales presentation should always be on ways the salesperson, her goods and services, and her company can add value to the customer (and in a business-to-business setting, to the customer's company). It is important for the salesperson to present this value proposition clearly and to invite the customer's involvement in the conversation. Let the customer ask questions, give feedback, and discuss her needs. Canned approaches to sales presentations are a poor choice for salespeople who want to build long-term relationships. In fact, sales managers rate *listening* skills, not talking skills, as the single most important attribute they look for when they hire relationship salespeople.[17]

Step 5: Handle Objections

It's rare when a prospect accepts everything the salesperson offers without question. The effective salesperson anticipates *objections*—reasons why the prospect is reluctant to make a commitment—and she's prepared to respond with additional information or persuasive arguments. Actually, the salesperson should welcome objections because they show that the prospect is at least interested enough to consider the offer and seriously weigh its pros and cons. Handling the objection successfully can move a prospect to the decision stage. For example, the salesperson might say, "Ms. Pellerano, you've said before that you don't have room to carry our new line of trail bikes although you mentioned that you may be losing some sales by carrying only one brand with very few different models. If we could come up with an estimate of how much business you're losing, I'll bet you'd consider making room for our line, wouldn't you?"

sales presentation
The part of the selling process in which the salesperson directly communicates the value proposition to the customer and invites two-way communication.

Step 6: Close the Sale

The win-win nature of relationship selling should take some of the pressure off salespeople to make "the dreaded close." But there still comes a point in the sales call at which one or the other party has to move toward gaining commitment to the objectives of the call—presumably a purchase. This is the decision stage, or **close**. Directly asking the customer for her business doesn't need to be painful or awkward: If the salesperson has done a great job in the previous five steps of the creative selling process, closing the sale should be a natural progression of the dialogue between the buyer and seller.

There are a variety of approaches salespeople use to close the sale:

close
The stage of the selling process in which the salesperson actually asks the customer to buy the product.

- A *last objection close* asks customers if they are ready to purchase, providing the salesperson can address any concerns they have about the product: "Are you ready to order if we can prove our delivery time frames meet your expectations?"

- An *assumptive* or *minor points close* mean the salesperson acts as if the purchase is inevitable with only a small detail or two to be settled: "What quantity would you like to order?"

- A *standing-room-only* or *buy-now close* injects some urgency when the salesperson suggests the customer might miss an opportunity if she hesitates: "This price is good through Saturday only, so to save 20 percent we should book the order now." When making such closes, salespeople must be sure the basis they state for buying now is truthful or they'll lose a valuable relationship for the price of a one-time sale!

Step 7: Follow-up

Understanding that the process doesn't end after the salesperson earns the client's business is basic to a relationship selling perspective that emphasizes the importance of long-term satisfaction. The **follow-up** after the sale includes arranging for delivery, payment, and purchase terms. It also means the salesperson makes sure the customer received delivery and is satisfied. Follow-up also allows the salesperson to *bridge* to the next purchase. Once a relationship develops, the selling process is only beginning. Even as one cycle of purchasing draws to a close, a good salesperson already lays the foundation for the next one.

follow-up
Activities after the sale that provide important services to customers.

OBJECTIVE
Explain the role of sales management.
(pp. 449–452)

Sales Management

Few, if any, firms succeed with just one star salesperson. Personal selling is a team effort that requires careful planning to be sure that the organization makes salespeople available when and where customers need them. **Sales management** is the process of planning, implementing, and controlling the personal selling function. Let's review some of the major decisions sales managers who oversee this function must make as Figure 14.2 outlines.

sales management
The process of planning, implementing, and controlling the personal selling function of an organization.

Set Sales Force Objectives

Sales force objectives state what management expects the sales force to accomplish and when. Sales managers develop sales force performance objectives such as "acquire 100 new customers," "generate $100 million in sales," or even "reduce travel expenses by 5 percent." Firms that engage in relationship selling also state objectives that relate to customer satisfaction, loyalty, and retention (or turnover). Other common objectives are new customer development, new product suggestions, training, reporting on competitive activity, and community involvement.

Sales managers also work with their salespeople to develop *individual* objectives. There are two types of individual objectives. *Performance objectives* are readily measurable outcomes, such as total sales and total profits per salesperson. *Behavioral objectives* specify the actions salespeople must accomplish, such as the number of prospects she should identify, the number of sales calls, and the number of follow-up contacts she should make.

sales territory
A set of customers, often defined by geographic boundaries, for whom a particular salesperson is responsible.

Figure 14.2 | The Sales Force Management Process

Sales management includes four major areas of decision making.

Create a Sales Force Strategy

A sales force strategy establishes important specifics such as the structure and size of a firm's sales force. Each salesperson is responsible for a set group of customers—her **sales territory**. The territory structure allows salespeople to have an in-depth understanding of customers and their needs through frequent contact, both business and personal. The most common way to allot territories is geographic to minimize travel and other field expenses. The firm usually defines a *geographic sales force*

Joseph F.
Rocereto

a professor at Monmouth University

My Advice for Woodtronics would be to choose

Option

real people, **Other Voices**

I would choose **Option 2** because the true essence of professional selling is to provide the best possible solution to a particular client's unique needs, while creating a salesperson–client relationship that is based upon mutual trust and commitment. Therefore, if Jeffrey truly believes that the Evolution platform would provide a better solution to the needs of his Jersey City prospect than would the former product, then this belief takes precedent over the possible risk of damaging his relationship with the architect. Jeffrey needs to remember that he, not the architect, is the expert in providing solutions to his clients' needs. Therefore, the wise decision, as a salesperson, would be to recommend the best possible product to his client even in the face of potential negative consequences outside of his relationship with the client. Besides, if Jeffrey truly is the expert regarding the needs of his clients and, therefore, decides to recommend the Evolution platform, then not only will his Jersey City prospect become a satisfied client who may provide Jeffrey with future referrals, but it is likely that the architect will observe the increased benefits of the new platform and become even more confident in recommending Jeffrey to his future clients. ➤

structure according to how many customers reside in a given area. If the product line is diverse or technically complex however, a better approach may be to structure sales territories in terms of different classes of goods and services; this approach enables the sales force to provide more focused product expertise to customers. Kraft Foods has separate sales forces for its major product areas, such as beverages, cheese and dairy, and grocery items.

Still another sales structure is *industry specialization* in which salespeople focus on a single industry or a small number of industries. Firms often refer to such large clients as *key accounts* or *major accounts*. Procter & Gamble uses cross-functional key account teams to focus on each of its major customers. For Lakeland, Florida based Publix Supermarkets (the number three ranked supermarket in the United States by revenue), P&G fields a team of over 100 people a top-level executive heads—customer managers, accountants, logistics people, and more—all of whom work in Central Florida. The idea behind this concentration is the old *80/20 rule* we discussed in Chapter 7—that is, if 20 percent of your customers account for 80 percent of your sales (and profits) those 20 percent deserve the bulk of your personal selling attention.[18]

Putting salespeople out into the field is a very expensive proposition that greatly impacts a company's profitability. Remember, cost-per-customer-contact is higher for personal selling than for any other form of promotion. Thus, it's really important to determine the optimal number of salespeople you put into the field. A larger sales force may increase sales, but at what cost? A smaller sales force will keep costs down. But this lean and mean approach could backfire if competitors move in with larger teams; they will be in a better position to develop strong customer relationships because each of their salespeople doesn't have to call on as many customers.

A key contributor to the success of a sales force is to keep salespeople in front of customers as much of the time as possible—as opposed to making them spend their time traveling, in meetings, doing paperwork, or otherwise engaging in nonselling activities. Fortunately, the advent of *virtual meetings* (or *videoconferencing*) cuts down substantially on nonselling time for salespeople. Also, the ability to videoconference—to have members of a geographically diverse sales team hold meetings from their home offices—can cut non-customer-related travel costs quite a bit. Along the same lines, more and more companies allow salespeople to work from virtual offices by *telecommuting*. This trend keeps salespeople from having to make trips back and forth from home to an office location, so they can use more of this precious travel time to visit customers.[19]

Recruit, Train, and Reward the Sales Force

Because the quality of a sales force can make or break a firm, a top priority for sales managers is to recruit and hire the right set of people to do the job. The ideal candidates exhibit good listening skills, effective follow-up skills, the ability to adapt their sales style from situation to situation, tenacity (sticking with a task), and a high level of personal organization.[20]

Companies screen potential salespeople to reveal these skills, along with useful information about interests and capabilities. Pencil-and-paper tests determine quantitative skills and competencies in areas interviews can't easily assess.

Are successful salespeople born or made? Probably elements of both inherent ability and trainable skills contribute to career success. *Sales training* teaches salespeople about the organization and its goods and services and helps them to develop the skills, knowledge, and attitudes they require to succeed. And training doesn't end once a person "graduates" into the organization. *Professional development* activities continually prepare salespeople personally and professionally for new challenges such as promotions and management responsibilities. They try to develop the salesperson more broadly than knowledge or skills training. Many sales organizations turn to outside consultants to help them develop sales force training and development programs. Sometimes a boost in creative thinking from the outside can do wonders to develop more productive salespeople. Today, with budgets tighter than ever, sales organizations expect identifiable returns on investments in training, and outside firms often deliver these quantifiable results.[21]

Of course, a good way to motivate salespeople is to pay them well. This can mean tying compensation to performance. A *straight commission plan* is based solely on a percentage of sales the person closes. Under a *commission-with-draw plan*, earnings come from commission plus a regular payment, or "draw," that may be charged against future commissions if current sales are inadequate to cover the draw. With a *straight salary plan*, the salesperson is paid a set amount regardless of sales performance. Sometimes a company augments a straight salary plan with a *quota-bonus plan*, in which it pays salespeople a salary *plus* a bonus for her sales that exceed an assigned quota or if she sells certain goods and services that are new or relatively more profitable. Table 14.2 shows some average sales compensation figures. If you haven't yet decided to pursue a sales career, this table may tip you over the edge.

Sales contests provide prizes (cash or otherwise) for selling specific goods and services during a specific period and can kick-start a short-term sales boost. Popular prizes for contest winners include cruises, resort vacations and products winners select from prize catalogs. However, it's easy for a firm to overuse sales contests; these incentives might motivate salespeople to simply wait to sell some goods and services until the contest period kicks in so in reality there is no net increase in sales.

Although many salespeople like to work independently, supervision is essential to an effective sales force. Sales managers often require salespeople to develop monthly, weekly, or daily *call reports*, where they document information about customers they called on and how the call went. Today most salespeople generate these call reports electronically, often on laptop computers or even as a part of the firm's overall CRM initiative. They allow the sales manager to track what the salespeople do in the field, and they provide marketing managers with timely information about customers' responses, competitive activity, and any changes in the firm's customer base.

Table14.2 | Average Salaries for Sales Personnel

	Total Compensation	Base Salary	Bonus plus Commissions
Executive	$147,824	$99,800	$48,440
Top performer	$161,501	$91,452	$74,539
Mid-level performer	$ 99,501	$62,625	$36,772
Low-level performer	$70,994	$47,702	$20,835
Average of all sales representatives	$119,637	$75,905	$44,888

Source: "2007 Compensation Survey," *Sales and Marketing Management*, May 2007, pp. 27–39. Table used by permission of Nielsen Business, Inc.

Sales organizations desiring to improve performance often turn to firms such as Synygy, which provides software and services designed to create performance-driven organizations. Here it advertises that its clients achieve a return on investment of up to 173 percent by investing in its solutions.

Evaluate the Sales Force

A sales manager's job isn't complete until she evaluates the total effort of the sales force. First, it is important to determine whether the sales force meets its objectives. If it is not, the sales manager must figure out the causes. Is the problem due to flaws in the design and/or implementation of the sales force strategy? Or did uncontrollable factors contribute? An overall downturn in the economy such as the one that began in 2008 with the subprime mortgage loan crisis, a big drop in housing prices, and a huge escalation in the price of gasoline, can make it impossible for the best sales force to meet its original sales objectives.

Managers normally measure individual salesperson performance against sales quotas for individual sales territories, even when compensation plans do not include bonuses or commissions based on the quotas. They may also include quantitative measures such as number of sales calls and sales reports the group completed when they evaluate performance. In addition to quantitative measures, many firms also evaluate their salespeople on qualitative indicators of performance, such as salesperson attitude, product knowledge, and communication skills. Increasingly, as firms focus on relationship selling, several important customer metrics such as customer satisfaction, loyalty, and retention/turnover are key measures of superior salesperson performance.

Finally, the company can consider the salesperson's expense account for travel and entertainment since the best sales record can mean little to a company's bottom line if the salesperson gouges the company with outrageous expenses. You think *you're* creative when you spend money? Here are some expenses a few salespeople actually submitted, according to *Sales and Marketing Management* magazine:[22]

- Chartering a private plane to make an appointment after missing a regularly scheduled flight

- A $2,300 round of golf for four people

- A set of china for a salesperson's wife to use for a client dinner party

- Season baseball tickets for $6,000

- A three-day houseboat rental with a crew and chef for $30,000

Metrics Moment

How does a firm know whether a salesperson is effective? Obviously, the short answer is that she produces high sales volume and meets or exceeds sales goals. But just increasing total dollar or unit sales volume is not always a good indicator of salesperson success. The problem is, everything else being equal, salespeople who are compensated strictly on sales volume will simply sell whatever products are easiest to sell to maximize total sales. But these may not be the products with the highest profit margins, and they may not be the goods and services the firm identifies as key to future success in the market.

Because of the problems with using raw sales volume as the sole indicator of salesperson success, some firms turn to a variety of other metrics, including input and output measures. Input measures are *effort* measures—things that go into selling, such as the number and type of sales calls, expense account management, and a variety of nonselling activities such as follow-up work and client service. Output measures, or the *results* of the salesperson's efforts, include sales volume but these also can be the number of orders, size of orders, number of new accounts, level of repeat business, customer profitability, and customer satisfaction.

Ultimately, the best approach to measure salesperson success is to use a variety of metrics that are consistent with the goals of the firm, to ensure the salesperson understands the goals and related metrics, and to link rewards to the achievement of those goals.

7 Direct Marketing

OBJECTIVE

Understand the elements of direct marketing.

(pp. 452–456)

Are you one of those people who love to get lots of catalogs in the mail, pore over them for hours, and then order just exactly what you want without leaving home? Do you download music from iTunes or order books from

Amazon.com? Have you ever responded to an infomercial on TV? All these are examples of direct marketing, the fastest-growing type of marketing communication.

Direct marketing refers to "any direct communication to a consumer or business recipient that is designed to generate a response in the form of an order, a request for further information, or a visit to a store or other place of business for purchase of a product."[23] The Direct Marketing Association (DMA) reports that direct-marketing-driven sales represent about 10 percent of the total U.S. gross domestic product (GDP)—an astounding figure! In 2007, the DMS tells us that direct-to-consumer commerce totaled $400 billion, of which $160 billion was on-line, $40 billion was via radio, and $160 billion was via television. The DMA forecasts that sales direct marketing drives will grow by 6.4 percent through 2009.[24]

Clearly, direct marketing has the potential for high impact. Let's look at the most popular types of direct marketing, starting with the oldest—buying through the mail.

Mail Order

In 1872, Aaron Montgomery Ward and two partners put up $1,600 to mail a one-page flyer that listed their merchandise with prices, hoping to spur a few more sales for their retail store.[25] The mail-order industry was born, and today consumers can buy just about anything through the mail. Mail order comes in two forms: catalogs and direct mail.

Catalogs

A **catalog** is a collection of products offered for sale in book form, usually consisting of product descriptions accompanied by photos of the items. Catalogs came on the scene within a few decades of the invention of movable type over 500 years ago, but they've come a long way since then.[26]

The early catalogs Montgomery Ward and other innovators such as Sears and JCPenney pioneered targeted people in remote areas who lacked access to stores. Today, the catalog customer is likely to be an affluent career woman with access to more than enough stores but without the time or desire to go to them. According to the DMA, over two-thirds of U.S. adults order from a catalog at least once a year.[27] Catalog mania extends well beyond clothing and cosmetics purchases. PC marketers HP and Dell both aggressively send out promotional catalogs that feature their own products along with accessories from a variety of manufacturers.

Many stores use catalogs to complement their in-store efforts—Neiman-Marcus is famous for featuring one-of-a-kind items like diamond-encrusted bras or miniature working versions of Hummers in its mailings as a way to maintain the store's image as a purveyor of unique and upscale merchandise. These upscale features change regularly, and avid Neiman's fans love to get the new catalog to find out what the next one is.

A catalog strategy allows the store to reach people in the United States who live in areas too small to support a store. But also, more and more U.S. firms use catalogs to reach overseas markets as well. Companies like Lands' End and Eddie Bauer do brisk

direct marketing
Any direct communication to a consumer or business recipient designed to generate a response in the form of an order, a request for further information, and/or a visit to a store or other place of business for purchase of a product.

catalog
A collection of products offered for sale in book form, usually consisting of product descriptions accompanied by photos of the items.

Michael S.
Munro
a professor at Florida International University
My Advice for Woodtronics would be to choose

Option

real people, **Other Voices**

I would choose **Option 3** because the original product does not exactly fit the project's needs and the Evolution platform is the best

state of the art product. It is critical to retain the support of the architect who made the referral because the architect can be the source of continuing sales leads in the future. Jeffrey Brechman needs to stress the importance of matching the trading room configuration to the new flat screen technology, which, in turn, can become a show piece for new business for the architect as well. ➤

sales in Europe and Asia where consumers tend to buy more goods and services through the mail in the first place than do Americans. Lands' End opened up a central warehouse in Berlin and attacked the German market with catalogs. The company trained phone operators in customer service and friendliness and launched an aggressive marketing campaign to let consumers know of the Lands' End lifetime warranty (German catalog companies require customers to return defective merchandise within two weeks to receive a refund). Although local competitors protested and even took the company to court, the case was settled in the American company's favor, and the Yankee invasion continues.

Catalog Choice started in 2007 as a Web site that enabled consumers to opt out of receiving catalogs by big companies (much like a "do not call" list for telemarketers). Part of the site's motivation is to reduce the waste unwanted catalogs create. However, when the 2007 holiday season came around, many catalog marketers initially didn't heed the requests of the consumers who signed up at Catalog Choice and mailed to them anyway. Since then, additional pressure has been put on the catalogers to comply and the Direct Marketing Association (DMA) itself has begun an initiative to help industry firms better police their own practices.[28]

Direct Mail

direct mail
A brochure or pamphlet that offers a specific good or service at one point in time.

Unlike a catalog retailer that offers a variety of merchandise through the mail, **direct mail** is a brochure or pamphlet that offers a specific good or service at one point in time. A direct-mail offer has an advantage over a catalog because the sender can personalize it. Charities, political groups, and other not-for-profit organizations also use a lot of direct mail.

Just as with e-mail spamming, many Americans are overwhelmed with direct-mail offers—"junk mail"—that mostly end up in the trash. This problem was amplified following the anthrax scare of 2001, when a lot of people became more reluctant to open mail from a source they couldn't identify. Procter & Gamble halted shipments of samples of Always Maxi Pads because consumers received lumpy packages without a clearly identified sender. Nissan once canceled a direct-mail push for its Altima model because the unusual packages spurred calls from fearful consumers.[29] The direct-mail industry constantly works on ways to monitor what companies send through the mail and provides some help when it allows consumers to "opt out" of at least some mailing lists.

Telemarketing

telemarketing
The use of the telephone to sell directly to consumers and business customers.

Telemarketing is direct marketing an organization conducts over the telephone (but why do they always have to call during dinner?). It might surprise you to learn that telemarketing actually is more profitable for business markets than for consumer markets. When business-to-business marketers use the telephone to keep in contact with smaller customers, it costs far less than a face-to-face sales call yet still lets small customers know they are important to the company.

The Federal Trade Commission (FTC) established the *National Do Not Call Registry* to allow consumers to limit the number of telemarketing calls they receive. The idea is that telemarketing firms check the registry at least every 31 days and clean their phone lists accordingly. Consumers responded very positively to the regulation, and over 100 million have posted their numbers on the Registry to date. Some direct marketers initially challenged this action; they argued that it would put legitimate companies out of business while unethical companies would not abide by the regulation and continue to harass consumers. However, the National Do Not Call Registry, along with similar operations at the state level, now is an accepted part of doing business through direct marketing. The FTC maintains a list of violators on its Web site.[30]

The major issue on the horizon for telemarketers is whether they will be able to access cell phone numbers, as many consumers fear. In fact, rumors crop up from time to time that it's now necessary to place your cell number on the Do Not Call lists to avoid telemarketing calls (so far, that's not true). Especially for many young people, their cell phone often is their *only* phone, which makes the lack of penetration of this media a glaring hole in a tele-marketing strategy.[31]

Direct-Response Advertising

Direct-response advertising allows the consumer to respond to a message by immediately contacting the provider to ask questions or order the product. This form of direct market-ing can be very successful. While the Internet has for many companies become the medium of choice for direct marketing, direct advertising in magazines, newspapers, and television is still alive and well.

As early as 1950, the Television Department Stores channel brought the retailing envi-ronment into the television viewer's living room when it offered a limited number of prod-ucts the viewer could buy when she called the advertised company. Television sales picked up in the 1970s when two companies, Ronco Incorporated (you may have seen Ron Popeil on TV) and K-Tel International began to hawk products such as the Kitchen Magician, the Mince-O-Matic, and the Miracle Broom on television sets around the world.[32] Make a sim-ple phone call and one of these wonders could be yours. **Direct-response TV (DRTV)** includes short commercials of less than two minutes, 30-minute or longer infomercials, and the shows home shopping networks such as QVC and HSN broadcast. Top-selling DRTV product categories include exercise equipment, self-improvement products, diet and health products, kitchen appliances, and music.

The primitive sales pitches of the old days have largely given way to slick **infomercials**. These are half-hour- or hour-long commercials that resemble a talk show but they really are sales pitches. Although some infomercials still carry a low-class, sleazy stereotype, in fact, over the years numerous heavyweights from Apple Computer to Volkswagen have used this format.

direct-response advertising
A direct marketing approach that allows the consumer to respond to a message by immediately contacting the provider to ask questions or order the product.

direct-response TV (DRTV)
Advertising on TV that seeks a direct response, including short commercials of less than two minutes, 30-minute or longer infomercials, and home shopping networks.

infomercials
Half-hour or hour-long commercials that resemble a talk show but actually are sales pitches.

By the **People**, For the **People**

Personal selling and direct marketing are widely-used selling strategies in addition to advertising and public relations. Traditionally, firms largely dictate what we learn about their products via the information we get from their salespeople, infomercials, or catalogs. However, Web 2.0 changes this equation as many of us increasingly rely as much — or more so — on what other consumers have to say about a product. If these other users like it, they become a (free) extension of the firm's sales force. If they don't... well, that's another story. Consumer review Web sites like ConsumerReview.com and Epinions.com provide unvarnished evaluations of a huge range of products.

Now, there's even a source that lets consumers do a "reality check" on all those infomercials they see for miracle workouts that tighten abs or magically reduce the maximus of the gluteus. At *Justin Leonard's Fitness Infomercial Review*, people post reviews of the infomercials they see on TV—including horror stories based on their experiences after they order the gadgets. This is a real hot potato for direct marketers because one tainted review (fair or unfair) can turn off large numbers of potential customers. Indeed, some consumer review sites (such as Amazon.com) reserve the right to edit or remove user-generated content. Others like TripAdvisor allow restau-rant and hotel managers to talk back—they can actually respond to specific comments people make about their establishments. Whether anyone will pay attention is another matter.[33]

The *Fitness Infomercial Review* Web site lets real consumers share their experi-ences about the fitness products they order from infomercials.

Ethical Decisions in the Real World

Almost two-thirds of Americans have had some experience with mobile Internet use, and the adoption trend is most pronounced among teens and young adults, according to the Pew Research Center. About 60 percent of adults 18 to 29 use text messaging every day, compared with only 14 percent of their parents. Nearly one-third of young adults use mobile Internet. This is the future, because people take their media habits with them as they age.

This brings up one of the biggest implications of wider use of the mobile Web—marketers will increasingly rely on personalization. Already, collections of Web sites known as *ad networks* track consumer behavior across multiple sites and then shoot targeted ads to users. This customized technology works well; often yields ad response rates 5 to 10 times higher than standard banner ads.

ETHICS CHECK:

Find out what other students taking this course **would do** and **why** on **www.mypearsonmarketinglab.com**

Microsoft wants to jump on the personalization bandwagon. It recently filed a patent application that would use off-line data such as credit card transactions, estimated physical location (from cell-phone towers), and TV viewing habits to serve you a customized ad the next time you go on-line. The fact that you bought cleats for your soccer shoes this morning, went to a sports bar for a burger at lunch, and turned on ESPN when you got home would conceivably trigger a personalized sports ad on your cell phone. What's not to like about such a great marketing opportunity, right?

Is Microsoft crossing an ethical line with its "extreme personalization" aimed at mobile Internet usage by young people? Should it move ahead with its plan? Is your feeling about this different for college-age consumers versus younger ones? What would you do?

Ripped from the Headlines! See what happened in the Real World at **www.mypearsonmarketinglab.com**

Do you approve of companies that track what teenagers buy so they can send them personalized ad messages on their cellphones?

☐YES ☐NO

m-commerce
Promotional and other e-commerce activities transmitted over mobile phones and other mobile devices, such as Smart phones and personal digital assistants (PDAs).

M-Commerce

One final type of direct marketing is m-commerce. The "m" stands for "mobile," and **m-commerce** refers to the promotional and other e-commerce activities mobile phones and other mobile devices such as Smartphones and PDAs deliver. With over 3 billion mobile phones in use worldwide—more and more of them Internet-enabled—it makes sense that marketers would want to reach out and touch this large audience.[34]

M-commerce is certainly catching on in the United States, but it is on fire in Europe and Asia. For example, over half of Japan's 30-million-plus Internet users gain access to the Web by using their wireless phones because that's a cheaper way to do it there.[35] Young people worldwide are particularly big users of cell phones (walk your school halls—how many students have a phone glued to their ear?), which of course explains why all the cell phone companies advertise aggressively on high-school and college campuses.

M-commerce through text messages (such as an ad for a concert or a new restaurant) is known as *short-messaging system* (SMS) marketing. As with e-mail, m-commerce has a dark side. Some unscrupulous marketers have figured out a new scam called *spim* (the instant messaging version of spam). In some cases when your America Online Buddy List sends you a link to a hot news flash, instead you're taken to an advertising site or to a place to download a game. Clicking on the link not only installs the game but (unbeknownst to you) also sends the program to contacts on your buddy list. You may also wind up installing *adware*—software that runs undetected as it tracks your Web habits and then presents pop-up advertisements or even resets your home page to serve up content that relates to places you've surfed.[36]

Infomercials, or program-length advertisements, are widely used to promote goods ranging from fitness products and kitchen knives to luxury items and real estate.

Real People, Real Choices

Jeffrey Brechman

Jeffrey chose:

Option

How it Worked out at Woodtronics

Jeffrey chose **Option 2**. He reasoned that as a salesperson his goal is to uncover customers' needs and bring them the correct solutions. He went directly to the client with a mock up of the new Evolution platform. He didn't let the architect know he had done this until he was confident that the client was completely satisfied with the new alternative. The client was impressed with the product's ability to handle his Jersey City project's technical needs such as the heat transfer, which was a critical element in the client's requirements.

Woodtronics got the sale; what's more, the client decided to purchase the new product within a week of seeing the demo. This is highly unusual in an industry where the typical time from demo to decision is as much as six months. And, in the long run, Jeffrey's relationship with the architect improved greatly because he realized that Jeffrey's product was going to help the project and make it more likely that the architect's client would be happy with the end result. This was a win-win situation for all involved.

How Woodtronics Measures Success

The most powerful measure of success in a sales situation is of course—sales! The new client is now a major account for the company. But, professional selling is all about building ongoing relationships in addition to making a sale today. Woodtronics went on to do other projects for the client in the United States, and Jeffrey is now pursuing an opportunity to provide additional trading room furniture for them in London. In addition, this solution worked so well that Jeffrey is able to use it as a great example when he makes sales presentations about the new Evolution platform to prospective clients.

The Evolution trading desk.

Refer back to **page 439** for Jeffrey's story ➡

Brand **YOU**!

Personal selling works!

No one can sell your brand better than you can. Sell yourself by connecting with people you know. Networking is the hidden job market—80 percent of jobs are filled through networking. You know more people than you realize. And it is those people who can lead you to more people. Before you know it, you'll be interviewing! Master the skill of networking in Chapter 14 of the *Brand You* supplement.

Objective Summary ➡ Key Terms ➡ Apply

1. Objective Summary (pp. 440–442)

Understand the important role of personal selling and how it fits into the promotion mix.

Personal selling occurs when a company representative interacts directly with a prospect or customer to communicate about a good or service. Many organizations rely heavily on this approach because at times the "personal touch" can carry more weight than mass-media material. Generally, a personal selling effort is more important when a firm engages in a push strategy, in which the goal is to "push" the product through the channel of distribution so that it is available to consumers. Today's salespeople are less likely to use transactional selling (hard-sell tactics) in favor of relationship selling, in which they pursue win-win relationships with customers.

Key Term

personal selling, p. 440

2. Objective Summary (pp. 442–443)

Explain how technology enhances the personal selling effort.

All sorts of technologies are available to enhance the personal selling process. However, as anyone making sales calls knows, technology cannot and should not *replace* personal selling. Customer relationship management (CRM) software and related approaches aid salespeople in managing their business with clients. Voice-over Internet protocol (VoIP) is coming into play more and more, as are wireless technologies and especially Smart phones.

3. Objective Summary (p. 444)

Identify the different types of sales jobs.

Order takers process transactions that the customer initiates. *Technical specialists* are very involved in giving product demonstrations, giving advice and recommendations, and product setup. *Missionary salespeople* work to stimulate purchase, but don't take actual orders. *New-business salespeople*, or *order getters*, are responsible for finding new customers and calling on them to present the company's products. And finally, *team selling* has become very prevalent in many industries as a way to bring together the expertise needed to better satisfy customer needs.

Key Terms

order taker, p. 444

technical specialist, p. 444

missionary salesperson, p. 444

new-business salesperson, p. 444

order getter, p. 444

team selling, p. 444

4. Objective Summary (pp. 444–445)

Describe the two approaches to personal selling.

Transactional selling focuses on making an immediate sale with little concern for developing a long-term relationship with the customer. It is sometimes called the "hard sell" approach. In contrast, *relationship selling* involves securing, developing, and maintaining long-term relationships with profitable customers. Developing a customer relationship means ensuring that you and the customer find more ways to add value over time.

Key Terms

transactional selling, p. 445

relationship selling, p. 445

5. Objective Summary (pp. 446–449)

List the steps in the creative selling process.

The steps in the personal selling process include prospecting and qualifying, preapproach, approach, sales presentation, handling objections, close, and follow-up. These steps combine to form the basis for communicating the company's message to the customer. Learning the intricacies of each step can aid the salesperson in developing successful relationships with clients and in bringing in the business for their companies.

Key Terms

creative selling process, p. 446 (Figure 14.1, p. 446)

prospecting, p. 446

preapproach, p. 447

approach, p. 447

sales presentation, p. 448

close, p. 448

follow-up, p. 449

6. Objective Summary (pp. 449–452)

Explain the role of sales management.

Sales management includes planning, implementing, and controlling the selling function. The responsibilities of a sales manager include the following: creating a sales force strategy, including the structure and size of the sales force; recruiting, training, and compensating the sales force; and evaluating the sales force.

Key Terms

sales management, p. 449 (Figure 14.2, p. 449)

sales territory, p. 449

7. Objective Summary (pp. 452–456)

Understand the elements of direct marketing.

Direct marketing refers to any direct communication designed to generate a response from a consumer or business customer. Some of the types of direct marketing activities are mail order (catalogs and direct mail), telemarketing, and direct-response advertising, including infomercials and home shopping networks.

Key Terms

direct marketing, p. 453

catalog, p. 453

direct mail, p. 454

telemarketing, p. 454

direct-response advertising, p. 455

direct-response TV (DRTV), p. 455

infomercials, p. 455

m-commerce, p. 456 (Ethical Decisions in the Real World, p. 456)

Chapter **Questions** and **Activities**

Concepts: Test Your Knowledge

1. What role does personal selling play within the marketing function?
2. What is relationship selling? How does it differ from transactional selling?
3. What is prospecting? What does it mean to qualify the prospect? What is the preapproach? Why are these steps in the creative selling process that occur before you ever even contact the buyer so important to the sale?
4. What are some ways you might approach a customer? Would some work better in one situation or another?
5. What is the objective of the sales presentation? How might you overcome buyer objections?
6. Why is follow-up after the sale so important in relationship selling?
7. Describe the role of sales managers. What key functions do they perform?
8. What is direct marketing? Describe the more popular types of direct marketing.
9. What is m-commerce?

Choices and Ethical Issues: You Decide

1. In general, professional selling has evolved from hard-sell to relationship selling. Do organizations still use the hard-sell style? If so, what types? What do you think the future holds for these organizations? Will the hard sell continue to succeed—that is, are there instances in which transactional selling is still appropriate? If so, when?
2. One reason experts cite for the increase in consumer catalog shopping is the poor quality of service available at retail stores. What do you think about the quality of service you get from most retail salespeople with whom you come into contact? What are some ways retailers can improve the quality of their sales associates?
3. Based on the salesperson compensation figures the chapter supplies, do you think professional salespeople are appropriately paid? Why or why not? What is it that salespeople do that warrants their compensation?

4. Would training and development needs of salespeople vary depending on how long they have been in the business? Why or why not? Would it be possible (and feasible) to have different training programs for salespeople who are at different career stages?
5. What would be the best approach for a sales manager to determine the appropriate rewards program to implement for her salespeople? What issues are important when she decides what rewards to offer?
6. M-commerce allows marketers to engage in *location commerce* when they can identify where consumers are and send them messages about a local store. Do you think consumers will respond positively to this? What do you think are the benefits for consumers of location commerce? Do you see any drawbacks (such as invasion of privacy)?

Practice: Apply What You've Learned

1. Assume a firm that publishes university textbooks has just hired you as a field salesperson. Your job requires that you call on university faculty members to persuade them to adopt your textbooks for their classes. As part of your training, your sales manager has asked you to develop an outline of what you will say in a typical sales presentation. Write that outline.
2. This chapter introduced you to several key success factors sales managers look for when hiring relationship salespeople. Are there other key success factors you can identify for relationship salespeople? Explain why each is important.
3. For you personally, what are the pros and cons of personal selling as a career choice? Make a list under the two columns and be as specific as you can in explaining each pro and con.
4. Consider carefully the potentially annoying downsides of various forms of direct marketing to consumers. As a marketer, what would you do to ensure that your firm's direct marketing efforts don't turn customers off to your product?

Miniproject: Learn by Doing

The purpose of this miniproject is to help you understand the advantages of following the creative selling process.

1. With several of your classmates, create a new product in a category that most college students buy regularly (for example, toothpaste, shampoo, pens, pencils, soft drinks ... anything that interests you that might be sold through a drugstore like Walgreens). Make up a new brand name and some creative features and benefits of the new product you come up with.

2. Develop a plan for executing each of the steps in the creative selling process. Carefully ensure that you cover all the bases of how you would go about selling your product to an organizational buyer at Walgreens for distribution to all stores.

3. Report on your plan to your class, and ask the other students for feedback on whether or not your approach will convince the Walgreens buyer to make a purchase.

Real people, **real surfers**: explore the web

A critical part of successful selling today is the effective use of technology and information by salespeople. Sometimes salespeople feel like they have information and technology "overload"—just too much to cope with. A well-run CRM system can go a long way toward organizing these important elements of selling.

Visit the Web sites you'll find at **www.customerthink. com** and **www.salesforce.com**. Peruse some of the content and then answer the following questions:

1. What are some of the most important issues surrounding successful use of CRM?

2. Pick any two experts featured on the sites and briefly summarize their key messages.

3. How do you suppose CRM can help link the marketing and sales functions in a firm? Hint: Consider the information needed by both groups, and how that information is collected, analyzed, and distributed for use.

4. Assume that you have been hired as a sales manager for a small firm with 20 outside salespeople. Would CRM be useful in such a setting? Why or why not?

Marketing Plan Exercise

Assume for a moment that you are Jeffrey Brechman at Woodtronics. Consider the nature of his business—its products and solutions, and the markets in which he competes for business. In developing his marketing plan, Jeffrey must be very careful to use the elements of the marketing communication mix (1) in an integrated way so that he communicates a consistent message and (2) in a way that represents the best investment of promotional dollars that will give Woodtronics the greatest returns.

1. Would personal selling be a high priority Jeffrey in his marketing plan? Why or why not?

2. What approach to personal selling would you recommend he build into his plan? Why do you recommend this approach?

3. Is there any place for direct marketing within Jeffrey's marketing plan? Justify your answer. If you believe direct marketing is called for, what type(s) do you recommend, and why?

Marketing in Action Case

Real **Choices** at **Eli Lilly**

Consider the following two opposing points of view on the value of pharmaceutical sales representatives (reps) to the medical community. One viewpoint is that reps provide valuable information about their products so they help keep physicians up-to-date. Because reps supply detailed information about drugs to doctors, they are often referred to as "detail salespeople" or simply "detailers." Providing this information helps save doctors the time of looking it up themselves. In addition, reps provide physicians with product samples.

An alternative and opposing view is that because there are so many pharmaceutical sales reps—over 100,000 at last count—that they do nothing more than drive up the cost of prescription drugs without providing much more information than what doctors can easily discover on their own on-line. In addition, pharmaceutical reps are notorious for the giveaways they provide doctors and office staff. Freebies not only include product samples but also all sorts of gifts, office supplies, and catered lunches to influence decision making that's not necessarily in patients' best interests. As evidence of the potential excess of such gifts, in the tiny state of Vermont alone drug makers spent nearly $778,000 in 2006 to buy food for doctors. Furthermore, pharmaceutical companies often invite doctors to speaker programs at lavish restaurants or even vacation resorts for a day or two of "professional development" activities. Unfortunately, these junkets have caused the entire pharmaceutical industry to come under considerable public and government scrutiny and criticism.

Which of the viewpoints do *you* believe? Probably most people feel that the reality is somewhere between the two extreme positions. Eli Lilly, a large manufacturer and distributor of pharmaceuticals, adopted such a middle-ground position. The increasingly adversarial environment toward the pharmaceutical industry caused Eli Lilly to implement a strategic change in its sales force it calls "the sales force of the future." Highlights include 1) the company gives reps smaller territories to cover so they can learn more about each doctor and develop a stronger professional relationship, 2) Lilly cross-trains reps on more drugs so the firm can reduce the number of different reps who call on the same doctor, 3) it emphasizes customer service and gives reps more time to respond to doctors' requests for information, and 4) it pays bonuses based partly on a rep's level of customer service to doctors. The company hopes that doctors will view their reps as an invaluable resource to help them tailor treatments for patients. At the same time, Lilly hopes to reduce its sales force costs so it can keep drug prices down.

But questions remain as to the potential effectiveness of Lilly's changes. One problem is that Lilly's sales force represents less than 4 percent of the entire population of pharmaceutical sales reps. What will happen to Lilly's business if other companies do not follow suit? In addition, what will Eli Lilly do if it finds that the changes it made actually result in reduced sales? Will the company revert back to its old ways and rehire more sales reps? One critic of the industry, who worked as a drug rep herself for nine years, said: "I was able to keep my job by how many pills I could push through my territory. All that mattered was pushing of pills. Companies are not going to change something that works even if they are under public relations fire."

Finally, some doctors' offices, clinics, and hospitals have begun to implement limits on what they allow pharmaceutical sales reps to give their doctors. Minnesota recently passed a law to forbid drug companies from giving doctors in the state more than $50 worth of food or other gifts per year. As a result, reps are more likely to offer doctors a Styrofoam cup full of M&Ms than a lobster lunch. Other states may follow. New Jersey, for example, has established a task force to look at ways to limit pharmaceutical company gifts and money.

Clearly, the pharmaceutical industry is badly in need of some self-policing before the government steps in and further polices the business for them.

You Make the Call

1. What is the decision Eli Lilly faces?
2. What factors are important to understand this decision situation?
3. What are the alternatives?
4. What decision(s) do you recommend?
5. What are some ways to implement your recommendation?

Based on: Gardiner Harris, "Minnesota Limit on Gifts to Doctors May Catch On," *New York Times*, October 12, 2007, http://www.nytimes.com/2007/10/12/us/12gift.html?scp=1&sq=pharmaceutical+sales+reps&st=nyt (accessed May 10, 2008); Jeff Swiatek, "Lilly Sales Force Stresses Its Service, Knowledge," *The Indianapolis Star*, May 18, 2006; Joann Loviglio, "Medical Centers Cracking Down on Freebies From Drug Reps," *The Associated Press State & Local Wire*, May 28, 2006; Tom Murphy, "Selling Change at Lilly; Company Overhauls Strategy Its Thousands of Sales Reps Use to Tout Drugs to Doctors," *Indianapolis Business Journal*, May 15, 2006, 1.

Chapter 15

Part 1   Make Marketing Value Decisions (Chapters 1, 2, 3)
Part 2   Understand Consumers' Value Needs (Chapters 4, 5, 6, 7)
Part 3   Create the Value Proposition (Chapters 8, 9, 10, 11)
Part 4   Communicate the Value Proposition (Chapters 12, 13, 14)
Part 5   Deliver the Value Proposition (Chapters 15, 16)

Deliver Value through Supply Chain Management, Channels of Distribution, and Logistics

DARDEN
RESTAURANTS.
DARDEN DIRECT DISTRIBUTION

Bahama Breeze.   Olive Garden ITALIAN RESTAURANT   Red Lobster

Jim
Lawrence
Profile ▼

▼ Q & A with Jim Lawrence

Q) **What I do when I'm not working?**
A) Sailing, exercise, travel, music, family outings.

Q) **First job?**
A) Drugstore soda clerk. ... I learned quickly about customer service!

Q) **Career high?**
A) Being promoted to my current position at Darden Restaurants.

Q) **My motto to live by?**
A) The golden rule.... Treat others as you want to be treated.

Q) **My management style?**
A) Open, collaborative, results-driven.

Q) **Don't do this when interviewing with me?**
A) Be unprepared.

Q) **My pet peeve?**
A) Pettiness.

A Decision Maker at Darden Restaurants

Jim Lawrence is Senior Vice President, Supply Management & Purchasing for Darden Restaurants. In this position, Jim leads Darden's Supply Management team with responsibility for food and beverage procurement, e-commerce, and purchasing support for the organization. Darden Restaurants, Inc. is the world's largest casual dining operator, with annual revenues in excess of $5.5 billion. The company owns and operates over 1,400 restaurants under the brands Red Lobster, Olive Garden, Bahama Breeze, and Seasons 52.

Previously, Jim was Vice President of Supply Management for the company, where he directed the efforts of Darden's distribution partners, Smallwares Resupply operations, Capital Equipment Logistics, Building Services for Darden's Support Center campus, and all Seafood Distribution functions.

Jim joined Darden in 1995 as Manager of Transportation, and fewer than two years later was promoted to Director of Seafood Inventory Management and Distribution. He then became Director of Restaurant Distribution Services, where he successfully managed transportation costs related to delivering products to Darden's restaurants, effectively managed seafood inventory levels for Red Lobster and the company's other brands, and led the company's conversion to a new distribution network supplier. In October 2000, Jim was promoted to Vice President of Supply Management.

Before joining Darden, Jim held numerous sales and distribution positions with Mobil Corporation and RJR Nabisco, Inc. He holds a bachelor of business administration in marketing from the University of Georgia and a master of business administration from the Crummer Graduate School of Business at Rollins College. Jim is a past executive board member of the Orlando Festival of Orchestras; a past executive board member of Efficient Foodservice Response, an industry consortium of suppliers, distributors, and operators; and is currently serving as a board member of Second Harvest Food Bank of Central Florida.

real people, **Real Choices**

Decision Time at Darden Restaurants

In 2000, Darden Restaurant's supply chain experienced significant disruption when its exclusive food distributor declared bankruptcy. This unfortunate situation not only caused tremendous service challenges with its restaurants (late deliveries, product shortages, etc.), but it also created instability within the supply chain regarding supplier management. Many suppliers discontinued shipments or curtailed production because of the uncertainty of working with such a volatile distributor. In mid-2000, Darden converted its distribution support to two national distributors. Within 18 months, one of the new distributors decided to exit the business because of a change in its business strategy.

The volatility of the chain distributor component of the foodservice industry forced the company to evaluate the model it had traditionally used to support food distribution to its restaurants. Darden needed to take steps to protect its supply chain by ensuring that its restaurants would always have access to the volume and quality of food it needed. In addition, the Darden executive team realized that this disruption in fact created a significant opportunity to work with supply chain partners in a more innovative, collaborative way *if* the company could develop a new way to do business.

> **Things to remember:**
>
> Darden depends on a stable distribution system to supply its restaurants. If menu items aren't available or the food is of inferior quality, diners won't blame the distributors — they will blame the restaurant. Jim needs a solution that will minimize the company's dependence on other companies or at least he has to insure that there is a backup in place if a key distributor encounters business problems.

There were two major requirements for this new operating model. First, the model had to provide supply chain protection for Darden Restaurants both from a corporate perspective and from a local-restaurant perspective. For example, Darden would need to own all inventory to guard against any supply chain disruptions associated with bankruptcies. Second, the model needed to provide the infrastructure to enable Darden and its supply chain partners to work in more collaborative ways so that they could more easily develop and implement supply chain innovation. By finding a way to erase the traditional barriers to collaboration (business silos, limited trust between trading partners) between the firm and its suppliers, Jim and his team felt they could realize these objectives.

Jim considered his Options 1·2·3

1 Option **Internalize the food delivery function by developing a food distribution network owned and operated by Darden that would support all of its restaurants.** This increased internal control would lead to higher service levels (on-time deliveries, case fill, overall restaurant satisfaction levels). And this approach would protect the supply chain from disruptive, external influences like those Darden had recently experienced. In addition, internal control and structure could allow for greater visibility of all synergistic opportunities regarding the entire supply chain. For example, since all of the costs/revenues would be fully visible to the organization in a privately-held enterprise, cost/benefit decision making would be more effective. Since the entity would be 100 percent owned and operated by Darden, the company could more easily obtain collaboration with the supplier community. On the other hand, this option would take Darden into a business function in which it did not have core competencies. There might be some costs associated with learning this end of the business—which might in return result

in just the kinds of supply chain disruptions Darden was trying to avoid. Also, as a stand-alone entity, Darden would be somewhat isolated from established systems distributors that possess food distribution experience and expertise. In addition, this path would be more costly than other options because of higher capital costs and significant human resource cost implications.

2 Option **Work with third-party logistics (3PL) providers to establish a food distributor network.** This option would allow Darden to work with strong 3PL companies with tremendous expertise in other industries (grocery retail, consumer products, industrial, etc.) but limited experience working with chain operators in the casual dining sector. Darden could take advantage of the best-practice approaches in the industry. This form of minimized engagement would mean that Darden would limit human resource efforts as compared with a wholly owned option. And the economies of scale for 3PLs that deal in greater volume for multiple clients could result in lower costs because these firms would have greater power to negotiate their prices with vendors. On the other hand, since 3PL companies typically work with consumer products, industrial, and retail companies, they have little to no experience providing food distribution support to casual dining operators. Service, especially in the early stages of the conversion, could be negatively impacted. Converting from current, traditional distribution networks to an internal network could also result in supply chain disruptions.

3 Option **Work with traditional systems distributors under a new operating model.** This model would provide support from distributors with the experience and expertise in casual dining while using an operating model that would protect the supply chain. Under this model, the traditional foodservice distributor would manage the warehousing and transportation components, while Darden would manage inventory control and customer service. Darden could provide higher levels of service to its restaurants by working with established, proven service providers with strong relationships with and knowledge of these establishments. Converting to this system would be strictly strategic/structural; no physical conversions (warehousing locations, employee changes, etc.) would occur. This continuity would ensure that Darden would avoid supply chain disruptions. On the other hand, foodservice systems distributors lack the knowledge and experience of working in other industries, so these companies do not have the ability to apply best-practice approaches. These distributors would be forced to develop new linkages/systems elements to support this new way of doing business and all employees would have to accept the new approach.

Now, put yourself in Jim's shoes: Which option would you choose, and why?

You Choose

Which **Option** would you choose, and **why**?

1. ☐YES ☐NO   **2.** ☐YES ☐NO   **3.** ☐YES ☐NO

See what **option** Jim chose and its success on **page 493**

1

OBJECTIVE

Understand the concept of the value chain and the key elements in a supply chain. (pp. 464–468)

Place: The Final Frontier

As the management that runs Darden's restaurant chains knows, you can cook the best food in the world, but if you're missing the raw ingredients to make Capellini Pomodoro at Olive Garden or West Indies Ribs at Bahama Breeze in the right quantities when diners order these dishes, the competition will eat your lunch.

Distribution may be the "final frontier" for marketing success. After years of hype, many consumers no longer believe that "new and improved" products really *are* new and improved. Nearly everyone, even upscale manufacturers and retailers, tries to gain market share through aggressive pricing strategies. Advertising and other forms of promotion are so commonplace they have lost some of their impact. Marketers know that *place* may be the only one of the *Four Ps* to offer an opportunity for competitive advantage—especially since many consumers now expect "instant gratification" by getting just what they want when the urge strikes.

That's why savvy marketers are always on the lookout for novel ways to distribute their products. In 2007, Microsoft had been pushing its own Microsoft Game Studios to produce more video games for its Xbox console. Throughout the Xbox's history up to that point, Microsoft's contracted developers created its core exclusive game franchises. These included such hits as *Halo* by Bungie, *Dead or Alive 3*, by Techmo, and *Star Wars: Knights of the Old Republic*, by Bioware/LucasArts. In 2007, one of Microsoft's first, big, completely in-house development efforts produced *Crackdown*, a game that features a free-roaming "sandbox" gameplay environment (a la *Grand Theft Auto*) and a futuristic backdrop where you play the role of a genetically-engineered super soldier/cop that pretty much stops all the crime in the city *Terminator*-style.

But Microsoft was concerned that the finicky gaming public wouldn't accept *Crackdown*. If the game flopped, that would be a huge blow to its in-house studio. What was its solution to this problem? Very creative *distribution*—specifically, capitalizing on the strong circulation of a franchise it owned the rights to, but did not develop, to sell copies of the game. The *Crackdown* package included software that also enabled players to go onto Xbox Live and download the beta demo of the highly-anticipated Bungie-developed game, *Halo 3*. This distribution ploy worked like gangbusters and the company sold enough copies of the *Crackdown* title to warrant the development of a sequel—a great launch for Microsoft's first in-house developed game. Also, the distribution approach introduced many people to Xbox Live who had never had a reason to go there before.[1]

In another novel distribution approach, Apple's iTunes and Pepsi partnered on a deal where select 20 oz. bottles of Pepsi sodas had a redemption code under the cap that the buyer could use for one free iTunes music download (yes, believe it or not there once was a time when Apple needed to get people to try out the service for the first time). In this case though, the combined distribution and promotional effort "went flat" with only 5 million of the 100 million songs redeemed. Also, there was a "one-in-three" chance of being a winner, but many wily fans discovered that if they simply tilted the bottle, the text under the cap was legible enough to tell if it was a winning bottle or not. The concept fizzled, but venerable Apple chief Steve Jobs said he was happy with it nonetheless because it "introduced a lot more people to iTunes."[2] Indeed, at this point it's hard to find anyone (at least under 90) who is not familiar with the successful iTunes on-line distribution strategy that has shaken up the music industry.

The Microsoft and Apple examples remind us that distribution is not just about trucks and warehouses. This chapter is about the science and art of getting goods and services to customers. As you'll see in Figure 15.1, we are now in Part 5 of the book: "Deliver the Value Proposition." A large part of the marketer's ability to deliver a value proposition rests on his ability to understand and develop effective distribution strategies. In this chapter, we will begin with a broad view of the company through the lens of the value chain concept.

Recall from Chapter 1 that the **value chain** is a useful way to appreciate all the players that typically work together to create value. This term refers to a series of activities involved in the design, production, marketing, delivery, and support of any product or service. In addition to marketing activities, the value chain includes business functions such as human resource management and R&D (research and development).

Each link in the chain has the potential to either add or remove value from the product the customer eventually buys. Then we focus on the supply chain, which spans activities across multiple firms. The **supply chain** includes all the activities necessary to turn raw materials into a good or service and put it into the hands of the consumer or business customer. Often, of course, firms like Darden may decide to bring in outside companies to accomplish these activities—firms with whom the company has likely developed some form of partnership or cooperative business arrangement.

Next, we talk about *distribution channels*, which are a subset of the supply chain. Distribution channels are important because a large part of the marketer's ability to deliver the value proposition rests on his ability to understand and develop effective distribution strategies. Finally, we look at *logistics management*, which is the process of actually moving goods through the supply chain. We will define each of these terms in greater detail in subsequent sections of this chapter, but for now let's look at the broader activities of the value chain.

The Value Chain and Supply Chain Management

Delivering value to the customer is of primary importance. As we saw in Chapter 1, the value chain concept is a way to look at how firms deliver benefits to consumers. They do this when they coordinate a range of activities that result in the customer's receipt of a satisfactory good or service. As we can see in Figure 15.2, the value chain consists of five primary activities (inbound logistics, operations, outbound logistics, marketing and sales, and service) and four support activities (procurement, technology development, human resource management, and firm infrastructure).

Figure 15.1 | Make and Deliver Value

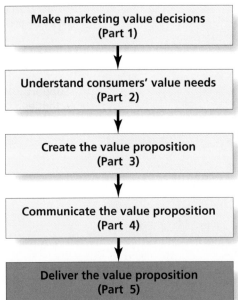

- Make marketing value decisions (Part 1)
- Understand consumers' value needs (Part 2)
- Create the value proposition (Part 3)
- Communicate the value proposition (Part 4)
- Deliver the value proposition (Part 5)

value chain
A series of activities involved in designing, producing, marketing, delivering, and supporting any product. Each link in the chain has the potential to either add or remove value from the product the customer eventually buys.

supply chain
All the activities necessary to turn raw materials into a good or service and put it in the hands of the consumer or business customer.

A.J.
Otjen
a professor at Montana State University–Billings
My Advice for Darden Restaurants would be to choose

1
Option

real people, **Other** Voices

I would choose a variation of **Option 1**. Jim should be vertically integrated across the entire value chain of the food industry. Each element could become volatile or profitable depending on how

well it is managed, and thus it is worth owning each piece of pie of the chain, and also contracting with more of each piece of the pie where necessary. Geographically, where the company lacks core competencies, he can build a hybrid system of warehousing and transportation. Direct or indirect corporate or local relationships would be determined by costs/benefits management and periodically reviewed. And he needs to recruit personnel expertise from the best practices of the other industries to gain ongoing knowledge of continued improvement. ➤

Figure 15.2 | The Generic Value Chain

The value chain (a concept first proposed by Professor Michael Porter) encompasses all the activities a firm does to create goods and services that in turn create value for the consumer and make a profit for the company.

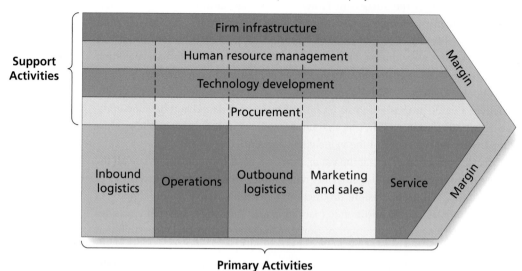

Source: Reprinted with the permission of the Free Press, a Division of Simon & Schuster Adult Publishing Group, from Michael E. Porter, *Competitive Advantage: Creating and Sustaining Superior Performance*. Copyright 1985-1998 by Michael Porter.

Specifically, during the stage of *inbound logistics* activity, the company receives materials it needs to manufacture its products. This activity includes taking delivery of the input materials, warehousing, and inventory control. In *operations*, activities transform the materials into final product form, such as by machining, packaging, and assembly. *Outbound logistics* activities ship the product out to customers, while *marketing and sales* handle advertising, promotion, channel selection, and pricing. *Service* activities enhance or maintain the value of the product, such as by installation or repair. We call this process a *value chain* because each of these activities adds value to the product the customer eventually buys.

Links in the Supply Chain

The value chain is an overarching concept of how firms create value. Similarly, the supply chain also encompasses components external to the firm itself, including all activities necessary to convert raw materials into a good or service and put it in the hands of the consumer or business customer. Thus, **supply chain management** is the coordination of flows among the firms in a supply chain to maximize total profitability. These "flows" include not only the physical movement of goods but also the sharing of information about the goods—that is, supply chain partners must synchronize their activities with one another. For example, they need to communicate information about which goods they want to purchase (the procurement function), about which marketing campaigns they plan to execute (so that the supply chain partners can ensure there will be enough product to supply the increased demand that results from the promotion), and about logistics (such as sending advance shipping notices to alert their partners that products are on their way). Through these information flows, a company can effectively manage all the links in its supply chain, from sourcing to retailing.

In his book *The World Is Flat: A Brief History of the Twenty-First Century* that we discussed way back in Chapter 3, Thomas Friedman addresses a number of high-impact trends in global supply chain management.[3] One such development is the trend whereby companies we traditionally know for other things remake themselves as specialists who take over the coordination of clients' supply chains for them. UPS is a great example of this trend. UPS, which used to be "just" a package delivery service, today is much, much more because it

supply chain management
The management of flows among firms in the supply chain to maximize total profitability.

specializes in **insourcing**. This process occurs when companies contract with a specialist who services their supply chains. Unlike the *outsourcing process* we reviewed in Chapter 3 where a company delegates nonessential tasks to subcontractors, insourcing means that the client company brings in an external company to run its essential operations. While we tend to associate UPS with those little brown trucks zipping around town delivering boxes, the company now also performs the following functions for some of its clients:

- If your Toshiba laptop needs repair, you drop it off at a UPS store. It's shipped to a UPS unit where UPS employees (not Toshiba technicians) actually get your machine booted back up.

- When you order a pizza from Papa John's, it's UPS that dispatches the drivers and schedules the delivery of pizza sauce, dough, and so on that the local store uses to make your "everything except anchovies."

- Order a pair of shoes at Nike.com and a UPS employee fills the order, bags it, labels it, and delivers it to your house.

The major difference between a supply chain and a channel of distribution (a term we also introduced in Chapter 1) is the number of members and their functions. A supply chain is broader; it consists of those firms that supply the raw materials, component parts, and supplies necessary for a firm to produce a good or service <u>plus</u> the firms that facilitate the movement of that product to the ultimate users of the product. This last part—the firms that get the product to the ultimate users—is the **channel of distribution**. (There will be more on channels of distribution in a bit.)

Now, let's take a closer look at one company's supply chain—Hewlett-Packard's Pavilion line of notebook computers we show in Figure 15.3. HP Pavilion uses hundreds of suppliers to manufacture its notebooks, and it sells those items at hundreds of on-line and off-line retailers worldwide. And it's noteworthy that the role of individual firms within the supply chain depends on your perspective. If we look at Hewlett-Packard's supply chain, Intel is a supplier, and Best Buy is a member of its channel of distribution. From Intel's perspective, however, Hewlett-Packard is a customer. From the perspective of Best Buy, Hewlett-Packard is a supplier.

In our example, Intel takes raw materials such as silicon and adds value when it turns them into chips, which it brands as "Core," "Centurion," "Celeron," and "Pentium." Intel then ships chips to Hewlett-Packard, which combines them with the other components of a computer (and places the famous "Intel Inside" stickers on the outside), again adding

insourcing
A practice in which a company contracts with a specialist firm to handle all or part of its supply chain operations.

channel of distribution
The series of firms or individuals that facilitates the movement of a product from the producer to the final customer.

Figure 15.3 | HP's Supply Chain

The supply chain for computer maker HP's line of notebooks includes firms that supply component parts for the machines as well as retailers such as Best Buy and Circuit City. Each firm in the chain adds value through its inputs to provide the notebook the consumer wants at the lowest cost.

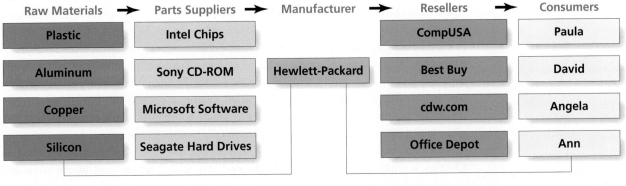

value. Best Buy takes the finished product and adds value when it provides display, sales support, repair service, and financing for the customer.

Now that you understand the basics of the value chain and the supply chain, let's dig into the nitty-gritty and understand how products actually get from point A to point B.

2

OBJECTIVE

Explain what a distribution channel is and what functions distribution channels perform.

(pp. 468–472)

Distribution is Important Because... You Can't Sell What Isn't There!

So you've created your product—priced it, too. And you've done the research to understand your target market and created a marketing message. Sorry, you're still not done—now you need to get what you make out into the marketplace. As we noted earlier, a channel of distribution is a series of firms or individuals that facilitates the movement of a product from the producer to the final customer. In many cases, these channels include an organized network of producers (or manufacturers), wholesalers, and retailers that develop relationships and work together to make products conveniently available to eager buyers.

Distribution channels come in different shapes and sizes. The bakery around the corner where you buy your cinnamon rolls is a member of a channel, as is the baked goods section at the local supermarket, the Starbucks that sells biscotti to go with your double mocha cappuccino, and the bakery outlet store that sells day-old rolls at a discount.

A channel of distribution consists of, at a minimum, a producer—the individual or firm that manufactures or produces a good or service—and a customer. This is a *direct channel*. For example, when you buy a loaf of bread at a mom-and-pop bakery, you're buying through a direct channel. Firms that sell their own products through Web sites, catalogs, toll-free numbers, or factory outlet stores use direct channels.

But life (and marketing) usually isn't that simple: Channels often are *indirect* because they include one or more **channel intermediaries**—firms or individuals such as wholesalers, agents, brokers, and retailers who in some way help move the product to the consumer or business user. For example, a baker may choose to sell his cinnamon buns to a wholesaler that will in turn sell boxes of buns to supermarkets and restaurants that in turn sell them to consumers.

Functions of Distribution Channels

Distribution channels perform a number of functions that make possible the flow of goods from the producer to the customer. Someone must handle these functions, be it the producer or a channel intermediary. Sometimes firms even "delegate" part of the distribution function to the customer, such as the venturesome shopper who picks up a new 60-inch HD TV from Circuit City's loading dock to avoid paying for home delivery.

Channels that include one or more organizations or intermediaries often can accomplish certain distribution functions more effectively and efficiently than can a single organization. As we saw in Chapter 3, this is especially true in international distribution channels where differences among countries' customs, beliefs, and infrastructures can make global marketing a nightmare. Even small companies can succeed in complex global markets when they rely on distributors that know local customs and laws.

Overall, channels provide the time, place, and ownership utility we described in Chapter 1. They make desired products available when, where, and in the sizes and quantities that customers desire. Suppose, for example, you want to buy that perfect bouquet of flowers for a special someone. You *could* grow them yourself or even "liberate"

channel intermediaries
Firms or individuals such as wholesalers, agents, brokers, or retailers who help move a product from the producer to the consumer or business user.

them from a cemetery if you were *really* desperate (very classy!). Fortunately, you can probably just accomplish this task with a simple phone call or a few mouse clicks, and "like magic" a local florist delivers a bouquet to your honey's door. Now, think about what just happened behind the scenes to make this possible. These days, large growers harvest and electronically sort acres of flowers, then auction them to buyers at a huge wholesale flower market such as the one in Amsterdam. From there they ship the flowers by air to importers in New York, who inspect them for insects and disease and in turn transport them to over 170 wholesalers

Supermarkets like this one are channel intermediaries. They buy fresh fruits and vegetables from farmers and make them available to consumers on a daily basis.

around the country. These wholesalers distribute the cut flowers to local florists who combine them into bouquets for their customers. The channel members—the growers, the auction house, the importers, the wholesalers, and the local florists—all work together to create just the gifts for budding lovers—and save you a lot of time and hassles (not to mention letting you score all those brownie points for sending the flowers in the first place).

Distribution channels provide a number of logistics or physical distribution functions that increase the efficiency of the flow of goods from producer to customer. How would we buy groceries without our modern system of supermarkets? We'd have to get our milk from a dairy, our bread from a bakery, our tomatoes and corn from a local farmer, and our flour from a flour mill. And forget about specialty items such as Twinkies or Coca-Cola. The companies that make these items would have to handle literally millions of transactions to sell to every individual who craves a junk-food fix.

Distribution channels create *efficiencies* because they reduce the number of transactions necessary for goods to flow from many different manufacturers to large numbers of customers. This occurs in two ways. The first is **breaking bulk**. Wholesalers and retailers purchase large quantities (usually cases) of goods from manufacturers but sell only one or a few at a time to many different customers. Second, channel intermediaries reduce the number of transactions when they **create assortments**—they provide a variety of products in one location—so that customers can conveniently buy many different items from one seller at one time.

Figure 15.4 provides a simple example of how distribution channels work. This simplified illustration includes five producers and five customers. If each producer sold its product to each individual customer, 25 different transactions would have to occur—not exactly an efficient way to distribute products. But with a single intermediary who buys from all five manufacturers and sells to all five customers, we quickly cut the number of transactions to 10. If there were 10 manufacturers and 10 customers, an intermediary would reduce the number of transactions from 100 to just 20. Do the math: Channels are efficient.

breaking bulk
Dividing larger quantities of goods into smaller lots in order to meet the needs of buyers.

creating assortments
Providing a variety of products in one location to meet the needs of buyers.

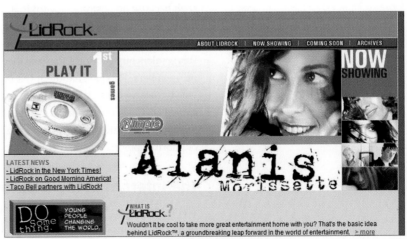

A company called LidRock discovered a competitive advantage by devising a novel way for record companies and movie studios to distribute samples—mini CDs stuck in the lids of beverage cups.

Figure 15.4 | Reducing Transactions via Intermediaries

One of the functions of distribution channels is to provide an assortment of products. Because the customers can buy a number of different products at the same location, this reduces the total costs of obtaining a product.

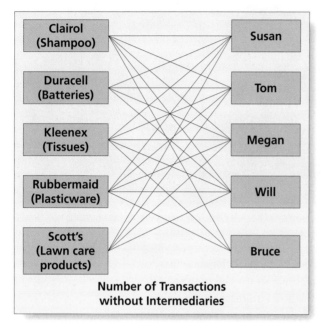

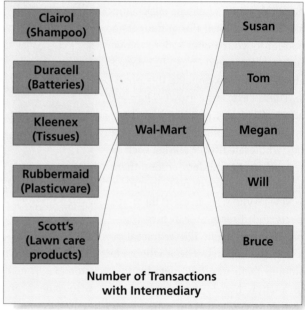

The transportation and storage of goods is another type of physical distribution function. Retailers and other channel members move the goods from the production point to other locations where they can hold them until consumers want them. Channel intermediaries also perform a number of **facilitating functions** that make the purchase process easier for customers and manufacturers. For example, intermediaries often provide customer services such as offering credit to buyers. Many of us like to shop at department stores because if we are not happy with the product we can take it back to the store where cheerful customer service personnel are happy to give us a refund (at least in theory). These same customer services are even more important in business-to-business markets where customers purchase larger quantities of higher-priced products.

Some wholesalers and retailers assist the manufacturer when they provide setup, repair, and maintenance service for products they handle. For example, Best Buy has its Geek Squad and Circuit City offers its own breed of geeks it calls Firedog. And channel members perform a risk-taking function. If a retailer buys a product from a manufacturer and it just sits on the shelf because no customers want it, he is stuck with the item and must take a loss. Perishable items present an even greater risk of spoilage.

Finally, intermediaries perform a variety of communication and transaction functions. Wholesalers buy products to make them available for retailers and sell products to other channel members. Retailers handle transactions with final consumers. Channel members can provide two-way communication for manufacturers. They may supply the sales force, advertising, and other types of marketing communication necessary to inform consumers and persuade them that a product will meet their needs. And the channel members can be invaluable sources of information on consumer complaints, changing tastes, and new competitors in the market.

facilitating functions
Functions of channel intermediaries that make the purchase process easier for customers and manufacturers.

The Internet in the Distribution Channel

The Internet has become an important place for consumers to shop for everything from tulip bulbs to exotic vacations. By using the Internet, even small firms with limited resources enjoy the same market opportunities as their largest competitors to make their products available to customers around the globe.

E-commerce creates radical changes in distribution strategies. Manufacturing firms like Dell, HP, and Apple in the personal computer space rely heavily on Internet-driven direct-to-end-user distribution strategies, although all three are very active outside this channel (consider Apple Stores and Dell Kiosks). In most cases, though, end users still don't obtain products directly from manufacturers. Rather, goods flow from manufacturers to intermediaries and then on to the final customers.

With the Internet, this need for intermediaries and much of what we assume about the need and benefits of channels changes. As you know, an increasing number of consumers buy (or pirate?) their music as an Internet download, making retail music stores less necessary. Then too, as more and more consumers have access to faster broadband Internet service, downloadable movies soon will become the norm. In the spirit of "if you can't beat 'em, join 'em," Netflix has become a champion of downloadable movies straight to your PC.[4]

In the future, channel intermediaries that physically handle the product may become obsolete. Already companies are eliminating many traditional intermediaries because they find that they don't add enough value in the distribution channel—a process we call **disintermediation (of the channel of distribution)**. For marketers, disintermediation reduces costs in many ways: fewer employees, no need to buy or lease expensive retail property in high-traffic locations, and no need to furnish a store with fancy fixtures and decor. You can also see this process at work when you pump your own gas, withdraw cash from an ATM, or use your electronic pass for expressway tolls instead of forking over your money to a flesh-and-blood attendant who sits in a toll booth.

Some companies use the Internet to make coordination among members of a supply chain more effective in ways that end consumers never see. These firms develop better ways to implement **knowledge management**, which refers to a comprehensive approach that collects, organizes, stores, and retrieves a firm's information assets. These assets include both databases and company documents and the practical knowledge of employees whose past experience may be relevant to solving a new problem. If a firm shares this knowledge with other supply chain members, this more strategic management of information results in a win-win situation for all the partners.

But as with most things cyber, the Internet as a distribution channel brings pain with pleasure. One of the more vexing problems with Internet distribution is the potential for

Many distribution channel members provide customer services. Appliance and electronics retailers like Best Buy offer repair and warranty services for many of the products they sell.

Chris Carlson/AP Wide World Photos

disintermediation (of the channel of distribution)
The elimination of some layers of the channel of distribution in order to cut costs and improve the efficiency of the channel.

knowledge management
A comprehensive approach to collecting, organizing, storing, and retrieving a firm's information assets.

Debra A.
Laverie
a professor at Texas Tech University

My Advice for Darden Restaurants would be to choose

1
Option

real people, Other Voices

I would select **Option 3** because it provides the needed service, with limited disruption, and keeps Darden focused on its core competencies. Option 1 would take a great deal of time and money.

Option 2 is dangerous because of possible service disruptions. By building strong relationships with established service partners, Darden will have a solid distribution system in place. This option will need to be marketed to employees so they understand the new way of doing business. ➤

Ethical Decisions in the Real World

Before it got kicked off Facebook in July 2008, Scrabulous, a virtual knockoff of the Scrabble board game, attracted over 700,000 players a day and boasted nearly 3 million registered users. Scrabulous features a board that looks just like Scrabble including the same number of letter tiles with the same point values. Fabulous now has its own self-contained Web site, but when it was on Facebook players could send invitations to others on Facebook or search for strangers to play with by posting messages.

Everyone seems to love the on-line game—everyone, that is, except the companies that own the rights to Scrabble: Hasbro and Mattel, which sell it in North America and elsewhere respectively. They have denounced Scrabulous as distribution piracy and threaten legal action against its creators: two brothers in Calcutta named Rajat and Jayant Agarwalla who run a software development company and collect about $25,000 a month from on-line advertising.

ETHICS CHECK: ↖
Find out what other students taking this course **would do** and **why** on **www.mypearsonmarketinglab.com**

The threat of legal action has not gained the companies many admirers. Many Scrabulous fans, some of whom say they bought the board game for the first time after they played the on-line version on Facebook, call their approach heavy-handed and out of touch. Dozens of other Web sites offer unauthorized versions of Scrabble, but most force users to play in real time or require clunky downloads to play. Groups devoted to saving the game have been created on Facebook, and tens of thousands of fans threaten to boycott Hasbro and Mattel products.

Hasbro, meanwhile, said in a statement that Electronic Arts planned to release an on-line version of Scrabble soon. And Mattel, which signed a deal with RealNetworks last July, says that settling with the Agarwallas would set a bad precedent.

Is Scrabulous on-line distribution piracy? Is it ethical for the Agarwallas to accept advertising revenue from it? Should Hasbro and Mattel pursue the law suits? What would you do?

Ripped from the Headlines! See what happened in the Real World at **www.mypearsonmarketinglab.com**

Is it ethical for the creators of Scrabulous to accept advertising revenue from the game when people play it on Facebook even if it's a knockoff of the Scrabble board game?

☐ **YES** ☐ **NO**

on-line distribution piracy
The theft and unauthorized repurposing of intellectual property via the Internet.

on-line distribution piracy, which is the theft and unauthorized repurposing of intellectual property via the Internet. The college textbook industry has high potential for on-line piracy. It's not uncommon for U.S.-produced textbooks to make their way to unscrupulous individuals outside the country who translate the core content into the native language and post it on-line for distribution. And obviously, unauthorized downloads of music is a predominant issue for the "recording" industry—to the point where the whole nature of the industry has turned topsy-turvy. Many in the music business are rethinking exactly what—and where—is the value-added for what they do. If the value is just to sell CDs in plastic cases, the industry is likely doomed. More and more musical artists opt to defect from traditional record labels and introduce their tunes on-line, effectively taking control of the channel of distribution themselves.[5]

So far, we've learned what a distribution channel is and about some of the functions it performs. Now let's find out about different types of channel intermediaries and channel structures.

3

OBJECTIVE

Describe the types of wholesaling intermediaries found in distribution channels.
(pp. 472–476)

Channel Composition: Types of Wholesaling Intermediaries

How can you get your hands on a new Jack Johnson T-shirt? You could pick one up at your local music store, at a trendy clothing store like Hot Topic or maybe at its on-line store. You might buy an "official Jack Johnson concert T-shirt" from vendors during a show. Alternatively, you might get a "deal" on a bootlegged, unauthorized version of the same shirt a shady guy who stands *outside* the concert venue sells from a battered suitcase. Perhaps you shop on-line at **www.jackjohnsonmusic.com**. Each of these distribution alternatives traces a different path from producer to consumer. Let's look at the different types of wholesaling intermediaries and at different channel structures. We'll hold off focusing on retailers, which are usually the last link in the chain, until the next chapter.

Wholesaling intermediaries are firms that handle the flow of products from the manufacturer to the retailer or business user. There are many different types of consumer and business-to-business wholesaling intermediaries. Some of these are independent, but manufacturers and retailers can own them, too. Table 15.1 summarizes the important characteristics of each.

Independent Intermediaries

Independent intermediaries do business with many different manufacturers and many different customers. Because no manufacturer owns or controls them, they make it possible for many manufacturers to serve customers throughout the world while they keep prices low.

Merchant Wholesalers

Merchant wholesalers are independent intermediaries that buy goods from manufacturers and sell to retailers and other business-to-business customers. Because merchant wholesalers **take title** to the goods (that is, they legally own them), they assume certain risks and can suffer losses if products are damaged, become outdated or obsolete, are stolen, or just don't sell. On the other hand, because they own the products, they are free to develop their own marketing strategies, including setting the prices they charge their customers.

- *Full-service merchant wholesalers* provide a wide range of services for their customers, including delivery, credit, product-use assistance, repairs, advertising, and other promotional support—even market research. Full-service wholesalers often have their own sales force to call on businesses and organizational customers. Some general merchandise wholesalers carry a large variety of different items, whereas specialty wholesalers carry an extensive assortment of a single product line. For example, a candy wholesaler carries only candy and gum products, but he stocks enough different varieties to give your dentist nightmares for a year.

- In contrast, *limited-service merchant wholesalers* provide fewer services for their customers. Like full-service wholesalers, limited-service wholesalers *take title* to merchandise but are less likely to provide services such as delivery, credit, or marketing assistance to retailers. Specific types of limited-service wholesalers include the following:

  o *Cash-and-carry wholesalers* provide low-cost merchandise for retailers and industrial customers that are too small for other wholesalers' sales representatives to call on. Customers pay cash for products and provide their own delivery. Some popular cash-and-carry product categories include groceries, office supplies, and building materials.

  o *Truck jobbers* carry their products to small business customer locations for their inspection and selection. Truck jobbers often supply perishable items such as fruit and vegetables to small grocery stores. For example, a bakery truck jobber calls on supermarkets, checks the stock of bread on the shelves, removes outdated items, and suggests how much bread the store needs to reorder.

  o *Drop shippers* are limited-function wholesalers that take title to the merchandise but never actually take possession of it. Drop shippers take orders from and bill retailers and industrial buyers, but the merchandise is shipped directly from the manufacturer. Because they take title to the merchandise, they assume the same risks as other merchant wholesalers. Drop shippers are important to both the producers and the customers of bulky products, such as coal, oil, or lumber.

  o *Mail-order wholesalers* sell products to small retailers and other industrial customers, often located in remote areas, through catalogs rather than a sales force. They usually carry products in inventory and require payment in cash or by credit card before shipment. Mail-order wholesalers supply products such as cosmetics, hardware, and sporting goods.

wholesaling intermediaries
Firms that handle the flow of products from the manufacturer to the retailer or business user.

independent intermediaries
Channel intermediaries that are not controlled by any manufacturer but instead do business with many different manufacturers and many different customers.

merchant wholesalers
Intermediaries that buy goods from manufacturers (take title to them) and sell to retailers and other business-to-business customers.

take title
To accept legal ownership of a product and assume the accompanying rights and responsibilities of ownership.

Table 15.1 | Types of Intermediaries

Intermediary Type	Description	Advantages
INDEPENDENT INTERMEDIARIES	Do business with many different manufacturers and many different customers	Used by most small- to medium-sized firms
• **Merchant Wholesalers**	Buy (take title to) goods from producers and sell to organizational customers; either full or limited function	Allow small manufacturers to serve customers throughout the world they keep costs low
○ Cash-and-carry wholesalers	Provide products for small-business customers who purchase at wholesaler's location	Distribute low-cost merchandise for small retailers and other business customers
○ Truck jobbers	Deliver perishable food and tobacco items to retailers	Ensure perishable items are delivered and sold efficiently
○ Drop shippers	Take orders from and bill retailers for products drop-shipped from manufacturer	Facilitate transactions for bulky products
○ Mail-order wholesalers	Sell through catalogs, telephone, or mail order	Provide reasonably priced sales options to small organizational customers
○ Rack jobbers	Provide retailers with display units, check inventories, and replace merchandise for the retailers	Provide merchandising services to retailers
• **Merchandise Agents and Brokers**	Provide services in exchange for commissions	Maintain legal ownership of product by the seller
○ Manufacturers' agents	Use independent salespeople; carry several lines of noncompeting products	Supply sales function for small and new firms
○ Selling agents, including export/import agents	Handle entire output of one or more products	Handle all marketing functions for small manufacturers
○ Commission merchants	Receive commission on sales price of product	Provide efficiency primarily in agricultural products market
○ Merchandise brokers, including export/import brokers	Identify likely buyers and bring buyers and sellers together	Enhance efficiency in markets where there are many small buyers and sellers
• **MANUFACTURER-OWNED INTERMEDIARIES**	Limit operations to one manufacturer	Create efficiencies for large firms
○ Sales branches	Maintain some inventory in different geographic areas (similar to wholesalers)	Provide service to customers in different geographic areas
○ Sales offices	Carry no inventory; availability in different geographic areas	Reduce selling costs and provide better customer service
○ Manufacturers' showrooms	Display products attractively for customers to visit	Facilitate examination of merchandise by customers at a central location

○ *Rack jobbers* supply retailers with specialty items such as health and beauty products and magazines. Rack jobbers get their name because they own and maintain the product display racks in grocery stores, drugstores, and variety stores. These wholesalers visit retail customers on a regular basis to maintain levels of stock and refill their racks with merchandise. Think about how quickly magazines turn over on the rack—without an expert who pulls old titles and inserts new ones, retailers would have great difficulty ensuring you can buy the current issue of *US* magazine on on the first day it hits the streets.

Merchandise Agents or Brokers

Merchandise agents or brokers are a second major type of independent intermediary. Agents and brokers provide services in exchange for commissions. They may or may not take possession of the product, but they <u>never</u> take title; that is, they do not accept legal ownership of the product. Agents normally represent buyers or sellers on an ongoing basis, whereas clients employ brokers for a short period of time.

- *Manufacturers' agents*, or *manufacturers' reps*, are independent salespeople who carry several lines of noncompeting products. They have contractual arrangements with manufacturers that outline territories, selling prices, and other specific aspects of the relationship but provide little if any supervision. Manufacturers normally compensate agents with commissions based on a percentage of what they sell. Manufacturers' agents often develop strong customer relationships and provide an important sales function for small and new companies.

Rack jobbers are limited-service merchant wholesalers. These intermediaries own and maintain product display racks in retail stores.

- *Selling agents*, including *export/import agents*, market a whole product line or one manufacturer's total output. They often work like an independent marketing department because they perform the same functions as full-service wholesalers but do not take title to products. Unlike manufacturers' agents, selling agents have unlimited territories, and control the pricing, promotion, and distribution of their products. We find selling agents in industries such as furniture, clothing, and textiles.

- *Commission merchants* are sales agents who receive goods, primarily agricultural products such as grain or livestock, on *consignment*—that is, they take possession of products without taking title. Although sellers may state a minimum price they are willing to take for their products, commission merchants are free to sell the product for the highest price they can get. Commission merchants receive a commission on the sales price of the product.

- *Merchandise brokers*, including export/import brokers, are intermediaries that facilitate transactions in markets such as real estate, food, and used equipment, in which there are lots of small buyers and sellers. Brokers identify likely buyers and sellers and bring the two together in return for a fee they receive when the transaction is completed.

merchandise agents or brokers
Channel intermediaries that provide services in exchange for commissions but never take title to the product.

Manufacturer-Owned Intermediaries

Sometimes manufacturers set up their own channel intermediaries. In this way, they can operate separate business units that perform all the functions of independent intermediaries while at the same time they can still maintain complete control over the channel.

- *Sales branches* are manufacturer-owned facilities that, like independent wholesalers, carry inventory and provide sales and service to customers in a specific geographic area. We find sales branches in industries such as petroleum products, industrial machinery and equipment, and motor vehicles.

- *Sales offices* are manufacturer-owned facilities that, like agents, do not carry inventory but provide selling functions for the manufacturer in a specific geographic area. Because they allow members of the sales force to locate close to customers, they reduce selling costs and provide better customer service.

- *Manufacturers' showrooms* are manufacturer-owned or leased facilities in which products are permanently displayed for customers to visit. We often find manufacturers' showrooms in or near large merchandise marts, such as the furniture market in High Point, North Carolina. Merchandise marts are often multiple buildings in which one or more industries hold trade shows and many manufacturers have permanent showrooms. Retailers can visit either during a show or all year long to see the manufacturer's merchandise and make business-to-business purchases.

4 Types of Distribution Channels

OBJECTIVE

Describe the types of distribution channels and how *place* fits in with the other three Ps in the marketing mix.
(pp. 476–481)

Firms face many choices when they structure distribution channels. Should they sell directly to consumers and business users? Would they benefit if they included wholesalers, retailers, or both in the channel? Would it make sense to sell directly to some customers but use retailers to sell to others? Of course, there is no single best channel for all products. The marketing manager must select a channel structure that creates a competitive advantage for the firm and its products based on the size and needs of the target market. Let's consider some of the factors these managers need to think about.

When they develop distribution (place) strategies, marketers first consider different **channel levels**. This refers to the number of distinct categories of intermediaries that make up a channel of distribution. Many factors have an impact on this decision. What channel members are available? How large is the market? How frequently do consumers purchase the product? What services do consumers require? Figure 15.5 summarizes the different structures a distribution channel can take. The producer and the customer are always members, so the shortest channel possible has two levels. Using a retailer adds a third level, a wholesaler adds a fourth level, and so on. Different channel structures exist for both consumer and business-to-business markets.

And what about services? As we saw in Chapter 11, services are intangible, so there is no need to worry about storage, transportation, and the other functions of physical distribution. In most cases, the service travels directly from the producer to the customer. However, an intermediary we call an *agent* can enhance the distribution of some services when he helps the parties complete the transaction. Examples of these agents include insurance agents, stockbrokers, and travel agents (no, not everyone books their travel on-line).

Consumer Channels

As we noted earlier, the simplest channel is a direct channel. Why do some producers sell directly to customers? One reason is that a direct channel may allow the producer to serve its customers better and at a lower price than is possible if it included a retailer. A baker who uses a direct channel makes sure his customers have fresher bread than if he sells the loaves through a local supermarket. Furthermore, if the baker sells the bread through a supermarket, the price will be higher because of the supermarket's costs of doing business

channel levels
The number of distinct categories of intermediaries that populate a channel of distribution.

and its need to make its own profit on the bread. In fact, sometimes this is the *only* way to sell the product, because using channel intermediaries may boost the price above what consumers are willing to pay.

Figure 15.5 | Different Types of Channels of Distribution

Channels differ in the number of channel members that participate.

Major Types of Channels of Distribution

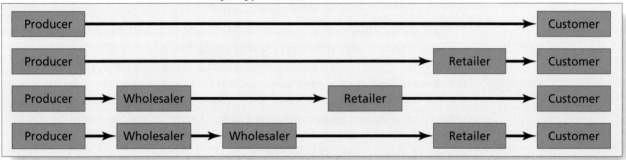

Typical Consumer Channels

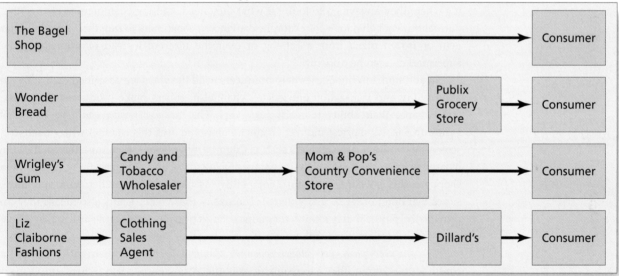

Business-to-Business Channels

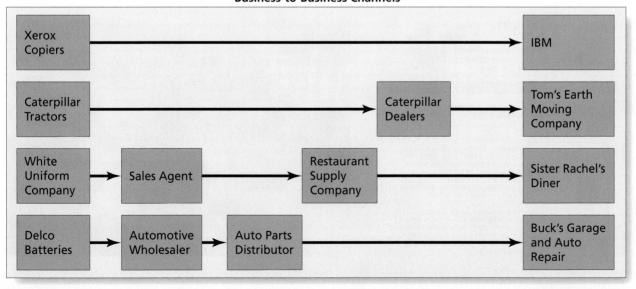

As we mentioned earlier, for many firms one of the most effective direct channels is to sell through the Internet. For example, small entrepreneurs Richie Lodico and Vinny Barbieri, owners of Eastern Meat Farms, Inc., discovered in the very early days of the Internet (they started their on-line business in 1995) that an on-line direct channel is a great way to continually expand their business globally. For years prior to going on-line, Lodico and Barbieri shipped sausages and cheeses across the country, but they didn't feel there was enough volume to justify the expense of direct marketing. However, with the advent of the Internet, **www.salami.com** was born (the URL alone must be worth a fortune today!). The company ships each order using Styrofoam and ice packs to ensure that customers from around the globe receive high-quality, fresh products, often for less than half the price they would have to pay for similar delicacies locally. Hot dog![6]

Another reason to use a direct channel is *control*. When the producer handles distribution, it maintains control of pricing, service, and delivery—all elements of the transaction. Because distributors and dealers carry many products, it can be difficult to get their sales forces to focus on selling one product. In a direct channel, a producer works directly with customers so it gains insights into trends, customer needs and complaints, and the effectiveness of its marketing strategies.

Why do producers choose to use indirect channels to reach consumers? A reason in many cases is that customers are familiar with certain retailers or other intermediaries—it's where they always go to look for what they need. Getting customers to change their normal buying behavior—for example, convincing consumers to buy their laundry detergent or frozen pizza from a catalog or over the Internet instead of from the corner supermarket—can be difficult.

In addition, intermediaries help producers in all the ways we described earlier. By creating utility and transaction efficiencies, channel members make producers' lives easier and enhance their ability to reach customers. The *producer–retailer–consumer channel* in Figure 15.5 is the shortest indirect channel. Panasonic uses this channel when it sells big-screen TVs through large retailers such as Circuit City or Best Buy. Because the retailers buy in large volume, they can obtain inventory at a low price and then pass these savings on to shoppers (this is what gives them a competitive advantage over smaller, more specialized stores that don't order so many items). The size of these retail giants also means they can provide the physical distribution functions such as transportation and storage that wholesalers handle for smaller retail outlets.

The *producer–wholesaler–retailer–consumer channel* is a common distribution channel in consumer marketing. Take ice cream, for example. A single ice-cream factory supplies, say, four or five regional wholesalers. These wholesalers then sell to 400 or more retailers such

Richard Lodico and Vinny Barbieri, owners of New York Italian Specialties, used the Internet to expand their business as Salami.com. It's turned out to be a meaty distribution strategy.

as grocery stores. The retailers, in turn, each sell the ice cream to thousands of customers. In this channel, the regional wholesalers combine many manufacturers' products to supply grocery stores. Because the grocery stores do business with many wholesalers, this arrangement results in a broad selection of products.

Business-to-Business Channels

Business-to-business distribution channels, as the name suggests, facilitate the flow of goods from a producer to an organizational or business customer. Generally, business-to-business channels parallel consumer channels in that they may be direct or indirect. For example, the simplest indirect channel in industrial markets occurs when the single intermediary—a merchant wholesaler we refer to as an *industrial distributor* rather than a retailer—buys products from a manufacturer and sells them to business customers.

Direct channels are more common to business-to-business markets than to consumer markets. As we saw in Chapter 6, this is because business-to-business marketing often means a firm sells high-dollar, high-profit items (a single piece of industrial equipment may cost hundreds of thousands of dollars) to a market made up of only a few customers. In such markets, it makes sense financially for a company to develop its own sales force and sell directly to customers—in this case the investment in an in-house sales force pays off.

Dual Distribution Systems

Figure 15.5 shows simple distribution channels. Well, once again we are reminded that life (or marketing) is rarely that simple: Producers, dealers, wholesalers, retailers, and customers alike may actually participate in more than one type of channel. We call these *dual* or *multiple distribution systems.*

The pharmaceutical industry provides a good example of multiple-channel usage. Pharmaceutical companies distribute their products in at least three types of channels.

By the **People**, For the **People**

Mass customization technologies involve customers in the distribution channel to a much greater extent than ever before. Today, the customer isn't necessarily just the last link in the chain who buys whatever products she finds in stores or on-line. These processes turn consumers into *co-designers* as they turn specific preferences into unique products tailored just for them. Every product made from scratch just for you? Not quite, unless you're Donald Trump. But, mass customization essentially lets you specify the size or appearance of each component in a product that the manufacturer then assembles for you. Want to design your own engagement ring? You can specify the stone type and size, the setting, and other features from a pre-existing inventory. Want a pair of jeans that fits perfectly even though one of your legs is an inch longer than the other? No problem; Levi Strauss can do it for you.

Dell is one of the oldest players in the mass customization distribution channel. Instead of assembling and selling standardized computers, *Dell's Choiceboards* technology allows consumers to design their own personal customer. It provides a menu of attributes, components, prices, and delivery options, and encourages consumers to specify the mix that exactly suits them. This Web-based direct ordering system is catching on in other industries as well: At VermontTeddyBears.com kids customize their teddy bear with a wide variety of add-ons such as shoes and glasses. Point.com helps customers identify service plans and wireless phones based on their budget and service profile. With Web 2.0, the distribution channel is no longer a one-way street.[7]

Kids can customize their teddy bears at the Vermont Teddy Bears Web site.

First, they sell to hospitals, clinics, and other organizational customers directly. These customers buy in quantity, and they purchase a wide variety of products. Because hospitals and clinics dispense pills one at a time rather than in bottles of 50, these outlets require different product packaging than when the manufacturer sells medications to other types of customers. Pharmaceuticals' second channel is an indirect consumer channel where the manufacturer sells to large drug store chains, like Walgreens, that distribute the medicines to their stores across the country. Alternatively, some of us would rather purchase our prescriptions in a more personal manner from the local independent drugstore where we can still get an ice-cream soda while we wait. In this version of the indirect consumer channel, the manufacturer sells to drug wholesalers that, in turn, supply these independents. Finally, third-party payers such as HMOs, PPOs, and insurance companies represent a third type of channel to which pharmaceutical companies also sell directly.

A recent development in the drug arena is the emergence of on-line sales of drugs from Canadian companies that offer pharmaceuticals at much lower prices than those available in the United States. U.S. drug manufacturers continue to aggressively push to halt this practice, but for now, Googling the words "Canadian drugs" yields hundreds of sellers including the likes of candrugstore.com, canadiandrugs.ca, canadapharmacychoice.com, and mapleleafpharmacy.com. And each of these home pages mentions the benefits of buying drugs from them to be shipped to the United States within the first paragraph!

Hybrid Marketing Systems

hybrid marketing system
A marketing system that uses a number of different channels and communication methods to serve a target market.

Instead of serving a target market with a single channel, some companies combine channels—direct sales, distributors, retail sales, and direct mail to create a **hybrid marketing system**.[8] For example, at one time you could buy a Xerox copier only directly through a Xerox salesperson. Today, unless you are a very large business customer, you likely will purchase a Xerox machine from a local Xerox authorized dealer, or possibly through the Xerox "Online Store." Xerox turned to an enhanced dealer network for distribution because such hybrid marketing systems offer companies certain competitive advantages, including increased coverage of the market, lower marketing costs, and a greater potential for customization of service for local markets.

Distribution Channels and the Marketing Mix

How do decisions regarding place relate to the other *Three Ps*? For one, place decisions affect pricing. Marketers that distribute products through low-priced retailers such as Wal-Mart, T.J. Maxx, and Marshalls will have different pricing objectives and strategies than will those that sell to specialty stores.

Distribution decisions can sometimes give a product a distinct position in its market. For example, Enterprise Rent-a-Car avoids being overly dependent on the cutthroat airport rental car market as it opens retail outlets in primary locations in residential areas and local business centers. This strategy takes advantage of the preferences of customers who are not flying and who want short-term use of a rental vehicle, such as when their primary vehicle is in the repair shop. Enterprise built such a successful following around this business model that loyal customers began to clamor for more Enterprise counters at airports. Now the company is a rising competitive threat to traditional airport car rental agencies such as Hertz and Avis.

And of course the nature of the product itself influences the retailers and intermediaries that we use. Manufacturers select mass merchandisers to sell mid-price-range products while they distribute top-of-the-line products such as expensive jewelry through high-end department and specialty stores.

Now we know what distribution channels and channel intermediaries are and the role of channel members in the distribution of goods and services. We also know that not all channels are alike. Some channels are direct while others are indirect, and indirect channels can be quite complex. And we've thought about how place fits in with the three other Ps in the marketing mix. The next section is about how marketers plan channel strategies to meet customer needs better than the competition—that is, how they seek the all-important competitive advantage.

Ethics in the Distribution Channel

The steps companies take to make their products available to consumers through distribution channels can create ethical dilemmas. For example, because their size gives them great bargaining power when negotiating with manufacturers, many large retail chains force manufacturers to pay a **slotting allowance**—a fee paid in exchange for agreeing to place a manufacturer's products on a retailer's valuable shelf space. Although the retailers claim that such fees pay the cost of adding products to their inventory, many manufacturers feel that slotting fees are more akin to highway robbery. Certainly, the practice prevents smaller manufacturers that cannot afford the slotting allowances from getting their products into the hands of consumers.

Another ethical issue involves the sheer size of a particular channel intermediary—be it manufacturer, wholesaler, retailer, or other intermediary. Giant retailer Wal-Mart, increasingly criticized for forcing scores of independent competitors (i.e., "mom-and-pop stores") to go out of business, has begun a very visible program to help its smaller rivals. The program offers hardware stores, dress shops, and bakeries near its new urban stores financial grants, training on how to survive with Wal-Mart in town, and even free advertising in Wal-Mart stores. Of course, Wal-Mart hopes to benefit from the program in cities like Los Angeles and New York, where its plan to build new stores in urban neighborhoods has met high resistance.[9]

Overall, it is important for all channel intermediaries to behave and treat each other in a professional, ethical manner—and, to do no harm to consumers (financially or otherwise) through their channel activities. Every intermediary in the channel wants to make money, but behavior by one to maximize its financial success at the expense of others' success is a doomed approach, as ultimately cooperation in the channel will break down. Instead, it behooves intermediaries to work cooperatively in the channel to distribute products to consumers in an efficient manner—making the channel a success for everybody participating in it (including consumers)!

slotting allowance
A fee paid in exchange for agreeing to place a manufacturer's products on a retailer's valuable shelf space.

5

OBJECTIVE

Understand the steps to plan a distribution channel strategy.
(pp. 481–487)

Plan a Channel Strategy

Do customers want products in large or small quantities? Do they insist on buying them locally, or will they purchase from a distant supplier? How long are they willing to wait to get the product? Inquiring marketers want to know!

Distribution planning works best when marketers follow the steps in Figure 15.6. In this section, we will first look at how manufacturers decide on distribution objectives and then examine what influences distribution decisions. Finally, we'll talk about how firms select different distribution strategies and tactics.

Firms that operate within a channel of distribution—manufacturers, wholesalers, and retailers—do *distribution planning*. In this section, our perspective focuses on distribution planning by producers and manufacturers rather than intermediaries because they, more often than intermediaries, take a leadership role to create a successful distribution channel.

Figure 15.6 | Steps in Distribution Planning

Distribution planning begins with setting channel objectives and includes developing channel strategies and tactics.

```
┌─────────────────────────────────────┐
│ Step 1: Develop distribution objectives │
└─────────────────────────────────────┘
                  │
                  ▼
┌─────────────────────────────────────┐
│ Step 2: Evaluate internal and external │
│      environmental influences          │
└─────────────────────────────────────┘
                  │
                  ▼
┌─────────────────────────────────────┐
│ Step 3: Choose a distribution strategy │
│ • Number of channel levels            │
│ • Conventional, vertical, or          │
│   horizontal marketing system         │
│ • Intensive, exclusive, or selective  │
│   distribution                        │
└─────────────────────────────────────┘
                  │
                  ▼
┌─────────────────────────────────────┐
│ Step 4: Develop Distribution Tactics  │
│ • Select channel partners             │
│ • Manage the channel                  │
│ • Develop logistics strategies        │
│    – Order processing                 │
│    – Warehousing                      │
│    – Materials handling               │
│    – Transportation                   │
│    – Inventory control                │
└─────────────────────────────────────┘
```

Step 1: Develop Distribution Objectives

The first step to decide on a distribution plan is to develop objectives that support the organization's overall marketing goals. How can distribution work with the other elements of the marketing mix to increase profits? To increase market share? To increase sales volume? In general, the overall objective of any distribution plan is to make a firm's product available when, where, and in the quantities customers want at the minimum cost. More specific distribution objectives, however, depend on the characteristics of the product and the market.

For example, if the product is bulky, a primary distribution objective may be to minimize shipping costs. If the product is fragile, a goal may be to develop a channel that minimizes handling. In introducing a new product to a mass market, a channel objective may be to provide maximum product exposure or to make the product available close to where customers live and work. Sometimes marketers make their product available where similar products are sold so that consumers can compare prices.

Step 2: Evaluate Internal and External Environmental Influences

After setting their distribution objectives, marketers must consider their internal and external environments to develop the best channel structure. Should the channel be long or short? Is intensive, selective, or exclusive distribution best? Short, often direct channels may be better suited for business-to-business marketers for whom customers are geographically concentrated and require high levels of technical know-how and service. Companies frequently sell expensive or complex products directly to final customers. Short channels with selective distribution also make more sense with perishable products, since getting the product to the final user quickly is a priority. However, longer channels with more intensive distribution are generally best for inexpensive, standardized consumer goods that need to be distributed broadly and that require little technical expertise.

The organization must also examine issues such as its own ability to handle distribution functions, what channel intermediaries are available, the ability of customers to access these intermediaries, and how the competition distributes its products. Should a firm use the same retailers as its competitors? It depends. Sometimes, to ensure customers' undivided attention, a firm sells its products in outlets that don't carry the competitors' products. In other cases, a firm uses the same intermediaries as its competitors because customers expect to find the product there. For example, you will find Harley-Davidson bikes only in selected Harley "boutiques" and Piaggio's Vespa scooters only at Vespa dealers (no sales through Wal-Mart for those two!), but you can expect to find Coca-Cola, Colgate toothpaste, and a Snickers bar in every possible outlet that sells these types of items.

Finally, when they study competitors' distribution strategies, marketers learn from their successes and failures. If the biggest complaint of competitors' customers is delivery speed, developing a system that allows same-day delivery can make the competition pale in comparison.

Step 3: Choose a Distribution Strategy

Planning distribution strategies means making at least three decisions. First, of course, distribution planning includes decisions about the number of levels in the distribution channel. We discussed these options earlier in the section on consumer and business-to-business channels and Figure 15.5 illustrates them again. Beyond the number of levels, distribution strategies also involve decisions about channel relationships—that is, whether a conventional system or a highly integrated system will work best—and the distribution intensity or the number of intermediaries at each level of the channel.

Conventional, Vertical, or Horizontal Marketing System?

Participants in any distribution channel form an interrelated system. In general, these marketing systems take one of three forms: conventional, vertical, or horizontal.

1. A **conventional marketing system** is a multilevel distribution channel in which members work independently of one another. Their relationships are limited to simply buying and selling from one another. Each firm seeks to benefit, with little concern for other channel members. Even though channel members work independently, most conventional channels are highly successful. For one thing, all members of the channel work toward the same goals—to build demand, reduce costs, and improve customer satisfaction. And each channel member knows that it's in everyone's best interest to treat other channel members fairly.

2. A **vertical marketing system (VMS)** is a channel in which there is formal cooperation among channel members at two or more different levels: manufacturing, wholesaling, and retailing. Firms develop vertical marketing systems as a way to meet customer needs better by reducing costs incurred in channel activities. Often, a vertical marketing system can provide a level of cooperation and efficiency not possible with a conventional channel, maximizing the effectiveness of the channel while also maximizing efficiency and keeping costs low. Members share information and provide services to other members; they recognize that such coordination makes everyone more successful when they want to reach a desired target market.

In turn there are three types of vertical marketing systems: administered, corporate, and contractual:

3a. In an *administered VMS*, channel members remain independent but voluntarily work together because of the power of a single channel member. Strong brands are able to manage an administered VMS because resellers are eager to work with the manufacturer so they will be allowed to carry the product.

3b. In a *corporate VMS*, a single firm owns manufacturing, wholesaling, and retailing operations. Thus, the firm has complete control over all channel operations. Retail giant Sears, for example, owns a nationwide network of distribution centers and retail stores.

3c. In a *contractual VMS*, cooperation is enforced by contracts (legal agreements) that spell out each member's rights and responsibilities and how they will cooperate. This arrangement means that the channel members can have more impact as a group than they could alone. In a wholesaler-sponsored VMS, wholesalers get retailers to work together under their leadership in a voluntary chain. Retail members of the chain use a common name, cooperate in advertising and other promotion, and even develop their own private-label products. Examples of wholesaler-sponsored chains are IGA (Independent Grocers' Alliance) food stores and Ace Hardware stores.

In other cases, retailers themselves organize a cooperative marketing channel system. A *retailer cooperative* is a group of retailers that establish a wholesaling operation to help them compete more effectively with the large chains. Each retailer owns shares in the wholesaler operation and is obligated to purchase a certain percentage of its inventory from the cooperative operation. Associated Grocers and True Value Hardware stores are examples of retailer cooperatives.

conventional marketing system
A multiple-level distribution channel in which channel members work independently of one another.

vertical marketing system (VMS)
A channel of distribution in which there is formal cooperation among members at the manufacturing, wholesaling, and retailing levels.

Jim
Lawrence

APPLYING Vertical Marketing System

Darden Restaurants had been relying on a conventional marketing system where its distributors were independent. Jim needs to decide if the company should shift gears and develop a VMS instead. ➡

ABOUT BLUE DIAMOND

Blue Diamond® Growers is the world's largest tree nut processing and marketing company. Founded in 1910, the cooperative celebrated its 90th anniversary in 2000. Blue Diamond® led the development of California's almond industry from a minor domestic specialty crop to the world leader in almond production and marketing. We continue to build markets and create new products, new uses, and new opportunities for members of Blue Diamond® Growers.

Headquartered in Sacramento, California, nearly 4000 California almond growers deliver over one-third of California's almonds annually to their cooperative. The crop is marketed to all 50 states and more than 90 foreign countries, making almonds California's largest food export, and the sixth largest U.S. food export. The California crop is valued annually at about $1 billion dollars.

Blue Diamond is a cooperative of over 4,000 almond growers who market together.

Franchise organizations are a third type of contractual VMS. Franchise organizations include a *franchiser* (a manufacturer or a service provider) who allows an entrepreneur (the *franchisee*) to use the franchise name and marketing plan for a fee. In these organizations, contractual arrangements explicitly define and strictly enforce channel cooperation. In most franchise agreements, the franchiser provides a variety of services for the franchisee, such as helping to train employees, giving access to lower prices for needed materials, and selecting a good location. In return, the franchiser receives a percentage of revenue from the franchisee. Usually the franchisees are obligated to follow the franchiser's business format very closely in order to maintain the franchise.

From the manufacturer's perspective, franchising a business is a way to develop widespread product distribution with minimal financial risk while at the same time maintaining control over product quality. From the entrepreneur's perspective, franchises are a helpful way to get a start in business.

horizontal marketing system
An arrangement within a channel of distribution in which two or more firms at the same channel level work together for a common purpose.

In a **horizontal marketing system**, two or more firms at the same channel level agree to work together to get their product to the customer. Sometimes unrelated businesses forge these agreements. For example, many 7-Eleven locations feature a Citibank Vcom electronic banking kiosk complete with ATM services, check cashing, bill paying, and Western Union money transfers. 7-Eleven leases the space to Citibank, and customers like it because they can do their shopping and their banking in one stop.

Most airlines today are members of a horizontal alliance that allows them to cooperate when they provide passenger air service. For example, American Airlines is a member of the **oneworld**® alliance which also includes British Airways, Cathay Pacific, Finnair, Iberia, JAL, LAN, Malev, Qantas, and Royal Jordanian Airways. These alliances increase passenger volume for all airlines because travel agents who book passengers on one of the airline's flights will be more likely to book a connecting flight on the other airline. To increase customer benefits, they also share frequent-flyer programs and airport clubs.[10]

Intensive, Exclusive, or Selective Distribution?

How many wholesalers and retailers should carry the product within a given market? This may seem like an easy decision: distribute the product through as many intermediaries as possible. But guess again. If the product goes to too many outlets, there may be inefficiency and duplication of efforts. For example, if there are too many Honda dealerships in town, there will be a lot of unsold Hondas sitting on dealer lots and no single dealer will be successful. But if there are not enough wholesalers or retailers to carry a product, this will fail to maximize total sales of the manufacturer's products (and its profits). If customers have to drive hundreds of miles to find a Honda dealer, they may instead opt for a Toyota, Mazda, or Nissan. Thus, a distribution objective may be to either increase or decrease the level of distribution in the market.

The three basic choices are intensive, exclusive, and selective distribution. Table 15.2 summarizes five decision factors—company, customers, channels, constraints, and competition—and how they help marketers determine the best fit between distribution system and marketing goals.

Intensive distribution aims to maximize market coverage by selling a product through all wholesalers or retailers that will stock and sell the product. Marketers use intensive distribution for products such as chewing gum, soft drinks, milk, and bread that consumers quickly consume and must replace frequently. Intensive distribution is necessary for these products because availability is more important than any other consideration in customers' purchase decisions.

In contrast to intensive distribution, **exclusive distribution** means to limit distribution to a single outlet in a particular region. Marketers often sell pianos, cars, executive training programs, television programs, and many other products with high price tags through exclusive distribution arrangements. They typically use these strategies with products that are high-priced and have considerable service requirements, and when a limited number of buyers exist in any single geographic area. Exclusive distribution enables wholesalers and retailers to better recoup the costs associated with long-selling processes for each customer and, in some cases, extensive after-sale service.

Of course, not every situation neatly fits a category in Table 15.2. (You didn't *really* think it would be that simple, did you?) For example, consider professional sports. Customers might not shop for games in the same way they shop for pianos. They might go to a game on impulse, and they don't require much individualized service. Nevertheless, professional sports use exclusive distribution. A team's cost of serving customers is high because of those million-dollar player salaries and multimillion-dollar stadiums. The alert reader (and/or sports fan) may note that there are some exceptions to the exclusive distribution of sports teams. New York has two football teams and two baseball teams, Chicago fields two baseball teams, and so on. We call market coverage that is less than intensive distribution but more than exclusive distribution **selective distribution**. This model fits when demand is so large that exclusive distribution is inadequate, but selling costs, service requirements, or other factors make intensive distribution a poor fit. Although a White Sox baseball fan may not believe that the Cubs franchise is necessary (and vice versa), Major League Baseball and even some baseball fans think the Chicago market is large enough to support both teams.

Selective distribution strategies are suitable for so-called *shopping products*, such as household appliances and electronic equipment for which consumers are willing to spend time visiting different retail outlets to compare alternatives. For producers, selective distribution means freedom to choose only those wholesalers and retailers that have a good credit rating, provide good market coverage, serve customers well, and cooperate effectively. Wholesalers and retailers like selective distribution because it results in higher profits than are possible with intensive distribution, in which sellers often have to compete on price.

intensive distribution
Selling a product through all suitable wholesalers or retailers that are willing to stock and sell the product.

exclusive distribution
Selling a product only through a single outlet in a particular region.

selective distribution
Distribution using fewer outlets than intensive distribution but more than exclusive distribution.

New Yorkers get to debate the merits of the Mets versus the Yankees because of selective distribution in that market.

Table15.2	Characteristics That Favor Intensive over Exclusive Distribution	
Decision Factor	**Intensive Distribution**	**Exclusive Distribution**
Company	Oriented toward mass markets	Oriented toward specialized markets
Customers	High customer density	Low customer density
	Price and convenience are priorities	Service and cooperation are priorities
Channels	Overlapping market coverage	Nonoverlapping market coverage
Constraints	Cost of serving individual customers is low	Cost of serving individual customers is high
Competition	Based on a strong market presence, often through advertising and promotion	Based on individualized attention to customers, often through relationship marketing

Step 4: Develop Distribution Tactics

As with planning for the other marketing Ps, the final step in distribution planning is to develop the distribution tactics necessary to implement the distribution strategy. These decisions are usually about the type of distribution system to use, such as a direct or indirect channel or a conventional or an integrated channel. Distribution tactics relate to the implementation of these strategies, such as how to select individual channel members and how to manage the channel.

These decisions are important because they often have a direct impact on customer satisfaction—nobody wants to have to wait for something they've bought! When Toyota first introduced the now wildly successful Scion, the company wisely came up with a new approach to distribute this youth-oriented vehicle that differs from its traditional Toyota distribution system. The company's overall goal was to cut delivery time to its impatient young customers to no more than a week by offering fewer model variations and doing more customization *at the dealer* rather than at the factory. The continuing resounding success of the Scion brand shows the power of tailoring distribution tactics differently for different markets.[11]

Select Channel Partners

When firms agree to work together in a channel relationship, they become partners in what is normally a long-term commitment. Like a marriage, it is important to both manufacturers and intermediaries to select channel partners wisely, or they'll regret the match-up later (and a divorce can be really expensive!). In evaluating intermediaries, manufacturers try to answer questions such as the following: Will the channel member contribute substantially to our profitability? Does the channel member have the ability to provide the services customers want? What impact will a potential intermediary have on channel control?

For example, what small to midsize firm wouldn't jump at the chance to have retail giant Wal-Mart distribute its products? With Wal-Mart as a channel partner, a small firm could double, triple, or quadruple its business. Actually, some firms that recognize size means power in the channel decided against selling to Wal-Mart because they are not willing to relinquish control of their marketing decision making. There is also a downside to choosing one retailer and selling only through that one retailer. If that retailer stops carrying the product, for example, the company will lose all its customers and it will be back to square one.

Another consideration in selecting channel members is competitors' channel partners. Because people spend time comparing different brands when purchasing a shopping product, firms need to make sure they display their products near similar competitors' products. If most competitors distribute their electric drills through mass merchandisers, a manufacturer has to make sure its brand is there also.

A firm's dedication to social responsibility may also be an important determining factor in the selection of channel partners. Many firms run extensive programs to recruit minority-owned channel members. Starbucks' famous organizationwide commitment to good corporate citizenship translates in one way into its "supplier diversity program" that works to help minority-owned business thrive.[12]

The new, youth-oriented Scion brand, a new line of vehicles from Toyota, gets delivered faster because the car company's new streamlined distribution strategy lets buyers customize the car on-line.

Manage the Channel

Once a manufacturer develops a channel strategy and aligns channel members, the day-to-day job of managing the channel begins. The **channel leader**, sometimes called a *channel captain*, is the dominant firm that controls the channel. A firm becomes the channel leader because it has power relative to other channel members. This power comes from different sources:

- A firm has *economic power* when it has the ability to control resources.

- A firm such as a franchiser has *legitimate power* if it has legal authority to call the shots.

- A producer firm has *reward* or *coercive power* if it engages in exclusive distribution and has the ability to give profitable products and to take them away from the channel intermediaries.

In the past, producers traditionally held the role of channel captain. Procter & Gamble, for example, developed customer-oriented marketing programs, tracked market trends, and advised retailers on the mix of products most likely to build sales. As large retail chains evolved, giant retailers such as Target and Wal-Mart began to assume a leadership role because of the sheer size of their operations. Today it is much more common for the big retailers to dictate their needs to producers instead of producers controlling what product is available to retailers.

Because producers, wholesalers, and retailers depend on one another for success, channel cooperation helps everyone. Channel cooperation is also stimulated when the channel leader takes actions that make its partners more successful. High intermediary profit margins, training programs, cooperative advertising, and expert marketing advice are invisible to end customers but are motivating factors in the eyes of wholesalers and retailers. Haggar Apparel, for example, finds ways to help its retail channel partners—especially the smaller ones—become more successful. By improving the speed and accuracy of reorders, retailers are able to maintain inventory levels necessary to satisfy customers while avoiding ordering errors.

Of course, relations among members in a channel are not always full of sweetness and light. Because each firm has its own objectives, channel conflict may threaten a manufacturer's distribution strategy. Such conflict most often occurs between firms at different levels of the same distribution channel. Incompatible goals, poor communication, and disagreement over roles, responsibilities, and functions cause conflict. For example, a producer is likely to feel the firm would enjoy greater success and profitability if intermediaries carry only its brands, but many intermediaries believe they will do better if they carry a variety of brands.

In this section, we've been concerned with the distribution channels firms use to get their products to customers. In the next section, we'll look at the area of logistics—physically moving products through the supply chain.

Logistics: Implement the Supply Chain

OBJECTIVE

Explain logistics and how it fits into the supply chain concept.
(pp. 487–492)

Some marketing textbooks tend to depict the practice of marketing as 90 percent planning and 10 percent implementation. Not so! In the "real world," many managers argue that this ratio should be reversed. Marketing success is very much the art of getting the timing right and delivering on promises—*implementation*.

That's why marketers place so much emphasis on efficient **logistics**; the process of designing, managing, and improving the movement of products through the supply chain. Logistics includes purchasing, manufacturing, storage, and transport. From a company's viewpoint, logistics takes place both *inbound* to the firm (raw

channel leader
A firm at one level of distribution that takes a leadership role, establishing operating norms and processes based on its power relative to other channel members.

logistics
The process of designing, managing, and improving the movement of products through the supply chain. Logistics includes purchasing, manufacturing, storage, and transport.

Jim
Lawrence

Logistics is a crucial aspect of the food business because many of the items a restaurant needs are perishable. Jim needs to select an option that will be most likely to get menu items to Darden's restaurants around the country quickly and in the right quantities.

physical distribution
The activities that move finished goods from manufacturers to final customers, including order processing, warehousing, materials handling, transportation, and inventory control.

Transporting and storing products requires companies to carefully track the movement of goods through the supply chain.

materials, parts, components, and supplies) and *outbound* from the firm (work-in-process and finished goods). Logistics is also a relevant consideration regarding product returns, recycling and material reuse, and waste disposal—*reverse logistics*.[13] As we saw in earlier chapters, that's becoming even more important as firms start to more seriously consider *sustainability* as a competitive advantage and put more effort into maximizing the efficiency of recycling to save money and the environment at the same time. So you can see logistics is an important issue across all elements of the supply chain. Let's examine this process more closely.

The Lowdown on Logistics

Have you ever heard the saying, "An army travels on its stomach"? *Logistics* was originally a term the military used to describe everything needed to deliver troops and equipment to the right place, at the right time, and in the right condition. In business, logistics is similar in that its objective is to deliver exactly what the customer wants—at the right time, in the right place, and at the right price. The application of logistics is essential to the efficient management of the supply chain.

The delivery of goods to customers involves **physical distribution**, which refers to the activities that move finished goods from manufacturers to final customers. Physical distribution activities include order processing, warehousing, materials handling, transportation, and inventory control. This process impacts how marketers physically get products where they need to be, when they need to be there, and at the lowest possible cost. Effective physical distribution is at the core of successful logistics.

When a firm does logistics planning, however, the focus also should be on the customer. When managers thought of logistics as physical distribution only, the objective was to deliver the product at the lowest cost. Today, forward-thinking firms consider the needs of the customer first. The customer's goals become the logistics provider's goals. And this means that when they make most logistics decisions, firms must decide on the best trade-off between low costs and high customer service. The appropriate goal is not just to deliver what the market needs at the lowest cost but rather to provide the product at the lowest cost possible *as long as the firm meets delivery requirements*. Although it would be nice to transport all goods quickly by air, that is certainly not practical. But sometimes air transport is necessary to meet the needs of the customer, no matter the cost.

Logistics Functions

When they develop logistics strategies, marketers must make decisions related to the five functions of logistics: order processing, warehousing, materials handling, transportation, and inventory control. For each decision, managers need to consider how to minimize costs while maintaining the service customers want.

Order Processing

Order processing includes the series of activities that occurs between the time an order comes into the organization and the time a product goes out the door. After a firm receives an order it typically sends it electronically to an office for record keeping and then on to the warehouse to fill it. When the order reaches the warehouse, personnel there check to see if the item is in stock. If it is not, they put the order on back-order status. That information goes to the office and then to the customer. If the item is available, the company locates it in the warehouse, packages it for shipment, and schedules it for pickup by either in-house or external shippers.

Fortunately, many firms automate this process with **enterprise resource planning (ERP) systems**. An ERP system is a software solution that integrates information from across the entire company, including finance, order fulfillment, manufacturing, and transportation. Data need to be entered into the system only once, and then the organization automatically shares this information and links it to other related data. For example, an ERP system ties information on product inventories to sales information so that a sales representative can immediately tell a customer whether the product is in stock.

Warehousing

Whether we deal with fresh-cut flowers, canned goods, or computer chips, at some point goods (unlike services) must be stored. Storing goods allows marketers to match supply with demand. For example, toys and other gift items are big sellers at Christmas, but toy factories operate 12 months of the year. **Warehousing**—storing goods in anticipation of sale or transfer to another member of the channel of distribution—enables marketers to provide *time utility* to consumers by holding on to products until consumers need them.

Part of developing effective logistics means making decisions about how many warehouses we need and where and what type of warehouse each should be. A firm determines the location of its warehouse(s) by the location of customers and access to major highways, airports, or rail transportation. The number of warehouses often depends on the level of service customers require. If customers generally demand fast delivery (today or tomorrow at the latest), then it may be necessary to store products in a number of different locations from which the company can quickly the goods to the customer.

Firms use private and public warehouses to store goods. Those that use *private warehouses* have a high initial investment, but they also lose less of their inventory due to damage. *Public warehouses* are an alternative; they allow firms to pay for a portion of warehouse space rather than having to own an entire storage facility. Most countries offer public warehouses in all large cities and many smaller cities to support domestic and international trade. A *distribution center* is a warehouse that stores goods for short periods of time and that provides other functions, such as breaking bulk.

Materials Handling

Materials handling is the moving of products into, within, and out of warehouses. When goods come into the warehouse, they must be physically identified, checked for damage, sorted, and labeled. Next they are taken to a location for storage. Finally, they are recovered from the storage area for packaging and shipment. All in all, the goods may be handled over a dozen separate times. Procedures that limit the number of times a product must be handled decrease the likelihood of damage and reduce the cost of materials handling.

Transportation

Logistics decisions take into consideration options for **transportation**, the mode by which products move among channel members. Again, making transportation decisions entails a compromise between minimizing cost and providing the service customers want. As Table 15.3 shows, modes of transportation, including railroads, water transportation, trucks, airways, pipelines, and the Internet, differ in the following ways:

- **Dependability:** The ability of the carrier to deliver goods safely and on time

- **Cost:** The total transportation costs to move a product from one location to another, including any charges for loading, unloading, and in-transit storage

- **Speed of delivery:** The total time to move a product from one location to another, including loading and unloading

- **Accessibility:** The number of different locations the carrier serves

- **Capability:** The ability of the carrier to handle a variety of different products such as large or small, fragile, or bulky

- **Traceability:** The ability of the carrier to locate goods in shipment

---

order processing
The series of activities that occurs between the time an order comes into the organization and the time a product goes out the door.

enterprise resource planning (ERP) systems
A software system that integrates information from across the entire company, including finance, order fulfillment, manufacturing, and transportation and then facilitates sharing of the data throughout the firm.

warehousing
Storing goods in anticipation of sale or transfer to another member of the channel of distribution.

materials handling
The moving of products into, within, and out of warehouses.

transportation
The mode by which products move among channel members.

Each mode of transportation has strengths and weaknesses that make it a good choice for different transportation needs. Table 15.3 summarizes the pros and cons of each mode.

- **Railroads:** Railroads are best to carry heavy or bulky items, such as coal and other mining products, over long distances. Railroads are about average in their cost and provide moderate speed of delivery. Although rail transportation provides dependable, low-cost service to many locations, trains cannot carry goods to every community.

- **Water:** Ships and barges carry large, bulky goods and are very important in international trade. Water transportation is relatively low in cost but can be slow.

- **Trucks:** Trucks or motor carriers are the most important transportation mode for consumer goods, especially for shorter hauls. Motor carrier transport allows flexibility because trucks can travel to locations missed by boats, trains, and planes. Trucks also carry a wide variety of products, including perishable items. Although costs are fairly high for longer-distance shipping, trucks are economical for shorter deliveries. Because trucks provide door-to-door service, product handling is minimal, and this reduces the chance of product damage.

- **Air:** Air transportation is the fastest and also the most expensive transportation mode. It is ideal to move high-value items such as important mail, fresh-cut flowers, and live lobsters. Passenger airlines, air-freight carriers, and express delivery firms, such as FedEx, provide air transportation. Ships remain the major mover of international

Table 15.3 | A Comparison of Transportation Modes

Transportation Mode	Dependability	Cost	Speed of Delivery	Accessibility	Capability	Traceability	Most Suitable Products
Railroads	Average	Average	Moderate	High	High	Low	Heavy or bulky goods, such as automobiles, grain, and steel
Water	Low	Low	Slow	Low	Moderate	Low	Bulky, nonperishable goods, such as automobiles
Trucks	High	High for long distances; low for short distances	Fast	High	High	High	A wide variety of products, including those that need refrigeration
Air	High	High	Very fast	Low	Moderate	High	High-value items, such as electronic goods and fresh flowers
Pipeline	High	Low	Slow	Low	Low	Moderate	Petroleum products and other chemicals
Internet	High	Low	Very fast	Potentially very high	Low	High	Services such as banking, information, and entertainment

cargo, but air transportation networks are becoming more important as international markets continue to develop.

- **Pipeline:** Pipelines carry petroleum products such as oil and natural gas and a few other chemicals. Pipelines flow primarily from oil or gas fields to refineries. They are very low in cost, require little energy, and are not subject to disruption by weather.

- **The Internet:** As we discussed earlier in this chapter, marketers of services such as banking, news, and entertainment take advantage of distribution opportunities the Internet provides.

Inventory Control: JIT and Fast Fashion

Another component of logistics is **inventory control**, which means developing and implementing a process to ensure that the firm always has sufficient quantities of goods available to meet customers' demands—no more and no less. That explains why firms work so hard to track merchandise so they know where their products are and where they are needed in case a low-inventory situation appears imminent.

Some companies are even phasing in a sophisticated technology (similar to the EZ Pass system many drivers use to speed through tollbooths) known as **radio frequency identification (RFID)**. RFID lets firms tag clothes, pharmaceuticals, or virtually any kind of product with tiny chips that contain information about the item's content, origin, and destination. This new technology has the potential to revolutionize inventory control and help marketers ensure that their products are on the shelves when people want to buy them. Great for manufacturers and retailers, right? But some consumer groups are creating a backlash against RFID, which they refer to as "spy chips." Through blogs, boycotts, and other anticompany initiatives, these groups proclaim RFID a personification of the privacy violations George Orwell predicted in his classic book *1984*.[15]

Firms store goods (that is, they create an *inventory*) for many reasons. For manufacturers the pace of production may not match seasonal demand. It may be more economical to produce snow skis year-round than to produce them only during the winter season. For channel members that purchase goods from manufacturers or other channel intermediaries, it may be economical to order a product in quantities that don't exactly parallel demand. For example, delivery costs make it prohibitive for a retail gas station to place daily orders for just the amount of gas people will use that day. Instead, stations usually order truckloads of gasoline, holding their inventory in underground tanks. The consequences of stockouts may be very negative. Hospitals must keep adequate supplies of blood, IV fluids, drugs, and other supplies on hand to meet emergencies, even if some items go to waste.

Inventory control has a major impact on the overall costs of a firm's logistics initiatives. If supplies of products are too low to meet fluctuations in customer demand, a firm may have to make expensive emergency deliveries or lose customers to competitors. If inventories are above demand, unnecessary storage expenses and the possibility of damage or deterioration occur. To balance these two opposing needs, manufacturers turn to **just in time (JIT)** inventory techniques with their suppliers. JIT sets up delivery of goods just as they are needed on the production floor. This minimizes the cost of holding inventory

MAERSK SEALAND

A new dimension in shipping

Unmatched in experience
Resourceful
Dedicated to giving customers value for money

MAERSK EGYPT S.A.E.
For Maritime Transport

Cairo office: 68, El Merghany St., 3rd floor, Heliopolis
                       Tel: 20-24144950 Fax: 20-24144974
Alexandria office: 9, El Fawatem St., 5th floor, Azarita
                       Tel: 20-34843315 Fax: 20-34143319

Transportation by water, such as that provided by Maersk Sealand, is best for large, bulky, nonperishable goods and is vital to international trade.

inventory control
Activities to ensure that goods are always available to meet customers' demands.

radio frequency identification (RFID)
Product tags with tiny chips containing information about the item's content, origin, and destination.

just in time (JIT)
Inventory management and purchasing processes that manufacturers and resellers use to reduce inventory to very low levels and ensure that deliveries from suppliers arrive only when needed.

Metrics Moment

Companies track a wide range of metrics within the supply chain area. Some of the most common ones are the following:

- On-time delivery
- Forecast accuracy
- Value-added productivity per employee
- Returns processing cost as a percentage of product revenue
- Customer order actual cycle time
- Perfect order measurement

Let's take a look at the last measure in more detail. The *perfect order measurement* calculates the error-free rate of each stage of a purchase order.[14] This measure helps managers track the multiple steps involved in getting a product from a manufacturer to a customer so that they can pinpoint processes they need to improve. For example, a company can calculate its error rate at each stage and then combine these rates to create an overall metric of order quality. Suppose the company identifies the following error rates:

- Order entry accuracy: 99.95 percent correct (five errors per 1,000 order lines)
- Warehouse pick accuracy: 99.2 percent
- Delivered on time: 96 percent
- Shipped without damage: 99 percent
- Invoiced correctly: 99.8 percent

The company can then combine these individual rates into an overall perfect order measurement by multiplying them together: $99.95 \times 99.2 \times 96 \times 99 \times 99.8 = 94.04$ percent.

One of the keys to Zara's success is the store chain's fast-fashion supply chain that replenishes its inventory quickly.

while it ensures the inventory will be there when customers need it.

A supplier's ability to make on-time deliveries is the critical factor in the selection process for firms that adopt this kind of system. JIT systems reduce stock to very low levels, or even zero, and time deliveries very carefully to maintain just the right amount of inventory. The advantage of JIT systems is the reduced cost of warehousing. For both manufacturers and resellers that use JIT systems, the choice of supplier may come down to one whose location is nearest. To win a large customer, a supplier may even have to be willing to set up production facilities close to the customer to guarantee JIT delivery.[16]

Most JIT systems are largely invisible to you as an end consumer. But if you're a clotheshorse, you have probably encountered this cutting-edge supply chain approach up close and personal. Several retail apparel chains such as H&M, Benetton, and Zara rocketed to success recently because they consistently offer up-to-date styles at affordable prices. Their secret? A concept the industry calls *fast fashion*—which is really another way to say JIT. Zara (based in Spain) offers customers a constant supply of new products but only a limited supply of each garment. This means that the store has to constantly send small batches of new styles through its supply chain. Zara's system depends on a constant exchange of information among supply chain members so that the company can keep track of which specific styles and colors are selling at which stores in order to replenish stock very quickly. The retailer's fast fashion system has to follow about 300,000 new *stock-keeping units (SKUs)* every year to be sure that its customers continue to get their new fashion fix no matter how many times they visit a store.[17]

Now that you've learned about creating value through supply chain management, read "Real People, Real Choices: How It Worked Out" to see which model of food distribution Jim selected for Darden Restaurants.

real people, **Real Choices**

Jim
Lawrence

Jim chose:

3

Option

How It Worked Out at Darden Restaurants

Jim and his team selected Option 3. The company developed a new model for distribution, Darden Direct Distribution, which allows it to protect its supply chain while working with its supply chain partners to develop competitive advantages. This entity uses traditional chain foodservice distributors through the use of a new third-party model. The organization now has approximately 35 percent of its restaurants engaged in this new model and plans to continue to transition more of its restaurants into this network during the next three to five years.

During the initial stages of the conversion, restaurants experienced greater satisfaction with the overall performance of the new operating entity and enjoyed significant savings related to the collaborative efforts of all supply chain partners. This new model provides for greater visibility to costs/revenues, which allows for heightened decision-making abilities. This enhanced efficiency puts success on the menu for Darden Restaurants.

Marketing Metrics: How Darden Restaurants Measures Success

Darden uses standard service metrics to ensure that the new model for distribution is successful in managing the needs of the restaurant. These include:

- On-time delivery: Percentage of the time supplies are received when promised
- Case fill: The number of cases of supplies delivered versus the number of cases ordered. Darden's goal for this metric is 99.7 percent.
- Satisfaction scores: Darden surveys its restaurants twice per year to assess managers' overall level of satisfaction regarding foodservice distribution. Since implementing the new system, satisfaction scores improved by 20 percent over one year.

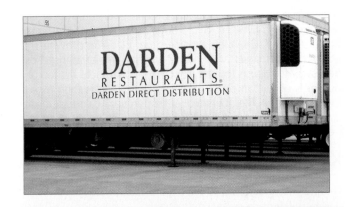

Refer back to **page 463** for Jims story ➡

Brand **YOU**!

Special delivery.

Deliver value to your prospective employer starting with your interview. Uncover some of the best secrets to a successful interview from employers and executives. Impress your interviewer with the exact balance of research, preparation personality and all the right questions. Get the inside track in Chapter 15 of the *Brand You* supplement.

Objective Summary ➡ Key Terms ➡ Apply

CHAPTER 15
Study Map

1. Objective Summary (pp. 464–468)

Understand the concept of the value chain and the key elements in a supply chain.

The value chain consists of five primary activities (inbound logistics, operations, outbound logistics, marketing and sales, and service) and four support activities (procurement, technology development, human resource management, and firm infrastructure). The process is called a value chain because each of these activities adds value to the product the customer eventually buys. Whereas the value chain is an overarching concept of how firms create value, the supply chain also encompasses components external to the firm itself, including all activities that are necessary to convert raw materials into a good or service and put it in the hands of the consumer or business customer.

Key Terms

value chain, p. 465 (Figure 15.2, p. 466)

supply chain, p. 465 (Figure 15.3, p. 467)

supply chain management, p. 466

insourcing, p. 467

channel of distribution, p. 467 (Figure 15.5, p. 477)

2. Objective Summary (pp. 468–472)

Explain what a distribution channel is and what functions distribution channels perform.

A distribution channel is a series of firms or individuals that facilitates the movement of a product from the producer to the final customer. Channels provide time, place, and ownership utility for customers and reduce the number of transactions necessary for goods to flow from many manufacturers to large numbers of customers by breaking bulk and creating assortments. Channel members make the purchasing process easier by providing important customer services. Today the Internet is becoming an important player in distribution channels.

Key Terms

channel intermediaries, p. 468 (Figure 15.5, p. 477)

breaking bulk, p. 469

create assortments, p. 469 (Figure 15.4, p. 470)

facilitating functions, p. 470

disintermediation (of the channel of distribution), p. 471

knowledge management, p. 471

on-line distribution piracy, p. 472 (Ethical Decisions in the Real World, p. 472)

3. Objective Summary (pp. 472–476)

Describe the types of wholesaling intermediaries found in distribution channels.

Wholesaling intermediaries are firms that handle the flow of products from the manufacturer to the retailer or business user. Merchant wholesalers are independent intermediaries that take title to a product and include both full-function wholesalers and limited-function wholesalers. Merchandise agents and brokers are independent intermediaries that do not take title to products. Manufacturer-owned channel members include sales branches, sales offices, and manufacturers' showrooms.

Key Terms

wholesaling intermediaries, p. 473 (Table 15.1, p. 474)

independent intermediaries, p. 473

merchant wholesalers, p. 473 (Table 15.1, p. 474)

take title, p. 473

merchandise agents or brokers, p. 475 (Table 15.1, p. 474)

4. Objective Summary (pp. 476–481)

Describe the types of distribution channels and how *place* fits in with the other three Ps in the marketing mix.

Distribution channels vary in length from the simplest two-level channel to longer channels with three or more channel levels. Distribution channels include direct distribution in which the producer sells directly to consumers, and indirect channels, which may include a retailer, wholesaler, or other intermediary. Decisions on what channels to utilize affect the price you can charge as well as overall positioning strategy for a product. The marketing mix is called a "mix" because each ingredient impacts the others as well as the whole marketing strategy.

Key Terms

channel levels, p. 476 (Figure 15.5, p. 477)

hybrid marketing system, p. 480

slotting allowance, p. 481

5. Objective Summary (pp. 481–487)

Understand the steps marketers use to plan a distribution channel strategy.

Marketers begin channel planning by developing channel objectives and considering important environmental factors. The next step is to decide on a distribution strategy, which involves determining the type of distribution channel that is best. Distribution tactics include the selection of individual channel members and management of the channel.

Key Terms

conventional marketing system, p. 483

vertical marketing system (VMS), p. 483

horizontal marketing system, p. 484

intensive distribution, p. 485

exclusive distribution, p. 485

selective distribution, p. 485

channel leader, p. 487

6. Objective Summary (pp. 487–492)

Explain logistics and how it fits into the supply chain concept.

Logistics is the process of designing, managing, and improving supply chains, including all the activities that are required to move products through the supply chain. Logistics contributes to the overall supply chain through activities including order processing, warehousing, materials handling, transportation, and inventory control.

Key Terms

logistics, p. 487

physical distribution, p. 488

order processing, p. 488

enterprise resource planning (ERP) systems, p. 488

warehousing, p. 489

materials handling, p. 489

transportation, p. 489

inventory control, p. 491

radio frequency identification (RFID), p. 491

just in time (JIT), p. 491

Chapter **Questions** and **Activities**

Concepts: Test Your Knowledge

1. What is a value chain?
2. What is a supply chain, and how is it different from a channel of distribution?
3. What is a channel of distribution? What are channel intermediaries?
4. Explain the functions of distribution channels.
5. List and explain the types of independent and manufacturer-owned wholesaling intermediaries.
6. What factors are important in determining whether a manufacturer should choose a direct or indirect channel? Why do some firms use hybrid marketing systems?
7. What are conventional, vertical, and horizontal marketing systems?
8. Explain intensive, exclusive, and selective forms of distribution.
9. Explain the steps in distribution planning.
10. What is logistics? Explain the functions of logistics.
11. What are the advantages and disadvantages of shipping by rail? By air? By ship? By truck?

Choices and Ethical Issues: You Decide

1. The supply chain concept looks at both the inputs of a firm and the firms that facilitate the movement of the product from the manufacturer to the consumer. Do you think *marketers* should be concerned with the total supply chain concept? Why or why not?
2. Sometimes people will say, "The reason products cost so much is because of all the intermediaries." Do intermediaries increase the cost of products? Would consumers be better off or worse off without intermediaries?
3. Many entrepreneurs choose to start a franchise business rather than "go it alone." Do you think franchises offer the typical businessperson good opportunities? What are some positive and negative aspects of purchasing a franchise?
4. As colleges and universities are looking for better ways to satisfy their customers, an area of increasing interest is the distribution of their product—education. Describe the characteristics of your school's channel(s) of distribution. What types of innovative distribution might make sense for your school to try?
5. "Music, video, or textbook downloading (even when done clandestinely) is just a way to create a more efficient supply chain because it 'cuts out the middleman' (stores that sell music, video, and books, for example)." Do you agree? Why or why not?

Practice: Apply What You've Learned

1. Assume that you have recently been hired by a firm that manufactures furniture. You feel that marketing should have an input into supplier selection for the firm's products, but the purchasing department says that should not be a concern for marketing. You need to explain to the department head the importance of the value chain perspective. In a role-playing exercise, explain to the purchasing agent the value chain concept, why it is of concern to marketing, and why the two of you should work together.
2. Assume that you are the director of marketing for a firm that manufactures cleaning chemicals used in industries. You have traditionally sold these products through manufacturer's reps. You are considering adding a direct Internet channel to your distribution strategy, but you aren't sure whether this will create channel conflict. Make a list of the pros and cons of this move. What do you think is the best decision?
3. As the one-person marketing department for a candy manufacturer (your firm makes high-quality, hand-dipped chocolates using only natural ingredients), you are considering making changes in your distribution strategy. Your products have previously been sold through a network of food brokers that call on specialty food and gift stores. But you think that perhaps it would be good for your firm to develop a corporate vertical marketing system (that is, vertical integration). In such a plan, a number of company-owned retail outlets would be opened across the country. The president of your company has asked that you present your ideas to the company executives. In a role-playing situation with one of your classmates, present your ideas to your boss, including the advantages and disadvantages of the new plan compared to the current distribution method.
4. Assume that your firm recently gave you a new marketing assignment. You are to head up development of a distribution plan for a new product line—a series of do-it-yourself instruction videos for home gardeners. These videos would show consumers how to plant trees, shrubbery, and bulbs; how to care for their plants; how to prune; and so on. You know that as you develop a distribution plan it is essential that you understand and consider a number of internal and external environmental factors. Make a list of the information you will need before you can begin to write the distribution plan. How will you adapt your plan based on each of these factors?

Miniproject: Learn by Doing

In the United States, the distribution of most products is fairly easy. There are many independent intermediaries (wholesalers, dealers, distributors, and retailers) that are willing to cooperate to get the product to the final customer. Our elaborate interstate highway system combines with rail, air, and water transportation to provide excellent means for moving goods from one part of the country to another. In many other countries, the means for distribution of products are far less efficient and effective.

For this miniproject, you and one or more of your classmates should first select a consumer product, probably one you normally purchase. Then use either library sources or other people or both (retailers, manufacturers, dealers, classmates, and so on) to gather information to do the following:

1. Describe the path the product takes to get from the producer to you. Draw a model to show each of the steps the product takes. Include as much as you can about transportation, warehousing, materials handling, order processing, inventory control, and so on.
2. Select another country in which the same or a similar product is sold. Describe the path the product takes to get from the producer to the customer in that country.
3. Determine if the differences between the two countries cause differences in price, availability, or quality of the product.
4. Make a presentation to your class on your findings.

Real people, **real surfers**: explore the web

Visit the Web site for UPS (**www.ups.com**). UPS has positioned itself as a full-service provider of logistics solutions. After reviewing its Web site, answer the following questions:

1. What logistics services does UPS offer its customers?

2. What does UPS say to convince prospective customers that its services are better than those of the competition?

Marketing Plan Exercise

Dell is a company that, for years, used one fairly simple supply chain system—direct sales over the Internet or by phone to both business and consumer users. In planning for the future, Dell began to experiment with making use of other distribution channels and outlets. It is already using kiosks at major airports to demonstrate and sell products as well as distribution in Best Buy stores. Yet, in considering expanding its channels it certainly doesn't want to overly impact the backbone of its supply chain process—the direct channel—because that channel carries the highest profit potential in the long run.

1. If you were a marketing executive at Dell, what other supply chain options would you suggest in designing a marketing plan beyond its traditional distribution model?
2. Over the long run, can Dell successfully coexist in retail store distribution and in distribution through its traditional direct means? Justify your answer.
3. Assume that your plan recommends Dell become more aggressive in pursuing distribution through other retail stores and other means beyond its traditional direct channel. What intermediaries do you recommend become part of its supply chain? Why?

Marketing in Action Case

Real **Choices** at **Cott**

Have you ever enjoyed a Red Rain, Red Rooster, or Throwdown energy drink? What about a bottle of Ben Shaws Lychee Juice? The Cott Corporation, one of the world's largest nonalcoholic beverage companies, makes all of these beverages and a lot more. While Cott may not be the name you see on the label, there's a good chance you've enjoyed a Cott beverage without realizing it.

Cott's beverage business includes both company-owned brands such as, Cott, RC, Vintage, Vess, Stars & Stripes, Ben Shaws, Carters, Red Rooster, Red Rain and So Clear, and over 200 retailer and licensed brands. Cott's vision to be a global leader in value beverages focuses on three key priorities:

1. Become the lowest cost producer in the industry
2. Become the retailers' best partner
3. Drive a pipeline of innovation

Cott's product portfolio includes carbonated soft drinks such as the leading RC brand; a variety of waters from purified drinking water and seltzers to flavored and fitness waters; Red Rain, Red Rooster, Throwdown™ and Aftershock brands of energy drinks; sports drinks; juices, juice drinks and smoothies; ready-to-drink teas; and other noncarbonated beverages.

Much of Cott's business strategy is based on partnerships with the largest retailers in the world, including Wal-Mart, HEB, Tesco, and Metro. For example, Cott derives 38 percent of its sales of $1.78 billion from retail giant Wal-Mart. In addition, Cott generates a large portion of its business from producing licensed beverage products. Recently Cott signed a licensing agreement with Twentieth Century Fox to launch a branded stimulation drink called 24-CTU, a spin-off from the hit U.S. drama, *24*.

But even good channel partnerships can turn sour. In spring of 2008, Cott faced a potentially crushing setback. Cott's biggest customer Wal-Mart decided to shrink the shelf space it devotes to Cott products to just four feet, a loss of $100 million in annual sales. Even worse news followed: Wal-Mart replaced the Cott products with beverages from rival Cadbury Schweppes.

For Cott Corporation, it may be time to question its channel strategy and the hazards of being too closely aligned with the world's largest retailers. What will happen to the company if other giant retail partners make similar decisions? Because of the size of Wal-Mart's global business, it is the channel leader in its distribution partnerships and it wields unequaled power in the channel. Cott, unlike soft drink leaders Coke and Pepsi, has no mega brands and thus has very little channel power. The relationship truly is a double-edged sword: While there's no doubt Cott benefited greatly from the rapid growth of Wal-Mart, dealing with a company that has so much channel power can be hazardous to a firm's health. Is it time for Cott to reevaluate its channel strategy and how its choice of channel partners may contribute to the future health of the company? Is it necessary for Cott to reinvent itself and become a strong branded company, or can it maintain its position in the industry by continuing to focus on being the global leader in value beverages and the "retailer's best partner"?

You Make the Call

1. What is the decision facing Cott?
2. What factors are important to understand this decision situation?
3. What are the alternatives?
4. What decision(s) do you recommend?
5. What are some ways to implement your recommendation?

Based on: Andy Georgiades, "Cott Plans to Refocus on Retailer-Branded Drinks," *The Wall Street Journal* (June 16, 2008), p C5; "Cott Experience Unsettling to Suppliers," *Wal-Mart News Now*, March 3, 2008; Jason Kirby, "How Canada's Pop Titan Got Crushed," *Macleans*, March 17, 2008, p 39.; Jemima Bokaie, "Twentieth Century Fox to Launch '24' Soft Drink," *Marketing*, September 19, 2007, p 4.

Retailing: Bricks and Clicks

Stan
Clark
Profile ▼

A Decision Maker at Eskimo Joe's

Stan Clark is a native of Tulsa, Oklahoma. He graduated from Oklahoma State University in May 1975 with a bachelor of science degree in business administration. For more than a decade, Stan's entrepreneurial success story has captivated audiences all over Oklahoma and across the country. Among other honors he was a Regional Finalist for *Inc.* magazine's Entrepreneur of the Year.

▼ **Q** & **A** with Stan Clark

Q) First job out of school?
A) Eskimo Joe's. I graduated from OSU in May 1975 and opened Joe's about two weeks later. To do that, I turned down an assistantship to go into the OSU MBA program!

Q) Career high?
A) During his 1990 commencement address in Lewis Field at OSU, President George Bush mentioned Eskimo Joe's in his speech. In 2006, George W. Bush did the same thing.

Q) A job-related mistake I wish I hadn't made?
A) Killing the annual Joe's Anniversary Party in 1993. It attracted tens of thousands of people but was getting unwieldy.

Q) Business book I'm reading now?
A) *Hug Your Customers* by Jack Mitchell and *Discovering the Soul of Service* by Len Berry.

Q) My hero?
A) My dad, who inspired me to be an entrepreneur, and my mom, who gave me a positive outlook on life.

Q) My motto to live by?
A) Live passionately, and make a difference.

real people, **Real Choices**

Decision Time at at Eskimo Joe's

Stan Clark, the colorful entrepreneur behind the toothy grin of the Eskimo Joe caricature and his dog Buffy, faced a big problem. In 1975, Stan opened Eskimo Joe's bar in Stillwater, Oklahoma—the home of Oklahoma State University. By the mid-1980s the watering hole had become a huge favorite among OSU students. Situated right across from the OSU campus, Joe's carved out a niche as "the" place to go for beer, music, pool, and foosball in this college town. Trading on the popularity of the bar as well as its quirky logo, Stan had also begun to sell some logo apparel over the counter. Before long, students, friends, parents, alums, and other visitors simply couldn't get enough of the T-shirts sporting the wide smiles by the boy and his faithful dog. For Stan, life was good and also lots of fun.

So what could possibly go wrong? Try the fact that Oklahoma had just passed a statewide "liquor by the drink" law. Prior to this, Oklahoma had a patchwork quilt of post–Prohibition era liquor laws including "club card" requirements at bars and bring-your-own-bottle rules. Liquor by the drink opened up normal serving of beer, wine, and spirits at any establishment with a proper state liquor license—however, part of the new law was an increase in the legal drinking age from 18 to 21. Oops ... a beer bar in a college town when you have to be 21 to drink? Not exactly an attractive business proposition. But, in the eight years since Eskimo Joe's opening, Stan had come to understand that the place represented a whole lot more to people than just pitchers of cold Bud on hot summer nights. There was a certain mystique and a strong sense of community around the brand that made it more than just a place to drink. Brisk sales of T-shirts and other clothing over the counter were evidence that people saw something else in the retailer—something that made them want to wear these items again and again. The affection and interest reached almost cult-like proportions and were not limited to Stillwater or even to Oklahoma. Stan had hit on something big, but what could he do? Big Brother in the person of the State of Oklahoma was about to regulate him right out of his core business.

Stan had to take a couple of steps back, take a new look at his business, and think about what he might do to ensure that his retail enterprise would survive the new law. The situation could be life or death for Eskimo Joe's.

Stan considered his Options 1·2·3

1 Option
Convert the beer bar into a full-service restaurant that focuses on selling great food. This option assumes that the equity of the Eskimo Joe's brand would transfer into a brand new market and product space. To accomplish this transformation, Stan would have to extensively remodel the facility. He would have to figure out who the new target market is and what type of menu fare would be most appealing to that customer. This was a risky proposition, since restaurants open and close all the time. On the other hand, if Stan could morph the location into a restaurant that also happens to serve alcohol (which, under the new liquor law would be legal—and potentially quite profitable), he would hopefully be able to continue to build the fledgling logo apparel business around the new restaurant theme, à la the Hard Rock Café.

2 Option
Continue operating as a beer bar at the core and work to offset declining beer sales with an increase in apparel sales. From 1975 to 1984, Joe's was "Stillwater's Jumpin' Little Juke Joint." It was by far one of the highest-volume beer bars in the region, and it had built its entire reputation on this image. As the number one competitor in its market space, Stan had every reason to believe that the weaker competitors would be forced out of business by the law change, leaving their share of the market to him. Stan could continue to operate the bar in much the way it had always been operated, and if he liked he could use it as a cash cow to generate revenues and then invest the money elsewhere for growth. The upside of this plan is that any attempt to rebrand Eskimo Joe's as something other than what it has always been would be risky. However, the downside is the unknown of what it would mean to a retailer over the long run to lose its primary customer base of 18-to 20-year-olds in a town brimming with college students.

3 Option
Close Eskimo Joe's bar and refocus resources on building the growing apparel business. The cult-like status of the Eskimo Joe's brand and image may have begun at the physical location of the bar in Stillwater, but the way to replicate and perpetrate it on a national or international scale is by marketing the now-hip logo. Stan could build a small retail clothing boutique in Stillwater but turn primarily to direct marketing through catalogs focused on his target primary age and demographic groups. A key benefit of this approach is avoiding any unexpected problems with the bar that might occur in the liquor law transition, especially the very negative publicity that would result if Joe's got caught selling beer to underage drinkers. The Eskimo Joe spirit would be maintained through the direct marketing and also through accompanying word of mouth. On the downside, to Joe's loyal fans, closing Stillwater's "Jumpin' Little Juke Joint" would be like Harley-Davidson ceasing to make motorcycles: Who wants the logo apparel when there's no product or place that still sports it? However, this option was tempting in that it would redirect Stan's resources to the high-growth (and high-profit-margin) apparel retailing sector.

Now, put yourself in Stan's shoes: Which option would you choose, and why?

You Choose

Which **Option** would you choose, and **why**?
1. ☐YES ☐NO 2. ☐YES ☐NO 3. ☐YES ☐NO

See what **option** Stan chose and its success on **page 527** ⟹

Check out chapter 16 **Study Map** on page 528

1

OBJECTIVE

Define retailing; understand how retailing evolves and some ethical issues in retailing. (pp. 500–507)

Retailing: Special Delivery

Shop 'til you drop! For many people, obtaining the product is only half the fun. Others, of course, would rather walk over hot coals than spend time in a store. Marketers like Stan Clark need to find ways to deliver goods and services that please both types of consumers. **Retailing** is the final stop on the distribution path—the process by which organizations sell goods and services to consumers for their personal use.

A retail outlet is more than a place to buy something. The retailer adds or subtracts value from the offering with its image, inventory, service quality, location, and pricing policy. In many cases, the shopping experience *is* what we buy as well as the products we take home. For example, Bass Pro Shops, a chain of outdoor sports equipment stores, features giant aquariums, waterfalls, trout ponds, archery and rifle ranges, putting greens, and free classes on topics from ice fishing to conservation.[1]

This chapter will explore the many different types of retailers, keeping one question in mind: How does a retailer—whether store or nonstore (selling via television, phone, or the Internet)—lure the consumer? The answer to this question isn't getting any easier as the competition for customers continues to heat up, fueled by the explosion of Web sites that sell branded merchandise (or that auction it like eBay), the "overstoring" of many areas as developers continue to build elaborate malls and strip shopping centers, and improvements in communications and distribution that make it possible for retailers from around the world to enter local markets. So, this chapter has plenty "in store" for us. Let's start with an overview of where retailing has been and where it's going.

Retailing: A Mixed (Shopping) Bag

Retailing is big business. In 2007 U.S. retail sales totaled more than $4.5 trillion.[2] Over 1.1 million retail businesses employ more than 15 million—more than 1 of every 10 U.S. workers.[3] Although we tend to associate huge stores such as Wal-Mart and Sears with retailing activity, in reality most retailers are small businesses. Certain retailers, such as Home Depot, also are wholesalers, because they provide goods and services to businesses as well as to end consumers.

As we said in Chapter 15, retailers belong to a channel of distribution, and as such provide time, place, and ownership utility to customers. Some retailers save people time or money when they provide an assortment of merchandise under one roof. Others search the world for the most exotic delicacies, allowing shoppers access to goods they would otherwise never see. Still others, such as Barnes & Noble café/bookstores, provide us with interesting environments in which to spend our leisure time and, they hope, our money.

Globally, retailing may have a very different face. In some European countries, don't even think about squeezing a tomato to see if it's too soft or picking up a cantaloupe to see if it smells ripe. Such mistakes will quickly gain you a reprimand from the store clerk who will choose which oranges and bananas you should have. In developing countries like Egypt, retailing often includes many small butcher shops where sides of beef and lamb proudly hang in store windows so everyone will be assured that the meat comes from healthy animals; vendors sell lettuce, tomatoes, and cucumbers on the sidewalk or neatly stack watermelons on a donkey cart; and women sell small breakfast items they have cooked out of the front of their homes for workers and school children who pass by in the mornings. Neat store shelves stacked with bottles of shampoo may be replaced by hanging displays that hold one-use size sachets of shampoo—the only size that a woman can afford to buy and then only for special occasions. Street vendors may sell cigarettes one at a time. The local pharmacist also gives customers injections and recommends antibiotics and other medicines for patients who come in with a complaint and who can't afford to see a doctor. Don't feel like cooking tonight? There's no drive-through window for pick up but even better—delivery from McDonald's, Hardees, KFC, Pizza Hut, Fuddruckers, Chili's, and a host of local restaurants via motor scooters that dangerously dash in and out of traffic is just a few minutes away. You can even order your Big Mac for delivery on-line through sites such as Egypt's **www.otlob.com**.

The Evolution of Retailing

Retailing has taken many forms over time, including the peddler who hawked his wares from a horse-drawn cart, a majestic urban department store, an intimate boutique, and a huge "hyperstore" that sells everything from potato chips to snow tires. But now the cart you see at your local mall that sells new-age jewelry or monogrammed golf balls to passersby has replaced the horse-drawn cart. As the economic, social, and cultural times change, different types of retailers emerge—and they often squeeze out older, outmoded types. How can marketers know what the dominant types of retailing will be tomorrow or 10 years from now?

The Wheel of Retailing

One of the oldest and simplest explanations for these changes is the **wheel-of-retailing hypothesis**. This proposition states that new types of retailers find it easiest to enter the market when they offer goods at lower prices than their competitors.[4] After they gain a foothold they gradually trade up, improve their facilities, increase the quality and assortment of merchandise, and offer amenities such as parking and gift wrapping. Upscaling results in greater investment and operating costs, so the store must raise its prices to remain profitable, which then makes it vulnerable to still newer entrants that can afford to charge lower prices. And so the wheel turns.

That's the story behind Pier 1 Imports. Pier 1 started as a single store in San Mateo, California that sold low-priced beanbags, love beads, and incense to post–World War II baby boomers. These days it sells quality home furnishings and decorative accessories to the same customers, who are now the most affluent segment of the American population.[5] Today, even low-cost retailer Wal-Mart is moving up, as it tries to broaden its appeal to upscale shoppers. The retail giant opened a new upscale supercenter in Plano, Texas, that boasts a Wi-Fi-enabled coffee shop, a sushi bar, quieter cash registers, and grocery selections that include more than 1,200 choices of wine and gourmet cheeses.[6]

Retailers, however, must be careful not to move too quickly and too far from their roots. Earlier attempts by Wal-Mart to upgrade its clothing lines from basic T-shirts, tank tops, and tube socks to brand name apparel alienated many of its loyal core cus-

retailing
The final stop in the distribution channel in which organizations sell goods and services to consumers for their personal use.

wheel-of-retailing hypothesis
A theory that explains how retail firms change, becoming more upscale as they go through their life cycle.

Pier 1 Imports exemplifies the wheel of retailing. The stores initially sold low-priced beanbags and love beads, but today shoppers can find quality home furnishings.

tomers who found the new items out of reach. Today Wal-Mart is reinventing its clothing offerings with higher fashion apparel while it maintains its focus on everyday apparel.[7]

The wheel of retailing helps us explain the development of some but not all forms of retailing. For example, some retailers never trade up; they simply continue to occupy a niche as discounters. Others, such as upscale specialty stores, start out at the high end. Of course, some retailers move down after experiencing success at the high end. Sometimes they open sister divisions that sell lower-priced products (as when Gap Stores opened Old Navy), or they develop outlets that sell lower-priced versions of their own products (as when Nordstrom creates the Nordstrom Rack or Anne Taylor opens Anne Taylor Loft).

The Retail Life Cycle

Of course, retailers sell products. But in a way retailers also *are* products because they provide benefits such as convenience or status to consumers, and they must offer a competitive advantage over other retailers to survive. And sometimes where a product is bought either adds to or takes away from its allure (which explains why some people secretly replace shopping bags from bargain stores with those from upscale stores to create the "right" impression).

From the value-chain perspective, a manufacturer's selection of a retail location adds value in two ways: by the utility the retailer provides and by the extent to which the store enhances the product's image. When a manufacturer makes its product available at Wal-Mart, the value the retailer adds is primarily time, place, and ownership utility. But when a product is available at Neiman-Marcus or Saks Fifth Avenue, the value of the product also increases because the high-end image of the retailer transfers to the product.

retail life cycle
A theory that focuses on the various stages that retailers pass through from introduction to decline.

So, another way to understand how retailers evolve is the **retail life cycle**. Like the *product life cycle* we discussed in Chapter 9, this perspective recognizes that (like people, soft-drink brands, and vacation destinations) retailers are born, they grow and mature, and eventually most die or become obsolete. The life cycle approach allows us to categorize retail stores by the conditions they face at different points in the cycle.[8]

In the *introduction* stage, the new retailer often is an aggressive entrepreneur who takes a unique approach to doing business. This may mean it competes on the basis of low price, as the wheel of retailing suggests. However, the new guy on the block may also enter the market by offering a distinctive assortment or a different way to distribute items, such as through the Internet. That's what Samuel Wurtzel did in 1949 when he opened Richmond, Virginia's first retail television store. Today, Circuit City has over 600 stores and sells a wide variety of electronics and home appliances.[9]

pop-up retailing
A retail strategy in which a store deliberately opens and then closes after a short period of time.

Or how about a store that plans to close even as it opens? That's just what happened recently in Berlin with the launch of a new concept called the Comme des Garçons Guerrilla Store. The store closed in a year—deliberately! Instead of spending millions to build or renovate a building, Comme des Garçons spent just $2,500 to fix up a former bookshop. This "here today, gone tomorrow" strategy (that insiders call **pop-up retailing**) acknowledges consumers' desires to have different shopping experiences all the time in a unique way.[10]

In the introduction stage, profits usually are low because of high development costs (pop-up stores are an exception!). As the business enters the *growth* stage, the retailer (hopefully) catches on with shoppers, and sales and profits rise. But a new idea doesn't stay new for long. Others start to copy it and competition increases, so the store needs to expand what it offers. Often the retailer responds by opening more outlets and develops systems to distribute goods to these new stores—which may in turn cut profits, as the firm invests in new buildings and fixtures.

Eric
Newman
a professor at California State University – San Bernardino

My Advice for Eskimo Joe's would be to choose **Option 2**

real people, **Other Voices**

I would choose Option 2 because Eskimo Joe's bar is already branded as a beer bar and to change the branded image could also hurt the apparel sales. Even though the drinking age has been changed from 18 to 21 there is still opportunity with the college seniors, graduate students, faculty, and alumni. Many of the apparel sales could be driven by the nostalgia of experiencing "Stillwater's Jumping' Little Juke Joint" and Oklahoma State University. Later, as the market changes, Stan can look at adding burgers or other college-style food depending on market demand. ➤

By the time the business reaches the *maturity* stage, many other individual retailers have copied the unique idea of the original entrepreneur to form an entire industry. The industry probably has overexpanded and intense competition makes it difficult to maintain customer loyalty. Profits decline as competitors resort to price cutting to keep their customers. We observe this pattern in department stores like Macy's and fast-food chains like McDonald's.

During the maturity stage, firms seek to increase their share of the market or to attract new customers. That has been the case with fast food retailers for a number of years. In order to meet changing customers tastes, KFC is considering a "nonfried chicken" menu as part of a brand transformation that will include new KFC signature beverages and a variety of grilled foods. McDonald's recently introduced a chicken wrap. Pizza Hut is also reinventing itself with new pasta, chicken, and everyday pizza value items, while Taco Bell offers customers a new line of "Fruitista Freeze" beverages.[11]

In the *decline* stage, retail businesses, like the general store or the peddler, become obsolete as newer ways of doing business emerge. Of course, the outmoded retailer does not have to fold its tent at this stage. Marketers who anticipate these shifts can avert decline by changing to meet the times. Some retailers, such as Starbucks, find growth opportunities in foreign markets. Starbucks now operates over 11,000 stores in the United States. There are over 4,500 additional Starbucks locations in 43 countries around the globe.[12] Of course, the competition quickly followed. Coffee Bean & Tea Leaf now has over 400 locations in 14 countries.[13]

The Evolution Continues: What's "In Store" for the Future?

As our world continues to change rapidly, retailers are scrambling to keep up. Three factors motivate innovative merchants to reinvent the way they do business: demographics, technology, and globalization.

Demographics

As we noted in Chapter 7, keeping up with changes in population characteristics is at the heart of many marketing efforts. Retailers can no longer afford to stand by and assume that their customer base is the same as it has always been. They must come up with new ways to sell their products to diverse groups.

For example, although many retailers chase after the same set of affluent customers, others carve out new markets when they target lower-income households. Stores like Dollar General, Dollar Tree, and Family Dollar profit as they serve the needs of the four out of ten U.S. households that earn less than $25,000 per year. These *value retailers* operate stores with

Starbucks is now a household name in Japan.

bare-bones fixtures and some offer cash-and-carry checkout only (no credit cards); they rack up total sales of over $8 billion in merchandise per year.

Here are some of the ways changing demographics are altering the face of retailing:

- **Convenience for working consumers:** Some retailers are expanding their operating hours because consumers no longer have time to shop during the day. Other retailers, including dry cleaners and pharmacies, add drive-up windows. In areas from financial services to interior decorating, enterprising individuals turn time shortage into a business opportunity when they become shopping consultants for busy consumers. In some areas, mobile furniture stores replace design studios; designers pick out 8 or 10 sofas from their large inventories and bring them to your home so you can see how each will actually look in your living room. Many major department stores offer in-house consultants at no charge. And walk-in medical clinics located at retailer, pharmacy, or grocery stores not only provide convenience but also save both patients and insurers money on routine care.[14]

- **Cater to specific age segments:** Retailers see benefits of serving specific age groups. For example, several companies, such as Pacific Sunwear and Hot Topic, prosper when they target suburban teenagers who prowl the mall for the latest in cool fashions. More recently, Pacific Sunwear opened a new chain called d.e.m.o. that's intended to deliver a hip-hop flavor to the mainstream youth market. The stores stock brands such as Ecko Unlimited, Enyce, Sean John, and Phat Farm. As one analyst observed, "You have to realize that teenagers are bored, and mainstream American mall culture is mostly boring. Hip hop, and to a different degree, snowboard and surf life, have an exciting, rebellious quality that kids in the suburbs may not be able to access where they live."[15] It's the job of retailers to provide that excitement—and sell a lot of products while doing so.

- **Recognize ethnic diversity:** Although members of every ethnic group can usually find local retailers that cater to their specific needs, larger companies must tailor their strategies to the cultural makeup of specific areas. For example, in Texas, California, and Florida, where there are large numbers of customers who speak only Spanish, many retailers make sure that there are sales associates who *habla Español*.

Technology

In addition to demographics, technology is revolutionizing retailing. As we all know, the Internet has brought us the age of e-tailing. Whether it's a store that sells only on the Web or a traditional retailer such as Banana Republic, J. Crew, or Eskimo Joe's that also sells on the Web, retailing is steadily evolving from bricks to clicks. Our personal computers have turned our homes into virtual malls. There are other technological advances that have little to do with the Internet that are also helping to change our shopping experiences.

point-of-sale (POS) systems
Retail computer systems that collect sales data and are hooked directly into the store's inventory-control system.

Some of the most profound changes are not even visible to shoppers, such as advanced electronic **point-of-sale (POS) systems**. These devices contain computer brains that collect sales data and connect directly into the store's inventory-control system (like the ones we read about in Chapter 6 that NCR makes). JCPenney stores led in the use of technology with its Point-of-Sale System. Every day JCPenney stores across the United States send data to corporate headquarters in Dallas. From there, computer programs analyze patterns of demand for different products and automatically send orders to vendors.[16] This makes stores more efficient. If shoppers in your area buy a lot of wide-legged jeans, for example, the company can be sure that its store there will offer an ample selection for every hip-hop shopper.

Today, customers who want to wear designer Nanette Lepore's fashions can use cutting-edge technology for "social-shopping." They can try on the designer garments and then send a video message to their friends' computers or mobile phones to get their green light before they buy. At Borders book stores, customers can print out a sample recipe from a cookbook and try it before they buy the book.[17]

The store of the future will use RFID tags (which we discussed in Chapters 13 and 15) and other technology to assist the shopper in ways we haven't even thought of. For example, an RFID tag on a bottle of wine can tip off a nearby plasma screen that will project an ad for Barilla pasta and provide a neat recipe for fettuccini with bell peppers and shrimp. Don't remember what number printer ink cartridge you need? No problem. In-store kiosks will allow consumers to ask questions of a product "expert" in another city via a video-enabled screen, alleviating customer complaints about lack of knowledgeable store personnel while creating a cost efficient way to provide expertise to dozens of customers at one time.[18]

Some restaurants already use technology to let diners order their food tableside directly from a screen complete with photos of the dishes it offers. The *e-menus* help customers because they can see what every item on the menu will look like and, hopefully, avoid a surprise when the waiter arrives.[19] This innovation also increases sales for the restaurant—who can avoid that mouth-watering picture of the four-layer chocolate cake with peppermint stick ice cream on top?

Globalization

As we saw in Chapter 3, the world is becoming a much smaller (and flatter) place. Retailers are busy expanding to other countries and they bring with them innovations and new management philosophies. McDonald's, T.G.I. Friday's, and Starbucks join the Hard Rock Café as they become global success stories for U.S. retailers. Similarly, Spanish fashion retailers Zara and Mango are now global brands, while Swedish home goods company IKEA furnishes homes around the world. Even French hyperstore chain Carrefours has stores in the United States.

Still, retailers need to adjust to different conditions around the world. In countries in the Middle East with large Muslim populations, you won't find the riblet basket on Applebee's menu, and McDonald's offers customers McArabia Kofta sandwiches. And some countries require that a certain percentage, often over half, of goods sold in retail stores are locally produced.

While Wal-Mart's global sales now account for 20 percent of the company's sales, the retail giant has made mistakes and suffered some losses. Some mishaps include promoting golf clubs in Brazil where consumers are crazy about soccer, and pushing ice skates in sweltering Mexico. In Germany, consumers were suspicious that smiling Wal-Mart clerks were flirting.[20] Wal-Mart was even less successful in South Korea—where the economy is dominated by a few family-controlled local firms that were better able to

Robert A.
Bergman
a professor at Lewis University

My Advice for Eskimo Joe's would
be to choose

Option

real people, **Other Voices**

I would choose Option 2. Stan's competitors, in terms of beer bars, are all in the same boat in terms of losing beer sales from the lucrative 18–20 college crowd. But Stan's core business isn't selling

beer. Yeah, that's how he makes money, but his customers come because it's "the" place to go. Patrons are almost guaranteed a hopping place with "good-time energy" and fun things to do every time they stop by. I wouldn't underestimate the competition and assume the weaker ones would be forced out of business. They may surprise him and draw customers away from Eskimo Joe's with new and different "beer drinking, hang-out" type entertainment. Stan needs to capitalize on the fun customers have, as well as offer non-alcoholic "brews" for the 18–20 crowd so that they can "fit in" to the beer drinking environment. In this way, beer (and nonalcoholic beer) sales remain high and apparel sales will continue to grow. ➤

keep costs down and to offer what Koreans wanted—and recently sold its 16 stores to its biggest competitor.[21]

Ethical Problems in Retailing

shrinkage

Losses experienced by retailers due to shoplifting, employee theft, and damage to merchandise.

Retailers must deal with ethical problems that involve both their customers and their employees. Particularly problematic are losses due to **shrinkage**: the term retailers use to describe losses due to shoplifting, employee theft, and damage to merchandise. Analysts estimate that shrinkage during 2005–2006 was 2.76 percent of overall retail sales.[22]

Shoplifting

Shoplifting has grown in recent years to giant proportions. In 2006, 23 major retailers reported that they apprehended over 530,000 shoplifters and dishonest employees—but they still suffered losses of over $6 billion due to "disappearing" merchandise.[23] These thefts in turn drive consumer prices up and hurt the economy and sometimes even cause smaller retailers to go out of business. For department stores, discount stores, and specialty stores, the items lifted include high price tag electronics, clothing, and jewelry. For food stores, razor blades, condoms, pregnancy tests, cigarettes, and pain relievers are shoplifters' common targets. The problem is so bad that many small stores now keep high theft items such as analgesics under lock and key.

At its worst, shoplifting can be an organized criminal activity where groups of thieves that use store floor plans and foil-lined bags to evade security sensors get away with thousands of dollars in goods in a single day. When Mervyn's stores in Los Angeles found that their inventories of Levi's jeans were mysteriously shrinking, surveillance cameras filmed organized gangs of thieves who whisked the jeans off shelves to waiting cars. Mervyn's estimated the stores lost more than $1 million before the company stopped the thieves.[24]

Ironically, the growth of on-line retailing boosts shoplifting from bricks and mortar stores because it facilitates a wide distribution of stolen goods—no longer do thieves have to fence their loot in the local market. One Houston, Texas, theft ring unloaded $258,000 worth of goods it stole from Target before it was caught.[25] Of course, some shoplifting is more amateurish and nakedly obvious—as when a nude man walked into a Missouri convenience store on a hot August day and did a hula dance to divert attention while his partner stole a case of beer from the store.[26] (Do not try this at home!)

Employee Theft

A second major source of shrinkage in retail stores is employee theft of both merchandise and cash. On a case by case basis, dishonest employees steal 6.6 times the amount shoplifters do.[27] Employees not only have access to products, but they also are familiar with the store's security measures. "Sweethearting" is an employee practice in which a cashier consciously undercharges, gives a cash refund, or allows a friend to walk away without paying for items.[28] Sometimes a dishonest employee simply carries merchandise out the back door to a friend's waiting car.

Retail Borrowing

A third source of shrinkage is an unethical consumer practice the industry calls *retail borrowing*. Merchants over recent decades have developed liberal policies of accepting returns from customers because the product performs unsatisfactorily or even if the customer simply changes her mind. Retail borrowing is the return of non-defective merchandise for a refund after it has fulfilled the purpose for which it was purchased.[29] Popular objects for retail borrowing include a dress for a high school prom, a new suit for a job interview, and a boom box for a weekend picnic on the beach. One study suggests that 12 percent of merchandise returns involve an intent to deceive the retailer. For the consumer the practice

Ethical Decisions in the Real World

Many college students like you work 20, 30, or more hours a week as a retail employee or even a store manager. Assume you are employed by a local electronics and media retailer. A great new video game has been released this week—but it has met with controversy. Consumer groups complain that it is violent and that it glorifies criminal behavior. The game maker has recommended—and even says on the label—that it is only for consumers aged 17 or over. But you know that it's the younger crowd that is the greatest market for games. And it is 12-, 13-, and 14-year-old kids who come into the store in droves to buy the game. These kids want you to overlook the store's policy about selling to underage consumers.

What would you do?

Ripped from the Headlines! See what happened in the Real World at **www. mypearsonmarketinglab.com**

ETHICS CHECK: ↖
Find out what other students taking this course **would do** and **why** on **www. mypearsonmarketinglab. com**

↓

Would you rent or sell a video or videogame that's rated "17 or over" to consumers who are a year or two younger than 17?

☐**YES** ☐**NO**

provides short term use of a product for a specific occasion at no cost. For the retailer, the practice results in lower total sales and often in damaged merchandise, unsuitable for resale.

Ethical Treatment of Customers

On the other side of the retail ethics issue is how retailers and their employees treat customers. While not providing equal access to consumers of different ethnic groups may be illegal, behavior that discourages customers who appear economically disadvantaged or socially unacceptable is not. As a classic scene in the movie *Pretty Woman* starring Julia Roberts depicted, stores that seek to maintain an image of elite sophistication may not offer assistance to customers who enter the premises not meeting the requirements for that image—or they may actually ask the customer to leave.

Similarly, many would suggest that retailers have an obligation not to sell products to customers if the products can be harmful. For example, for many years some teens and young adults abused potentially harmful over-the-counter medicines. While government regulations removed many of these drug products from store shelves in recent years, retailers still have to carefully police their distribution. The same is true for products such as alcohol and cigarettes, which are by law limited to sale to adult customers.

2

OBJECTIVE

Understand how we classify retailers.

(pp. 507–512)

From Mom-and-Pop to Super Wal-Mart: How Marketers Classify Retail Stores

The field of retailing covers a lot of ground—from mammoth department stores to sidewalk vendors to Web sites to bars like Eskimo Joe's. Retail marketers need to understand all the possible ways they might offer their products in the market, and they also need a way to benchmark their performance relative to other similar retailers.

Classify Retailers by What They Sell

Stan Clark's dilemma boils down to what Eskimo Joe's should sell—beer, food, clothing, some mixture of these? One of the most important strategic decisions a retailer makes is *what* to sell—its **merchandise mix**. This choice is similar to settling on a market segment (as we discussed in Chapter 7): If a store's merchandise mix is too limited, it may not have enough potential customers, whereas if it is too broad the retailer runs the risk of being a "jack of all trades, master of none." Because what the retailer sells is central to its identity, one way we describe retailers is in terms of their merchandise mix.

merchandise mix
The total set of all products offered for sale by a retailer, including all product lines sold to all consumer groups.

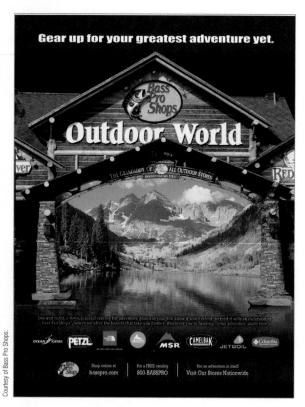

Bass Pro Shops competes directly against other retailers that sell outdoor products, such as REI and Patagonia.

While we learned in Chapter 9 that a manufacturer's product line consists of product offerings that satisfy a single need, in retailing a *product line* is a set of related products a retailer offers, such as kitchen appliances or leather goods. The *Census of Retail Trade* that the U.S. Bureau of the Census conducts classifies all retailers by North American Industry Classification System (NAICS) codes (the same system we described in Chapter 6 that classifies industrial firms). A retailer that wants to identify direct competition simply looks for other firms with the same NAICS classification codes.

However, a word of caution: As retailers experiment with different merchandise mixes, it's getting harder to make these direct comparisons. For example, even though marketers like to distinguish between food and nonfood retailers, in reality these lines are blurring. Supermarkets are adding hardware product lines, and some department stores offer gourmet food. In Japan, the major department stores have one floor that, like freestanding supermarkets, sells meats, vegetables, and other fresh food items, while another entire floor offers store customers a wide range of prepared foods ready for the modern Japanese working woman (or man) to carry home for dinner.

Classify Retailers by Level of Service

Retailers differ in the amount of service they provide for consumers. Firms recognize that there is a trade-off between service and low prices, so they tailor their strategies to the level of service they offer. Customers who demand higher levels of service must be willing to pay for that service, and those who want lower prices must be willing to give up services. Unfortunately, some consumers don't understand this trade-off and still insist on top-level service while they pay bottom-dollar prices!

Retailers like Sam's Club that promise cut-rate prices often are self-service operations. When customers shop at *self-service retailers*, they make their product selection without any assistance, they often must bring their own bags or containers to carry their purchases, and they may even handle the checkout process with self-service scanners.

Contrast that experience to visiting a *full-service retailer*. Many of us prefer to shop at major department stores like Bloomingdale's and specialty stores like Victoria's Secret because they provide supporting services such as gift wrapping, and they offer trained sales associates who can help us select that perfect gift. Other specialized services are available based on the merchandise the store offers. For example, many full-service clothing retailers will provide alteration services. Retailers like Macy's that carry china, silver, housewares, and other items brides might want also offer special bridal consultants and bridal gift registries.

Limited-service retailers fall in between self-service and full-service retailers. Stores like Wal-Mart, Target, Old Navy, and Kohl's offer credit and merchandise return but little else. Customers select merchandise without much assistance, preferring to pay a bit less rather than be waited on a bit more.

Classify Retailers by Merchandise Selection

Another way to classify retailers is in terms of the selection they offer. A retailer's **merchandise assortment**, or selection of products it sells, has two dimensions: breadth and depth. **Merchandise breadth**, or variety, is the number of different product lines available. A *narrow assortment*, such as that we encounter in convenience stores, means that shoppers will find only a limited selection of product lines such as candy, cigarettes, and soft drinks. A *broad assortment*, such as that a warehouse store like COSTCO or Sam's Club offers, means there is a wide range of items from eyeglasses to barbecue grills.

merchandise assortment
The range of products a store sells.

merchandise breadth
The number of different product lines available.

Stan
Clark

APPLYING **Merchandise Assortment**

Eskimo Joe's sells food and beverages, but also T-shirts, caps, and other merchandise bearing its distinctive logo. How would you describe the bar's merchandise assortment? ➡

Figure 16.1 | Classification of Retailers by Merchandise Selection

Marketers often classify retail stores on the breadth and depth of their merchandise assortment. In this figure, we use the two dimensions to classify types of bookstores that carry science fiction books.

	Breadth	
	Narrow	Broad
Shallow	**Airport Bookstore:** A few *Lord of the Rings* books	**Sam's Club:** A few *Lord of the Rings* books and a limited assortment of *Lord of the Rings* T-shirts and toys
Deep	**www.legendaryheroes.com:** Internet retailer selling only merchandise for *Lord of the Rings, The Highlander, Zena: Warrior Princess, Legendary Swords, Conan,* and *Hercules*	**www.Amazon.com:** Literally millions of current and out-of-print books plus a long list of other product lines including electronics, toys, apparel, musical instruments, jewelry, motorcycles and ATVs

(Depth is the vertical axis labeled on the left)

Merchandise depth is the variety of choices available within each specific product line. A *shallow assortment* means that the selection within a product category is limited, so a factory outlet store may sell only white and blue men's dress shirts (all made by the same manufacturer, of course) and only in standard sizes. In contrast, a men's specialty store may feature a *deep assortment* of dress shirts (but not much else) in varying shades and in hard-to-find sizes. Figure 16.1 illustrates these assortment differences for one product, science fiction books.

Now that we've seen how retailers differ in the breadth and depth of their assortments, let's review some of the major forms these retailers take.

merchandise depth
The variety of choices available for each specific product line.

Convenience Stores

Convenience stores carry a limited number of frequently purchased items, including basic food products, newspapers, and sundries. They cater to consumers willing to pay a premium for the ease of buying staple items close to home. In other words, convenience stores meet the needs of those who are pressed for time, who buy items in smaller quantities, or who shop at irregular hours. But these stores are starting to change, especially in urban areas, where many time-pressed shoppers prefer to visit these outlets even for specialty items.

A new design for 7-Eleven stores illustrates that convenience stores aren't just for Slurpee drinks anymore. The chain, whose stores rack up $43 billion in sales worldwide and a daily average of 6 million customers in the United States alone, decided to pull out all the stops when it opened its 25,000th store. The new "urban" version boasts a huge coffee bar, flanked by cases of fresh-made deli sandwiches and pastries delivered fresh every day of the year. The wall is painted in "grasslands," not

convenience stores
Neighborhood retailers that carry a limited number of frequently purchased items and cater to consumers willing to pay a premium for the ease of buying close to home.

7-Eleven's new "urban store" concept upgrades the convenience store experience for a new generation of sophisticated customers who want more than just Slurpees and speed.

off-white. Pendant lamps hang from faux tin ceilings, and the porcelain-tile floors look like wood. At the opening, waiters in tuxedos served doughnut centers and taquitos while a high school choir belted out "Oh Thank Heaven" (for 7-Eleven...).[30] And just to make the 7-Eleven stores even more convenient, the chain introduced a radio-frequency-based payment system so that customers can pay for purchases of $25 or less simply by passing a card with a radio-frequency identification (RFID) chip within inches of a specialized scanner before they leave the store.[31]

Supermarkets

supermarkets
Food stores that carry a wide selection of edibles and related products.

Supermarkets are food stores that carry a wide selection of edible and nonedible products. Although the large supermarket is a fixture in the United States, it has not caught on to the same extent in other parts of the world. In many European countries, for example, consumers walk or bike to small stores near their homes. They tend to have smaller food orders per trip and to shop more frequently, partly because many lack the freezer space to store a huge inventory of products at home. Although wide variety is less important than quality and local ambiance to Europeans, their shopping habits are starting to change as huge hypermarkets become popular around the globe.

Specialty Stores

specialty stores
Retailers that carry only a few product lines but offer good selection within the lines that they sell.

Specialty stores have narrow and deep inventories. They do not sell a lot of product lines, but they offer a good selection of brands within the lines they do sell. For many women with less-than-perfect figures, shopping at a store that sells only swimsuits means there will be an adequate selection to find a suit that really fits. The same is true for larger, taller men who can't find suits that fit in regular department stores but have lots of choices in stores that cater to big-and-tall guys. Specialty stores can tailor their assortment to the specific needs of a targeted consumer, and they often offer a high level of knowledgeable service.

Discount Stores

general merchandise discount stores
Retailers that offer a broad assortment of items at low prices with minimal service.

General merchandise discount stores, such as Target, Kmart, and Wal-Mart, offer a broad assortment of items at low prices and with minimal service and are the dominant outlet for many products. Discounters are tearing up the retail landscape because they appeal to price-conscious shoppers who want easy access to a lot of merchandise. Kohl's, for example, is one of the nation's fastest-growing retailers. These stores increasingly carry designer-name clothing at bargain prices as companies like Liz Claiborne create new lines just for discount stores.[32] Recently, Kohl's became the exclusive vendor for Candies branded apparel, sportswear, accessories, and intimate apparel.[33]

off-price retailers
Retailers that buy excess merchandise from well-known manufacturers and pass the savings on to customers.

Some discount stores, such as Loehmann's, are **off-price retailers**. These stores obtain surplus merchandise from manufacturers and offer brand-name, fashion-oriented goods at low prices.

warehouse clubs
Discount retailers that charge a modest membership fee to consumers who buy a broad assortment of food and nonfood items in bulk and in a warehouse environment.

Warehouse clubs such as COSTCO and BJ's are a newer version of the discount store. These establishments do not even pretend to offer any of the amenities of a full-service store; they reinforce a bargain mentality when they display merchandise (often in its original box) in a cavernous, bare-bones facility. These clubs often charge a membership fee to consumers and small businesses. A recent survey showed that the typical warehouse shopper shops about once a month, is intrigued by bulk buying, hates long lines, and is likely drawn to the club retailer because of specific product areas such as fresh groceries.[34] Nothing like laying in a three-year supply of paper towels or five-pound boxes of pretzels even if you have to build an extra room in your house to store all this stuff! And, consistent with the wheel of retailing, even these stores "trade up" in terms of what they sell today; shoppers can purchase fine jewelry and other luxury items at many warehouse clubs. COSTCO sells fine art, including limited-edition lithographs by Pablo Picasso, Marc Chagall, and Joan Miró.[35] Take a few masterpieces home along with that 20-pound bag of pretzels today!

The **factory outlet store** is still another type of discount retailer. A manufacturer owns these stores. Some factory outlets enable the manufacturer to sell off defective merchandise or excess inventory, while others carry items not available at full-price retail outlets, and are designed to provide an additional distribution channel for the manufacturer. Although the assortment is not wide because a store carries products only one manufacturer makes, we find most factory outlet stores in *outlet malls* where a large number of factory outlet stores cluster together in the same location. And, in keeping with the wheel-of-retailing idea, we are starting to see outlet malls adding amenities such as elaborate food courts and local entertainment.

Department Stores

Department stores sell a broad range of items and offer a deep selection organized into different sections of the store. Grand department stores dominated urban centers in the early part of the twentieth century. In their heyday, these stores sold airplanes and auctioned fine art. Lord & Taylor even offered its customers a mechanical horse to ensure the perfect fit of riding habits.

Warehouse clubs continue to expand their range of offerings. Today shoppers can stock up on doughnuts, deodorants, dust ruffles, and even expensive watches and diamonds on the same trip.

In many countries, department stores continue to thrive and they remain consumers' primary place to shop. In Japan, department stores are always crowded with shoppers who buy everything from a takeaway sushi dinner to a string of fine pearls. In Spain, a single department store chain, El Corte Inglés, dominates retailing. Its branch stores include store-size departments for electronics, books, music, and gourmet foods, and each has a vast supermarket covering one or two floors of the store.

In the United States, however, department stores have struggled in recent years. On the one hand, specialty stores lure department-store shoppers away with deeper, more cutting-edge fashion selections and better service. On the other hand, department stores have also been squeezed by discount stores and catalogs that offer the same items at lower prices because they don't have the expense of rent, elaborate store displays and fixtures, or high salaries for salespeople.

Because of these recent problems, department stores are searching for different strategies to compete. Federated Department Stores, for example, replaced a number of old retail branded stores including Bullock's, Filene's, Foley's, Hecht's, Marshall Field's, and Strawbridge, with just two brands. Since the end of 2006, all of Federated's stores operate either as Macy's or Bloomingdale's.[36] Some retail stores have pruned their assortments to concentrate more on *soft goods*, such as clothing and home furnishings, and less on *hard goods*, such as appliances. Macy's dropped its electronics department altogether and used the space instead to create its highly successful Macy's Cellar, which features tastefully displayed cooking items and food.

Some department stores try to go upscale by introducing amenities such as valet parking; others compete more directly with discount stores when they provide shopping carts. Nordstrom and Saks Fifth Avenue are cutting prices, while May Company targets specific types of customers such as brides. Federated is trying still a different strategy: To increase sales for young women's clothing, the chain is enhancing young women's departments

factory outlet store
A discount retailer, owned by a manufacturer, that sells off defective merchandise and excess inventory.

department stores
Retailers that sell a broad range of items and offer a good selection within each product line.

Samuel A.
Spralls III
a professor at Central Michigan University

My Advice for Eskimo Joe's would
be to choose

Option 2

real people, **Other Voices**

I would choose Option 2 for four reasons. First, Eskimo Joe's Bar has established a strong brand image as "Stillwater's Jumpin' Little Juke Joint" and its reputation is linked to that brand image. Positioned as "'the' place to go for beer, music, pool and foosball,"

the retailer has developed substantial brand equity that should be maintained. Second, Eskimo Joe's has created brand loyalty that goes beyond frequent patronization. Joe's, which is "more than just a place to drink," has captured psychological and emotional loyalty as well. Third, there is a significant possibility that Joe's will gain market share as weaker retailers are forced out of business by the new law. This, in turn, could offset the loss of Joe's traditional 18- to 20-year old customer base. Finally, there is the opportunity under this scenario to invest in the fast-growing apparel business and begin the process of morphing into a full-service restaurant, which would likely appeal to a broader segment of the Stillwater market and position the business for both domestic and global expansion. ➤

with new sound systems and Internet access. The chain also places these departments near the young men's department to create more of a social atmosphere.

Hypermarkets

hypermarkets

Retailers with the characteristics of both warehouse stores and supermarkets; hypermarkets are several times larger than other stores and offer virtually everything from grocery items to electronics.

Hypermarkets combine the characteristics of warehouse stores and supermarkets. Originally introduced in Europe, these are huge establishments several times larger than other stores. A supermarket might be 40,000 to 50,000 square feet, whereas a hypermarket takes up 200,000 to 300,000 square feet, or four football fields. They offer one-stop shopping, often for over 50,000 items, and feature restaurants, beauty salons, and children's play areas. Hypermarkets, such as those the French firm Carrefours runs, are popular in Europe and Latin America where big stores are somewhat of a novelty. More recently, Carrefours is expanding to developing countries such as China where a burgeoning population and a lack of large retailers provide hyper-opportunities. Hypermarkets have been less successful in the United States where many other shopping options including discount stores, malls, and supermarkets are available. Consumers in the United States find the hypermarkets to be too large and shopping in them too time-consuming.

Stan
Clark

APPLYING Nonstore Retailing

Eskimo Joe's started out as a bar, but over time an increasing proportion of its revenues come from merchandise the company sells over the Internet. This evolution illustrates how the Web can transform a small business in a college town to a global presence. ➡

3

OBJECTIVE

Describe the more common forms of nonstore retailing.

(pp. 512–514)

Nonstore Retailing

Stores like the Limited succeed because they put cool merchandise in the hands of young shoppers who can't get it elsewhere. But competition for shoppers' dollars comes from sources other than traditional stores that range from bulky catalogs to dynamic Web sites. Debbie in Dubuque can easily log on to alloy.com at 3:00 AM and order the latest belly-baring fashions without leaving home.

As the founder of the Neiman-Marcus department store once noted, "If customers don't want to get off their butts and go to your stores, you've got to go to them."[37] Indeed, many products are readily available in places other than stores. Think of the familiar Avon lady who sells beauty products to millions of women around the world. Avon allows customers to place orders by phone, fax, or catalog or through a sales representative.

nonstore retailing

Any method used to complete an exchange with a product end user that does not require a customer visit to a store.

Avon's success at giving customers alternatives to traditional store outlets illustrates the increasing importance of **nonstore retailing**, which is any method a firm uses to complete an exchange that does not require a customer to visit a store. Indeed, many conventional retailers—from upscale specialty stores such as Tiffany's to discounter Wal-Mart—offer nonstore alternatives such as catalogs and Web sites for customers who want to buy their merchandise. For other companies, such as Internet retailer Amazon.com, nonstore retailing is their entire business. Catalog companies have, perhaps, had the easiest time making the transition to the Web. Many have been able to use their experience delivering goods directly to consumers and make a successful jump to on-line sales.

In Chapter 14 we talked about direct marketing done through the mail, telephone, and television. In this section, we'll look at two other types of nonstore retailing: direct selling and automatic vending.

Direct Selling

Direct selling occurs when a salesperson presents a product to one individual or a small group, takes orders, and delivers the merchandise. The Direct Selling Association reported that in 2006, 15.2 million people engaged in direct selling in the United States and these activities generated $32.18 billion in sales. Of this, 75.2 percent of revenues came from face-to-face sales and 66.9 percent of those interactions took place in people's homes. Female salespeople accounted for 85.2 percent of all direct salespeople. The major product categories for direct sales include personal care products such as cosmetics, jewelry, and skin care products (33.7 percent), and home/family care products such as cleaning products, cookware, and cutlery (26.7 percent).[38]

direct selling
An interactive sales process in which a salesperson presents a product to one individual or a small group, takes orders, and delivers the merchandise.

Door-to-Door Sales

Door-to-door selling is still popular in some countries, such as China. But, it's declining in the United States, where two-income households are the norm, because fewer people are home during the day, and those who *are* home are reluctant to open their doors to strangers. Companies that used to rely on door-to-door sales have had to adapt their retailing strategies. Avon now sells to women at the office during lunch and coffee breaks.

Parties and Networks

Home shopping parties generate nearly 30 percent of direct sales; in these situations a company representative makes a sales presentation to a group of people who have gathered in the home of a friend.[39] One reason that these parties are so effective is that people who attend may get caught up in the "group spirit," and buy things they would not normally purchase if they were alone—even Botox injections to get rid of those nasty wrinkles. We call this sales technique a **party plan system**.

party plan system
A sales technique that relies heavily on people getting caught up in the "group spirit," buying things they would not normally buy if they were alone.

Perhaps the most famous party products are Tupperware; we associate Tupperware parties with American suburban life in the 1950s (along with wholesome TV shows like *Leave it to Beaver*).[40] Today Tupperware has over a million salespeople in more than 100 countries (80 percent of sales are from outside the United States) and the company sells its plastic ware through the Internet, infomercials, and mall kiosks. Tupperware parties are now more likely to be a rush-hour office event at the end of the workday.

Another form of nonstore retailing, which the Amway Company epitomizes, is a **multilevel network**, or *network marketing*. In this system, a *master distributor* recruits other people to become distributors. The master distributor sells the company's products to the people she entices to join, and then she receives commissions on all the merchandise sold by the people she recruits. Today, Amway has over 3 million independent business owners who distribute personal care, home care, and nutrition and commercial products in more than 80 countries and territories.[41] Amway and other similar network marketers use revival-like techniques to motivate distributors to sell products and find new recruits.[42]

multilevel network
A system in which a master distributor recruits other people to become distributors, sells the company's product to the recruits, and receives a commission on all the merchandise sold by the people recruited.

One of the advantages of *multilevel marketing* is that it allows firms to reach consumers who belong to tightly knit groups that are not so easy to reach. Salt Lake City–based Nu Skin Enterprises relies on Mormons to sell its products in Mormon communities. Shaklee (which sells food supplements, cleaning products, and personal care items) recruits salespeople in isolated religious communities, including Amish and Mennonite people (who receive "bonus buggies" instead of cars as prizes for superior salesmanship).[43]

pyramid schemes
An illegal sales technique that promises consumers or investors large profits from recruiting others to join the program rather than from any real investment or sale of goods to the public.

Modern vending machines are capable of selling a broad range of products. The bait machine on the top dispenses prepackaged minnows, night crawlers, red wigglers, and crickets in Styrofoam containers that keep bait fresh for up to one week. The image on the bottom dispenses cigars, and it features a direct line customers can use to order boxes of the cigars they purchase from the vending machine. Important: Do not mix up these

Despite the growing popularity of this technique, some network systems are illegal. They are really **pyramid schemes**: illegal scams which promise consumers or investors large profits from recruiting others to join the program rather than from any real investment or sale of good to the public. Often large numbers of people at the bottom of the pyramid pay money to advance to the top and to profit from others who might join. At recruiting meetings, pyramid promoters create a frenzied, enthusiastic atmosphere complete with promises of easy money. Some pyramid schemes are disguised as multilevel marketing—that is, people entering the pyramid do not pay fees to advance but they are forced to buy large costly quantities of merchandise. Of course, in these organizations, little or no effort ever goes into actually marketing the products.[44] That's one of the crucial differences between pyramid schemes and legitimate network marketers.

Automatic Vending

Coin-operated vending machines are a tried-and-true way to sell convenience goods, especially cigarettes and drinks. These machines are appealing because they require minimal space and personnel to maintain and operate. Some of the most interesting innovations are state-of-the-art vending machines that dispense everything from Ore-Ida French fries to software. French consumers purchase Levi's jeans from a machine called Libre Service that offers the pants in 10 different sizes. In the United States, vending machines that utilize touch screens and credit cards dispense pricey items like digital cameras and Elizabeth Arden cosmetics.[45] Macy's department stores offer consumers self-serve "Zoom Stores" in 400 of its locations. The Zoom Stores offer Macy's customers iPods and accessories that shoppers pay for with credit cards, debit cards, or Macy's gift cards. The giant vending machines allow Macy's to offer electronics without the expense of full electronics departments.[46]

In general, however, vending machines are best suited to the sales of inexpensive merchandise and food and beverages. Most consumers are reluctant to buy pricey items from a machine. New vending machines may spur more interest, however, as technological developments loom on the horizon, including video kiosk machines that let people see the product in use, have the ability to accept credit cards as payment, and have inventory systems that signal the operator when malfunctions or stockouts occur.

4

OBJECTIVE

Describe B2C e-commerce and its benefits, limitations, and future promise.
(pp. 514–519)

B2C E-Commerce

Business-to-consumer (B2C) e-commerce is on-line exchange between companies and individual consumers. Forrester Research reports that in 2007 total non-travel on-line sales were $175 billion; it expects revenues to grow by approximately $30 billion in each of the next five years. Furthermore, the vast majority (88 percent) of on-line consumers say they have purchased on-line in the past. The majority of consumers who did not purchase on-line told Forrester that they were concerned about sharing financial information on-line or that they wanted to see items before they bought. And even those consumers who shop on-line still prefer traditional off-line stores over the Internet.[47]

What is powering this on-line retail growth? As more people shop, more retailers enter the Web marketplace, which makes more types of products available. At the same time, enhanced technology and improvements in delivery and security entice even more consumers to shop on-line. Table 16.1 shows 2007 and predicted 2012 B2C sales in various product categories.

A number of factors prevent on-line sales from growing even more. Most consumers prefer stores where they can touch and feel items and avoid issues with returns and

Table 16.1	B2C Sales by Product Category	

Product Category	2007 On-line Sales (in $billions)	Projected 2012 On-line Sales (in $billions)
Total U.S. Internet Retail Sales (excluding travel)	$174.5	$334.7
Apparel, accessories, and footwear	$22.7	$41.8
Computer hardware and software	$20.7	$37.1
Auto/auto parts	$16.8	$30.9
Consumer electronics	$13.5	$29.5
Music/video	$8.2	$11.7
Books	$7.6	$9.5
Toys/video games	$6.7	$13.2
Jewelry	$6.4	$12.6
Food/beverage/grocery	$6.2	$13.7
Flowers/cards	$3.3	$6.4
Over-the-counter medicines and personal care	$1.8	$4.2
Cosmetics/fragrances	$1.0	$2.0

Source: Adapted from Sucharita Mulpuru with Carrie Johnson, Brendan McGowan, and Scott Wright, "US eCommerce Forecast: 2008 To 2012," January 18, 2008, Forrester Research, Inc.

shipping costs. Also, many consumers don't like to buy on-line because they want the product immediately. To address some of these issues, retailers such as Best Buy are merging their on-line and instore sales functions. Consumers can select an item and pay for it on-line and have it ready for pickup at their local store within hours—no wandering over the store to find the item or waiting in line to pay and no concerns about stockouts. We'll talk more about these limitations of B2C e-commerce later in this section.

Electronic commerce in retailing has enormous potential. The continued success of this nonstore format will depend on the ability of retailers to offer sites that are entertaining and informative and that are worth surfing to even after the novelty wears off. Lands' End, for example, offers a virtual model on its Web site that you can customize to your own body type as you let it "try on" that blouse or pair of shorts before you buy.

business-to-consumer (B2C) e-commerce
On-line exchanges between companies and individual consumers.

Benefits of B2C E-Commerce

For both consumers and marketers, B2C e-commerce provides a host of benefits and some limitations. Table 16.2 lists some of these. E-commerce allows consumers and marketers to easily find and make exchanges in a global marketplace. Consumers can choose from hundreds of thousands of sellers worldwide, while marketers can tap into consumer and business markets with virtually no geographic limitations.

From the consumer's perspective, electronic marketing increases convenience as it breaks down many of the barriers time and location cause. You can shop 24/7 without leaving home. Consumers in even the smallest of communities can purchase funky shoes or a hot swimsuit from Bloomingdales.com just like big-city dwellers. In less-developed countries, the Internet lets consumers purchase products that may not be available at all in local markets. The Web site Ideeli offers its customers the chance to buy heavily discounted luxury items in a kind on on-line "blue-light special" on your cell phone. Thus, the Internet can improve the quality of life without the necessity of developing costly infrastructure, such as opening retail stores in remote locations.

Ideeli is one of a new breed of social networking sites that lets users dish about fashion items as well as buy them.

| Table 16.2 | Benefits and Limitations of E-Commerce |

Benefits	Limitations
For the consumer:	**For the consumer:**
Shop 24 hours a day	Lack of security
Less traveling	Fraud
Can receive relevant information in seconds from any location	Can't touch items
More product choices	Exact colors may not reproduce on computer monitors
More products available to less developed countries	Expensive to order and then return
Greater price information	Potential breakdown of human relationships
Lower prices, so less affluent can purchase	**For the marketer:**
Participate in virtual auctions	Lack of security
Fast delivery	Must maintain site to reap benefits
Electronic communities	Fierce price competition
For the marketer:	Conflicts with conventional retailers
The world is your marketplace	Legal issues not resolved
Decreases costs of doing business	
Very specialized businesses can be successful	
Real-time pricing	

experiential shoppers
Consumers who engage in on-line shopping because of the experiential benefits they receive.

Understanding just what on-line shoppers really desire and why they are shopping on-line makes marketers more successful. For some consumers, on-line shopping provides an additional benefit because it fulfills their experiential needs, that is, their desire to shop for fun. Consumers who are collectors or who enjoy hobbies are most likely to be **experiential shoppers**. While most on-line consumers engage in goal-directed behavior—they wish to satisfy their shopping goal as quickly as possible—between 20 and 30 percent of on-line consumers shop on-line because they enjoy the "thrill of the hunt" as much as or more than the actual acquisition of the item. Experiential shoppers linger at sites longer and a desire to be entertained is what motivates them. Consequently, marketers who wish to attract these customers must design Web sites that offer surprise, uniqueness, and excitement. LandsEnd.com gives frequent markdowns on overstock items, which encourages bargain-hunter experiential shoppers to visit the site more frequently. How well a site satisfies experiential needs helps to determine how much money consumers will choose to spend at that site.

Marketers realize equally important benefits from e-commerce. Because an organization can reach such a large number of consumers via electronic commerce, it is possible to develop very specialized businesses that could not be profitable if limited by geographic constraints. The Internet provides an excellent opportunity to bring merchants with excess merchandise and bargain-hunting consumers together.[48] The Web site Ideeli, which we mentioned earlier, offers members a chance to buy heavily discounted luxury items, which—if they act fast enough to take advantage of the site's special offers. When retailers become concerned that, due to economic downturns or other factors, consumers may not buy enough, they may utilize on-line liquidators such as Overstock.com and Bluefly that offer consumers great bargains on apparel and accessories, items that retailers refer to as "distressed inventory."

Even high fashion designers whose retail outlets we associate with Rodeo Drive in Los Angeles, Fifth Avenue in New York, and the Magnificent Mile in Chicago are setting up shop on the Internet to sell $3,000 skirts and $5,000 suits.[49] Forrester Research predicts that soon luxury apparel on-line sales will approach $1 billion per year. Armani, for example, offers its entire Emporio collection at EmporioArmani.com. The high-end Neiman Marcus department store finds it can easily sell items like $7,900 Valentino gowns and $5,500 Carolina Herrera jackets on-line.

Web sites also allow the retailer to meet the needs of shoppers who don't live near the company's stores. For example, although your town may not have enough fanatic dog owners to support a doggie toy store, there are a number of sites on the Web, including Dogtoys.com and FuturePets.com, that cater to the needs of pampered pooches.

As we discussed in Chapter 11, one of the biggest advantages of e-commerce is that it's easy to get price information. Want to buy a new Hellboy action figure, a mountain bike, an MP3 player, or just about anything else you can think of? Instead of plodding from store to store to compare prices, many Web surfers use search engines or "shop bots" like Ask. com that compile and compare prices from multiple vendors. With readily available pricing information, shoppers can browse brands, features, reviews, and information on where to buy that particular product. This means that consumers can find all of this information in one central location, which makes shopping more efficient.

E-commerce also allows businesses to reduce costs. Compared to traditional bricks-and-mortar retailers, e-tailers' costs are minimal—no expensive mall sites to maintain and no sales associates to pay. And, for some products, such as computer software and digitized music, e-commerce provides fast, almost instantaneous delivery. Beginning in 2000, consumers could download music at no charge, thanks to the infamous Napster program 19-year-old college dropout Shawn Fanning created. Although Napster didn't store music on its own servers, the software allowed its members to download music that other Napster members had on their computers. After the Recording Industry Association of America as well as the heavy-metal band Metallica sued the service, Napster closed in July 2001. In 2003, after years of dealing with such digital piracy, the music industry began to license music to a host of legal download services. Music fans responded by buying over 30 million downloads from sites including iTunes (an Apple Computer site), Dell, and Wal-Mart Stores, Inc. Now, Napster is open for business once again—although today the downloads no longer are free.[50] Newer entertainment downloads have gone a step further with sites such as iTunes that offer on-line shoppers the opportunity to purchase or rent movies. Just download a flick to your iPod, plug it into your new flatscreen TV and pop some corn. You're set for the evening.

Limitations of B2C E-Commerce

But, all is not perfect in the virtual world. E-commerce does have its limitations. One drawback compared to shopping in a store is that customers must wait a few days to receive most products, which are often sent via private delivery services, so shoppers can't achieve instant gratification by walking out of a store clutching their latest "finds." And many e-commerce sites still suffer from poor design that people find confusing or irritating. One study found that 65 percent of on-line shoppers empty their carts before they complete their purchase because they find the process hard to follow and there are no "flesh and blood" customer service people available to answer questions. To make matters worse, 30 percent of on-line shoppers who have problems with a Web site say they won't shop there again, and 10 percent say they won't shop on-line at all anymore.[51]

Security is a concern to both consumers and marketers. We hear horror stories of consumers whose credit cards and other identity information have been stolen. Although in the United States an individual's financial liability in most theft cases is limited because credit card companies usually absorb most or all of the loss, the damage to one's credit rating can last for years.

Consumers also are concerned about Internet fraud. Although most of us feel competent to judge a local bricks-and-mortar business by its physical presence, by how long it's been around, and from the reports of friends and neighbors who shop there, we have little or no information on the millions of Internet sites offering their products for sale—even though sites like eBay and the Better Business Bureau try to address these concerns by posting extensive information about the reliability of individual vendors.

Metrics Moment

E-commerce marketers often try to look at a metric they call the *conversion rate*, which is the percentage of visitors to an on-line store who purchase from it. This is a useful metric, but if this rate is low, it doesn't help the retailer understand the problems that might affect the Web site's performance. So, in addition to knowing the conversion rate, researchers at IBM compute other metrics that they call *microconversion rates* to pinpoint more precisely what companies may need to improve in their on-line shopping process.[52] This technique breaks down the shopping experience into the stages that occur from the time a customer visits a site to if or when she actually makes a transaction:

- **Product impression:** Viewing a hyperlink to a Web page that presents a product
- **Click-through:** Clicking on the hyperlink and viewing the product's Web page
- **Basket placement:** Placing the item in the "shopping basket"
- **Purchase:** Actually buying the item

These researchers calculate microconversion rates for each adjacent pair of measures to come up with additional metrics that can pinpoint specific problems in the shopping process:

- **Look-to-click rate:** How many product impressions convert to click-throughs? This can help the e-tailer determine if the products it features on the Web site are the ones that customers want to see.
- **Click-to-basket rate:** How many click-throughs result in the shopper placing a product in the shopping basket? This metric helps to determine if the detailed information the site provides about the product is appropriate.
- **Basket-to-buy rate:** How many basket placements convert to purchases? This metric can tell the e-tailer which kinds of products shoppers are more likely to abandon in the shopping cart instead of buying them. It can also pinpoint possible problems with the checkout process, such as forcing the shopper to answer too many questions or making her wait too long for her credit card to be approved.

Another problem is that people need "touch-and-feel" information before they buy many products. Although it may be satisfactory to buy a computer or a book on the Internet, buying clothing and other items for which touching the item or trying it on is essential may be less attractive. As with catalogs, even though most on-line companies have liberal return policies consumers can still get stuck with large delivery and return shipping charges for items that don't fit or simply aren't the right color. In some cases, ingenious businesspeople find ways to combine electronic retailing with traditional shopping to overcome this barrier. For example, Peapod.com, the leading Internet grocer in the United States, offers home delivery of groceries to 12,700,000 households in 18 metropolitan areas. A "personal shopper" selects the groceries so they are based on customers' exact preferences; she even squeezes fruit to be sure it corresponds to the customer's exact ripeness requirements.

Developing countries with primarily cash economies pose yet another obstacle to the global success of B2C e-commerce. In these countries, few people use credit cards, so they can't easily pay for items they purchase over the Internet. Furthermore, banks are far less likely to offer consumers protection against fraudulent use of their cards so a hacked card number can literally wipe you out. *Digital cash* is a payment alternative that may become more popular in the future. Currently, this option is available on prepaid cards and smart cards such as a prepaid phone card.

Another alternative is e-cash, developed by Digicash of Amsterdam. E-cash provides secure payments between computers using e-mail or the Internet. You can use e-cash to buy a pizza or to get money from home. To do so, you need e-cash client software and a *digital bank account*, a Web-based account that allows you to make payments to Internet retailers directly from the account while on-line. You withdraw money from your bank account, store it on your computer, and spend it when you need to. When the going gets tough, the tough go shopping!

As major marketers beef up their presence on the Web, they worry that inventory they sell on-line will *cannibalize* their store sales (we discussed the strategic problem of cannibalization in Chapter 9). This is a big problem for companies like bookseller Barnes & Noble, which has to be careful as it steers customers toward its Web site and away from its chain of stores bursting with inventory. Barnes & Noble has to deal with competitors such as Amazon.com (with 40 million worldwide customers and annual sales of not only books but myriad products from apparel to cell phones of over $14.84 billion in 2007), which sells its books and music exclusively over its six global Web sites and so doesn't have to worry about this problem.[53]

B2C's Effect on the Future of Retailing

Does the growth of B2C e-commerce mean the death of bricks-and-mortar stores as we know them? Don't plan any funerals for your local stores prematurely. Although some argue that virtual distribution channels will completely replace traditional ones because of their cost advantages, this is unlikely. For example, although a bank saves 80 percent of its costs when customers do business on-line from their home computers, Wells Fargo found that it could not force its customers to use PC-based banking services. At least in the short term, too many people are accustomed to obtaining goods and services from stores—and, of course, shopping provides a social outlet that solitary surfing can't replace. For now, clicks will have to coexist with bricks.

However, this doesn't mean that physical retailers can rest easy. Stores as we know them will continue to evolve to lure shoppers away from their computer screens. In the future, the trend will be *destination retail*; that is, consumers will visit retailers not so much to buy a product but for the entertainment they receive from the total experience. Many retailers are already developing ways to make the shopping in bricks-and-mortar stores an experience rather than just a place to pick up stuff. For example, Levi Strauss opened a retail store in San Francisco that features a "shrink-to-fit" hot tub, fabric painting and ornamentation services, and a showcase of new music, art, and Levi's product samples from around the world.[54] At the General Mills Cereal Adventure in the Mall of America, children of all ages cavort in the Cheerios Play Park and the Lucky Charms Magical Forest. Sony's Metreon in San Francisco is a high-tech mall that features futuristic computer games and cutting-edge electronics.[55]

5

Develop a Store Positioning Strategy:
Retailing as Theater

A "destination retail" strategy reminds us that shopping often is part buying, part entertainment, and part social outlet. So far we've seen that we distinguish stores in several ways, including the types of products they carry and the breadth and depth of their assortments. But recall that a store is itself a product that adds to or subtracts from the goods the shopper came to buy there.

When we decide which store to patronize, many of us are less likely to say, "I'll go there because their assortment is broad," and more likely to say, "That place is so cool. I really like hanging out there." Stores can entertain us, bore us, make us angry, or even make us sad (unless it's a funeral parlor, that last kind probably won't be in business for long). In today's competitive marketplace, retailers have to do more than offer good inventory at reasonable prices. They need to position their stores so that they offer a competitive advantage over other stores that also vie for the shopper's attention—not to mention the catalogs, Web sites, and shopping channels that may offer the same or similar merchandise. Let's see next how bricks-and-mortar retailers compete against these alternatives.

Walk into REI, a Seattle-based retailer with over 70 stores in 24 states, and you'll find gear for camping, climbing, cycling, skiing, outdoor cross-training, paddling, snow sports, and travel. REI is more than that,

Cutting-edge retailers and mall developers understand that stores of the future will double as entertainment centers and social hubs that will let shoppers hungry for stimulation shop, eat, network, and have a good time all at once. This is the CocoWalk mall in Coconut Grove, Florida.

REI creates a stimulating, interactive shopping environment. Some stores, like this one in Seattle, even include a rockclimbing pinnacle.

though. The Seattle store, for example, features a 65-foot-high, artificial climbing rock, while other REI stores include a vented area for testing camp stoves and an outdoor trail to check out mountain bikes. Buying a water pump? Test it in an indoor river. Want to try out those boots before you walk in them? Take a walk on hiking boot test trails.[56]

In Chapter 10, we saw that staging a service is much like putting on a play. Similarly, many retailers recognize that much of what they do is theater. At a time when it is possible to pick up a phone or log on to a computer to buy many items, a customer must have a reason to make a trip to a store instead. True, you can probably buy that jacket over the Web, but try getting your computer to rain on it.

Shoppers are an audience to entertain. The "play" can cleverly use stage sets (store design) and actors (salespeople) that together create a "scene." For example, think about buying a pair of sneakers. Athletic shoe stores are a far cry from the old days, when a tired shoe salesman (much like Al Bundy in the TV show *Married with Children*) waded through box after box of shoes as kids ran amuck across dingy floors.

Now salespeople (actors) dress in costumes such as black-striped referee outfits. Stores like Foot Locker are ablaze with neon, and they display their shoes in clear acrylic walls so they appear to be floating.[57] All these special effects make the buying occasion less about buying and more about having an experience. As one marketing strategist commented, "The line between retail and entertainment is blurring. Even traditionally stodgy banks are getting on board and are revamping their buildings to look more like coffeehouses and retail boutiques. Some branch banks now offer customers amenities such as comfortable couches, Wi-Fi Internet access, movie screens, and even yoga classes."[58] In this section, we'll review some of the tools available to the retailing playwright.

Store Image

store image
The way the marketplace perceives a retailer relative to the competition.

When people think of a store, they often have no trouble describing it in the same terms they might use to describe a person. They might come up with labels like *exciting, boring, old-fashioned, tacky,* or *elegant.* **Store image** is how the target market perceives the store—its market position relative to the competition. Even stores the same parent company such as Federated operates can be quite different from one another; many shoppers see Bloomingdale's department stores as chic and fashionable, especially compared to its sister stores that do business under the Macy's name. Eskimo Joe's distinctive personality as "Stillwater's Jumpin' Little Juke Joint" is probably the retailer's strongest asset. But these images don't just happen. Just as brand managers do for products, store managers work hard to create a distinctive and appealing personality.

To appreciate this idea, consider the dramatic makeover now in place at Selfridges, long a well-known but dowdy British department store chain. At the newly renovated flagship store in London, shoppers can wander over to a body-piercing salon where store associates are teenagers in dreadlocks. Periodic events that scream cutting-edge accent the store's makeover, including the "Body Craze" promotion when thousands of shoppers flocked to see 650 naked people ride the escalators.[59]

Not every store can (or wants) to have naked people running around the store, but even more modest strategies to enliven the atmosphere make a big difference. When a retailer decides to create a desirable store image, it has many tools at its disposal. Ideally, all these elements work together to create a clear, coherent picture that meets consumers' expectations of what that particular shopping experience should be. Figure 16.2 illustrates one early attempt to identify and compare the store images of eight different department stores in the New York City area (some of which are now defunct).

Atmospherics is the use of color, lighting, scents, furnishings, sounds, and other design elements to create a desired setting. Marketers manipulate these elements to create a certain "feeling" for the retail environment.[60]

Think convenience stores are just for convenience and a late night gallon of milk? Maverik Country Stores, Inc., doesn't think so. The 187-store chain transformed itself from an Old West country store to match its slogan, "Adventure's First Stop." Customers from soccer moms to mountain bikers think it's a fun place. Inspired by the Walt Disney Co. theme parks that entertain visitors both on the rides and in waiting lines, Maverikland combines the typical convenience-store merchandise with a one-of-a-kind shopping experience, a sense of adventure customers can't get anywhere else. The Adventure First Stop stores feature cascading waterfalls of fountain drinks, a winding river of coffee, and snowy mountains made of frozen yogurt. Unique names are also a part of the fun. Destination areas of the stores include Bodacious Bean coffee stations, Fountain Falls beverage dispensers, Big Moon restrooms (no comment), Big Bear Bakery, and Room with a Brew walk-in beer coolers. Even the three levels of Maverik's loyalty program have adventure-related names: Action Level, Expert Level, and Extreme Level. Employees are called "Adventure Guides." Vivid graphics add to the atmosphere: Store décor includes brightly colored, action-packed 3-D murals, lifelike mannequins, trees with real branches, blue sky ceilings, and stained concrete floors that make you think you're walking in the great outdoors. The stores even wrap their fuel pumps and tanker delivery trucks in murals of sports images such as jet skis and snowmobiles.[61]

Store Design: Set the Stage

The elements of store design should correspond to management's desired image. A bank lobby needs to convey respectability and security because people need to be reassured

atmospherics
The use of color, lighting, scents, furnishings, and other design elements to create a desired store image.

Figure 16.2 | Mapping a Store's Personality

Marketers use perceptual mapping to chart the personality of retail stores.
Source: Adapted from BBDO, Stephanie from, "Image and Attitude Are Department Stores' Draw," *New York Times*, August 12, 1993, B1.

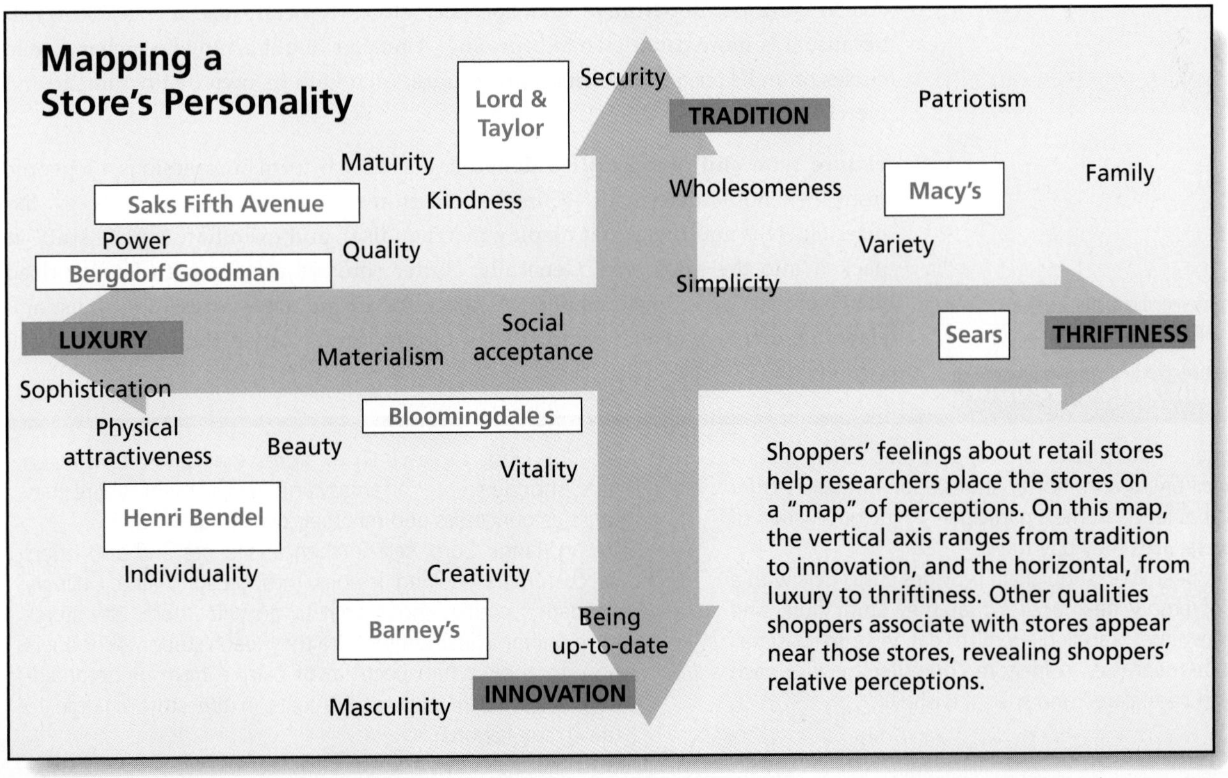

Mapping a Store's Personality

Security · TRADITION · Patriotism
Lord & Taylor
Maturity · Wholesomeness · Macy's · Family
Saks Fifth Avenue · Kindness
Power · Quality · Variety
Bergdorf Goodman · Simplicity
Social
LUXURY · Materialism · acceptance · Sears · THRIFTINESS
Sophistication
Physical attractiveness · Beauty · Bloomingdale s · Vitality
Henri Bendel
Individuality · Creativity
Barney's · Being up-to-date
Masculinity · INNOVATION

Shoppers' feelings about retail stores help researchers place the stores on a "map" of perceptions. On this map, the vertical axis ranges from tradition to innovation, and the horizontal, from luxury to thriftiness. Other qualities shoppers associate with stores appear near those stores, revealing shoppers' relative perceptions.

Stan
Clark

APPLYING **Store Positioning Strategy**

Stan employs the elements of atmospherics to create a distinctive personality for each of his restaurants. These include employees' behavior and appearance as well as décor and the physical design of each operation. ➡

traffic flow
The direction in which shoppers will move through the store and which areas they will pass or avoid.

activity stores
Experiential retailing environments that involve customers in the creation of the products they buy.

about the safety of their money. In contrast, a used bookstore might create a disorderly look so that shoppers think treasures lie buried beneath piles of tattered novels.

Today many retailers seek to create a "playground" for adults in their stores, often through sophisticated use of lighting, more intimate retail spaces and even strategic smells they pump into the space.[62] The Nova Scotia Liquor Corp. scents its wine section with the smell of baked bread to suggest the paring of bread and wine. The beer section offers consumers the scent of fresh cut grass to remind customers of summer even in the dead of winter. Drom Fragrances International offers customers the chance to check out its products in "Smelling Booths."[63] At Levi's Stores and other retailers, consumers can enjoy a Jetsons-like virtual fitting room. A shopper steps into the cylindrical unit where holographic imaging technology performs a 360-degree body scan in less than 10 seconds. The customer then gets a printout with the store's styles and sizes that will best fit his particular body type.[64]

Here are some other design factors that retailers consider:

- **Store layout:** This is the arrangement of merchandise in the store. The placement of fixtures such as shelves, racks, and cash registers is important because store layout determines **traffic flow**—how shoppers will move through the store and which areas they will pass or avoid. A *grid layout*, which we usually find in supermarkets and discount stores, consists of rows of neatly spaced shelves that are at right angles or parallel to one another. This configuration is useful when management wants to move shoppers systematically down each aisle, being sure that they pass through such high-margin sections as deli and meat. Figure 16.3 illustrates how a grid layout in a supermarket helps regulate traffic flow.

  A typical strategy is to place staple goods in more remote areas. The designers know that traffic will move to these areas because shoppers need to purchase these items frequently. They try to place impulse goods in spots shoppers will pass on their way to look for something else to encourage them to stop and check them out. Then they place eye-catching displays to rope people in, such as the signs for Mountain Dew that PepsiCo puts above the cash registers in convenience stores that look like a mountain biker dropped through the ceiling.

  In contrast, department and specialty stores typically use a *free-flow layout* because it is more conducive to browsing. A retailer might arrange merchandise in circles or arches or perhaps in separate areas, each with its own distinct image and merchandise mix.

- **Fixture type and merchandise density:** Just as we form impressions of people from their home decor, our feelings about stores are affected by furnishings, fixtures (shelves and racks that display merchandise), and even how much "stuff" is packed into the sales area. Generally, clutter conveys a store with lower-priced merchandise. Upscale stores allocate space for sitting areas, dressing rooms, and elaborate displays of merchandise. A shopping center called the Lab in southern

By the **People**, For the **People**

To boost the entertainment value of shopping (and to lure on-line shoppers back to bricks-and-mortar stores), some retailers offer **activity stores** that let consumers participate in the production of the products or services they buy there:[65]

- The Build-A-Bear Workshop chain provides customers with a selection of empty bear bodies that they stuff, fluff, and dress in costumes ranging from bridal veils to baseball gloves. Customers use an in-store computer to print each bear's "birth certificate" and special wish.

- At Club Libby Lu, a chain of stores that caters to preteen girls, shoppers enter a fantasyland environment where they dress as princesses and mix their own fragrances.
- Viking Range Corp. sells kitchen appliances and also offers its customers cooking lessons through its Viking Culinary Academy so they know what to do with them. The stores have built-in classrooms where they teach students/shoppers how to cook a full spectrum of cuisine from gingerbread-houses to Indian cuisine. Products in the store change to match the lessons.

Figure 16.3 | Grid Layout

A grid layout encourages customers to move up and down the aisles, passing many different products, and supermarkets and discount stores often use it.

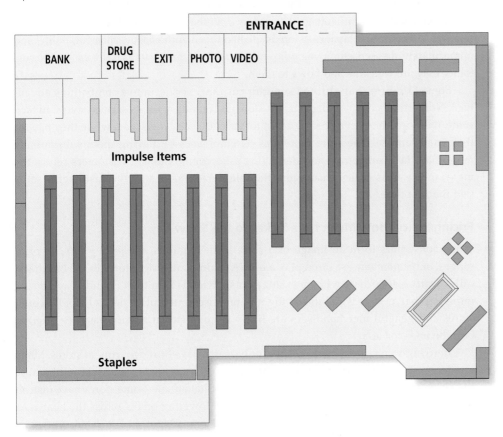

California attracts a target audience of mall rats aged 18 to 30 as it incorporates unusual furnishings such as concrete walls, a fountain made of oil drums, and an open-air living room filled with thrift-shop furniture to craft a laid-back image its patrons call "the antimall."

- **The sound of music:** An elegant restaurant softly playing Mozart in the background is worlds apart from a raucous place such as the Hard Rock Café, where loud rock-and-roll is essential to the atmosphere. The music playing in a store has become so central to its personality that many retailers, including Ralph Lauren, Victoria's Secret, Au Bon Pain, Starbucks, and Pottery Barn, even sell the sound-tracks specially designed for them.[66]

- **Color and lighting:** Marketers use color and lighting to set a mood. Red, yellow, and orange are warm colors (fast-food chains use a lot of orange to stimulate hunger), whereas blue, green, and violet signify elegance and cleanliness. Light colors make one feel more serene, whereas bright colors convey excitement. Fashion designer Norma Kamali replaced fluorescent lights with pink ones after its managers discovered that pink lighting creates a more flattering reflection in dressing room mirrors, so female customers were more willing to try on bathing suits.[67]

Store Personnel

Store personnel (the actors) should complement a store's image. Each employee has a part to play, complete with props and costumes. Movie theaters often dress ushers in tuxedos, and many stores provide employees with scripts to use when they present products to customers.

Although the presence of knowledgeable sales personnel is important to shoppers, they generally rate the quality of service they receive from retail personnel as low, often because stores don't hire enough people to wait on their customers.[68] Retailers work hard to maintain service quality, though they often find that the rapid turnover of salespeople makes this a difficult goal to achieve. Perhaps they can learn from Japanese retailers. A visitor to a Japanese store is greeted by an enthusiastic, cheerful, polite, and immaculately dressed employee who, no matter how busy she is, tells each new customer they are welcome and bows to them.

Some U.S. firms have turned superior customer service into a competitive advantage. Nordstrom's chain of department stores is legendary for its service levels. In fact, some "Nordies" have even been known to warm up customers' cars while they pay for their merchandise! The store motivates its employees by paying them substantially more than the average rate and deducting sales commissions if customers return the merchandise. This policy encourages the salesperson to be sure the customer is satisfied the first time.

Pricing Policy: How Much for a Ticket to the Show?

When consumers form an image of a store in their minds, the *price points*, or price ranges, of its merchandise often play a role. A chain of off-price stores in the Northeast called Daffy's advertises with such slogans as, "Friends Don't Let Friends Pay Retail," implying that anyone who buys at the full, nondiscounted price needs help. Discount stores and general merchandisers are likely to compete on a price basis by offering brand names for less.

In recent years, consumers' desires for bargains have hurt department stores. Many retailers responded by running frequent sales, a strategy that often backfired because they trained consumers to buy *only* when the store held a sale. Some stores have instead reduced the number of sales they run in favor of lowering prices across the board. As we saw in Chapter 11, some stores, including Home Depot and Wal-Mart, offer an *everyday-low-pricing (EDLP) strategy*; they set prices that are between the list price the manufacturer suggests and the deeply discounted price stores that compete on price only offer.

Build the Theater: Store Location

Any real estate agent will tell you the three most important factors when they sell a home are "location, location, and location." The same is true in retailing. Wal-Mart's success is due not only to what it is but also to *where* it is. It was the first large discount retailer to locate in small and rural markets. When they choose a site, Wal-Mart's planners consider factors such as proximity to highways and major traffic routes. By carefully selecting "undiscovered" areas, the company has been able to negotiate cheap leases in towns with expanding populations. This is an important strategic advantage for Wal-Mart because it means access to markets hungry for a store that offers such a wide assortment of household goods. In this section we'll review some important aspects of retail locations.

Types of Store Locations

As Figure 16.4 shows, there are four basic types of retail locations. Stores locate in a business district, in a shopping center, as a freestanding entity, or in a nontraditional location.

central business district (CBD)
The traditional downtown business area found in a town or city.

- **Business districts:** A **central business district (CBD)** is the traditional downtown business area you'll find in a town or city. Many people are drawn to the area to shop or work, and public transportation is usually available. CBDs have suffered in recent years because of concerns about security, lack of parking, and the lack of customer traffic on evenings and weekends. To combat these problems, many cities provide incentives

Figure 16.4 | Types of Store Locations

Different types of store locations are best for different types of retailers. Retailers choose from among central business districts, shopping centers, freestanding stores, and nontraditional locations.

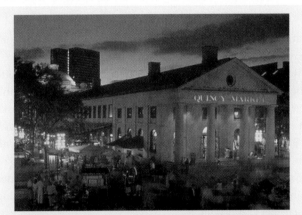

A central business district is often found in downtown areas. Although U.S. retailers have been deserting impoverished center cities in droves for the past 20 years, these downtown areas are now staging a comeback. Sophisticated developments such as festival marketplaces including New York City's South Street Seaport, Union Station in St. Louis, Harborplace in Baltimore, and Boston's Fanueil Hall (shown here) are contributing to the renaissance of American cities.

A shopping center is a group of commercial establishments owned and managed as a single property. They range in size from strip centers to superregional centers such as the Mall of America, which covers 4.2 million square feet of shopping space. Shopping malls offer the ability to combine shopping with entertainment.

A freestanding store is not located near other stores. This locational strategy, used by some big chains like Kids "R" Us, has the advantage of offering a lack of direct competition, lower rents, and adaptability. The store has the freedom to alter its selling space to accommodate its own needs. On the other hand, the store had better be popular because it cannot rely on the drawing power of neighbor stores to provide it with customer traffic.

A nontraditional location offers products to shoppers in convenient places. For example, Taco Bell now has locations inside Target stores, tempting shoppers to take a taquito break.

such as tax breaks to encourage the opening of stores and entertainment areas such as Boston's Quincy Marketplace. These vibrant developments or *festival marketplaces* have done a lot to reverse the fortunes of aging downtown areas from Boston to Baltimore.

- **Shopping centers:** A **shopping center** is a group of commercial establishments owned and managed as a single property. They range in size and scope from *strip centers* to massive *superregional centers* such as Minneapolis's Mall of America, which offers 4.2 million square feet of shopping plus such attractions as a seven-acre Knott's Camp Snoopy Theme Park. Strip centers offer quick and easy access to basic conveniences such as dry cleaners and video rentals, though shoppers seeking more exotic goods need to look elsewhere. Shopping malls offer variety and the ability to combine shopping with entertainment. Rents tend to be high in shopping malls, making it difficult for many stores to be profitable. In addition, small specialty stores may find it hard to compete with a mall's *anchor stores*, the major department stores that typically draw many shoppers.

  A *lifestyle center* combines the feel of a neighborhood park with the convenience of a strip mall. Typically located in affluent neighborhoods and featuring expensive landscaping, these more intimate centers are an appealing way for retailers to blend in to residential areas. Retailers including Williams-Sonoma and Talbot's invest heavily in this concept.[69]

shopping center
A group of commercial establishments owned and managed as a single property.

- **Freestanding retailers:** Some stores, usually larger ones such as IKEA, are freestanding, located by themselves in a separate building. These retailers benefit from lower rents and fewer parking problems. However, the store must be attractive enough on its own to be a destination point for shoppers because it can't rely on spillover from consumers visiting other stores at the same place.

- **Nontraditional store locations:** Innovative retailers find new ways to reach consumers. For example, many entrepreneurs use *carts* or *kiosks*, to sell their products. Carts are small, movable stores that can be set up in many locations including inside malls, in airports, or in other public facilities. Kiosks are slightly larger than carts and offer store-like facilities, including telephone hookups and electricity. Carts and kiosks are relatively inexpensive and a good way for new businesses to get started. Even hotels are getting mobile. SuiteMovil sells pop-up motel units called the Hotelmovil. The units look very much like a normal 18-wheel semi truck but at the press of a remote control, four legs lower to the ground, a second story rises, the first floor slides out, and just like that you have 11 bedrooms, each with its own private bath, heating and air conditioning, flat-screen TV, and WiFi.[70]

Site Selection: Choose Where to Build

A story from the past is that Sam Walton, the founder of Wal-Mart, used to fly over an area in a small plane until he found a spot that appealed to him. Now factors such as long-term population patterns, the location of competitors, and the demographic makeup of an area enter into retailers' decisions. The choice of where to open a new store should reflect the company's overall growth strategy. It should be consistent with long-term goals and be in a place that allows the company to best support the outlet. For example, a chain with stores and an extensive warehouse system in the Northeast may not be wise to open a new store in California because the store would be an "orphan," cut off from the company's supply lines.

trade area
A geographic zone that accounts for the majority of a store's sales and customers.

Location planners look at many factors when they select a site. They want to find a place that is convenient to customers in the store's **trade area**, the geographic zone that accounts for the majority of its sales and customers.[71] A *site evaluation* considers specific factors such as traffic flow; number of parking spaces available; ease of delivery access; visibility from the street; local zoning laws that determine the types of buildings, parking, and signage allowed; and cost factors such as the length of the lease and the amount of local taxes.

Planners also consider population characteristics such as age profile (is the area witnessing an influx of new families?), community life cycle (is the community relatively new, stable, or in decline?), and mobility (how often do people move into and out of the area?). This information is available from a variety of sources, including the U.S. Bureau of the Census, the buying power index (BPI) the trade magazine *Sales & Marketing Management* publishes each year, and research firms such as Urban Decision Systems and Claritas that analyze many forms of demographic data to create profiles of selected areas.

Planners also have to consider the degree of competition they will encounter if they locate in one place versus another. One strategy that fast-food outlets, for example, follow is to locate in a *saturated trade area*. This is a site where a sufficient number of stores already exist so that high customer traffic is present but where the retailer believes it can compete successfully by going head to head with the competition. As one fast-food industry executive put it, "Customers are lazybones. They absolutely will not walk one more step. You literally have to put a store where people are going to smack their face against it." However, that task is getting harder and harder because at this point many of the good sites are already taken: The United States has 277,208 fast-food outlets from coast to coast—one for every 1,000 people in the country. Subway Restaurants opens a new store in the United States every three hours on average. Starbucks unveils a new store every 11 hours, and Quiznos Sub opens a new door every 16 hours.[72]

Another strategy is to find an *understored trade area*, where too few stores exist to satisfy the needs of the population (this was Wal-Mart's strategy) and the retailer can establish itself as a dominant presence in the community. Over time, these areas may become *overstored* so that too many stores exist to sell the same goods. Those that can't compete are forced to move or close, as has happened to many small mom-and-pop stores that can't beat the Wal-Marts of the world at their sophisticated retailing games.

A store's targeted consumer segment also determines where it locates. For example, a new, growing community appeals to hardware stores that can supply hammers and drywall to home owners, while upscale dress stores and travel agencies might find better locations in more established areas because people living there have the income to spend on fashion items and vacations. The Buckle, a clothing store chain, successfully sells designer clothing in 200 small towns across the United States. This retailer specifically targets high school and college students who want cutting-edge fashion but who live in relatively isolated areas.[73]

Now that you've learned about retailing, read "Real People, Real Choices: How It Worked Out" to see which strategy Stan Clark of Eskimo Joe's selected.

© Eskimo Joe's Clothes. www.eskimojoes.com

real people, **Real Choices**

Stan
Clark
Stan chose:

Option

How It Worked Out at Eskimo Joe's

Stan chose Option 1. He gave himself six months to completely convert the facility, and he reopened Eskimo Joe's as a trendy restaurant. The success was immediate, and Stan credits the result with paying close attention to the quality of food and service. In fact, his business philosophy revolves around hiring people who embody both fun and attention to customers and quality. To this day Stan participates in almost every job interview, regardless of the position. He looks for applicants that personify the Eskimo Joe's values of customers and fun first. His success is as infectious as Eskimo Joe's smile, and today the company consists of three restaurants that locals call "The Three Amigos." The original Eskimo Joe's, located right across from campus, still serves up burgers, cheese fries, and other fun fare, while Mexico Joe's offers south-of-the-border food and Joseppi's is a family-style Italian place. On the apparel side, the rise of on-line shopping and continued cult-like status of the logo have driven Stan's Eskimo Joe's clothing business to unanticipated heights. It may be an urban legend that only Hard Rock Café sells more nonathletic emblem logo apparel than Eskimo Joe's, but still it's inevitable that if you travel around enough you will spot Joe's grinning face on shirts all over the world. The apparel is sold in a store right at Eskimo Joe's, in outlets in Tulsa and Oklahoma City, and also via a thriving catalog and on-line business (check out **www.eskimojoes.com**). And recently, Stan has further expanded the business by developing logo merchandise for other businesses that want to offer promotional products.

Marketing Metrics: How Eskimo Joe's Measures Success

To measure how well its bricks-and-mortar (restaurant and apparel store) operations are doing, Eskimo Joe's uses metrics that are standard in these businesses. These include table turnover and average sale per customer for the restaurants and profit per square foot for clothing sales. And, like other e-commerce retailers, Eskimo Joe's assesses its on-line logo merchandise business by calculating metrics such as click-through percentage (that is, the number of browsers who hit the site and then buy from it) and the percentage of repeat purchases by the same customers. In addition, Stan has developed a very sophisticated, integrated CRM system (like those we discussed in Chapter 7) that identifies and tracks his customers for targeted promotions.

Refer back to **page 499** for Stans story ➡

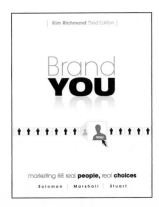

Kim Richmond Third Edition

Brand
YOU

marketing 6E real **people**, real **choices**
Solomon | Marshall | Stuart

Brand **YOU**!

You're hired!

You successfully created and communicated your personal brand. Now you have job offers to consider. How do you orchestrate the timing so you get all your offers at the same time? How do you determine which offer is really best for you? How do you finalize the offer you want? Enjoy reading Chapter 16 in the *Brand You* supplement where your job search comes together.

Objective Summary ➡ **Key Terms** ➡ **Apply**

1. Objective Summary (pp. 500–507)

Define retailing; understand how retailing evolves and appreciate some ethical issues in retailing.

Retailing is the process by which goods and services are sold to consumers for their personal use. The wheel-of-retailing hypothesis suggests that new retailers compete on price and over time become more upscale, leaving room for other new, low-price entrants. The retail life cycle theory suggests that retailing institutions are introduced, grow, reach maturity, and then decline. Three factors that motivate retailers to evolve are changing demographics, technology, and globalization. Some of the ethical issues retailers face include shrinkage due to shoplifting, employee theft, and retail borrowing. Retailers and their employees must also be cognizant of the ethical treatment of customers.

Key Terms

retailing, p. 500

wheel-of-retailing hypothesis, p. 501

retail life cycle, p. 502

pop-up retailing, p. 502

point-of-sale (POS) systems, p. 504

shrinkage, p. 506

2. Objective Summary (pp. 507–512)

Describe how we classify retailers.

Retailers are classified by NAICS codes based on product lines sold. Retailers may also be classified by the level of service offered (self-service, full-service, and limited-service retailers) and by the merchandise assortment offered. Merchandise assortment is described in terms of breadth and depth, which refer to the number of product lines sold and the amount of variety available for each. Thus, stores are classified as convenience stores, supermarkets, specialty stores, discount stores (including warehouse clubs and factory outlets), department stores, and hypermarkets.

Key Terms

merchandise mix, p. 507

merchandise assortment, p. 508

merchandise breadth, p. 508 (Figure 16.1, p. 509)

merchandise depth, p. 509 (Figure 16.1, p. 509)

convenience stores, p. 509

supermarkets, p. 510

specialty stores, p. 510

general merchandise discount stores, p. 510

off-price retailers, p. 510

warehouse clubs, p. 510

factory outlet store, p. 511

department stores, p. 511

hypermarkets, p. 512

3. Objective Summary (pp. 512–514)

Describe the more common forms of nonstore retailing.

The two more common types of nonstore retailing are direct selling and automatic vending machines. In direct selling, a salesperson presents a product to one individual or a small group, takes orders, and delivers the merchandise. Direct selling includes door-to-door sales and party or network sales. State-of-the-art self-service vending machines can dispense products from French fries to iPods.

Key Terms

nonstore retailing, p. 512

direct selling, p. 513

party plan system, p. 513

multilevel network, p. 513

pyramid schemes, p. 514

4. Objective Summary (pp. 514–519)

Describe B2C e-commerce and its benefits, limitations, and future promise.

B2C e-commerce, on-line exchanges between companies and consumers, is growing rapidly. B2C benefits include greater convenience and greater product variety for consumers and opportunities for specialized businesses, lower business costs, and lower cost of doing business for marketers. For consumers, the downside of B2C e-commerce includes having to wait to receive products, security issues, and the inability to touch and feel products. For Internet-only marketers, success on the Internet may be difficult to achieve, whereas cannibalization may be a problem with traditional retailers' on-line operations.

Key Terms

business-to-consumer (B2C) e-commerce, p. 514 (Table 16.1, p. 515)

experiential shoppers, p. 516

5. Objective Summary (pp. 519–527)

Understand the importance of store image to a retail positioning strategy and explain how a retailer can create an image in the marketplace.

Store image is how the target market perceives the store relative to the competition and results from many different elements working together to create the most desirable shopping experience and to ensure that shoppers view a store favorably relative to the competition. Color, lighting, scents, furnishings, and other design elements, called atmospherics, are used to create a "feel" for a store environment. Use of atmospherics includes decisions on (1) store layout, which determines traffic flow and influences the desired customer behavior in the store; (2) the use of store fixtures and open space; (3) the use of sound to attract (or repel) certain types of customers; and (4) the use of color and lighting that can influence customers' moods. The number and type of store personnel, pricing of products sold in the store, and store location contribute to a store's image. The major types of retail locations include central business districts, shopping centers, freestanding retailers, and nontraditional locations such as kiosks.

Key Terms

store image, p. 520 (Figure 16.2, p. 521)

atmospherics, p. 521

traffic flow, p. 522 (Figure 16.3, p. 523)

activity stores, p. 522

central business district (CBD), p. 524 (Figure 16.4, p. 525)

shopping center, p. 525 (Figure 16.4, p. 525)

trade area, p. 526

Chapter Questions and Activities

Concepts: Test Your Knowledge

1. Define retailing. What is the role of retailing in today's world?
2. How do the wheel-of-retailing and retail life cycle theories explain the evolution of retailing? How do demographics, technology, and globalization affect the future of retailing?
3. Explain retail store shrinkage and the ways shrinkage normally occurs. What are some of the ethical issues in retailers' treatment of consumers? What is "sweethearting"?
4. How do marketers classify retail stores? Describe the differences in merchandise assortments for convenience stores, supermarkets, specialty stores, discount stores, department stores, and hypermarkets.
5. Explain the different types of direct selling. What is the difference between a multilevel network and a pyramid scheme?
6. What is the role of automatic vending in retailing?
7. What is B2C e-commerce? What are some benefits of B2C e-commerce for consumers and for marketers? What are the limitations of B2C e-commerce?
8. What are some possible effects of B2C e-commerce on traditional retailing?
9. How is store-positioning strategy like theater?
10. What is store image? Why is it important?
11. What is meant by store atmospherics? How can the elements of atmospherics be used to increase the store's success? How are store personnel a part of store image?
12. What are some of the different types of store locations? What are their advantages and disadvantages?

Choices and Ethical Issues: You Decide

1. The wheel-of-retailing theory suggests that the normal path for a retailer is to enter the marketplace with lower-priced goods and then to increase quality, services, and prices. Why do you think this happens? Is it the right path for all retailers? Why or why not?
2. Most retail store shrinkage can be attributed to shoplifting, employee theft, and retail borrowing. What are some ways that retail store managers can limit or stop shrinkage? What are some problems inherent in security practices? Should retailers create stricter merchandise return policies?
3. Pyramid-scheme promoters specialize in recruiting new members of the pyramid with exciting, even frenzied, meetings where potential members are made fearful that they may pass up a great opportunity if they don't join. Why do people continue to be lured into these schemes? What do you think should be done to stop these unethical promoters?
4. Macy's and other stores are using vending machines to sell electronics such as iPods. What are some other opportunities for vending-machine sales? What are the negative and positive elements of vending-machine sales?
5. Wal-Mart has become a dominant retailer in the American marketplace, accounting for over 30 percent of the total sales of some products. Is this a good thing for consumers? For the retail industry as a whole? Some communities try to prevent Wal-Mart from building a store in their area. Why do you think people feel this way?
6. Experts predict the future of B2C e-commerce to be very rosy indeed, with exponential increases in Internet sales of some product categories within the next few years. What effect do you think the growth of e-retailing will have on traditional retailing? In what ways will this be good for consumers, and in what ways will it not be so good?

Practice: Apply What You've Learned

1. Assume you are a business consultant for a chain of 37 traditional department stores located in 12 Midwestern U.S. cities. In recent years, the stores have seen declining revenues as specialty stores and hypermarkets have begun to squeeze the department stores out. The chain has asked you for suggestions on how to increase its business. Develop an outline of your recommendations and present your plan to your class.

2. As a college graduate, you and a friend think the career you really would enjoy means being your own boss—you want to start your own business. You feel that e-commerce is the place for you to make your fortune. You and your friend are considering two options: (1) an on-line business that sells custom-made blue jeans based on customers' measurements and (2) an on-line business that sells gourmet foods from around the world. In a role-playing exercise, debate with your friend the pros and cons of each of these two on-line retail businesses and make a decision about which is better.

3. All your life you've wanted to be an entrepreneur and to own your own business. Now you're ready to graduate from college, and you've decided to open a combination coffee shop and bookstore in a location near your college. You know that to attract both the college-student market and other customers from the local community, it will be necessary to carefully design the store image. Develop a detailed plan that specifies how you will use atmospherics to create the image you desire.

4. In your job with a marketing consulting firm, you often are asked to make recommendations for store location. Your current client is a local caterer that is planning to open a new retail outlet for selling take-out gourmet dinners. You are examining the possible types of locations: the central business district, a shopping center, a freestanding entity, or some nontraditional location. Outline the advantages and disadvantages of each type of location. In a role-playing exercise, present your recommendations to your client.

5. Assume that you are the director of marketing for a national chain of convenience stores. Your firm has about 200 stores located in 43 states. The stores are fairly traditional both in design and in the merchandise they carry. Because you want to be proactive in your marketing planning, you are concerned that your firm may need to consider making significant changes because of the current demographic, technological, and global trends in the marketplace. You think it is important to discuss these things with the other executives at your firm. Develop a presentation that includes the following:
   a. A discussion of the demographic changes that will impact your stores
   b. A discussion of the technological changes that will impact your stores
   c. A discussion of how global changes may provide problems and opportunities for your organization
   d. Your recommendations for how your firm might meet the challenges faced in each of these areas

Miniproject: Learn by Doing

This project is designed to help you understand how store atmospherics play an important role in consumers' perceptions of a retail store.

1. First, select two retail outlets where students in your college are likely to shop. It will be good if you can select two outlets that you feel are quite different in terms of store image but that sell the same types of products. You might consider two specialty women's clothing stores, two jewelry stores, two department stores, or two coffee shops.

2. Visit each of the stores, and write a detailed description of the store atmosphere—colors, materials used, types of displays, lighting fixtures, product displays, store personnel, and so on.

3. Survey some of the students in your college. Develop a brief questionnaire asking about the perceptions of the two stores you are studying. You may want to ask about things such as the quality of merchandise, prices, competence and friendliness of the store personnel, the attitude of management toward customer service, and so on. What is the "personality" of each store?

4. Develop a report of your findings. Compare the description of the stores with the results of the survey. Attempt to explain how the different elements of the store atmosphere create each store's unique image.

Real people, **real surfers**: explore the web

Many traditional retailers now have Internet sites. Other on-line retailers such as Amazon.com do not have actual stores but practice only direct selling. Visit the sites of one or two popular retailers such as Gap, Pottery Barn, Williams-Sonoma, J. Crew, Banana Republic, or others. Then visit the site of a direct-only retailer.

1. Describe each retailer's Web site. What information is available on each site? How easy was each to navigate? What information did you find interesting and useful on each site? What did you find that you didn't expect to find at a retailer site? What did you find lacking at each site?

2. What differences are there between sites that have traditional bricks-and-mortar stores and those that do not? Does the site encourage consumers to visit the physical store or just to remain an on-line shopper?

3. How do the retailers' Web sites communicate the image or personality of their stores? How are they alike? How are they different? If you had no information except that available on the Web, would you know what types of products are sold; whether the products sold are expensive, prestige products, or low-priced products; and what types of consumers each retailer is attempting to attract to its stores? How does each site use graphics or other design elements to represent the "setting" as retailers do in their stores? How do they communicate the type of consumer they consider their primary market?

4. What recommendations would you make to each retailer to improve its Web site?

Marketing Plan Exercise

The wheel of retailing suggests that new retailers enter the marketplace by offering goods at lower prices than those of their competitors and that after they gain a foothold they "trade up," improving their facilities and their merchandise assortment. Think about a new retail venture, a specialty store that sells timepieces, such as men's and ladies' watches and clocks.

1. What retailing strategies do you recommend for the new retailer for their first two years in business—what merchandise, what store image, and what location(s)?
2. What long-term retailing strategies do you recommend?

Marketing in Action Case

Real Choices at IKEA

How would you go about becoming one of the wealthiest people in the world? Ingvar Kamprad did it by flying coach, taking public transportation, driving 10-year-old automobiles, moving from Sweden to Switzerland (for lower taxes) ... oh, and incidentally, founding IKEA—now the world's largest furniture store.

Kamprad founded IKEA in Sweden in 1943 when he was just 17 years old and while the world was caught up in World War II. He began by dealing pens, picture frames, wallets, and other bargain items out of a catalog. In 1951 he started to sell furniture made by local carpenters and in 1957 he opened his first IKEA furniture store in Sweden. Today, IKEA, with €19.8 billion ($31.2 billion) in sales and 270 retail outlets in 36 countries, is the world's largest home furnishing company that is known for its contemporary designs, affordable prices, and loyal customers.

IKEA retail locations are gigantic—roughly three times the size of a typical Home Depot—and they focus exclusively on the furniture and home decorating market. IKEA's size and focus limit the *breadth* of items it offers, but they do provide a great deal of merchandise *depth* including furniture, decorative accessories, and lighting fixtures for all rooms of the house. While the company has historically made only low-priced, flat-packed furniture, it recently introduced a new 82-piece collection it calls Stockholm to offer its shoppers more expensive furniture made from higher quality materials.

In designing its store layout, IKEA is responding to consumer interest in one-stop shopping—finding what the consumer wants in one store rather than having to visit numerous stores. Also, IKEA makes it easier for customers to shop once they enter the store. It sets up furniture displays in "lifestyle" themes that show the type of furniture that singles, couples, or young families might need. The company also uses vignette displays to suggest how a customer can put together various items to create a certain look. These types of displays are perfect for the generation that is no longer interested in buying furniture to last a lifetime but rather that fits their lifestyle now.

IKEA has enjoyed great success throughout its history, and that success has not come by accident—IKEA got to where it is today through great marketing planning. Presently, one of the most important decisions facing IKEA is how and where it should look to expand its business and its revenues. The company has announced its desire to add new store locations in Russia, Germany, France China, Italy, Japan, U.K., Finland, Spain, and Switzerland.

But IKEA is more than just a bricks-and-mortar retailer. In recent years the firm has also become a popular on-line store. Its Web site is very popular; it got 450 million hits during the year 2007 alone. Despite its renown among on-line furniture shoppers, IKEA recently announced plans to focus on the in-store experience as "the only sales channel." It doesn't plan to invest more money in home shopping or on-line sales channels. The company bases this decision on its belief that the chain can give customers the best offers and the lowest prices when it makes its products available only through its bricks-and-mortar stores. Despite IKEA's successful history, there are no guarantees for the future in the hyper-competitive world of retailing. Is focusing solely on the in-store experience the right decision? Can IKEA reach its growth and revenue goals without on-line sales? In the U.S. alone, internet sales of home furnishings are over $150 billion a year and industry experts forecast continued annual growth at double digit rates. Would IKEA be better advised to continue to push on-line sales at least in some areas of the world?

You Make the Call

1. What is the decision facing IKEA?
2. What factors are important to understand this decision situation?
3. What are the alternatives?
4. What decision(s) do you recommend?
5. What are some ways to implement your recommendation?

Based on: Cora Daniels and Adam Edström, "Create IKEA, Make Billions, Take Bus," *Fortune*, May 3, 2004, 44; Emma Hall and Normandy Madden, "IKEA Courts Buyers with Offbeat Ideas," *Advertising Age*, April 12, 2004, 10; "IKEA Report," Datamonitor, February 10, 2008, **www. datamonitor.com**; Jon Ortiz, "Customers Drawn to IKEA Experience," *The Sacramento Bee*, February 26, 2006, D1; Luisa Kroll and Allison Fass, "The World's Billionaires," Forbes.com, **http://www.forbes.com/billionaires** (accessed June 19, 2006); Marianne Rohrlich, "Currents: Furniture; IKEA for the Post-Collegiate Crowd: Fancier Finishes and Less Work," *New York Times*, April 26, 2007, **http://query.nytimes.com/gst/fullpage.html?res=9D00E4DF153EF935A15757C0A9619C8B63&scp=3&sq=ikea&st=nyt** (accessed May 1, 2008); Mei Fong, "IKEA Hits Home in China," *Wall Street Journal Online*, March 3, 2006, B1; Mike Duff, "IKEA Eyes Aggressive Growth," *DSN Retailing Today*, January 27, 2003, 3, 22; "News," *Chain Store Age*, February 2008, p. 50

Marketing Plan: The S&S Smoothie Company

Executive Summary

Situation Analysis

S&S Smoothie Company is an entrepreneurial organization that produces fruit-and-yogurt-based beverages with superior flavor and nutritional content and unique packaging. Within the United States, S&S has targeted a consumer market of younger, health-conscious, upscale consumers who frequent gyms and health clubs, and two broad reseller markets: (1) gyms and health clubs and (2) smaller upscale food markets. S&S distributes its product through manufacturers' agents in the United States, Canada, and the United Kingdom and through Internet sales. An analysis of the internal and external environments indicates the firm enjoys important strengths in its product, its employees, and its reputation, while weaknesses are apparent in its limited size, financial resources, and product capabilities. S&S faces a supportive external environment, highlighted by a growing interest in healthy living, and limited threats, primarily from potential competitive growth.

Marketing Objectives

The S&S marketing objectives are to increase awareness, gross sales (50 percent), and distribution, and to introduce two new product lines over the next three years:

- A line of low-carb smoothies

- A line of gourmet flavored smoothies

Marketing Strategies

To accomplish its growth goals, S&S will direct its marketing activites toward the following strategies:

1. *Target Market Strategy:* S&S will continue to target its existing consumer markets while expanding its organizational markets to include hotels and resorts, golf and tennis clubs, and university campuses.

2. *Positioning Strategy:* S&S will continue to position its products as the first-choice smoothie beverage for the serious health-conscious consumer, including those who are seeking to lower their carbohydrate intake.

3. *Product Strategy:* S&S will introduce two new product lines, each identifiable through unique packaging/labeling:
    a. **S&S Smoothie Gold:** a product similar to the original S&S Smoothie beverages but in six unique flavors
    b. **Low-Carb S&S Smoothie:** a product with 50 percent fewer grams of carbohydrates

4. *Pricing Strategy:* S&S will maintain the current pricing strategy for existing and new products.

5. *Promotion Strategy:* S&S will augment current personal selling efforts with television and magazine advertising, with sponsorships of marathons in major cities, and with a sampling program.

6. *Supply Chain Strategy:* S&S will expand its distribution network to include the organizational markets targeted. In addition, to encourage a high level of inventory in larger health clubs, S&S Smoothie will offer free refrigerated display units.

Implementation and Control

The Action Plan details how the marketing strategies will be implemented including the individual(s) responsible, the timing of each activity, and the budget necessary. The measurement and control strategies provide a means of measurement of the success of the plan.

Situation Analysis

The S&S Smoothie Company[1] was founded in September 2001 in New York with the goal of creating and marketing healthy "smoothie" beverages for sale to health-conscious consumers. S&S Smoothie expects to take advantage of an increasing desire for healthy foods both in the United States and internationally—and to ride the wave of consumer interest in low-carb alternatives. While there are other companies both large and small competing in this market, S&S Smoothie feels it has the expertise to create and market superior products that will appeal to its target market.

Internal Environment

Mission Statement

The strategic direction and actions of the S&S Smoothie Company are driven by its mission:

> S&S Smoothie seeks to meet the needs of discriminating, health-conscious consumers for high-quality, superior-tasting smoothie beverages and other similar products.

Organizational Structure

As an entrepreneurial company, S&S Smoothie does not have a very sophisticated organizational structure. Key personnel include the following:

- Patrick Small, founder and co-president. Small is responsible for the creation, design, packaging, and production management of all S&S Smoothie products.

- William "Bill" Sartens, founder and co-president. Sartens is responsible for international and domestic distribution and marketing.

- Gayle Humphries, chief financial officer. Humphries develops financial strategy and keeps the company's books.

- Alex Johnson, national sales manager. Johnson is responsible for maintaining the sales force of independent sales reps. He also advises on product development.

---

[1] S&S Smoothie Company is a fictitious company created to illustrate a sample marketing plan.

- Bob LeMay, Pam Sartens, and Paul Sartens, shareholders. Next to Patrick Small and William Sartens, Bob, Pam, and Paul own the largest number of shares. They consult and sit on the company's board of directors. Bob is a lawyer and also provides legal services.

Corporate Culture

S&S Smoothie is an entrepreneurial organization. Thus, a key element of the internal environment is a culture that encourages innovation, risk taking, and individual creativity. The company's beginning was based on a desire to provide a unique, superior product, and company decisions have consistently emphasized this mission.

Products

The original S&S Smoothie, introduced in mid-2002, was a fruit-and-yogurt-based beverage that contained only natural ingredients (no additives) and was high in essential nutrients. Table A.1 provides nutritional information for the 12-ounce size S&S Smoothie beverage. Because of the company's patented manufacturing process, S&S Smoothie beverages

Table A.1	Nutritional Information: S&S Smoothie Beverage

Serving Size: 12 ounces
For 20-ounce sizes, multiply the amounts by 1.67.

	Amount per Serving	% Daily Value
Calories	140	
Calories from fat	6	
Total fat	<0.5 g	1%
Saturated fat	<0.5 g	2%
Cholesterol	6 mg	2%
Sodium	70 mg	3%
Potassium	100 mg	3%
Total carbs	10 g	3%
Dietary fiber	5 g	20%
Sugar	1 g	
Protein	25 g	50%
Vitamin A		50%
Vitamin C		50%
Calcium		20%
Iron		30%
Vitamin D		40%
Vitamin E		50%
Thiamin		50%
Riboflavin		50%
Niacin		50%
Vitamin B^6		50%
Vitamin B^{12}		50%
Biotin		50%
Pantothenic acid		50%
Phosphorus		10%
Iodine		50%
Chromium		50%
Zinc		50%
Folic acid		50%

do not have to be refrigerated and have a shelf life of over a year. Therefore, the product can be shipped and delivered via nonrefrigerated carriers. S&S Smoothie currently sells its beverages exclusively through gyms, health clubs, and smaller upscale food markets.

As a producer of dairy-based beverages, S&S Smoothie's NAICS (North American Industry Classification System) classification is 311511, Fluid Milk Manufacturers. At present, the single product line is the S&S Smoothie fruit and yogurt beverage. This healthy beverage product has a flavor and nutritional content that makes it superior to competing products. The present product comes in five flavors: strawberry, blueberry, banana, peach, and cherry. S&S offers each in a 12-ounce and a 20-ounce size. S&S packages the product in a unique hourglass-shaped, frosted glass bottle with a screw-off cap. The bottle design makes the product easy to hold, even with sweaty hands after workouts. The frosted glass allows the color of the beverage to be seen, but at the same time it communicates an upscale image. The labeling and lid visually denote the flavor with an appropriate color. Labeling includes complete nutritional information. In the future, S&S Smoothie plans to expand its line of products to grow its market share of the health drink market.

Pricing of S&S Smoothie beverages is as follows:

	12 oz.	20 oz.
Suggested retail price	$4.00	$6.00
Price to retail outlets (health clubs, etc.)	$2.00	$3.00
Price to distributor/discount to sales agent	$1.00	$1.50

Thus, S&S Smoothie receives $1.00 in revenue for each 12-ounce bottle and $1.50 in revenue for each 20-ounce bottle it sells.

At present, S&S Smoothie outsources actual production of the product. Still, the company takes care to oversee the entire production process to ensure consistent quality of its unique product. With this method of production, variable costs for the 12-ounce S&S Smoothie beverages are $0.63, and variable costs for the 20-ounce size are $0.71. Current annual fixed costs for S&S Smoothie office space, management salaries, and professional services are as follows:

Salaries and employee benefits	$275,000
Office rental, equipment, and supplies	$24,600
Expenses related to sales (travel, etc.)	$32,000
Advertising and other marketing communications	$50,000
Total fixed costs	**$381,600**

Sales of the two sizes of the product are approximately equal; that is, half of sales are for the 12-ounce size and half are for the 20-ounce size. Thus, there is an average contribution margin of $0.58 per bottle. Based on this, to achieve break even, S&S Smoothie must sell

$$\frac{\$381,600}{.58} = 657,931 \text{ units}$$

Again, assuming equal sales of the two size products, the break-even point in dollars is $822,413.

Previous Sales

Sales of S&S Smoothie products have continued to grow since their introduction to the market in 2002. Actual sales figures for 2002 through 2007 are shown in Table A.2.

Markets

The consumer market for S&S Smoothie products is made up of anyone who is interested in healthy food and a healthy lifestyle. Although according to published research nearly 70 percent of American consumers say they are interested in living a healthy lifestyle, the

Table A.2	Company Sales Performance
Year	**Gross Sales**
2002	$ 87,000
2003	$238,000
2004	$311,000
2005	$436,000
2006	$618,000
2007	$650,000

number of those who actually work to achieve that goal is much smaller. It is estimated that approximately 80 million Americans actually engage in exercise and/or follow nutritional plans that would be described as healthy. As experts expect the trend toward healthier living to grow globally, the domestic market and the international market for S&S Smoothie products are expected to expand for some time.

Within the U.S. consumer market, S&S Smoothie targets upscale consumers who frequent gyms and health clubs. While these consumers are primarily younger, there is also an older segment that seeks to be physically fit and that also patronizes health clubs.

Distribution

In order to reach its target market, S&S Smoothie places primary distribution emphasis on health clubs and other physical fitness facilities and small, upscale specialty food markets. The company began developing channel relationships with these outlets through individual contacts by company personnel. As sales developed, the company solicited the services of manufacturers' agents and specialty food distributors. Manufacturers' agents are individuals who sell products for a number of different noncompeting manufacturers. By contracting with these agents in various geographic regions, the company can expand its product distribution to a significant portion of the United States and Canada. Similar arrangements with agents in the United Kingdom have allowed it to begin distribution in that country.

The company handles large accounts such as Gold's Gym and World Gyms directly. While total sales to these chains are fairly substantial, when considering the large number of facilities within each chain the sales are very small with much room for growth.

The Internet is a secondary channel for S&S Smoothie. On-line retail outlets currently account for only five percent of S&S Smoothie sales. While this channel is useful for individuals who wish to purchase S&S Smoothie products in larger quantities, S&S does not expect that on-line sales will become a significant part of the business in the near future.

External Environment

Competitive Environment

S&S Smoothie faces several different levels of competition. Direct competitors are companies that also market smoothie-type beverages and include the following:

1. Franchise smoothie retail operations
2. On-line-only smoothie outlets
3. Other smaller manufacturers
4. Larger companies such as Nestlé that produce similar products

Indirect competition comes from the following:

1. Homemade smoothie drinks made from powders sold in retail outlets and over the Internet

2. Homemade smoothie drinks made using a multitude of available recipes

3. Other healthy beverages, such as juices

Economic Environment

S&S Smoothie first introduced its products during a period of economic downturn following the dot.com bust and 9/11. Despite this, the product quickly gained momentum and sales steadily increased. As the economy of the United States has remained stable during recent years, sales have correspondingly begun to increase. Analysts estimate that the total U.S. gross domestic product (GDP) will increase only a little over two percent annually for the next three years with a similar percentage increase anticipated for the European Union, while Canada's GDP will grow slightly over three percent annually.

Technological Environment

Because S&S Smoothie produces a simple food product, technological advances have minimum impact on the firm's operations. Nevertheless, the use of current technology enables and enhances many of the company's operations. For example, S&S Smoothie uses the Internet to enhance its operations in two ways. First, the Internet provides an additional venue for sales. In addition, manufacturers' agents and channel members can keep in contact with the company, allowing for fewer problems with deliveries, orders, and so on.

Political and Legal Environment

Because they are advertised as nutritional products, all S&S Smoothie products must be approved by the FDA. Labeling must include ingredients and nutritional information also regulated by the FDA. In addition, S&S Smoothie products are regulated by the U.S. Department of Agriculture.

While there are no specific regulations about labeling or advertising products as low-carb, there is potential for such regulations to come into play in the future. In addition, there are numerous regulations that are country-specific in current and prospective global markets of which the company must constantly remain aware. Any future advertising campaigns developed by S&S Smoothie will have to conform to regulatory guidelines both in the United States and internationally.

Sociocultural Environment

The social and cultural environment continues to provide an important opportunity for S&S Smoothie. The trend toward healthy foods and a healthier lifestyle has grown dramatically for the past decade or longer. In response to this, the number of health clubs across the country and the number of independent resorts and spas that offer patrons a healthy holiday have also grown. In addition, many travelers demand that hotels offer health club facilities.

During the past three years, consumers around the globe have become aware of the advantages of a low-carbohydrate diet. Low-carb menu items abound in restaurants, including fast-food chains such as McDonald's. A vast number of low-carb foods, including low-carb candy, fill supermarket shelves.

There are approximately 125 million American adults aged 15 to 44. Demographers project that this age group will remain stable for the foreseeable future, with an increase of less than eight percent projected to 2025. Similarly, incomes should neither decrease nor increase significantly in the near future in this segment of the population.

SWOT Analysis

The SWOT analysis provides a summary of the strengths, weaknesses, opportunities, and threats identified by S&S Smoothie through the analysis of its internal and external environments.

Strengths

The following are the strengths identified by S&S Smoothie:

- A creative and skilled employee team

- A high-quality product recipe that provides exceptional flavor with high levels of nutrition

- Because of its entrepreneurial spirit, the ability to remain flexible and to adapt quickly to environmental changes

- A strong network of manufacturers' agents and distributors

- The growth of a reputation of a high-quality product among health clubs, other retail outlets, and targeted consumer groups

Weaknesses

The following are the weaknesses identified by S&S Smoothie:

- Limited financial resources for growth and for advertising and other marketing communications

- Little flexibility in terms of personnel due to size of the firm

- Reliance on external production to maintain quality standards and to meet any unanticipated surges in demand for the product

Opportunities

The following are the opportunities identified by S&S Smoothie:

- A strong and growing interest in healthy living, among both young, upscale consumers and older consumers

- Continuing consumer interest in low-carb alternatives that offers opportunities for additional product lines

Threats

The following are the threats identified by S&S Smoothie:

- The potential for competitors, especially those with large financial resources who can invest more in promotion, to develop products that consumers may find superior

- A major economic downturn that might affect potential sales

- Fizzling of the low-carb craze if other forms of dieting gain in popularity

- Increase in market for energy drinks like Rockstar, etc.

Marketing Objectives

The following are the marketing objectives set by S&S Smoothie:

- To increase the awareness of S&S Smoothie products among the target market

- To increase gross sales by 50 percent over the next two years

- To introduce two new product lines over the next three years: a line of low-carb smoothies and a line of gourmet flavored smoothies

- To increase distribution of S&S Smoothie products to include new retail outlets both in the United States and globally

Marketing Strategies

Target Markets

Consumer Markets

S&S Smoothies will continue to target its existing consumer markets. The primary consumer target market for S&S Smoothie beverages can be described as follows:

Demographics

- Male and female teens and young adults

- Ages: 15–39

- Household income: $50,000 and above

- Education of head of household: College degree or above

- Primarily located in midsize to large urban areas or college towns

Psychographics

- Health-conscious, interested in living a healthy lifestyle

- Spend much time and money taking care of their bodies

- Enjoy holidays that include physical activities

- Live very busy lives and need to use time wisely to enjoy all they want to do

- Enjoy spending time with friends

- According to the VALS2™ typology, many are in the Achievers and Experiencers categories

Media Habits

- Individuals in the target market are more likely to get their news from television or the Internet than from newspapers. They are likely to view not only the news channels but also the financial news networks.

- The consumers prefer watching edgier shows such as *Weeds* and *Californication*.

- They are likely to have satellite radio installed in their automobiles.

- Magazines frequently read include *Men's Health*, *BusinessWeek*, *Sports Illustrated*, and the *New Yorker*.

Organizational Markets

In the past, S&S Smoothie has targeted two categories of reseller markets: (1) health clubs and gyms and (2) small upscale specialty food markets. To increase distribution and sales of its products, S&S Smoothie will target the following in the future:

1. Hotels and resorts in the United States and in selected international markets
2. Golf and tennis clubs
3. College and university campuses

Upscale young professionals frequently visit hotels and resorts, and they demand that even business travel should include quality accommodations and first-rate health club facilities. The membership of golf and tennis clubs, while including many older consumers, also is an excellent means of providing products conveniently for the targeted groups. College and university students, probably more than any other consumer group, are interested in health and in their bodies. In fact, many universities have built large, fairly elaborate health and recreational facilities as a means of attracting students. Thus, providing S&S Smoothie beverages on college campuses is an excellent means of meeting the health beverage needs of this group.

Positioning the Product

S&S Smoothie seeks to position its products as the first-choice smoothie beverage for the serious health-conscious consumer, including those who are seeking to lower their carbohydrate intake. The justification for this positioning is as follows: Many smoothie beverages are available. The S&S Smoothie formula provides superior flavor and nutrition in a shelf-stable form. S&S Smoothie has developed its product, packaging, pricing and promotion to communicate a superior, prestige image. This positioning is thus supported by all its marketing strategies.

Product Strategies

To increase its leverage in the market and to meet its sales objectives, S&S Smoothie needs additional products. Two new product lines are planned:

1. *S&S Smoothie Gold:* This product will be similar to the original S&S Smoothie beverage but will come in six unique flavors:
   a. Piña colada
   b. Chocolate banana
   c. Apricot nectarine madness
   d. Pineapple berry crush
   e. Tropical tofu cherry
   f. Peaches and dreams

   To set the product apart from the original-flavor Smoothie beverages in store refrigerator cases, labels will include the name of the beverage and the logo in gold lettering. The bottle cap will be black.

2. *Low-Carb S&S Smoothie:* The Low-Carb S&S Smoothie beverage will have approximately 50 percent fewer grams of carbohydrates than the original Smoothie beverage or the S&S Smoothie Gold. Low-Carb S&S Smoothie will come in the following four flavors:
   a. Strawberry
   b. Blueberry
   c. Banana
   d. Peach

   Packaging for the Low-Carb S&S Smoothie will be similar to other S&S Smoothie beverages but will include the term "Low-Carb" in large type. The label will state that the beverage has 50 percent fewer carbs than regular smoothies.

Pricing Strategies

The current pricing strategy will be maintained for existing and new products. This pricing is appropriate for communicating a high-quality product image for all S&S Smoothie products. The company feels that creating different pricing for the new beverages would be confusing and create negative attitudes among consumers. Thus, there is no justification for increasing the price of the new products.

Promotion Strategies

In the past, S&S Smoothie has used mainly personal selling to promote its products to the trade channel. To support this effort, signage has been provided for the resellers to promote the product at the point of purchase. Posters and stand-alone table cards show appealing photographs of the product in the different flavors and communicate the brand name and the healthy benefits of the product. Similar signage will be developed for use by resellers who choose to stock the S&S Smoothie Gold and the Low-Carb Smoothies.

Selling has previously been handled by a team of over 75 manufacturers' agents who sell to resellers. In addition, in some geographic areas, an independent distributor does the selling. To support this personal selling approach, S&S Smoothie plans for additional promotional activities to introduce its new products and meet its other marketing objectives. These include the following:

1. *Television advertising:* S&S Smoothie will purchase a limited amount of relatively inexpensive and targeted cable channel advertising. A small number of commercials will be shown during prime-time programs with high viewer ratings by the target market. Television advertising can be an important means of not only creating awareness of the product, but also enhancing the image of the product. Indeed, consumers are prone to feel that if a product is advertised on prime-time TV, it must be a good product.

2. *Magazine advertising:* Because consumers in the target market are not avid magazine readers, magazine advertising will be limited and will supplement other promotion activities. During the next year, S&S Smoothie will experiment with limited magazine advertising in such titles as *Sports Illustrated*. The company will also investigate the potential of advertising in university newspapers.

3. *Sponsorships:* S&S Smoothie will attempt to sponsor several marathons in major cities. The advantage of sponsorships is that they provide visibility for the product while at the same time showing that the company supports activities of interest to the target market.

4. *Sampling:* Sampling of S&S Smoothie beverages at select venues will provide an opportunity for prospective customers to become aware of the product and to taste the great flavors. Sampling will include only the two new products being introduced. Venues for sampling will include the following:
   a. Marathons
   b. Weight-lifting competitions
   c. Gymnastics meets
   d. Student unions located on select college campuses

Supply Chain Strategies

As noted earlier, S&S Smoothie distributes its beverages primarily through health clubs and gyms, and small upscale specialty food stores. S&S Smoothie plans to expand its target reseller market to include the following:

1. Hotels and resorts in the United States and in targeted international markets

2. Golf and tennis clubs

3. College campuses

To increase leverage in larger health clubs, S&S Smoothie will offer free refrigerated display units. This will encourage the facility to maintain a high level of inventory of S&S Smoothie beverages.

Implementation

The Action Plan details the activities necessary to implement all marketing strategies. In addition, the Action Plan includes the timing for each item, the individual(s) responsible, and the budgetary requirements. Table A.3 shows an example of one objective (to increase distribution venues) and the action items S&S Smoothie will use to accomplish it.[2]

| Table A.3 | Action Items to Accomplish Marketing Objective Regarding Supply Chain |

OBJECTIVE: INCREASE DISTRIBUTION VENUES

Action Items	Beginning Date	Ending Date	Responsible Party	Cost	Remarks
1. Identify key hotels and resorts, golf clubs, and tennis clubs where S&S Smoothies might be sold	July 1	September 1	Bill Sartens (consulting firm will be engaged to assist in this effort)	$25,000	Key to this strategy is to selectively choose resellers so that maximum results are obtained from sales activities. Because health club use is greater during the months of January to May, efforts will be timed to have product in stock no later than January 15.
2. Identify 25 key universities where S&S Smoothies might be sold	July 1	August 1	Bill Sartens	0	Information about colleges and universities and their health club facilities should be available on the university Web pages.
3. Make initial contact with larger hotel and resort chains	September 1	November 1	Bill Sartens	Travel: $10,000	
4. Make initial contact with larger individual (nonchain) facilities	September 1	November 1	Bill Sartens	Travel: $5,000	
5. Make initial contact with universities	August 15	September 15	Manufacturers' agents	0	Agents will be assigned to the 25 universities and required to make an initial contact and report back to Bill Sartens on promising prospects.
6. Follow up initial contacts with all potential resellers and obtain contracts for coming six months	September 15	Ongoing	Bill Sartens, manufacturers' agents	$10,000	$10,000 is budgeted for this item, although actual expenditures will be on an as-needed basis, as follow-up travel cannot be preplanned.

---

[2] Note that the final marketing plan should include objectives, action items, timing information, and budget information necessary to accomplish all marketing strategies. We have only one objective in this sample marketing plan.

Measurement and Control Strategies

A variety of activities will ensure effective measurement of the success of the marketing plan and allow the firm to make adjustments as necessary. These include market research and trend analysis.

Research

Firms need continuous market research to understand brand awareness and brand attitudes among their target markets. S&S Smoothie will therefore commission exploratory research and descriptive benchmark studies of its target consumer and reseller markets.

Trend Analysis

S&S Smoothie will do a monthly trend analysis to examine sales by reseller type, geographic area, chain, agent, and distributor. These analyses will allow S&S Smoothie to take corrective action when necessary.

MARKETING MATH

To develop marketing strategies to meet the goals of an organization effectively and efficiently, it is essential that marketers understand and use a variety of financial analyses. This appendix provides some of these basic financial analyses, including a review of the income statement and balance sheet, as well as some basic performance ratios. In addition, this appendix includes an explanation of some of the specific calculations that marketers use routinely to set prices for their goods and services.

Income Statement and Balance Sheet

The two most important documents used to analyze the financial situation of a company are the income statement and the balance sheet. The *income statement* (which is sometimes referred to as the *profit and loss statement* or the *P&L*) provides a summary of the revenues and expenses of a firm—that is, the amount of income a company received from sales or other sources, the amount of money it spent, and the resulting income or loss that the company experienced.

The major elements of the income statement are as follows:

- **Gross sales** are the total of all income the firm receives from the sales of goods and services.

- **Net sales revenue** is the gross sales minus the amount for returns and promotional or other allowances given to customers.

- **Cost of goods sold** (sometimes called the *cost of sales*) is the cost of inventory or goods that the firm has sold.

- **Gross margin** (also called *gross profit*) is the amount of sales revenue that is in excess of the cost of goods sold.

- **Operating expenses** are expenses other than the cost of goods sold that are necessary for conducting business. These may include salaries, rent, depreciation on buildings and equipment, insurance, utilities, supplies, and property taxes.

- **Operating income** (sometimes called *income from operations*) is the gross margin minus the operating expenses. Sometimes accountants prepare an *operating statement*, which is similar to the income statement except that the final calculation is the operating income—that is, other revenues or expenses and taxes are not included.

- **Other revenue and expenses** are income and/or expenses other than those required for conducting the business. These may include items such as interest income/expenses and any gain or loss experienced on the sale of property or plant assets.

- **Taxes** are the amount of income tax the firm owes calculated as a percentage of income.

- **Net income** (sometimes called *net earnings* or *net profit*) is the excess of total revenue over total expenses.

Table B.1 shows the income statement for an imaginary company, DLL Incorporated. DLL is a typical merchandising firm. Note that the income statement is for a specific year and includes income and expenses inclusively from January 1 through December 31. The following comments explain the meaning of some of the important entries included in this statement.

- DLL Inc. has total or gross sales during the year of $253,950. This figure was adjusted, however, by deducting the $3,000 worth of goods returned and special allowances given to customers and by $2,100 in special discounts. Thus, the actual or net sales generated by sales is $248,850.

Table B.1 | **DLL Income Statement for the Year Ended December 31, 2008**

Gross Sales		$253,950	
Less: Sales Returns and Allowances	$ 3,000		
Sales Discounts	2,100	5,100	
Net Sales Revenue			$ 248,850
Cost of Goods Sold			
Inventory, January 1, 2008		60,750	
Purchases	135,550		
Less: Purchase Returns and Allowances	1,500		
Purchase Discounts	750		
Net Purchases	133,300		
Plus: Freight-In	2,450	135,750	
Goods Available for Sale		196,500	
Less: Inventory, December 31, 2008		60,300	
Cost of Goods Sold			136,200
Gross Margin			112,650
Operating Expenses			
Salaries and Commissions		15,300	
Rent		12,600	
Insurance		1,500	
Depreciation		900	
Supplies		825	
Total Operating Expenses			31,125
Operating Income			81,525
Other Revenue and (Expenses)			
Interest Revenue		1,500	
Interest Expense		(2,250)	(750)
Income Before Tax			80,775
Taxes (40%)			32,310
Net Income			$ 48,465

- The cost of goods sold is calculated by adding the inventory of goods on January 1 to the amount purchased during the year and then subtracting the inventory of goods on December 31. In this case, DLL had $60,750 worth of inventory on hand on January 1. During the year the firm made purchases in the amount of $135,550. This amount, however, was reduced by purchase returns and allowances of $1,500 and by purchase discounts of $750, so the net purchases are only $133,300.

There is also an amount on the statement labeled "Freight-In." This is the amount spent by the firm in shipping charges to get goods to its facility from suppliers. Any expenses for freight from DLL to its customers (Freight-Out) would be an operating expense. In this case, the Freight-In expense of $2,450 is added to net purchase costs. Then these costs of current purchases are added to the beginning inventory to show that during the year the firm had a total of $196,500 in goods available for sale. Finally, the inventory of goods held on December 31 is subtracted from the goods available for sale, to reveal the total cost of goods sold of $136,200.

We mentioned that DLL Inc. is a merchandising firm—a retailer of some type. If DLL were instead a manufacturer, calculation of the cost of goods sold would be a bit more complicated and would probably include separate figures for items such as inventory of finished goods, the "work-in-process" inventory, the raw materials inventory, and the cost of goods delivered to customers during the year. Continuing down the previous income statement we have the following:

- The cost of goods sold is subtracted from the net sales revenue to get a gross margin of $112,650.

- Operating expenses for DLL include the salaries and commissions paid to its employees, rent on facilities and/or equipment, insurance, depreciation of capital items, and the cost of operating supplies. DLL has a total of $31,125 in operating expenses, which is deducted from the gross margin. Thus, DLL has an operating income of $81,525.

- DLL had both other income and expenses in the form of interest revenues of $1,500 and interest expenses of $2,250, making a total other expense of $750, which was subtracted from the operating income, leaving an income before taxes of $80,775.

- Finally, the income before taxes is reduced by 40 percent ($32,310) for taxes, leaving a net income of $48,465. The 40 percent is an average amount for federal and state corporate income taxes incurred by most firms.

The *balance sheet* lists the assets, liabilities, and stockholders' equity of the firm. Whereas the income statement represents what happened during an entire year, the balance sheet is like a snapshot; it shows the firm's financial situation at one point in time. For this reason, the balance sheet is sometimes called the *statement of financial position*.

Table B.2 shows DLL Inc.'s balance sheet for December 31. Assets include any economic resource that is expected to benefit the firm in the short or long term. *Current assets* are items that are normally expected to be turned into cash or used up during the next 12 months or during the firm's normal operating cycle. Current assets for DLL include cash, securities, accounts receivable (money owed to the firm and not yet paid), inventory on hand, prepaid insurance, and supplies: a total of $84,525. *Long-term assets* include all assets that are not current assets. For DLL, these are furniture and fixtures (less an amount for depreciation) and land, or $45,300. The *total assets* for DLL are $129,825.

A firm's *liabilities* are its economic obligations, or debts that are payable to individuals or organizations outside the firm. *Current liabilities* are debts due to be paid in the coming year or during the firm's normal operating cycle. For DLL, the current liabilities—the accounts payable, unearned sales revenue, wages payable, and interest payable—total $72,450. *Long-term liabilities* (in the case of DLL, a note in the amount of $18,900) are all liabilities that are not due to be paid during the coming cycle. *Stockholders' equity* is the value

Table B.2	DLL Inc. Balance Sheet: December 31, 2008		

Assets

Current assets

Cash		$ 4,275	
Marketable securities		12,000	
Accounts receivable		6,900	
Inventory		60,300	
Prepaid insurance		300	
Supplies		150	
Total current assets			84,525

Long-term assets—property, plant and equipment

Furniture and fixtures	$42,300		
Less: accumulated depreciation	4,500	37,800	
Land		7,500	
Total long-term assets			45,300
Total assets			$129,825

Liabilities

Current liabilities

Accounts payable	$70,500		
Unearned sales revenue	1,050		
Wages payable	600		
Interest payable	300		
Total current liabilities		72,450	

Long-term liabilities

Note payable		18,900	
Total liabilities			91,350

Stockholders' equity

Common stock		15,000	
Retained earnings		23,475	
Total stockholders' equity			38,475
Total liabilities and stockholders' equity			$129,825

of the stock and the corporation's capital or retained earnings. DLL has $15,000 in common stock and $23,475 in retained earnings for a total stockholders' equity of $38,475. Total liabilities always equal total assets—in this case $129,825.

Important Financial Performance Ratios

How do managers and financial analysts compare the performance of a firm from one year to the next? How do investors compare the performance of one firm with that of another? As the book notes, managers often rely upon various metrics to measure performance.

Often a number of different financial ratios provide important information for such comparisons. Such *ratios* are percentage figures comparing various income statement items to net sales. Ratios provide a better way to compare performance than simple dollar sales or cost figures for two reasons. They enable analysts to compare the performance of large and small firms, and they provide a fair way to compare performance over time without having to take inflation and other changes into account. In this section, we will explain the basic operating ratios. Other measures of performance that marketers frequently use and that are also explained here are the inventory turnover rate and return on investment (ROI).

Operating Ratios

Measures of performance calculated directly from the information in a firm's income statement (sometimes called an operating statement) are called the *operating ratios*. Each ratio compares some income statement item to net sales. The most useful of these are the *gross margin ratio*, the *net income ratio*, the *operating expense ratio*, and the *returns and allowances ratio*. These ratios vary widely by industry but tend to be important indicators of how a firm is doing within its industry. The ratios for DLL Inc. are shown in Table B.3.

- **Gross margin ratio** shows what percentage of sales revenues is available for operating and other expenses and for profit. With DLL, this means that 45 percent, or nearly half, of every sales dollar is available for operating costs and for profits.

- **Net income ratio** (sometimes called the *net profit ratio*) shows what percentage of sales revenues is income or profit. For DLL, the net income ratio is 19.5 percent. This means that the firm's profit before taxes is about 20 cents of every dollar.

- **Operating expense ratio** is the percentage of sales needed for operating expenses. DLL has an operating expense ratio of 12.5 percent. Tracking operating expense ratios from one year to the next or comparing them with an industry average gives a firm important information about the efficiency of its operations.

- **Returns and allowances ratio** shows what percentage of all sales is being returned, probably by unhappy customers. DLL's returns and allowances ratio shows that only a little over 1 percent of sales are being returned.

Table B.3	Hypothetical Operating Ratios for DLL Inc.					
Gross margin ratio	=	$\dfrac{\text{gross margin}}{\text{net sales}}$	=	$\dfrac{\$112,650}{248,850}$	=	45.3%
Net income ratio	=	$\dfrac{\text{net income}}{\text{net sales}}$	=	$\dfrac{\$48,465}{248,850}$	=	19.5%
Operating expense ratio	=	$\dfrac{\text{total operating expenses}}{\text{net sales}}$	=	$\dfrac{\$31,125}{248,850}$	=	12.5%
Returns and allowances ratio	=	$\dfrac{\text{returns and allowances}}{\text{net sales}}$	=	$\dfrac{\$3,000}{248,850}$	=	1.2%

Inventory Turnover Rate

The *inventory turnover rate*, also referred to as the stockturn rate, is the number of times inventory or stock is turned over (sold and replaced) during a specified time period, usually a year. Inventory turnover rates are usually calculated on the basis of inventory costs, sometimes on the basis of inventory selling prices, and sometimes by number of units.

In our example, for DLL Inc. we know that for the year the cost of goods sold was $136,200. Information on the balance sheet enables us to find the average inventory. By adding the value of the beginning inventory to the ending inventory and dividing by 2, we can compute an average inventory. In the case of DLL, this would be as follows:

$$\frac{\$60,750 + \$60,300}{2} = \$60,525$$

Thus,

$$\text{Inventory turnover rate} \atop \text{(in cost of goods sold)} = \frac{\text{costs of goods sold}}{\text{average inventory at cost}} = \frac{\$136,200}{\$60,525} = 2.25 \text{ times}$$

Return on Investment

Firms often develop business objectives in terms of *return on investment (ROI)*, and ROI is often used to determine how effective (and efficient) the firm's management has been. First, however, we need to define exactly what a firm means by investment. In most cases, firms define investment as the total assets of the firm. To calculate the ROI, we need the net income found in the income statement and the total assets (or investment) found in the firm's balance sheet.

Return on investment is calculated as follows:

$$\text{ROI} = \frac{\text{net income}}{\text{total investment}}$$

For DLL Inc., if the total assets are $129,825 then the ROI is as follows:

$$\frac{\$48,465}{\$129,825} = 37.3\%$$

Sometimes return on investment is calculated by using an expanded formula:

$$\text{ROI} = \frac{\text{net profit}}{\text{sales}} \times \frac{\text{sales}}{\text{investment}}$$

$$= \frac{\$48,465}{\$248,850} \times \frac{\$248,850}{\$129,825} = 37.3\%$$

This formula makes it easy to show how ROI can be increased and what might reduce ROI. For example, there are different ways to increase ROI. First, if the management focuses on cutting costs and increasing efficiency, profits may be increased while sales remain the same:

$$\text{ROI} = \frac{\text{net profit}}{\text{sales}} \times \frac{\text{sales}}{\text{investment}}$$

$$= \frac{\$53,277}{\$248,850} \times \frac{\$248,850}{\$129,825} = 41.0\%$$

But ROI can be increased just as much without improving performance simply by reducing the investment—by maintaining less inventory:

$$\text{ROI} = \frac{\text{net profit}}{\text{sales}} \times \frac{\text{sales}}{\text{investment}}$$

$$= \frac{\$48,465}{\$248,850} \times \frac{\$248,850}{\$114,825} = 42.2\%$$

Sometimes, however, differences among the total assets of firms may be related to the age of the firm or the type of industry, which makes ROI a poor indicator of performance. For this reason, some firms have replaced the traditional ROI measures with *return on assets managed* (ROAM), *return on net assets* (RONA), or *return on stockholders' equity* (ROE).

Price Elasticity

Price elasticity, discussed in Chapter 11, is a measure of the sensitivity of customers to changes in price. Price elasticity is calculated by comparing the percentage change in quantity to the percentage change in price:

$$\text{Price elasticity of demand} = \frac{\text{percentage change in quantity}}{\text{percentage change in price}}$$

$$E = \frac{(Q_2 - Q_1)/Q_1}{(P_2 - P_1)/P_1}$$

where Q = quantity and P = price

For example, suppose a manufacturer of jeans increased its price for a pair of jeans from $30.00 to $35.00. But instead of 40,000 pairs being sold, sales declined to only 38,000 pairs. The price elasticity would be calculated as follows:

$$E = \frac{(38,000 - 40,000)/40,000}{(\$35.00 - 30.00)/\$30.00} = \frac{-0.05}{0.167} = 0.30$$

Note that elasticity is usually expressed as a positive number even though the calculations create a negative value.

In this case, a relatively small change in demand (5 percent) resulted from a fairly large change in price (16.7 percent), indicating that demand is inelastic. At 0.30, the elasticity is less than 1.

On the other hand, what if the same change in price resulted in a reduction in demand to 30,000 pairs of jeans? Then the elasticity would be as follows:

$$E = \frac{(30,000 - 40,000)/40,000}{(\$35.00 - 30.00)/\$30.00} = \frac{-0.25}{0.167} = 1.50$$

In this case, because the 16.7 percent change in price resulted in an even larger change in demand (25 percent), demand is elastic. The elasticity of 1.50 is greater than 1.

Note: Elasticity may also be calculated by dividing the change in quantity by the average of Q_1 and Q_2 and dividing the change in price by the average of the two prices. However, we have chosen to include the formula that uses the initial quantity and price rather than the average.

Cost-Plus Pricing

As noted in Chapter 11, the most common cost-based approach to pricing a product is *cost-plus pricing*, in which a marketer figures all costs for the product and then adds an amount to cover profit and, in some cases, any costs of doing business that are not assigned to specific products. The most frequently used type of cost-plus pricing is *straight markup pricing*. The price is calculated by adding a predetermined percentage to the cost. Most retailers and wholesalers use markup pricing exclusively because of its simplicity—users need only estimate the unit cost and add the markup.

The first step requires that the unit cost be easy to estimate accurately and that production rates are fairly consistent. As Table B.4 shows, we will assume that a jeans manufacturer has fixed costs (the cost of the factory, advertising, managers' salaries, etc.) of $2,000,000. The variable cost, per pair of jeans (the cost of fabric, zipper, thread, and labor) is $20.00. With the current plant, the firm can produce a total of 400,000 pairs of jeans, so the fixed cost per pair is $5.00. Combining the fixed and variable costs per pair means that the jeans are produced at a total cost of $25.00 per pair and the total cost of producing 400,000 pairs of jeans is $10,000,000.

The second step is to calculate the markup. There are two methods for calculating the markup percentage: markup on cost and markup on selling price. For *markup on cost pricing*, just as the name implies, a percentage of the cost is added to the cost to determine the firm's selling price. As you can see, we have included both methods in our example shown in Table B.4.

Markup on Cost

For markup on cost, the calculation is as follows:

$$\text{Price} = \text{total cost} + (\text{total cost} \times \text{markup percentage})$$

But how does the manufacturer or reseller know which markup percentage to use? One way is to base the markup on the total income needed for profits, for shareholder dividends, and for investment in the business. In our jeans example, the total cost of producing the 400,000 pairs of jeans is $10,000,000. If the manufacturer wants a profit of $2,000,000, what markup percentage would it use? The $2,000,000 is 20 percent of the $10 million total cost, so 20 percent. To find the price, the calculations would be as follows:

$$\text{Price} = \$25.00 + (\$25.00 \times 0.20) = \$25.0 + \$5.00 = \$30.00$$

Note that in the calculations, the markup percentage is expressed as a decimal; that is, 20% = 0.20, 25% = 0.25, 30% = 0.30, and so on.

Markup on Selling Price

Wholesalers and retailers more generally use markup on selling price. The markup percentage here is the seller's gross margin, the difference between the cost to the wholesaler or retailer and the price needed to cover overhead items such as salaries, rent, utility bills, advertising, and profit. For example, if the wholesaler or retailer knows that it needs a margin of 40 percent to cover its overhead and reach its target profits, that margin becomes the markup on the manufacturer's selling price.

So now let's say a retailer buys the jeans from the supplier (wholesaler or manufacturer) for $30.00 per pair. If the retailer requires a margin of 40 percent, it would calculate the price as a 40 percent markup on selling price. The calculation would be as follows:

$$\text{Price} = \frac{\text{total cost}}{(1.00 - \text{markup percentage})}$$

$$\text{Price} = \frac{\$30.00}{(1.00 - 0.40)} = \frac{\$30.00}{.60} = \$50.00$$

Therefore, the price of the jeans with the markup on selling price is $50.00.

Just to compare the difference in the final prices of the two markup methods, Table B.4 also shows what would happen if the retailer uses a markup on cost method. Using the same product cost and price with a 40 percent markup on cost would yield $42.00, a much

---

Table B.4	Markup Pricing Using Jeans as an Example	

Step 1: Determine Costs		
1.a: Determine total fixed costs		
Management and other nonproduction-related salaries	$750,000	
Rental of factory	600,000	
Insurance	50,000	
Depreciation on equipment	100,000	
Advertising	500,000	
Total fixed costs	**$2,000,000**	
1.b: Determine fixed costs per unit		
Number of units produced = 400,000		
Fixed cost per unit ($2,000,000/400,000)		**$5.00**
1.c: Determine variable costs per unit		
Cost of materials (fabric, zipper, thread, etc.)	$7.00	
Cost of production labor	10.00	
Cost of utilities and supplies used in production process	3.00	
Variable cost per unit		**$20.00**
1.d: Determine total cost per unit		
$20.00 + $5.00 = $25.00		
Total cost per unit		**$25.00**
Total cost for producing 400,000 units = $10,000,000		
Step 2: Determine markup and price		
***Manufacturer's markup on cost* (assuming 20% markup)**		
Formula: Price = total cost + (total cost × markup percentage)		
Manufacturer's Price to the Retailer		
= $25.00 + ($25.00 × .20) = $25.00 + $5.00 =		**$30.00**
***Retailer's markup on selling price* (assuming 40% markup)**		
Formula: Price = $\dfrac{\text{total cost}}{(1.00\ -\ \text{markup percentage})}$		
Retailer's Price to the Consumer		
= $\dfrac{\$30.00}{(1.00\ -\ .40)} = \dfrac{\$30.00}{.60} =$		**$50.00**
***Retailer's alternative markup on cost* (assuming 40% markup)**		
Formula: Price = total cost + (total cost × markup percentage)		
Retailer's Price to the Consumer		
= $30.00 + ($30.00 × .40) = $30.00 + $12.00 =		**$42.00**

lower price. The markup on selling price gives you the percentage of the selling price that the markup is. The markup on cost gives you the percentage of the cost that the markup is. In the markup on selling price the markup amount is $20.00, which is 40 percent of the selling price of $50.00. In the markup on cost, the markup is $12.00, which is 40 percent of the cost of $30.00.

Economic Order Quantity

The amount a firm should order at one time is the *economic order quantity* (EOQ). Every time a firm places an order, there are additional costs. By ordering larger quantities less frequently, the firm saves on these costs. But it also costs money to maintain large inventories of needed materials. The EOQ is the order volume that provides both the lowest processing costs and the lowest inventory costs. The EOQ can be calculated as follows:

1. Determine the *order processing cost*. This is the total amount it costs a firm to place an order from beginning to end. Typically, this might include the operating expenses for the purchasing department, costs for follow-up, costs of record keeping of orders (data processing), costs for the receiving department, and costs for the processing and paying of invoices from suppliers. The simplest way to calculate this is to add up all these yearly costs and then divide by the number of orders placed during the year.

2. Next, calculate the *inventory carrying cost*. This is the total of all costs involved in carrying inventory. These costs include the costs of capital tied up in inventory, the cost of waste (merchandise that becomes obsolete or unusable), depreciation costs, storage costs, insurance premiums, property taxes, and opportunity costs.

The formula for calculating EOQ is as follows:

$$EOQ = \sqrt{\frac{2 \times \text{units sold (or annual usage)} \times \text{order processing cost}}{\text{unit cost} \times \text{inventory carrying cost (\%)}}}$$

For example, suppose an office supply store sells 6,000 cases of pens a year at a cost of $12.00 a case. The cost to the store for each order placed is $60.00. The cost of carrying the pens in the warehouse is 24 percent per year. (This is a typical inventory carrying cost in many businesses.) Thus, the calculation is as follows:

$$EOQ = \sqrt{\frac{2 \times 6,000 \times \$60}{\$12 \times 0.24}} = \sqrt{\frac{\$720,000}{\$2.88}} = 500$$

The firm should order pens about once a month (it sells 6,000 cases a year, or 500 cases a month).

▶ **Notes**

CHAPTER 1

1. John W. Schouten, "Selves in Transition: Symbolic Consumption in Personal Rites of Passage and Identity Reconstruction," *Journal of Consumer Research*, March 17, 1991, 412–25; Michael R. Solomon, "The Wardrobe Consultant: Exploring the Role of a New Retailing Partner," *Journal of Retailing* 63 (1987): 110–28; Michael R. Solomon and Susan P. Douglas, "Diversity in Product Symbolism: The Case of Female Executive Clothing," *Psychology & Marketing* 4 (1987): 189–212; Joseph Z. Wisenblit, "Person Positioning: Empirical Evidence and a New Paradigm," *Journal of Professional Services Marketing* 4, no. 2 (1989): 51–82.

2. "Marketing Definitions," MarketingPower.com, http://www.marketingpower.com/AboutAMA/Pages/DefinitionofMarketing.aspx (accessed September 19, 2008).

3. Michael R. Solomon, "Deep-Seated Materialism: The Case of Levi's 501 Jeans," in *Advances in Consumer Research*, ed. Richard Lutz (Las Vegas, NV.: Association for Consumer Research, 1986), 13: 619–22.

4. Peter F. Drucker, *Management: Tasks, Responsibilities, Practices* (New York: Harper & Row, 1972), 64–65.

5. Evan Shannon, "3BR w/VU of Asteroid Belt," *Wired* (April 2006): 130.

6. "Henry Ford and the Model T," in *Forbes Greatest Business Stories* (New York: Wiley, 1996), www.wiley.com/legacy/products/subject/business/forbes/ford.html.

7. Theodore Levitt, "Marketing Myopia," *Harvard Business Review*, July–August 1960, 45–56.

8. Rahul Jacob, "How to Retread Customers," *Fortune*, Autumn/Winter 1993, 23–24.

9. Ian Mount, "Rise of the Instapreneur," *Wired*, December 2007, 129.

10. Englis, P. D., Englis, B., Solomon, M.S., and Groen, A. (2006), "Strategic Sustainability and Triple Bottom Line Performance in Textiles: Implications of the Eco-Label for the EU And Beyond," Business as an Agent of World Benefit Conference, United Nations and the Academy of Management, Cleveland, OH.

11. Gabriel Sherman, "Green on the Outside," *Wired*, December 2007, 126.

12. Bob Tedeschi, "Brand Building on the Internet," *New York Times Online* (August 25, 2003), http://www.nytimes.com/2003/08/25/technology/25ECOM.html?ei=5007&en=0c6702f4bc5c2a9d&ex=1377230400&adxnnl=1&partner=USERLAND&adxnnlx=1210698904-VtYXZvlWoRZjxZHgDoTTsA.

13. Cf. M. K., Khoo, S.G., Lee, S.W. Lye, "A Design Methodology for the Strategic Assessment of a Product's Eco-efficiency," *International Journal of Production Research*, 39 (2001): 245–74; C. Chen, "Design for the Environment: A Quality-Based Model for Green Product Development," *Management Science*, 47(2) (2001): 250–64; McDonough Braungart Design *Chemistry's Design Paradigm*. Retrieved April 15, 2006, from http://www.mbdc.com/c2c_home.htm; Elizabeth Corcoran, "Thinking Green," *Scientific American*, 267:6 (1992): 44–46; Amitai Etzioni, "The Good Society: Goals Beyond Money." *The Futurist*, (2001): 68–69; M.H. Olson, "Charting a Course for Sustainability." *Environment*, 38:4,(1996) 10–23.

14. Kate Fitzgerald, "Avon Adds 3 Venues to Anti-Cancer Walk," *Advertising Age*, May 1, 2000, 54.

15. Jeff Lowe, *The Marketing Dashboard: Measuring Marketing Effectiveness* (Venture Communications, February 2003), www.brandchannel.com/images/papers/dashboard.pdf; G. A. Wyner, "Scorecards and More: The Value Is in How You Use Them," *Marketing Research*, Summer, 6–7; C. F. Lundby and C. Rasinowich, "The Missing Link: Cause and Effect Linkages Make Marketing Scorecards More Valuable," *Marketing Research*, Winter 2003, 14–19.

16. Sal Randazzo, "Advertising as Myth-Maker; Brands as Gods and Heroes," *Advertising Age*, November 8, 1993, 32.

17. Lee D. Dahringer, "Marketing Services Internationally: Barriers and Management Strategies," *Journal of Service Marketing* 5 (1991): 5–17.

18. Stuart Elliott, "Introducing Kentucky, the Brand," June 9, 2004, *New York Times Online*, www.nyt.com.

19. Clive Thompson, "Almost Famous," *Wired*, December 2007; 84.

20. Jean Halliday, "Mustang Fans Help Ford Give New Model Free Ride," *Advertising Age*, May 24, 2004, 4.

21. Michael E. Porter, *Competitive Advantage: Creating and Sustaining Superior Performance* (New York: Free Press, 1985).

22. Suzanne Vranica, "Marketers' New Idea: Get the Consumer to Design the Ads," *Wall Street Journal*, December 14, 2005, B1.

23. James Yang, "Here's an Idea: Let Everyone Have Ideas," *New York Times Online*, March 30, 2006.

24. *Snakes on a Plane*, Wikipedia.org, (accessed April 16, 2006).

25. Kevin Kelleher, "Social Networks Grow Up," *Wired*, December 2007, 124.

26. Some material adapted from a presentation by Matt Leavey, Prentice Hall Business Publishing, July 18, 2007.

27. This section adapted from Michael R. Solomon, *Consumer Behavior: Buying, Having and Being* 8/e, Upper Saddle River, NJ: Pearson Education, 2008.

28. Jeff Surowiecki, *The Wisdom of Crowds* (New York: Anchor, 2005); Jeff Howe, "The Rise of Crowdsourcing," *Wired* (June 2006): http://www.wired.com/wired/archive/14.06/crowds.html, (accessed October 3, 2007).

29. Mark Weingarten, "Designed to Grow," *Business 2.0* (June 2007): 35–37.

30. Daniel Roth, 'Open Source Tycoons,' *Wired* December 2007, 122 2 pp.

31. "Dear Chrysler: Outsiders' Advice on Handling the Odometer Charge," *Wall Street Journal*, June 26, 1987, 19.

32. Larry Edwards, "The Decision Was Easy," *Advertising Age*, August 26, 1987, 106. For research and discussion related to public policy issues, see Paul N. Bloom and Stephen A. Greyser, "The Maturing of Consumerism," *Harvard Business Review*, November/December 1981, 130–39; George S. Day, "Assessing the Effect of Information Disclosure Requirements," *Journal of Marketing*, April 1976, 42–52; Dennis E. Garrett, "The Effectiveness of Marketing Policy Boycotts: Environmental Opposition to Marketing," *Journal of Marketing* 51 (January 1987): 44–53; Michael Houston and Michael Rothschild, "Policy-Related Experiments on Information Provision: A Normative Model and Explication," *Journal of Marketing Research* 17 (November 1980): 432–49; Jacob Jacoby, Wayne D. Hoyer, and David A. Sheluga, *Misperception of Televised Communications* (New York: American Association of Advertising Agencies, 1980); Gene R. Laczniak and Patrick E. Murphy, *Marketing Ethics: Guidelines for Managers* (Lexington, MA: Lexington Books, 1985): 117–23; Lynn Phillips and Bobby Calder, "Evaluating Consumer Protection Laws: Promising Methods," *Journal of Consumer Affairs* 14 (Summer 1980): 9–36; Donald P. Robin and Eric Reidenbach, "Social Responsibility, Ethics, and Marketing Strategy: Closing the Gap between Concept and Application," *Journal of Marketing* 51 (January 1987): 44–58; Howard Schutz and Marianne Casey, "Consumer Perceptions of Advertising as Misleading," *Journal of Consumer Affairs* 15 (Winter 1981): 340–57; and Darlene Brannigan Smith and Paul N. Bloom, "Is Consumerism Dead or Alive? Some New Evidence," in *Advances in Consumer Research*, ed. Thomas C. Kinnear (Provo, UT: Association for Consumer Research, 1984): 569–73.

33. This section adapted from Michael R. Solomon, *Consumer Behavior: Buying, Having and Being* 8/e, Upper Saddle River, NJ: Pearson Education, 2008.

34. William Leiss, Stephen Kline, and Sut Jhally, *Social Communication in Advertising: Persons, Products, and Images of Well-Being* (Toronto: Methuen, 1986); Jerry Mander, *Four Arguments for the Elimination of Television* (New York: William Morrow, 1977).

35. William Leiss, Stephen Kline, and Sut Jhally, *Social Communication in Advertising: Persons, Products, and Images of Well-Being* (Toronto: Methuen, 1986).

36. Quoted in Leiss et al., *Social Communication*, 11 (Toronto: Methuen, 1986).

37. Parts of this section are adapted from Michael R. Solomon, *Consumer Behavior: Buying, Having, and Being*, 7th ed. (Upper Saddle River, NJ: Prentice Hall, 2007).

38. Thomas C. O'Guinn and Ronald J. Faber, "Compulsive Buying: A Phenomenological Explanation," *Journal of Consumer Research* 16 (September 1989): 154.

39. Samantha Manas, "Addicted to Chapstick: The World of Chapstick Addicts Revealed," *Associated Content* (July 5, 2006): http://www.associatedcontent.com/article/41148/addicted_to_chapstick.html, (accessed May 13, 2008).

40. "Advertisers Face Up to the New Morality: Making the Pitch," *Bloomberg* (July 8, 1997).

41. Gerry Khermouch, "Virgin's 'Va Va' Bottle Has 'Voom'; First Ads via Long Haymes Carr," *Brandweek*, July 10, 2000, 13.

42. Michael McCarthy, "Adidas Puts Computer on New Footing," *USA Today.com* (March 3, 2005): http://www.usatoday.com/money/industries/2005-03-02-smart-usat_x.htm (accessed May 13, 2008).

CHAPTER 2

1. Bloomberg News, "Margin Calls Forced Lay to Sell Stock, Witness Says," *New York Times*, May 5, 2006, www.nytimes.com/2006/05/05/business/businessspecial3/05enron.html (accessed December 22, 2007).

2. "Government Lifts Ban on Contracts with MCI," *USA Today*, www.usatoday.com/money/industries/telecom/2004-01-07-mci-contracts_x.htm (accessed December 22, 2007).

3. Krysten Crawford, "Martha, Out and About," CNNMoney.com, http://money.cnn.com/2005/03/03/news/newsmakers/martha_walkup (accessed December 22, 2007).

4. Mara Der Hovanesian and Christopher Palmeri, "That Sinking Feeling," *BusinessWeek*, October 15, 2007, 32–38.

5. "Dow Chemical Company Code of Business Conduct," Dow, http://www.dow.com/about/aboutdow/code_conduct/ethics_conduct.htm (accessed December 31, 2007).

6. MADD, www.madd.org (accessed May 30, 2006).

7. "About Xerox," Xerox, http://www.xerox.com/go/xrx/portal/STServlet?projectID=ST_About_Xerox&pageID=Landing&Xcntry=USA&Xlang=en_US (accessed December 20, 2007).

8. Kevin Freiberg and Jackie Freiberg, *NUTS! Southwest Airlines' Crazy Recipe for Business and Personal Success* (New York: Broadway Books, 1998).

9. Dan Reed, "Southwest Plans New Seating Policy, Schedule Changes," *USA Today*, June 27, 2007 http://www.usatoday.com/travel/flights/2007-06-27-southwest-plans_N.htm (accessed December 21, 2007); http://www.swamedia.com/about_swa/press/070919_boarding.html (accessed December 21, 2007).

10. "Get the Power of Oats Working for You," Cheerios, http://www.cheerios.com/forAdults/cholesterol/PowerOfOats.aspx (accessed December 19, 2007); http://www.quakeroatmeal.com/qo_heartHealthy/oatmealAndHeartHealth/index.cfm (accessed December 19, 2007).

11. Anath Hartman, "Senior Citizens Wowed by Nintendo's Wii," *Gazette.Net*, December 20, 2007, http://www.gazette.net/stories/122007/laurnew142319_32358.shtml (accessed December 29, 2007).

12. Christina Binkley, "Hotels? 'Go to the Mattresses'; Marriott is Latest to Make Huge Bet on Better Bedding," *Wall Street Journal*, January 25, 2005, D1.

13. Michael Arndt, "McDonald's 24/7," *BusinessWeek*, February 5, 2007, 64–72.

14. Freiberg and Freiberg, *NUTS! Southwest Airlines' Crazy Recipe for Business and Personal Success* (New York: Broadway Books, 1998).

15. Gordon A. Wyner, "Beyond ROI: Make Sure the Analytics Address Strategic Issues," *Marketing Management* 15 (May/June 2006), 8–9.

16. Tim Ambler, "Don't Cave in to Cave Dwellers," *Marketing Management*, September/October 2006, 25–29.

17. "Fortune 100 Best Companies to Work for in 2007," *CNNMoney.com*, http://money.cnn.com/magazines/fortune/bestcompanies/2007/ (accessed December 31, 2007).

CHAPTER 3

1. Keith Naughton, "The Great Wal-Mart Of China; To move into China, America's biggest and most successful retailer had to learn its business all over again," *Newsweek*, U.S. Edition, October 30, 2006, Vol. 148, Issue 16, p. 50.

2. Jonathan Birchall, "Wal-Mart plans big expansion outside US," *Financial Times*, London: Oct 24, 2007, pg. 20.

3. Keith Naughton, "The Great Wal-Mart Of China; To move into China, America's biggest and most successful retailer had to learn its business all over again," *Newsweek*, October 30, 2006, http://www.newsweek.com/id/45140 (accessed May 15, 2008).

4. *Ibid*.

5. World Trade Organization, "International Trade Statistics 2007," http://www.wto.org/english/res_e/statis_e/its2007_e/its2007_e.pdf (accessed May 15, 2008).

6. "The Philippines Imports Vietnam Rice on Countertrade," *Thanhniem News.com*, http://www.thanhniennews.com/business/?catid=2&newsid=6395 (accessed August 1, 2006).

7. "Key Dates in China Export Scares," *Wall Street Journal*, October 21, 2007, http://online.wsj.com/article/SB118606827156686195.html (accessed Jan 10, 2008).

8. Walt Bogdanich, "Toxic Toothpaste Made in China is Found in U.S.," *New York Times*, June 2, 2007, http://www.nytimes.com/2007/06/02/us/02toothpaste.html?sq=toothpaste%20china&scp=3&pagewanted=print (accessed January 10, 2008).

9. "Key Dates in China Export Scares," *Wall Street Journal*, October 21, 2007, http://online.wsj.com/article/SB118606827156686195.html (accessed Jan 10, 2008).

10. "Key Dates in China Export Scares," *Wall Street Journal*, October 21, 2007, http://online.wsj.com/article/SB118606827156686195.html (accessed Jan 10, 2008).

11. "Key Dates in China Export Scares," *Wall Street Journal*, October 21, 2007, http://online.wsj.com/article/SB118606827156686195.html (accessed Jan 10, 2008).

12. Walt Mogdanich, "Chinese Chemicals Flow Unchecked Onto World Drug Market," *New York Times*, October 31, 2007, http://www.nytimes.com/2007/10/31/world/asia/31chemical.html?scp=1&sq=pharmaceutical+chemicals (accessed January 10, 2008).

13. Mark Bursa, "China automotive market review: Management briefing: Major developments at other Chinese automakers," *Just-Auto*, October 2007, pp 20–23.

14. "Chinese Automaker Coming to the U.S.," MSN.com, http://autos.msn.com/as/article.aspx?xml=Geely&shw=autoshow2006 (accessed May 15, 2008).

15. "Losing their vrrooom?" *The Economist*, February 24, 2007, p 77.

16. Michael R. Czinkota and Masaaki Kotabe, "America's New World Trade Order," *Marketing Management* 1, no. 3 (1992): 47–54.

17. Guy Chazam, "Russian Meat Import Quotas Imperil WTO Bid," *Wall Street Journal — Eastern Edition*, February 3, 2003, page A12.

18. "U.S. Moves to Limit Textile Imports from China," November 19, 2003, *New York Times*, http://query.nytimes.com/gst/fullpage.html?res=9E0DEFDC163BF93AA25752C1A9659C8B63.

19. Jane Wardell, Associated Press Worldwide, "U.S., China Sign Deal on Imports of Chinese Clothing, Textiles into U.S." Highbeam Research http://www.highbeam.com/doc/1P1-114998802.html (accessed May 1, 2008).

20. "Bill Aims for 27.5% Tariff on China Textiles," *Home Textiles Today*, High Point: July 30, 2007, p 31.

21. World Trade Organization, "The WTO in Brief." http://www.wto.org/english/res_e/doload_e/inbr_e.pdf (accessed May 15, 2008).

22. Nic Hopkins, "Software Piracy Microsoft's Big Threat," *CNN.com*, February 7, 2001, www.cnn.com/2001/WORLD/asiapcf/east/02/07/hongkong.microsoft.

23. Geri Smith, Elisabeth Malkin, Jonathan Wheatley, Paul Magnusson, and Michael Arnds, "Betting on Free Trade," *BusinessWeek*, April 23, 2001, 60–62; "Antecedents of the FTAA Process," Free Trade Area of the Americas, http://www.ftaa-alca.org/View_e.asp (accessed May 25, 2008).

24. Peter Fuhrman and Michael Schuman, "Where Are the Indians? The Russians?" *Forbes*, July 17, 1995, 126–27.

25. "Peru: Privatization Is Principal Policy for Attracting Foreign Investment," *Wall Street Journal*, October 27, 1993, B7.

26. Bruce Einhorn, Frederik Balfour, and Andy Reinhardt, "Cell Phones: The Big Boys Are Back in China," *BusinessWeek*, September 27, 2004, http://www.businessweek.com/magazine/content/04_39/b3901066.htm (accessed July 27, 2006).

27. Deborah Ball, "Lattes Lure Brits to Coffee; Tea Sales Fall as Starbucks Draws the Young," *Wall Street Journal*, October 20, 2005: B1.

28. "Corporate Facts: Wal-Mart by the Numbers," Walmart, http://www.walmartfacts.com/FactSheets/Corporate_Facts.pdf (accessed November 26, 2007).

29. EB Eggs, "About Eggland's Best" http://www.egglandsbest.com/egglands-eggs/why-egglands/about-us.aspx (accessed September 19, 2008).

30. Jason Leow and Jane Zhang, "Product-Safety Pacts Put Greater Burden on Beijing," *Wall Street Journal*, December 12, 2007, p A13.

31. "KFC's Claims That Fried Chicken Is a Way to 'Eat Better' Don't Fly: National Fast Food Chain, KFC, Settles FTC Charges That It Made False Claims About Fried Chicken's Nutritional Value and Compatibility with Popular Weight-Loss Programs," *Federal Trade Commission*, http://www.ftc.gov/opa/2004/06/kfccorp.shtm (accessed November 19, 2007).

32. "United States: Tightening a loose noose; Iran," *The Economist*, November 3, 2007, p 57.

33. Sara Hope Franks, "Overseas, It's What's Inside That Sells," *Washington Post National Weekly Edition*, December 5–11, 1994, 21.

34. William C. Symonds, "Border Crossings," *BusinessWeek*, November 22, 1993, 40.

35. April Wortham, "BMW is OK with lowish N.A. parts content; Company will raise Spartanburg output to combat rising euro," *Automotive News*, May 14, 2007, p 46D.

36. Thomas L. Friedman, "U.S. Prods Indonesia on Rights," *New York Times*, January 18, 1994, D1(2).

37. Amy Merrick, "Gap Offers Unusual Look at Factory Conditions," *Wall Street Journal-Eastern Edition*, May 12, 2004, pages A1–A12.

38. "Gap: Report of kids' sweatshop 'deeply disturbing,'" *CNN.com*, http://www.cnn.com/2007/WORLD/asiapcf/10/29/gap.labor/index.html (accessed January 10, 2008); Amelia Gentleman, "Gap Campaigns Against Child Labor," *New York Times*, November 16, 2007, http://www.nytimes.com/2007/11/16/business/worldbusiness/16gap.html (accessed Jan 10, 2008).

39. "Apple: No Sweatshop iPod Labor," *Associated Press* 08.18.06 | 9:00 AM, http://www.wired.com/science/discoveries/news/2006/08/71619 (accessed November 19, 2007).

40. David Barboza, "In Chinese FActories, Lost Finger and Low Pay," *New York Times*, January 5, 2008, http://www.nytimes.com/2008/01/05/business/worldbusiness/05sweatshop.html?pagewanted=print (accessed January 14, 2008).

41. Adapted from Michael R. Solomon, *Consumer Behavior: Buying, Having, and Being*, 7th ed. (Upper Saddle River, NJ: Prentice Hall, 2007).

42. David Carr, "Romance, In *Cosmo's* World, Is Translated in Many Ways," May 26, 2002, *New York Times*, sec. 1, 1, adapted from Michael R. Solomon, *Consumer Behavior: Buying, Having, and Being*, 6th ed. (Upper Saddle River, NJ: Prentice Hall, 2003).

43. Richard W. Pollay, "Measuring the Cultural Values Manifest in Advertising," *Current Issues and Research in Advertising* 6 (1983): 71–92.

44. Deborah Ball, "Women in Italy Like to Clean but Shun the Quick and Easy," *Wall Street Journal*, April 25, 2006, A1.

45. Daniel Goleman, "The Group and the Self: New Focus on a Cultural Rift," December 25, 1990, *New York Times Online*, http://query.nytimes.com/gst/fullpage.html?res=9C0CE3DD1330F936A15751C1A966958260&scp=1&sq=The+Group+and+the+Self%3A+New+Focus+on+a+Cultural+Rift&st=nyt, 37; Harry C. Triandis, "The Self and Social Behavior in Differing Cultural Contexts," *Psychological Review* 96 (July 1989): 506; Harry C. Triandis et al., "Individualism and Collectivism: Cross-Cultural Perspectives on Self-Ingroup Relationships," *Journal of Personality and Social Psychology* 54 (February 1988): 323.

46. "The VALS™ Segments," SRI Consulting Business Intelligence The VALS™ Survey http://www.sric-bi.com/VALS/types.shtml (accessed December 14, 2007).

47. "Japan-VALS™," SRI Consulting Business Intelligence Japan-VALS™, http://www.sric-bi.com/VALS/JVALS.shtml (accessed December 14, 2007).

48. George J. McCall and J. L. Simmons, *Social Psychology: A Sociological Approach* (New York: Free Press, 1982).

49. Adapted from Michael R. Solomon, *Consumer Behavior*.

50. Philip R. Cateora, *Strategic International Marketing* (Homewood, IL: Dow Jones-Irwin, 1985).

51. "Foreign Corrupt Practices Act of 1977 (As Amended)," U.S. Department of Justice, http://www.usdoj.gov/usao/eousa/foia_reading_room/usam/title9/47mcrm.htm (accessed May 15, 2008).

52. Tom Gilbert, "An 'Idol' By Any Other Name," *Television Week*, May 29, 2006, page 2.

53. Michael Skapinker, "Brand Strength Proves Its Worth," *Financial Times*, January 20, 2004, http://search.ft.com/ftArticle?queryText=brand+strength+proves+its+worth&y=0&aje=true&x=0&id=040119006365&ct=0&nclick_check=1.

54. Alexander Hiam and Charles D. Schewe, *The Portable MBA in Marketing* (New York: Wiley, 1992).

55. Harvey S. James Jr. and Murray Weidenbaum, *When Businesses Cross International Borders* (Westport, CT: Praeger, 1993).

56. Duncan Freeman, "EU Fights for Share of China's Cheese Market," Asia Times Online, July 12, 2005, http://www.atimes.com/atimes/China/GG12Ad02.html.

57. McDonald's Corporation, "About McDonald's" www.mcdonalds.com/corp/about.html (accessed May 15, 2008).

58. Saritha Rai, "Tastes of India in U.S. Wrappers," *New York Times*, April 29, 2003, http://query.nytimes.com/gst/fullpage.html?res=9C03E6D6133DF93AA15757C0A9659C8B63.

59. "The Company," General Motors, www.gm.com/company/corp_info/profiles (accessed March 21, 2006); "Keith Naughton, "Battle in the Boardroom," *Newsweek* [on-line], July 12, 2006, http://www.msnbc.msn.com/id/13816350/site/newsweek/ (accessed July 23, 2006).

60. Goh Bee Kuan, "Haier aims higher," *New Straits Times*, May 8, 2007, p 44.

61. Sak Onkvisit and John J. Shaw, *International Marketing: Analysis and Strategy*, 2nd ed. (New York: Macmillan, 1993).

62. Quoted in Teri Agins, "Costume Change: For U.S. Fashion Firms, a Global Makeover," WSJ Online, February 2, 2007; Page A1, http://blogs.wsj.com/runway/2007/02/02/for-us-fashion-firms-a-global-makeover/?mod=WSJBlog (accessed February 10, 2008).

63. Jeremy Kahn, "The World's Most Admired Companies," *Fortune*, October 26, 1998, 206–16.

64. One of the most influential arguments for this perspective can be found in Theodore Levitt, "The Globalization of Markets," *Harvard Business Review*, May–June 1983, 92–102.

65. Juliana Koranteng, "Reebok Finds Its Second Wind as It Pursues Global Presence," *Advertising Age International*, January 1998, 18.

66. Terry Clark, "International Marketing and National Character: A Review and Proposal for an Integrative Theory," *Journal of Marketing* 54 (October 1990): 66–79.

67. Norihiko Shirouzu, "Snapple in Japan: How a Splash Dried Up," the *Wall Street Journal*, April 15, 1996, B1(2).

68. Richard C. Morais, "The Color of Beauty," *Forbes*, November 27, 2000, 170–86.

69. Ben Charny, "Apple's iPhone Approach in Europe: Be Proactive," *Wall Street Journal*, November 14, 2007, http://online.wsj.com/article/SB119499624370691953.html?apl=y&r=79676D (accessed November 19, 2007).

70. Sara Hope Franks, "Overseas, It's What's Inside That Sells," *Washington Post National Weekly Edition*, December 5–11, 1994, 21.

71. Aaron O. Patrick, "World Cup's Advertisers Hope One Size Fits All: Month-Long Tournament Sets Off Scramble to Reach Huge Global TV Audience," *Wall Street Journal*, March 28, 2006: B7.

72. Sheryl Wu Dunn, "An Uphill Journey to Japan," *New York Times*, May 16, 1995, D1(2).

73. Diana Ransom, "Tip of the Week: Try to Avoid 'Gray' Goods," *Wall Street Journal*, June 4, 2006, 1.

74. "Kodak Alleges Fuji Photo Is Dumping Color Photographic Paper in the U.S.," *Wall Street Journal*, February 22, 1993, B6.

75. Choe Sang-Hun, "Wal-Mart Selling Stores and Leaving South Korea," *New York Times Online*, May 23, 2006.

76. Jennifer Corbett Dooren, "Alcohol Ads Impact Consumption among the Young, Study Shows," *Wall Street Journal Interactive Edition*, January 2, 2006.

CHAPTER 4

1. Alan J. Greco and Jack T. Hogue, "Developing Marketing Decision Support Systems in Consumer Goods Firms," *Journal of Consumer Marketing* 7 (1990): 55–64.

2. "The Simply Everything Plan," Sprint.com, www.sprintspecialoffers.com/everything/?id12=UHP_Masthead_040708_SimplyEverything (accessed April 1, 2008).

3. Hollywood Stock Exchange, www.hsx.com (accessed April 15, 2008); Glenn Boyle and Steen Videbeck, "Want to Predict the Future? Ask the Market," Policy, Vol. 22, No. 2 (Winter 2006), pp. 39–42; Mark Henricks, "Forward," *Entrepreneur* (February 2007), pp. 17–8; Teck-Hua Ho and Kay-Yut Chen, "New Product Blockbusters: The Magic and Science of Prediction Markets," *California Management Review*, Vol. 50, No. 1 (Fall 2007), pp. 144–58.

4. Marketing Evaluations Inc., "The Q Scores Company," www.qscores.com (accessed February 15, 2006).

5. Tan, Pan-Ning, Michael Steinbach, and Vipin Kumar, *Introduction to Data Mining* (New York: Addison Wesley, 2005).

6. Catherine Holahan, "Battling Data Monsters at Yahoo!" *BusinessWeek*, 14 December 2007, www.businessweek.com/technology/content/dec2007/tc20071213_341756.htm?chan=search (accessed January 28, 2008); Catherine Holahan, "Facebook: Marketers Are Your 'Friends,'" *BusinessWeek*, 7 November 2007, www.businessweek.com/technology/content/nov2007/tc2007116_289111.htm?chan=search (accessed January 28, 2007).

7. Tan et al., *Introduction to Data Mining*.

8. Frederick F. Reichheld, *Loyalty Rules! How Leaders Build Lasting Relationships in the Digital Age* (Cambridge, MA: Harvard Business School Press, 2001).

9. Robert Nelson, "Sprint may cancel your service if you call customer service too often," 6 July 2007, http://www.gadgetell.com/tech/comment/sprint-may-cancel-your-service-if-you-call-customer-service-to-often/ (accessed February 24, 2008); Samar Srivasta, "Sprint Drops Clients Over Excessive Inquiries" 7 July 2007, *Wall Street Journal*, http://online.wsj.com/public/article_print/SB118376389957059668-IpRTFYVQbLGbXKvlbPELi83M_8A_20080710.html (accessed September 19, 2008).

10. Vanessa Fuhrmans, "Bedside Manner: An Insurer Tries A New Strategy: Listen to Patients," *Wall Street Journal*, 11 April 2006, http://online.wsj.com/article/SB114472468261322626-search.html?KEYWORDS=humana&COLLECTION=wsjie/6month (accessed March 12, 2008).

11. Hamilton Nolan, "Mercedes Launches PR Push," *PR Week*, February 6, 2006, 3.

12. Michael R. Solomon, *Conquering Consumerspace: Marketing Strategies for a Branded World* (New York: AMACOM Books, 2003).

13. Michael R. Solomon, *Consumer Behavior: Buying, Having, and Being*, 8th ed. (Upper Saddle River, NJ: Prentice Hall, 2009).

14. Jean Halliday, "Nissan Delves into Truck Owner Psyche," *Advertising Age*, December 1, 2003, 11.

15. Jack Neff, "Six-Blade Blitz," *Advertising Age*, September 19, 2005, 3.

16. Srikumar Rao, "Diaper–Beer Syndrome," *Forbes*, April 6, 1998, 128 (3).

17. Clive Thompson, "There's a Sucker Born in Every Medial Prefrontal Cortex," *NYTimes.com*, October 26, 2003, http://www.nytimes.com/2003/10/26/magazine/26BRAINS.html?pagewanted=2&ei=5007&en=f2f892dad7b173aa&ex=1382500800&partner=USERLAND (accessed September 19, 2008).

18. Direct Marketing Association, "Where Marketers Can Obtain State Do-Not-Call Lists," www.the-dma.org/government/donotcalllists.shtml (accessed February 7, 2006).

19. Kim Bartel Sheehan, "Online Research Methodology: Reflections and Speculations," *Journal of Interactive Advertising* 3:1 (Fall 2002) http://www.websm.org/index.php?fl=2&lact=1&bid=631&cat=351&p1=1123&p2=82&id=520&page=1&parent=12 (accessed February 7, 2006).

20. Basil G. Englis and Michael R. Solomon, "Life/Style OnLine ©: A Web-Based Methodology for Visually-Oriented Consumer Research," *Journal of Interactive Marketing* 14:1 (2000): 2–14; Basil G. Englis, Michael R. Solomon, and Paula D. Harveston, "Web-Based, Visually Oriented Consumer Research Tools," *Online Consumer Psychology: Understanding and Influencing Consumer Behavior in the Virtual World*, ed. Curt Haugtvedt, Karen Machleit, and Richard Yalch (Hillsdale, NJ: Lawrence Erlbaum Associates, 2005).

21. Matt Richtel, "A New On-the-Job Hazard: Turning into a Mall Rat," *NYTimes.com*, May 3, 2004, http://www.nytimes.com/2004/05/03/technology/03wifi.html?ex=1398916800&en=f6432461e01b5bf7&ei=5007&partner=USERLAND (accessed February 7, 2006).

22. Tim Callahan, "Building on Success to Deliver Better Insights," http://us.acnielsen.com/pubs/2004_q4_ci_building.shtml (accessed June 10, 2008).

23. Abbey Klaassen and Matthew Creamer, "Facebook to add shopping service to its menu," Advertising Age, 5 November 2007, www.highbeam.com/doc/1G1-171075422.html (accessed April 3, 2008); "Facebook Purchase Feed Draws User Criticism," TradingMarkets.com, 28 November 2007, www.tradingmarkets.com/.site/news/Stock%20News/862644/ (accessed April 3, 2008).

24. Jean Halliday, "Automakers Involve Consumers," *Advertising Age*, http://www.highbeam.com/doc/1G1-59214691.html (accessed April 11, 2008).

25. Manu Kaushik, "Rock for Jocks: The Nike + iPod," *Wall Street Journal Online*, 18 November 2007, http://online.wsj.com/article/SB119612230607104594.html?mod=yahoo_hs&ru=yahoo (accessed March 12, 2008).

26. James Heckman, "Turning the Focus Online," *Marketing News*, February 28, 2000, 15; Judith Langer, "'On' and 'Offline' Focus Groups: Claims, Questions," *Marketing News*, June 5, 2000, H38.

27. Deborah L. Vence, "In an Instant: More Researchers Use IM for Fast, Reliable Results," *Marketing News*, March 1, 2006, 55 (3).

28. Bruce L. Stern and Ray Ashmun, "Methodological Disclosure: The Foundation for Effective Use of Survey Research," *Journal of Applied Business Research* 7 (1991): 77–82.

29. Alan E. Wolf, "Most Colas Branded Alike by Testy Magazine," *Beverage World*, August 31, 1991, 8.

30. Gary Levin, "New Adventures in Children's Research," *Advertising Age*, August 9, 1993, 17.

31. 2007 Honomichl Top 25 Report, *Marketing News*, August 15, 2007.

32. ESOMAR, Amsterdam, Netherlands, as reported in Marketing News, July 15, 2005.

33. Tara Parker-Pope, "Nonalcoholic Beer Hits the Spot in Mideast," *Wall Street Journal*, December 6, 1995, B1(2).

CHAPTER 5

1. James R. Bettman, "The Decision Maker Who Came in from the Cold," Presidential Address, in *Advances in Consumer Research*, vol. 20, ed. Leigh McAllister and Michael Rothschild (Provo, UT: Association for Consumer Research, 1990); John W. Payne, James R. Bettman, and Eric J. Johnson, "Behavioral Decision Research: A Constructive Processing Perspective," *Annual Review of Psychology* 4 (1992): 87–131; for an overview of recent developments in individual choice models, see Robert J. Meyer and Barbara E. Kahn, "Probabilistic Models of Consumer Choice Behavior," in *Handbook of Consumer Behavior*, ed. Thomas S. Robertson and Harold H. Kassarjian (Englewood Cliffs, NJ: Prentice Hall, 1991), 85–123.

2. Graham Donoghue, "Content is King and Users are in Control," *Travel Trade Gazette* (20 September 2006), p. 13; Jennifer Merritt, "Advancing Online with Web 2.0," *TravelAgent* (August 27, 2007), pp. 18–20; Lodging Hospitality, "Embrace the Customer," *Lodging Hospitality* (December 2007), p. 110; "Fact Sheet," TripAdvisor, http://www.tripadvisor.com/PressCenter-c4-Fact_Sheet.html.

3. Aaron O. Patrick, "Microsoft Ad Push Is All about You: 'Behavioral Targeting' Aims to Use Customer Preferences to Hone Marketing Pitches," *Wall Street Journal* (December 26, 2006): B3; Brian Steinberg, "Next Up on Fox: Ads That Can Change Pitch," *Wall Street Journal* (April 21, 2005): B1; Bob Tedeschi, "Every Click You Make, They'll Be Watching You," *New York Times Online* (April 3, 2006); David Kesmodel, "Marketers Push Online Ads Based on Your Surfing Habits," *Wall Street Journal on the Web* (April 5 2005).

4. Sarah McBride and Vauhini Vara, "We Know What You Ought To Be Watching This Summer," *Wall Street Journal* (July 31, 2007): p. D1.

5. Louise Story, "Company Will Monitor Phone Calls to Tailor Ads," *New York Times Online* (September 24, 2007), http://www.nytimes.com/2007/09/24/business/media/24adcol.html?scp=1&sq=company%20will%20monitor%20phone%20calls&st=cse (accessed September 24, 2007).

6. Michael R. Solomon, *Consumer Behavior: Buying, Having, and Being*, 7th ed. (Upper Saddle River, NJ: Prentice Hall, 2007).

7. Christopher Lawton, "Pushing Faux Foreign Beer in U.S.: Can Anheuser-Busch Tap Imports' Growth with Beers Produced in Land of Budweiser?" *Wall Street Journal*, June 30, 2003, section B, Page 1.

8. Adapted from Paul W. Farris, Neil T. Bendle, Phillip E. Pfeifer, and David J. Reibstein, *Marketing Metrics: 50+ Metrics Every Executive Should Master*, Pearson Education, 2006.

9. "Touch Looms Large as a Sense That Drives Sales," *Brand Packaging*, May/June 1999, 39–40.

10. Michael Lev, "No Hidden Meaning Here: Survey Sees Subliminal Ads," *New York Times*, May 3, 1991, D7.

11. "ABC Rejects KFC Commercial, Citing Subliminal Advertising," *The Wall Street Journal Interactive Edition*, March 2, 2006.

12. Stuart Elliott, "TV Commercials Adjust to a Shorter Attention Span," *New York Times Online*, April 8, 2005.

13. Brian Sternberg, "Next Up on Fox: Ads That Can Change Pitch," *Wall Street Journal*, April 21, 2005, B1.

14. Robert M. McMath, "Image Counts," *American Demographics*, May 1998, 64.

15. Abraham H. Maslow, *Motivation and Personality*, 2nd ed. (New York: Harper & Row, 1970).

16. Robert A. Baron and Donn Byrne, *Social Psychology: Understanding Human Interaction*, 5th ed. (Boston: Allyn & Bacon, 1987).

17. Jeffrey Zaslow, "Happiness Inc.: Science Is Exploring the Roots of Joy—And Companies Are Putting the Findings to Work. How It's Changing Your Appliances and Cheering Up Your Sales Clerks," *Wall Street Journal* (March 18, 2006): P1.

18. Stuart Elliott, "Pepsi's New Campaign Leaves Left Brain for Right," *New York Times*, November 20, 2003, http://www.nytimes.com/2003/11/20/business/media/20adco.html?ex=1384750800&en=cedefc056e741021&ei=5007&partner=USERLAND.

19. Richard E. Petty and John T. Cacioppo, "Need for Cognition and Advertising: Understanding the Role of Personality Variables in Consumer Behavior," *Journal of Consumer Psychology* 1, no. 3 (1992): 239–60.

20. Mercedes M. Cardona, "Kenra Restyles Idea of 'Good/Bad' Hair," *Advertising Age*, August 16, 1999, 27.

21. Jeffrey F. Durgee, "Self-Esteem Advertising," *Journal of Advertising* 14 (1986): 4–21.

22. Stuart Elliott, "Flower Power in Ad Land," *New York Times Online*, April 11, 2006 http://www.nytimes.com/2006/04/11/business/retirement/11marketing.html (accessed May 14, 2008).

23. Nat Ives, "Creating Ads for Older Lads," *New York Times Online*, April 25, 2005, http://www.nytimes.com/2005/04/25/business/media/25adco.html?n=Top/News/Business/Companies/NBC%20Universal (accessed May 15, 2008).

24. Benjamin D. Zablocki and Rosabeth Moss Kanter, "The Differentiation of Life-Styles," *Annual Review of Sociology* (1976): 269–97.

25. Ben Detrick, "Skateboarding Rolls Out of the Suburbs," *New York Times*, November 11, 2007, http://www.nytimes.com/2007/11/11/fashion/11skaters.html?scp=1&sq=skateboarding&st=nyt (accessed February 10, 2008).

26. Damien Cave, "Dogtown U.S.A.," *New York Times Online*, June 12, 2005, http://www.nytimes.com/2005/06/12/fashion/sundaystyles/12skate.html.

27. Brian Sternberg, "Pioneer's Hot-Rod Ads Too Cool for Mainstream," *The Wall Street Journal* (March 14, 2003): B1.

28. Alfred S. Boote, "Psychographics: Mind Over Matter," *American Demographics*, April 1980, 26–29; William D. Wells, "Psychographics: A Critical Review," *Journal of Marketing Research*, 12 (May 1975): 196–213.

29. Alan R. Hirsch, "Effects of Ambient Odors on Slot-Machine Usage in a Las Vegas Casino," *Psychology & Marketing* 12, no. 7 (October 1995): 585–94.

30. James Vlahos, "Scent and Sensibility," *New York Times*, September 9, 2007, http://query.nytimes.com/gst/fullpage.html?res=9D07EFDC1E3AF93AA3575AC0A9619C8B63&scp=1&sq=scent%20and%20sensibility&st=cse (accessed February 1, 2008).

31. Marianne Meyer, "Attention Shoppers!" *Marketing and Media Decisions* 23 (May 1988): 67.

32. Eben Shapiro, "Need a Little Fantasy? A Bevy of New Companies Can Help," *New York Times*, March 10, 1991, F4.

33. Janet Ginsburg, "Xtreme Retailing," *BusinessWeek*, December 20, 1999, 120(7).

34. John P. Cortez, "Media Pioneers Try to Corral On-the-Go Consumers," *Advertising Age*, August 17, 1992, 25.

35. Quoted in John P. Cortez, "Ads Head for Bathroom," *Advertising Age*, May 18, 1992, 24.

36. John P. Robinson, "Time Squeeze," *Advertising Age*, February 1990, 30–33.

37. Leonard L. Berry, "Market to the Perception," *American Demographics*, February 1990, 32.

38. Kerry Capel, "The Arab World Wants Its MTV," *Business Week*, October 11, 2007, http://www.businessweek.com/globalbiz/content/oct2007/gb20071011_342851.htm.

39. Adapted from Michael R. Solomon, *Consumer Behavior*.

40. Adapted from Michael R. Solomon, *Consumer Behavior*.

41. Adapted from Michael R. Solomon, *Consumer Behavior*.

42. Richard W. Pollay, "Measuring the Cultural Values Manifest in Advertising," *Current Issues and Research in Advertising* (1983): 71–92.

43. Adapted from Michael R. Solomon, *Consumer Behavior: Buying, Having, and Being*.

44. Bob Jones, "Black Gold," *Entrepreneur*, July 1994, 62–65; Fred Thompson, "Blacks Spending Potential Up 54 Percent since 1990," *Montgomery Advertiser*, May 9, 1997, 1.

45. Richard Gibson, "Wendy's Moves to Eliminate Most Trans Fats from Menu," *Wall Street Journal* (June 9, 2006): A13.

46. Michael Barbaro, "Home Depot to Display an Environmental Label," *New York Times Online* (April 17, 2007), http://www.nytimes.com/2007/04/17/business/17depot.html (accessed May 14, 2008).

47. Leonora Openheim, "H&M's New Organic Cotton Collection," Treehugger, http://www.treehugger.com/files/2007/02/hennes-organic-cotton.php (accessed May 14, 2008).

48. "P&G Going Green: Liquid Detergents Will Come in Smaller Packaging with Double Concentrate as the Company Moves to Become Enviro-friendly, According to a Published Report," *CNNMoney.com*, http://money.cnn.com/2007/05/02/news/companies/procter_gamble/index.htm (accessed May 2, 2007).

49. Emily Lambert, "Marketing, Organic Miracle," *Forbes* (September 4, 2006): 68.

50. Tim Hepher, "Our Superjumbo Will Save the Planet, Airbus Says," Reuters, http://www.reuters.com/article/environmentNews/idUSL1981306620070619 (accessed May 14, 2008).

51. "Interface Sustainability," http://www.interfacesustainability.com/whatis.html (accessed May 14, 2008); "Sustainability," Wikipedia, http://en.wikipedia.org/wiki/Sustainability (accessed May 14, 2008).

52. Laurie Young, "Creating Value: Service Strategy from Aristocrats to Aviation," *Market Leader*, Winter 2007, 28–32.

53. J. Michael Munson and W. Austin Spivey, "Product and Brand-User Stereotypes among Social Classes: Implications for Advertising Strategy," *Journal of Advertising Research* 21 (August 1981): 37–45.

54. Stuart U. Rich and Subhash C. Jain, "Social Class and Life Cycle as Predictors of Shopping Behavior," *Journal of Marketing Research* 5 (February 1968): 41–49.

55. Ray A. Smith, "'Life After Lasik' A Clear-Eyed Urge To Wear Glasses," *Wall Street Journal*, April 26, 2008, http://online.wsj.com/article/SB120915416195645623.html (accessed May 13, 2008).

56. Adapted from Michael R. Solomon, *Consumer Behavior*.

57. Nathan Kogan and Michael A. Wallach, "Risky Shift Phenomenon in Small Decision-Making Groups: A Test of the Information Exchange Hypothesis," *Journal of Experimental Social Psychology* 3 (January 1967): 75–84; Arch G. Woodside and M. Wayne DeLozier, "Effects of Word-of-Mouth Advertising on Consumer Risk Taking," *Journal of Advertising* (Fall 1976): 12–19.

58. Carlo Dellaverson, "Tailgating: It's Bigger Business Than You Think," CNBC.com, December 21, 2006, http://www.cnbc.com/id/16315025/for/cnbc (accessed May 6, 2008).

59. Everett M. Rogers, *Diffusion of Innovations*, 3rd ed. (New York: Free Press, 1983).

60. Kathleen Debevec and Easwar Iyer, "Sex Roles and Consumer Perceptions of Promotions, Products, and Self: What Do We Know and Where Should We Be Headed," in *Advances in Consumer Research*, vol. 13, ed. Richard J. Lutz (Provo, UT: Association for Consumer Research, 1986), 210–14; Lynn J. Jaffe and Paul D. Berger, "Impact on Purchase Intent of Sex-Role Identity and Product Positioning," *Psychology & Marketing* (Fall 1988): 259–71.

61. Becky Ebenkamp, "Battle of the Sexes," *Brandweek*, April 17, 2000, www.findarticles.com/p/articles/mi_m0BDW/is_16_41/ai_61860406.

62. Debevec and Iyer, "Sex Roles and Consumer Perceptions of Promotions, Products and Self"; Deborah E. S. Frable, "Sex Typing and Gender Ideology: Two Facets of the Individual's Gender Psychology That Go Together," *Journal of Personality and Social Psychology* 56 (1989): 95–108; Jaffe and Berger, "Impact on Purchase Intent of Sex-Role Identity and Product Positioning"; Keren A. Johnson, Mary R. Zimmer, and Linda L. Golden, "Object Relations Theory: Male and Female Differences in Visual Information Processing," in *Advances in Consumer Research*, vol. 14, ed. Melanie Wallendorf and Paul Anderson (Provo, UT: Association for Consumer Research, 1986), 83–87; Leila T. Worth, Jeanne Smith, and Diane M. Mackie, "Gender Schematicity and Preference for Gender-Typed Products," *Psychology & Marketing* 9 (January 1992): 17–30.

63. Kara K. Choquette, "Not All Approve of Barbie's MasterCard," *U.S.A Today*, March 30, 1998, 6B.

64. Jennie Yabroff, "Girls Going Mild(er): A New 'Modesty Movement' Aims to Teach Young Women They Don't Have to Be Bad, or Semiclad," *Newsweek* (July 23, 2007), http://boards.youthnoise.com/eve/forums/a/tpc/f/573295355/m/38310644 (accessed July 18, 2007).

65. Vivian Manning-Schaffel, "Metrosexuals: A Well-Groomed Market?" brandchannel.com, http://brandchannel.com/features_effect.asp?pf_id=315 (accessed May 22, 2006).

66. "Defining Metro Sexuality" *Metrosource* (September/October/November 2003).

67. Rinallo, Diego, "Metro/Fashion/Tribes of Men: Negotiating the Boundaries of Men's Legitimate Consumption" in B. Cova, R. Kozinets, and A. Shankar, eds., *Consumer Tribes: Theory, Practice and Prospects* (Burlington MA Oxford: Elsevier/Butterworth-Heinemann, 2007); Susan Kaiser, Michael R. Solomon, Janet Hethorn, Basil Englis, Van Dyk Lewis, and Wi-Suk Kwon, "Menswear, Fashion, and Subjectivity," paper presented in Special Session: Susan Kaiser, Michael Solomon, Janet Hethorn, and Basil Englis (Chairs), "What Do Men Want? Media Representations, Subjectivity, and Consumption," at the ACR Gender Conference, Edinburgh, Scotland, June 2006.

68. Catharine Skipp and Arian Campo-Flores, "Looks: A Manly Comeback," *Newsweek* (August 20, 2007), http://services.newsweek.com/search.aspx?offset=0&pageSize=10&sortField=pubdatetime&sortDirection=descending&mode=summary&q=Looks%2C+a+manly+comeback (accessed August 17, 2007).

69. "National Poll Reveals the Emergence of a 'New Man,'" Miller Brewing Co., PR Newswire, http://goliath.ecnext.com/coms2/summary_0199-5364500_ITM (accessed May 14, 2008).

70. Adam Lashinsky, "Meg and the Machine" *Fortune*, August 11, 2–3.

71. "Fast Facts As of March 31, 2008," http://news.ebay.com/fastfacts.cfm (accessed May 14, 2008).

72. This section adapted from Michael R. Solomon, *Consumer Behavior: Buying, Having and Being*, 5th ed. (Upper Saddle River, NJ: Prentice Hall, 2001).

73. "Facebook," Wikipedia, http://en.wikipedia.org/wiki/Facebook (accessed February 26, 2008).

74. This section adapted from Michael R. Solomon, *Consumer Behavior: Buying, Having, and Being 7/e*, Upper Saddle River, NJ: Prentice Hall, 2007.

75. "April 2007 Trend Briefing," Trendwatching.com, http://www.trendwatching.com/briefing/ (accessed March 13, 2007).

76. Susanna Hamner, "Cashing in on Doctor's, Thinking," *Business 2.0* (June 2006): 40.

77. "Shopmobbing," *Fast Company* (April 2007): 31.

78. Veronique Cova and Bernard Cova, "Tribal Aspects of Postmodern Consumption Research: The Case of French In-Line Roller Skaters," *Journal of Consumer Behavior* 1 (June 2001): 67–76.

79. Laurie Petersen, "Pontiac Goes Underground to Tap Fans," *Marketing Daily* (February 8, 2007), http://publications.mediapost.com/index.cfm?fuseaction=Articles.printEdition&art_send_date=2007-2-8&art_type=16 (accessed May 14, 2008).

80. Quoted in Rob Walker, "McDonald's: When a Brand Becomes a Stand-In for a Nation," *New York Times Online*, March 30, 2003. http://query.nytimes.com/gst/fullpage.html?res=9E01E5D81639F933A05750C0A9659C8B63&scp=1&sq=When%20a%20brand%20becomes%20a%20stand%20%20in%20for%20a%20nation&st=cse.

CHAPTER 6

1. F. Robert Dwyer and John F. Tanner, *Business Marketing: Connecting Strategy, Relationships, and Learning* (Boston: McGraw-Hill, 2008); Edward F. Fern and James R. Brown, "The Industrial/Consumer Marketing Dichotomy: A Case of Insufficient Justification," *Journal of Marketing*, Spring 1984, 68–77.

2. Porche, "All Boxter Models," www.porsche.com/usa/models/boxster/ (accessed April 17, 2008).

3. *The 2008 Statistical Abstract of the United States*, U.S. Census Bureau, "The 2008 Statistical Abstract," www.census.gov/compendia/statab/ (accessed March 29, 2008).

4. U.S. Census Bureau, "North America Industry Classification System (NAICS)," www.census.gov/epcd/www/naics.html (accessed March 31, 2008).

5. Aflac, "Aflac for Business," www.aflac.com/us/en/aflacforbusiness/default.aspx (accessed April 18, 2008).

6. Carol Krol, "Companies use fun and games to find serious business." B to B, December 10, 2007, www.btobonline.com/apps/pbcs.dll/article?AID=/20071210/FREE/71210001/1109/FREE&template=printart (accessed May 3, 2008); Andy Sernovits and Guy Kawasaki, *Word of Mouth Marketing: How Smart Companies Get People Talking*, (New York: Kaplan Publishing, 2006).

7. Sun Microsystems, "Customer Reference Program Overview," www.sun.com/customers/overview.html (accessed April 21, 2008).

8. Innocentive, www.innocentive.com (accessed April 25, 2008); Jeff Howe, "The Rise of Crowdsourcing," *Wired* (June 2006): 176(8).

9. *The Computer & Internet Lawyer*, "Sun Microsystems Contributes Key Java Implementations to Open Source," *The Computer & Internet Lawyer*, 24 (2), p. 24; *eWeek*, "Cashing in on Open Source," *eWeek* (March 6, 2006), p. D6, D8; Larry Dignan, "Open-Source Java," *eWeek* (May 15, 2006), p. 34.

10. Patrick LaPointe, *Marketing by the Dashboard Light: How to Get More Insight, Foresight, and Accountability from Your Marketing Investments*, (New York: ANA, 2005).

11. Steven J. Kafka, Bruce D. Temkin, Matthew R. Sanders, Jeremy Sharrard, and Tobias O. Brown, "eMarketplaces Boost B2B Trade," The Forrester Report, February 2000.

12. Intranet Journal, "The Whole Enchilada: Java-Based Document Sharing Software Keeps Taco Bell's Franchisees in Touch," www.intranetjournal. com/rweb/tacobell.shtml (accessed April 29, 2008).

CHAPTER 7

1. Ellen Neuborne and Kathleen Kerwin, "Generation Y," *BusinessWeek Online* February 15, 1999, http://www.businessweek.com/1999/99_07/b3616001. htm (accessed May 23, 2008).

2. "Converse's All-Star Image," *BusinessWeek Online* April 25, 2008, www.businessweek.com/innovate/content/apr2008/id20080425_383266. htm?chan=search (accessed April 25, 2008).

3. Stanley C. Hollander and Richard Germain, *Was There a Pepsi Generation before Pepsi Discovered It? Youth-Based Segmentation in Marketing* (New York: NTC Business Books, 1992).

4. Conway Lackman and John M. Lanasa, "Family Decision-Making Theory: An Overview and Assessment," *Psychology & Marketing* 10 (March/April 1993): 81–93.

5. Christopher Palmeri, "Holiday Hits: Music, Toys, and Games," *BusinessWeek Online* December 19, 2007, www.businessweek.com/ bwdaily/dnflash/content/dec2007/db20071218_252797.htm?chan=search (accessed April 18, 2008).

6. Mary Beth Grover, "Teenage Wasteland," *Forbes*, July 28, 1997, 44–45.

7. Amy Barrett, "To Reach the Unreachable Teen," *BusinessWeek*, September 18, 2000, 78–80.

8. Anastasia Goodstein, "Teen Marketing: Apple's the Master," *BusinessWeek Online* August 16, 2007, http://www.businessweek.com/technology/ content/aug2007/tc20070815_636359.htm?chan=search (accessed March 3, 2008).

9. Tracy A. Rickman and Michael R. Solomon, "Anomie Goes Online: The Emo Microculture," presented at the Association for Consumer Research, October 2006.

10. Bruce Horovitz, "Gen Y: A Tough Crowd to Sell," *USA Today*, May 21, 2002 www. usatoday.com/money/covers/2002-04-22-geny.htm (accessed March 22, 2006).

11. Alan Cohen, "Swimming Against the Tide," *Fast Company*, January 2005, 80–84.

12. Douglas Coupland, *Generation X: Tales for an Accelerated Culture* (New York: St. Martin's Press, 1991).

13. Quoted in Karen Lowry Miller, "You Just Can't Talk to These Kids," *BusinessWeek*, April 19, 1993, 104.

14. Robert Scally, "The Customer Connection: Gen X Grows Up, They're in Their 30s Now," *Discount Store News*, archived in *Bnet.com*, October 25, 1999, 38 http://findarticles.com/p/articles/mi_m3092/is_20_38/ai_57443548?tag= content;col1 (accessed June 25, 2008).

15. Scally, "The Customer Connection: Gen X Grows Up, They're in Their 30s Now," *Discount Store News*, archived in *Bnet.com*, October 25, 1999, 38 http://findarticles.com/p/articles/mi_m3092/is_20_38/ai_57443548?tag= content;col1 (accessed June 25, 2008).

16. Alex Williams, "What Women Want: More Horses," *New York Times Online* www.nytimes.com/2005/06/12/fashion/sundaystyles/12cars.html?ex= 1276228800&en=7ea4473d0aa65bb0&ei=5090&partner=rssuserland&emc= rss (accessed June 12, 2008).

17. Jonathan Welsh, "The Manwagon," *Wall Street Journal*, February 24, 2006, W1, http://online.wsj.com/article/SB114073775464081884.html?mod= mostpop (accessed March 12, 2008); www.mercedes-benz.com; www.audi. com; www.bmw.com.

18. U.S. Census Bureau, "Resident Population by Age and Sex 1980–2006," www. census.gov/compendia/statab/tables/08s0007.pdf (accessed March 31, 2008).

19. Jennifer Lawrence, "Gender-Specific Works for Diapers-Almost Too Well," *Advertising Age*, February 8, 1993, S–10.

20. Michael Flocker, *The Metrosexual Guide to Style: A Handbook for the Modern Man* (Cambridge, MA: Da Capo Press, 2003).

21. "Metrosexual," Urban Dictionary, www.urbandictionary.com/define. php?term=metrosexual (accessed May 1, 2008).

22. Adam Tschorn, "Men Can Wear Jewelry Too," *LA Times Online* April 27, 2008, www.latimes.com/features/lifestyle/la-ig-mens27apr27, 1,245137.story?track=rss (accessed May 1, 2008); Teri Agins, "Men Say Bling It On: Retailers Court Modern Guys with Baubles All Their Own; Brad Pitt Gives Tiffany a Lift," *Wall Street Journal*, November 30, 2005, B1.

23. "Glass Baby Bottles in Demand," *BrandPackaging.com*, June 1, 2008, www. brandpackaging.com/CDA/Articles/Trends_Next_Now/BNP_GUID_ 9-5-2006_A_10000000000000352222 (accessed June 25, 2008).

24. "Water," Voss of Norway, www.vosswater.com (accessed March 22, 2006).

25. Lola Ogunnaike, "Satirical Superheroes for the Rude Set," *New York Times Online* March 16, 2006, www.nytimes.com/2006/03/18/arts/television/ 18mino.html?ei=5088&en=bd25716390bac434&ex=1300338000&partner= rssnyt&emc=rss&pagewanted=all (accessed June 25, 2008).

26. Michael E. Ross, "At Newsstands, Black Is Plentiful," *New York Times*, December 26, 1993, F6.

27. Brad Edmondson, "Asian Americans in 2001," *American Demographics*, February 1997, 16–17.

28. Greg Johnson and Edgar Sandoval, "Advertisers Court Growing Asian Population: Marketing, Wide Range of Promotions Tied to New Year Typify Corporate Interest in Ethnic Community," *Los Angeles Times* (February 4, 2000): C1.

29. Alice Z. Cuneo and Jean Halliday Ford, "Penney's Targeting California's Asian Populations," *Advertising Age* (January 4, 1999): 28.

30. Dorinda Elliott, "Objects of Desire," *Newsweek* (February 12, 1996): 41.

31. "United States Census 2000," U.S. Census Bureau, www.census.gov/main/ www/cen2000.html (accessed March 22, 2006).

32. Carolyn Shea, "The New Face of America," *PROMO*, January 1996, 53.

33. Lucette B. Comer and J. A. F. Nicholls, "Communication between Hispanic Salespeople and Their Customers: A First Look," *Journal of Personal Selling & Sales Management* 20 (Summer 2000): 121–27.

34. See Lewis Alpert and Ronald Gatty, "Product Positioning by Behavioral Life Styles," *Journal of Marketing* 33 (April 1969): 65–69; Emanuel H. Demby, "Psychographics Revisited: The Birth of a Technique," *Marketing News*, January 2, 1989, 21; and William D. Wells, "Backward Segmentation," in *Insights into Consumer Behavior*, ed. Johan Arndt (Boston: Allyn & Bacon, 1968), 85–100.

35. Tara Weingarten, "Life in the Fastest Lane," *Newsweek*, February 21, 2000, 60–61.

36. For other examples of applications see "Representative VALS™ Projects," SRI Consulting Business Intelligence, http://www.sric-bi.com/VALS/projects. shtml#positioning (accessed February 29, 2008).

37. Neal E. Boudette, "Navigating Curves: BMW's Push to Broaden Line Hits Some Bumps in the Road," *Wall Street Journal*, January 10, 2005, A1.

38. Judann Pollack, "Kraft's Miracle Whip Targets Core Consumers with '97 Ads," *Advertising Age*, February 3, 1997, 12.

39. Chris Anderson, *The Long Tail: Why the Future of Business Is Selling Less of More* (New York: Hyperion, 2006).

40. "Lesson 3c: Language & Location Targeting," Google Learning Center, www. google.com/adwords/learningcenter/text/print-19158.html (accessed March 12, 2008).

41. www.geaviation.com/engines/index.html (accessed June 25, 2008).

42. Anthony Ramirez, "New Cigarettes Raising Issue of Target Market," *New York Times*, February 18, 1990, 28.

43. "Our Brands," L'Oréal, www.loreal.com/_en/_ww/index.aspx (accessed March 31, 2008).

44. "Our Business," Toyota, http://www.toyota.com/about/our_business/ index.html (accessed May 1, 2008).

45. www.blacksocks.com (accessed March 22, 2008); Jack Ewing, "A Web Outfit with Socks Appeal," *BusinessWeek Online* July 24, 2002, http://www. businessweek.com/technology/content/jul2002/tc20020724_9718.htm? chan=search (accessed March 22, 2008).

46. "Build You Own 'IdeaStorm' with UserVoice," Web Strategies by Jeremiah, http://www.web-strategist.com/blog/2008/05/02/build-your-own-ideastorm-with-uservoice/; David Sidman "What Customers Want," *MediaWeek*, Vol. 17, Issue 45 (December 10, 2007), p. 45; Liane Cassavoy, "Ads Get Flashier, More Personal," *PC World* (February 2005), p. 22; Media Buying/Planning, "Jaffe Juice: Finally, a Smart Biz Model," *iMedia Connection* (December 5, 2002) http://www.imediaconnection.com/printpage/ printpage.aspx?id=1127; Susie Harwood, "Behavioral Targeting," *NMA Explains* (March 31, 2005), pp. 6–7.

47. Chip Bayers, "The Promise of One to One (a Love Story)," *Wired*, May 1998, 130.

48. Amanda Mark, "Under Armour's Star Presence," *Multichannel Merchant* (November 1, 2000), http://multichannelmerchant.com/news/marketing_ armours_star_presence/ (accessed May 1, 2008).

49. Arundhati Parmar, "Where Are They Now? Revived, Repositioned Products Gain New Life," *Marketing News* (April 14, 2003): 1 (3).

50. For an example of how consumers associate food brands with a range of female body shapes, see Martin R. Lautman, "End-Benefit Segmentation and Prototypical Bonding," *Journal of Advertising Research*, June/July 1991, 9–18.

51. "SoBe,", South Beach Beverage Co., www.sobebev.com/gateway_flash.html (accessed March 22, 2006).

52. "A Crash Course in Customer Relationship Management," *Harvard Management Update*, March 2000 (Harvard Business School reprint U003B).

53. Don Peppers and Martha Rogers, *The One-to-One Future* (New York: Doubleday, 1996).

54. Don Peppers, Martha Rogers, and Bob Dorf, "Is Your Company Ready for One-to-One Marketing?" *Harvard Business Review*, January–February 1999, 151–60.

55. Quoted in Cara B. DiPasquale, "Navigate the Maze," Special Report on 1:1 Marketing, *Advertising Age*, October 29, 2001, S1(2).

56. Leonard L. Berry, *On Great Service: A Framework for Action*, (New York: The Free Press, 1995); Paul T. Ringenbach, *USAA: A Tradition of Service*, (San Antonio, TX: The Donning Company, 1997).

57. Barney Beal, "CRM, Customer Service Still Driving Technology Spending," SearchCRM.com, January 18, 2007, http://searchcrm.techtarget.com/news/article/0,289142,sid11_gci1239727,00.html (accessed April 10, 2008).

58. Kelly Shermach, "Travel Disruptions: Using CRM to Soften the Blow," CRM Buyer September 7, 2006, http://www.crmbuyer.com/story/52854.html (accessed May 2, 2008).

59. Jeff Kang, "Amazon.com and Customer Relationship Management," Iconocast, www.iconocast.com/ZZZZResearch/eMarketing_amazon.pdf (accessed April 8, 2008).

60. Susan Fournier, Susan Dobscha, and David Glen Mick, "Preventing the Premature Death of Relationship Marketing," *Harvard Business Review*, January–February 1998, 42–4.

61. Ian Ayers, *Super Crunchers: Why Thinking-by-Numbers Is the New Way To Be Smart*, (New York: Bantam, 2007); Jerry Adler, "Era of the Super Cruncher," *Newsweek*, September 3, 2007, 42; "The Short Life of the Chief Marketing Officer," *BusinessWeek*, December 10, 2007, 63–5.

62. Robert C. Blattberg, Gary Getz, and Mark Pelofsky, "Want to Build Your Business? Grow Your Customer Equity," *Harvard Management Update*, August 2001 (Harvard Business School reprint U0108B), 3.

63. Bernd Schmitt, *Customer Experience Management: A Revolutionary Approach to Connecting with your Customers*, (Hoboken, NJ: Wiley, 2003); Shaun Smith and Joe Wheeler, *Managing the Customer Experience: Turning Customers into Advocates*, (Upper Saddle River, NJ: FT Press, 2002).

64. "SPAR Saves a Six-Figure Sum Using a Virtualized Environment for SAP ERP with IBM System p," IBM, March 21, 2008, www-01.ibm.com/software/success/cssdb.nsf/CS/STRD-7D3GXL?OpenDocument&Site=, (accessed May 3, 2008).

65. Quoted in Miriam Jordan, "Cerveza, Sí o No?: The Beer Industry's Embrace of Hispanic Market Prompts a Backlash from Activists," *Wall Street Journal*, March 29, 2006, B1.

CHAPTER 8

1. Woodstream Corp., *Victor*, www.victorpest.com (accessed March 27, 2006).

2. Microsoft Corp., "Communities," www.microsoft.com/communities/default.mspx (accessed April 3, 2006).

3. Walter S. Mossberg, "Lots of Laptop Choices Mean Shoppers Have to Identify Their Needs," *Wall Street Journal*, April 29, 2004, B1.

4. iRobot Corp., *iRobot*, www.irobot.com/sp.cfm?pageid=316 (accessed May 5, 2008).

5. "The Story of Cotton," Cotton's Journey, www.cottonsjourney.com/Storyofcotton/page7.asp (accessed May 7, 2008).

6. "Pharmaceuticals No Longer Good Investment, Says Forbes," *Networking for a Better Future*, December 9, 2003, www.newmediaexplorer.org/sepp/2003/12/09/pharmaceuticals_no_longer_good_investment_says_forbes.htm (accessed June 25, 2008).

7. Yo Takatsuki, "Cost Headache for Game Developers," *BBC News Online* December 27, 2007, http://news.bbc.co.uk/2/hi/business/7151961.stm (accessed May 1, 2008).

8. "The Replacements," *Newsweek*, June 25, 2001, 50.

9. "Milestone for Unique Bionic Hand," *BBC News Online*, July 17, 2007, http://news.bbc.co.uk/2/hi/uk_news/scotland/edinburgh_and_east/6901231.stm (accessed April 29, 2008).

10. "Lexus Self Parking Car Video and Review," GIZMODO http://gizmodo.com/gadgets/clips/lexus-self-parking-car-video-and-review-196551.php (accessed May 3, 2008).

11. "Radar Car Collision Systems Put to Test," *Gizmag*, February 25, 2008, www.gizmag.com/radar-car-collision-prevention-systems-put-to-the-test/8813/ (accessed April 23, 2008).

12. Kermit Whitfield, "Touch and Go – Design – BMW's iDrive System," *bNet*, June 2002, http://findarticles.com/p/articles/mi_m0KJI/is_6_114/ai_87421719 (accessed May 1, 2008).

13. Steve Traiman, "Goin' Digital," *Billboard*, May 1, 2004, 45(2); John Markoff, "Oh, Yeah, He Also Sells Computers," *New York Times*, April 25, 2004, Section 3, 1; Devin Leonard, "Songs in the Key of Steve," *Fortune*, May 12, 2003, 52+; Apple Computer, "The New iPod," www.apple.com/pr/library/2005/oct/12ipod.html (accessed March 29, 2006).

14. Palm Inc., *The Treo Store*, http://web.palm.com/index.jhtml?requestid=278572 (accessed March 30, 2006).

15. A. G., "The Sound and the Wiki," *PC Magazine* (October 2, 2007), p. 19; Elizabeth Woyke and Deborah Stead, "A Dark and Stormy Site," *BusinessWeek*, Issue 4024 (March 5, 2007), p. 10: Jeffrey Burt, "The Buzz," *eWeek* (February 12/19, 2007), p. 47; Penguin Wiki, "About Penguin Wiki," http://www.amillionpenguins.com/wiki/index.php/About.

16. Tim Ambler, *Marketing and the Bottom Line* 2nd ed., Edinburgh Gate, UK: Pearson/Financial Times, p.172.

17. Becky Worley, "Marriage-Saving Technology: Simple Devices Help Achieve Marital Bliss," *ABC News*, http://abcnews.go.com/GMA/Technology/story?id=1390155 (accessed April 1, 2006).

18. F. Keenan, "G.I. Joe Heroics at Hasbro," *BusinessWeek*, November 26, 2001, 16.

19. CBS Broadcasting Inc., "Getting Products on Store Shelves," *CBS Evening News*, www.cbsnews.com/stories/2000/09/14/eveningnews/main233535.shtml (accessed March 28, 2006).

20. Quoted in Brendan I. Koerner, "Geeks in Toyland," *Wired* (February 2006): 105 (9).

21. Mary Bellis, "History of Sony Playstation," About.com: Inventors, http://inventors.about.com/library/inventors/bl_playstation.htm (accessed May 7, 2008); "Sony Playstation," CyberiaPC.com, www.cyberiapc.com/vgg/sony_ps.htm (accessed May 7, 2008); Steven L. Ken, *The Ultimate History of Video Games: From Pong to Pokemon – The Story Behind the Craze that Touched Our Lives and Changed the World*, Pittsburgh, PA: Three Rivers Press, 2001.

22. James Dao, "From a Collector of Turkeys, a Tour of a Supermarket Zoo," *New York Times*, September 24, 1995, F12.

23. Fara Warner, "Chop. Purée. Liquefy. (The Ideas, That Is.)," *New York Times*, September 7, 2003, http://query.nytimes.com/gst/fullpage.html?res=9C07E4DC1138F934A3575AC0A9659C8B63 (accessed June 25, 2008).

24. Quoted in Jack Neff, "P&G Boosts Design's Role in Marketing," *Advertising Age*, February 9, 2004, 1 (2): 52; Jessie Scanlon, "Wanted: VPs of Design," *BusinessWeek*, August 28, 2007, www.businessweek.com/innovate/content/aug2007/id20070829_407662.htm?chan=search (accessed May 7, 2008).

25. Robert Berner, "Why P&G's Smile Is So Bright," *BusinessWeek*, August 12, 2002, 58–60; Procter & Gamble Co., "Crest SpinBrush," www.spinbrush.com (accessed March 28, 2006).

26. Dan Cray and Maggie Sieger, "Inside the Food Labs," *Time*, October 6, 2003, 56–60; James Norton, "The McGriddle," *flakmagazine*, http://flakmag.com/misc/mcgriddle.html (accessed April 5, 2006); "McDonald's Breakfast Items," McDonald's Corporation, http://www.mcdonalds.com/corp/news/media/multi/Prod/breakfast_menu.html (accessed April 27, 2008).

27. Simon Pitman, "Pfizer Sues P&G over Mouthwash Ad Claims," *CosmeticsDesign.com*, March 6, 2006, www.cosmeticsdesign.com/news/ng.asp?n=66236-pfizer-proctor-gamble-lawsuit-mouthwash (accessed April 19, 2008).

28. Andrew Pollack, "Nasal Spray Mishaps," Boston.com, November 19, 2003, www.boston.com/yourlife/health/other/articles/2003/11/19/nasal_spray_mishaps?mode=PF (accessed June 25, 2008).

29. Malcolm Gladwell, *The Tipping Point* (Newport Beach, CA: Back Bay Books, 2002).

30. Staples, www.staples.com/webapp/wcs/stores/servlet/CategoryDisplay?&secondlevelCategoryId=10103&firstlevelCatName=Technology&firstlevelCategoryId=10912&langId=1&storeId=10001&pCategoryId=10103&splCatType=1&catalogId=10051&categoryId=12054&secondlevelCatName=Copiers+%26+Fax.

31. Alice Z. Cuneo, "Microsoft Taps 'Puffy' for Xbox," *Advertising Age*, October 20, 2004, 4.

32. "Jetta," VW, http://www.vw.com/jetta/en/us/ (accessed May 8, 2008); Neal E. Boudette and Lee Hawkins, "Volkswagen Eyes Young Parents with Newest Version of Jetta," *Wall Street Journal*, January 11, 2005, D.9.

33. "Products," Tamagotchi Connections, www.tamagotchi.com (accessed April 5, 2008).

34. Bill Gerba, "Gamestop Trials Dell Kiosks," Interactive Kiosk News, September 30, 2005, http://kiosknews.blogspot.com/2005/09/gamestop-trials-dell-kiosks.html (accessed April 1, 2008); "Dell Completes Acquision of Alienware," Dell, May 9, 2006, www.dell.com (accessed April 1, 2008).

35. Amy Gilroy, "More Players Enter Portable Nav Market," TWICE, April 5, 2004, 28(2); Pioneer Electronics Co., "XM NavTraffic," Pioneer: Car Electronics, www.pioneerelectronics.com/pna/article/0,,2076_3149_269505659,00.html (accessed April 4, 2006).

36. Everett Rogers, Diffusion of Innovations (New York: Free Press, 1983), 247–51.

37. Sources used in this section: "Wi-Fi's Big Brother," Economist, March 13, 2004, 65; William J. Gurley, "Why Wi-Fi Is the Next Big Thing," Fortune, March 5, 2001, 184; Joshua Quittner, "Cordless Capers," Time, May 1, 2000, 85; Scott Van Camp, "Intel Switches Centrino's Gears," Brandweek, April 26, 2004, 16; Benny Evangelista, "SBC Park a Hot Spot for Fans Lugging Laptops," San Francisco Chronicle, April 26, 2004, A1; Todd Wallack, "Santa Clara Ready for Wireless," San Francisco Chronicle, April 19, 2004, D1; Glenn Fleishman, "Three Essays on Muni-Fi You Should Read," WNN Wi-Fi Net News, http://wifinetnews.com.

38. Christine Chen and Tim Carvell, "Hall of Shame," Fortune, November 22, 1999, 140.

39. Rogers, Diffusion of Innovations, Chapter 6.

40. Deere & Co., "Gator High-Performance Utility Vehicles," John Deere, www.deere.com/en_US/ProductCatalog/HO/series/HO_gator_hp_series.html (accessed March 28, 2006).

CHAPTER 9

1. Joseph B. White, "Lexus Tries to Redefine Hybrids," Wall Street Journal Online, March 20, 2006, http://online.wsj.com/article/SB114252707250600173.html (accessed May 8, 2008); Joseph B. White, "Lexus Tries to Redefine 'Top of the Line,'" Wall Street Journal Online, April 23, 2007, http://online.wsj.com/article/SB117708381282476998.html?mod=googlenews_wsj, (accessed May 8, 2008).

2. Anthony Vagnoni, "Overused and Misunderstood," Print, November–December 2003, 42(2).

3. David Kiley, "The MINI Bulks Up," BusinessWeek Online, January 17, 2006, www.businessweek.com/autos/content/jan2006/bw20060117_818487.htm?chan=search (accessed May 8, 2008).

4. Pepperidge Farm, http://www.pfgoldfish.com (accessed June 13, 2006).

5. Dawn, http://www.dawn-dish.com/en_US/home.do (accessed May 5, 2008).

6. Rolls-Royce Motor Cars, www.rolls-roycemotorcars.com (accessed May 8, 2008).

7. Matt Stone, "First Drive: 2009 Hyundai Sonata," MoterTrend Online, http://www.motortrend.com/roadtests/sedans/112_0804_2009_hyundai_sonata/index.html (access April 29, 2008); Joann Muller and Robyn Meredity, "Last Laugh," Forbes, April 18, 2005, 98.

8. Daniel Thomas, "Relaunches: New Life or Last Gasps?" Marketing Week, January 29, 2004, 20(2).

9. Lea Goldman, "Big Gulp," Forbes, January 10, 2005, 68.

10. Material adapted from a presentation by Glenn H. Mazur, QFD Institute, 2002.

11. Geoffrey Colvin, "The Ultimate Manager," Fortune, November 22, 1999, 185–87.

12. Baldrige National Quality Program, www.quality.nist.gov (accessed June 14, 2006).

13. "General Information on ISO," ISO, www.iso.org/iso/support/faqs/faqs_general_information_on_iso.htm (accessed May 5, 2008).

14. "The Sabre System of the Appliance Service Industry," Appliance, March 2004, 69(2).

15. Thomas L. Friedman, The World Is Flat (New York: Picador, 2007).

16. Erik Sherman, "Heavy Lifting," Chief Executive, March 2004, 52(4).

17. Mohanbir Sawhney et al., "Creating Growth with Services," MIT Sloan Management Review, Winter 2004, 34(10).

18. Al Ries and Laura Ries, The Origin of Brands (New York: Collins, 2005).

19. Philip H. Francis, "New Product Development—the Soul of the Enterprise," Mechanical Engineering Online, March 14, 2003, http://memagazine.org/contents/current/webonly/webex.html (accessed May 4, 2008).

20. "Today's Buzzword: Low-Carb," Chain Drug Review, February 2, 2004, 40.

21. "Our Products," Promise, http://www.promisehealthyheart.com/products_buttery_spreads.asp (accessed May 6, 2008).

22. "Getting Emerson Humming Again," BusinessWeek, April 11, 2005, 1.

23. Olay, www.olay.com (accessed May 1, 2008).

24. Julian Hunt, "Making Great Ideas Pay Off," Grocer, March 27, 2004, 2; Glen L. Urban, Digital Marketing Strategies (Englewood Cliffs, NJ: Prentice Hall, 2004).

25. Gail Tom, Teresa Barnett, William Lew, and Jodean Selmonts, "Cueing the Consumer: The Role of Salient Cues in Consumer Perception," Journal of Consumer Marketing (1987): 23–27; "Snow Commander Series," Toro, www.toro.com/home/snowthrowers/snowcommander/index.html (accessed May 3, 2008).

26. "Jell-O Sugar Free Gelatin," Product Alert, May 10, 2004, 34(9), 0.

27. "'Apple' wins logo lawsuit against Beatles," MacNN.com, May 8, 2006, www.macnn.com/articles/06/05/08/apple.wins.logo.lawsuit (accessed April 28, 2008).

28. Joan Johnson, "Manufacturers are letting consumers personalize their purchases," Colorado Springs Business Journal (August 18, 2006); Kevin T. Higgins, "Meeting the Challenges of Customized Manufacturing," Food Engineering (August 2007), pp. 42–9.

29. Suzanne Vranica, "McDonald's Vintage T-Shirts Sizzle," Wall Street Journal Online (April 27, 2006), http://www.post-gazette.com/pg/06117/685629-28.stm (accessed June 8, 2008).

30. Susan Fournier, "Consumers and Their Brands: Developing Relationship Theory in Consumer Research," Journal of Consumer Research 24 (March 1998): 343–73.

31. "The Most Famous Name in Music," Music Trades, September 2003, 118(12).

32. Kevin Lane Keller, "The Brand Report Card," Harvard Business Review, January–February 2000 (Harvard Business School reprint R00104).

33. "The Idea for Häagen-Dazs Dates Back to the Early 1920s," Häagen-Dazs http://www.haagen-dazs.com/company/history.aspx (accessed May 17, 2008).

34. Nicholas Casey, "Can New Quiksilver Line Reach Beyond the Beach," Wall Street Journal Online, March 6, 2008, http://online.wsj.com/article_email/SB120476311128015043-lMyQjAxMDI4MDA0NjcwNjYzWj.html (accessed May 2, 2008).

35. John D. Stoll, "Eight-Brand Pileup Dents GM's Turnaround Efforts, Wall Street Journal Online, March 4, 2008, www.emailthis.clickability.com/et/emailThis?clickMap=viewThis&etMailToID=2096463462&pt=Y (accessed May 1, 2008).

36. "EquiTrend," Harris Interactive, http://www.harrisinteractive.com/services/equitrend.asp (accessed May 11, 2008).

37. "The Top 100 Global Brands Scorecard for 2007," BusinessWeek Online, http://bwnt.businessweek.com/interactive_reports/top_brands/index.asp (accessed April 15, 2008).

38. Kusum L. Ailawadi, Donald R. Lehmann, and Scott A. Neslin, "Revenue Premium as an Outcome Measure of Brand Equity," Journal of Marketing 67 (October 2003): 1–17.

39. "Why Not Try a Nurse in a Box," Clarkhoward, January 11, 2007, http://clarkhoward.com/shownotes/category/11/65/315/ (accessed April 19, 2008); "Pharmacy," Walmart.com, www.walmart.com/pharmacy (accessed April 19, 2008).

40. "Psst! Wanna See Loblaws' New Products?" Private Label Buyer, January 2003, 10(1); Len Lewis, "Turf War!" Grocery Headquarters, November 2002, 13(6).

41. "Friday's Complete Menu," TGI Fridays, www.tgifridays.com/menu/menu_jackdaniels.htm (accessed May 1, 2008); "Ultimate Recipe Showdown Menu," TGI Fridays, http://74.6.239.67/search/cache?ei=UTF-8&p=Ultimate+Recipe+Showdown+Menu&y=Search&fr=yfp-t-501&u=www.tgifridays.com/menu/E208_stf.htm&w=ultimate+recipe+recipes+showdown+menu+menus&d=G-KtgvReRXbS&icp=1&.intl=us (accessed September 19, 2008).

42. "Harry Potter," Lego, http://parents.lego.com/awards/awards.aspx?id=legoharrypotter (accessed April 22, 2008).

43. D. C. Denison, "The Boston Globe Business Intelligence Column," Boston Globe, May 26, 2002.

44. "Putting Zoom into Your Life," Time International, March 8, 2004, 54.

45. Stephanie Thompson, "Brand Buddies," Brandweek, February 23, 1998, 26–30; Jean Halliday, "L.L. Bean, Subaru Pair for Co-Branding," Advertising Age, February 21, 2000, 21.

46. Ed Brown, "I Scream You Scream—Saaay, Nice Carton!" Fortune, October 26, 1998, 60.

47. Pringles, http://www.pringles.com/pages/index.shtml (accessed May 2, 2008).

48. "A Package that Lights Up the Shelf," New York Times online, March 4, 2008, http://www.nytimes.com/2008/03/04/business/media/04adco.html?ex=1205298000&en=844d46791650b628&ei=5070&emc=etal (accessed April 10, 2008).

49. "Labels to Include Trans Fat," San Fernando Valley Business Journal, January 19, 2004, 15.

50. Professor Jakki Mohr, University of Montana, personal communication (April 2004).

CHAPTER 10

1. Deborah L. Vence, "Boston Orchestra Tunes Up Net Campaign," Marketing News, June 23, 2003, 5–6.

2. "Season at a Glance," Colorado Symphony Orchestra, http://www.coloradosymphony.org/media/EDocs/Season_at_a_Glance1.pdf (accessed May 10, 2008).

3. Ross Kerber and Benjamin A. Holden, "Power Struggle: Deregulation Sparks Marketing Battle," *Wall Street Journal*, May 13, 1996, B1(2); Rebecca Piirto Heath, "The Marketing of Power," *American Demographics*, September 1997, 59–63.

4. "Kentucky Utility Companies Help Restore Power after Katrina," *BusinessFirst*, September 12, 2005, www.bizjournals.com/louisville/stories/2005/09/12/daily6.html (accessed May 9, 2008).

5. "Giving and Volunteering in the United States 2001: Independent Sector Survey Measures the Everyday Generosity of Americans," Independent Sector, http://www.independentsector.org/programs/research/GV01main.html (accessed August 21, 2006).

6. www.salvationarmyusa.org/usn/www_usn_2.nsf/vw-text-dynamic-arrays/401D2B4D64792DF58525743300516F7B?openDocument (accessed June 30, 2008).

7. "Clerk of Courts Launches Pay Online Service," *Orlando Business Journal*, July 21, 2005, http://orlando.bizjournals.com/orlando/stories/2005/07/18/daily40.html (accessed May 8, 2008).

8. Bureau of Labor Statistics, "Employment Situation Summary: The Employment Situation: April 2008," www.bls.gov/news.release/empsit.nr0.htm (accessed May 10, 2008).

9. Eleena de Lisser, "Rock 'n' Roll Hits the Multiplex," *Wall Street Journal*, March 25, 2004, www.wsj.com; "Garth Brooks to Simulcast Concert in Movie Theaters," *FoxNews.com*, October 16, 2007, http://www.foxnews.com/story/0,2933,302506,00.html (accessed September 19, 2008).

10. John A. Czepiel, Michael R. Solomon, and Carol F. Surprenant, eds., *The Service Encounter: Managing Employee/Customer Interaction in Service Businesses* (Lexington, MAS: D.C. Heath and Company, 1985).

11. "Can Business Analytics Deliver Home Runs," Cognos, May 1, 2006, www.cognos.com/newsletter/business/st_060206_02.html (accessed May 13, 2008); J. A. Quelch, "Ambidextrous Marketing," *Wall Street Journal* (October 2005), B2.

12. Lou W. Turley and Douglas L. Fugate, "The Multidimensional Nature of Service Facilities: Viewpoints and Recommendations," *Journal of Services Marketing* 6 (Summer 1992): 37–45.

13. David H. Maister, "The Psychology of Waiting Lines," in Czepiel et al., *The Service Encounter*, 113–24.

14. Alex Frankel, "Zipcar makes the Leap," *Fast Company*, Issue 123 (March 2008), pp. 48–50; Mary Morse, "Hourcar Puts Green Slant on Car Sharing," *In Business* (September/October 2007), pp. 10–11; Susan A. Shaheen, Adam P. Cohen, and J. Darius Roberts, "Carsharing in North America: Market Growth, Current Developments, and Future Potential," *Transportation Research Record*, Volume 1986, Issue 17 (2006), pp. 116–124; nuride, www.nuride.com (accessed May 16, 2008).

15. Bigleague, www.bigleagueonline.com (accessed May 1, 2008).

16. Jennifer Chao, "Airports Open Their Gates to Profits," *Montgomery Advertiser*, January 26, 1997, 16A.

17. Greg Winter, "Jacuzzi U.? A Battle of Perks to Lure Students," *New York Times*, October 5, 2003, http://query.nytimes.com/gst/fullpage.html?res=9B07E0D8123CF936A35753C1A9659C8B63&scp=2&sq=Jacuzzi+U&st=nyt (accessed January 21, 2004).

18. "Disney's Magical Express Service," *DisneyMeetings.com*, http://disneymeetings.disney.go.com/dwm/services/detail?name=DMEAttendeesDetailPage (accessed May 13, 2008); "When Art Meets Science: The challenge of ROI Marketing. Knowledge at Wharton: Strategy and Business," *Strategy+Business*, www.strategy-business.com/sbkwarticle/sbkw031217?pg=1 (accessed May 11, 2008).

19. Jim Kerstetter and Jay Greene, "Pay-As-You-Go Is Up and Running," *BusinessWeek*, January 12, 2004, 69–70.

20. Aaron Ricadella, "Computing Heads for the Clouds," *BusinessWeek* Online, November 16, 2007, www.businessweek.com/technology/content/nov2007/tc20071116_379585.htm (accessed May 1, 2008).

21. Heather Green, "Downloads: The Next Generation," *BusinessWeek*, February 16, 2004, 54.

22. "True Love? Let a Computer Matchmaker Decide," *ChinaDaily.com*, May 31, 2004, www.chinadaily.com.cn/english/doc/2004-05/31/content_335169.htm (accessed June 30, 2008).

23. "Relationship Central," Chemistry, http://www.chemistry.com/relationshipcentral/rcindex.aspx (accessed May 10, 2008).

24. AskPhysicians.com, www.AskPhysicians.com (accessed July 7, 2006).

25. WebMD, http://www.webmd.com/content/pages/22/107831 (accessed May 10, 2008).

26. Cengiz Haksever, Barry Render, Roberta S. Russell, and Robert G. Murdick, *Service Management and Operations* (Englewood Cliffs, NJ: Prentice Hall, 2000), 25–26.

27. Stephen J. Grove, Raymond P. Fisk, and Joby John, "Surviving in the Age of Rage," *Marketing Management*, March/April 2004, 41–45.

28. FedEx, www.fedex.com (accessed April 29, 2008).

29. Wendy Zellner, "Is JetBlue's Flight Plan Flawed?" *BusinessWeek*, February 16, 2004, 56–58.

30. Joe Kleinsasser, "Air Tran Tales Top AQR Spot; Industry Score Falls to New Low," *WSU Online—This Is Wichita State*, April 16, 2008, www.wichita.edu/thisis/wsunews/news/?nid=182 (accessed May 15, 2008); Jeff Bailey, "JetBlue's CEO is `Mortified' after Travelers are Stranded," *New York Times Online*, February 29, 2007, www.nytimes.com/2007/02/19/business/19jetblue.html (accessed May 15, 2008).

31. Cynthia Webster, "Influences upon Consumer Expectations of Services," *Journal of Services Marketing* 5 (Winter 1991): 5–17.

32. Lewis P. Carbone and Stephan H. Haeckel, "Engineering Customer Experiences," *Marketing Management* 3 (Winter 1994).

33. Valarie A. Zeithaml, Mary Jo Bitner, and Dwayne Gremler, *Services Marketing*, 4th ed. (Englewood Cliffs, NJ: Prentice Hall, 2005).

34. A. Parasuraman, Leonard L. Barry, and Valarie A. Zeithaml, "SERVQUAL: A Multiple-Item Scale for Measuring Consumer Perceptions of Service Quality," *Journal of Retailing* 64 (1, 1988): 12–40; A. Parasuraman, Leonard L. Barry, and Valarie A. Zeithaml, "Refinement and Reassessment of the SERVQUAL Scale," *Journal of Retailing* 67 (4, 1991): 420–50.

35. Valarie A. Zeithaml, Leonard L. Berry, and A. Parasuraman, "Communication and Control Processes in the Delivery of Service Quality," *Journal of Marketing* 52 (April 1988): 35–48.

36. Jody D. Nyquist, Mary F. Bitner, and Bernard H. Booms, "Identifying Communication Difficulties in the Service Encounter: A Critical Incident Approach," in Czepiel et al., *The Service Encounter*, 195–212.

37. Nyquist et al., "Identifying Communication Difficulties in the Service Encounter," 195–212.

38. "MMHI Winners," *MarketMetrix*, www.marketmetrix.com/en/default.aspx?s=products&u=mmhi&p=1winners (accessed May 11, 2008).

39. Kristin Anderson and Ron Zemke, *Delivering Knock Your Socks Off Service* (New York: American Management Association, 1998).

40. Haksever et al., *Service Management and Operations*, 342–43.

41. Stephen J. Grove, Raymond P. Fisk, and Joby John, "Surviving in the Age of Rage," *Marketing Management*, March/April 2004, 41–5.

42. Stephen L. Vargo and Robert F. Lusch, "Evolving to a New Dominant Logic for Marketing," *Journal of Marketing* 68 (January 2004): 1–17.

43. Frederik Balfour, Manjeet Kripalani, Kerry Capell, and Laura Cohn, "Over the Sea, Then Under the Knife," *BusinessWeek*, February 16, 2004, 20–22.

44. "Search Hyatt Hotels & Resorts," Hyatt, www.hyatt.com/hyatt/features/hotel-search-results.jsp?No=10&type=clear&N=409 (accessed May 22, 2008).

45. Michael R. Solomon, "The Wardrobe Consultant: Exploring the Role of a New Retailing Partner," *Journal of Retailing* 63 (Summer 1987): 110–28.

46. Irving J. Rein, Philip Kotler, and Martin R. Stoller, *High Visibility* (New York: Dodd, Mead, 1987).

47. "Million Back Comic for President," *BBC News Online*, October 29, 2007, http://news.bbc.co.uk/1/hi/world/americas/7068040.stm, (accessed May 8, 2008).

48. Michael R. Solomon, "Celebritization and Commodification in the Interpersonal Marketplace," unpublished manuscript, Rutgers University, 1991.

49. "New York Rolls Out Tourism Ad Campaign," *CNN.com*, November 8, 2001, http://cnn.com/travel.

50. "Annual Report 2004–2005," *NYC & Company Online*, www.nycvisit.com/_uploads/docs/AnnualReport2004-2005.pdf (accessed April 30, 2008).

51. Gustav Niebuhr, "Where Religion Gets a Big Dose of Shopping-Mall Culture," *New York Times*, April 16, 1995, 1(2).

52. Antonio Regaldo, "Marketers Urge Small, 'Green' Steps," *Wall Street Journal*, May 17, 2005, B5.

CHAPTER 11

1. Leslie Vreeland, "How to Be a Smart Shopper," *Black Enterprise*, August 1993, 88.

2. Kenneth Labich, "What Will Save the U.S. Airlines," *Fortune*, June 14, 1993, 98–101.

3. "Higher Airfares to Help Offset Fuel Costs in '06," *Wall Street Journal*, March 23, 2006; Kevin Dome, "Airlines Blame High Oil Price for Forecast Dollars 7bn in Annual Losses," *Financial Times*, September 13, 2005, 4. Andrew Ross Sorkin and Jeff Bailey, "Northwest and Delta Talk Merger," *New York Times*, February 7, 2008, http://www.nytimes.com/2008/02/07/business/07air.html?scp=4&sq=airlines+losses&st=nyt (accessed March 12).

4. http://en.wikipedia.org/wiki/Teen_Buzz (accessed June 30, 2006).

5. Wendy Zellner, "Is JetBlue's Flight Plan Flawed?" *BusinessWeek*, February 16, 2004, 56–58.

6. Chris Woodyard, "High-tech gear disables car if borrower misses payment," *USA Today*, March 31, 2008, http://www.usatoday.com/money/autos/2008-03-30-repo-device-car-loans_n.htm (accessed March 31, 2008).

7. Quoted in Mercedes M. Cardonna, "Affluent Shoppers Like Their Luxe Goods Cheap," *Advertising Age*, December 1, 2003, 6.

8. Steward Washburn, "Pricing Basics: Establishing Strategy and Determining Costs in the Pricing Decision," *Business Marketing*, July 1985, reprinted in Valerie Kijewski, Bob Donath, and David T. Wilson, eds., *The Best Readings from Business Marketing Magazine* (Boston: PWS-Kent, 1993), 257–69.

9. Robin Cooper and W. Bruce Chew, "Control Tomorrow's Costs through Today's Design," *Harvard Business Review*, January–February 1996, 88–97.

10. Nikki Swartz, "Rate-Plan Wisdom," *Telephony Online*, June 15, 2000, http://telephonyonline.com/wireless/mag/wireless_rateplan_wisdom/ (accessed May 28, 2008).

11. Nikki Swartz, "Rate-Plan Wisdom," *Telephony Online*, June 15, 2000, http://telephonyonline.com/wireless/mag/wireless_rateplan_wisdom/ (accessed May 28, 2008).

12. Anthony Bianco, Wendy Zellner, Diane Brady, Mike France, Tom Lowry, Nanette Byrnes, Susan Zegel, Michael Arndt, Robert Berner, and Ann Therese Palmer, "Is Wal-Mart Too Powerful?" *BusinessWeek*, October 6, 2003, 100–10.

13. Carol Angrisani, "How Low Can You Go?" *Supermarket News*, August 6, 2007, pp 37–38; Al Heller, "The New Science of Pricing," *Supermarket News*, March 19, 2007, pp 14–18.

14. Jennifer Merritt, "The Belle of the Golf Balls," *BusinessWeek*, July 29, 1996, 6.

15. "HP 17bII+ Financial Business Calculator – overview and features," HP United States http://h10010.www1.hp.com/wwpc/us/en/sm/WF05a/215348-215348-64232-20036-215349-384708.html (accessed March 20 2008).

16. Douglas Lavin, "Goodbye to Haggling: Savvy Consumers Are Buying Their Cars Like Refrigerators," *Wall Street Journal*, August 20, 1993, B1, B3.

17. "International Commercial Terms," Export 911, http://www.export911.com/e911/export/comTerm.htm (accessed May 27, 2008).

18. Amy E. Cortese and Marcia Stepanek, "Good-Bye to Fixed Pricing?" *BusinessWeek*, May 4, 1998, 71–84.

19. "iTunes Music Store Downloads Top a Quarter Billion Songs," press release, January 24, 2005, Apple http://www.apple.com/pr/library/2005/jan/24itms.html (accessed ay 25, 2008).

20. Emma Ritch, "Mobile Music is Shooting Up the Charts," *San Jose Business Journal*, March 31, 2008, http://www.mlive.com/business/ambizdaily/bizjournals/index.ssf?/base/abd-3/1206949203163950.xml (accessed March 30, 2008).

21. Heather Green, "Downloads: The Next Generation," *BusinessWeek*, February 16, 2004, 54; Peter Burrows, Ronald Grover, and Jay Greene, "Tuning Up Like Nobody's Business," *BusinessWeek*, October 13, 2003, 48.

22. Walter Baker, Mike Marn, and Craig Zawada, "Price Smarter on the Net," *Harvard Business Review*, February 2001.

23. This section is adapted from Chris Anderson, "Free! Why $0.00 is the Future of Business" *Wired*, March 2008, 140 (10).

24. David Ackerman and Gerald Tellis, "Can Culture Affect Prices? A Cross-Cultural Study of Shopping and Retail Prices," *Journal of Retailing* 77 (2001): 57–82.

25. Shankar Vedantam, "Eliot Spitzer and the Price-Placebo Effect," *WashingtonPost.com*, March 17, 2008, http://www.washingtonpost.com/wp-dyn/content/article/2008/03/16/AR2008031602168.html (accessed May 27, 2008).

26. Robert M. Schindler and Thomas M. Kibarian, "Increased Consumer Sales Response through Use of 99-Ending Prices," *Journal of Retailing* 72 (1996): 187–99.

27. Edmund L. Andrews, "Europe to Seek Uniformity in Car Pricing," February 5, 2002, http://query.nytimes.com/gst/fullpage.html?res=9502E5DB103DF936A35751C0A9649C8B63.

28. Warren St. John, "Behind the Catwalk, Suspicion and Suits," *New York Times*, April 8, 2004, http://query.nytimes.com/gst/fullpage.html?res=9E02EED9123BF93BA25757C0A9629C8B63&scp=1&sq=Behind%20the%20Catwalk&st=cse.

29. Janet Frankston Lorin, "Regulators Investigate Chocolate Price Fixing Claims," *USA Today*, February 13, 2008, http://www.usatoday.com/money/industries/food/2008-02-13-chocolate_N.htm (accessed March 25).

30. Adam Bryant, "Aisle Seat Bully?" *Newsweek*, May 24, 1999, 56.

31. Greg Small, "Aloha Air Files for Bankruptcy, Cites Rival's 'Predatory Pricing,'" *USA Today*, March 21, 2008, http://www.usatoday.com/travel/flights/2008-03-21-aloha-air_N.htm (accessed March 28).

CHAPTER 12

1. Leiss et al., *Social Communication*; George Stigler, "The Economics of Information," *Journal of Political Economy* (1961): 69.

2. Burt Helm, "Who Should Pitch, Angelina or Dylan?" *BusinessWeek*, March 5, 2007, p 73–74.

3. Fara Weiner, "A New Campaign for Mercedes-Benz," *New York Times*, March 24, 2004, www.nytimes.com/2004/03/24/business/media/24adco.html (accessed March 24, 2004).

4. Steve Miller, "Fram Testimonial Ads Filtered Through Web," *Brandweek*, May 15, 2006, 6.

5. Gert Assmus, "An Empirical Investigation into the Perception of Vehicle Source Effects," *Journal of Advertising* 7 (Winter 1978): 4–10; for a more thorough discussion of the pros and cons of different media, see Stephen Baker, *Systematic Approach to Advertising Creativity* (New York: McGraw-Hill, 1979).

6. Quoted in Brian Steinberg, "Bob Dylan Gets Tangled Up in Pink," *Wall Street Journal-Eastern Edition*, April 2, 2004, p. B3.

7. A. S. Mitchell, "P&G Creates a Tremor in Word-of-Mouth Marketing," *New Media Age* (November 20, 2003), p. 19; Jack Neff, "P&G Provides Product Launchpad, A Buzz Networks of Moms," *Advertising Age*, Volume 77, Issue 12 (March 20, 2006), pp. 1 and 40; Richard H. Levey, "P&G Relies on Teens for Viral Marketing," *Direct*, Volume 15, Issue 10 (August 2003), p. 57.

8. Stuart Elliott, "For a New Brand, Pepsi Starts the Buzz Online," *New York Times*, March 14, 2008, http://www.nytimes.com/2008/03/14/business/media/14adco.html?scp=16&sq=buzz++marketing&st=nyt (accessed April 14, 2008).

9. Catharine P. Taylor, "What's In a Word?" *Brandweek*, October 24, 2005, p 30.

10. Lois Geller, "Wow—What a Buzz," *Target Marketing*, June 2005, 21.

11. Matthew Creamer, "In Era of Consumer Control, Marketers Crave the Potency of Word of Mouth," *Advertising Age*, November 28, 2005, 32.

12. Todd Wasserman, "Word Games," *Brandweek*, April 24, 2006, 24.

13. "Word of Mouth: Brands of the Unexpected," *Brand Strategy*, December 5, 2005, 24.

14. "Word of Mouth: Brands of the Unexpected," *Brand Strategy*, December 5, 2005, 24.

15. "Word of Mouth: Brands of the Unexpected," *Brand Strategy*, December 5, 2005, 24.

16. "Word of Mouth: Brands of the Unexpected," *Brand Strategy*, December 5, 2005, 24.

17. "Word of Mouth: Brands of the Unexpected," *Brand Strategy*, December 5, 2005, 24.

18. Todd Wasserman, "Blogs Cause Word of Mouth Business to Spread Quickly," *Brandweek*, Oct 3, 2005, p 9.

19. Todd Wasserman, "Word Games," *Brandweek*, April 24, 2006, p 24.

20. Suzanne Vranica, "Getting Buzz Marketers to Fess Up," *Wall Street Journal*, February 9, 2005, p B9.

21. Suzanne Vranica, "Getting Buzz Marketers to Fess Up," *Wall Street Journal*, February 9, 2005, p B9.

22. Todd Wasserman, "Blogs Cause Word of Mouth Business to Spread Quickly," *Brandweek*, October 3, 2005, 9.

23. Karen J. Bannan, "Online Chat Is a Gerapevine That Yields Precious Fruit," *New York Times*, December 26, 2006, http://www.nytimes.com/2006/12/25/business/media/25buzz.html?scp=18&sq=buzz++marketing&st=nyt (accessed April 14, 2008).

24. Wasserman, "Word Games."

25. Wasserman, "Blogs Cause Word of Mouth Business to Spread Quickly."

26. Wasserman, "Blogs Cause Word of Mouth Business to Spread Quickly."

27. T. L. Stanley, "Guerrilla Marketers of the Year," *Brandweek*, March 27, 2000, 28; Jeff Green, "Down with the Dirt Devils," *Brandweek*, March 27, 2000, 41–44; Stephanie Thompson, "Pepsi Favors Sampling over Ads for Fruit Drink," *Advertising Age*, January 24, 2000, 8.

28. Jaimie Seaton, "Burger King Guns for Rivals in Guerilla Push," *Media*, September 9, 2005, 6.

29. Quoted in Michelle Kessler, "IBM Graffiti Ads Gain Notoriety," *USA Today*, April 26, 2001, 3B.

30. Erik Hauser, "Experiential Marketing," *Brandweek*, July 26, 2007, http://www.experientialforum.com/content/view/112/48/ (accessed April 14, 2008).

31. Stuare Elliott, "Show and Tell Moves into Living Rooms," *New York Times*, April 4, 2008, http://www.nytimes.com/2008/04/04/business/media/04adco.html?scp=5&sq=buzz++marketing&st=nyt (accessed April 14, 2008).

32. "CGM Overview," Neilsen BuzzMetrics, http://www.nielsenbuzzmetrics.com/cgm.

33. Keith Schneider, "Brands for the Chattering Masses," *New York Times*, December 17, 2006, http://www.nytimes.com/2006/12/17/business/yourmoney/17buzz.html (accessed April 14, 2008); Nielsen Buzzmetrics, http://www.nielsenbuzzmetrics.com/products (accessed April 14, 2008).

34. Suzanne Vranica, "Getting Buzz Marketers to Fess Up," *Wall Street Journal*, February 9, 2005, p B9.

35. Todd Wasserman, "Word Games," *Brandweek*, April 24, 2006, p 24.

36. Tom Eppes, "From Theory to Practice," Price/McNabb corporate presentation, Charlotte, NC, 2002.

37. John Burnett and Sandra Moriarty, *Marketing Communications: An Integrated Approach* (Upper Saddle River, NJ: Prentice Hall, 1998).

38. Danny Kucharsky, "Ads on Demand," *Marketing*, May 15, 2006, 9.

39. "Friends' Fans Can Choose Favorite Episodes to Air on NBC This Spring by Voting on America Online; AOL, Warner Bros. Television and NBC Team Up in Unique Promotion," *Business Wire*, Jan 8, 2004, http://findarticles.com/p/articles/mi_m0EIN/is_2004_Jan_8/ai_111973646.

40. Martin Everett, "This One's Just for You," *Sales and Marketing Management*, June 1992, 119–26.

41. Martin Everett, "This One's Just for You," *Sales and Marketing Management*, June 1992, 119–26.

42. John Borland, "All Eyes on New DVDs' Format War," *CNET News.com* http://news.cnet.com/All-eyes-on-new-DVDs-format-war/2100-1026_3-5783387.html, July 11, 2005 (accessed July 1, 2006).

43. Jean Halliday, "Staff Discounts It Ain't, But GM Gas Ploy Pumps Up Sales," *Advertising Age*, June 19, 2006, 3–4.

44. Jack Neff, "P&G Trims Fat Off its $2B Trade-Promotion System," *Advertising Age*, June 5, 2006, 8.

45. Bill Britt, "Volkswagen Waxes Poetic to Stir Up Emotions and Sales," *Advertising Age*, September 29, 2003, 8.

46. Linda L. Golden and Mark I. Alpert, "Comparative Analysis of the Relative Effectiveness of One- and Two-Sided Communication for Contrasting Products," *Journal of Advertising* 16 (1987): 18–25; Robert B. Settle and Linda L. Golden, "Attribution Theory and Advertiser Credibility," *Journal of Marketing Research* 11 (May 1974): 181–85.

47. Paul Tolme, "Sponsoring the Slopes," *Newsweek*, December 8, 2003, 10.

48. Khanh T. L. Tran, "Lifting the Velvet Rope: Nightclubs Draw Virtual Throngs with Webcasts," *Wall Street Journa-Eastern Edition* (August 30, 1999), p. B1.

CHAPTER 13

1. Zachary Rodgers, "Watchdog Calls on FTC to Investigate Tremor," ClickZ.com, October 19, 2005.

2. "U.S. Advertising Expenditures by Medium," *Advertising Age*, June 21, 2007, http://adage.com/datacenter/article?article_id=118678&search_phrase=ad+expenditures+2007 (accessed April 20, 2008).

3. Gail Schiller, "Survey: Alternative Media Surges," Adweek.com http://www.adweek.com/aw/content_display/news/nontraditional/e3i7d4936f8e5dd3cf6dad2f8be0abb548f (accessed June 9, 2008).

4. "A Snapshot of America's Viewing Habits," *Television Week*, March 5, 2007, Section: Media&Tech, pg 14.

5. Stuart Elliott, "On ABC, Sears Pays to Be Star of New Series," *New York Times*, December 3, 2003, http://query.nytimes.com/gst/fullpage.html?res=9F06E0D81F3AF930A35751C1A9659C8B63&scp=1&sq=sears+pays+to+be+a+star&st=nyt; Brian Steinberg and Suzanne Vranica, "Prime-Time TV's New Guest Stars: Products," *Wall Street Journal*, January 12, 2004, www.wsj.com; "IAG Top 10 Most Recalled IN-Program Product Placements: Reality, *Advertising Age*, April 17, 2008, http://adage.com/madisonandvine/article?article_id=126483&search_phrase=product+placements (accessed June 9, 2008).

6. Brian Steinberg and Suzanne Vranica, "Five Key Issues Could Alter the Ad Industry," *Wall Street Journal*, January 4, 2004, p. B1.

7. William Wells, John Burnett, and Sandra Moriarty, *Advertising: Principles and Practice*, 5th ed. (Englewood Cliffs, NJ: Prentice Hall, 2000).

8. "Index to the 100 Leading National Advertisers," *Advertising Age*, June 20, 2007, http://adage.com/datacenter/article?article_id=118652&search_phrase=top+ad+spenders+2007 (accessed April 21, 2008).

9. John M. Broder, "Governors Join in Creating Regional Pacts on Climate Change," *New York Times*, November 15, 2007, http://www.nytimes.com/2007/11/15/washington/15climate.html?scp=1&sq=governors+join+in+creating+regional&st=nyt (accessed June 9, 2008).

10. Bob Garfield, "PSA Won't Change Perennial Parental Bleacher Creatures," *Advertising Age*, April 14, 2008, http://adage.com/garfield/post?article_id=126354&search_phrase=PSA (accessed April 19, 2008).

11. Julie Bosman, "Chevy Tries a Write-Your-Own-Ad Approach, and the Potshots Fly," *New York Times*, April 4, 2006, Section C, 1.

12. "Customer-Made," Trend-watching.com www.trendwatching.com/briefing/; "Generation C," http://www.trendwatching.com/trends/GENERATION_C.htm.

13. Constantine von Hoffman, "GM's CGM Wins at Big Game," *Brandweek*, February 12, 2007, page 28.

14. Karen E. Klein, "Should Your Customers Make Your Ads?" *Business Week Online*, January 3, 2008, page 9.

15. Stuart Elliott, "A Consumer's Spot for Apple Grows Up," *New York Times*, October 31, 2007, http://www.nytimes.com/2007/10/31/business/media/31adco.html?scp=1&sq=&st=cse (accessed April 21, 2008).

16. Eleftheria Parpis, "Your Ad Here," *Adweek*, Volume 47, Issue 39 (October 23, 2006), p. 24; Karen E. Klein, "Should Your Customers Make Your Ads?" *Business Week Online* (January 3, 2008), p. 9, http://www.businessweek.com/smallbiz/content/jan2008/sb2008012_248465.htm?chan=search, "Cary Super Bowl Ad Ranked No. 4 by USA Today, *the News and observer*, February 5, 2007, http://images.google.com/imgres?imgurl=http://blogs.newsobserver.com/media/doritos-large.jpg&imgrefurl=http://blogs.newsobserver.com/tv/index.php%3Fm%3D20070205&h=343&w=490&sz=22&hl=en&start=8&sig2=wwZiR49ORBPBkhquLMRdKw&um=1&tbnid=QHFYLpc2LoGg6M:&tbnh=91&tbnw=130&ei=MUQTSJbOD6HAerPhnbsC&prev=/images%3Fq%3DDoritos%2BSuper%2BBowl%2Bcommercial%2B2007%26um%3D1%26hl%3Den%26rlz%3DT4HPIA_en___US241%26sa%3DN (accessed April 26, 2008).

17. Quoted in Stuart Elliott, "Chevy Tries a Write-Your-Own-Ad Approach, and the Potshots Fly," *New York Times Online*, April 6, 2006. http://www.nytimes.com/2006/04/04/business/media/04adco.html?scp=1&sq=chevy+tries+a+write-your.own&st=nyt (accessed June 9, 2008).

18. Alice G. Cuneo, "LG Partners with Iron Man to Break Out of Niche," *Advertising Age*, April 16, 2008, http://adage.com/madisonandvine/article?article_id=126453&search_phrase=magazine+ad+campaign (accessed April 21, 2008).

20. "Agency Report 2007 Index," *Advertising Age*, April 25, 2007, http://adage.com/article?article_id=116344 (accessed April 18, 2008).

21. Federal Trade Commission, *FTC Policy Statement on Deception*, October 14, 1983, www.ftc.gov/bcp/policystmt/ad-decept.htm (accessed July 2, 2006); Dorothy Cohen, *Legal Issues in Marketing Decision Making* (Cincinnati: South-Western College Publishing, 1995).

22. "Appeals Court Backs FTC Call for Changes to Doan's Pills Ads," *Wall Street Journal*, August 21, 2000, 1.

23. Leslie Kaufman, "Enough Talk," *Newsweek*, August 18, 1997, 48–49.

24. "Index to the 100 Leading National Advertisers," *Advertising Age*, June 20, 2007, http://adage.com/datacenter/article?article_id=118652&search_phrase=top+ad+spenders+2007 (accessed April 21, 2008).

25. Kate Macarthur, "Why Big Brands Are Getting Into the Ring," *Advertising Age*, May 22, 2007, http://adage.com/print?article_id=116722 (accessed April 21, 2008).

26. Geoffrey A. Fowler, "For P&G in China, It's Wash, Rinse, Don't Repeat," *Wall Street Journal*, April 7, 2006, p. B3.

27. Jonathan Lemonnier, "Big Players in Diet Industry Shift Focus to Online Presences," *Advertising Age*, February 18, 2008, p. 18,

28. Jeremy Lee, "Ofcom Bans Follow-Up Renault Megane Spot," *Campaign*, August 6, 2004, p 10.

29. Stephanie Kant, "Magic of Clorox Sells for a Song," *Wall Street Journal*, March 28, 2008, http://online.wsj.com/article/SB120666813235770629.html (accessed April 17, 2008).

30. "Who Owns What," *Columbia Journalism Review*, http://www.cjr.org/resources/ (accessed April 18, 2008).

31. Christopher Rocchio, "Report: Writers strike spikes 'American Idol' ad rates to $1 million plus," Radio-TV World, January 14, 2008, http://www.realitytvworld.com/news/report-writers-strike-spikes-american-idol-ad-rates-1-million-plus-6390.php (accessed April 21, 2008).

32. "TV Advertising Is Less Effective: Survey," *PROMO Magazine*, www.promomagazine.com/news/tvadvertising_survey_032406/index/html (accessed July 29, 2006).

33. Phil Hall, "Make Listeners Your Customers," *Nation's Business*, June 1994, 53R.

34. Jack Neff, "Viva Viva! K-C Boosts Brand's Marketing," *Advertising Age*, June 11, 2007, p. 4.

35. "Internet Advertising Revenues Again Reach New Highs, Estimated to Pass $21 Billion in 2007 and Hit Nearly $6 Billion in Q4 2007, February 25, 2008," press release, Interactive Advertising Bureau, http://www.iab.net/about_the_iab/recent_press_releases/press_release_archive/press_release/195115 (accessed April 21, 2008).

36. Kevin J. Delaney, "Once Wary Industry Giants Embrace Internet Advertising," *Wall Street Journal*, April 17, 2006, p A1.

37. Louise Story, "Online Pitches Made Just for You," *New York Times*, March 6, 2008, p 7.

38. Michael McCarthy, "Companies Are Sold on Interactive Ad Strategy," *USA Today*, March 3, 2000, 1B.

39. Ann M. Mack, "Got E-Mail," *Brandweek*, March 20, 2000, 84–88.

40. "Interactive Advertising Revenues to Reach $147B Globally, $62.4B in US," The Kelsey Group, http://www.marketingcharts.com/direct/interactive-advertising-revenues-to-reach-147b-globally-624b-in-us-3567/ (accessed April 21, 2008).

41. Lisa Marie Petersen, "Outside Chance," *Mediaweek*, June 15, 1992, 20–23.

42. Lisa Marie Petersen, "Outside Chance," *Mediaweek*, June 15, 1992, 20–23.

43. Doreen Carvajal, "Advertiser Counts on Sheep to Pull Eyes over the Wool," *New York Times*, April 24, 2006, www.nytimes.com (accessed July 29, 2006).

44. Louise Story, "Away From Home, TV Ads Are Inescapable," *New York Times*, March 2, 2007, p. 6.

45. Jeremy Wagstaff, "Loose Wire — Bootleg Backlash: Software industry groups are snooping for people using pirated software; But their assumptions about who's a pirate seem awfully mixed up," July 31, 2003, *Far Eastern Economic Review* p. 31.

46. Shahnaz Mahmud, "PQ: Branded Entertainment to Surge in '08," *Adweek.com*, February 12, 2008, http://www.adweek.com/aw/content_display/news/media/e3i11eaec8a171fba4996f6f978d0da75ec (accessed June 6, 2008).

47. Karl Greenberg, "Audi Ties R8 to Promotion Of "Iron Man," Due out May 2," *Marketing Daily*, Apr 23, 2008, http://publications.mediapost.com/index.cfm?fuseaction=Articles.san&s=81185&Nid=41887&p=941737 (accessed April 23, 2008).

48. Andrew Hampp, "In This Year's Upfront, It's All About Branded Entertainment," *Advertising Age*, May 26, 2008, http://adage.com/print?article_id=127312 (accessed June 6, 2008).

49. Bristol Voss, "Measuring the Effectiveness of Advertising and PR," *Sales & Marketing Management*, October 1992, 123–24.

50. This remark has also been credited to a British businessman named Lord Leverhulme; see Charles Goodrum and Helen Dalrymple, *Advertising in America: The First 200 Years* (New York: Harry N. Abrams, 1990).

51. Stuart Elliott, "New Survey on Ad Effectiveness," April 14, 2004, http://query.nytimes.com/search/query?frow=0&n=10&srcht=s&query=new+survey+on+ad+effectiveness&srchst=nyt&submit.x=0&submit.y=0&submit=sub&hdlquery=&bylquery=&daterange=full&mon1=01&day1=01&year1=1981&mon2=06&day2=09&year2=2008.

52. Charles Goodrum and Helen Dalrymple, *Advertising in America: The First 200 Years* (New York: Harry N. Abrams, 1990).

53. Quoted in Kevin Goldman, "Knock, Knock. Who's There? The Same Old Funny Ad Again," *Wall Street Journal*, November 2, 1993, B10.

54. Howard Stumpf and John M. Kawula, "Point of Purchase Advertising," in *Handbook of Sales Promotion*, ed. S. Ulanoff (New York: McGraw-Hill, 1985); Karen A. Berger, *The Rising Importance of Point-of-Purchase Advertising in the Marketing Mix* (Englewood Cliffs, NJ: Point-of-Purchase Advertising Institute).

55. "Bausch & Lomb Makes Eyes with Consumers in Spain," *PROMO Magazine*, October 1994, 93.

56. Gardiner Harris, "Drug Makers Offer Consumers Coupons for Free Prescriptions–But Patients Still Have to Get Their Physician's Approval, And Most Don't Pay for Pills," *The Wall Street Journal*, March 13, 2002, p. B1.

57. Bob Tedeschi, "E-Commerce Report; More consumers are using online coupons as companies begin to offer them for a wider array of products.," May 17, 2003, http://query.nytimes.com/gst/fullpage.html?res=9D04E5DA1631F934A25750C0A9659C8B63&scp=1&sq=smartsource.com&st=nyt (accessed June 9, 2008).

58. "Virgin Atlantic Rolls Out Space Miles," *PROMO Magazine*, http://promomagazine.com/incentives/virgin_atlantic_miles_011106/index.html (accessed June 12, 2006).

59. "Six Flags Launches Kids Loyalty Club," *PROMO Magazine*, http://promomagazine.com/entertainmentmarketing/news/sixflagskids/index.html (accessed June 12, 2006).

60. This section based on material presented in Don E. Schultz, William A. Robinson, and Lisa A. Petrison, *Sales Promotion Essentials*, 2nd ed. (Lincolnwood, IL: NTC Business Books, 1993).

61. "Ben & Jerry's Launches Ice Cream Flavor Contest," *PROMO Magazine*, http://promomagazine.com/news/benjerry_contest_031606/index.html (accessed March 16, 2006).

62. "Lengthy Research Leads Disney to Global 'Dreams' Theme," *PROMO Magazine*, http://promomagazine.com/research/disney_research_061206/index.html (accessed June 12, 2006).

63. "Consumers Vote for Oreo Idol," *PROMO Magazine*, http://promomagazine.com/contests/news/oreo_idol_contest_061206/index.html (accessed June 9, 2008).

64. Kerry J. Smith, "It's for You," *PROMO Magazine*, August 1994, 41(4); Sharon Moshavi, "Please Deposit No Cents," *Forbes*, August 16, 1993, 102.

65. Emily Bryson York, "Starbucks Offers Free Cups of New Blend," *Advertising Age*, April 7, 2008, http://adage.com/print?article_id=126232 (accessed April 21, 2008); Emily Bryson York, "Starbucks Seeks Jolt From Another Mass Tactic," *Advertising Age*, April 21, 2008, pp. 3, 32.

66. Amanda Beeler, "Package-Goods Marketers Tune in Free-Sampling Sites," *Advertising Age*, June 12, 2000, 58.

67. Kate Fitzgerald, "Homemade Bikini Contest Hits Bars, Beach for 10th Year," *Advertising Age*, April 13, 1998, p. 18.

68. Melissa Marr, "Publicity, PR and 'Passion,'" *Wall Street Journal*, February 20, 2004, B.1.

69. Willie Vogt, "Shaping Public Perception," *Agri Marketing*, June 1992, 72–75.

70. Alan J. Liddle, "Guilty Pleas End Wendy's Finger-Pointing, but Will They Inspire Leniency in Sentencing," *Nation's Restaurant News*, September 19, 2005, 202; Jonathan Birchall, "Jail For Wendy's Finger Claim Couple," *Financial Times*, January 19, 2006, 25.

71. "Jail for Wendy's Finger Scam Couple," CBSNews, January 18, 2006, http://www.cbsnews.com/stories/2006/01/18/national/main1218315.shtml (accessed June 9, 2008).

72. "Man Who Put Dead Mouse in Burrito at Taco Bell Given Prison Time," *FoxNews.com*, http://www.foxnews.com/story/0,2933,197993,00.html (accessed June 9, 2008).

73. Steve Jarvis, "How the Internet Is Changing Fundamentals of Publicity," *Marketing News*, July 17, 2000, 6–7.

74. Dana James, "When Your Company Goes Code Blue," *Marketing News*, November 6, 2000, 1, 15.

75. Judy A. Gordon, "Print Campaign Generates Sales Leads for Biotechnology Product," *Public Relations Journal*, July 1991, 21.

76. Lindsay Chappell, "PR Makes Impressions, Sales," *Advertising Age*, March 22, 1993, S–18, S–32.

77. Andy Pasztor, "FAA Ruling on Long-Haul Routes Would Boost Boeing's Designs," *Wall Street Journal*, June 5, 2006, p A.3.

78. Amy Chozick, "Star Power: The LPGA Is Counting on a New Marketing Push to Take Women's Golf to the Next Level," *Wall Street Journal*, June 12, 2006, R.6.

79. Ni Chen and Hugh M. Culbertson, "Two Contrasting Approaches of Government Public Relations in Mainland China," *Public Relations Quarterly*, Fall 1992, 36–41.

80. John Nardone and Ed See, Measure Sponsorships to Drive Sales; Shift Gears: Move Beyond Perceiving Sponsorships as Mere Brand Builders and Instead Assess ROI," *Advertising Age*, March 5, 2007, Page 20.

81. "McDonald's Celebrates World Cup Fever with Global Campaign," *PROMO Magazine*, http://promomagazine.com/eventmarketing/news/mcds_worldcup_campaign_060906/index.html (accessed June 12, 2006).

82. "Unilever Airs Laundry in NYC," *PROMO Magazine*, http://promomagazine.com/contests/unileverairs/index.html (accessed July 30, 2006).

CHAPTER 14

1. James B. Arndorfer, "Models to Troll Taverns for Pricey French Vodka," *Advertising Age*, May 5, 1997, 8.

2. Bureau of Labor Statistics, *Occupational Outlook Handbook* 2008–09, www.bls.gov/oco/ocos119.htm#outlook (accessed May 13, 2008).

3. Quoted in Jaclyn Fierman, "The Death and Rebirth of the Salesman," *Fortune*, July 25, 1994, 38(7), 88.

4. "Super Bowl Commercials Cost Plenty, Deliver Little," *TransWorldNews*, February 4, 2008, www.transworldnews.com/NewsStory.aspx?id=35308&cat=2 (accessed May 11, 2008).

5. Direct Selling Association, www.dsa.org (accessed May 16, 2008); Scott Reeves, "'Do Not Call' Revives Door-to-Door Sales," *Marketing News*, December 8, 2003, 13; Maria Puente, "Direct Selling Brings It All Home," *USA Today*, October 28, 2003, 5D.

6. Salesforce.com, www.salesforce.com (accessed May 11, 2008); Daniel Tynan, "CRM Software: Who Needs It?" *Sales & Marketing Management*, July 2003, 30; Daniel Tynan, "CRM: Buy or Rent?" *Sales & Marketing Management*, March 2004, 41–45.

7. Skype, www.skype.com (accessed May 11, 2008); Daniel Tynan, "Tech Advantage," *Sales & Marketing Management*, April 2004, 47–51.

8. T-Mobil Hotspot, http://hotspot.t-mobile.com/services_need.htm (accessed May 15, 2008).

9. Jennifer Gilbert, "No Strings Attached," *Sales & Marketing Management*, July 2004, 22–27.

10. "U.S. Locations," T-Mobil Hotspot, https://selfcare.hotspot.t-mobile.com/locations/viewLocationMap.do (accessed May 15, 2008).

11. Tim Carpenter, "Nationwide Uses Analytics, Metrics to Hone Internet Delivery Strategies," *Insurance & Technology*, May 21, 2003, www.insurancetech.com/story/news/IST20030521S0002, accessed May 15, 2008.

12. Dan C. Weilbaker, "The Identification of Selling Abilities Needed for Missionary Type Sales," *Journal of Personal Selling & Sales Management*, 10 (Summer 1990), 45–58.

13. Derek A. Newton, *Sales Force Performance and Turnover* (Cambridge, MA: Marketing Science Institute, 1973), 3.

14. Mark W. Johnston and Greg W. Marshall, *Relationship Selling*, 2nd ed. (Boston: McGraw-Hill, 2008).

15. Accela Communications, www.accelacommunications.com (accessed May 16, 2008).

16. Linked in, www.linkedin.com (accessed May 16, 2008).

17. Greg W. Marshall, Daniel J. Goebel, and William C. Moncrief, "Hiring for Success at the Buyer-Seller Interface," *Journal of Business Research* 56 (April 2003): 247–55.

18. "2007 Fortune 500 Ranking of America's Largest Corporations," *CNNMoney.com*, http://money.cnn.com/magazines/fortune/fortune500/2007/snapshots/1092.html (accessed May 10, 2008).

19. Andy Cohen, "Selling from Home Base," *Sales & Marketing Management*, November 2003, 12.

20. Marshall et al., "Hiring for Success at the Buyer-Seller Interface."

21. Julia Chang, "Making the Grade," *Sales & Marketing Management*, March 2004, 24–29.

22. Adapted from Erin Strout, "The Top 10 Most Outrageous T&E Expenses," *Sales & Marketing Management*, February 2001, 60.

23. Direct Marketing Association, www.the-dma.org (accessed May 12, 2008); "Industry Research, Facts & Figures," Electronic Retailing Association, http://63.117.125.183/new_site/memresources/research/facts_figures.htm. (accessed September 19, 2008).

24. *DMA Statistical Fact Book*, 30th Edition, (New York: Direct Marketing Association, 2008).

25. Frances Huffman, "Special Delivery," *Entrepreneur*, February 1993, 81(3).

26. Paul Hughes, "Profits Due," *Entrepreneur*, February 1994, 74(4).

27. *DMA Statistical Fact Book*, 2008.

28. Burt Helm, "Cutting the Stack of Catalogs," *BusinessWeek* Online, December 20, 2007, http://www.businessweek.com/magazine/content/07_53/b4065035213195.htm?chan=search (accessed May 15, 2008).

29. C. B. DiPasquale, "Direct Hit after Anthrax Threat," *Advertising Age*, October 22, 2001, 1, 60.

30. Federal Trade Commission, National Do Not Call Registry, www.ftc.gov/donotcall (accessed May 8, 2008).

31. Robert Longley, "Truth About Cell Phones and the Do Not Call Registry," *About.com: U.S. Government Information*, April 2005, http://www.ftc.gov/donotcall (accessed May 10, 2008).

32. Alison J. Clarke, "'As Seen on TV': Socialization of the Tele-Visual Consumer," (paper presented at the Fifth Interdisciplinary Conference on Research in Consumption, University of Lund, Sweden, August 1995).

33. Elizabeth A. Sullivan, "Consider Your Source," *Marketing News* (February 15, 2008), pp. 16–19; Judith A. Chevalier and Dina Mayzlin, "Online User Reviews Influence Consumers' Decision to Purchase," *Marketing News* (August 15, 2006), p. 17; Justin Leonard's Fitness Infomercial Review, www.fitnessinfomercialreview.com (accessed May 17, 2008); TripAdvisor, www.tripadvisor.com (accessed May 17, 2008).

34. "Mobile Phone Use Reaches 50% Worldwide," *Romow Shopping Blog*, February 28, 2008, http://www.romow.com/shopping-blog/mobile-phone-use-reaches-50-worldwide/ (accessed April 30, 2008).

35. Randall Frost, "M-Commerce: Is the Line Dead," BrandChannel.com, March 8, 2004, www.brandchannel.com/features_effect.asp?pf_id=200 (accessed May 12, 2008).

36. Sandeep Junnarkar, "When Instant Messages Come Bearing Malice," *New York Times* Online, March 25, 2004, www.nytimes.com/2004/03/25/technology/circuits/25mess.html?ex=1395550800&en=5a97ae410187d88c&ei=5007&partner=USERLAND (accessed May 1, 2008).

CHAPTER 15

1. Aaron Linde, "Microsoft Considering Crackdown Sequel," *ShackNews.com*, February 8, 2008, www.shacknews.com/onearticle.x/51227 (accessed May 15, 2008); Saleem Kahn, "Crackdown Battles Halo 3 as Freebies Excite, Raise Eyebrows," *CBC News Online*, February 27, 2007, www.cbc.ca/technology/technology-blog/2007/02/crackdown_battles_halo_3_as_fr.html (accessed May 15, 2008).

2. Ina Fried, "Pepsi iTunes Promotion Goes Flat," *CNET News.com*, April 28, 2004, www.news.com/2100-1025_3-5201676.html (accessed May 14, 2008).

3. Thomas L. Friedman, *The World Is Flat 3.0: A Brief History of the Twenty-First Century* (New York: Picador, 2007).

4. "How it Works," Netflix, www.netflix.com/HowItWorks (accessed May 17, 2008).

5. David Byrne, "David Byrne's Survival Strategies for Emerging Artists – and Megastars," *Wired*: Issue 16.01, December 18, 2007, www.wired.com/entertainment/music/magazine/16-01/ff_byrne/ (accessed May 16, 2008).

6. "About us," Eastern Meat Farms, Inc., www.salami.com/ordereze/AboutUs.aspx (accessed May 17, 2008).

7. Adrian J. Slywotzky, "The War of the Choiceboards," *Harvard Business Review* (January–February 2000) p. 41; Adrian J. Slywotzky, "Getting Rid of Guesswork," *Business Week* (August 21, 2000), p. 142; Praytyush Bharati and Abhijit Chaudhury, "Using Choiceboards to Create Business Value," *Communications of the ACM*, Vol. 47, No. 12 (December 2004), pp. 77–81.

8. Rowland T. Moriarty and Ursula Moran, "Managing Hybrid Marketing Systems," *Harvard Business Review*, November–December 1990, 2–11.

9. Michael Barbaro, "Wal-Mart Offers Aid to Rivals," *New York Times*, April 5, 2006, Section C, page 1.

10. Oneworld, www.oneworld.com/home.cfm (accessed May 16, 2008).

11. John Neff, "Scion May Break Promise to Itself, Add Fourth Model," *AutoBlog*, May 25, 2007, http://www.autoblog.com/2007/05/25/scion-may-break-promise-to-itself-add-fourth-model/ (accessed May 17, 2008).

12. "About us," Starbucks, www.starbucks.com/aboutus/sup_div.asp (accessed May 17, 2008).

13. Toby B. Gooley, "The Who, What, and Where of Reverse Logistics," *Logistics Management* 42 (February 2003), 38–44; James R. Stock, *Development and Implementation of Reverse Logistics Programs* (Oak Brook, IL: Council of Logistics Management, 1998, 20).

14. "Perfect Order Measure," Supply Chain Metric.com, www.supplychainmetric.com/perfect.htm (accessed May 15, 2008).

15. "Spychipped Levi's Brand Jeans Hit the U.S.," RFID Nineteen Eighty-Four, April 27, 2006, www.spychips.com/press-releases/levis-secret-testing.html (accessed May 10, 2008): Katherine Albrecht and Liz McIntyre, *Spychips: How Major Corporations and Government Plan to Track Your Every Purchase and Watch Your Every Move* (New York: Plume, 2006).

16. Faye W. Gilbert, Joyce A. Young, and Charles R. O'Neal, "Buyer-Seller Relationships in Just-in-Time Purchasing Environments," *Journal of Organizational Research*, February 1994, 29, 111–20.

17. Kasra Ferdows, Michael A. Lewis, and Jose A. D. Machuca, "Zara's Secret for Fast Fashion," *Harvard Business School – Working Knowledge for Business Leaders*, February 21, 2005, http://hbswk.hbs.edu/archive/4652.html (accessed May 8, 2008).

CHAPTER 16

1. Janet Ginsburg, "Xtreme Retailing," *BusinessWeek*, December 20, 1999, 120.

2. U.S. Department of Labor, "Employment Situation Summary," March 2008 http://www.bls.gov/news.release/empsit.nr0.htm (accessed April 26, 2008).

3. U.S. Census Bureau, "Advance Monthly Sales for Retail and Food Services, December 2007," http://www.census.gov/marts/www/download/pdf/adv0712.pdf (accessed April 26, 2008).

4. Stanley C. Hollander, "The Wheel of Retailing," *Journal of Retailing*, July 1960, 41.

5. "About Us," Pier 1 imports, www.pier1.com/company/history.aspx (accessed June 25, 2006).

6. "Wal-Mart Opens Supercenter for Upscale Shoppers," *PROMO Magazine*, http://promomagazine.com/news/wal-mart_supercenter_033006/index.html (accessed June 12, 2006); Stuart Elliott and Michael Barbaro, "Wal-Mart on the Hunt for an Extreme Makeover," *New York Times*, May 4, 2006, Section C, 1.

7. Ann Zimmerman and Cheryl Lu-Lien Tan, "After Misstep, Wal-Mart Revisits Fashion," *Wall Street Journal*, April 24, 2008 http://online.wsj.com/article/SB120899828876040063.html (accessed April 29, 2008).

8. William R. Davidson, Albert D. Bates, and Stephen J. Bass, "The Retail Life Cycle," *Harvard Business Review*, November-December 1976, 89.

9. "About Circuit City," Circuit City, http://www.circuitcity.com/ccd/lookLearn.do?cat=-13317&edOid=105485&c=1 (accessed June 25, 2006).

10. Cathy Horyn, "A Store Made for Right Now: You Shop until It's Dropped," *New York Times*, February 17, 2004, www.nytimes.com.

11. Richard Gibson, "KFC Tries to Teach an Old Chicken New Tricks," *Wall Street Journal*, February 6, 2008, http://online.wsj.com/article/SB120227503488747205.html (accessed April 29, 2008).

12. "Company Fact Sheet, February, 2008," Starbucks Coffee, http://www.starbucks.com/aboutus/Company_Factsheet.pdf (accessed April 29, 2008).

13. Emily Bryson York, "Starbucks Paved Way, and Now It Must Pay," *Advertising Age*, March 24, 2008, p 28.

14. Thomas M. Anderson, "Checkups on the Run," *Kiplinger Personal Finance,* May 2006, 96.

15. Quoted in Stephanie Kang, "Pacific Sunwear's d.e.m.o. Chain Sells Hip-Hop Lite to Teenagers," *Wall Street Journal,* February 20, 2004, p. A11.

16. Michael Levy and Barton A. Weitz, *Retailing Management,* 3rd ed. (Boston: Irwin/McGraw-Hill, 1998).

17. Abbey Klaassen, "Retailers Harness Digital Media for In-Store Experiences, Product Sampling," *Advertising Age,* March 19, 2008, p. 18.

18. Mya Frazier, "The Store of the Future," *Advertising Age,* January 16, 2006, pp. 1, 23.

19. Rebecca Harrison, "Restaurants Try E-Menus," *Reuters,* February 25, 2008, http://uk.reuters.com/article/internetNews/idUKL204599320080226.

20. Geraldo Samor, Cecillie Rohwedder, and Ann Zimmerman, "Innocents Abroad? Wal-Mart's Global Sales Rise as It Learns from Mistakes: No More Ice Skates in Mexico," *Wall Street Journal,* May 16, 2006, B1.

21. Evan Ramstad, "Wal-Mart Leaves South Korea by Selling Stores to Local Rival: Sale to Shinsegae Follows April Pullout by Carrefour as Domestic Firms Prevail," *Wall Street Journal,* May 23, 2006, A2.

22. Kelly Gates and Dan Alaimo, "Solving Shrink," *Supermarket News,* October 22, 2007, p. 43.

23. "Shoplifter and Dishonest Employee Theft on Rise," Jack L. Hayes International, Inc., http://www.hayesinternational.com/thft_srvys.html (accessed May 1, 2008).

24. Jessica Silver-Greenberg, "Shoplifters Get Smarter," *Business Week,* November 19, 2007, accessed May 1, 2008, at http://www.businessweek.com/magazine/content/07_47/b4059051.htm?chan=search (accessed May 1, 2008).

25. Jessica Silver-Greenberg, "Shoplifters Get Smarter," *Business Week,* November 19, 2007, accessed May 1, 2008, at http://www.businessweek.com/magazine/content/07_47/b4059051.htm?chan=search.

26. "Weird But True, The Naked Truth," *Convenience Store News,* October 22, 2007, p. 13.

27. "Shoplifter and Dishonest Employee Theft on Rise," Jack L. Hayes International, Inc., http://www.hayesinternational.com/thft_srvys.html (accessed May 1, 2008).

28. Kelly Gates and Dan Alaimo, "Solving Shrink," *Supermarket News,* October 22, 2007, p. 43.

29. Francis Piron and Murray Young, "Retail Borrowing: Insights and Implications on Returning Used Merchandise," *International Journal of Retail & Distribution Management,* Vol. 28, No. 1, 2000, pp. 27–36.

30. Jodi Wilgoren, "In the Urban 7-Eleven, the Slurpee Looks Sleeker," *New York Times,* July 31, 2003, http://query.nytimes.com/gst/fullpage.html?res=9903EFD7113DF930A25754C0A9659C8B63&scp=1&sq=In%20the%20Urban%207-Eleven,%20the%20Slurpee%20Looks%20Sleeker&st=cse.

31. Keith Morrow and Derek Top, "King of Convenience," *Optimize,* August 2005, 18–24.

32. Mark Albright, "Kohl's Debut With Fresh New Look," *The St. Petersburg Times,l,* September 28, 2006, p.1D.

33. Emily Scardino, "Kohl's Makes Sweet Deal for Exclusive Candie's Line," *DSN Retailing Today,* January 10, 2005, 5–6.

34. "Proof of Club Popularity in the 64-Ounce Pudding," *DSN Retailing Today,* December 19, 2005, 64.

35. Martin Forstenzer, "In Search of Fine Art amid the Paper Towels," *New York Times,* February 22, 2004, http://www.nytimes.com/2004/02/22/business/yourmoney/22cost.html?ex=1213156800&en=553d276643b52704&ei=5070.

36. "Federated Department Stores: King of Them All," *Journal of Commerce,* May 29, 2006, 1.

37. Quoted in Stratford Sherman, "Will the Information Superhighway Be the Death of Retailing?" *Fortune,* April 18, 1994, 99(5), 110.

38. "Direct Selling by the Numbers—Calendar Year 2006," Direct Selling Association, http://www.dsa.org/pubs/numbers/#PRODUCT (accessed April 30, 2008).

39. Direct Selling Association, "Direct Selling by the Numbers—Calendar Year 2006."

40. Janet K. Keeler, "Tupperware Kept Lives Fresh Too," *The St. Petersburg Times Online, February 9,* 2004, http://www.sptimes.com/2004/02/09/Tampabay/Tupperware_kept_lives.shtml (accessed June 27, 2008).

41. "About Amway," Amway, www.amway.com/en/General/About-Amway-10725.aspx (accessed June 25, 2006).

42. "Amway Corporation Company Profile," Yahoo Finance, http://biz.yahoo.com/ic/103/103441.html (accessed June 27, 2008).

43. H. J. Shrager, "Close Social Networks of Hasidic Women, Other Tight Groups, Boost Shaklee Sales," *Wall Street Journal,* November 19, 2001, www.wsj.

44. "Pyramid Schemes," Direct Selling Association, www.dsa.org/aboutselling/consumer/dis_pyramid.cfm (accessed June 25, 2006).

45. Aili McConnon, "Vending Machines Go Luxe," *Business Week,* January 29, 2008, p. 17.

46. "Macy's Readies iPod Vending Machines," *PROMO Magazine,* http://promomagazine.com/news/macys_ipod_machines_05232006/index.html (accessed June 12, 2006).

47. Sucharita Mulpuru with Carrie Johnson, Brendan McGowan, and Scott Wright, "U.S. eCommerce Forecast: 2008 To 2012," Forrester Research, Inc.

48. Bob Tedeschi, "A Quicker Resort This Year to Deep Discounting," *New York Times,* December 17, 2007, http://www.nytimes.com/2007/12/17/technology/17ecom.html?scp=41&sq=forrester+research&st=nyt (accessed May 1, 2008).

49. Bob Tedeschi, "$7,900 Valentino Gowns, a Click Away," *New York Times,* November 5, 2007, http://www.nytimes.com/2007/12/17/technology/17ecom.html?_r=1&scp=41&sq=forrester+research&st=nyt&oref=slogin (accessed May 1, 2008).

50. Heather Green, "Downloads: The Next Generation," *BusinessWeek,* February 16, 2004, 54.

51. Juhnyoung Lee, Robert Hoch, Mark Podlaseck, Edith Schonberg, and Stephen Gomory, "Analysis and Visualization of Metrics for Online Merchandising," *Lecture Notes in computer Science,* Vol 1836, 1999, pp. 126–141.

52. Joan Raymond, "No More Shoppus Interruptus," *American Demographics* (May 2001): 39.

53. "Amazon.com Announces Fourth Quarter Sales up 42% to $5.7 Billion; 2007 Free Cash Flow More Than Doubles, Surpassing $1 Billion for the First Time" Press Releases, Amazon.com, http://phx.corporate-ir.net/phoenix.zhtml?c=176060&p=irol-newsArticle&ID=1102343&highlight= (accessed June 27, 2008).

54. Kathryn Waskom, "Destination Retail Is on Its Way," *Marketing News,* March 13, 2000, 15.

55. Sonia Reyes, "Brand Builders," *Brandweek,* p. 14.

56. Randy Hurlow, "REI To Open Store in Pittsburg," Industry News, Outdoor Industry Association, June 22, 2004, February 28, 1998, http://outdoorindustry.com/media.outdoor.php?news_id=640&sort_year=2006 (accessed June 27, 2008).

57. "A Wide World of Sports Shoes: Fixtures Enhance Appeal of World Foot Locker," *Chain Store Age Executive,* January 1993, 176–81.

58. Jane J. Kim, "A Latte with Your Loan?" *Wall Street Journal,* May 17, 2006, D1.

59. Tracie Rozhon, "High Fashion, from Front Door to the Top Floor," *New York Times,* July 31, 2003, http://query.nytimes.com/gst/fullpage.html?res=9C00E5DA143EF932A05754C0A9659C8B63&scp=1&sq=High+Fashion%2C+from+Front+Door+to+the+Top+Floor&st=nyt.

60. L. W. Turley and Ronald E. Milliman, "Atmospheric Effects on Shopping Behavior: A Review of the Experimental Evidence," *Journal of Business Research* 49 (2000): 193–211.

61. Linda Lisanti, "Adventure's Next Stop," *Convenience Store News,* March 3, 2008, pp. 28–34; Michael Browne, "Maverik's Big Adventure," *Convenience Store News,* November 15, 2005, pp. 50–54.

62. Eric Newman, "Retail Design for 2008: Thinking Outside the Big Box," *Brandweek,* December 17, 2007, p. 26.

63. RoxAnna Sway and Jessie Bove, "New York's Stylish New Stores," *Display & Design Ideas,* December, 2006, pp. 38–40.

64. Samantha Murphy, "A Contemporary Future," *Chain Store Age,* April 2007, p. 62.

65. Alice Z. Cuneo, "Malls Seek Boost with 'Activity' Stores," *Advertising Age* (July 21, 2003): 6.

66. Julie Flaherty, "Music to a Retailer's Ears; Sorry. Springsteen Won't Be Playing at Pottery Barn Today.," *New York Times,* July 4, 2001, http://query.nytimes.com/gst/fullpage.html?res=9F00E6DB1F39F937A35754C0A9679C8B63&scp=3&sq=ambient+music+has+moved&st=nyt.

67. Deborah Blumenthal, "Scenic Design for In-Store Try-Ons," *New York Times,* April 1988.

68. "Service: Retail's No. 1 Problem," *Chain Store Age,* January 19, 1987.

69. Lorrie Grant, "Shopping in the Great Outdoors," *USAToday,* August 3, 2004, http://www.usatoday.com/money/industries/retail/2004-08-03-lifestyle-center_x.htm.

70. Lindsay Blakely, "New Hotels Start Popping Up," *Business 2.0,* August 2007, p. 32.

71. Michael Levy and Barton A. Weitz, *Retailing Management,* 3rd ed. (Boston: Irwin/McGraw-Hill, 1998).

72. Quoted in Shirley Leung, "A Glutted Market Is Leaving Food Chains Hungry for Sites," *Wall Street Journal,* September 1, 2003, www.wsj.com.

73. Rekha Balu, "The Buckle Finds Rural Kids Will Pay Dearly for Hip Clothes," *Wall Street Journal,* January 14, 1998, www.wsj.com.

Glossary

80/20 rule A marketing rule of thumb that 20 percent of purchasers account for 80 percent of a product's sales.

A

action plans Individual support plans included in a marketing plan that provide the guidance for implementation and control of the various marketing strategies within the plan. Action plans are sometimes referred to as "marketing programs."

activity stores Experiential retailing environments that involve customers in the creation of the products they buy.

actual product The physical good or the delivered service that supplies the desired benefit.

advergaming Brand placements in video games.

advertising Nonpersonal communication an identified sponsor pays for that uses mass media to persuade or inform an audience.

advertising appeal The central idea or theme of an advertising message.

advertising campaign A coordinated, comprehensive plan that carries out promotion objectives and results in a series of advertisements placed in media over a period of time.

advertising exposure The degree to which the target market will see an advertising message placed in a specific vehicle.

advocacy advertising A type of public service advertising an organization provides that seeks to influence public opinion on an issue because it has some stake in the outcome.

affect The feeling component of attitudes; refers to the overall emotional response a person has to a product.

AIDA model The communication goals of attention, interest, desire, and action.

aided recall A research technique that uses clues to prompt answers from people about advertisements they might have seen.

aperture The best place and time to reach a person in the target market group.

approach The first step of the actual sales presentation in which the salesperson tries to learn more about the customer's needs, create a good impression, and build rapport.

atmospherics The use of color, lighting, scents, furnishings, and other design elements to create a desired store image.

attention The extent to which a person devotes mental processing to a particular stimulus.

attitude A learned predisposition to respond favorably or unfavorably to stimuli on the basis of relatively enduring evaluations of people, objects, and issues.

attitudinal measures A research technique that probes a consumer's beliefs or feelings about a product before and after being exposed to messages about it.

augmented product The actual product plus other supporting features such as a warranty, credit, delivery, installation, and repair service after the sale.

augmented services The core service plus additional services provided to enhance value.

average fixed cost The fixed cost per unit produced.

B

baby boomers The segment of people born between 1946 and 1964.

back-translation The process of translating material to a foreign language and then back to the original language.

bait-and-switch An illegal marketing practice in which an advertised price special is used as bait to get customers into the store with the intention of switching them to a higher-priced item.

banners Internet advertising in the form of rectangular graphics at the top or bottom of Web pages.

basing-point pricing A pricing tactic in which customers pay shipping charges from set basing-point locations, whether the goods are actually shipped from these points or not.

BCG growth-market share matrix A portfolio analysis model developed by the Boston Consulting Group that assesses the potential of successful products to generate cash that a firm can then use to invest in new products.

behavior The doing component of attitudes; involves a consumer's intention to do something, such as the intention to purchase or use a certain product.

behavioral learning theories Theories of learning that focus on how consumer behavior is changed by external events or stimuli.

behavioral segmentation A technique that divides consumers into segments on the basis of how they act toward, feel about, or use a good or service.

behavioral targeting The marketing practice by which marketers deliver advertisements for products a consumer is looking for by watching what the consumer does on-line.

benefit The outcome sought by a customer that motivates buying behavior—that satisfies a need or want.

blog On-line personal journals similar to Web pages, but a different technology that lets people upload a few sentences without going through the more elaborate process of updating a Web site.

born-global firms Companies that try to sell their products in multiple countries from the moment they're created.

bottom-up budgeting techniques Allocation of the promotion budget based on identifying promotion goals and allocating enough money to accomplish them.

brand A name, a term, a symbol, or any other unique element of a product that identifies one firm's product(s) and sets it apart from the competition.

brand community A group of consumers who share a set of social relationships based upon usage or interest in a product.

brand competition When firms offering similar goods or services compete on the basis of their brand's reputation or perceived benefits.

brand equity The value of a brand to an organization.

brand extensions A new product sold with the same brand name as a strong existing brand.

brand loyalty A pattern of repeat product purchases, accompanied by an underlying positive attitude toward the brand, that is based on the belief that the brand makes products superior to those of its competition.

brand manager An individual who is responsible for developing and implementing the marketing plan for a single brand.

brand personality A distinctive image that captures a good's or service's character and benefits.

branded entertainment A form of advertising in which marketers integrate products into entertainment venues.

break-even analysis A method for determining the number of units that a firm must produce and sell at a given price to cover all its costs.

break-even point The point at which the total revenue and total costs are equal and beyond which the company makes a profit; below that point, the firm will suffer a loss.

breaking bulk Dividing larger quantities of goods into smaller lots in order to meet the needs of buyers.

bribery When someone voluntarily offers payment to get an illegal advantage.

business analysis The step in the product development process in which marketers assess a product's commercial viability.

business cycle The overall patterns of change in the economy—including periods of prosperity, recession, depression, and recovery—that affect consumer and business purchasing power.

business ethics Rules of conduct for an organization.

business plan A plan that includes the decisions that guide the entire organization.

business planning An ongoing process of making decisions that guides the firm both in the short term and for the long term.

business portfolio The group of different products or brands owned by an organization and characterized by different income-generating and growth capabilities.

business-to-business (B2B) e-commerce Internet exchanges between two or more businesses or organizations.

business-to-business marketing The marketing of goods and services that business and organizational customers need to produce other goods and services for resale or to support their operations.

business-to-business markets The group of customers that include manufacturers, wholesalers, retailers, and other organizations.

business-to-consumer (B2C) e-commerce On-line exchanges between companies and individual consumers.

buttons Small banner-type advertisements that can be placed anywhere on a Web page.

buyclass One of three classifications of business buying situations that characterizes the degree of time and effort required to make a decision.

buying center The group of people in an organization who participate in a purchasing decision.

buzz Word of mouth communication that customers view as authentic.

buzz marketing Using high-profile entertainment or news to get people to talk about your brand.

C

cannibalization The loss of sales of an existing brand when a new item in a product line or product family is introduced.

capacity management The process by which organizations adjust their offerings in an attempt to match demand.

captive pricing A pricing tactic for two items that must be used together; one item is priced very low, and the firm makes its profit on another, high-margin item essential to the operation of the first item.

case allowance A discount to the retailer or wholesaler based on the volume of product ordered.

case study A comprehensive examination of a particular firm or organization.

cash cows SBUs with a dominant market share in a low-growth-potential market.

catalog A collection of products offered for sale in book form, usually consisting of product descriptions accompanied by photos of the items.

causal research A technique that attempts to understand cause-and-effect relationships.

central business district (CBD) The traditional downtown business area found in a town or city.

channel intermediaries Firms or individuals such as wholesalers, agents, brokers, or retailers who help move a product from the producer to the consumer or business user.

channel leader A firm at one level of distribution that takes a leadership role, establishing operating norms and processes based on its power relative to other channel members.

channel levels The number of distinct categories of intermediaries that populate a channel of distribution.

channel of distribution The series of firms or individuals that facilitates the movement of a product from the producer to the final customer.

classical conditioning The learning that occurs when a stimulus eliciting a response is paired with another stimulus that initially does not elicit a response on its own but will cause a similar response over time because of its association with the first stimulus.

close The stage of the selling process in which the salesperson actually asks the customer to buy the product.

co-op advertising A sales promotion where the manufacturer and the retailer share the cost

cobranding An agreement between two brands to work together to market a new product.

code of ethics Written standards of behavior to which everyone in the organization must subscribe.

cognition The knowing component of attitudes; refers to the beliefs or knowledge a person has about a product and its important characteristics.

cognitive dissonance The anxiety or regret a consumer may feel after choosing from among several similar attractive choices.

cognitive learning theory The theory of learning that stresses the importance of internal mental processes and that views people as problem solvers who actively use information from the world around them to master their environment.

collectivist cultures Cultures in which people subordinate their personal goals to those of a stable community.

commercialization The final step in the product development process in which a new product is launched into the market.

communication model The process whereby meaning is transferred from a source to a receiver.

compatibility The extent to which a new product is consistent with existing cultural values, customs, and practices.

competitive intelligence (CI) The process of gathering and analyzing publicly available information about rivals.

competitive-parity method A promotion budgeting method in which an organization matches whatever competitors are spending.

complexity The degree to which consumers find a new product or its use difficult to understand.

component parts Manufactured goods or subassemblies of finished items that organizations need to complete their own products.

concentrated targeting strategy Focusing a firm's efforts on offering one or more products to a single segment.

conformity A change in beliefs or actions as a reaction to real or imagined group pressure.

consumer The ultimate user of a good or service.

consumer addiction A physiological or psychological dependency on goods or services.

consumer behavior   The process involved when individuals or groups select, purchase, use, and dispose of goods, services, ideas, or experiences to satisfy their needs and desires.

consumer goods   The goods individual consumers purchase for personal or family use.

consumer interview   One-on-one discussion between a consumer and a researcher.

consumer orientation   A management philosophy that focuses on ways to satisfy customers' needs and wants.

consumer satisfaction/dissatisfaction   The overall feelings or attitude a person has about a product after purchasing it.

consumer tribe   A group of people who share a lifestyle and who can identify with each other because of a shared allegiance to an activity or a product.

consumer-generated media   The on-line consumer-generated comments, opinions, and product-related stories available to other consumers through digital technology.

consumer-generated value   Everyday people functioning in marketing roles, such as participating in creating advertisements, providing input to new product development, or serving as wholesalers or retailers.

consumer-to-consumer (C2C) e-commerce   Communications and purchases that occur among individuals without directly involving the manufacturer or retailer.

consumerism   A social movement that attempts to protect consumers from harmful business practices.

continuous innovation   A modification of an existing product that sets one brand apart from its competitors.

contribution per unit   The difference between the price the firm charges for a product and the variable costs.

control   A process that entails measuring actual performance, comparing this performance to the established marketing objectives, and then making adjustments to the strategies or objectives on the basis of this analysis.

convenience product   A consumer good or service that is usually low-priced, widely available, and purchased frequently with a minimum of comparison and effort.

convenience sample   A nonprobability sample composed of individuals who just happen to be available when and where the data are being collected.

convenience stores   Neighborhood retailers that carry a limited number of frequently purchased items and cater to consumers willing to pay a premium for the ease of buying close to home.

conventional marketing system   A multiple-level distribution channel in which channel members work independently of one another.

conventions   Norms regarding the conduct of everyday life.

convergence   The coming together of two or more technologies to create a new system with greater benefits than its separate parts.

cookie   Text file inserted by a Web site sponsor into a Web surfer's hard drive that allows the site to track the surfer's moves.

core product   All the benefits the product will provide for consumers or business customers.

core service   The basic benefit of having a service performed.

corporate culture   The set of values, norms, and beliefs that influence the behavior of everyone in the organization.

corrective advertising   Advertising that clarifies or qualifies previous deceptive advertising claims.

cost per thousand (CPM)   A measure used to compare the relative cost-effectiveness of different media vehicles that have different exposure rates; the cost to deliver a message to 1,000 people or homes.

cost-plus pricing   A method of setting prices in which the seller totals all the costs for the product and then adds an amount to arrive at the selling price.

countertrade   A type of trade in which goods are paid for with other items instead of with cash.

creating assortments   Providing a variety of products in one location to meet the needs of buyers.

creative selling process   The process of seeking out potential customers, analyzing needs, determining how product attributes might provide benefits for the customer, and then communicating that information.

creative strategy   The process that turns a concept into an advertisement.

credence qualities   Product characteristics that are difficult to evaluate even after they have been experienced.

critical incident technique   A method for measuring service quality in which marketers use customer complaints to identify critical incidents—specifically face-to-face contacts between consumer and service providers that cause problems and lead to dissatisfaction.

cross-elasticity of demand   When changes in the price of one product affect the demand for another item.

cross-sectional design   A type of descriptive technique that involves the systematic collection of quantitative information.

crowdsourcing   Through a formal network, pulling together expertise from around the globe put to work on solving a particular problem for a firm.

cultural diversity   A management practice that actively seeks to include people of different sexes, races, ethnic groups, and religions in an organization's employees, customers, suppliers, and distribution channel partners.

cultural values   A society's deeply held beliefs about right and wrong ways to live.

culture   The values, beliefs, customs, and tastes a group of people values.

custom   A norm handed down from the past that controls basic behaviors.

custom marketing strategy   An approach that tailors specific products and the messages about them to individual customers.

custom research   Research conducted for a single firm to provide specific information its managers need.

customer equity   The financial value of a customer relationship throughout the lifetime of the relationship.

customer experience management (CEM)   The concept of holistically aligning a firm's people, processes, systems, and strategies to maximize the customer's experience with all aspects of your firm and its brands.

customer reference program   A formalized process by which customers formally share success stories and actively recommend products to other potential clients, usually facilitated through an on-line community.

customer relationship management (CRM)   A systematic tracking of consumers' preferences and behaviors over time in order to tailor the value proposition as closely as possible to each individual's unique wants and needs. CRM allows firms to talk to individual customers and to adjust elements of their marketing programs in light of how each customer reacts.

D

data mining   Sophisticated analysis techniques that take advantage of the massive amount of transaction information now available.

database marketing   The creation of an ongoing relationship with a set of customers who have an identifiable interest in a good or service and whose responses to promotional efforts become part of future communication attempts.

decline stage   The final stage in the product life cycle, during which sales decrease as customer needs change.

decoding   The process by which a receiver assigns meaning to the message.

demand Customers' desires for products coupled with the resources needed to obtain them.

demand-based pricing A price-setting method based on estimates of demand at different prices.

demographics Statistics that measure observable aspects of a population, including size, age, gender, ethnic group, income, education, occupation, and family structure.

department stores Retailers that sell a broad range of items and offer a good selection within each product line.

derived demand Demand for business or organizational products caused by demand for consumer goods or services.

descriptive research A tool that probes more systematically into the problem and bases its conclusions on large numbers of observations.

developed country A country that boasts sophisticated marketing systems, strong private enterprise, and bountiful market potential for many goods and services.

developing countries Countries in which the economy is shifting its emphasis from agriculture to industry.

differential benefit Properties of products that set them apart from competitors' products by providing unique customer benefits.

differentiated targeting strategy Developing one or more products for each of several distinct customer groups and making sure these offerings are kept separate in the marketplace.

diffusion The process by which the use of a product spreads throughout a population.

direct mail A brochure or pamphlet that offers a specific good or service at one point in time.

direct marketing Any direct communication to a consumer or business recipient designed to generate a response in the form of an order, a request for further information, and/or a visit to a store or other place of business for purchase of a product.

direct selling An interactive sales process in which a salesperson presents a product to one individual or a small group, takes orders, and delivers the merchandise.

direct-response advertising A direct marketing approach that allows the consumer to respond to a message by immediately contacting the provider to ask questions or order the product.

direct-response TV (DRTV) Advertising on TV that seeks a direct response, including short commercials of less than two minutes, 30-minute or longer infomercials, and home shopping networks.

discontinuous innovation A totally new product that creates major changes in the way we live.

discretionary income The portion of income people have left over after paying for necessities such as housing, utilities, food, and clothing.

disintermediation Eliminating the interaction between customers and salespeople so as to minimize negative service encounters and reduce costs.

disintermediation (of the channel of distribution) The elimination of some layers of the channel of distribution in order to cut costs and improve the efficiency of the channel.

distinctive competency A superior capability of a firm in comparison to its direct competitors.

diversification strategies Growth strategies that emphasize both new products and new markets.

dogs SBUs with a small share of a slow-growth market. They are businesses that offer specialized products in limited markets that are not likely to grow quickly.

dumping A company tries to get a toehold in a foreign market by pricing its products lower than it offers them at home.

durable goods Consumer products that provide benefits over a long period of time, such as cars, furniture, and appliances.

dynamic pricing A pricing strategy in which the price can easily be adjusted to meet changes in the marketplace.

dynamically continuous innovation A change in an existing product that requires a moderate amount of learning or behavior change.

E

e-commerce The buying or selling of goods and services electronically, usually over the Internet.

early adopters Those who adopt an innovation early in the diffusion process, but after the innovators.

early majority Those whose adoption of a new product signals a general acceptance of the innovation.

economic communities Groups of countries that band together to promote trade among themselves and to make it easier for member nations to compete elsewhere.

economic infrastructure The quality of a country's distribution, financial, and communications systems.

elastic demand Demand in which changes in price have large effects on the amount demanded.

embargo A quota completely prohibiting specified goods from entering or leaving a country.

emergency products Products we purchase when we're in dire need.

encoding The process of translating an idea into a form of communication that will convey meaning.

enterprise resource planning (ERP) systems A software system that integrates information from across the entire company, including finance, order fulfillment, manufacturing, and transportation and then facilitates sharing of the data throughout the firm.

environmental stewardship A position taken by an organization to protect or enhance the natural environment as it conducts its business activities.

environmentalism A broad philosophy and social movement that seeks conservation and improvement of the natural environment.

equipment Expensive goods that an organization uses in its daily operations that last for a long time.

ethnocentrism The tendency to prefer products or people of one's own culture.

ethnography An approach to research based on observations of people in their own homes or communities.

evaluative criteria The dimensions consumers use to compare competing product alternatives.

exchange The process by which some transfer of value occurs between a buyer and a seller.

exclusive distribution Selling a product only through a single outlet in a particular region.

experience qualities Product characteristics that customers can determine during or after consumption.

experiential marketing Marketing activities that attempt to give customers an opportunity to actually interact with brands, thus enabling them to make more intelligent and informed purchase decisions.

experiential shoppers Consumers who engage in on-line shopping because of the experiential benefits they receive.

experiment A technique that tests prespecified relationships among variables in a controlled environment.

exploratory research A technique that marketers use to generate insights for future, more rigorous studies.

export merchants Intermediaries a firm uses to represent it in other countries.

exposure The extent to which a stimulus is capable of being registered by a person's sensory receptors.

external environment The uncontrollable elements outside an organization that may affect its performance either positively or negatively.

extortion When someone in authority extracts payment under duress.

extranet A private, corporate computer network that links company departments, employees, and databases to suppliers, customers, and others outside the organization.

F

F.O.B. delivered pricing A pricing tactic in which the cost of loading and transporting the product to the customer is included in the selling price and is paid by the manufacturer.

F.O.B. origin pricing A pricing tactic in which the cost of transporting the product from the factory to the customer's location is the responsibility of the customer.

facilitating functions Functions of channel intermediaries that make the purchase process easier for customers and manufacturers.

factory outlet store A discount retailer, owned by a manufacturer, that sells off defective merchandise and excess inventory.

family brand A brand that a group of individual products or individual brands share.

family life cycle A means of characterizing consumers within a family structure on the basis of different stages through which people pass as they grow older.

fast-moving consumer goods (FMCG) Products that exhibit consistently high velocity of sales in the consumer marketplace.

feedback Receivers' reactions to the message.

fixed costs Costs of production that do not change with the number of units produced.

focus group A product-oriented discussion among a small group of consumers led by a trained moderator.

follow-up Activities after the sale that provide important services to customers.

Four Ps Product, price, promotion, and place.

franchising A form of licensing involving the right to adapt an entire system of doing business.

freenomics A business model that encourages giving products away for free because of the increase in profits that can be achieved by getting more people to participate in a market.

freight absorption pricing A pricing tactic in which the seller absorbs the total cost of transportation.

frequency The average number of times a person in the target group will be exposed to the message.

frequency programs Consumer sales promotion programs that offer a discount or free product for multiple purchases over time; also referred to as loyalty or continuity programs.

full-service agency An agency that provides most or all of the services needed to mount a campaign, including research, creation of ad copy and art, media selection, and production of the final messages.

functional planning A decision process that concentrates on developing detailed plans for strategies and tactics for the short term, supporting an organization's long-term strategic plan.

G

gap analysis A marketing research method that measures the difference between a customer's expectation of a service quality and what actually occurred.

gender roles Society's expectations regarding the appropriate attitudes, behaviors, and appearances of men and women.

General Agreement on Tariffs and Trade (GATT) International treaty to reduce import tax levels and trade restrictions.

general merchandise discount stores Retailers that offer a broad assortment of items at low prices with minimal service.

Generation X The group of consumers born between 1965 and 1978.

Generation Y The group of consumers born between 1979 and 1994.

generational marketing Marketing to members of a generation, who tend to share the same outlook and priorities.

generic branding A strategy in which products are not branded and are sold at the lowest price possible.

geocoding Customizing Web advertising so that people who log on in different places will see ad banners for local businesses.

geodemography A segmentation technique that combines geography with demographics.

good A tangible product that we can see, touch, smell, hear, or taste.

government markets The federal, state, county, and local governments that buy goods and services to carry out public objectives and to support their operations.

gray market goods Items manufactured outside a country and then imported without the consent of the trademark holder.

green marketing The development of marketing strategies that support environmental stewardship by creating an environmentally-founded differential benefit in the minds of consumers.

greenwashing Environmentally-friendly claims that are exaggerated or untrue.

gross domestic product (GDP) The total dollar value of goods and services produced by a nation within its borders in a year.

gross national product (GNP) The value of all goods and services produced by a country's citizens or organizations, whether located within the country's borders or not.

gross rating points (GRPs) A measure used for comparing the effectiveness of different media vehicles: average reach × frequency.

growth stage The second stage in the product life cycle, during which consumers accept the product and sales rapidly increase.

guerrilla marketing Marketing activity in which a firm "ambushes" consumers with promotional content in places they are not expecting to encounter this kind of activity.

H

heuristics A mental rule of thumb that leads to a speedy decision by simplifying the process.

hierarchy of effects A series of steps prospective customers move through, from initial awareness of a product to brand loyalty.

hierarchy of needs An approach that categorizes motives according to five levels of importance, the more basic needs being on the bottom of the hierarchy and the higher needs at the top.

horizontal marketing system An arrangement within a channel of distribution in which two or more firms at the same channel level work together for a common purpose.

hybrid marketing system A marketing system that uses a number of different channels and communication methods to serve a target market.

hypermarkets Retailers with the characteristics of both warehouse stores and supermarkets; hypermarkets are several times larger than other stores and offer virtually everything from grocery items to electronics.

I

idea generation The first step of product development in which marketers brainstorm for products that provide customer benefits and are compatible with the company mission.

idea marketing Marketing activities that seek to gain market share for a concept, philosophy, belief, or issue by using elements of the marketing mix to create or change a target market's attitude or behavior.

import quotas Limitations set by a government on the amount of a product allowed to enter or leave a country.

impressions The number of people who will be exposed to a message placed in one or more media vehicles.

impulse product A product people often buy on the spur of the moment.

impulse purchase A purchase made without any planning or search effort.

independent intermediaries Channel intermediaries that are not controlled by any manufacturer, but instead do business with many different manufacturers and many different customers.

individualist cultures Cultures in which people tend to attach more importance to personal goals than to those of the larger community.

industrial goods Goods individuals or organizations buy for further processing or for their own use when they do business.

inelastic demand Demand in which changes in price have little or no effect on the amount demanded.

infomercials Half-hour or hour-long commercials that resemble a talk show but actually are sales pitches.

information search The process whereby a consumer searches for appropriate information to make a reasonable decision.

ingredient branding A form of cobranding that uses branded materials as ingredients or component parts in other branded products.

innovation A product that consumers perceive to be new and different from existing products.

innovators The first segment (roughly 2.5 percent) of a population to adopt a new product.

inseparability The characteristic of a service that means that it is impossible to separate the production of a service from the consumption of that service.

insourcing A practice in which a company contracts with a specialist firm to handle all or part of its supply chain operations.

instapreneur A business person who only produces a product when it is ordered.

institutional advertising An advertising message that promotes the activities, personality, or point of view of an organization or company.

intangibility The characteristic of a service that means customers can't see, touch, or smell good service.

intangibles Experience-based products.

integrated marketing communication (IMC) A strategic business process that marketers use to plan, develop, execute, and evaluate coordinated, measurable, persuasive brand communication programs over time to targeted audiences.

intelligent agents Computer programs that find sites selling a particular product.

intensive distribution Selling a product through all suitable wholesalers or retailers that are willing to stock and sell the product.

internal environment The controllable elements inside an organization, including its people, its facilities, and how it does things that influence the operations of the organization.

internal reference price A set price or a price range in consumers' minds that they refer to in evaluating a product's price.

interpretation The process of assigning meaning to a stimulus based on prior associations a person has with it and assumptions he makes about it.

intranet An internal corporate communication network that uses Internet technology to link company departments, employees, and databases.

introduction stage The first stage of the product life cycle in which slow growth follows the introduction of a new product in the marketplace.

inventory control Activities to ensure that goods are always available to meet customers' demands.

involvement The relative importance of perceived consequences of the purchase to a consumer.

ISO 14000 Standards of the International Organization for Standardization concerned with "environmental management" aimed at minimizing harmful effects on the environment.

ISO 9000 Criteria developed by the International Organization for Standardization to regulate product quality in Europe.

J

joint demand Demand for two or more goods that are used together to create a product.

joint venture A strategic alliance in which a new entity owned by two or more firms allows the partners to pool their resources for common goals.

just in time (JIT) Inventory management and purchasing processes that manufacturers and resellers use to reduce inventory to very low levels and ensure that deliveries from suppliers arrive only when needed.

K

Kansei engineering A Japanese philosophy that translates customers' feelings into design elements.

knockoff A new product that copies, with slight modification, the design of an original product.

knowledge management A comprehensive approach to collecting, organizing, storing, and retrieving a firm's information assets.

Kyoto Protocol A global agreement among countries that aims at reducing greenhouse gasses that create climate change.

L

laggards The last consumers to adopt an innovation.

late majority The adopters who are willing to try new products when there is little or no risk associated with the purchase, when the purchase becomes an economic necessity, or when there is social pressure to purchase.

learning A relatively permanent change in behavior caused by acquired information or experience.

least developed country (LDC) A country at the lowest stage of economic development.

level of economic development The broader economic picture of a country.

licensing An agreement in which one firm sells another firm the right to use a brand name for a specific purpose and for a specific period of time.

lifestyle The pattern of living that determines how people choose to spend their time, money, and energy and that reflects their values, tastes, and preferences.

lifetime value of a customer How much profit companies expect to make from a particular customer, including each and every purchase he will make from them now and in the future. To calculate lifetime value, companies estimate the amount the person will spend and then subtract what it will cost the company to maintain this relationship.

limited-service agency An agency that provides one or more specialized services, such as media buying or creative development.

list price The price the end customer is expected to pay as determined by the manufacturer; also referred to as the suggested retail price.

lobbying talking with and providing information to government officials in order to influence their activities relating to an organization.

local content rules A form of protectionism stipulating that a certain proportion of a product must consist of components supplied by industries in the host country or economic community.

logistics The process of designing, managing, and improving the movement of products through the supply chain. Logistics include purchasing, manufacturing, storage, and transport.

long tail A new approach to segmentation based on the idea that companies can make money by selling small amounts of items that only a few people want, provided they sell enough different items.

longitudinal design A technique that tracks the responses of the same sample of respondents over time.

loss leader pricing The pricing policy of setting prices very low or even below cost to attract customers into a store.

M

m-commerce Promotional and other e-commerce activities transmitted over mobile phones and other mobile devices, such as Smart phones and personal digital assistants (PDAs).

maintenance, repair, and operating (MRO) products Goods that a business customer consumes in a relatively short time.

mall-intercept A study in which researchers recruit shoppers in malls or other public areas.

marginal analysis A method that uses cost and demand to identify the price that will maximize profits.

marginal cost The increase in total cost that results from producing one additional unit of a product.

marginal revenue The increase in total income or revenue that results from selling one additional unit of a product.

market All the customers and potential customers who share a common need that can be satisfied by a specific product, who have the resources to exchange for it, who are willing to make the exchange, and who have the authority to make the exchange.

market development strategies Growth strategies that introduce existing products to new markets.

market fragmentation The creation of many consumer groups due to a diversity of distinct needs and wants in modern society.

market manager An individual who is responsible for developing and implementing the marketing plans for products sold to a particular customer group.

market penetration strategies Growth strategies designed to increase sales of existing products to current customers, nonusers, and users of competitive brands in served markets.

market position The way in which the target market perceives the product in comparison to competitors' brands.

market segment A distinct group of customers within a larger market who are similar to one another in some way and whose needs differ from other customers in the larger market.

marketing An organizational function and a set of processes for creating, communicating, and delivering value to customers and for managing customer relationships in ways that benefit the organization and its stakeholders.

marketing concept A management orientation that focuses on identifying and satisfying consumer needs to ensure the organization's long-term profitability.

marketing decision support system (MDSS) The data, analysis software, and interactive software that allow managers to conduct analyses and find the information they need.

marketing information system (MIS) A process that first determines what information marketing managers need and then gathers, sorts, analyzes, stores, and distributes relevant and timely marketing information to system users.

marketing intelligence system A method by which marketers get information about everyday happenings in the marketing environment.

marketing mix A combination of the product itself, the price of the product, the place where it is made available, and the activities that introduce it to consumers that creates a desired response among a set of predefined consumers.

marketing plan A document that describes the marketing environment, outlines the marketing objectives and strategy, and identifies who will be responsible for carrying out each part of the marketing strategy.

marketing research The process of collecting, analyzing, and interpreting data about customers, competitors, and the business environment in order to improve marketing effectiveness.

marketing research ethics Taking an ethical and above-board approach to conducting marketing research that does no harm to the participant in the process of conducting the research.

marketplace Any location or medium used to conduct an exchange.

mass customization An approach that modifies a basic good or service to meet the needs of an individual.

mass market All possible customers in a market, regardless of the differences in their specific needs and wants.

mass-class The hundreds of millions of global consumers who now enjoy a level of purchasing power that's sufficient to let them afford high-quality products—except for big-ticket items like college educations, housing, or luxury cars.

materials handling The moving of products into, within, and out of warehouses.

maturity stage The third and longest stage in the product life cycle, during which sales peak and profit margins narrow.

media blitz A massive advertising campaign that occurs over a relatively short time frame.

media planning The process of developing media objectives, strategies, and tactics for use in an advertising campaign.

media schedule The plan that specifies the exact media to use and when to use it.

medium A communication vehicle through which a message is transmitted to a target audience.

merchandise agents or brokers Channel intermediaries that provide services in exchange for commissions but never take title to the product.

merchandise assortment The range of products a store sells.

merchandise breadth The number of different product lines available.

merchandise depth The variety of choices available for each specific product line.

merchandise mix The total set of all products offered for sale by a retailer, including all product lines sold to all consumer groups.

merchandising allowance Reimburses the retailer for in-store support of the product.

merchant wholesalers Intermediaries that buy goods from manufacturers (take title to them) and sell to retailers and other business-to-business customers.

message The communication in physical form that goes from a sender to a receiver.

metrosexual A straight, urban male who is keenly interested in fashion, home design, gourmet cooking, and personal care.

mission statement A formal statement in an organization's strategic plan that describes the overall purpose of the organization and what it intends to achieve in terms of its customers, products, and resources.

missionary salesperson A salesperson who promotes the firm and tries to stimulate demand for a product but does not actually complete a sale.

modified rebuy A buying situation classification used by business buyers to categorize a previously made purchase that involves some change and that requires limited decision making.

monopolistic competition A market structure in which many firms, each having slightly different products, offer unique consumer benefits.

monopoly A market situation in which one firm, the only supplier of a particular product, is able to control the price, quality, and supply of that product.

mores Customs with a strong moral overtone.

motivation An internal state that drives us to satisfy needs by activating goal-oriented behavior.

multilevel network A system in which a master distributor recruits other people to become distributors, sells the company's product to the recruits, and receives a commission on all the merchandise sold by the people recruited.

multiple sourcing The business practice of buying a particular product from several different suppliers.

myths Stories containing symbolic elements that express the shared emotions and ideals of a culture.

N

national or manufacturer brands Brands that the product manufacturer owns.

need The recognition of any difference between a consumer's actual state and some ideal or desired state.

new dominant logic for marketing A reconceptualization of traditional marketing to redefine service as the central (core) deliverable and the actual physical products purveyed as comparatively incidental to the value proposition.

new-business salesperson The person responsible for finding new customers and calling on them to present the company's products.

new-task buy A new business-to-business purchase that is complex or risky and that requires extensive decision making.

noise Anything that interferes with effective communication.

nondurable goods Consumer products that provide benefits for a short time because they are consumed (such as food) or are no longer useful (such as newspapers).

nonprobability sample A sample in which personal judgment is used to select respondents.

nonstore retailing Any method used to complete an exchange with a product end user that does not require a customer visit to a store.

norms Specific rules dictating what is right or wrong, acceptable or unacceptable.

North American Industry Classification System (NAICS) The numerical coding system that the United States, Canada, and Mexico use to classify firms into detailed categories according to their business activities.

not-for-profit institutions/organizations The organizations with charitable, educational, community, and other public service goals that buy goods and services to support their functions and to attract and serve their members.

O

objective-task method A promotion budgeting method in which an organization first defines the specific communication goals it hopes to achieve and then tries to calculate what kind of promotional efforts it will take to meet these goals.

observability How visible a new product and its benefits are to others who might adopt it.

observational learning Learning that occurs when people watch the actions of others and note what happens to them as a result.

off-price retailers Retailers that buy excess merchandise from well-known manufacturers and pass the savings on to customers.

oligopoly A market structure in which a relatively small number of sellers, each holding a substantial share of the market, compete in a market with many buyers.

on-line auctions E-commerce that allows shoppers to purchase products through on-line bidding.

on-line distribution piracy The theft and unauthorized repurposing of intellectual property via the Internet.

open source model A practice used in the software industry in which companies share their software codes with anyone to assist in the development of a better product.

operant conditioning Learning that occurs as the result of rewards or punishments.

operational planning A decision process that focuses on developing detailed plans for day-to-day activities that carry out an organization's functional plans.

operational plans Plans that focus on the day-to-day execution of the marketing plan. Operational plans include detailed directions for the specific activities to be carried out, who will be responsible for them, and time lines for accomplishing the tasks.

opinion leader A person who is frequently able to influence others' attitudes or behaviors by virtue of his active interest and expertise in one or more product categories.

order getter A salesperson who works to develop long-term relationships with particular customers or to generate new sales.

order processing The series of activities that occurs between the time an order comes into the organization and the time a product goes out the door.

order taker A salesperson whose primary function is to facilitate transactions that the customer initiates.

organizational markets Another name for business-to-business markets.

out-of-home media A communication medium that reaches people in public places.

outsourcing The business buying process of obtaining outside vendors to provide goods or services that otherwise might be supplied in-house.

P

package The covering or container for a product that provides product protection, facilitates product use and storage, and supplies important marketing communication.

party plan system A sales technique that relies heavily on people getting caught up in the "group spirit," buying things they would not normally buy if they were alone.

patent Legal documentation granting an individual or firm exclusive rights to produce and sell a particular invention.

penetration pricing A pricing strategy in which a firm introduces a new product at a very low price to encourage more customers to purchase it.

perceived risk The belief that choice of a product has potentially negative consequences, whether financial, physical, and/or social.

percentage-of-sales method A method for promotion budgeting that is based on a certain percentage of either last year's sales or on estimates for the present year's sales.

perception The process by which people select, organize, and interpret information from the outside world.

perceptual map A technique to visually describe where brands are "located" in consumers' minds relative to competing brands.

perfect competition A market structure in which many small sellers, all of whom offer similar products, are unable to have an impact on the quality, price, or supply of a product.

perishability The characteristic of a service that makes it impossible to store for later sale or consumption.

permission marketing E-mail advertising in which on-line consumers have the opportunity to accept or refuse the unsolicited e-mail.

personal selling Marketing communication by which a company representative interacts directly with a customer or prospective customer to communicate about a good or service.

personality The set of unique psychological characteristics that consistently influences the way a person responds to situations in the environment.

physical distribution The activities that move finished goods from manufacturers to final customers, including order processing, warehousing, materials handling, transportation, and inventory control.

place The availability of the product to the customer at the desired time and location.

place marketing Marketing activities that seek to attract new businesses, residents, or visitors to a town, state, country, or some other site.

place-based media Advertising media that transmit messages in public places, such as doctors' offices and airports, where certain types of people congregate.

point of purchase (POP) displays In-store displays and signs.

point-of-sale (POS) systems Retail computer systems that collect sales data and are hooked directly into the store's inventory-control system.

pop-up retailing A retail strategy in which a store deliberately opens and then closes after a short period of time.

popular culture The music, movies, sports, books, celebrities, and other forms of entertainment consumed by the mass market.

portfolio analysis A management tool for evaluating a firm's business mix and assessing the potential of an organization's strategic business units.

positioning Developing a marketing strategy to influence how a particular market segment perceives a good or service in comparison to the competition.

posttesting Research conducted on consumers' responses to actual advertising messages they have seen or heard.

preapproach A part of the selling process that includes developing information about prospective customers and planning the sales interview.

predatory pricing Illegal pricing strategy in which a company sets a very low price for the purpose of driving competitors out of business.

prediction markets Approach to forecasting and trend identification that pools opinions from a group of knowledgeable people about a product or service.

premiums Items offered free to people who have purchased a product.

press release Information that an organization distributes to the media intended to win publicity.

prestige products Products that have a high price and that appeal to status-conscious consumers.

pretesting A research method that seeks to minimize mistakes by getting consumer reactions to ad messages before they appear in the media.

price The assignment of value, or the amount the consumer must exchange to receive the offering.

price bundling Selling two or more goods or services as a single package for one price.

price elasticity of demand The percentage change in unit sales that results from a percentage change in price.

price leadership A pricing strategy in which one firm first sets its price and other firms in the industry follow with the same or very similar prices.

price lining The practice of setting a limited number of different specific prices, called price points, for items in a product line.

price-fixing The collaboration of two or more firms in setting prices, usually to keep prices high.

primary data Data from research conducted to help make a specific decision.

private exchanges Systems that link an invited group of suppliers and partners over the Web.

private-label brands Brands that a certain retailer or distributor owns and sells.

probability sample A sample in which each member of the population has some known chance of being included.

problem recognition The process that occurs whenever the consumer sees a significant difference between his current state of affairs and some desired or ideal state; this recognition initiates the decision-making process.

processed materials Products created when firms transform raw materials from their original state.

producers The individuals or organizations that purchase products for use in the production of other goods and services.

product A tangible good, service, idea, or some combination of these that satisfies consumer or business customer needs through the exchange process; a bundle of attributes including features, functions, benefits, and uses.

product adaptation strategy Product strategy in which a firm offers the a similar but modified product in foreign markets.

product adoption The process by which a consumer or business customer begins to buy and use a new good, service, or idea.

product advertising An advertising message that focuses on a specific good or service.

product category managers Individuals who are responsible for developing and implementing the marketing plan for all the brands and products within a product category.

product competition When firms offering different products compete to satisfy the same consumer needs and wants.

product concept development and screening The second step of product development in which marketers test product ideas for technical and commercial success.

product development strategies   Growth strategies that focus on selling new products in existing markets.

product invention strategy   Product strategy in which a firm develops a new product for foreign markets.

product life cycle   A concept that explains how products go through four distinct stages from birth to death: introduction, growth, maturity, and decline.

product line   A firm's total product offering designed to satisfy a single need or desire of target customers.

product mix   The total set of all products a firm offers for sale.

product sampling   Distributing free trial-size versions of a product to consumers.

product specifications   A written description of the quality, size, weight, and so forth required of a product purchase.

product/brand placement   Marketing communication activity in which companies have their products embedded in movies, TV shows, and other entertainment vehicles.

production orientation   A management philosophy that emphasizes the most efficient ways to produce and distribute products.

projective technique   A test that marketers use to explore people's underlying feelings about a product; especially appropriate when consumers are unable or unwilling to express their true reactions.

promotion   The coordination of a marketer's marketing communications efforts to influence attitudes or behavior; the coordination of efforts by a marketer to inform or persuade consumers or organizations about goods, services, or ideas.

promotion mix   The major elements of marketer-controlled communication, including advertising, sales promotion, public relations, personal selling, and direct marketing.

promotional products   Goodies such as coffee mugs, T-shirts, and magnets given away to build awareness for a sponsor. Some freebies are distributed directly to consumers and business customers; others are intended for channel partners such as retailers and vendors.

prospecting   A part of the selling process that includes identifying and developing a list of potential or prospective customers.

protectionism   A policy adopted by a government to give domestic companies an advantage.

prototypes   Test versions of a proposed product.

psychographics   The use of psychological, sociological, and anthropological factors to construct market segments.

public relations (PR)   Communication function that seeks to build good relationships with an organization's publics, including consumers, stockholders, and legislators.

public relations campaign   A coordinated effort to communicate with one or more of the firm's publics.

public service advertisements (PSAs)   Advertising run by the media without charge for not-for-profit organizations or to champion a particular cause.

publicity   Unpaid communication about an organization that appears in the mass media.

puffery   Claims made in advertising of product superiority that cannot be proven true or untrue.

pull strategy   The company tries to move its products through the channel by building desire for the products among consumers, thus convincing retailers to respond to this demand by stocking these items.

push money   A bonus paid by a manufacturer to a salesperson, customer, or distributor for selling its product.

push strategy   The company tries to move its products through the channel by convincing channel members to offer them.

pyramid schemes   An illegal sales technique that promises consumers or investors large profits from recruiting others to join the program rather than from any real investment or sale of goods to the public.

Q

quantity discounts   A pricing tactic of charging reduced prices for purchases of larger quantities of a product.

question marks   SBUs with low market shares in fast-growth markets.

R

radio frequency identification (RFID)   Product tags with tiny chips containing information about the item's content, origin, and destination.

raw materials   Products of the fishing, lumber, agricultural, and mining industries that organizational customers purchase to use in their finished products.

reach   The percentage of the target market that will be exposed to the media vehicle.

rebates   Sales promotions that allow the customer to recover part of the product's cost from the manufacturer.

receiver   The organization or individual that intercepts and interprets the message.

reciprocity   A trading partnership in which two firms agree to buy from one another.

reference group   An actual or imaginary individual or group that has a significant effect on an individual's evaluations, aspirations, or behavior.

relationship selling   A form of personal selling that involves securing, developing, and maintaining long-term relationships with profitable customers.

relative advantage   The degree to which a consumer perceives that a new product provides superior benefits.

reliability   The extent to which research measurement techniques are free of errors.

repositioning   Redoing a product's position to respond to marketplace changes.

representativeness   The extent to which consumers in a study are similar to a larger group in which the organization has an interest.

research design   A plan that specifies what information marketers will collect and what type of study they will do.

resellers   The individuals or organizations that buy finished goods for the purpose of reselling, renting, or leasing to others to make a profit and to maintain their business operations.

retail life cycle   A theory that focuses on the various stages that retailers pass through from introduction to decline.

retailing   The final stop in the distribution channel in which organizations sell goods and services to consumers for their personal use.

retro brand   A once-popular brand that has been revived to experience a popularity comeback, often by riding a wave of nostalgia.

return on investment (ROI)   The direct financial impact of a firm's expenditure of a resource such as time or money.

return on marketing investment (ROMI)   Quantifying just how an investment in marketing has an impact on the firm's success, financially and otherwise.

reverse marketing   A business practice in which a buyer firm attempts to identify suppliers who will produce products according to the buyer firm's specifications.

S

sales management The process of planning, implementing, and controlling the personal selling function of an organization.

sales presentation The part of the selling process in which the salesperson directly communicates the value proposition to the customer and invites two-way communication.

sales promotion Programs designed to build interest in or encourage purchase of a product during a specified period.

sales territory A set of customers, often defined by geographic boundaries, for whom a particular salesperson is responsible.

sampling The process of selecting respondents for a study.

scenario Possible future situation that futurists use to assess the likely impact of alternative marketing strategies.

search engine optimization (SEO) A systematic process of ensuring that your firm comes up at or near the top of lists of typical search phrases related to your business.

search qualities Product characteristics that the consumer can examine prior to purchase.

secondary data Data that have been collected for some purpose other than the problem at hand.

segment profile A description of the "typical" customer in a segment.

segmentation The process of dividing a larger market into smaller pieces based on one or more meaningfully shared characteristics.

segmentation variables Dimensions that divide the total market into fairly homogeneous groups, each with different needs and preferences.

selective distribution Distribution using fewer outlets than intensive distribution but more than exclusive distribution.

self-concept An individual's self-image that is composed of a mixture of beliefs, observations, and feelings about personal attributes.

selling orientation A managerial view of marketing as a sales function, or a way to move products out of warehouses to reduce inventory.

service encounter The actual interaction between the customer and the service provider.

services Intangible products that are exchanged directly between the producer and the customer.

servicescape The actual physical facility where the service is performed, delivered, and consumed.

SERVQUAL A multiple-item scale used to measure service quality across dimensions of tangibles, reliability, responsiveness, assurance, and empathy.

share of customer The percentage of an individual customer's purchase of a product that is a single brand.

shopping center A group of commercial establishments owned and managed as a single property.

shopping product A good or service for which consumers spend considerable time and effort gathering information and comparing alternatives before making a purchase.

shrinkage Losses experienced by retailers due to shoplifting, employee theft, and damage to merchandise.

single sourcing The business practice of buying a particular product from only one supplier.

situation analysis An assessment of a firm's internal and external environments.

Six Sigma A process whereby firms work to limit product defects to 3.4 per million or fewer.

skimming price A very high, premium price that a firm charges for its new, highly desirable product.

slotting allowance A fee paid in exchange for agreeing to place a manufacturer's products on a retailer's valuable shelf space.

social class The overall rank or social standing of groups of people within a society according to the value assigned to factors such as family background, education, occupation, and income.

social marketing concept A management philosophy that marketers must satisfy customers' needs in ways that also benefit society and also deliver profit to the firm.

social network services On-line applications that use software to build on-line communities of people who share interests and activities.

source An organization or individual that sends a message.

specialty product A good or service that has unique characteristics and is important to the buyer and for which she will devote significant effort to acquire.

specialty stores Retailers that carry only a few product lines but offer good selection within the lines that they sell.

sponsorships PR activities through which companies provide financial support to help fund an event in return for publicized recognition of the company's contribution.

stakeholders Buyers, sellers, or investors in a company, community residents, and even citizens of the nations where goods and services are made or sold—in other words, any person or organization that has a "stake" in the outcome.

standard of living An indicator of the average quality and quantity of goods and services consumed in a country.

staples Basic or necessary items that are available almost everywhere.

stars SBUs with products that have a dominant market share in high-growth markets.

status symbols Visible markers that provide a way for people to flaunt their membership in higher social classes (or at least to make others believe they are members).

stimulus generalization Behavior caused by a reaction to one stimulus occurs in the presence of other similar stimuli.

store image The way the marketplace perceives a retailer relative to the competition.

straight extension strategy Product strategy in which a firm offers the same product in both domestic and foreign markets.

straight rebuy A buying situation in which business buyers make routine purchases that require minimal decision making.

strategic alliance Relationship developed between a firm seeking a deeper commitment to a foreign market and a domestic firm in the target country.

strategic business units (SBUs) Individual units within the firm that operate like separate businesses, with each having its own mission, business objectives, resources, managers, and competitors.

strategic planning A managerial decision process that matches an organization's resources and capabilities to its market opportunities for long-term growth and survival.

subculture A group within a society whose members share a distinctive set of beliefs, characteristics, or common experiences.

subliminal advertising Supposedly hidden messages in marketers' communications.

supermarkets Food stores that carry a wide selection of edibles and related products.

supply chain All the activities necessary to turn raw materials into a good or service and put it in the hands of the consumer or business customer.

supply chain management   The management of flows among firms in the supply chain to maximize total profitability.

sustainability   A product design focus that seeks to create products that meet present consumer needs without compromising the ability of future generations to meet their needs.

SWOT analysis   An analysis of an organization's strengths and weaknesses and the opportunities and threats in its external environment.

syndicated research   Research by firms that collect data on a regular basis and sell the reports to multiple firms.

T

take title   To accept legal ownership of a product and assume the accompanying rights and responsibilities of ownership.

target costing   A process in which firms identify the quality and functionality needed to satisfy customers and what price they are willing to pay before the product is designed; the product is manufactured only if the firm can control costs to meet the required price.

target market   The market segments on which an organization focuses its marketing plan and toward which it directs its marketing efforts.

target marketing strategy   Dividing the total market into different segments on the basis of customer characteristics, selecting one or more segments, and developing products to meet the needs of those specific segments.

targeting   A strategy in which marketers evaluate the attractiveness of each potential segment and decide in which of these groups they will invest resources to try to turn them into customers.

tariffs   Taxes on imported goods.

team selling   The sales function when handled by a team that may consist of a salesperson, a technical specialist, and others.

technical development   The step in the product development process in which company engineers refine and perfect a new product.

technical specialist   A sales support person with a high level of technical expertise who assists in product demonstrations.

telemarketing   The use of the telephone to sell directly to consumers and business customers.

test marketing   Testing the complete marketing plan in a small geographic area that is similar to the larger market the firm hopes to enter.

tipping point   In the context of product diffusion, the point when a product's sales spike from a slow climb to an unprecedented new level, often accompanied by a steep price decline.

top-down budgeting techniques   Allocation of the promotion budget based on management's determination of the total amount to be devoted to marketing communication.

total costs   The total of the fixed costs and the variable costs for a set number of units produced.

total quality management (TQM)   A management philosophy that focuses on satisfying customers through empowering employees to be an active part of continuous quality improvement.

touchpoint   Any point of direct interface between customers and a company (on-line, by phone, or in person).

trade area   A geographic zone that accounts for the majority of a store's sales and customers.

trade or functional discounts   Discounts off list price of products to members of the channel of distribution who perform various marketing functions.

trade promotions   Promotions that focus on members of the "trade," which include distribution channel members, such as retail

salespeople or wholesale distributors, that a firm must work with in order to sell its products.

trade shows   Events at which many companies set up elaborate exhibits to show their products, give away samples, distribute product literature, and troll for new business contacts.

trademark   The legal term for a brand name, brand mark, or trade character; trademarks legally registered by a government obtain protection for exclusive use in that country.

traffic flow   The direction in which shoppers will move through the store and which areas they will pass or avoid.

transactional selling   A form of personal selling that focuses on making an immediate sale with little or no attempt to develop a relationship with the customer.

transportation   The mode by which products move among channel members.

trial pricing   Pricing a new product low for a limited period of time in order to lower the risk for a customer.

trialability   The ease of sampling a new product and its benefits.

triple bottom line orientation   A business orientation that looks at financial profits, the community in which the organization operates, and creating sustainable business practices.

U

U.S. Generalized System of Preferences (GSP)   A program to promote economic growth in developing countries by allowing duty-free entry of goods into the U.S.

unaided recall   A research technique conducted by telephone survey or personal interview that asks whether a person remembers seeing an ad during a specified period without giving the person the name of the brand.

undifferentiated targeting strategy   Appealing to a broad spectrum of people.

unfair sales acts   State laws that prohibit suppliers from selling products below cost to protect small businesses from larger competitors.

uniform delivered pricing   A pricing tactic in which a firm adds a standard shipping charge to the price for all customers regardless of location.

unique selling proposition (USP)   An advertising appeal that focuses on one clear reason why a particular product is superior.

Universal Product Code (UPC)   The set of black bars or lines printed on the side or bottom of most items sold in grocery stores and other mass-merchandising outlets. The UPC, readable by scanners, creates a national system of product identification.

unobtrusive measure   Measuring traces of physical evidence that remain after some action has been taken.

unsought products   Goods or services for which a consumer has little awareness or interest until the product or a need for the product is brought to her attention.

usage occasions   An indicator used in behavioral market segmentation based on when consumers use a product most.

utility   The usefulness or benefit consumers receive from a product.

V

validity   The extent to which research actually measures what it was intended to measure.

VALS2™ (Values and Lifestyles)   A psychographic system that divides the entire U.S. population into eight segments.

value   The benefits a customer receives from buying a good or service.

value chain   A series of activities involved in designing, producing, marketing, delivering, and supporting any product. Each link in the chain has the potential to either add or remove value from the product the customer eventually buys.

value pricing or **everyday low pricing (EDLP)**   A pricing strategy in which a firm sets prices that provide ultimate value to customers.

value proposition   A marketplace offering that fairly and accurately sums up the value that will be realized if the good or service is purchased.

variability   The characteristic of a service that means that even the same service performed by the same individual for the same customer can vary.

variable costs   The costs of production (raw and processed materials, parts, and labor) that are tied to and vary depending on the number of units produced.

venture teams   Groups of people within an organization who work together to focus exclusively on the development of a new product.

vertical marketing system (VMS)   A channel of distribution in which there is formal cooperation among members at the manufacturing, wholesaling, and retailing levels.

viral marketing   Creating entertaining or informative messages that are designed to be passed along in an exponential fashion, often electronically or by e-mail.

W

want   The desire to satisfy needs in specific ways that are culturally and socially influenced.

warehouse clubs   Discount retailers that charge a modest membership fee to consumers who buy a broad assortment of food and nonfood items in bulk and in a warehouse environment.

warehousing   Storing goods in anticipation of sale or transfer to another member of the channel of distribution.

Web 2.0   The new generation of the World Wide Web that incorporates social networking and user interactivity.

wheel-of-retailing hypothesis   A theory that explains how retail firms change, becoming more upscale as they go through their life cycle.

wholesaling intermediaries   Firms that handle the flow of products from the manufacturer to the retailer or business user.

wisdom of crowds   Under the right circumstances, groups are smarter than the smartest people in them meaning that large numbers of consumers can predict successful products.

word of mouth (WOM)   When consumers provide information about products to other consumers.

word of mouth marketing   Giving people a reason to talk about your products and making it easier for that conversation to take place.

world trade   The flow of goods and services among different countries—the value of all the exports and imports of the world's nations.

World Trade Organization (WTO)   An organization that replaced GATT, the WTO sets trade rules for its member nations and mediates disputes between nations.

Y

yield management pricing   A practice of charging different prices to different customers in order to manage capacity while maximizing revenues.

▶Index

SUBJECT INDEX